EUROPEAN UNION LAW

European Union Law

Fifth Edition

EDITED BY

CATHERINE BARNARD

AND

STEVE PEERS

OXFORD
UNIVERSITY PRESS

OXFORD
UNIVERSITY PRESS

Great Clarendon Street, Oxford, OX2 6DP,
United Kingdom

Oxford University Press is a department of the University of Oxford.
It furthers the University's objective of excellence in research, scholarship,
and education by publishing worldwide. Oxford is a registered trade mark of
Oxford University Press in the UK and in certain other countries.

Second Edition 2017
Third Edition 2020
Fourth Edition 2023

Published in the United States of America by Oxford University Press
546 Fifth Avenue, New York, NY 10036, United States of America

British Library Cataloguing in Publication Data
Data available

Library of Congress Control Number: 2026942056

ISBN 9780198988182

Printed in the UK by Bell & Bain Ltd., Glasgow

The manufacturer's authorized representative in the EU for product safety is
Oxford University Press España S.A. of Parque Empresarial San Fernando de Henares,
Avenida de Castilla, 2 – 28830 Madrid (www.oup.es/en or product.safety@oup.com).
OUP España S.A. also acts as importer into Spain of products made by the manufacturer.

MIX
Paper | Supporting responsible forestry
FSC® C007785

Preface

It is hard to be neutral about the EU. It provokes strong views and passions. Yet in the tumult of Treaty reform, Brexit, case law, legislation, theory, and empirical research lies a core subject that thousands of students wish to study. So for us, as editors, the question is how to fashion a book in a way that is engaging and accessible. How is it possible in one course to convey, for example, EU constitutional, administrative, and criminal law, subjects that command whole courses of their own in domestic legal systems? This book tries to address the conundrum in two ways.

First, it provides thorough but realistic coverage of the main topics taught on undergraduate courses (constitutional and institutional law, remedies, four freedoms, competition law). However, it then supplements those topics with chapters on specific subjects (eg consumer law, health law, social law, environmental law, criminal law) which are intended to illustrate how the core topics apply to those specific subject areas, as well as whetting the readers' appetite for more.

Secondly, the book brings a range of voices to the subject. This makes it unique in textbooks on EU law. Each chapter is written by a different author, enabling readers to learn from the experts within each specialist area. Some of the chapter authors also work for (or have worked for) EU institutions. This brings a different perspective to their work. The authors are also all experienced teachers. Between them, they have decades of practice explaining complex subjects to students. This experience has shaped their presentation of each topic. The authors are also distinguished researchers and their research has helped to frame the themes which are woven into each chapter. The authors come from a number of different countries (Belgium, the Czech Republic, Finland, Germany, Ireland, Italy, Luxembourg, the Netherlands, Spain, Sweden, the UK). This reflects the diverse legal heritage into which EU law must fit and from which EU law develops.

Of course, with such diversity comes the risk of lacunae or repetition. Our job, as editors, has been to minimize such risks, by coordinating the different contributions to keep overlaps, conflicts, and omissions to a minimum. We have also benefited from the substantial input of Abbey Nelms, the publishing editor of the first edition at OUP, Emily Hoyland, the publishing editor of the second edition, Amy Chard, the publishing editor of the third and fourth edition, later joined by Sera Singh, Sarah Jacobs for the fifth edition, and their team of anonymous referees, both academic and student, who have commented on every chapter, and helped to check not only for quality but also that the coverage is thorough but manageable.

That said, the close connections between the subject matter of the different chapters means that some crossover between chapters is inevitable. We thought it was useful, for instance, that some chapters included a case study of the same case, but from different perspectives, to allow the same issue to be viewed through various lenses. Our aim was to balance the twin objectives of uniformity and diversity. And while each author has painted a different picture of their particular aspect of EU law, we have assembled these separate images into a mosaic depicting the subject as a whole.

The Brexit vote occurred as the second edition of this book was being prepared; Brexit itself happened on 31 January 2020 as the third edition was being put to bed and the UK moved into transition. The UK has now fully left the EU and the fourth edition was written against the backcloth of the evolving new relationship between the UK and the EU and the fifth edition has been against the backcloth of the UK 'reset' of its relations with the EU under a Labour government. The decision of a major Member State to leave has profoundly shaken the EU; the UK is still working through the legal, economic, and political implications of the Brexit vote. What is becoming abundantly clear is that UK students will continue to need a deep knowledge of EU law to understand the Withdrawal Agreement (the divorce text based on Article 50 which contains important provisions on citizens' rights and the unique position of Northern Ireland under the Ireland/Northern Ireland Protocol now supplemented by the Windsor Framework), retained, now assimilated, EU law, and how EU law will still continue to affect those wishing to trade with the EU post-Brexit. The Brexit chapter has been revised to address some of these issues. However, this book has not become a book about Brexit. It is and continues to be a book about EU law, with reference to Brexit where and when it is relevant.

This book has been written with the image of the student firmly in mind. So each chapter has an introduction which sets out the main themes relevant on the topic and an outline of what is to follow, and a list of further reading at the end of each chapter enabling the student to take the material further. Each chapter also contains one or more case studies which may develop the ideas in the chapter or highlight a particular topic which merits further attention. Where appropriate, diagrams have also been included to provide a visual summary of complex points of law. This book does not, however, constitute legal advice.

We are hugely grateful to the editorial team at OUP, to Aswini Ashokkumar, our production contact, to Joy Ruskin-Tompkins for her excellent work as our copy editor on the first edition and this edition, Marie Gill as copy editor of the second and third editions, and to Julie Rowbotham on the fourth edition. We also owe a debt of gratitude to the authors for taking on the challenge of writing for this book and who have patiently put up with our streams of emails and questions, to the many referees for doing such a thorough job, and to our long-suffering families who have put up with us.

CSB and SP
December 2025

Outline contents

Detailed contents

Notes on contributors

Editors

Catherine Barnard is Professor of European Union Law and Employment Law and Senior Tutor Trinity College, University of Cambridge. She specializes in European Union law, labour and discrimination law, and competition law.

Steve Peers is a an expert on the European Union. He is a Professor in the School of Law at Royal Holloway, University of London. He is also the author of the popular blog *EU Law Analysis* which offers his, and a variety of well-respected contributors', views on all the key developments in EU law.

Contributors

Albertina Albors-Llorens is a Professor of European Union Law and Fellow of St John's College, University of Cambridge.

Michal Bobek is president of chamber at the Supreme Administrative Court, the Czech Republic, and Visiting Professor at the University of Vienna Law Faculty and the College of Europe in Bruges.

Kieran Bradley is a judge in a number of international administrative tribunals, an Adjunct Professor at Trinity College, Dublin, and a Visiting Professor at the Global School of Law, Lisbon, and the Autonomous University of Barcelona. He was formerly a judge of the European Union Civil Service Tribunal, the special adviser on Brexit to the Court of Justice, and a Director in the Legal Service of the European Parliament.

Paul Craig is Emeritus Professor of English Law, St John's College, University of Oxford.

András Csúri is a Senior Researcher at the Vienna University of Economics and Business.

Geert De Baere is a judge at the General Court of the European Union and currently serves as a President of Chamber. He is also an Associate Professor of International Law and EU Law at the University of Leuven, Belgium.

Leo Flynn is a Principal Legal Adviser at the European Commission and Visiting Professor at King's College London.

Darren Harvey is a Senior Lecturer in Law and Director of Undergraduate Studies at the Dickson Poon School of Law at King's College London.

Tamara K Hervey is Jean Monnet Professor of EU Law at City St George's, University of London.

Alicia Hinarejos is James McGill Professor of Law and Jean Monnet Chair in European Union Law at McGill University, Canada.

Herwig CH Hofmann is Professor of European and Transnational Public Law at the University of Luxembourg.

Geraint Howells is Established Professor, School of Law, University of Galway, and Visiting Professor at the University of Manchester.

Alison Jones is Professor of Law at King's College London and a solicitor at Freshfields Bruckhaus Deringer LLP.

Kati Kulovesi is Professor of International Law and Co-Director of the Centre for Climate Change, Energy and Environmental Law at the University of Eastern Finland.

Martín Martínez Navarro is a member of the European Commission's Legal Service and Visiting Professor at the Université Libre de Bruxelles and the College of Europe, Bruges.

Elisa Morgera is Professor of International Law and Sustainability, University of Durham Law School, UK, Professor of International and EU Environmental Law, University of Eastern Finland, and UN Special Rapporteur on Climate Change and Human Rights.

Niamh Nic Shuibhne is Professor of European Union Law at the University of Edinburgh.

Okeoghene Odudu is a Fellow of Emmanuel College and Professor of Competition Law in the Faculty of Law at the University of Cambridge.

Mia Rönnmar is Vice-Chancellor of Malmö University and Professor in Private and Labour Law at Lund University, Sweden.

Albert Sanchez-Graells is Professor of Economic Law at the University of Bristol.

Robert Schütze is Professor of European Union and Comparative Constitutional Law at Durham University and Luiss University (Rome).

Jukka Snell is Professor of European Law at the University of Turku, Finland.

Eleanor Spaventa is Professor of Law at Bocconi University, Italy, and Director of the Bocconi Lab in European Studies.

John R Spencer is Emeritus Professor, University of Cambridge.

Seita Vesa is Professor of Environmental Law at the University of Eastern Finland Law School, and a Principal Researcher at the Finnish Environment Institute.

Jenny Julén Votinius is Professor in Private and Labour Law at Lund University, Sweden.

Jonathon Watson has held various research positions, including at the WWU Münster in Germany, King's College London, and the Jagiellonian University in Poland.

Bruno de Witte is Professor Emeritus of European Union Law at Maastricht University, the Netherlands.

Table of abbreviations

ACTA	Anti-Counterfeiting Trade Agreement
AFSJ	Area of Freedom, Security and Justice
AG	Advocate General
AI	artificial intelligence
All	ER All England Law Reports
ATC	average total costs
ATP	absolute territorial protection
AVC	average variable costs
BER	block exemption regulation
BVerfG	Bundesverfassungsgericht (German Federal Constitutional Court)
BVerfGE	Entscheidungen des Bundesverfassungsgerichts (Reports of the Decisions of the [German] Federal Constitutional Court)
CAT	Competition Appeal Tribunal
CBAM	Carbon Border Adjustment Mechanism
CBD	Convention on Biological Diversity
CCP	Common Commercial Policy
CDDH	Steering Committee for Human Rights
CEAS	Common European Asylum System
CEE	charge of equivalent effect
CEN	European Committee for Standardization
CENELEC	European Committee for Electrotechnical Standardization
CFE	Conference on the Future of Europe
CFSP	Common Foreign and Security Policy
Ch	Chancery Division Reports
CIS	Common Implementation Strategy
CISA	Convention Implementing the Schengen Agreement
CJEU	Court of Justice of the European Union
CMLR	Common Market Law Reports
CORSIA	Carbon Offsetting and Reduction Scheme for Aviation
CRD	Citizens' Rights Directive 2004/38
CSDP	Common Security and Defence Policy
DMA	Digital Markets Act
DSA	Digital Services Act
DTC	Double Taxation Convention
EAEC	European Atomic Energy Community
EAW	European Arrest Warrant
EC	European Community
ECB	European Central Bank
ECHA	European Chemicals Agency
ECHR	European Convention on Human Rights
ECI	European Citizens' Initiative
ECJ	European Court of Justice
ECmHRR	European Commission on Human Rights Reports
ECN	European Competition Network
ECR	European Court Reports

ECSC	European Coal and Steel Community
ECtHR	European Court of Human Rights
EDC	European Defence Community
EDPB	European Data Protection Board
EEA	European Economic Area
EEAS	European External Action Service
EEC	European Economic Community
EES	European Employment Strategy
EFSF	European Financial Stability Fund
EFSM	European Financial Stability Mechanism
EFTA	European Free Trade Association
EIO	European Investigation Order
EMA	European Medicines Agency
EMS	European Monetary System
EMU	Economic and Monetary Union
ENISA	European Network and Information Security Agency
EPC	European Political Community
EPF	European Peace Facility
EPPO	European Public Prosecutor's Office
ESA	European Supervisory Authority
ESCB	European System of Central Banks
ESM	European Stability Mechanism
ESMA	European Securities and Markets Authority
ETS	Emission Trading Scheme
ETUC	European Trade Union Confederation
EU	European Union
EUIPO	European Union Intellectual Property Office
Euratom	European Atomic Energy Community
Eurojust	European Union Agency for Criminal Justice Cooperation
Europol	European Police Office
EUSS	EU Settlement Scheme
EWCA	Civ England and Wales Court of Appeal (Civil Division) Reports
EWCA	Crim England and Wales Court of Appeal (Criminal Division) Reports
EWHC	(Admin) England and Wales High Court (Administrative Division) Reports
EWHC	(QB) England and Wales High Court (Queen's Bench Division) Reports
FAO	United Nations Food and Agriculture Organization
FF55	Fit for 55
FHR	fundamental human rights
Frontex	European Border and Coast Guard Agency
GATS	General Agreement on Trade in Services
GATT	General Agreement on Tariffs and Trade
GBER	General Block Exemption Regulation
GDP	gross domestic product
GDPR	General Data Protection Regulation 2016/679
GPSD	General Product Safety Directive
HERA	Health Emergency Preparedness and Response Authority
ICAO	International Civil Aviation Organization

ICH	International Conference on Harmonisation of Technical Requirements for Registration of Pharmaceuticals for Human Use
ICJ	International Court of Justice
IGC	intergovernmental conference
ILM	International Legal Materials
ILO	International Labour Organization
IMA	Independent Monitoring Authority
IMF	International Monetary Fund
IMO	International Maritime Organization
INP	innominate non-legislative procedure
ITLOS	International Tribunal for the Law of the Sea
JHA	Justice and Home Affairs
JIT	joint investigation team
MEE	measure of equivalent effect
MEP	Member of the European Parliament
MFN	most favoured nation
MLA	mutual lega assistance
NATO	North Atlantic Treaty Organization
NCA	national competition authority
NDICI—Global	Europe Neighbourhood, Development and International Cooperation Instrument—Global Europe
NGEU	2020 Next Generation EU programme
NGO	non-government organization
NICA	Court of Appeal in Northern Ireland Decisions
NIKB	High Court of Justice in Northern Ireland King's Bench Division Decisions
nyr	not yet reported
OCT	overseas country or territory
OECD	Organisation for Economic Co-operation and Development
OEEC	Organisation for European Economic Co-operation
OGH	Oberster Gerichtshof (Austrian Supreme Court)
OJ	*Official Journal of the European Union*
OLAF	l'Office européen de lutte anti-fraude (European Anti-Fraud Office)
OLP	ordinary legislative procedure
OMT	Outright Monetary Transactions
ORRPI	overriding reason in the public interest
PCT	Primary Care Trust
PEPP	Public Emergency Purchase Programme
PIF	protection des intérêts financiers
PIM	person of independent means
PJCCM	Police and Judicial Cooperation in Criminal Matters
POP	Persistent Organic Pollutant
PSO	public service obligation
PSPP	Public Sector Purchase Programme
QB	Queen's Bench Reports
QMV	qualified majority voting
QR	quantitative restriction
REIO	regional economic international organization
RES	renewable energy sources
RRF	Recovery and Resilience Facility
SA	social assistance

SEA	Single European Act
SG	or L student grants or loans
SGEI	service of general economic interest
SIS	Schengen Information System
SLP	special legislative procedure
SME	small and medium enterprise
SOLAS	Convention States of the International Convention for the Safety of Life at Sea
SPS	sanitary and phytosanitary measures
SRM	Single Resolution Mechanism
SSGI	social service of general interest
SSM	Single Supervisory Mechanism
Stat	Statutes at Large
SURE	Support to mitigate Unemployment Risks in an Emergency
TBT	Technical Barriers to Trade
TCA	Trade and Cooperation Agreement
TCN	third-country national
TEU	Treaty on European Union
TFEU	Treaty on the Functioning of the European Union
TRIPS	Trade-Related Aspects of Intellectual Property Rights
TSCG	Treaty on Stability, Coordination and Governance in the EMU
UAF	Ukraine Assistance Fund
UCLAF	Unité de coordination de la lutte anti-fraude
UKSC	United Kingdom Supreme Court Reports
UN	United Nations
UNECE	UN Economic Commission for Europe
UNEP	United Nations Environment Program
UNFCCC	UN Framework Convention on Climate Change
UNTS	United Nations Treaty Series
VCLT	Vienna Convention on the Law of Treaties
VIS	Visa Information System
WEU	Western European Union
WHO	World Health Organization
WLR	Weekly Law Reports
WLUK	Westlaw United Kingdom Reports
WTO	World Trade Organization

Table of legislation

European Union

EU Treaties, Conventions and Agreements

Acts of the other EU Institutions

Directives

Regulations

Rules

Decisions

Recommendations

Opinions

National Jurisdictions

Czech Republic

France

Germany

Italy

Malta

Poland

Spain

United Kingdom statutes

United Kingdom Statutory Instruments

United States of America

International Instruments

World Trade Organization

Table of cases

European Cases – alphabetical

European Court of Justice–Numerical

Commission Cases

Competition Appeal Tribunal (CAT)

European Committee of Social Rights

European Court of Human Rights Cases

EFTA Court of Justice Cases

International Court of Justice

National Jurisdictions

Czech Republic

Denmark

France

Germany

1

Introduction

Catherine Barnard and Steve Peers

1 Introduction

For some people European Union (EU) law interferes with too many aspects of their lives. This was summed up by the headline in a UK paper: 'Bog standard: Brussels demands the same toilet flush across the Continent after discovering Brits use the most water.'[1] This story has it all: mad Brussels bureaucrats excessively regulating even how we go to the toilet; 'Loo couldn't make it up', cried one tabloid newspaper. Yet a closer look reveals a different picture. As the European Commission pointed out, toilet flushing accounts for about a third of total household water consumption.[2] Much of this water use is unnecessary. So an eco-label can help buyers purchase toilets that will save water and money. Eco-labelling measures already existed for washing machines and dishwashers, and it was perfectly logical to take steps to help people buy more water-efficient toilets. In a single market where products are being sold across borders, this is best done at EU level.[3] The question, then, is who is right: the tabloid press or the European Commission?

The story about the loo flush raises in microcosm some of the biggest questions facing the EU today: what should it be doing, how should it be doing it, and how should it be communicating what it is doing? A bottom-up approach (no pun intended) would suggest that loo flushing should be a matter for national law; a top-down single market perspective would suggest that the EU should intervene when the movement of goods across borders is affected.

Let's assume that the Commission is right and the EU should act. If so, how intensive should that action be? The eco-labelling award scheme reveals an imaginative approach to regulation. The use of these eco-labels is voluntary:[4] industries apply for the label if they

[1] www.dailymail.co.uk/news/article-2480829/Bog-standard-Brussels-demands-toilet-flush-Continent-discovering-Brits-use-water.html#ixzz2llsEoH4v.

[2] https://www.nidirect.gov.uk/articles/saving-water-home.

[3] A Commission study estimates that even with only 10 per cent market penetration for eco-label toilets, the cumulative savings for households alone across the EU would exceed £330 million (€388.5 million). With 20 per cent market penetration, that figure would roughly double.

[4] http://ec.europa.eu/environment/ecolabel/information-and-contacts.html.

choose to benefit from the kudos that goes with it. They may choose not to. However, if they do apply, their product needs to comply with the criteria set for each product group (eg a decision[5] adopted under powers conferred by European Parliament and Council Regulation 66/2010 on the EU Ecolabel).[6]

Thus, contrary to popular misconception, EU rules are not all of the command and control kind ('all bananas must be straight'). The EU has experimented with different types of regulation to create flexibility in the operation of its rules. This flexibility is provided by the law and, as this book will show, the law is central to the operation of the EU.

Indeed, the EU itself is a legal construct.[7] It was born out of treaties and its subsequent development has been marked by successive Treaty amendments. One of the earliest major research projects on the EU described the process of its evolution as 'integration through law';[8] and the Court of Justice, the supreme court of the EU, has been at the heart of that process. Of course, law and politics go hand in hand, and no lawyer would deny the important role played by politicians in both driving forward and shaping the development of the EU, particularly faced with seismic forces—the fall of the Berlin Wall, 9/11, the sovereign debt crisis, the refugee crisis, the decision of the British voters to leave the EU (Brexit), the rule of law crisis (see later in this chapter), the consequences of the war in Ukraine, and an increasingly hostile geopolitical climate. Although the hegemony of law may have waned somewhat over recent years, as problems have arisen which are not immediately amenable to legal resolution (eg how to deal with very high levels of youth unemployment, how to get funding to Ukraine), law remains central to the EU project. And it is the law, set in this broader political context, which is the subject matter of this book.

2 The development of EU law

In the early days, the EU focused upon economic integration: the free movement of goods, persons, capital, and services,[9] collectively known as the four freedoms, along with competition law and control of government support to industry, known as 'State aid'.[10] The basic idea was simple but fundamental: due to closer trade ties, States would become dependent on each other and thus the imperative to go to war would be reduced.

However, the material scope (ie the subject matter) of EU law has been widening beyond these issues for many years.[11] For example, while the original Treaty establishing what was then the European Economic Community (EEC) made some reference to social policy, due to concerns about the impact of economic integration upon social standards, the EU has since developed a significant body of law in this area.[12] Owing to growing concern about the environment and consumers, including the possible impact of economic integration upon national environment and consumer law, the EU has also developed law in these areas too.[13] Even an area of law which in principle the EU largely leaves to

[5] See eg Commission Decision 2013/641 establishing the ecological criteria for the award of the EU Ecolabel for flushing toilets and urinals (OJ [2013] L299/38).

[6] OJ [2010] L27/1.

[7] This phrase was used by the then British Attorney General, Dominic Grieve, in a newspaper interview (http://www.telegraph.co.uk/news/politics/10469453/Dominic-Grieve-were-a-changing-nation-but-Im-an-optimist.html).

[8] M Cappelletti, M Seccombe, and JHH Weiler (eds), *Integration through Law* (Berlin: De Gruyter, 1985); cf R Schuetze, '"Integration-through-Law": Grand Theory, Revisionist History' (2025) 4 *European Law Open* 162.

[9] For details, see chapters 11–16.

[10] See respectively chapters 17 and 18.

[11] For a more detailed overview of the development of the EU, see chapter 2.

[12] For details, see chapter 19. See also Case C-19/23 *Denmark* v *Council and Parliament (minimum wages)* EU:C:2025:865.

[13] For details, see chapters 22 and 23.

the Member States to regulate—health care—is significantly affected by the economic integration process.[14] This is the 'spillover' effect which Jean Monnet, one of the founding fathers of the EU project, hoped would occur once the process of integration had started. As the theory of neofunctionalism describes it, integration in one sector necessitates integration in another sector to ensure that the advantage of integration in the first sector is maximized. To give a concrete example, Member States could legitimately obstruct the free movement of goods (such as magazines coming from Germany to Austria, magazines which contain adverts for tobacco products where those adverts are allowed in Germany but not in Austria) due to concerns about consumer protection.[15] The EU, witnessing this legitimate obstruction to trade, would argue that it, the EU, should harmonize rules in this area (eg a directive banning tobacco advertising) in order to facilitate free movement of goods. In this way the EU's powers extend beyond just regulating technical standards of, say, lightbulbs, and touch on more sensitive matters, like the regulation of advertising which in turn affects fundamental rights.

Taking this spillover effect one stage further, if exporters of goods within the EU are really to benefit from the economies of scale offered by the single market, then they need to enjoy the certainty offered by having a single currency. It was this biggest step of all that was launched by the Maastricht Treaty in 1992, which set out a framework for the EU to create an economic and monetary union (EMU). The majority of Member States now share a single currency and, in connection with this, the EU coordinates Member States' fiscal and economic policies. The intensity of this coordination has strengthened since the single currency project began to face increasing difficulties in light of the economic crisis, beginning in 2008, and it became necessary for some Member States effectively to 'bail out' other Member States in order for the currency to survive.

In the same vein, the EU agreed to further integration of Member States' economic policies and greater political control of those policies by the EU institutions, as regards eurozone States.[16] The centripetal forces at play point to ever-greater centralization—at the very time when citizens (and populist parties) in a number of countries are calling for a repatriation of powers to the Member States. This tension between the need for effective governance of the European project while respecting State autonomy and diversity at national level has tormented the EU since its inception. For some, this tension is creative and leads to better solutions in the longer term, preventing the EU from overreaching itself. For others, it has handicapped the EU in its ability to respond to the crisis—the German refusal to agree to Eurobonds (the joint pooling of some or all of the eurozone States' government debt), widely seen as an important potential mechanism for resolving the financial crisis, was a case in point. The German refusal, wholly comprehensible in terms of domestic politics, shows that neofunctionalism is too simplistic a theory to describe the complex interactions in the EU. Governments, particularly in Germany and France, continue to call the shots when it really matters, and this intergovernmentalism is reflected in the role of the European Council, now one of the most important EU institutions.[17] In its strongest form, objection to EU integration led to the UK vote to leave the EU—despite that country's many opt-outs from EU rules.

The EU has also become a major forum for integration as regards issues which, at first sight, are non-economic. While the EU always had a common policy on trade with third (ie non-EU) countries, known as the 'common commercial policy', and many of its internal policies have a significant external dimension (eg EU environment and digital policies), the EU has also taken steps towards creating a Common Foreign and Security

[14] For details, see chapter 21.

[15] For details, see chapters 12 and 16. For more on the concept of neofunctionalism, see chapter 2.

[16] For details, see chapter 19.

[17] For details, see chapter 3.

Policy, including defence issues,[18] a policy which has become ever more significant in the light of the war in Ukraine.[19] In addition, the EU has increasingly addressed issues within the scope of justice and home affairs, matters traditionally seen as lying at the heart of national sovereignty, in particular criminal law and immigration and asylum matters.[20] In practice, even these issues have important links with economic integration, since the abolition of border controls between most Member States has meant that it is easier for alleged criminals to flee from one Member State to another, and harder to apply a purely national policy on asylum and immigration.

Along with this widening of the material scope of EU law, the EU's territorial scope has increased greatly too, with its membership expanding from 6 to 28 Member States (now 27 Member States);[21] many argue that this process should go further and faster to include countries such as Serbia, Macedonia, and Ukraine. Others say that the EU is in no position to enlarge further. Serious Treaty reform is needed first—improving the operation of the institutions, the functioning of the eurozone, greater use of qualified majority voting—but at the moment this seems impossible to deliver due to the requirement for unanimous agreement of all the Member States and referenda in some countries. Following the Brexit referendum, Member States are wary of referenda.

Over the years, EU law has not just widened its material and territorial scope, but it has also developed a complex institutional framework for the adoption and enforcement of its law, establishing both a political and a judicial system to that end.[22] Like any complex legal system, the EU has recognized basic principles that govern the application of that system, as well as rules which govern its administration.[23] One of these key principles is the requirement to protect human rights,[24] which became increasingly important as (for example) EU law concerned itself with issues (eg criminal law and asylum) that impact upon civil liberties,[25] and as EU austerity policies (which were intended to address the economic and financial crisis linked to EMU) had an impact upon social rights.[26] Another fundamental value of the EU is respect for democracy and the rule of law, principles which have been facing significant challenges in certain Member States and causing major problems for the institutions to address them.[27] The disrespect of the rule of law by some Member States undermines the values espoused in Article 2 TEU which the Member States are committed to upholding, and has created deep tension in the EU and between the Member States. This had led the Court to find in *Commission* v *Hungary* that Article 2 TEU is a free standing provision and legally binding in the case of 'manifest and particularly serious breaches of one or more values common to the Member States.[28]

More broadly, the constitutional and administrative law of the EU as a whole poses questions about the nature of national sovereignty within the EU legal order and the EU's fidelity to basic constitutional principles, such as the separation of powers.[29] The ever-growing impact of EU law has also been accelerated by the very nature of EU law, because (for many Member States) EU law has a much greater force within national legal systems than most other international treaties.[30] Indeed, there is an important debate as

[18] On all of these issues, see chapter 26.

[19] F Fabbrini, *The EU Constitution in Time of War: Legal Responses to Russia's Aggression Against Ukraine* (Oxford: Oxford University Press, 2025).

[20] For details, see respectively chapters 24 and 25.

[21] For an overview of EU enlargement, see chapter 2.

[22] On the political system, see chapter 3; on the judicial system, see chapter 10; and on the decision-making process, see chapter 5.

[23] For details, see chapter 8.

[24] For details, see chapter 9.

[25] See chapters 24 and 25.

[26] See chapters 19 and 20.

[27] See eg chapter 9.

[28] See eg Case C-448/23 *Commission v Poland* (*Ultra vires review of the case law of the Court—Primacy of EU law*), EU:C:2025:975; Case C-769/22 *Commission v Hungary* ('*Values of the European Union*'), EU:C:2026:326.

[29] For a detailed discussion, see chapter 4.

[30] For details, see chapter 6.

to whether EU law can still be regarded as a form of international law at all, or whether it has become *sui generis* (meaning, 'in a class by itself').[31] For the Court, the answer is clear: 'unlike standard international treaties, the Community Treaties established a new legal order, integrated into the legal systems of the Member States on their entry into force and which is binding on their courts'.[32] Crucially, and in recognition of the sovereignty-limiting function of EU membership, the Court continued: 'The Member States have limited, in the fields defined by the Treaties, their sovereign rights, for the benefit of that new legal order possessing its own institutions and whose subjects comprise not only Member States but also their nationals.'

This raises even more fundamental questions—does the EU have a constitution, following the demise of the Constitutional Treaty in 2005,[33] and if so, what sort? The formal answer is yes. As the Court has said, the EU legal order 'created and developed by the subsequent treaties, most recently by the Treaty of Lisbon, has its own constitutional framework and founding principles, a particularly sophisticated institutional structure and a complete set of legal rules which ensure its functioning, and enjoys autonomy from the law of the Member States and from international law'.[34] However, as the book will show, the EU has a special brand of constitutionalism which accommodates uniformity and diversity, as well as the role of the centre and that of national and sub-national actors. This has led to an increasingly sophisticated debate about the role of multi-level governance (the idea that there are various interacting authority structures at work) *within* the EU. This stems in turn from the EU's judicial system, which is likewise more advanced than that of many international bodies.[35] And the growth of EU agencies, and the parallel development of EU administrative law, also aim to give stronger effect to EU rules.[36] But all of these developments challenge national legal, administrative, and judicial autonomy—just as national autonomy over *substantive* law in many fields is challenged by the EU's integration process.

But it also raises questions as to how the EU relates to other major international bodies *outside*.[37] How open can and should the EU be to these external bodies? This brings us to the question of autonomy, an increasingly important tenet of EU law. The EU talks about the autonomy of the EU: economic, security, and, most importantly for the purposes of this book, legal autonomy. We return to this in the next section.

3 Themes

The chapters of this book are linked by overarching themes, which can be introduced in the form of two questions: 'What should the EU be doing?' and 'How should the EU go about doing it?'

The question of *what* the EU should do is linked to the concept of '*output* legitimacy', that is, the EU proving its value to the public by showing that it is effective in contributing to the achievement of objectives which have wide public support (eg economic growth and job creation). The question of *how* the EU should accomplish these

[31] For details of this debate, see chapter 7.

[32] Case C-448/23 *Commission v Poland*, EU:C:2025:975, para 165 citing Case 26/62 *van Gend & Loos*, EU:C:1963:1, p 12; Case C-430/21 *RS* (*Effect of the decisions of a constitutional court*), EU:C:2022:99, para 47.

[33] On the failed attempt to draw up a Constitutional Treaty for the EU, see further chapter 2.

[34] Case C-448/23 *Commission v Poland*, EU:C:2025:975, para 166, citing Opinion 2/13 (*Accession of the European Union to the ECHR*), EU:C:2014:2454, paras 158 and 170; and Case C-157/21 *Poland v Parliament and Council*, EU:C:2022:98, para 143).

[35] See chapter 10. [36] See chapter 8.

[37] See further chapter 26 and the case studies in chapters 8 and 9.

tasks is linked to the concept of '*input* legitimacy', that is, how fair and democratic is the process by which the EU takes decisions. These two types of legitimacy are linked, because if the EU tries to do more things, more questions are likely to be raised about its democratic credentials.[38] Indeed, the two forms of legitimacy might come into direct conflict, where, for instance, an attempt to make the EU more effective by removing Member States' vetoes over a policy area (which will make it easier for the EU to take decisions) could be seen as a reduction in democratic legitimacy, from the point of view of a national parliament (which will no longer have full sovereignty over decisions in that policy area).

The successive crises in recent years (the financial crisis, the refugee crisis, terrorism fears, Brexit, Covid-19, war in Ukraine, climate change, geopolitical instability) have exacerbated the tensions between these aspects of legitimacy. The EU's initial response to these crises has pushed in opposite directions. Some have been addressed by more EU regulation, to ensure output legitimacy: more EU laws on banking regulation, economic governance, counterterrorism, immigration, and asylum; and more powers for EU bodies such as the European Central Bank, Europol, and the EU border control agency.[39] But this reaction prompts a parallel concern about input legitimacy—in that individual Member States (and, by extension, their voters) have even less control over these politically sensitive issues. When the chips are down, as we saw during the pandemic, most voters look to their own States to step in and help out.

3.1 **Input legitimacy**

The EU has various systems in place to help achieve input legitimacy: the doctrines of separation of powers,[40] the vertical division of competences between the States and the EU,[41] and a powerful judicial system[42] which has been active in developing the 'general principles of EU law' (including the principles of proportionality, the rule of law (transparency, legality, legal certainty, and legitimate expectations), good administration, information-related rights (freedom of information and data protection), and procedural rights (the right to be heard, the right to an effective judicial remedy, and additional rights of the defence)) as tools to review the activities of the EU legislature and executive, as well as those of the Member States when acting within the scope of EU law.[43] The EU is also highly conscious that it needs to ensure that EU law is operational in the individual Member States which led to the creation of the key principles of direct effect (the enforceability of EU law in the national courts) and supremacy or primacy of EU law (EU law takes precedence over all conflicting national law, including provisions of the national constitutions). These principles are described as 'the essential characteristics of the EU legal order arising from that autonomous nature'.[44] The Court says that these essential characteristics of EU law have given rise to 'a structured network of principles, rules and mutually interdependent legal relations binding the European Union and its Member States reciprocally and binding its Member States to each other'. In other words, when acceding to the EU, the Member States accept the rules of membership including the autonomy of EU law but in so doing are able to enjoy the benefits of membership, including full participation in the single market.

But what happens when one or more Member States do not comply with those rules? This brings us to 'the rule of law' crisis. Discussed in various chapters of this book, the rule of law crisis concerns certain Member States deliberately disregarding the rule of law

[38] For details, see chapter 2.
[39] See chapters 19, 24, and 25.
[40] For details, see chapter 4.
[41] For details, see chapter 5.
[42] For details, see chapter 10.
[43] For details, see chapter 8.
[44] Case C-448/23 *Commission v Poland*, EU:C:2025:975, para 167.

by, for example, interfering with the appointment of the judiciary, by stacking the courts with their supporters. Not only does this undermine the independence of the judiciary it also means there is a lack of trust in the State's ability to enforce EU rules at domestic level.

The other essential element of EU law is the growing protection of human rights in the EU legal order, which was restructured in 2009 to provide for a binding EU Charter of Fundamental Rights and an obligation for the EU to sign up to the European Convention on Human Rights (ECHR), which resulted in a draft treaty to this end (though the EU Courts then stalled the ECHR accession process, at least for a while).[45] Specific tensions between human rights and security objectives can be seen in the regulation of immigration and asylum law (ie the entry and residence of non-EU citizens) by the EU[46] and between human rights and the power for national authorities to decide which citizens of other EU Member States can come into the territory and stay there.[47] The protection of human rights has become directly linked to the creation of EU citizenship: the introduction of EU citizenship has had an impact on the way in which the Court of Justice has viewed nationals of one Member State who move to another Member State.[48] This, in itself, has raised further questions about the legitimacy of the Court of Justice within the EU system, a system based on notions of separation of powers.

Moreover, these fundamental questions about the EU's legitimacy raise a further set of questions, in particular: 'How much should the EU do, as compared to its Member States?' and 'How should EU law reconcile tensions between different objectives—particularly between economic and non-economic objectives?' Of course, the answers to these questions might change over time, or be different in the various policy fields. Again, the two questions are necessarily linked: the more that the EU gets involved with a particular policy area, the less capacity for Member States to make their own individual decisions about how to balance economic and non-economic objectives in that area. These questions could be described as raising respectively a *vertical* issue—the 'division of powers' between the EU and its Member States—and a *horizontal* issue—regarding the relative priority of economic over non-economic objectives.

If the EU does act and a Member State objects, then it is the Court of Justice which polices the boundary. Its decisions have influenced the level of EU intervention: the more the Court checks whether the criteria for EU action have been satisfied, the more likely it is to strike down a measure. In practice, its review has been generally light touch, with one notable exception, the decision in *Tobacco Advertising I*.[49] This decision highlights the tension between input and output legitimacy: if the EU wants to deliver in a particular policy area, it needs to have the powers and the ability to exercise them in the way that it chooses. However, this may come at the price of national sovereignty.

What if individuals object to what the EU is doing? Do they have a voice? If that voice means bringing a case to court to challenge the EU's use of its powers, the Court of Justice has made it difficult for individuals to do so directly before the EU Courts.[50] If that voice means voting in parliamentary elections, then many think their voice is drowned out or the politicians are not responding to what they want. In some Member States, like France, the Netherlands, and Hungary, this has led to growing support for populist parties, and in the UK it led to Brexit.[51] The EU has failed to inspire much loyalty or love among many of its citizens. This may be because it is hard to love a customs union or a common market on which much of the EU's output legitimacy is based.

[45] For further details, see chapter 9. [46] For further details, see chapter 25.
[47] For further details, see chapters 13 and 16. [48] For further details, see chapter 13.
[49] For details, see chapter 11. [50] For details, see chapter 10. [51] See chapter 27.

3.2 **Output legitimacy**

The EU's output legitimacy is explicitly or implicitly linked to its achievements in substantive EU law—beginning with the original core issues of economic integration,[52] as extended to economic and monetary union,[53] and to other policy areas such as health care and social policy.[54] Successful delivery of these policies has been backed up by the creation—by the Court of Justice—of a system of remedies at domestic level,[55] now significantly expanded by the use of Article 47 of the Charter. For some, this is judicial activism; for others, this is necessary to ensure the effective application of the rules Member States voluntarily signed up to.

And the EU has reinforced its internal policies through parallel action on the external stage. Reforms to the EU's competence in this field have strengthened the EU's ability to negotiate international agreements, particularly as regards international trade.[56] Paradoxically, the EU's success in achieving the four freedoms (free movement of goods, persons, services, and capital) has raised fundamental questions as to the ability of nation-States to control their own borders and keep out goods (horsemeat), persons (large-scale immigration from Central and Eastern Europe, the Polish plumber), and capital (foreign ownership of key industries) they do not want.[57] Nationals in some Member States want to pull up the drawbridge and keep out all that is foreign. EU law stops their governments from doing this. However, with the growing power of Russia and China, the EU's position is beginning to change. States, enabled by the EU, are increasingly focusing on economic security and EU rules, like the Foreign Direct Investment Regulation,[58] permit this.

However, the major challenge to the EU's biggest claim for output legitimacy—that it is able to deliver growth and prosperity—came with the financial crisis. Some blamed EU policies for contributing to the crisis in the first place; others criticized the EU's laggard, piecemeal response to the crisis for making a bad situation worse. Those living in countries in receipt of a 'bailout' blamed the EU/IMF (International Monetary Fund) for the pain they suffered as a result of the austerity policies which were imposed on them as a condition of receiving financial assistance. Nevertheless, even in these countries the majority view was that they would prefer to remain within the EU than out. This must say something about the safety net the EU continues to offer to many countries.

The crisis also posed major challenges to the welfare state. Traditionally seen as an area of national competence, EU law and policies are increasingly having a direct or indirect impact. First, austerity measures led to significant cuts in pension and social welfare provision, whether it be care for the elderly, social benefits, or health care.

Secondly, eurozone countries which are no longer free to devalue their currencies in order to regain competitiveness were forced into a cycle of 'internal devaluation', a euphemism for cuts to wages and labour standards; standards which have often been the result of decades of struggle by the trade union movement and the International Labour Organization (ILO). This is a direct challenge to the European Social Model, which has long been regarded as one of the proudest achievements of EU Member States.[59] This is not the first challenge to the EU's social model. The enlargement of the EU to include the Central and Eastern European States created opportunities for workers from those States but risks for workers from wealthier States who saw their wages being undercut by EU migrant workers.[60] The advent of the Covid-19 pandemic posed even greater challenges for welfare states and ultimately the EU.

[52] For details, see chapters 11–17.
[53] For details, see chapter 19.
[54] For details, see chapters 20–26.
[55] For details, see chapter 6.
[56] For details, see chapter 26.
[57] For details, see chapter 16.
[58] Regulation 2019/452 (OJ [2019] L791/1). A revised version is pending.
[59] For details, see chapter 20.
[60] See further F Vandenbroucke, C Barnard, and G De Baere (eds), *A European Social Union after the Crisis* (Cambridge: Cambridge University Press, 2017).

Thirdly, as the control on the use of public money gets tighter, there is ever-greater pressure from the EU for States to open up the provision of public services to competition in order to obtain value for money. For some States, this has long been public policy; for others it is a recent development. Increasingly the Court of Justice has been applying pressure on national systems: it has ruled that the four freedoms and competition rules, including State aid, apply to public services where those services are seen as an economic activity.[61] However, there has been some sensitivity to the necessity, particularly in the case of SSGIs—social services of general interest (eg home care for the elderly)—that EU law should not interrupt the provision of quality services. So EU law has carved out some exceptions to the rules.[62]

This tension between the economic and non-economic objectives of the EU can be seen played out in other areas too. For example, in the field of environmental law, where initially there was a perceived conflict between environmental and economic objectives, EU law now attempts to reconcile these objectives, either by trying to strike a balance between competing environmental and economic objectives or by integrating environmental and economic objectives through market-based mechanisms and other innovative regulatory approaches, in particular as regards climate change.[63] However, there are also concerns that the rush to greening is putting significant pressure on the budgets of Member States. The breadth and complexity of the regulation has also drawn considerable criticism.[64] Similar criticisms have been made of its digital policy: the relevant legislation, while groundbreaking, is too much and too complex.[65] This has led to the adoption of 'Omnibus' measures removing some of the regulatory burden created by EU legislation,[66] which in turn have attracted criticism for reducing the level of ambition.

4 Conclusion

The EU has fundamentally changed the relationship between States and their citizens. It has also delivered reforms in major policy areas and improved the daily quality of life for individuals—just think about low-cost air travel; and the ready availability of abundant, good, varied food (pasta, panettone, pancetta). However, national politicians have been woefully bad at explaining the benefits of EU membership; and very quick to blame the EU for things that go wrong.

The EU, too, has also been poor at making a successful case for its own existence (and financial skulduggery has sullied its own image and undermined trust in the EU). The justification for the existence of the EU based on delivering peace in Europe[67] no longer seems relevant to younger generations. So a case based on output legitimacy needs to be made all the more strongly for the EU to have legitimacy. And when the EU fails to deliver on this, this precipitates a crisis in confidence in the EU: 'What has the EU ever done for me?'

But let's consider the counterfactual. What if the EU ceased to exist, would there be a need for an equivalent body? In a highly globalized world with two power blocs, the US and China, and now with Russia proving a serious threat, European states would need to form some kind of unit to get their voice heard on the global stage. It may be that if the EU had to be recreated, it wouldn't look the same as it does now. But it is very likely that some pan-European body would be created (as can be seen with newly created customs unions

[61] For details, see chapter 18. [62] See chapters 18 and 21.
[63] For further details, see chapter 22.
[64] https://www.ft.com/content/076945ae-e7cb-4336-b0c5-a0fb33432a6e.
[65] https://www.ft.com/content/cbfd8af4-b3a8-4ade-9831-6cb7cf836745.
[66] https://finance.ec.europa.eu/news/omnibus-package-2025-04-01_en. [67] cf xx.

emerging across the globe, such as the one between Russia, Belarus, and Kazakhstan, and the East African Community). The question then is, what would the European version look like—and how different would it be from the EU we have today? While the EU could be better, would EU citizens be worse off without it? The aim of this book is to help readers understand what the EU is and why.

The book covers a range of issues, crudely divided into 'constitutional law' issues and 'substantive law' issues. The former concerns the constitution of the EU (the foundation Treaties, the Charter of Fundamental Rights, the EU's institutions and agencies, their powers), but also the effect that EU law has on national law (the principles of direct effect, supremacy, and state liability when things go wrong). It also looks at the 'remedies' provided by EU law, enabling judicial challenges of EU acts directly but also of national acts which operate in the field of EU law.

The substantive law of the EU concerns the so-called four freedoms (free movement of goods, persons, services, and capital), which are in essence about negative integration, stopping Member States from interfering with trade unless they have very good reasons for doing so. But it also covers the EU's positive action in ever-growing areas—such as health care, social policy, the environment, consumer protection, and crucially monetary union.

This book cannot hope to be comprehensive, but it aims to provide a good grounding for all students wishing to understand more about the EU's legal system. Students can then decide for themselves whether the EU is a good thing—or not.

2

Development of the EU

Paul Craig

1 Introduction

This chapter charts the development of what is now the EU. It is a complex and interesting story, and one that is still unfolding. It cannot be understood without an appreciation of the proximate connection between the rise of nationalism in the nineteenth century, its excesses in the twentieth, and the movement towards European integration. This is considered in the next section, which is followed by the first concrete steps towards European integration in the form of the European Coal and Steel Community in 1951 and the way in which this led towards the European Economic Community in 1957, after the failure of more ambitious attempts at integration in the mid-1950s. The period thereafter was relatively stable, since there were no major amendments to the original EEC Treaty until the passage of the Single European Act 1986 (SEA). The rationale for this reform is examined in section 4, and is followed in section 5 by consideration of the Treaty amendments that occurred between 1986 and the end of the millennium, the Maastricht Treaty, the Treaty of Amsterdam, and the Treaty of Nice. The dawn of the new century seemed to herald yet more piecemeal Treaty reform, but this expectation was undermined by efforts at more comprehensive Treaty reform. The story of these reform efforts, including the drafting and demise of the Constitutional Treaty in 2004, followed by the successful ratification of the Lisbon Treaty in 2009, is told in section 6. The hope that an expanded EU might develop in relative calm was, however, undermined by the financial crisis, Brexit (the UK's decision to leave the EU), and the migration crisis, which are discussed in section 7. The chapter concludes by introducing theories that seek to explain why integration has occurred.

There are a number of related themes that are central to the emergence and development of the EEC from its inception to the EU as it currently exists. Three are especially noteworthy.

There is, first, discourse concerning the motivation behind European integration, and the relative influence of Member States and the very institutions they created, which has been at the centre of much theorizing concerning the EU.

A second theme concerns the relative importance of what are termed output legitimacy and input legitimacy. The former sees the EU's legitimacy primarily in terms of the beneficial outcomes that flow from its existence. This was the traditional conception of legitimacy that underpinned the vision of those who created the EEC, with peace and prosperity being seen as the positive outcomes of integration. By the 1980s, political and academic commentators were increasingly concerned with input legitimacy. It was clear that the European Community (EC) was wielding considerable power over significant areas, which was not purely economic. This led to greater attention on democratic legitimacy. There was a growing literature on the EC's democratic deficit, and the extent to which an increase in the power of the European Parliament might alleviate this problem. Enlargement from an EEC with 6 Member States to an EU of 27 was another factor in the shift to concern over input legitimacy, with discussion as to how EU decision-making procedures would have to be modified to render the EU governable and workable. The relative shift in focus from output to input legitimacy has been further fuelled by the financial crisis, which cast a long shadow over the promise that the EU will deliver prosperity, and, albeit in different ways, by Brexit and the migration crisis.

The third theme is related to the second, albeit distinct. It concerns the balance between economic and social objectives within EU integration. The initial focus of the EEC was on economic integration, as evidenced by the very name European Economic Community. However, the original Treaty of Rome that established the EEC was not solely concerned with economic matters, and this has been reinforced by many subsequent Treaty amendments, which deal with matters that are as much social as they are economic, and by the subsequent change in nomenclature from EEC to EC, European Community, and then to EU, European Union. The balance between the economic and the social within the EU nonetheless remains contestable, ever more so in light of the financial crisis, where austerity measures at EU and national levels have had a significant impact on the social dimension of EU policies.

Alongside the five major amendments to the Treaties that are the foundation of EU law (and previously EEC/EC law), there have been seven enlargements of the EU over the years. These key steps in the EU's development can be visualized in the form of a timeline (see Fig. 2.1).[1]

2 Nationalism and the origins of the EU

There is no doubt that ideas of European unity can be traced to the late seventeenth century, when a prominent English Quaker, William Penn, called for a European Parliament.[2] There is, however, also little doubt that the more immediate push for European integration can be dated to the nineteenth century. It is worth recalling that, for example, Germany and Italy only became unified States in 1871, drawing together what had hitherto been groups of smaller States, duchies, or principalities, some of which were ruled by foreign powers. A powerful factor in the unification process in both countries was the surge in nationalist sentiment, which resonated in politics, philosophy, and

[1] For more detail, see the interactive map and timeline of the EU's development, which can be found in the online resources which accompany this book.

[2] D Urwin, *The Community of Europe: A History of European Integration* (2nd edn, London: Longman, 1995); J Pinder and S Usherwood, *The European Union: A Very Short Introduction* (3rd edn, Oxford: Oxford University Press, 2013).

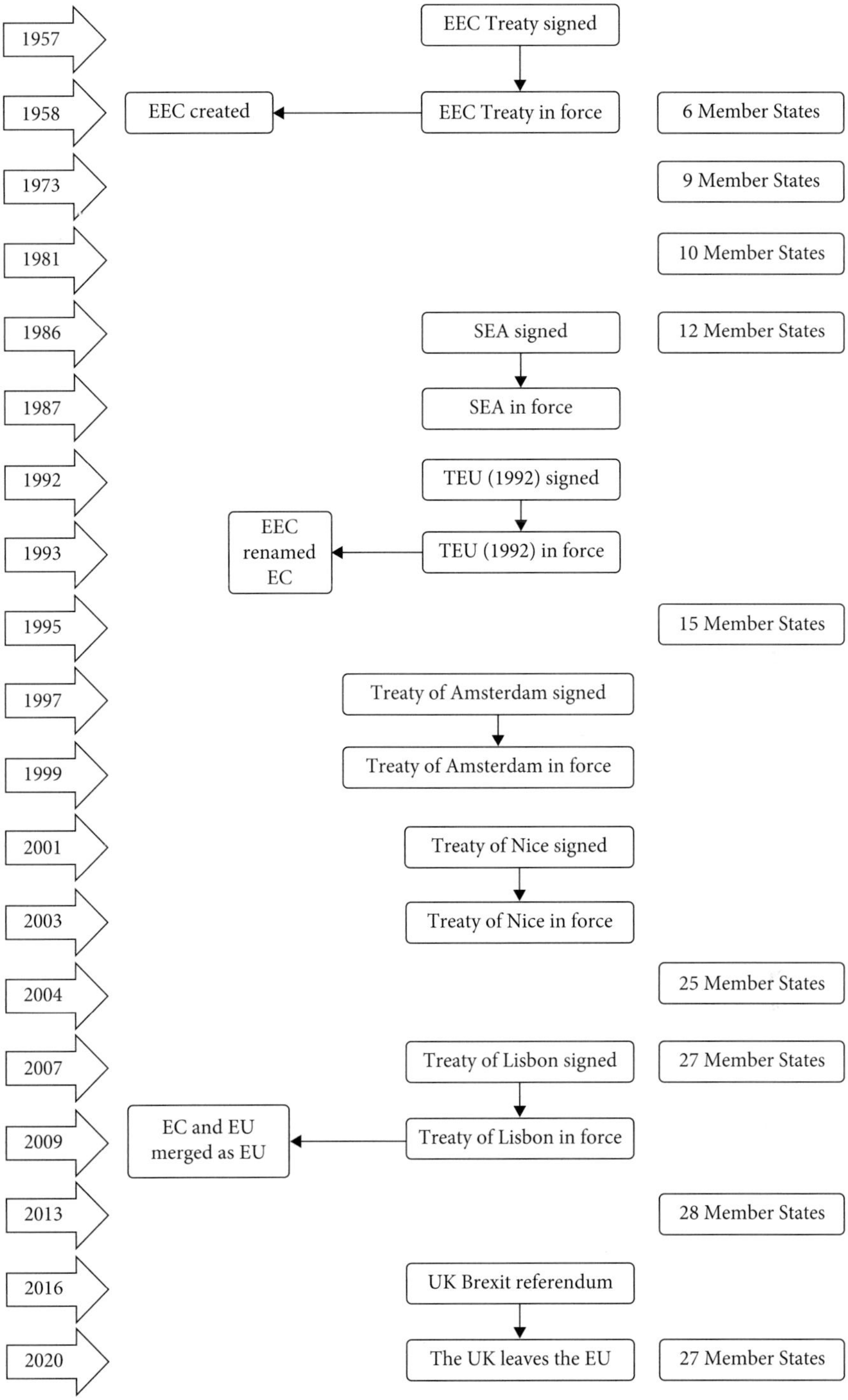

Fig. 2.1 Timeline of the EU's development

literature. Fichte in Germany and Manzoni in Italy were but two prominent proponents of this nationalist ethos. It can be traced back to the beginning of the nineteenth century, in reaction to French dominance of Europe and the privations that resulted from Napoleonic campaigns in Central Europe.

There was much that was positive about this nationalist sentiment, which was initially directed towards attainment of unified States from disparate principalities and the like, combined with the desire to be free from foreign control. It was also driven by the strong feeling that those who shared a common language and culture should naturally coexist in a single political entity, the corollary being that pre-existing boundaries between principalities were 'unnatural'.

The darker side of nationalism became apparent towards the end of the nineteenth and the beginning of the twentieth centuries. It was driven in part by economic imperatives, but in part also by the desire to assert the prominence of a particular national identity. The battles were initially fought on borrowed terrain, with nation-States in Europe engaged in the carving up of Africa. The First and Second World Wars brought the clash of nation-States to the very forefront of the European stage. While there is considerable debate about the causes of both conflicts, the aggressive and external effects of nationalism were significant in relation to both conflicts.

The culmination of the Second World War generated a widespread feeling that there had to be a way of organizing international affairs to reduce, if not eradicate, the possibility of such national conflict recurring. This explains the founding of the United Nations in 1945, where the guiding rationale was to resolve disputes through dialogue rather than conflict, and to institutionalize international peacekeeping and dispute settlement where force was required.

The founding of the EEC was another response to the horrors of two world wars. During the war, the Resistance movement had strongly supported the idea of a united Europe, to replace the destructive forces of nationalism.[3] However, the integration movement faltered after the war, especially after the electoral defeat in the UK of Churchill, who had been a strong proponent of European unity. There were, nonetheless, moves towards European cooperation. The US in 1947 introduced the Marshall Plan to provide financial aid for Europe, which was administered in 1948 by the Organisation for European Economic Co-operation (OEEC) and in 1960 the Organisation for Economic Co-operation and Development (OECD). Cooperation in defence was furthered by the creation of the North Atlantic Treaty Organization (NATO) in 1948 and the Western European Union (WEU) in 1954. The Statute on the Council of Europe was signed in 1949, providing for a Committee of Ministers and a Parliamentary Assembly. The international organization is best-known for the European Convention on Human Rights (ECHR), which was signed in 1950 and came into force in 1953. We can now consider the more concrete moves towards the founding of the EEC.

3 From ECSC to EEC

3.1 European Coal and Steel Community: ECSC

The UK was unwilling to participate in potentially far-reaching plans for European integration in 1948, and this led to more modest, albeit important, proposals advanced by the French foreign minister that France and Germany should administer their coal and steel resources pursuant to an international agreement in which supervisory authority

[3] W Lipgens (ed), *Documents of the History of European Integration* (Florence: European University Institute, 1985).

was given to a body termed the High Authority. The proposal was framed so that other States could also join the international agreement. The detailed plan was drafted by Jean Monnet, a committed federalist. The focus on coal and steel was in part economic, but also in large part political. Coal and steel were still the principal materials for waging war. Placing production of such material under an international body was consciously designed to assuage fears that Germany might covertly rearm. By assuaging such fears, it was hoped to bring Germany back into the mainstream European fold, more especially because the political architecture in Europe had changed dramatically after 1945, with Russian dominance of Eastern Europe and the emergence of the cold war.

The European Coal and Steel Community (ECSC) Treaty was signed in 1951 by France, Germany, Italy, Belgium, Netherlands, and Luxembourg. It had a lifespan of 50 years to expire in 2002, and established a common market in coal and steel. There were four principal institutions. The High Authority, composed of nine independent appointees of the six Member State governments, was the main executive institution with decision-making power; an Assembly made up of national parliaments' delegates had supervisory and advisory powers; a Council composed of a representative from each national government had limited decision-making powers and a broader consultative role; the fourth institution was the Court of Justice composed of nine judges. Although the remit of the ECSC was limited to coal and steel, its proponents always saw it as a supranational authority, in which the High Authority could adopt decisions other than by unanimity, which could then serve as the first step towards broader European integration.[4]

3.2 **European Defence Community and European Political Community: EDC and EPC**

The 1950s also witnessed setbacks in the moves towards European integration, which were nonetheless important in the overall story of the creation of the EEC. The central proposals that failed were the European Defence Community (EDC) and the European Political Community (EPC).

The proposal for the EDC had its origins in French opposition to German membership of NATO. The French alternative outlined in the Pleven Plan in 1950 was for the EDC, which would have a European army, a common budget, and joint institutions. The EDC Treaty was signed in 1952 by the six ECSC States, but Britain refused to participate, and progress towards ratification was slow. It was felt that a European army required some form of common European foreign policy, and this was the catalyst for plans to establish the EPC. The 1953 EPC draft statute was crafted by the ECSC Assembly as reinforced by certain additional members, with the principal work being carried out by a Constitutional Committee. It produced far-reaching plans for a federal, parliamentary-style form of European integration, in which there would be a bicameral ('two-level') parliament, with one chamber elected by direct universal suffrage, and the other senate-type body being appointed by national parliaments. The parliament would have real legislative power. There was also to be an Executive Council, which would have been the government of the EPC, with responsibility to the Parliament. The draft statute also contained provision for a Court of Justice and an Economic and Social Council. Although the draft received almost unanimous support in the ECSC Assembly, the reaction of the six foreign ministers of the ECSC was more circumspect, and there was significant opposition to the degree of parliamentary power in the draft EPC statute.

The fate of the EPC was inextricably linked with that of the EDC. The latter failed when the French National Assembly refused to ratify the EDC in 1954, opposition coming from

[4] F Duchêne, *Jean Monnet: The First Statesman of Interdependence* (London: Norton, 1994) 239.

both the French right and left wings, albeit for very different reasons.[5] This resulted in a major setback for the integration process and the shelving of plans for defence and political union.

3.3 European Economic Community: EEC

Movement towards European integration was not halted by the failure of the EDC/EPC. Indeed, the very demise of these ambitious projects led proponents of European integration to focus more directly on the economic rather than the political, while drawing on ideas that had been discussed when the EPC was being drafted. Thus, the Netherlands had sought to include in the EPC proposals the idea of a common market in which products would be able to move freely under the guarantee of a supranational authority. This was felt to be too risky for several countries in the early 1950s, since they had protectionist traditions that they were unwilling to relinquish. It was this very idea of a common market in which goods and services would be traded freely across the Member States that was to resurface. A conference of foreign ministers of the six Member States of the ECSC was held in Messina in Italy in 1955. A committee chaired by Paul-Henri Spaak, Belgian Prime Minister and a strong advocate of integration, published its report in 1956, which contained the basic plan for what became the European Atomic Energy Community (Euratom) and the EEC. The underlying long-term objective may well have been political, but the initial focus was economic. There was no temporal limit to the EEC Treaty. The Treaty of Rome was signed in March 1957 and came into effect in January 1958. There were six Member States: France, Germany, the Netherlands, Belgium, Italy, and Luxembourg. The same Member States were signatories of the Euratom Treaty, which came into effect at the same time as the EEC Treaty.

In economic terms, the idea of a common market connotes the removal of barriers to trade, such as tariffs, which increase the cost of imports, or quotas, which limit the imports of a product. These barriers to trade were to be abolished and a common customs tariff was to be set up. The common market was to be established over a transitional period, during which tariff barriers would be removed and the common external customs tariff established. A common market connoted more than the removal of tariffs and quotas. It also entailed the free movement of the economic factors of production to ensure that they were being used most efficiently throughout the Community. This explains the centrality to the Community of the 'four freedoms', which are often regarded as the core of its economic constitution: free movement of goods, workers, capital, and establishment and the provision of services (see further chapters 11 to 16). The idea was that if, for example, a worker could not obtain a job in a particular country because unemployment levels were high, he or she could move freely within the EEC to search for employment within another country where there might be an excess of demand over the supply for labour, with the consequence that the value of the labour resource within the Community was enhanced. The Treaty also contained key provisions to ensure that the idea of a level playing field was not undermined by the anticompetitive actions of private parties, or by national action that favoured domestic industry (see further chapter 17). The Treaty of Rome was in addition designed to approximate the economic policies of the Member States, to promote harmonious development of economic activities throughout the Community, to increase stability and raise the standard of living, and to promote closer relations between the Member States. There were common policies in agriculture

[5] J Pinder, *The Building of the European Union* (3rd edn, Oxford: Oxford University Press, 1998).

and transport. A European Social Fund was established to improve employment opportunities, and an Investment Bank to give loans and guarantees and to help less developed regions or sectors. A European Development Fund for overseas countries and territories of some Member States was also established.

In institutional terms, the Treaty of Rome was a mixture of continuity with the ECSC, combined with novel arrangements for the EEC. The Parliamentary Assembly and the Court of Justice were shared with the ECSC. There was, however, a separate Council of Ministers consisting of a national representative from each Member State, and a separate executive authority, the Commission, which was composed of members drawn from the Member States, who had an obligation of independence and who were to represent the Community rather than the national interest. It was not until the Merger Treaty in 1965 that these institutions were shared by the three Communities. An Economic and Social Committee with advisory status was set up, to be shared with the Euratom Community.

The location of legislative and executive power was crucial to the Treaty of Rome (on the institutions, see further chapters 3 and 4). The draft statute for the European Political Community gave very considerable power to the proposed bicameral legislature, but this aroused considerable opposition from the Member States of the ECSC. The same unwillingness to accord power to parliamentary institutions was evident in the Treaty of Rome. The legal and political reality was that legislative power was divided between the Commission, which proposed legislative initiatives, and the Council of Ministers, which voted on them. The Parliamentary Assembly, which changed its name to the European Parliament in 1962, had a bare right to be consulted only where a particular Treaty article mandated such consultation. Voting procedure varied according to the nature of the issue: in some limited instances voting was by simple majority, in many others it was by 'qualified majority', while in yet others unanimity was required. Where qualified majority voting applied, voting in the Council was weighted to give greater weight to the larger Member States than the smaller.

Executive power was also divided in the original Treaty of Rome, although the Commission was given considerable power in this respect. The Commission was accorded the role of 'watchdog' to ensure that Member States complied with the Treaty; it had responsibility to ensure that regulations, directives, and decisions enacted pursuant to the Treaty were effectively implemented; and it was the principal negotiator of international agreements on behalf of the Community. The Council nonetheless exercised certain executive responsibilities in relation to, for example, the conclusion of international agreements, the planning of the overall policy agenda, and the Community budget. The Assembly was also given some power over the budget, and in addition possessed a strong but never-used power of censure, despite the tabling of many motions of censure over the years.[6]

4 From EEC to the Single European Act

4.1 Tensions within the Community

The Treaty of Rome continued to provide the legal framework for the EEC for almost 30 years, subject to the Merger Treaty of 1965, which came into effect in 1967, and which merged the executive organs of the ECSC, Euratom, and the EEC. There were nonetheless important developments between the EEC Treaty and the SEA.

[6] K Bradley, 'The Institutional Law of the EU in 1999' (1999/2000) 19 *Yearbook of European Law* 547, 584.

The Community expanded through accession of new Member States. The UK had chosen to remain outside the EEC when it was initially established. It made its first application to join in 1961, but the French President, Charles de Gaulle, vetoed UK membership in 1963, and in 1967. It was not until de Gaulle's resignation that Britain's application for membership was accepted, together with those of Ireland and Denmark in 1973. Greece became a member of the EEC in 1981, followed by Spain and Portugal in 1986.

The almost 30-year period between the EEC and the SEA revealed tensions between an intergovernmental view of the Community, championed initially by President de Gaulle of France, in which State interests were regarded as paramount, and a more supranational perspective espoused initially by Walter Hallstein, the Commission President, in which the overall Community good was perceived as the primary objective. The tension surfaced in 1965, at the time when the transitional provisions of the Treaty dictated a move from unanimous to qualified majority voting in the Council. De Gaulle objected to a Commission proposal that the Community should be able to raise its own resources from agricultural levies and external tariffs, rather than national contributions.[7] When compromise in the Council proved to be impossible, France refused to attend further Council meetings and adopted what became known as the 'empty-chair' policy. This lasted for seven months, from June 1965 until January 1966, after which a settlement was reached, which became known as the Luxembourg Compromise or the Luxembourg Accords. They were essentially an agreement to disagree over voting methods in the Council. The French asserted that even where the Treaty provided for majority decision-making, discussion must continue until unanimity was reached whenever important national interests were at stake. The other five Member States declared that in such circumstances the Council would 'endeavour, within a reasonable time, to reach solutions which can be adopted by all'.[8] It seems nonetheless that the French view prevailed, such that if a State pleaded that its 'very important interests' were at stake, then this was akin to a veto, which the other Member States would respect.

The period between the EEC Treaty and the SEA also saw other developments that enhanced Member State power over decision-making and intergovernmentalism. In 1970, the Davignon Report recommended the holding of quarterly meetings of the foreign ministers of the Member States, which became an intergovernmental forum for cooperation in foreign policy. In 1973, this became known as European Political Co-operation, which enabled the EEC to be represented as one voice in other international organizations in which all Member States participated, but also enhanced intergovernmentalism.

In 1974, the European Council was established to regularize the practice of holding summits. It consists of the heads of government of the Member States, with the President of the Commission attending its biannual meetings. The European Council's 'summitry' provided the Community with much needed direction, but represented to some a weakening in the supranational elements of the Community. This body was not within the framework created by the Treaties, and it was not until the SEA that it was recognized in a formal instrument. European Political Co-operation and the European Council enabled Member State interests at the highest level to impact on matters of political or economic concern, and their decisions, while not formally binding, normally constituted the frame for binding Community initiatives. The Member States also assumed greater control over the detail of Community secondary legislation, through the creation of what became known as Comitology. This enabled Member States to influence the content of secondary Community legislation. Commentators lamented the dilution of the EEC's

[7] The EEC achieved its own resources through the Treaty of Luxembourg 1970 (known as 'the first budgetary treaty'), which entered into force in 1971.

[8] Bull EC 3–1966, 9.

supranational dimension and regarded it as a principal reason why legislative initiatives were not enacted.[9]

There were, however, also developments during the period between the EEC and the SEA that enhanced supranationalism. Thus, 1976 saw agreement on direct elections to the Assembly, with the first such elections in 1979. It provided the EEC with a direct electoral mandate, but voter turnout was low, and elections were often fought on national rather than Community issues.[10] Moreover, the direct electoral mandate served to highlight the Assembly's limited power in the legislative process. The supranational dimension to the Community was enhanced by developments relating to resources and the budget. In 1969, agreement was reached on funding from the Community's own resources rather than from national contributions, and on the expansion of the Parliament's role in the budgetary process. This gave the Community greater financial independence and strengthened Parliament's role as a decision-maker. These developments were furthered in 1975 when a second budgetary treaty was adopted. The European Court of Justice (ECJ) also made important contributions to the supranational dynamic of the Community during this period. It used the doctrine of direct effect in the 1960s and 1970s to make Community policies more effective. It interpreted Treaty provisions broadly to foster the overall aims of the Community, such as the free movement of goods. It created the primacy of Community law over national law to reinforce these judicial strategies (see further chapter 6; on the Court of Justice generally, see chapter 10).

While there were positive developments relating to the Community from a supranational perspective, the mid-1970s to the mid-1980s was nonetheless perceived as a period of relative political stagnation in the EEC. This was epitomized by the Commission's difficulty in securing the passage of legislation through the Council, with the consequence that Community objectives were left unfulfilled or that progress was extremely slow. The malaise was recognized in high-level reports from the mid-1970s onwards, such as the Tindemans Report 1974–5 and that of the 'Three Wise Men' in 1978,[11] both of which recommended strengthening the supranational elements of the Community, but neither was acted on. The European Parliament proposed radical reform in 1984 in a 'Draft Treaty on European Union', but it too was largely ignored. The catalyst for change came from a meeting of the heads of State in the Fontainebleau European Council in 1984, which established two committees to consider Treaty revision and political integration. This led the 1985 European Council in Milan to establish an intergovernmental conference (IGC) to discuss Treaty amendment. It was this IGC that generated the SEA. The impetus for reform was furthered by an extensive Commission 'White Paper' that set out a timetable for completion of the internal market, and barriers to be removed before a deadline of 1992.[12]

4.2 **Single European Act: SEA**

The SEA 1986 was a disappointment to those who advocated far-reaching reform of the kind posited by the European Parliament in its Draft Treaty on European Union. It nonetheless had a far-reaching significance because of the institutional and substantive changes that it introduced.

In institutional terms, the SEA made several changes. It gave a legal basis to European Political Co-operation and formal recognition to the European Council, although not

[9] P Dankert, 'The EC: Past, Present and Future' in L Tsoukalis (ed), *The EC: Past, Present and Future* (Oxford: Basil Blackwell, 1983). For more on the European Council as an EU Institution, see chapter 3, and for more on the comitology procedure, see chapter 5.

[10] M Holland, *European Integration from Community to Union* (London: Pinter, 1994) 42.

[11] Bull EC 11–1979, 1.5.2. [12] COM(85) 310.

within the Community Treaties. A Court of First Instance was created to assist the Court of Justice. Lastly, the so-called 'comitology' procedure, under which the Council delegates powers to the Commission on certain conditions, was formally included within what was Article 202 EC.[13]

The most significant institutional change was that the SEA began the transformation in the role of the European Parliament. In the Rome Treaty, its role in the legislative process was limited to a right to be consulted and then only where a particular Treaty article so mandated. The SEA created a new legislative procedure, the 'cooperation' procedure, which applied to specified Treaty articles. It transformed the Community decision-making process. Prior to the SEA, the approach to the passage of legislation was captured by the aphorism that the 'Commission proposes, and the Council disposes', revealing the Commission's role as initiator of legislation and the Council's role in voting on such measures. After the SEA, the Commission had to take seriously the views of the European Parliament in the areas where the cooperation procedure applied. The enactment of legislation required input from three players, not two, because the cooperation procedure meant that the European Parliament could in effect block legislative proposals provided that it had some support in the Council.

The impact of the cooperation procedure was enhanced because of the substantive changes made by the SEA, in particular the creation of what was Article 100a EEC and is now Article 114 TFEU, which is the main Treaty provision conferring power upon the EU to adopt legislation concerning the internal market. The completion of a common market requires not merely that trade barriers are prohibited, what is termed negative integration, but also that there should be European regulation of certain issues instead of national regulation, what is termed positive integration or harmonization. The latter is required because each country will have certain rules on, for example, banking that embody important public interests, such as the prevention of fraud, the safeguarding of deposits, and the like. These rules cannot be eradicated, nor should they be. The very multiplicity of such national rules can hamper the creation of a common market, because traders must satisfy different rules in each Member State, thereby adding significantly to the costs of business (see further chapter 11). A way of meeting this difficulty is for there to be one set of Community rules on such issues. This was recognized in the original Treaty of Rome, but the provision conferring power to adopt legislation concerning the common market, what was Article 100 EEC and is now Article 115 TFEU, required unanimity in the Council, which was difficult to secure. This was the rationale for Article 100a EEC, now Article 114 TFEU, which provided for measures to approximate the laws of the Member States. The cooperation procedure was applicable to this article and voting within the Council was by qualified majority, rather than unanimity. The European Parliament was thereby accorded a role in the legislative process and this role was applicable to the very Treaty article that was the foundation for measures to complete the internal market. The SEA amended the Treaty of Rome to provide that the Community should adopt measures with the aim of 'progressively establishing the internal market over a period expiring on 31 December 1992', and defined the internal market as 'an area without internal frontiers in which the free movement of goods, persons, services and capital is ensured'.[14] What is now Article 114 TFEU became the principal vehicle for measures to complete the internal market through legislation approximating Member State laws.

[13] The legal regime for dealing with these measures was altered by the Lisbon Treaty, Arts 290–291 TFEU. See further chapter 5.

[14] Art 8a EEC.

The substantive impact of the SEA was also evident in new areas of Community competence, some of which had already been asserted by the institutions and supported by the Court, without any express Treaty basis. The additions covered cooperation in economic and monetary union (see chapter 19), social policy (see chapter 20), economic and social cohesion, research and technological development, and environmental policy (see chapter 22).

5 From the SEA to the Nice Treaty

5.1 Maastricht Treaty: the Treaty on European Union

The SEA reinvigorated the Community and many measures to complete the internal market were enacted between 1986 and 1992. However, the internal market could not truly be 'completed' by 1992, or indeed any particular date thereafter, because technological change, industrial innovation, and changing patterns of consumer behaviour can generate the need for new EU measures to eradicate or reduce obstacles to interstate trade. The momentum generated by the SEA continued after its adoption. A committee chaired by the President of the Commission, Jacques Delors, on economic and monetary union (EMU) reported in 1989 and set out a three-stage plan for reaching EMU. The European Council held an IGC on the subject, and a second IGC on political union. This led to a draft Treaty in 1991 and the Treaty on European Union (TEU) was signed by the Member States in Maastricht in February 1992.[15] It entered into force in November 1993 having survived constitutional challenge before the German Federal Constitutional Court.[16]

5.1.1 The three-pillar system

The TEU made several important changes to the Treaty of Rome, in both institutional and substantive terms. It was also significant in terms of the overall legal architecture, because it introduced what was known as the 'three-pillar' structure for what was to be the European Union, with the Communities as the first pillar, and the EEC Treaty was officially renamed the European Community Treaty.[17] The Second Pillar dealt with Common Foreign and Security Policy (CFSP) and built on earlier mechanisms for European Political Cooperation. The Third Pillar dealt with Justice and Home Affairs (JHA) and built on earlier informal initiatives in this area (see chapters 24 and 25). The pillar structure was preserved in subsequent Treaty amendments, but removed by the Lisbon Treaty, although distinct rules still apply to the CFSP (see chapter 26). Title I of the TEU contained common provisions, which laid down basic principles for the 'Union', and set out its objectives.[18]

The EU was given new responsibilities in relation to CFSP and JHA. The key issue is why these new competences were not simply added to those already existing, as with earlier Treaty amendments, such as those in the SEA. The principal rationale for creating separate pillars for the CFSP and JHA was as follows. The Member States wished for some established mechanism through which they could cooperate in relation to CFSP and JHA, since it was time-consuming and cumbersome to set up a meeting for each new problem.

[15] R Corbett, *The Treaty of Maastricht* (London: Longman, 1993).

[16] Cases 2 BvR 2134/92 and 2159/92 *Brunner v The European Union Treaty* [1994] 1 CMLR 57.

[17] D Curtin, 'The Constitutional Structure of the Union: A Europe of Bits and Pieces' (1993) 30 *Common Market Law Review* 17.

[18] There were originally seven titles in the TEU: Title I included the 'common provisions', which set out the basic objectives of the TEU. Titles II, III, and IV covered the First Pillar amendments to the EEC, ECSC, and Euratom Treaties respectively. Title V created the Second Pillar of the Common Foreign and Security Policy, Title VI the Third Pillar of Justice and Home Affairs, and Title VII contained the final provisions.

However, the Member States were not willing to subject these areas to the normal supranational methods of decision-making that characterized the Community Pillar. They did not wish the Commission and the ECJ to have the powers they had under the Community Pillar, because the Second and Third Pillars concerned sensitive areas of policy at the core of national sovereignty. The central distinguishing feature of decision-making under the Second and Third Pillars is that it was more intergovernmental, with the Member States in the Council and European Council retaining the primary reins of power. The other Community institutions, the Commission, European Parliament, and ECJ, either had no role, or one that was much reduced by way of comparison with the Community Pillar.

5.1.2 The Community Treaties

The Maastricht Treaty made several institutional changes to the Treaty of Rome, the most significant being the further increase in the Parliament's legislative involvement, through the co-decision procedure, which was amended and strengthened by the Treaty of Amsterdam. This allowed the European Parliament to block legislation of which it disapproved, if it was subject to this procedure. The Parliament was also given the right to request the Commission to initiate legislation and the power to block the appointment of the new Commission. There were other significant institutional changes: provision was made for a European System of Central Banks (ESCB) and a European Central Bank (ECB) to oversee economic and monetary union (see chapter 19), for a Parliamentary Ombudsman, and for a 'Committee of the Regions'.

The Maastricht Treaty also made significant substantive changes. It established the principle of subsidiarity, which was introduced to alleviate fears that the EC was becoming too 'federal' by distinguishing areas where action was best taken at Community level and national level.[19] A new concept of European citizenship was introduced.[20] There were new provisions on economic and monetary union,[21] which laid the foundations for the introduction of the single currency.[22] The Maastricht Treaty also added new areas of competence to the EC, with new titles added in areas such as culture, public health (see chapter 21), consumer protection (see chapter 23), trans-European networks, and development cooperation; and significant modifications made in relation to the titles on, for example, the environment (see chapter 22).

5.1.3 Common foreign and security policy

The CFSP Pillar created by the Maastricht Treaty was distinct from the Community institutional and legal structure, such that decision-making was more intergovernmental and less supranational than under the Community Pillar. The CFSP Pillar established the objectives of EU action in this area, which included preservation of peace and international security, respect for human rights, and development of democracy. Each Member State had an obligation to inform and consult each other on any matter of common foreign and security policy that was of general interest, to ensure that the Member States' combined influence could be exercised as effectively as possible through concerted and convergent action. Provision was made for the Council to define a 'common position' for the Member States on such issues. However, it was the European Council, consisting of the heads of State and government of the Member States, which defined the principles and general guidelines for the CFSP, with the Council having responsibility for decisions to implement them. The CFSP included all questions related to the security of the Union,

[19] Art 5 EC. For more on the principle of subsidiarity, see chapter 5.

[20] Arts 17–21 EC. See chapter 13.

[21] Arts 98–124 EC. See chapter 19.

[22] J Pipkorn, 'Legal Arrangements in the Treaty of Maastricht for the Effectiveness of the Economic and Monetary Union' (1994) 31 *Common Market Law Review* 263.

including the eventual framing of a common defence policy. While decision-making was concentrated in the hands of the Council and the European Council, there was nonetheless provision for the European Parliament to be kept informed about foreign and security policy, and the Commission was to be fully associated with work in this area.

5.1.4 **Justice and home affairs**

The JHA Pillar originally governed policies such as asylum, immigration, and 'third country' (non-EU) nationals, which were integrated into the EC Treaty by the Treaty of Amsterdam (see chapter 25). However, prior to the Lisbon Treaty the Third Pillar also included cooperation on a range of international crime issues and various forms of judicial, customs, and police cooperation, including the establishment of a European Police Office (Europol) for exchanging information (see chapter 24). National sensitivity about such issues meant that the Member States were not willing for them to be included within the ordinary Community Pillar. Decision-making was dominated by the Council, and the ECJ's powers were limited. The Lisbon Treaty has now brought the entirety of what was the Third Pillar into the general fabric of the Treaty.[23]

5.2 **Treaty of Amsterdam**

The process of Treaty amendment did not halt other important developments. Membership of the EU expanded shortly after the Maastricht Treaty, with Austria, Sweden, and Finland joining in 1995. An accession agreement was also negotiated with Norway, but a national referendum opposed membership of the EU, as it had done in 1973. An Agreement on the European Economic Area (EEA) was also made between the EC and the States that were party to the European Free Trade Association (EFTA), and came into force in 1994.[24]

The ink was nonetheless scarcely dry on the Maastricht Treaty before plans were being made for an IGC between the Member States that would pave the way for the next round of Treaty reform, which was the Treaty of Amsterdam. It was signed in 1997 and came into effect on 1 May 1999. It was initially intended to prepare the Union for enlargement through accession of Eastern European countries, but this issue was postponed until the Nice Treaty. The result was that the Treaty of Amsterdam was a modest exercise in Treaty reform, but it did delete obsolete provisions from the EC Treaty, and renumber all the articles, titles, and sections of the TEU and the EC Treaty.

The 1990s saw a surge in debate, political and academic, concerning the legitimacy of the EU. This is the rationale for amendments introduced by the Treaty of Amsterdam designed to enhance the EU's legitimacy. The principle of openness was added, such that decisions were to be taken 'as openly as possible' and as closely as possible to the citizen.[25] Promotion of a high level of employment and the establishment of the area of 'freedom, security and justice' were added to the EU's objectives.[26] There were amendments the effect of which was that the Union was said to be founded on respect for human rights, democracy, and the rule of law.[27] Respect for these principles was a condition

[23] Arts 67–89 TFEU.

[24] It provided for free-movement provisions similar to those in the EC Treaty, analogous rules on competition policy, and 'close cooperation' in other policy areas, having been declared compatible with the EC Treaty by the ECJ, Opinion 1/91 [1991] ECR I-6079; Opinion 1/92 [1992] ECR I-2821; J Forman, 'The EEA Agreement Five Years On: Dynamic Homogeneity in Practice and Its Implementation by the Two EEA Courts' (1999) 36 *Common Market Law Review* 751. Since 1995, the non-EU parties to the EEA have been Iceland, Norway, and Liechtenstein. One country (Switzerland) remains a member of EFTA, but decided not to join the EEA; it has, however, entered into a number of separate bilateral treaties with the EU.

[25] Art 1 EU. On the transparency of the EU decision-making process, see chapters 3 and 8.

[26] Art 2 EU. [27] Art 6 EU.

for EU membership.[28] On a related note, the Treaty of Amsterdam declared that the EU should respect the fundamental rights protected in the ECHR and in national constitutions,[29] and there was provision that if the Council found a 'serious and persistent breach' by a Member State of principles concerning the rule of law, human rights, and democracy, it could suspend some of that State's rights under the Treaty.[30]

The institutional changes made by the Treaty of Amsterdam were an extension and consolidation of a reform process begun with the SEA. The co-decision procedure was amended to increase the European Parliament's power and the number of Treaty articles to which it was applicable was expanded. The cooperation procedure introduced by the SEA was virtually eliminated, apart from provisions on EMU. The increase in the European Parliament's power was also evident in the amendment whereby its assent was required for appointment of the Commission President.[31] There were changes designed to enhance the Community's legitimacy in relation to its citizens. The scope of Community power was further enhanced through new heads of competence, or the modification of existing heads.[32] There was also a new provision that conferred legislative competence on the Community to combat discrimination based on sex, racial or ethnic origin, religion or belief, disability, age, or sexual orientation.[33]

The Treaty of Amsterdam also amended the Second and Third Pillars. The changes made to the Second Pillar were modest, including the fact that the Secretary-General of the Council was nominated as 'High Representative' for the CFSP to assist the Council Presidency, and the Council was given power to 'conclude' international agreements,[34] whenever this was necessary in implementing the CFSP.

The changes made to the Third Pillar were more significant. The decision-making structure had been criticized on the ground that many JHA policies, such as immigration, asylum, and border controls, were unsuited to the intergovernmental processes established. The parts of JHA dealing with visas, asylum, immigration, and other aspects of free movement of persons were incorporated into Title IV EC, although decision-making was still more intergovernmental than in other areas for a certain period of time (see chapter 25). The remaining Third Pillar provisions were subjected to institutional controls closer to those under the Community Pillar, and the Third Pillar was renamed 'Police and Judicial Cooperation in Criminal Matters'. The aim of the remodelled Third Pillar was to provide citizens with a high level of safety in an area of freedom, security, and justice, by developing 'common action' in three areas: police cooperation in criminal matters, judicial cooperation in criminal matters, and the prevention and combating of racism and xenophobia.[35] These objectives were pursued through legal instruments specific to the Third Pillar:[36] common positions, framework decisions, decisions, and conventions. The ECJ had some jurisdiction over certain measures adopted under this pillar,[37] thereby further eroding the distinction between the Community Pillar and the Third Pillar, although it was not equivalent to its jurisdiction under the Community Pillar.

[28] Art 49 EU.

[29] Art 6(2) EU. This was subject to judicial oversight through Art 46 EU. See further chapter 9.

[30] Art 7 EU. [31] Art 214(2) EC. See chapter 3.

[32] There was a new title on employment, the provisions on social policy were modified, the title on public health was replaced and enhanced, and that on consumer protection was amended. See chapters 20, 21, and 23.

[33] Art 13 EC. See chapter 20.

[34] Art 24 EU; JW de Zwaan, 'Legal Personality of the European Communities and the European Union' (1999) 30 *Netherlands Yearbook of International Law* 75; K Lenaerts and E de Smijter, 'The European Union as an Actor under International Law' (1999/2000) 19 *Yearbook of European Law* 95. On the CFSP, see further chapter 26.

[35] Art 29 EU. On the revised Third Pillar, see further chapter 24.

[36] Art 34 EU. [37] Art 35 EU.

5.3 **Treaty of Nice**

The period from the mid-1980s onwards was dominated by Treaty reform or discussion about such reform.[38] The very fact that the Treaty of Amsterdam failed to address the institutional structure pending enlargement meant that a further IGC was inevitable. It was convened in 1999 to consider composition of the Commission, the weighting of votes in the Council, and the extension of qualified majority voting. The Treaty of Nice was concluded in December 2000, and entered into force on 1 February 2003.[39]

The Treaty of Nice made several changes to the Community's institutional structure. This had been devised for a Community of six Member States, which had now expanded to 15. There was consensus on the need for reform of institutional arrangements pending enlargement. This was achieved and the Treaty provisions concerning the weighting of votes in the Council, the distribution of seats in the European Parliament, and the composition of the Commission were amended. The debates concerning reform were often fierce, because the issues raised broader considerations concerning the relative power of large, medium, and small States in the Community, and the balance of power between the EU institutions (see further chapter 3). The detailed provisions on these matters were superseded by the Lisbon Treaty.

5.4 **Charter of Rights**

Parallel to the discussion that led to the Treaty of Nice, there was discourse that led to the EU Charter of Rights. The initial catalyst came from the European Council in 1999, which conceived of the Charter as important in itself and as a mechanism for enhancing the legitimacy of the EU. It established a 'body' which included national parliamentarians, European parliamentarians, and national government representatives to draft a Charter of fundamental rights for the EU.[40] This body, which renamed itself a 'Convention', began work early in 2000 and drew up a Charter by the end of 2000. The Charter received political approval of the Member States at the Nice European Council in December 2000.[41] It was drafted so as to be legally binding. The Charter's legal status was not, however, resolved in Nice, and the decision on its legal status was placed on the 'post-Nice agenda' and postponed until the 2004 IGC.

6 **From Nice to Lisbon**

6.1 **The Laeken Declaration**

The initial expectation following the Treaty of Nice was that there would be yet another round of piecemeal Treaty reform four years later in 2004 to consider issues not resolved in the Treaty of Nice. These included the status of the Charter of Rights, the scope of Community competence, and the role to be played by national parliaments in the

[38] B de Witte, 'The Closest Thing to a Constitutional Conversation in Europe: The Semi-Permanent Treaty Revision Process' in P Beaumont, C Lyons, and N Walker (eds), *Convergence and Divergence in European Public Law* (Oxford: Hart Publishing, 2002) ch 3.

[39] OJ [2001] C80/1; K Bradley, 'Institutional Design in the Treaty of Nice' (2001) 38 *Common Market Law Review* 1095; R Barents, 'Some Observations on the Treaty of Nice' (2001) 8 *Maastricht Journal of European and Comparative Law* 121.

[40] G de Búrca, 'The Drafting of the EU Charter of Fundamental Rights' (2001) 26 *European Law Review* 126. See further chapter 9.

[41] OJ [2000] C364/1.

Community decision-making process. These issues were to be considered further at the Laeken European Council scheduled for December 2001. The reform process was, however, transformed during 2000, which was then reflected in the conclusions of the Laeken European Council.[42]

It came to be accepted that the topics left over from the Treaty of Nice were not discrete, but resonated with other issues concerning the institutional balance of power within the EU, and the distribution of authority between the EU and the Member States. This led to a growing feeling that there should be a more profound rethinking of the fundamentals of the EU. It was also accepted that if a broad range of issues was to be discussed, then the result should be legitimated by input from a broader 'constituency' than hitherto. This emerging consensus was reflected in the Laeken European Council,[43] which gave formal approval, through the Laeken Declaration, to the broadening of the issues left open post-Nice. These issues became the 'headings' within which a plethora of other questions were posed, concerning virtually every issue of importance for the EU. The Laeken Declaration also formally embraced the Convention model used to draw up the Charter of Rights, and established a Convention on the Future of Europe, with a composition designed to enhance the legitimacy of its results.

6.2 **Constitutional Treaty**

The Convention[44] was composed of representatives from national governments, national parliaments, the European Parliament, and the Commission. The accession countries were also represented. The Convention was chaired by former French President Giscard d'Estaing, and there were two vice-chairmen, Giuliano Amato and Jean-Luc Dehaene. The executive role in the Convention was undertaken by the Praesidium.[45] It began work in 2002, making extensive use of Working Groups for particular topics.[46] The end result in 2003 was a proposal for a Constitutional Treaty, but this was not preordained. The possibility of a constitutional text was mentioned only at the end of the Laeken Declaration, in the context of Treaty simplification, and the language was cautious. Many Member States felt that the Convention might just be a talking shop which produced recommendations.[47] It was therefore something of a surprise when Giscard d'Estaing, in the Convention opening ceremony, announced that he sought consensus on a Constitutional Treaty for Europe. The idea took hold that the Convention should produce a Constitutional Treaty. The Draft Treaty Establishing a Constitution for Europe[48] was duly agreed by the Convention in June 2003 and submitted to the European Council in July.[49]

[42] P Craig, 'Constitutional Process and Reform in the EU: Nice, Laeken, the Convention and the IGC' (2004) 10 *European Public Law* 653.

[43] Laeken European Council, 14–15 December 2001.

[44] www.europeansources.info/record/the-convention-on-the-future-of-europe-march-2002/.

[45] It was composed of the Convention Chairman and Vice-Chairmen, and nine other members.

[46] Working Groups were established on subsidiarity; Charter of Rights; legal personality; national parliaments; competence; economic governance; external action; defence; Treaty simplification; freedom, security, and justice; and social Europe. The decision to create the first six groups was taken in May 2002; the remaining five groups were created later in autumn 2002.

[47] P Norman, 'From the Convention to the IGC (Institutions)' (2003) Federal Trust for Education and Research, Online Paper 28/03, 2.

[48] The Constitutional Treaty was divided into four parts: Part I dealt with the basic objectives and values of the EU, fundamental rights, competences, forms of law-making, institutional division of power, and the like; Part II contained the Charter of Rights, which had been made binding by Part I; Part III concerned the policies and functions of the EU; and Part IV contained the final provisions.

[49] CONV 850/03, Draft Treaty establishing a Constitution for Europe, Brussels, 18 July 2003.

The Member States in the European Council were, however, divided on certain issues and agreement on the Constitutional Treaty was only secured at the European Council meeting in June 2004.[50] It was still necessary for the Constitutional Treaty[51] to be ratified in accord with the constitutional requirements of each Member State. Fifteen Member States ratified the Treaty, but progress with ratification came to an abrupt halt when France and the Netherlands rejected the Constitutional Treaty in their referenda.[52] Several Member States then postponed their ratification process. The European Council in 2005 decided it was best for there to be a time for 'reflection'. The Constitutional Treaty never 'recovered' from the negative votes in France and the Netherlands, and did not become law. However, the major changes in the Lisbon Treaty were taken over from the Constitutional Treaty without further debate.

6.3 **Lisbon Treaty**

The failure of the Constitutional Treaty meant that the EU continued to be based on the Treaty of Rome as amended by later Treaties, including the Treaty of Nice. This Treaty architecture had to regulate an EU of 25 Member States, the result of the 2004 enlargement that brought ten further States into the EU: Cyprus, the Czech Republic, Estonia, Hungary, Latvia, Lithuania, Malta, Poland, Slovakia, and Slovenia. Bulgaria and Romania joined the EU in 2007, and Croatia acceded in 2013, making 28 States.

Case study 2.1: Negotiation of the Lisbon Treaty

The preceding discussion revealed the delicate negotiations that often accompany Treaty reform. This was evident also in relation to the Lisbon Treaty, more especially so given the negative reaction to the Constitutional Treaty, which generated academic debate as to what should happen to the 'constitutional' project.[53] The decision that there should be a 'period of reflection' after the negative results in the French and Dutch referenda was sensible, given the concern that more States might vote against the Constitutional Treaty. The Member States were not, however, willing to allow the work on the Constitutional Treaty to be lost. To this end, the European Council in 2006 commissioned Germany, which held the Presidency of the European Council in the first half of 2007, to report on the prospects for Treaty reform. Germany engaged in a series of bilateral discussions with other Member States, to determine whether an agreement could be brokered that would lead to some revised Treaty reform. Germany's Presidency of the European Council culminated with the June 2007 European Council,[54] which considered a detailed mandate of the changes that should be made to the Constitutional Treaty, in order that a revised Treaty could successfully be concluded.

This led to the Reform Treaty.[55] It was agreed to convene an IGC,[56] which was complete its deliberations by the end of 2007.[57] The Reform Treaty was to contain two principal clauses,

[50] Brussels European Council, 17–18 June 2004, paras 4–5.

[51] Treaty Establishing a Constitution for Europe (OJ [2004] C316/1).

[52] R Dehousse, 'The Unmaking of a Constitution: Lessons from the European Referenda' (2006) 13 *Constellations* 151.

[53] G de Búrca, 'The European Constitution Project after the Referenda' (2006) 13 *Constellations* 205; A Duff, 'Plan B: How to Rescue the European Constitution' (2006) Notre Europe, Studies and Research No 52; J Ziller, 'Une constitution courte et obscure ou claire et détaillée? Perspectives pour la simplification des traites et la rationalisation de l'ordre juridique de l'union européenne' (2006) EUI Working Papers, Law 2006/31.

[54] Brussels European Council, 21–22 June 2007.

[55] Ibid, para 8. [56] Ibid, para 10. [57] Ibid, para 11.

which amended respectively the TEU, and the EC Treaty, the latter of which would be renamed the Treaty on the Functioning of the European Union, TFEU. The Union should have a single legal personality and the word 'Community' throughout would be replaced by the word 'Union'.[58] There was a conscious decision to remove mention of the word 'constitution' from the Reform Treaty. The constitutional terminology of the Constitutional Treaty was problematic for some Member States and was dropped. This was also the rationale for other changes where the wording in the Constitutional Treaty was felt, whether correctly or not,[59] to connote the idea of the EU as a State entity. Thus the title 'Union Minister for Foreign Affairs' was replaced by 'High Representative of the Union for Foreign Affairs and Security Policy'; the terms 'law' and 'framework law' were abandoned; there was no flag, anthem, or motto; and the clause in the Constitutional Treaty concerning the primacy of EU law was replaced by a declaration.

Portugal held the Presidency of the European Council in the second half of 2007 and developments were rapid. There was scant time for detailed discussion or input into the draft Treaty that emerged from the IGC. What became the Lisbon Treaty was forged hurriedly by the Member States and Community institutions, since they were keen to conclude a process that had started shortly after the beginning of the new millennium. As noted earlier, the Lisbon Treaty was the same in most important respects as the Constitutional Treaty. The issues had been debated in detail in the Convention on the Future of Europe, and were considered again in the IGC in 2004. There was therefore little appetite for those engaged in the 2007 IGC to reopen Pandora's box.[60] This could not be admitted too explicitly since it could lead to criticism that the IGC was largely repackaging provisions rejected by voters in two prominent Member States, although the negative votes in the French and Dutch referenda had relatively little to do with anything new in the Constitutional Treaty.[61]

The 2007 IGC produced a document that was signed by the Member States on 13 December 2007,[62] and the title was changed from the Reform Treaty to the Lisbon Treaty in recognition of the place of signature. The finishing post was in sight, but the Treaty required ratification by each Member State, and Ireland rejected it in a referendum. This obstacle was overcome by a second Irish referendum in October 2009, after concessions were made to Ireland. The final hurdle was the unwillingness of the Czech President to ratify the Lisbon Treaty, but he did so reluctantly after a constitutional challenge to the Treaty had been rejected by the Czech Constitutional Court, and after other Member States agreed to add at a later date a Protocol to the Treaties relating to the Czech Republic and the Charter of Rights (see chapter 9). The Lisbon Treaty entered into force on 1 December 2009.

6.3.1 **Form**

The Lisbon Treaty amends the TEU and the EC Treaty.[63] The Lisbon Treaty has seven articles, of which Articles 1 and 2 are the most important, plus numerous Protocols and declarations. Article 1 amended the TEU, and contained some principles that govern

[58] Ibid, Annex I, para 2.

[59] S Griller, 'Is This a Constitution? Remarks on a Contested Concept' in S Griller and J Ziller (eds), *The Lisbon Treaty: EU Constitutionalism without a Constitutional Treaty?* (Vienna: Springer, 2008).

[60] G Tsebelis, 'Thinking about the Recent Past and Future of the EU' (2008) 46 *Journal of Common Market Studies* 265.

[61] See in general, Dehousse (n 52) 151.

[62] Conference of the Representatives of the Governments of the Member States, Treaty of Lisbon Amending the Treaty on European Union and the Treaty Establishing the European Community, CIG 14/07, Brussels, 3 December 2007 (OJ [2007] C306/1).

[63] J-C Piris, *The Lisbon Treaty: A Legal and Political Analysis* (Cambridge: Cambridge University Press, 2010); P Craig, *The Lisbon Treaty: Law, Politics and Treaty Reform* (Oxford: Oxford University Press, 2010).

the EU, as well as revised provisions concerning the CFSP and enhanced cooperation. Article 2 amended the EC Treaty, which was renamed the Treaty on the Functioning of the European Union. The EU is henceforth to be founded on the TEU and the TFEU, and the two Treaties have the same legal value.[64] The Union replaces and succeeds the EC.[65] A consolidated version of the Lisbon Treaty contains the new numbering and references to the old provisions where appropriate.[66]

6.3.2 **Substance**

Part I of the Constitutional Treaty contained principles of a constitutional nature that governed the EU. The Lisbon Treaty is less clear in this respect, although the revised TEU has some constitutional principles for the EU. This is especially true in relation to Title I—Common Provisions, Title II—Democratic Principles, and Title III—Provisions on the Institutions. There are, nonetheless, matters not included in the revised TEU, which had properly been in Part I of the Constitutional Treaty. Thus, for example, the main rules concerning competence are in the TFEU,[67] as are the provisions concerning the hierarchy of norms,[68] and those relating to budgetary planning.[69]

However, the Lisbon Treaty did improve the architecture of the TFEU. The latter Treaty is divided into seven parts. Part One, entitled Principles, contains two titles, the first of which deals with Categories of Competence, the second of which covers Provisions having General Application. Part Two deals with Discrimination and Citizenship of the Union. Part Three, which covers Policies and Internal Actions of the Union, is the largest Part of the TFEU with 24 titles.[70] The provisions on Police and Judicial Cooperation in Criminal Matters, the Third Pillar of the old TEU, have been moved into the new TFEU.[71] Part Four of the TFEU covers Association of Overseas Countries and Territories. Part Five deals with EU External Action. Part Six is concerned with Institutional and Budgetary Provisions, while Part Seven covers General and Final Provisions.

The Lisbon Treaty is not built on the pillar system, and the Treaty architecture that had prevailed since the Maastricht Treaty has now gone. There are nonetheless distinctive rules relating to the CFSP, which means that there is still something akin to a separate 'pillar' for such matters. The approach to the CFSP in the Lisbon Treaty largely replicates that in the Constitutional Treaty, subject to the change of nomenclature, from 'Union Minister for Foreign Affairs' to 'High Representative of the Union for Foreign Affairs and Security Policy'. Executive authority continues to reside principally with the European Council and the Council.[72] The ECJ continues to be largely excluded from the CFSP.[73]

[64] Art 1, para 3 TEU. [65] Art 1, para 3 TEU.

[66] Consolidated Versions of the Treaty on European Union and the Treaty on the Functioning of the European Union (OJ [2008] C115/1, OJ [2010] C83/1).

[67] Arts 2–6 TFEU. See further chapter 5. [68] Arts 288–292 TFEU. See further chapter 5.

[69] Art 312 TFEU.

[70] I—Internal Market; II—Free Movement of Goods; III—Agriculture and Fisheries; IV—Free Movement of Persons, Services and Capital; V—Area of Freedom, Security and Justice; VI—Transport; VII—Common Rules on Competition, Taxation and Approximation of Laws; VIII—Economic and Monetary Policy; IX—Employment; X—Social Policy; XI—The European Social Fund; XII—Education, Vocational Training, Youth and Sport; XIII—Culture; XIV—Public Health; XV—Consumer Protection; XVI—Trans-European Networks; XVII—Industry; XVIII—Economic, Social and Territorial Cohesion; XIX—Research and Technological Development and Space; XX—Environment; XXI—Energy; XXII—Tourism; XXIII—Civil Protection; XXIV—Administrative Cooperation.

[71] Part Three, Title V TFEU. See chapter 24.

[72] Arts 22, 24 TEU. On the CFSP, see further chapter 26.

[73] Art 24 TEU, Art 275 TFEU. It does, however, have jurisdiction in relation to Art 40 TEU, which is designed to ensure that exercise of CFSP powers does not impinge on the general competences of the EU, and vice versa; the ECJ also has jurisdiction under Art 275 TFEU to review the legality of decisions imposing restrictive measures on natural or legal persons adopted by the Council under Chapter 2 of Title V TEU.

7 Recent challenges for the EU

7.1 The financial crisis

It was hoped that with the ratification of the Lisbon Treaty there could be a period of relative calm. This was not to be. Ratification of the Lisbon Treaty overlapped with the beginnings of the financial crisis, which had a profound political, economic, and social impact on the EU.[74]

The reasons for the crisis are complex and cannot be examined in detail here (see instead chapter 19).[75] Suffice it to say the following. The Maastricht Treaty introduced the legal framework for economic and monetary union. The latter connotes the idea of a single currency overseen by a European Central Bank. The former captures the idea of control over national fiscal and budgetary policy, to ensure that a Member State does not spend more than it earns. The stability of the euro could be undermined if the economies of the Member States that subscribed to the currency were weak, and the financial markets might reach this conclusion if some Member States persistently spent more than they earned. The problem was that the two parts of the Maastricht settlement were out of sync.[76] The EU could not exert the requisite control over national economic policy.

The problem for the EU began in earnest with the fact that Greece's credit rating to repay its debt was downgraded. This then led to problems for the euro, and to concerns about the budgetary health of some other countries that used the currency. This led to downward pressure on the euro, which was only alleviated when euro countries provided a support package for Greece that satisfied the financial markets. The sovereign debt crisis interacted with the banking crisis that affected some lending institutions that were heavily committed to economic sectors, such as housing, which were hit badly by the downturn in the economic markets.[77] The net effect was that several countries, in particular Greece, Ireland, and Portugal, required very large amounts of assistance provided from funds financed by other Member States. Italy and Spain were also on the 'danger list'. The assistance was subject to 'strict conditionality', which means that the funding to the recipient States was contingent on their introducing far-reaching economic and social reforms, which could increase unemployment when the general economic outlook was bleak.

The financial crisis had profound effects on the EU, including its constitutional architecture.[78] It generated a complex array of political responses to assist ailing States and increase oversight of national economic policy. The measures assumed varying legal forms, ranging from the enactment of ordinary EU legislation, to intergovernmental agreements made outside the formal confines of the Treaties. These developments had

[74] M Adams, F Fabbrini, and P Larouche (eds), *The Constitutionalization of European Budgetary Constraints* (Oxford: Hart Publishing, 2014); M Markakis, *Accountability in the Economic and Monetary Union: Foundations, Policy, and Governance* (Oxford: Oxford University Press, 2020); F Amtenbrink and C Herrmann (eds), *EU Law of Economic and Monetary Union* (Oxford: Oxford University Press, 2020); A Hinarejos, 'Economic and Monetary Union: Evolution and Conflict' in P Craig and G de Búrca (eds), *The Evolution of EU Law* (3rd edn, Oxford: Oxford University Press, 2021) ch 22.

[75] H James, H-W Micklitz, and H Schweitzer, 'The Impact of the Financial Crisis on the European Economic Constitution' (2010) EUI Working Papers, Law 2010/05.

[76] J-V Louis, 'Guest Editorial: The No-Bailout Clause and Rescue Packages' (2010) 47 *Common Market Law Review* 971.

[77] M Maduro, 'A New Governance for the European Union and the Euro: Democracy and Justice' (2012) European Parliament, Directorate-General for Internal Policies, Policy Department C: Citizens' Rights and Constitutional Affairs, PE 462.484.

[78] P Craig, 'Economic Governance and the Euro Crisis: Constitutional Architecture and Constitutional Implications' in Adams, Fabbrini, and Larouche (n 74).

profound consequences for the legal, economic, and political dimensions of the EU, and indeed for the balance between the 'economic' and the 'social' within the EU. The social dimension of EU policy has been markedly affected by austerity policies at both EU and national levels.

7.2 **Brexit**

The EEC continued to expand since its inception. Prior to the Lisbon Treaty, there was no Treaty article dealing with the possibility that a state might wish to leave. This issue is now governed by Article 50 TEU. The UK voted to leave the EU in the referendum held on 23 June 2016. The implications are dealt with in more detail in chapter 27.

Suffice it to say for the present context that David Cameron, the then UK Prime Minister, promised in June 2013 to hold a referendum after the next election on whether the UK should remain in the EU. The promise was made because of pressure from Eurosceptic Conservative MPs, and because it was thought to be a way of keeping the UK Independence Party at bay. Electoral success in 2015 brought renewed pressure to honour the promise to hold a referendum, which was duly held on 23 June 2016. The referendum contest was fought fiercely, and four issues dominated the debate: the economic implications of leaving the EU; control over immigration; sovereignty; and a populist/anti-establishment sentiment prevalent in some parts of the electorate.

The decision to leave was the beginning of the UK's withdrawal process, which is regulated by Article 50 TEU. It requires a Member State to notify the European Council of its intention to withdraw. It stipulates that a withdrawal agreement shall be made within two years from the date of this notification. If this does not happen, the Member State leaves without an agreement, unless the other Member States agree with the withdrawing State to extend the time line.

The Article 50 notification was duly given on 29 March 2017, and the European Union (Notification of Withdrawal) Act 2017 gave the Prime Minister power to notify the European Council of the UK's intention to withdraw from the EU under Article 50(2).

There then followed over two years of protracted negotiations between the UK and the EU to secure a Withdrawal Agreement. This was agreed by European leaders on 25 November 2018, and then laid before the UK Parliament on 26 November 2018. Section 13 of the European Union (Withdrawal) Act 2018 required that the Withdrawal Agreement should be approved by Parliament. However, the government failed to secure the requisite majority in votes on 15 January 2019, 12 March 2019, and 29 March 2019. The failure to secure parliamentary approval for the Withdrawal Agreement led to the UK making two requests for extension of the two-year period in Article 50. These requests were granted, so that the new deadline became 31 October 2019.

However, the Prime Minister, Theresa May, resigned on 23 May 2019, following pressure from her own party. Boris Johnson succeeded her as Prime Minister, and negotiated a revised Withdrawal Agreement. European leaders agreed to this at the European Council on 17 October 2019. Boris Johnson initially failed to secure parliamentary authorization for his revised Withdrawal Agreement. However, he achieved a significant majority in the election held on 12 December 2019. This enabled him to complete the process whereby the UK left the EU with the revised Agreement, which was completed on 31 January 2020. There was a transitional period, which lasted until 31 December 2020, during which the UK remained bound by EU law.

Brexit entailed multiple pieces of domestic legislation, but there were two principal statutes. The European Union (Withdrawal) Act 2018 became law on 26 June 2018 and was designed to ensure that the UK had a functioning statute book when the UK left the

EU. The European Union (Withdrawal Agreement) Act 2020 gave effect in UK law to the revised Withdrawal Agreement. The UK is a dualist country, such that treaties have no effect in domestic law until they have statutory authorization.

The EU and the UK then negotiated a Trade and Cooperation Agreement to regulate trade in a post-Brexit world.[79] This was given legal effect in the UK by the European Union (Future Relationship) Act 2020.

The EU now has 27 Member States. There is no doubt that Brexit had profound implications for the EU. The very idea that a State should seek to leave, when hitherto the momentum had been in the other direction, with States seeking to join, was a significant jolt to the EU. However, Brexit also led the other Member States to pull together during the Brexit negotiations, and revealed the difficulties that would be encountered by a State that sought to leave the EU.

7.3 **Migration crisis**

The pressures on the EU have been exacerbated by the migration crisis, which has seen very large numbers of people from Africa and the Middle East seeking to move to the EU. Some are asylum seekers fleeing from war-torn countries such as Syria and Iraq, others are economic migrants in search of a better life.

This has placed a tremendous strain on the EU, and more particularly Member States such as Italy and Greece, which have borne the brunt of those making the journey by sea. There is an EU asylum policy, which is discussed in chapter 25, but it was never initially designed to deal with such mass movements of people. It is predicated on the assumption that in most cases the Member State first entered by the migrant has the obligation to process the claim and grant asylum if the conditions are met. The EU has attempted to modify the existing asylum regime, such that each State would be obliged to accept a quota of asylum seekers, but it has proven difficult to generate political support to enact such measures. The danger is then that States will resort to unilateral measures, which fly in the face of EU and international law.

7.4 **'Rule of law' crisis**

The EU has also had to face further difficulties, which are commonly labelled the 'rule of law' crisis. The concerns were raised by governmental behaviour in certain Member States—Hungary, Romania, and Poland—whereby changes were made which undermined the independence of the judiciary. The EU can address such issues through Article 7 TEU, but there are political and legal difficulties with application of this Treaty article (see chapter 9). The ways in which the EU has responded to the rule of law problems are considered in later chapters of the book. There are three rationales for EU involvement in this area.

First, compliance with the rule of law is seen as a prerequisite for the protection of all fundamental values listed in Article 2 TEU: respect for human dignity, freedom, democracy, equality, and human rights. Secondly, compliance with the rule of law is perceived as a prerequisite for upholding all rights and obligations derived from the Treaties and from international law. Thirdly, such compliance is required to ensure the mutual trust on which the area of freedom, security, and justice is grounded. The Area of Freedom, Security and Justice (AFSJ) schema demands that a European Arrest Warrant against an alleged criminal issued in one Member State should be executed in other Member States.

[79] [2021] OJ L149/10.

If there are concerns as to the rule of law in an EU country related to its judicial system, then this undermines the trust that is a necessary precondition for such mutual recognition to operate.

7.5 **Pandemic crisis**

The Coronavirus hit the EU in 2020. Its effects were felt especially strongly in Italy, Spain, and the UK, but all Member States were affected to some degree. There were multiple dimensions to the crisis, as attested to by its impact on health, free movement, and macroeconomic policy. The EU's competence differs in each area. Thus, in relation to health, the EU's competence is to complement that of the Member States,[80] while its competence in relation to EMU is bounded by the proscription of bailouts.[81] The Court of Justice of the European Union (CJEU) interpreted the salient provisions teleologically to help save the euro during the financial crisis,[82] but there were nonetheless limits as to what could be done by the ECB and other EU institutions. The EU nonetheless did a considerable amount within the legal limits of its competence, and within the political constraints of what the Member States were willing to accept.[83]

The initiatives were far-reaching. This is especially so in relation to the Next Generation EU programme (NGEU 2020), which provides EU financial assistance to the Member States. The EURI Regulation, based on Article 122 TFEU, established an EU fund of €750 billion to support recovery, broadly conceived, from the difficulties caused by the Covid-19 crisis.[84] It allocated the resources among the various NGEU programmes, with the great majority going to the Recovery and Resilience Facility, RRF, which was assigned €312.5 billion of grants and €360 billion of loans.[85] The third component of the NGEU package was an amendment to the EU's Own Resources Decision, which allowed the €750 billion to be raised by EU borrowing on the financial markets, with the sums to be fully repaid by 31 December 2058 at the latest.[86] These measures are important, and have implications for the fiscal capacity of the EU, connoting in this context its ability to incur debt on the financial markets to be repaid in due course.[87]

[80] Art 168 TFEU. [81] Art 123 TFEU, Art 125 TFEU.

[82] Case C-370/12 *Pringle v Government of Ireland, Ireland and the Attorney General*, EU:C:2012:756; Case C-62/14 *Gauweiler v Deutsche Bundestag*, EU:C:2015:400; Case C-493/17 *Weiss*, EU:C:2018:1000. See chapter 19. On the impact of EU funding in specific fields, see particularly chapters 25 and 26.

[83] See eg K Purnhagen et al, 'More Competences Than You Knew? The Web of Health Competences for Union Action in Response to the COVID-19 Outbreak', Amsterdam Law School Legal Studies Research Paper No 2020-13; T Tesche, 'The European Union's Response to the Coronavirus Emergency: An Early Assessment', LEQS Paper No 157/2020; A Barbier-Gauchard et al, 'Towards a More Resilient European Union after the COVID-19 Crisis', BETA No 2020-33.

[84] Council Regulation (EU) 2020/2094, of 14 December 2020, establishing a European Union Recovery Instrument to support the recovery in the aftermath of the COVID-19 crisis (OJ [2020] L433 I/23).

[85] Regulation (EU) 2021/241 of the European Parliament and of the Council of 12 February 2021 establishing the Recovery and Resilience Facility (OJ [2021] L57/17).

[86] Council Decision (EU, Euratom) 2020/2053, of 14 December 2020, on the system of own resources of the European Union and repealing Decision 2014/335/EU, Euratom (OJ [2020] L424/1).

[87] B de Witte, 'The European Union's COVID-19 Recovery Plan: The Legal Engineering of an Economic Policy Shift' (2021) 58 *Common Market Law Review* 635; P Leino-Sandberg and M Ruffert, 'Next Generation EU and its Constitutional Ramifications: A Critical Assessment' (2022) 59 *Common Market Law Review* 433; F Fabbrini, 'Next Generation EU: Legal Structure and Constitutional Consequences' (2022) REBUILD Centre—Working Paper 3; F Amtenbrink and M Markakis, 'Never Waste a Good Crisis: On the Emergence of an EU Fiscal Capacity' in A Hinarejos and R Schütze (eds), *EU Fiscal Federalism: Past, Present, Future* (Oxford: Oxford University Press, 2023) ch 7.

7.6 **Conference on the Future of Europe**

The advent of the 2019 European Parliament and Commission brought EU reform back on the table. The catalyst for this was in part an earlier Commission White Paper on the future of Europe.[88] The idea was supported by the European Parliament,[89] and the European Council.[90] The new Commission President, Ursula von der Leyen, committed in her political guidelines to establish 'a Conference on the Future of Europe'.[91] It was to be a two-year process, which would begin on Europe Day, 9 May 2020,[92] the objective being to revitalize the EU post-Brexit.

The Conference on the Future of Europe (CFE) engaged in a broad array of consultations.[93] It contained 49 proposals and 326 more specific measure structured around nine themes:[94] climate change and the environment; health; a stronger economy, social justice, and jobs; EU in the world; values and rights, rule of law, and security; digital transformation; European democracy; migration; and education, culture, youth, and sport.

The Commission responded rapidly to the CFE Report.[95] Its response was divided into four categories: existing Commission initiatives that addressed the CFE proposals; Commission proposals currently under consideration that did so; areas where the Commission intended to make proposals and would consider suggestions made by the CFE; and areas where CFE proposals required new Commission initiatives. The Commission responses included an admixture of legislative and non-legislative action, either because of limited legislative competence or because it was the best way to reach the desired outcome. The Commission also noted that not all CFE proposals fell within its competence, and that some could be best initiated by other EU institutions. It was, moreover, clear that while many proposals could be accommodated within the Lisbon Treaty, there were some that would require Treaty change.

7.7 **War in Ukraine**

The challenges faced by the EU are not purely internal, in the sense of being related to its political and institutional ordering. There are also external challenges, most notably in relation to the Russian invasion and war in Ukraine. The EU has supported Ukraine with significant financial assistance, and sanctions against Russia (see further chapter 26). The EU's response has been rendered more complicated because a small group of EU Member States take a different view concerning responsibility for the conflict. This division of opinion has in turn made talks concerning possible Ukrainian accession to the EU more difficult, given that unanimity among the Member States in the Council is necessary for accession of a new State to the EU under Article 49 TEU.

[88] The Future of Europe, 1 March 2017.

[89] European Parliament resolution of 16 February 2017 on possible evolutions of and adjustments to the current institutional set-up of the European Union, P8_TA(2017)0048.

[90] Sibiu Declaration, 9 May 2019.

[91] Commission President candidate Ursula von der Leyen, 'A Union that strives for more: My Agenda for Europe, Political Guidelines for the Next European Commission 2019–2024', 16 July 2019, 19.

[92] Shaping the Conference on the Future of Europe, COM(2020) 27 final.

[93] Conference on the Future of Europe (archive-it.org).

[94] Conference on the Future of Europe, Report on the Final Outcome, May 2022, 2po250fn174z62m8g-8c9ya9e62m7 (archive-it.org).

[95] Conference on the Future of Europe, 'Putting Vision into Concrete Action', COM(2022) 404 final; Conference on the Future of Europe—European Commission (europa.eu).

8 Theories of integration

The preceding discussion has shown how the EEC has changed since its inception. There is a related but distinct issue, which is the rationale for this integration. The original EEC Treaty has been amended on many occasions, and the subject matter over which the EU has competence has expanded very considerably. It is important to consider the rationale for this. There is a wealth of literature, principally from political science, and there is not surprisingly debate as to the causes of integration (see also chapter 11).

8.1 Neofunctionalism

Neofunctionalism was the early ideology of Community integration.[96] The central tenet of neofunctionalism was the concept of 'spillover'. Functional spillover was based on the interconnectedness of the economy. Integration in one sphere created pressure for integration in other areas. Thus, for example, removal of formal tariff barriers would generate a need to deal with non-tariff barriers, which could equally inhibit realization of a single market. Political spillover was equally important and involved the build-up of political pressure in favour of further integration. In integrated areas, interest groups would be expected to concentrate their attention on the Community, and apply pressure on those with regulatory power. Such groups would become mindful of remaining barriers to interstate trade, which prevented them from reaping the rewards of existing integration, thereby adding to the pressure for further integration. The Commission was seen as a major player in this political spillover, since it would encourage the beliefs of the State players. Neofunctionalism was to be the vehicle through which Community integration, conceived of as technocratic, elite-led gradualism, was to be realized. The idea of spillover reinforced the view that gradualism was a meaningful strategy for integration. Legitimacy was conceived of in terms of outcomes, increased prosperity, which was to be secured through technocracy, even if this meant a marginal role for elected bodies.[97]

Neofunctionalism was challenged empirically and theoretically. The empirical challenge was based on its failure to explain the Community's development. The 1965 Luxembourg crisis had a profound impact. The resulting de facto unanimity principle signalled that Member States were not willing to allow Community development inconsistent with their vital interests. Decision-making was conducted in the shadow of the veto. The Commission's role changed from emerging government for the Community to a more cautious bureaucracy.[98] Moreover, evidence of interest-group pressure for greater integration was found to be equivocal.[99]

The theoretical challenge to neofunctionalism was based on the fact that its failure to accord with political reality led to theoretical modification that rendered it increasingly indeterminate,[100] and on neofunctionalism's failure to relate to general themes within

[96] E Haas, *The Uniting of Europe: Political, Social and Economic Forces 1950–1957* (Stanford, CA: Stanford University Press, 1958); L Lindberg, *The Political Dynamics of European Economic Integration* (Stanford, CA: Stanford University Press, 1963); L Lindberg and S Scheingold, *Europe's Would-Be Polity: Patterns of Change in the European Community* (Upper Saddle River, NJ: Prentice Hall, 1970); L Lindberg and S Scheingold, *Regional Integration* (Cambridge, MA: Harvard University Press, 1970).

[97] Lindberg and Scheingold, *Europe's Would-Be Polity* (n 96) 268–269.

[98] K Neunreither, 'Transformation of a Political Role: The Case of the Commission of the European Communities' (1971–2) 10 *Journal of Common Market Studies* 233.

[99] S George, *Politics and Policy in the European Union* (3rd edn, Oxford: Oxford University Press, 1996) 41–43.

[100] A Moravcsik, 'Preferences and Power in the European Community: A Liberal Intergovernmentalist Approach' (1993) 31 *Journal of Common Market Studies* 473, 476.

international relations, which sought to explain why States engaged in international cooperation. It would, nonetheless, be wrong to conclude that neofunctionalism has no explanatory value for EU integration, and it is arguable that functional spillover created impetus for further integration.[101]

8.2 **Liberal intergovernmentalism**

An alternative theory of integration is known as liberal intergovernmentalism, championed by Moravcsik.[102] His thesis is rooted in a branch of international relations theory. The central thesis is that States are the driving forces behind integration, that supranational actors are there largely at their behest, and that such actors have little independent impact on the pace of integration.

The demand for integration is said to depend on national preferences, which are aggregated through their political institutions.[103] The increase in cross-border flows of goods and services create what are termed 'international policy externalities' among nations, which can have negative side effects on other States, thereby creating an incentive for policy coordination. The supply of integration is said to be a function of interstate bargaining and strategic interaction. Domestic preferences define 'a "bargaining space" of potentially viable agreements, each of which generates gains for one or more participants'.[104] Governments choose one such agreement, normally through negotiation. Integration is pursued through a supranational institution because it is felt to be more efficient. Constructing individual ad hoc bargains between States can be costly.[105] This problem is obviated by a supranational structure such as the EU. The same basic driving force of efficiency is said to explain decision-making procedures in the EU. Thus Member States carry out a cost–benefit calculation, with the decision to delegate or pool sovereignty signalling the willingness of national governments to accept an increased risk of being outvoted or overruled on any individual issue in exchange for more efficient collective decision-making.[106]

8.3 **Multi-level governance**

Liberal intergovernmentalism was predicated on the assumption that supranational institutions enabled national governments to attain policy goals that could not be obtained by independent action.[107] This State-centric view was challenged by those who saw the EU in terms of multi-level governance.

Thus Marks, Hooghe, and Blank argued that integration was a process in which authority and policymaking were shared across multiple levels of government—sub-national,

[101] George (n 99) 40–41.

[102] Moravcsik, 'Preferences and Power' (n 100); A Moravcsik, *National Preference Formation and Interstate Bargaining in the European Community, 1955–86* (Cambridge, MA: Harvard University Press, 1992); A Moravcsik, 'Negotiating the Single European Act: National Interests and Conventional Statecraft in the European Community' (1991) 45 *International Organization* 19.

[103] Moravcsik, 'Preferences and Power' (n 100) 481.

[104] Ibid, 497.

[105] J Buchanan and G Tullock, *The Calculus of Consent: Logical Foundations of Constitutional Democracy* (Ann Arbor, MI: University of Michigan Press, 1962).

[106] Moravcsik, 'Preferences and Power' (n 100) 509–510.

[107] A Milward, *The European Rescue of the Nation State* (Berkeley, CA: University of California Press, 1992); A Milward and V Sorensen, 'Independence or Integration? A National Choice' in A Milward, R Ranieri, F Romero, and V Sorensen (eds), *The Frontier of National Sovereignty: History and Theory, 1945–1992* (London: Routledge, 1993); P Taylor, 'The European Community and the State: Assumptions, Theories and Propositions' (1991) 17 *Review of International Studies* 109.

national, and supranational.[108] National governments were major players, but did not have a monopoly of control. Supranational institutions, including the Commission, the European Parliament, and the ECJ, had influence in policymaking and could not merely be regarded as agents of national governments.[109] When competence over a certain subject matter has been transferred to the EU, proponents of multi-level governance contend that there are real limits to the degree of individual and collective State control over EU decisions.[110] Thus while Member States may play the decisive role in the Treaty-making process, they do not exert a monopoly of influence. The ability of the 'principals', the Member States, to control the 'agents', the Commission, and the Court of Justice, is limited by several factors, including the 'multiplicity of principals, the mistrust that exists among them, impediments to coherent principal action, informational asymmetries between principals and agents, and by the unintended consequences of institutional change'.[111]

8.4 **Rational choice institutionalism**

Rational choice institutionalism is a derivative of rational choice theory. The latter is premised on methodological individualism, whereby individuals have preferences, and choose the course of action that is the optimal method of securing them.[112] Rational choice institutionalists were critical of liberal intergovernmentalism because of the minimal role that the latter accorded to EU institutions,[113] although the gap between the two theories became narrower in the late 1990s.[114]

Proponents of rational choice institutionalism acknowledged that institutions were important. Institutions constituted the rules of the game, thereby enhancing equilibrium, and they exemplified principal–agent analysis. Member State 'principals' delegated to supranational 'agents' to enhance the credibility of their commitments, and to deal with incomplete contracting, since Treaty provisions are often open to a spectrum of possible interpretations. Principal–agent literature focused on the controls that the principal might use to ensure that the agent did not deviate from the desired goals of the principal.[115]

8.5 **Constructivism**

Constructivists agree with rational choice institutionalists that institutions matter. They nonetheless dispute the foundations of much rational choice literature, more especially methodological individualism and the idea that individual or State preferences are 'given'. Constructivists contend that the relevant environment in which preferences are formed

[108] G Marks, L Hooghe, and K Blank, 'European Integration from the 1980s: State-Centric v Multiple-Level Governance' (1996) 34 *Journal of Common Market Studies* 341, 342.

[109] Ibid, 346. [110] Ibid, 350–351. [111] Ibid, 353–354.

[112] J Jupille, J Caporaso, and J Checkel, 'Integrating Institutions: Rationalism, Constructivism, and the Study of the European Union' (2003) 36 *Comparative Political Studies* 7.

[113] M Pollack, 'International Relations Theory and European Integration' (2000) EUI Working Papers, RSC 2000/55.

[114] This was primarily because Moravcsik modified his theory to acknowledge that supranational institutions might have greater powers over agenda-setting and the making of EU law outside major Treaty negotiations than he had posited in his earlier work: A Moravcsik, *The Choice for Europe: Social Purpose and State Power from Messina to Maastricht* (Ithaca, NY: Cornell University Press, 1998) 8.

[115] M Pollack, *The Engines of European Integration: Delegation, Agency, and Agenda Setting in the EU* (Oxford: Oxford University Press, 2003); Pollack (n 113).

is inescapably social.[116] This impacts on, and thus constitutes, a person's understanding of their own interests. Institutions embody social norms and affect a person's interests and identity.

Thus, whereas rational choice institutionalism regards institutions as rules of the game that provide incentives within which players pursue their given preferences, constructivists regard institutions more broadly to include 'informal rules and intersubjective understandings as well as formal rules, and posit a more important and fundamental role for institutions, which constitute actors and shape not simply their incentives but their preferences and identities as well'.[117]

There have been attempts to soften the divide between rational choice institutionalism and constructivism.[118] Many rational choice theorists accept that preferences may well be altruistic as opposed to egoistic, and that preferences may be constrained by social structure. There have also been efforts to test the relative cogency of the two approaches through carefully crafted case studies.[119]

9 Conclusion

There will be no attempt to summarize the preceding analysis. Two more general points should be borne in mind concerning this material when reading later chapters in this book.

First, there have always been debates, both political and academic, as to why the EU has the array of powers that it currently possesses. This has been a theme in the contending theories of integration, and it has surfaced repeatedly in conflicting claims as to the relative degree of influence of the ECJ (now Court of Justice) in furthering the integration process. A simple fact should nonetheless be borne in mind when thinking about this issue. It was the Member States acting by unanimity through a series of Treaty amendments spanning 30 years that decided to accord new heads of power to the EU. This should again be borne firmly in mind when claims are made that the current disposition of power is the result of some unwarranted arrogation of power by EU institutions.

Secondly, the balance between the 'economic' and the 'social' dimension of the EU has always been contentious. The successive Treaty amendments accorded the EU power over a broad array of subject matter—economic, social, and political in nature. While the EEC began with primarily economic aims, the establishment of a common market, the founding Member States were always alive to the interconnection between the economic, social, and political facets of society. They did not imagine that the economic dimension could be hermetically sealed, and this was symbolically reflected in the shift of nomenclature from EEC to EC. It also serves to explain the grant of social power to the EU, this being justified in part in order to prevent the balance between the economic and the social within the EU being tilted too greatly in favour of the former. A danger of the financial crisis is that the social dimension will be sidelined as a result of the prominence given to resolution of economic problems.

[116] T Risse, 'Exploring the Nature of the Beast: International Relations Theory and Comparative Policy Analysis Meet the European Union' (1996) 34 *Journal of Common Market Studies* 53; J Checkel, 'The Constructivist Turn in International Relations Theory' (1998) 50 *World Politics* 324; T Christiansen, K Jorgensen, and A Wiener, 'The Social Construction of Europe' (1999) 6 *Journal of European Public Policy* 528.

[117] Pollack (n 113) 14–15.

[118] J Checkel, 'Bridging the Rational-Choice/Constructivist Gap? Theorizing Social Interaction in European Institutions' (2000) University of Oslo, ARENA Working Papers, WP 00/11.

[119] See eg the essays in (2003) 36 *Comparative Political Studies*.

Further reading

M Bond and K Feus, *The Treaty of Nice Explained* (London: Federal Trust, 2001)

D Chryssochoou, *Theorizing European Integration* (Thousand Oaks, CA: Sage, 2001)

R Corbett, *The Treaty of Maastricht* (London: Longman, 1993)

P Craig, *The Lisbon Treaty: Law, Politics, and Treaty Reform* (Oxford: Oxford University Press, 2010)

A Duff (ed), *The Treaty of Amsterdam* (London: Sweet & Maxwell, 1997)

N MacCormick, *Who's Afraid of a European Constitution?* (Exeter: Imprint Academic, 2005)

A Moravcsik, *The Choice for Europe* (London: University College London Press, 1999)

P Norman, *The Accidental Constitution: The Making of Europe's Constitutional Treaty* (Brussels: EuroComment, 2005)

D O'Keefe and P Twomey (eds), *Legal Issues of the Amsterdam Treaty* (Oxford: Hart Publishing, 1999)

J-C Piris, *The Lisbon Treaty: A Legal and Political Analysis* (Cambridge: Cambridge University Press, 2010)

J-C Piris, *The Constitution for Europe: A Legal Analysis* (Cambridge: Cambridge University Press, 2006)

A Wiener, T Borzel, and T Risse (eds), *European Integration Theory* (3rd edn, Oxford: Oxford University Press, 2018)

J Winter, D Curtin, A Kellermann, and B de Witte, *Reforming the Treaty on European Union: The Legal Debate* (Alphen aan den Rijn: Kluwer, 1996)

J Ziller, *La nouvelle Constitution Européenne* (Paris: La Découverte, 2005)

3

The EU's political institutions

Steve Peers

1 Introduction

All of the EU's Member States are representative democracies. Furthermore, according to Article 10(1) TEU, as revised by the Treaty of Lisbon, 'the functioning of the Union shall be founded on representative democracy' (ie the concept that decisions are taken by politicians who have a democratic mandate). More precisely, Article 10(2) TEU specifies that the European Parliament is directly elected, the Council consists of Member States' ministers, and the European Council (which should be distinguished from the Council) consists of heads of State or government—the latter two groups being accountable to the voters or parliament of each individual Member State. But, despite this, there is a widespread perception that the EU is highly undemocratic.

This potentially raises tensions with another key feature of the EU's system: the attempt to ensure that EU law is effective. Effectiveness depends on there being EU measures in existence in the first place—and therefore upon the effective functioning of the EU's political institutions, since they are the main source of such EU measures. To that end, the Treaties provide that Member States' governments usually do not have a veto over the adoption of EU measures. But, for those citizens who believe that, at least for some matters, only the decisions of their *national* politicians can be regarded as democratic, this is a fundamental problem. Indeed, it was one of the features of EU law that led to the UK vote to leave the EU (on which, see chapter 27). Again, as discussed in chapter 1, we see a conflict, at least on some occasions, between different concepts of legitimacy: input legitimacy (public acceptance of the procedures which lead to the adoption of decisions) on the one hand, and output legitimacy (public approval of the substantive outcome of the decision-making process) on the other.

This chapter examines this possible tension between democracy and effectiveness in the context of the EU's political institutions: the European Parliament, the European Council, the Council, and the Commission. To this end, it examines in turn the composition, powers, and functioning of each of these institutions, comparing them to national systems and assessing their democratic accountability and the effectiveness of their functioning. Some key aspects of their powers (the adoption of legislation and other measures) are discussed in more detail in chapter 5,[1] and the details of their functioning in certain specific areas are discussed in other chapters (eg chapter 17 as regards competition law).

It will be seen that, largely to address concerns about democratic accountability, the role of various EU institutions has evolved over time—in particular to strengthen the legislative function of the European Parliament, and that body's control over the Commission. Similarly, the European Council has been enhancing its position as an EU institution, at the Commission's expense. These developments might have cumulatively increased the democratic legitimacy of the EU system, but decreased its efficiency. Conversely, as regards the Council, there has been a long-term shift towards increasingly using a form of majority voting instead of unanimous voting of Member States, thereby increasing the efficiency of the EU (ie its capacity to take decisions) at the possible cost of democratic legitimacy (because the democratic governments of Member States can be outvoted more often, and they are perceived by many to be more legitimate than the EU's institutions).

Although, according to Article 13(1) TEU, there are three other official EU institutions—the Court of Justice, the European Central Bank, and the Court of Auditors—this chapter focuses on the institutions which have essentially political tasks. The rules governing some of the EU's other institutions, and the EU's offices, bodies, and agencies generally, are discussed elsewhere in this book.[2]

2 The concept of representative democracy

In theory, representative democracy is simple. The public decides which politicians (who usually group themselves into political parties) they wish to vote for at each election, judge the performance of the successful politicians (ie the public's representatives) while in government, and then decide at the next election whether they wish to re-elect the same politicians or to vote for someone else.

But, in practice, when it comes to designing a system for representative democracy, questions soon arise. What voting system should be used? Who gets to vote in elections? In the modern day, few now argue that women should be denied the right to vote, or that people should be excluded from voting because they do not have enough property, but what about foreigners? When should they be allowed to vote—if ever?

Furthermore, most modern political systems are more complex than the simple example given earlier—comprising only a single level of government with one legislative chamber. The larger and more diverse the groups of people voting (ie the electorate), the more likely that these groups (as defined, eg by language, region, class, or ethnicity) have a conflicting point of view on some key issues. If the country being governed is fairly large and/or diverse, an obvious way to address this is by providing for multiple levels of

[1] On the democratic context of the EU's decision-making rules, see particularly section 11 of that chapter.

[2] On the Court of Justice, see chapter 10; on the European Central Bank, see chapter 19; on the agencies, see generally chapter 8. The EU also has two advisory bodies, the Economic and Social Committee and the Committee of the Regions (see Art 13(4) TEU and Arts 300–307 TFEU), which are not further discussed here.

government, so that at least as regards some issues (eg education or criminal law) different parts of the country can decide to have different policies if the electorates vote for this. So, a country can be established as a federal State like Germany (or, outside the EU, the US, Canada, or Australia). As discussed further in chapter 4, a 'federal' State is one which divides powers between the central ('federal') government level and the sub-federal level (known, eg, as states, provinces, or Länder). The opposite situation, where all powers in principle are held by the central government, is known as a 'unitary' State—for example, Ireland or the Netherlands.

However, there are other ways of dividing power between different levels of government. While the UK is in principle a unitary State, it has devolved power to some of its nations (Scotland, Wales, and Northern Ireland), and many unitary States give a significant role to local governments (ie the governments of cities, towns, and counties). Having said that, at least in principle, the central governments of unitary States could take such powers away from devolved or local governments, although that might prove difficult in practice. For instance, any attempt by the UK's central government to abolish the Scottish parliament without the consent of the Scottish people in a referendum would probably lead to increased support for Scottish independence. On the other hand, the division of powers between the two levels of government in federal States is, as discussed in chapter 4, entrenched by a constitution which has a higher rank than ordinary law, and cannot be amended without the consent of (usually) both levels of government.

Another way of addressing regional concerns, or the concerns of other diverse groups in society, is by establishing a second parliamentary chamber (ie a 'bicameral legislature'; again see further chapter 4). Like the UK (ie the House of Commons and the House of Lords), the majority of EU States, such as Germany (the Bundestag and Bundesrat) and France (the National Assembly and the Senate), have established such a two-chamber legislature. As the German example shows, it is common for federal States to have a bicameral legislature.

Moreover, as discussed in chapter 4, government does not consist of legislatures only, but has two other branches: the executive and the judiciary (on the latter, see further chapter 10). Political systems usually make some form of attempt to allocate specific functions between these three branches (the principle of separation of powers). The executive is made up of a core group of individuals, namely a president or prime minister, along with a cabinet and support staff. The executive (usually) drafts bills for the parliament to vote on, and determines the detail of government policy on a day-to-day basis. It includes a permanent administration (ie a bureaucracy, or civil service), with the task of advising the government and applying the law on an individual basis—for instance, processing applications for passports and student loans. This brings us to the question of how representative democracy works in the EU.

2.1 **Representative democracy and the EU**

As a rough starting point, it is useful to compare the EU's political institutions to the political institutions of States on a practical level (for a more theoretical version of this comparison, see chapter 4). The Commission can broadly be compared to the executive and administration (civil service) of the EU, while the Council and European Parliament can be compared to a two-chamber (bicameral) legislature, as described in the previous section. As in many bicameral systems, the lower house, in this case the European Parliament, is directly elected (like the House of Commons in the UK, or the Bundestag in Germany), but the upper house, in this case the Council, is not directly elected (like the House of Lords in the UK, or the Bundesrat in Germany). However, some executive powers have been conferred upon the Council and European Council.

Furthermore, as we will see in chapter 4, a key feature of the EU's political and legal system is that the division of powers between the EU and its Member States is comparable to the division of powers within federal States, as described previously. The system for the division of powers between the EU and its Member States is referred to as the rules on EU 'competences', and this system is discussed in detail in chapter 5. This current chapter sets out the institutional context of the EU's system of divided powers: in other words, how does the EU exercise its powers?

Another key feature of the EU system is that EU law is almost entirely administered by Member States—that is, it is national civil servants who, for instance, take action to enforce environmental law (see chapter 22), even though the substantive decisions which they make are largely determined by EU law. This is different to the approach in most federal States, although it is similar to the system in Germany, the EU's biggest federal State. For example, in the US the laws adopted by the federal government are often applied by federal agencies—the individual states cannot be ordered to act by the federal government (although they can be encouraged through the use of financial incentives). Within the EU system, an analogous obligation is instead recognized expressly by the Treaty, which states that 'Member States shall adopt all measures of national law necessary to implement legally binding Union acts'.[3] It is also reflected by the use of directives (which must be implemented by means of national law) to apply many EU policies,[4] and the role of national courts in the implementation of EU law.[5] Even where the EU institutions have traditionally taken the main role in administering EU law, in recent years that administration has also been decentralized.[6]

The relationship between the EU institutions can be seen in Fig. 3.1.

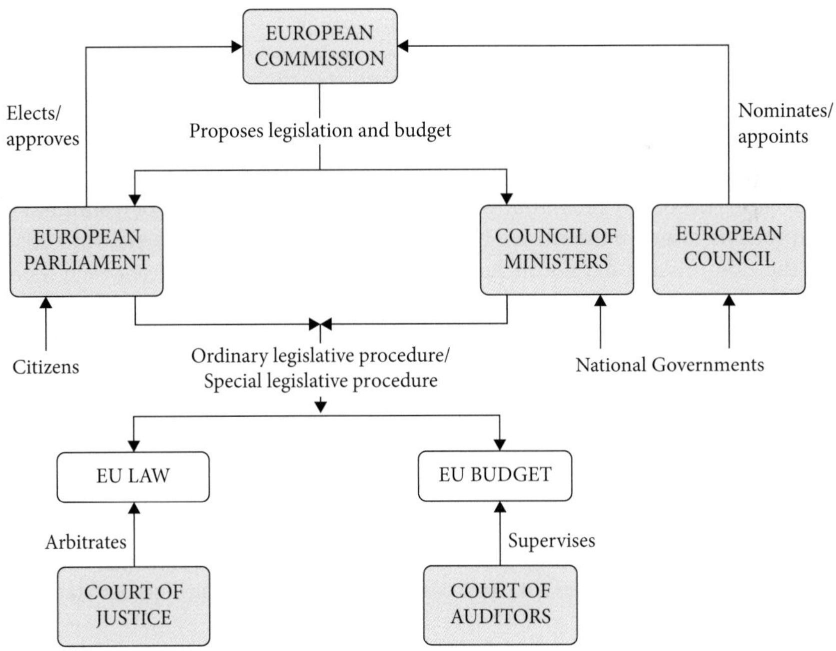

Fig. 3.1 The relationship between the EU institutions

[3] Art 291(1) TFEU. [4] See further chapters 5 and 6.
[5] See further chapter 10. [6] See eg chapter 17, as regards competition law.

3 Commission

3.1 Introduction

Our examination of the EU's political institutions starts with the Commission, since most EU measures (as we will see) are either adopted by the Commission, or begin life as a Commission proposal. The Commission's role in the EU political system often attracts strong criticism. This is because it has a great deal of power—although the extent of that power is often misunderstood and overstated—and because many believe that it is not sufficiently democratically accountable. In particular, as noted already in section 2.1, the Commission constitutes an important part of the executive, and is responsible for almost all of the day-to-day administration of the EU (ie applying EU law to individual cases)—although it should not be forgotten that most EU law is administered by Member States. The key provisions on the composition, powers, and functioning of the Commission are in Article 17 TEU, and further rules are set out in Article 18 TEU, as regards the EU's High Representative for its common foreign and security policy (the 'High Representative'), and Articles 244 to 250 TFEU.

3.2 Composition

The Commission consists first and foremost of a 'college of Commissioners', which includes two particularly important Commissioners discussed separately—its President (section 3.2.2) and the EU's High Representative for its common foreign and security policy (section 3.2.3). But the Commission also consists of thousands of permanent administrative staff (see further later in the section).

3.2.1 Number of members

The Commission initially consisted of one member from each Member State and one extra member from each of the five largest Member States (the pre-Brexit UK, France, Germany, Italy, and Spain). However, there were concerns that the number of Commissioners would become unmanageable after the extensive enlargement planned to the East (which was ultimately carried out in 2004). But while a reduction in the number of Commissioners would probably improve the efficiency of that institution, there was a contrary concern that if the Commission did not include at least one Commissioner from each Member State, it would lose some of its legitimacy.

The debate concerning the number of Commissioners ultimately became bound up with the even more difficult debate concerning the weighting of Member States' votes in the Council (see section 5), because the larger Member States did not want to give up their extra Commissioner unless they were given extra votes in the Council as a quid pro quo. It proved impossible to agree on these two issues during the negotiation of the Treaty of Amsterdam (in force 1999), so instead a Protocol was attached to the Treaties, stating that as of the next enlargement of the EU, there would be one Commissioner per Member State, provided that the weighting of votes in the Council had been adjusted 'in a manner acceptable to all Member States', in particular 'compensating' those Member States which lost a Commissioner.

It was no longer possible to put off this issue when negotiating the Treaty of Nice (in force 2003), given the imminence of EU enlargement. So this Treaty provided that there would be only one Commissioner per Member State as of 1 November 2004 (the start of the next Commission's term).[7] To increase efficiency, once the EU had 27 Member States

[7] On the parallel changes to Council voting, see section 5.

(which occurred in 2007), the next Commission to take office (ie as of 1 November 2009) would have fewer Commissioners than the number of Member States. But the Treaty negotiators could not agree how this would take place, so left it up to the Council to decide on the details, including the exact number of Commissioners and which Member States would lose a Commissioner at any given time.

However, the rules providing for a further reduction in the number of Commissioners from 2009 never came into effect, because the relevant provisions in the Treaties were amended again with the Treaty of Lisbon (in force 2009). Now the Treaties provide that the Commission remained at one Commissioner per Member State until 1 November 2014.[8] After that point, the number of Commissioners was meant to be reduced so that only two-thirds of Member States would have a Commissioner at any one time, with the European Council adopting detailed rules on the exact system of rotation of Commissioners between Member States.

But this plan never came into force either, because the European Council used its power to alter the number of Commissioners,[9] in order to address the concerns of Irish voters (who initially voted against the Treaty of Lisbon in 2008) about losing a permanent Commissioner. So as part of the deal to encourage Irish voters to vote in favour of the Treaty, EU leaders promised in December 2008 that if the Treaty of Lisbon were ratified, the European Council would decide to retain one Commissioner per Member State even after November 2014. Following the positive vote of the Irish public in a second referendum on that Treaty, and the subsequent entry into force of the Treaty of Lisbon, the decision to this effect was formally adopted in 2013.[10]

3.2.2 **The President**

As noted already, a key role in the Commission is the job of President.[11] According to the Treaty, he or she lays down the guidelines for the Commission's work; decides on the internal organization of the Commission, ensuring its efficiency, consistency, and collegiality; and appoints Vice-Presidents from among the Commission's members. These Vice-Presidents are in addition to the High Representative for the EU's foreign policy, who is always a Vice-President.

The President can reshuffle the Commission, and require a Commissioner to resign, so on paper at least he or she has powers similar to a prime minister over his or her cabinet (ie the executive of a Member State). But historically the President did not have such powers,[12] and in fact there has never been a major reshuffle of the sort seen in (for instance) British politics. The President does not have any kind of veto over Commission proposals, or over anything else. Having said that, the President usually has significant influence over the rest of the Commission, and some Presidents (Walter Hallstein, President from 1958 to 1967, and Jacques Delors, President from 1995 to 2005) have had a major impact on the EU integration process (although some end up in disgrace, eg the Santer Commission in 1999). Indeed, each Commission is named in practice after its President (at the time of writing, the 'Von der Leyen Commission', serving a second term from 2024 to 2029).

3.2.3 **High Representative**

The job of High Representative[13] was created, in its initial form, by the Treaty of Amsterdam in 1999. At this point, the post was part of the Council, not the Commission. The creation of the post was intended to simplify the Union's representation as regards foreign policy,

[8] Art 17(4) TEU. [9] Art 17(5) TEU; see also Art 244 TFEU. [10] OJ [2013] L165/98.
[11] Art 17(6) TEU and Art 248 TFEU. [12] They only date back to the Treaty of Nice.
[13] See Art 18 TEU.

which had previously been in the hands of the rotating Council Presidency (see section 5). However, this just raised more questions, since the rotating Council Presidency continued to exist, and there was also a Commissioner for external relations.

To reduce the complexity of the system, the Treaty of Lisbon recast the role of the High Representative. He or she is a Commissioner (indeed a Commission Vice-President) but is also, as regards his or her foreign policy tasks, answerable to the Council (on those tasks and on the High Representative's appointment and role in practice, see the following section and chapter 26).

3.2.4 **Appointment**

Historically, the Commission President, and then the rest of the Commission, was appointed by the Member States 'by common accord' (ie unanimously, with no abstentions possible). In practice, the only debate was over the name of the Commission President; otherwise Member States just accepted each other's nominees. After all, if (for example) the pre-Brexit UK had vetoed a French nominee, the French government would, in all likelihood, have vetoed a British nominee in retaliation. Each Member State normally nominated an individual from the governing political party (or the main governing party, in the event of a coalition). Due to the Commission's independence, however (see section 3.4), that individual would remain a Commissioner for the Commission's full term even if the appointing government changed hands.

There is also the question of which portfolios go to which Commissioner, given that some jobs in the Commission (eg being in charge of competition or external trade) are perceived to be better jobs than others (eg being in charge of administration). The appointment system meant (and still means) that the Commissioners came from diverse political backgrounds, as compared to national politics, where cabinet ministers are all members of the party (or coalition parties) which has (or have) a parliamentary majority. Usually, Commissioners are (or have recently been) senior cabinet ministers in their national governments; indeed, between 1995 and 2019, Commission Presidents were all sitting prime ministers in a Member State at their time of election.[14] For that reason, Commissioners are sometimes described derisively as 'failed politicians', although some of them do return to national political life after their term(s) in the Commission. In fact, there is usually a mini-exodus of Commissioners in the final year of a Commission's term, as cabinet posts and other desirable appointments in their respective national political systems become available.

Over the years, in order to address concerns about the Commission's democratic accountability, the role of the European Parliament in the Commission's appointment was enhanced considerably. The Parliament was first given the power to approve the appointment of the Commission as a whole (Maastricht Treaty), and then the Commission President (Treaty of Amsterdam). In 1995, the Commission's term of office (originally four years) was changed to five years,[15] in order to align it with the European Parliament terms. So a new Commission takes office every five years (at the time of writing the next Commission will take office on 1 November 2029), not long after the election of a new European Parliament (as discussed in section 4, the next election at the time of writing is in spring 2029).

Since the Treaty of Lisbon, the Treaties state that the Parliament, by a majority of its members (not just a majority of the votes), has the power to 'elect' the Commission President, although the European Council must first (by a qualified majority vote) nominate a single candidate for the Parliament's approval, 'taking account of' the results of

[14] eg the Commission President from 2014–19 was the sitting Prime Minister of Luxembourg.

[15] See now Art 17(3) TEU.

the European Parliament election which has just been held.[16] From one point of view, the revised procedure looks the same as the previous rules (where the European Parliament approved an appointment to be made by the European Council), but the reference to the Parliament electing the Commission President and taking account of the results of the elections to the Parliament suggests that a stronger link between those election results and the selection of the Commission President can be made.

In practice, it was already assumed in 1999, 2004, and 2009 that, in light of the Parliament's veto power over the appointment, the next Commission President had to come from the same political background as the largest party in the Parliament. But the names of potential candidates were only really discussed *after* the elections to the Parliament—meaning that the public voted in those elections without any discussion of who the next Commission President might be.[17] For the 2014 elections, though, the largest parties decided in advance who their preferred candidates were for the post of the Commission President.[18] This can obviously be compared to the election process in many Member States, where voters know that their (collective) vote for a particular political party will in effect determine who becomes (or remains) the prime minister after the elections. In the event, the European Parliament then insisted that the candidate nominated by the party which won the most seats (the European People's Party) should be elected as Commission President, by threatening to vote down any other nominee, and the European Council reluctantly conceded. However, although the parties nominated their preferred candidates for Commission President in 2019, the European Parliament did not insist this time that the candidate nominated by the party which won the most seats (the European People's Party again) should be elected as Commission President. But for 2024, the nominee of the party that won the most seats retained the post of Commission President.

After the election of the President, the other Commissioners are then appointed, on the basis of Member States' proposals, by agreement with the Commission President, by a qualified majority vote of the European Council and the approval of the European Parliament. The current Commissioners were appointed as of 1 December 2024.[19]

A special rule applies to the appointment of the High Representative. The holder of this post is selected by the European Council by a qualified majority vote, with the agreement of the Commission President. The High Representative is also subject to the vote of the European Parliament as regards the entire Commission. The most recent person to hold this post (Kaja Kallas) was appointed by the European Council with effect from 1 December 2024.[20]

Since the Treaty of Lisbon, there have been three important EU posts to fill at the same time, every five years (Commission President, High Representative, and European Council President—on which, see section 6). The posts are decided as part of a 'package deal'. Declaration 6 to the Treaty of Lisbon refers to the need to consider 'geographical and demographic diversity' (ie the size and location of Member States) when making the appointments, but in practice the European Council also considers political background (ie ensuring major posts are held from candidates from both the left and right of

[16] Art 17(7) TEU.

[17] One of the leading candidates *was* known in the 2009 elections—but only because he was the sitting President, and it was clear that the national governments where his party, the 'European People's Party', was in power, would nominate him for a new term if (as happened) that party was again the largest party following the elections.

[18] See the Commission recommendation on the conduct of the elections (OJ [2013] L79/29).

[19] OJ [2024] L 29.11.2024.

[20] OJ [2024] L 26.7.2024. On the terms of the job, see OJ [2009] L322/36.

the political spectrum) and gender (ie ensuring there are both men and women holding major posts).

While technically the European Parliament can only choose whether to vote for the entire Commission, not individual Commissioners, since 2004 it has found a way of rejecting individual nominees. When it was unsatisfied with the credentials or policies of a few of the would-be Commissioners, the Parliament simply threatened to reject the whole lot, and the targeted individuals then withdrew their names from contention.[21]

3.2.5 **Control of the Commission**

The basic question as regards political accountability can be summarized simply as, 'Can we throw the rascals out?' So how can the Commission be removed? Within the Member States (or the UK), a government usually has to resign if it loses a no-confidence vote in parliament. Following that, fresh elections are held, or another party or parties (or another potential prime minister) is/are given a chance to form a government. Similarly, the EU Treaties have always provided for the possibility for the European Parliament (but not the Council, or the European Council) to remove the entire Commission, by means of a 'censure' vote. But this is difficult to apply, as it requires a two-thirds vote of Members of the European Parliament (MEPs) in favour, including a majority of the members of the Parliament (ie an absence or abstention effectively counts as a vote to keep the Commission in office).[22] Even if one were passed, the High Representative would remain in office as regards his or her responsibilities to the Council.

Indeed, no censure vote has ever been passed. On the one occasion (the Santer Commission in 1999, as mentioned earlier) when a censure vote was absolutely certain to pass—every political party in the Parliament having declared its support, due to concerns that allegations about fraud and nepotism (the 'nepo baby' in question being one Commissioner's dentist[23]) as regards certain Commissioners had not been adequately investigated—the Commission simply jumped before it was pushed, with the Commissioners resigning en masse before they could be censured. The Treaties provide that in the event of censure or mass resignation, the Commissioners continue to remain in office until they are replaced.[24] This might take some time, and it potentially damages the EU's legitimacy that such 'guilty' individuals still retain their jobs. While it is sometimes claimed that the European Council could then simply reappoint the same 'censured' Commissioners again, this is clearly not politically realistic—as the Parliament would then obviously use its powers to reject a proposed Commission consisting wholly of individuals who it had just censured.[25]

Sometimes, of course, individual Commissioners are considered to be poor at their job, or otherwise unsuitable for it. In fact, the Parliament's planned censure vote of 1999 was essentially aimed at only a small number of the Commissioners then in office. But there was no way for the Parliament to remove those individual Commissioners. The Treaties do provide for the removal of individual Commissioners who are 'guilty of serious misconduct' or cannot do their job, by the Court of Justice on application by the Council or Commission, but this procedure was not used in 1999 or since.[26]

[21] eg compare the final list of Commissioners in 2019 ([2019] OJ L 304/16) to the initial nominations (OJ [2019] L231I/1). For the first time since 2004, in 2024 the European Parliament did not de facto reject any proposed Commissioners.

[22] See Art 17(8) TEU and Art 234 TFEU.

[23] Case C-432/04 *Commission v Cresson* [2006] ECR I-6387.

[24] Arts 234 and 246 TFEU.

[25] Even before it obtained such powers, the Parliament would obviously have used its powers to *censure* that reappointed Commission again as soon as it could.

[26] See Art 17(8) TEU and Art 234 TFEU.

It is now possible, as mentioned already, for the Commission President to force a Commissioner to resign, or to reshuffle the Commission. This is equivalent to the powers enjoyed by prime ministers over their cabinets; and in national politics, sustained serious criticism of a particular cabinet minister will probably sooner or later lead to his or her (forced) resignation, sacking by the prime minister, or removal from the cabinet or demotion to a lesser job at the time of the next reshuffle. But as noted already, no Commission President has ever reshuffled the Commission in a major way. Nor has any Commission President fired an individual Commissioner—although the issue has been litigated. When a Maltese Commissioner facing a public scandal resigned in 2012, he argued that he had in effect been dismissed, and tried to challenge his alleged dismissal in the EU Courts. But the Courts concluded (rather unconvincingly) that he had not been dismissed, but rather chose to resign.[27] Moreover, the European Parliament still cannot demand the removal of individual Commissioners. Yet perhaps a threat to use the censure vote would, by analogy with its threats to block the appointment of a new Commission, induce the Commission President to fire the Commissioner(s) concerned. By way of exception, the High Representative can lose their job, as the European Council can end their term of office by the same procedure which applies to their appointment.[28]

An individual vacancy in the Commission is filled by the Council, after consulting the European Parliament, with the agreement of the Commission President.[29]

3.3 **Powers**

Article 17(1) TEU sets out a very lengthy list of the Commission's tasks:

- to 'promote the general interest' of the EU and 'take appropriate initiatives to that end';
- to 'ensure the application of the Treaties' and measures giving effect to them;
- to 'oversee the application' of EU law, subject to the Court of Justice;
- to 'execute the budget and manage programmes';
- to exercise 'coordinating, executive and management functions';
- to 'ensure the Union's external representation', except as regards EU foreign policy (where the High Representative has this task);
- to 'initiate the Union's annual and multi-annual programming'.

Starting with the Commission's executive tasks, first of all, as Article 17(2) TEU provides, it has a near-monopoly on introducing proposals for EU legislation, meaning that EU legislation cannot be adopted unless the Commission initially proposed it.[30] The proposed legislative acts must then be agreed by the Council and the European Parliament.

Similarly, the Commission has a monopoly on negotiating most international treaties on behalf of the EU, and otherwise representing the Union on the international level, with the exceptions of foreign policy (mentioned already) and treaties related to monetary issues (where the Council decides on a case-by-case basis who the negotiator will be).[31]

[27] Case T-562/12 *Dalli*, EU:T:2015:270. The appeal was dismissed: Case C-394/15 P, EU:C:2016:262. A subsequent action for damages also failed: Case T-399/17 *Dalli*, EU:T:2019:384, also dismissed on appeal: Case C-615/19 P, EU:C:2021:133.

[28] Art 18(1) TEU. [29] Art 247 TFEU.

[30] There are limited derogations from the Commission's monopoly on making legislative proposals. For further discussion, see chapter 5.

[31] Arts 218 and 219 TFEU. For further discussion, see chapter 26. The Council conferred power on the Commission to negotiate the Brexit withdrawal agreement with the UK: see Art 50(2) TEU, discussed in chapter 27.

Again, however, any treaties negotiated by the Commission must then be approved by the Council (and usually also the European Parliament) to come into force, and before the Commission can start to negotiate, it must be granted authority to do so by the Council.

Another key executive task is the power to adopt delegated acts or implementing measures, that is, sub-legislative acts which set out further details of EU policies. Delegated acts, which 'supplement or amend' non-essential elements of EU legislative acts, can only be adopted by the Commission, although its adoption of such measures is subject to control by the Council and the European Parliament.[32] Implementing measures can be adopted when 'uniform conditions for implementing [EU acts] are needed'. Usually implementing measures can only be adopted by the Commission as well, but the Council adopts such measures as regards foreign policy and possibly as an exception in other cases.[33] The Commission's adoption of implementing measures is controlled by committees composed of Member States' officials.

These two tasks can be compared to the powers that are delegated to the executive and to civil servants in the Member States by acts of parliament in order to implement legislation (often known as 'secondary legislation', although that term is not used as regards the EU measures). However, the grant of power to the Commission is not usually as far-reaching as the grant of power to national executives and administrations. After all, as mentioned already, it is primarily up to Member States to implement EU law.

Next, the Commission has the legal right to take infringement actions against Member States which have not met their obligations under EU law.[34] This is an important means of ensuring the effective application of EU law, although it is also possible for individuals to use other means to enforce their EU law rights in the national courts (see chapter 6).

As for its administrative tasks, the Commission has the role of administering the EU's budget,[35] although the amount of each annual budget, and the multi-annual budget framework, is decided on first by the Council and the European Parliament.[36] The Commission is also subject to financial regulations adopted by those legislative bodies, and is supervised by the European Parliament as regards its budgetary management.[37]

Another key administrative job is to apply EU law in individual cases—for example, as regards EU competition law, where the Commission investigates cartels (ie groups of companies setting prices etc together) and monopolies (a single company controlling most or all of a market), and EU law on State aid (ie money given by governments to companies), where the Commission has the power to decide that such money must be repaid. But as noted already, the power to apply EU competition law has been partly decentralized, and most areas of EU law are implemented entirely by Member States.[38]

As for the High Representative, his or her job is to conduct the EU's foreign policy, and to make proposals regarding that policy, 'as mandated by the Council'.[39] In addition, he or she chairs the EU's Foreign Affairs Council (ie meetings of Member States' foreign ministers; see section 5).[40] But the High Representative also sits in the Commission and coordinates the Commission's overall external activity (ie trade, development, enlargement, etc).[41]

[32] Art 290 TFEU. For further discussion, see chapter 5.

[33] Art 291 TFEU. For further discussion, see chapter 5.

[34] Arts 258 and 260 TFEU; see further chapter 10. [35] Art 317 TFEU.

[36] Arts 311, 312, and 314 TFEU. [37] Arts 319 and 322 TFEU.

[38] eg the Commission cannot issue injunctions to enforce EU consumer law (see chapter 23), or European Arrest Warrants (see chapter 24).

[39] Art 18(2) TEU. [40] Art 18(3) TEU. [41] Art 18(4) TEU.

3.4 Functioning

The key feature of the Commission's functioning is that it is 'completely independent' and cannot take instructions from governments or any other body.[42] There is an obvious tension between this rule and the objective of ensuring the Commission's accountability, but its independence does not constrain the other EU institutions as regards whether to accept Commission proposals (for instance). Nor does it prevent the application of the rules (discussed previously) which provide that individual Commissioners could possibly be fired, or that the entire Commission could be censured. In any event, it is widely believed that many individual Commissioners have a closer relationship with the Member State that nominated them than the letter of the Treaty would allow.

As an exception, as noted already, the High Representative is accountable to the Council, as far as foreign policy is concerned, but as regards his or her other tasks, must be as independent as the rest of the Commission.

The college of Commissioners makes decisions by a majority, and in accordance with the Commission's rules of procedure.[43] For its administrative tasks, the Commission is organized into Directorates-General, each responsible for a particular subject, and usually presided over by a particular Commissioner. Since Commission proposals often have an impact on more than one subject, there are sometimes 'turf battles' between the Commissioners and Directorates-General. In some cases, these battles are resolved by two Commissioners making a joint proposal.[44] In these and many more cases, there are extensive 'inter-service consultations' between different Directorates-General before a proposal is made. For instance, the 2013 proposal for new EU legislation on the admission of students, researchers, and other persons from non-EU countries was made by the Home Affairs Commissioner,[45] but doubtless was discussed with the Commissioners responsible for education and research (among others) beforehand.

As regards the High Representative, a special rule in the Treaties requires a particular administration—the European External Action Service—to be set up (see further chapter 26).

4 European Parliament

4.1 Introduction

The European Parliament is perhaps the most familiar EU political institution for those searching for parallels between the EU political system and national political systems. Like the lower legislative chamber (if there are two legislative chambers) or the only legislative chamber (if there is only one such chamber) of every democratic country, it is elected by popular vote at regular intervals. Indeed, from the very foundation of the European Communities (as they then were) in the 1950s, the intention was to elect the members of the European Parliament—although the first such elections were not arranged until 1979. Before that point, the Parliament was made up of part-time members whose main job was serving in national parliaments.

Also, like national parliaments, the European Parliament's main tasks are to participate in the legislative and budgetary process and to hold the executive to account—although

42 Art 17(3) TEU and Art 245 TFEU.

43 Arts 249 and 250 TFEU. For the current rules of procedure of the Commission, see OJ [2010] L308/26.

44 eg the proposal for legislation on fraud against EU financial interests (COM(2012) 363, 11 July 2012).

45 COM(2013) 151, 25 March 2013. On this legislation, see further chapter 25.

the latter task in particular is complicated by the complex structure of the EU, where the tasks of the executive are spread among three different institutions.

In addition to the Treaty provisions on the European Parliament,[46] there are also some important secondary measures which regulate its composition and functioning. In particular:

(a) Article 223 TFEU provides for the adoption of a Council decision on the procedure for elections to the European Parliament and for European Parliament regulations on the statute of its members (ie the pay and expenses of those members);[47]

(b) Article 14(2) TEU provides for the European Council to adopt a decision on the 'composition' of the European Parliament (ie allocating the number of seats per Member State); and

(c) Article 22(2) TFEU provides that every EU citizen living in another Member State can vote or stand for election to the European Parliament, subject to the adoption of detailed measures to that end by the Council.

Also, Article 224 TFEU provides for the adoption of regulations on European political parties, which broadly correspond to the political groups which sit in the European Parliament. Although the political parties as such do not impact on the functioning of the European Parliament, the political groups are a crucial part of the Parliament's day-to-day activities (as discussed in section 4.4). According to the Treaties, European political parties 'contribute to forming European political awareness and to expressing the will of citizens of the Union'.[48] The legal rules governing the parties' functioning are set out in legislation adopted in 2004, and amended subsequently.[49]

4.2 Composition

4.2.1 Number of members

As the EU enlarged, the number of MEPs was adjusted upwards over the years to match (then the number of MEPs was reduced following Brexit). The Treaty of Lisbon raised the normal ceiling to 751 MEPs. A key question is the distribution of the seats in the European Parliament between Member States. The Treaties require the seats to be allocated on the basis of 'degressive proportionality', that is, giving small Member States more weight (relative to their population) than large Member States, with no Member State having more than 96 seats or fewer than 6 seats.[50] As discussed in chapter 4, this has been criticized in some quarters because it does not adhere to the principle of 'representation by population' (ie the equal voting weight of each voter) which usually applies to the election of the lower house of parliament in federal systems. The exact allocation of seats between Member States is decided by the European Council.[51]

4.2.2 Elections

As Article 14(3) TEU states, the European Parliament is elected for five-year terms. This electoral term has been applied since the first direct election in 1979, and so the next election (at the time of writing) is due in spring 2029. Also, the European Parliament's term is fixed, meaning that it is not possible to dissolve the entire parliament and hold

[46] Art 14 TEU and Arts 223–234 TFEU.

[47] For the text of this statute, see OJ [2005] L262/1.

[48] Art 10(4) TEU.

[49] Regulation 2004/2003 (OJ [2004] L297/1), as later replaced by Regulation 1141/2014 (OJ [2014] L317/1), since amended by Regulation 2019/493 (OJ [2019] L85 I/7). See Art 224 TFEU.

[50] Art 14(2) TEU.

[51] OJ [2023] L238/114.

early elections, even if the Commission has had to resign due to a vote of censure by the Parliament (see section 3). This is different from the rules in most national political systems, which usually require fresh parliamentary elections if a government loses a 'no-confidence' vote and no alternative government can be formed (see eg the early elections following no-confidence votes in Ireland in 2011, Germany in 2005, and the Netherlands in 2012).

Originally, the Treaties provided for the adoption of a 'uniform procedure' for elections to the European Parliament.[52] While a Council Act on the election of MEPs was adopted in 1976,[53] this measure left open the adoption of a common electoral procedure for a later date, confining itself to defining issues like the dates of elections, and leaving the electoral system to be defined by 'national provisions' until then.[54]

The Treaty of Amsterdam (in force 1999) changed the rules so that the electoral law could instead be based on 'principles common' to all Member States.[55] This allowed for the amendment of the Council Act in 2002.[56] The 2002 measure provides that voting must take place on the basis of 'proportional representation', that is, the seats must be allocated in principle according to the percentage of the vote obtained by each political party, rather than the first-past-the-post system used in the UK for general elections (where the winning candidate in each constituency is the person with the greatest number of votes, meaning that a party can win a majority of the seats in parliament with only a minority of the votes in the election).

However, there is still flexibility for Member States as to whether to have several large constituencies in that Member State, as long as the system is still proportional,[57] and as regards other aspects of the voting system.[58] The fixed date of elections can be altered slightly, by deciding to hold an election up to two months before or one month after the normal period in early June.[59] Elections take place between Thursday and Sunday of the same week, reflecting the different polling traditions of Member States, but results cannot be made public in any Member State until all voting is finished.[60]

Being an MEP is incompatible with holding posts in other EU institutions or certain EU bodies, holding a national government post, or (since the 2002 amendments to the electoral act) being a member of a national parliament.[61]

While, as noted previously, there are European political parties, voting in European Parliament elections takes place on the basis of national political party affiliation, and is often seen as a verdict by voters on the performance of national governments.[62] Before 2019, the voter turnout for European Parliament elections dropped at every election, even as the European Parliament's powers (see section 4.3) increased. This may have been because, in the absence of a direct link between the result of the European Parliament elections and the government of the EU, it was hard for voters to understand what they were voting for. However, the turnout increased in 2019 and again (slightly) in 2024.

Turnout is lower than for national elections, possibly because of the remoteness of the European Parliament, both literally (ie the distant location of its meetings) and as regards individual MEPs (ie the much larger size of the European Parliament's constituencies as compared to the size of national parliamentary constituencies). Another factor may be

[52] See Art 138 of the original EEC Treaty, since repealed. [53] OJ [1976] L278/1.

[54] Arts 7 and 9, 1976 Act. [55] Art 223(1) TFEU.

[56] Decision 2002/772/EC (OJ [2002] L283/1). A further amendment was agreed in 2018 (Decision 2018/994, OJ [2018] L178/1), but was not in force yet for the 2019 or 2024 elections.

[57] Art 2, 1976 Act as amended. [58] Arts 1(1) and (2) and 3, 1976 Act as amended.

[59] Art 11, 1976 Act as amended. [60] Art 10, 1976 Act as amended.

[61] Art 7, 1976 Act as amended.

[62] Art 3b of the 1976 Act, as amended in 2018, gives Member States the option to permit the display of the logo of the affiliated European political party on the ballot paper in future elections.

public irritation about the cost of the European Parliament, since the Treaty requires it to meet in both Strasbourg and Brussels, and there are well-publicized scandals about the expenses of MEPs—although, of course, national parliamentarians are not scandal-free either.

The eligibility to vote in European Parliament elections and to run for office in the European Parliament is partly defined by EU law, which specifies that EU citizens who live in another Member State can in principle vote and run for election in European Parliament elections in that State, on the same conditions as nationals of that State.[63] Otherwise, the Court of Justice has ruled that the eligibility to vote and stand for election is defined by national law, subject to compliance with EU law. So while Member States may confine the right to vote in European Parliament elections to their national residents, they cannot discriminate by giving their citizens who reside in third countries the right to vote in those elections, while denying that right to their citizens who reside in their associated territories.[64] Member States also have discretion to allow citizens of third countries to vote in European Parliament elections.[65] In addition, they have obligations pursuant to the European Convention on Human Rights to permit the residents of their quasi-colonies to vote in European Parliament elections, if a sufficient proportion of EU law applies to the territory of those entities.[66] Finally, the reference to the right to vote in European Parliament elections in the EU Charter of Fundamental Rights limits Member States' ability to restrict prisoners and convicts from voting in those elections.[67]

4.3 **Powers**

Article 14(1) TEU lists two main categories of powers for the European Parliament: 'legislative and budgetary functions', which it exercises 'jointly with the Council'; and powers of 'political control and consultation'. The first category of powers is paralleled by the description of the first category of powers conferred upon the Council (see Article 16(1) TEU, discussed in section 5.3). As noted in the introduction, this wording reflects the two-chamber parliamentary system which the EU has developed.

Originally, the European Parliament was only consulted on a selection of draft measures. Following the first direct elections to the chamber in 1979, all five subsequent major Treaty amendments have expanded the Parliament's decision-making powers considerably, so that it now has equal legislative and budgetary power with the Council in a large majority of areas.[68]

First of all, the Single European Act (SEA) (in force 1987) created a procedure called the 'cooperation procedure', which gave the Parliament some additional influence over the legislative process in some fields. Secondly, the Maastricht Treaty (in force 1993)

[63] Art 22(1) TFEU; see Directive 93/109 (OJ [1993] L329/34), as amended by Directive 2013/1 (OJ [2013] L26/27) and Directive 2025/1788 (OJ [2025] L 8.9.2025). The CJEU has ruled that Member States cannot ban citizens of other Member States from joining political parties: Cases C-814/21 *Commission v Poland*, EU:C:2024:963 and C-808/21 *Commission v Czech Republic*, EU:C:2024:962.

[64] Case C-300/04 *Eman and Sevinger* [2006] ECR I-8055. Art 9a of the 1976 Act, as amended in 2018, expressly confirms that a Member State may permit its citizens living in non-EU countries to vote in European Parliament elections. See also Case T-388/19 *Puigdemont*, EU:C:2022:421, on Member State certification of election winners.

[65] Case C-145/04 *Spain v UK* [2006] ECR I-7917.

[66] *Matthews v UK* (Appl No 24833/94), ECtHR, 1999.

[67] Case C-650/13 *Delvigne*, EU:C:2015:648.

[68] Although Arts 14(1) and 16(1) TEU refer to legislative and budgetary functions, in fact EU measures on the annual budget and multi-annual budget framework are legislative acts (see Arts 311, 312, and 314 TFEU), so are not discussed here separately. The European Parliament has the main role giving discharge to the Commission as regards its implementation of the budget (see Art 319 TFEU).

created a new procedure, known in practice as the 'co-decision' procedure, which put the Parliament and the Council broadly on the same footing as regards legislation in certain areas. That Treaty also extended the cooperation procedure to new areas.

Thirdly, the Treaty of Amsterdam (in force 1999) both extended the co-decision procedure to many new areas and streamlined that procedure, putting the Council and Parliament on an entirely equal footing within it.[69] That Treaty also curtailed the use of the cooperation procedure.

Fourthly, the Treaty of Nice (in force 2003) extended the co-decision procedure to a small number of new areas.

Finally, the Treaty of Lisbon (in force 2009) dramatically expanded the use of the co-decision procedure, renaming it the 'ordinary legislative procedure' (OLP) and specifying that a number of residual cases with different rules for adopting legislative acts had to be regarded as 'special legislative procedures' (SLPs).[70] Although most special legislative procedures entail consultation of the European Parliament only (and thus its views can be disregarded by the Council), in some cases it has the power of 'consent'—that is, it can veto the proposal in question.

As for the second category of the Parliament's powers ('political control and consultation'), its most important power of political control—as regards the appointment and dismissal of the Commission President and the rest of the Commission—has already been discussed in section 3. The Parliament also has political control as regards the Commission's delegated acts, as discussed already in section 3. In addition, it has political control, in the form of the power of consent, as regards the following decisions:

- sanctions against Member States for breach of human rights;[71]
- the European Council's decision on the Parliament's own composition;[72]
- some aspects of Treaty amendment;[73]
- enlargement of the EU;[74]
- treaties concerning the withdrawal of a Member State from the EU;[75]
- extensions of EU competence over criminal law;[76]
- the conclusion of most international agreements;[77]
- approval of enhanced cooperation (ie a group of some Member States going ahead without some others to adopt EU law).[78]

Further, the Parliament attempts to exert its power of control via means of parliamentary questions, committees of enquiry, petitions, and the European Ombudsman, who can investigate alleged maladministration by the EU's institutions, offices, bodies, and agencies (Articles 226 to 228 TFEU).

As for the Parliament's power of consultation, it applies to various other 'innominate non-legislative procedures' (ie cases where the Treaties provide for the EU institutions to

[69] So unlike, eg the UK's Parliament Acts, it is not possible for either legislative chamber in the EU system to overrule the other one, where the co-decision system (now the ordinary legislative procedure) applies.

[70] On legislative procedures generally, see Art 289 TFEU; on the ordinary legislative procedure, see Art 294 TFEU. For discussion of the details of these procedures, see chapter 5.

[71] Art 7(1) and (2) TEU. [72] Art 14(2) TEU.

[73] The Parliament has to consent if the European Council does not want to hold a 'convention' before amending the Treaty according to the ordinary Treaty amendment procedure (Art 48(3) TEU), and to any simplified Treaty amendments extending the use of qualified majority voting or the ordinary legislative procedure (Art 48(7) TEU). For more discussion of the Treaty amendment procedures, see chapter 5.

[74] Art 49 TEU. [75] Art 50(2) TEU. See further chapter 27.

[76] Arts 82(2)(d), 83(1), and 86(4) TFEU. [77] Art 218(6)(a) TFEU. See further chapter 26.

[78] Art 329(1) TFEU. See further chapter 5.

adopt non-legislative acts)[79]—for instance, as regards appointments, the adoption of rules on competition or State aid law, the creation of committees, or changes in decision-making rules.[80] In some cases, there is only an obligation to inform the European Parliament once measures are adopted.[81] The European Parliament's role in relation to EU foreign policy is particularly weak: there is only an obligation for the High Representative to consult it on 'the main aspects and the basic choices' of EU foreign policies, and to inform it of 'how those policies evolve'.[82]

It should be noted, however, that like national parliaments, the European Parliament has long found ways of enhancing its powers beyond the strict letter of the law.[83] For instance, often closely related EU measures are proposed and adopted in a 'package', which sometimes includes non-legislative measures and measures subject to a SLP alongside measures subject to the OLP. When this happens, the European Parliament invariably tries to use its leverage over the measures which must be adopted pursuant to the OLP to influence the content of the other measures as well.[84] As regards international treaties, the Parliament's lack of power over the authorization and content of negotiations, and over the decision to sign the treaty (and perhaps apply it provisionally), is compensated for by its power (in most cases) to veto the final conclusion of the treaty concerned by the EU. If the Parliament indicates in a non-binding vote, while the treaty is being negotiated, that it is inclined to vote against the treaty when the time comes, or at least that it objects to that treaty unless certain changes are made to the intended text, the EU's negotiators (and the Council) must logically consider the Parliament's point of view, or risk the rejection of that treaty by the Parliament.

When negotiations with the Council are particularly tough, but the Parliament is chiefly committed to achieving its objectives, it sometimes 'freezes' EU funds, or other proposed legislation, in order to place pressure on the other EU institutions. For instance, when negotiating the 'Returns Directive' on the legal position of unauthorized (sometimes called 'illegal') immigrants, it blocked the release of EU money intended to help the Member States with the cost of dealing with returnees, until the negotiations were completed.[85] Subsequently, when negotiating legislation on the possible reintroduction of internal border controls by 'Schengen' Member States, the Parliament objected both to the content of changes to the Commission's proposals made by the Council, and the Council's decision to reclassify a proposal covered by the OLP as a non-legislative act on which the Parliament would only be consulted. It therefore refused to adopt legislation on five other security-related measures until it reached an agreement on these proposals with the Council.[86]

Furthermore, the Parliament is able and willing to resort to court action in order to pursue its legal arguments about EU measures.[87] Most obviously, it has brought

[79] On this concept, see further chapter 5. I am grateful to the author of that chapter, Kieran Bradley, for coining this term.

[80] Arts 74, 78(3), 81(3), 95(3), 103(1), 109, 125(2), 126(14), 128(2), 129(4), 140(2), 148(2), 150, 153(2), 160, 188, 192(2), 203, 218(6)(b), 219(1), 246, 283(2), 286(2), 322(2), 332, and 333(2) TFEU, and Arts 27(3), 41(3), 48(3), and 48(6) TEU. On the substance of the competition rules, see chapter 17.

[81] Arts 70, 71, 121(2), 122(2), 126(11), 134(3), 155(2), 156, 168(2), 173(2), 181(2), 215(1), 218(10), 219(2), 222(3), and 329(2) TFEU.

[82] Art 36 TEU.

[83] See similarly the Parliament's use of its powers as regards appointments to the Commission, discussed in section 3.

[84] A good example is the 'six-pack' legislation on economic governance, discussed in chapter 19.

[85] On the content of this legislation, see case study 25.1 in chapter 25.

[86] In practice, this was known as the 'Schengen freeze'. On the content of the border control legislation, see again chapter 25.

[87] See further chapter 10.

cases arguing that EU measures were adopted on the wrong 'legal basis', that is, that the Council adopted a measure on the basis of an article in the Treaties that gave the Parliament limited powers, but it should have instead adopted a measure on the basis of a clause in the Treaties which gives the Parliament more powers.[88] It has also challenged non-legislative measures that it believed should have been adopted as legislative measures.[89]

4.4 **Functioning**

Even though (as discussed in section 3) the European Parliament must approve the appointment of the Commission, and can remove the Commission by means of a censure motion, the link between the parliament and the executive in the EU system is much weaker than in most national systems. Put simply, unlike in many countries, the European Parliament does not need to 'support' the Commission as the government of the EU, because the removal of the Commission will not result in early elections to the European Parliament.

The consequence of this is that there is no parliamentary majority party (or parties), and therefore no 'opposition parties'. Instead, there are 'political groups', which bring together MEPs who are members of similar national parties in different Member States. For instance, the 'Progressive Alliance of Socialists and Democrats' political group consists of MEPs affiliated with the German Social Democratic Party, the Spanish PSOE, and a number of other centre-left parties across the EU. Although, due to the Commission's near-monopoly on proposing legislation (see section 3), MEPs do not have the right of legislative initiative (ie there are no 'private member's bills'),[90] each political group decides whether it will vote in favour of 'government bills' (ie Commission proposals) or not, on a case-by-case basis (although sometimes some MEPs split with the party line on voting for a proposal in each group, ie equivalent to being a 'rebel' in UK politics). This means that a large number of political groups often work together to achieve the necessary majorities, even if the MEPs in those groups are linked to national political parties (eg the main socialist and conservative parties), which rarely form coalitions at a national level.

As with many national parliaments, the day-to-day work of the European Parliament is largely carried out in committees. The Parliament's committees broadly reflect the tasks of individual Commissioners and Directorates-General (see section 3) and Council configurations (see section 5), and again there are sometimes turf battles.

Shortly after each legislative proposal or other measure which the Parliament examines, it allocates a 'rapporteur' in the relevant committee for the subject. The rapporteur is responsible for drafting the European Parliament's position on the measure and will be (where relevant) in charge of negotiations with the Council. These positions are allocated based on each political group's share of the seats in the Parliament, although, of course, each rapporteur will need to obtain support from other political groups (by taking account of their opinions when drafting a position and negotiating with the Council, and by accepting some proposed amendments suggested by other political groups) in order to obtain a majority in support of a proposal.

[88] For examples of successful and unsuccessful claims of this sort, see respectively Case C-490/10 *European Parliament v Council*, EU:C:2012:525, and Case C-130/10 *European Parliament v Council*, EU:C:2012:472. On the concept of 'legal basis', see further chapter 5.

[89] For an example of a successful claim of this sort, see Case C-355/10 *European Parliament v Council* (*Frontex*), EU:C:2012:516, which is the subject of case study 5.2 in chapter 5.

[90] However, the Parliament as a whole can propose legislation in a few areas: for details, see chapter 5. It can also request the Commission to make a legislative proposal (Art 225 TFEU).

5 Council

5.1 Introduction

The Council is the EU's main decision-making organ, although to a large extent it now shares this role with the European Parliament. It is usually made up of ministers from Member States' governments,[91] so unsurprisingly it is one of the most 'intergovernmental' institutions (ie an institution dominated by Member States' governments). As mentioned at the outset of this chapter, it is crucial to keep in mind that the Council is a distinct body from the *European* Council, which is made up of Member States' presidents and prime ministers (see section 6). The basic rules on the composition and functioning of the Council are set out in Article 16 TEU, and further detailed rules are set out in Articles 237 to 243 TFEU and in the Council's rules of procedure.[92]

As noted already, the Council is, to a certain extent, comparable to the upper chamber of a two-chamber legislative system. In particular, it can be compared to the upper chamber in countries such as Germany (the Bundestag) and the US (the Senate), where membership of the chamber is directly linked to the division of the country into Länder (Germany) or states (the US). However, this comparison is only partly useful, since the Council has executive functions as well as legislative ones, and the members of the Council do not sit in Brussels as full-time 'senators'. Rather, their main job is as ministers in their national governments. Moreover, as we shall see, different ministers serve in the Council depending on the subject matter of the issues under discussion.

As we saw at the outset of this chapter, Article 10(2) TEU states that the Council's democratic legitimacy is based on each *individual* minister's democratic accountability to the electorate or parliament of each Member State. There is no collective legitimacy of the Council as regards the EU as a whole.[93]

5.2 Composition

The Council consists of national ministers who represent their Member State's government, who can commit their government and cast a vote on its behalf.[94] It is therefore for the government of each Member State to decide who will appear in the Council to represent that government; this will depend on the results of elections, coalition negotiations, and cabinet reshuffles.

As noted already, the Council does not have a fixed membership. Rather, it is made up of different ministers depending on the subject matter being discussed. In this context, Article 16(6) TEU refers to the different 'configurations' of the Council. This Treaty provision refers to two specific such configurations. First of all, the General Affairs Council (usually made up of Member States' European Affairs Ministers), which is:

> responsible for overall coordination of policies, institutional and administrative questions, horizontal dossiers which affect several of the European Union's policies, such as the multiannual financial framework and enlargement, and any dossier entrusted to it by the European Council.[95]

[91] It is possible that ministers from regional or state governments can attend the Council, although in that case they are still representing that Member State as a whole (Art 16(2) TEU).

[92] OJ [2009] L325/35.

[93] On the implications of this for the democratic credentials of the EU, see further chapter 4.

[94] Art 16(2) TEU.

[95] Art 2(2), Council rules of procedure. The General Affairs Council also has a role preparing and following up the European Council: see further section 6.

Secondly, the Foreign Affairs Council (obviously made up of Member States' foreign ministers), 'elaborates' the EU's external actions. More precisely, it is:

> responsible for the whole of the European Union's external action, namely common foreign and security policy, common security and defence policy, common commercial policy, development cooperation and humanitarian aid.[96]

Otherwise, the list of Council configurations is adopted by the European Council.[97] Currently, there are eight other configurations: Agriculture and Fisheries; Justice and Home Affairs; Economic and Financial Affairs; Employment, Social Policy, Health and Consumer Affairs; Competitiveness (Internal Market, Industry, Research and Space); Education, Youth, Culture and Sport; Transport, Telecoms and Energy; and Environment. In practice, some are subdivided (ie transport, telecoms, and energy ministers actually meet separately). The subject matter that each of these configurations deals with is not precisely defined, and there are occasionally 'turf battles' as to which Council configuration is in charge of a particular 'dossier'.

In practice, the General Affairs, Foreign Affairs, Agriculture and Fisheries, and Economic and Financial Affairs Councils usually meet every month, while the other Councils meet every two or three months.

5.3 **Powers**

Article 16(1) TEU says that the Council has two main categories of powers: 'legislative and budgetary functions', which it exercises 'jointly with the European Parliament', and 'policy-making and coordinating functions'. As we have seen (section 4), the first of these powers matches the first of the European Parliament's main powers (as described in Article 14(1) TEU), but the second category of powers is obviously rather different from the Parliament's further powers of 'political control and consultation'.[98]

The Council's role in legislative procedures is discussed in detail in chapter 5, but it should be recalled (as discussed in section 4) that its role in the ordinary legislative procedure is exactly equal to that of the European Parliament. As regards special legislative procedures, most of these provide for the Council to adopt legislation with a requirement only to *consult* the Parliament. Article 16(8) TEU requires the Council to meet in public when discussing legislative acts,[99] and to divide the agenda of each of its meetings between legislative and non-legislative acts.

As regards its 'policy-making and coordinating' functions, the Council's policymaking role is most obviously manifest in relation to the areas where it can adopt 'innominate non-legislative acts', that is, where the Treaties provide for the Council to adopt acts which are not legislative, in areas such as competition and State aid rules, or foreign policy measures.[100] It also has the lead role regarding international treaties, deciding on whether to give the Commission a mandate to negotiate, deciding on the content of that mandate, overseeing the negotiations in a special committee, and then deciding to sign and conclude the agreement. But the European Parliament's power to consent to most such treaties, and the Commission's (or High Representative's) power to negotiate them, cannot

[96] Art 2(5), Council rules of procedure.

[97] Art 236(a) TFEU. For this list, see OJ [2009] L315/46, amended by OJ [2010] L263/12.

[98] Yet it should be recalled that the Council, like the Parliament, has the power of political control as regards delegated acts of the Commission: see section 3.

[99] For more on the transparency of the legislative process, see section 7.

[100] On this concept, see chapter 5. On the substance of such rules, see eg chapters 17 and 26.

be forgotten.[101] The Council also has the power to suspend such treaties and to define the EU's position as regards implementing them.

In a limited number of cases, the Council also has the power to adopt implementing measures—namely, where the EU acts concerned confer such power upon it, and concerning the implementation of foreign policy acts.[102]

As regards its coordination power, the Council has the power to coordinate, in particular, Member States' economic, employment, and social policies (see Article 5 TFEU). This process is often referred to as the 'open method of coordination', and results in measures which are often called 'soft law'.[103] In the area of economic policy coordination, however, the legal effect of the coordination has in principle been enhanced since 2011, following the economic and financial crisis.[104]

5.4 **Functioning**

5.4.1 **Voting in the Council**

The most controversial question concerning the functioning of the Council has been its voting procedures. There are two key issues here: (a) whether the Council votes by unanimity, or by a 'qualified majority' (ie a majority vote in which Member States have different weights due to the size of their population); and (b) how to calculate a 'qualified majority' when such a vote must be held. A qualified majority vote is the default rule;[105] but there are also a few minor cases where only a simple majority of Member States (ie 14 out of 27 at present) can adopt a measure.[106]

On the first point, it is obviously difficult to obtain unanimity in the Council, and inevitably it has been getting more difficult as the EU has enlarged. To address this, all five major Treaty amendments have expanded the use of qualified majority voting (QMV) in the Council. For instance, the SEA (in force 1987) introduced QMV for many measures related to completion of the internal market (eg Article 114 TFEU), including in flanking areas such as sea and air transport (see now Article 100 TFEU). This has facilitated (inter alia) the adoption of most of the legislation on consumer law discussed in chapter 23—when unanimity had applied, it had taken many years to negotiate measures such as the Product Liability Directive. The Maastricht Treaty introduced QMV as regards (inter alia) environmental law, facilitating the adoption of much of the legislation discussed in chapter 22, while the Treaties of Amsterdam, Nice, and Lisbon gradually extended QMV as regards (inter alia) immigration law, facilitating the adoption of much of the legislation discussed in chapter 25. The Treaty of Lisbon introduced QMV for (inter alia) most criminal law and policing measures, making it easier in particular to adopt legislation on criminal suspects' rights, which had previously been blocked by national vetoes (see further chapter 24).

However, unanimous voting still remains in the Council for sensitive issues such as taxation, as well as certain aspects of employment law and environmental law (see further chapters 20 and 22), or the creation of a European Public Prosecutor (see further chapter 24). While QMV is always used in the context of the ordinary legislative procedure, and

[101] On Art 218 TFEU, see further sections 3.3 and 4.3, and the analysis in chapter 26.

[102] According to Art 291(2) TFEU, the Council can only be given such powers in 'duly justified specific cases', and as regards foreign policy. An example is the power for the Council (conferred by a directive) to create 'temporary protection' for a mass influx of people, which has been used once, following the invasion of Ukraine (see chapter 25) The Council cannot create new types of legislative procedures which give it further power to adopt measures: see Case C-133/06 *European Parliament v Council* [2008] ECR I-3189. For more on implementing measures, see chapter 5.

[103] For more detail, see chapter 5.

[104] For more detail, see chapter 19.

[105] Art 16(3) TEU.

[106] Art 238(1) TFEU.

usually applies when the Council adopts innominate non-legislative procedures (which were explained in section 4), unanimity usually applies as regards special legislative procedures. Abstentions do not prevent the adoption of acts by unanimity.[107]

Sometimes a Member State which has been outvoted pursuant to a qualified majority vote argues that the measure concerned was adopted on the wrong 'legal basis' (see section 4), and so unanimous voting should have applied. Then again, sometimes the argument is the other way around—that a legal basis entailing a qualified majority should have been used, instead of a legal basis entailing unanimity (usually it is the Commission which makes this argument). These disputes often lead to legal challenges to the measures concerned, which are brought before the Court of Justice. For instance, the UK government brought a challenge (unsuccessfully) against the adoption of the EU's 'Working Time' Directive, which provides (among other things) for a maximum 48-hour week for workers in the Member States. The UK argued that this directive should have been adopted under Article 100 EC rather than 118a EC (under the 'old' Treaty numbers). Article 100 EC would have given the UK a veto.[108]

In the event of a persistent veto, it is possible for a group of the Member States in favour of the measure in question to circumvent that veto by adopting the measure pursuant to the rules on 'enhanced cooperation'—for instance, as regards the adoption of legislation on EU patents in 2011 (despite Spanish and Italian opposition)—provided that there is a qualified majority vote in Council in favour of using this process and other procedural and substantive rules are satisfied.[109] If the law is ultimately agreed, it will apply only to those Member States that wish to sign up to it.

On the second point, as with the European Parliament (see section 4), votes have always been weighted in the Council in the form of 'degressive proportionality'—that is, giving small Member States more weight (relative to their population) than large Member States. The crucial question was always how to put together a 'blocking minority' in the case where qualified majority voting is required, that is, a combination of Member States with enough votes to block a decision from being adopted.

For many years, the Member States had between two votes (Luxembourg) and ten votes (the four biggest Member States) in the Council, with the blocking minority adjusted with every enlargement of the EU.[110] So, for instance, between 1995 and 2004, 26 votes were needed to block a decision. This could consist of two large Member States (which had ten votes each) plus Spain (which had eight votes), or two large Member States plus (in most cases) two smaller Member States. However, with the planned enlargement to include a number of small and medium-sized Member States in the East and the Mediterranean, the larger Member States were concerned that they would no longer be able to form blocking minorities as easily as they had in the past. So, before this major enlargement could go ahead, the larger Member States insisted that the system of Council voting should be reweighted, to give them more relative weight than they would enjoy if the then-current system were simply extended to cover the new Member States *mutatis mutandis*. In particular, Germany preferred to switch to a 'dual majority' system, meaning a measure would need to receive backing from a majority of Member States which also represent

[107] Art 238(4) TFEU.

[108] Case C-84/94 *UK v Council* [1996] ECR I-5755, concerning Directive 93/104 (OJ [1993] L307/18). On this directive, see further chapter 20. The relevant Treaty provisions are now Arts 115 and 153 TFEU.

[109] For more on this process, see chapter 5. In a few cases, enhanced cooperation can be 'fast-tracked' in the event of a veto, dispensing with these additional requirements: see Arts 86 and 87 TFEU.

[110] Before the first enlargement in 1973, Luxembourg had one vote and the largest Member States had four. Upon that enlargement, the numbers of votes were changed to benefit the medium-sized and large Member States slightly.

a majority of the total EU population; this would reflect Germany's de facto increase in population since its unification in 1990.

As noted previously (section 3.2), this dispute became connected with the question of the number of Commissioners, since the large Member States did not want to give up their extra Commissioners without an increase in their relative voting weight in the Council. We have seen already that it was impossible to agree on these issues when negotiating the Treaty of Amsterdam, but a deal was reached as part of the Treaty of Nice.

This reweighting, which took effect from 1 November 2004, provided that (as adjusted for the 2007 and 2013 enlargements) a 'qualified majority' was achieved when there were 260 votes in favour out of 352 votes cast (so 93 votes were needed for a blocking minority).[111] As before, large Member States had more votes than small Member States, but the distribution of the votes was not fully proportionate to population. However, that distribution was more proportionate than it was previously. For instance, there were 29 votes each for the UK, Germany, France, and Italy; 27 votes for Spain and Poland; 4 votes each for Luxembourg, Latvia, Estonia, Slovenia, and Cyprus; and 3 votes for Malta. It can be seen that a blocking minority could consist of (for instance) three large Member States plus any other Member State opposed (unless the other Member State was one of the six States with only three or four votes).

In addition, there was a requirement of 'dual majority' in favour of a measure: a proposal also had to be supported by a majority of Member States, and by Member States representing 62 per cent of the EU population. Usually, the latter criterion only came into play if Germany (and several other countries) opposed a proposal.

Due to concerns (which were not borne out in practice) that these rules would make it too difficult to adopt EU measures, the Treaty of Lisbon altered the Council voting rules again, as of 1 November 2014. In principle, since then a simple dual majority system has applied: a proposal needs the support of 55 per cent of Member States (currently 15 out of 27 Member States) with 65 per cent of the EU population. A blocking minority has to consist of at least four Member States.[112]

In principle, the post-2014 rules have made it easier to adopt measures. However, there was a transitional rule: until 31 March 2017, any Member State could insist that the old rules applied when a vote was taken. Effectively, the new and old rules coexisted until then.[113] This benefited particularly Poland and Spain (in fact, Poland insisted upon this rule), which had a larger share of the votes under the pre-2014 rules.

A further limit on the use of the revised QMV rules after November 2014 is a Council decision which provides that discussions must continue if a proportion of Member States falling short of a blocking minority insist upon this.[114] The Council must try to reach a 'satisfactory solution' to these States' concerns within a 'reasonable time'.

There are also two variants on QMV. First of all, where the proposal in question was not made by the Commission (eg it was proposed by a group of Member States, or another EU institution or body: see chapter 5, section 7.1.1), 72 per cent of Member States (currently 20 countries) must vote in favour.[115]

Secondly, where not all Member States participate in an EU measure, due to opt-outs or the use of enhanced cooperation (see further chapter 5, section 9), the relevant Member

[111] For details, see Art 16(5) TEU and Art 3(3), Protocol 36 on transitional provisions. Note that an abstention effectively counts as a vote *against*.

[112] Art 16(4) TEU. [113] Art 3(2), transitional Protocol.

[114] OJ [2009] L314/73. Before 31 March 2017, this clause could have been triggered by a group of Member States which had either 75 per cent of the population or 75 per cent of the numbers necessary to constitute a blocking minority. After that date, these percentages dropped to 55 per cent.

[115] Art 238(2) TFEU. Before 1 November 2014, two-thirds of Member States had to vote in favour (Art 3(3), transitional Protocol).

States do not participate in the Council vote, so the voting rules have to be recalculated to apply to the participating Member States only.[116]

Finally, it should be noted that in a few sensitive cases (social security, foreign policy implementing measures, and aspects of criminal law), Member States with profound objections to a measure which could be adopted by a qualified majority can stop its adoption by means of a so-called 'emergency brake' procedure.[117]

5.4.2 Council Presidencies

A key feature of the functioning of the Council is its Presidency. Historically, before the entry into force of the Treaty of Lisbon, the Presidency was held by each Member State in turn for a period of six months. This system was then amended by the Treaty of Lisbon to provide that the Foreign Affairs Council is chaired by the High Representative (see section 3).[118] Similarly, before the Treaty of Lisbon, each Member State holding the Council Presidency also chaired the European Council, but now that body has its own full-time President (see section 6.2).

For the remaining Council configurations, according to Article 16(9) TEU, this role must still be taken by Member States on the basis of 'equal rotation', in accordance with a decision adopted by the European Council by a qualified majority.[119] According to this European Council decision, the Presidency is nominally held by groups of three Member States working together; these groups are chosen on the basis of their 'diversity and geographical balance'.[120] This means that each group of three contains a large, medium, and small State, and States from different parts of the EU; obvious groupings like the Baltic States or the Benelux States are avoided. However, in practice (as before) each of these three States takes the main role for a period of six months (ie Ireland in the second half of 2026, Lithuania in the first half of 2027, and Greece in the second half of 2027), on a revolving basis, with the other members of the group assisting the lead Member State on the basis of a common programme.[121]

Holding the Presidency means that the Member State in question is responsible for scheduling and chairing all of the Council meetings planned for the six-month period (except for the Foreign Affairs Council), as well as the meetings of the Council's 'preparatory bodies', that is, its committees and working parties (see section 5.4.3).[122] As an exception, a representative of the High Representative chairs those preparatory bodies which are related to the foreign policy and defence aspects of the Foreign Affairs Council,[123] and certain other working groups or committees have a fixed chair who is elected (ie by his or her peers on that committee) or are chaired by the Council's General Secretariat (on which, see later).[124] Before the Treaty of Lisbon, the Council Presidency also had a significant role as regards EU foreign policy (ie representing the EU at the United Nations and other international meetings relating to foreign policy), but this task has effectively been taken over by the High Representative.

116 Art 3(4), transitional Protocol and Art 238(3)(a) TFEU. Where both of these variants apply simultaneously (ie where a group of Member States make a criminal law proposal, and not all Member States participate in it), see the rule in Art 238(3)(b) TFEU.

117 See further chapter 5, section 7.1.2.

118 However, a footnote to Art 2(5) of the Council's rules of procedure indicates that when discussing trade issues, the High Representative will delegate chairing the Foreign Affairs Council to the rotating Council Presidency.

119 Art 236(a) TFEU. For this decision, see OJ [2009] L315/50. A further Council decision sets out additional details: OJ [2009] L322/28, as amended to remove the UK in light of Brexit (OJ [2016] L208/42).

120 Art 1(1), European Council Decision OJ [2009] L315/50.

121 Ibid, Art 1(2) and Annex I, Council Decision OJ [2009] L322/28 as amended (OJ [2016] L208/42).

122 Art 2, European Council Decision OJ [2009] L315/50.

123 Annex II, Council Decision OJ [2009] L322/28.

124 Ibid, Annex III.

Even though the Treaty of Lisbon reduced its significance, the Council Presidency is in practice still an important part of the EU. The Member State which holds the Presidency is able to set the agenda for six months and usually selects certain outstanding disputes over policy or legislation that it will try to solve, between Member States and/or between the Council and the European Parliament (the Presidency is in charge of negotiating legislation with the European Parliament on behalf of the Council). In practice, though, the Presidency's flexibility is usually constrained by the agenda and deadlines set by the European Council (see section 6), as well as by the timetable of events. The following case study of a successful Council Presidency illustrates the continuing importance of this office.

Case study 3.1: The Irish Council Presidency of 2013

The Irish government held the office of Council Presidency in the first half of 2013, following Denmark and Cyprus in 2012, and before Greece and Lithuania in 2013–14. The most crucial task for the Presidency was to reach agreement between the Council and European Parliament over the proposed legislation establishing the EU's multi-annual spending and revenue, since the existing multi-annual budget rules expired at the end of 2013. A failure to reach a deal would not have quite as drastic an effect as the periodic shutdowns of the US government over budget disputes, since it is legally possible for the EU to continue with the previous multi-annual budget framework if no new framework can be agreed (see Article 312(4) TFEU). But it is much easier for the EU to function with a new multi-annual financial framework, and it has adopted such new frameworks at regular intervals since the mid-1980s.

Negotiations for the new multi-year financial framework first of all took place between Member States, since the framework takes the form of a 'special legislative procedure' which has to be agreed unanimously in the Council. This section of the talks was in part conducted by the Council Presidency, and in part by the President of the European Council (see section 6), given that in practice the final, most controversial, details of these frameworks are always agreed by the European Council. The European Council reached a deal in February 2013, but this was not the end of the story, because the European Parliament had to give its consent to the adoption of the legislation concerned. It was up to the Irish Presidency to reach a deal between the Parliament and the Council, which it did by June 2013. However, the Parliament then imposed a 'freeze' (see section 4.3) and delayed its formal vote of approval of this legislation, because it wanted to plug gaps in the 2013 budget and influence the content of the 2014 annual budget too. So it fell to the subsequent Lithuanian Presidency to negotiate these issues with the European Parliament, and it reached a deal finally in November 2013.[125]

The negotiation of the multi-annual financial framework was only part of the picture. About 70 more legislative measures set out the details of the EU's multi-annual spending in specific fields (eg agriculture, fisheries, and research). So the Council Presidency was also responsible for concluding negotiations on as much as possible of this legislation. It was able to reach agreement between the European Parliament and the Council on a large majority of the measures concerned, with the main exceptions of external relations and Justice and Home Affairs spending, which the Lithuanian Presidency then had to negotiate on.

The Irish Presidency completed negotiations between the Council and European Parliament on other major issues as well. These included the reform of the EU's fisheries and agricultural

[125] OJ [2013] L347/884.

policies, which were closely linked to the revision of the EU's funding legislation on those issues. It also negotiated a deal on the remaining legislation to establish the second phase of the Common European Asylum System, which had been under discussion since 2008–9. Furthermore, the Presidency agreed a deal with the European Parliament on reform of the 'Schengen' rules on external border controls (see further chapter 25), thereby 'unfreezing' the legislative proposals which the European Parliament had been blocking (see section 4). In the area of economic and monetary union, the Presidency negotiated deals on the transfer of banking supervision tasks to the European Central Bank, and on the 'two-pack' legislation on the fiscal policies of eurozone Member States (see further chapter 19).

The Presidency also reached deals within the Council on new legislation on winding up failing banks and on a mandate for the Commission, on behalf of the EU, to negotiate a free trade deal with the US (see further chapters 19 and 26). But in the former case, it then fell to the subsequent Presidency (Lithuania) to negotiate a deal with the European Parliament on the legislation to wind up banks, and to a succession of future presidencies to address disputes that arose during the trade negotiations with the US (which ultimately failed at the end of President Obama's tenure).

While the Irish Presidency's achievements reflect that country's interests as an agricultural exporter, its good relations with the US, and its troubled banking industry,[126] any Member State holding the Presidency at that time would probably have tried to address the same issues. It is notable that some of the Presidency's successes concern issues in which it did not even participate at the time (asylum and border control legislation); perhaps in those cases it was successful precisely because Ireland did *not* have a national interest at stake, and so could be a neutral mediator.

The EU judges Council Presidencies by how much EU business they are able to conclude successfully, that is, how efficient they are. By that standard, the Irish Presidency was judged a great success. For comparison's sake, it is useful to contrast it to a particularly *un*successful Presidency. The Italian Presidency in the second half of 2003 not only failed to agree legislation establishing the *first* phase of the Common European Asylum System,[127] but also presided over the collapse of both the EU's economic governance system[128] and of negotiations to amend the Treaties to establish a Constitutional Treaty.[129]

5.4.3 **Other aspects**

For all EU measures, the Council is assisted by a Committee of Permanent Representatives (ambassadors) of the Member States to the EU, known as 'Coreper'.[130] Coreper meets in two different formats: Coreper II deals with the business of the General Affairs, Foreign Affairs, Justice and Home Affairs, and Economic and Financial Affairs Council (ie the economic, foreign policy, political, and security issues that political scientists often refer

[126] On the link between the European Central Bank supervision of banks and the debt which Ireland incurred to bail out its banking system, see further chapter 19.

[127] These negotiations were then concluded successfully under the following Irish Presidency in the first half of 2004. For the substance of the law, see chapter 25.

[128] This led to a weakened system for control of Member States' excessive deficit spending, which some blame (at least in part) for the difficulties faced by the EU's economic and monetary union since 2008. See further chapter 19.

[129] As noted in chapter 2, these negotiations were resumed successfully under the following Presidency (the Irish again!), but the ensuing Constitutional Treaty was then not ratified by all Member States, and so did not come into force. However, the Treaty of Lisbon, which included much of the same text as the Constitutional Treaty, was later negotiated and ratified instead.

[130] Art 240(1) TFEU.

to as 'high politics'), while Coreper I deals with the subject matter of the six other Council configurations[131] (ie the issues that political scientists often refer to as 'low politics'). Both Coreper I and Coreper II meet most weeks for one or two days each. Coreper cannot take legally binding decisions, but can take purely procedural decisions.[132] The national civil servants from the permanent representations in Brussels who deal with specific subjects sometimes meet separately to discuss those issues (eg in the form of 'Justice and Home Affairs Counsellors').

Beneath the level of Coreper, the Council is assisted by a number of working groups and committees; some (but not all) of the committees are referred to expressly in the Treaty. For instance, Article 207 TFEU refers to a committee on external trade matters, which plays a key role in the development of the EU's common commercial policy (see chapter 26). Like Coreper, the working groups and committees prepare the Council's work, and cannot take legally binding decisions. They agree in principle on the large majority of the texts of proposed EU measures. The provisions of those texts which are politically more difficult to agree are discussed by Coreper, which usually reaches agreement upon them. If Coreper cannot agree due to the great political sensitivity of a particular issue, then Member States' ministers must discuss that issue in Council. Of course, it should not be forgotten that if the measure concerned is subject to the ordinary legislative procedure, the Council must also negotiate a deal with the European Parliament.

The Council has a permanent staff who assist it with its tasks. They are organized in the form of a General Secretariat, which is divided into Directorates-General, rather like the Commission (see section 3). This administration is presided over by a Secretary-General.[133]

6 European Council

6.1 Introduction

The final political institution is the European Council, which consists primarily of the heads of State or government of each Member State. Like the Council (which, as pointed out previously, is comprised of national *ministers*), the members of the European Council can each individually refer back to a democratic mandate conferred by the voters or parliament of each individual Member State, but they do not have any collective mandate conferred by the EU electorate as a whole.[134] As we shall see, while the European Council is a weak institution in legal terms, its role is far more significant in political practice. The rules governing the European Council are set out in Article 15 TEU and Articles 235 to 236 TFEU.

6.2 Composition

As with the Council, it is up to each Member State to decide who attends as its representative in the European Council.[135] Since the European Council is a working political institution, those heads of State whose job is purely or largely ceremonial (eg the monarch, in the

[131] The configurations dealt with by Coreper I are Agriculture and Fisheries; Employment, Social Policy, Health and Consumer Affairs; Competitiveness (Internal Market, Industry, Research and Space); Education, Youth, Culture and Sport; Transport, Telecoms and Energy; and Environment. See section 5.2.

[132] See Case C-25/94 *Commission v Council* [1996] ECR I-1469. See the Council's rules of procedure (OJ [2009] L325/35).

[133] Art 240(2) TFEU. For details of the current organization of the Secretariat-General, see www.consilium.europa.eu/en/general-secretariat/.

[134] See Art 10(2) TEU.

[135] See Case T-715/19 *Wagenknecht v European Council*, EU:T:2020:340.

case of several Member States, or the presidents of Ireland and Germany) do not attend. Instead, the European Council consists of prime ministers or their equivalents (eg the German chancellor, the Irish Taoiseach) and the presidents of those countries (like France) where the president is the most important politician.

The High Representative (see section 4.3.2) also takes part in the work of the European Council,[136] and the President of the European Council (see later) and the President of the Commission are also members of it. However, only the Member States' heads of State or government can vote.[137]

Up until the Treaty of Lisbon, the Presidency of the European Council was held by a rotation of Member States for six-month periods (with the Member State holding both the Presidency of the Council (see section 5.4.2) and the Presidency of the European Council). The Treaty of Lisbon created the post of President of the European Council, which replaced this rotation system. The President is appointed by the European Council for two-and-a-half years, renewable once, by a qualified majority vote;[138] there is no role for any other EU institution (or the general public) in his or her appointment. The first full-time President, appointed as of 1 December 2009 when the Treaty of Lisbon entered into force, was Herman van Rompuy, the former Prime Minister of Belgium; his term was renewed in 2012, so expired at the end of November 2014.[139] Subsequently, Donald Tusk, the previous Prime Minister of Poland, became the second person to hold the job; his term was renewed over the objections of his home Member State, which by 2017 had a different government.[140] The post has since been held by Charles Michel, another former Prime Minister of Belgium (2019–24) and António Costa, former Prime Minister of Portugal (since 2024).[141]

It should be noted that, despite some confusion in the press, the President of the European Council is not the 'President of the EU', but only the President of one of its institutions. As compared to powerful presidencies like those in France or the US, the powers of the President of the European Council are quite limited.[142] As noted already, the President does not vote at the European Council; and since the European Council does not have a legislative role, the President of the European Council cannot veto legislation (eg unlike the President of the US). Nor can he or she issue instructions to the European Council (or other EU institutions), or adopt binding measures (although the European Council *itself* can adopt binding acts, as discussed later). Rather, the President chairs the European Council and drives forward its work,[143] ensures its preparation and continuity,[144] aims to facilitate 'cohesion and consensus', reports regularly to the European Parliament, and represents the EU 'at his [or her] level' as regards foreign policy, without prejudice to the role of the High Representative (discussed in section 3). In practice, in light of the economic and financial crisis since van Rompuy took office, the external role

[136] Art 15(2) TEU. [137] Art 235(1) TFEU.

[138] Art 15(5) TEU. This vote is calculated the same way as for the Council (see section 5). The European Council can dismiss its President (by the same voting rule) in the event of 'impediment or serious misconduct'.

[139] OJ [2009] L315/48; OJ [2012] L77/17. On the President's terms of office, see OJ [2009] L322/35.

[140] OJ [2014] L262/5; OJ [2017] L67/87. [141] OJ [2019] L179 I/1 and OJ [2024] L 1.7.2024.

[142] Art 15(6) TEU.

[143] The President of the European Council sets the agenda of meetings and draws up draft conclusions and decisions, but these must be discussed first in the General Affairs Council (see Art 3, European Council rules of procedure).

[144] On this point, the President of the European Council must cooperate with the President of the European Commission and acts 'on the basis of the work of the General Affairs Council'. See also Art 16(6) TEU, which provides for the General Affairs Council to ensure the follow-up to European Council meetings, in conjunction with the President of the European Council.

of the first full-time President of the European Council was limited. The refugee crisis and Brexit in turn limited the external role of Donald Tusk.

While the President of the European Council cannot hold a national office, he or she is not banned from holding another EU post, although it would be awkward to hold the presidencies of both the European Council and the Commission simultaneously—due to the differences in the appointment process and the degree of independence of these two offices. Similarly, it would be difficult in practice for the President of the European Council to hold another post in the Commission or the European Parliament.

In the absence of any legal powers for the President of the European Council, it is hard to judge the impact of creating the post. But it is clear that the post is not purely ceremonial: Presidents van Rompuy and Tusk in particular were politically highly involved, and can hardly be compared to the UK's monarch, or the President of Germany. The European Council became intensively involved in crisis management relating to the EU's economic and monetary union and refugee and migrant influx, and the President played a role in facilitating agreement on the measures to be taken. Under the pre-Lisbon system, the president or prime minister of the rotating Member State which held the Presidency would of course have tried to achieve the same results, but given the length and complexity of the crisis, it is probable that the EU benefited from having a single individual focus largely on such tasks for a longer period.

Conversely, the prime minister or president of the Member State which holds the Council Presidency has very little to do,[145] as compared to the pre-Lisbon situation, when he or she chaired the meetings of the European Council. The foreign minister of the Member State holding the Council Presidency also now has little to do, given that the Presidency no longer has an external relations role (see section 5.3).

6.3 **Powers**

6.3.1 **Historical background**

Unlike the EU's other political institutions, the European Council has not existed from the very beginning of the EU's Treaties. Rather, after several sporadic previous summit meetings of heads of State and government, it was created in 1974, but on an informal basis (ie not on the basis of a treaty or any legally binding text). The original intention of these summit meetings was to adopt 'an overall approach to the internal problems involved in achieving European unity and the external problems facing Europe', and 'to ensure progress and overall consistency in the activities of the Communities and in the work on political cooperation (ie foreign policy)'.[146]

Despite its informal basis, the European Council quickly became the main venue for discussing and deciding upon the key issues facing the EU, such as enlargement, budget disputes, Treaty amendments, high-profile external relations issues, and major political initiatives. It met at least twice a year and, until the Treaty of Lisbon, the Presidency of the European Council matched the Presidency of the Council (see section 5.4.2).

[145] The prime minister or president of the Member State holding the Council Presidency can fill in for the President of the European Council only in limited circumstances (see Art 2(4) European Council rules of procedure), namely where the President is ill, has died, or been removed from office, and only until the European Council selects a replacement. Also, he or she reports to the European Council on the work of the Council (Art 4(1), European Council rules of procedure).

[146] Final communique of Paris summit, 9–10 December 1974.

In purely legal terms, the role of the European Council before the Treaty of Lisbon was modest. This body was formally established in the SEA (in force 1987), which simply provided for the existence of the European Council in the form of heads of State and government, assisted by the Commission President and Member States' foreign ministers, to meet at least twice a year.[147] Subsequently, the original Treaty on European Union (Maastricht Treaty) specified that the task of the European Council 'shall provide the Union with the necessary impetus for its development and shall define the general political guidelines thereof'. It also confirmed that the European Council was chaired by the Member State holding the Council Presidency (which was already the existing practice), and that it would send the European Parliament a report after each of its meetings and an annual report on the development of the EU.[148] The Maastricht Treaty also provided for a few formal roles for the European Council—for instance, to 'define the principles of and general guidelines for the common foreign and security policy'[149] and to discuss the broad guidelines for Member States' and the EU's economic policy.[150] However, it was still left to the Council to adopt binding decisions, although as regards the start of economic and monetary union (EMU) (and admitting new States to the EMU) the Council had to do so in the formation of heads of State and government.[151] Moreover, some decisions were to be made by the heads of State and government as such, as distinct from the European Council.[152]

Subsequently, the Treaty of Amsterdam gave the European Council the power to adopt 'common strategies' in the area of foreign policy (although the legal status of these acts was not defined),[153] a decision establishing a 'common defence' for the EU (subject to ratification by Member States),[154] and decisions settling a dispute over the start of 'closer cooperation' (now called 'enhanced cooperation') in the field of policing and criminal law.[155] However, the Treaty of Amsterdam still also provided for action by the Council, meeting at the level of heads of State and government,[156] and for mere 'conclusions' of the European Council on the employment situation.[157]

Next, the Treaty of Nice (in force 2003) included a declaration on the 'venue' of European Councils, providing that once the EU had 18 or more Member States (ie from May 2004), all its meetings would be held in Brussels, rather than (as before) in the Member State holding the Presidency. This was a precursor to the Treaty of Lisbon, which broke the link between the European Council Presidency and Member States.

[147] Art 2 SEA.

[148] Art D TEU (OJ [1992] C191), renumbered Art 4 TEU by the Treaty of Amsterdam (OJ [1997] C340), in force 1999.

[149] Art J.8(1) TEU, renumbered Art 13(1) TEU by the Treaty of Amsterdam.

[150] Art 103 EC, renumbered Art 99 EC by the Treaty of Amsterdam.

[151] Arts 109j and 109k EC, renumbered Arts 121 and 122 EC by the Treaty of Amsterdam.

[152] Arts 109a and 109f EC, renumbered Arts 112 and 117 EC by the Treaty of Amsterdam, concerning appointments to the European Central Bank and its precursor body, the European Monetary Institute.

[153] Art 13(2) TEU (Treaty of Amsterdam version). Only three such measures were ever adopted, concerning Russia, Ukraine, and the Mediterranean (for the last such measure, see OJ [2004] L337/72).

[154] Art 17(1) TEU (Treaty of Amsterdam version). On the EU's defence policy, see chapter 26.

[155] Art 40(1) TEU (Treaty of Amsterdam version). For more on enhanced cooperation, see chapter 5.

[156] Art 11(2) EC (Treaty of Amsterdam version), which applied in the event of a dispute over launching 'closer cooperation' as regards EC law. In that case, the Council, in that special composition, could take a decision unanimously. Also, Art 7(1) TEU (Treaty of Amsterdam version), provided for the Council, in that special composition, to adopt decisions sanctioning Member States for serious and persistent breaches of human rights.

[157] Art 128 EC (Treaty of Amsterdam version).

6.3.2 **Treaty of Lisbon**

In total, the Treaty of Lisbon made three significant changes to the status and functioning of the European Council. First of all, that Treaty made the European Council an official Institution of the EU.[158] This means that the European Council can sue and be sued,[159] and has its own rules of procedure.[160]

Secondly, the role of the European Council was enhanced, by providing that it could adopt a much wider array of formal decisions, including decisions previously taken by heads of State and government (or by the Council in that composition). These mainly comprise decisions on major appointments,[161] its own functioning,[162] the composition and functioning of other institutions,[163] and the Treaty amendment process,[164] along with other sundry powers.[165]

The European Council also retained its power to decide on sanctions against Member States and to adopt strategic foreign policy decisions and a decision establishing a common defence.[166] Its role in giving general guidance (as distinct from binding decisions) has also been retained, as regards the discussion of economic policy guidelines, its involvement in the adoption of the euro by more Member States, and the adoption of conclusions on the employment situation.[167] This general guidance power has also been enhanced, both generally[168] and as regards the specific areas of foreign policy,[169] justice and home affairs,[170] dispute settlement in sensitive areas,[171] enlargement,[172] and problematic Treaty ratifications.[173]

[158] See the list of institutions in Art 13(2) TEU.

[159] Arts 263 and 265 TFEU (on actions for annulment and failure to act) refer expressly to the European Council. Implicitly, it is one of the 'institutions' whose acts can be the subject of references from national courts to the Court of Justice, for a ruling on those acts' validity and interpretation (Art 267(b) TFEU); this has been confirmed by the Court (Case C-370/12 *Pringle*, EU:C:2012:756). On the Court's jurisdiction, see further chapter 10.

[160] OJ [2009] L315/51.

[161] See Art 17(7) TEU (nomination of candidate for Commission President, appointment of Commission); Art 18(1) TEU (appointment of High Representative); and Art 283(2) TFEU (appointments to the European Central Bank). On the Commission, see section 3; on the Central Bank, see most recently OJ [2019] L267/1.

[162] Art 15(5) TEU (appointment of its President); Art 235(3) TFEU (adoption of rules of procedure).

[163] See Art 14(2) TEU (composition of the European Parliament); Art 17(5) TEU (number of members of the European Commission); Art 236 TFEU (list of Council configurations and rotating Council Presidencies); and Art 244 TFEU (system for rotation of Commissioners). See sections 3, 4, and 5.

[164] See, in particular, Art 48 TEU, and the discussion of the Treaty amendment process in chapter 5.

[165] The European Council must be informed as regards the withdrawal of a Member State from the EU, and can decide to extend the time period to negotiate a withdrawal agreement (Art 50 TEU; see chapter 27). It can also extend the scope of crimes over which the European Public Prosecutor has jurisdiction (Art 86(4) TFEU), and decide on removing Ireland from its participation in certain Justice and Home Affairs matters (Art 5(4) Protocol on the Schengen *acquis*). The first of these powers has been used, as discussed further in chapter 27.

[166] See respectively Arts 7(2), 22(1), and 42(2) TEU.

[167] See respectively Arts 121(2), 140(2), and 148(1) TFEU.

[168] In place of the previous reference to 'general political guidelines', Art 15(1) TEU now provides for the European Council to 'define the general political direction and priorities' of the EU.

[169] Art 15(1) TEU.

[170] Art 68 TFEU provides for the European Council to 'define the strategic guidelines for legislative and operational planning within the area of freedom, security and justice'. These guidelines are not legally binding, and do not prevent the use of qualified majority voting in the Council: Joined Cases C-643/15 and C-647/15, *Slovakia and Hungary v Council*, EU:C:2017:641, paras 136–150.

[171] While there is no longer a role for the European Council as regards disputes over launching enhanced cooperation, it has a formal role in the event of disputes over proposed legislation concerning social security (Art 48 TFEU) or aspects of criminal law and policing (Arts 82(3), 83(3), 86(1), and 87(3) TFEU).

[172] Art 49 TEU now requires the Council to take into account the 'conditions of eligibility' for EU membership which the European Council has agreed upon. This confirms the prior practice as regards the so-called 'Copenhagen criteria' for membership, which were agreed in 2002.

[173] See Art 48(5) TEU. This confirms the European Council's prior role as a venue for resolving problems relating to the ratification of the Maastricht, Nice, and Lisbon Treaties, and for restarting the Treaty amendment process after the failure of the Constitutional Treaty. See further chapter 2.

Significantly, the Treaties also set out one thing the European Council *cannot* do: it 'shall not exercise legislative functions'.[174] So, formally at least, the legislative process only involves the other three political institutions (the Commission, the European Parliament, and the Council). However, the work of the European Council necessarily impacts on the legislative process—for instance, as regards multi-annual budget legislation (as seen in case study 3.1), and the European Council sometimes sets deadlines to adopt legislation or adopts broad guidelines as to its content (eg as regards much of the post-financial crisis legislation on EMU, discussed in chapter 19).

Despite the significant changes to the Treaty provisions on the role of the European Council, the legal position according to the Treaty still understates its practical significance. For instance, in relation to enlargement, the European Council does not merely decide on eligibility criteria, but in practice decides when the EU is willing to open negotiations for particular countries to join. For instance, the European Council of June 2022 decided that Ukraine and Moldova could be candidates for EU membership, and the European Council of December 2023 decided to start negotiations with both countries. As regards major Treaty amendments, the European Council is the venue for the final phase of the negotiations in each intergovernmental conference, where the most difficult issues are settled. For the multi-year EU budget process, the European Council is (as noted already) the venue for agreeing the most difficult issues between Member States.

Since the Treaty of Lisbon, though, the European Council has mainly focused on addressing the results of the ongoing economic and financial crisis, and in particular its effect on EMU.

Finally, the third major change brought about by the Treaty of Lisbon was the appointment of a full-time President of the European Council (discussed at section 6.2).

Taken as a whole, then, the Treaty of Lisbon has increased the efficiency of the European Council by creating the office of full-time President and by conferring more legal powers upon that body. However, the effect of these changes is to detach individual Member States from the workings of the EU, by divesting the prime ministers of the Member State holding the Council Presidency from their previous role. This is accentuated by the reduction in the role of the foreign minister of the Member State holding the Council Presidency, and by the previous decision to stop the European Council meeting in the Member State holding that Presidency. So there is a risk that while these changes enhanced the effectiveness of this institution, they decreased its legitimacy.

6.4 **Functioning**

The basic rule is that the European Council must act by 'consensus', which is not precisely defined, except where the Treaties provide otherwise.[175] In fact, the Treaties frequently provide otherwise, providing for a voting rule as regards the adoption of any formal decisions; for instance, unanimity is required for the adoption of Treaty amendments by a simplified procedure, QMV is required for appointments, and simple majority voting as regards the European Council's own rules of procedure. Meetings of the European Council are not public,[176] although they are often high-profile affairs attracting much press and public attention, and some of them have been significant turning points in the European integration process.

[174] Art 49 TEU now requires the Council to take into account the 'conditions of eligibility' for EU membership which the European Council has agreed upon. This confirms the prior practice as regards the so-called 'Copenhagen criteria' for membership, which were agreed in 2002.

[175] Art 15(4) TEU. [176] Art 4(3) European Council rules of procedure.

7 Transparency of the EU's political institutions

Intertwined with the concern about the democratic credentials of the EU institutions have been concerns about the openness and transparency of their decision-making. This was addressed first of all in the mid-1990s by the insertion of provisions on public meetings and access to documents in the rules of procedure of these three EU institutions. Subsequently, the Treaty of Amsterdam required general rules to be adopted, pursuant to the co-decision procedure (as it was then), regulating access to their documents (see now Article 15 TFEU).

This legislation, adopted in 2001,[177] has been the source of fertile litigation before the courts of the EU. Broadly speaking, that case law has followed the legislative/non-legislative divide between the types of EU activity that the Treaty of Lisbon confirmed and elaborated upon. Therefore, where the Council and European Parliament are legislating, they are not only obliged to meet in public (Article 15(2) TFEU). Beyond this, as previously described in sections 4 and 5, given that those institutions prepare their decisions at an earlier stage (particularly working groups, committees, and Coreper, for the Council), it is also necessary to ensure public access to the documents generated at an earlier stage, in order to ensure democratic accountability of the EU legislative process. So even though the 2001 legislation on access to documents provides for an exception related to the decision-making process, the Court of Justice has been unwilling to accept its application as regards any aspect of legislative activity, on the ground that the right of access to documents is linked to the democratic accountability of the EU institutions.[178]

On the other hand, as regards the non-legislative activity of the EU, the Court has been willing to accept a blanket presumption that whole categories of documents fall within the scope of one or more exceptions in the 2001 legislation, for instance as regards infringement proceedings, merger control, and State aid investigations.[179] The assumption in these cases is rather that the efficiency of the decision-making procedure might be affected unduly by making it public.

8 Conclusion

As we have seen, the application of the principle of representative democracy to the EU is complex. Even though the 'lower house' of the EU's two-chamber legislature, the European Parliament, has been elected directly by the public since 1979, this has not alleviated a public perception that the EU is undemocratic, despite the significant growth in powers for this elected body. This manifested itself in steadily lower turnouts to elections (although this was reversed in 2019), and probably had many different causes: indifference or hostility to the EU in general; the lack of representation by population; a perception that the Parliament still had no real powers; a lack of understanding of the EU political system—that is, the practical impact of casting a vote in these elections; the costs and remoteness of the Parliament; and reduced interest in politics in general. The increased turnout since 2019 may, on the other hand, suggest an increase in public engagement with European Union politics.

On the other hand, the Union's legislative 'upper house', the Council, has (like the European Council) a direct connection back to national democratic politics. But this is

[177] Regulation 1049/2001 (OJ [2001] L145/43).

[178] See particularly Joined Cases C-39/05 P and C-52/05 P *Turco v Council* [2008] ECR I-4273 and Case C-280/11 *Access Info Europe v Council*, EU:C:2013:671.

[179] See, eg, Joined Cases C-514/11 P and C-605/11 P *LPN v Commission*, EU:C:2013:738.

not perceived to solve the democratic problem either. This may be because of (again) a lack of understanding of the EU political system (there is a widespread belief that the *Commission* adopts legislation), or conversely because of the public's objection to the possibility that each Member State's democratically elected government might be outvoted on many issues. On this point, the trade-off between efficiency and (national) democratic accountability is self-evident, since the EU's interest in achieving its objectives will take priority over the view of the democratically elected government of one or more Member States, if they are outvoted.

Interestingly, by keeping the number of members in the Commission equal to the number of Member States, the EU has instead chosen to prioritize legitimacy over efficiency. This is consistent with a long-term trend that has seen the profile and authority of the EU's most efficient institution reduced in favour of the other political institutions, each of which can claim a far stronger EU-wide or national democratic mandate, and whose powers over the appointment and removal of Commissioners and to influence or control the Commission's actions has steadily increased.

In any event, the institutional development of the European Union did not prevent the UK vote to leave the EU—and the extension of qualified majority voting and powers of the European Parliament may well have contributed to that result.

Further reading

A Arnull and D Willcott (eds), *Accountability and Legitimacy in the European Union* (Oxford: Oxford University Press, 2003)

C Barnard and J Adams-Prassl, 'The Making of the EU Platform Work Directive' (2025) 50 *European Law Review* 655

R Corbett, F Jacobs, and M Shackleton, *The European Parliament* (8th edn, London: John Harper, 2011)

H de Waele and H Broeksteeg, 'The Semi-Permanent European Council Presidency: Some Reflections on the Law and Early Practice' (2012) 49 *Common Market Law Review* 1039

S Hix and B Høyland, *The Political System of the European Union* (4th edn, Oxford: Oxford University Press, 2022)

D Naurin and H Wallace (eds), *Unveiling the Council of the European Union: Games Governments Play in Brussels* (Basingstoke: Palgrave Macmillan, 2010)

D Spence (ed), *The European Commission* (3rd edn, London: John Harper, 2006)

H Wallace et al (eds), *Policy-Making in the European Union* (8th edn, Oxford: Oxford University Press, 2020)

Chapter acknowledgements

My thanks to Kieran Bradley for his comments on a draft of this chapter. The usual disclaimer applies.

4

Constitutionalism and the European Union

Robert Schütze

1 Introduction: constitutionalism(s)

Constitutionalism is the set of ideas that defines what a constitution is or ought to be. Various conceptions of constitutionalism have developed in legal history. According to a 'descriptive' constitutionalism, a constitution is the factual description of the institutions and powers of government.[1] By contrast, normative constitutionalism insists that constitutions do not merely *describe* the existing governmental structures, but *prescribe* their composition and powers.[2] Standing above all ordinary laws, constitutional laws are identified with those norms that represent the highest laws within a society. This *formal* definition has in the last 200 years competed with a *material* understanding of what a constitution ought to be. This material constitutionalism links the—legal—concept of constitution with a particular *political* philosophy. According to a 'democratic' constitutionalism, a genuine constitution only exists where it is based on the idea of a 'government of the people, by the people, for the people'.[3] A 'liberal' constitutionalism, on the other hand, believes that a constitution is only a true constitution if it sets limits to the powers of government,[4] and the two traditional constitutional limits here are the separation of powers and fundamental rights (see Fig. 4.1).[5]

[1] In this 'descriptive' sense, there is no distinction between the 'government' and the 'constitution'. Cf E Zoller, *Droit Constitutionnel* (Paris: Presses Universitaires de France, 1998) 10.

[2] cf T Paine, 'Rights of Man' in *Political Writings* (Cambridge: Cambridge University Press, 1997) 89: 'A Constitution is a thing antecedent to a government, and a government is only the creature of a constitution.'

[3] A Lincoln, 'Gettysburg Address, 1863' in HS Commager and M Cantor (eds), *Documents of American History*, vol I (Upper Saddle River, NJ: Prentice Hall, 1988) 429.

[4] cf CH McIlwain, *Constitutionalism: Ancient and Modern* (Ithaca, NY: Cornell University Press, 1947).

[5] cf 1789 Declaration of the Rights of Man and of the Citizen, Art 16 of which states: 'Toute Société dans laquelle la garantie des Droits n'est pas assurée, ni la séparation des Pouvoirs déterminée, n'a point de Constitution.'

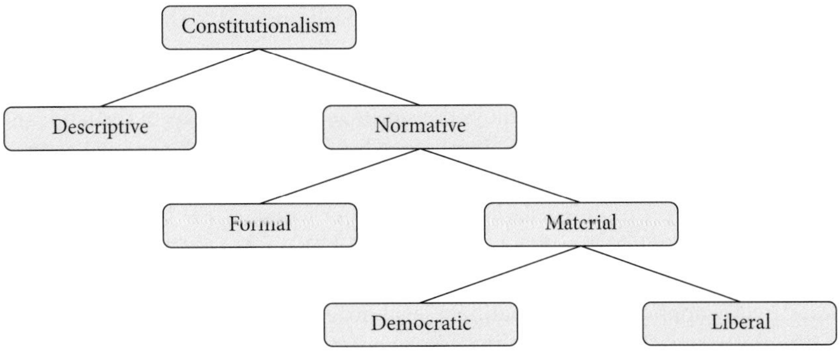

Fig. 4.1 Concepts of constitutionalism

Is there an EU constitution? This question has plagued EU law ever since its birth.[6] From a descriptive point of view, the EU undoubtedly has a constitution, since it has a set of institutions that engage in the business of government.[7] However, could the same be said from the perspective of normative constitutionalism? Does the EU have a formal constitution; and, if so, what is the political philosophy that underpins that formal constitution? Section 2 explores the formal constitutional credentials of the Union legal order. We shall see there that the Union has claimed that the EU Treaties constitute the highest law in Europe. Sections 3 and 4 subsequently explore the constitutional nature of the Union from a democratic perspective. Should the EU Treaties be denied their constitutional law status because they have not had a (nation-like) democratic foundation, or because they have not established a (nation-like) democratic system of representation? Sections 5 and 6 finally evaluate the Union legal order through the lens of liberal constitutionalism. This classic school of constitutionalism assesses the constitutional character of the EU Treaties through the separation of powers and the existence of fundamental rights.

2 **Formal constitutionalism: contested primacy**

Formal constitutionalism defines a constitution as the set of those norms that stand at the apex of a legal hierarchy. Constitutional norms are the highest norms within a legal order and as such enjoy absolute—legal—'primacy' over all other norms. Standing on top, their validity cannot be legally derived from other norms.[8] Norms that are socially 'given' such a constitutional status can, however, be produced in a variety of ways: they may be

[6] The EU legal order is not the only one suffering from this doubt. For the question of whether the UK has a legal constitution, see E Barendt, 'Is There a United Kingdom Constitution?' (1997) 12 *Oxford Journal of Legal Studies* 137.

[7] On the Union institutions and overall governmental system, see chapter 3.

[8] H Kelsen, *General Theory of the State* (Piscataway, NJ: Transaction Publishers, 2005) 115–116:

> If we ask why the constitution is valid, perhaps we come upon an older constitution. Ultimately we reach some constitution that is the first historically and that was laid down by an individual usurper or by some kind of assembly. The validity of this first construction is the last presupposition, the final postulate, upon which the validity of all the norms of our legal order depends. ... This is the basic norm of the legal order under consideration. ... The basic norm is not created in a legal procedure by a law-creating organ. It is not—as a positive legal norm is—valid because it is created in a certain way by a legal act, but it is valid because without this presupposition no human act could be interpreted as a legal, especially as a norm-creating act.

granted by a monarch,[9] they may be adopted by a parliament,[10] or they may result from a treaty between States.[11] From a formal constitutionalist perspective, the historical origin or material content of a norm that is 'given' constitutional status is secondary. All that counts for a constitution is that it enjoys the *status* as the highest law of the land; and this legal status is not granted by another legal norm but is postulated by a social convention.

What are the highest norms in the EU legal order? It is generally accepted that the EU Treaties stand above Union legislation and all other forms of *EU* law.[12] However, what about the relationship between EU and national law? This question became relevant once the Union legal order insisted—and the Member States generally accepted—that EU law was directly applicable in the national legal orders.[13] For by integrating the EU legal order into the national legal orders, the question arose as to which legal norms would be 'supreme' in the case of a conflict.

Modern federal states typically resolve conflicts between federal and state law in favour of the former: federal law reigns supreme over state law.[14] However, the Union is not a federal state and when the Union was born, the EU Treaties, did not expressly mention the primacy of EU law.[15] Did this mean that primacy was a matter to be determined by the national legal orders (decentralized solution); or was there a Union doctrine of primacy (centralized solution)? The question has never been definitively resolved. Two competing perspectives thus coexist within the EU: one national, one European. What does this mean for the constitutional credentials of the EU Treaties? Let us look at both aspects in turn.

2.1 **Legal primacy: two perspectives**

Early on, the European Court of Justice tried to centralize the question of primacy by turning it into a principle of EU law. In *Costa v ENEL*,[16] the EU judiciary had been asked whether national legislation adopted after 1957 could prevail over the EU Treaties. Italy had claimed that the EU Treaties—like ordinary international law—had been transposed into the Italian legal order by national legislation, which could therefore be derogated by subsequent national legislation. The Court rejected this presumption of the primacy of national law in the following way:

> By contrast with ordinary international treaties, the E[U] Treaty has created its own legal system which, on the entry into force of the Treaty, became an integral part of the legal systems of the Member States and which their courts are bound to apply . . . [T]he law stemming from the Treaty, an independent source of law, could not, because of its special and original nature,

[9] For illustrations of monarchic constitutions, see the 1814 French Charte, as well as the 1820 Vienna Final Act: 'the entire authority of the state must, according to the basic concepts provided thereby, remain united within the head of state, and the sovereign can therefore only in the exercise of particular rights be constitutionally bound to the participation of the estates' (ibid, Art 57).

[10] On this (indirect) democratic creation, see section 3.1.

[11] On this form of international creation, see section 3.2.

[12] cf Art 263 TFEU and Case 294/83 *Parti écologiste 'Les Verts' v European Parliament* [1986] ECR 1339.

[13] cf Case 26/62 *Van Gend en Loos v Netherlands Inland Revenue Administration* [1963] ECR 1. On the doctrines of direct applicability and direct effect, see chapter 6.

[14] eg Art VI, cl 2 of the US Constitution states: 'This Constitution, and the Laws of the United States which shall be made in pursuance thereof; and all treaties made, or which shall be made, under the Authority of the United States, shall be the supreme Law of the Land.'

[15] The (failed) EU Constitutional Treaty (2004) would have added an express provision (Art I-6 CT): 'The Constitution and law adopted by the institutions of the Union in exercising competences conferred on it shall have primacy over the law of the Member States.' However, the provision was not taken over by the Lisbon Treaty.

[16] Case 6/64 Costa v ENEL [1964] ECR 585.

be overridden by domestic legal provisions, however framed, without being deprived of its character as [European] law and without the legal basis of the [Union] itself being called into question.[17]

EU law was thus supreme over national law. But how supreme was EU law? The fact that the EU Treaties prevailed over national legislation did not automatically imply that all EU law would prevail over all national law. Would the Court, for example, accept a relative solution for a State's own highest (constitutional) norms? This issue was clarified in *Internationale Handelsgesellschaft*.[18] A German court had doubted that EU legislation could violate national fundamental rights granted by the German Constitution and raised this very question with the European Court of Justice. Were the fundamental principles of national constitutions, including human rights, beyond the scope of EU primacy? The Court disagreed. The validity of EU law could never be affected by national law—even by the most fundamental norms within the Member States. The Court's vision of the primacy of EU law over national law was thus an absolute one: 'The whole of [EU] law prevails over the whole of national law.'[19]

From an EU perspective, the European Treaties are thus constitutional treaties.[20] Yet this perspective is—unsurprisingly—not fully shared by the Member States. Indeed, a competing national view coexists with an EU view; and this national perspective only accepts the relative primacy of EU law over *some* national law. While accepting that the EU constitutes a 'new legal order' distinct from classic international law, many Member States still insist that its validity ultimately derives from the national decision to accede to the EU (see further chapter 7). This national perspective has, in the past, been expressed in two traditional contexts. First, some Member States—in particular their supreme courts[21]—have fought a battle over fundamental rights within the Union legal order. It was claimed that EU law could not violate national fundamental rights. A similar constitutional contest also arose in a second context: ultra vires control. This constitutional battleground became prominent in light of the expansive use of legislative and judicial competences by the Union. In denying the Union a competence to create or exclusively interpret its own competences, some Member States here insist on the last word with regard to the competences of the Union.[22]

[17] Ibid, 593–594.

[18] Case 11/70 *Internationale Handelsgesellschaft mbH v Einfuhr- und Vorratsstelle für Getreide und Futtermittel* [1970] ECR 1125.

[19] R Kovar, 'The Relationship between Community Law and National Law' in EC Commission (ed), *Thirty Years of Community Law* (EC Commission, 1981) 112–113. On the implications for the protection of human rights within EU law, see further chapter 9.

[20] Case 294/83 *Parti Ecologiste 'Les Verts' v Parliament* [1986] ECR 1339, 1365, para 23: 'a [Union] based on the rule of law, inasmuch as neither its Member States nor its institutions can avoid a review of the question whether the measures adopted by them are in conformity with the basic constitutional charter, the Treaty'.

[21] For an historical overview of the relationship between EU and national law, see A Oppenheimer, *The Relationship between European Community Law and National Law: The Cases* (Cambridge: Cambridge University Press, 1994); as well as W Sadurski, '"Solange, Chapter 3": Constitutional Courts in Central Europe—Democracy—European Union' (2008) 14 *European Law Journal* 1.

[22] On the (strange) German notion of 'competence-competence', see R Schütze, *From Dual to Cooperative Federalism: The Changing Structure of European Law* (Oxford: Oxford University Press, 2009) 34–36 and 151–156.

Case study 4.1: Constitutional conflicts and the German Federal Constitutional Court

A strong national view on the primacy issue first crystallized around *Internationale Handelsgesellschaft*.[23] For after the European Court of Justice had espoused its absolute view on the primacy of European law over national law, the case moved back to the German Federal Constitutional Court.[24] The Constitutional Court here clarified its perspective on the primacy question and famously replaced the European Court's vision with its countertheory of relative primacy. The reasoning of the German court was as follows: while the German Constitution expressly allowed for the transfer of sovereign powers to the EU, such a transfer was itself limited and controlled by national constitutional law. Did this mean that national law would prevail over EU law? The response of the German Federal Constitutional Court was the famous *So-Long* Doctrine.

> [I]n the hypothetical case of a conflict between [EU] law and a part of national constitutional law or, more precisely, of the guarantees of fundamental rights in the Constitution, there arises the question of which system of law takes precedence, that is, ousts the other. In this conflict of norms, the guarantee of *fundamental rights in the [German] Constitution prevails so long as the competent organs of the [Union] have not removed the conflict of norms in accordance with the Treaty mechanism.*[25]

The Union legal order did indeed subsequently develop extensive human rights bill(s).[26] Yet with the constitutional conflict over fundamental rights settled, a second concern emerged: the ever-growing competences of the EU.

Who was to control and limit the scope of EU law? Was it enough to have the EU legislator be centrally controlled by the European Court of Justice? Or should the national constitutional courts be entitled to a decentralized ultra vires review? The EU view on this problem is crystal clear: national courts cannot disapply—let alone invalidate—EU law.[27] A national vision on the ultra vires issue was, however, expressed by the German Federal Constitutional Court's *Maastricht* decision.[28] The court here held as follows:

> [I]f European institutions or agencies were to treat or develop the Union Treaty in a way that was no longer covered by the Treaty in the form that is the basis for the [German] Act of Accession, the resultant legislative instruments would not be legally binding within the sphere of German sovereignty. The German state organs would be prevented for constitutional reasons from applying them in Germany.[29]

The German Federal Constitutional Court thus threatened to disapply EU law that it considered to have been adopted ultra vires.

2.2 **Contested hierarchies: federalism and constitutional pluralism**

If constitutional law is the highest law within a legal order, will it not follow from the continued existence of *national* constitutional law that there cannot be any coexistent *European* constitutional law? Traditionally, classic constitutionalism indeed draws this

[23] *Internationale Handelsgesellschaft mbH* (n 18).

[24] BVerfGE 37, 271 (*Solange I (Re Internationale Handelsgesellschaft)*). For an English translation, see [1974] 2 CMLR 540.

[25] Ibid, 550–551, paras 23 and 24 (emphasis added).

[26] On this point, see section 6.

[27] Case 314/85 *Foto-Frost v Hauptzollamt Lübeck-Ost* [1987] ECR 4199. On the EU's judicial architecture, see further chapter 10.

[28] BVerfGE 89, 155 (*Maastricht* decision). For an English translation, see [1994] 1 CMLR 57.

[29] Ibid, 105.

conclusion: there can only be *one* supreme constitution within a legal order—be it either the national or the EU constitution.

However, this 'unitary' or 'monistic' standard has never lived up to the constitutional practice of federal orders—like the United States, where both the Union *and* the states were seen to have 'constitutional' claims.[30] Unlike the unitary constitutionalism within unitary States,[31] many federal unions have thus developed a federal or pluralist constitutionalism. Each of the two political bodies—the Union and its Member States—will have constitutional claims that may even sometimes come into conflict with each other.[32] Unlike unitary States in which the primacy and sovereignty issue is settled, in federal unions the locus of sovereignty remains 'suspended'.[33] For wherever the sovereignty question is—eventually—answered in favour of the Union, the 'Union' is transformed into a sovereign State. (This is what gradually happened to the US after the Civil War.[34]) Conversely, wherever the sovereignty question is—eventually—answered in favour of the Member States, the political existence of the federation disappears and the Union dissolves into an international organization. The normative ambivalence surrounding the location of sovereignty, and the consequent potential for constitutional conflicts, are the core of all—real—federations.[35]

This fundamental insight into the pluralist nature of unions of states as 'multi-level' or 'federal' constitutional orders has been rediscovered by an academic movement called 'constitutional pluralism'.[36] The central claim behind this 'new' school is this:

> EU law . . . poses the most pressing paradigm-challenging test to what we might call constitutional monism. Constitutional monism merely grants a label to the defining assumption of constitutionalism in the Westphalian age . . ., namely the idea that the sole centres or units of constitutional authorities are states. Constitutional pluralism, by contrast, recognizes that the European legal order inaugurated by the Treaty of Rome has developed beyond the traditional confines of inter-*national* law and now makes its own independent constitutional claims exist alongside the continuing claims of states.[37]

The idea of constitutional pluralism thus accepts—like that of federalism—the coexistence of multiple constitutional orders that are not hierarchically ordered but may

[30] cf E Zoeller, 'Aspects internationaux du droit constitutionnel: Contribution à la théorie de la féderation d'états' (2002) 194 *Recueil des Cours de l'Académie de la Haye* 43. The same is true for Germany, where the 'Länder' have their own 'constitutions'.

[31] Traditional unitary States are France and the UK; and even if the latter has increasingly recognized a degree of administrative 'devolution', this devolution does not recognize the 'constitutional' autonomy of the decentralized regions.

[32] On the existence of constitutional conflicts in the US before and after the Civil War, see R Schütze, 'Federalism as Constitutional Pluralism: Letter from America' in M Avbelj and J Komárek (eds), *Constitutional Pluralism in the European Union and Beyond* (Oxford: Hart Publishing, 2012).

[33] C Schmitt, *Verfassungslehre* (Berlin: Duncker & Humblot, 1993) 376–378 (trans R Schütze).

[34] cf E Katz, 'The Development of American Federalism, 1763–1865' in A Bosco (ed), *The Federal Idea*, vol I (London: Lothian Foundation Press, 1992).

[35] Schmitt, *Verfassungslehre* (n 33) 378.

[36] The movement gained momentum in the aftermath of the *Maastricht* decision by the German Federal Constitutional Court (cf J Baquero-Cruz, 'The Legacy of the Maastricht-Urteil and the Pluralist Movement' (2008) 14 *European Law Journal* 389). One of the strongest proponents of this movement has claimed that '[c]onstitutional pluralism has been, perhaps, the most successful attempt at theorizing the nature of European constitutionalism' (MP Maduro, 'Three Claims of Constitutional Pluralism' in Avbelj and Komárek (n 32) 68). Personally, I share the much more sceptical opposite views of G Davies, 'Constitutional Disagreement in Europe and the Search of Pluralism' in ibid, 269: 'the investment in constitutional pluralism by scholars has not brought satisfactory returns'.

[37] cf N Walker, 'The Idea of Constitutional Pluralism' (2002) 65 *Modern Law Review* 317, 337.

interact in a *heterarchical* way.[38] However, the absence of an 'Archimedean point' from which all legal authority can be explained is here—wrongly—hailed as a *sui generis* quality of the EU.[39] The theory of constitutional pluralism indeed speaks federal prose without being aware of it. For unlike the unitary and hierarchical constitutionalism that was developed for the modern sovereign State, both federal constitutionalism and constitutional pluralism accept the existence of two alternative answers to the primacy question and insist that sovereignty within a union of states is shared or suspended. And as we shall see in the next section, the distinction between State (unitary) constitutionalism and federal (pluralist) constitutionalism also helps us to analyse the democratic credentials of the EU.

3 Democratic constitutionalism I: popular sovereignty

3.1 Unitary constitutionalism: 'We, the People'

Democratic constitutional theory insists that since 'the people' are sovereign, they must create the constitution. Popular sovereignty can thereby express itself either directly or indirectly. The former means that the people directly adopt their constitution through a referendum.[40] The softer version of popular sovereignty, by contrast, allows this task to be delegated to an elected assembly,[41] which adopts the constitution 'on behalf' of the people.

What happens if we apply this unitary theory of popular sovereignty to the EU? Under this doctrine, only 'a people' can democratically constitute itself into a legal sovereign. A constitution is thus regarded as a unilateral act of a democratic '*pouvoir constituant*':

> [I]t is inherent in a constitution in the full sense of the term that it goes back to an act taken by or at least attributed to the people, in which they attribute political capacity to themselves. There is no such source for primary Union law. It goes back not to a European people but to the individual Member States, and remains dependent on them even after its entry into force. While nations give themselves a constitution, the European Union is given a constitution by third parties.[42]

In short, the EU would only have a constitution if the latter were adopted by 'the people'; and in the absence of an EU 'people'—or demos—the EU cannot have a European Constitution.

[38] In the words of Maduro, 'Three Claims of Constitutional Pluralism' (n 36) 75: 'While the empirical thesis of constitutional pluralism limits itself to state that the question of final authority remains open, the normative claim is that the question of final authority ought to be left open. Heterarchy is superior to hierarchy as a normative ideal in circumstances of competing constitutional claims of final authority.'

[39] In particular Walker, 'The Idea of Constitutional Pluralism' (n 37) 338. His—'Eurocentric'—views strikingly ignore the American experience, in which the Union and the states were seen to have 'constitutional' claims and in which the 'Union' was—traditionally—not(!) conceived in statist terms (cf Zoeller (n 30) 43).

[40] For advocates of this direct democratic source, see Paine (n 2) 89: 'The constitution of a country is not the act of its government, but of the people constituting its government.' For the French expression of the same thought, see EJ Sieyes, 'What Is the Third Estate' in *Political Writings* (Indianapolis, IN: Hackett Publishing, 2003).

[41] For illustrations of this indirect democratic source, see the 1791 French Constitution and the 1919 (Weimar) Constitution of Germany. The 1949 German Constitution was also originally adopted by the state parliaments.

[42] D Grimm, 'Does Europe Need a Constitution?' (1995) 1 *European Law Journal* 282, 290. For a severe and brilliant early criticism of this view, see J Habermas, 'Remarks on Dieter Grimms's "Does Europe Need a Constitution?"' (1995) 1 *European Law Journal* 303.

A softer version of this argument has not denied that there 'is' a European Constitution but ultimately rejects the material legitimacy—the 'ought' to be—of that constitution:

> In federations, whether American or Australian, German or Canadian, the institutions of a federal state are situated in a constitutional framework which presupposes the existence of a 'constitutional demos', a single *pouvoir constituant* made of the citizens of the federation in whose sovereignty, as a constituent power, and by whose supreme authority the specific constitutional arrangement is rooted. . . . In Europe, that precondition does not exist. Simply put, *Europe's constitutional architecture has never been validated by a process of constitutional adoption by a European constitutional demos . . . It is a constitution without some of the classic conditions of constitutionalism.*[43]

But is this—unitary—standard for what counts as a democratic 'validation' of the EU 'constitution' the right standard for the EU? Unitary constitutionalism insists on a unitary perspective: *one* people must form *one* State on the basis of *one* constitution. But what about federal or pluralist arrangements between peoples, States, and constitutions? Unitary constitutionalism is simply unable to envisage *two* peoples living in the same territory—yet, this is generally the case in federal unions.[44] It is unable to envisage two 'sovereigns' operating in the same territory—yet, this is generally the case in federal unions. It is unable to envisage *two* constitutional orders existing within the same territory—yet, this is generally the case in federal unions.[45] And, finally, it is unable to envisage a pluralist *pouvoir constituant*—yet, this is generally the case in federal unions.[46]

In sum, if unitary constitutionalism is not the right theoretical 'fit' for the non-unitary EU, let us see how a federal standard can explain the democratic credentials of the EU constitution.

3.2 **Federal constitutionalism: 'We, the Peoples'**

Who is or are the popular sovereign(s) and who embodies the 'constituent power' within a federal or pluralist legal order? What are the historical and theoretical alternatives to the unitary focus on popular sovereignty?

We do find historical alternatives to unitary popular sovereignty in the constitutional history of the US. Believing that the 1787 US Constitution had 'split the atom of sovereignty',[47] early American constitutionalism was based on the idea that the constituent power underlying the American Union was exercised by a plurality of peoples. The 1787 Constitution had indeed been ratified 'by the people, *not as individuals composing one entire nation*, but as composing the distinct and independent States to which they respectively belong'.[48] 'Each State, in ratifying the Constitution, [was] considered as a sovereign

[43] JHH Weiler, 'Federalism without Constitutionalism: Europe's Sonderweg' in K Nikolaidis and R Howse (eds), *The Federal Vision: Legitimacy and Levels of Governance in the United States and the European Union* (Oxford: Oxford University Press, 2001) 56–57 (emphasis added). In my opinion, Professor Weiler seriously mistakes the American case. For neither of the two constitutions of the United States was ratified by a 'federal demos' in the form of 'the' American people.

[44] cf O Beaud, 'The Question of Nationality within a Federation: A Neglected Issue in Nationality Law' in R Hansen and P Weil (eds), *Dual Nationality, Social Rights, and Federal Citizenship in the US and Europe* (Oxford: Berghahn Books, 2002).

[45] On this point, see section 2.

[46] On this point, see section 3.2.

[47] *US Term Limits, Inc v Thornton*, 514 US 779 (1995), 838 (Justice Kennedy).

[48] J Madison, 'Federalist No 39' in J Madison et al, *The Federalist*, ed T Ball (Cambridge: Cambridge University Press, 2003) 184 (emphasis added).

body, independent of all others, and only to be bound by its own voluntary act.' The 1787 Constitution was therefore 'a[n] [international], and not a national act'.[49]

Yet the American Union had not been based on an ordinary international treaty. For instead of the ordinary state legislatures, the ratification of the 1787 US Constitution was achieved through constitutional 'Conventions' within the states.[50] The famous US constitutional phrase 'We, the People' must therefore be read with two qualifications in mind. First, it did not refer to a national referendum; and, secondly, it also did not refer to the 'American people' but instead to the peoples of the several states.[51]

The best theoretical generalization of this pluralist conception of the constituent power has come from Carl Schmitt.[52] According to his federal theory, the normative foundation of every union of states is a 'federal treaty'. This federal treaty is an international treaty of a constitutional nature.[53] 'Its conclusion is an act of the *pouvoir constituant*. Its content establishes the federal constitution and forms, at the same time, a part of the constitution of every member state.'[54] Each union of states is here seen as a creature of international and national law.[55] Unlike unitary constitutionalism, a federal constitutional theory thus replaces the idea of a *single* sovereign subject with that of a pluralist constituent power. From the perspective of democratic constitutionalism, the constituent power behind a union of states will be the state *peoples* instead of a single national 'demos'. This is also the reason why in true federal orders, there is a right of withdrawal from the Union—a right that, with regard to the European Union, can be found in Article 50 TEU.

How should the democratic validation of a federal constitution take place? The most direct expression would be a series of constitutional referenda in the Member States. A less direct democratic expression would be the ratification of the federal constitution through state conventions. (This is what happened, as was mentioned above, to the 1787 US Constitution.) The least direct expression of popular sovereignty is to leave the ratification decision to the 'ordinary' state legislatures. And it is this third—parliamentary—version that is commonly used in the constitutional practice of the EU. Genetically, therefore, the EU Treaties are *not* constitutional treaties,[56] because from a democratic

[49] Ibid, 185.

[50] On the novel (American) technique of constitutional 'Conventions', see G Wood, *The Creation of the American Republic: 1776–87* (Chapel Hill, NC: University of North Carolina Press, 1998) ch 8. These Conventions were composed of delegates who were elected to represent(!) their constituency. Unlike popular referenda, they operate as single-issue 'parliaments' that are solely called into being to decide whether the Constitution should be adopted.

[51] The original 1787 draft preamble indeed read: 'We, the people of the States of New Hampshire, Massachusetts, Rhode-Island and Providence Plantations, Connecticut, New-York, New-Jersey, Pennsylvania, Delaware, Maryland, Virginia, North-Carolina, South-Carolina, and Georgia, do ordain, declare and establish the following constitution for the government of ourselves and our posterity.' However, due to the uncertainty about which of the 13 states would succeed in the ratification (according to Art VII of the Constitution-to-be, only nine states were required for the document to enter into force), the enumeration of the individual states was dropped by the 'Committee of Style'. Cf M Farrand, *The Framing of the Constitution of the United States* (New Haven, CT: Yale University Press, 1913) 190–191.

[52] Schmitt, *Verfassungslehre* (n 33) esp Part IV.

[53] Ibid, 367 and 368 (trans R Schütze).

[54] Ibid. This idea was subsequently taken up by Pernice's concept of 'Verfassungsverbund' or 'multi-level constitutionalism'. Cf I Pernice, 'Multilevel Constitutionalism and the Treaty of Amsterdam: European Constitution-Making Revisited?' (1999) 36 *Common Market Law Review* 703.

[55] Schmitt, *Verfassungslehre* (n 33) 379.

[56] It is difficult—if not impossible—to accept that 'the founding treaties as well as each amendment agreed upon by the governments appear as the *direct* expression of the common will of the [national] peoples of the Union' (Pernice (n 54) 717 (emphasis added)). National ratifications are—with the exception of a few Member States—only indirect expressions of the common will of the national peoples of the Union. National consent is typically expressed through national legislatures.

point of view, they lack the 'higher' democratic validation that theoretically legitimizes a constitution's normative position above ordinary (state) legislation.

The EU is, however, not alone in this 'democratic deficit' with regard to the adoption of its constitution;[57] and in any event, before we come to the conclusion that the Union falls short of its constitutional aspirations from a democratic point of view, we need to explore its second aspect: the democratic structure of its government.

4 Democratic constitutionalism II: popular representation

The historical origin of a constitution can only be one aspect of democratic constitutionalism: indeed, an undemocratically created constitution might still set up democratic institutions,[58] while a popular referendum might create an undemocratic regime.[59]

A governmental system is traditionally regarded as democratic when each governmental function reflects the will of the people. The modern 'translation' of this (ancient) democratic ideal is representative democracy.[60] Within a representational government, democracy means that the legislature, or even the executive and the judiciary, should be *elected* by the people. In essence, modern democracy means that the constitution delegates power to elected officials, which exercise public power 'in the name of the people'.

Hardly any existing State constitution has created a completely democratic structure for all governmental powers. Not only is the judiciary often not elected, non-democratic elements can often be found even within the legislative branch.[61] However, the democratic credentials of a governmental system will typically be measured by means of the powers possessed by 'parliament'. Democratic constitutionalism here simply means 'parliamentarism', that is, a governmental regime in which parliament is the central and dominant actor. But what about the executive branch? Two models of democratic government have here historically developed: the parliamentary model and the presidential model. The parliamentary system is a model in which the (governing) executive—like the British prime minister and the cabinet—will be elected and controlled by parliament. By contrast, a presidential system will typically invest the—independent—executive with its own direct democratic legitimacy. This idea stands behind the election of the US President.[62]

What are the democratic credentials of the European Union's system of government? Article 10 TEU unambiguously demands: 'The functioning of the Union shall be founded on representative democracy.'[63] But how democratic or representative are its legislative and executive branches?

4.1 Democratic legitimacy and the Union legislature

Within a unitary State with one people, parliamentary democracy demands that all legislative power should be placed in a parliament that is elected on the principle of 'one person, one vote'. The British 'Westminster system' has come to be identified with this unitary standard.

[57] On the adoption of the 1949 German Constitution by the state legislatures, see n 41.

[58] The 1949 German Constitution is again a case in point.

[59] The 1852 Constitution of the Second French Empire was ratified by a plebiscite; and yet it established an undemocratic government.

[60] M Loughlin, *Foundations of Public Law* (Oxford: Oxford University Press, 2012) 284.

[61] eg in the UK, the second chamber (the House of Lords) is not elected.

[62] Another illustration of a presidential (democratic) system is the 1958 Constitution of the French Republic.

[63] Art 10(1) TEU.

But is this—unitary—standard the appropriate yardstick for a federal polity that is characterized by a plurality of peoples? In a union of states, there will always be two democratic constituencies: each state will have its own 'demos', while the union will also have a 'demos' that is constructed out of the various state populations. Each of these democratic constituencies thereby offers an independent source of democratic legitimacy; and a federal constitutionalism will have to take account of this dual democracy.

Within a union of states, one *institutional* expression of this dual democracy is the compound nature of the union legislator. It is typically made up of two chambers: a state chamber representing the state peoples is joined to a parliamentary chamber representing the union citizens as a whole.[64] Every union law is thus —ideally—legitimized by reference to two democratic sources: the consent of the state peoples and the consent of the union population as represented in the union parliament. As we have seen in chapter 3, the EU is based on this dual democratic legitimacy. Its legislative branch consists of two chambers: the European Parliament is formed through elections by the totality of the Union's citizens, whereas the Council indirectly represents the Member States' democratically organized peoples. When measured against a—federal—standard, the Union consequently does not suffer from a democratic deficit simply because one part of its legislative branch is not directly elected.[65]

But what about the democratic credentials of the European Parliament as such? How 'democratic' is its composition? Despite the insistence of the EU Treaties that the 'Citizens are directly represented at Union level in the European Parliament',[66] the distribution of seats within the European Parliament continues to be partly based on national 'quotas'. Instead of 'one person, one vote', the Union legal order has a system that is according to Article 14 TEU 'degressively proportional'.[67] This means that the distribution of seats is proportionate to the size of the national populations; yet this proportionate system is qualified so as to allow smaller States' populations to have some representation within the European Parliament. Each Member State will have a minimum number of 6 European parliamentarians, while the maximum number of 'national' seats is limited to 96.[68] The European Council originally offered the following definition of the Union's degressive proportionality system:

> In the application of the principle of degressive proportionality provided for in the first subparagraph of Article 14(2) of the Treaty on European Union, the following principles shall apply:
>
> - the allocation of seats in the European Parliament shall fully utilise the minimum and maximum numbers set by the Treaty on European Union in order to reflect as closely as possible the sizes of the respective populations of Member States;
> - the ratio between the population and the number of seats of each Member State before rounding to whole numbers shall vary in relation to their respective populations in such a way that each Member of the European Parliament from a more populous Member State represents more citizens than each Member from a less populous Member State and, conversely, that the larger the population of a Member State, the greater its entitlement to a large number of seats.[69]

[64] cf A Gerber, 'Les Notions de Représentation et de Participation des Régions dans les Etats Fédéraux', LLM thesis (European University Institute, 1993).

[65] In this sense also, see RA Dahl, 'Federalism and the Democratic Process' in JR Pennock and JW Chapman (eds), *Nomos XXV: Liberal Democracy* (New York: New York University Press, 1983).

[66] Art 10(2) TEU.

[67] Art 14(2) TEU. See European Council, Decision establishing the composition of the European Parliament (OJ [2013] L181/57); and now for the 2024–29 term, see European Council, Decision 2023/2061 establishing the composition of the European Parliament (OJ [2023] L238/114).

[68] Art 14(2) TEU.

[69] European Council (2013) Decision establishing the composition of the European Parliament (n 67) Art 1.

While the idea of national 'quotas' for parliamentary seats is designed to protect smaller Member States, it distorts the democratic principle of 'one person, one vote'. The preference of a *degressively* proportionate system over a *purely* proportionate system therefore does constitute a—minor—democratic deficit of the Union. For since the EU Treaties charge the European Parliament to represent the Union citizens *directly*, its composition should not be mediated by the political existence of the Member States as States. This distortion in the democratic credentials has been subject to judicial scrutiny by the German Federal Constitutional Court. In its *Lisbon* decision,[70] the court here held that the composition of the European Parliament meant that it still represented the peoples of the Member States as opposed to the EU citizens as such.

Case study 4.2: The democratic deficit and the *Lisbon* decision of the German Federal Constitutional Court

The German Federal Constitutional Court has reviewed the democratic structures of the Union in a number of famous cases—the most important of which are its *Maastricht* and *Lisbon* judgments. In *Maastricht*,[71] the court explored how EU laws could be regarded as legitimized through national democracy. This exploration was continued in its *Lisbon* decision.[72] The court here held that in a Union with 'clear elements of executive and governmental cooperation' the primacy of national democratic legitimation could be justified; yet, were the Union to move towards a (federal) State, the national route would be blocked and a 'structural democratic deficit' would arise.[73]

Why would the Union fail the democratic standard of a (federal) State? The court answered this question by concentrating on the democratic principle of 'one person, one vote'; and held that the Union—even after Lisbon—'lacks a political decision-making body created in equal elections by all citizens of the Union and with the ability to uniformly represent the will of the people'.[74] 'Even in the wording of Article 14.2 Lisbon TEU, and contrary to the claim that Article 10.1 Lisbon TEU seems to make according to its wording, the European Parliament is not a representative body of a sovereign European people.'[75] In light of the degressively proportionate allocation of seats, 'the European Parliament factually remains a representation of the peoples of the Member States'.[76] Democratic representation within the Union was primarily *indirect* representation via the national States and peoples.[77]

Did this mean the court identified a democratic deficit within the Union? It did not. For the court admitted that it should not judge Union democracy by a state standard, but by a democratic standard 'commensurate with the status and the function of the Union'.[78] And: 'In the present state of integration, it is therefore not required to democratically develop the system of the European institutions in analogy to that of a state.' This meant, in particular, that 'the composition of the European Parliament does not need to do justice to equality in such a way that differences in the weight of the votes of the citizens of the Union depending on the Member States' population figures are eliminated'.[79]

[70] BVerfGE 123, 267 (*Lisbon* decision). For an English translation, see http://www.bundesverfassungsgericht.de/entscheidungen/es20090630_2bve000208en.html.

[71] BVerfGE 89, 155 (*Maastricht* decision). The following discussion refers to the English translation of the judgment: [1994] CMLR 57 (*Maastricht* decision).

[72] *Lisbon* decision (n 70). [73] Ibid, para 264. [74] Ibid, para 280. [75] Ibid.

[76] Ibid, para 284. [77] Ibid, para 286.

[78] Ibid, para 266. In the words of para 271: 'Because and in so far as the European Union itself only exercises derived public authority, it need not fully comply with the requirements.'

[79] Ibid, para 278.

What about the governmental powers of the European Parliament? The TEU today defines the powers of the Parliament in Article 14 TEU as follows: 'The European Parliament shall, jointly with the Council, exercise legislative and budgetary functions. It shall exercise functions of political control and consultation as laid down in the Treaties. It shall elect the President of the Commission.'[80] This definition distinguishes between four types of powers: legislative and budgetary powers as well as supervisory and elective powers.

What are the legislative powers of parliament? Parliament may informally propose new legislation.[81] However, it is not—unlike national parliaments—formally entitled to propose legislative bills. The task of making these proposals is, with minor exceptions, a constitutional prerogative of the Commission. Like other federal legal orders, the Union legal order also acknowledges a number of different legislative procedures (see further chapter 5). The Treaties now textually distinguish between the 'ordinary' legislative procedure and a number of 'special' legislative procedures.[82] The former is defined as 'the joint adoption [of legislation] by the European Parliament and the Council'.[83] This procedure thus reflects the federal idea of dual democracy with the European Parliament (more or less) *directly* representing the European people and the Council *indirectly* representing the national peoples.

4.2 **Democratic legitimacy and the Union executive**

What are the democratic credentials of the Union's executive branch? Modern constitutionalism typically distinguishes between 'parliamentary' and 'presidential' systems. Within the former the executive is elected by parliament, whereas in the latter the executive is elected independently from parliament. The EU's governmental regime sits somewhere in between both constitutional models. It has a dual executive composed of the European Council and the Commission.[84] The former is composed of the heads of State or government, which—as a body—is not dependent on any parliamentary election, yet whose members will have received direct or indirect *national* democratic legitimation. As regards the Commission as the second branch of the Union executive, it is the European Parliament that has increasingly come to give *supranational* democratic legitimacy to that body. Article 17 TEU describes the involvement of the European Parliament in the appointment of the Commission as follows:

> Taking into account the elections to the European Parliament and after having held the appropriate consultations, the European Council, acting by a qualified majority, shall propose to the European Parliament a candidate for President of the Commission. This candidate shall be elected by the European Parliament by a majority of its component members . . . The Council, by common accord with the President-elect, shall adopt the list of the other persons whom it proposes for appointment as members of the Commission. They shall be selected, on the basis of the suggestions made by Member States . . . The President, the High Representative of the Union for Foreign Affairs and Security Policy and the other members of the Commission shall be subject as a body to a vote of consent by the European Parliament. On the basis of this consent the Commission shall be appointed by the European Council, acting by a qualified majority.[85]

[80] Art 14(1) TEU. [81] Art 225 TFEU.

[82] Special legislative procedures cover various degrees of parliamentary participation. These procedures will be discussed in more detail in chapter 5 below.

[83] Art 289(1) TFEU.

[84] In the past, there was a third institution—the Council—that was heavily involved in the executive function. This has changed with the Lisbon Treaty (see further chapter 3), although the latter continues to contain elements of the former regime (cf the possibility of Council implementing acts, as set out in Art 291(2) TFEU; on this, see further chapter 5).

[85] Art 17(7) TEU.

The appointment of the second branch of the EU executive is consequently built on a dual parliamentary consent. Parliament must—first—'elect' the President of the Commission. And it must—secondly—confirm the Commission as a collective body.[86] Once appointed, the Commission will continue to remain 'responsible to the European Parliament'.[87] It must enjoy the 'confidence' of the European Parliament; and where this parliamentary confidence is lost, Parliament may vote on a motion of censure. If this vote of mistrust is carried, the Commission must resign as a body. (The motion of collective censure thus mirrors Parliament's appointment power, which is also focused on the Commission as a collective body.[88]) In light of the European Parliament's elective and censuring power, one is therefore justified in characterizing the Union's governmental system as a '*semi*-parliamentary democracy'.[89]

What about the governmental functions exercised by the Union executive? The traditional task of the executive branch is to enforce legislation; and in discharging this task the executive will generally act *under* the Union legislature. Moreover, due to its more indirect democratic credentials, democratic constitutionalism has traditionally insisted that the executive should not be given—autonomous or delegated—law-making powers. However, with the advent and expansion of the 'administrative state' in the twentieth century, executive law-making has today become the norm in many legal orders and the Union legal order has followed this evolution. But like many other constitutional orders, it has imposed constitutional safeguards to control the delegation of legislative power to the executive.[90]

What are the constitutional or political safeguards of democracy imposed on delegated legislation? Constitutionally, the Union legislator is prohibited from delegating *essential* political choices to the executive.[91] Yet even for *non*-essential powers, the Union legislator has been unwilling to delegate power without political control. These political safeguards of democracy can now be found in Article 290 TFEU. The provision allows the European Parliament or the Council to revoke the delegation or to veto the adoption of a specific delegated act. In establishing an alternative—as opposed to cumulative—veto power for the two branches of the Union legislator, the EU's political safeguards for delegated legislation are here democratically stronger than their equivalent in the US.[92] A less democratic system of executive law-making has been created for 'implementing acts' under Article 291 TFEU. However, the constitutional logic here is not to protect the powers of the EU legislator but rather to protect the Member States within the Union's system of executive federalism according to which the power to implement EU law in principle belongs to the Member States.[93]

[86] However, Parliament may request each nominated Commissioner to appear before Parliament and to 'present' his or her views. This practice thus comes close to 'confirmation hearings' (D Judge and D Earnshaw, *The European Parliament* (2nd edn, Basingstoke: Palgrave Macmillan, 2008) 5).

[87] Art 17(8) TEU.

[88] However, unlike the appointment power, Parliament has been able to sharpen its tools of censure significantly by concluding a political agreement with the Commission. Accordingly, if Parliament expresses lack of confidence in an individual member of the Commission, the President of the Commission 'shall either require the resignation of that Member' or, after 'serious' consideration, explain its refusal to do so before Parliament. On this point, see Framework Agreement on Relations between the European Parliament and the European Commission (OJ [2010] L304/47), para 5.

[89] P Dann, 'European Parliament and Executive Federalism: Approaching a Parliament in a Semi-Parliamentary Democracy' (2003) 9 *European Law Journal* 549 (emphasis added).

[90] B Schwartz, 'Delegated Legislation in America: Procedure and Safeguards' (1948) 11 *Modern Law Review* 449.

[91] On the constitutional limits imposed on a delegation of legislative power, see R Schütze, '"Delegated" Legislation in the (New) European Union: A Constitutional Analysis' (2011) 74 Modern Law Review 661, 669 *et seq*. See further chapter 5.

[92] Ibid, 663 *et seq*.

[93] R Schütze, 'From Rome to Lisbon: "Executive Federalism" in the (New) European Union' (2010) 47 *Common Market Law Review* 1385. On implementing acts, see further chapter 5.

5 Liberal constitutionalism I: separation of powers

5.1 The 'classic' separation of powers principle(s)

The central task of liberal constitutionalism is to establish limits to 'the [i]nconveniences of [a]bsolute power'.[94] It aims to protect freedom by establishing a 'government of laws, and not of men'.[95] For all governmental power, even democratic governmental power is dangerous when used arbitrarily.[96] One of the oldest constitutional devices of limiting absolute power is to split it, that is 'balance[ing] the [p]ower of [g]overnment, by placing several parts of it in different hands'.[97]

However, the central question behind the separation of powers doctrine is this: which governmental *parts* should be placed into which governmental *hands*? Liberal constitutionalism has here built on a tripartite division that was originally developed by a French aristocrat: Baron Charles de Montesquieu. When he published *The Spirit of Laws* in 1748,[98] three powers were famously identified:

> In every government there are three sorts of power: the legislative; the executive in respect to things dependent on the law of nations; and the executive in regard to matters that depend on the civil law. By virtue of the first, the prince or magistrate enacts temporary or perpetual laws, and amends or abrogates those that have been already enacted. By the second, he makes peace or war, sends or receives embassies, establishes the public security, and provides against invasions. By the third, he punishes criminals, or determines the disputes that arise between individuals. The latter we shall call the judiciary power.[99]

Having acknowledged three governmental 'powers' or functions, Montesquieu then moved on to advocate their 'distribution' between different institutions:

> When the legislative and executive powers are united in the same person, or in the same body of magistrates, there can be no liberty; because apprehensions may arise, lest the same monarch or senate should enact tyrannical laws, to execute them in a tyrannical manner. Again, there is no liberty, if the judicial power be not separated from the legislative and executive. Were it joined with the legislative, the life and liberty of the subject would be exposed to arbitrary control; for the judge would be then the legislator. Were it joined to the executive power, the judge might behave with violence and oppression.[100]

But did distribution here mean that each 'separate' power would need to be given to a 'separate' institution? Liberal constitutionalism has given two distinct answers to this question.

[94] J Locke, *Two Treatises of Government* (Cambridge: Cambridge University Press, 2005) § 107 = 338.

[95] J Harrington as quoted in WB Gwyn, *The Meaning of the Separation of Powers* (Leiden: Martinus Nijhoff, 1965) 13.

[96] In the famous words of J Madison in 'Federalist No 51' (see n 48):

> If men were angels, no government would be necessary. If angels were to govern men, neither external nor internal controls on government would be necessary. In framing a government which is to be administered by men over men, the great difficulty lies in this: you must first enable the government to control the governed; and in the next place oblige it to control itself. A dependence on the people is, no doubt, the primary control on the government; but experience has taught mankind the necessity of auxiliary precautions.

[97] Locke (n 94) § 107 = 338.

[98] Charles de Secondat, Baron de Montesquieu, *The Spirit of Laws*, trans and ed T Nugent, rev J Prichard (London: Bell, 1914), available at http://www.constitution.org/cm/sol.htm.

[99] Ibid, Book XI, ch 6. [100] Ibid.

According to the *functional separation* version, each governmental institution must not be given more than one governmental function.[101] This reading appears—at first sight—to be chosen by the founding fathers of the US. For all legislative power seems exclusively vested in 'Congress',[102] the executive power solely vested in a 'President',[103] while the judicial power is reserved to the 'Supreme Court'.[104] The heart of this version of the separation of power is the distinction between law-creation and law-application. The separation between the making of laws and their (administrative or judicial) execution is designed to create a 'rule of law' in which the men who made the law would also be subject to it. This idea stands behind the liberal prohibition on the legislature not to pass 'individual laws'—that is, laws that are tailored for a single individual or a limited group of individuals.[105] The insistence on the general nature of parliamentary laws was to prevent the legislative branch from overreaching into the executive domain. At the same time, the executive is—theoretically—not allowed to exercise any law-making power, as this is an exclusive prerogative of the legislature.

By contrast: according to the *institutional cooperation* version, each governmental function should be distributed over more than one institution. 'To form a moderate government, it is necessary to combine the several powers; to regulate, temper, and set them in motion; to give, as it were, ballast to one, in order to enable it to counterpoise the other.'[106] The exercise of the legislative function should thus ideally involve more than one institution: 'The legislative body being composed of two parts, they check one another by the mutual privilege of rejecting. They are both restrained by the executive power, as the executive is by the legislative.'[107] The core idea behind this second conception is a system of checks and balances; and it is this—second—version of the separation of powers principle that truly informs the 1787 US Constitution.[108] American constitutionalism even went beyond Montesquieu by introducing the idea of judicial 'checks' on the legislative power.[109]

What do the two versions of the separation of powers doctrine have in common? Both versions require that there exist *distinct* governmental *institutions*; and in order to be distinct institutions, there must be a *personal* independence from one another. The simplest expression of this principle is a constitutional prohibition that the same person(s) are part of two or more separate institutions.[110] Liberal constitutionalism

[101] The theory of a functional separation of powers finds (almost) no matching constitutional practice. It has been said to contradict the British constitutional idea of parliamentary sovereignty: cf AV Dicey, *Introduction to the Study of the Law of the Constitution* (Indianapolis, IN: Liberty Fund, 1992) 3–10.

[102] Art I, Section 1 US Constitution: 'All legislative Powers herein granted shall be vested in a Congress of the United States, which shall consist of a Senate and House of Representatives.'

[103] Ibid, Art II, Section 1: 'The executive Power shall be vested in a President of the United States of America.'

[104] Ibid, Art III, Section 1: 'The judicial Power of the United States, shall be vested in one Supreme Court, and in such inferior Courts as the Congress may from time to time ordain and establish.'

[105] For the US Constitution, see Art I, Section 9: 'No Bill of Attainder or ex post facto Law shall be passed.' For C Schmitt, the prohibition for the legislature not to pass individual laws represents the cornerstone of the liberal State (*Verfassungslehre* (n 33) 146).

[106] De Montesquieu (n 98) Book V, ch 14.

[107] Ibid.

[108] cf Madison, 'Federalist No 47' (n 48) 234 *et seq.*

[109] *Marbury v Madison*, 5 US 137 (1803).

[110] cf de Montesquieu (n 98): 'There would be an end of everything, were the same man or the same body, whether of the nobles or of the people, to exercise those three powers, that of enacting laws, that of executing the public resolutions, and of trying the causes of individuals.'

may, however, go even further and require the *political* independence of each institution from all the others:

> In order to lay a due foundation for that separate and distinct exercise of the different powers of government, which to a certain extent is admitted on all hands to be essential to the preservation of liberty, *it is evident that each department should have a will of its own; and consequently should be so constituted that the members of each should have as little agency as possible in the appointment of the members of the others.*[111]

For liberal constitutionalism, as propagated by the US founding fathers (and de Montesquieu),[112] the selection of the executive by parliament represents a serious breach of the separation of powers doctrine. The modern English 'parliamentary system' would thus violate the separation of powers doctrine, since it is based on a 'fusion'—not a separation—of the legislative and executive branch.[113] A 'thick' liberal constitutionalism consequently recommends a 'presidential system', a system in which the executive branch is elected *independently*.

In light of this historical exegesis, what are the liberal constitutionalist credentials of the EU Treaties? Is there a separation of powers doctrine; and, if so, which one?

5.2 **Separating 'powers' in the EU**

When born in 1958 with the genetic code of an international organization, the EU could hardly be viewed in light of the classic *trias politica*.[114] For while it had executive and judicial powers, its 'regulatory' competences were not immediately regarded as of a 'legislative' quality.[115] The subsequent ascendancy of the European Parliament changed this dramatically; and today the EU Treaties formally acknowledge 'legislative' procedure(s) in the EU legal order.[116] The legislative powers of the Union do, however, appear to allow for the adoption of legislative 'decisions',[117] and the Treaties also allow for the delegation

[111] Madison, 'Federalist No 51' (n 48) 251 (emphasis added).

[112] De Montesquieu (n 98): 'But if there were no monarch, and the executive power should be committed to a certain number of persons selected from the legislative body, there would be an end then of liberty; by reason the two powers would be united, as the same persons would sometimes possess, and would be always able to possess, a share in both.'

[113] W Bagehot, *The English Constitution* (Oxford: Oxford University Press, 2001) esp 11.

[114] For the literature on the separation of powers in the Union legal order, see P Pescatore, 'L'executif communautaire: justification des traités de Paris et de Rome' (1978) 4 *Cahiers de droit européen* 387; W Hummer, 'Das institutionelle Gleichgewicht als Strukturdeterminante der Europäischen Gemeinschaften' in H Miehsler et al (eds), *Ius Humanitatis: Festschrift zum 90. Geburtstag von Alfred Verdross* (Berlin: Duncker & Humblot, 1980); K Lenaerts, 'Some Reflections on the Separation of Powers in the European Community' (1991) 28 *Common Market Law Review* 11; P Huber, 'Das institutionelle Gleichgewicht zwischen Rat und dem Europäischen Parlament in der künftigen Verfassung für Europa' (2003) *Europarecht* 574; JP Jacqué, 'The Principle of Institutional Balance' (2004) 41 *Common Market Law Review* 383; and G Conway, 'Recovering a Separation of Powers in the European Union' (2011) 17 *European Law Journal* 304.

[115] Early commentators therefore speak of the 'decision law' of the Community (see H Wagner, *Grundbegriffe des Beschlußrechts der Europäische Gemeinschaft* (Cologne: C Heymanns, 1965)). This argument has had a (partial) renaissance in the work of G Majone and his disciple P Lindseth (see *Power and Legitimacy: Reconciling Europe and the Nation-State* (Oxford: Oxford University Press, 2010)). The main error within these recent works appears to me to be the absence of any conceptualization of the notion of 'legislation' and 'legislative power'.

[116] Art 289 TFEU.

[117] According to Art 289(1) TFEU, the acts that can be adopted under the Union's legislative procedure(s) include the instrument of 'regulation, directive *or decision*' (emphasis added). This wording seems to suggest that the adoption of individual decisions by the Union legislature is possible.

of legislative power to the executive;[118] and in making these constitutional choices, the Union legal order seems to have rejected the functional version of the separation of powers doctrine.

Has the Union nonetheless adopted the second version of the doctrine and, if so, how? The Union legal order has indeed followed the institutional cooperation version of the 'separation of powers' principle; and the EU Treaties make this constitutional choice even clearer than the US Constitution. For while each Union institution also has 'its' article in the TEU, the latter expressly describes the various governmental functions in which each Union institution partakes.[119] The European Commission will, for example, be involved in the legislative,[120] executive,[121] and judicial process.[122] Institutional cooperation is indeed required in the exercise of most governmental functions. The Treaties have thus 'set up a system for distributing powers among different [Union] institutions, assigning to each institution its own role in the institutional structure of the [Union] and the accomplishment of the tasks entrusted to the [Union]'.[123]

This conception of the separation of powers principle informs Article 13(2) TEU. The provision is known as the principle of institutional balance and reads:

> Each institution shall act within the limits of the powers conferred on it in the Treaties, and in conformity with the procedures, conditions and objectives set out in them. The institutions shall practice mutual sincere cooperation.[124]

Article 13(2) TEU thereby contains two constitutional commands. First, each institution must act within its powers as defined by the Treaties. This ultra vires doctrine is the horizontal expression of the vertical principle of conferral.[125] It is consequently not possible for an institution to extend its powers unilaterally through constitutional practice.[126] Nor may an institution transfer its powers to another institution—unless the Treaties expressly allow for such delegations of power. Secondly: 'Observance of the institutional balance means that each of the institutions must exercise its powers with due regard for the powers of the other institutions.'[127] This principle of 'mutual sincere cooperation' between the institutions in Article 13(2) TEU is the horizontal extension of the principle of sincere—vertical—cooperation in Article 4(3) TEU.[128]

[118] On this point, see section 4.2.

[119] This is normally the first section of the TEU article dealing with the (respective) institution. See further chapter 3.

[120] Art 17(2) TEU: 'Union legislative acts may only be adopted on the basis of a Commission proposal, except where the Treaties provide otherwise.'

[121] Art 17(1) TEU: 'The Commission shall promote the general interest of the Union and take appropriate initiatives to that end. It shall ensure the application of the Treaties, and of measures adopted by the institutions pursuant to them. It shall oversee the application of Union law under the control of the Court of Justice of the European Union. It shall execute the budget and manage programmes. It shall exercise coordinating, executive and management functions, as laid down in the Treaties.'

[122] Art 258 TFEU.

[123] Case C-70/88 *Parliament v Council (Chernobyl)* [1990] ECR I-2041, para 21.

[124] Art 13(2) TEU.

[125] Jacqué, 'The Principle of Institutional Balance' (n 114) 383: 'From a legal point of view, the principle of institutional balance is one manifestation of the rule that the institutions have to act within the limits of their competences.' On the concept of conferral, see further chapter 5.

[126] Case 149/85 *Wybot v Faure* [1986] ECR 2391, esp para 23.

[127] Case C-70/88 *Parliament v Council (Chernobyl)* [1990] ECR I-2041, para 22.

[128] See generally chapter 5.

Case study 4.3: The European Parliament and judicial review

When the EU was born in 1958, the Treaty of Rome (the original treaty establishing the European Economic Community) only granted the European Parliament 'advisory and supervisory powers'.[129] Its advisory powers permitted Parliament to be consulted on Commission proposals before their adoption by the Council. The authors of the Treaty had, however, felt that the right to be consulted was not 'active' enough to justify giving Parliament a constitutional right to judicially challenge Union acts that violated its prerogatives. The original provision on judicial review in the 1957 Treaty of Rome (ex Article 173 EEC) consequently only allowed two Union institutions—the Commission and the Council—to challenge the legality of Union acts before the European Court. This exclusion of the European Parliament remained in place even after the Single European Act (in force 1987)—despite the fact that the latter had provided Parliament in some instances with the active right to cooperate in the adoption of Union legislation.

Should the principle of institutional balance entitle Parliament to bring an action before the Court? In *Parliament v Council (Comitology)*,[130] the Court at first rejected this idea. While recognizing the new role of the Parliament in the legislative sphere, the Court felt that the EEC Treaty had conferred 'specifically on the Commission the responsibility for ensuring that the Parliament's prerogatives are respected and for bringing for that purpose such actions for annulment as might prove to be necessary'.[131] This constitutional rationale assumed that the institutional interests of the Commission and the Parliament were always aligned—an assumption that soon proved mistaken. In *Parliament v Council (Chernobyl)*,[132] the Court therefore changed its view and gave Parliament legal standing judicially to enforce its prerogatives.

According to the Court, the principle of institutional balance meant that each institution 'must exercise its powers with due regard for the powers of the other institutions', and this 'require[d] that it should be possible to penalize any breach of that rule which may occur'.[133] The principle of institutional balance mandated that 'Parliament's prerogatives, like those of the other institutions, cannot be breached without *it* having available a legal remedy'. The parliamentary prerogative to participate actively in the drafting of legislative measures would consequently imply the power to ask the Court to 'check' and 'control' the other institutions. This constitutional solution was subsequently codified in the Maastricht Treaty (in force 1993); and ever since the Treaty of Nice (in force 2003) Parliament is recognized as a fully privileged applicant under Article 263 TFEU.

Finally, what about the—personal and political—independence of the Union institutions? With regard to their 'personal' independence, this is generally guaranteed by the Treaties; yet as regards their political independence, this is not always the case. For some EU institutions are involved in the selection of another: Parliament, for example, is involved in the election of the President of the European Commission and also needs to consent to the appointment of the entire Commission.[134] The Commission's political dependence on another EU institution—Parliament—goes, as we saw previously, beyond parliamentary approval, since the Commission continues to 'be responsible to the European Parliament'.[135] From a 'thick' liberal constitutionalist perspective, this constitutes a serious—albeit democratic—breach of the separation of powers principle.

[129] Art 137 EEC.
[130] Case 302/87 *Parliament v Council (Comitology)* [1988] ECR 5615.
[131] Ibid, para 27.
[132] *Parliament v Council (Chernobyl)* (n 127).
[133] Ibid, para 22.
[134] Art 17(7) TEU. For an analysis of this point, see earlier in the text.
[135] Art 17(8) TEU.

6 Liberal constitutionalism II: fundamental rights

The idea of fundamental rights is an achievement of liberal constitutionalism. They are based on the discovery of the 'individual'—a discovery that ultimately led to the protection of an inviolable private sphere.[136] This philosophical idea was first minted into constitutional form in the aftermath of the American Revolutionary War. The 1776 Virginia Declaration of Rights stated. 'That all men are by nature equally free and independent and have certain inherent rights, of which, when they enter into a state of society, they cannot, by any compact, deprive or divest their posterity.'[137] This philosophy of inalienable rights was to inspire the adoption of the 'Bill of Rights' attached to the 1787 US Constitution; and it was subsequently expressed in the 1789 (French) Declaration of the Rights of Man and of the Citizen.[138] The Declaration insisted on 'natural' rights that even bound the constitution-makers;[139] and it soon became the symbol and stimulus for the liberal constitutionalism of nineteenth-century Europe.

Since the twentieth century, the protection of fundamental rights has become a central task of most constitutions.[140] Unlike the separation of powers principle that operates as a *political* safeguard of liberalism, the protection of human rights is typically conceived of as a *judicial* safeguard of liberalism that involves the judicial review of governmental action.[141] A thin liberal constitutionalism thereby restricts judicial review to actions of the executive.[142] A thick liberal constitutionalism, on the other hand, insists that even parliamentary legislation must be judicially reviewed in light of possible violations of fundamental rights.[143]

The EU follows this second constitutional tradition.[144] But what are the sources of fundamental rights in the Union legal order? Originally, there was no 'bill of rights' in the EU Treaties. Two *constitutional* sources for fundamental rights were, however, subsequently developed. The European Court of Justice at first began distilling fundamental rights from the general principles of EU law. This unwritten bill of rights was—despite the reference to 'general principles'—not grounded in a natural rights philosophy. For as we shall see later, the European Court identifies the source of these fundamental rights in the *constitutional* traditions of the *Member States*. With the Lisbon Treaty, a second constitutional source has been added: the Charter of Fundamental Rights of the European Union. Yet again, the Charter proclaims no 'inalienable' natural rights but—modestly—'reaffirms' the fundamental rights as they result, inter alia, 'from the constitutional traditions and international obligations common to the Member States'.[145] EU fundamental rights are thus constitutional—not natural—rights.

6.1 Fundamental rights as 'general principles'

The birth of EU fundamental rights did not happen overnight. The Court had been invited—as long ago as 1958—to review the constitutionality of an EU act in light of fundamental rights. In *Stork*,[146] the applicant had challenged a European Commission

[136] E Wolgast, *Geschichte der Menschen- und Bürgerrechte* (Stuttgart: Kohlhammer, 2009) 33.

[137] 1776 Virginia Declaration of Rights, Art 1.

[138] For an analysis and historical interpretation of the declaration, see Wolgast (n 136) ch 2.

[139] These rights were not 'founded' but simply 'declared'—hence the title: 'Declaration'—by the constitutional assembly.

[140] On human rights as constitutional rights, see A Sajó, *Limiting Government* (Budapest: Central European University Press, 1999) ch 8.

[141] See M Cappelletti, *Judicial Review in the Contemporary World* (Indianapolis, IN: Bobbs-Merrill, 1971).

[142] Traditionally, this is the case for the UK.

[143] The classic example here is the US.

[144] On the power of constitutional/judicial review, see chapter 10.

[145] EU Charter, Preamble 5.

[146] Case 1/58 *Stork & Cie v High Authority of the European Coal and Steel Community* [1958] ECR English Special Edition 17.

decision on the ground that the Commission had infringed *German* fundamental rights. In the absence of an EU bill of rights, this claim drew on the so-called 'mortgage theory'. According to this theory, the powers conferred on the EU were tied to a national human rights 'mortgage'. National fundamental rights would bind the EU, since the Member States could not have created an organization with more powers than themselves.[147] This argument was—correctly[148]—rejected by the Court. The task of the EU institutions was to apply EU laws 'without regard for their validity under national law'.[149] Thus, national fundamental rights could not be the direct source of EU human rights.

This position of the EU towards national fundamental rights has never changed. However, the Court's view evolved with regard to the existence of implied EU fundamental rights. Having originally found that EU law did '*not* contain any general principle, express or otherwise, guaranteeing the maintenance of vested rights',[150] the Court subsequently discovered 'fundamental human rights enshrined in the general principles of [EU] law'.[151] This new position was spelled out in *Internationale Handelsgesellschaft*.[152] The judgment confirmed the existence of an 'analogous guarantee inherent in [EU] law'.[153] And accordingly, 'respect for fundamental rights forms an integral part of the general principles of law protected by the Court of Justice'.[154]

Whence did the Court derive these fundamental rights? The famous answer here was that the Union's fundamental rights would be '*inspired* by the constitutional traditions common to the Member States'.[155] While thus not a direct source, national constitutional rights constituted an indirect source for the Union's fundamental rights. What was the nature of this indirect relationship between national rights and EU rights? How would the former influence the latter? A constitutional clarification was offered in *Nold*.[156] Drawing on its previous jurisprudence, the Court held:

> [F]undamental rights form an integral part of the general principles of law, the observance of which it ensures. In safeguarding these rights, the Court is bound to draw inspiration from constitutional traditions common to the Member States, and it cannot therefore uphold measures which are incompatible with fundamental rights recognised and protected by the constitutions of those States. Similarly, international treaties for the protection of human rights on which the Member States have collaborated or of which they are signatories, can supply guidelines which should be followed within the framework of [European] law.[157]

In searching for fundamental rights inside the general principles of EU law, the Court thus draws 'inspiration' from the common constitutional traditions of the Member States. The Court also uses international agreements of the Member States to identify EU fundamental rights, and one such international agreement is the European Convention

[147] As the Latin legal proverb makes clear: '*Nemo dat quod non habet*'.

[148] For a criticism of the 'mortgage theory', see R Schütze, 'EC Law and International Agreements of the Member States—An Ambivalent Relationship?' (2006–07) 9 *Cambridge Yearbook of European Legal Studies* 387, 399–402.

[149] Case 1/58 *Stork v High Authority* (n 146) 26.

[150] Ibid, 439 (emphasis added).

[151] Case 29/69 *Stauder v City of Ulm* [1969] ECR 419, para 7.

[152] Case 11/70 *Internationale Handelsgesellschaft mbH v Einfuhr- und Vorratsstelle für Getreide und Futtermittel* [1979] ECR 1125.

[153] Ibid, para 4.

[154] Ibid.

[155] Ibid (emphasis added).

[156] Case 4/73 *Nold v Commission* [1974] ECR 491.

[157] Ibid, para 13.

on Human Rights (ECHR). The Convention, indeed, soon assumed a 'particular significance' in identifying fundamental rights for the EU.[158] The Lisbon Treaty goes even further and requires the EU itself to accede to the ECHR.[159] Once this happens, the Union will be directly bound by the Convention; yet this binding effect will not be of a constitutional nature.[160]

6.2 **The EU Charter of Fundamental Rights**

The desire for a written bill of rights for the EU was first expressed in arguments favouring the Union's accession to the ECHR.[161] Yet an alternative strategy became prominent in the late twentieth century: the Union's own bill of rights.

The initiative for a 'Charter of Fundamental Rights' came from the European Council, which transferred the drafting mandate to a 'European Convention'.[162] The idea behind an internal codification was to strengthen the protection of fundamental rights in Europe 'by making those rights more visible in a Charter'.[163] The Charter was proclaimed in 2000, but it was not at first legally binding. Its status (as regards the Union) was similar to the ECHR. It provided an informal inspiration but imposed no formal obligation on the EU institutions.[164] This ambivalent status was immediately perceived as a constitutional problem.[165] With the Lisbon Treaty, the Charter is today recognized as having 'the same legal value as the Treaties'. Article 6(1) TEU in effect 'appends' the—slightly amended original—Charter to the Treaties.

What fundamental rights are listed in the Charter? The Charter 'reaffirms' the rights that result 'in particular' from the constitutional traditions common to the Member States, the ECHR, and the general principles of EU law.[166] This formulation suggested two things. First, the Charter aims to codify existing fundamental rights and is not intended to create 'new' ones.[167] And, secondly, it codifies EU rights from various sources—and thus not solely the general principles found in the Treaties. A closer analysis of all these points will take place in chapter 9.

[158] See Joined Cases 46/87 and 227/88 *Höchst v Commission* [1989] ECR 2859, para 13.

[159] Art 6(2) TEU states: 'The Union shall accede to the European Convention for the Protection of Human Rights and Fundamental Freedoms. Such accession shall not affect the Union's competences as defined in the Treaties.'

[160] On the status of international treaties concluded by the Union, see chapter 26.

[161] Commission, 'Memorandum on the Accession of the European Communities to the European Convention for the Protection of Human Rights and Fundamental Freedoms' (1979) *Bulletin of the European Communities*, Supplement 2/79, esp 11 *et seq*.

[162] On the drafting process, see chapter 9, and further G de Búrca, 'The Drafting of the European Union Charter of Fundamental Rights' (2001) 26 *European Law Review* 126.

[163] EU Charter, Preamble 4.

[164] See Case C-540/03 *Parliament v Council* [2006] ECR I-5769, para 38: 'the Charter is not a legally binding instrument'.

[165] The Charter was announced at the Nice European Council in December 2000, and its status was one of the questions in the 2000 Nice Declaration on the Future of the Union.

[166] EU Charter, Preamble 5.

[167] See Protocol (No 30) on the application of the Charter of Fundamental Rights of the European Union to Poland and to the United Kingdom, Preamble 6: 'the Charter reaffirms the rights, freedoms and principles recognised in the Union and makes those rights more visible, but does not create new rights or principles'.

7 Conclusion

The EU's constitutional theory must be derived from its own constitutional principles and values—or else become a banal metaphysical formalism.[168] This chapter has tried to analyse the EU legal order, as established by the European Treaties, against three versions of constitutionalism: formal constitutionalism, democratic constitutionalism, and liberal constitutionalism. The liberal constitutional claim is the most easily satisfied: the Union has adopted a version of the separation of powers principle and also constitutionally protects fundamental rights. With regard to formal and democratic constitutionalism, on the other hand, the Union has had trouble in staking its constitutional claim. As we saw previously, this is, however, mainly due to the 'unitary' standard traditionally adopted by classic constitutionalism. When viewed in light of a 'federal' standard, this dramatically changes. For a federal standard is able to recognize the existence of two constitutional claims—the national and the European claim—alongside one another; and it can also account for a pluralist version of popular sovereignty ('We, the Peoples') as well as the bicameral structure of the Union legislator. Table 4.1 provides a brief summary of the—respective—constitutionalist claims when read across a unitary and a federal standard.

Table 4.1 Unitary and federal constitutionalism: an overview

	Unitary standard	**Federal standard**
Formal constitutionalism	There is *one* constitution in *one* polity, where the primacy issue has *one* solution.	There are *two* (or *more*) constitutional levels in a *compound* polity, where the primacy issue has *multiple* solutions.
Democratic constitutionalism		
(a) Foundational origin	The Constitution is founded by *one* people ('We, the People').	The Constitution is founded on the basis of a *treaty* between multiple *peoples* ('We, the Peoples').
(b) Parliamentary structure	The legislator is (ideally) composed of *one* Parliament and represents *one* people.	The legislator is composed of *two* chambers, whereby the first represents the federal *people* and the second the State *peoples*.
Liberal constitutionalism		
(a) Separation of powers	There is *one* horizontal separation of powers.	There is a horizontal *and* a vertical separation of powers.
(b) Human rights	There is (typically) *one* Bill of Rights.	There is (typically) *one* federal and *one* State Bill of Rights.

168 The problem with much contemporary European 'constitutionalism' is that it has escaped into the realm of the metaphysical and mysterious. For the perfect example of this imperfect constitutional theory, see N Walker, 'Postnational Constitutionalism and the Problem of Translation' in JHH Weiler et al (eds), *European Constitutionalism Beyond the State* (Cambridge: Cambridge University Press, 2003). In the words of N Krisch, 'Europe's Constitutional Monstrosity' (2005) 25 *Oxford Journal of Legal Studies* 321, 326: 'at [Walker's] level of generality, all the particular content of constitutionalism, all its connections to particular historical and social circumstances, are lost'.

Further reading

A von Bogdandy and J Bast, *Principles of European Constitutional Law* (Oxford: Hart Publishing, 2011)

P Craig, 'Constitutions, Constitutionalism, and the European Union' (2001) 7 *European Law Journal* 125

G Duke, 'European Constitutionalism and Constituent Power' (2019) 44 *European Law Review* 50

P Eleftheriadis, *A Union of Peoples* (Oxford: Oxford University Press, 2020)

T Isiksel, *Europe's Functional Constitution: A Theory of Constitutionalism Beyond the State* (Oxford: Oxford University Press, 2016)

M Maduro, 'Contrapunctual Law: Europe's Constitutional Pluralism in Action' in N Walker (ed), *Sovereignty in Transition* (Oxford: Hart Publishing, 2003) 501

S Rehling Larsen, *The Constitutional Theory of the Federation and the European Union* (Oxford: Oxford University Press, 2021)

C Schmitt, *Constitutional Theory* (Durham, NC: Duke University Press, 2008)

R Schütze, 'Constitutionalism(s)' in R Masterman and R Schütze (eds), *Cambridge Companion to Comparative Constitutional Law* (Cambridge: Cambridge University Press, 2019) 40

R Schütze, *European Constitutional Law* (Cambridge: Cambridge University Press, 2021)

R Schütze, 'Demoicracy in Europe: Some Preliminary Thoughts' (2022) 47 *European Law Review* 24

JHH Weiler, *The Constitution of Europe* (Cambridge: Cambridge University Press, 1999)

5

Legislating in the European Union

Kieran Bradley

1 Introduction

The European Union is emphatically not a State,[1] though it exercises certain powers which are normally exercised by States. It is instead a 'common legal order', whose identity is defined by the 'values . . . which are common to the Member States' as set out in Article 2 TEU: 'respect for human dignity, freedom, democracy, equality, the rule of law and respect for human rights, including the rights of persons belonging to minorities . . . in a society in which pluralism, non-discrimination, tolerance, justice, solidarity and equality between women and men prevail'. The Union legislature must pursue these values within the scope of its activities.[2]

The Union exercises its powers through institutions of government and decision-making procedures whose design is modelled to a large extent on that of federal States, and which seek to balance the necessary freedom of action of the Union with the preservation of those powers the Member States have retained. The Union institutions enjoy a wide degree of functional autonomy and have been vested with extensive decision-making

[1] The Union is 'precluded by its very nature from being considered a State' (Opinion 2/13, *ECHR Accession II*, EU:C:2014:2454, para 156).

[2] Case C-157/21 *Poland v Parliament and Council* (*Conditionality*), EU:C:2022:98, paras 142 and 145; for convenience, the largely identical companion case, C-156/21 *Hungary v Parliament and Council*, EU:C:2022:97 is not considered here.

competences, which they exercise independently of, and at times against, the Member States. The exercise of these competences is subject to various constraints, both procedural and substantive, and, subject to one important exception,[3] is fully amenable to judicial review by the Court of Justice of the European Union.[4]

This chapter examines the procedures for the adoption of legislative and other normative measures in the European Union. It touches on a wide variety of subjects: forms of legal act, law-making competences and choice of procedure, delegation of normative powers, and the application of the constitutional principles of conferral, subsidiarity, and proportionality, as well as a number of more abstract matters, such as the hierarchy of norms and the Union's democratic credentials. While each subject is treated separately for the sake of a simpler presentation, it should be understood from the outset that these matters are closely related, both in legal theory and in the daily practice of the Union institutions.

The chapter thus describes the legal structures and the rules governing the allocation of powers between the Union and the Member States, and the distribution of powers between the different organs of Union government. It is political law of the highest order, in the sense that the principal parties concerned are the political actors of the Union (Member State governments[5] and the Union institutions), and the judgments of the Court of Justice regularly both involve an appreciation of politically sensitive matters and have major implications for the conduct of the political process; it has even been suggested that the Union legislature is a mere 'Agent of the European Court of Justice'. [6] This area of law has evolved more significantly over time than many areas of material law;[7] all of the major Treaty revisions in the history of the Community, now Union,[8] have entailed reforms of the decision-making procedures of greater or lesser scope. The Court is in effect engaged in an ongoing dialogue with the Treaty authors; its interpretations of the relevant institutional provisions tend to influence the drafting of subsequent provisions, and are often incorporated in whole or in part into the Treaties.[9]

Of particular note is the proliferation, reformulation, and clarification under the 2009 Lisbon Treaty[10] of rules seeking to constrain Union action which has accompanied the granting of new powers to the Union. This might give the impression that the powers of the Member States are protected from Union encroachment essentially by legal rules and judicial process. Nothing could be further from the truth; the fact that ministers from the Member States make up one of the branches of the legislature, and also exercise many executive functions, such as appointments to office in certain of the Union institutions, always has been, and remains, the principal, and very effective, 'political safeguard of federalism'.

[3] The Common Foreign and Security Policy (CFSP); see section 4.4.4 and chapter 26.

[4] For brevity, 'the Court [of Justice]', including when referring to the General Court.

[5] Member State parliaments also play a specific role in scrutinizing decision-making and Treaty reform: see respectively sections 5.2 and 10.

[6] G Davies, 'The European Union Legislature as an Agent of the European Court of Justice', (2016) 54 *Journal of Common Market Studies* 846, 846.

[7] See generally JHH Weiler, 'The Transformation of Europe' (1991) 100 *Yale Law Journal* 2403.

[8] For convenience, the term 'Union' will henceforth be used throughout, however anachronistic it may be in some contexts, unless it is necessary to distinguish between 'Union' and 'Community'.

[9] See eg Arts 3(2) and 216(1) TFEU, which are based on the voluminous case law of the Court on the extent of the Union's competence in the field of external relations, starting with the *ERTA* judgment (Case 22/70 *Commission v Council*, EU:C:1971:32).

[10] For treaties amending the Union Treaties, the date indicated is that on which the treaty entered into force; see further chapter 2.

That said, the Treaty provisions governing the intense web of relations between the political institutions of the Union are relatively scant, with the exception of those laying down the procedures for the adoption of legislation and the Union budget. It was left to the Court of Justice to develop the notion of the 'institutional balance' intended by the Treaty, on the basis of the injunction that '[e]ach institution ... act within the limits of the powers conferred on it in the Treaties'.[11] While this was originally identified as a guarantee for the protection of the interests of individuals, it is now used as a touchstone for the interpretation of provisions governing interinstitutional relations.[12] In accordance with this principle, 'each of the institutions must exercise its powers with due regard for the powers of the other institutions'.[13] The institutional balance is reflected, for example, in the Commission's power of legislative initiative and its freedom to refuse to submit a proposal when requested to do so by Parliament or the Council, or to give effect to a European Citizens' Initiative (ECI).[14] Similarly, when Parliament and the Council are exercising their legislative power, it is 'for those institutions alone to decide the content of a measure', independently of any position the European Council or the college of Member State governments may have adopted.[15] For its part, the Court has held that it is empowered to ensure the institutional balance is respected, even in the absence of a specific jurisdictional clause permitting it to do so;[16] that said, the second paragraph of Article 19(1) TEU does provide support for the Court's approach.

While the institutional balance determines the distribution of powers, the related duty of 'mutual sincere cooperation', also developed by the Court and now set out explicitly in the TEU, disciplines the exercise by the institutions of their respective powers.[17] Thus, for example, in the *Macro-financial Assistance* case, the Council's complaint that the Commission had breached the principle of sincere cooperation by withdrawing a legislative proposal belatedly and without any prior warning or verifying whether the Council was unanimous was treated as a separate plea from that alleging the Commission had no power to withdraw the proposal; a breach of this principle in the course of the legislative procedure may be relied on to challenge the validity of the act finally adopted.[18] In the *ITLOS statement* case, the Court held that sincere cooperation is 'exercised within the limits of the powers conferred by the Treaties on each institution ... [and is] not such as to change those powers'.[19]

[11] Art 4(1), second indent, EEC, now Art 13(2), first sentence, TEU; see also section 4.2.

[12] Case 9/56 *Meroni v High Authority*, EU:C:1958:7, 152, and, more recently, Case C-551/21 *Commission v Council* (*Agreement with the Gabonese Republic*), EU:C:2024:281, para 80. For an overview of the development of this doctrine, see K Bradley, 'Institutions' in *European Union Law Reporter* (Bicester: CCH Editions, 1997) para 4400.

[13] Case C-70/88 *Parliament v Council* (*Chernobyl—admissibility*), EU:C:1990:217, para 22; see also Case C-409/13 *Council v Commission* (*Macro-financial Assistance*), EU:C:2015:217, para 64, and Case C-24/20 *Commission v Council* (*Geneva Act*) EU:C:2022:911, para 92.

[14] Case C-418/18 P *Puppinck and Others v Commission*, EU:C:2019:1113, para 60; see section 11.3.

[15] Case C-5/16 *Poland v Parliament and Council* (*Market Stability Reserve*), EU:C:2018:483, para 84, and Joined Cases C-106/19 and C-232/19, *Italy and Comune di Milano v Parliament and the Council* (*Seat of EMA*), EU:C:2022: 568, para 146.

[16] Case C-70/88 (n 13) paras 23–27.

[17] Art 13(2), second sentence, TEU; an equivalent duty applies to relations between the Member States and the Union, Art 4(3), first sentence, TEU.

[18] Case C-409/13, *Macro-financial Assistance* (n 13) paras 47–49 and 97–105 and Case C-128/17 *Poland v Parliament and Council* (*Atmospheric pollutants*), EU:C:2019:194, paras 66–82; see also section 7.

[19] Case C-73/14, *Council v Commission*, EU:C:2015:663, para 84.

2 Forms of legislative and other normative acts

2.1 Principal forms of normative act

The main forms of normative act adopted by the institutions in implementing the Union's policy objectives are regulations and directives.[20] The institutions may also adopt rule-making decisions and international agreements, which are legally binding, and guidelines and recommendations, which have the legal effects attributed to them in their respective specific contexts, as well as opinions, which are neither normative nor have binding legal effects.[21]

The Treaty prescribes the form of legal act that Union action may take in a small number of areas, such as regulations for common commercial policy, or directives to facilitate freedom of establishment and freedom to provide services.[22] Some provisions even restrict the material content of the Union's action, for example by limiting its competence to 'incentive measures', which normally take the form of decisions.[23] For the most part, however, the institutions may choose the form of legal act they use to attain a particular objective; they must do so on a case-by-case basis and opt for the least intrusive form which will allow them to achieve their desired aim, in accordance with the principle of proportionality.[24] Normative measures adopted on the basis of provisions of legislative acts also take the form of regulations, directives, or decisions, though they need not specify the form of the legal act.[25]

2.2 Regulations

Regulations are the most easily recognizable form of normative act at the disposal of the Union. A regulation 'shall have general application [and is] binding in its entirety and directly applicable in all Member States';[26] it is in effect the equivalent of a 'statute' or 'law' in a national legal order. Regulation 261/2004, for example, famously establishes a charter of the rights of air passengers in difficulty.[27] The Member States need not adopt any national measures to give effect to a regulation in national law, and indeed they may not do so, as this would disguise the Union character of the act, though they may on occasion be required to adopt national provisions to implement a regulation. Regulations are the legal instrument of choice for the implementation of the common policies, as distinct from, say, internal market measures, which usually take the form of directives, though there is no hard-and-fast rule in this regard.

2.3 Directives

Directives are normative acts addressed to the Member States, which are then required, within a specified deadline, to adopt into national law ('transpose') the necessary provisions to give effect to the policy objectives set out in the directive, and to notify the

[20] Art 288 TFEU provides a definition of different legal acts of the Union, though the list is incomplete.

[21] See eg Art 121(4) TFEU (broad guidelines on economic policy) or Art 126(7)–(9) TFEU (recommendations on the reduction of an excessive deficit).

[22] See respectively Art 207(2) TFEU and Arts 50(1) and 59(1) TFEU.

[23] See eg Parliament and Council Decision 1145/2002/EC of 10 June 2002 on Community incentive measures in the field of employment (OJ [2002] L170/1).

[24] Art 296, first para, TFEU; on proportionality, see section 6.

[25] Case C-440/14 P *National Iranian Oil Company v Council*, EU:C:2016:128, para 18.

[26] Art 288, second para, TFEU.

[27] OJ [2004] L46/1; the validity of the Regulation was vigorously but unsuccessfully contested by IATA and an association of low-cost airlines (Case C-344/04 *IATA and ELFAA*, EU:C:2006:10); see also chapter 23.

Commission of their transposition measures. A directive is therefore 'binding as to the result to be achieved' while 'leav[ing] to the national authorities the choice of form and methods';[28] the equivalent term in certain other languages translates back into English as 'guideline', though it is in effect a framework law.[29] The instrument of the directive is said to reflect the principle of subsidiarity,[30] in that the Union is supposed to lay down only the rules and procedures which are strictly necessary to define and pursue its policy objectives, entrusting the Member States to adapt their national laws and procedures accordingly. Union policy is therefore applied through national legal forms, which are more familiar to both the citizen and the administrative authorities responsible for its concrete application. The directive is a particularly appropriate legal instrument for the pursuit of Union objectives in areas which are already subject to a developed legal framework in the Member States, for example rules governing the provision of services.[31]

The political reality is somewhat different from the legal theory. In practice, directives often regulate a policy area in great detail, leaving the Member States precious little discretion, even as regards 'the form and methods', particularly where the matter being regulated is highly technical in character. While often attributed to a thirst for power on the part of 'Brussels', in reality the level of detail often reflects instead, at least in part, the limited extent to which the governments of the Member States trust each other faithfully to pursue the policy objectives they agreed on in adopting the particular directive. The factual evidence would, moreover, tend to support the doubters; more or less all the Member States have been guilty, though not equally so, of failing properly to transpose, and/or to implement, Union directives.[32]

The Union's response to this state of affairs has been twofold. In the first place, the Court of Justice has recognized that, where a Member State has not implemented a directive by the deadline set, an individual may rely on those provisions of the directive which are unconditional and sufficiently precise in order to defeat the application of the conflicting national provisions. This direct effect of unimplemented provisions of directives is based on the idea that a Member State may not rely on its own turpitude to deny individuals rights deriving from Union law. It follows from this legal foundation that neither individuals nor public authorities may rely on such unimplemented provisions of directives in their dealings with (other) individuals.[33]

The second response came in the form of a special judicial procedure, introduced by the Maastricht Treaty in 1993,[34] under which the Court may impose financial penalties on a Member State which fails to comply with a previous judgment finding that the Member State has infringed Union law. In practice, a large proportion of the proceedings initiated under this heading have concerned failures to transpose and/or to apply directives properly. The Lisbon Treaty introduced a specific provision allowing the Court to impose a financial penalty on the Member State directly in infringement proceedings concerning its failure to notify the Commission of the national measures taken to transpose a directive adopted under a legislative procedure;[35] this has the advantage of allowing the Commission and the Court to concentrate on a single question of fact and law, and, of course, a Member State cannot notify transposition measures unless it has adopted them.

[28] Art 288, third para, TFEU. [29] eg in German 'directive' is 'Richtlinie' and in Dutch 'richtlijn'.

[30] See section 5. [31] Directive 2006/123/EC (OJ [2006] L376/36).

[32] See eg the Commission's annual reports on the monitoring of the application of EU law: https://ec.europa.eu/info/publications/annual-reports-monitoring-application-eu-law_en.

[33] See further chapter 6.

[34] Though formally known as the 'Treaty on European Union', this Treaty has been completely overhauled since; the 'Maastricht Treaty' therefore refers to the instrument as it came into force on 1 November 1993.

[35] Art 260(3) TFEU.

Once the Commission has sight of the transposition measures, it can proceed with the more substantive task of verifying whether or not the measures implement the directive.

2.4 'Rule-making decisions'

The original Treaty definition of a 'decision' is an act which is 'binding in its entirety upon those to whom it is addressed'.[36] However, the Union institutions discovered long ago that certain policy measures, or measures laying down institutional arrangements, for example, could best be formulated in a decision rather than a regulation or directive, an instrument often referred to by the German term *Beschluß*, in contradistinction to the individual decision, the *Entscheidung*. As such a rule-making decision[37] was addressed to no one in particular, it was theoretically devoid of legal effect. This type of decision was nonetheless a useful legal instrument; for example, the original Erasmus programme on the mobility of students was set up by such a decision in 1987,[38] and prior to the Lisbon Treaty reforms, the arrangements by which the exercise by the Commission of its implementing powers was supervised had been laid down in Council decisions.[39] It is for this reason that the Treaty now specifies that, while decisions are 'binding in [their] entirety', a 'decision which specifies those to whom it is addressed' is only binding on its addressees.[40]

2.5 International agreements

International agreements concluded by the Union are incorporated into its legal order by a Council decision, following a specific (non-legislative) procedure.[41] Such agreements are binding on the institutions of the Union and the Member States and therefore, subject to a few important exceptions, provide a criterion for the validity of Union acts.[42]

2.6 Interinstitutional agreements

In order to facilitate the smooth application of the institutional and budgetary provisions of the Treaties, over the years the political institutions have concluded a large number of so-called 'interinstitutional agreements'. While these might be considered more contractual than normative, they may nonetheless have important policy and even legal effects, and successive reforms have transformed the functional necessity to conclude agreements on certain specific matters into a Treaty obligation; one such is the multi-annual financial framework which, with the Lisbon Treaty, crossed over from agreement to regulation.[43] Such interinstitutional agreements may be general in scope or limited to a particular field, and may be concluded by Union institutions with bodies other than institutions strictly so called.[44]

[36] Art 249, fourth para, EC.

[37] K Lenaerts and P Van Nuffel refer to the *sui generis* decision (*EU Constitutional Law* (Oxford: Oxford University Press, 2021) para 27-038, 739), while R Schütze calls it the 'non-addressed' decision (*European Constitutional Law* (3rd edn, Cambridge: Cambridge University Press, 2021) 167); neither denomination clearly indicates the legal characteristics of the measure.

[38] Council Decision 87/327/EEC (OJ [1987] L166/1).

[39] On secondary normative acts, see section 8.

[40] Art 288, third para, TFEU.

[41] Art 218(2)–(8) and (10) TFEU.

[42] Arts 218 and 216(2) TFEU respectively; the General Agreement on Tariffs and Trade (GATT) and the World Trade Organization (WTO) Agreements comprise the most important exceptions. See chapter 26.

[43] Compare Art 161, third para, EC with Art 312(2) TFEU.

[44] See eg Agreement between Parliament, the Council, and the Commission on Better Law-Making (OJ [2016] L123/1), and Agreement between Parliament and the Single Resolution Board on the practical modalities of Parliament's supervision of the Board's activities (OJ [2015] L339/58).

The Court has recognized that interinstitutional agreements can be a useful supplement to the Treaty provisions themselves, and that certain delicate political questions can better be resolved by the application of an agreement between the main players than intervention by the judicial authority.[45] It will thus give legal effect to the substantive content of such an agreement, where the institutions intended to enter into a binding commitment in an area where they are under a duty to cooperate with each other.[46] Moreover, the Treaty now obliges Parliament, the Council, and the Commission to 'consult with each other and by common agreement make arrangements for their cooperation'; the resulting interinstitutional agreements would in principle be binding and may be relied upon by the Court as a criterion of validity of a normative act.[47]

Even where an agreement is not formally binding, the institutions would be expected to keep their word.[48]

2.7 **Recommendations, opinions, and other non-binding acts**

A recommendation, which may be either targeted or normative in scope, is designed 'to exhort and to persuade'.[49] An opinion is the expression of a position on a specific issue. According to the fifth paragraph of Article 288 TFEU, recommendations and opinions have no binding force.

There are, however, important exceptions to this rule. National courts are 'obliged to take [recommendations] into consideration with a view to resolving the disputes submitted to them, in particular when they are intended to supplement binding European Union provisions'.[50] In the specific area of economic and monetary policy, the procedure for dealing with a Member State's excessive deficit requires the Council first to address 'recommendations' to the Member State concerned; if the Member State does not put these into practice, the Council may in effect order it to take deficit-reduction measures, failing which the Council itself may adopt the necessary measures.[51] Even 'broad guidelines' on economic policy may have some legal effects, in that non-compliance provides the basis for a Commission warning, followed by Council recommendations.[52]

The 'opinion' the Court provides on the compatibility with Union law of an 'envisaged' international agreement is wholly binding; a negative opinion requires the renegotiation or abandonment of the agreement, or an amendment to the Treaties.[53] While the content of the opinion of an institution or body which is consulted on a proposed normative act is not binding, respect for the consultation procedure is a substantive procedural requirement, breach of which justifies the annulment of the act.[54] Where Parliament and the Council have been granted the power to adopt legislative acts, they may not adopt other, non-legislative, acts, such as declarations and recommendations.[55]

[45] See in particular Case 34/86 *Council v Parliament (1986 Budget)* [1986] ECR 2155, para 50.

[46] Case C-25/94 *Commission v Council*, EU:C:1996:114, para 49.

[47] Art 295 TFEU; see eg the Better Law-Making Agreement (n 44) and Case C-482/17 *Czech Republic v Parliament and Council* (*Gun control*), EU:C:2019:1035, para 84.

[48] See eg AG Sharpston, Opinion in Joined Cases C-457–460/11 *Verwertungsgesellschaft Wort* (*VG Wort*), EU:C:2013:34, para 32.

[49] Case C-501/18 *BT v Balgarska Narodna Banka*, EU:C:2021:249, para 80.

[50] Ibid. [51] Art 126(7)–(11) TFEU. [52] Art 121(4) TFEU; see further chapter 19.

[53] Art 218(11) TFEU. The term 'opinion' is clearly a misnomer; Art 104, third para, Euratom, provides that the Court adopts a 'ruling'.

[54] See section 7.4.

[55] Art 296, third para, TFEU; unless reflected in the text of the legal act, declarations by the legislature in any case have no legal effect, even as a guide to interpretation of the act (Case C-292/89 *Antonissen*, EU:C:1991:80).

The institutions also adopt various forms of what is loosely called 'soft law', which does not fit in the 'binary black and white distinction between binding and non-binding legal effects'.[56] Arguably, insofar as certain of these acts do not have binding legal effects, they should in principle not be called 'law' at all. This is notably the case of the 'open method of coordination', a substitute for, or addition to, normative Union action which has been applied in areas of regulation where traditional 'command and control' mechanisms are considered inappropriate, such as certain aspects of economic, social, and employment policies. Under this method, the Union sets guidelines which are to be implemented by national action plans; the fulfilment of these action plans is monitored through benchmarking and peer review. The process is intended to be participative; regional and local government, management and labour, and civil society are to be actively involved in the planning and review stages, and the private sector in its implementation.[57]

On the other hand, where a purported act of 'soft law', such as a Commission communication, has the effect of creating legal rights or obligations, it is not 'soft'; it is subject to judicial review and may be annulled. Thus, for example, in *France v Commission*, the Commission had issued a communication which restated, ostensibly as its 'general approach', the substantive provisions of a proposal for a directive on pension funds which had not been adopted by the legislature. The Court held that the communication created new obligations for the Member States and annulled it.[58]

There is a wide variety of normative instruments, apart from recommendations and opinions, whose provisions may have legal effects within the Union's legal order, notwithstanding their putatively non-binding character and/or the fact that they are not adopted by bodies belonging to the Union's institutional structures. Such is the case, for example, of the harmonized technical standards adopted by the European Committee for Standardisation, which is a private, not-for-profit association established under Belgian law; compliance with such standards is voluntary. In *James Elliot Construction*, the Court held that it had jurisdiction to interpret such standards in the framework of a request for a preliminary ruling, albeit that a national court is not bound to give effect to these standards in proceedings between two private parties.[59]

3 Hierarchy of norms

Within a national legal system, it is generally quite easy to identify the respective places of different legal instruments in the hierarchy of norms, particularly where the State in question operates under a written constitution. Thus, at its simplest, statutes are subordinate to the constitution, while statutory instruments (or their equivalent) must comply with the statute under which they are adopted. Moreover, the name of the particular legal act, and/or the procedure for its adoption, usually indicates its place in this hierarchy.

At the apex of the pyramid of European Union norms are the Treaties, including the Charter of Fundamental Rights, which has 'the same legal value as the Treaties',[60] and the fundamental principles of Union law developed in the case law of the Court, including

[56] In Case C-16/16 P *Belgium v Commission*, AG Bobek distinguished between 'legal effect' and 'binding effect' (EU:C:2017:959, paras 55–82); the Court held that the recommendation in question did not have binding legal effect and could not be challenged (EU:C:2018:79).

[57] European Council, Lisbon, March 2000; see eg K Armstrong, 'The Open Method of Coordination: Obstinate or Obsolete?' in R Schütze and T Tridimas (eds), *Oxford Principles of European Union Law* (Oxford: Oxford University Press, 2018) 777.

[58] Case C-57/95 *France v Commission*, EU:C:1997:164; see also the judgment in Case C-16/16 P (n 58).

[59] Case C-613/14 *James Elliot Construction Ltd v Irish Asphalt Ltd*, EU:C:2016:821.

[60] Art 6(1), first subpara, TEU. See further section 8 and chapter 9.

the requirement to protect fundamental rights; collectively these may be termed 'primary law'. Acts which are based directly on the Treaty, including, in particular, Union legislation and similar normative measures, may be termed 'secondary law'. The denomination of an act as a 'regulation', 'directive', or 'decision' does not in itself determine its place in the hierarchy of norms. There is no hierarchy between acts of secondary law, unless the later act is implementing an existing binding act; a directive may thus derogate from a regulation, and a regulation may implement a decision. Under conditions laid down in the Treaty and/or secondary law, the Commission (and, in very limited cases, the Council) may adopt regulatory acts, which are based either on the Treaty or on enabling provisions in acts of secondary law.[61]

Obviously, the Court is not empowered to rule on the validity of provisions of the founding Treaties.[62] In *Pringle*, the Court examined the question of whether an amendment to the Treaty had been validly adopted in accordance with one of the simplified revision procedures available since the Lisbon reforms, which allows the European Council to adopt amendments under certain procedural and substantive conditions.[63]

The hierarchical relationship between primary and secondary law is relatively simple. A normative act based directly on the Treaty must comply with the Treaty itself, the Charter, and the general principles of Union law. By the same token, a delegated or implementing act, which seeks to give effect to a measure of secondary law, must respect the conditions and limitations of the enabling provision of that measure, failing which the delegated or implementing act is deemed ultra vires and may be annulled.[64] An enabling provision in an act of secondary law may itself be challenged for failing to respect the Treaty rules defining the conditions under which such delegations of power may be made—for example, by delegating to the Commission the power to adopt essential elements of the matter being regulated.[65]

4 Competences and conferral

4.1 'Competence' as ability and 'competence' as power

The EU Treaties use the term 'competence' as a synonym for both 'legal authority' or 'power' and in its more quotidian meaning of 'personal ability'. The latter usage is to be found particularly in the provisions governing the qualifications for appointment to office as a member of an institution or ancillary body; thus Commissioners are selected, inter alia, on grounds of their 'general competence', while 'jurisconsults of recognised competence' may be appointed to the Court of Justice.[66] It is, however, the former usage of the term which is primarily relevant for the present chapter.

In its original English version, the EEC Treaty used 'competence' to mean power in only one, albeit highly relevant, provision; Article 173, second paragraph, EEC, identified 'lack of competence' as the first ground on which an act of the Council or the Commission could be annulled. The term was a direct translation of the word '*incompétence*', previously used in Article 33, first paragraph, of the 1951 Treaty of Paris establishing the European Coal and Steel Community (ECSC), which was only authentic in the French language. The idea is equivalent to ultra vires in the administrative law terminology of

[61] See further sections 7.3 and 8.

[62] See Cases C-235/94 P *Roujansky v Council*, EU:C:1995:376 and C-167/94 *Grau Gomis*, EU:C:1995:113.

[63] Case C-370/12 *Pringle v Ireland*, EU:C:2012:756; see further section 10.2.1.

[64] See section 8.

[65] See Case C-359/92 *Germany v Council* (*Product safety*), EU:C:1994:306.

[66] See respectively Art 17(3), second subpara, TEU and Art 253, first para, TFEU.

the common law jurisdictions. The term 'power' was preferred in the remainder of the EEC Treaty.

Both the Single European Act (1987) and the Maastricht Treaty (1993) used the term 'competence', in preference to 'power', at the same time as they significantly extended the formal powers of the Community and established the European Union, which was also endowed with extensive decision-making powers. The Treaty of Lisbon sought to classify the competences of the Union into three categories: exclusive, shared, and ancillary, incidentally providing a definition of 'competence' as being the power to 'legislate and adopt legally binding acts'.[67] Like the witches in *Macbeth* around their cauldron, the three principles of conferral, subsidiarity, and proportionality watch over the Union's competences on behalf of the Member States. Conferral determines what competences the Union enjoys, subsidiarity provides a test as to whether or not they should be exercised in a given case, and proportionality seeks to ensure the competences are exercised in such a manner as to encroach on the competences of the Member States, and the rights of individuals, as little as possible.[68]

4.2 **Conferral**

The principle underlying the division of competences between the Union and the Member States is set out in the first paragraph of Article 1 TEU, which states that 'the Member States confer competences [on the Union] to attain objectives they have in common'. This paragraph establishes the centrality of the principle of conferral (also referred to as the principle of 'attributed powers') in the first substantive provision of the Treaties and identifies the very *raison d'être* of the Union.

The principle of conferral is repeated insistently throughout the Union Treaties. Article 4(1) TEU thus declares that 'competences not conferred upon the Union in the Treaties remain with the Member States'; Article 5(1) TEU stipulates that '[the] limits of Union competences are governed by the principle of conferral'; while Article 5(2) TEU provides that 'the Union shall act only within the limits of the competences conferred on it by the Member States in the Treaties to attain the objectives set out therein'. In addition, Article 13(2) TEU requires each of the institutions to act 'within the limits of the powers conferred on it in the Treaties'. The authors of the Lisbon Treaty did not, however, discover the moon; the same principle underlay all the previous Union and Community Treaties, right from the ECSC Treaty, which explicitly enjoined the institutions to act within the limits of their powers and vested the Court of Justice with jurisdiction to ensure they did so.[69]

The Court is occasionally called on to evaluate the validity of Union legislation against the principle of conferral, and relied on it, for example, in striking down the first Tobacco Advertising Directive as being incorrectly classified as an internal market measure.[70] As Member States are expected to comply with the common values of the Union, the defence of such values in a legislative act does not offend the principle of conferral.[71] The same is true of the protection of 'other fundamental interests' which may be affected by measures adopted by the legislature in a given area of regulation, as the legislature is charged with safeguarding the general interests of the Union and its overarching objectives.[72]

[67] Art 2(1) TFEU. [68] See respectively sections 4.2–4.4, 5, and 6.

[69] Art 6, para 4, and Art 33, first para, ECSC; on the institutional balance, see section 1.

[70] Case C-376/98 *Germany v Parliament and the Council* (*Tobacco advertising I*), EU:C:2000:544; see also Case C-482/17 *Gun control* (n 47) paras 21–29.

[71] Case C-157/21 *Conditionality* (n 2) paras 143 and 146.

[72] Case C-620/18 *Hungary v Parliament and Council* (*Posting of workers*), EU:C:2020:1001, para 42.

4.3 **Grants of legislative power ('legal bases')**

Unlike the equivalent provisions of the US Constitution, the Treaties do not provide a list of areas of policy activity in which the Union enjoys the plenitude of legislative power, and authorize the Union to act in those areas. Instead, the Treaty grants the Union legislative competence in a number of discrete areas;[73] though the Union's competences are often widely drawn, they are nonetheless hedged about in most cases by material restrictions and procedural requirements of different kinds, which are designed to protect the competences of the Member States. In two cases, the Union's legislative competence is phrased primarily in terms of pursuing objectives, those of establishing and ensuring the functioning of the internal market (Article 114 TFEU), and of attaining Union objectives where the necessary powers have not been provided elsewhere (Article 352 TFEU). The Court has regularly been called upon to ensure that the institutions respect the boundaries of the former legal basis, while the requirement of a unanimous vote in the Council ensures that the question of the legality of recourse to the latter arises only rarely.[74]

In accordance with the principle of conferral, every binding act the Union adopts must have a legal foundation either in the Treaties or in a valid pre-existing normative act, the 'legal basis' of the act. This provision indicates who may adopt the act, what the act may contain, and what procedure must be followed to adopt it. Disputes on whether or not the Union has exceeded its competences tend to take the form of a challenge to the choice of legal basis for the particular act, rather than an allegation that the Union has no competence whatsoever; this is because Union competence to act on the particular matter may be available under another legal basis than the legal basis chosen, in particular, as a last resort, Article 352 TFEU.[75]

Since the Single European Act in 1987, the Court has built up a vast body of case law on the matter of the determination of the legal basis of Union acts.[76] The legislature is obliged to indicate the legal basis of binding acts; its choice is amenable to judicial review.[77] The identification of the legal basis is required to comply with the obligation to provide a proper statement of reasons and demonstrate adherence to the principles of conferral and institutional balance; however, a failure to identify the relevant Treaty article explicitly in the preamble would not justify the annulment of the measure if the legal basis can be gleaned from other parts of the measure.[78]

The aim and material content of a measure are the principal criteria for the determination of its legal basis.[79] Where the measure in question amends an existing measure,

[73] According to Davies, the Member States have 'constitutionalized . . . [the Union's] policy goals and legislative capacities' (n 6) 846. It has been plausibly suggested that the term 'area' is used in the context of the division of competences between the Union and the Member States, while 'field' is used for that between the institutions (AG Sharpston, Opinion in Joined Cases C-103/12 and C-165/12 *Parliament and Commission v Council* (*Venezuela Fishing*), EU:C:2014:334, para 152).

[74] Regarding the internal market, see eg *Tobacco advertising I* (n 70), Case C-377/98 *Netherlands v Parliament and Council* (*Biotechnological patents*), EU:C:2001:523, and Case C-58/08 *Vodafone v Secretary of State for Business, Enterprise and Regulatory Reform*, EU:C:2010:321 (see case study 5.1), and on Art 352 TFEU (then Art 235 EEC), see Opinion 2/94, *ECHR Accession I*, EU:C:1996:140.

[75] See Case C-157/21 *Conditionality* (n 2) paras 111–120 and, for Art 352 TFEU, Case 45/86 *Commission v Council* (*1986 GSP*), EU:C:1987:163, and Opinion 2/94 (n 74).

[76] See K Bradley, 'Powers and Procedures in the EU Constitution: Legal Bases and the Court' in P Craig and G de Búrca (eds), *The Evolution of EU Law* (2nd edn, Oxford: Oxford University Press, 2011), and the references provided.

[77] Case 45/86 *1986 GSP* (n 75).

[78] Case C-600/14 *Germany v Council*, EU:C:2017:935, paras 80–84.

[79] Case C-300/89 *Commission v Council* (*Titanium dioxide*), EU:C:1991:244; ironically, the application of these criteria was not sufficient for the Court to determine the legal basis of the contested directive in this case. See also *Conditionality* (n 2) para 121.

the earlier measure may be taken into account, in particular to assess the objective of the rules in question.[80] On the other hand, an institutional practice 'however consistent, cannot alter the rules of the Treaties' which dictate recourse to a particular legal basis.[81] As the legal bases in the Treaties are many and are often widely drafted, there is a significant possibility of overlap, where more than one legal basis might apply. In such a case, the more specific provision should be preferred.[82] Where a measure has 'a twofold purpose or . . . comprises two components', the legal basis should be chosen in function of the 'main or predominant purpose or component'; it is only exceptionally, where 'the measure simultaneously pursues a number of objectives or has several components that are inextricably linked, without one being incidental to the other', that the legislature may resort to more than one legal basis for a single act.[83] The legal basis for an international agreement 'must be assessed with regard to that agreement as a whole . . . having regard to its essential object and not in terms of its individual clauses'.[84] The combination of legal bases may not lead to the application of legislative procedures which are incompatible *inter se*. The splitting of a measure into two distinct acts with different legal bases is not justified where the measure could properly have been adopted on a single legal basis.[85]

The Court has acknowledged that '[t]he choice of the appropriate legal basis has constitutional significance',[86] a finding fully internalized by the Union's political institutions; European Parliament committees, for example, are required to verify the legal basis of every proposal referred to them, while its Committee on Legal Affairs may raise the question of its own motion.[87] Successive rounds of Treaty reform since the Single Act have added numerous new legal bases and amended or deleted others. The legal basis for an act 'must . . . be in force when the act is adopted', and the 'procedure for adopting that act must be carried out in accordance with the rules in force at the time of adoption'.[88]

Successful Member State challenges to Union legislation on grounds of lack of competence in legal bases disputes are in practice very rare; even in the case of tobacco advertising, the validity of a second directive, carefully crafted to take account of the judgment of the Court in the first case, was subsequently upheld.[89] Where grants of power to the Union are framed in terms of achieving certain objectives, it may adopt measures affecting areas of regulation which are in principle reserved to the Member States. This is particularly striking in the area of the internal market. Thus, for example, while the Member States may in principle adopt their own rules on tobacco advertising in pursuit of public health objectives, the Union may harmonize these national provisions in order to ensure the proper functioning of the internal market in the relevant goods and services.[90] Even where an existing measure has already removed obstacles to trade, 'the EU legislature may not be denied the possibility

[80] Case C-157/21 *Conditionality* (n 2) para 122.

[81] Case C-551/21 *Commission v Council* (*Agreement with the Gabonese Republic*) (n 12) para 82.

[82] Case C-61/22 *RL*, EU:C:2024:251; each of the competing legal bases only applied 'where the Treaties have not provided the necessary powers'.

[83] Case C-180/20 *Commission v Council* (*Armenia Agreement*), EU:C:2021:658, para 34.

[84] Ibid, paras 38 and 45. [85] Ibid, para 58.

[86] Opinion 2/00, *Cartagena Protocol on the Transfer of Living Modified Organisms*, EU:C:2001:664, para 5.

[87] Art 39(1) and (3), EP Rules of Procedure.

[88] Case C-361/14 P *Commission v McBride and Others*, EU:C:2016:434, para 40.

[89] Case C-380/03 *Germany v Parliament and Council II*, EU:C:2006:772; see also Case C-358/14 *Poland v Parliament and Council* (*Menthol cigarettes*), EU:C:2016:323. This is equally true of Member State challenges to legislation on other grounds; see eg Joined Cases C-541–555/20, *Lithuania et al v Parliament and Council*, EU:C:2024:818; in a judgment running to some 1,500 paragraphs, not one of the dozens of grounds of annulment was successful.

[90] See also the Opinion of AG Poiares Maduro in Case C-58/08 *Vodafone v Secretary of State for Business, Enterprise and Regulatory Reform*, EU:C:2009:596, para 1. As regards the defence of the rule of law in the Member States, see Case C-157/21 *Conditionality* (n 2).

of adapting that act to any change in circumstances or development of knowledge having regard to its task of safeguarding the general interests recognized by the Treaty', such as the fight against international terrorism and serious crime or successive enlargements of the Union.[91] Where the conditions for recourse to the relevant legal basis are fulfilled, the fact that the safeguarding of such interests is the 'decisive factor' in the determination of the content of the measure does not invalidate the choice of legal basis.[92]

The Court has repeatedly held that the 'rules regarding the manner in which the EU institutions arrive at their decisions are laid down in the Treaties and are not within the discretion of the Member States or of the institutions themselves'.[93] Allowing an institution to establish 'secondary legal bases' alleviating or strengthening the Treaty rules for the adoption of an act would be 'tantamount to according that institution a legislative power which exceeds that provided for by the Treaties'.[94] The 'sensitive nature of the matter concerned cannot warrant the adoption of a secondary legal basis establishing a special procedure'.[95] Nor may the institutions adopt through legislation a mechanism with the same objective, and allowing the adoption of the same measures, as a mechanism provided in the Treaties.[96]

4.4 **Classification of competences**

The TFEU classifies the various domains of activity of the Union into 'categories and areas of Union competence', each 'category' being comprised of a number of 'areas'.[97] The different lists of categories of competence set out in Articles 2 to 6 TFEU complete and replace, in effect, the list of 'activities of the Community' formerly set out in Article 3 EC. The three categories of competence already mentioned (exclusive, shared, and ancillary) are supplemented by two areas of competences which are excluded from these categories because of the specific character of the matters concerned—that is, the power to adopt 'arrangements' for the coordination of the Member States' economic and employment policies, and the competence under the TEU to define and implement a common foreign and security policy.[98] Arguably, this categorization does not in any way affect the material scope of the competences themselves, which are regulated by the terms of the respective legal bases provided in the remainder of that Treaty and in the TEU. While it was suggested that '[legal] consequences flow from [the] categorization' of competences,[99] the classification set out in Articles 2 to 6 TFEU does not represent a radical change from the pre-Lisbon situation as it arose from the case law of the Court of Justice.

4.4.1 **Exclusive competence**

The mark of an exclusive competence is that it is one which the Union is legally obliged to exercise, where Member State action would render Union action ineffective;[100] thus in such areas 'only the Union may legislate and adopt legally binding acts', though the

[91] Respectively Case C-482/17 *Gun control* (n 47) paras 38 and 40 and Case C-620/18 *Posting of workers* (n 72) para 62.

[92] Case C-482/17 *Gun control* (n 47) para 36.

[93] See eg Case C-275/20 *Commission v Council* (*Agreement with the Korean Republic*), para 32; the principle was first stated in Case 68/86 *United Kingdom v Council* (*Hormones*), EU:C:1988:85, para 38.

[94] *Agreement with the Gabonese Republic*, ibid; see section 8.2.

[95] Case C-275/20 *Commission v Council* (n 93), para 50.

[96] Case C-157/21 *Conditionality* (n 2) para 206.

[97] See generally S Garben and I Govaere, *The Division of Competences between the EU and the Member States* (Oxford: Hart/Bloomsbury, 2017).

[98] On the CFSP, see section 4.4.4; on economic policy coordination, see chapter 19.

[99] P Craig and G de Búrca, *EU Law* (7th edn, Oxford: Oxford University Press, 2020) 102.

[100] JP Jacqué, *Droit institutionnel de l'Union européenne* (7th edn, Paris: Dalloz, 2012) para 23.

Member States may be required to adopt national measures to implement the Union acts in such areas. The 'exclusive' character of a Union competence is not absolute, however; the Union may authorize the Member States to adopt legislation and other measures.[101]

Prior to the Lisbon Treaty, the Court had recognized that, notwithstanding the 'total and definitive' transfer of competences to the Union, the Member States could be authorized to adopt national measures which were necessary to avoid a legislative lacuna, where the Union had failed, for one reason or another, to exercise an exclusive competence. In such cases, the Member States were considered to be acting as 'trustees of the common interest'.[102]

The list of exclusive competences provided in Article 3 TFEU is intended to be exhaustive: the customs union, 'competition rules necessary for the functioning of the internal market', monetary policy for the eurozone, 'the conservation of marine biological resources' (essentially the fixing of fishing quotas), the common commercial policy, and the adoption of international agreements to give effect to the Union's internal policies. Most of these categories of competence had been identified as exclusive in the Court's case law, or are inherently exclusive. Though not listed, it is clear that competences relating to the functioning of the Union are exclusive.[103]

There are other matters within the area of the Union's shared competences which might at first blush be thought to be inherently exclusive, notably the power to harmonize national rules to ensure the establishment and functioning of the internal market, though the Court has not accepted this view.

4.4.2 Shared competences

The bulk of Union competences fall within the category described as 'shared'. This is a residual category, in that any competence not listed as being exclusive or ancillary is considered shared,[104] and the list provided in Article 4(2) TFEU is that of the 'principal areas'. Thus, for example, the 2010 and 2012 directives on the rights of accused persons to interpretation and translation and on information in criminal proceedings lay down Union-level rules in specific areas of criminal procedure, for which the Member States are otherwise fully responsible.[105]

The use of the term 'shared' is not obviously appropriate, in that it implies that the Member States remain competent to act in respect of matters which are already governed by Union legislation, whereas this is not the case. While the term 'concurrent' might have been more accurate, the choice of 'shared' in the Lisbon Treaty was almost certainly motivated by the same political concerns as led to the repetition of the principle of conferral in the opening provision of the Union Treaties.[106] In these areas, Member States may 'exercise their competence to the extent the Union has not exercised its competence [or] . . . has decided to cease exercising its competence'; once the Union has adopted rules on a particular matter, action by the Member State is said to be pre-empted, and it may no longer legislate.[107] Given the nature of Union competences, however, pre-emption only concerns 'those elements of the Union action in question' and not the 'whole area' of the activity being regulated.[108]

[101] Art 2(1) TFEU; see eg Regulation 1219/2012 on transitional arrangements for bilateral investment agreements, OJ [2012] L351/40. For the pre-Lisbon situation, see Case 804/79 *Commission v United Kingdom (Fisheries policy)*, EU:C:1981:93 and Case 174/84 *Bulk Oil*, EU:C:1986:60.

[102] Case 804/79 *Commission v United Kingdom (Fisheries policy)* (n 101); see also Case 174/84 *Bulk Oil*, EU:C:1986:60.

[103] Case C-157/21 *Conditionality* (n 2) para 241.

[104] Art 4(1) TFEU.

[105] Respectively Directive 2010/64/EU (OJ [2010] L280/1) and Directive 2012/13/EU (OJ [2012] L142/1). See further chapter 24.

[106] See section 4.2.

[107] Art 2(2) TFEU; see also Art 4(3), third para, TEU.

[108] Protocol No 25 on the exercise of shared competences.

To avoid pre-emption in the areas of research, technological development and space, and development cooperation and humanitarian aid, Article 4(3) and (4) TFEU provides explicitly that the exercise of Union competence in these areas does not have the effect of preventing the Member States exercising their competence. Furthermore, in a small number of areas, such as the mutual recognition of judgments of criminal courts, the definition of serious trans-border crimes, and social policy, the material scope of Union competence is limited to setting minimum standards.[109]

4.4.3 Ancillary (or 'complementary') competences

In certain areas, the Union may 'carry out actions to support, coordinate, or supplement actions of the Member States'; its action is thus ancillary to that of the Member States and takes the form of promoting cooperation between them, along with the adoption of Union-level incentive measures, which may include the provision of funding, to tackle particular problems. The exercise of an ancillary competence may not itself lead to the harmonization of national provisions; on the other hand, the fact that the Union has an ancillary competence in a given area does not preclude harmonization in the name of the internal market, where the conditions for recourse to the internal market legal basis are fulfilled.[110] The areas listed in Article 6 TFEU are all matters of shared concern between the Member States, where the pursuit of national (or indeed local) policy objectives is inevitably affected by Union measures in areas of shared or exclusive competence, but where the matters regulated are considered too close to national or local interests, or even national identity,[111] or otherwise too politically sensitive, to grant the Union any more extensive influence. One of the most successful such actions is the Erasmus programme to encourage student mobility which was set up in 1987 and under which several million students have completed periods of study in a Member State other than their home Member State.[112]

4.4.4 Common Foreign and Security Policy (CFSP)

The CFSP is given separate treatment compared to all other Union policies. The relevant provisions are located in the TEU rather than the TFEU, and the decision-making procedures and legal instruments differ significantly from those which obtain under the general regime.[113] Legislation is expressly excluded, in preference to guidelines, decisions defining Union actions, positions, and implementing arrangements, and systematic cooperation between the Member States. The policy is defined and implemented by the European Council and the Council, and put into effect by the High Representative for Foreign Affairs and Security Policy, with Parliament, the Commission, and the Court of Justice each playing correspondingly lesser, not to say rather marginal, roles. Though the provisions of the TEU on the fundamental constitutional and democratic principles apply to the CFSP, the rule of law as defined and defended in the general Union regime to a large extent does not.[114] Article 218 TFEU nonetheless provides a 'single procedure of general application . . . [for] the negotiation and conclusion of international agreements', including those within the domain of the CFSP, 'except where the Treaties lay down special procedures'.[115]

[109] Respectively Arts 82(2), 83(1) and (2), and 153(2)(b) TFEU; the social policy measures may, moreover, only be implemented gradually. See also chapters 20 (social policy) and 24 (criminal law).

[110] See *Tobacco advertising I* (n 70) paras 78 and 79.

[111] Art 4(2) TEU requires the Union to respect, inter alia, the national identities of the Member States.

[112] See now Regulation (EU) 2021/817 (OJ [2021] L189/1).

[113] Art 24(1), second para, TEU.

[114] See Arts 23–46 TEU and chapter 26; see also Case C-72/15 *Rosneft v HM Treasury*, EU:C:2017:236 and K Lenaerts, 'New Horizons for the Rule of Law within the EU' (2020) 21 *German Law Journal* 29.

[115] Case C-180/20 *Armenia Agreement* (n 83) para 27.

5 Subsidiarity

In its most general meaning, as a principle of constitutional design, subsidiarity requires that public power be attributed to the level of government (local, regional, national, etc) where it can most effectively be exercised. In the constitutional design of the Union, subsidiarity is a concrete manifestation of the Member States' aspiration that 'decisions [be] taken as closely as possible to the citizen' set out in the first article of the TEU. That said, both the Union Treaties and the Court are rigorously neutral as regards the distribution of governmental powers within the Member States.[116]

As formulated in Article 5(3) TEU, the principle of subsidiarity provides a test which is intended to act as a brake, under certain conditions, on the exercise of competence which has been conferred on the Union. It is for this reason that subsidiarity is sandwiched between the principles of conferral and proportionality. The primary function of the subsidiarity test is to provide a yardstick against which the political institutions evaluate whether or not the Union should exercise its competence in a particular area. It also serves as a criterion of the validity of measures adopted, in the context of judicial review under Articles 263 and 267 TFEU.

From its first introduction into the Treaty as a modest qualification of the exercise of the then new Community competence in the field of environmental protection, the subsidiarity principle has been expanded, extended, and transformed into a principle of general application, of which each of the Union institutions is bound to ensure 'constant respect'.[117] The Treaty principle has been supplemented by Protocol No 2, which lays down procedural requirements to reinforce respect for subsidiarity, including provisions which allow the national parliaments to express their views on whether proposed legislation complies with this principle or not—the so-called 'early warning' mechanism.

5.1 The subsidiarity test

The test does not apply to Union action in areas where it enjoys exclusive competence; while these are now listed in Article 3 TFEU, the interpretation of this notion, and hence the scope of application of the subsidiarity test, are not entirely free from uncertainty.[118]

The first, negative, condition for Union action is that 'the objectives of the proposed action cannot be sufficiently achieved by the Member States, either at central level or at regional and local level' (the 'necessity test'). The legislature must assess the capacity of the Member States to achieve the particular (Union) objectives of the proposed action. In this context, it is not obliged to rely solely on the assessment put forward by its usual interlocutors, the national governments; in the 'wide consultations' which it carries out in preparing legislative proposals, the Commission must 'take into account the regional and local dimension of the action envisaged'.[119] Within their respective institutions, both members of the European Parliament and ministers of sub-national governments, such as those of the German Länder, who participate in the work of the Council may argue that the particular objectives can be better achieved at the Member State level. Where consulted, the Committee of the Regions will also be able to make a subsidiarity case against, or indeed for, Union action.

[116] See Case C-359/92 *Product safety* (n 65).
[117] Art 1, Protocol No 2 on the application of the principles of subsidiarity and proportionality.
[118] See section 5.4; the list of exclusive competences is set out at section 4.4.1.
[119] Art 2, Protocol No 2.

The second, positive, condition is that 'by reason of the scale or effects of the proposed action, [the Union objectives can] be better achieved at Union level'; in other words, the Union action would provide added value compared to action by the Member States acting individually.[120] It is difficult to see how this branch of the test would, in practice, operate as an autonomous impediment to Union action where the first branch of the test was satisfied. Where the 'scale or effects' of the action are shown to be too small or only minor, then the objectives can prima facie be achieved by the Member States at some level of government. On the other hand, where under the necessity test the Member States cannot achieve the Union objectives, it follows that these can be 'better achieved at Union level', unless it is shown that the objectives can be better achieved at a different, third, level, such as by means of an international agreement.[121]

It is also difficult to imagine, as a matter of law, a legislative initiative which would fully comply with the requirements of its legal basis, including the condition (which is part of the proportionality test) that the action be suitable to achieve the aims of the measure, but fail because the scale or effects would be either so small or so large that the particular objectives cannot be better achieved at Union level.[122]

5.2 **Protocol No 2: the 'early warning mechanism'**

The so-called 'early warning mechanism', with its suggestion of impending hostilities, is ostensibly designed to allow national parliaments to ensure Union legislation complies with the subsidiarity test. In the first stage, the national parliaments receive draft legislative acts, whatever the originating institution or body,[123] as well as the subsequently amended drafts; the drafts must be accompanied by a 'detailed statement making it possible to appraise compliance with the principles of subsidiarity and proportionality', including 'qualitative and wherever possible quantitative indicators', as well as certain other information, such as their financial impact and repercussions for the law of the Member States.[124]

The national parliaments, or in the case of bicameral parliaments, their component chambers, then have an eight-week period in which to produce a 'reasoned opinion' on why the draft fails to comply with the subsidiarity principle, which is sent to the Presidents of the European Parliament, the Council, and the Commission. In practice, the national parliamentary participants occasionally take a position on other matters than subsidiarity strictly so called, such as the choice of legal basis or even the existence of a Union competence in the first place.[125] In such cases, the initiator will only be obliged to respond to the parliamentary opinions which deal with subsidiarity; equally, only these opinions will count in verifying which, if any, threshold has been attained.

[120] European Commission, 'Annual Report 2015 on Subsidiarity and Proportionality', COM(2016) 469 final, 15 July 2016, 3.

[121] The Netherlands argued this point, unsuccessfully, in its challenge to the 1998 directive on biotechnological patents (n 74).

[122] For a critical view, see G Davies, 'Subsidiarity: The Wrong Idea, in the Wrong Place, at the Wrong Time' (2006) 43 *Common Market Law Review* 63.

[123] Both the ordinary and the special legislative procedures can be initiated in limited circumstances by institutions other than the Commission, or by a group of Member States; sections 7.1 and 7.2.

[124] Art 5, Protocol No 2; see generally A Cygan, '"Collective" Subsidiarity Monitoring by National Parliaments after Lisbon: The Operation of the Early Warning Mechanism' in M Trybus and L Rubini (eds), *The Treaty of Lisbon and the Future of European Law and Politics* (Cheltenham: Edward Elgar, 2012) 55.

[125] See eg the variety of views expressed on the 'Monti II' proposal, which triggered the first collective opinion: section 3, Commission, 'Annual Report 2012 on subsidiarity and proportionality', COM(2013) 566 final.

Reasoned opinions come in three varieties: the individual opinion, the collective opinion, and the special legislative opinion. The level of support for each type of opinion determines its formal impact on the legislative process. Each national parliament has two votes at its disposal, which are cast separately by the two chambers of a bicameral parliament or together by a unicameral parliament; in this context, the Luxembourg Chambre des députés and the Maltese Kamra tad-Deputati each wield double the voting power of the German Bundestag or the French Assemblée nationale.

5.2.1 **Opinion of individual parliaments or chambers**

The institutions are obliged to 'take account of' the reasoned opinions issued by an individual national parliament or chamber. In the absence of any indication to the contrary in the Treaty, however, they are not obliged to follow such opinion or take any further action.

5.2.2 **Collective opinion**

A collective opinion can only be adopted by at least one-third of the total votes (at present 18 out of 54); the threshold is lowered to a quarter of the votes (14) where the initiative falls within the area of freedom, security, and justice. In fact, the 'collective opinion' is not a single document but comprises the aggregate of the reasoned opinions of all the national parliamentary bodies which have concluded that the draft act does not comply with the subsidiarity test. Where the number of negative votes reaches the threshold, the draft legislation must be reviewed; however, after the review, the initiator of the draft act is free to maintain, amend, or withdraw it, though it must provide reasons for its decision.

5.2.3 **Special legislative opinion**

The national parliaments may adopt a special legislative opinion only when they are examining a Commission proposal under the ordinary legislative procedure; the threshold for adopting such an opinion is a simple majority of the total votes available (28). As before, the Commission may choose to maintain, amend, or withdraw the proposal. Where it maintains the proposal, it must once again explain, this time in light of the national parliaments' contrary positions, how the proposal complies with the subsidiarity test; the Commission's position, confusingly also called a 'reasoned opinion', and those of the national parliaments (including, presumably, any positive opinions), are referred to the European Parliament and the Council. The two branches of the legislature are obliged to take 'particular account'—presumably something more than 'account' *simpliciter*—of the various opinions washing around; where a majority of the members of the European Parliament who take part in the vote, or a 55 per cent majority of the members of the Council, reject the proposal for reasons of subsidiarity compliance, it is dead in the water.

5.3 **Scope of the early warning mechanism**

While trumpeted in Article 12(b) TEU as allowing the national parliaments to 'see . . . to it that the principle of subsidiarity is respected', the early warning mechanism is subject to a number of important limitations. In the first place, it only applies to legislation properly so called, excluding, in particular, measures adopted by an innominate non-legislative procedure, some of which are legislative in all but name, as well as delegated and implementing acts.[126] It is also limited to the initial proposal and amended versions of that proposal; it does not, therefore, allow the Member States' parliaments to examine, even briefly, the different preparatory acts which make their appearance later in the course

[126] See sections 7.3, 8.1, and 8.2 respectively.

of a legislative procedure. As noted elsewhere,[127] in the ordinary legislative procedure, the European Parliament and the Council no longer act on the basis of the Commission proposal after the first reading stage. Perhaps it is hoped that the legislature would nonetheless not ignore the views of the national parliaments during the remainder of the procedure.

Even where it applies, however, the mechanism appears to promise more than it delivers; at its strongest, there is no formal guarantee that the impact the community of national parliaments can make on a determined Union legislature is more than negligible. Under any scenario, the initiator can press on with its draft legislation; the requirement that it, and the legislature under the ordinary legislative procedure, provide reasons for doing so, or take account, or indeed 'particular account', of a contrary position does not appear to be a significant impediment to Union action, even where a large number of national parliaments oppose this on subsidiarity grounds. When faced with the first collective opinion in 2012, comprising 19 negative votes from 12 parliaments, the Commission maintained its view that the principle of subsidiarity had not been breached, but withdrew its proposal largely on the ground that this was 'unlikely to gather the necessary political support' in the legislature, particularly as the adoption of the proposed regulation would have required a unanimous vote in the Council.[128] The procedure was also applied in the case of the proposal to establish a European Public Prosecutor's Office, which provoked 18 negative votes from 13 parliaments.[129] This time the Commission stuck to its guns, issuing a robust defence of its proposal and of the sufficiency of the reasons it had provided to justify compliance with the subsidiary principle; the proposal was nonetheless adopted by 22 Member States under enhanced cooperation.[130] Likewise, the 14 reasoned opinions against the proposed amendment to the 1996 directive on posted workers did not prevent its adoption.[131]

In any case, the referral of the matter back to the legislature as a last resort may prove to be of little or no assistance to those who oppose the proposed measure. The provision that a majority of the votes cast in the European Parliament may kill off the proposal is, to all intents and purposes, the same rule as that which applies under Parliament's first reading in the ordinary legislative procedure.[132] Paradoxically, the voting requirement for the Council to block a proposal under the early warning mechanism may prove to be higher than the normal threshold; whereas the negative votes of 13 Member States are in principle sufficient to block a legislative proposal under the ordinary legislative procedure whatever the reasons for the minority's opposition, under Protocol No 2 the opposition of at least 15 Member States (55 per cent) to the proposed measure is required in order to prevent its adoption on the ground of non-compliance with the subsidiarity principle.[133] In other words, if it were ever to be applied, the voting rule in the Council would actually

[127] See section 7.1.1.

[128] Section 3, Commission, *Annual Report 2012 on subsidiarity and proportionality* (n 125). The subject matter of the proposal, the relationship in EU law between economic freedoms and the right to strike, was in any case highly controversial; see F Fabbrini and K Granat, 'Yellow Card But No Foul' (2013) 50 *Common Market Law Review* 115.

[129] Proposal, COM(2013) 534 final, 17 July 2013; reasoned opinions, 'Annual Report 2013 on subsidiarity and proportionality', COM(2014) 506 final, 5 August 2014.

[130] Communication COM(2013) 851 final, 27 November 2013 and Council Regulation (EU) 2017/1939 (n 284); see A Csúri, 'The Proposed European Public Prosecutor's Office: From a Trojan Horse to a White Elephant' (2016) 18 *Cambridge Yearbook of European Legal Studies* 122, and chapter 24.

[131] Directive (EU) 2018/957 (OJ [2018] L173/16).

[132] See Arts 294(3) and 231 TFEU, and section 7.1.1.

[133] Respectively Art 238(3)(a) TFEU (if the number includes the minimum number of Member States representing 35 per cent of the Union's population, plus one) and Art 7(3)(b), Protocol No 2.

make it more difficult for the Council to oppose a measure on subsidiarity grounds than for any other reason. The number of reasoned opinions appears to fluctuate significantly from year to year, though not necessarily in function of the number of Commission proposals presented.[134]

Bringing the national parliaments in on the act of adopting Union legislation might, at first blush, appear like a useful idea which strikes another blow for democratic decision-making. A slightly less charitable view would be that the prime utility of the early warning mechanism is to ensure that the national parliaments are informed about forthcoming Union legislation, to enable them to influence the position their own minister and her officials will be defending in Brussels, should they choose to do so. The question then arises as to why a set of Treaty provisions was required in order to regulate relations between the national governments and the national parliaments to which they are, at least according to Article 10(2) TEU, 'democratically accountable'. Might not this particular objective have been better achieved by the Member States acting individually?

5.4 **Judicial review of compliance with the subsidiarity test**

By including a subsidiarity test in the Treaty as a general principle, the Member States clearly intended respect for this principle to be justiciable, despite the highly political character of the questions it raises—in particular, the respective capacity of the Union and the Member States (at different levels of government) to achieve defined policy objectives. Perhaps for this reason, some of the Member States which were among the keenest supporters of subsidiarity at the time of its incorporation into the Union legal order themselves hesitated to rely on a substantive breach of this principle when challenging legislation on which they had been outvoted; instead they preferred to plead that the legislature had failed to explain how the principle had been respected in the given case, or that a particular legal basis should be interpreted in light of the requirements of subsidiarity.[135] In any case, the Court reviews compliance with both 'the substantive conditions set out in Article 5(3) TEU and . . . the procedural safeguards provided for by [the] Protocol'.[136]

One of the most keenly argued questions has been whether, and if so how, the subsidiary test applies in the context of the adoption of internal market measures. In the *Working Time* case, the Court had held that once the legislature had found it was necessary to pursue a particular (here, social policy) objective, 'achievement of that objective . . . necessarily presupposes Community-wide action'.[137] This was interpreted in some quarters as indicating that the principle of subsidiarity did not apply to internal market measures, on the ground that 'the Member States simply cannot harmonise each other's laws, regulations or administrative action in fields which come within the scope of application of the Treaty'.[138] At first, the Court appeared to rally to this view, noting in

[134] See https://ec.europa.eu/info/law/law-making-process/adopting-eu-law/relations-national-parliaments/annual-reports-application-principles-subsidiarity-and-proportionality-and-relations-national-parliaments_en.

[135] Case C-426/93 *Germany v Parliament and Council* (*Business register for statistical purposes*), EU:C:1995:367; Case C-84/94 *UK v Council* (*Working time*), EU:C:1996:431.

[136] Case C-358/14 *Menthol cigarettes* (n 89) para 113; on the case law generally, see D Wyatt, 'Is the European Union an Organisation of Limited Powers' in A Arnull et al (eds), *A Constitutional Order of States? Essays in EU Law in Honour of Alan Dashwood* (Oxford: Hart Publishing, 2011) 3.

[137] Case C-84/94 *Working time* (n 135).

[138] Opinion of AG Fennelly in '*Tobacco advertising I*', EU:C:2000:234, para 136; R Schütze, 'Dual Federalism Constitutionalised: The Emergence of Exclusive Competences in the EC Legal Order' (2007) 32 *European Law Review* 3, 522.

the *Biotechnological Patent* case that harmonization in this area 'could not be achieved by action taken by the Member States alone'.[139]

However, in *British American Tobacco*, the Court clarified that, as the Union does not have exclusive competence to regulate economic activity on the internal market, the principle of subsidiarity applies to measures in this area, before examining 'whether the objective of the proposed action could be better achieved at [Union] level'.[140] The Court noted that the objectives of the contested directive 'cannot be sufficiently achieved by the Member States individually' and that '[it] follows that . . . the objective of the proposed action could be better achieved at [Union] level'.[141] In *Vodafone*, on the other hand, the Court concluded that the objectives of the contested regulation 'could be best achieved at [Union] level', not because of the Member States' inability to achieve those objectives but 'by reason of the [Union-wide] effects of the . . . approach laid down in [the] Regulation'.[142] The Court therefore appears to favour a single test, 'better achievement at the Union level', though taking account of both the positive and the negative elements of the test as formulated in Article 5(3) TEU.

Where a measure seeks to achieve two interdependent objectives, the fact that one of these can be better achieved at Member State level is not sufficient to show a breach of the principle of subsidiarity. Equally, '[t]he subsidiarity principle is not intended to limit the EU's competence on the basis of the situation of any particular Member State taken individually, but requires only that the proposed action can, by reason of its scale or effects, be better achieved at EU level, given [the Union's] objectives' and competences.[143]

The setting up of the early warning mechanism described earlier was accompanied by special provisions on judicial review at the suit of the national parliaments, restricted *ratione materiae* to alleged breaches of the subsidiarity principle. Such proceedings are merely 'notified' by the national government on behalf of the parliament or chamber 'in accordance with their legal order'.[144] Some of the Member States allow a minority in the national parliament or chamber to initiate such actions; this is clearly consistent with the logic of the special provision, as a parliamentary majority would in any case be able to force the government to bring a normal annulment action act under Article 263 TFEU. Where the Committee of the Regions must be consulted on a particular proposal for legislation, it may under Article 8 of Protocol No 2 also challenge on subsidiarity grounds the act subsequently adopted.

6 **Proportionality**

Though first incorporated into the Treaty as a generally applicable principle at the same time as subsidiarity, the proportionality requirement had long been recognized as a legal constraint on legislative and administrative action.[145] According to Article 5(4) TEU

[139] Judgment in *Biotechnological patents* (n 74) para 32.

[140] Case C-491/01 *British American Tobacco* (*BAT*), EU:C:2002:741, para 180; see also Art 114(4)–(8) and (10) TFEU, acknowledging and regulating the Member States' right to legislate in a particular area which has already been harmonized by internal market legislation.

[141] Case C-491/01 *BAT* (n 140) paras 182 and 183.

[142] Case C-58/08 *Vodafone* (n 74) para 78; see case study 5.1.

[143] Case C-508/13 *Estonia v Parliament and Council*, EU:C:2015:403, respectively paras 47 and 48, and 53.

[144] See Case C-553/24 *Assemblée nationale v Parliament and Council* (pending). The Dutch government had led the way well before the Lisbon Treaty in the *Biotechnological patents* case, which it initiated at the behest of the lower house of parliament (n 74).

[145] The Court's case law on the application of the principle of proportionality is correspondingly vast; for an overview, see eg Case C-482/17 *Gun control* (n 47) paras 76–93.

'[the] content and form of Union action shall not exceed what is necessary to achieve the objectives of the Treaties'.

The Union Courts exercise only a marginal review of respect for the proportionality principle in the context of legislation; they are not the judges of the expediency of a measure.[146] The legislature enjoys wide discretion, as it must make political, economic, and social choices on the basis of complex assessments. Its discretion includes 'to some extent, the finding of the basic facts' as well as the content of measures it adopts.[147] That said, the legislature must base its choice on objective criteria and seek to minimize any substantial negative burdens on economic operators; to this end, the institutions 'must at the very least be able to produce and set out . . . the basic facts' on which they relied.[148] Relying on the interinstitutional Better Law-Making Agreement, the Court has held that as a rule an impact assessment should be carried out; however, failure to do so does not violate the principle of proportionality 'where the EU legislature is in a particular situation requiring it to be dispensed with and has sufficient information enabling it to assess the proportionality of an adopted measure'.[149] In the *Spanish cotton subsidies* case, for example, the Court found that by omitting to calculate labour costs in cotton production, the Council had not taken all the relevant factors into account as it was required to in order to achieve the objectives of the regulation, and had hence failed to comply with the principle of proportionality.[150] The principle of proportionality plays a particularly important role in challenges to legislation on grounds of failure to respect fundamental rights.[151]

In order to show that the principle of proportionality has not been respected in these circumstances, a party would have to demonstrate either that the objective of the measure was not one the legislature could pursue under the Treaty, or that 'the measure was manifestly inappropriate having regard to the objective': it is not necessary that this be 'the only or best possible measure'.[152] The Court may thus be led to quite a concrete examination of other possible policy solutions, and an evaluation of whether the solutions chosen are appropriate to achieve the measure's objectives, and do not go beyond what is required to achieve those objectives. In *British American Tobacco*, for example, the Court had to rule on the validity of a ban on the manufacture within the Union of cigarettes for export to third States, where the cigarettes did not comply with the standards set by the legislation for sale within the Union.[153] The Court found that the legislature could validly take the view that the ban was a more efficient means to combat illegal trafficking in cigarettes than the mere reinforcement of import controls.

As with subsidiarity, each of the institutions is duty-bound to 'ensure constant respect' for the principle of proportionality, which respect must be justified in a 'detailed statement' accompanying draft legislative acts; the Commission considers proportionality, along with subsidiarity, to be 'core elements of [its] better regulation agenda which underpins how [it] prepares its policy proposals'.[154] However, the principle of proportionality does not benefit from the same early warning mechanism or special provisions on judicial review as subsidiarity.

[146] Case C-157/21 *Conditionality* (n 2) para 136.

[147] Agreement on Better Law-Making (n 44); Case C-482/17 *Gun control* (n 47) para 84; see generally A Meuwese, *Impact Assessments in EU Lawmaking* (The Hague: Kluwer Law International, 2006).

[148] Case C-482/17 *Gun control* (n 47) paras 79–81.

[149] Ibid, paras 84 and 85, and *Atmospheric pollutants* (n 18) para 31.

[150] Case C-310/04 *Spain v Council* (*Spanish cotton subsidies*), EU:C:2006:521.

[151] Case C-694/20 *Orde van Vlaamse Balies*, EU:C:2022:963.

[152] Case C-157/21 *Conditionality* (n 2) para 354.

[153] Case C-482/17 *Gun control* (n 47) paras 122–141.

[154] Respectively Art 5, Protocol No 2, and Commission Communication on 'The principles of subsidiarity and proportionality: Strengthening their role in the EU's policymaking', COM(2018) 703 final, Brussels, 23 October 2018.

Case study 5.1: Vodafone

The 2007 Roaming Regulation[155] brought down the prices paid by consumers for mobile phone calls made or received in a Member State other than their home Member State ('roaming') by putting a cap on both wholesale prices—that is, those charged by the foreign host network operator to the customer's home provider, and retail prices, that is, those charged to the customer by his home provider for roaming calls. The Regulation was challenged in the UK courts by a number of mobile phone operators on the grounds that it was founded on an incorrect legal basis and that it breached the principles of subsidiarity and proportionality.[156]

The Court of Justice first restated the fundamental tenets of its case law on recourse to the internal market legal basis:

- the object of the measure must be genuinely to improve the conditions for the establishment and functioning of the internal market;
- the legislature may only act where the differences in the national rules are such as to obstruct the fundamental freedoms and have a direct and appreciable effect on the functioning of the internal market in goods and services, or where such differences are likely to emerge;
- the legislature may amend existing internal market legislation to take account of a change in circumstances or the development of knowledge;
- the legislature enjoys a discretion, depending on the general context and the specific circumstances of the matter to be harmonized, as regards the method of approximation of national laws;
- provided that the conditions for using the internal market legal basis are fulfilled, the fact that other considerations (here consumer protection) may be decisive does not prevent the legislature's relying on that legal basis.[157]

The Court noted the 'unique characteristics of the roaming markets', and in particular the fact that retail prices were excessive compared to the costs of providing the service, because of the high wholesale charges levied by the foreign host providers and the high retail mark-ups charged by the home provider. The individual national regulatory authorities had no means of controlling the wholesale prices of operators in other Member States, and in order to bring consumer prices down were likely to fix retail prices, which would lead to divergent national laws and distortions of the conditions of competition. In these circumstances, the adoption of a 'single coherent regulatory framework' was justified with a view to maintaining competition among operators of mobile networks.[158]

The Court's reasoning on recourse to the internal market legal basis largely dealt with the question of subsidiarity too. Given the interdependence between wholesale and retail charges, the Court found that 'reduc[ing] retail charges alone without affecting the level of costs for the wholesale supply of Community-wide roaming services would have been liable to disrupt the smooth functioning of the Community-wide roaming market'. 'Thus,' continued the Court, 'by reason of the effects of the common approach laid down by [the] Regulation . . . the objective pursued by that regulation could best be achieved at Community level.'[159]

[155] Regulation 717/2007 (OJ [2007] L171/32); this has now been replaced by Regulation 2022/612 (OJ [2022] L115/1).

[156] Case C-58/08 *Vodafone* (n 74).

[157] Ibid, paras 32–36.

[158] Ibid, paras 42 and 38 respectively.

[159] Ibid, paras 77 and 78.

As to proportionality, the legislature's wide discretion means that the criterion of legality is not whether the measure adopted was the best possible measure, but whether it is 'manifestly inappropriate having regard to the objective which the competent institution is seeking to pursue'. The legislature must nonetheless base its choice on objective criteria and evaluate 'whether the objectives pursued by the measure chosen are such as to justify even substantial negative economic consequences for certain operators'.[160]

The main issue as regards proportionality was whether consumer prices could have been brought down by imposing ceilings on wholesale charges only. The Court noted that the average retail charge for a roaming call was more than five times the cost of providing the wholesale service; setting a common ceiling on retail charges was obviously appropriate as a means of bringing these charges down. As to the necessity of capping retail as well as wholesale charges, the Court noted that in effect the only competition on retail prices took place in the form of complete retail packages, of which the rates of roaming charges were a minor element. This meant that there was no competitive pressure on operators to pass on to consumers any reduction in wholesale charges which would result from the setting of a ceiling on these charges alone; as a result, capping wholesale charges would not have had any effect on retail prices, which are those the consumer pays. In these circumstances, the legislature was entitled directly to set ceilings on retail prices as well, particularly as the system was limited in time and applied to a market which was subject to competition.

The *Vodafone* case is a textbook example of a substantive challenge to a controversial policy measure adopted by the Union legislature. Given the inherently cross-border character of the activity being regulated, and the practical impossibility for the national regulators to deal with the problem of high consumer prices without dividing up the market in roaming services into Member State blocks, the Court had little difficulty in finding that the Regulation was correctly classified as an internal market measure and that it passed the subsidiarity test. Respect for proportionality did not detain the Court very long either, though it did check that the institutions had studied the existing market conditions thoroughly and had considered other possibilities of dealing with the problem, such as regulating wholesale prices only or retail prices only. The Court also noted the impact that the Regulation could have on mobile phone operators. It is not surprising, however, that the operators' interest in charging customers five times the actual cost of providing a roaming service did not weigh heavily in the balance.

7 Legislative and other decision-making procedures

Decision-making procedures are the means by which the Union exercises its competences in a given case. The procedure, which is dictated by the legal basis of the act,[161] determines precisely the degree of formal influence each institutional actor (institution or consultative body, Member State government or parliament) may exercise on the outcome. Formal influence is, of course, not the full story, but other aspects of that story fall outside the compass of the present chapter.

Union law makes an explicit distinction between 'legislation' and other forms of normative act, and between primary and secondary normative measures. 'Legislation' refers to any act adopted on the basis of a procedure identified in the Treaty legal basis as being a legislative procedure, either 'ordinary' or 'special'; the fact that the European Parliament participates in a decision-making procedure not explicitly so described does not make that

[160] Ibid, paras 52 and 53, judgment.

[161] See section 4.3.

procedure 'legislative'.[162] Legislation is necessarily adopted in public, and the Court has held that 'it is precisely openness in the legislative process that contributes to conferring greater legitimacy on the institutions in the eyes of EU citizens and increasing their confidence in them by allowing divergences between various points of view to be openly debated'.[163] The distinction between legislative and non-legislative acts is important in other respects as well, notably as regards the participation of national parliaments.[164] Moreover, under long-standing constitutional doctrine, the legislature must lay down the 'essential elements of the matter to be dealt with', and may not delegate the power to regulate these elements.[165]

A certain number of normative acts are adopted directly on the basis of Treaty provisions by procedures not described as 'legislative'.[166] Normative measures which are based on enabling provisions contained in acts of secondary law (adopted on the basis of legislative and assimilated procedures) take the form of 'delegated' or 'implementing' acts.[167]

7.1 **Legislative and assimilated procedures**

These are of three kinds: the ordinary legislative procedure (OLP), the special legislative procedures (SLPs), and the various innominate non-legislative procedures (INPs). Of these, the OLP is by far the most important in practical terms, as it applies for the adoption of the bulk of the Union's policy measures.

7.1.1 **The ordinary legislative procedure**

The details of the OLP are set out in Article 294 TFEU.[168] Subject to a number of important, if limited, exceptions, the procedure may only be initiated by the Commission's submitting a proposal.[169] The Commission's right of initiative is 'inextricably linked' to its task of promoting the general interest of the Union in accordance with Article 17(1) TEU.[170] As this prerogative 'reflects the principle of conferred powers . . . and more broadly, the principle of institutional balance', the Commission alone decides whether or not to propose a legislative act, and cannot be constrained in the exercise of its discretion by conclusions of the European Council.[171] The Commission may be invited to submit legislative proposals by the European Parliament, by the Council, or by a million citizens from a minimum of a quarter of the Member States (7);[172] though not obliged to respond favourably, in each case the Commission must explain its reasons for not so doing.

The term 'proposal' is a term of art, which carries certain legal consequences, notably for the position of the Commission.[173] Prior to submitting proposals, the Commission

[162] Joined Cases C-643/15 and C-647/15 *Slovak Republic and Hungary v Council* (*International protection*), EU:C:2017:631, paras 59–63.

[163] Art 289(3) TFEU and Case T-540/15 *De Capitani v Parliament*, EU:T:2018:167, para 78.

[164] See respectively sections 8 and 5.2.

[165] Case 25/70 *Köster*, EU:C:1970:115; see now Art 290(1) TFEU, Case C-355/10 *Parliament v Council* (*Frontex*), EU:C: 2012:516, and section 8.1.

[166] See section 7.3. [167] See section 8.

[168] Both Parliament and the Council have published helpful guides to the OLP on their respective websites, including in each case lists of the articles to which the OLP applies and diagrams on how the procedure operates: www.europarl.europa.eu/ordinary-legislative-procedure/en/home, and www.consilium.europa.eu/en/documents-publications/publications/guide-ordinary-legislative-procedure.

[169] Art 17(2) TEU; the Commission may also take other forms of initiative (Art 17(1) TEU).

[170] Case C-24/20 *Commission v Council* (*Geneva Act*) (n 13) para 88.

[171] Case C-643/15 *International protection* (n 162) para 145; see also Case C-928/19 P *EPSU and Goudriaan v Commission*, EU:2021:656, para 48.

[172] Respectively Arts 225 and 241 TFEU and Art 11(4) TEU; see section 11.3.

[173] The reference to a European Parliament 'proposal' in the English-language version of Art 223(1) TFEU is anomalous; the French version correctly uses the term '*projet*' (draft).

is obliged to 'carry out broad consultations with parties concerned in order to ensure that the Union's actions are coherent and transparent', under the 'democratic principles' which govern 'all its activities'. More generally, in common with the other institutions, the Commission is obliged to engage with citizens and representative associations, and 'maintain an open, transparent and regular dialogue with representative associations and civil society'.[174]

Having initiated the OLP, the Commission may amend its proposal 'at any time during the procedure leading to the adoption of a Union act', as long as the Council has not acted;[175] this allows the Commission to modify its initial proposal to garner the support of a qualified majority which has emerged in the Council discussions.[176] Moreover, where the Council does not accept Parliament's first reading position, the Commission makes known its position on the state of play; this allows it the opportunity to suggest a compromise which the other two participants might accept, or at least a policy measure in line with its own thinking. The Commission's right to amend its proposal in effect disappears, however, after the first reading once the Council has acted.[177] Subsequent readings take as their subject matter 'the Council's position' (on first reading), the 'European Parliament's amendments' (on second reading), 'the positions of the European Parliament and the Council at second reading' (in conciliation), and 'the joint text' (on third reading). Thus, in the OLP, the Commission may only alter its proposal before the Council's first reading, though, of course, the rule is fully applicable to the adoption of Council acts under other procedures.

This does not mean that the Commission is excluded from the procedure after the first reading. On second reading, the Council must act unanimously, rather than by a qualified majority, if it wishes to adopt a European Parliament amendment on which the Commission has given a negative opinion. The Commission takes part in the proceedings of any conciliation committee convened to prepare for a third reading and, in practice, in any informal negotiations, where its expertise is often appreciated, particularly where it facilitates agreement between the principal parties.

Institutions and bodies other than the Commission may initiate the OLP where the Treaty so provides, essentially in areas of their special competence. The Court of Justice may propose amendments to its Statute, except regarding the status of its members and the Court's language regime.[178] In March 2011, for example, the Court proposed amendments which eventually led to the doubling of the number of judges of the General Court and the abolition of the Civil Service Tribunal.[179] The European Central Bank may submit recommendations for the amendment, under the OLP, of various provisions of the Statute of the European System of Central Banks and of the European Central Bank.[180]

Legislative measures in the field of judicial cooperation in criminal matters and police cooperation may be initiated by a quarter (7) of the Member States, or by the Commission. While this situation may appear somewhat anomalous, given the inclusion of this policy field within the general regime of Union decision-making, it still represents an advance

[174] Arts 11(3) and 9 TEU respectively; see also section 11. [175] Art 293(2) TFEU.

[176] Opinion of AG Lenz in Case 45/86 *1986 GSP* (n 75) para 32.

[177] Art 294(3) TFEU and Case C-409/13 *Macro-financial Assistance* (n 13).

[178] Art 281, second para, TFEU.

[179] Respectively Regulation (EU, Euratom) 2015/2422 (OJ [2015] L341/14) and Regulation (EU, Euratom) 2016/1192 (OJ [2016] L200/137). See A Cartier-Bresson and D Bugny, *Les réformes de la Cour de justice: Bilan et Perspectives* (Brussels: Editions Bruylant, 2020).

[180] See Art 40(1) of that Statute; the rules on voting in the Bank's Governing Council may be amended, on a recommendation of the Bank, by the European Council, though the amendment is subject to national ratification (Art 40(2)).

on the pre-Lisbon position, where any single Member State, or all of them individually, could initiate such measures.

Where the OLP is not initiated by the Commission, Parliament's first reading takes place on the basis of an 'initiative' (of the Member States), a 'request' (from the Court of Justice), or a 'recommendation' (from the European Central Bank). The OLP is brought to a close in all cases by the signature of the legislative act by the Presidents of the European Parliament and the Council.[181]

Two related Treaty rules are important in this context for the protection of the Commission's position: the Council acts by a qualified majority unless the Treaty provides otherwise and, except in very limited circumstances, it may only amend a Commission proposal if acting unanimously.[182] This latter safeguard applies in respect of acts in the field of the Union's external action as well as its internal action.[183] The Council would not be obliged to follow the position proposed by the Commission where this is not in conformity with international law.[184]

In essence, the adoption of a legislative act under the OLP requires the complete agreement of the European Parliament and the Council on a text, which agreement may be reached in a number of different ways: Council approval of Parliament's first reading position, mutual acceptance by Parliament and the Council of each other's amendments on second reading, or the convening of a conciliation committee of equal numbers of members of each institution to hammer out a joint text which the two institutions approve on third reading.

Each of the institutions can prevent the adoption of the legislation proposed, at different stages of the procedure. The Commission's power to submit a proposal, and to determine its subject matter, objective, and content, includes a concomitant power to withdraw it 'as long as the Council has not acted'; the Commission is not restricted thereafter to merely assisting the legislature to adopt the act proposed. The Court has held that this is not a right of veto, in that the Commission must provide reasons for the withdrawal decision 'supported by cogent evidence or arguments', which is then amenable to judicial review.[185] In particular, the fact that the legislature intends to adopt an act which would prevent the achievement of the objectives of the Commission proposal justifies its withdrawal. Equally, a first reading rejection of the proposal by Parliament, which only requires a majority of the members voting, could in turn be refused by the Council; in these circumstances, Parliament would require a vote by a majority of its component members, rather than a simple majority, to prevent the adoption of the legislation, though in practice it would not be difficult to achieve this level of parliamentary support for reasons of institutional pride, whatever the merits of the proposal.

In practice, a large proportion of such legislative acts are adopted in first reading, on the basis of a text negotiated between the parliamentary committee, represented by its rapporteur, and the Council formation responsible, represented by its president, in informal 'trilogue' meetings, with the Commission making up the threesome.[186]

In accordance with the principle of sincere cooperation of Article 4(3) TEU, Member States also have rights to participate in the legislative process, and in particular the right of access to the information on which the legislature bases its decision, the right to be

[181] Art 297(1), second para, TFEU. [182] Arts 16(3) TEU and 293(1) TFEU respectively.

[183] Case C-24/20 *Commission v Council* (*Geneva Act*) (n 13) para 79.

[184] Case C-161/20 *Commission v Council (IMO)*, EU:C:2022:260; the position here was a proposed 'submission' to an international organization rather than a legislative proposal.

[185] *Macro-financial Assistance* (n 13).

[186] See generally the *Joint Declaration on practical arrangements for the co-decision procedure adopted by the European Parliament, the Council, and the Commission* of 13 June 2007 (OJ [2007] C145/5), and Case T-540/15 *De Capitani v Parliament* (n 163) para 68.

heard during the procedure, and the right to a statement of the basic facts the legislature has taken into account.[187] The adoption of a legislative act against the wishes of a Member State does not contravene the duty of sincere cooperation.

7.1.2 **'Emergency brakes'**

For the adoption of three categories of measure, a supplementary procedure grafted on the OLP allows a single Member State to call a 'time out' during the adoption procedure, and have the question referred to the European Council for a period for reflection. This so-called 'emergency brake' may only be applied if the Member State considers that the legislation being proposed would affect 'important' or 'fundamental' aspects of its existing national system.[188] In the area of social security for those who have worked in other Member States, the European Council may block the adoption of the legislation either by taking no action or requesting the Commission to submit a new proposal.[189] The equivalent provisions in certain areas of criminal justice appear to be even more intrusive, in that the European Council may only refer the draft back to the Council for the OLP to continue 'in case of a consensus'; in such cases, however, it is specified that a group of at least nine Member States may go ahead with the proposal on the basis of enhanced cooperation.[190] There is no evidence that the emergency brake mechanism is widely used, though its very existence may influence legislative debate in the Council.[191]

The Court has also acknowledged that where it is considering a mixed agreement, the Council may seek the 'common accord' of the Member States, where this is justified by 'institutional and political considerations liable to affect the perceived legitimacy and effectiveness' of the Union's action, though it may not make the conclusion of the agreement 'contingent on the prior establishment of such a "common accord"'.[192]

7.2 **Special legislative procedures**

There is no single special legislative procedure (SLP), but a wide variety of such procedures which differ as regards who can initiate the procedure, who participates in the procedure, and what voting rules apply. While this plethora of procedural permutations detracts from the legibility of the Treaty, each SLP is in fact restricted to a specific area of policy or institutional decision.

A large majority of SLPs are derogations from the application of the OLP in a particular area, to take account of national sensibilities of different kinds (notably political, budgetary, economic, and social). Thus, for example, measures to facilitate the exercise of the right to free movement of citizens are adopted under the OLP, with the exception of those concerning social security and social protection, for which an SLP applies.[193] Similarly, while measures on judicial cooperation in civil matters are generally subject to the OLP, those concerning family law with cross-border implications are subject to an SLP.[194] In these 'derogation' cases, the SLP is initiated by a Commission proposal, the European Parliament is consulted, and the Council adopts the legislative act by unanimous vote.

[187] Case C-128/19 *Atmospheric pollutants* (n 18) paras 66–76.

[188] This mechanism appears to be a revenant of the 1966 Luxembourg Compromise.

[189] Art 48(2) TFEU.

[190] Arts 82(3) and 83(3) TFEU. On enhanced cooperation, see section 9.

[191] J Öberg, 'Exit, Voice and Consensus: A Legal and Political Analysis of the Emergency Brake in EU Criminal Law', *European Law Blog*, 11 October 2021.

[192] Opinion 1/19, *Istanbul Convention*, EU:C:2021:198, paras 254 and 249. Three Member State governments had stated their intention not to ratify the Convention.

[193] Art 21(2) and (3) TFEU.

[194] Art 81(2) and (3) TFEU.

In other areas, Parliament may be asked for its consent to a Council measure—for example, on Union action to combat discrimination on grounds other than nationality where no more specific legal bases are available, or on certain decisions which have an impact on the Union's budget such as measures implementing the own resources decision, and the regulation establishing the multi-annual financial framework.[195] The combination of consent and an SLP does not 'effectively amount[ ] to codecision between the Council and the Parliament'.[196]

Parliament may itself both initiate and adopt legislative measures on most matters concerning its own functioning (though not its seat or working places), or within its specific responsibility (eg the Statute of Ombudsman), by means of a special legislative procedure, with the Commission giving an opinion and subject to the consent of the Council.[197] The Union budget is adopted under a somewhat complex special legislative procedure.[198] Similarly, the European Investment Bank may initiate the procedure for the amendment of its own Statute, a right it shares with the Commission.[199]

7.3 **Innominate non-legislative procedures**

A number of normative measures are adopted directly on the basis of the Treaty in accordance with procedures which are not described as being 'legislative'; these may be dubbed 'innominate non-legislative procedures' (INPs). The procedural requirements tend to be minimal; in many cases, the Council adopts the measure by a qualified majority on the basis of a Commission proposal, often without any participation of the European Parliament or at most after requesting its opinion. In some cases, the measures might arguably be considered executive in character, such as the fixing of agricultural prices and fishing quotas; in others, the exclusion of the OLP is more difficult to justify, such as the adoption of rules on private and public sector competition.[200] The latter examples may reflect nothing more than an unwillingness to change an institutional arrangement which is as old as the Treaty of Rome itself. Certain emergency measures may be adopted by an INP—for example, where a Member State is suffering from difficulties in obtaining oil supplies or from a sudden influx of third-country nationals.[201]

An INP may be required by derogation from the OLP for the adoption of particularly sensitive measures in a 'normal' policy field—for example, recommendations in some areas of ancillary competence,[202] as well as for the adoption of a small number of decisions in the area of economic and monetary union, or decisions with a foreign policy aspect.[203] Thus, for example, the rules on personal data protection in the foreign policy domain are laid down by the Council, apparently acting without a Commission proposal or any participation of the European Parliament, whereas the general data protection provisions are adopted under an OLP.[204] An act adopted under an INP may even, in effect,

[195] Respectively Arts 19(1), 311, fourth para, and 312(2) TFEU.

[196] Case C-24/20 *Commission v Council* (*Geneva Act*) (n 13) paras 39 and 42–45; the 'codecision' procedure had been abolished more than a decade previously.

[197] eg Arts 223(2), 226, third para, and 228(4) TFEU.

[198] Art 314 TFEU; see also Case C-77/11 *Council v Parliament*, EU:C:2013:559.

[199] Art 308, third para, TFEU.

[200] Respectively Art 43(3) TFEU and Arts 103(1) and 109 TFEU (and in the field of transport, Art 95(3) TFEU).

[201] Respectively Arts 122(1) and 78(3) TFEU.

[202] See eg Arts 167(6) and 168(6) TFEU, on culture and public health respectively.

[203] Respectively Art 121(2) and (4) TFEU, and Arts 26(2) and 29 TEU.

[204] See respectively Arts 39 TEU and 16 TFEU.

allow for a minor amendment of the Treaty.[205] The European Council, the Commission, and the European Central Bank also adopt measures directly on the basis of the Treaty in a small number of instances.[206]

The character of INP acts is best illustrated by the dividing line between the agricultural policy measures the legislature adopts on the basis of Article 43(2) TFEU, and the fixing of agricultural prices and similar measures which the Council adopts on the basis of Article 43(3) TFEU. The former entail a policy decision which is reserved to the legislature, while the latter are 'of a primarily technical nature and are intended to be taken in order to implement [legislative] provisions'.[207] Each of these legal bases has a specific field of application and may hence be used separately for measures under the common agricultural policy. Such INP measures are not to be assimilated to 'implementing acts' adopted under Article 291 TFEU; provided they do not entail a policy choice, they may do more than merely fix prices or allocate fishing opportunities.[208] Just as the Council may not encroach on the legislature's powers under Article 43(2) TFEU, the legislature may not encroach on the powers reserved to the Council to adopt INPs under Article 43(3) TFEU.[209]

Provided it complies with the limitations laid down in its own legal basis, an act adopted under an INP may derogate from a legislative act governing the same matter.[210]

7.4 **Consultation and assimilated requirements**

The consultation of different institutions and ancillary bodies, particularly the European Parliament, the Economic and Social Committee, and the Committee of the Regions, may be required in the context of an SLP or INP, or (obviously excluding Parliament) in the first reading of the OLP. The content of the opinion provided does not bind the institution(s) participating in the decision-making procedure, but consultation is a substantive procedural requirement, the breach of which justifies the annulment of the act, except where the Court considers that the institution being consulted contributed to the breach of such requirement.[211] The Court has held that the reliance by the Council on a legal basis which provided for voluntary, rather than obligatory, consultation of Parliament was a purely formal defect if the Council had in fact consulted Parliament, unless it is 'shown that the Council's error prevented the effective participation of the Parliament in the procedure in question or interfered with the conditions in which the Parliament performs its duties'.[212]

Parliament must be 'immediately and fully informed at all stages of the procedure' for negotiating and concluding international agreements, including those relating exclusively to the CFSP.[213] The rationale of the requirement is to allow Parliament to exercise democratic control over the Union's external action and exercise its own powers in

[205] See eg Art 83(1), third subpara, TFEU, authorizing the Council to add to the material scope of the Union's competences to define certain criminal offences and sanctions.

[206] See respectively Art 14(2), second para, TEU; Arts 45(3)(d), 105(3), 106(3), and 108(4) TFEU; and Art 132(1) TFEU.

[207] See case study 5.2, and Joined Cases C-124/13 and C-125/13 *Parliament and Commission v Council*, EU:C:2015:790.

[208] Ibid, paras 52 and 59; see also section 8.2.

[209] Case C-113/14 *Germany v Parliament and Council*, EU:C:2016:635; acting in its capacity as a branch of the bicephalous legislature, the Council had in effect encroached on its own autonomous powers, and was only 'saved' by the action of a Member State.

[210] Case C-482/17 *Gun control* (n 47) para 78.

[211] See, as regards the European Parliament, Cases 138/79 *Roquette Frères v Council* (*Isoglucose*), EU:C:1980:249, and C-65/93 *Parliament v Council* (*1993 GSP*), EU:C:1995:91.

[212] Case C-363/14 *Parliament v Council* (*Europol agreements*), EU:C:2015:579, respectively paras 96 and 91.

[213] Art 218(10) TFEU.

full knowledge of such action, and in particular to verify the choice of legal basis.[214] The Council (rather than the Union's High Representative for Foreign Affairs and Security Policy, who is a member of the Commission) must therefore inform Parliament on the progress of negotiations; it is not enough to do so only when these are commenced and concluded. The publication of the decision on the signature of an agreement in the *Official Journal* does not remedy the Council's failure to keep Parliament informed. An information requirement applies in a handful of areas within the general regime (as distinct from the CFSP).[215]

8 Delegated and implementing acts

8.1 Notion of 'delegated acts'

'Delegated act' is a term of art in EU law, designating the particular type of measures which the Commission adopts in accordance with the conditions laid down in Article 290 TFEU; it must be so designated in its title. They are 'non-legislative acts of general application which supplement or amend non-essential aspects of the legislative act' or, in pre-Lisbon jargon, 'quasi-legislative' measures. Delegated acts lay down provisions which the legislature itself could in principle have adopted but in respect of which it has chosen for different reasons—complexity of the subject matter, need to take account of changing conditions, etc—to delegate the power to adopt to the Commission. Such delegation 'aims to enable the legislature to focus on the essential elements of a piece of legislation and the non-essential elements in respect of which it deems it appropriate to legislate'.[216]

A delegated act may therefore not regulate the 'essential elements' of a matter under consideration, that is those involving political choices.[217] A delegated act may 'amend or supplement' a basic (legislative) act; the 'purpose of granting a delegated power is to achieve the adoption of rules coming within the regulatory framework as defined by the basic legislative act'.[218] The notion of 'amend' may be understood as referring to the formal amendment of a provision of, or annex to, the basic legislation, while 'supplement' means the addition of new (non-essential) elements. A clear distinction should be drawn between these two types of delegated acts. As 'supplement' means only 'to flesh out' the legislation, in adopting such an act the Commission must comply with the entirety of the legislative act, whereas a power to 'amend' the basic legislation allows it 'to modify or repeal non-essential elements laid down by the legislature . . . the Commission is not [here] required to act in compliance with the elements that the authority conferred on it aims precisely to "amend"'.[219]

It also follows that the legislative measure must determine which of the two powers it is conferring on the Commission, rather than leaving it to the Commission to choose; where the Commission is granted a power to adopt a delegated act supplementing the legislation, 'for reasons of regulatory clarity and transparency of the legislative process', it may not amend the legislation by adding a new element.[220] Moreover, a delegated act supplementing a legislative measure must remain a separate act which does not formally amend that measure.[221] The modification of the framework or the definitions laid down in the basic legislation would, on the other hand, be a bridge too far.[222]

[214] Case C-263/14 *Parliament v Council* (*Tanzania pirates*), EU:C:2016:435, paras 70 and 71.
[215] See in particular Art 215(1) TFEU.
[216] Case C-286/14 *Parliament v Commission* (*Connecting Europe Facility*), EU:C:2016:83, para 54.
[217] Case C-759/23 *PJ Carroll et al*, EU:C:2025:477: see case study 5.2.
[218] *PJ Carroll et al* (n 217) para 26. [219] Case C-286/14 *Connecting Europe Facility* (n 216) para 41.
[220] Ibid, para 53. [221] Ibid, para 63. [222] *Frontex* (n 165).

The wording of Article 290(1) TFEU is hardly a model of constitutional drafting; it is unnecessary to describe these as 'non-legislative acts', as they are not adopted under a legislative procedure. Equally, it was unnecessary to specify that only non-essential elements may be supplemented or amended by derived measures, as the legal duty of the legislature to lay down the essential elements of legislation is a long-established canon of EU constitutional law.[223]

8.1.1 The Common Understanding

Article 290 TFEU is complete in itself and does not require any implementing measure in order to be applied; all that is required is that the legislature determine in each individual case the objectives, content, scope, and duration of the delegation, and the supervisory mechanism(s) which apply to the exercise of delegated powers. Largely to pre-empt possible disputes on the application of this provision to legislation adopted under the OLP, however, Parliament, the Council, and the Commission concluded a Common Understanding on Delegated Acts.[224] In June 2019, the institutions adopted supplementary non-binding criteria for the application of Articles 290 and 291 TFEU, taking account of the case law of the Court on the choice of secondary normative act.[225]

Such delegations may only be effected in legislative measures, and not in any other form of normative act; by contrast, implementing acts can be adopted on the basis of 'any legally binding Union act'.[226] As regards their duration, while Article 290(1) TFEU leaves the legislature entirely free to delegate powers for a fixed term or an indefinite duration, the institutions have agreed, essentially in the interests of efficiency, that where a fixed-term delegation is provided, the basic act 'should in principle provide for the delegation of powers to be tacitly extended for periods of an identical duration', unless either Parliament or the Council objects at least three months in advance.[227]

8.1.2 Forms of supervision of delegated acts

Article 290(1) TFEU provides for two forms of supervision: either branch of the legislature may revoke the delegation ('right of revocation') or prevent the entry into force of individual delegated acts ('right of objection'). The legislature may apply both forms of supervisory mechanism to the same delegation.[228] The wording of Article 290(2) TFEU ('those [supervisory] conditions may be as follows') is strikingly ambiguous as to whether the legislature could resort to other types of supervisory mechanism than the two expressly mentioned, as the European Parliament has suggested it may.[229] No other form of supervision is mentioned in the Common Understanding, which merely commits the institutions to using 'as far as possible' the standard clauses for revocation and objection appended to the agreement.[230]

Under one interpretation, Article 290(2) TFEU would allow the Council, where it is acting under an SLP, to exclude Parliament from the supervision of the relevant delegated acts. That said, nothing in the Treaty would prevent Parliament from supervising delegated acts adopted on the basis of a legislative measure adopted by the Council alone in accordance with an SLP, or vice versa, if the adopting institution were so minded.

223 See *Köster* and *Frontex* (n 165), and *PJ Carroll*, case study 5.2.

224 Section V of, and the Annex to, the Agreement on 'Better Law-Making' (n 44).

225 OJ [2019] C223/1. 226 Art 291(2) TFEU; see section 8.2.

227 Common Understanding (n 224) para 17.

228 See eg the basic legislation at issue in Case C-286/14 *Connecting Europe Facility* (n 216).

229 European Parliament Resolution of 5 May 2010 on the power of legislative delegation, P7_TA-PROV(2010)0127, para 2.

230 Common Understanding (n 224) para 3.

In adopting provisions on the procedure for elections to the European Parliament, for example, the Council acts under an SLP with Parliament's consent. It would be consistent with this procedure, and with the wording of Article 290(2) TFEU (which refers to all 'legislative acts' without distinction), that Parliament be entitled to supervise the exercise of any powers delegated to the Commission under such provisions.[231]

Under the objection procedure, the delegated act does not enter into force until the two-month objection period has expired; either institution may extend the period on its own initiative for a further two months. Where both institutions inform the Commission they have no objection, the delegated act may come into force immediately on publication in the *Official Journal*. Even though it has been 'adopted' by the Commission, a delegated act may not be challenged in annulment proceedings until the expiry of the objection period, as the act will not yet have entered into force or have produced binding legal effects.[232] Under the 'urgency procedure', however, the delegated act may enter into force before the expiry of the objection period and be applied until and unless either Parliament or the Council lodges an objection.[233]

While the delegation arrangements were intended to abandon comitology once and for all in the context of the adoption of this category of third-level policy measure, the Commission is obliged under paragraph II.4 of the Common Understanding to 'consult experts designated by each Member State in the preparation of draft delegated acts', and to state in its conclusions on the meeting 'how they will take the experts' views into consideration and how [it] intends to proceed'. This procedure bears more than a passing resemblance to the advisory procedure for the adoption of implementing acts; it could be seen as reintroducing comitology by the back door for delegated acts.[234]

8.2 **Notion of 'implementing acts'**

An 'implementing act', which must also be identified as such in its title, allows the Commission (or exceptionally the Council) to 'provide further detail in relation to the content of the legislative act, in order to ensure that it is implemented under uniform conditions in all Member States'.[235] It 'merely specif[ies] the content of that act, in compliance with the essential general aims pursued by that act'.[236] As such, it must comply with both Article 291(2) TFEU and the provision of the legislative measure conferring the power to adopt such an act; the enabling provision of the legislative act is, moreover, to be interpreted in the light of Article 291(2) TFEU.[237] When acting under such a power, the Commission may adopt 'all the measures which are necessary or appropriate for the implementation of [the legislation], provided they are not contrary to it', though it may neither amend nor supplement the legislative measure.[238] 'Implementation' covers both the adoption of implementing rules and the application of rules in specific cases.[239] Given the legislature's discretion to choose between delegated and implementing acts, judicial review of the choice of an implementing measure is limited in effect to the questions

[231] K Bradley, 'Delegation of Powers in the European Union: Political Problems, Legal Solutions?' in CF Bergström and D Ritleng (eds), *Rulemaking by the European Commission: The New System for Delegation of Powers* (Oxford: Oxford University Press, 2016) 55, 68–70.

[232] Case C-310/21 P *Aquind v Commission*, EU:C:2022:615.

[233] ***Common Understanding*** **(n 224)** paras 18, 19, and 22 respectively; Parliament and Council experts may also attend meetings of the Commission expert groups along with Member State experts (para 11).

[234] Ibid, para 4; comitology *redivivus*, Bradley, 'Delegation of Powers in the European Union' (n 231) 81–84.

[235] Case C-65/13 *Parliament v Commission* (*EURES*), EU:C:2014:2289, para 43.

[236] **Case C-695/20 *Fenix*, EU:C:2023:127**, para 37.

[237] Ibid, paras 43 and 60.

[238] Ibid, paras 44 and 45.

[239] Case C-440/14 P *National Iranian Oil Company v Council*, EU:C:2016:128, para. 49.

of whether the legal framework being implemented 'needs only the addition of further detail, without its non-essential elements having to be amended or supplemented and, secondly, whether the provisions of the [basic legislation] require uniform conditions for implementation'.[240]

When such uniform conditions are required, the conferral of implementing powers becomes obligatory, in accordance with Article 291(2) TFEU. The Commission remains answerable to the European Parliament for its policy choices in this domain, notably by means of parliamentary questions and the (remote) possibility of a parliamentary motion of censure.[241]

The conferral of implementing powers on the Council 'requires a detailed statement of the reasons why that institution is entrusted with the adoption of measures implementing a legally binding act of the Union'; moreover, the Council's powers to adopt implementing acts are no different from those the Commission enjoys and it may not supplement or amend the non-essential elements of the legislative act, even where it had adopted the basic act.[242]

The arrangements for the adoption of implementing acts laid down in Article 291 TFEU are the second part of the comitology legacy; as implementation falls in principle within the responsibility of the Member States, the Union should only adopt implementing measures when 'uniform conditions for implementing legally binding Union acts are needed'. This restriction on the conferral of implementing powers is designed to safeguard the prerogatives of the Member States, and it is they, rather than Parliament or the Council, who are charged with supervising the exercise of such powers. The exclusion of the Council from the supervisory arrangements may, however, prove illusory in practice, as the legal distinction between Member States' governments, which make up the Council, and national civil servants, who act on behalf of the Member States' governments, may have little real significance.[243] Moreover, old habits die hard, and Parliament and the Council have jointly insisted on some form of supervisory role, albeit rather modest, over the Commission's implementation of primary legal acts.

8.2.1 **Conferral of implementing powers and Regulation 182/2011**

Article 291 TFEU does not specify which institution may confer implementing powers; such powers may be conferred in 'any legally binding Union act', including legislation. Outside the domain of the OLP, this power of conferral falls almost exclusively in practice to the Council, which adopts the vast majority of acts under both SLPs and INPs, though Parliament adopts a limited number of legislative acts concerning its own functioning. Implementing powers 'in duly justified specific cases'[244] may, and in the area of the CFSP must, be conferred on the Council, which would therefore be conferring implementing powers on itself.[245]

The mechanisms for control by the Member States of the Commission's exercise of implementing powers are defined by Parliament and Council Regulation 182/2011.[246] This provides for two principal supervisory mechanisms, the advisory procedure and the examination procedure; these have a number of common features, while the examination

[240] Case C-427/12 *Commission v Parliament and Council* (*Biocides*), EU:C:2014:170, para 40.

[241] See further chapter 3, section 3.2.5.

[242] *Fenix*, respectively paras 37 and 46–48.

[243] For an alternative view, see AM Fernández Pasarín and N Font, 'Unveiling Inconsistency: Consensus and Contestation along the Council–Comitology of EU Policy-Making' (2021) 60 *Journal of Common Market Studies* 427.

[244] This criterion was taken from the Court's judgment in Case 16/88 *Commission v Council*, EU:C:1989:397.

[245] For the legal situation prior to the Lisbon Treaty, see Case C-133/06 *Parliament v Council*, EU:C:2008:257.

[246] OJ [2011] L55/13.

procedure has a large number of variants. In essence, however, the Commission is obliged to refer its draft implementing measure to a committee, which can, depending on the applicable procedure (or variant), require the Commission to reconsider or amend its draft measure, or even prevent the Commission adopting the measure. Unlike the situation prior to the Lisbon Treaty, the new arrangements do not provide for any reversion of the power to decide, in the case of a negative committee vote, to the Council. The institutions concerned have agreed to refrain from adding 'procedural requirements which would alter the mechanisms for control set out in Regulation (EU) No 182/2011'.[247]

The 2017 Commission proposal to amend Regulation 182/2011 was withdrawn on 6 October 2025.[248]

8.2.2 Common features of the supervisory procedures

Article 3 of Regulation 182/2011 lays down common provisions regarding the composition and procedure of the different committees, including as regards time limits and referral to the Appeal Committee. All of the committees which participate in the supervisory mechanisms are composed of 'representatives of the Member States'. The Member States are free to choose the level and professional background of their representatives in such committees: civil servants, academic experts, professional experts, members of professional associations, and so forth. Each committee adopts its own rules of procedure on the basis of a model issued by the Commission.[249] The time limits laid down in Article 3(3) of Regulation 182/2011 comprise essential procedural requirements, breach of which justify the annulment of the act so adopted. [250]

Under both the advisory and the examination procedures, the Commission submits a draft implementing measure; individual members of the committee may present amendments and the Commission is charged with 'find[ing] solutions which command the widest possible support within the committee', notably by presenting an amended draft. The Commission also fixes the timetable for consideration of its draft measures, subject to certain minimum deadlines and the possibility of applying a procedure for urgent consideration in 'duly justified cases'. The voting requirements of the committees are, naturally, modelled on those of the Council.

8.2.3 Choice of supervisory procedure

Article 2 of Regulation 182/2011 lays down a number of rather flexible guidelines regarding the choice of appropriate procedure for each category of implementing measure, a matter which the first comitology decision of 1987 had signally failed to tackle, and which remained controversial right up to the Lisbon Treaty reforms.[251] While the choice of procedure should take account of 'the nature [and] the impact of the implementing act', the examination procedure applies for acts of general scope and certain types of implementing act which may be sensitive in the Member States, such as those concerning 'programmes with substantial implications' (particularly budgetary), taxation, and certain policy areas where the Union enjoys very wide powers (agriculture and fisheries; protection of human, animal, and plant health, and the environment; and the common commercial policy). The advisory procedure is therefore the default procedure, and the legislature may apply it to the 'sensitive' areas too, again 'in duly justified cases'.

[247] Better Law-Making Agreement (n 44) para 30.

[248] Proposal COM(2017)085 final, 14 February 2017; withdrawal OJ [2025] C5423/3.

[249] OJ [2011] C206/11; the appeal committee (see section 8.2.6) has its own rules of procedure, OJ [2011] C183/13.

[250] Case C-118/16 P *Tilly-SabcoSAS v Commission*, EU:C:2017:704, para 114.

[251] Joined Cases C-378/00 and C-122/04, both *Commission v Parliament and Council*, respectively EU:C:2003:42 and EU:C:2006:555.

8.2.4 **The advisory procedure**

The advisory procedure[252] is simple; the Commission submits a proposal, the committee gives its opinion, either by consensus or by a simple majority vote of its component members, and the Commission proceeds, 'taking the utmost account of the conclusions drawn from the discussions . . . and the opinion'. In other words, the Commission is not bound by anything the committee says under this procedure; the 'utmost account' requirement recalls the so called 'aerosol formula' invented in the 1960s as a sop to the Member States under a supervisory procedure which provided them with negligible formal powers. That said, the consultation of the committee is a substantial procedural requirement, non-compliance with which would justify the annulment of the implementing act;[253] moreover, given that the implementation in practice of Union measures is carried out by the national administrations in all but a handful of areas, it is in principle helpful for the Commission to know their views in advance.

8.2.5 **The examination procedure**

The examination procedure is anything but simple, and is only presented here in its broad outlines.[254] It provides that:

- if the draft implementing act is supported by a qualified majority of the committee, the Commission may then adopt it;
- a negative committee opinion prevents the Commission adopting that measure; it may either submit an amended version or refer the matter to the appeal committee.

Where the committee fails to adopt an opinion, the Commission may adopt the implementing measure, except in four cases:

- where the basic act provides it may not do so;
- where a simple majority of the component members of the committee opposes the draft measure;
- in certain 'sensitive' policy areas; or
- where the measure lays down anti-dumping or countervailing duties (ie measures to respond to unfair trade measures of third countries) *and* a simple majority of the members of the committee opposes adoption.

In the first three cases, the Commission may submit an amended version of the draft measure or refer the matter to the appeal committee; in the fourth case, the Commission is obliged to submit the matter to the appeal committee.

In 'exceptional cases', the Commission may override the opposition of an examination committee, where the adoption of the measure is required 'without delay', in order to 'avoid creating a significant disruption of the [agricultural] markets or a risk for the [Union's] financial interests'. The Commission must submit the measure immediately to the appeal committee, and repeal it immediately where the committee adopts a negative opinion; in other cases, the measure remains in force.

8.2.6 **The appeal committee**

In certain circumstances under the examination procedure, if the adoption of the draft measure is blocked by the committee, the draft must be submitted for consideration to an 'appeal committee'.[255] According to the preamble to Regulation 182/2011, the appeal

252 Arts 2(3) and 4, Regulation 182/2011.

253 See eg Case C-212/91 *Angelopharm*, EU:C:1994:21.

254 Arts 2(2), 5, 6, and 7, Regulation 182/2011.

255 Art 6, Regulation 182/2011.

committee 'should meet at the appropriate level', meaning in effect national representatives at a higher level than those who carry out the advisory or examination procedure. Whatever its personal composition, the committee would not be legally identical to the committee of permanent representatives of the Member State governments ('Coreper'), as the Commission may attend, but does not chair, meetings of Coreper, as it does of the appeal committee.[256]

Under the appeal committee procedure, committee members may propose amendments to the draft implementing measure referred to it, in which case the Commission is enjoined to 'endeavour to find solutions which command the widest possible support', and to inform the committee how it has taken account of the suggested amendments or why it has rejected them. The committee acts by a qualified majority; a positive opinion means that the Commission must adopt the measure, no opinion means the Commission may do so, while a negative opinion means it may not adopt the measure.

8.2.7 **'Immediately applicable implementing acts'**

The basic act may also allow the Commission to adopt an implementing measure before the draft measure is submitted to the committee under the advisory or examination procedure, on 'duly justified imperative grounds of urgency'.[257] The measure is applied for up to six months (or longer if the basic act so provides). The Commission submits the measure to the relevant committee within 14 days of its adoption; a negative committee opinion obliges the Commission to repeal the measure immediately, otherwise it stays in force until the expiry date indicated.

8.2.8 **Openness in committee governance**

The Regulation seeks to ensure a certain degree of open government[258] in an area once characterized by systemic obscurity.[259] Thus the different committees are to publish their rules of procedure, their documents are subject to the Union rules on access to documents held by the institutions,[260] and the Commission is to keep a register of committee proceedings, to which Parliament and the Council may have access. Parliament and the Council also receive, at the same time as the committees themselves, the meeting agendas and the draft implementing acts on which the committees are consulted, as well as the final draft of the implementing act following the delivery of the committee's opinion. This rule facilitates the exercise by each of the institutions concerned of their so-called 'right of scrutiny', though the right is limited to expressing the opinion that the implementing act is ultra vires the basic act, in which case the Commission must review the draft act, and inform the two institutions whether it will maintain, amend, or withdraw its draft. While the Commission has expressed the view that neither of these institutions should be involved in supervising the exercise of its implementing powers, the right of scrutiny imposes little appreciable restriction on the Commission's freedom of movement, and may even serve its interests by reducing the risk of subsequent legal proceedings.

As against this, there is no requirement in the Regulation for the publication of the names and/or professional affiliations of the members of the committees. Such information might in any case be considered personal data under the Union's data protection rules which also apply to the committees.[261]

[256] Art 240(1) TFEU; see further chapter 3, section 5.4.3.

[257] Art 8, Regulation 182/2011.

[258] Arts 10 and 11, Regulation 182/2011.

[259] K Bradley, 'Comitology and the Law: Through a Glass, Darkly' (1992) 29 *Common Market Law Review* 693.

[260] Regulation 1049/2001 (OJ [2001] L145/43); see also Case T-188/97 *Rothmans v Commission*, EU:T:1999:156.

[261] Regulation 2018/1725 (OJ [2018] L295/39); see also Case C-28/08 P *Bavarian Lager v Commission*, EU:C:2010:378.

8.3 **Borderline between delegated and implementing acts**

While the notions of 'delegated act' and 'implementing act' were both born out of the pre-Lisbon Treaty concept of implementing act,[262] the borderline between these two types of act has not always been clear.[263] Whereas the Treaty defines a 'delegated act' in terms of its content ('non-legislative acts of general application [which] supplement or amend certain non-essential elements of the legislative act'), it defines 'implementing act' in terms of its rationale, that is, the necessity to lay down 'uniform conditions for implementing legally binding Union acts'.[264] It is therefore possible to imagine a measure which is a delegated act as to its content, but an implementing act as to its objective. As a measure described as an 'implementing act' may 'neither amend nor supplement the legislative act', such a hybrid act would perforce have to be adopted as a 'delegated act'.

The principal parties responsible for classifying such derived measures have diametrically opposing interests; being largely excluded from the supervision of implementing acts, the European Parliament has a natural preference for delegated acts, while the Council favours implementing acts, as the Member State officials who participate in the adoption procedures can in effect escape from parliamentary scrutiny of all kinds. The fact is, however, that whenever the OLP applies, Parliament and the Council must agree on the choice of derived measure, failing which they may opt for the relatively safe course of a full legislative procedure.[265] The legislature enjoys wide discretion in choosing between the two categories of act, and judicial review of this choice is limited to manifest errors of assessment.[266] The Court has rejected the view, espoused by the Commission and at least part of the academic community, that the choice between a delegated and an implementing act depends on that institution's discretion: 'neither the existence nor the extent of the discretion conferred on [the Commission] by the legislative act is relevant for determining whether the act to be adopted ... comes under Article 290 TFEU or Article 291 TFEU'.[267] As noted above, the political institutions supplemented the Common Understanding with 'non-binding criteria for the application of Articles 290 and 291 [TFEU]'.[268]

The articulation of these notions is illustrated, for example, by the Commission delegated regulation amending Annex I to Regulation 211/2011 on the citizens' initiative[269] adjusting the minimum number of signatories per Member State to the modified composition of the European Parliament, and its implementing regulation laying down the technical specifications for the online collection of signatures.[270]

[262] Arts 202, third indent, and 211, fourth indent, EC referred to 'powers ... for the implementation of [Council] rules'.

[263] See generally E Tauschinsky and W Weiß, *The Legislative Choice Between Delegated and Implementing Acts in EU Law: Walking a Labyrinth* (Cheltenham: Edward Elgar, 2018).

[264] T Christiansen and M Dobbels, 'Comitology and Delegated Acts after Lisbon: How the European Parliament Lost the Implementation Game' (2012) 16, *European Integration online Papers* (EIoP), http://eiop.or.at/eiop/texte/2012-013a.htm, p 8.

[265] Though the Commission may object to this course of action; see eg, Case C-88/14 *Commission v Parliament and Council* (*Visa exemption*), EU:C:2015:499.

[266] Case C-427/12 *Biocides* (n 240) para 40. Though deeply unhappy at the Council's insistence that the secondary measures at issue be adopted as implementing rather than delegated acts, Parliament nonetheless defended the validity of the contested Regulation with its customary vigour and, indeed, successfully.

[267] *Visa exemption* (n 265) para 32; see eg D Ritleng, 'The Dividing Line between Delegated Acts and Implementing Acts' (2015) 52 *Common Market Law Review* 243.

[268] n 225. [269] OJ [2011] L65/1.

[270] Respectively Regulation 268/2012 (OJ [2012] L89/1) and Regulation 1179/2011 (OJ [2011] L301/3).

For all the attention lavished on the design and operation of the committee system, it has not prevented the Commission on occasion adopting measures which are eye-wateringly incompatible with the basic act and for which it has been unable to provide any plausible legal explanation.[271]

Case study 5.2: PJ Carroll

As appears from its title, Parliament and Council Directive 2014/40/EU (the 'basic Directive') lays down quite a comprehensive set of rules on 'the manufacture, presentation and sale of tobacco and related products'.[272] The basic Directive replaces the equivalent directive of 2001 in order 'to reflect [intervening] scientific, market and international developments' and provides the Commission with powers to adopt the necessary delegated acts accordingly. Substantively, the basic Directive prohibits the use of 'characterising flavours' or flavourings in tobacco and components of tobacco products; it then exempts tobacco products other than cigarettes and roll-your-own tobacco from this prohibition, but requires the Commission by delegated acts to withdraw the exemption if there is 'a substantial change of circumstances', that is, an increase in sales of 'a particular product category' as demonstrated by indicators laid down in an implementing act (Article 7(12) of the basic Directive). The basic Directive also imposes certain labelling requirements, notably health warnings, for the packaging of tobacco products; in this case, the Member States are allowed to exempt cigarettes, roll-your-own tobacco, and waterpipe tobacco from these requirements. Once again, in case of 'a substantial change of circumstances', the Commission is required to withdraw the exemption option in respect of 'particular product categories' (Article 11(6)).[273]

Unlike the 2001 legislation, the basic Directive laid down provisions on 'novel tobacco products', which it defined as tobacco products not falling within any of the nine categories of tobacco product listed in Article 2(14)(a) and which are placed on the market after 19 May 2014. Manufacturers and importers are required to notify the competent national authority before launching the product on the market; the Member States, should they so choose, may introduce a system of authorization of such products.[274] While it is explicitly stated that novel tobacco products 'shall respect the requirements of th[e] Directive', it is also provided that '[w]hich of the provisions of th[e] Directive apply to novel products depends on whether those products fall under the definition of a smokeless tobacco product or of a tobacco product for smoking'.[275]

'Heated tobacco products' (HTPs) are a novel tobacco product. Rather than burning the tobacco, the HTP device heats a portion of tobacco to 'produce an emission containing nicotine and other chemicals which is then inhaled by the user and that depending on its characteristics, is a smokeless tobacco product or a tobacco product for smoking'.[276] Proponents of HTPs claim that the amount of tobacco thus consumed is half that of a cigarette.

On the basis of sales figures of the number of units sold, the Commission established in 2022 that 'a substantial change in circumstances' had taken place for HTPs. The delegated Directive amended the basic Directive to apply it to HTPs, and to withdraw both the exemption from the ban on the use of characterizing flavours or components in respect of such

[271] Joined Cases C-14/06 and C-295/06 *Parliament and Denmark v Commission* (*DecaDBE*), EU:C:2008:176 and more recently Case C-144/21 *Parliament v Commission* (*Chromium trioxide*), EU:C:2023:302.

[272] OJ [2014] L127/1.

[273] Arts 7(12) and 11(6) respectively of the basic Directive.

[274] Art 19(1) and (3) respectively.

[275] Art 19(4).

[276] Preamble to Commission Delegated Directive (EU) 2022/2100, the 'delegated Directive' (OJ [2022] L283/4).

products, and the option to exempt them from the labelling requirements. The delegated Directive was challenged directly before the General Court, while the Regulations transposing this Directive into Irish law were challenged in the High Court by major importers and manufacturers of HTPs.[277]

The applicants in *PJ Carroll* were intending to sell HTPs, including HTPs with characterizing flavours or components containing flavourings, in Ireland and other Member States. They contended that the delegated Directive was invalid primarily on the ground that the delegations operated by the basic Directive were limited to the 'particular product categories' which existed at the time this measure was adopted, and that the Commission had made 'policy choices' in respect of products on which the legislature had not deliberated. The Commission had thereby acted ultra vires the delegations provided for in the basic Directive, whose objectives, content, and scope had not included the regulation of HTPs, and in breach of Article 290 TFEU.

The Court held as follows as regards the notion of delegated powers:

- the purpose of granting a delegated power is to achieve the adoption of rules coming within the regulatory framework as defined by the basic legislative act;
- the 'political choices' reflected in the 'essential elements' which only the legislature may adopt are those which either entail the weighing up of 'the conflicting interests at issue . . . on the basis of a number of assessments' or where 'the fundamental rights of the persons concerned may be interfered with to such an extent that the involvement of the EU legislature is required'.[278]

For his part, the Advocate General had suggested that the essential elements of a legislative act should not be given an 'overly broad scope', and must be reserved for 'provisions which are intended to give concrete shape to the fundamental guidelines of [the relevant EU] policy', before proposing the two-part the test the Court then adopted.[279]

The Court went on to outline the regulatory framework in which the relevant delegated powers were to be exercised: the general regime for the use of flavourings and labelling obligations, the exemption in respect of 'certain tobacco products which are mainly consumed by older consumers and small groups of the population', and the application of the Directive to novel tobacco products. It held that the Commission had acted in compliance with this regulatory framework; the contested Directive 'meets the twofold objective of' the basic Directive, 'to facilitate the smooth functioning of the internal market in tobacco products and related products, while ensuring a high level of protection for human health, especially for young people'.[280]

The applicants had a second string to their bow, arguing that the Commission had used an improper criterion in establishing whether or not there had been 'a substantial change in circumstances' for HTPs. Given the focus of the basic Directive to regulate the health effects of tobacco, in order to calculate the market share of HTPs the Commission should have relied on the weight of tobacco sold rather than the number of units. Had it done so, the market share of HTPs would not have reached the 2.5 per cent threshold.

[277] Respectively Case T-706/22 *Nicoventures Trading and Others v Commission*, EU:T:2023:39, now on appeal as C-731/23 P (pending), and Case C-759/23 *PJ Carroll & Company Ltd and Nicoventures Trading Ltd v Minister for Health, Ireland et al*, EU:C:2025:477.

[278] *PJ Carroll*, paras 26 and 27; see, however, Case C-130/10 *Parliament v Councils* (*Listing procedures*), EU:C:2012:472, para 83.

[279] Opinion of AG Emiliou, EU:C:2025:44, para 31.

[280] *PJ Carroll*, paras 29–37.

The Court noted that the definition of 'substantial change in circumstances' in the basic Directive did not refer either to the weight of tobacco or the quantity of tobacco in a particular product category, while it did require manufacturers and importers to report annual sales volumes 'in sticks or kilograms'. The Commission was therefore free to choose the method of calculation of market share. Moreover, the preamble to the basic Directive showed that the exemptions should not apply in the case of a change in the 'consumption patterns of young people'; as 'any product that consists, even partly, of tobacco has the potential to cause mortality, morbidity and disability', the Commission was under no obligation to rely on the overall tobacco content of HTPs in assessing the existence or not of a substantial change in circumstances.

The judgment in *PJ Carroll* provides a concise overview of the conditions for the exercise of, and limits to, delegated powers. Both the basic and delegated Directives illustrate the necessity, at least in certain fields, that Union legislation be adapted to keep up with changing social and economic conditions and more particularly, in the present case, with the inventiveness of the purveyors of tobacco products and containing the potential for harm to different segments of the population from products which did not exist a handful of years ago. Requiring the full panoply of the ordinary legislative procedure for such updating would significantly undermine the effectiveness of the Union in pursuing its policy objectives. At the same time, the Advocate General underlined that policing the exercise of delegated powers is 'an issue of constitutional significance since the institutional balance . . . requires that each of the institutions exercise its power with due regard for the powers of the other institutions'.[281]

9 Enhanced cooperation

The increasing heterogeneity of economic, social, and political conditions in the Member States making up the Union which results from successive enlargements has inevitably meant that certain Member States, while continuing to subscribe to the ideals and the values of the Union as a whole, are unwilling to participate in specific projects, even rather major ones. This has led to a variety of formal opt-outs from parts of the Treaties; some of these are permanent, subject to a possible abrogation of the relevant Protocol, such as the non-participation of Denmark in the euro, while others allow the non-participating Member State to opt back into individual policy measures, such as Ireland in the area of freedom, security, and justice.[282] Conversely, where support for a given measure, particularly one requiring unanimity in the Council, is insufficient for its adoption as a normal Union act, the Treaty allows a coalition of the willing to proceed with the measure using the forms, procedures, and institutions of the Union, adapting the calculation of voting majorities within the Council as required. This technique of policymaking is known as 'enhanced cooperation' and is available over the entire gamut of the Union's activities except in the area of its exclusive competences; special rules apply for enhanced cooperation in CFSP. Such cooperation is 'enhanced' in the sense that it necessarily has a pro-Union flavour, and cannot be used as a means of avoiding the obligations of the Union method of policymaking.

Both recourse to enhanced cooperation and the conduct of such cooperation are subject to compliance with a large number of legal requirements.[283] The preliminary decision to authorize enhanced cooperation is taken by the Council 'as a last resort, when it has

[281] Opinion, para 5. [282] See further chapters 20, 25, and 27.
[283] Art 20 TEU and Arts 326–334 TFEU.

established that the objectives of such cooperation cannot be attained within a reasonable time by the Union as a whole'. The non-participating Member States may take part in deliberations and the vote on authorizing enhanced cooperation, but only Member States intending to participate in such cooperation may vote upon and are bound by the resulting legal acts. The decision authorizing enhanced cooperation and any subsequent decision implementing such cooperation are each subject to judicial review.[284]

Enhanced cooperation must 'aim to further the objectives of the Union, protect its interests and reinforce the integration process'; it may not 'undermine the internal market or economic, social and territorial cohesion [or] constitute a barrier to, or discrimination in trade between Member States nor ... distort competition between them', and must respect the 'competences, rights and obligations' of non-participating Member States. While the coalition of the willing may be as few as nine Member States, such cooperation must be 'open at any time to all Member States'. Non-participating Member States for their part may not impede the implementation of acts adopted under enhanced cooperation.

The Schengen Protocol (No 19) authorizes the establishment of enhanced cooperation between all the Member States excluding Ireland, which may only take part in the Schengen *acquis* by means of the procedure laid down in the Protocol. It may, however, be permitted to engage in other more limited forms of cooperation, short of 'taking part' per se, by means of ordinary legislative provisions.[285]

10 Treaty revision

The Treaties, including the Euratom Treaty, may now be amended under either the 'ordinary' revision procedure (which comes in two variants), a generally applicable simplified revision procedure, or one or other of a series of specific simplified revision procedures, depending on the character and the extent of the modifications being undertaken.[286]

10.1 Ordinary revision procedures

The ordinary revision procedure, which is largely inspired by the procedure which produced the 'Constitution for Europe' in 2004, is unrestricted in material scope, and is hence available for any Treaty amendment, though it would presumably not be used where a less cumbersome procedure is available.[287] Amendments may be proposed by Parliament, the Commission, or any Member State government, and are notified to the national parliaments. After consulting the European Parliament and the Commission and, where the amendments concern 'institutional changes in the monetary area', the European Central Bank, the European Council decides by a simple majority whether or not the procedure should continue. If so, the President of the European Council convenes a convention comprising representatives of the national parliaments and the European Parliament, the heads of State or government of the Member States, and the Commission.

Acting 'by consensus', the convention may recommend Treaty amendments to a conference of the representatives of the Member States' governments ('intergovernmental

[284] Respectively Joined Cases C-274/11 and C-295/11 *Spain and Italy v Council*, EU:C:2013:240, and Case C-146/13 *Spain v Parliament and Council*, EU:C:2015:298. For an example of enhanced cooperation in action, see eg Council Regulation (EU) 2017/1939 establishing the European Public Prosecutor's Office (OJ [2017] L283/1).

[285] Case C-44/14 *Spain v Parliament and Council*, EU:C:2015:554.

[286] See S Peers, 'The Future of EU Treaty Amendments' (2012) 31 *Yearbook of European Law* 17.

[287] Art 48(2)–(5) TEU.

conference' (IGC)), which adopts the amendments 'by common accord'. The matter does not end there, as the amendments still require ratification by the Member States; should this final stage of the procedure not be completed within two years of the adoption of the amendments, and providing four-fifths of the Member States (22) have ratified these, the question is referred to the European Council. While the Treaty is silent on what this last-gasp step may entail, the European Council has been quite successful in the past in coming up with astute, if legally obscure, solutions for the Member States unable to cross the finishing line (usually Ireland or, on one occasion, Denmark).

A variant of this procedure allows a simple majority of the European Council, with the consent of the European Parliament, to dispense with the convention stage entirely and move straight to the IGC, should none of the simplified procedures be available and should the scope of the proposed amendments not justify the convening of the convention.[288] Once it consents to bypassing the convention stage, the European Parliament may not object to the content of the amendments adopted. On the other hand, the national parliaments may still register their disagreement with the procedure used, as well as the content of the amendment, at the ratification stage.

10.2 Simplified revision procedures

There are three generally applicable 'simplified revision procedures' for amending the Treaties without recourse to the ordinary revision procedures; these are laid down respectively in Article 48(6) TEU, Article 48(7), first subparagraph, TEU, and Article 48(7), second subparagraph, TEU. Various Treaty provisions also allow limited Treaty amendments in specific areas.

10.2.1 Article 48(6) TEU procedure

The application of the Article 48(6) TEU procedure is subject to two material restrictions: it may not be used to increase the competences conferred on the Union, and it may only be used to amend Part Three of the TFEU, which contains all the policy provisions of the old EC Treaty (except those relating to external relations), along with those on the area of freedom, security, and justice formerly located in the TEU.

Amendments may be proposed by a Member State, the European Parliament, or the Commission. The European Council decides, unanimously, on the amendments to the Treaties, after consulting Parliament, the Commission, and, in the case of institutional changes in the monetary area, the European Central Bank. The amendments still need national ratification before they can come into force.

The European Stability Mechanism was established following the addition of a new paragraph to Article 136 TFEU using this procedure. The decision was unsuccessfully challenged in *Pringle*.[289]

10.2.2 The general passerelle procedures

The procedure laid down in Article 48(7), first subparagraph, TEU, allows the European Council, again acting unanimously, to replace a Treaty requirement for Council unanimity with a qualified majority voting rule, either for the adoption of a particular act or generally, except for decisions with defence or military implications. Similarly, the procedure under Article 48(7), second subparagraph, TEU, allows the European Council to replace an SLP in which the Council is the adopting institution with an OLP, though a number of specific matters are excluded from the scope of this provision: decisions on the

[288] Art 48(3), second subpara, TEU.

[289] Case C-370/12 *Pringle* (n 63).

Union's budgetary resources and the multi-annual financial framework, the application of the flexibility clause, and the suspension of a Member State's voting rights where it fails to respect the Union's fundamental values.[290]

In each case, these institutional reforms require the consent of the European Parliament, acting by a majority of its component members, and may be vetoed by any of the national parliaments within six months of the notification of the proposed amendment. In the absence of any contrary indication in the text, the two houses of any bicameral parliament would presumably have to agree on the exercise of such a veto. These procedures, known familiarly as the 'general passerelle clauses',[291] do not allow the substitution of unanimity for a qualified majority rule or an SLP where the Treaty already provides for an OLP.

By analogy with *Pringle*, the Court would presumably have jurisdiction to verify whether the Union was entitled to use these procedures and that the procedure has been correctly applied.[292]

10.2.3 **Sector-specific passerelles**

In a number of instances where the ordinary legislative procedure does not apply, the Treaty nonetheless provides for a specific passerelle allowing either the substitution of the ordinary legislative procedure for a special legislative procedure (cross-border measures on family law; certain social policy matters; selected environmental policy matters; measures under enhanced cooperation which require a special legislative procedure), or the replacement of a unanimity requirement for Council voting by qualified majority voting (common foreign and security policy, except for decisions having military or defence implications; the adoption of the multi-annual financial framework).[293] For the passage to the ordinary legislative procedure, the application of the passerelle may be decided by the Council, acting unanimously, whereas for the move to qualified majority voting, the decision is taken by the European Council.

10.2.4 **Miscellaneous revision procedures**

Though not identified as such, other forms of specific simplified revision procedure are scattered throughout the Treaty. The Council may thus strengthen or add to the rights of Union citizens set out in Article 20(2) TFEU, acting under a special legislative procedure, though in this case Member State approval is required before the modification enters into force. The Council may also amend the Treaty on certain matters without requiring such approval, for example amending the Protocol on the excessive deficit procedure, while the Statute of the Court of Justice may be amended under an OLP.[294] The European Council may also amend the Treaty by simple decision, for example extending the powers which can be conferred on the European Public Prosecutor.[295] These may be considered specific provisions (*leges speciales*) which render inapplicable the general requirements of other procedures laid down in Article 48(6) and (7) TEU.

The application of Article 50 TEU, which can only be triggered by a Member State, in effect brings about an amendment to the Treaties by reducing the size of the Union,

[290] Respectively Art 311, third and fourth paras; Art 312(2), first subpara; Art 352; and Art 354 TFEU. The derogations from Art 48(7) TEU are set out in Art 353 TFEU.

[291] From the French for 'footbridge'.

[292] Case 370/12 *Pringle v Ireland* (n 63).

[293] Respectively Arts 81(3), 153(2), 192(2), and 333(2) TFEU, and Art 31(3) and (4) TEU and Art 312(2) TFEU.

[294] Respectively Arts 81(3), second subpara, and 281, second para, TFEU.

[295] Art 86(4) TFEU.

though unlike Article 49 TEU this provision does not provide a legal basis for any concomitant amendments to the Treaties.[296]

10.2.5 **The 'lost treasure' initiatives**

The passerelle clauses lay dormant for most of the first decade which followed their introduction into the Treaties. Starting in September 2017, the then Commission President, Jean-Claude Juncker, began advocating that what he dubbed the 'lost treasure clause of the Lisbon Treaty' be used 'as an important tool for achieving a stronger, more efficient and more democratic Union'.[297] The Commission subsequently proposed recourse to the general and/or specific passerelles in different areas of the common foreign and security policy, taxation, energy and climate, and social policy.[298] It also proposed that the Euratom Treaty be amended to apply the ordinary legislative procedure within the framework of this Treaty.[299] The European Parliament has also called for the implementation of the passerelle provisions of the Treaties.[300]

10.3 **Accession and withdrawal**

Specific rules govern the accession of a State to the Union, and the withdrawal of a Member State from the Union.

Accession to the Union is in principle available to '[any] European State which respects the [Union's] values and is committed to promoting them', under a two-stage procedure.[301] The decision on the application to accede is taken by the Council, unanimously, after informing the national parliaments, consulting the Commission, and obtaining the consent of the European Parliament acting by a majority of its component members. The conditions of accession, including any modifications of the Treaties, are then laid down in an agreement between the acceding State and the Member States (not the Union), which is in turn ratified by the Member States under their national procedures and by the acceding State; this latter condition paves the way for the inclusion in the Act of Accession of 'adjustments to the Treaties . . . which such admission entails'. The Treaty does not define what the term 'European' designates.

Article 50 TEU both declares that a Member State may withdraw from the Union and provides a procedure which is designed to ensure that the withdrawal is orderly. After deciding to withdraw 'in accordance with its own constitutional requirements', the State must notify the European Council of its intention to do so; the notification starts the process for the negotiation of an agreement between the Union and that State, setting out the 'arrangements for its withdrawal'. Should no such agreement be reached, the Treaties will cease to apply to that Member State two years after notification, unless there is unanimous agreement to extend this time period. The Court has held that the Member State has a more or less unconditional right, not mentioned in the Treaty, to revoke the notification.[302] The decision by the United Kingdom to withdraw from the Union ('Brexit')

[296] See section 10.3.

[297] EPSC Brief, *A Union that Delivers: Making Use of the Lisbon Treaty's Passerelle Clauses*, European Commission, 14 January 2019.

[298] Respectively COM(2018) 647 final, 12 September 2018; COM(2019) 8 final, 15 January 2019; COM(2019) 177 final, 9 April 2019; and COM(2019) 186 final, 16 April 2019.

[299] COM(2019) 177 final.

[300] Resolution of 13 July 2023, P9_TA(2023)0269.

[301] Art 49 TEU.

[302] Case C-621/18 *Wightman and Others*, EU:C:2018:999. Art 50 could conceivably be interpreted as precluding any right of revocation, though this was not argued before the Court: K Bradley 'Disintegration through Law: Brexit, Article 50 TEU and the Court' in C Kilpatrick and J Scott (eds), *Contemporary Challenges to EU Legality* (Oxford: Oxford University Press, 2021) 123, 137–151.

dominated European Union and United Kingdom politics from the referendum of June 2016 to the date of actual withdrawal on 31 January 2020.[303]

With the exception of certain overseas countries and territories which have special relationships with Member States,[304] the Treaty does not make explicit provision for the withdrawal from the Union, or secession, of part of a Member State. In 1984, Greenland withdrew from the Communities in accordance with a special treaty, though remaining part of Denmark,[305] while Algeria ceased to be part of the European Communities when it gained its independence from France in 1962.

11 The democratic credentials of the European Union

11.1 Case law origins

The Union's 'democratic deficit', much debated in political and academic circles, refers in large part to the purported lesser accountability of the Union institutions compared to that of the governments of the Member States. While it is hence more a political than a legal concept, traces of concern regarding the Union's democratic credentials may be found in the case law of the Court of Justice, going back at least as far as *Van Gend en Loos*.[306] There the Court relied, inter alia, on the fact that citizens participated in the functioning of the Community through the intermediary of the European Parliament in order to justify the autonomy of the Community's legal order and the direct effect under specific conditions of Treaty provisions.

In proceedings which arose directly from the organization of the first direct elections to Parliament in 1979, the Court again relied on the principle of democratic participation in Community decision-making both to interpret the scope of the right of that institution to intervene in judicial proceedings, and to evaluate the nature of the requirement that the European Parliament be consulted on draft legislation.[307] More controversially, in its *Titanium dioxide* ruling more than a decade later, the Court gave priority to the Community-level democratic participation in the legislative procedure of the European Parliament over the competing right of individual Member States to exercise a veto in the name of national democracy.[308]

The Court's recourse to democratic principles as a significant factor in its judgments has been irregular, but on occasion significant. In *Wightman*, for example, it relied on the Union's adherence to the values of democracy and liberty as requiring an interpretation of Article 50 TEU which allows a Member State unilaterally to revoke its intention to withdraw from the Union in the absence of any clear textual indications to this effect.[309]

11.2 Reform of decision-making procedures and principles

The Member States' shared concern with the democratic character of the Union manifested itself in Treaty reforms which over time increased the formal powers of the European Parliament quite dramatically, first as regards the adoption and supervision of

[303] See chapter 27. [304] See Art 355(6) TFEU.

[305] Treaty amending, with regard to Greenland, the Treaties establishing the European Communities (OJ [1985] L29/1).

[306] Case 26/62 *Van Gend en Loos*, EU:C:1963:1. [307] Case 138/79 *Isoglucose* (n 211).

[308] Case C-300/89 *Titanium dioxide* (n 79); see also see K Lenaerts, 'The Principle of Democracy in the Case Law of the European Court of Justice' (2013) 62 *International and Comparative Law Quarterly* 271.

[309] Case C-621/18 *Wightman* (n 302); see also Case C-263/14 *Tanzania pirates* (n 214).

the Union budget, and subsequently both in policymaking generally and in institutional matters such as the appointment of the Commission. At the same time, the Member States made more explicit their understanding, which was always inherent in the structures of the Union, that the Union would be guided by principles such as conferral, subsidiarity, and proportionality, which seek to ensure that policy decisions are only taken by the Union where this is more appropriate than action at the national level. While the scope for national parliamentary supervision over the decisions of their ministers in Council meetings has been attenuated by qualified majority voting and the sharing of legislative power between the Council and the European Parliament, the national parliaments, indeed individual parliamentary chambers, have been given certain powers to supervise and possibly influence the adoption of Union legislation.

11.3 **Treaty provisions on democratic principles**

The insertion of the new 'provisions on democratic principles' into the TEU by the Lisbon Treaty[310] should be seen in the context of the ongoing debate on the Union's purported democratic deficit. Having declared unreservedly that '[the] functioning of the Union shall be founded on representative democracy', the Treaty identifies two components of that democracy: representation of the citizens at the Union level in the European Parliament, and representation of the Member States in the European Council by heads of State/government, and in the Council by governments which are themselves democratically accountable. The rules on qualified majority voting in the Council are seen as ensuring '[i]n accordance with the value of democracy contained in Article 2 TEU . . . that the Council's decisions are sufficiently representative of both the Member States and the population of the European Union'.[311]

The 'right of [every citizen] to participate in the democratic life of the Union' is formally declared in Article 10(3) TEU, along with the aspiration that decisions be 'taken as openly and as closely as possible to the citizen'. To give effect to the former, the Treaty lays down provisions on voting rights for (non-national) Union citizens in local and European Parliament elections in their Member State of residence, on open Union government, and on the dialogue between the institutions and civil society, and recognizes the contribution of political parties at 'the European level'.[312] Article 12 TEU also lists different ways by which national parliaments 'contribute actively to the good functioning of the Union', though this is prima facie descriptive rather than prescriptive. The right of citizens to obtain access to documents held by the institutions, and in particular those concerning the legislative process, should be considered another element in the Union's aspiration to democratic respectability.[313]

Potentially the most high-profile of these new provisions is that providing for the European Citizens' Initiative (ECI), which allows a million citizens from at least seven Member States to request the Commission to take a policy initiative; the right of initiative is 'intended to reinforce citizenship of the Union and enhance [its] democratic functioning'.[314] According to the Court, 'the particular added value of the ECI mechanism resides . . . in the possibilities and opportunities that it creates for Union citizens to initiate debate on policy';

310 See Arts 9–12 TEU.

311 Case C-157/21 *Conditionality* (n 2) para 309.

312 Respectively, Art 20(2)(b) TFEU, Art 15 TFEU, Art 11(2) TEU, and Art 10(4) TEU.

313 Art 15(3) TFEU and Case T-540/15 *De Capitani* (n 163) paras 58 and 59; see also Case C-57/16 P *ClientEarth v Commission*, EU:C:2018:660.

314 Art 11(4) TEU, and preamble to Regulation 211/2011 (n 269); see generally F Mendez and M Mendez, 'The Promise and Perils of Direct Democracy for the European Union' (2017) 19 *Cambridge Yearbook of European Legal Studies* 48.

it is designed to invite the Commission to act, but not to oblige it to do so.[315] In short, the ECI mechanism is intended to make the Union more accessible to its citizens.[316] That said, it is not designed to initiate a 'dialogue' between the Commission and the proposers but to 'request[ ] the Commission, within the framework of its powers, to submit a proposal for an act'.[317]

Under these arrangements, the Commission must refuse to register a proposed citizens' initiative if it 'manifestly [falls] outside the framework of the Commission's powers to submit a proposal for a legal act'.[318] The application of this test does not require the initiators to provide facts or evidence 'subject as such to the rules on the burden of proof, but [is] essentially a question of the interpretation and application of the relevant provisions of the Treaties' and 'whether [the] measures envisaged in the abstract could be adopted on the basis of the Treaties'.[319] However, a general reference to a series of Treaty articles without any explanation of how they related to the proposed initiative would be insufficient, as would the evocation of a principle of international law where this is not reflected in any relevant provision of the Treaties.[320] While it is open to the proposers to request an act based on the so-called 'flexibility clause', Article 352 TFEU, 'the objective of democratic participation ... underlying the ECI mechanism cannot frustrate the principle of conferred powers and authorise the Union to legislate in a field for which no power has been accorded to it'.[321] In this regard, though they are not obliged to demonstrate that the act is 'necessary' within the meaning of this provision, the proposers must at least show that it would fall within the policies and the objectives of the Treaty.[322]

The lodging of an ECI 'imposes a series of specific obligations on the Commission', set out in Articles 10 and 11 of Regulation 211/2011; it must 'examine [the] information [provided] with care and impartiality' and 'provide assistance and advice to the organisers of an ECI, particularly with regard to registration criteria'.[323] These 'strict conditions and ... specific procedural safeguards' distinguish the treatment of an ECI from that of a petition submitted to the European Parliament.[324] Should the Commission refuse to register an ECI, its decision must be fully reasoned and is amenable to judicial review, as such a refusal 'impinges upon the very effectiveness of the right of Union citizens to submit a citizens' initiative'.[325]

In *Romania v Commission*, the General Court rejected on its merits, without examining the admissibility of the action, a challenge to a Commission decision registering an ECI.[326] The judgment was upheld on appeal, again without any consideration of the admissibility of the action.[327]

12 Conclusion: Union law and Union politics

It is in the nature of constitutions to grant powers to institutions of government and at the same time create devices and rules to limit the exercise of those powers. In a federal-type entity, these devices and rules seek to facilitate the policing of the boundaries both

[315] Case C-418/18 P *Puppinck* (n 14) para 60.
[316] Case C-420/16 P *Izsák and Dabis v Commission*, EU:C:2019:177, para 53.
[317] Case T-44/14 *Cosantini v Commission*, EU:T:2016:232, para 31.
[318] Art 4(2)(b), Regulation 211/2011 (n 269).
[319] Case C-420/16 *Izsák and Dabis* (n 316) paras 61 and 62.
[320] Case C-589/15 P *Anagnostakis v Commission*, EU:C:2017:663, paras 36–41 and 100.
[321] Ibid, para 53.
[322] Case T-44/14 *Cosantini* (n 317) para 54.
[323] Case C-589/15 P *Anagnostakis* (n 320) paras 35 and 46.
[324] Case C-418/18 P *Puppinck* (n 14) para 91.
[325] Case C-589/15 P *Anagnostakis* (n 320).
[326] Case T-391/17 *Romania v Commission*, EU:T:2019:672.
[327] Case C-899/19 P *Romania v Commission*, EU:C:2022:41.

vertically, between the central government and the component states, and horizontally, between the different institutions or branches of government. While not formally a constitution, the European Union Treaties clearly perform these functions by means of the rules on competence and on decision-making, both legislative and non-legislative, which they lay down.

It falls at first instance to the political institutions of the Union to ensure these boundaries are respected. This has always been so, owing to the design of these institutions, and in particular their composition and respective roles in Union governance. Since the Single European Act, which was as substantively modest as it was psychologically radical, the Member States have dramatically increased the policymaking powers of the Union. At the same time, they have established new legal rules and procedures which bring the Court of Justice more directly and more frequently centre stage in the political controversies of the day. It is called upon not only to arbitrate boundary disputes between the Union and the Member States, and between the institutional actors *inter se*, but also to act as the court of last instance, in effect, for certain questions in very sensitive areas of litigation, such as the organization of the national judiciary, the legality of the detention of accused persons, custody disputes between couples, the protection of the rights of those whose assets have been frozen in pursuit of decisions taken outside the Union legal framework, and even the composition of the Union itself; in *Wightman*, the Court's ruling could potentially have determined whether the United Kingdom remained a Member State of the Union or not.[328]

As a result, disputes on competence matters and the proper conduct of the decision-making procedures laid down in, or on the basis of, the Treaties become ever more fraught with political consequences. Time was when the principal issue of debate regarding competences was whether the Treaty, read as a whole, allowed the then European (Economic) Community to regulate a particular matter not expressly provided for; now the Court is obliged to weigh up a variety of factors which are not obviously legal in character, such as the capacity of the Member States to deal with a particular matter, or the potential impact of Union action on private parties. This is not necessarily a negative development, but it has modified the role of the Court in the political life of the Union. It has been suggested in this regard that, 'faced with an ever-evolving scope of Union activities, the Court attempts to fit the square peg of allowing the Union to adapt to such evolutions into the round hole of compliance with the principle of conferral and with the institutional balance', sometimes with mixed results.[329]

In its early case law on the proper conduct of decision-making, the Court occasionally displayed a certain insouciance. The 1973 judgments in *Massey-Ferguson* and *Balkan Import*, for example, respectively allowed the Council, in effect, to ignore the substantive requirements of Article 235 EEC (now Article 352 TFEU) and to bypass the requirement to consult the European Parliament on agricultural measures.[330] Both of these judgments have subsequently been overruled on these points, albeit *sub silentio* in each case.[331] Again since the Single Act, the Court has taken the institutional bull by the horns; it has firmly established that this is an area which is fully subject to judicial review, rather than one which is left to the political institutions, or the most powerful among them, alone.[332] Its more robust attitude is particularly evident, for example, in its case law on the determination of

[328] Case C-621/18 *Wightman* (n 302).

[329] E Sharpston and G De Baere, 'The Court of Justice as a Constitutional Adjudicator' in A Arnull et al (eds), *A Constitutional Order of States? Essays in EU Law in Honour of Alan Dashwood* (Oxford: Hart Publishing, 2011) 123, 149.

[330] Case 8/73 *Massey-Ferguson*, EU:C:1973:90 and Case 5/73 *Balkan Import*, EU:C:1973:109.

[331] See respectively sections 4.4 and 7.3.

[332] See eg Case 68/86 *United Kingdom v Council* (n 93).

the legal basis of legislative acts, the strict respect of procedural requirements in decision-making, and the delimitation between legislative and sub-legislative acts,[333] matters which are regularly raised by the institutions and, increasingly, by Member States which find themselves on the wrong side of a vote in Council.[334]

Despite being dragged into what might be considered essentially power struggles between institutional actors, the Court has demonstrated an acute sense of the limitations on its own role and a good deal of sensitivity to the different interests at stake. In this area at least, its decisions have not attracted the type or degree of controversy which has been provoked by rulings on certain substantive questions.[335] The Court has managed to oversee a significant degree of judicialization of political decision-making, without admitting the politicization of judicial activity.[336]

Further reading

CF Bergström and D Ritleng (eds), *Rulemaking by the European Commission: The New System for Delegation of Powers* (Oxford: Oxford University Press, 2016)

A Biondi et al (eds), *EU Law after Lisbon* (Oxford: Oxford University Press, 2012) chs 2, 4, 5, 10, and 12

P Craig, 'Delegated and Implementing Acts Legislation' in R Schütze and T Tridimas (eds), *Oxford Principles of European Union Law* (Oxford: Oxford University Press, 2018) 716

P Craig, *The Lisbon Treaty: Law, Politics, and Treaty Reform* (Oxford: Oxford University Press, 2010) chs 2, 5, 7, and 11

P Craig and G de Búrca, *EU Law* (7th edn, Oxford: Oxford University Press, 2020) chs 3–6

G Davies, 'Legislative Control of the European Court of Justice' (2014) 51 *Common Market Law Review* 1579

S Garben and I Govaere (eds), *The Division of Competences Between the EU and the Member States* (London: Bloomsbury, 2017)

H Hofmann, 'Legislation, Delegation and Implementation under the Treaty of Lisbon: Typology Meets Reality' (2009) 15 *European Law Journal* 482

D Jančič (ed), *National Parliaments after the Lisbon Treaty and the Euro Crisis* (Oxford: Oxford University Press, 2017)

C Joerges and C Glinska (eds), *The Euro Crisis and the Transformation of Transnational Governance* (Oxford: Bloomsbury, 2014)

P Kiiver, *The National Parliaments in the European Union* (The Hague: Kluwer Law International, 2006)

P Kjaer, *Between Governing and Governance* (Oxford: Hart Publishing, 2010)

K Lenaerts and JA Gutiérrez-fons, 'The Constitutional Allocation of Powers and General Principles of EU Law' (2010) 47 *Common Market Law Review* 1629

K Lenaerts and P Van Nuffel, *EU Constitutional Law* (Oxford: Oxford University Press, 2021) part IV

[333] See respectively sections 4.3, 7, and 8.3.

[334] Examples of the former are scattered throughout the annals of the Court; regarding the latter, see eg Joined Cases C-643/15 and C-647/15 *International protection* (n 162), Case C-128/17 *Atmospheric pollutants* (n 18), Case C-482/17 *Gun control* (n 47), and, most blatantly, Case C-157/21 *Conditionality* (n 2).

[335] For a sample, see J Weiler, 'Epilogue: Judging the Judge: Apology and Critique' in M Adams et al (eds), *Judging Europe's Judges: The Legitimacy of the Case Law of the European Court of Justice* (Oxford: Hart Publishing, 2013).

[336] See generally R Hirschl, 'The Judicialization of Politics' in K Whittington et al (eds), *The Oxford Handbook of Law and Politics* (Oxford: Oxford University Press, 2008).

J-C Piris, *The Lisbon Treaty: A Legal and Political Analysis* (Cambridge: Cambridge University Press, 2012) chs 7, 8, 11, and 12

R Schütze, *European Constitutional Law* (2nd edn, Cambridge: Cambridge University Press, 2015) chs 7 and 9

R Schütze, 'Subsidiarity after Lisbon: Reinforcing the Safeguards of Federalism?' (2009) 68 *Cambridge Law Journal* 525

K Shaw, *The Court of Justice of the European Union: Subsidiarity and Proportionality* (Leiden/Boston: Brill, 2018)

S Smismans, *Law, Legitimacy, and European Governance* (Oxford: Oxford University Press, 2004)

A Türk, 'Primary Legislation and Legislative Procedures' in R Schütze and T Tridimas (eds), *Oxford Principles of European Union Law* (Oxford: Oxford University Press, 2018) 689

6

The effects of EU law in the national legal systems

Michal Bobek

1 Introduction

EU law has many dimensions. There is the grand Brussels (Luxembourg/Strasbourg) world of EU institutions: policies, competences, types of legislative procedures, institutional balance, democratic deficit(s), Union's external action, and so on. Connected to this world are various international undertakings, law firms, interest groups, and lobbyists. There is, however, also another, arguably more important, dimension to EU law: the national one. At first sight perhaps less glamorous, sometimes even dull, this world is concerned with the application of EU law in individual cases and to concrete people: a pension claim of a migrant worker, the enforcement of a civil decision rendered in another Member State, a consumer protection dispute, a workplace discrimination case, the question of valid consent given to a merchant for the processing of one's personal data when shopping online, to name just a few examples.

It is at the national level that most of the law students studying this book (and future practitioners in whatever legal profession) are likely, sooner or later, to encounter EU law. The study and the teaching of EU law remain remarkably centralist and Court-focused: the Court of Justice of the European Union (the Court) interpreted this provision or the Court failed to annul that piece of EU legislation. However, in reality, the vast majority of cases of actual application of EU law happen quietly at the national level with no involvement of the Court, or any other EU institutions, for that matter.

This chapter explains the basic principles of how the national world of EU law is supposed to operate, at least from the point of view of EU law. It shows how EU law enters the national legal systems and how the provisions of the two normative legal systems interact.

The chapter starts by explaining the default rules for the national application of EU law. It then focuses on four key principles: direct effect, indirect effect, primacy, and state liability. The chapter closes with a case study, in which the interplay among the rules and principles introduced is illustrated.

The principles discussed in this chapter represent the backbone of the entire legal system of the EU. Without them, the Union could hardly aspire to be more than (yet) another international organization. But still, in spite of their importance (or perhaps, later on, *because of* their importance), these principles are in fact nowhere enacted. But for a non-binding declaration No 17 annexed to the Treaty of Lisbon, there is no mention of primacy or direct effect in the Treaties. The principles discussed in this chapter are of judicial origin. They have been brought to life and upheld by the case law of the Court.

The fact that the key principles of national enforcement of EU law are almost entirely of judicial origin has its strengths and weaknesses. On the one hand, the system develops organically, in constant interaction between the national courts and the Court. The Court can help in ensuring effective enforcement of EU law and EU law-derived individual rights in the Member States in individual cases. On the other hand, as any case law-based system, a purely judicial world of remedies may suffer from lack of clarity, internal contradictions, and hidden reversals, which result in a lack of foreseeability of the law. An ongoing tension between these two interests is the characteristic element of this entire area of law.

2 EU law in the Member States: institutions, procedures, principles

Imagine a passion: football, for example. Imagine a number of football clubs becoming increasingly unhappy with the state and quality of the game: poor quality, doping, rampant corruption, unclear managerial and governance structures etc. The clubs wish to join forces and do something about it. They have a number of options.

First, they could sign an agreement. They might call it the 'Fair Football Charter'. In the Charter, they would set out minimum requirements for each of the problems identified. These would be, however, just substantive rules. Their implementation and enforcement by and within the clubs would be left entirely to the individual clubs. Thus, some of the clubs might indeed faithfully implement the Charter, reflecting its provisions in the club's articles of association and rigorously enforcing it by all the club's organs. In other clubs, however, the Charter might just be put in a deep drawer in the president's office and scarcely looked at again.

Secondly, the clubs could be much more ambitious. They might wish not only to set some minimal rules, but also to provide for their enforcement. They establish an organization and name it the 'Fair Football Federation'. The Federation becomes entitled to pass rules binding upon its members. Moreover, it is also asked to supervise the enforcement of these rules. Within each of the clubs, representatives of the Federation are stationed to defend the interests and to enforce the rules of the Federation. The Federation representatives supervising the individual clubs act according to the Federation's own rules on administration and dispute settlement. Finally, a decision of a Federation representative or a judicial pronouncement by one of the Federation courts on matters falling within the scope of the Federation powers is final.

Today, EU law finds itself somewhere in the middle between these two scenarios. The first scenario represents the traditional way in which public international law obligations may be enforced within the States. The second scenario outlines a certain type of a fully-fledged federal structure, in which the federation lays down not only substantive rules, but also provides for their enforcement within its member units, both substantively and institutionally.

There are three important elements which need to be outlined in order to understand the nature of the current constitutional settlement within the EU and the issues raised in this chapter: *institutions*, *procedures*, and *principles*. In other words, *who* enforces EU law in the Member States, and *how*, following what procedures and guided by *what principles*.

On the *institutional* plane, unless explicitly provided otherwise, EU law in the Member States is carried out by the existing national institutions. All the national institutions, be it the executive, the courts, or even the legislator, become de facto EU institutions when acting *within the scope of EU law*. The Union sets up no own network of decentralized agencies within the Member States, which would be present in the Member States and would enforce 'federal' EU law.[1] For this purpose, the Union relies on the existing institutional structures of its Member States.

On the *procedural* plane, again, unless explicitly provided otherwise, EU law is enforced according to existing national rules of procedure. Also here, the Union relies primarily on the procedures already extant in the Member States, to which it nonetheless attaches some further conditions, which will be explained later in this chapter.

National institutions thus become servants of two masters: the national States and the EU. It is the subject matter of the case or problem at hand which decides which master the national institution is supposed to serve at a given moment. Imagine, for instance, a civil servant deciding on social security claims in a national social security administration in, say, the Netherlands. At one moment, she decides on a pension claim of one person, who has spent her entire life in the Netherlands. Applicable substantive law is Dutch, applicable procedure would be the Dutch law on administrative procedure. The ensuing decision is a purely national one. However, 15 minutes later, when deciding on the next pension claim submitted by a different person, who spent 15 years working in the Netherlands, but also 10 years working in Germany and a further 7 years working in Belgium, the very same official suddenly becomes an EU official. She is applying EU law[2] to the case at hand. The overall procedure will still follow the Dutch administrative procedure. However, the decision issued by the same official sitting in the same office became a decision *under EU law*, rendered *within the scope of EU law*.

The Member States thus put their national institutions and procedures at the disposal of the national enforcement of EU law. If the EU provides otherwise, the (default) national choice in this regard will be pre-empted by the Union. The perhaps most significant pre-emption of Member States' autonomy occurred not on the level of procedures or institutions, but on the level of *principles*, which provide for the overall status of EU law in the Member States. Principles like direct effect, primacy, or indirect effect are the overall rules of engagement between the systems: EU law and the national law. They do not determine which particular institution shall implement EU law or according to which procedure it shall be applied; they determine what happens in cases of divergence or even collisions between national law and EU law. The logic of the evolution of these principles is nonetheless the same as the one of 'mere' institutions and procedures according to

[1] For the sake of completeness: the European Union has, over the years, established over 40 further bodies or agencies, which are physically located in various Member States. These agencies are, however, *concentrated* in one place and *specialized* as to the subject matter they are tasked to deal with, typically under the overall supervision of the Commission. Thus, eg, there is one European Chemicals Agency (located in Helsinki), one European Environment Agency (in Copenhagen), or one European Banking Agency (in Paris). They are competent for the entire EU, with no further branches in other Member States.

[2] Regulation (EC) No 883/2004 of the European Parliament and of the Council of 29 April 2004 on the coordination of social security systems (OJ [2004] L166/1) and further implementing legislation.

which EU law is enforced in the Member States. In its key decisions in *Van Gend en Loos*[3] and *Costa*,[4] the Court pre-empted the potential national choice and diversity with respect to the overall status of EU law in the Member States.

Thus, the current stage of the Union could be called a type of 'cooperative federalism'.[5] On the one hand, through progressive unification or harmonization, the Union has over the years clearly moved away from a public international model (the Fair Football Charter). Important principles of national application of EU law became unified. So did certain procedures and remedies, and institutional structures of the Member States. On the other hand, the Union remains far from a fully-fledged federal structure (the Fair Football Federation), in which a federal institutional structure and procedures would be set up and the ultimate question of primacy and final word resolved. Often, in facing difficulty in classifying the Union, the notional escape route taken at this stage is to call the Union either an international organization *sui generis* or a federation *sui generis*, depending on the ideological outlook of the observer and the yardstick chosen. There is, however, at least agreement that the Union is *sui generis*, that is, of its own kind, even if we may not be precisely sure what kind it is.

2.1 **National rules, unless . . .**

In the words of the Court, the general rule is that:

> in the absence of Community rules governing the matter, it is for the domestic legal system of each Member State to designate the courts and tribunals having jurisdiction and to lay down the detailed procedural rules governing actions for safeguarding rights which individuals derive from Community law . . . the detailed procedural rules governing actions for safeguarding an individual's rights under Community law must be no less favourable than those governing similar domestic actions (principle of equivalence) and must not render practically impossible or excessively difficult the exercise of rights conferred by Community law (principle of effectiveness).[6]

The Court is essentially saying:

(a) if the EU has enacted its own procedural rules, they are to be applied instead of national rules;

(b) if there are no EU rules on the matter, it is the national procedural responsibility to enforce EU law following the general national rules and procedures;

(c) *but*, there are two qualifications to such full national procedural autonomy:

   (i) requirement of equivalence;

   (ii) requirement of effectiveness.

The first step is hardly a surprise: the 'federal' choice, if exercised, pre-empts local choices. Over the years, there are more and more areas within which the Union has unified or

[3] Case 26/62 *Van Gend en Loos* [1963] ECR English Special Edition 1.

[4] Case 6/64 *Costa* [1964] ECR English Special Edition 585.

[5] See further R Schütze, *From Dual to Cooperative Federalism: The Changing Structure of European Law* (Oxford: Oxford University Press, 2009) and the discussion in chapter 4 of this volume.

[6] Case C-268/06 *Impact* [2008] ECR I-2483, paras 44–46. This is a more recent statement of the rule going back to Case 33/76 *Rewe-Zentralfinanz* [1976] ECR 1989, para 5 and Case 45/76 *Comet* [1976] ECR 2043, para 13; since then repeated in dozens of cases, such as Case C-432/05 *Unibet* [2007] ECR I-2271, para 39; Case C-40/08 *Asturcom* [2009] ECR I-9579, para 41.

harmonized institutional or procedural rules in a given area. The rules issued there can be of *legislative* or *judicial* origin.

Legislative *unification* of national procedures ensues by regulations which provide for a special regime in certain specific areas of procedure or institutional set-up. Examples in this category may include Regulation 1215/2012 (Brussels Regulation recast)[7] or the General Data Protection Regulation.[8] Such regulations cover the specific subject matter in question and exclude the parallel application of national laws governing the same issues. Thus, for instance, a German judge who is asked to enforce a final judgment issued by an Irish court in a commercial dispute ought to proceed by applying the relevant provisions of the Brussels Regulation and not the general German provisions on the enforcement of foreign judgments. The latter naturally remains valid law. But it will be only applicable to the enforcement of civil judgments coming from courts outside the European Union.

Legislative *harmonization* in the area of national procedures for enforcement of EU law typically proceeds by directives. It seeks to approximate, but not to wholly replace, national procedural rules.[9] Thus, for instance, a Czech administrative authority enforcing a tax decision for a Finnish administrative authority will proceed on the basis of the Czech code of tax procedure. However, the national procedure applied is likely to be, to a great extent, just the transposition of one and the same directive[10] in both Member States.

Finally, EU procedural rules can also be of *judicial* origin. Over the years, the case law of the Court has touched upon a number of elements of national procedural rules: access to court; standing; legal aid; time limits; interim relief, and injunctions in particular; *ex officio* application of EU law by national judges; evidence; finality of decisions (*res iudicata*); and many others. The key principles discussed in this chapter, such as direct effect, primacy, or State liability, are equally examples of judicial harmonization of the way EU and national laws are supposed to interact. In the world of traditional public international law, it would be for national constitutional rules to state under which conditions and at what level international legal rules are allowed to enter a domestic legal system. That choice has, however, been pre-empted and unified for all Member States by the early case law on direct effect and primacy, which effectively superseded the national constitutional choices on that matter.

2.2 **The not-so-autonomous national procedural autonomy**

The fact that unless EU law provides otherwise, it is the national procedures which will govern the enforcement of EU law in the Member States, is often referred to as the principle of 'national procedural autonomy'. The use of such a notion may be somewhat unfortunate: it implies freedom and choice for the Member States, which is in fact not present. When it comes to national enforcement of EU law, there is no fully 'autonomous' space free of EU law on the national level.

[7] Regulation (EU) 1215/2012 (OJ [2012] L351/1).

[8] Regulation (EU) 2016/679 (OJ [2016] L119/1).

[9] Examples include Council Directive 89/665/EEC of 21 December 1989 on the coordination of the laws, regulations and administrative provisions relating to the application of review procedures to the award of public supply and public works contracts (OJ [1989] L395/33) or Directive 2004/48/EC of 29 April 2004 on the enforcement of intellectual property rights (OJ [2004] L157/45). Before the entry into force of the Treaty of Lisbon, a number of such harmonizing instruments were adopted under the former Third Pillar (Justice and Home Affairs) and were called framework decisions—eg Council Framework Decision 2002/584/JHA of 13 June 2002 on the European arrest warrant and the surrender procedures between Member States (OJ [2002] L190/1; see chapter 24).

[10] Council Directive 2008/55/EC of 26 May 2008 on mutual assistance for the recovery of claims relating to certain levies, duties, taxes and other measures (OJ [2008] L150/28).

It is important to understand in this context that in contrast to the *legislative* unification or harmonization of national procedural rules, the *judicial* reach—that is, unification by the case law of the Court—is limitless. The exercise of EU legislative competence is governed by the principle of conferral. The Union can legislate only in specific areas attributed to it by the Treaties (in detail, see chapter 5). No such limitation is, however, present for national application of EU law. The Member States are tasked with effective enforcement of EU law, without any area or field of law limitation as to where that enforcement is (or is not) to happen. The case law of the Court can touch upon any aspect of national procedure, provided that the question relates to national enforcement of EU law-based rights and it has been submitted to the Court on a preliminary ruling.

It is thus important to underline that major difference which exists in the national enforcement of EU law. Indeed, the logic of EU legislation is one of *area-specific, conferred* competence: in order to become active, the Union must have a concrete legal basis. In contrast, the logic of the Court's engagement with national enforcement of EU law is just *functional* and *incidental*, but as to its scope *transversal*. Any and all questions of national law, provided that they serve for the enforcement of EU law-derived claims at the national level, thereby enter the *scope of national application of EU law*. The latter logic is not limited to any field or area of law.[11] Put differently again: the attributed competence limitation is fully applicable for *adopting* original legislation in Brussels. However, once that legislation has been adopted, it enters the national legal order to be implemented and applied. Any and all national rules serving the *enforcement* of that legislation are an EU law matter.

All national procedural rules may therefore be subject to the dual requirement of equivalence and/or effectiveness, provided that EU law is applicable in the individual case at hand. They may involve any part of the national administrative or judicial process: from rules on jurisdiction through access to court, fees, representation, to finality of judgments and their binding force. Seen from this perspective, it might be somewhat misplaced to refer to the original national procedural choice as 'national procedural autonomy', at least if we understand 'autonomy' in its dictionary sense as the ability to act and make decisions without being controlled by anyone else.[12]

2.3 **From equivalence/effectiveness to the principle of effective judicial protection**

The current form of national procedures for enforcing EU law on the national level is a somewhat odd mongrel. The default provisions will be the national procedural provisions. These might, however, be altered in specific sectors or in relation to specific questions by pieces of EU legislation or requirements formulated by the Court. Furthermore, the degree of unification/harmonization with respect to individual questions might also differ considerably: from full-scale unification to just a few accidental provisions relating to procedure hidden in a directive chiefly dealing with substantive issues. All this will remain interlinked with national provisions, without which national enforcement of EU law could not operate.

[11] The examples from various areas of EU law include judgment of 24 October 2018, Case C-234/17 *XC and Others*, EU:C:2018:853; judgment of 4 October 2018, Case C-571/16 *Kantarev*, EU:C:2018:807; or judgment of 13 December 2017, Case C-403/16 *El Hassani*, EU:C:2017:960.

[12] See further M Bobek, 'Why There Is No Principle of "Procedural Autonomy" of the Member States' in H-W Micklitz and B de Witte (eds), *The European Court of Justice and the Autonomy of the Member States* (Antwerp: Intersentia, 2012).

Most importantly, however, any other non-harmonized questions of national procedure are subject to the dual requirement of equivalence and/or effectiveness. *Equivalence* is in essence a prohibition of discrimination: EU law-based claims cannot be treated less favourably than comparable 'purely national' claims. Thus, for instance, a national law cannot provide that the time limit for requesting the repayment of overpaid value added tax (which is an EU-harmonized tax) is six weeks, whereas the requests for the reimbursement of overpaid income tax (which is the competence of the Member States) can be made within two years following the end of the taxable period in question.

Effectiveness is more difficult to capture. It requires not only that the enforcement of EU law-based claims cannot be rendered *practically impossible*, but also not *excessively difficult*. Impossible means impossible. It refers to situations where, for instance, an appropriate remedy would not be available at all. It would be equally unavailable for both EU law-based as well as purely national claims. Excessively difficult, on the other hand, relies on (by its nature by definition a rather subjective) view of the appropriate level of 'difficulty' claimants ought (not) to be facing when vindicating their rights under EU law. Moreover, 'excessively difficult' might mean something quite different to a multinational company with a dedicated litigation department than to a small high street business, even if both legal persons would be bringing an identical legal claim.

The more recent case law of the Court[13] has begun to discuss issues concerning national remedies more frequently in terms of *effective judicial protection*.[14] The dual requirement of equivalence and/or effectiveness is still present, but the rhetoric has shifted.[15] This terminological move corresponds to the changes brought about by the Treaty of Lisbon. First, Article 47 of the Charter of Fundamental Rights of the European Union, which became binding primary law following the Treaty of Lisbon, guarantees the 'right to an effective remedy and to a fair trial'. Secondly, the Treaty of Lisbon inserted a new provision into Article 19(1) TFEU, which reads 'Member States shall provide remedies sufficient to ensure effective legal protection in the fields covered by Union law'.

3 Within the scope of EU law?

Within such shared institutional structures at the national level, the delineation as to when a Member State's authority is in the individual case acting *within the scope of EU law* becomes of crucial importance. It logically precedes any potential discussion as to how Union law might interact with the national law in the individual case. If a case before a national authority is not within the scope of EU law, then none of the principles discussed further in this chapter are applicable. True, if the national authority wishes, it might still take EU law into account as a non-mandatory source of inspiration. But then, that source is persuasive only, as any other comparative or foreign inspiration in law.

[13] eg *Impact* (n 6) paras 43–48; Case C-279/09 *DEB* [2010] ECR I-13880, paras 29–33; Case C-177/10 *Rosado Santana* [2011] ECR I-7907, paras 87–89.

[14] Further see eg J Krommendijk, 'Is There Light on the Horizon? The Distinction between "Rewe Effectiveness" and the Principle of Effective Judicial Protection in Article 47 of the Charter after Orizzonte' (2016) 53 *Common Market Law Review* 1395.

[15] On the discussion of how much is actually new under the heading of effective judicial protection as opposed to the previous category of effectiveness, see Opinion of AG Bobek in Case C-89/17 *Banger*, EU:C:2018:225, points 99–101.

When is a national case within the scope of EU law? From the point of view of national authorities (judicial or administrative), that will typically be the case in three scenarios:

(a) The national authority is directly applying an EU legal source at the national level (*direct application of an EU source of law*). The subject matter of the case at hand is covered by an EU law act, which the national authority applies, such as the previously cited Coordination Regulation[16] and the example of a case involving an issue of social security (pension) of a migrant worker.

(b) The national authority is applying rules of national origin, which are, however, the national implementation of an EU law obligation (*implementation of an EU obligation*). That will typically be the case of directives. While formally, the national authority is likely to apply provisions of national law, there are EU law rules in the background that are being transposed and upheld by the Member State at the national level.

(c) Although not initially covered by an EU law legislative act, national rules in question enter into conflict with EU law rules, typically with those of primary law origin, such as the four fundamental freedoms—the free movement of goods, persons, services, or capital (*the conflict with EU law scenario*). Within such a scenario, however, there typically needs to be a transborder element to the free movement in order for the case to enter within the scope of EU law.[17]

Two points are to be underlined. First, in contrast to popular belief, in the first and second of the outlined scenarios, there need not be any transborder element for EU law to be applicable. Unless the given secondary law act that is being applied would explicitly require it in its text, EU law may be applicable at the national level even if there is no transborder element whatsoever. Take, for instance, a workplace discrimination dispute—EU legislation on the matter will be applicable, at present under the second scenario outlined earlier because the subject matter is regulated directives,[18] equally (or rather mostly) in purely domestic cases, concerning a national employer and employee. The same is true of the already mentioned General Data Protection Regulation, that would be directly applicable under the first scenario. Equally there, the data controller and the data subject concerned may both be from within the same Member State.

Secondly, a concern common to both, the second and third scenarios, that has arisen in particular in the past decade, is the issue *of proximity* (or reasonable, close enough connection) between EU law rules and national ones that are said to implement them or to enter into conflict with them. Could any and every national rule, however distant from the original Union obligation, be potentially within the scope of EU law at the national level? As the example of the early case law on free movement of goods demonstrates, with the approach like that in *Dassonville*, if any national rules, which are capable of *hindering, directly or indirectly, actually or potentially, intra-Community trade*,[19] were to be caught, then the reach of EU rules at the national level would indeed be limitless. The entire national legal order would simply become the transposition of EU law.

The more recent case law of the Court became therefore more circumspect in this regard, albeit specifically within the free movement of goods,[20] but equally with regard

[16] See n 2.

[17] See in particular judgment of 15 November 2016, Case C-268/15 *Ullens de Schooten*, EU:C:2016:874.

[18] Such as Directive 2006/54/EC on equal treatment of men and women in the workplace (OJ [2006] L204/23), or Directive 2000/43/EC on racial discrimination (OJ [2000] L180/22).

[19] Case 8/74 *Dassonville* [1974] ECR 837, p 852. Further see chapter 12.

[20] Already Joined Cases C-267/91 and C-268/91 *Keck and Mithouard*, EU:C:1993:905.

to the scope of EU law in general. The Court insists that there must be a direct connection between the EU obligation and its national implementation or the national conflicting rules. Thus, while 'dual purpose' national rules, which were not adopted specifically for transposing an EU law obligation, but are still occasionally used for its enforcement, will come within the scope of EU law,[21] that is not the case in a situation where the link between an EU obligation and the national rules in question is too remote or uncertain.[22] The same is true of national rules that are within the subject matter covered by a Union act, but then go clearly beyond the minimum requirements of EU law, extending the rules of the latter to situations or scenarios not foreseen by the latter.[23] It is nonetheless fair to admit that although possible to state in abstract terms, the infinite variety of factual situations may render the assessment as to whether a specific case finds itself within the scope of EU law rather complex.[24]

Finally, the rule of law backsliding or an outright rule of law crisis in several Member States has forced the Court to add what effectively amounts to an exception to the general rules on the national case needing to be within the scope of EU law.[25] Under Article 19(1) TEU, the Member States are obliged to ensure effective legal protection in the fields covered by EU law. That obligation extends *to all cases at the national level, irrespective of* whether the Member States are implementing Union law within the meaning of Article 51(1) of the Charter. It suffices that a national *court or tribunal could rule on questions concerning the application or interpretation of EU law* in general, not necessarily in the individual case, for such a situation to come under Article 19(1) TFEU.[26]

Thus, when structural, transversal issues of judicial independence are at stake, EU law may also reach into cases which may not be within the scope of EU law in the traditional sense outlined in this section. However, that extraordinary remedy should indeed remain limited to extraordinary situations.[27]

[21] Such as national rules on sanctions for tax evasion, that will be, under national law, applicable for evasion of VAT (an EU harmonized tax) as well as evasion of income tax (national one)—see already judgment of 26 February 2013, Case C-617/10 *Hans Åkerberg Fransson*, EU:C:2013:105.

[22] For the conflict with EU law scenarios, that will be the case when for a potential conflict with EU law to materialize there are several hypotheses or inferences necessary in order to make the connection ('what ... if, and if, and if')—see for illustration judgments of 7 June 2012, Case C-27/11 *Vinkov*, EU:C:2012:236; of 25 January 2007, Case C-302/06 *Koval'ský*, EU:C:2007:64; of 6 October 2006, Case C-328/04 *Vajnai*, EU:C:2005:596. With regard to the implementation scenario, see eg judgments of 11 June 2020, Case C-581/18 *TÜV Rheinland*, EU:C:2020:453 or of 10 December 2020, Case C-620/19 *J&S Services*, EU:C:2020:1011.

[23] See eg judgments of 10 July 2014, Case C-198/13 *Julián Hernández and Others*, EU:C:2014:2055; of 17 March 2015, Case C-533/13 *Auto- ja Kuljetusalan Työntekijäliitto AKT ry*, EU:C:2015:173, of 14 January 2021, Case C-826/18 *Stichting Varkens in Nood*, EU:C:2021:7.

[24] See in this regard Opinion of AG Bobek in Case C-298/16 *Ispas*, EU:C:2017:650 (particularly points 26–65), suggesting, in view of the difficulty finding in EU law as it stands a clear-cut rule, a certain 'lighthouse approach' instead, later further developed in Opinion of AG Bobek in Case C-310/16 *Dzivev*, EU:C:2018:623.

[25] See in particular judgment of 27 February 2018, Case C-64/16 *Associação Sindical dos Juízes Portugueses*, EU:C:2018:117; judgment of 24 June 2019, Case C-619/18 *Commission v Poland* (*Independence of the Supreme Court*), EU:C:2019:531; judgment of 19 November 2019, Joined Cases C-585/18, C-624/18, and C-625/18 *AK and Others* (*Independence of the Disciplinary Chamber of the Supreme Court*), EU:C:2019:982.

[26] Judgment of 19 November 2019, Joined Cases C-585/18, C-624/18, and C-625/18 *AK and Others* (*Independence of the Disciplinary Chamber of the Supreme Court*), EU:C:2019:982, paras 82 and 83.

[27] For a structural justification, see the Opinion of AG Bobek of 30 April 2019, Case C-556/17 *Torubarov*, EU:C:2019:339, points 54–56; for a concrete application, see Opinion of AG Bobek of 20 May 2021, Joined Cases C-748–754/19 *Prokuratura Rejonowa v Mińsku Mazowieckim*, EU:C:2021:403, points 130ff.

4 Direct effect

Direct effect means that an EU provision becomes the immediate source of law for the national court or administrator. No further implementing act is necessary for its application within the national legal order. EU provisions enlarge the pool of sources of law available to national authorities in deciding cases. Metaphorically speaking, directly effective EU law speaks by itself to the national judge or administrator in an unmediated way, without there being any need for its 'translation' by national law.

4.1 *Van Gend en Loos*

The principle of direct effect made its first appearance in 1963.[28] A company based in the Netherlands, Van Gend en Loos, imported a quantity of urea-formaldehyde from Germany. The company disagreed with the amount of duty charged by the Dutch Inland Revenue on this importation. It suggested that the Netherlands had in fact increased the amount of the duty by changing the tariff classification for urea-formaldehyde. Van Gend en Loos claimed that this was contrary to the then (now repealed) Article 12 EEC, which read:

> Member States shall refrain from introducing between themselves any new customs duties on import or exports or any charges having equivalent effect, and from increasing those which they already apply in their trade with each other.

The question was soon raised whether such a standstill provision, which was contained in an international agreement (the then EEC Treaty) signed by States and binding between them, has any legal effects *within those States*. Can a private party invoke such provisions directly in the courts of a signatory party?

To this question, the Court, in spite of the united opposition of all the Member States intervening (the Netherlands, Belgium, Germany), and against the Opinion of Advocate General Roemer issued in the case, answered 'yes'. As put by the Court:

> The objective of the EEC Treaty, which is to establish a Common Market, the functioning of which is of direct concern to interested parties in the Community, implies that this Treaty is more than an agreement which merely creates mutual obligations between the contracting states. . . .
>
> The conclusion to be drawn from this is that the Community constitutes a new legal order of international law for the benefit of which the states have limited their sovereign rights, albeit within limited fields, and the subjects of which comprise not only Member States but also their nationals. Independently of the legislation of Member States, Community law therefore not only imposes obligations on individuals but is also intended to confer upon them rights which become part of their legal heritage. These rights arise not only where they are expressly granted by the Treaty, but also by reason of obligations which the Treaty imposes in a clearly defined way upon individuals as well as upon the Member States and upon the institutions of the Community.[29]

[28] *Van Gend en Loos* (n 3). [29] Ibid, para 12.

Drawing on these general statements, the Court further held with respect to Article 12 EEC:

> The wording of Article 12 contains a clear and unconditional prohibition which is not a positive but a negative obligation. This obligation, moreover, is not qualified by any reservation on the part of states which would make its implementation conditional upon a positive legislative measure enacted under national law. The very nature of this prohibition makes it ideally adapted to produce direct effects in the legal relationship between Member States and their subjects.
>
> The implementation of Article 12 does not require any legislative intervention on the part of the states. The fact that under this Article it is the Member States who are made the subject of the negative obligation does not imply that their nationals cannot benefit from this obligation.[30]

In the view of the Court, a clear and unconditional prohibition such as Article 12 EEC, which does not necessitate any further implementation by the Member States, is capable of producing direct effect in the Member States' legal orders. What matters is the wording of the Treaty provision itself, *not the original intent* of its signatories. Thus, Treaty provisions could be directly effective even if the Member States did not intend it or, at best, were indifferent to such an idea when signing the Treaties. By opting for such an *objective* test of direct effect, the Court cut the cord with traditional public international law, where the intent of the signatories is relevant for the later interpretation of a treaty.[31]

Moreover, by stipulating that EU law is to be directly effective in all the Member States' legal systems *irrespective of* what their individual national constitutions state in relation to the domestic status of international law, the Court *pre-empted* national choices in that regard. By combining both of these points in one stroke, the Court indeed carved out *a new legal order*, independent of both international law as well as national constitutions.

4.2 **The conditions and the real test**

In *Van Gend en Loos*, the Court stated that a Treaty provision may produce direct effects in the Member States if it is:

(a) clear;

(b) unconditional in the sense of not allowing for any reservations on the part of the Member States; and

(c) not dependent on any subsequent further implementation measures to be adopted by the Member States or the Community.

However, subsequent case law obscured these conditions in two ways. First, even Treaty articles which were conditional or dependent on further implementation measures were eventually deemed to be directly effective.[32] Secondly, direct effect was expanded to other sources of EU law: regulations, decisions, directives, as well as provisions of

[30] Ibid, para 13.

[31] cf Art 31 of the Vienna Convention on the Law of Treaties (1969), UN Treaty Series, vol 1155, p 331.

[32] See notably Case 2/74 *Reyners* [1974] ECR 631; Case 41/74 *Van Duyn* [1974] ECR 1337; Case 43/75 *Defrenne* [1976] ECR 455. It is quite telling that, eg in *Defrenne*, where the Court found that Art 119 EC (now Art 157 TFEU—equal pay for equal work) is directly effective, the conditions laid down in *Van Gend en Loos* for direct effect are neither discussed nor even cited.

international agreements to which the EU is a party. The conditions for direct effect of these other sources, however, vary. Their application in practice, in particular with respect to potential direct effect of international agreements, is even more divergent. Thus, it is open to debate whether there is one 'direct effect' of EU law or rather several 'direct effects'.

The standard formula used by the Court for direct effect (of directives) today includes three conditions. A provision of a directive may be directly effective if it is:

(a) sufficiently (clear and) precise;
(b) unconditional;
(c) the Member State in question failed to implement the directive by the end of the period prescribed therein or failed to implement the directive correctly.[33]

The changing nature of the conditions for direct effect brings to the fore the true nature of the test. In spite of being labelled differently and sometimes even not being labelled at all, the test has, on the level of the basic question it poses, perhaps always been the same: does the EU law provision in question contain *an understandable and justiciable rule of behaviour*, which can be applied directly by national authorities? It suffices if such a rule is recognizable and extractable from a broader or more detailed EU provision. It does not need to be expressed verbatim in the provision itself. That is why EU provisions, which leave much to be desired in terms of clarity of their literal expression, can in fact be directly effective, as long as there is a clear rule of behaviour which can be extracted from such provisions.[34] Thus, in spite of the EU legal order since its very beginnings insisting on being something more than 'mere' international law (see further chapter 7), direct effect remains a type of centrally imposed general 'self-execution' command for EU law in national legal orders in all but name.

To provide an example: Article 34 TFEU reads, 'Quantitative restrictions on imports and all measures having equivalent effect shall be prohibited between Member States.' This provision is directly effective, in spite of containing two indeterminate legal notions ('quantitative restrictions' and 'measures having equivalent effect') which, as decades of the case law of the Court on the free movement of goods evidence, are in dire need of interpretation (see further chapter 12).

EU law provisions which are not directly effective are those from which such an extraction exercise of an immediately applicable rule is impossible. These instances tend to be limited to provisions which are wholly incapable of direct judicial application. They include mere programme or aim-setting norms[35] or provisions which themselves were supposed to establish new legal constructs or institutions in the Member States,[36] subject to considerable discretion to be exercised by the Member States in relation to choice and implementation.[37]

[33] More recently, eg Case C-268/06 *Impact* [2008] ECR I-2483, para 57; Joined Cases C-397–403/01 *Pfeiffer* [2004] ECR I-8835, para 103; judgment of 6 November 2018, Case C-684/16 *Max-Planck-Gesellschaft zur Förderung der Wissenschaften*, EU:C:2018:874, para 63; judgment of 8 March 2022, Case C-205/20 *Bezirkshauptmannschaft Hartberg-Fürstenfeld*, EU:C:2022:168, para 17.

[34] This rule of thumb is, however, applicable only to EU *internal* sources—Treaties and EU legislation. Direct effect of international agreements is a case apart. Further see chapter 26.

[35] See eg Joined Cases C-72/91 and C-73/91 *Sloman Neptun* [1993] ECR I-887 or Case 126/86 *Zaera* [1987] ECR 3697.

[36] eg setting up a new and quite complex mechanism for protection of employees in the event of the insolvency of their employer—see Joined Cases C-6/90 and C-9/90 *Francovich and Bonifaci* [1991] ECR I-5357.

[37] Further see eg judgments of 5 February 2004, Case C-157/02 *Rieser Internationale Transporte*, EU:C:2004:76, para 40; of 5 September 2012, Case C-83/11 *Rahman ea*, EU:C:2012:519, para 25; or of 15 February 2017, Case C-592/15 *British Film Institute*, EU:C:2017:117, paras 14–24.

4.3 **Direct effect in action**

A directly effective provision of EU law may function in a number of ways. Two of them are frequent. First, a directly effective EU provision may *create a new rule* which did not previously exist in national law, and which will then be applied in the case at hand. Secondly, together with the principle of primacy of EU law, it may exclude the application of an *existing* but contrary national *rule*.

To illustrate the difference: imagine a fictitious EU directive on judicial education. The aim of the directive is to facilitate judicial cooperation between the Member States in civil, commercial, and criminal matters. Apart from providing for systemic education of judges in EU law, it also grants all judges five days of additional paid leave annually for the purpose of further study. Member State A, we may call it Brutalia, did not implement this directive at all. Judges have a right to the same benefits as all other State employees. However, Brutalian State employees have no right to study leave in general. Member State B, which might be called Exceptia, has implemented the directive. However, it denied the five days' study leave to all national judges dealing with family cases. Exceptia stated that it suffers from a chronic shortage of family judges. Taking into account its constitutional as well as international human rights obligations to deal with family cases, especially those relating to minor children in an expedient manner, Exceptia maintains that it cannot provide all family judges with five days of extra study leave every year.

Assume that the provision of the directive providing for the five extra days is directly effective. In Brutalia, judges invoking this provision against the State will ask the national court to apply it directly in the national legal order, thus *substituting* the directive for a non-existent (non-implemented) provision of national law. In Exceptia, family judges seeking to rely on the same provision will ask for the conflicting national rule which denies the five days' study leave to them to be *excluded* from the national legal order. Both of these examples are instances of direct effect, which can either substitute a national rule which is lacking, or exclude a conflicting one.[38]

There are two further important characteristics of the operation of the principle of direct effect which ought to be mentioned.[39] First, the test for direct effect is carried out with respect to individual provisions of EU law. Thus, even a single section or indent of a Treaty article or a directive may be directly effective. Secondly, even EU provisions which do not grant any individual, subjective rights may be directly effective. Direct effect is concerned with objective justiciability of an EU provision. Granting individual rights is not a *condition* for direct effect. Subjective rights and their vindication might be *the cause* for an individual invoking EU law in the first place. Granting some individual rights will also be the logical consequence if the individual action was successful.[40] Moreover, as we will see in the immediately following sections, in certain types of legal relationships, individual rights may bar an otherwise directly effective provision of a directive from being

[38] The debate between the proponents of a narrow notion of direct effect (substitution only) or the broad notion of direct effect (substitution and exclusion) may be said to be resolved in favour of the latter by the Grand Chamber of the Court in *Pfeiffer* (n 33), more recently confirmed in the judgment of 24 June 2019, Case C-573/17 *Popławski*, EU:C:2019:530. In any case, that debate had been rather academic, as both sides recognize that EU law requires the exclusion of a conflicting national rule. They thus both arrive at the same outcome. They differ only in the argument whether the reason for exclusion is direct effect or, rather, the primacy of EU law.

[39] For a more detailed analysis, see Opinion of AG Bobek in Case C-167/17 *Klohn*, EU:C:2018:387, points 36–46.

[40] In general, see also JHH Weiler, '*Van Gend en Loos*: The Individual as Subject and Object and the Dilemma of European Legitimacy' (2014) 12 *ICON* 94.

applied to the detriment of the individual. That said, however, granting of individual rights is in itself not one of the general conditions for direct effect.[41]

4.4 **Differentiation I: types of legal acts**

Subsequent case law of the Court expanded direct effect to other sources of EU law. However, as already mentioned, with this expansion also came differentiation between the various direct effects, their conditions, and their scope. The first type of differentiation relates to the *type of source* of EU law which may be directly effective. The second type of differentiation is based on the *nature of the parties* to a legal relationship for which the EU provision is supposed to be directly effective. The second differentiation makes the national application of EU law somewhat 'directional'. It distinguishes between *vertical* (an individual—ie physical or legal person—suing the State; also known as ascending vertical), *reverse vertical* (the State suing, or rather punishing, the individual; also known as descending vertical), and *horizontal* types of legal relationship (involving just private individuals—physical or legal persons—on both sides).

4.4.1 **Treaty and Charter provisions**

Van Gend en Loos and subsequent case law[42] established the direct effect of Treaty provisions. Over the years, the case law of the Court has confirmed the direct effect of the key Treaty provisions, such those relating to the free movement of goods, persons, or capital; competition law; State aid; and equal pay. Moreover, directly effective Treaty provisions can be invoked in any type of legal relationship: vertical, including reverse vertical, as well as horizontal.[43]

Since 2009, the EU Charter of Fundamental Rights has become part of primary law. Article 6(1) TEU states that the Charter shall have the same legal value as the Treaties. Charter provisions can be directly effective in the sense of their invoking against the Union institutions and the Member States when they are implementing EU law (Article 51(1) of the Charter). Thus, ascending vertical direct effect of fundamental rights provisions is common practice. After all, fundamental rights catalogues are there to be relied upon against the public power. Limiting the public power is their very purpose. The more complex and contested issue has been the horizontal direct effect of the Charter: could the Charter, or certain of its provisions, apply horizontally, in situations between two private parties? After initial hesitation,[44] the case law of the Court confirmed the (horizontal) direct effect of a number of Charter provisions, in particular its Article 21 (various types of prohibition of discrimination),[45] Article 31(2) (right to annual paid leave),[46] Article 47 (right to an effective remedy),[47] or Article 50 (prohibition of *non bis in idem*).[48]

[41] See, in general, eg judgment of 25 July 2008, Case C-237/07 *Janecek*, EU:C:2008:447, paras 37–39. The granting of individual rights is, however, as will be shown in section 7 of this chapter, one of the conditions for State liability for breaches of EU law. Naturally, however, direct effect and State liability are distinct remedies.

[42] See nn 3 and 32.

[43] Already *Defrenne* (n 32) and Case 36/74 *Walrave and Koch* [1974] ECR 1405; later, eg Case C-281/98 *Angonese* [2000] ECR I-4139 or Case C-438/05 *Viking* [2007] ECR I-10779.

[44] See notably Case C-176/12 *Association de médiation sociale*, EU:C:2014:2, paras 44–49.

[45] Judgment of 17 April 2018, Case C-414/16 *Egenberger*, EU:C:2018:257; judgment of 11 September 2018, Case C-68/17 *IR*, EU:C:2018:696; judgment of 22 January 2019, Case C-193/17 *Cresco Investigation*, EU:C:2019:43.

[46] Judgment of 6 November 2018, Case C-619/16 *Kreuziger*, EU:C:2018:872; judgment of 6 November 2018, Cases C-569/16 and C-570/16 *Bauer and Willmeroth*, EU:C:2018:871; judgment of 6 November 2018, Case C-684/16 *Max-Planck-Gesellschaft zur Förderung der Wissenschaften*, EU:C:2018:874.

[47] Judgment of 17 April 2018, Case C-414/16 *Egenberger*, EU:C:2018:257; judgment of 29 July 2019, Case C-556/17 *Torubarov*, EU:C:2019:626; or judgment of 19 November 2019, Joined Cases C-585/18, C-624/18, and C-625/18 *AK and Others (Independence of the Disciplinary Chamber of the Supreme Court)*, EU:C:2019:982.

[48] Judgment of 20 March 2018, Case C-537/16 *Garlsson Real Estate and Others*, EU:C:2018:193.

If measured against the traditional criteria of clear, unconditional, and in no need of further implementation, Charter provisions are not good candidates for direct effect: they tend to be rather abstract, vague, and in need of further legislative implementation. Moreover, bills of rights and fundamental rights charters are addressed to the State or public power, not to other individuals. For similar reasons, most of the national legal orders, even those with rather robust catalogues of fundamental rights, deny direct horizontal applicability to their fundamental rights catalogues. They allow instead for a variety of conforming interpretation, the radiating effect of fundamental rights, into private relationships and disputes.[49]

4.4.2 **Regulations**

Regulations were the optimal candidate for direct effect. From the very beginnings of the EEC, the Treaty stated that a regulation 'shall be binding in its entirety and directly applicable in all Member States'.[50] This original Treaty-based distinction between the effects of individual sources of EU law was, however, soon blurred by the Court's robust vision of direct effect. If Treaty provisions and directives can also produce direct effects in the Member States, what is then the difference between 'direct effect' and 'direct applicability' of regulations?

In earlier case law, the Court simply equated direct effect with direct applicability.[51] Later, however, this position became nuanced, separating the two categories again.[52] *Direct applicability* means that unless expressly requested by the regulation itself,[53] no national implementing act is by default necessary. A regulation, once it has entered into force, will be immediately applicable in all the Member States. *Direct effect*, on the other hand, aims at the justiciability of a provision: can it be applied by a national authority directly?

The Court further stated that the direct effect of regulations is generally *presumed* and need not be specifically examined.[54] There might nonetheless be rare cases in which a provision of a directly applicable regulation is not directly effective.[55] Imagine a regulation which is so abstract or conditional upon a number of other further legislative acts that it contains simply no 'executable' rules which could be applied judicially.

Finally, a regulation is applicable and directly effective in any type of legal relationship: vertical as well as horizontal. Equally, the enforcement of a regulation may naturally include sanctions imposed by a State against individuals. Competition law might provide examples in this respect. In this area of EU law, it frequently occurs that the Commission or the national authorities impose (considerable) sanctions on individual undertakings for violating their obligations provided for by EU regulations or Treaty articles.

4.4.3 **Decisions**

Decisions under Article 288 TFEU are of two kinds: addressed and non-addressed (see further chapter 5).[56] An addressed decision is an individual act, stating its concrete addressee(s). A non-addressed decision amounts in practice to a legislative act in all but

[49] In general, see eg R Alexy, *Theorie der Grundrechte* (Baden-Baden: Nomos, 1985) 473ff or A Sajó and R Uitz (eds), *The Constitution in Private Relations: Expanding Constitutionalism* (The Hague: Eleven, 2005).

[50] Now Art 288 TFEU.

[51] Case 43/71 *Politi* [1971] ECR 1039, para 9.

[52] See the Opinion of AG Geelhoed in Case C-253/00 *Muñoz and Superior Fruiticola* [2002] ECR I-7289, paras 22ff.

[53] See eg Case C-592/11 *Ketelä*, EU:C:2012:673, para 35 or Case C-316/10 *Danske Svineproducenter*, EU:C:2011:863, paras 39 and 40.

[54] Case C-367/09 *SGB Belgium* [2010] ECR I-10761, para 32; Case C-278/02 *Handlbauer* [2004] ECR I-6171, para 25. See also Case C-375/09 *Tele2 Polska* [2011] ECR I-3055, paras 31–35.

[55] Case C-403/98 *Monte Arcosu* [2001] ECR I-103.

[56] For the sake of completeness, it might be recalled that decisions as named (or typical) sources of EU law under Art 288 TFEU are different from 'framework decisions', adopted under the pre-Lisbon 'Third' Pillar (AFSJ pillar). On direct effect of framework decisions, see judgment of 24 June 2019, Case C-573/17 *Popławski*, EU:C:2019:530.

name. Although labelled a 'decision', it does not expressly name its addressees, but provides a set of abstract and general rules. This dual nature and use of decisions is also reflected with respect to their potential direct effect. A decision addressed to concrete person(s) other than a Member State will be binding on those persons in its entirety. This is due, however, to the binding nature of an individual administrative decision. A decision addressed to a Member State or several Member States might produce direct effect with respect to individuals within those Member States in question, provided its provisions are sufficiently clear, precise, and unconditional.[57]

Direct effect of a decision is, however, limited to vertical situations, in which an individual is invoking a directly effective provision of a decision against the Member State to which it was addressed. Similarly to directives, the Court has refused to consider decisions as horizontally directly applicable. They cannot be invoked in a dispute between two individuals to whom the decision was addressed before the courts of their Member State.[58]

Finally, over the years the Court has examined and expanded direct effect to other sources of EU law, including international agreements to which the Union is party;[59] measures previously adopted under other 'pillars' (see chapter 2), and equally to general principles of EU law.[60] Our attention in the ensuing section will, however, turn to the most complicated yet the most frequently used instance of direct effect: the case of directives.

4.5 **Differentiation II: types of legal relationship**

If it were not for directives, direct effect could have become a rather marginal topic of academic interest to EU constitutional lawyers. The default rule for a national judge would be directly to engage with EU law provided that its provisions are justiciable.[61] It was, however, the direct effect of directives and in particular the differentiation the Court introduced with respect to various types of legal relationship, followed by a number of exceptions to the exception itself, which made the case law difficult to navigate.

As already mentioned in the previous section with respect to regulations and directly applicable Treaty provisions, their infusion into the national legal order is complete. They may be applied in any type of legal relationship: vertical, reverse vertical, as well as horizontal. On the other hand, for directives and, by extension also for decisions, the type of legal relationship, or rather the direction within, matters.

In *Van Duyn*,[62] the Court stated that directives may be vertically directly effective. The case involved a Dutch national, Mrs Van Duyn, who was refused leave to enter the UK to take up employment as a secretary with the Church of Scientology. The UK considered the activities of the said church to be socially harmful. Appealing the decision of the UK authorities, Mrs Van Duyn wished to rely, inter alia, on provisions of a directive.[63]

The Court stated that individuals may rely on a directive's provisions to vindicate their rights against the Member State. In order to do so, however, the provision of a directive must

[57] Case C-18/08 *Foselev* [2008] ECR I-8745, para 11; Case C-156/91 *Hansa Fleisch Ernst Mundt* [1992] ECR I-5567, paras 12 and 13; Case 9/70 *Grad* [1970] ECR 825, para 5.

[58] Case C-80/06 *Carp* [2007] ECR I-4473, paras 19–22.

[59] For an introduction in this very complex area, see chapter 26.

[60] Case C-144/04 *Mangold* [2005] ECR I-9981 and Case C-555/07 *Kücükdeveci* [2010] ECR I-365. For another illustration, see judgment of 22 November 2017, Case C-251/16 *Cussens*, EU:C:2017:881.

[61] Thereby fulfilling the vision presented in P Pescatore, 'The Doctrine of "Direct Effect": An Infant Disease of Community Law' (1983) 8 *European Law Review* 155.

[62] Case 41/74 *Van Duyn* [1974] ECR 1337.

[63] Council Directive 64/221/EEC (OJ [1964] L56, English special edition, Series I, vol 1963–4, p 117).

be sufficiently clear and precise, unconditional,[64] and the implementation period the Member State had for transposing the directive into the national legal order must have already passed.

There was no textual support in the Treaty for the conclusion reached by the Court. The Treaty stated[65] that directives are, in contrast to regulations, binding upon each Member State as to the results to be achieved, leaving to the national authorities the choice of form and method for their implementation. Thus, there was a strong argument suggesting that a directive is an obligation of result, binding the Member States but, in contrast to regulations, not directly applicable within their legal orders.

The perhaps strongest argument the Court offered for overriding the text of the Treaty was not in fact articulated in *Van Duyn* itself, but later.[66] It became known as the 'estoppel argument': a Member State that has failed to implement a directive cannot rely on that failure as a defence against an individual who is invoking the directive. In other words, direct effect may be seen as a certain type of 'sanction' against a defaulting Member State. If the Member State had implemented the directive on time and/or correctly, it could have exercised its choice as to how it wished to do so, how far it wanted to go, and by what means. However, because it had failed to do so, it had forfeited that choice.

The estoppel rationale for direct effect has been contested.[67] It nonetheless puts the direct effect of directives on a solid, albeit perhaps one-sided, footing. The argument that no one should be allowed to profit from their own wrong has a universal moral appeal. The same argument, however, also decisively framed the ensuing direction-based differentiation within the direct effect of directives. First, if a Member State cannot prevent an individual's reliance on a sufficiently clear and precise provision of a directive after the time for its implementation has elapsed, then that Member State is precluded from enforcing the non-implemented directive against its own nationals. Thus, *reverse vertical* direct effect of directives is excluded.[68] A Member State must first transpose the directive into its national law and only then can it enforce it against individuals.

Secondly, and more importantly, the State-centred rationale within the estoppel argument does not answer the question whether or not a directive can be directly effective in *horizontal* relationships between two private individuals. The Court addressed this question in *Marshall*.[69] Mrs Marshall challenged the compulsory retirement age for women in the UK, which was set at 62 at that time, as discriminatory. She wished to continue working, which would have been possible for a man, as the retirement age for men was set at 65. The question arose whether she could rely on the provisions of a directive prohibiting sex discrimination as against her employer. The Court stated that:

> the binding nature of a directive, which constitutes the basis for the possibility of relying on the directive before a national court, exists only in relation to 'each Member State to which it is addressed'. It follows that a directive may not of itself impose obligations on an individual and that a provision of a directive may not be relied upon as such against such a person.[70]

[64] For more recent examples in which those conditions are not met with regard to provisions of a directive, see eg Joined Cases C-165–167/09 *Stichting Natuur en Milieu and Others*, EU:C:2011:348, paras 92–98; or judgment of 16 July 2015, Joined Cases C-108/14 and C-109/14 *Larentia + Minerva and Marenave Schiffahrt*, EU:C:2015:496, paras 50–52.

[65] As it still does today in the third intent of Art 288 TFEU.

[66] Case 148/78 *Ratti* [1979] ECR 1629, para 22. See also Case 152/84 *Marshall* [1986] ECR 737, para 47 or judgment of 14 July 1994, Case C-91/92 *Faccini Dori*, EU:C:1994:292, point 24.

[67] eg S Prechal, *Directives in EC Law* (2nd edn, Oxford: Oxford University Press, 2005) 223–226.

[68] Case C-80/86 *Kolpinghuis Nijmegen* [1987] ECR 3969, paras 9 and 13; Case C-168/95 *Arcaro* [1996] ECR I-4705, paras 36 and 37; Joined Cases C-387/02, C-391/02, and C-403/02 *Berlusconi* [2005] ECR I-3565, paras 73 and 74.

[69] *Marshall* (n 66).

[70] Ibid, para 48.

In *Marshall*, as well as subsequent case law, a number of arguments were offered for not extending the direct effect of directives to horizontal situations. One of the prominent arguments was that of legal certainty: individuals are not the addressees of directives.[71] They are not obliged to follow directives in order to know their legal obligations. Therefore, directives cannot directly impose obligations upon them. Moreover, the key argument that served for the expansion of the principle of direct effect to directives in the first place, the estoppel argument, cannot be stretched so far as to justify the direct effect of directives in horizontal situations.[72]

4.6 **No horizontal direct effect of directives: the rule and the exceptions**

The original choice made by the Court with respect to the horizontal direct effect of directives might be criticized. The greatest problem this area of case law has been facing is nonetheless not the choice the Court made in *Marshall*. The real issue is that the Court has not been ready to adhere to that choice *in substance*. In its subsequent case law, while verbally upholding the 'no-horizontal-direct-effect-of-directives' rule established in *Marshall*, the Court created a number of alternative avenues for reaching into horizontal relationships. These exceptions in fact undermined the original position taken. When taken together, they make a curious observer wonder what is the rule and what are the exceptions in fact.

The original rule is that EU law provisions generally are capable of direct effect. The exception to this rule is that in certain types of legal relationship, in particular in horizontal relationships, a directive or a decision is precluded from becoming directly effective. However, the subsequent case law of the Court has created further exceptions to the latter exception, thus somewhat silently reaffirming the original rule, in a number of ways.

First, *Marshall* itself already started with viewing what is a 'Member State' in a rather expansionist view. The subsequent case law expanded the notion of the 'State' to encompass any organization or body which is subject to the authority or control of the State *or* has special powers beyond those which result from the normal rules applicable to relations between individuals. Therefore, all bodies or entities which are subject to the authority or control of a public authority or the State will, for the purpose of direct effect of directives, be considered to be part of the Member State.[73] This category includes, for instance, public hospitals, State-owned companies, or any private bodies which have been entrusted with the exercise of any aspect of a 'public authority'.

The Court has further held that even when a State is acting in a 'private capacity', for example as a normal employer, exercising no sovereign power or authority in a legal relationship, the relationship will, for the purpose of the direct effect of directives, still be deemed as vertical and not horizontal.[74] That would include, for instance, staff employed by a State-run hospital or school. The staff (eg nurses, doctors, teachers) have normal,

[71] See the Opinion of AG Slynn of 18 September 1985 in Case C-152/84 *Marshall*, EU:C:1986:84, pp 734–735.

[72] As the Court indicated in Case C-91/92 *Faccini Dori* [1994] ECR I-3325, paras 20–24, and more recently restated eg in judgment of 7 August 2018, Case C-122/17 *Smith*, EU:C:2018:631, para 45. For further discussion, see P Craig, 'The Legal Effects of Directives: Policy, Rules and Exceptions' (2009) 34 *European Law Review* 349 or A Dashwood, 'From *Van Duyn* to *Mangold* via *Marshall*: Reducing Direct Effect to Absurdity' (2006–7) 9 *Cambridge Yearbook of European Legal Studies* 81.

[73] Judgment of 12 July 1990, Case C-188/89 *Foster*, EU:C:1990:313, paras 18 and 20; with an important clarification about the nature of both conditions (being connected by a disjunctive 'or') finally coming in judgment of 10 October 2017, Case C-413/15 *Farrell*, EU:C:2017:745, para 28.

[74] Judgment of 26 February 1986, Case 152/84 *Marshall*, EU:C:1986:84, para 49; or judgment of 18 November 2010, Joined Cases C-250/09 and C-268/09 *Georgiev*, EU:C:2009:549, para 70.

private law contracts of employment. They are not civil servants. For the Court, however, even such, technically speaking, 'horizontal' and private law contractual relationships would be a type of ascending vertical relationship, as one of the parties is the State, even if acting as a normal 'private' employer. The employees could therefore rely on directly effective provisions of directives as against the employer.[75]

Secondly, the Court has allowed Member States' failure to notify technical standards and regulations to spill over into private relationships, affecting individuals who were not only not to blame, but unlikely to even be aware of the failure of the Member State.[76] One may imagine two Austrian companies that conclude an otherwise perfectly valid contract for the delivery of several thousand plastic toys. At the time of delivery, the buyer refuses to accept the toys, claiming that although the products are in compliance with all the applicable Austrian legislation, a piece of national legislation adopted two years previously lays down the maximum content of polymer additives for children's toys is a technical standard that should have been notified to the Commission. Because the Austrian government failed to do so two years earlier, the private law contract concluded between the buyer and seller cannot be enforced.[77]

Thirdly, the Court affirmed that general principles of law are applicable in horizontal relationships without any limitations.[78] Thus, an employment contract concluded between an individual and a private company (ie a company that is indeed not a 'Member State', even on the broad reading of that notion under the first point made earlier). Suppose that the employer believes that in the employment contract there is a provision which constitutes discrimination on the basis of age: for instance, there is a different retirement age for men and women or there is an age-based differentiation in the amount of occupational pension premiums to be paid by the employer and employee respectively.[79] As both parties to the contract are private individuals, the direct effect of directives is said to be excluded. However, no such limitation applies to the general principle of discrimination on the basis of age, the existence of which the Court has confirmed in *Mangold*.[80] Such a general principle will then be applicable horizontally, with exactly the same (or, in fact, even broader) results as if the directive itself were horizontally directly applicable.

Fourthly, as already explained in section 4.4.1 of this chapter, over the past decade, the Court has held that a number of Charter provisions can be relied upon directly (ie are, for

[75] See judgment of 12 December 2013, Case C-425/12 *Portgás*, EU:C:2013:829, paras 23–38 or judgment of 12 September 2013, Case C-614/11 *Anneliese Kuso*, EU:C:2013:544, para 32.

[76] The line of case law starting with the judgment of 30 April 1996, Case C-194/94 *CIA Security International*, EU:C:1996:172 and culminating in judgment of 26 September 2000, Case C-443/98 *Unilever Italia*, EU:C:2000:496. Subsequent case law has sought to contain this line of cases, with respect to its reach (see eg judgment of 16 June 1998, Case C-226/97 *Lemmens*, EU:C:1998:296) as well as its impact on the validity of private contracts (judgment of 6 June 2002, Case C-159/00 *Sapod Audic*, EU:C:2002:343).

[77] Intriguingly, the same discussion might be reignited with regard to Regulation (EU) 2019/515 of the European Parliament and of the Council of 19 March 2019 on the mutual recognition of goods lawfully marketed in another Member State and repealing Regulation (EC) No 764/2008 (OJ [2019] L91/1), which established a notification obligation similar to technical standards for market authorizations, without clearly setting out the procedural consequences for a failure to notify.

[78] Judgment of 22 November 2005, Case C-144/04 *Mangold*, EU:C:2005:709 and judgment of 19 January 2010, Case C-555/07 *Kücükdeveci*, EU:C:2010:21. But contrast also judgment of 11 July 2006, Case C-13/05 *Chacón Navas*, EU:C:2006:456 or judgment of 15 October 2009, Case C-101/08 *Audiolux*, EU:C:2009:626. Outside the prohibition of discrimination, see eg judgment of 22 November 2017, Case C-251/16 *Cussens and Others*, EU:C:2017:881 (with the Irish Supreme Court enquiring about the temporal applicability of the general principle of the prohibition of abuse of law in tax law).

[79] Recently, eg judgment of 26 September 2013, Case C-476/11 *HK Danmark*, EU:C:2013:590, as well as judgment of 12 October 2010, Case C-499/08 *Ingeniørforeningen i Danmark*, EU:C:2010:600, followed up by the judgment of 19 April 2016, Case C-441/14 *Dansk Industri*, EU:C:2016:278.

[80] Judgment of 22 November 2005, Case C-144/04 *Mangold*, EU:C:2005:709.

all practical purposes, horizontally directly applicable) in disputes between two individuals. In practice, in particular in relation to social rights, but also prohibition of discrimination, directly effective Charter rights are fuelled by the content of secondary legislation, in particular by the relevant (but not directly effective) directive. Of course, not every provision of a directive will make it into a Charter-guaranteed right. But it is precisely the selectivity of that transition that poses issues in terms of predictability.

Fifthly, in *Popławski II*, after some previous hesitations,[81] the Court explicitly confirmed that 'a provision of EU law which does not have direct effect may not be relied on, as such, in a dispute coming under EU law in order to disapply a provision of national law that conflicts with it'.[82] The Court thus explicitly tied the setting aside of national conflicting norms to an EU law provision having direct effect. Setting aside cannot therefore be the consequence of the principle of primacy of EU law alone.[83] *Popławski II* concerned framework decisions. However, subsequent case law has confirmed that the same is applicable also to Treaties and Charter provisions.[84]

Such a seemingly abstract constitutional statement is of practical significance for the issue of direct effect. In order to be effectively able to reach into a case before a national court, an EU law rule of whatever nature needs to be directly effective. Certainly, direct effect is not a precondition for conform interpretation, which could always serve as a substitute in an individual case. However, in practice, it is unlikely to happen frequently that a provision of a directive is either not sufficiently clear, precise, or unconditional, and therefore cannot be directly effective, while the same provision would be sufficiently clear as to allow the national judge to determine which of the possible interpretations she should choose from among the range of possible options. If a provision lacks the basic clarity to be justiciable, it is unlikely, although in a particular constellation certainly not fully excluded, that it will be clear enough to instruct a national judge as to the conform interpretation of national law.[85]

However, all that means that, within such a broad vision of direct effect, where it is only directly effective provisions that will really 'bite' at the national level, there will be a natural tendency of declaring every provision of EU law directly effective. Thus, the trend that has existed in the past decade with regard to the Charter provisions, will only be further enhanced with regard to any and every provision of EU law.[86] Otherwise, EU law would

[81] The issue would appear to had been settled in judgment of 5 October 2004, Joined Cases C-379–403/01 *Pfeiffer*, EU:C:2004:584, only to resurge again as indeed open in judgment of 4 October 2018, Case C-384/17 *Link Logistic*, EU:C:2018:810.

[82] Judgment of 24 June 2019, Case C-573/17 *Poplawski II*, EU:C:2019:530, point 62.

[83] Contrast section 4.3 and in particular n 38.

[84] See eg judgments of 19 November 2019, Joined Cases C-585/18, C-624/18, and C-625/18 *AK and Others (Independence of the Disciplinary Chamber of the Supreme Court)*, EU:C:2019:982, para 161; of 19 December 2019, Case C-752/18 *Deutsche Umwelthilfe*, EU:C:2019:1114, para 42; of 14 May 2020, Case C-615/18 *Staatsanwaltschaft Offenburg*, EU:C:2020:376, para 69; of 30 September 2020, Case C-233/19 *Liège*, EU:C:2020:757, para 54; of 15 April 2021, Case C-30/19 *Braathens Regional Aviation*, EU:C:2021:269, para 58; and of 18 May 2021, Joined Cases C-83/19, C-127/19, C-195/19, C-291/19, C-355/19, and C-397/19 *Asociația 'Forumul Judecătorilor din România' and Others*, EU:C:2021:393, para 248.

[85] For illustration, see the Opinion of AG Bobek of 5 June 2018, Case C-167/17 *Volkmar Klohn*, EU:C:2018:387, points 69ff, where the same issue (and the choice between potentially direct effect and indirect effect) arose with regard to a rule that litigation in environmental matters is *not to be prohibitively expensive*. If such a rule was, in the context of a given case, not sufficiently clear, precise, and unconditional as to be directly applied (because the national judge would allegedly not understand what she is supposed to do in a given case), it is difficult to see how exactly the same rule would possess the necessary clarity for conform interpretation of national law.

[86] See eg the judgment of 8 March 2022, Case C-205/20 *Bezirkhauptmannschaft Hartberg-Fürstenberg*, EU:C:2022:168, by which the Grand Chamber of the Court explicitly overruled *Link Logistic* and stated that the principle of proportionality of sanctions has direct effect.

effectively remain *ante portas* of national legal order, with potential conform interpretation or State liability being the only remedies in an individual case.

Sixthly and finally, the Court has promoted a very robust vision of indirect effect/conform interpretation (see section 5 of this chapter) as a way for directives to reach into horizontal relationships. Conform interpretation is therefore the alternative and very powerful tool to reach into horizontal, private relationships.

In sum, the combined effect of all the outlined exceptions to the rule of 'no-horizontal-direct-effect-of-directives' comes close to reversing the relationship between the rule and the exception. Or it in fact goes even further: secondary legislation, such as directives, would at least have some textual limits. What might be inserted into a vague and indeterminate fundamental right under the Charter, or reborn as a general principle of EU law applicable without any temporal constraints, has hardly any limits at all.[87]

5 Indirect effect

The principle of indirect effect is also known as conform interpretation, consistent interpretation, harmonious interpretation, or EU-consistent interpretation. It means the duty of all national bodies to interpret, as far as possible, all national law in light of and in conformity with EU law.

The requirement of consistent interpretation is certainly not a novel concept or unique to EU law. It has been employed in a number of other legal orders for achieving consistency between independent sets of norms by the fiat of interpretation. Some municipal legal systems employ consistent interpretation as a way of implementing their international law obligations. A similar duty of constitutionally consistent interpretation has been imposed by a number of constitutional courts, thus expanding constitutional and human rights considerations into all types of legal relationship.[88]

In EU law, indirect effect became an important, or in fact perhaps even the most important, principle for the national application of EU law, both quantitatively and qualitatively. Although academic attention would typically focus on direct effect and in particular on hair-splitting taxonomic discussions of the direct effect of directives, the vast majority of instances in which sources of EU law are taken into account directly at the national level is in fact likely to occur under the heading of consistent interpretation.

5.1 The notion

The Court first articulated the principle of indirect effect in *Von Colson*,[89] Since then, and repeated in a number of other decisions, there has been a restatement of the case law in *Pfeiffer*, where the Court held that:

> the Member States' obligation arising from a directive to achieve the result envisaged by the directive and their duty under Article 10 EC to take all appropriate measures, whether general or particular, to ensure the fulfilment of that obligation is binding on all the authorities of Member States including, for matters within their jurisdiction, the courts . . .

[87] Critically see the Opinion of AG Bobek in Case C-193/17 *Cresco Investigation*, EU:C:2018:614, in particular points 131–149.

[88] A notable example is the case law of the German Federal Constitutional Court, which inspired a number of other constitutional courts around Europe. See BVerfGE 7, 198 (207) (*Lüth*); BVerfGE 30, 173 (187) (*Mephisto*); BVerfGE 34, 269 (280) (*Soraya*).

[89] Case 14/83 *Von Colson and Kamann* [1984] ECR 1891.

> . . . when it applies domestic law, and in particular legislative provisions specifically adopted for the purpose of implementing the requirements of a directive, the national court is bound to interpret national law, so far as possible, in the light of the wording and the purpose of the directive concerned in order to achieve the result sought by the directive . . .
>
> Although the principle that national law must be interpreted in conformity with Community law concerns chiefly domestic provisions enacted in order to implement the directive in question, it does not entail an interpretation merely of those provisions but requires the national court to consider national law as a whole in order to assess to what extent it may be applied so as not to produce a result contrary to that sought by the directive.[90]

The scope of indirect effect in the vision of the Court is very ambitious: *all* national law must be interpreted in accordance with *all* EU law by *all* national authorities. In contrast to direct effect, there are no source-based exceptions to this requirement, at least from the point of view of the Court. All national law, even that adopted prior to the EU legislation in question, must be interpreted in conformity with the latter.[91] There is, however, no duty of consistent interpretation before the lapse of the implementation period in the case of directives.[92]

Indirect effect covers *all* EU law and *all* national law. Thus, although it is directives that are likely to be invoked most frequently for the purpose of consistent interpretation, Treaty provisions or regulations may also produce indirect effect. Consistent interpretation is not limited to EU law sources which cannot, for whatever reason, be directly effective. Also, directly effective sources, such as regulations or Treaty provisions, might be used only for consistent interpretation, if appropriate under the circumstances of the case. Moreover, even EU acts of a non-binding nature, such as recommendations,[93] may produce indirect effect.[94] On the national side, *all national* law naturally covers not only national laws enacted specifically for the implementation of a directive or other EU act, but all national law of whatever legal force, including the national constitution, adopted prior or subsequently to the EU law source in question.

5.2 **The scope**

Given the breadth of the indirect effect in the Court's case law, the real operation of the principle can hardly be put into one doctrinal box. It is, rather, a continuous scale of potential arguments of varying strength used in national adjudication and based on an EU law source. Thus, consistent interpretation may include, depending on the particular strength of the argument drawn from EU law in the individual case:

(a) *weak indirect effect*: an EU law provision is simply used as a *confirming* argument for a result which could safely be reached on the basis of national legal sources. The EU provision(s) provides an additional, subsidiary authority. The typical reasoning of a national court in such cases would be: the result we reach is X because national

[90] *Pfeiffer* (n 33) paras 110–115.

[91] Case C-106/89 *Marleasing* [1990] ECR I-4135, para 8.

[92] Case C-212/04 *Adeneler* [2006] ECR I-6057, para 115. However, even before the lapse of the implementation period, Member States must refrain from taking any measures liable seriously to compromise the attainment of the result prescribed by the directive. This so-called 'blocking effect' of directives was established in Case C-129/96 *Inter-Environnement Wallonie* [1997] ECR I-7411. See further Case C-157/02 *Rieser* [2004] ECR I-1477 or Case C-422/05 *Commission v Belgium* [2007] ECR I-4749.

[93] Judgment of 13 December 1989, Case C-322/88 *Grimaldi*, EU:C:1989:646, para 13. See also judgment of 15 July 2021, Case C-911/19 *Fédération bancaire française*, EU:C:2021:599, para 71.

[94] Case C-207/01 *Altair Chimica* [2003] ECR I-8875, para 41 or Joined Cases C-317–320/08 *Alassini* [2010] ECR I-2213, para 40.

law says probably X, our constitutional case law requires X, moreover X is a fair and equitable solution, and, *by the way*, X is also in conformity with EU directive Z, as interpreted by the Court in cases A and B;

(b) *medium indirect effect*: an EU law provision typically determines *the choice* between several interpretative options, which are all plausible—the meaning of national statute X might be X^1, X^2, or even perhaps X^3. After consulting an EU law provision, typically a directive and its recitals, the national court decides that it is in fact X^2 that best reflects the aims and the purpose of the directive; or

(c) *strong indirect effect*: the wording of a national law provision starts to be bent, sometimes even considerably, in order to achieve conformity with an EU law provision. In similar cases, the national court typically steps outside the literal meaning of a provision and, relying more on systematic, purposive reasoning of national law in conjunction with EU law, begins to modify the text or the established interpretation of a national provision. The decision of the Czech Constitutional Court in the *European Arrest Warrant* (EAW) case[95] may provide an example of such a strong indirect effect. Article 14(4) of the Czech Constitution states that 'No citizen may be forced to leave his homeland.' In the view of the Constitutional Court, however, even such a categorical provision does not preclude Czech citizens from being surrendered on the basis of an EAW to other EU Member States. Naturally, this is likely to happen against the will of the citizen concerned. Thus, it is hard to argue that a Czech citizen would not be *forced to leave his homeland* if put on a plane and sent off to face trial or serve a prison term in another Member State, unless of course one were to suggest that by now EU citizens consider the Union as their homeland, and that they are indifferent as to whether they will face trial in Luxembourg, Sweden, Bulgaria, or Italy. However, even in view of such constitutional text, the Constitutional Court 'interpreted' the Czech Constitution in conformity with EU law. In contrast, the German as well as Polish constitutional courts that faced similar constitutional provisions in their respective constitutions declared that the national constitutions were incompatible with the EU law requirement of extraditing their citizens. They stated that Germany and Poland respectively might participate in the EAW system but, in order to do so, the national law should first be amended.[96]

There is no clear borderline between instances of such strong consistent interpretation and direct effect. Arguments made on the basis of EU law represent a continuous line. On one side of the line are instances of weak indirect effect, in which the weight of an EU law argument borders on the irrelevant. On the other side, the strong interpretative bending of a national provision gradually slides into directly applying EU law without, in fact, openly acknowledging the fact. The difference between a strong 'conform interpretation', where a provision of national law is bent in order to reach a solution compatible with EU law, and direct application of the EU law norm requiring the same, is in practice very thin. Often, one has to rely on what the national court says that it is doing.

With respect to the potential choice between direct effect and (strong) indirect effect, it is often the case that consistent interpretation can be better reconciled, certainly in

[95] Judgment of 3 May 2006, Case No Pl ÚS 66/04, No 434/2006 Coll. An English translation of the decision is available at www.usoud.cz/en/decisions.

[96] See also eg J Komárek, 'European Constitutionalism and the European Arrest Warrant: In Search of the Limits of "Contrapunctual Principles"' (2007) 44 *Common Market Law Review* 9.

diplomatic terms, with the integrity of the national system.[97] As we saw in section 4, direct effect means the exclusion or substitution of a national rule. It requires an open acknowledgement on the part of the judge or administrator that she is disregarding otherwise perfectly binding national law, a statute, or even a constitution. Conversely, indirect effect is much less controversial. It superficially preserves the integrity of the national legal system (nothing is being disregarded, it is only 'interpretation' happening here), even if in substance the outcome of the case is the same.

5.3 **Interpretation unbounded?**

Seen from such a realist perspective, indirect effect offers quite a robust alternative to the previously discussed prohibition of the horizontal direct effect of directives. It might also reach into reverse vertical situations, in particular in administrative law but, as far as the interpretation of indeterminate legal notions is concerned, also in tax or criminal law. The only thing needed is a national law provision that could reasonably be claimed to be interpreted in conformity with EU law. If there is such a provision, all the previously discussed limitations, in particular those relating to the prohibition of horizontal direct effect of directives or decisions, fall away.

Imagine the following scenario: a Member State has incorrectly implemented the Unfair Terms in Consumer Contracts Directive.[98] It has not implemented the indicative list of prohibited terms contained in Annex 1 to the Directive. There is, however, in the national civil code, a general provision stating that consumers are the vulnerable party and as such are to be protected. Any provision in a contract between a consumer and a seller which creates a considerable imbalance in mutual obligations may be challenged by the weaker party.

A Mr X has concluded a consumer contract with a seller Y that provides, inter alia, that all disputes arising under the contract are to be settled exclusively by arbitration. Furthermore, the seat of the arbitrators is in the city where the seller has its main office. When the case comes to court, a national judge will declare this contractual term void, relying on the national general civil code provision *interpreted in conformity* with the Directive.[99]

Would such a case represent an instance of consistent interpretation of national law with a directive or an example of the prohibited horizontal direct effect of a directive? Both can be plausibly argued. It depends on the level of abstraction chosen. On the one hand, there is some textual basis in national law in the form of a general consumer protection clause. Thus, declaring the just stated unfair arbitration clause void is a *concretization of* the general prohibition, for which EU law provided just inspiration. On the other hand, the seller might object stating that the concrete rule which was in fact applied to his case and which just imposed a new obligation on him came straight from the annex of the directive. It has no concrete textual foundation in national law.

Finally, the same applies to the prohibition of reverse vertical direct effect. For the purposes of direct effect, the Member State cannot rely on a non-implemented or wrongly

[97] The Court has never prescribed any assessment order in which the national court shall proceed or choose between direct effect and conform interpretation. That is quite logical, since their use is deeply case and context dependent. For illustration, see the Opinion of AG Bobek of 23 September 2021, Case C-205/20 *Bezirkshauptmannschaft Hartberg-Fürstenfeld*, EU:C:2021:759, points 112–117.

[98] Council Directive 93/13/EEC of 5 April 1993 on unfair terms in consumer contracts (OJ [1993] L95/29). On the substance of this Directive, see further chapter 23.

[99] Point (q) of the annex to the Directive, which was not, however, implemented in national law.

implemented directive to the detriment of the individual.[100] In other words, the directive cannot, *in itself and independently of a national law* adopted by a Member State for its implementation, impose obligations on an individual.

But what if a Member State uses a provision of a directive for the purpose of consistent interpretation of national law, which in its outcome nonetheless disadvantages or even burdens the individual? For instance, imagine the interpretation of indeterminate legal notions in national tax law: who is a taxable person with respect to value added tax? What is a taxable transaction? Suppose that a Member State wishes to respect the autonomous nature of EU law notions, as it ought to. Thus, in order to interpret the notions in EU tax law, it reaches into other areas of EU law, perhaps into another directive. By doing so and interpreting the notion in conformity, the Member State reaches the conclusion that person X is not subject to the tax, whereas person Y is. In consequence, one party has just been forced to pay a tax which he would not have been obliged to pay if the Member State had not resorted to consistent interpretation. In this way, the Member State has applied EU law in a vertical situation to the detriment of an individual.[101]

5.4 **Introducing some limits**

In reaction to the apparently boundless potential of indirect effect, the attention of the Court has turned to the question of its limits. The Court progressively formulated three limits to the originally vast duty of consistent interpretation. These are:[102]

(a) interpretative methods recognized by national law;
(b) general principles of law; and
(c) no interpretation *contra legem*.

The first limit may appear redundant. When interpreting national law, a national authority is bound to limit itself to the interpretative methods recognized under national law. What else should it be doing in fact? At the same time, however, such a condition may not be that odd if viewed in the broader context of the Court's case law. In the past, the Court has not hesitated to expand the powers of national authorities in the name of effective enforcement of EU law at the national level. Thus, with respect to the scope of indirect effect, such a condition should perhaps be read as a soothing message: interpretation of law ought to remain interpretation, even in the face of the requirement of 'full effectiveness' of EU law.

The second limit, general principles of law, particularly those of legal certainty, legitimate expectation, and non-retroactivity, have more teeth. General principles put an equitable brake on far-reaching interpretative adventures in individual cases. They might be triggered if the interpretative outcome were to be rather unexpected and to the detriment of the individual in both horizontal relationships (the other party could not have reasonably expected such an interpretation) as well as in cases of reverse vertical relationships (eg a national administrative authority suddenly changing its established administrative

[100] See n 68.

[101] See Case C-168/95 *Arcaro* [1996] ECR I-4705 or judgment of 14 May 2019, Case C-55/18 *CCOO*, EU:C:2019:402. Specifically in a criminal law context, see also Case C-105/03 *Pupino* [2005] ECR I-5285, para 45 or judgment of 12 February 2019, Case C-492/18 PPU *TC*, EU:C:2019:108.

[102] Case C-212/04 *Adeneler* [2006] ECR I-6057, paras 110 and 111. See also Case C-268/06 *Impact* [2008] ECR I-2483, paras 100 and 101; Joined Cases C-378–380/07 *Angelidaki* [2009] ECR I-3071, para 199; judgment of 15 January 2014, Case C-176/12 *Association de médiation sociale*, EU:C:2014:2, para 39; judgment of 18 January 2022, Case C-261/20 *Thelen Technopark Berlin*, EU:C:2022:33, para 28.

practice by relying on an EU law argument, without prior legislation to that effect in order that the results are foreseeable to those affected).[103]

Thirdly, the prohibition of reaching an interpretative outcome *contra legem* comes from continental, in particular German, legal doctrine. There, a traditional distinction has been drawn between judicial decision-making within the law but outside its clear text (*praeter legem*) and decision-making against the law/statute (*contra legem*). In adjudication, the former is said to be possible, the latter is out of bounds.[104]

What precisely might be reading of a provision *contra legem*? Does it mean only that a national authority cannot interpret a specific national provision as to amount to the textual denial of the original rule (an 'A' cannot become 'non-A' by the fiat of interpretation)? Or does it also mean that a national interpreter cannot start twisting and extensively modifying national law generally in order to reach 'an artificial or strained interpretation of national law'[105] only to achieve consistency with EU law?

From the leading judgment on that issue in *Impact*,[106] it would appear that the Court had the latter, broader limit in mind. In that case, conformity of Irish law with EU law could be achieved by interpretation if retrospective effects of the national implementing Act were allowed. However, Irish law contains a general rule that precludes the retrospective application of legislation unless there is a clear and unambiguous indication to the contrary. The national implementing Act contained, however, no such express provision. The Court concluded that:

> In the absence of such a provision, Community law—in particular the requirement for national law to be interpreted in conformity with Community law—cannot be interpreted as requiring the referring court to give [the relevant section of the national implementing Act] retrospective effect to the date by which [the Directive] should have been transposed, as the referring court would otherwise be constrained to interpret national law *contra legem*.[107]

In conclusion, indirect effect has been construed as a very robust duty incumbent upon all national authorities to ensure conformity with EU law in the process of interpretation. Originally perhaps construed as an alternative to direct effect, it soon became arguably more important than direct effect itself. Indirect effect can reach into situations and relationships where direct effect cannot. In quantitative terms, consistent interpretation became the most important avenue for EU law penetration of the national legal orders in the process of adjudication. The Court has thus begun to set some boundaries to this originally limitless principle.

6 Primacy

The principle of primacy of EU law means that in the case of conflict, EU law prevails over national law. In contrast to some aspects of direct effect, the principle of primacy poses political rather than legal difficulties. In any type of large structure, in which the norms of multiple systems are supposed to coexist, sooner or later the question of their mutual hierarchy arises. What is striking with respect to the EU is the fact that, even

[103] For a controversy on this limit, see judgment of 8 September 2015, Case C-105/14 *Taricco and Others*, EU:C:2015:555, and its reversal in judgment of 5 December 2017, Case C-42/17 *MAS and MB*, EU:C:2017:936.

[104] See eg judgment of 17 April 2018, Case C-414/16 *Egenberger*, EU:C:2018:257, para 73.

[105] Opinion of AG Sharpston of 30 November 2006 in Case C-432/05 *Unibet* [2007] ECR I-2271, para 55.

[106] Case C-268/06 *Impact* [2008] ECR I-2483.

[107] Ibid, para 103.

today, questions of hierarchy, sovereignty, and the ultimate word remain unresolved. Both the Union and the Member States have different views on why and to what extent EU law is allowed to prevail over national law. Both of these views will be discussed in this section.

6.1 **The Court's view**

In *Van Gend en Loos*,[108] direct effect enabled the new legal order to penetrate independently into the national legal systems. The ensuing question that had already surfaced in *Van Gend en Loos* was, however, with what legal force this occurs. Furthermore, what happens in the case of conflict between the directly effective Treaty provisions and national law?

6.1.1 **Costa**

The Court gave the answers to these questions a year later, in *Costa*.[109] The case concerned Italian legislation which was incompatible with the Treaty, but which was adopted after Italy joined the EEC. The question posed was whether such subsequent national legislation, encapsulating a clear expression of will of the national legislator, may unilaterally derogate from Treaty obligations.

The resounding 'no' pronounced by the Court in reply to this question deserves to be repeated, as it equally announces the ideological dimension of the European project:

> By contrast with ordinary international treaties, the EEC Treaty has created its own legal system which, on the entry into force of the Treaty, became an integral part of the legal systems of the Member States and which their courts are bound to apply.
>
> By creating a Community of unlimited duration, having its own institutions, its own personality, its own legal capacity and capacity of representation on the international plane and, more particularly, real powers stemming from a limitation of sovereignty or a transfer of powers from the States to the Community, the Member States have limited their sovereign rights, albeit within limited fields, and have thus created a body of law which binds both their nationals and themselves.
>
> The integration into the laws of each Member State of provisions which derive from the Community, and more generally the terms and the spirit of the Treaty, make it impossible for the States, as a corollary, to accord precedence to a unilateral and subsequent measure over a legal system accepted by them on a basis of reciprocity. Such a measure cannot therefore be inconsistent with that legal system. The executive force of Community law cannot vary from one State to another in deference to subsequent domestic laws, without jeopardizing the attainment of the objectives of the Treaty . . .
>
> It follows from all these observations that the law stemming from the Treaty, an independent source of law, could not, because of its special and original nature, be overridden by domestic legal provisions, however framed, without being deprived of its character as Community law and without the legal basis of the Community itself being called into question.
>
> The transfer by the States from their domestic legal system to the Community legal system of the rights and obligations arising under the Treaty carries with it a permanent limitation of their sovereign rights, against which a subsequent unilateral act incompatible with the concept of the Community cannot prevail.[110]

[108] See n 3. [109] Case 6/64 *Costa* [1964] ECR English Special Edition 585.
[110] Ibid, 593–594.

What the Court stated in *Costa* and further elaborated on in subsequent case law[111] is a claim for an unreserved, absolute EU law primacy: *all* EU law prevails over *all* national law. The basis for such a sweeping claim was, in the view of the Court, the *special and original nature* of the law stemming from the Treaty. Absent any textual foundation to this effect in the Treaties themselves, the reasoning of the Court became somewhat circular: the special and original nature of the new Community requires the Community to have these special and original characteristics.

Primacy in combination with direct effect nonetheless provides for a very efficient enforcement mechanism for EU law in national legal systems. The key to success is the *synergic effect* of both principles. One does not necessarily follow from the other but, together, they constitute a strong combination. This statement is best demonstrated by a thought experiment in which one were to dissociate the two principles. Imagine: to have only primacy without direct effect would amount to something that is nominally supreme but in practice left outside the gates of the national legal order. To have direct effect without primacy would mean that the rank of EU law in the national legal systems would be left to the discretion of the individual national constitutions. Member State A could thus state that EU law takes precedence over national statutes but not the constitution, whereas Member State B might position EU law under the level of statutes, on the same level as derived legislation (statutory instruments).

To provide for both principles in almost one breath was a defining moment for EU law. Similarly to Christopher Columbus and his egg, the Court elegantly redefined the nature of the problem. It is said that when challenged that his journey to the Americas was no great accomplishment, Columbus asked his critics to try to make an egg balance on its tip. After they had failed to do so, Columbus tapped the tip of the egg and made it stand on the crack. In a similar vein, instead of trying to explain to the Member States in future individual cases what is and what is not an effective enforcement of their international obligations, the Court pre-empted any national choice in this matter. It cracked national constitutional choices and gave EU law the same effects everywhere. Thus, in all the Member States, EU law is to have the same type of primacy over national law, irrespective of what the national constitution states with respect to the status of international law obligations in the national legal order. The choice made in *Costa* and *Van Gend en Loos* was perhaps not a legal revolution or a *coup d'état*,[112] but it was certainly a courageous choice which became *the* key element of the entire EU legal system.

The importance of this initial choice may be highlighted by contrasting the EU legal order with another advanced system of international cooperation in Europe, namely the European Convention on Human Rights. Absent any similar bold, original choice by the European Court of Human Rights that would have redefined the rules of the game, the status and effectiveness of domestic implementation and enforcement of the Convention is left to the constitutional systems of the signatory parties. This means that for some signatory parties the Convention has the status of a national constitutional act, in others it is below the constitution but above statutory law, yet in others it is implemented by a simple statute. In Ireland, up until 2003, the Convention was not domestically implemented at all.[113]

[111] Notably Case 11/70 *Internationale Handelsgesellschaft* [1970] ECR 1125; Case 106/77 *Simmenthal* [1978] ECR 629; Case C-213/89 *Factortame* [1990] ECR I-2433; Case C-314/08 *Filipiak* [2009] ECR I-11049; Case C-409/06 *Winner Wetten* [2010] ECR I-8015; Case C-399/11 *Melloni*, EU:C:2013:107; and Case C-614/14 *Ognyanov*, EU:C:2016:514.

[112] See the discussion of *Costa* as the 'juridical *coup d'état*' by A Stone Sweet in M Poiares Maduro and L Azoulai (eds), *The Past and Future of EU Law* (Oxford: Hart Publishing, 2010) 202.

[113] For further discussion of fundamental rights and the ECHR, see chapter 9.

6.1.2 The scope and effect of primacy

There are three important aspects of the primacy principle which ought to be highlighted. First, primacy of EU law over national law means *primacy in application* in the individual case at hand. Primacy *does not affect the validity* of the national law provision in question. The principle of primacy of EU law requires only that the conflicting national provision is set aside. It shall be left non-applied in the individual case. The national provision, however, continues to be a valid part of the national legal order unless it is amended or repealed by the competent national authorities,[114] for example the legislator or the national constitutional court if the latter has such power under national law.

The underlying logic of primacy in application is one of two independent sets of norms: EU law and national law. Both sets influence each other, they interact, but neither of them is hierarchically supreme.[115] Norms of either set can be created or annulled exclusively by the institutions of that given set.[116] In general, national law can only be invalidated by the national institutions and EU law by the EU institutions.[117]

Therefore, a national provision that was declared incompatible with EU law in a case falling within the scope of EU law and set aside by a national court or administrator can later be applied in purely national situations outside the scope of EU law. Until repealed, it remains a valid part of national law. Equally, in less fortunate scenarios, one court within one Member State may reach the conclusion that a provision of national law is incompatible with EU law and set it aside. Deciding in a parallel or even later case, a different court within the same legal system may decide that the same national law is compatible with EU law. Until there is a decision by a higher court within the national judicial hierarchy which binds both lower courts involved or a decision of the Court given on a preliminary ruling, neither of the lower courts is per se wrong.

Secondly, as already apparent from *Costa*, the primacy in application is, at least from the point of view of the Court, *unreserved and absolute*, certainly with respect to the *internal* acts of the Member States.[118] It is absolute in two dimensions: hierarchical and temporal. All EU law includes, indeed, all potential sources of EU law: primary law, including since the Lisbon Treaty also the Charter; general principles of EU law; and all sources of binding EU secondary law, such as directives. Any of these sources then prevails over all national law, including national constitutional provisions.[119] Furthermore, as was already apparent from *Costa*, from the point of view of the Court, EU law also prevails over subsequent national legislation.

[114] Joined Cases C-1022/97 *IN.CO.GE* [1998] ECR I-6307, para 21; Case C-314/08 *Filipiak* [2009] ECR I-11049, para 83.

[115] That is also why this chapter uses the notion of 'primacy' and not 'supremacy'. Apart from the fact that the case law of the Court consistently refers to 'primacy' and not to 'supremacy' of EU law, the term primacy also better captures the nature of the principle, which is *primacy in application* in cases involving EU law, not *hierarchical supremacy*.

[116] With respect to judicial challenges to validity, only the Court can invalidate EU acts—Case 314/85 *Foto-Frost* [1987] ECR 4199. On the other hand, the Court can only declare a national rule incompatible with EU law. It cannot annul it.

[117] But see, for specific cases, eg judgment of 26 February 2019, Joined Cases C-202/18 and C-238/18 *Rimšēvičs and ECB v Latvia*, EU:C:2019:139 (on the competence of the Court of Justice to annul, in a specific case foreseen by the Treaties, directly a national measure).

[118] A specific exception to the unreserved primacy of EU law is provided by Art 351 TFEU with respect to international agreements concluded with third countries by a Member State before its accession to the EU. This traditional exception was, however, considerably narrowed by the Court in Joined Cases C-402/05 P and C-415/05 P *Kadi* [2008] ECR I-6351.

[119] Case C-285/98 *Kreil* [2000] ECR I-69 offers an example in which a provision of EU secondary law (directive) prevailed over a national constitutional provision.

Thirdly, the primacy of EU law empowers all national judges, from a court of first instance to the supreme jurisdiction, to set aside incompatible national laws. They can do so of their own motion, at whatever stage of procedure, and irrespective of what national law states in that regard.[120] They do not have to ask the Court before doing so.[121] However, what is perhaps more significant from a constitutional point of view is that the Court has extended the same powers to all bodies of the Member States, which means also to *national administrators*. National administrative authorities may also disregard national law in order to enforce directly effective provisions of EU law.[122]

The rise of 'omnipotent administrators' may cause concern. In the liberal rule of law tradition, the national administration/executive is the bound power. It is allowed to act only and exclusively on the basis and within the law, to which it is subordinate. From the point of view of the requirement of (strict) legality of all administrative action, there is something perturbing about the idea that, for instance, every tax commissioner in every district town is entitled to disregard whenever she pleases (of her own motion) an act of parliament or even the national constitution, simply because she thinks that it is not compatible with a provision of the EU Value Added Tax Directive.

On the other hand, extending such powers to administrators is no doubt logical from the point of view of EU law. The Court proceeds from an international law holistic conception of a State: all Member State bodies are obliged to enforce EU law effectively within their respective competence. The fear that also extending the principles of primacy and direct effect to national administrations would amount to administration getting out of control is normatively as well as empirically unwarranted. Normatively, membership of the EU means that 'national' legality became 'European' legality, as the pool of sources of law has enlarged. Empirically and pragmatically, even if applying EU law to its fullest and occasionally getting it wrong, national administrative authorities would hardly be doing anything other than that which occurs with respect to national law. Finally, in the same way as national law and its application, and also with respect to the administrative (mis)application of EU law, national administrations remain subject to full national judicial review, which naturally also includes questions of EU law.[123]

6.2 **The national views**

The story told so far was the Court's version, capturing the origins, justification, as well as effects of the principle of primacy of EU law through the case law of the Court. However, the nobility (or perhaps the plight, depending on the point of view) of the European project is the unresolved nature of the question of ultimate sovereignty: who has the last word within the Union? Is it the EU or the Member States?

This unresolved issue surfaces when views concerning the primacy of EU law and the therein-lurking question of sovereignty are articulated. On the one hand is the robust vision of the Court postulating that EU law must have primacy owing to its special and original nature stemming directly from the Treaties. On the other hand, the approach of the Member States articulated in the decisions of their constitutional and/or supreme courts provides a different narrative and overall justification.

[120] *Simmenthal* (n 111) para 21; *Filipiak* (n 111) para 81; *Winner Wetten* (n 111) para 56.

[121] Case C-555/07 *Kücükdeveci* [2010] ECR I-365, paras 53–55.

[122] Notably Case 103/88 *Costanzo* [1989] ECR 1839, para 31 or Case C-198/01 *CIF* [2003] ECR I-8055, paras 49–58. See also judgment of 4 December 2018, Case C-378/17 *Minister for Justice and Equality and Commissioner of An Garda Síochána*, EU:C:2018:979.

[123] See further, with a discussion of examples, M Bobek, 'Thou Shalt Have Two Masters: The Application of European Law by Administrative Authorities in the New Member States' (2008) 1 *Review of European Administrative Law* 62.

6.2.1 **Different foundations, same outcome**

The national responses to the Court's claims for absolute primacy of EU law reflect the richness of national constitutional traditions as well as nation-specific concerns. Still, the premises on which most of the national systems base their answers are, with the exception of monist systems such as the Netherlands or Estonia, similar.[124] This is perhaps not that surprising for two reasons. First, a national constitutional or supreme court naturally perceives its role as the guardian of the integrity of the *national* constitutional system. Thus, responses given from such a position to claims for absolute primacy of EU law formulated by the Court are likely to start from similar assumptions and voice similar concerns. Secondly, a number of constitutional courts in 'old' as well as 'new' Europe have been under the distinct influence of the German Federal Constitutional Court[125] and its position vis-à-vis primacy of EU law articulated early in the 1970s.[126] The same ideas 'migrate' horizontally around Europe, with national courts being well versed in the reservations expressed by others.

In a nutshell, the common themes of national responses to the Court's absolute primacy claim could be formulated as follows:

(a) The basis for the system of EU law is not its 'special and original nature', but the Treaties signed by the Member States as an obligation under *international* law. The last word in shaping the Union and its law rests with the Member States; so does sovereignty. They remain, in the term coined by the German Federal Constitutional Court, the 'Masters of the Treaties'. The Member States simply decided to transfer the exercise of some competences to an advanced international organization.[127] They have not given carte blanche to any irreversible 'Union of destiny'.

(b) Internally within a given Member State, the reason for application of EU law on the national territory, including its primacy and direct effect, is the national constitutional mandate with which the constitution-maker expressed the wish to join the EU and/or is encapsulated in the respective 'Euro-article' of the national constitution. Therefore, in the eyes of the national constitution, EU law is hierarchically either *under* or *beyond* the national constitution, but not above it. EU law having primacy over the national constitution might be silently accepted as the outcome in an individual case, but hardly in conceptual terms. Consequently, a clear constitutional wish to negate an obligation stemming from EU law or even a constitutional command to withdraw from the Union would take precedence over any EU law obligations.[128]

[124] See further eg A-M Slaughter, A Stone Sweet, and JHH Weiler (eds), *The European Court of Justice and National Courts: Doctrine and Jurisprudence* (Oxford: Hart Publishing, 1998); for the new Member States, see eg A Łazowski (ed), *Brave New World: The Application of EU Law in the New Member States* (The Hague: TMC Asser Press, 2010) and A Albi and S Bardutzky (eds), *National Constitutions in European and Global Governance: Democracy, Rights, and the Rule of Law* (The Hague: TMC Asser Press, 2019).

[125] For detail, see M Bobek, *Comparative Reasoning in European Supreme Courts* (Oxford: Oxford University Press, 2013) 159, 255–257.

[126] In particular BVerfGE 37, 271 (*Solange I*) (in English [1974] CMLR 540). See also BVerfGE 73, 339 (*Solange II*) ([1987] 3 CMLR 225); BVerfGE 89, 155 (*Maastricht*) ([1994] 1 CMLR 57); BVerfGE 123, 267 (*Lisbon*) ([2010] 3 CMLR 276); and BVerfGE 126, 286 (*Honeywell*) ([2011] 1 CMLR 1067).

[127] Resonating also with the characterization provided by the Court itself, albeit in a different context, in Opinion 2/13 (*Accession of the European Union to the ECHR*) of 18 December 2014, EU:C:2014:2454, para 156.

[128] As evidenced by the Brexit process, with the Court acknowledging that possibility in judgment of 10 December 2018, Case C-621/18 *Wightman and Others*, EU:C:2018:999.

(c) If it is the 'Euro-article' in the national constitution that opens the gates for domestic application of EU law, then a national guardian of constitutionality is entitled to check whether or not the Union remains within the powers conferred upon it by the national constitution. With such reasoning, most of the national constitutional courts assumed the power to review, for the purposes of the application of EU law on their territory, whether an EU act remained within the powers transferred to the Union (*intra vires*) or whether it went beyond (*ultra vires*). Assuming such power of review of EU acts in principle may not mean that it will be effectively exercised in individual cases. The national courts will frequently reserve such residual review for repetitive or manifest violations of the principle of conferral.

There are, of course, many national variations of these three starting assumptions that focus on the political ontology, constitutional hierarchy, and the question of control/review. Furthermore, around these three points, the themes have changed over the years. The motive for original reservations on the part of the Member States back in the 1970s was the lack of protection of fundamental rights by the then EEC. Later, in the 1990s, the main theme became finality of the integration process itself and the nature of the Union, especially after the Maastricht Treaty. With further expansion of the Union's competences after Maastricht and Amsterdam, the concerns voiced in the national constitutional jurisprudence moved on to setting limits to further integration. 'Hardcore' or 'unalterable' cores of national constitutions began to be emphasized, later to merge with concerns about the preservation of the national constitutional identity.

With the rule of law crises raging in some Member States over the last decade, the question of genuine protection of fundamental rights within the Union has surfaced again, this time in a somewhat different garb. It is primarily perhaps not the Union itself which would not be able to protect individuals against the EU institutions, but the multitude of mutual assistance and horizontal enforcement mechanisms in criminal, administrative, or civil matters introduced over the last two decades.[129] With the EU and the Court pushing for long-ranging horizontal mutual recognition in these areas, the individual and her fundamental rights protection may get lost in the cracks between the systems, or potentially even outright disregarded in a Member State, where because of systemic deficiencies in the quality of the rule of law, there is no longer any guarantee of an independent trial following the surrender of a person to that State.[130]

6.2.2 **The last decade: different foundations, different outcomes**

For almost half a century, the beauty of the European Union constitutional project lay in its ability to function on the basis of mutual respect and voluntary compliance, not on blunt coercion. Although both the Court and national courts see primacy and sovereignty in quite different lights, as to the concrete outcome in the individual case, both agreed that EU law is to be given primacy. Both thus arrived at the same outcome, however following very different reasoning. The last decade has witnessed an erosion of that understanding. It came from two directions.

[129] See notably Joined Cases C-411/10 and C-493/10 *NS*, EU:C:2011:865; Joined Cases C-404/15 and C-659/15 PPU *Aranyosi and Căldăraru*, EU:C:2016:198; judgment of 25 July 2018; Case C-220/18 PPU *Generalstaatsanwaltschaft* (*Conditions of detention in Hungary*), EU:C:2018:589; or judgment of 15 October 2019, Case C-128/18 *Dorobantu*, EU:C:2019:857.

[130] See in particular judgments of 25 July 2018, Case C-216/18 PPU *Celmer*, EU:C:2018:586; of 17 December 2020, Joined Cases C-354/20 PPU and C-412/20 PPU *Openbaar Ministerie* (*Independence of the issuing judicial authority*), EU:C:2020:1033, and of 22 February 2022, Joined Cases C-562/21 and C-563/21 *Openbaar Ministerie* (*Court established by law in the issuing Member State*), EU:C:2022:100.

First, since 1970s, the idea that a national (constitutional) court could declare a Union act *ultra vires* has remained a matter for heated theoretical discussions in constitutional law textbooks. Indeed, commenting upon the repetitive warnings issued notably by the German Federal Constitutional Court, some academic commentators called that court a dog which barks but never bites.[131] It was widely believed that triggering the *ultra vires* review would be the 'nuclear option' for a national constitutional court, leading to 'mutual assured destruction' of the entire European judicial architecture, if expressed in cold war terminology.

To the surprise of many, it was not the German Federal Constitutional Court, but a completely different animal, that delivered the first bite. In a curious decision of 21 January 2012,[132] it was the Czech Constitutional Court that declared, for the first time ever openly,[133] an EU law act (*in casu* a decision of the Court of Justice) *ultra vires*.[134] In 2016, another declaration came from the Danish Supreme Court.[135] In 2020, the German Federal Constitutional Court joined the biting as well.[136] Furthermore, other national highest courts, in particular the French ones,[137] started articulating stronger reservations regarding unconditional primacy of certain provisions of EU law or case law of the Court, without, however, going as far as declaring an EU law act *ultra vires*.

Secondly, a wholly unprecedented dimension in *ultra vires* declarations has been reached in Member States suffering from the ongoing rule of law crisis and the effective hijacking of the highest courts, including constitutional courts, by a given political party. The Polish Constitutional Tribunal, in a somewhat twisted Star Trek scenario, boldly went where nobody had gone before by declaring not only decisions of the Court of Justice *ultra vires*, but also key provisions of the EU Treaties as incompatible with the Polish Constitution.[138] Subsequently, that (former) court equally declared decisions of the European Court of Human Rights incompatible with the Polish Constitution,[139] thus achieving the questionable primacy of being the first body ever to declare both systems of European law incompatible with what appears to be the current interpretation of a national constitution.

It remains to be seen whether all this is just a temporal deviation, or indeed an ongoing reshaping of the European constitutional and judicial space, within which the

[131] See eg U Schmid, 'All Bark and No Bite: Notes on the Federal Constitutional Court Banana Decision' (2001) 7 *European Law Journal* 95.

[132] Decision of 21 January 2012, Case No Pl ÚS 5/12 (N 24/64 SbNU 237).

[133] Certainly, there has been resistance from the national courts to different strands of EU case law in the past. These were, however, happening in different and more subtle terms—for illustration, see B Davies, *Resisting the European Court of Justice: West Germany's Confrontation with European Law, 1949–1979* (Cambridge: Cambridge University Press, 2012).

[134] For detail, see M Bobek, 'Landtová, Holubec, and the Problem of an Uncooperative Court: Implications for the Preliminary Rulings Procedure' (2014) 10 *European Constitutional Law Review* 54.

[135] Judgment of 6 December 2016, 15/2014, *Ajos A/S*. Further see eg MR Madsen, HP Olsen, and U Šadl, 'Competing Supremacies and Clashing Institutional Rationalities: The Danish Supreme Court's Decision in the *Ajos* Case and the National Limits of Judicial Cooperation' (2017) 23 *European Law Journal* 140.

[136] Decision of 5 May 2020, Case No 2 BvR 859/15 (English translation online at: www.bverfg.de/e/rs20200505_2bvr085915en.html).

[137] See notably the plenary decision of the French Council of State of 21 May 2021, No 393099 (FR:CEASS:2021:393099.20210421) or the decision of the French Constitutional Council of 15 October 2021, no 2021–940 QPC, Société Air France (JORF no 0242 du 16 octobre 2021).

[138] Decision of 7 October 2021, Case No K 3/21, where the Polish Constitutional Tribunal declared Arts 1, 4(3), and 19(1) TEU wholly or partly incompatible with the Polish Constitution. Decision of 10 June 2025, Case No K 10/24, then declared Arts 192(1) and 192(2)(c) TFEU, as far as they limited the sovereign choice of Poland in the structure of its energy supply in the framework of the Green Deal legislation, incompatible with the Polish Constitution.

[139] Decision of 24 November 2021, Case No K 6/21.

declaring of decisions that do not fit as 'inexistent' is becoming part of standard discourse. The moderately positive news is that, in retrospect, at least with regard to the normally operating Member States, the past ultra vires declarations cited here, such as the German, Danish, or Czech ones, appear to amount to just very strongly worded but isolated objections to one particular decision or line of case law of the Court of Justice. Their *ultra vires* declarations were apparently not meant to amount to the structural and lasting denial of primacy or authority of EU law and case law in those Member States, but perhaps the continuation of judicial discourse by different, indeed more assertive, means.

7 State liability

Liability of the Member State for breaches of EU law is an example of a more advanced judicial unification of a type of remedy before national courts.[140] The case law of the Court has unified the conditions for State liability. However, the national realization of State liability, including designation of the competent courts, procedures, time limits and so on, is a matter for national law, provided naturally that the dual requirement of equivalence and effectiveness is preserved.[141]

The principle made its first appearance in *Francovich*, where the Court stated that:

> the principle of State liability for harm caused to individuals by breaches of Community law for which the State can be held responsible is inherent in the system of the Treaty.[142]

Since then, the conditions for State liability have been slightly reformulated by the Court. The current test, as articulated in *Brasserie du Pêcheur/Factortame*, reads:

> Community law confers a right to reparation where three conditions are met: the rule of law infringed must be intended to confer rights on individuals; the breach must be sufficiently serious; and there must be a direct causal link between the breach of the obligation resting on the State and the damage sustained by the injured parties.[143]

Restating the test in a more accessible way reflecting the traditional categories of non-contractual (tortious) liability, present in the laws of a number of Member States, there are in fact five conditions in the test announced by the Court:

(a) a wrong (an act or an omission violating EU law):
   (i) of a legal provision which was intended to confer rights on individuals, and
   (ii) the wrong was sufficiently serious;
(b) damage;
(c) causal link between the wrong and the damage.

140 In the structural classification outlined in section 2.1 of this chapter.

141 The judicially unified conditions for State liability are the minimal threshold, under which the Member States cannot go. The Member States are nonetheless entitled, as in other areas of EU law, to go above and to provide for more favourable conditions than those set out in EU law. See eg judgments of 29 July 2019, Case C-620/17 *Hochtief Solutions*, EU:C:2019:630, para 38; of 4 October 2018, Case C-571/16, *Kantarev*, EU:C:2018:807, para 121.

142 Joined Cases C-6/90 and C-9/90 *Francovich and Bonifaci* [1991] ECR I-5357, para 35.

143 Joined Cases C-46/93 and C-48/93 *Brasserie du Pêcheur/Factortame* [1996] ECR I-1029, para 51; Case C-278/05 *Robins* [2007] ECR I-1059, para 69; Case C-445/06 *Danske Slagterier* [2009] ECR I-2119, para 20; and Case C-429/09 *Fuß* [2010] ECR I-12167, para 47.

Conditions (a), (b), and (c) constitute the essence of any regime of tortious liability (non-contractual liability in civil law terms).[144] The two EU-specific conditions are (i) and (ii). They represent qualifying factors with respect to the types of wrongs for which a State may incur liability. Not all violations of EU law committed by Member States will qualify, only those committed with respect to EU law provisions conferring rights on individuals and (cumulatively) those which are sufficiently serious.

Since *Francovich*, the case law of the Court has expressly confirmed that the Member State may be liable for violations of EU law committed by any branch of government (State organ). The fact that the administration may be liable for public wrongs was perhaps not that contentious.[145] The more contested scenarios, at least in some Member States, included the statement that a Member State may be liable for the acts or omissions attributable to the (sovereign) legislator.[146] The same applies to judicial violations of EU law, committed by lower courts as well as by national courts of last instance.[147] The Court proceeds from an international law holistic point of view: the duty correctly to implement and enforce EU law rests on the Member State as a unity. Equally, a potential violation of the primary duty may be committed by any body of the State.

Finally, liability for breaches of EU law is not limited to the Member States. The Union may also incur non-contractual liability. The conditions are the same as those with respect to wrongs committed by the Member States.[148] Conversely, potential violations of EU law committed by individuals (private persons) are subject to general national regimes of non-contractual liability. The case law of the Court has so far been limited to mandating the Member States to allow for such type of liability, without, however, unifying its conditions.[149]

8 Connecting the dots: the interplay of the different principles

After having introduced the rules and the key principles for the application of EU law in the Member States, this section illustrates their interplay in greater detail. The following case study is based on *Audiolux*,[150] a 2009 decision of the Court. However, the facts of the original case have been *modified* for the purpose of this case study.

[144] For the application of those conditions, with particular emphasis on causality, see eg judgment of 5 September 2019, Case C-417/18 *AW and Others* (*Calls to 112*), EU:C:2019:671 or judgment of 4 October 2018, Case C-571/16 *Kantarev*, EU:C:2018:807.

[145] See eg *Danske Slagterier* (n 143) or Case C-5/94 *Hedley Lomas* [1996] ECR I-2553.

[146] Typically for a failure to implement a directive or for implementing it incorrectly. See eg Case C-178/94 *Dillenkofer* [1996] ECR I-4845; Case C-392/93 *British Telecommunications* [1996] ECR I-1631; or judgment of 9 September 2015, Case C-160/14 *Ferreira da Silva e Brito and Others*, EU:C:2015:565.

[147] Case C-224/01 *Köbler* [2003] ECR I-10239; Case C-173/03 *Traghetti del Mediterraneo* [2006] ECR I-5177; judgment of 28 July 2016, Case C-168/15 *Tomášová*, EU:C:2016:602; judgment of 29 July 2019, Case C-620/17 *Hochtief Solutions*, EU:C:2019:630.

[148] Art 340 TFEU and Case C-352/98 P *Bergaderm* [2000] ECR I-5291, para 41. But see judgment of 31 October 2019, Case C-391/17 *Commission v United Kingdom*, EU:C:2019:919 and judgment of 31 October 2019, Case C-395/17 *Commission v Netherlands*, EU:C:2019:918, which would hint at a silent departure from *Bergaderm* in cases when a liability action against a Member State is launched by the Commission under Art 258 TFEU.

[149] Case C-453/99 *Courage* [2001] ECR I-6297, paras 26–28; Joined Cases C-295–298/04 *Manfredi* [2006] ECR I-6619, paras 60–64; Case C-536/11 *Donau Chemie*, EU:C:2013:366, paras 22–25.

[150] Case C-101/08 *Audiolux* [2009] ECR I-9823. For further background and insightful analysis, see also the Opinion of AG Trstenjak of 30 June 2009 in this case.

Case study 6.1: Audiolux

Audiolux was a minority shareholder in the RTL Group, a public limited company having its registered office in Luxembourg. RTL's shares were traded on the stock exchanges in Luxembourg, Brussels, and London. In the course of several stock market operations in 2001, the Bertelsmann company acquired most of the RTL shares. One of these operations included a shares swap, whereby Groupe Bruxelles Lambert transferred its holding of 30 per cent of the RTL shares in exchange for 25 per cent of Bertelsmann shares. Later, Bertelsmann bought a further 22 per cent of RTL shares from the British group Pearson Television. Finally, once Bertelsmann had acquired control of RTL, it removed RTL shares from the London stock exchange. At the same time, Bertelsmann also decreased the basic capital of RTL.

Audiolux and other RTL minority shareholders disagreed with the steps taken by Bertelsmann. They brought a number of actions in (national) Luxembourg courts against Bertelsmann. In one of the actions, Audiolux asked the Luxembourg court seized of the dispute to order Bertelsmann to offer Audiolux the opportunity to exchange its shares in RTL for shares in Bertelsmann *under the same conditions* as those offered to Groupe Bruxelles Lambert. Audiolux suggested that when a major shareholder transfers its shares to another, minority shareholders are entitled to *equal treatment* by the majority shareholder. The key question which arose was thus, simply put, is there anything in EU law that would oblige Bertelsmann to treat all shareholders in the same way and offer them the same conditions?

The area of company law has been extensively harmonized by EU law. There are a number of binding as well as non-binding EU acts in this area,[151] which also regulate the question of trade in shares and the position of minority shareholders. Most importantly, Article 42 of Directive 77/91/EEC[152] provides that, 'For the purposes of the implementation of this Directive, the laws of the Member States shall ensure equal treatment to all shareholders who are in the same position.' The fifth recital to the same Directive adds that:

> it is necessary . . . that the Member States' laws relating to the increase or reduction of capital ensure that the principles of equal treatment of shareholders in the same position and of protection of creditors whose claims exist prior to the decision on reduction are observed and harmonised.

Against such a factual and legal background, what would be the potential remedies open to Audiolux in the national legal system(s)?

First of all, Audiolux naturally needs to decide where and how to pursue its claim. In doing so, it will rely on existing national procedural rules in Luxembourg or potentially in another Member State concerned. The claim is *within the scope of EU law*: the just cited directive governs not only the subject matter (formation of and changes in public limited liability companies), but even the situation that arose in national proceedings (equal treatment of shareholders in cases of decrease in capital of a publicly traded company). Consequently, any national procedures, judicial or administrative, will be subject to the EU requirement of *effective judicial protection* (the dual requirement of *equivalence and/or effectiveness*). Thus, for instance, if the national legal system did not provide any type of remedy for the protection of minority shareholders, or made it subject to very onerous or impossible requirements relating to access to court, jurisdiction, standing, and so on, EU law would already be triggered.

[151] For a more detailed overview, which is not necessary for the purposes of this case study, see the Opinion of AG Trstenjak in *Audiolux* at paras 3–16 and 75–83.

[152] OJ [1977] L26/1.

Once in a court,[153] Audiolux might wish to rely directly on the provisions of the previously cited Directive 77/91/EC. It could suggest that Article 42 of the Directive is *directly effective*. Is Article 42 sufficiently clear, precise, and unconditional? With the implementation period for a directive from 1977 clearly passed, the question would turn on whether or not Article 42 contains a self-executing, justiciable rule of behaviour, which could be applied directly by a national court. Taking into account that Article 42 is a categorical, clear prohibition of discrimination between minority and majority shareholders, the answer would most likely be yes. Such a provision could produce direct effect.[154]

There is, however, a different problem. Both Audiolux as well as Bertelsmann are private undertakings. Even on the very extensive notion of 'State' adopted by the Court, it is impossible to claim that Bertelsmann would be an emanation of the Member State.[155] Thus, Audiolux finds itself in a horizontal situation, in which it cannot rely on the direct effect of directives as against another individual,[156] Bertelsmann.

With direct effect excluded, how else could Audiolux try to bring Article 42 of the Directive and/or other provisions of EU law back into the game? First, there is *indirect effect*. For this purpose, Audiolux would have to find a provision in national law which could be interpreted in conformity with Article 42 of the Directive. Such national provision could be even a general one, a general prohibition of discrimination, even of a constitutional nature.

If Audiolux were able to convince a national judge to interpret a national provision in conformity with the Directive, then Bertelsmann might indeed face a judicially imposed obligation of treating Audiolux in the same way as Groupe Bruxelles Lambert. All that a national court would do is apply its national constitution or statute *interpreted in conformity* with a provision of EU law. Bertelsmann might try to counter-suggest that such an interpretation violates legal certainty, thus reaching one of the limits introduced by the Court on indirect effect.[157] Such assessment would require a deeper immersion into previous national judicial and administrative practice in order to establish that such an interpretation would indeed be unexpected and unforeseeable. But, as there is no general ban on worsening an individual's position in horizontal relationships via consistent interpretation, indirect effect would be possible in a similar situation.

If a national judge were either unable or unwilling to interpret national law in conformity with EU law, Audiolux might try to invoke directly *Article 21(1) of the Charter and the prohibition of discrimination*. The list of prohibited grounds of discrimination in Article 21(1) is illustrative only, so prima facie it could be extended judicially. Invoking Article 21(1) of the Charter might be nonetheless problematic, in view of the fact that the Charter only became a binding part of primary law in 2009, and in view of the facts of the case, which clearly preceded that moment. Moreover, there might equally be the question whether or not fundamental rights, such as prohibition of discrimination, are without further ado transposable to (commercial) legal persons. The general answer tends to be yes, as far as reasonably applicable by analogy.[158] However, in the concrete case at hand, what ground of discrimination

[153] Or before an administrative authority, entrusted with supervision and regulation of a national securities market, as is the case in a number of Member States. However, as already previously discussed (text accompanying nn 123 and 124), the obligations of the national administrative authority would be largely the same.

[154] Leaving aside the substantive question which would have to be assessed next, namely whether Groupe Bruxelles Lambert and Audiolux were 'in the same position'.

[155] *Foster* and *Farrell* (n 73).

[156] *Marshall* and *Faccini Dori* (nn 66 and 72).

[157] See the text accompanying n 103.

[158] See in detail Opinion of AG Bobek of 13 July 2017, Case C-194/16 *Bolagsupplysningen*, EU:C:2017:554, points 41 to 60.

would be at play in the case of unequal treatment of shareholders when decreasing capital in a company? Discrimination 'on the basis of company size'? Or indirect discrimination on the basis of property?

Could, however, equal treatment of shareholders be seen as a *general principle of EU law*? As such, it would transcend any material or temporal limits to its application expressed in the Directive. It would become horizontally applicable across EU law, or certainly within all EU company law. The beauty as well as the danger of general principles is that they know no bounds: temporal, material, or personal. As the Court does not 'create' them, but just 'discovers' them, they apply to any type of legal relationship irrespective of the temporal applicability of mere directives or regulations.

In its judgment in *Audiolux*, the Court was faced with this precise question. After having canvassed a number of EU law instruments issued over the course of three decades, the Court concluded that there is no general principle of equal treatment of shareholders in EU law. Thus, relying on a general principle of EU law of equal treatment of shareholders would not be possible for Audiolux.

Finally, provided that Audiolux was not able to convince the national court in respect of any of the previous grounds, it may try to claim damages from the Member State for its failure properly to implement Directive 77/91/EC. Assume that Luxembourg or any other Member State had indeed failed to implement Article 42 of the Directive. Could a claim for *State liability* succeed?

Examining the conditions for State liability,[159] it could be argued that Audiolux suffered actual and certain damage, which would be calculated as the difference between the current value of its RTL shares and the price paid to the majority shareholder for the same shares. The damage is in causal link to the Luxembourg failure properly to implement the Directive (the wrong): if Article 42 of the Directive were transposed into national law, Audiolux should be treated the same. Thus, Article 42 of the Directive can be construed as conferring rights upon individuals (the guarantee of equal treatment).

The remaining question is whether or not the breach could be qualified as 'sufficiently serious'. The problem with this condition is its conceptual lack of clarity. In the practice of the Court, 'sufficiently serious breach' is a leftover category, which may include anything from subjective elements of liability (fault, contributory negligence, style of exercise of administrative discretion) to objective questions (clarity and precision of the EU provisions concerned). However, taking into account the categorical imperative of Article 42, which could even be construed as being directly effective, it could be suggested that the Member State had little discretion when implementing the Directive and that its failure to do so might indeed be sufficiently serious.

9 Conclusion

The 'remedial landscape' in national cases involving EU law outlined in this chapter is rather complex. It will also be highly contextual, depending on national legislation and the willingness of individual judges to engage with EU law. In some Member States, judges might be ready to set aside national rules or to twist them extensively in order to secure conformity with EU law. In other States, judges might perceive their role to be one

[159] *Brasserie du Pêcheur/Factortame* (n 143).

of much more self-restraint. The highly valued unity and the often invoked effectiveness of EU law might frequently represent just a glowing idea, hovering over the surface of the dark waters of the real life of EU law in national courts.

One of the problems, perhaps *the* problem of a system of remedies construed in such a way, is the lack of predictability. Imagine that you were asked to provide legal counsel to a company or individual, for instance in the case study to either Audiolux or Bertelsmann. Would you be able to advise your client as to what the courts would decide? The tension between the requirement of effectiveness of national enforcement of EU law and the requirement of legal certainty and also in respect of national procedural choices, already introduced at the beginning of this chapter, clearly rises to the surface.

This is unfortunate and somewhat paradoxical. One of the reasons for which the Court refused to allow the horizontal direct effect of directives was the argument of legal certainty. The simultaneous prohibition of the horizontal direct effect of directives and the massive building of alternative avenues for directives' reach into horizontal relationships, such as indirect effect or the possibility to invoke and rely directly on the Charter also in horizontal legal relationships, hardly help to safeguard legal certainty.

Finally, the ongoing rule of law crisis in several Member States, in particular in Poland and Hungary, has been rendering the entire system of remedies and enforcement of EU law at the national level even more complex. That is because the case law of the Court became confronted not only with normal cases (where the Member States' authorities act in good faith in just complex cases), but also with abnormal cases (situations in which Member States' authorities no longer play by the rules). But how can the latter situations be assessed and then translated into normative guidance within a system that is built on trust and cooperation?[160] Can there be two or even more layers of rules for national enforcement of EU law, based on whether or not a Member State is rule-of-law-compliant? Certainly, it is not reasonable to subject objectively different situations to the same conditions.[161] However, how may one account for the objective differences, without succumbing to hardly generalizable casuistic exceptions and exceptions to exceptions, while avoiding the effective imposition of double standards?

Further reading

M Avbelj and J Komárek (eds), *Constitutional Pluralism in the European Union and Beyond* (Oxford: Hart Publishing, 2012)

M Bobek and J Adams-Prassl (eds), *The EU Charter of Fundamental Rights in the Member States* (Oxford: Hart Publishing, 2020)

M Bonelli et al (eds), *Article 47 of the EU Charter and Effective Judicial Protection, Volume 1: The Court of Justice's Perspective* (Oxford: Hart Publishing, 2022)

M Botman and J Langer (eds), *National Courts and the Enforcement of EU Law: The Pivotal Role of National Courts in the EU Legal Order*. The XXIX FIDE Congress in the Hague. Vol 1 (The Hague: Eleven International Publishing, 2020)

[160] Starting with the very question what is supposed to be analysed before the Court in proceedings that are supposed to be concerned only with the interpretation of EU law, not with the examination of the specific instances of (mis)application of national law or even just problematic national practice that has no legal basis—further see Opinion of AG Bobek of 23 September 2020, Joined Cases C-83/19, C-127/19, and C-195/19 *Asociația 'Forumul Judecătorilor din România'*, EU:C:2020:746, points 240–248.

[161] Injustice is believed to arise not only when similar situations are treated differently, but also when objectively different situations are treated alike—RC Bartlett and SD Collins, *Aristotle's Nicomachean Ethics: A New Translation* (Chicago, IL: University of Chicago Press, 2011), Book 3.

Court of justice of the European Union, *50th Anniversary of the Judgment in Van Gen den Loos 1963–2013* (Luxembourg: Office for Official Publications, 2013)

P Craig, 'The Legal Effects of Directives: Policy, Rules and Exceptions' (2009) 34 *European Law Review* 349

A Dashwood, 'From *Van Duyn* to *Mangold* via *Marshall*: Reducing Direct Effect to Absurdity' (2006–7) 9 *Cambridge Yearbook of European Legal Studies* 81

B de Witte, 'Direct Effect, Supremacy and the Nature of the Legal Order' in P Craig and G de Búrca (eds), *The Evolution of EU Law* (3rd edn, Oxford: Oxford University Press, 2021)

M Dougan, 'Primacy and the Remedy of Disapplication' (2019) 56 *Common Market Law Review* 1459

M Dougan, 'When Worlds Collide! Competing Visions of the Relationship between Direct Effect and Supremacy' (2007) 44 *Common Market Law Review* 931

M Dougan, *National Remedies before the Court of Justice* (Oxford: Hart Publishing, 2004)

D Gallo, *Direct Effect in EU Law* (Oxford: Oxford University Press, 2025)

A Łazowski (ed), *Brave New World: The Application of EU Law in the New Member States* (The Hague: TMC Asser Press, 2010)

K Lenaerts and T Courthaut, 'Of Birds and Hedges: The Role of Primacy in Invoking Norms of EU Law' (2006) 31 *European Law Review* 287

T Lock, 'Is Private Enforcement of EU Law through State Liability a Myth? An Assessment 20 Years after *Francovich*' (2012) 49 *Common Market Law Review* 1675

H-W Micklitz and B de Witte (eds), *The European Court of Justice and the Autonomy of the Member States* (Antwerp: Intersentia, 2012)

P Pescatore, 'The Doctrine of "Direct Effect": An Infant Disease of Community Law' (1983) 8 *European Law Review* 155

M Poiares Maduro and L Azoulai, *The Past and Future of EU Law* (Oxford: Hart Publishing, 2010)

S Prechal, 'Direct Effect, Indirect Effect, Supremacy and the Evolving Constitution of the European Union' in C Barnard (ed), *The Fundamentals of EU Law Revisited: Assessing the Impact of the Constitutional Debate?* (Oxford: Oxford University Press, 2007)

S Prechal, 'Community Law in National Court: The Lessons from *Van Schijndel*' (1998) 35 *Common Market Law Review* 681

S Prechal, *Directives in EC Law* (2nd edn, Oxford: Oxford University Press, 2005)

A-M Slaughter, A Stone Sweet, and JHH Weiler (eds), *The European Court of Justice and National Courts: Doctrine and Jurisprudence* (Oxford: Hart Publishing, 1998)

W van Gerven, 'On Rights, Remedies and Procedures' (2000) 37 *Common Market Law Review* 501

Z Varga, *The Effectiveness of the Köbler Liability in National Courts* (Oxford: Hart Publishing, 2020)

7

EU law: is it international law?

Bruno de Witte

1 Introduction

The European Communities, and later the European Union, came into being as creatures of international law, as they were established by means of international treaties concluded by States. Today still, the TEU and the TFEU form the basic documents of the EU legal order. It logically follows from this that EU law is still part—albeit a very distinctive and advanced one—of international law. There are, however, also good reasons for thinking that the EU is now so different from any other international organization in the world that it has become 'something else', more like the central unit of a European federal State. This discussion on the proper 'legal nature' of the EU, and of EU law, has been going on for decades, and it is indeed a curious characteristic of EU law that its precise place within the legal universe is not firmly established. This is an illustration of how legal reality—in this case, the way in which European integration has been shaped in legal terms—puts pressure on the established categories of legal science. This chapter will present the terms of the discussion on the legal nature of EU law, to help the reader situate the 'place of EU law'[1] within the world of legal phenomena.

So, this chapter is not centrally concerned with another question which is sometimes dealt with under the same title of 'EU law and international law', namely the conditions under which norms of international law that are binding on the EU (in most cases, because the EU has concluded a treaty with non-Member States) are applied within the EU legal order. That different, though related, question will be briefly considered in section 4. Before that, section 2 will present the 'straightforward' view that EU law is a part (or 'sub-system') of international law, and section 3 will discuss the 'alternative' view that EU law, although originating in international law, is now so distinctive that it should no longer be considered to be part of international law.

[1] N Walker, 'The Place of European Law' in G de Búrca and JHH Weiler (eds), *The Worlds of European Constitutionalism* (Cambridge: Cambridge University Press, 2012).

2 EU law as a sub-system of international law

2.1 The EU as an international organization?

There is no disputing the fact that 'the EU has successfully expanded its substantive mandate and institutional prerogatives to a level without parallel among international organizations',[2] and this raises the question whether it is still situated 'among international organizations' or has ceased to belong to that category. In fact, if one reads the scholarly literature of international law and of EU law, we find remarkably contrasting views on this question. A large part of the EU law literature takes the view that the EU, while certainly not yet a federal State, is also no longer an international organization but rather a legal construct that is somewhere in between those two poles, in a category all of its own (this is often expressed by saying that the EU is a *sui generis* entity). If, however, one reads textbooks on international law or the law of international organizations, their authors unanimously agree that the EU is still an international organization and is still situated *within* international law. The legal education programmes of different European countries imply similarly contrasting conceptions. In the UK, for example, the Law of the European Union was, until recently, a mandatory core subject of the undergraduate law degree, whereas international law is typically considered as an altogether different subject, usually offered as an optional course for few students. In the Netherlands, by contrast, law students are usually confronted, in the mandatory part of their undergraduate degree, with a combined introduction course to international *and* European Union law, which highlights the close connection that is seen to exist between the two subjects.

There are two basic reasons why it makes sense—subject to later qualifications of this view—to view EU law as part of international law. The first reason is that EU law continues to find its origins in international treaties. The rule of recognition of EU law (ie the rule that allows us to decide whether a norm is part of EU law or not)[3] is whether a particular norm can be traced back, directly or indirectly, to the text of the TEU and the TFEU. We will highlight this continuing reliance on international law as the foundation of the EU legal order in the following subsections. The second reason is the extraordinary flexibility of international law. International law is made mainly by means of treaties between States, but there are no legal limits to the kinds of cooperation that States can undertake by means of treaties;[4] indeed, the content of some treaties puts major limitations on the sovereign powers of the participating States. This is especially so when States create an international organization, that is, a permanent institutional structure for cooperation at the international level with its own organs possessing independent decision-making powers. There is a wide variety of such international organizations. They range from the United Nations Organization, of which almost all countries of the world are members and which deals with vital matters of peace and security, to the *Office franco-allemand pour la jeunesse*, a small bilateral organization created in 1963 by France and Germany in order to stimulate youth exchanges between the two countries. Each such treaty creates a particular sub-system of international law with its own special rules. Although there is some

[2] A Moravcsik, 'The European Constitutional Settlement' in S Meunier and K McNamara (eds), *Making History: European Integration and Institutional Change at Fifty* (Oxford: Oxford University Press, 2007) 23.

[3] The notion of the 'rule of recognition' is a well-known element of the legal theory exposed by HLA Hart in his *The Concept of Law* (Oxford: Clarendon Press, 1972).

[4] Except for one, rather nebulous, limit, namely that States are not allowed to make treaties that would conflict with *jus cogens* norms; see Art 53 of the Vienna Convention on the Law of Treaties (1969).

controversy about the criteria to be used in deciding whether a legal entity can be called an international organization, there is no doubt that the European Communities first, and the European Union now, tick all the boxes. They were created by an international Treaty between States and possess organs (which are called 'institutions' in EU law) with a will distinct from the will of the Member States.[5]

This said, the European Communities were, right from the start, a very special kind of international organization (section 2.2), and this peculiarity has become more evident with the passage of time (section 2.3). Yet, even today, the EU's pedigree in international law remains. It reappears most forcefully when the Treaties on which the EU is based are being reformed, as they repeatedly have been in the past 30 years: those are major political events, which take the legal form of Treaty amendments, that is, acts of international law (case study 7.1).

2.2 **The international origins of the European integration process**

Between 1948 and 1951, three new international organizations were created in quick succession in Western Europe. The *Organisation for European Economic Co-operation* (OEEC; later named OECD) was established by a Treaty signed in Paris on 16 April 1948 by 16 European States and the three Western Commanders-in-Chief of the German occupation zones. The *Council of Europe* was created by a statute (taking the legal form of a Treaty) signed in London on 5 May 1949 by ten European States. In addition, a Treaty signed in Paris on 18 April 1951 by six European States established the European Coal and Steel Community (ECSC). The creation of new international organizations was common practice. Dozens of multilateral international organizations had been set up since the middle of the nineteenth century.[6] Most of them, though, had a universal remit, or at least an extra-European one, and the focus on creating ambitious multilateral entities responding to the 'need of a closer unity between all like-minded countries of Europe'[7] was a new development of the post-war period. All three organizations expressed, in their own way, the aspiration towards greater European unity, and they were often considered together in the legal scholarship of that period.[8]

In fact, during those immediate post-war years, active groups of European federalists had hoped to create a United Europe based on a federal constitution inspired by that of the US, and had sought to promote the adoption of federal solutions in the context of the various political initiatives taken in that period to reorganize the European political landscape. The European governments chose, instead, not to take the federal route and they rather shaped their new initiatives of European cooperation by using the age-old legal tool of the international Treaty. The OEEC, the Council of Europe, and the ECSC all took the form of an international organization based on a Treaty subject to ratification by the parliaments of their Member States. Both the OEEC and the Council of Europe were set up as rather old-fashioned and traditional international organizations, as their main

[5] On the legal definition of an international organization, see J Klabbers, *An Introduction to International Organizations Law* (4th edn, Cambridge: Cambridge University Press, 2022) 6–13.

[6] For a synthesis of this historical development, see A Peters and S Peter, 'International Organizations: Between Technocracy and Democracy' in B Fassbender and A Peters (eds), *The Oxford Handbook of the History of International Law* (Oxford: Oxford University Press, 2012).

[7] Statute of the Council of Europe, Preamble, para 4.

[8] In the English language literature, see eg AH Robertson, *European Institutions: Co-operation, Integration, Unification* (London: Stevens, 1959).

organs were kept under the close control of the Member State governments (the European Convention on Human Rights was a legal breakthrough within the Council of Europe, but it happened by means of a separate Treaty which entered into force only later).[9] The ECSC Treaty, by contrast, was an innovative endeavour; it created a *different*, functionally and politically more effective, international organization.

Indeed, whereas the ECSC was based on what seemed like an ordinary international Treaty, that Treaty was far from ordinary in terms of its content. A major, and at the time startling, innovation of the 'Schuman Plan',[10] contrasting with most pre-war and post-war cooperation projects, was that sovereign States should agree to transfer their powers to regulate the coal and steel industries to a common body, the High Authority. By signing the ECSC Treaty, as it emerged from the Schuman Plan through negotiations in 1950 and 1951, the governments of the six founding States agreed to relinquish national control over these two sectors of the economy and to allow the supranational High Authority to exercise State-like public authority in their stead.

The term *supranational*, itself, appeared only once in the ECSC Treaty, and not in a very prominent place, but it had been repeatedly used during the negotiations, and was rapidly adopted by political and legal commentators as the defining characteristic not only of the High Authority but also of the entire Community of which it was an organ. The supranational character of the ECSC Treaty did not spring so much from the substantive norms it contained, but from the way in which it distributed legal authority and organized the decision-making by its organs. The ECSC had three institutions composed of persons who were not government representatives (the High Authority, a parliamentary Assembly, and a Court of Justice). Its institutions (particularly the independent High Authority) had the power to adopt binding acts, often by a majority vote; some of those decisions were directly applicable to private individuals and firms; and compliance by both the institutions and the Member States with their obligations was subject to judicial enforcement. None of those features was unprecedented in international law, so that the novelty of the ECSC did not reside in one or other of those specific characteristics but rather in their cumulative presence.[11]

When the EEC and the European Atomic Energy Community (EAEC) were created in 1957, as a further stage of the European integration process, they were equipped with an institutional regime that was as supranational as that of the ECSC. It is true that the Commission had a less prominent place in the decision-making system of the EEC than the High Authority had in the ECSC. Yet, the Community's power to make directly applicable rules was now extended in its scope: broadly-based regulations could be adopted in a number of economic areas by the Council acting on a proposal by the Commission, in contrast with the limited decisions, relating solely to the coal and steel industries, which the High Authority could adopt under ECSC law. The EEC preserved all the other supranational characteristics of the earlier Treaty, with the interesting addition of the preliminary reference procedure before the European Court of Justice whose supranational potential went, however, largely unnoticed in 1957.

[9] On the extent to which the Statute of the Council of Europe, as agreed in 1949, constituted a dampener on the high hopes held by European federalists, see AJ Zurcher, *The Struggle to Unite Europe 1940–1958* (New York: New York University Press, 1958) ch 5.

[10] Thus named after the French minister of foreign affairs Robert Schuman who had launched the idea of the ECSC in a speech delivered in Paris on 9 May 1950.

[11] F Capotorti, 'Supranational Organizations' in *Encyclopedia of Public International Law*, vol 5 (Amsterdam: North-Holland, 1983) 263–264.

2.3 **The later evolution of the European Communities and the European Union**

The 'Treaty path' towards closer European integration, after having been confirmed when the EEC was established in 1957, was also followed during the later stages of the European integration process. Deliberate attempts to transform the European Communities into 'something else' (legally speaking) were made at several moments in the history of European integration, but none of those attempts resulted in a clear and explicit change of the legal nature of the organizations. Indeed, when the Maastricht Treaty, signed in February 1992, eventually created a new legal entity, called the European Union, along-side the European Communities, many considered this a *step back* in the European integration process. That new legal entity was created, by the then 12 Member States, to host two new forms of interstate cooperation, in common foreign and security policy (CFSP) and justice and home affairs (JHA), which were marked by a *lesser* degree of supranationalism than the existing European Communities. So, the creation of the EU in the early 1990s was not a jump forward towards a federal Europe, but a partial return to more traditional forms of intergovernmental cooperation—despite the fact that, in other ways, the Maastricht Treaty did indeed deepen the integration process: it created the Economic and Monetary Union, it coined the co-decision procedure for EC law-making, it introduced the concept of European citizenship, etc.

The curious 'legal architecture' resulting from Maastricht, consisting of two separate treaties corresponding to two separate but interconnected organizations (the EC and the EU), has now been replaced—through the Lisbon Treaty—by a new architecture. We now still have (at least[12]) two separate and legally equivalent Treaties (the TEU and the TFEU) but only a single organization, namely the European Union, which has now absorbed the European Community.[13] That single organization is still firmly rooted in international law. In fact, the first sentence of Article 1 TEU uses the traditional language of international law:

> By this Treaty, the HIGH CONTRACTING PARTIES establish among themselves a EUROPEAN UNION . . . on which the Member States confer competences to attain objectives they have in common.[14]

The evolution traced in the previous paragraphs would seem to lead to the logical conclusion that the EC, first, and the EU, now, remain creatures of international law, and therefore continue to belong to the legal category of international organizations. The European Treaties themselves do not contain express language to confirm this, but the EU Member States have accepted this qualification when operating in the broader international arena. Indeed, there are many multilateral Treaty provisions that use the terms 'international organization' or 'regional economic international organization' (REIO) where it is clear from the context that the (only) organization intended by that term is the EC or the EU.[15]

[12] ie without counting the EAEC Treaty, which continues to have a separate legal existence and is not subordinated to the TEU and TFEU; but its political importance has dwindled over the years.

[13] See M Cremona, 'The Two (or Three) Treaty Solution: The New Treaty Structure of the EU' in A Biondi, P Eeckhout, and S Ripley (eds), *EU Law after Lisbon* (Oxford: Oxford University Press, 2012).

[14] The capitalized words in the main text are printed in capitals in the version published by the *Official Journal of the European Union* (OJ [2008] C115/16).

[15] See, among many other examples, the Energy Charter Treaty (1991), Art 1(2) and (3); the Convention on Biological Diversity (1992), Art 35; the UN Framework Convention on Climate Change (1992), Art 20; the UNESCO Convention on the Protection and Promotion of the Diversity of Cultural Expressions (2005), Art 27. See, on the practice of making these 'REIO' references, E Paasivirta and PJ Kuijper, 'Does One Size Fit All? The European Community and the Responsibility of International Organizations' (2005) 36 *Netherlands Yearbook of International Law* 169, 206 *et seq.*

The EU Member States participate in drawing up those multilateral international conventions and could therefore object to the qualification of the EC or the EU as international organizations, but they do not.

The EU (or, previously, the EC) is also considered an international organization under the constitutional law of many of its Member States. Some national constitutions contain clauses dealing with the transfer of powers to the EU (such clauses were introduced by some 'old' members usually at the time of the Maastricht Treaty, and by 'new' members at the time they acceded to the EU). Other countries, however, continue to adopt a generic approach of allowing transfers of powers, or limitations of sovereignty, for the benefit of international organizations or international institutions without making special reference to the EU.[16] It is clear that those generic references to international organizations include the EU. Therefore, the prevalent view, from the perspective of national constitutional law, seems to be that the EU is indeed a creature of international law and therefore an international organization, and that State sovereignty has not been abandoned or shared, but rather is being 'exercised in common' within the framework of the Union.[17]

When we turn to the Court of Justice, which has the principal authority to interpret and apply EU law,[18] and therefore the authority to declare what the legal nature of the EU is, we find no conclusive views on the matter. It is true that the Court of Justice has regularly stated that 'the EEC Treaty has created its own legal system',[19] or similar language, but this, in itself, is nothing special: every other international organization has its own legal sub-system as defined by its founding Treaty. The Court never added that this legal system was situated *outside* the scope of international law. In its famous early judgments, *Van Gend en Loos* and *Costa*, the Court sought to differentiate the EEC Treaty from 'other' or 'ordinary' international Treaties, but that otherness was not pushed to the conclusion that the EEC Treaty had created something other than an international organization.[20] Much has been made of the fact that the Court held, in its *Van Gend en Loos* judgment of 1963, that the EEC Treaty had created 'a new legal order of international law', whereas it dropped the last three words one year later in *Costa* when it simply spoke of 'a new legal order'. This has been interpreted, by a number of commentators, as a deliberate tearing away of Community law from its international legal moorings. Yet, the way in which the Court described the peculiar characteristics of the EEC Treaty was very similar in both those early judgments. It would therefore be very odd if that description had led, in 1963, to the conclusion that this was a special legal order *still of international law*, and only one year later to the opposite conclusion that it was a special legal order *no longer of international law*.

In the many years since its *Costa* judgment, the Court of Justice did not seek to develop a doctrine affirming the specific *and* non-international nature of the EU. In the *Wightman*

[16] See M Claes, 'Constitutionalising Europe at Its Source: The "European Clauses" in the National Constitutions: Evolution and Typology' (2005) 24 *Yearbook of European Law* 81.

[17] See, on this question of the continuing relevance of the notion of sovereignty in the context of European integration, N Walker, 'Late Sovereignty in the European Union' in N Walker (ed), *Sovereignty in Transition* (Oxford: Hart Publishing, 2003) and B de Witte, 'Sovereignty and European Integration: The Weight of Legal Tradition' in A-M Slaughter, A Stone Sweet, and JHH Weiler (eds), *The European Court and National Courts: Doctrine and Jurisprudence* (Oxford: Hart Publishing, 1998).

[18] Art 19(1) TEU.

[19] eg in the European Court of Justice (ECJ), Joined Cases C-6/90 and C-9/90 *Francovich and Bonifaci v Italy* [1991] ECR I-5357, para 31.

[20] See, however, the Opinion of AG Poiares Maduro in the *Kadi* case, who stated that the ECJ, in *Van Gend en Loos*, had considered the EEC Treaty to form a new legal order which was 'beholden to, but distinct from the existing legal order of public international law' (Opinion of 23 January 2008 in Joined Cases C-402/05 P and C-415/05 P *Kadi and Al Barakaat v Council and Commission*, para 21). The ECJ, in fact, did not quite use those words in its 1963 judgment, nor later.

judgment, the Court stated that 'the founding Treaties, which constitute the basic constitutional charter of the European Union ... established, *unlike ordinary international treaties*, a *new legal order*, possessing its own institutions, for the benefit of which the Member States thereof have limited their sovereign rights, in ever wider fields'.[21] The Court hereby claims that the EU is not a simple sub-system within international law but a true 'legal order', and that the TEU and TFEU are not 'ordinary Treaties'. Yet, the Court still does not state in so many words that the EU legal order has ceased to be part of international law. In fact, there is no need for the Court to adopt the view that the European Union is 'something other' than an international organization in order to affirm and protect the advanced features of European Union law since, as we saw, international law is extraordinarily flexible as to the content of the cooperation between States. On the few occasions on which the Court gives an indication of the kind of legal entity the EU might be, it tends to use tautological categories, as when it described the EU as a '*union* based on the rule of law'.[22]

Case study 7.1: Revision Treaties

We have seen in the preceding discussion, the European Communities were founded, back in the 1950s, by means of international Treaties concluded between their Member States. Since then, the *deepening* of the European integration process has taken place essentially by means of new Treaties between the Member States 'revising' (or 'amending', which has the same meaning) the existing Treaties. The *widening* of the European integration process took the form of a series of accession Treaties between the existing and the acceding States, organizing the way in which the new Member States could join the existing organizations. The main revision Treaties were the Single European Act, the Maastricht Treaty, the Treaty of Amsterdam, the Treaty of Nice, and most recently the Lisbon Treaty. Seven accession Treaties were concluded so far: with the UK, Ireland, and Denmark; with Greece; with Spain and Portugal; with Austria, Finland, and Sweden; with eight Central and Eastern European countries, Malta and Cyprus; with Bulgaria and Romania; and most recently with Croatia.

Revision Treaties are, legally speaking, more interesting than accession Treaties. Whereas the latter tend to be based on the simple principle that the newcomers must accept the existing legal order with only little room for institutional accommodation and derogations, revision Treaties have led to major changes in the institutional set-up and policy scope of the European Communities and the EU.

It frequently happens, of course, that States may want to amend a Treaty that they have previously concluded. The rules relating to such operations are set out in Articles 39 to 41 of the Vienna Convention on the Law of Treaties (1969). Article 39 contains the very simple default rule that a Treaty may be amended by an agreement between all the parties, and that the normal rules on the conclusion of Treaties apply to this amending agreement. The parties may set aside that default rule when concluding the original (to-be-amended) Treaty.

[21] Case C-621/18 *Andy Wightman and others v Secretary of State for Exiting the European Union*, EU:C:2018:999, para 44 (emphasis added). The same formula was also used, a few years earlier, in Opinion 2/13, *Accession to the ECHR*, EU:C:2014:2454, para 157.

[22] Case C-583/11 P *Inuit Tapiriit Kanatami v Parliament and Council*, EU:C:2013:625, para 91 (emphasis added). Note the shift from 'Union' (the *species*) to 'union' (the *genus*). The small-u term is left undefined, and should not be read as denying that EU law belongs to international law. Curiously, the concept of 'international union' was of common usage in the nineteenth and early part of the twentieth centuries to describe the early international regimes for technical cooperation, eg for post, telegraphy, and copyright (A Peters and S Peter (n 6) 174–176).

The international legal regime of Treaty amendment is, thus, one of utmost flexibility; the contracting parties[23] are free to arrange for the later amendment of 'their' Treaty in the way they wish.[24] Indeed, a large and increasing number of multilateral Treaties contain such a special amendment procedure, generally aimed at facilitating adaptation to changing circumstances, often by allowing for the amendment of a Treaty without the agreement of all the States.[25] Article 48 EU, the amendment provision applying to changes of both the TEU and TFEU, is an example of a specific amendment clause but, contrary to most others, it does *not* provide more flexibility than the default rule of Article 39 Vienna Convention. It requires the agreement of *all* the parties (in this case, the Member States of the EU) for the valid adoption of the amendments and, *in addition*, it requires some involvement of the EU institutions in the preparatory phase and, in almost every case, the separate approval of the amendments by each State according to its own constitutional requirements.[26]

The EU's 'rule of change' is thus particularly rigid, not because this rigidity is prescribed by general rules of international law, but because its Member States have committed themselves to such a rigid mechanism. The original rule that the EC Treaties could only be revised with the agreement of all the Member States, which made perfect sense when the EC counted only six States, was left untouched on each later occasion, despite the fact that membership grew from 6 to 28. This has rendered the unanimity requirement an ever more cumbersome obstacle in the way of Treaty change.[27]

As to the *content* of the Treaty amendments, the Member States traditionally acted, to use a famous German expression, as the *Herren der Verträge* ('Masters of the Treaties'), bound by nothing else than the limits posed by their respective constitutions; they acted as 'independent and sovereign States having freely decided . . . to exercise in common some of their competences'.[28] The fact that the Member State governments acted as collective 'masters' of the Treaty text did not mean that they could also control what happened under the new Treaty once it had entered into force. The dynamic evolution of EU law in between Treaty revisions partly escaped their control, and they could correct unwanted evolutions only on the occasion of a further Treaty revision and on the unlikely condition that they found a consensus to overrule, say, a particular interpretation of the Treaty text adopted by the Court of Justice.

The close control exercised by the Member State governments on the revision process has now been diluted somewhat. Compared to the previous revision clauses, the new rules enacted by the Lisbon Treaty for future revisions of the European Treaties innovate in two limited respects: they prescribe the use of the 'Convention method' for future revisions, and they provide for two so-called simplified revision procedures, in addition to the ordinary revision procedure.

[23] 'Contracting parties' is the expression used in the practice of international law to denote the States (or international organizations) that have accepted to be bound by a particular treaty.

[24] See A Aust, *Modern Treaty Law and Practice* (Cambridge: Cambridge University Press, 2000) 214: 'It is wrong to think that the Vienna Convention is a rigid structure which places obstacles in the way of treaty modification: rather, it allows states to include in treaties such amendment provisions as they wish.'

[25] For a survey of the wide variety of those special amendment procedures, see J Brunnée, 'Treaty Amendments' in DB Hollis (ed), *The Oxford Guide to Treaties* (2nd edn, Oxford: Oxford University Press, 2020).

[26] On the current, post-Lisbon, EU Treaty amendment regime, see chapter 5, and for an overview of the content of the major revision Treaties, see chapter 2. For further discussion, see S Peers, 'The Future of EU Treaty Amendments' (2012) 31 *Yearbook of European Law* 17; B de Witte, 'Treaty Revision Procedures after Lisbon' in Biondi, Eeckhout, and Ripley, *EU Law after Lisbon* (n 13).

[27] For an analysis of how, in particular, the requirement that each Treaty revision should be separately ratified by each State has placed obstacles in the way of EU Treaty change on many occasions, see C Closa, *The Politics of Ratification of EU Treaties* (Abingdon: Routledge, 2013).

[28] The Member State governments used this phrase in the introductory part of the Decision on Denmark, adopted at the Edinburgh summit of 12 December 1992, but it referred back to their earlier adoption of the Maastricht Treaty.

The Convention method consists in the fact that all important Treaty revisions must, from now on, be preceded by a deliberative phase within a 'Convention' comprising representatives not only of the national governments but also of the national parliaments and of the EU institutions (especially the European Parliament). The model for this new body is the Convention that was convened on an experimental basis, in 2002–3, to prepare the adoption of the Constitutional Treaty. The debate on the direction of future Treaty reforms is thus no longer confined to traditional diplomatic exchanges between national governments but is opened up to a wider constituency. Still, the Convention can only express an opinion or make proposals. The actual decision to amend the Treaties will still take the form of an agreement between Member State governments laid down in an international treaty.

The new simplified procedures, which apply for certain kinds of amendments mentioned in Article 48(6) and (7) EU, allow for the text of the Treaties to be amended, not by another international Treaty but by a unilateral decision of an organ of the EU itself (ie the European Council). However, the Articles thus amended will then take their place among the other Articles of the TEU or TFEU, thereby sharing the international legal nature of those Treaties.[29]

Those innovations of the Lisbon Treaty do not affect the fundamental rule of the game, namely that all Member States must give their unanimous consent to future amendments of the Treaties. The EU's rules of change thereby continue to be much more rigid than the ones applying to national constitutions, but also more rigid than the ones applying to the founding instruments of other, less integrated, international organizations.[30] They are a powerful confirmation of the fact that EU law remains anchored in international law and that the Union's legal fate remains in the hands of the States that have created it, or joined it later on.

3 The specific features of EU law

Although the view that the EU is, and remains, a creature of international law may seem logical in view of the preceding discussion, it is, in fact, strongly contested in the legal literature. Many EU law scholars have argued, already since the 1960s, that the legal characteristics of Community law (and now Union law) are so peculiar and far removed from what one normally observes in the world of international relations that it does not make good sense to consider it to be part of international law.[31] The EU is then no longer an international organization at all, but 'something else', a *sui generis* legal system that does not fit in the traditional dichotomy between (federal) States and international organizations. To continue to refer to it as an international organization would be 'to try to push the toothpaste back in the tube'.[32]

[29] The possibility for a treaty establishing an international organization to be amended through a unilateral act of one of the organs of that organization is not unheard of in the practice of international law; see Brunnée (n 25) 362.

[30] For this comparison, see W Lehmann, 'Federal States and International Organisations: A Short Comparison of Their Amending Rules with the European Union', European Parliament note, December 2011.

[31] Among those scholars figure also some prominent former members of the European Court of Justice who defended this view in an extra-judicial capacity: P Pescatore, 'International Law and Community Law: A Comparative Analysis' (1970) 7 *Common Market Law Review* 167; GF Mancini, 'Europe: The Case for Statehood' (1998) 4 *European Law Journal* 29. As mentioned in the previous section, the Court itself, in its judgments, never expressed a clear position on this controversy.

[32] JHH Weiler and UR Haltern, 'Constitutional or International? The Foundations of the Community Legal Order and the Question of Judicial Kompetenz-Kompetenz' in Slaughter, Stone Sweet, and Weiler, *The European Court and National Courts* (n 17) 331, 342.

The legal features of EU law that could support this alternative view are manifold: the broad and flexible nature of EU competences which extend into many areas of law-making; the existence of a (partially) common currency and a common (though derivative) citizenship; the decision-making regime, marked by the involvement of some institutions not controlled by the Member State governments and by recourse to majority voting as the usual rule in the State-controlled Council of Ministers; the relatively effective mechanism of State compliance; the habit of obedience by national courts to their duty to apply EU law.

This raises the question whether any of these legal features are incompatible with the notion of an international organization, thereby placing EU law as a whole outside the scope of international law. One could also argue that the incomparability of the EU results not from any one of those features but from their combination, which makes the EU a unique phenomenon and makes it seem contrived to insist on the formal view of the EU as just another international organization. We will discuss these arguments in the following two subsections.

3.1 **The incomparability of the EU's legal features**

Advanced international organizations are created year after year, and display one or several of the characteristic features of the EU, mentioned previously. Many international organizations have organs possessing the power to adopt operational decisions that are binding on States, and occasionally such decisions can even be adopted by a majority vote, that is, against the wishes of single Member States of the organization.[33] It is true, though, that those decisions seldom deal with very sensitive policy matters; they tend to be about technical issues, with some well-known exceptions such as the UN's Security Council.

In the EU, by contrast, there is a constant stream of new legislation in a broad range of policy areas, typically adopted nowadays through what the Lisbon Treaty appropriately renamed the 'ordinary legislative procedure'.[34] This procedure is marked by the fact that the European Parliament and the Council must agree on the text, and that the Council can decide by a qualified majority of the represented Member States. Furthermore, in some key areas of EU law, such as competition law and monetary policy, supranational institutions (the European Commission and the European Central Bank, respectively) that are not controlled by the Member States exercise crucial decision-making powers. The European Parliament, which is directly elected by the European citizenry, exercises democratic control of the European Commission, and democratic input in the law-making process—this is, of course, unknown in any other international law regime.

If we move from law-making to considering judicial enforcement of the law, also there we can find some examples of international organizations equipped with international courts having compulsory jurisdiction to settle disputes between States.[35] It is rare, though, for international courts to provide for direct access by individual plaintiffs. Apart from the case of the European Court of Human Rights, we mostly find this in

[33] For a general view, see J von Bernstorff, 'Procedures of Decision-Making and the Role of Law in International Organizations' (2008) 9 *German Law Journal* 1939; ND White, 'Decision-Making' in J Klabbers and A Wallendahl (eds), *Research Handbook on the Law of International Organizations* (Cheltenham: Edward Elgar, 2011) 225; and J Wouters and P De Man, 'International Organizations as Law-Makers', ibid 190.

[34] Art 294 TFEU. See further chapter 5.

[35] C Baudenbacher and MJ Clifton, 'Courts of Regional Economic and Political Integration Agreements' in C Romano, K Alter, and Y Shany (eds), *The Oxford Handbook of International Adjudication* (Oxford: Oxford University Press, 2014).

the framework of regional integration organizations whose political and judicial institutions were deliberately modelled on the EU.[36] Examples include the Caribbean Court of Justice, and the Andean Tribunal of Justice (an organ of the Andean Community), which is engaged in an active dialogue with national courts through a preliminary reference mechanism comparable to that existing in the EU.

A feature of the EU's judicial enforcement regime which remains fairly unique is the power of the European Commission (an institution acting independently from the Member States) to sue the Member States before the Court of Justice for infringement of their EU law obligations. This mechanism has allowed the Court to state, very early on, that the general international rule allowing States to retaliate in the event of non-compliance by other parties to the same Treaty (*inadimplenti non est adimplendum*)[37] did not apply in the context of Union law. The Court deduced this innovative characteristic from a specific feature of the EEC Treaty itself, namely this power of the Commission to bring infringement actions against non-complying States.[38] There is, thus, a specific system of State responsibility in EU law which does not allow States to adopt countermeasures in the event of a violation of EU obligations by the other States; yet, this specificity follows logically from choices made by the Member States themselves when they created the EEC and in particular from their decision to vest the Commission with an independent power to take non-compliant Member States to court. It can therefore be seen as an example of the flexibility provided by international law: when creating an international organization, States can devise operational rules for their organization that derogate from (ie go further than) the general rules of international law.

As for the preliminary reference mechanism, through which national courts engage in a dialogue with the Court when dealing with the application of EU law norms, this mechanism has been imitated elsewhere (see earlier in this subsection). Yet, it has produced, in the EU legal system, some seemingly unique consequences, in particular the formulation of an obligation for national courts to recognize the *primacy* of EU law. Since this obligation is often cited as the most compelling evidence that EU law is no longer part of international law, it deserves a closer look in the next subsection.

3.2 **The primacy of EU law, a federal characteristic?**

The feature of Union law that is most widely mentioned as showing its remoteness from international law is its *primacy* within the national legal orders of its Member States. Indeed, whereas international Treaties take precedence over national law, this precedence operates at the international level rather than within the domestic legal orders. Already in 1930, the Permanent Court of International Justice held that it was 'a generally accepted principle of international law that in the relations between powers who are

[36] KJ Alter, 'The Global Spread of European Style International Courts' (2012) 35 *West European Politics* 135.

[37] See N White, 'Countermeasures and Sanctions' in ME Evans (ed), *International Law* (6th edn, Oxford: Oxford University Press, 2024).

[38] Joined Cases 90/63 and 91/63 *Commission v Luxembourg and Belgium* [1964] ECR English Special Edition 625:

> the [EEC] Treaty is not limited to creating reciprocal obligations between the different natural and legal persons to whom it is applicable, but establishes a new legal order which governs the powers, rights and obligations of the said persons, *as well as the necessary procedures for taking cognizance of and penalizing any breach of it*. Therefore . . . *the basic concept of the Treaty requires that the Member States shall not take the law in their own hands.* (emphasis added)

The same principle has been repeated by the Court many times since 1964; eg in Case C-111/03 *Commission v Sweden* [2005] ECR I-8789, para 66.

contracting parties to a treaty, the provisions of municipal law cannot prevail over those of the treaty'.[39] Yet, this statement is, in fact, limited to the 'relations between powers' on the international plane; it does not apply to the *internal* workings of the national legal systems, in respect of which international law does not seem to claim a priority of Treaty norms over conflicting national norms. Indeed, the received view among international law scholars is the following:

> From the standpoint of international law states are generally free as to the manner in which, domestically, they put themselves in the position to meet their international obligations; the choice between the direct reception and application of international law, or its transformation into national law by way of statute, is a matter of indifference . . . These are matters for each state to determine for itself according to its own constitutional practice.[40]

One finds this view repeated in all contemporary international law textbooks.[41] In practice, though, we can observe a tendency towards greater recognition of the primacy of international law over national law in the text of national constitutions or in the case law of national constitutional and supreme courts.[42] It is also possible for a particular Treaty to give specific guidance on the steps that States must take within their domestic legal order. The European Court of Justice noted this possibility in a judgment of 1999:

> According to the general rules of international law there must be *bona fide* performance of every agreement. Although each contracting party is responsible for executing fully the commitments which it has undertaken it is nevertheless free to determine the legal means appropriate for attaining that end in its legal system, ***unless the agreement, interpreted in the light of its subject-matter and purpose, itself specifies those means.***[43]

The TEU and TFEU (and their earlier pre-Lisbon versions) are agreements of the kind referred to in the sentence above. Their *wording* does not specify in any detail the means by which the Member States must comply with their commitments (except for the fact, recorded in what is now Article 267 TFEU, that they must allow their courts to refer preliminary questions to the Court on the interpretation of EU law), but, interpreting the Treaties in light of their *subject matter* and *purpose*, the Court came to the conclusion that some of their provisions should have direct effect in the domestic legal system (*Van Gend en Loos* and its progeny) and that all those norms that have direct effect should also have primacy over conflicting national law (*Costa* and its progeny).[44]

[39] Permanent Court of International Justice, *Greek and Bulgarian Communities*, PCIJ, Series B, No 17, p 32.

[40] RY Jennings and A Watts (eds), *Oppenheim's International Law*, vol I (9th edn, London: Longman, 1992) 82–83.

[41] For a more detailed treatment of the limited dictates of international law, and of divergent national constitutional practice, see M Mendez, *The Legal Effects of EU Agreements: Maximalist Treaty Enforcement and Judicial Avoidance Techniques* (Oxford: Oxford University Press, 2013) ch 1. See also E Denza, 'The Relationship between International and National Law' in ME Evans (ed), *International Law* (6th edn, Oxford: Oxford University Press, 2024) 383.

[42] See A Peters and UK Preuss, 'International Relations and International Law' in M Tushnet, F Fleiner, and C Saunders (eds), *Routledge Handbook of Constitutional Law* (Abingdon: Routledge, 2013) 36–40.

[43] Case C-149/96 *Portugal v Council* [1999] ECR I-8395, para 35 (emphasis added). Of course, the agreement to which the ECJ refers in this extract is not the EC Treaty or EU Treaty but an external agreement concluded by the EC.

[44] On the legal effect of EU law in national legal systems, see generally chapter 6. For more on the development of the direct effect and primacy doctrines by the Court of Justice and their acceptance at the national level, see M Claes, *The National Courts' Mandate in the European Constitution* (Oxford: Hart Publishing, 2006) and, for a shorter synthesis, B de Witte, 'Direct Effect, Primacy, and the Nature of the Legal Order' in P Craig and G de Búrca (eds), *The Evolution of EU Law* (3rd edn, Oxford: Oxford University Press, 2021).

The principle that EU law prevails, or should prevail, over national law even in cases decided by national courts is reminiscent of the supremacy of federal law over Member State law, which is entrenched in the constitutions of prominent federal States such as the US and Germany. It is not surprising, therefore, to find many EU law scholars who saw the primacy doctrine as a hallmark of the quasi-federal and non-international nature of European law. Writing very shortly after the foundational judgments *Van Gend en Loos* and *Costa*, Peter Hay devoted a chapter of his work on *Federalism and Supranational Organizations* to what he termed the 'Federal Relation of Community Law to National Law'.[45] In 1991, Joseph Weiler wrote, in his *Transformation of Europe*, that the doctrines of direct effect and primacy rendered the relationship between Community law and national law 'indistinguishable from analogous relationships in constitutions of federal states'.[46] Many other authors have expressed similar views until the present day.

On a closer look, though, the primacy of EU law is quite different from the supremacy of federal law in countries such as Germany, Switzerland, the US, or Canada. In all those countries, the supremacy of federal law is effectively guaranteed by the fact that its enforcement is largely in the hands of federal courts. In the EU legal order, the inconsistency of a national norm with an EU law norm can be directly examined by the Court of Justice only in the framework of an infringement action brought by the Commission under Article 258 EC, where the Court can make Union law prevail as a matter of course, just like any international court would give precedence to international law over the domestic laws of the States parties to an international dispute. Usually, however, inconsistencies between national law and EU law appear through litigation before national courts and have to be solved by them, with the possible guidance of a preliminary ruling by the Court of Justice. In contrast with all federal States, there is no right of appeal to the Court of Justice against judgments of national courts that fail to recognize the primacy of EU law. Therefore, it is crucially important that the national courts should faithfully absorb and apply the primacy doctrine laid down by the Court of Justice, since it falls to them to make the doctrine a living reality.

This institutional factor has important consequences for the operation of the primacy doctrine. Since national courts conceive themselves to be organs of their State, they try to fit their 'European mandate' within the framework of the powers attributed to them by their national legal system. For those courts and, indeed, for most constitutional law scholars throughout Europe, the authority of EU law is rooted in their constitution, and subject to restrictions that may be imposed by the constitution.[47] This situation is in stark contrast with the position prevailing in federal States where the primacy of federal law is based on the federal constitution whose authority as the fundamental norm of the State is uncontested. In the EU legal order, on the contrary, the hierarchical relationship between EU law and national law needs to be more heavily emphasized by the Court of Justice and its supporters because the ultimate hierarchy of norms is not settled in favour of EU law.

It is not so clear, therefore, that the doctrines of primacy and direct effect count as features of EU law that distinguish it from international law. The doctrine of primacy, as presently formulated by the Court and accepted by the Member State courts, has,

[45] P Hay, *Federalism and Supranational Organizations: Patterns for New Legal Structures* (Champaign, IL: University of Illinois Press, 1966).

[46] JHH Weiler, 'The Transformation of Europe' (1991) 100 *Yale Law Journal* 2403, 2413. On the concept of federalism in EU law, see further chapter 4.

[47] For the evidence backing this statement, see the various 'national reports' in Slaughter, Stone Sweet, and Weiler, *The European Court and National Courts* (n 17), the comparative analysis by Claes (n 44), and S Griller, L Papadopoulou, and R Puff (eds), *National Constitutions and EU Integration* (Oxford: Hart Publishing, 2022).

no doubt, a distinct federal flavour but it could also be termed a creative development of international law. The central rule of international treaty law is *pacta sunt servanda*: States are bound by their treaty obligations; and whenever a conflict between a treaty obligation and a norm of national law is brought before the International Court of Justice, or any other international court, the answer is clear: the Treaty rule will prevail. The originality of the EEC Treaty, when it was concluded back in 1957, was to grant to the newly established Court, the ECJ, a jurisdictional competence which was then unique in the panorama of international law, namely that of guiding the activity of national courts while they are applying EU law by means of the preliminary rulings procedure. By means of this procedure, the ECJ had a 'window' through which it could intervene in pending national court cases and direct those national courts to respect the precedence of EU law.[48]

Seen from this angle, the direct effect and primacy doctrines do not so much signal a shift away from international law; they rather illustrate the dynamic potential of international law. The fact that, as a rule, international law leaves to States a choice among various methods of domestic enforcement of international obligations does not prevent specific Treaties or international decisions from imposing specific requirements in this respect. The TEU and TFEU may no longer be the only Treaties that do this. Given appropriate circumstances, primacy within the domestic legal orders may be required by other international Treaties as well.

3.3 **Finding a name to describe the EU's specificity**

The preceding discussion does not lead to an unambiguous conclusion. There are, in fact, two credible options for explaining the legal nature of the EU. The first option consists in saying that, in view of its basis in a set of international Treaties, the EU is still an international organization and EU law is part of international law. This option must necessarily come with the recognition that the EU is an international organization unlike any other that has existed before, in view of the width and depth of the limitations imposed on the sovereignty of its Member States. However, this option allows for other experiments of international cooperation to adopt some or all of the distinctive features of EU law in order to create similarly advanced organizations elsewhere in the world. This explanatory option expresses, therefore, a belief in the flexibility and dynamic potential of international law.[49]

The second option consists in arguing that, because of its particular legal features, the 'European legal order has . . . cut the umbilical cord with the international legal order'.[50] There is no entity, anywhere in the world, that resembles the EU, and there is no realistic prospect for such an entity to appear any time soon. As it is not a credible option to argue that the EU has become a federal State, the authors defending this view argue that the EU finds itself on a middle ground. It is more than an international regime and not (yet) a federal State, but it possesses features stemming from both sides.[51]

[48] The importance of the preliminary rulings procedure in allowing for the emergence of the primacy doctrine was emphasized by D Wyatt, 'New Legal Order, or Old?' (1982) 7 *European Law Review* 147.

[49] For a fuller articulation of this view, see B de Witte, 'The European Union as an International Legal Experiment' in de Búrca and Weiler, *The Worlds of European Constitutionalism* (n 1); and TC Hartley, 'International Law and the Law of the European Union' (2001) 72 *British Yearbook of International Law* 1.

[50] R Schütze, *European Constitutional Law* (Cambridge: Cambridge University Press, 2012) 66.

[51] Among the authors who have expressed this view, we can mention Schütze (n 50) and M Avbelj, 'Theory of European Union' (2011) 36 *European Law Review* 818.

Under both these options, there is a strong urge to find new names and concepts to describe the specific nature of the EU. Under the first option, that denomination would serve to identify the sub-category of advanced international organizations of which the EU is the leading exemplar. Under the second option, the need for a new denomination is even more urgent. Since the proponents of that option argue that the EU is neither an international organization nor a federal State, they are hard pressed to find an appealing name for this intermediate category, beyond the rather feeble solution consisting in saying that the EU is simply *sui generis* (meaning: it is in a category all of its own).

The term *supranational organization* served the name-giving purpose for many years, in the early decades of European integration, but it has now fallen into disuse, partly because of its now unfashionable hierarchical overtones, and partly because it failed to reflect the intergovernmental mode of integration that prevailed in the Second and Third Pillars of the EU after the Maastricht Treaty.[52] The term *confederation* is occasionally proposed, but it bears the stigma of weakness and instability that derives from the historical examples of confederations, and is therefore rather unusual as a denomination for the EU.[53] Alternative terminology should, in order to be attractive *and* true to reality, encapsulate both the international roots of the EU and its uniquely massive pooling of Member State powers and constitutional mode of operation.

No such alternative terminology has obtained Europe-wide currency so far, but influential descriptions in this vein have been proposed in Germany (the *Staatenverbund*) and in France (the *fédération d'Etats-nations*). The latter is a rather paradoxical denomination, which is particularly popular among French authors.[54] It comes close to the German *Staatenverbund*, a term that was coined by Paul Kirchhof, and adopted in the Federal Constitutional Court judgment (the *Maastricht* judgment) which he helped to draft (as a member of that court) in 1993.[55] It was proposed as a deliberate neologism intended to occupy an intermediate space between the Bundesstaat (meaning: federal State) and the Staatenbund (meaning: confederation of States). According to Everling, a former German judge at the European Court of Justice, the term Staatenverbund 'stresses, *albeit in a fashion that is almost impossible to convey in other languages*, that the Member States are bound more tightly in the Union than in the traditional confederation of states'.[56] Other,

52 The term *supranational organization* is still used, occasionally, to describe the nature of the EU, for lack of a better term. See eg K Lenaerts and P Van Nuffel, *European Union Law* (3rd edn, London: Sweet & Maxwell, 2011) 16–17.

53 On the 'stigma of confederation', see M Burgess, *Federalism and European Union: The Building of Europe, 1950–2000* (Abingdon: Routledge, 2000) 259–260. Nevertheless, Burgess proposes rehabilitating and revitalizing the old concept as an adequate description of the EU (at 265–269). See also A Cuyvers, 'The Confederal Comeback: Rediscovering the Confederal Form for a Transnational World' (2013) 19 *European Law Journal* 711.

54 Among the French authors who have discussed or promoted the use of this concept in connection with the EU are: JL Quermonne, 'La "Fédération d'Etats nations": concept ou contradiction?' (2010) 84 *Revue française de droit constitutionnel* 677; V Constantinesco, 'Europe fédérale ou fédération d'Etats-nations' in R Dehousse (ed), *Une constitution pour l'Europe?* (Paris: Presses de Sciences Po, 2002); G Ricard-Nihoul, *Pour une Fédération européenne d'États-Nations: La vision de Jacques Delors revisitée* (Brussels: Larcier, 2012). A related concept is that of 'plurinational federation', proposed by A Bailleux and H Dumont, *Le pacte constitutionnel européen* (Brussels: Larcier, 2015) 226–233.

55 P Kirchhof later presented an updated version of his views, in English, in 'The Legal Structure of the European Union as a Union of States' in A von Bogdandy and J Bast (eds), *Principles of European Constitutional Law* (Oxford: Hart Publishing, 2005).

56 U Everling, 'The European Union between Community and National Policies and Legal Orders' in von Bogdandy and Bast, *Principles of European Constitutional Law* (n 55) 719 (emphasis added).

very similar, terms proposed in the legal literature are those of a *federation of States*,[57] a *commonwealth*,[58] or a *constitutional order of States*.[59]

This terminological discussion is, perhaps, not of great practical importance. One does not need to find a consensus on the best categorical denomination for the EU in order to study its law and its politics. However, the underlying discussion on the true legal nature of the EU is interesting from the perspective of the self-understanding of legal science. Legal science has traditionally been based on two crucial distinctions which were used to 'organize the world' of normative phenomena: between State law and non-State law (ie legal norms developed by groups in society outside the State structures); and between national law and international law. The latter dichotomous distinction, which slowly emerged through centuries of scholarship, is called into question by the 'unruly' phenomenon constituted by EU law. The question is whether we can continue to stick to the dichotomy (whereby EU law would be considered a sub-system within the category of international law) or whether we should recognize that the world of 'State law' should henceforth be divided in three: national law, international law, and EU law. However, would this not be a rather Eurocentric perspective?

3.4 **The constitutional perspective on EU law**

The controversy on the legal nature of the EU does not stand in the way of a widespread tendency, in the legal literature, to use constitutional terminology to describe and understand EU law. It is often claimed, also occasionally by the Court of Justice, that EU law forms a 'constitutional' legal order. Only a minority of scholars object to this usage, on the ground that constitutions are the basic legal instruments of sovereign States, and that constitutional terminology should therefore be reserved for States and not extended to non-State entities such as the EU.[60]

Around the turn of the century, the use of constitutional terminology to describe central features of the EU legal order had become commonplace in legal writing.[61] This approach was transferred from legal scholarship to practical politics in 2002–3, when the Convention on the Future of the Union set out to draft a new Treaty text that was called the Treaty establishing a Constitution for Europe. Most EU legal scholars applauded this project to formalize the EU's informal constitutional arrangements,[62] but it failed. During the so-called 'period of reflection' that followed the negative referenda in France and the Netherlands and the demise of the Constitutional Treaty, the Member State governments came to the conclusion that part of the Treaty's failure to take force was due to its

[57] Schütze (n 50) ch 2; SR Larsen, *The Constitutional Theory of the Federation and the European Union* (Oxford: Oxford University Press, 2021).

[58] N MacCormick, *Questioning Sovereignty: Law, State, and Nation in the European Commonwealth* (Oxford: Oxford University Press, 1999).

[59] A Dashwood, 'States in the European Union' (1998) 23 *European Law Review* 201.

[60] See eg D Grimm, 'Does Europe Need a Constitution?' (1995) 1 *European Law Journal* 282.

[61] Among the many writings of that period in which the terms constitution and constitutional were considered in relation to EU law, see JHH Weiler, *The Constitution of Europe* (Cambridge: Cambridge University Press, 1999); K Lenaerts, P Van Nuffel, and R Bray, *Constitutional Law of the European Union* (London: Sweet & Maxwell, 1999); J-C Piris, 'Does the European Union Have a Constitution? Does It Need One?' (1999) 24 *European Law Review* 557; P Craig, 'Constitutions, Constitutionalism, and the European Union' (2001) 7 *European Law Journal* 125; A Peters, *Elemente einer Theorie der Verfassung Europas* (Berlin: Duncker & Humblot, 2001).

[62] But see, for a critical voice, JHH Weiler, 'In Defence of the Status Quo: Europe's Constitutional *Sonderweg*' in JHH Weiler and M Wind (eds), *European Constitutionalism beyond the State* (Cambridge: Cambridge University Press, 2003).

overambitious constitutional design. In order to save most of the content of the reforms, they stated in June 2007 that 'the constitutional concept, which consisted in repealing all existing Treaties and replacing them by a single text called "Constitution" is abandoned'.[63] They also scrapped from the text of the Lisbon Treaty, which was subsequently agreed, some of the terminology used in the Constitutional Treaty that seemed too redolent of national constitutional texts, such as 'law' (instead of regulation or directive) or 'minister of foreign affairs' (instead of High Representative of the European Union) and 'primacy of European Union law' (see generally chapter 2).

Still, the constitutional perspective on EU law continues to make sense even after the demise of the Constitutional Treaty,[64] and we find several textbooks on EU law that flaunt constitutional terms in their titles.[65] By using constitutional language, these authors seek to emphasize that the Treaties perform many of the same functions as a national constitution: they establish public authority, and allocate powers between different political institutions; they establish a division of competences between the EU and the Member States, in a way which is reminiscent of similar delimitations of competences in federal constitutions; they set out the basic values of the EU legal order, and the fundamental rights of persons; they organize a system of judicial review for the enforcement of EU law obligations and for the review of the validity of EU action. In other words, the usage of constitutional terminology seeks to underline the close similarity (or analogy) between some of the legal issues that arise under EU law and those that arise in the constitutional law of States (especially federal States).

4 The EU as object and subject of international law

In this final section, attention is drawn to the complex situation that arises from the fact that the EU, while being a Treaty-based legal construct, can itself, in turn, conclude further Treaties in order to advance its policy objectives (and see further chapter 26). In other words, the EU is both an *object* of international law made by others (its Member States) and a *subject* entitled to make new international law. This is, once again, not a unique feature of the EU: other international organizations have the capacity to conclude Treaties;[66] indeed, some of them have concluded Treaties with the EC or the EU.

The EU contributes to the development of international law in the same three main ways as States do: through its unilateral practice (which may contribute to the emergence

[63] Those were the words used in the European Council's mandate for the intergovernmental conference that was to elaborate the Lisbon Treaty (Annex 1 to the European Council Conclusions of 21–22 June 2007, p 1).

[64] On the latter point there is a solid consensus in the EU law literature; see among others: G de Búrca, 'Reflections on the EU's Path from the Constitutional Treaty to the Lisbon Treaty' (2008) Jean Monnet Working Paper 03/08; N Walker, 'European Constitutionalism in the State Constitutional Tradition' (2006) 59 *Current Legal Problems* 51; L Besselink, 'The Notion and Nature of the European Constitution after the Lisbon Treaty' in J Wouters, L Verhey, and P Kiiver (eds), *European Constitutionalism beyond Lisbon* (Antwerp: Intersentia, 2009); S Griller, 'Is This a Constitution? Remarks on a Contested Concept' in S Griller and J Ziller (eds), *The Lisbon Treaty: EU Constitutionalism without a Constitutional Treaty?* (Vienna: Springer, 2008); K Lenaerts, 'De Rome à Lisbonne, la Constitution européenne en marche?' (2008) *Cahiers de droit européen* 229.

[65] A Rosas and L Armati, *EU Constitutional Law: An Introduction* (3rd edn, Oxford: Hart Publishing, 2018); Schütze (n 50); A von Bogdandy and J Bast (eds), *Principles of European Constitutional Law* (2nd edn, Oxford: Hart Publishing, 2011): K Tuori, *European Constitutionalism* (Cambridge: Cambridge University Press, 2015); U Haltern, *The Constitution of the European Union: A Contextual Analysis* (Oxford: Hart Publishing, 2025). See also the discussion of constitutionalism and EU law in chapter 4.

[66] See Klabbers (n 5) ch 12.

of rules of customary international law);[67] through concluding Treaties with non-EU States or international organizations; and through its activity as a member of some multilateral organizations, such as the World Trade Organization (WTO).[68] Of those three, Treaty making is particularly important. The EU, in fact, has replaced its Member States as an international actor in a number of policy fields, such as international trade or international fisheries regulation. The Member States have had to accept abandoning their power to conclude Treaties in those areas that are within the EU's exclusive competence.[69] In other areas, such as environmental protection or immigration, the EU and the Member States share their Treaty-making competence.

When the EU concludes an international agreement, then international law starts acting as a constraint on the EU. This constraint is simply expressed by the rule in the TFEU stating that EU agreements are binding on the institutions of the EU and also on its Member States.[70] The Court of Justice sees the relationship between EU law and other forms of international law as a relationship between distinct legal orders. Thus, the Court held that 'Security Council resolutions, on the one hand, and Council common positions and regulations, on the other hand, originate from distinct legal orders. Measures within the framework of the United Nations and the European Union are adopted by organs with autonomous powers, granted to them by their basic charters, that is to say, the treaties that created them.'[71]

The statement that the EU legal order is *autonomous* with regard to the surrounding international legal environment may, in fact, mean two rather different things: either that EU law, as a specialized international legal order, *deviates* from the general rules of international law on one or other point, or that the EU *fails to comply* with specific international obligations and gives priority instead to its own internal rules.[72]

The *first meaning of autonomy*, namely the capacity to adopt special legal rules that deviate from the general rules of international law, is unproblematic. The general rules of international law are default rules that States can set aside and replace by more suitable rules in their mutual relations. The *second* and stronger *meaning of autonomy* is the capacity for a particular system to give priority to its own internal rules over and above external international obligations. This form of autonomy is typical for those international organizations that are subjects of international law, and have used their capacity to conclude international agreements with States or other international organizations. When acting as subjects of international law, they may—just like States—incur obligations under international law that may appear, at some point in time, to conflict with their own internal rules. In view of the multiplication of such external legal commitments of the EU, it is quite likely that they may occasionally enter into conflict with the EU's own domestic law.

[67] See, on this aspect of the interaction between EU law and general international law, F Hoffmeister, 'The Contribution of EU Practice to International Law' in M Cremona (ed), *Developments in EU External Relations Law* (Oxford: Oxford University Press, 2008) 54 *et seq*.

[68] See G De Baere, 'EU Status in Other International Organizations' in R Schütze and T Tridimas (eds), *Oxford Principles of European Union Law*, vol I (Oxford: Oxford University Press, 2018).

[69] This is perhaps the characteristic that is most unusual from the point of view of general international law; see discussion in B de Witte, 'The Emergence of a European System of Public International Law: The EU and Its Member States as Strange Subjects' in J Wouters, A Nollkaemper, and E de Wet (eds), *The Europeanisation of International Law* (The Hague: TMC Asser Press, 2008).

[70] Art 216, second para, TFEU.

[71] Case C-380/09 P *Melli Bank v Council*, EU:C:2012:137, para 54. The term *autonomy* has repeatedly been used in the Court's case law. See also Opinion 2/13, *Accession of the EU to the ECHR*, EU:C:2014:2454, paras 170 and 183.

[72] For a similar distinction between the different meanings of the autonomy of EU law, see M Klamert, 'The Autonomy of the EU (and of EU Law): Through the Kaleidoscope' (2017) 42 *European Law Review* 815.

In *Kadi*, the European Court of Justice thus refused the application of 'external' international obligations in order to preserve fundamental norms of the 'internal' legal order of the EU, namely the right of defence and the right to property. The wisdom of the Court's attitude has been very widely discussed in the literature.[73] From the point of view that concerns us here, namely that of the relation between the EU legal order and the surrounding international legal environment, the Court held that international obligations concluded by the EU cannot prevail over the highest norms of the internal EU legal order. In defending that view, which is very similar to that adopted by national courts when confronted with a conflict between international and national constitutional law, the European Court of Justice appropriately highlighted the autonomy of the special legal order that the EU Member States have decided to carve out by using the instrument of an international Treaty.

5 Conclusion

The EU can be seen, as Wyatt and Dashwood aptly put it, as 'a developed form of international organization which displays characteristics of an embryonic federation'.[74] The various revision Treaties of the past decades (including the last one, the Lisbon Treaty) do not signal a change in this respect. They rather show that the Member State governments were not willing to contemplate a fundamental change of the EU's legal nature; on the contrary, they have actively experimented, in the Lisbon Treaty, with the toolkit of international Treaty law, with generous use of Protocols, declarations, transition clauses, derogations, opt-outs, etc. Still, as we have seen, many EU law scholars disagree with this assessment and propose a different view of the EU as an unprecedented type of non-State entity.

The fact that, in this matter, legal scholars keep disagreeing has never stopped EU law from evolving through repeated Treaty revisions and through the institutional practice of its institutions and the legal interpretations by its Court of Justice. Indeed, hardly any practical consequences derive from the choice of a given qualification. In particular, qualifying EU law as international law does not imply that one should interpret the text of the Treaties from an intergovernmental perspective and that limitations of sovereignty should be narrowly construed. The Court has convincingly shown, since *Van Gend en Loos*, why it could construe the EC Treaty in a broad and purpose-oriented way, and other international courts have followed the same jurisprudential line in interpreting 'their' Treaties. Still, the recognition that EU law is an advanced *species* of the *genus* international law explains more easily some crucial characteristics of the EU legal order without hindering its autonomous development. It has the added advantage of making the 'European way of law'[75] a more amenable source of inspiration for other States, in other parts of the world, when they devise their own forms of international cooperation. The progressive development of international law would be weakened if its conceptual links with EU law were cut off.

[73] See, for some contrasting views (among many others): T Tridimas and JA Gutierrez-Fons, 'EU Law, International Law, and Economic Sanctions against Terrorism: The Judiciary in Distress' (2009) 32 *Fordham International Law Journal* 660; and G de Búrca, 'The ECJ and the International Legal Order: A Re-Evaluation' in de Búrca and Weiler, *The Worlds of European Constitutionalism* (n 1).

[74] *Wyatt and Dashwood's European Union Law* (5th edn, London: Sweet & Maxwell, 2006) 132.

[75] A-M Slaughter and W Burke-White, 'The Future of International Law Is Domestic (or, the European Way of Law)' (2006) 47 *Harvard Journal of International Law* 327.

Further reading

B de Witte, 'The European Union as an International Legal Experiment' in G de Búrca and JHH Weiler (eds), *The Worlds of European Constitutionalism* (Cambridge: Cambridge University Press, 2012)

P Eleftheriadis, *A Union of Peoples: Europe as a Community of Principle* (Oxford: Oxford University Press, 2020)

J Klabbers, '*Sui Generis*? The European Union as an International Organization' in D Patterson and A Sodersten (eds), *A Companion to European Union Law and International Law* (Wiley: Blackwell, 2016)

J Klabbers, 'Straddling the Fence: The EU and International Law' in A Arnull and D Chalmers (eds), *The Oxford Handbook of European Union Law* (Oxford: Oxford University Press, 2015)

J Odermatt, *International Law and the European Union* (Cambridge: Cambridge University Press, 2021) ch 1

A Rosas and L Armati, *EU Constitutional Law: An Introduction* (3rd edn, Oxford: Hart Publishing, 2018) chs 2 and 3

R Schűtze, *European Constitutional Law* (3rd edn, Cambridge: Cambridge University Press, 2021)

D Simon and A Rigaux, 'Les Communautés et l'Union européenne comme organisations internationales' in E Lagrange and JM Sorel (eds), *Droit des organisations internationales* (Paris: LGDJ, 2013)

N Walker, 'The Place of European Law' in G de Búrca and JHH Weiler (eds), *The Worlds of European Constitutionalism* (Cambridge: Cambridge University Press, 2012)

8

General principles of EU law and EU administrative law

Herwig CH Hofmann

1 Introduction

The provisions of the Treaty and EU legislative acts defining the content of EU policies must be implemented in real life. This often requires some form of regulatory or administrative action by the European Union administration, consisting of the Union's institutions, bodies, offices, and agencies (Article 298(1) TFEU), as well as those of the Member States when implementing EU law.[1] Such action will be needed to provide further specification of the content of legislative acts or such measures as the creation of specific agencies to ensure coordination between Member States. This chapter explores two key questions in this context: Who does what and by what means to make sure that Union policies specified in the Treaties and EU legislative acts are implemented? Which rights and obligations exist in that context, and how can they be protected?

General principles of EU law play a crucial role in answering these two questions, as they serve as criteria for the legality of all forms of EU law, including those used for the implementation and enforcement of EU law. Next to the General principles of EU law, the legality of implementing actions also depends on legislation governing questions such as the creation of EU bodies, offices, and agencies, as well as administrative organization and procedures, for example the creation of networks between EU and Member State bodies implementing EU policies. This body of law is often referred to as European Union administrative law.[2] EU administrative law is a particularly dynamic field marked by the

[1] The latter are under the obligation to transpose and implement EU law under the principle of sincere cooperation. They 'shall take any appropriate measure, general or particular, to ensure fulfilment of the obligations arising out of the Treaties or resulting from the acts of the institutions of the Union' (Art 4(3) TEU).

[2] HCH Hofmann, GC Rowe, and A Türk, *Administrative Law and Policy of the European Union* (Oxford: Oxford University Press, 2011).

close interaction of legal sources arising from the international, EU, and national levels. Additionally, EU law and particularly its administrative law, must be flexible enough to accommodate the fact that many policy fields have varying constellations of participating Member States. For example, in the Economic and Monetary Union (EMU), only 21 of 27 EU Member States share the euro as their common currency. Or, consider the Schengen zone, which covers not all EU Member States but includes some non-EU Member States.

This chapter will first give an overview of the key institutions, offices, bodies, and agencies of the EU and what they do in terms of implementation of EU law (section 2), before then moving on to develop an understanding of the applicable law which is key to developing notions of accountability and the protection of rights in this field (section 3).

You are already familiar with some elements relevant for this chapter. You have, for example, read in the chapter on decision-making and competences about delegated and implementing acts under Articles 290 and 291 TFEU, as well as about the principle of conferral (Article 5 TEU), which limits the EU to the exercise of powers conferred upon it in the Treaties. In other contexts, you will have read about the separation of functions between the Member States and the EU—especially in the context of the principle of sincere cooperation (Article 4(3) TEU). You will have further read about EU agencies and the possibilities of delegating powers to agencies. These elements are brought together in this chapter to demonstrate how institutional, substantive, and procedural law, resulting from the rules and principles of EU law, shape the legal reality.

2 Organizational levels and the distribution of powers in implementing EU law

In the EU's legal system, the exercise of administrative functions is undertaken by a diverse range of actors, both at the EU level and within the Member States. These are institutions and bodies of the Union as well as those of its Member States. The following discussion concentrates on some central principles of law governing this distribution and holding the actors on various levels to account.

2.1 Conferral of powers on the Union

Under the principle of conferral, not only is the Union barred from enacting legislation in cases where it is not authorized to do so by the Treaties, it is also barred from passing implementing acts if not authorized. This results from the principle of conferral under Article 5(1) and (2) TEU. The result of the distribution of implementing powers in EU law is explicitly restated in Article 291(1) TFEU, according to which 'Member States shall adopt all measures of national law necessary to implement legally binding Union acts', a provision which is as much a restatement of powers remaining within the hands of Member States as a restatement of obligations of Member States under the principle of sincere cooperation in Article 4(3) TEU.

Where the Union is authorized to undertake the implementation of EU policies, administrative functions are carried out by the Commission (and, to a certain extent, also the Council) and, increasingly, by EU agencies. Comitology committees, comprising Member State experts, are designated to supervise and advise the Commission when undertaking implementing activities under Article 291 TFEU. These issues were already addressed and further explained in the context of chapter 5 on decision-making procedures.

Administrative powers conferred on the EU primarily consist of the authority to adopt acts with general content, such as non-legislative administrative rule-making in the form of directives, regulations, or decisions (Article 289 TFEU), as well as the issuance of guidance or the creation of standards. However, in an increasing number of areas of EU law, Union bodies have also been conferred with the power to take single-case decisions with binding force directly on individuals. Probably the best-known area where that is the case is the Commission's power to impose fines in the area of competition law (see further chapter 17). Increasingly, EU agencies are also being empowered to take individual decisions addressing issues of EU-wide concern, such as the granting of trademarks for the entire EU market (by the EUIPO, the European Intellectual Property Office), admitting chemical products as safe for use (by ECHA, the European Chemicals Agency), and other such regulatory activity. Where EU agencies have decision-making powers, they generally also have a board of appeal or a complaint board to address complaints regarding decisions.[3]

In most policy areas, however, even if the EU has adopted legislation and some common rules for implementing these rules have been established at the EU level, final decisions regarding the implementation of these rules are made by Member State bodies. An example of this approach to indirect administration is the EU's customs policy, where national customs officials adopt decisions with binding effect throughout the entire EU based on highly detailed EU legislation.

2.2 **Implementation of EU law by the Member States**

In the absence of EU law provisions conferring powers to implement EU law on EU institutions and bodies, Member States not only have the right to implement EU law through their administrative apparatus, but they are also obliged to do so.

Under the principle of 'sincere cooperation' in Article 4(3) TEU, Member States are obliged to:

> take any appropriate measure, general or particular, to ensure fulfilment of the obligations arising out of the Treaties or resulting from acts of the institutions of the Union.

They may do so by applying existing national legislation, but may also be obliged by EU law to enact specific national implementing legislation and adopt associated administrative regulations to create the necessary conditions for implementation at the national level. Member States, under this model, enjoy only limited institutional or procedural autonomy to implement and enforce EU law.[4]

Limitations on the Member States' autonomy, arise from the fact that, in the fields of Union policy, Member States' substantive and procedural administrative law is to be applied within the framework of EU law. This framework consists of three basic concepts:

First, Member States have the right to set their own standards for substantive and procedural law only in the absence of any explicit requirements in Union law. Therefore, insofar as Union law itself makes provision as regards procedures, criteria, or organizational requirements, national administrations are obliged to act in conformity with these.[5]

[3] Case C-46/21 P *ACER v Aquind*, EU:C:2023:182, paras 57, 67. In *Aquind*, the Court of Justice stated that boards must ensure a comprehensive review of agencies' decisions, as otherwise the guarantees of effective judicial protection in the EU legal system would be compromised.

[4] See Case 33/76 *Rewe*, EU:C:1976:188, para. 5.

[5] National law might turn out to be inconsistent or even incompatible with EU provisions in the area. The EU's conflicts rules applicable to such situations are the principle of primacy and the possibility of direct effect of EU law. These interpretative principles oblige the Member States' bodies to set aside national law which is in conflict with EU law provisions; see eg case law since Case 106/77 *Amministrazione delle Finanze dello Stato v Simmenthal SpA* ('*Simmenthal II*') EU:C:1978:49 and the discussion in chapter 6.

Secondly, in the area of indirect administration, the legality of Member States' rules and procedures will be measured by their compliance with General principles of EU law and the EU's Charter of Fundamental Rights (see further chapter 9).

Thirdly, the application of national procedural rules in the implementation of Union law must be exercised in strict compliance with the principles of *equivalence* and *effectiveness*.[6]

2.2.1 'Equivalence' and 'effectiveness'

Under the principle of equivalence, in the absence of applicable EU law, Member States must grant at least equivalent protection for violation of EU law to that available against violation of national law.[7] Provisions used under national law may not be 'less favourable than those governing similar domestic actions (principle of equivalence)'.[8] A rule must therefore 'be applied without distinction', whether the infringement arises from Union law or national law.[9]

Where there is no equivalent national law, or where its application does not lead to the result of enforcing or protecting a right under EU law, the principle of effectiveness will override the principle of equivalence. National courts are obliged to set aside:

> any provision of a national legal system and any legislative, administrative or judicial practice which might impair the effectiveness [of Union law].[10]

Even in cases where there is no equivalent form of protection of rights under national law, Member States, under the principle of effectiveness, may not make the exercise of rights conferred by Union law (even only temporarily) 'practically impossible or excessively difficult'.[11]

The obligations under the principles of equivalence and effectiveness apply not only to national courts but also directly to national administrations.[12] The latter are explicitly obliged under EU law to set aside national laws which conflict with directly effective EU law.[13]

2.2.2 Composite procedures and decision-making with 'trans-territorial' effect

In many cases, the implementation of EU law by Member States requires the national bodies to take decisions in cooperation with offices and bodies from other Member States or with input from EU agencies.

[6] See Case C-261/95 *Palmisani v INPS*, EU:C:1997:351, para 27. See also Case C-453/99 *Courage and Crehan*, EU:C:2001:465, para 25.

[7] Joined Cases C-205–215/82 *Deutsche Milchkontor*, EU:C:1983:233, para 17; *Courage* (n 6) para 29.

[8] *Courage* (n 6) para 29.

[9] Case C-231/96 *Edis*, EU:C:1998:401, para 36; Joined Cases 66/79, 127/79, and 128/79 *Salumi*, EU:C:1980:101, para 21. Whether a situation under EU law is sufficiently similar to a situation regulated under national law is subject to detailed case-by-case analysis, the Court looking at the purpose and effect of a national measure in question—see Case C-326/96 *Levez*, EU:C:1998:557, para 41.

[10] Case C-213/89 *Factortame*, EU:C:1990:257, paras 19 and 20.

[11] *Courage* (n 6) para 29. This is a standard formula which was initially developed in Case C-312/93 *Peterbroeck*, EU:C:1995:437, para 14, Joined Cases C-430 and C-431/93 *Van Schijndel*, EU:C:1995:441, para 19. This formula can be found in many cases and contexts, eg Case C-249/11 *Bykanov*, EU:C:2012:608, para 75.

[12] S Prechal, *Directives in EC Law* (2nd edn, Oxford: Oxford University Press, 2005) 65–72.

[13] See Case 103/88 *Fratelli Costanzo v Comune di Milano*, EU:C:1989:256; Case C-224/97 *Ciola* [1999] ECR I-2517; Case C-118/00 *Larsy v Inasti* [2001] ECR I-5063; Case C-453/00 *Kühne & Heitz*, EU:C:2004:17. These cases, for the basis of that obligation, refer to the principle of sincere cooperation under Art 4(3) TEU (but the cases still refer to the old Art 10 EC). For a critique of this approach by the Court of Justice, see eg Prechal (n 12) 65–72.

Case study 8.1: EU data protection law

An example of these commonplace 'composite procedures' is found in EU data protection law, which contains both horizontal cooperation procedures (between national authorities) and vertical and diagonal cooperation procedures (between national authorities in EU bodies). Horizontal cooperation, for example, occurs when a person files a complaint for a data privacy violation in the EU Member State where they reside. The 'lead' in handling the complaint will usually be taken by the data protection authority in the Member State where the company that committed the alleged violation is located (Article 55(1) GDPR—Regulation 2016/679—provides for the implementation of a so-called 'one-stop shop' mechanism based on a sharing of competences between the data protection authorities). These authorities cooperate in handling the complaint and the investigation. The GDPR also contains vertical and diagonal forms of cooperation when data protection authorities involved in handling a case disagree on the outcome. In that case, under Articles 60, 63, and 65 of the GDPR, the lead supervisory authority must obtain a binding decision from the European Data Protection Board (EDPB), a body established under EU law. The relevant national data protection authorities will then implement that binding EDPB decision.[14]

Composite procedures come with their own set of questions regarding the General principles of EU law, as they are also addressed in Article 41 of the Charter on Good Administration. These include how to ensure the rights of a fair hearing. There arise questions arise of which authority needs to hear a party and how the result of such a hearing can be taken into account based on which file, as well as how to address access to documents and whether the final decision-maker establishing a binding act has had full access to all relevant facts and findings. Overall, composite procedures raise problems with respect to judicial review, in that it is not always clear which court, within which Member State or the CJEU, is responsible for hearing a case. Such problems are reflected in cases such as *Berlioz*,[15] *Luxembourg v B*,[16] and *WhatsApp Ireland*,[17] which highlight several issues of judicial review and accountability within multi-jurisdictional composite procedures.[18]

Throughout EU administrative law, however, a phenomenon exists which we might refer to as the trans-territorial effect of administrative action. Some acts have an effect not only on the territory of that State but in the entire EU. This phenomenon is well illustrated by looking at EU customs law. For example, once a product from, say, Brazil has cleared customs via the port of Rotterdam in the Netherlands, that product can be sold throughout the Union without facing any further customs controls or duties; in other words, it can freely circulate in the Union. The Dutch customs officials will de facto act as customs officials of the entire Union when classifying the product according to the EU law's system of customs classifications and assessing the customs tariff due to be paid at the port of Rotterdam. The Dutch customs officials in this example act on a mix of applicable law: they are agents of the Kingdom of the Netherlands (subject eg to the Dutch civil service

[14] See for an example of that situation, Case T-183/23 *Ballmann v EDPB*, EU:T:2025:735.

[15] Case C-682/15 *Berlioz Investment Fund SA*, EU:C:2017:373.

[16] Joined Cases C-245/19 and C-246/19 *Etat Luxembourgeois v B and Others*, EU:C:2020:795.

[17] Case C-97/23 P *WhatsApp Ireland Ltd v European Data Protection Board*, case still pending.

[18] See HCH Hofmann, 'Multi-Jurisdictional Composite Procedures—the Backbone to the EU's Single Regulatory Space' (2019) University of Luxembourg Law Working Paper No 003-2019 26, 24; M Eliantonio, 'Composite Procedures, the Violation of Fundamental Rights, and the Availability of Sufficient Remedies in the Multi-Level EU Judicial Architecture' in M Fink (ed), *Redressing Fundamental Rights Violations by the EU* (Cambridge: Cambridge University Press, 2024) 345–365.

employment rules), yet in the exercise of their duties as customs officials—in our example, the act of classifying the goods which is a decision which has an effect within the entire EU—they act based on EU law.

To mitigate potential problems with the widespread phenomenon of what might be referred to as decision-making with trans-territorial effect (some authors call this transnational effect), in most policy areas, there is some form of common structure for the exchange of information and coordination of administrative action. These are sometimes referred to using the metaphor of administrative 'networks'. The objective of networked administration, establishing, for example, structures of information-exchange, is to reduce potential problems arising from decentralized administration. Information-exchange systems are generally established by EU legislation and linked to an EU agency. An example of such a system is the so-called 'Schengen Information System'[19] (see further chapters 24 and 25). It is actually difficult to identify a policy area within EU law where no information network exists. To name just a few examples, agencies have been created to deal with food safety,[20] the environment,[21] fisheries,[22] and maritime and ship safety.[23]

[19] The information exchange is based on a set of updated regulations from 2018 and 2019 including regulations covering the use of the Schengen Information System (SIS) for entry bans and the exchange of information on third-country nationals who have been refused entry (see Regulation (EU) 2018/1860 of the European Parliament and of the Council on the use of the Schengen Information System (SIS) for the return of illegally staying third-country nationals (OJ [2018] L312/1); Regulation (EU) 2018/1861 of the European Parliament and of the Council on the establishment, operation and use of the SIS in the field of border checks, and amending the Convention implementing the Schengen Agreement, and amending and repealing Regulation (EC) No 1987/2006 (OJ [2018] L312/14)). Other regulations focus on the exchange of information for police and judicial cooperation within the Schengen area (eg Regulation (EU) 2018/1862 of the European Parliament and of the Council on the establishment, operation and use of the SIS in the field of police cooperation and judicial cooperation in criminal matters, amending and repealing Council Decision 2007/533/JHA, and repealing Regulation (EC) No 1986/2006 of the European Parliament and of the Council and Commission Decision 2010/261/EU (OJ [2018] L312/56)). Several other regulations establish a framework for interoperability between large-scale IT systems, including SIS, enhancing information exchange and cooperation between different EU agencies and Member States (eg Regulation (EU) 2019/817 of the European Parliament and of the Council on establishing a framework for interoperability between EU information systems in the field of borders and visa and amending Regulations (EC) No 767/2008, (EU) 2016/399, (EU) 2017/2226, (EU) 2018/1240, (EU) 2018/1726 and (EU) 2018/1861 and Council Decisions 2004/512/EC and 2008/633/JHA (OJ [2019] L135/27); Regulation (EU) 2019/818 of the European Parliament and of the Council of 20 May 2019 on establishing a framework for interoperability between EU information systems in the field of police and judicial cooperation, asylum and migration (OJ [2019] L135/85).

[20] Regulation (EC) No 178/2002 of the European Parliament and of the Council of 28 January 2002 laying down the General Principles and requirements of food law, establishing the European Food Safety Authority and laying down procedures in matters of food safety (OJ [2002] L31/1) amended by Regulation (EU) 2019/1381 on the transparency and sustainability of the EU risk assessment in the food chain and amending Regulations (OJ [2019] L231/1) Commission Regulation (EU) No 16/2001 of 10 January 2011 laying down implementing measures for the rapid alert system for food and feed (OJ [2011] L6/7) and Regulation (EU) 2019/1381 of the European Parliament and of the Council of 20 June 2019 on the transparency and sustainability of the EU risk assessment in the food chain (OJ [2019] L231/1).

[21] Regulation (EC) No 401/2009 of the European Parliament and of the Council of 23 April 2009 on the European Environment Agency and the European Environment Information and Observation Network (OJ [2009] L126/13).

[22] Council Regulation (EC) No 1005/2008 of 29 September 2008 establishing a Community system to prevent, deter and eliminate illegal, unreported and unregulated fishing, amending Regulation (EEC) No 2847/93, (EC) No 1936/2001, and (EC) No 601/2004, and repealing Regulation (EC) No 1093/94 and (EC) No 1447/1999 (OJ [2008] L286/1).

[23] Regulation (EC) No 1406/2002 of the European Parliament and of the Council of 27 June 2002 establishing a European Maritime Safety Agency (OJ [2002] L208/1).

2.3 **Delegation of powers within the Union**

As discussed in chapter 3, delegation of powers from legislators to the executive constitutes an inevitable aspect of modern legal systems. Reasons include the technical complexity of many areas of regulation, the limited effectiveness of hierarchical command structures, and the highly pluralistic societies which require knowledge and balancing of very diverse interests. Delegation is not only a practical necessity but also a general phenomenon in the implementation of EU policies.

At first glance, the principle of attributed powers under Articles 5(2) and 13(2) TEU provides a presumption against delegation. Under these provisions, powers should be exercised in the EU by those entrusted with them by the Treaties, but the Treaty provisions on delegation of powers, set out in Articles 290 and 291 TFEU, do allow for delegation to the Commission (see further chapter 5).[24] In this system, no reference is made to EU agencies and other EU bodies as possible recipients of delegations—despite the express acknowledgement in the provisions on judicial review of acts (Article 263, paragraphs 1 and 5, TFEU) of EU agencies as potential decision-makers (see further chapter 10).[25] In the same vein, the 2011 Comitology Regulation sets out only the general rules on the conferment upon the Commission of the power to adopt measures implementing EU acts, pursuant to Article 291 TFEU.[26] It makes no mention of agencies and does not clarify the relation of decision-making with the help of comitology committees as opposed to agency decision-making.[27]

Agencies with decision-making powers are, however, an important part of the EU's administration. Some such agencies have a legal basis directly in the Treaties,[28] most are created by an legislative act. EU agencies have been entrusted with pursuing different tasks,[29] including the provision of information and the provision of services as a basis for the adoption of implementing acts, and even the exercise of specific implementing

[24] Art 290 TFEU allows conferring upon the Commission the power to adopt quasi-legislative 'delegated' acts under the oversight of the European Parliament and the Council. Under Art 291, paras 2 and 3, TFEU, implementing powers shall be conferred on the Commission—exceptionally on the Council—'where uniform conditions for implementing legally binding Union acts are needed'.

[25] Besides Art 263 TFEU, several other provisions in the TFEU directly take into consideration the importance and role played by agencies in the EU legal system. Among these, the most important are: Art 15 (transparency and access to documents), Art 16 (data protection), Art 228 (competence of the European Ombudsman), Art 265 (action for failure to act), Art 267 (reference for preliminary ruling), and Art 287 (jurisdiction of the European Court of Auditors). Also the EU's Charter of Fundamental Rights under Art 47 explicitly gives the right to an effective remedy, including against agencies. Agencies are further explicitly mentioned in Arts 41, 42, and 43 Charter.

[26] Regulation (EU) No 182/2011 of 16 February 2011, laying down the rules and General Principles concerning mechanisms for control by Member States of the Commission's exercise of implementing powers (OJ [2011] L55/13), is the legislative act that under Art 291, para 3, TFEU lays down 'mechanisms for control by Member States of the Commission's exercise of implementing powers'.

[27] Instead it might actually be read to exclude the possibilities of delegating decision-making powers to independent EU agencies since it allows explicitly only for delegating to the Commission of implementing powers either under what it defines as the 'advisory' or the 'examination' procedure. Regulation 182/2011 (OJ [2011] L55/13).

[28] eg the European Police Office, Europol, Art 88 TFEU; the agency in charge of cooperation of judicial cooperation, Eurojust, Art 85 TFEU. On these bodies, see further chapter 24.

[29] The basis for this classification can be found in E Vos, 'Reforming the European Commission: What Role to Play for EU Agencies' (2000) 37 *Common Market Law Review* 1113, 1120–1121. For a different classification of agencies, see E Chiti, 'The Emergence of a Community Administration: The Case of European Agencies' (2000) 37 *Common Market Law Review* 309, 315–317.

powers.[30] Therefore, some agencies support the Commission and the Member States by collecting information or processing applications, and other EU agencies have been delegated powers allowing them to adopt individually binding decisions.[31] In these cases, agencies exert discretion, sometimes qualified by the Courts as 'broad discretion',[32] but always under by the provisions of the relevant regulations.[33]

How, then, does an EU agency receive a mandate to exercise its powers, by whom, why, and within which limits? Delegation of powers in the EU is generally discussed in the context of the *Meroni* case from the very early days of European integration.[34] In *Meroni*, the Court explicitly allowed sub-delegation of Commission powers to private parties, despite the lack of explicit authorization in the ECSC Treaty. It did, however, set some conditions for such sub-delegation: first, the Commission could only sub-delegate powers which it had previously been granted. Thereby, the Court reconfirmed the principle of conferral and prohibited actions ultra vires.[35] Secondly, the Commission had to oversee and control the exercise of the sub-delegated powers.[36] Thirdly, the Commission was barred from delegating powers to adopt acts with quasi-legislative content since doing so would upset the 'institutional balance' established by the ECSC.[37] This reference to 'institutional balance'—a principle akin to the separation of powers—is the reason for also applying the standards set by *Meroni* today in the context of the EU.[38] Under current EU law, the delegation of clearly defined powers, if subject to supervision, is possible.[39] Today, most legislative acts of the Union establishing EU agencies are based on Treaty provisions that permit the adoption of 'measures' for the harmonization or approximation of national law, such as, most importantly, Article 114 TFEU (the general legal base for the adoption of internal market measures). Also, some policy-specific Treaty provisions exist allowing for the creation of structural 'measures' such as agencies.[40]

[30] Two examples of many: Art 42(5) of Council Regulation (EC) No 207/2009 of 26 February 2009 on the Community trade mark (codified version) (OJ [2009] L78/1) as amended by Regulation (EU) 2015/2424 of the European Parliament and the Council of 16 December 2015 (OJ [2015] L241/21); Art 62 of Council Regulation (EC) No 2100/94 of 22 July 1994 on Community plant variety rights (OJ [1994] L227/1), as amended.

[31] eg the Community Plant Variety Office—CPVO, the European Chemicals Agency—ECHA, and, in non-scientific fields, the European Union Intellectual Property Office—EUIPO.

[32] See eg with regard to the Community Plant Variety Office, Case C-38/09 P *Schräder v CPVO*, EU:C:2010:196, para 77; Case C-534/10 P *Brookfield New Zealand v CPVO*, EU:C:2012:813, para 50. For other policy areas, see eg C-281/10 P *PepsiCo*, EU:C:2011:679, para 67; Joined Cases C-101/11 and 102/11 P *Neuman and Galdeano*, EU:C:2012:641, para 41.

[33] This was, eg, a situation of confirmation upon appeal of Case T-187/06 *Schräder v Community Plant Variety Office* in Case C-38/09 P *Schräder v CPVO*, EU:C:2010:196.

[34] Joined Cases 9/56 and 10/56 *Meroni v ECSC High Authority*, EU:C:1958:7. There the Court examined the question whether and to what extent the Commission (which was then called the High Authority) could delegate powers under Art 53 of the Treaty establishing the European Coal and Steel Community (ECSC) for the operation of the supply of ferrous scrap to two bodies it had set up on the basis of Belgian private law—the 'Joint Bureau of Ferrous Scrap Consumers' and the 'Imported Ferrous Scrap Equalization Fund'.

[35] *Meroni* (n 34) para 150. [36] Ibid, para 152. [37] Ibid.

[38] See eg Case C-345/00 P *FNAB v Council* [2001] ECR I-3811, para 41 (on the relevance of the concept of institutional balance); on the limits to delegate by legislative act the right to amend an annex to such legislation by means of implementing acts (under the pre-Lisbon system), see Joined Cases C-154/04 and C-155/04 *Alliance for Natural Health* [2005] ECR I-6451, para 90; on the limits arising from institutional balance on delegation to agencies, see Case C-270/12 *UK v Parliament and Council* (*ESMA, Short Selling*), EU:C:2014:18.

[39] Case C-270/12 *UK v EP and Council* (*ESMA—Short Selling*), EU:C:2014:18.

[40] See eg in the area of research, Arts 182, fifth para, and 187 TFEU; in the environmental field, Art 192 TFEU (the legal basis for the European Environmental Agency (OJ [2009] L126/13)); in the air and maritime transport field, Art 100, second para TFEU; regarding border checks, asylum, and immigration in the context of the 'Area of Freedom, Security and Justice', Arts 74 and 77(2)d TFEU (the latter is the legal basis for the creation of the EU's external borders agency, Frontex (now Regulation 2019/1896 (OJ [2019] L295/1)); see further chapters 5 and 25).

In the past, many agencies were also established as 'measures' under the reserve clause of Article 352 TFEU.[41]

3 Criteria for legality

In the day-to-day application of EU law, one of the most central questions which needs to be asked—and answered—concerns the legality of an act or action of an institution, body, or agency. Criteria for the legality of acts of the EU exist primarily in the form of General principles of EU law.[42] These General principles of EU law[43] have a constitutional status in that they bind the Union institutions in the exercise of their legislative and administrative competences. Their function is to provide a guide to the interpretation of Union law, including the Treaties, to constitute grounds for the review of Union law, whether directly based on the Treaties themselves or subordinate acts, and to establish a basis for the non-contractual liability of the Union (Articles 268 and 340, second and third paragraphs, TFEU). In addition, such principles must also be observed by the Member States when they implement Union law,[44] where they derogate from it,[45] and in all other cases within the 'scope' of Union law.[46]

The following discussion addresses in greater detail the principle of proportionality (section 3.1); the rule of law—and its various sub-elements including transparency, legality, and the protection of legitimate expectations (section 3.2); principles of good administration—including the right to a fair hearing, reasoning, and rights of defence (section 3.3); information rights (section 3.4); and, finally, the right to an effective judicial remedy (section 3.5).

3.1 **Proportionality**

Under Article 5(4) TEU, 'the content and form of Union action, shall not exceed what is necessary to achieve the objectives of this Treaty'. The CJEU's concept of the general principle of proportionality is both older than the formulation in Article 5(4) TEU and much richer. Directly or indirectly, proportionality can be understood as the most widely used General principle of EU law. One of the reasons for this is that proportionality is a very versatile principle serving to review the legality of:

- acts of EU institutions and bodies when limiting or regulating the exercise of rights of individuals (eg the Commission adopts a decision fining a company for violation of EU antitrust law under Article 101 TFEU);[47]

[41] Which gives residual power for the EU to act to attain one of its objectives, if the Treaties have not set out the necessary powers.

[42] The European Parliament has repeatedly called on the Commission to present a legislative proposal for a regulation on EU administrative procedures (eg European Parliament resolution of 9 June 2016 for an open, efficient and independent European Union administration (2016/2610(RSP)) to remedy the lack of an EU 'administrative procedure act'. For a model, see P Craig, HCH Hofmann, J-P Schneider, and J Ziller (eds), *ReNEUAL Model Rules on EU Administrative Procedure* (Oxford: Oxford University Press, 2017), also published in French, German, Italian, Polish, Romanian, and Spanish language versions.

[43] General principles of law often include principles requiring standards of procedural justice in administrative procedures, eg the notions of proportionality, right of defence, and others.

[44] See Case 5/88 *Wachauf v Bundesamt für Ernährung und Forstwirtschaft*, EU:C:1989:32.

[45] Case C-260/89 *ERT v DEP*, EU:C:1991:254.

[46] Case C-617/10 *Åklagaren v Hans Åkerberg Fransson*, EU:C:2013:105; Case C-263/97 *First City Trading*, EU:C:1998:444.

[47] Joined Cases C-189, 202, 205–208, and 213/02 P *Dansk Rørindustri v Commission*, EU:C:2005:408. On EU competition law, see further chapter 17.

- acts of EU institutions and bodies when limiting Member State powers by adopting EU acts (eg an EU legislative directive on the maximum working time of workers per week);[48]
- indirectly, in the case of acts of Member State bodies transposing or implementing EU law (eg the Dutch veterinary authorities confiscate pet sheep in order to comply with an EU regulation on the limitation of the outbreak of viral veterinary diseases);[49]
- acts of Member States when limiting or regulating in the context of rights or freedoms guaranteed by EU law (eg Greek authorities decide not to grant a broadcasting licence to a private TV station).[50]

The Court of Justice has developed the review of compliance with the principle of proportionality as a three-step test:

- Under the first level, 'the principle of proportionality requires that measures adopted by European Union institutions do not exceed the limits of what is appropriate and necessary in order to attain the objectives legitimately pursued by the legislation in question'.[51]
- Secondly, 'when there is a choice between several appropriate measures, recourse must be had to the least onerous'.[52] The notion of 'least onerous' must be understood as the least restricting of the rights in question.
- Thirdly, 'the disadvantages caused must not be disproportionate to the aims pursued',[53] that is, there must be an overall reasonable ratio between means and outcome.

Case study 8.2: Broadcasting of sports events in news programmes

The use of the proportionality test is best explained using a practical example such as the *Sky Österreich* case.[54] This case concerned the legality of a provision of an EU directive requiring companies which had acquired exclusive broadcasting licences for sports events also to allow limited reporting of those events by other, competing, channels. In reviewing the compliance of this requirement with the 'freedom to conduct a business', a right under Article 16 of the EU Charter of Fundamental Rights, the Court found that this right needed to be balanced with the right to the freedom to receive information under Article 11(2) Charter. With regard to the first step of the proportionality test, the Court found that 'safeguarding of the freedoms protected under Article 11 of the Charter undoubtedly constitutes a legitimate aim in the general interest'.[55] The directive was also considered 'appropriate for the purpose of ensuring that the objective pursued is achieved' in that it allowed any broadcaster 'to be able to make short news reports and thus to inform the general public of events of high interest'.[56] In

[48] Case C-84/94 *UK v Council* ('*Working Time Directive*'), EU:C:1996:43. On this legislation, see further chapter 20.

[49] Case C-189/01 *Jippes* ,EU:C:2001:420.

[50] Case C-260/89 *ERT v DEP* (n 45).

[51] See eg Case C-343/09 *Afton Chemical* [2010] ECR I-7027, para 45, and Joined Cases C-581/10 and C-629/10 *Nelson*, EU:C:2012:657, para 71.

[52] See eg *Afton Chemical* (n 51) para 45, and *Nelson* (n 51) para 71.

[53] See eg *Afton Chemical* (n 51) para 45, and *Nelson* (n 51) para 71.

[54] Case C-283/11 *Sky Österreich*, EU:C:2013:28.

[55] Ibid, para 52. [56] Ibid, para 53.

its analysis of the second leg of the proportionality test, the Court first explored which measures would have been conceivable which were capable of reaching the legitimate legislative goal but were at the same time less restrictive for the rights of the plaintiff. It considered, for example, the possibility of granting the rights holder the right partially to recover the costs of acquisition of the exclusive sports broadcasting rights. The Court, however, found that this less restrictive option would not achieve the objective pursued by the directive. It would effectively further restrict the access of the general public to the information.[57] The Court then turned to the third step of the proportionality test regarding the overall disproportionality of the directive. The Court found that the EU legislature had struck a fair 'balance between' the rights of the parties involved by limiting the broadcasting rights of the short news reports only to specific types of general news programmes and by requiring them to cite the source of the information.[58] Thereby, the disadvantages resulting for the rights holder were 'not disproportionate in the light of the aims' which the directive pursues and were 'such as to ensure a fair balance between the various rights and fundamental freedoms at issue in the case'.[59]

As noted, the principle of proportionality is applied in many different contexts. Within these different contexts, the degree of judicial review varies. In some cases, the Court (as described in chapter 5) will apply only marginal review and thereby only check for manifest errors of assessment in the different steps of application of the proportionality test.[60] This is especially the case where the institutions enjoy wide legislative discretion. The reason for judicial self-restraint in these cases is that the Court is reluctant to replace the legislature's assessment with its own assessment of the politically desirable outcome, thereby respecting the separation of powers (Article 13(2) TEU). Increasingly, therefore, in the context of reviewing Union legislative acts, the Court does not examine the substance of an act but instead checks whether the institutions can demonstrate that they themselves assessed the proportionality of a measure before adopting it.[61]

In areas other than the review of EU legislation, the Court tends to exercise less judicial self-restraint and will conduct a more probing review of the proportionality of an act. Such cases include:

- those where the institutions have no or only limited discretion—as is often the case in matters of administrative acts implementing legislation;[62]

[57] Ibid, paras 55–57. [58] Ibid, paras 58–63.

[59] Ibid, paras 66 and 67.

[60] *Working Time Directive* (n 48) para 58:

> As to judicial review of those conditions, however, the *Council must be allowed a wide discretion* in an area which, as here, involves the legislature in making social *political choices* and requires it to *carry out complex assessments*. Judicial review of the exercise of that discretion must therefore be limited to examining whether it has been *vitiated by manifest error of misuse of powers*, or whether the institution concerned has *manifestly exceeded the limits* of its discretion. (Emphasis added)

That means that although the Court reviews the different elements of discretion, it only reviews manifest errors in each of the steps.

[61] One way for the legislature to do just that is to prove that it has undertaken an impact assessment study weighing the effects of various policy alternatives and analysing the cost–benefit relation between a measure and its disadvantages to other rights and principles. See eg Case C-58/08 *Vodafone*, EU:C:2010:321, paras 51 *et seq*; Case C-176/09 *Luxembourg v European Parliament and Council*, EU:C:2011:290, paras 56 *et seq*; Case C-128/17 *Republic of Poland v EP and Council*, EU:C:2019:194, paras 31–45, 100, 127, 136–139.

[62] Case T-170/06 *Alrosa v Commission*, EU:T:2007:220, paras 108–110; Case C-12/03 P *Commission v Tetra Laval*, EU:C:2005:87, paras 38–40.

- acts of Member States which limit EU fundamental rights or fundamental freedoms;[63]
- acts of the institutions which restrict the scope of applicability of a fundamental right or balance various rights and principles against each other.[64] This is an explicit obligation under Article 52(1) Charter, which reads: 'Subject to the principle of proportionality, limitations may be made only if they are necessary and genuinely meet objectives of general interest.' An example of this is the previously discussed *Sky Österreich* case in case study 8.2.

3.2 **Rule of law: transparency, legality, legal certainty, legitimate expectations**

The EU is established, as famously pronounced by the Court in *Les Verts*, as a 'Community based on the rule of law'.[65] Although there is a lively academic debate about what that actually means in practice for the EU legal system, most people would agree that the rule of law is an 'umbrella principle' with some core content and numerous (sub-)principles, many of which can in themselves be regarded as having a certain independent existence.[66] In this understanding, the rule of law contains both elements which arise primarily as criteria for the legality of legislative acts and others which relate more directly to the exercise of administrative functions. The following is a selection of some of the main sub-elements of the rule of law within the EU's legal system.

3.2.1 **Legality**

One requirement of the rule of law is that actions of public bodies of the EU take place *under* and *within* the law. This means that, first, a legal basis is required (the principle of conferral under Article 5(2) TEU), which can be traced to primary law: 'Public authorities must have a legal basis and be justified on the grounds laid down by law.'[67] Secondly, the institutions and bodies must act within the limits of the powers so conferred on them. They may not, therefore, act ultra vires and have to comply with the procedural rules spelt out in their specific legal basis. In other words, no act may violate higher-level Union law,[68] including fundamental rights and other General principles of EU law.[69]

A further consequence of the rule of law is the requirement of the correct exercise of discretionary power, where such discretionary powers are conferred on the institution or body.[70] In particular, the institution or body must take into account all relevant factors

[63] See for one of many examples: Case C-41/02 *Commission v Netherlands* ('*Vitamins drops*'), EU:C:2004:762, para 46: 'However, in exercising their discretion relating to the protection of public health, the Member States must comply with the principle of proportionality. The means which they choose must therefore be confined to what is actually necessary to ensure the safeguarding of public health; they must be proportional to the objective thus pursued, which could not have been attained by measures which are less restrictive of intra-Community trade.'

[64] eg *Sky Österreich* (n 54) paras 47–66.

[65] Case 294/83 *Les Verts v Parliament* [1986] ECR 1339, para 23.

[66] For many, see K Lenaerts, 'The Rule of Law and the Coherence of the Judicial System of the European Union' (2007) 44 *Common Market Law Review* 1625.

[67] Joined Cases 46/87 and 227/88 *Hoechst v Commission*, EU:C:1989:337, summary point 3.

[68] Case 1/54 *France v High Authority* [1954] ECR 7, 23; Case 38/70 *Deutsche Tradax GmbH v Einfuhr- und Vorratsstelle für Getreide und Futtermittel* [1971] ECR 145, para 10.

[69] See eg Case 240/83 *Procureur de la République v ADBHU*, EU:C:1985:59.

[70] Case 18/57 *Nold KG v ECSC High Authority*, EU:C:1959:6.

for decision-making[71] but is barred from acting on improper motives leading to misuse of its powers. As in any exercise of public powers, therefore, they must act in good faith and avoid any improper purpose.[72]

3.2.2 **Legal and institutional transparency**

Legal and institutional transparency is essential for the exercise of the rule of law and can be regarded as a precondition for establishing an accountable legal and political system.

Transparency, however, has multiple meanings and facts. On a narrow interpretation, it might be seen as referring to a minimal level of openness in the process, access to documents, and publication of official measures. With respect to transparency in the sense of access to documents and freedom of information, a key Treaty provision is Article 15 TFEU, which, inter alia, expressly requires that the proceedings of all bodies are transparent (paragraph (3), third sub-paragraph), for example by publication of 'documents relating to the legislative procedures'.[73] Additionally, the legislature, as per Article 297 TFEU, has the duty to publish all legislative measures and decisions. Access to documents is also restated in terms of an individual right in Article 42 Charter. Details are laid down by Regulation 1049/2001 on public access to documents.[74]

Case study 8.3: Tennis racquets on board planes?

Airport authorities at Vienna airport refused Mr Heinrich the right to board a plane because they found an item which was prohibited as cabin luggage—here, a tennis racquet. Mr Heinrich, outraged about missing his flight, brought a case before the competent Austrian administrative court asking for a declaration that it was illegal for the authorities to refuse to allow him to board his plane with a racquet in his luggage.[75]

The Austrian court noted that the authorities were acting on the basis of an EU regulation (622/2003) but that it was impossible for individuals to comply with that regulation since the annex to the regulation listing prohibited articles was not made public. This constituted, in the view of the Austrian court, a severe impairment of the most elementary principles of the rule of law. Such regulations should therefore be declared by the Court of Justice as legally non-existent and hence non-binding.

The CJEU, in a preliminary ruling, adopted a more differentiated position. It held that the annex to Regulation 622/2003 adapting the list of articles prohibited on board an aircraft, which was not published in the *Official Journal*, had no binding force insofar as it seeks

[71] This criteria is summarized in the case law of the CJEU as the 'duty of care'—an essential procedural requirement allowing for review of compliance with the rule of law. There is a host of case law specifying the duties of decision-makers under the duty of care, the seminal cases of which include: Case 6/54 *Netherlands v High Authority*, EU:C:1955:5; Case C-269/90 *Technische Universität München v Hauptzollamt München-Mitte*, EU:C:1991:438; Case C-367/95 P *Commission v Sytraval and Brinks France*, EU:C:1998:154, paras 60 and 62.

[72] Art 263, second para, TFEU, dealing with actions for annulment before the Court of Justice, makes the application of these principles explicit in providing that actions against all EU institutions in respect of measures having legal effects may be based on the grounds of 'lack of competence, infringement of an essential procedural requirement, infringement of the Treaties or of any rule of law relating to their application, or misuse of powers' (see further chapter 10).

[73] Case C-345/06 *Heinrich*, EU:C:2009:140, paras 41–47 and 64–66.

[74] Regulation (EC) No 1049/2001 of the European Parliament and the Council of 30 May 2001 regarding public access to European Parliament, Council and Commission documents (OJ [2001] L145/43). Replacement by a revised measure is currently being discussed among the institutions. See further chapter 3.

[75] See Case C-345/06 *Gottfried Heinrich*, EU:C:2009:140, paras 42–44 and 59–63.

to impose obligations on individuals and therefore cannot be enforced against individuals. Article 297(2) TFEU states clearly that EU law cannot take effect in law unless it has been published in the *Official Journal*. The Court held that:

> an act adopted by a Community institution cannot be enforced against natural and legal persons in a Member State before they have the opportunity to make themselves acquainted with it by its proper publication in the *Official Journal of the European Union*. In particular, the principle of legal certainly requires that Community rules enable those concerned to know precisely the extent of the obligations which are imposed on them. Individuals must be able to clearly understand their rights and obligations and take the necessary steps accordingly.

As a consequence, the Court declared that all the relevant implementing acts of the EU Regulation could not be enforced against individuals. Until proper publication, tennis racquets and other items listed in secret could be taken on board. The Vienna authorities' refusal to let Mr Heinrich board the plane with the racquet was therefore illegal.

In terms of administrative law, the often mixed enforcement of policies involving various Member States and EU bodies (eg in the field of data protection under the General Data Protection Regulation) may exacerbate transparency problems arising from a certain lack of clarity regarding who is responsible for decision-making. The transparency of a system is directly linked to the possibility of holding actors accountable and therefore interacts with certain other important precepts, such as legal and institutional responsibility.[76]

3.2.3 **Legal certainty and the protection of legitimate expectations**

The principle of legal certainty and the principle of the protection of legitimate expectations are both sub-concepts of the rule of law and are criteria for the legality of acts adopted on the basis of or in the scope of EU law.

Legal certainty

According to the CJEU, the principle of legal certainty is a General principle of EU law[77] essentially requiring that:

- 'Legal rules be clear and precise, and aim to ensure that situations and legal relationships governed by Community law remain foreseeable.'[78]
- 'Individuals must be able to ascertain unequivocally what their rights and obligations are and take steps accordingly.'[79]

Practically speaking, this has a series of consequences, for example:

- EU institutions are barred from applying rules to individuals which are inconsistent or contradictory;[80]

[76] See Case T-188/97 *Rothmans International BV v Commission*, EU:T:1999:156.

[77] Case 43/75 *Defrenne v SABENA*, EU:C:1976:56, paras 69 *et seq*; Joined Cases 205–215/82 *Deutsche Milchkontor v Germany*, EU:C:1983:233.

[78] Case C-199/03 *Ireland v Commission*, EU:C:2005:548, para 69.

[79] See eg Case C-158/06 *ROM-projecten*, EU:C:2007:370, para 25 with further references. This leg of legal certainty is thus directly related to the principle of transparency discussed above.

[80] Case T-115/94 *Opel Austria v Council*, EU:T:1997:3, para 125; Case C-143/93 *Gebroeders van Es Douane Agenten*, EU:C:1996:45, para 27; there the Commission was held to be 'under an obligation to amend those regulations' which were detrimental to the principle of legal certainty, which requires that an individual will be able 'to ascertain unequivocally what his rights and obligations are and take steps accordingly'.

- double jeopardy (also known as the principle of *ne bis in idem* in criminal law and embodied in Article 50 Charter in comparable terms) is prohibited;
- administrative proceedings must be conducted within a reasonable period of time;[81]
- there is a requirement of legal certainty with respect to legal charges and limitation periods;[82]
- retroactive effect of EU law is, in principle, prohibited.

The latter is, from a practical point of view, probably the most important consequence of the principle of legal certainty. Article 297(1) TFEU lays down that Union acts come into force only after publication, which implies that retroactive entry into force is in principle excluded.[83] Retroactive effect of Union law is exceptionally possible if such effect explicitly follows from Union law[84] and if the public interest in retroactive effect overrides the private interest in the maintenance of the existing legal situation.[85] This indicates that balancing of interests in maintenance of different principles, for example that of the public in upholding the law and that of private parties in legal certainty, is necessary.[86] This requirement for balancing of the public interest in upholding the law and the private interest in maintaining a previously acquired legal position can be well illustrated when looking at questions of revocation of acts and recovery of monies. These are instances of application of the principle of legal certainty which relate to acts of individual application.

The case law with regard to revocation of acts of Union institutions distinguishes *lawful* acts from those which have a legal defect (*unlawful* acts). It is important to recall that even unlawful acts, if not challenged and annulled (eg following an action for annulment before the Courts under Article 263 TFEU), are valid and have effect. This is one of the consequences of the principle of legal certainty.[87]

Lawful acts, in particular those creating rights for individuals or Member States, may not in principle be revoked since, generally, the interest of the individual in the continuous application of the act prevails over the public interest of revocation.[88]

On the other hand, the retroactive revocation of *unlawful* acts is:

> permissible provided that the withdrawal occurs within a reasonable time and provided that the institution from which it emanates has had sufficient regard to how far the applicant might have been led to rely on the lawfulness of the measure.[89]

[81] eg Case T-347/03 *Branco v Commission*, EU:T:2005:265, para 114.

[82] Case 41/69 *Chemiefarma v Commission*, EU:C:1970:71, para 16.

[83] Joined Cases T-64/01 and T-65/01 *Afrikanische Frucht-Compagnie v Council and Commission*, EU:T:2004:37, para 90; Case 98/78 *Racke v Hauptzollamt Mainz*, EU:C:1979:14, para 20. This fundamental approach is also recognized within the legal systems of the Member States (see by comparison Case 63/83 *Regina Kirk*, EU:C:1984:255, para 22) and established with regard to criminal sanctions in Art 49(1) Charter and Art 7 ECHR.

[84] See Case T-357/02 *Freistaat Sachsen v Commission*, EU:T:2011:376, para 98, where the Court stated that 'provisions of Community law have no retroactive effect unless, exceptionally, it clearly follows from their terms or general scheme that such was the intention of the legislature, that the purpose to be achieved so demands and that the legitimate expectations of those concerned are duly respected'.

[85] For the public interests recognized by the Court, see T Tridimas, *The General Principles of EU Law* (2nd edn, Oxford: Oxford University Press, 2006) 256–257.

[86] Joined Cases 42/59 and 49/59 *SNUPAT v High Authority*, EU:C:1961:5.

[87] See also chapter 10.

[88] See Joined Cases 7/56 and 3–7/57 *Algera v Common Assembly*, EU:C:1957:7. See also Case T-251/00 *Lagardère and Canal+ v Commission*, EU:T:2002:278, para 139.

[89] *Lagardère and Canal+* (n 88) para 140. Going back to Case 14/81 *Alpha Steel v Commission*, EU:C:1982:76.

Similar concerns govern the question of recovery of monies. This is important, for example, in the area of subsidies (so-called 'State aid').[90]

Legitimate expectations

The principle of the protection of legitimate expectations is a general legal principle of Union law, which has been recognized since the very early case law of the Court, particularly where an administrative decision is cancelled or revoked.[91] It is closely linked to that of legal certainty.[92] Three key elements must be satisfied:

- The existence of justifiable reliance[93] (this can arise from a valid legislative act,[94] but can also arise from any act of a Union official conferring individual rights or benefits, for example by giving precise assurances, which can give rise to protected 'legitimate expectations'[95]).
- An affected interest[96] (expectations of the continuous existence of a future legal situation are not protected under Union law, if the beneficiary knew that the situation or assurance was illegal,[97] for example due to incorrect facts which the potential beneficiary had given.[98] Also, legitimate expectations cannot arise if the alleged assurance was made contrary to Union law, for example in the form of a promise not to apply or enforce the law[99]).
- Priority for the protection of expectations over the interest of the Union.

3.3 **Good administration**

Principles of good administration have been subject to a particularly dynamic development. Good administration is best understood as an 'umbrella' concept containing numerous more specific rights, rules, and principles, the practically most relevant of which we will discuss in the following.

3.3.1 **General observations on good administration**

Good administration and its sub-principles are protected as General principles of EU law,[100] granting individuals rights also vis-à-vis Member States when implementing and

[90] Case C-24/95 *Land Rheinland-Pfalz v Alcan Deutschland*, EU:C:1997:163, paras 36 and 37. National aid granted to companies is in principle subject to authorization by the Commission. Could the principle of legal certainty be invoked by *Alcan* to avoid the sanction of repayment of the aid which was declared unlawful after payment? The Court, balancing the principles of legal certainty, on the one hand, preferred to give preference to the principle of effectiveness of EU law and requested repayment.

[91] See Case 111/63 *Lemmerz-Werke*, EU:C:1965:76, where the concept of protection of legitimate expectations was first explicitly enunciated. See also *Algera* (n 88) 118; *SNUPAT* (n 86) 103, 111, and 172 *et seq*; Case 14/61 *Hoogovens v ECSC High Authority*, EU:C:1962:28.

[92] Cases C-177/99 and C-181/99 *Ampafrance und Sanofi* [2000] ECR I-7013, para 67, where the Court regarded the principle of legitimate expectations as a 'corollary of the principle of legal certainty'.

[93] Case T-176/01 *Ferriere Nord Spa v Commission* [2004] ECR II-3931.

[94] See Case 120/86 *Mulder v Minister van Landbouw en Visserij* [1988] ECR 2321; Case 170/86 *Van Deetzen v Hauptzollamt Hamburg-Jonas* [1988] ECR 2355.

[95] Case T-283/02 *EnBW*, EU:T:2005:101, para 89.

[96] Case 74/74 *CNTA v Commission*, EU:C:1976:84, para 44.

[97] *EnBW* (n 95) para 113. See also Case T-13/99 *Pfizer Animal Health v Council*, EU:T:2002:209, para 501.

[98] Case 228/84 *Pauvert v Court of Auditors*, EU:C:1985:271, para 14.

[99] See Joined Cases 303/81 and 312/81 *Klöckner v Commission*, EU:C:1983:129, para 34.

[100] See eg Case C-337/15 P *European Ombudsman v Claire Stehlen*, EU:C:2017:256, para 34; Case C-556/14 P *Holcim (Romania) SA v European Commission*, EU:C:2016:207, para 80; Case C-534/10 P *Brookfield New Zealand and Elaris v CPVO*, EU:C:2012:813, para 51.

enforcing EU law.[101] Good administration is also recognized as a fundamental right binding EU institutions, bodies, offices, and agencies under Article 41 Charter.

Article 41 Charter reads:

1. Every person has the right to have his or her affairs handled impartially, fairly and within a reasonable time by the institutions, bodies, offices and agencies of the Union.
2. This right includes:
   a) the right of every person to be heard, before any individual measure which would affect him or her adversely is taken;
   b) the right of every person to have access to his or her file, while respecting the legitimate interests of confidentiality and of professional and business secrecy;
   c) the obligation of the administration to give reasons for its decisions.
3. Every person has the right to have the Union make good any damage caused by its institutions or by its servants in the performance of their duties, in accordance with the General Principles common to the laws of the Member States.
4. Every person may write to the institutions of the Union in one of the languages of the Treaties and must have an answer in the same language.

Principles of good administration are essential procedural requirements, and their violation may lead to an annulment of an act.[102] And possibly the right to damages.[103]

It is noteworthy that the material, institutional, and personal scope of the right to good administration as recognized in Article 41 Charter is more limited than that of the right to good administration as protected as a General principle of EU law (Article 6(3) TEU). Whether good administration will be invoked to exist under Article 41 Charter, as opposed to the same right as a General principle of law, may therefore change the outcome of a case. This can be illustrated by the following comparison:

- The wording of Article 41 Charter indicates that:
  - the material scope of protection of good administration is predominantly intended to cover 'single case decision-making' according to the formulations in Article 41 Charter which cover an 'individual measure', access of a person to 'his or her' (specific) file, and the obligation to give reasons for administrative decisions—as opposed to the broader obligation of stating reasons in all 'legal acts' of the Union in Article 296, first paragraph, TFEU;[104]

[101] Art 6(3) TEU. See eg Case C-166/13 *Sophie Mukarubega v Préfet de police, Préfet de la Seine-Saint-Denis*, EU:C:2014:2336, paras 44–48.

[102] Case T-211/02 *Tideland Signal v Commission*, EU:T:2002:232; *Tideland Signal* (n 102) para 37.

[103] Case C-337/15 P *European Ombudsman v Claire Staelen*, EU:C:2017:256, para 41; Case T-62/98 *Volkswagen*, EU:T:2000:180, para 607.

[104] J Ziller, 'Is a Law of Administrative Procedure for the Union Institutions Necessary?' (2011) 3 *Rivista italiana di diritto pubblico comunitario* 699, 718, however, notes that 'nothing impedes applying art. 41 of the Charter on the right to good administration also to rule making, including to consultation procedures by the Commission'. However, the Court of Justice in Case C-221/09 *AJD Tuna Ltd*, EU:C:2011:153, para 49, has consistently held that Art 41 Charter does not cover the process of enacting measures of general application and the General Court agrees eg in Case T-135/05 *Crampoli v Commission*, EU:T:2006:366, paras 149 and 150, in which it held that the Council when establishing acts of an abstract general nature was not subject to the obligations equivalent to what is now protected in Art 41 Charter, and that their violation could therefore not lead to the annulment of an act.

  - the institutional scope of the right to good administration under Article 41(1) Charter is limited to 'institutions, bodies, offices and agencies of the Union'.[105]

- The right to good administration as a General principle of EU law (Article 6(3) TEU), on the other hand, is also applicable:

  - to general acts, for example for the review of international association agreements,[106] as well as for non-legislative acts which, as the Court held, must be 'adopted by the Commission pursuant to the principle of sound administration and the duty of care';[107]
  - to Member State action in the scope of EU law;
  - under certain conditions to third parties if they have a qualified involvement in an administrative procedure.[108]

3.3.2 **Sub-principles of good administration**

Article 41(2) Charter lists an indicative set of principles useful for the definition of the general concept of good administration invoked in Article 41(1) Charter.

The right to have his or her affairs handled impartially, fairly, and within a reasonable time: the duty of care

The duty of care's (sometimes also referred to the duty of diligence) central feature is the obligation of any decision-maker to establish impartially and carefully all relevant factual and legal elements of a case, and to take these into account in decision-making.[109] A decision must be taken 'carefully and impartially',[110] in full recognition of the facts so assembled.[111] The duty of care binds EU institutions and bodies as well as Member States' authorities acting in the scope of EU law.[112]

The fairness dimension of the right to good administration also requires the absence of arbitrary action and unjustified preferential treatment, including the absence of a conflict of interest. At least for this reason, an interested party is entitled to know the identity of persons conducting investigations and making decisions.[113]

The notion of fairness in the wider sense is also relevant for the right to the treatment of an issue 'within a reasonable time'. After all, not only can overly hasty administration result in bad administration, but it is also widely accepted that 'slow administration is bad administration'[114] and might violate the principle of legal certainty.

[105] Still more limited are the formulations regarding damages and language rights (Art 41(3) and (4) Charter) which speak of 'institutions' and 'servants in the performance of their duties' respectively.

[106] Opinion of AG Trstenjak in Case C-204/07 P *CAS SpA v Commission*, EU:C:2008:175, para 146; Joined Cases T-186/97, T-187/97, T-190–192/97, T-210/97, T-211/97, T-216/97, T-217/97, T-218/97, T-279/97, T-280/97, T-293/97, and T-147/99 *Kaufring AG v Commission*, EU:T:2001:133, para 257.

[107] Case C-248/99 P *Monsanto*, EU:C:2002:1, paras 91–93.

[108] A good example of the analysis of this effect is Case T-260/94 *Air Inter SA v Commission*, EU:T:1994:265, with discussion by HP Nehl, *Principles of Administrative Procedure in EC Law* (Oxford: Hart Publishing, 1999) 91–94.

[109] See in that respect, AG Van Gerven in Case C-16/90 *Eugen Nölle v Hauptzollamt Bremen-Freihafen*, EU:C:1991:233.

[110] Case C-269/90 *TU München v Hauptzollamt München Mitte*, EU:C:1991:438, para 14.

[111] Case 6/54 *Netherlands v High Authority*, EU:C:1955:5, English language version p 112; Case C-12/03 P *Commission v Tetra Laval*, EU:C:2005:87, para 39.

[112] See eg Case C-166/13 *Mukarubega v Seine-Saint-Denis*, EU:C:2014:2336, paras 47–49; and Case C-362/14 *Schrems v Data Protection Commissioner*, EU:C:2015:650, para 63.

[113] Case T-305/94 *Limburgse Vinyl Maatschappij v Commission*, EU:T:1999:80, paras 317 *et seq*.

[114] AG Jacobs in Case C-270/99 P *Z v Parliament*, EU:C:2001:180, para 40, with reference to Art 41 Charter and claiming that this was 'a generally recognised principle'.

Hearing and access to one's file

Article 41(2)(a) and (b) Charter address the right to a fair hearing (*audi alteram partem* or *audiatur altera pars*) 'before any individual measure' which could affect a person 'adversely' is taken. Additionally, access to one's file contains:

- the right to full information which may affect a person's position in an administrative procedure, especially where sanctions may be involved;[115]
- the right to be informed of:
  - the administration's response to complaints or representations;[116]
  - the outcome of procedures and of decisions made;[117]
  - all matters necessary for their defence,[118] including rights of appeal.

The right to a fair hearing as a General principle of EU law 'cannot be excluded'[119] and must be observed 'in all proceedings initiated against a person which are liable to culminate in a measure adversely affecting that person'.[120] As a General principle of law, it thus supplements legislation, which does not explicitly provide for its exercise,[121] requiring that the party concerned:

- must receive an exact and complete statement of the claims or objections raised;
- must also be given the opportunity to make its views known 'on the truth and relevance of the facts and circumstances alleged and on the documents used';[122]
- must be given right of access to documents and the file (which can be limited in the case of confidential information of third parties).

In procedures using large databases and automated access to and processing of information, it will be necessary to reconsider the notion of the 'file' mentioned in Article 41 Charter and the under the General principle of law. Here, the traditional idea of a file will not contain all the information processed in decision-making and possibly not all of the facts leading to the decision with the help of an automated system. In view of the purpose of the right to a hearing to serve as a defence right, access rights under the principle of good administration will therefore need to be interpreted as giving access to the relevant information processed by the automated system in the preparation of decision-making.

115 eg Case 270/82 *Estel v Commission*, EU:C:1984:84, paras 13 *et seq*; Case C-54/95 *Germany v Commission*, EU:C:1999:11, para 118.

116 Case 179/82 *Lucchini Siderurgica v Commission*, EU:C:1983:280, para 27.

117 Case 120/73 *Lorenz v Germany*, EU:C:1973:152, para 5; Case 121/73 *Markmann v Germany*, EU:C:1973:153, para 5; see also R Bauer, *Das Recht auf eine gute Verwaltung im Europäischen Gemeinschaftsrecht* (Frankfurt am Main: Peter Lang, 2002) 64.

118 Case 41/69 *Chemiefarma v Commission*, EU:C:1970:71, para 27.

119 Case T-260/94 *Air Inter v Commission*, EU:T:1994:265, para 60; Case C-135/92 *Fiskano v Commission*, EU:C:1994:267, para 39.

120 Case T-306/01 *Yusuf and Al Barakaat International Foundation v Council and Commission*, EU:T:2005:331.

121 Case 234/84 *Belgium v Commission*, EU:C:1986:302, para 27; Case 259/85 *France v Commission*, EU:C:1987:478, para 12.

122 See eg Cases 100–103/80 *Musique Diffusion française v Commission*, EU:C:1983:158, para 10. In Joined Cases C-402/05 P and C-415/05 P *Kadi and Al Barakaat v Council and Commission* ('*Kadi I*'), EU:C:2008:461, paras 338–352, the Court held that overriding considerations of safety or the conduct of international relations might justify that certain matters may not be communicated to the persons concerned, but do not allow for evidence used against them to justify restrictive measures or for them not to be afforded the right to be informed of such evidence within a reasonable period after those measures were taken.

It is less clear when a right to a hearing might exist in situations where the proceedings lead to the adoption of an act of general application—such as a legislative act (Article 289 TFEU), a delegated act (Article 290 TFEU), or an implementing act with effect beyond a single case (Article 291 TFEU). Article 11(1) and (3) TEU requires Union institutions to hear views and opinions on Union measures and to enter into consultation procedures. This reinforces the view of the Court in *Denmark v Commission*,[123] which had found that a right to a hearing is not excluded simply because the basic act is of general application. It is, so far, not clear from the evolving case law whether the hearing in these cases is a subjective right of individuals or just a factor for review of the act.

Reasoning of decisions

The obligation to give reasons for decisions which is also restated in Article 41(2)(c) Charter, in other words, to provide grounds for the action taken, finds expression in the more general obligation under Article 296(2) TFEU to support all legal acts in the EU with reasons. The extent of the obligation to state reasons under Article 296 TFEU comprises an indication of the legal basis of the act, the general situation which led to its adoption, and the general objectives which it is intended to achieve:[124]

> the statement of reasons must disclose in a clear and unequivocal fashion the reasoning followed by the Community authority which adopted the measure in question in such a way as to make the persons concerned aware of the reasons for the measure and thus enable them to defend their rights and to enable the Court to exercise its supervisory jurisdiction.[125]

The lack of reasoning of an act is a ground for its annulment.

Where decision-making has been fully or partially automated, the purpose of reasoning should also be interpreted to require not only that there be transparency about the fact that an automated system has been used, but also to require that a detailed listing of the information taken into account in decision-making be provided in order to show that the duty of care has been complied with in the course of automated processing of data.

Damages

The right to good administration in Article 41(3) Charter contains an explicit reference to the right to receive compensation for damage under Article 340 TFEU. Article 41 Charter therefore cannot limit the obligation to pay damages only for violations of the principles listed in the provisions on good administration. The right to damages is discussed in greater detail in chapter 10 on judicial review.

Language rights

The entitlement to 'write' to the institutions of the Union in one of the languages of the Treaties and to receive an answer in the same language is a parallel provision to the right under Article 24(4) TFEU, with Article 342 TFEU giving the Council the authority to establish the language regime for the institutions.[126] The right of free choice of the language is applicable to communications with 'institutions' of the EU only. Agencies and

[123] Case C-3/00 *Denmark v Commission*, EU:C:2003:167.

[124] Case 5/67 *Beus GmbH v Hauptzollamt München*, EU:C:1968:13; see also Case T-13/99 *Pfizer Animal Health v Council*, EU:T:2002:209, para 501; Case C-342/03 *Spain v Council*, EU:C:2005:151, para 55.

[125] *TU München* (n 110) paras 14 and 26.

[126] This was done by one of the first legal acts issued by the Council, Regulation 1/58 determining the languages used by the European Economic Community (OJ [1952–8] English Special Edition, p 59).

other bodies may thus be subject to specific and possibly more limited language regimes, provided for by law.[127]

3.4 **Information-related rights: freedom of information and data protection**

The right of access to documents is a precondition for both a fair and accountable administration and a functioning, participatory democracy in which citizens are able to engage in an informed debate and to exert influence on public decision-making. It is thus of utmost importance in a system under the rule of law. The right of access to documents is explicitly protected as a fundamental individual right under Article 42 Charter and Article 15(3) TFEU.[128] Regulation 1049/2001 specifies conditions of access under Article 15 TFEU but when limiting this right must be interpreted in light of the principle of proportionality under Article 52(1) Charter.[129] Policy-specific legislation on access to documents exists in the field of environmental law[130] and in the field of food safety law obliging the EU food safety authority to proactively publish documents.[131]

Freedom of information rights must be balanced with other individual rights, most notably the right to the protection of personal data and privacy of individuals.[132] Case law of the CJEU has upheld access rights regarding documents arising from legislative procedures.[133] However, exceptions to the constitutionally guaranteed right of access to documents listed in Article 4(2) of Regulation 1049/2001 have been interpreted by the Court of Justice quite extensively, finding that important parts of the administrative activities of the Commission should 'enjoy a general presumption of confidentiality' and thus the exercise of the constitutionally guaranteed access rights requires proof that the individual interest of access would override any public interest in secrecy.[134]

Union law governing information contains not only rules on access to information but also on the protection of personal information data. Under Article 8 Charter, protection of personal information constitutes an individual right against the potential misuse of

[127] See eg Case T-120/99 *Kik v OHIM*, EU:T:2001:189, para 64.

[128] Art 15(3) TFEU lays down that 'Any citizen of the Union and any natural or legal person residing or having its registered office in a Member State, shall have a right of access to documents of the Union institutions, bodies, offices and agencies, whatever their medium, subject to the principles and the conditions to be defined in accordance with this paragraph.' Historically speaking, the right of access to documents, as a constitutional right, goes back to the Swedish and Finnish traditions.

[129] Regulation (EC) No 1049/2001 of the European Parliament and of the Council of 30 May 2001 regarding public access to European Parliament, Council and Commission documents (OJ [2001] L145/43).

[130] See Regulation (EC) No 1367/2006 of the European Parliament and of the Council of 6 September 2006 on the application of the provisions of the Aarhus Convention on Access to Information, Public Participation in Decision-making and Access to Justice in Environmental Matters to Community institutions and bodies (OJ [2006] L264/13).

[131] Regulation (EU) 2019/1381 of the European Parliament and of the Council of 20 June 2019 on the transparency and sustainability of the EU risk assessment in the food chain (OJ [2019] L231/1).

[132] See esp Case C-28/08 P *Commission v Bavarian Lager*, EU:C:2010:378 and Joined Cases C-92/09 and C-93/09 *Schecke*, EU:C:2009:284, para 85:

> It is necessary to bear in mind that the institutions are obliged to balance, before disclosing information relating to a natural person, the EU's interest in guaranteeing the transparency of its actions and the infringement of the rights recognised by Articles 7 and 8 of the Charter. No automatic priority can be conferred on the objective of transparency over the right to protection of personal data, even if important economic interests are at stake.

[133] See eg Joined Case C-39/05 P and 52/05 P *Sweden and Turco v Council*, EU:C:2008:374 (Grand Chamber), paras 35–41.

[134] Case C-612/13 P *Client Earth*, EU:C:2015:486. See especially para 77 of the judgment with many further references. As a result, de facto, an overriding interest in access must be argued without prior knowledge of the content of the documents to which access is sought.

information both by governments and non-governmental actors. Limitations on privacy rights to the extent 'necessary in a democratic society' are, for example, explicitly recognized in Article 8 of the European Convention on Human Rights (ECHR). Legal persons are protected with respect to their professional or business secrets. This is recognized, for example, in Article 339 TFEU and in secondary legislation.[135]

3.5 **The right to an effective judicial remedy and additional rights of defence**

The CJEU has held that 'the very existence of effective judicial review designed to ensure compliance with provisions of EU law is of the essence of the rule of law'.[136] Persons affected by measures of the Union or the Member States acting under Union law must therefore be able to challenge actions affecting their interests.[137] This is protected in Union law by the right to an effective remedy and additional rights of defence.

3.5.1 **Right to an effective remedy**

The existence of a right is linked to the existence of a remedy under the principle known as *ubi ius, ibi remedium*, which in Union terms might read: where there is a right under Union law, there is a remedy to ensure its enforcement. Accordingly, the 'right to obtain an effective remedy in a competent court' is protected as a fundamental right as a General principle of EU law,[138] and under Article 47 Charter. This right is also protected in Articles 6 and 13 ECHR.

Article 47, first paragraph, Charter, expanding the language of the Convention, grants a 'right to an effective remedy before a tribunal', where any right and freedom recognized under Union law are violated. Since first-line judicial protection of rights under EU law must be offered by the courts and tribunals of the Member States, certain provisions refer to the notion of the courts, such as Article 47, second paragraph, Charter clarifying that a tribunal be 'independent and impartial',[139] that hearings be 'fair and public', and that everyone 'ha[s] the possibility of being advised, defended and represented'.

A remedy under EU law, by analogy with Article 13 ECHR, 'must be "effective" both in law and in practice'.[140] Any act which fails to provide 'for any possibility for an individual

[135] See eg Art 16 of Commission Regulation (EC) No 773/2004 of 7 April 2004 relating to the conduct of proceedings by the Commission pursuant to Articles 81 and 82 of the EC Treaty (OJ [2004] L123/18); Art 28 of Council Regulation (EC) No 1/2003 of 16 December 2002 on the implementation of the rules on competition laid down in Articles 81 and 82 of the Treaty (OJ [2003] L1/1); Art 8 of Regulation (EC) No 1073/1999 of the European Parliament and of the Council of 25 May 1999 concerning investigations conducted by the European Anti-Fraud Office (OLAF) (OJ [1999] L136/1); Art 8(1) of Council Regulation (Euratom, EC) No 2185/96 of 11 November 1996 concerning on-the-spot checks and inspections carried out by the Commission in order to protect the European Communities' financial interests against fraud and other irregularities (OJ [1996] L292/2) of Regulation 1/2003 on antitrust enforcement. Art 28 of Regulation 1/2003 protects professional secrecy insofar as it provides that this information may only be used for purposes for which it was gathered by the Commission and within the competition network and that such information shall not be disclosed.

[136] Case C-72/15 *Rosneft*, EU:C:2017:236, paras 73–78; Case C-562/13 *Abdida*, EU:C:2014:2453, para 45; Case C-362/14 *Schrems I*, EU:C:2015:650, para 95.

[137] HCH Hofmann, GC Rowe, and A Türk, *Administrative Law and Policy of the European Union* (Oxford: Oxford University Press, 2011) 204.

[138] Case 85/76 *Hoffmann-La Roche v Commission*, EU:C:1979:36, para 9; Case 222/84 *Johnston*, EU:C:1986:206, para 19.

[139] Case C-506/04 *Wilson*, EU:C:2006:587, paras 60–62.

[140] *Kudla v Poland* (Appl No 30210/96), ECHR 2000-XI (Grand Chamber), para 157. Art 13 ECHR is, however, more limited than the right to effective judicial review under EU law. Art 13 ECHR protects only rights arising from the Convention—therefore only fundamental rights and freedoms. The General principle of EU law, by contrast, protects all rights arising from EU law in both a vertical and a horizontal level.

to pursue legal remedies' in order to protect her or his rights can be found to violate 'the essence of the fundamental right to effective judicial protection, as enshrined in Article 47 of the Charter'.[141] The right to an effective judicial remedy under EU law is also linked with the principle of effectiveness (flowing from Article 4(3) TEU as discussed previously). Under the *Factortame* formula, the right to an effective remedy offers protection against 'any provision of a national legal system and any legislative, administrative or judicial practice which might impair the effectiveness' of Union law.[142] That means that Member States:

- may 'not render virtually *impossible or excessively difficult* the exercise of rights'[143] conferred by EU law;
- are obliged to 'guarantee real and effective judicial protection';[144]
- are barred from applying any rule or applying any procedure which 'might prevent, even temporarily, Community rules from having full force and effect'.[145]

For a practical illustration of this, we turn to *Factortame*. The right to an effective judicial remedy resulted there in the obligation of the English High Court to offer interim relief measures to protect the plaintiff's interests under EU law, even though such measures were not available to that court under English law at the time.

Compliance with the right to an effective remedy, therefore, depends both on:

- the *procedural* aspect—whether the Member State offers procedural rules granting fair possibilities of bringing a case and that admissibility criteria allow actual access to a court;
- and the more *substantive* issue—whether success on the grounds of the claim of violation of a right under EU law would lead to a remedy which is capable of addressing the violation of the right.[146]

Additionally, remedies must be granted by courts or tribunals which enjoy independence. The conditions for what counts as an independent court in the sense of Article 19 TEU and thus Article 47 Charter have been developed by the CJEU in a series of cases.[147] The second sub-paragraph of Article 19(1) TEU requires Member States to 'provide remedies sufficient to ensure effective judicial protection for individual parties in the fields covered by EU law'. Therefore, Member States must ensure that the 'courts or tribunals' within the meaning of EU law 'meet the requirements of effective judicial protection'.[148] This is the case if a court or tribunal can exercise its judicial functions without being subject to any hierarchical constraint or subordinated to any other body and without taking orders or instructions from another source.[149] A 'court or tribunal', capable of granting effective

[141] Case C-362/14 *Schrems v Data Protection Commissioner*, EU:C:2015:650, para 95.

[142] Case C-213/89 *Factortame*, EU:C:1990:257, paras 19 and 20.

[143] See eg Case C-128/93 *Fisscher*, EU:C:1994:353, para 37; Case C-261/95 *Palmisani*, EU:C:1997:351, para 27; *Courage* (n 6) para 29; Joined Cases C-231–233/06 *Jonkman*, EU:C:2007:373, para 28 (emphasis added).

[144] Case 14/83 *Van Colson*, EU:C:1984:153, para 23.

[145] *Factortame* (n 142) paras 19 and 20.

[146] Correctly, the European Court of Human Rights has pointed out that with respect to Art 13 ECHR (in *MSS v Belgium and Greece* (Appl No 30696/09) [2011] ECHR 108 (Grand Chamber), paras 289 and 290) that 'the "effectiveness" of a "remedy" within the meaning of Article 13 does not depend on the certainty of a favourable outcome for the applicant'. Also, even if a single remedy does not by itself entirely satisfy the requirements of Art 13, the aggregate of remedies provided for under domestic law may do so.

[147] Case C-64/16 *Associação Sindical dos Juízes Portugueses (ASJP)*, EU:C:2018:117 paras 33–37; Case C-222/13 *TDC*, EU:C:2014:2265, para 32.

[148] Case C-284/16 *Achmea*, EU:C:2018:158, para 34.

[149] Case C-64/16 *ASJP*, EU:C:2018:117, paras 44–45.

judicial protection,[150] must be permanently established by law, its jurisdiction must be compulsory (excluding commercial arbitration), and it must apply procedural rules predefined by law providing for an adjudicatory (*inter partes*) procedure.[151] Courts must be independent and capable of acting with objectivity as a third party to a decision-maker.[152]

Independence under EU law, in limitation of Member State procedural autonomy, is further measured by rules establishing 'the composition of the body, the appointment, length of service and grounds for abstention, rejection and dismissal of its members'.[153] Any national disciplinary regime, including the procedures for removal from office concerning judges, must guarantee that it cannot be used as 'a system of political control of the content of judicial decisions', including guarantees against removal from office.[154] Impartiality also requires fairness in a procedure in the sense of a level playing field for the parties to the proceedings and the absence of a judge of any interest in the outcome of the proceedings. The requirement of independence of courts is, according to the CJEU, 'of cardinal importance as a guarantee that all the rights which individuals derive from EU law will be protected'[155] within a system under the rule of law, according to the EU's own 'constitutional structure'.[156]

3.5.2 **Additional rights of defence**

A guarantee of respect for 'the rights of the defence of anyone who has been charged' is provided in Article 48 Charter. But, more broadly, under EU law the rights of defence must be ensured not only in procedures before a court, but also in administrative procedures conducted by EU institutions and bodies or by Member State bodies implementing EU law. They are enforced even 'where there is no specific legislation and also where legislation exists which does not itself take account of that principle'.[157] The Court of Justice held that:

> Respect for the rights of the defence constitutes a fundamental principle and must therefore be ensured not only in administrative procedures which may lead to the imposition of penalties but also during preliminary inquiry procedures such as investigations.[158]

Some of the rights in administrative proceedings, such as the right to be heard and the right of access to one's file, have been enshrined in Article 41(2) Charter and were discussed previously. Generally speaking, rights of defence further include:

- rights of legal professional privilege,[159] concerning the right to confidentiality of communications with an external lawyer;[160]

[150] Case C-506/04 *Wilson v Ordre des avocats du barreau de Luxembourg*, EU:C:2006:587 (Grand Chamber), para 48 with further references; Case C-64/16 *ASJP*, EU:C:2018:117, paras 38, 40; Case C-503/15 *Margarit Panicello*, EU:C:2017:126, para 27.

[151] Case 14/86 *Pretore di Salò* v *Persons Unknown*, EU:C:1987:275, para 7; Case C-17/00 *De Coster*, EU:C:2001:651, para 17.

[152] Case C-506/04 *Wilson*, EU:C:2006:587, para 51; Case C-503/15 *Margarit Panicello*, EU:C:2017:126, para 37.

[153] This the CJEU refers to as factors protecting courts form external influences. See Case C-103/97 *Köllensperger and Atzwanger*, EU:C:1999:52, para 21; Case C-407/98 *Abrahamsson and Anderson*, EU:C:2000:367, para 36.

[154] Joined Cases C-9/97 and C-118/97 *Jokela and Pitkäranta*, EU:C:1998:497, para 20.

[155] Case C-216/18 PPU *LM*, EU:C:2018:586, para 48.

[156] Case C-284/16 *Achmea*, EU:C:2018:158, paras 33 and 36 with further references.

[157] Case 222/84 *Johnston v Chief Constabulary*, EU:C:1986:206. See also Case C-32/95 P *Commission v Lisrestal*, EU:C:1996:402, para 30.

[158] *Hoechst* (n 67) summary point 1.

[159] See Case 155/79 *AM&S*, EU:C:1982:157, paras 23–26; Case T-30/89 *Hilti v Commission*, EU:T:1991:70, para 18; Joined Cases T-125/03 and T-253/03 confirmed by Case C-550/07 P *Akzo*, EU:C:2010:512.

[160] *Hilti* (n 159).

- a right against self-incrimination[161]—this, for example, prohibits the Commission, in a request for information in competition proceedings, to require the undertaking 'to provide it with answers which might involve an admission on its part of the existence of an infringement'.[162]

Case study 8.4: Terrorism and rights

Following the September 2001 terrorist attacks on targets in the US, the United Nations introduced what it called 'smart sanctions'. The UN Security Council was authorized to establish lists of persons and entities accused by UN Security Council members of being in some way or another associated with terrorist organizations such as al-Qaeda. UN Member States were then required to freeze personal funds and economic resources, including access to bank accounts and other assets of these listed persons and entities.

The EU, not a member of the UN but acting within its competencies, implemented these decisions of the UN Security Council by various legal acts. As a result, Mr Yusuf and Mr Kadi, two Swedish citizens, woke up one morning to find that they could no longer withdraw money from their bank accounts. They brought cases before the General Court against the EU legal acts listing them among the persons and entities whose assets should be frozen.[163] Upon appeal against the General Court's judgment, the Court of Justice held in *Kadi I* that sanctions against Mr Yusuf had to be withdrawn. Some of the central legal questions arising in these cases were, aside from the jurisdiction of EU Courts and the degree of review of EU legal acts implementing UN Security Council decisions, whether the rights of defence and the right to an effective judicial review were violated by the EU legal acts. The Court of Justice, in the *Kadi I* and *Kadi II* cases, dismissed the notion of Union acts as capable of having some form of 'immunity' from judicial review.[164] It then went on also to address the issues of rights of defence and the right to an effective judicial review.

The General Court in *Yusuf* had already recalled that the right to a fair hearing required an individual to be able to 'learn about the accusations held against them, to be able to understand the evidence gathered against them and to be able to defend themselves against such accusations'.[165] The right to a fair hearing must be observed 'in all proceedings initiated against a person which are liable to culminate in a measure adversely affecting that person'.[166] Although 'the right to be heard cannot be extended to the context of a Community legislative process culminating in the enactment of legislation' applying generally, the right exists even if a legislative act also targets individuals.[167] However, according to the General Court, this standard under EU law was not applicable to the case. Rather, the impugned EU legal act

[161] See *Hoechst* (n 67); Case 374/87 *Orkem v Commission*, EU:C:1989:387. See also Case 27/88 *Solvay v Commission* [1989] ECR 3355; Case T-34/93 *Société Générale v Commission* [1995] ECR II-545, paras 72–74; Case C-407/04 P *Dalmine v Commission*, EU:C:2007:53, para 34.

[162] Case C-407/04 P *Dalmine v Commission*, EU:C:2007:53, para 35. The Court made it clear in Case C-60/92 *Otto v Postbank*, EU:C:1993:876, paras 15–17, that this limitation does not apply to civil proceedings in national courts.

[163] Case T-306/01 *Yusuf and Al Barakaat International Foundation v Council and Commission*, EU:T:2005:331; Case T-315/01 *Kadi v Council and Commission*, EU:T:2005:332.

[164] Joined Cases C-402/05 P and C-415/05 P *Kadi and Al Barakaat v Council and Commission* ('*Kadi I*'), EU:C:2008:46, esp paras 325–327.

[165] *Kadi I* (n 1564) paras 325–327.

[166] Case T-306/01 *Yusuf and Al Barakaat International Foundation v Council and Commission*, EU:T:2005:331, para 325.

[167] Ibid, para 327.

implementing a UN Security Council decision was only to be reviewed against compliance with standards of *jus cogens* arising from public international law.

On appeal in *Kadi I*, the Court of Justice set aside the General Court's decision and held that 'the rights of the defence, in particular the right to be heard, and the right to effective judicial review of those rights, were patently not respected' when the EU simply implemented the UN Security Council resolution without following a procedure allowing for compliance with fundamental rights.[168] Therefore, it annulled the regulation freezing Mr Kadi's assets. The Court held:

> that the Courts of the European Union must ensure the review, in principle the full review, of the lawfulness of all European Union acts in the light of fundamental rights, including where such acts are designed to implement Security Council resolutions, and that the General Court's reasoning was consequently vitiated by an error of law.[169]

The 'effectiveness of judicial review means that the competent European Union authority is bound to communicate the grounds for the contested listing decision to the person concerned and to provide that person with the opportunity to be heard in that regard'. The Court stated that, 'as regards a decision that a person's name should be listed for the first time, for reasons connected with the effectiveness of the restrictive measures at issue and with the objective of the regulation concerned, it was necessary that that disclosure and that hearing should occur not prior to the adoption of that decision but when that decision was adopted or as swiftly as possible thereafter'.[170] 'Since Mr Kadi had not been in a position effectively to make known his point of view in that regard, with the consequence that the rights of defence and the right to effective judicial review had been infringed.'[171]

The *Kadi II* case, decided by the Court of Justice in 2013,[172] arose from the UN Security Council's Sanctions Committee's attempts to remedy the situation by transferring a summary narrative of reasons for the listing of Mr Kadi (referred to as Mr Quadi) to him and publishing it on the UN website. Mr Kadi sent his statements to the Commission, requested the production of the evidence in support of the claims and assertions made in the UN's summary of reasons, and asked that he be allowed to submit comments on that evidence. Irrespective of these demands, the Commission adopted a new regulation continuing the freezing of Mr Kadi's assets without further commenting on the statements made by Mr Kadi in response to the allegations of the UN.

Again, Mr Kadi brought an action for annulment against this act before the General Court alleging, inter alia, breach of the right of defence and of the right to effective judicial protection. The Court, in view of *Kadi I*, had found that it was to ensure 'in principle the full review' of the lawfulness of the contested regulation in light of the fundamental rights guaranteed by the EU. This meant that:

> the Courts of the European Union must review the assessment made by the institution concerned of the facts and circumstances relied on in support of the restrictive measures at issue and determine whether the information and evidence on which that assessment is based is accurate, reliable and consistent.[173]

[168] *Kadi I* (n 164) followed the AG. It upheld the Community standards of fundamental rights protection in paras 281 *et seq*.

[169] Ibid, esp paras 326 and 327.

[170] Ibid, esp paras 336–342 in the summary given by Joined Cases C-584/10 P, C-593/10 P, and C-595/10 P *Commission and UK v Kadi* ('*Kadi II*'), EU:C:2013:518, para 24.

[171] *Kadi I* (n 164) paras 345–349 in the summary given in *Kadi II* (n 170) para 25.

[172] *Commission and UK v Kadi* (n 170).

[173] Ibid, paras 39–41.

The Court found that there was a breach of Mr Kadi's rights of defence because:

> those rights had been respected only in a purely formal and superficial sense, since the Commission considered itself strictly bound by the findings of the Sanctions Committee and at no time envisaged calling them into question in the light of Mr Kadi's comments or making any real effort to refute the exculpatory evidence adduced by Mr Kadi.
>
> *(a) No access to the evidence against him*
>
> Mr Kadi was refused access by the Commission to the evidence against him despite his express request, while no balance was struck between his interests and the need to protect the confidentiality of the information in question.
>
> *(b) Vague and insufficient allegations*
>
> The few pieces of information and the vague allegations in the summary of reasons relating to the listing of Mr Kadi . . . for example, that Mr Kadi was a shareholder in a Bosnian bank in which planning sessions for an attack on a United States facility in Saudi Arabia 'may have' taken place, were clearly insufficient to enable Mr Kadi to mount an effective [defence against allegations].[174]

The General Court also found 'that the principle of effective judicial protection had been infringed' on the grounds that neither was Mr Kadi afforded proper access to the information and evidence used against him, nor had he been able to 'defend his rights with regard to that information and evidence in satisfactory conditions'. Further, no evidence of that kind or any indication of the evidence relied on against Mr Kadi had been disclosed to the Court.[175]

On appeal, the Court of Justice in its *Kadi II* judgment confirmed the General Court's interpretation of the violation of the right of defence and of an effective judicial review.[176] The right of defence arises from both the General principles of EU law affirmed, inter alia, by Articles 42(2) and 47 Charter. However, limitations on the exercise of the right are possible, as set out in Article 52(1) Charter. This requires that limitations respect the essence of the right in question and are proportionate. It also requires analysis of the specific circumstances of the particular case, including the nature of the act at issue, the context of its adoption, and the legal rules governing the matter in question.[177]

One of the obligations which arises in the context of the right to good administration and is also related to the right of defence is the obligation of the Union administration regarding the 'duty of care'. In the words of the Court of Justice, when 'comments are made by the individual concerned on the summary of reasons, the competent European Union authority is under an obligation to examine, carefully and impartially, whether the alleged reasons are well founded, in the light of those comments and any exculpatory evidence provided with those comments'.[178]

The duty to state reasons for a decision arising from Article 296 TFEU and the right to an effective judicial review 'entails in all circumstances' 'that that statement of reasons identifies the individual, specific and concrete reasons why the competent authorities consider that the individual concerned must be subject to restrictive measures'.[179] The reason for this is that

[174] Case T-85/09 *Kadi v Commission* [2010] ECR II-5177 (General Court), paras 171–180 as cited by *Kadi II* (n 170) para 43.

[175] *Kadi II* (n 170) para 44.

[176] Ibid, paras 97–134.

[177] Ibid, para 102.

[178] Ibid, para 114 with references to Case C-269/90 *Technische Universität München*, EU:C:1991:438, para 14; Case C-525/04 P *Spain v Lenzing*, EU:C:2007:698, para 58.

[179] *Kadi II* (n 170) para 116; Joined Cases C-539/10 P and C-550/10 P *Al-Aqsa v Council and Netherlands v Al-Aqsa*, EU:C:2012:711, paras 140 and 142.

effective judicial review requires verification of the allegations and a review of whether 'those reasons, or, at the very least, one of those reasons, deemed sufficient in itself to support that decision, is substantiated'.[180] In the absence of sufficient reasoning of the act, the Courts will base their review 'solely on the material which has been disclosed to them' and if 'that material is insufficient to allow a finding that a reason is well founded, the Courts of the European Union shall disregard that reason'.[181] The reason behind this is that 'the essence of effective judicial protection must be that it should enable the person concerned to obtain . . . annulment' of the contested measure.[182]

The Court of Justice therefore concluded that it:

> follows from the criteria analysed above that, for the rights of the defence and the right to effective judicial protection to be respected first, the competent European Union authority must (i) disclose to the person concerned the summary of reasons provided by the Sanctions Committee which is the basis for listing or maintaining the listing of that person's name in Annex I to Regulation No 881/2002, (ii) enable him effectively to make known his observations on that subject and (iii) examine, carefully and impartially, whether the reasons alleged are well founded, in the light of the observations presented by that person and any exculpatory evidence that may be produced by him.[183]

The *Kadi* and *Al Barakaat* cases, as well as the *Ahmed Ali Yusuf* case, have become central reference points for several central issues of EU law. They address not only the relation between EU law and public international law obligations of the Member States in general, but they also clarify that it is inconceivable that any exercise of public authority by the EU could fail to comply with fundamental rights and EU General principles protecting both substantive and procedural rights of individuals. Procedural rights, especially regarding the rights of defence and of good administration including the right to a fair hearing, the right to access to one's file, and many other rule of law-related principles, were enforced by the Court of Justice in a highly publicized case.

4 Conclusion

In summary, with the entry into force of the Charter of Fundamental Rights of the European Union under the Treaty of Lisbon (Article 6(1) TEU) many of the rights and principles which were initially established under the case law of the Court of Justice only, are now also restated in positive law. This adds to the prominence of principles which might initially not have been known to the wider public, such as the right to good administration in Article 41 Charter. Importantly, however, this has not led to the discarding of the pre-Treaty of Lisbon approach of case law-led developments of rights as General principles. To the contrary, under Article 6(3) TEU, rights are also protected as General principles of EU law. There is no hierarchy between the different sources of Article 6(1) TEU versus Article 6(3) TEU. This contributes to the dynamism of the EU legal system, which continues to be capable of adapting to new challenges arising from policy areas increasingly becoming subject to 'Europeanization' and new influences, such as the drive towards more transparency of the legal system which took on board some of the more 'Nordic' legal traditions of the EU. A general administrative procedure act for the EU might clarify, to a much greater degree than Article 41 Charter was capable of doing, the

[180] *Kadi II* (n 170) para 119. [181] Ibid, para 123. [182] Ibid, para 134.
[183] Ibid, para 135.

rights of individuals and obligations of administrations implementing EU law. Especially in the context of a highly integrated system of implementation of EU law in which Member States and EU institutions and bodies are involved, such clarification of applicable procedural provisions would add much to the transparency of the system, compliance with principles under the rule of law, and good administration in general.

Further reading

There is much literature on General principles of EU law, less so on EU administrative law. As always, it is important to study EU law by taking into account contributions from the different language groups which often discuss EU law from varying experiences and with a focus sometimes different from that chosen by authors of another.

J-B Auby and J Dutheil de la Rochère (eds), *Traité de Droit Administratif Européen* (2nd edn, Brussels: Bruylant, 2014)

M Chiti (ed), *Diritto amministrativo europeo* (Milan: Guiffrè Editore, 2013)

P Craig, *EU Administrative Law* (4th edn, Oxford: Oxford University Press, 2026)

D-U Galetta and J Ziller, *EU Administrative Law* (Cheltenham: Elgar 2024)

HCH Hofmann, GC Rowe, and AH Türk, *Administrative Law and Policy of the European Union* (Oxford: Oxford University Press, 2011)

JE Soriano García (ed), *Procedimiento Administrativo Europeo* (Navarra: Thomson Reuters, 2012)

JP Terhechte (ed), *Verwaltungsrecht der Europäischen Union* (2nd edn, Baden-Baden: Nomos, 2021)

9

Fundamental rights in the European Union

Eleanor Spaventa

1 Introduction

In this chapter we are going to look at fundamental rights in the EU. As we shall see, the original Treaties did not contain any specific reference to fundamental rights. For this reason it fell upon the Court of Justice to develop a fundamental rights jurisprudence to ensure that individuals would be adequately protected. Eventually this gap was remedied and the EU 'proclaimed' its own catalogue of rights, the Charter of Fundamental Rights of the European Union, which became 'legally binding' following the entry into force of the Lisbon Treaty. The Lisbon Treaty also provided for competence for the EU to accede to the European Convention on Human Rights (ECHR), a fundamental rights document adopted in the context of the Council of Europe (which is a separate organization from the EU). A first Accession Agreement had been concluded in 2013; however, accession stalled following a ruling by the Court of Justice which found the proposed agreement incompatible with the Treaty.[1] The Court's objections were far-reaching and negotiations restarted only in 2019 and a provisional agreement was finalized in 2023. However, as we shall see, it is only after the Court of Justice expanded its jurisdiction in the area of Common Foreign and Security Policy in 2025 that the remaining outstanding objection might have been overcome. The Commission has now requested a new opinion from the

[1] Opinion 2/13 on *the Accession of the European Union to the European Convention for the Protection of Human Rights and Fundamental Freedoms*, EU:C:2014:2454 (hereinafter Opinion 2/13); on the Opinion, see eg B de Witte and Š Imamovic, 'Opinion 2/13 on Accession to the ECHR: Defending the EU Legal Order against a Foreign Human Rights Court' (2015) 40 *European Law Review* 683; E Spaventa, 'A Very Fearful Court? The Protection of Fundamental Rights in the European Union after Opinion 2/13' (2015) 22 *Maastricht Journal of European and Comparative Law* 35.

Court as to the compatibility of the revised Draft Revised Accession Agreement with the Treaties.[2]

The protection of fundamental rights in the EU is a rich, and at times contested, area of EU law and it has become increasingly important with the expansion of the powers of the EU, especially in the field of criminal law. However, when reflecting on the debate on fundamental rights you should bear in mind the bigger picture: the more extensive the jurisdiction of the Court, the more enthusiastic its protection of individuals, the more pronounced the intrusion in national law.[3] Here, consider that once the Court of Justice has asserted jurisdiction, the national courts must relinquish it—if the Court decides that it is for itself to assess whether, for example, a national immigration rule falling within the scope of EU law is compatible with fundamental rights, it will then be only for the Court to balance the competing interests (ie the desire to curtail immigration vis-à-vis the rights of the migrant). Those incursions in what is felt to be the national jurisdiction might lead to problems, especially when national courts disagree with the level of protection afforded by the Court. Moreover, further judicial review of national legislation might be perceived as an unwelcome intrusion into the sovereignty of national parliaments. The same problem arises in the context of the so-called rule of law crisis, where some Member States are failing to uphold the EU's foundational values. On the one hand, because of its multi-layered and *sui generis* nature, the EU had found it difficult to enforce its values against Member States. On the other hand, a threat to democracy, fundamental rights, and rule of law, even in just one Member State, considerably weakens and endangers the functioning (and the existence) of the EU.

This chapter will start by analysing the historical background and the development of the case law on fundamental rights since, despite the introduction of the Charter, an understanding of the previous case law is vital to appreciate when and how fundamental rights apply in the EU. We will then analyse the main Treaty provisions relating to fundamental rights protection, including Article 7 TEU and its inability to successfully address the rule of law crisis, to then turn to the Charter of Fundamental Rights of the EU. In the last section, we will look at the relationship between the EU and the ECHR, including the extent to which the European Court of Human Rights (ECtHR) accepts to scrutinize EU acts. We will then look at the first draft agreement on the EU's accession to the ECHR, the Court's objections to that agreement together with the solutions proposed by the contracting parties to overcome such objections in the Draft Revised Accession Agreement.

[2] Commission Decision on a request for an opinion (1/25) of the Court of Justice pursuant to Art 218(11)TFEU in relation to the draft agreement providing for the accession of the European Union to the Convention for the Protection of Human Rights and Fundamental Freedoms, C(2025)3950, https://ec.europa.eu/transparency/documents-register/detail?ref=C(2025)3950&lang=en. It is utterly regrettable that the content of the decision has not been made public.

[3] In some instances, national courts are concerned about the fact that the standard of protection guaranteed by the Court of Justice is insufficient; see eg *Internationale Handelsgesellschaft* ('*Solange I*') [1974] 2 CMLR 540; the 'bananas saga' triggered by the ruling in Case C-280/93 *Germany v Council* [1994] ECR I-4973, N Reich 'Judge-Made "Europe à la Carte": Some Remarks on Recent Conflicts between European and German Constitutional Law Provoked by the Banana Litigation' (1996) *European Journal of International Law* 103–111; and, more recently, and in the context of the Charter, see Case C-399/11 *Melloni v Ministerio Fiscal*, EU:2013:107, discussed further in section 4.3.5. In relation to the problems raised by differing standards of protection in the context of the European Arrest Warrant, see the order of the Bundesverfassungsgericht (German Constitutional Court) of 15 December 2015, 2 BvR 2735/14; the Court of Justice then 'relaxed' its stance as to the presumption of equivalence in fundamental rights protection in the EU in relation to the European Arrest Warrant in Joined Cases C-404/15 *Aranyosi* and C-659/15 *Robert Căldăraru*, EU:2016:198.

2 Historical background and development of the case law

We have seen in chapter 2 how in the aftermath of the Second World War there was a drive towards international cooperation, which also laid the roots for the creation and development of the European Communities. Not surprisingly, the atrocities committed during the war provoked a reaction aimed at ensuring that the past could not repeat itself and, as a result, the codification and protection of fundamental rights became of paramount importance both at international[4] and national level.[5] In particular, in the European context, State parties created a new international instrument, the ECHR. The Convention is a catalogue of civil and political fundamental rights and States parties accepted not only to be bound by its rules but also to establish a supervisory mechanism through the European Commission of Human Rights and the ECtHR;[6] this would ensure that good intentions would not remain unfulfilled ideals. Given this background, it might come as a surprise that fundamental rights were largely absent from the founding European Treaties;[7] the reason for such a gap is that, according to the original plans, European cooperation was to be part of a much broader political project which also comprised a European Defence Community Treaty and a European Political Community Treaty. The latter, provided as its first aim 'to contribute towards the protection of human rights and fundamental freedoms in the Member States'.[8] Furthermore, it incorporated the rights and freedoms contained in the ECHR (in Part I),[9] and it limited accession to the Political Community to those European States that guaranteed fundamental rights as provided in the ECHR.[10] However (and as seen in chapter 2), both the Defence and the Political Community Treaties were abandoned in 1954 as the French national assembly would not ratify the former. As a result, fundamental rights remained largely absent from the founding Treaties establishing the three Communities.[11]

2.1 The development of the case law of the Court of Justice

This fundamental rights gap became all too apparent at a very early stage in the life of the Communities: in particular, national courts feared that Member States could use the Communities in order to circumvent the fundamental rights guarantees that had been at the centre of the post-war constitutionalizing effort. If the Communities had been given regulatory powers which could directly affect individuals, and those powers were not

[4] Universal Declaration of Human Rights 1948; and ECHR (n 6).

[5] See eg the German and Italian Constitutions; the commitment to fundamental rights protection, including through international cooperation, is now being challenged by some political forces; take for instance the structural changes and attacks on the judiciary in Hungary and Poland, examined later in section 3.1.

[6] Until 1998, the European Commission of Human Rights acted as gatekeeper and decided on the admissibility of cases. Following the entry into force of Protocol 11 ECHR, the Commission has been abolished. The system was further restructured following the entry into force of Protocol 14 ECHR in 2010; this Protocol also provides for the possibility for the EU to join the Convention, subject (according to the explanatory report to the Convention) to the negotiation of a separate treaty to this effect (on which, see section 5.2).

[7] With the exception of the right not to be discriminated against on grounds of sex in relation to pay which was included from the start.

[8] See Information and Official Documents of the Constitutional Committee of the Ad Hoc Assembly (Paris 1953) 53 *et seq* (Art 2).

[9] See ibid, 53 *et seq* (Art 3). [10] Ibid (Art 116).

[11] See G de Búrca, 'The Evolution of EU Human Rights Law' in P Craig and G de Búrca, *The Evolution of EU Law* (2nd edn, Oxford: Oxford University Press, 2011).

curtailed by fundamental rights, then individuals might see their fundamental rights limited beyond what was permissible under their own constitutional arrangements.

In an initial stage, individuals sought to enforce domestic fundamental rights against the (then) Communities' institutions.[12] However, those attempts failed since EU law (and previously EEC/EC law) can only be measured according to its own constitutional standards, otherwise the principle of supremacy would be compromised and the application of EU law would vary from one country to the other. The problem then was a serious one: national courts were not willing to allow executive action, even if exercised through international cooperation, to go unchecked, rather declaring that ultimately they would exercise jurisdiction to assess compatibility with (domestic) fundamental rights.[13] In this way, one of the very foundations of the emerging European building—the principle of supremacy of EU law—was at risk of being compromised.[14] It did not take long for the Court of Justice to find that fundamental rights were part of the 'general principles of Community law' which the Court would protect (on the broader context of the general principles, see chapter 8).

In the case of *Stauder*,[15] Mr Stauder attacked a Commission decision which made the distribution of butter at reduced prices conditional upon the identification of the recipient; he claimed that having to be identified by name breached his right to dignity as protected by the German Constitution. The German court referred a question to the Court of Justice to assess the validity of the Commission's decision. However, this time the national court did not enquire as to the compatibility of a Community act with its own national constitutional fundamental rights; rather, it enquired whether the regime provided by the decision was 'compatible with the *general principles* of Community law in force'.[16] Having examined different language versions of the Commission's decision, the Court of Justice found that identification by name was not required by the Community act. It then continued:

> Interpreted in this way the provision at issue contains nothing capable of ***prejudicing the fundamental human rights enshrined in the general principles of Community law*** and protected by the Court.[17]

The Court therefore made clear that:

- it considered fundamental rights unwritten general principles applicable to the acts of the Communities' institutions;
- it would protect such rights, so that an act of the Communities adopted in breach of fundamental rights would be declared void; and
- if more than one interpretation of a legal instrument was possible, that which did not infringe fundamental rights would have to be adopted.

[12] Case 1/58 *Stork v High Authority* [1959] ECR 17; Joined Cases 36–40/59 *Geitling v High Authority* [1960] ECR 425; Case 40/64 *Sgarlata v Commission* [1965] ECR 215.

[13] *Solange I* (n 3); see also *Steinike und Weinling* [1980] 2 CMLR 531; and cf also the Italian Constitutional Court rulings Sentenza 7/3/64, no 14 (in F Sorrentino, *Profili Costituzionali dell'Integrazione Comunitaria* (2nd edn, Turin: Giappichelli Editore, 1996) 61 *et seq*) and *Societá Acciaierie San Michele v High Authority* (27 December 1965, no 98) [1967] CMLR 160.

[14] Some authors (eg P Craig and G de Búrca, *EU Law: Text, Cases, and Materials* (5th edn, Oxford: Oxford University Press, 2011) 364) believe that the recognition of fundamental rights as general principles was due primarily to pressure from national courts; however, it should be pointed out that it is unlikely that experienced judges and jurists coming from countries with a strong constitutional ethos would be insensitive to such a major constitutional gap.

[15] Case 29/69 *Stauder* [1969] ECR 419.

[16] Ibid, para 1 (emphasis added).

[17] Ibid, para 7 (emphasis added).

In subsequent case law the Court clarified that in deciding which fundamental rights formed part of the general principles of Community law it would draw inspiration from constitutional traditions common to the Member States[18] and from international Treaties for the protection of human rights to which Member States were signatory or had collaborated;[19] of those, the most significant is without doubt the ECHR.[20]

As mentioned previously, the gap-filling function of general principles was of paramount importance not only to ensure that the Communities would be a constitutionally complete system, but also to assuage the fears of national courts in relation to fundamental rights protection. While at first, some national courts, and especially the German Federal Constitutional Court, were cautious in relinquishing jurisdiction,[21] with time it was accepted that the standard of protection afforded by the Court of Justice could be considered equivalent (never identical) to that afforded by domestic courts, so that the latter could entrust the review of the validity of Community/Union acts to the judgment of the Court of Justice.[22] This approach was therefore compatible with the *Foto-Frost* ruling,[23] where the Court made clear that it had sole jurisdiction to declare an act of the EU invalid.

3 The response of the political institutions: from the 1977 Declaration to the Lisbon Treaty

It was mentioned previously that the gap in the Treaties concerning fundamental rights protection was largely coincidental; it is not surprising then that the developments in the case law of the Court met with the approval of the political institutions. In 1977, just eight years after the ruling in *Stauder* and once the case law was 'settled', the European

[18] Case 11/70 *Internationale Handelsgesellschaft* [1970] ECR 1125, para 4.

[19] Case 4/73 *Nold* [1974] ECR 491, para 13.

[20] See eg Case 222/84 *Johnston v Royal Ulster Constabulary* [1986] ECR 1651; Case C-260/89 *Elliniki Radiophonia Tiléorassi AE (ERT) v Dimotiki Etairia Pliroforissis* [1991] ECR I-2925; Opinion 2/94 [1996] ECR I-1783; Case C-299/95 *Kremzow v Austria* [1997] ECR I-2629.

[21] *Solange I* (n 3); see also *Steinike und Weinling* [1980] 2 CMLR 531; see also the Italian Constitutional Court rulings Sentenza 7/3/64, no 14 (in Sorrentino, *Profili Costituzionali dell'Integrazione Comunitaria* (n 13) 61 *et seq*) and *Societá Acciaierie San Michele* (n 13). On the *Solange* decision, see chapter 4, case study 4.1.

[22] *Wünsche Handelsgesellschaft* ('*Solange II*') [1987] 3 CMLR 225; this said the relationship between national supreme courts and the Court of Justice in relation to fundamental rights protection is a complex one; see eg *Maastricht* decision (*Brunner v EU Treaty* [1994] 1 CMLR 57); German Federal Constitutional Court, decision 7 June 2000 [2000] *Human Rights Law Journal* 251; and *Treaty of Lisbon* decision [2010] 3 CMLR 13; French Conseil Constitutionnel, Decision No 2004–496 (10 June 2004); Decision No 2004–497 (1 July 2004); the Polish Constitutional Court ruling in *Trybunal Konstytucyjny, arrêt du 27.04.05, P 1/05, Dziennik Ustaw 2005.77.680*, as reported by *Réflets-Informations rapides sur les développements juridiques présentant un intérêt communautaire*, no 2/2005, p 16, also available at https://isap.sejm.gov.pl/isap.nsf/DocDetails.xsp?id=WDU20050770680. See A Pliakos and G Anagnostaras, 'Who Is the Ultimate Arbiter? The Battle over Judicial Supremacy in the EU' (2011) 26 *European Law Review* 109. More recently, see the controversy sparked by the *Taricco* (Case C-105/14, EU.C:2015:555) ruling in Italy which gave rise to the first preliminary reference by the Italian Constitutional Court, Ordinanza 24/2017, available on www.cortecostituzionale.it/actionSchedaPronuncia.do?anno=2017&numero=24, then settled by the Court of Justice in Case C-42/17 *MAS and MB*, EU:C:2017:936; controversies continued though in the light of an obiter of the Italian Constitutional Court in Sentenza 269/2017, which indicated that where both domestic and EU fundamental rights could apply, national courts would have to refer the matter first to the Italian Constitutional Court to assess whether protection was available in the Italian Constitution before referring the case to the Court of Justice. This would have put the Italian Constitutional Court at odds with the case law of the Court of Justice. The Italian Constitutional Court then changed its course in Sentenza 20/2019. On these issues, see G Martinico and G Repetto, 'Fundamental Rights and Constitutional Duels in Europe: An Italian Perspective on Case 269/2017 and Its Aftermath' (2019) 15 *European Constitutional Law Review* 731.

[23] Case 314/85 *Foto-Frost* [1987] ECR 4199, and see chapter 10.

Parliament, the Council, and the Commission issued a joint declaration to the effect that they considered themselves bound by fundamental rights as general principles of (then) Community law.[24] After that, every Treaty revision strengthened the protection of fundamental rights in the EU.[25] In particular, following the expansion of Union competences in the field of asylum, immigration, and criminal law, the protection of fundamental rights in the EU became of paramount importance for many of the Member States. The process of codification of the Court's case law, and the ongoing attention to fundamental rights, culminated in 2000 with the drafting of the Charter of Fundamental Rights of the European Union.[26] While at first the Charter was 'merely' proclaimed by the three political institutions, almost mirroring the 1977 Declaration, the Lisbon Treaty subsequently gave it the 'same legal value' as the Treaties themselves (Article 6(1) TEU). Furthermore, and as we shall see in more detail later, the debate as to whether the Union should become a party to the ECHR has finally received a positive answer and Article 6(2) TEU provides not only the competence for accession but also a legal obligation to do so.[27]

Article 6 TEU also recognizes the continued relevance of the case law preceding the Charter; Article 6(3) TEU provides that:

> Fundamental rights, as guaranteed by the European Convention for the Protection of Human Rights and Fundamental Freedoms and as they result from the constitutional traditions common to the Member States, shall constitute general principles of the Union's law.

Thus, even after the incorporation of the Charter in the primary law of the EU, the Treaty restates the centrality of fundamental rights, the ECHR, and the common constitutional traditions, as general principles of Union law.[28] Article 6(3) therefore allows the Court of Justice to go beyond the rights contained in the Charter, should the need ever arise.[29]

Besides Article 6 TEU, the Lisbon Treaty further enhanced the protection of fundamental rights in several fields. Thus, for instance, it provides for (almost) full jurisdiction of the Court of Justice in the field of cooperation in criminal law;[30] for the Court's jurisdiction to review Common Foreign and Security Policy (CFSP) decisions that provide for

[24] OJ [1977] C103/1.

[25] See Preamble to the Single European Act; Art F(2) TEU (Maastricht version); Arts 7, 46, and 49 TEU as modified and renumbered by the Treaty of Amsterdam; and the modification to Art 7 TEU introduced by the Treaty of Nice.

[26] Charter of Fundamental Rights (OJ [2000] C364/1); other initiatives in the field of fundamental rights include the establishment of an EU Fundamental Rights Agency, Regulation (EC) No 168/2007 establishing a European Union Agency for Fundamental Rights (OJ [2007] L53/1).

[27] However, see later on the obstacles to accession to the ECHR following the ruling of the Court of Justice in Opinion 2/13.

[28] On the 'multiple' sources of fundamental rights, see HCH Hofmann and BC Mihaescu, 'The Relation between the Charter's Fundamental Rights and the Unwritten General Principles of EU Law: Good Administration as the Test Case' (2013) 9 *European Constitutional Law Review* 73; on the post-Lisbon fundamental rights landscape, see S Morano-Foadi and S Andreadakis, 'Reflections on the Architecture of the EU after the Treaty of Lisbon: The European Judicial Approach to Fundamental Rights' (2011) 17 *European Law Journal* 595.

[29] eg while the right to good administration in Art 41 of the Charter only applies to EU bodies, the Court has confirmed that this right remains a general principle of EU law as regards national authorities. See eg Case C-166/13 *Mukarubega*, EU:C:2014:2336, paras 44 and 45 and more recently Case C-230/18 *PI v Landespolizeidirektion Tirol*, EU:C:2019:383.

[30] See chapter 24. However, Art 276 TFEU excludes jurisdiction for the Court of Justice to review the validity and proportionality of police and law enforcement operations of a Member State, or the exercise of Member States' responsibilities as regards law and order and internal security.

measures against natural or legal persons;[31] and for slightly relaxed conditions for standing before the Union Courts.[32]

Finally, respect for fundamental rights, as well as the other values listed in Article 2 TEU, is a precondition for accession to the EU,[33] and relevant for participation in the EU. For this reason, Article 7 TEU provides for a procedure to police and react to the risk of serious breaches of those values, which we shall now examine in more detail.

3.1 Article 7 TEU and the rule of law crisis

As we shall see later in this chapter, the Charter applies to Member States whenever they are 'implementing' EU law, that is to say when they give effect to EU law or limit one of the free movement rights. Furthermore, and as already mentioned, respect for fundamental rights, the rule of law, and democracy is a precondition for accession to the EU. However, the EU does not have general fundamental rights competence: this means that the Commission (in particular) cannot bring infringement proceedings against a Member State that is violating fundamental rights, unless a connection with EU law can be established.[34]

In a European Union which is founded on fundamental rights, democracy, and the rule of law (Article 2 TEU) this creates considerable tension since the EU cannot force its Member States to respect those same rights and values. It is for this reason that the Amsterdam Treaty introduced a procedure (now contained in Article 7 TEU) to allow the EU to react to a 'serious and persistent breach' of the values contained in Article 2 TEU by one of its Member States. However, following the election in Austria of Mr Haider, the leader of a far-right political party, the limits of that provision became all too apparent: the EU could only react to a breach of Article 2 TEU values *after* it had occurred; it was not empowered to act to prevent such breach from occurring in the first place.[35] As a result, Article 7 TEU was amended by the Nice Treaty, to empower the EU to act also when there is a 'clear risk' of breach of Article 2 TEU values. In its current version, then, Article 7 TEU provides two 'safeguard' mechanisms to ensure compliance with the foundational values by the Member States:

- In case of a 'clear risk' of breach of foundational values the Council can issue recommendations to the Member State in question and it can monitor the situation. The procedure can be triggered by a reasoned proposal of one third of the Member States (excluding the vote of the Member State under scrutiny), by the European Parliament, or by the Commission. In order to make the finding the Council must vote with a four-fifths majority.
- On the other hand, the determination of a 'serious and persistent' breach of the foundational values must be agreed by the European Council, that is, by the heads of State or government, unanimously (minus the vote of the Member State in question), with the consent of the European Parliament. In this case, though, the procedure can only be initiated by one-third of the Member States or by the Commission, and not by the European

[31] Art 275(2) TFEU; furthermore, the Court has greatly expanded the scope of its own jurisdiction in CFSP thus paving the way to accession to the ECHR; see below and chapter 26.

[32] See chapter 10. [33] Art 49 TEU. [34] See section 3.1.1.

[35] The Haider affair was admittedly handled very badly by the Member States and following criticism it led to the so-called wise men report: M Ahtisaari, J Frowein, and M Oreja, 'Report on the Austrian government's commitment to the common European values, in particular concerning the rights of minorities, refugees and immigrants, and the evolution of the political nature of the FPÖ (The Wise Men Report)' (2001) 20 *International Legal Materials* 102. The report recommended an amendment to Art 7 TEU, creating a Fundamental Rights Agency, and giving legal value to the Charter.

Parliament. After this determination is made, the Council, by qualified majority, might adopt 'sanctions' including the suspension of the voting rights of the Member State concerned, and the suspension of some of the rights deriving from the Treaties. However, the Council must also take into account the consequences of such deliberations on the rights of natural and legal persons.

Article 7 TEU might seem at first sight a very balanced compromise between the need to respect the separation of powers of the EU and its Member States, while at the same time ensuring that all the members of the EU respect the EU foundational values. It is for this reason that Article 7 TEU has been devised as a political mechanism, and not one that gives competence to the Commission to just 'go after' non-compliant Member States. And yet, the political nature of the Article 7 TEU procedure is the reason why it has been ineffective in dealing with threats to the foundational values which have occurred in the past decade, in particular (but not only) in Hungary and Poland.[36] In both countries, the rule of law has been under serious and sustained attack by governments aiming to ensure a compliant judiciary. It took several years before Article 7(1) TEU was triggered, by the European Parliament in relation to Hungary and the Commission in relation to Poland.[37] Despite this however, there has not yet been a vote in Council to support an Article 7(1) decision—the majority required is so high that it has proven impossible to secure sufficient backing for the procedure.[38] Furthermore, there is no prospect of any sanctions ex Article 7(2) TEU being imposed since, in order to do so, a prior unanimous European Council decision is necessary. Thus, de facto, the EU has been unable to react to increasingly authoritarian governments within its Member States. This situation has led to two, parallel, developments: first of all, a series of sectoral challenges against single pieces of legislation relying on whatever piece of EU law available, including through the activation of other Treaty provisions, most notably Article 19 TEU and Article 2 TEU.[39] Secondly, a series of proposals aimed at addressing the structural inadequacy of Article 7 TEU without the need of a Treaty amendment (which would require unanimity and hence it is inconceivable while the rule of law crisis persists). We shall look at both in turn.

3.1.1 **Addressing the rule of law crisis: the case law and the proposals**

As said earlier in this chapter, the Commission has used every tool in its armoury to challenge single offending measures: for instance it has brought proceedings against Hungary on the grounds that by imposing a new mandatory retirement age for judges it breached age discrimination rules; it relied on the free movement of capital and services to challenge restrictions on

[36] For a comprehensive overview of the threat and challenges also in other EU Member States, see the Annual Rule of Law Cycle and the Commission Rule of Law Reports, with country-by-country chapters.

[37] European Parliament resolution of 12 September 2018 on a proposal calling on the Council to determine, pursuant to Article 7(1) of the Treaty on European Union, the existence of a clear risk of a serious breach by Hungary of the values on which the Union is founded (2017/2131(INL)), P8_TA(2018)0340; European Commission, Reasoned proposal in accordance with Article 7(1) of the Treaty on European Union regarding the Rule of Law in Poland, COM(2017)835 final, 20 December 2017.

[38] See more recently European Parliament Resolution, Ongoing hearings under Article 7(1) TEU regarding Poland and Hungary, 5 May 2022 P9_TA(2022)0204; see also the joint urgent opinion of the Venice Commission and the Directorate General of Human Rights and Rule of Law of the Council of Europe on amendments to the law on the common courts, the law on the supreme court, and some other laws (CDL-PI (2020)002-e), www.venice.coe.int/webforms/documents/?pdf=CDL-PI(2020)002-e.

[39] See Case C-192/18 *Commission v Poland (Independence of ordinary courts)*, EU:C:2019:529 and ensuing case law discussed below; Art 2 TEU is becoming increasingly relevant; at the time of writing, the Court has not yet delivered its ruling in Case C-769/22 *European Commission v Hungary (Valeurs de l'Union)*, which will clarify the extent to which this provision can be relied upon to challenge breaches of EU foundational values; see AG Ćapeta, EU:C:2025:408.

the operation of NGOs, and on the General Agreement on Trade in Services (GATS) to challenge the de facto expulsion of the Central European University from Hungary.[40]

However, by far the most important constitutional development in this respect stems from the *Commission v Poland* case on the independence of the judiciary. It has been mentioned earlier that both Poland and Hungary have attempted to curtail judicial independence through sweeping reforms. Building on a previous case,[41] the Commission challenged judicial reforms in Poland by relying on a breach of Article 19(1) TEU. The latter states that Member States have to 'provide remedies that are sufficient to ensure effective legal protection in the fields covered by Union law'.[42] The Commission successfully argued that failure to ensure the independence of the judiciary inherently affects legal protection in fields covered by EU law. In this way, even lacking a more general fundamental rights competence, reforms that weaken significantly judicial independence can be challenged, and even sanctioned since the Court of Justice can impose fines for failure to comply with its rulings.[43] Furthermore, in subsequent cases,[44] the Court refined its reasoning, by imposing on the (new?) Member States a non-regression obligation, at least in terms of the independence of the judiciary. In particular, in the *Republika* case, the issue related to whether changes in the Maltese Constitution in relation to the appointment of judges threatened judicial independence by giving excessive discretion to the executive. Whereas the Court of Justice found that the new rules did not constitute a threat to judicial independence, it used the case to provide a more nuanced, and detailed, ruling on the obligations bestowed upon Member States by EU membership. In particular, the Court linked the process of accession to the need to ensure the independence of the judiciary (a core element of the rule of law). Thus, the Court reasoned, given that States' accession to the EU is conditional upon certain criteria being met, among which adherence and promotion of the values enshrined in Article 2 TEU,[45] then a Member State cannot regress in

[40] eg Case C-286/12 *Commission v Hungary (Mandatory retirement of judges)*, EU:C:2012:687; Case C-288/12 *Commission v Hungary*, EU:C:2014:237 (*Mandatory retirement of data protection supervisory authority*); Case C-78/18 *Commission v Hungary* (*NGOs*), EU:C:2020:476; Case C-66/18 *Commission v Hungary* (*lex CEU*), EU:C:2020:792.

[41] Case C-64/16 *Associação Sindical dos Juízes Portugueses v Tribunal de Contas*, EU:C:2018:117.

[42] Case C-619/18 *Commission v Poland* (*Independence of the Supreme Court*), EU:C:2019:615; and from the ECHR perspective, *Xero Flor w Polsce sp z oo v Poland* (Appl No 4907/18), ECtHR, judgment of 7 August 2021. On the use of infringement actions as part of the Commission's rule of law toolkit, see M Bonelli, 'Infringement Actions 2.0: How to Protect EU Values before the Court of Justice' (2022) 18 *European Constitutional Law Review* 30; and for a broader analysis, see P Van Elsuwege and F Gremmelprez, 'Protecting the Rule of Law in the EU Legal Order: A Constitutional Role for the European Court of Justice' (2020) 16 *European Constitutional Law Review* 8.

[43] Fines of €1 million per day had been imposed on Poland for non-compliance with the Court's ruling, see Case C-204/21 R *Commission v Poland*, EU:C:2021:978. There is now a growing body of case law on Art 19(1) TEU; see eg Joined Cases C-615 and 617/20 *JP and Others* (C-615/20), *MM* (C-671/20), intervening parties: *Prokuratura Okręgowa w Warszawie, Komisja Nadzoru Finansowego and Others*, EU:C:2023:562; Case C430/21 *RS*, EU:C:2022:99; Case C-487/19 *W Ż*, EU:C:2021:798.

[44] Case C-896/19 *Republika*, EU:C:2021:311; Joined Cases C-83/19, C-127/19, C-195/19, C-291/19, C-355/19, and C-397/19 *Asociația 'Forumul Judecătorilor din România*, EU:C:2021:393, and see M Moraru and R Bercea, 'The First Episode in the Romanian Rule of Law Saga: Joined Cases C-83/19, C-127/19, C-195/19, C-291/19, C-355/19 and C-397/19, *Asociatia Forumul Judecatoril or din Romania*, and their follow-up' (2022) 18 *European Constitutional Law Review* 82; C Rizcallah and V Davio, 'The Requirement That Tribunals Be Established by Law: A Valuable Principle Safeguarding the Rule of Law and the Separation of Powers in the Context of Trust' (2021) 17 *European Constitutional Law Review* 581; M Leloup, 'Who Safeguards the Guardians? A Subjective Right of Judges to Their Independence under Article 6(1) ECHR' (2021) 17 *European Constitutional Law Review* 394.

[45] Art 2 TEU provides: 'The Union is founded on the values of respect for human dignity, freedom, democracy, equality, the *rule of law* and respect for human rights, including the rights of persons belonging to minorities. These values are common to the Member States in a society in which pluralism, non-discrimination, tolerance, justice, solidarity and equality between women and men prevail' (emphasis added).

relation to the organization of justice from the situation at the time of accession and upon which accession was based. In this way, the Court provides an objective benchmark, the situation at the time of accession, vis-à-vis which to judge reforms to the organization of justice. In *LG*,[46] the Court, building on its own case law and relying on the findings of the ECtHR,[47] clarified that it will refuse a preliminary ruling request from a court that does not satisfy the criterion of independence.

This said, whereas this case law has major constitutional implications,[48] both in relation to upholding some of the values of the EU and in redrawing the boundaries of Member States' discretion in determining their judicial system,[49] in practice it has limited effects given that it is for the Member States themselves to ensure compliance with the rulings of the Court of Justice. For this reason, the Commission has also sought to develop other tools to address the rule of law crisis. In particular, after instituting a rule of law framework to guide its own action in relation to Article 7 TEU proceedings,[50] the Commission has articulated its action around three key concepts; *promotion*, *prevention*, and *response*.[51]

The rule of law is promoted through building knowledge and rule of law culture; prevention is achieved especially through a rule of law cycle, including an annual rule of law report with discrete chapters for each country; and response entails a strategic approach to infringement proceedings as well as the possibility to limit access to certain European funds in case of rule of law breaches which affect the integrity of the EU budget (so-called rule of law conditionality Regulation).[52] In the writer's opinion, of the rule of law toolkit, Regulation 2020/2092 might perhaps be the most effective, so it is worth looking at it in detail.

The Commission first proposed a Regulation to protect the Union's budget from 'generalised deficiencies as regards the rule of law' in 2018, and its remit was broader than the compromised reached in the adopted Regulation.[53] It is important to note that the Regulation, being adopted under qualified majority voting, would have bypassed the veto of those Member States where the rule of law was already backsliding (notably Hungary and Poland, but not only). Yet, between the first proposal for the Regulation and its adoption, the Covid-19 pandemic occurred: as discussed in chapter 2, the EU reacted comparatively swiftly to support its Member States by means of the NextGeneration EU plan. The latter, as is well known, made available to Member States a considerable amount of funds, through both grants and loans, and its rapid approval

[46] Case C-718/21 *LG v Krajowa Rada Sądownictwa*, EU:C:2023:1015.

[47] Case C-187/19 *WŻ* (*Chamber of Extraordinary Control and Public Affairs of the Supreme Court—Appointment*), EU:C:2021:798; Case C-132/20 *BN, DM, EN v Getin Noble Bank SA*, EU:C:2022:235; *Dolińska-Ficek and Ozimek v Poland* (CE:ECHR:2021:1108JUD004986819)

[48] See also K Lenaerts, 'New Horizons for the Rule of Law within the EU' (2020) 21 *German Law Journal* 29.

[49] Art 19(1) TEU, together with Art 47 CFR, has now acquired a strategic importance to ensure effective judicial protection in all fields; see eg Case C-600/23 *Royal Football Club Seraing SA*, EU:C:2025:617; Case C-292/23 *IRO, FJLR* (*EPPO*), EU:C:2025:255; Case C-430/21 *RS*, EU:C:2022:99; Joined Cases C-354/20 PPU and C-412/20 PPU *Openbaar Ministerie* (*Indépendance de l'autorité judiciaire d'émission*), EU:C:2020:1033.

[50] Commission Communication, 'A new EU Framework to Strengthen the Rule of Law', COM(2014) 158 final; Council Legal Service believes there was no legal basis for the Commission's framework, see Council Legal Service Opinion on Commission's rule of law framework (http://data.consilium.europa.eu/doc/document/ST-10296-2014-INIT/en/pdf).

[51] See Communication from the Commission to the European Parliament, the European Council, the Council, the European Economic and Social Committee and the Committee of the Regions strengthening the rule of law within the Union. A blueprint for action, COM/2019/343 final.

[52] Regulation 2020/2092 on a general regime of conditionality for the protection of the Union budget (OJ [2020] L433 I/1), hereinafter Regulation 2020/2092 or the 'conditionality Regulation'.

[53] (COM(2018) 324); as we shall see, Regulation 2092/2020 is limited to instances where rule of law breaches affect the Union budget in a '*sufficiently direct way*'.

was crucial to ensure the post-pandemic recovery. Because of the novelty and magnitude of the recovery plan, the operation was linked to the own resources decision,[54] the approval of which requires the unanimous consent of the Member States as well as ratification at national level pursuant to the domestic constitutional requirements. The unanimity requirement was then used as a bargaining chip for the amendment, and watering down, of the conditionality Regulation. Furthermore, as part of this compromise, the European Council conclusions of December 2020 held that the Commission would adopt guidelines on the way it would apply the Regulation (although no such requirement is contained in the Regulation itself), and that those guidelines would not be adopted until any potential action for annulment of the Regulation would be decided by the European Court of Justice. The conclusions also clarified that the Commission would not propose any measure under the Regulation until the guidelines were published,[55] hence determining a de facto (and legally dubious) delay in the operation of the conditionality Regulation.[56] Not surprisingly, Hungary and Poland challenged the Regulation,[57] but were unsuccessful in their pursuit, and the Commission has now published the guidelines for the application of Regulation 2092/2020, taking into account the above-mentioned rulings.[58]

In brief, the conditionality Regulation allows for the withholding and suspension of EU funds when breaches of the rule of law by a Member State 'affect or seriously risk affecting the sound financial management of the Union budget or the protection of the financial interests of the Union in *a sufficiently direct way*'.[59] The Regulation also offers a definition of the rule of law, linking it clearly with the foundational values in Article 2 TEU, and gives a non-exhaustive list of examples of breaches relevant for the purposes of the Regulation. The initiation of the procedure is in the hands of the Commission, so that it falls upon the latter, when it has 'reasonable grounds' to believe that the conditions provided for in the Regulation are satisfied, to send a written notification to the Member State in question. The Member State has a duty to provide the Commission with the information requested (if any) and a right to make observations within a time-limit, decided by the Commission itself, of between one and three months. The Member State also has the

[54] See generally B de Witte, 'The European Union's Covid-19 Recovery Plan: The Legal Engineering of an Economic Policy Shift' (2021) 58 *Common Market Law Review* 635.

[55] See European Council Conclusions 11 December 2020, EUCO 22/20, I(2)(c). On the legislative history of Regulation 2092/2020 as well as the political context, see S Platon, 'Bringing a Knife to a Gunfight: The European Parliament, the Rule of Law Conditionality, and the Action for Failure to Act', VerfBlog, 2021/6/11, https://verfassungsblog.de/bringing-a-knife-to-a-gunfight/, DOI: 10.17176/20210611-193356-0.

[56] The European Parliament brought an action against the Commission for failure to act, Case C-657/21 *European Parliament v Commission*, which it then decided to discontinue (see Order of the President of the Court, 8 June 2022).

[57] Case C-156/21 *Hungary v European Parliament and Council* (*Conditionality Regulation*), EU:C:2022:97; Case C-157/21 *Poland v European Parliament and Council* (*Conditionality Regulation*), EU:C:2022:98; and on the rulings, see F Weber, 'The Pluralism of Values in an Identity-Framed Verbund: Federal Belonging in the European Union after the Rule of Law Conditionality Judgments' (2022) 47 *European Law Review* 514; M Fisicaro 'Protection of the Rule of Law and "Competence Creep" via the Budget: The Court of Justice on the Legality of the Conditionality Regulation: ECJ judgments of 16 February 2022, Cases C-156/21, *Hungary v Parliament and Council* and C-157/21, *Poland v Parliament and Council*' (2022) 18 *European Constitutional Law Review* 334.

[58] Communication from the Commission Guidelines on the application of the Regulation (EU, EURATOM) 2020/2092 on a general regime of conditionality for the protection of the Union budget (OJ [2022] C123/02).

[59] Art 4, Regulation 2092/2020.

right to submit observations on the next stage of the procedure, when the Commission proposes the sanctioning measures. After that the Commission submits a proposal for an implementing decision to the Council. The Council must adopt the implementing decision, but it can amend it by qualified majority.[60]

The conditionality Regulation introduces a real financial incentive to reverse reforms that are incompatible with the rule of law. However, it remains a political mechanism in the hands of the Commission and Council, with very limited involvement for the European Parliament, and little guarantee that it will be used consistently. Furthermore, there is a risk that counter-backsliding reforms might be cosmetic and/or ineffective, and/or evaluated positively because of competing concerns. For instance, significant doubts have been raised in relation to the Commission's decision that sufficient progress had been made by Hungary justifying the release of funding previously held up pursuant to the Conditionality Regulation.[61] The European Parliament has therefore brought annulment proceedings arguing, inter alia, that the Commission had misused its power in order to ensure that Hungary would lift its veto in relation to European Council decisions relating to Ukraine.[62]

4 The Charter of Fundamental Rights

The adoption of the EU's Charter of Fundamental Rights is one of the most significant constitutional steps in the history of the EU.[63] This is particularly so for two reasons: first of all, the Charter was drafted using a new (and some might say revolutionary) procedure which involved not only representatives of national governments but also representatives of national and European parliaments.

Secondly, the fact that Member States felt the need to adopt a fundamental rights document (even though there is no general fundamental rights competence for the EU) is a further step in the long process of the constitutional evolution of the EU. We will first analyse the way the Charter was drafted and explain, in broad terms, its content, before turning to its scope of application.

[60] At the time of writing, the European Commission has triggered the conditionality mechanism in relation to Hungary (www.reuters.com/world/europe/eu-gives-hungary-month-act-before-moving-suspend-funds-2022-07-22/) which was then amended (https://www.consilium.europa.eu/en/press/press-releases/2022/12/12/rule-of-law-conditionality-mechanism/), but not in relation to Poland. In relation to the latter, the Council has now approved the Polish recovery plan so as to authorize the release of funds. In an unprecedented move, four associations of European judges brought annulment proceedings against the Council decision approving the release of the recovery funds on the grounds that Poland has failed to effectively implement the rulings of the Court of Justice to ensure an impartial judiciary. However, the case was held to be inadmissible for lack of standing of the associations, see Case T-530/22 *Medel v Council*, EU:T:2024:363 appeal pending at the time of writing (Case C-555/24 P) and see https://www.politico.eu/article/european-judges-sue-council-over-polish-recovery-plan/.

[61] Commission Implementing Decision C(2023) 9014 of 13 December 2023 on the approval and signature of the Commission assessment, in accordance with Art 15(4) of Regulation (EU) 2021/1060, of the fulfilment of the horizontal enabling condition '3. Effective application and implementation of the Charter of Fundamental Rights' with regard to the deficiencies in judicial independence in Hungary.

[62] Case C-225/24 *European Parliament v Commission* (*Funding to Hungary*), case pending at the time of writing. See also European Parliament, Press Release, 25 November 2025, 'Parliament sounds the alarm over Hungary's deepening rule of law crisis', https://www.europarl.europa.eu/news/en/press-room/20251120IPR31492/parliament-sounds-the-alarm-over-hungary-s-deepening-rule-of-law-crisis.

[63] For a detailed article-by-article analysis of the Charter, see S Peers, T Hervey, J Kenner, and A Ward (eds), *The EU Charter of Fundamental Rights: A Commentary* (2nd edn, Oxford: Hart Publishing, 2021).

4.1 The structure of the Charter

We have mentioned that the inclusion of national and European Parliamentarians in the drafting of the Charter was novel, being if anything more reminiscent of national constitution drafting than of international Treaty-making; equally novel was the choice made by the Convention to depart from the traditional dichotomy of civil and political rights/economic and social rights, instead approaching fundamental rights as an indivisible whole, hence placing all rights, at least theoretically, on the same level. The Charter is thus divided into titles according to six fundamental values: dignity, freedom, equality, solidarity, citizens' rights, and justice. The substantive provisions are then complemented by the Preamble and by the so-called horizontal provisions (Articles 51 to 54), which are general provisions that set out the scope of application of the Charter, the legitimate grounds of limits on, and derogations from, Charter rights, as well as the relationship with the ECHR, national constitutions, and international human rights treaties. As we shall see, the scope of application of the Charter mirrors that of the general principles so that the Charter applies to the Union institutions as well as to the Member States when they implement or act within the scope of Union law. The Charter is also complemented by 'explanations' which clarify the scope and, most importantly, the source of each of the Charter rights/provisions.[64] The identification of the 'origin' of Charter rights is of paramount importance for understanding their scope, since the Charter incorporates rights contained in other documents and in particular in the ECHR and in the TEU/TFEU. The Convention-derived rights must be interpreted to give *at least* the same protection granted by the Convention (Article 52(3)), while Treaty-derived rights must be given the same scope as their Treaty counterparts (Article 52(2)).

4.2 The substantive provisions of the Charter

4.2.1 Title I *Dignity* (Articles 1 to 5)

Title I contains those rights which are essential to the enjoyment of any other right: the right to human dignity;[65] the right to life; the right to the integrity of the person, which contains new generation rights such as the principle of informed consent in relation to medical intervention and the prohibition of eugenic practices; the prohibition of torture and inhuman and degrading treatment; and the prohibition of slavery and forced labour. As we shall see, in the *NS* case the prohibition of torture and inhuman treatment was relied upon to curtail the discretion of the UK and prevent it from deporting the claimants (asylum seekers) to Greece.[66]

[64] Explanations relating to the Charter of Fundamental Rights (OJ [2007] C303/02). Art 52(7) Charter provides that the explanations must be given 'due regard' by the courts of the Union and of the Member States; Art 6(1), third subpara, TEU provides that the Charter must be interpreted having due regard to the explanations: see eg Case C-198/13 *Hernández and others*, EU:C:2014:2055, para 33.

[65] See eg Case C-709/20 *CG*, EU:C:2021:602; Case C-233/18 *Haqbin*, EU:C:2019:956; Case C-377/98 *Netherlands v Council* (*'Biotechnology Directive'*) [2001] ECR I-7079; see also Case C-36/02 *Omega* [2004] ECR I-9609, esp para 34. Even though it is not expressly mentioned in the Convention, the right to dignity informs the interpretation of all Convention rights; eg *Tyrer v UK* (Appl No 5856/72) (1979–80) 2 EHRR 1.

[66] Joined Cases C-411/10 and C-493/10 *NS v Secretary of State for the Home Department*, EU:C:2011:13905. See section 4.4.2.

4.2.2 **Title II** ***Freedom*** **(Articles 6 to 19)**

This heading contains some of the traditional civil and political rights, such as the right to liberty;[67] the right to private life;[68] the right to freedom of expression; the right to property; some new generation rights, such as the right to the protection of personal data;[69] as well as some socio-economic rights, such as the right to work and the right to education. In the *Kadi* case, the Court addressed the legality of a Regulation, intended to fight international terrorism, freezing the assets of (inter alia) Mr Kadi. The Court held that while the freezing of Mr Kadi's assets could in principle have been justified, in the case at issue it violated his right to property because it did not provide for sufficient procedural guarantees.[70] In the *Alemo-Herron* case,[71] the Court held that the freedom to conduct a business provided for in Article 16 Charter could be relied upon to limit the discretion of a Member State to provide enhanced protection for employees in the case of a transfer of undertaking. Thus, the Court held that the employer's freedom to contract (part of the freedom to conduct a business) would be compromised by a dynamic clause that imposed contractual obligations without the business having been able to participate in the negotiations leading to its obligations. Similarly, in *Achbita* the Court found that Article 16 Charter could act as a counterweight to an individual's right not to be discriminated against on grounds of religion.[72]

4.2.3 **Title III** ***Equality*** **(Articles 20 to 26)**

Title III contains traditional equality rights (non-discrimination on grounds of sex, race, sexual orientation, religion, belief, etc),[73] together with the right not to be discriminated against on grounds of nationality within the scope of application of the Treaty and the rights of more vulnerable members of society such as children, the elderly, and disabled people. As we shall see further later, Article 21—the right not to be discriminated against—is capable in certain circumstances and for grounds covered in secondary legislation, of having horizontal direct effect (ie it can be invoked against a private party). For more on the application of these rights in EU law, see chapter 20.

4.2.4 **Title IV** ***Solidarity*** **(Articles 27 to 38)**

Title IV contains traditional social rights and 'principles', such as the right to collective bargaining and action, including the right to strike and protection against unjustified dismissal; the right to fair working conditions as well as protection for children and young

[67] For a rather restrictive interpretation, see eg Case C-294/16 PPU *JZ*, EU:C:2016:610.

[68] See eg Joined Cases C-593/12 and 594/12 *Digital Rights Ireland*, EU:C:2014:238, discussed later and Case C-362/14 *Schrems*, EU:C:2015:650.

[69] Now disciplined by Regulation 2016/679 on the protection of natural persons with regard to the processing of personal data and on the free movement of such data, and repealing Directive 95/46/EC (General Data Protection Regulation or GDPR) (OJ [2016] L119/1).

[70] Joined Cases C-402/05 P and C-415/05 P *Kadi and Al Barakaat v Council* ('*Kadi I*') [2008] ECR I-6351; see also the rulings in Case T-85/09 *Kadi II* [2010] ECR II-5177, and Joined Cases C-584/10, C-593/10, and C-595/10 P *Commission and UK v Kadi*, EU:C:2013:518.

[71] Case C-426/11 *Alemo-Herron*, EU:C:2013:521; see also eg Case C-201/15 *AGET Iraklis*, EU:C:2016:972; Case C-254/23 *INTERZERO Trajnostne rešitve za svet brez odpadkov doo and Others, Surovina, družba za predelavo odpadkov doo and Others*, EU:C:2025:569.

[72] Case C-157/15 *Samira Achbita v G4S Secure Solutions*, EU:C:2017:203.

[73] On freedom of religion, as protected by Directive 2000/78 establishing a general framework for equal treatment in employment and occupation (OJ [2000] L303/16), see eg Case C-188/15 *Bougnaoui and ADDH*, EU:C:2017:204; Case C-157/15 *Achbita*, EU:C:2017:203; Case C-414/16 *Egenberger*, EU:C:2018:257; Case C-193/17 *Cresco Investigation*, EU:C:2019:43; and for a more nuanced approach, see Joined Cases C-848/18 and C-341/19 *IX v WABE eV and MH Müller Handels GmbH v MJ*, EU:C:2021:594; Case C-344/20 *LF v SCRL*, EU:C:2022:774.

people at work, and protection for the family, including protection against dismissal linked to maternity. It also includes 'recognition' of social security and social assistance; access to services of general economic interests; and the 'right' to health care, as well as the obligation for the Union to ensure a high level of environmental and consumer protection in its policies. It should be noted that some of these rights are entirely dependent on national laws and practices; while others are 'principles', that is, not self-standing rights, rather instructions that establish the principles the Union legislature must respect.[74] Again, and as we shall see, some of those rights are capable of having horizontal direct effect. For more on the application of these rights in EU law, refer again to chapter 20.

4.2.5 **Title V *Citizens' rights* (Articles 39 to 46)**

Title V reproduces rights contained in the TFEU and mainly benefits only Union citizens. It includes the right to vote[75] and stand for elections in the European Parliament and in municipal elections in the Member State of residence, the right to move and reside freely in the territory of the Member States, and the right to consular and diplomatic protection, all limited to Union citizens. The 'administrative rights' in this title, such as the right to good administration, the right to access documents, the right to complain to the Ombudsman, and the right to petition, are also available to non-EU citizens resident or, in the case of legal persons, to companies having their registered office in the EU. As an example of how the rights in Title V apply in practice, see chapter 13 regarding the free movement of persons.

4.2.6 **Title VI *Justice* (Articles 47 to 50)**

Title VI is concerned with the administration of justice and draws mainly on the ECHR and on the common constitutional traditions of the Member States. It includes the right to an effective remedy and a fair trial; the right to be presumed innocent and the right of defence; the principle of legality and proportionality of criminal offences and penalties;[76] and the principle of *ne bis in idem*, which is to say the right not to be tried or punished twice for the same offence.[77] These rights were relevant, for instance, in the *Kadi* and *Fransson* cases discussed in this chapter. Furthermore, the right to an effective remedy has become pivotal in strengthening judicial protection in the EU and in its Member States.[78]

4.3 **The horizontal provisions**

As mentioned previously, Articles 51 to 54 set out the scope of application of the Charter, clarifying its field of application (Article 51), the scope and interpretation of rights and principles (Article 52),[79] the level of protection (Article 53), and the prohibition of abuse

[74] On the distinction between principles and rights, see also discussion on Art 52(5) in section 4.3.5.

[75] On the fact that the franchise for the European Parliament falls within the scope of EU law for the purposes of application of the Charter, see Case C-650/13 *Delvigne*, EU:C:2015:648.

[76] See eg Case C-42/17 *MAS and MB*, EU:C:2017:936.

[77] See eg Joined Cases C-596 and C-597/16 *Enzo di Puma*, EU:C:2018:192; Case C-537/16 *Garlsson Real Estate Sa*, EU:C:2018:193.

[78] eg in relation to the Court of Justice's jurisdiction in CFSP, Joined Cases C-29/22 and C-44/22 P *KS and KD*, EU:C:2024:725 and Case C-351/22 *Neves 77 Solutions SRL v Agenția Națională de Administrare Fiscală—Direcția Generală Antifraudă Fiscală*, EU:C:2024:723; and see discussion above in relation to the protection of the rule of law, and the independence of the judiciary.

[79] See generally K Lenaerts, 'Exploring the Limits of the EU Charter of Fundamental Rights' (2012) 8 *European Constitutional Law Review* 375.

of rights (Article 54). Those are, without doubt, the most complex and difficult provisions of the Charter since they reflect anxieties and divisions among Member States in relation not only to what the Charter should achieve, but also in relation to the direction of the EU. In particular, some Member States fear that fundamental rights might become a vehicle for further intrusion into national sovereignty, even in those fields which Member States have reserved to themselves; that the Charter might eventually have the effect of granting the Court of Justice broad and general fundamental rights jurisdiction; and that the Charter is a further step towards a more integrated, and federal, EU. We shall now consider some of these issues.

4.3.1 The scope of application of the Charter

As we have seen, the Charter codifies existing case law making rights more visible to the citizen. Its primary addressee is the EU, so that EU institutions, bodies, and agencies are bound by the Charter and, as such, can never escape its provisions, regardless of the capacity in which they act, whether as legislators, as administrators, as employers, or in any other capacity. For instance, in *Ledra Advertising*,[80] the Court of Justice (on appeal) found that the Commission is always bound by the Charter, even when it is acting outside the EU framework, in that case signing a memorandum of understanding within the European Stability Mechanism.[81] In the above-mentioned case of *Kadi I*, the Court found that EU institutions are bound by EU fundamental rights even when giving effect to a UN Security Council Resolution—that is, mandatory international law.[82] In reviewing acts of the institutions, the Court will, wherever possible, interpret the act in question so as to comply with fundamental rights.[83] However, where that is not possible, the Court will annul an act of the EU institutions infringing the Charter, A good example of this, is case study 9.1 on *Digital Rights Ireland*.

Case study 9.1: Digital Rights Ireland

In *Digital Rights Ireland*,[84] two national courts, one in Ireland and the other one in Germany, raised questions as to the validity of the data retention directive,[85] and in particular its compatibility with the right to private and family life, the right to the protection of personal data and freedom of expression (Arts 7, 8, and 11 Charter). The directive imposed

[80] Joined Cases C-8/15 and 10/15 P *Ledra Advertising*, EU:C:2016:701; see also Case C-258/14, *Florescu*, EU:C:2017:448, although, of course, a non-binding act can only be challenged through a preliminary ruling and not through direct action.

[81] The opposite also applies, so the General Court held that the EU–Turkey statement, which provides for a system of return to Turkey of irregular migrants landed on Greek islands, and whose asylum claim has failed, was not in fact an act of the EU: Case T-192/16 *NF v Council*, EU:T:2017:128, confirmed on appeal in Joined Cases C-208–210/17 P, EU:C:2018:705.

[82] See also Case C-351/22 *Neves 77 Solutions SRL v Agenția Națională de Administrare Fiscală—Direcția Generală Antifraudă Fiscală*, EU:C:2024:723, for positive duties of the Council to act to give effect to a decision in CFSP, which in turns justifies the exercise of the Court's jurisdiction in relation to the decision in CFSP when the Council has failed to act.

[83] Consistent case law from the outset; see eg Case 29/69 *Stauder* [1969] ECR 419.

[84] Joined Cases C-293/12 and 594/12 *Digital Rights Ireland*, EU:C:2014:238.

[85] Directive 2006/24 on the retention of data generated or processed in connection with the provision of publicly available electronic communications services or of public communications networks and amending Directive 2002/58/EC (OJ [2006] L105/54).

on providers a duty to retain all data from phone, mobile, and internet communication for at least six months. First, the Court found that the Directive entailed an interference with both the right to private life and protection of personal data. Secondly, it turned to assess whether such interference was justified. The Court found that the reason for the interference was to combat particularly serious crime and contribute to public security, a legitimate public interest. Thirdly, the Court proceeded to analyse whether the interference with individual rights was proportionate. In this regard it found that the scope of the Directive was too wide ranging and indiscriminate, entailing an interference with the fundamental rights of 'practically the entire European population'. Furthermore, the Directive failed to lay down objective criteria for access to the data by public authorities, and just indicated a window for retention of between 6 and 24 months without specifying that the period of retention should be based on objective criteria so as to be limited to what is strictly necessary. The Court held:

> It must therefore be held that Directive 2006/24 entails a wide-ranging and particularly serious interference with those fundamental rights in the legal order of the EU, without such an interference being precisely circumscribed by provisions to ensure that it is actually limited to what is strictly necessary.[86]

The Directive was therefore annulled. However, this did not exhaust the issue since some Member States decided to adopt/retain similar provisions as provided for in the Directive but in national law. In *Tele2 Severige Ab*,[87] the national authorities required communication providers to retain data in a similar way to what was provided by the data retention directive. The Court held that the national rules were not compatible with the EU data protection directive (now replaced by the General Data Protection Regulation (GDPR)) as read in the light of the Charter, hence basically extending the limits imposed on the EU legislature also to national authorities.[88]

The limits imposed on the EU institutions by EU data protection legislation, secondary legislation, and the Charter, are extensive and curtail the discretion of the decision-maker in all fields, including external relations. For instance, in *Schrems II* the Court,[89] once again,[90] annulled the Commission's Privacy Shield Decision which allowed the transfer of data to the US. The Court held that the Commission had not taken into due account the GDPR interpreted in the light of Article 7 (private life), Article 8 (personal data), and Article 47 (effective remedies) of the Charter.[91] Similarly, in the PNR case, the Court set clear limits to the data that could be transferred to a non-EU State.[92]

It is clear, then, that the EU institutions must make sure they act compatibly with the Charter or risk seeing their action annulled. For this reason, the Commission, according to its own guidance, should carry out a fundamental rights impact assessment in all its

[86] Joined Cases C-593/12 and 594/12 *Digital Rights Ireland*, EU:C:2014:238, para 65.
[87] Joined Cases C-203/15 and C-698/15, EU:C:2016:970.
[88] See also eg Case C-140/20 *GD*, EU:C:2022:258.
[89] Case C-311/18 *Data Protection Commissioner, Facebook Ireland and Schrems*, EU:C:2020:559.
[90] Case C-362/14 *Schrems I*, EU:C:2015:650.
[91] Case C-311/18 *Data Protection Commissioner, Facebook Ireland and Schrems*, EU:C:2020:559.
[92] Opinion 1/15 (Passenger Name Record Agreement with Canada), EU:C:2017:592; pre-Lisbon and in relation to the Passenger Name Record Agreement with the US, Joined Cases C-317/04 and C-318/04 *Parliament v Council*, EU:C:2015:190.

proposals.[93] However, unfortunately, in recent times this has not always been the case, especially in the field of migration.[94]

4.3.2 **The application of the Charter to the Member States**

Member States are also bound by EU fundamental rights when they exercise a discretion which has either been conferred by Union law (ie when they implement a Union law instrument) or when they bring themselves within the scope of EU law by limiting or derogating from one of the free movement rights conferred by the Treaties.[95] The basic principle behind this interpretation is that when Member States implement Union law, or act within its scope by limiting one of the rights granted by the Treaties, they have to comply with all of the constitutional principles of the EU, including fundamental rights protection.

Article 51(1) therefore states that the provisions of the Charter are addressed to the Member States 'only' when they implement Union law.[96] It should be noted, however, that the interpretation of what constitutes 'implementation' for the purposes of Article 51(1) is at times very broad. It covers cases in which the Member State is implementing or giving effect to a directive, regulation, or decision, as well as cases where the Member State is limiting one of the rights granted by the Treaty.[97] It also covers cases in which the Member States exercise a power that was 'reserved' to them in a piece of secondary legislation. For instance, in *NS*,[98] the case related to the application of (then) Regulation 343/2003,[99] known as the 'Dublin II Regulation', which provided the criteria for allocating

[93] See also Commission's Strategy to strengthen the application of the Charter of Fundamental Rights in the EU, COM(2020) 711 final, https://eur-lex.europa.eu/legal-content/EN/TXT/?uri=CELEX%3A52020DC0711; and Communication from the Commission, 'Revised operational guidance on taking account of fundamental rights in European Commission impact assessments', C(2025) 8354 final. See generally M Dawson, *The Governance of Fundamental Rights* (Cambridge: Cambridge University Press, 2017).

[94] See eg Ombudsman Decision, 'Decision in case 1409/2014/MHZ on the European Commission's failure to carry out a prior human rights impact assessment of the envisaged EU-Vietnam free trade agreement', https://www.ombudsman.europa.eu/en/decision/en/64308; Ombudsman Decision, 'Decision on how the European Commission intends to guarantee respect for human rights in the context of the EU–Tunisia Memorandum of Understanding (OI/2/2024/MHZ)'; https://www.ombudsman.europa.eu/en/decision/en/193851; Ombudsman Recommendation on the European Commission's compliance with 'Better Regulation' rules and other procedural requirements in preparing legislative proposals that it considered to be urgent (983/2025/MAS—the 'Omnibus' case, 2031/2024/VB—the 'migration' case, and 1379/2024/MIK—the 'CAP' case), www.ombudsman.europa.eu/en/recommendation/en/215920. See generally Editorial Comments, 'Diplomacy by Press Release: Externalising Border Control, Forgetting EU Values' (2025) 62 *Common Market Law Review* 315.

[95] See eg Case C-235/17 *Commission v Hungary* (*Expropriation*), EU:C:2019:432.

[96] To start with, there was some confusion about the fact that while fundamental rights as general principles apply when the Member States implement EU law or *act within their scope* (see previously), Art 51 only referred to the former. However, the explanations to the Charter refer to Member States acting within the scope of EU law, and the Court, rightly, has adopted an integrated reading so that the reference to 'implement' in Art 51 also includes Member States acting within the scope of EU law; see eg Case C-256/11 *Dereci* [2011] ECR I-11315, para 72.

[97] Charter, see eg Case C-390/12 *Pfleger*, EU:C:2014:281; on the intersection between citizenship and fundamental rights, see eg Cases C-182/15 *Petruhhin*, EU:C:2016:630; C-650/13 *Delvigne*, EU:C:2015:648; and C-221/17 *Tjebbes*, EU:C:2019:189.

[98] Joined Cases C-411/10 and C-493/10 *NS v Secretary of State for the Home Department*, EU:C:2011:13905; and see more recently Case C-753/22 *QY v Bundesrepublik Deutschland*, EU:C:2024:524.

[99] Council Regulation (EC) No 343/2003 (OJ [2003] L50/1), repealed and substituted by Regulation 604/2013 (OJ [2013] L108/31), known as the Dublin III Regulation, repealed by Regulation (EU) 2024/1351 on Asylum and Migration Management (OJ [2024] L 22.5.2024). On EU asylum law (including later developments on this issue), see further chapter 25.

the Member State responsible to examine asylum claims: lacking other connecting factors this would be the country where the asylum seeker first entered the territory of the Union. However, the Regulation also contained the so-called sovereignty clause according to which Member States retained the discretion to examine claims, even when such examination was not their responsibility pursuant to the Regulation. In the *NS* case the claimants were challenging their deportation from the UK, the country where they were present, to Greece, which was responsible for their application (being the first port of entry). In particular, they argued that given the conditions under which asylum applications were dealt with in Greece, deportation would entail a breach of their right not to be subjected to degrading treatment as protected by Article 4 of the Charter and Article 3 ECHR.[100] The issue was then whether the discretion of the Member State should be subjected to review pursuant to EU fundamental rights: the Court found that the exercise of discretion still constituted 'implementation' of EU law and that therefore EU fundamental rights were (at least to a certain extent) applicable. The UK could not therefore deport the applicants if it could not be unaware of the systemic deficiencies of the asylum system in the country of destination (Greece).

Member States are also implementing EU law when they seek to limit one of the free movement rights conferred by the Treaties. Thus, for instance, in *Familiapress* the Court held that when limiting the free movement of goods, the Member States are bound to respect freedom of expression as guaranteed by Article 10 ECHR (the case was pre-Charter).[101] At times the application of fundamental rights to acts of the Member States is more contested, such as is the case in particular in relation to politically sensitive situations.[102] This can also be seen in case study 9.2 on the decision in *Carpenter*.

Case study 9.2: Immigration, sovereignty, and fundamental rights: the case of Mr and Mrs Carpenter

Mrs Carpenter was a national of the Philippines living in the UK; she married Mr Carpenter, who was a British citizen also living in the UK, and applied for a residence permit as the spouse of a British national.[103] Her application was denied on the grounds that she had overstayed her visa and she was asked to leave the country and apply for a new visa from

[100] The ECtHR had examined a similar issue in *MSS v Belgium and Greece* (Appl No 30696/09), judgment of 21 January 2011, esp paras 358, 360, and 367, and found that, as a matter of ECHR law, Member States could not deport asylum seekers to the Member State responsible under the EU rules when they knew that the country of destination would not examine the application properly, and that the asylum seeker would be exposed to living conditions that amounted to degrading treatment.

[101] Case C-368/95 *Familiapress* [1997] ECR I-3689, esp para 24; see also Case C-36/02 *Omega Spielhallen-und Automatenaufstellungs-GmbH v Oberbürgermeisterin der Bundesstadt Bonn* [2004] ECR I-9609.

[102] See eg Case C-673/16 *Coman*, EU:C:2018:385; Case C-490/20 *VMA*, EU:C:2021:1008; Case C-709/20 *CG v The Department for Communities in Northern Ireland*, EU:C:2021:602; Case C-836/18 *Subdelegación del Gobierno en Ciudad Real v RH*, EU:C:2020:119; Joined Cases C-451/19 and C-532/19 *Subdelegación del Gobierno en Toledo v XU and QP*, EU:C:2022:354; Case C-82/16 *KA and others*, EU:C:2018:308; Case C-133/15 *HC Chavez-Vilchez*, EU:C:2017:354; Case C-304/14 *CS*, EU:C:2016:674; Case C-165/14 *Rendón Marín*, EU:C:2016:675; Case C-221/17 *Tjebbes*, EU:2019:189; and Case C-118/20 *JY v Wiener Landesregierung*, EU:C:2022:34. On these issues, see E Spaventa, 'The Relationship between Free Movement of Persons and Fundamental Rights' in J Adams-Prassl, A Ezrachi, S Bogojević, and D Leczykiewicz (eds), *The Internal Market Idea—Essays in Honor of Steve Weatherill* (Oxford: Oxford University Press, 2024) ch 8.

[103] Case C-60/00 *Carpenter* [2002] ECR I-6279. See subsequently Case C-457/12 *S and G*, EU:C:2014:136.

the Philippines. The immigration authorities accepted that the marriage of Mr and Mrs Carpenter was genuine—that is, it was not a sham entered into only to avoid the application of immigration rules. The refusal of leave to remain therefore constituted an interference with Mr and Mrs Carpenter's right to family life, as deportation would result in the forced separation of Mr and Mrs Carpenter. The issue was then whether this interference was legitimate, in that it constituted a proportionate interference with the right to family life justified by the policy aim of curtailing illegal immigration by discouraging overstays on visas. The most obvious route would have been to invoke the Human Rights Act 1998, which incorporates the ECHR in British law. However, according to a consistent body of case law, immigration policy, as long as it is applied proportionately, constitutes a legitimate ground to limit the right to family life; the claim was therefore unlikely to succeed by invoking the Human Rights Act.

Counsel for Mr and Mrs Carpenter therefore chose a different strategy: he sought to transform the case into an EU law case so that EU fundamental rights could be invoked. This strategy had two advantages: first of all, if EU law was applicable, the Court of Justice would have jurisdiction to assess the case. Since Convention rights are a minimum standard, he was hoping that the Court would be willing to grant more extensive protection to the right to family life. Secondly, if EU law could be invoked when balancing the right to family life with the immigration policy of the Member State, the Court of Justice (and the national court) would also take into account the right to move granted by the Treaty. As a result, the balance might be tilted in favour of the claimants. But how did counsel manage to establish a sufficient link with EU law? After all, the case was linked exclusively to the UK: Mr Carpenter was British; his wife had overstayed the visa granted by British authorities; neither party had moved to, or was returning from, another Member State. From an EU law perspective, the case seemed prima facie purely internal. As a result, as you will see in chapter 13, the EU rules on the free movement of persons would not apply, and so the UK would be free to apply its own restrictions on immigration.

Counsel argued that Mr Carpenter, who ran a business selling advertising space, provided services to clients in other EU States; he also occasionally had to travel to France on business. He was therefore a service provider covered by Article 56 TFEU. Further, Counsel argued that when Mr Carpenter was travelling on business his wife would take care of his children; her deportation would therefore constitute a hindrance to his ability to travel to provide services. In order to assess whether this hindrance was justified, due recourse should be had to his family rights. Counsel thus suggested that deportation was a disproportionate interference with the Carpenters' family life and therefore an unjustified restriction on Mr Carpenter's right to provide services in the EU as protected (now) by the TFEU. The Court, broadly speaking and with marginal differences, accepted this reasoning. Regardless of the subtleties of the free movement issues, it should be noted that by linking the case to EU law, and by ensuring that EU fundamental rights were applicable, Mr and Mrs Carpenter obtained what they would have been denied had they relied solely on UK immigration rules and the Human Rights Act: Mrs Carpenter obtained leave to remain without having to return to the Philippines and apply from there.[104]

[104] As you will see in chapters 13 and 20, another delicate situation arises when Treaty freedoms clash with fundamental rights so that the enjoyment of the former results in the limitation of another claimant's fundamental right. See Case C-112/00 *Schmidberger* [2003] ECR I-5659; Case C-438/05 *International Transport Workers' Federation and Finnish Seamen's Union v Viking Line* [2007] ECR I-10779; Case C-341/05 *Laval un Partneri* [2007] ECR I-11767.

The applicability of EU fundamental rights through the free movement provisions has also been of crucial importance in relation to the protection of personal autonomy,[105] contributing to enhance the effectiveness of rulings of the ECtHR. For instance, in *Mirin*, the Court applied the Charter, read in light of the ECHR below which protection the Charter cannot fall, to demand that the recognition by the home Member State of the new name and gender identity occurred in another Member State.[106] In *Trojan*,[107] the Court held that Member States must ensure the recognition of a same-sex marriage lawfully concluded by two own citizens in another Member State, in the exercise of the right to free movement, even when the home State does not recognise same-sex marriage.

4.3.3 **The notion of 'implementation' of EU law for the purposes of Article 51(1) Charter**

In recent years, the Court has also sought to draw the limits of the application of the Charter more precisely by outlining the proximity with EU law necessary before the Charter can apply to acts of the Member States.[108] We shall now look at three strands of case law: first, *Åkerberg Fransson*, where the Court gave a broad definition of the scope of the Charter; secondly, the slightly more nuanced application of the Charter in cases relating to procedural coordination; and, thirdly, those cases in which the Charter did not apply as there was insufficient connection between European Union law and the national rules at issue.

(i) Åkerberg Fransson: a broad definition of 'implementing'

In cases which have a stronger connection with European interests, and especially the internal market, the Court is more ready to find that the Charter applies to acts of the Member States.[109]

In *Åkerberg Fransson*,[110] the issue concerned whether the principle of *ne bis in idem* provided for in Article 50 Charter, applied to proceedings brought against Mr Åkerberg Fransson on charges of serious tax offences, including providing false information in

[105] See E Spaventa, 'Free Movement and Public Policy: The European Space as a Guarantee for Self-Determination' in MA Panascì and E Spaventa (eds), *Handbook on Free Movement Law* (Cheltenham: Elgar, forthcoming 2026).

[106] Case C-4/23 *Mirin*, EU:C:2024:845, noted by F Ristuccia and A Marcia, 'Trans* EU Citizens: Free beyond Movement? The Grand Chamber in Case C-4/23 *Mirin*' (2025) 32 *Maastricht Journal of European and Comparative Law* 505; see also Case C-490/20 *Stolichna obshtina, rayon 'Pancharevo'*, EU:C:2021:1008; and LD Spieker, 'Pushing for Trans Rights: How the Court of Justice Can Turn the EU into a "Freedom Zone" for Trans Citizens' (2025) 62 *Common Market Law Review* 1337.

[107] Case C-713/23 *Jakub Cupriak-Trojan, Mateusz Trojan v Wojewoda Mazowiecki*, EU:C:2025:917; see also Case C-673/16 *Coman and Others*, EU:C:2018:385.

[108] See M Dougan, 'Judicial Review of Member State Action under the General Principles and the Charter: Defining the "Scope of Union Law"' (2015) *Common Market Law Review* 1201; and, less optimistic, E Spaventa, 'The Interpretation of Article 51 of the EU Charter of Fundamental Rights', Study on behalf of the PETI Committee, European Parliament, www.europarl.europa.eu/RegData/etudes/STUD/2016/556930/IPOL_STU(2016)556930_EN.pdf.

[109] See also Case C-218/15 *Paoletti and Others*, EU:C:2016748; and Case C-540/16 *Spika' UAB*, EU:C:2018:565, where the Court clarified that when the Member State is exercising a competence expressly attributed to them by EU law then they are implementing EU law for the purposes of Art 51(1) Charter.

[110] Case C-617/10 *Åklagaren v Hans Åkerberg Fransson*, EU:C:2013:105; noted by E Hancox, 'The Meaning of "Implementing" EU Law under Article 51(1) of the Charter: *Åkerberg Fransson*' (2013) 50 *Common Market Law Review* 1411; on this case and the reaction it provoked in the German Federal Constitutional Court, see F Fontanelli, '*Hic Sunt Nationes*: The Elusive Limits of the EU Charter and the German Constitutional Watchdog' (2013) 9 *European Constitutional Law Review* 315; and 'Ultra Vires: Has the Bundesverfassungsgericht Shown Its Teeth?', editorial (2013) 50 *Common Market Law Review* 925; D Sarmiento, 'Who Is Afraid of the Charter? The Court of Justice, National Courts and the New Framework of Fundamental Rights Protection in the EU' (2013) 50 *Common Market Law Review* 1267.

relation to VAT. Several intervening Member States, together with the Commission, argued that the Charter was not applicable since the legislation which formed the basis for the proceedings was not implementing EU law. The Court disagreed: it found that the tax penalties and the criminal proceedings to which Mr Åkerberg Fransson was subjected were in part connected to his obligations to declare VAT. The Court then found that it followed from Directive 2006/112,[111] as well as from the principle of loyal cooperation, that Member States have an obligation to take 'all legislative and administrative measures' to ensure collection of VAT due on their territory. Furthermore, since part of the VAT revenue is destined to the EU's own resources, a lacuna in collection of the tax would also determine a reduction in the revenues of the EU. Since Article 325 TFEU obliges Member States to counter illegal activities affecting the financial interests of the EU, the tax penalties at issue also constituted implementation of that provision of the Treaty. For these reasons, and even though the proceedings also related to the collection of income tax, which is not harmonized at EU level, the Court found that the tax penalties and the criminal proceedings constituted 'implementation' of EU law and therefore fell within the scope of application of the Charter.[112] In the case of *Alemo-Herron* the Court found that the Charter applies also to the discretion of the Member State to provide more protective rules in relation to a minimum harmonization directive.[113] In particular, minimum harmonization directives (and in this case the transfer of undertaking directive) set a minimum floor of protection, leaving Member States free to provide more extensive rights, which was exactly what the UK had done in the case at issue. As mentioned earlier, the Court found that the Charter limited the discretion of the Member States to provide more protective rules, so that the rights of the employers to freedom to contract as protected by the Charter limited the discretion of Member States to protect employees beyond the provisions of the Directive in case of transfer of undertakings. It should be noted, however, that it is not always that the Charter applies to rules which go beyond rights conferred in the Directive. Rather, as first noted by De Cecco,[114] whether the Charter applies will depend on the policy area and its connection with the internal market.[115]

(ii) McB: EU rules coordinating national procedural rules

A more limited application of the Charter arises in those cases where the EU rules aim at coordinating rather than harmonizing national rules. In this respect, it should be recalled that Article 51(1) states that institutions and Member States apply the Charter

[111] Directive 2006/112 on the common system of value added tax (OJ [2006] L347/1).

[112] The ruling might be also seen in the context of the strategic importance of VAT collection for the EU budget; see also Case C-42/17 *MAS and MB*, EU:C:2017:936; Case C-105/14 *Taricco*, EU:C:2015:555; Joined Cases C-286/94, C-340/95, C-401/95, and C-47/96 *Garage Molenheide*, EU:C:1997:623.

[113] Case C-426/11 *Alemo-Herron*, EU:C:2013:521; the decision has given rise to much criticism for weakening the protection of employees; see eg M Bartl and C Leone, 'Minimum Harmonization after Alemo-Herron: The Janus Face of EU Fundamental Rights Review' (2015) 11 *European Constitutional Law Review* 140; J Prassl, 'Freedom of Contract as a General Principle of EU Law? Transfers of Undertakings and the Protection of Employer Rights in EU Labour Law' (2013) 42 *Industrial Law Journal* 434; S Weatherill, 'Use and Abuse of the Charter of Fundamental Rights: On the Improper Veneration of "Freedom of Contract"' (2014) 14 *European Review of Contract Law* 167; R Babayev, 'Private Autonomy at Union level: On Article 16 CFREU and Free Movement Rights' (2016) 53 *Common Market Law Review* 979.

[114] F De Cecco, 'Room to Move? Minimum Harmonization and Fundamental Rights' (2006) 43 *Common Market Law Review* 9.

[115] But see Joined Cases C-609 and 610/17 *TSN and AKT*, EU:C:2019:98, noted by R Král and P Mádr, 'On the (In)Applicability of the EU Charter of Fundamental Rights to National Measures Exceeding the Requirements of Minimum Harmonisation Directives' (2021) 46 *European Law Review* 81; see also E Spaventa, 'Should We "Harmonize" Fundamental Rights in the EU? Some Reflections about Minimum Standards and Fundamental Rights Protection in the EU Composite Constitutional System' (2018) *Common Market Law Review* 997–1023.

'in accordance with their respective powers and respecting the limits of the powers of the Union as conferred in the Treaties', hence reinforcing the separation between Union and national competences. This is further restated in Article 51(2), which clarifies that:

> The Charter does not extend the field of application of Union law beyond the powers of the Union or establish any new power or task for the Union, or modify powers and tasks as defined in the Treaties.

As we mentioned previously, Article 51 reflects a certain anxiety on behalf of the Member States that the Charter might become a vehicle to establish general fundamental rights jurisdiction for the Court of Justice.[116] These fears were duly taken into account by the Court in the ruling in *McB*.[117]

In *McB* the issue related to Irish rules on custody rights according to which, while the mother obtains automatic custody of her children, the unmarried father, lacking an agreement, must apply to a court to see his right recognized. When the McB couple separated, Mr McB applied for custody to the Irish courts; the mother, however, removed the children from the jurisdiction of the Irish courts before custody had been granted. Pursuant to Regulation 2201/2003 on the recognition of judgments in matters of parental responsibility, if children are wrongfully removed from their country of residence the jurisdiction is maintained by the latter's courts.[118] However, the Irish court denied jurisdiction on the ground that when the removal took place the father had not yet acquired custody rights. The Irish Supreme Court then referred a question to enquire whether the Regulation, read in light of the Charter, precluded the national rule that, in the case of unmarried fathers, subordinated custody rights to agreement between the parents or to judicial pronouncement. Mr McB argued that the Irish rules were inconsistent with his right to private and family life as guaranteed by Article 7 Charter, and Article 8 ECHR.

The question was very sensitive: family law is, broadly speaking, reserved to the Member States. As a result, Regulation 2201/2003, which merely coordinates national rules and does not harmonize them, refers to the law of the Member States to determine when removal of the child has been wrongful, thereby resulting in abduction. However, Mr McB was seeking through the medium of EU law a review of the national rules on custody: in this way a matter reserved to the Member State would become open to scrutiny by the Union judicature. The Court relied on Article 51 to limit the effects of the Charter, and it held:

> 52. It follows that, in the context of this case, the Charter should be taken into consideration solely for the purposes of interpreting Regulation no 2201/2003, and there *should be no assessment of national law as such*.[119]

The Court then performed an indirect review of national law by focusing on its own interpretation of the Regulation. In this way it sought to respect the letter and the spirit of Article 51 Charter and to balance the need to respect the competencies of the Member States, with the need to ensure that the rights of individuals are protected.

[116] On the duty of national courts in relation to the Charter, see again *Åklagaren v Hans Åkerberg Fransson* (n 110).

[117] Case C-400/10 PPU *McB* [2010] ECR I-8965.

[118] OJ [2003] L338/1.

[119] Emphasis added.

(iii) Cases in which the Charter does not apply

The Charter applies only in those instances where Member States are 'implementing' EU law; for instance in the *Ledra Advertising* case mentioned earlier, the Court clarified that if the Member States are giving effect to an instrument that has been adopted outside the institutional framework of the EU, they are not bound by the Charter.[120] In some cases it is not easy to determine whether the national rules constitute implementation of EU law or not. This is because EU rules cover and/or impact on ever increasing fields; to impose the application of the Charter on national authorities simply because the subject matter has been the focus of EU rules would extend the scope of application of the Charter considerably. For this reason, the Court has attempted to draw some guidelines on the degree of proximity between EU and national rules required before the Charter can apply.[121] In the case of *Siragusa*, Mr Siragusa made modifications to buildings in a conservation area and then applied for retrospective planning permission. This was denied and an order made for the buildings to be restored to their original state. The national court enquired, inter alia, as to whether the conservation rules in Italy were compatible with Article 17 Charter guaranteeing the right to property. It stated that the connection with EU law was present since the national legislation sought to protect the landscape, and as such contributed to environmental protection, a field where the EU had legislated extensively. The Court, however, found that the concept of 'implementation' in Article 51(1) Charter required a certain 'degree of connection above and beyond the matters covered being closely related or one of those matters having an indirect impact on the other'.[122] The Court then explained the factors to be taken into consideration to determine whether that connection was sufficient to trigger the application of the Charter.

> 25. In order to determine whether national legislation involves the implementation of EU law for the purposes of Article 51 of the Charter, some of the points to be determined are whether that legislation is intended to implement a provision of EU law; the nature of that legislation and whether it pursues objectives other than those covered by EU law, even if it is capable of indirectly affecting EU law; and also whether there are specific rules of EU law on the matter or capable of affecting it.
>
> 26. In particular, the Court has found that fundamental EU rights could not be applied in relation to national legislation because the provisions of EU law in the subject area concerned did not impose any obligation on Member States with regard to the situation at issue in the main proceedings.

In subsequent case law the Court reaffirmed the *Siragusa* test: for instance in *Hernández* the Court excluded the relevance of the Charter in relation to a situation which partially fell within the scope of Union law.[123] And, in *Torralbo Marcos*,[124] the Court found that the

[120] Joined Cases C-8/15 and 10/15 P *Ledra Advertising*, EU:C:2016:701.

[121] The Court had already given some indication as to the boundaries of Art 51(1) Charter in Case C-40/11 *Iida v Stadt Ulm*, EU:C:2012:691, para 81; see also Case C-87/12 *Ymeraga v Ministre du Travail, de l'Emploi et de l'Immigration*, EU:C:2013:291.

[122] Case C-206/13 *Siragusa*, EU:C:2014:126, para 24; now consistent case law, see eg Case C-218/15 *Paoletti et al*, EU:C:2016:748; Case C-177/18 *Almudena Baldonedo Martín v Ayuntamiento de Madrid*, EU:C:2020:26; Case C-481/19 *LH v Profi Credit Slovakia sro*, EU:C:2021:313.

[123] Case C-198/13 *Hernández and others*, EU:C:2014:2055; here the Court gave great weight to the fact that the legislation at issue was pursuing an aim other than that pursued by the relevant directive (see esp para 41).

[124] Case C-265/13 *Torralbo Marcos*, EU:C:2014:187; on the lack of applicability of the Charter, see also Case C-638/16 PPU *X and X*, EU:C:2017:173 and Case C-219/24 *A and Others v Tallinna linn*, EU:C:2025:442.

Charter could not be applied to rules regulating access to justice, even when the claimant was trying to enforce a Directive.

4.3.4 **The horizontal application of the Charter**

We have mentioned earlier that the Charter is addressed to Union institutions and Member States when they implement EU law; the Charter is, however, silent as to whether it also binds individuals, and if yes, in which circumstances. Here, it is necessary to recall some general principles of EU law regarding horizontal application (ie the possibility to invoke EU law against a private party). Whereas Directives do not impose duties on individuals and therefore cannot be invoked against a private party, Treaty provisions, even when apparently addressed to Member States, can have horizontal direct effect. This is the case, for instance, for those provisions which enshrine fundamental principles of the EU such as the prohibition of unequal pay for equal work performed by men and women,[125] and the prohibition on discrimination on grounds of nationality.[126] The issue arose then as to whether the Charter could be invoked by individuals against other individuals: on the one hand, allowing for horizontal application might maximize the effect of the Charter, and would be consistent with the interpretation given to those Treaty provisions which enshrine fundamental EU rights. On the other hand, and as mentioned earlier, the Charter is formally addressed only to institutional actors. Furthermore, the Charter is not a standard constitutional document as it applies in the national context only insofar as the Member State is implementing EU law.

Both in case of Treaty provisions having horizontal direct effect and Regulations (which are always capable of having horizontal effect), the applicability of the Charter to individuals can be easily justified. After all, if a Regulation applies to an individual that same Regulation, according to EU constitutional principles, cannot be interpreted in a way that would be incompatible with fundamental rights. It is the Regulation, in that case, that applies to individuals, and it is by means of the Regulation that the Charter applies. Matters are rather more complex in the case of Directives since those are not capable, per se, of having horizontal direct effect.[127] The question then arises as to whether the Charter can be invoked against an individual if the only reason why the litigation falls within the scope of EU law is by virtue of a Directive which, in itself, cannot be invoked against an individual (see chapter 6). The Court has answered this question in the affirmative, at least in some cases. In particular, when there is a Directive which details rights also contained in the Charter, then the Charter is capable of applying in full even if the Directive cannot be invoked against a private party. For instance, in the *Max-Planck* and *Bauer* cases,[128] the Court held that Article 31(2) Charter which provides for the right to maximum working periods, rest and paid holiday, could be applied in relation to a dispute between private parties by virtue, and within the limits set by, the working time directive.[129] This was the case, even if (and because) the Directive itself was not applicable for lack of horizontal direct effect. In prior case law, the Court had reached a similar conclusion in relation to age discrimination cases, where the framework discrimination directive could not apply

[125] Case C-43/75 *Defrenne v SABENA*, EU:C:1976:56.

[126] eg Case C-281/98 *Angonese*, EU:C:2000:296.

[127] Consistent case law, see for all Case C-91/92 *Faccini Dori v Recreb*, EU:C:1994:292.

[128] Case C-569/16 *Bauer*, EU:C:2018:871; and Case C-684/16 *Max-Planck-Gesellschaft zur Förderung der Wissenschaften eV*, EU:C:2018:874. See also Case C-55/18 *CCOO v Deutsche Bank*, EU:C:2019:402; Case C-233/20 *WD*, EU:C:2021:960; see eg A Colombi Ciacchi, 'The *Direct Horizontal Effect* of EU Fundamental Rights' (2019) 15 *European Constitutional Law Review* 254.

[129] Directive 2003/88/EC concerning certain aspects of the organization of working time (OJ [2003] L299/9).

for lack of horizontal direct effect, whereas the general principle of non-discrimination on grounds of age first and Article 21 Charter later was found applicable.[130]

In these cases, the Court has de facto applied the Directives through the Charter, by interpreting the Charter rights as coinciding in full with secondary legislation. Moreover, at least in those cases and with the exception of the ruling in *Mangold*, the Court has limited the possibility to invoke the Charter horizontally to those situations that fell within the scope of the Directives detailing the rights at issue (ie situations which fell within the scope of the non-discrimination directives, or the working time directive). The reason for this is that, given the hierarchy of norms, the Court perceives the rights in the Charter to have been sufficiently detailed in secondary legislation:[131] whether we interpret this as an undeclared horizontal application of certain directives, or as true horizontal application of the Charter, is a matter for debate.

4.3.5 **The scope and interpretation of the Charter**

Very few fundamental rights are absolute; the vast majority of fundamental rights can be limited in order to protect the rights of others and/or to ensure that public policy objectives can be carried out. Take, for instance, the right to liberty on the one hand, and the need to impose custodial sentences for given crimes on the other; or the need to respect other people's property when enjoying one's own. In order to ensure that a balance can be struck between competing private or public interests, fundamental rights documents often contain derogation and limitation clauses:[132] thus, for instance, the ECHR contains the permissible grounds of limitation in each of the right-granting Articles which are subject to limitations, and a general power to derogate from most of the Convention in emergencies (Article 15). By contrast, the Charter provides for just one general derogation and limitation clause. Article 52(1) states that limitations on the exercise of Charter rights must:

- be provided by law;
- respect the essence of those rights;[133]
- respect the principle of proportionality; and
- be necessary to meet the objectives of general interest recognised by the Union or the need to protect the rights and freedoms of others.

Furthermore, in order to ensure consistency, Article 52(2) clarifies that Treaty-derived rights are to be exercised according to the conditions and limits defined by the Treaties (eg Union citizenship rights can be legitimately detailed/limited in Directive 2004/38;

[130] See eg Case C-144/04 *Mangold* [2005] ECR I-9981; Case C-555/07 *Kücükdeveci v Swedex* [2010] ECR I-365; see generally E Spaventa, 'The Horizontal Application of Fundamental Rights as General Principles of EU Law' and M Dougan, 'In Defence of *Mangold*?', both in A Arnull, C Barnard, M Dougan, and E Spaventa, *A Constitutional Order of States? Essays in EU Law in Honour of Alan Dashwood* (Oxford: Hart Publishing, 2011).

[131] However, if the rights contained in a directive cannot be inferred from the provisions of the Charter, eg because the latter are generic, then the Charter rights cannot have horizontal direct effect; see eg Case C-196/23 *Plamaro*, EU:C:2024:596.

[132] In those cases in which derogations are not expressly provided, the courts will interpret the content of the rights to reflect the need to balance them against conflicting legitimate interests. For an example of how the Court of Justice applies the limitation clause, see Case C-291/12 *Schwarz*, EU:C:2013:270.

[133] For an example of the application of the 'essence' of the right doctrine vis-à-vis proportionality, see eg Joined Cases C 245/19 and C 246/19 *État luxembourgeois v B*, EU:C:2020:795; and see F De Cecco, 'The Trouble with Trumps, or How (Not) to Approach the Essence of EU Fundamental Rights' (2023) 60 *Common Market Law Review* 1515; and on essence of rights in EU law, see generally the special issue of the *German Law Journal* (2019), Vol 20, Issue 06.

see further chapter 16). More importantly, in order to ensure adequate protection, paragraph 3 of the same Article provides that insofar as Charter rights correspond to ECHR rights, their meaning and scope must be the same as those laid down by the Convention, even though it is open to the Union to afford more generous protection (eg in immigration cases the Union might legitimately give a more generous interpretation of the right to family life; see case study 9.2 on the *Carpenter* judgment). Article 52(4) provides that rights resulting from common constitutional traditions must be interpreted in harmony with those traditions.

These latter provisions are complemented by Article 53, which ensures that:

> Nothing in this Charter shall be interpreted as restricting or adversely affecting human rights and fundamental freedoms as recognised, ***in their respective fields of application***, by Union law and international law and by international agreements to which the Union or all the Member States are party, including the European Convention for the Protection of Human Rights and Fundamental Freedoms, and by the Member States' constitutions. (Emphasis added)

The reference to national constitutions proved somewhat confusing: in particular, it was unclear whether Article 53 would amend the status quo according to which in relation to EU legislation the only fundamental rights standard which is relevant is that set by the EU constitutional order.[134] In *Melloni*,[135] the Court of Justice clarified that Article 53 cannot be used to apply national fundamental rights (even when more protective than the Charter) to EU law which complies with the Charter. In that case, the issue related to the execution of a European Arrest Warrant;[136] this is an instrument pursuant to which Member States can request another Member State to surrender a suspect for the purposes of criminal prosecution; or to surrender a convicted person in order to execute a custodial sentence. Unlike extradition, the execution of a European Arrest Warrant is, besides a few listed exceptions, automatic. Mr Melloni had been convicted *in absentia* (ie he was not present at the trial); however, even though he was not physically present during the trials because he had fled, he was legally represented by lawyers of his choosing. Once the conviction was final, the Italian authorities issued a European Arrest Warrant for its execution. Mr Melloni was then arrested by the Spanish authorities. In an attempt to resist surrender to the Italian authorities, Mr Melloni argued, inter alia, that his conviction *in absentia* breached his right to a fair trial inasmuch as Italian procedural law did not allow appeal against (final) judgments imposed *in absentia*. He therefore argued that his surrender should be made conditional upon the possibility to appeal the Italian judgment or else his rights as guaranteed by the Spanish Constitution would be violated.

The national court made a reference to the Court of Justice enquiring, amongst other things, whether Article 53 Charter allowed a Member State to make surrender conditional upon further review of the conviction *in absentia*, therefore providing protection of the right to fair trial and defence more generous than that afforded by the Charter but in line with its own national constitutional standard. In other words, the national court

[134] On the interpretation of the Charter, see G de Búrca, 'After the EU Charter of Fundamental Rights: The Court of Justice as a Human Rights Adjudicator?' (2013) 20 *Maastricht Journal of European and Comparative Law* 168; P Popelier, C Van de Heyning, and P Van Nuffel (eds), *Human Rights Protection in the European Legal Order: The Interaction between the European and the National Courts* (Cambridge: Intersentia, 2011).

[135] Case C-399/11 *Melloni v Ministerio Fiscal*, EU:C:2013:107, noted in N de Boer (2013) 50 *Common Market Law Review* 1083.

[136] Council Framework Decision 2002/584/JHA on the European Arrest Warrant and the surrender procedures between Member States (OJ [2002] L190/1), consolidated version 28 March 2009.

was enquiring whether, if the standard of protection afforded by the national constitution is higher than that afforded by the Charter, national courts can enforce the former. While this is not a new question, having been discussed in cases such as *Internationale Handelsgesellschaft*,[137] it acquired a new poignancy given that Article 53 Charter provides that nothing therein can be interpreted as restricting or adversely affecting human rights as guaranteed by national constitutions. An affirmative answer would possibly maximize protection of human rights in the EU, always allowing the highest standard to prevail; however, it would jeopardize the principle of supremacy since the application of EU law would differ from country to country according to national fundamental rights standards. The Court of Justice, not surprisingly, held that:

> It is settled case law that, by virtue of the principle of primacy of EU law, which is an essential feature of the EU legal order . . ., rules of national law, even of a constitutional order, cannot be allowed to undermine the effectiveness of EU law on the territory of that State . . .
>
> It is true that article 53 of the Charter confirms that, where an EU legal act calls for national implementing measures, national authorities and courts remain free to apply national standards of protection of fundamental rights, ***provided*** that the level of protection provided for by the Charter, as interpreted by the Court, and the ***primacy, unity*** and ***effectiveness*** of EU law are not thereby compromised.[138]

As a result, national courts are prevented from imposing their own constitutional standards in those cases in which to do so would affect the uniform application of EU law, that is, when EU law leaves no discretion to Member States.[139] On the other hand, and in the same way as was the case before the Charter, when EU law leaves space for the exercise of discretion by national authorities, the Charter only provides Member States with a floor of rights leaving national authorities (and national courts) the freedom to apply their own (higher or differing) constitutional standards.[140]

Article 52(5) introduces a distinction between rights and principles: the latter are judicially cognizable only in the interpretation of legislative and executive acts and in the assessment of their validity.[141] This basically means that programmatic provisions, such as Article 37, which provides that a high level of environmental protection must be integrated into Union policies, might not grant a free-standing right.[142] In any event, though,

[137] Case 11/70 *Internationale Handelsgesellschaft* [1970] ECR 1125, and discussion in section 2.1; cf also, eg *Biotechnology Directive* (n 65).

[138] *Melloni* (n 135) paras 59 and 60.

[139] But see Joined Cases C-404/15 *Aranyosi* and C-659/15 *Robert Căldăraru*, EU:2016:198; this case law has now been consolidated, see eg Case C-128/18 *Dumitru-Tudor Dorobantu*, EU:C:2019:857. As we shall see, the ECtHR has imposed some limits on the operability of the so-called mutual trust doctrine: *Avotiņš v Latvia* (Appl No 17502/07), judgment of 23 May 2016.

[140] On this point, see eg Case C-476/17 *Pelham et al*, EU:C:2019:624; Case C-469/17 *Funke Medien NRW GmbH v Bundesrepublik Deutschland*, EU:C:2019:623; Joined Cases C-609 and 610/17 *Terveys- ja sosiaalialan neuvottelujärjestö (TSN) ryi*, EU:C:2019:981.

[141] See generally T Lock, 'Rights and Principles in the EU Charter of Fundamental Rights' (2019) 56 *Common Market Law Review* 1201; J Krommendijk, 'Principled Silence or Mere Silence on Principles: The Role of the EU Charter's Principles in the Case Law of the Court of Justice' (2015) 11 *European Competition Law Review* 321; see Case C-626/22 *CZ and Others v Ilva SpA in Amministrazione Straordinaria, Acciaierie d'Italia Holding SpA*, EU:C:2024:542 interpreting secondary legislation in line with Art 37 Charter, and see R Zorzos, '*Ilva and others*: Ethical Judgement, or an Unethical Judgment?' (2025) 62 *Common Market Law Review* 1579.

[142] See eg Case C-565/19 P *Carvalho v Parliament and Council*, EU:C::2021:252; A Rocha and PF Martins, 'Standing for the Environment? Locus Standi of Associations Before the ECtHR and the CJEU' (2025) 5 *European Human Rights Law Review* 591.

the Court is able to use Article 37 to interpret existing legislation as well as annul acts of the Union which clearly disregard the principles enshrined in that Article.[143]

Article 52(6) restates that full account must be taken of national law and practices specified in the Charter, while Article 52(7) instructs the courts to have due regard to the Charter explanations when interpreting the Charter.

Finally, Article 54 provides a prohibition on abuse of rights, and it is almost identical to Article 17 ECHR. It is aimed at ensuring that the Charter rights cannot be used in order to deprive individuals of rights conferred therein.[144]

Very few people would take Articles 51, 52, and 53 Charter as examples of clear and unambiguous drafting; rather, those provisions reflect the tensions and anxieties pertaining to EU fundamental rights. Be that as it may, the Charter is a remarkable document—it took over 30 years following the *Stauder* judgment to provide Union citizens with a proper catalogue of rights in order to ensure, at least theoretically, better awareness and therefore increased protection of fundamental rights.[145]

5 The EU and the ECHR

The Lisbon Treaty introduced a new Article 6(2) TEU, which provides:

> The Union shall accede to the European Convention for the Protection of Human Rights and Fundamental Freedoms. Such accession shall not affect the Union's competences as defined in the Treaties.

The first negotiations for accession started in June 2010 and ended in April 2013. However, and as mentioned at the beginning of this chapter, in December 2014 the Court of Justice declared the proposed agreement incompatible with the Treaties, and the process was therefore abruptly halted until October 2019 when the Council agreed to restart the negotiations and provided a new mandate for the Commission. We will first look at the background to accession, including the case law of the ECtHR on acts of the EU, to then turn to the first Draft Accession Agreement together with the Court ruling in Opinion 2/13, also looking at how the Court's objections have been overcome in the new Draft Revised Accession Agreement.

[143] Although, see L Besselink, 'The National and EU Targets for Reduction of Greenhouse Gas Emissions Infringe the ECHR: The Judicial Review of General Policy Objectives' (2022) 18 *European Constitutional Law Review* 155, discussing a Dutch case imposing an emission reduction target for the Dutch government: *Urgenda Foundation v Netherlands*, unreported 20 December 2019 (HR (NL)); and see in the ECtHR *Verein Klimaseniorinnen Schweiz and Others v Switzerland* (Appl No 53600/20), judgment of 9 April 2024.

[144] See in the ECHR context, eg *Lawless v Ireland (No 3)* (1979–80) 1 EHRR 15.

[145] A mention should be made of Protocol 30 on the application of the Charter to Poland (and formerly the UK); this Protocol (re)states that the Charter does not 'extend' the powers of the Court of Justice or national judiciary to find national rules incompatible with the Charter. Given that the Charter only codifies existing rights, this provision has been deemed legally irrelevant in *NS* (n 66) paras 116 *et seq*; Art 1(2) of the Protocol on the other hand provides that Title IV (Solidarity), which contains social rights, does not create 'justiciable rights' applicable in Poland (or in the UK), except insofar as 'Poland (or the UK) has provided for such rights in national law'. It is open to doubt whether there is any right in Title IV which is not already provided for in Union law and therefore also in the laws of Poland (and the UK). Art 2 also restates the obvious: if the Charter refers to national laws and practices, it shall apply to Poland (and the UK) only to the extent to which those two countries recognize in their laws and practices the rights and principles therein.

5.1 **Background to accession**

The European Convention on Human Rights (ECHR or Convention) is a charter of rights adopted in the aftermath of the Second World War by the Council of Europe, a body distinct from, and of much wider composition than, the EU. In order to ensure that the Convention would have 'teeth', the contracting parties set up an international court, the ECtHR, entrusted with interpreting the ECHR and holding the contracting parties to account.[146] Uniquely for the time, cases before the ECtHR can be brought by individual parties; however, since the Convention is a 'safety net', setting only the minimum standard of fundamental rights for contracting Parties, individuals must have exhausted domestic remedies before being able to bring a case before the ECtHR.[147]

It has been mentioned previously that, from the very first cases concerning human rights protection in the (then) EEC, the Court of Justice stated that it would draw inspiration also from the ECHR, and that this document had special importance for the EU. Furthermore, in interpreting fundamental rights, the Court of Justice looks at the jurisprudence of the ECtHR and while discrepancies in the interpretation given by the two courts have occurred, those have not been intentional.[148] And, starting with the Maastricht Treaty, the centrality of the ECHR in the system of fundamental rights protection in the EU has also been restated at Treaty level.[149]

In many respects, then, the ECHR is already part of EU public law: it is mentioned in the Treaties and Article 52(3) of the Charter clarifies that the EU can only improve on the protection afforded by the ECHR. Yet, the fact that the EU is not a party to the Convention raises very serious legal and political issues, and especially:

- it excludes the jurisdiction of the ECtHR over the EU;
- it introduces an idiosyncrasy as regards the EU Member States, in that respect for human rights is a precondition for joining the EU and yet the EU does not subject itself to any external scrutiny of its fundamental rights compliance; and
- it leads to accusations of double standards as regards non-EU States, since the EU often imposes human rights conditionality clauses in international Treaties.

For these reasons, discussions as to whether the EU should accede to the Convention have been long-running and in 1994 the Court of Justice was asked for an Opinion (2/94) on whether accession would be legally possible. The Court declared that, as the Treaties stood at the time, there was no competence for the Union to accede to the ECHR.[150] This eventually led to the adoption of Article 6(2) TEU.

Before turning to the problem of accession to the ECHR we shall briefly analyse the case law of the ECtHR in relation to EU law.

[146] The ECtHR is based in Strasbourg and for this reason is at times referred to as the Strasbourg Court; the Court of Justice is instead at times referred to as the Luxembourg Court.

[147] Protocol 16 ECHR provides for the possibility for the highest national courts to request an advisory opinion to the ECtHR; the Protocol was adopted in 2013 and entered into force for the ratifying countries in 2018.

[148] See eg Joined Cases 46/87 and 227/88 *Hoechst AG v Commission* [1989] ECR 2859 and cf *Niemietz v Germany* (1993) Series A, Vol 251, 16 EHRR 97; note that the European Court of Justice ruling predates the ECtHR interpretation; this divergence was corrected at the earliest possible opportunity, see Case C-94/00 *Roquette Frères SA v Directeur général de la concurrence, de la consomation et de la répression des fraudes* [2002] ECR I-9011. On the relationship between the Court and ECtHR, see generally C Timmermans, 'The Relationship between the European Court of Justice and the European Court of Human Rights' in Arnull, Barnard, Dougan, and Spaventa (n 130) ch 8.

[149] Art F(2) TEU, Maastricht Treaty; and now Art 6(3) TEU.

[150] Opinion 2/94 (n 20).

5.1.1 **The case law of the European Court of Human Rights: the doctrine of equivalent protection**

When thinking about the relationship between EU and ECHR law we should distinguish two situations according to whether the challenged act arises out of the discretion of the Member State or whether it is mandated by EU law. In the first case, when the national authorities implement EU law but have a discretion,[151] the application of the ECHR and the jurisdiction of the ECtHR do not concern EU law per se, but rather what the Member State has autonomously decided to do (see Fig. 9.1 at the end of this chapter).

In the second case, the threat to fundamental rights arises directly and solely by virtue of EU law: this is the case when the individual sphere is affected directly by an EU law rule and/or when the individual sphere is affected by action of a Member State which is implementing a mandatory rule of EU law, ie when the Member State, under EU law, has no discretion as to whether or not to act in a certain way. It is this latter situation which creates a tension between the ECHR and the EU, since the latter is not party to the Convention, and yet it would be inconsistent with the very purpose of the Convention to allow the Member States collectively through the EU to pierce the safety net so carefully crafted after the war.

In this respect we see an evolution in the case law of the ECtHR, seeking a balance between these two conflicting interests. In *M & Co*, the first case to raise the issue of compatibility of EU law with the Convention, the claimant attacked the acts of German authorities which were enforcing a European Commission decision taken within the field of competition law. The company argued that the ECHR was applicable, and the ECtHR had jurisdiction, since the obligations imposed by the ECHR on the German authorities did not cease just because the authorities were giving effect to a decision of the European Commission. Otherwise, it was argued, it would be all too easy for contracting parties to evade their obligations by acting through the medium of Union law rather than national law. The European Commission of Human Rights (then in charge of deciding on the admissibility of the case before the ECtHR), partially rejected such reasoning. It first noted that according to Article 1 ECHR, Member States are responsible for *any* violation of the Convention, whether it is a consequence of domestic or international law. However, it also found that the EU system both secured and controlled compliance with fundamental rights. To require the Member State to check whether the Convention rights had been respected in each individual case would be contrary to the very idea of transferring powers to an international organization.[152] This non-interventionist stance was successfully challenged in the case of *Matthews*.[153]

Ms Matthews, a resident of Gibraltar, a British overseas territory, was denied the possibility of voting in the European Parliament elections on the ground that franchise for such elections was reserved to British nationals resident in the UK. Residents in Gibraltar were

[151] See eg *Ilias and Ahmed v Hungary* (Appl No 47287/15), judgment of 21 November 2019, esp para 96; *MSS v Belgium and Greece* (n 100) esp para 338; this ruling had important effects in relation to the European asylum system framework, see *NS* (n 66), discussed at section 4.4.2. The ECtHR has left open the question as to whether in certain circumstances a ruling of the CJEU might have the effects of leaving no discretion to the Member State for the purposes of the application of the Bosphorus presumption, *Case of O'Sullivan McCarthy Mussel Development Ltd v Ireland* (Appl No 44460/16), judgment of 7 June 2018, paras 110–114.

[152] *M & Co v Germany*, decision of the European Commission of Human Rights, 9 February 1990 (1990) 64 ECmHRR 138; see also *Pafitis v Greece*, decision of the ECtHR, 26 February 1998; in *Cantoni v France* ECtHR 1996-V 1614, the ECtHR held that the fact that a piece of national legislation reproduced word by word the provision of a Community directive did not subtract it from the scope of application of the Convention.

[153] *Matthews v UK* (Appl No 24833/94), ECtHR 1999-I.

therefore excluded, even though most of EU law applied to that territory. Ms Matthews then complained that her disenfranchisement was a violation of Article 3 Protocol 1 of the Convention, which guarantees the right to free elections. The issue was therefore a thorny one: at stake was the very foundation of the democratic process, the principle of democratic representation. However, the case related to the elections to the European Parliament, which, in this matter, were regulated by the 1976 Act on direct elections, a measure having the same value as the Treaties.[154] For this reason, the UK argued that the ECtHR did not have jurisdiction; and that the UK could not be held responsible for a potential violation arising from a collective act of the (then) 15 Member States, since it was unable to amend that act unilaterally.

The ECtHR found that acts of the (then) European Community were not subject to its scrutiny since the EC was not a contracting party to the Convention, and the latter did not exclude transfer of competences to international organizations provided Convention rights continued to be 'secured'. However, in the case of EC primary legislation, where the Court of Justice has no jurisdiction to assess compliance with fundamental rights, the UK, together with the other EC Member States would be responsible for violations of the Convention.

Matthews is a seminal case in that it lays the foundations for the subsequent evolution of the case law of the ECtHR on the relationship between the Convention and EU law. In particular, it makes clear that gaps in fundamental rights protection cannot be tolerated, so that when the Court of Justice is unable to protect those rights then the ECtHR is willing to step in and hold the Member States collectively responsible for upholding/violating Convention rights. In the case of *Bosphorus*,[155] the ECtHR further clarified that, even when the Court of Justice has jurisdiction, the review of the ECtHR is not altogether excluded. Rather, the ECtHR will refrain from exercising its jurisdiction over the act of an international institution (eg the EU) as implemented by a Member State (ie the contracting party to the Convention) only to the extent to which it deems that:

> the relevant organisation is considered to protect fundamental rights, as regards both the substantive guarantees offered and the mechanisms controlling their observance, in a manner which can be considered at least ***equivalent*** to that for which the Convention provides . . .
>
> . . .
>
> 156. If such equivalent protection is considered to be provided by the organisation, the presumption will be that a State has not departed from the requirements of the Convention when it does no more than implement legal obligations flowing from its membership of the organisation.
>
> However, any such presumption can be rebutted if, in the circumstances of a particular case, it is considered that the protection of Convention rights was ***manifestly deficient***. In such cases, the interest of international cooperation would be outweighed by the Convention's role as a 'constitutional instrument of European public order' in the field of human rights. (Emphasis added)

[154] Act concerning the election of the representatives of the European Parliament by direct universal suffrage, annexed to Decision 76/787/ECSC, EEC, Euratom. This was later amended partly as a result of the ruling in *Matthews* (n 153), see Council Decision 2002/772/EC Euratom (OJ [2002] L283/1); the UK then changed its rules and faced a challenge before the Court of Justice in Case C-145/04 *Spain v UK* [2006] ECR I-7917.

[155] *Bosphorus v Ireland* (Appl No 45036/98), ECtHR 2005-VI, noted in (2005) *European Human Rights Law Review* 649.

The ruling in *Bosphorus* then ensures that the safety net provided by the Convention remains in place even when the contested act can be ascribed to the EU rather than to its Member State; however, *Bosphorus* only provides protection against significant gaps in the safety net, since:

- it establishes a presumption of equivalent protection of EU law with the ECHR;
- it is for the claimant to prove that such equivalent protection is not only lacking but manifestly deficient.

That said, in later case law the Court elaborated the notion of 'equivalent' protection; in *Michaud v France*,[156] the ECtHR clarified that the presumption of equivalent protection applies only when the control mechanism provided for by EU law has been fully brought into play. This is not the case where a national court refuses to make a reference on the compatibility between EU law and fundamental rights.[157] In *Avotiņš*,[158] the ECtHR went a step further: the case concerned mutual recognition that applies in relation to certain coordinating pieces of EU legislation, such as the European Arrest Warrant,[159] the Dublin system,[160] and the Brussels Regulations.[161] Pursuant to the case law of the Court of Justice, in executing a decision to transfer an individual or recognize an act of another Member State, the executing authority should not normally assess whether the requesting or issuing Member State complies with fundamental rights. Rather, unless there is a real and demonstrable risk that the individual concerned might see her fundamental rights compromised,[162] the national authority should *trust* all of the other Member States in the EU to be respecting the standards set by the Charter and by the ECHR.

In *Avotiņš*, then, the ECtHR had to decide the extent to which it had jurisdiction in cases where mutual recognition, required in this case by the Brussels I Regulation,[163] might come at the expense of fundamental rights. The Court therefore set a series of tests to decide when it would assert jurisdiction over national authorities implementing mandatory rules of EU law.[164]

In line with previous case law, it held that if the protection afforded by EU law is equivalent to that afforded by the ECHR, then the ECtHR would intervene only if it was proven in the case in front of it, that the protection had nonetheless been manifestly deficient (a very high bar).

156 *Michaud v France* (Appl No 12323/11), judgment of 6 December 2012, paras 114 *et seq.*

157 On the duty of national courts of last instance to make a reference to the Court of Justice pursuant to Art 267 TFEU, see *Ullens de Schooten and Rezabek v Belgium* (Appl Nos 3989/07 and 38353/07), judgment of 20 September 2011.

158 *Avotiņš v Latvia* (Appl No 17502/07), judgment of 23 May 2016. See also *Bivolaru and Moldovan v France* (Appl Nos 40324/16 and 12623/17), judgment of 25 March 2021.

159 Council Framework Decision 2002/584/JHA on the European Arrest Warrant and the surrender procedures between Member States (OJ [2002] L190/1), consolidated version 28 March 2009.

160 Regulation 604/2013 (OJ [2013] L108/31), known as the Dublin III Regulation.

161 Regulation 1215/2012 on jurisdiction and the recognition and enforcement of judgments in civil and commercial matters (recast) (OJ [2012] L351/1); Regulation 2201/2003 concerning jurisdiction and the recognition and enforcement of judgments in matrimonial matters and the matters of parental responsibility (OJ [2003] L338/1).

162 eg Joined Cases C-411/10 and C-493/10 *NS v Secretary of State for the Home Department*, EU:C:2011:13905; Joined Cases C-404/15 *Aranyosi* and C-659/15 *Robert Căldăraru*, EU:2016:198; Case C-216/18 PPU *LM*, EU:C:2018:586; Joined Cases C-562 and 563/21 PPU *X and Y*, EU:C:2022:100.

163 Now Regulation 1215/2012 on jurisdiction and the recognition and enforcement of judgments in civil and commercial matters (recast) (OJ [2012] L351/1).

164 It should be remembered that if the Member State has discretion in the implementation of EU law then the ECHR and the jurisdiction of the Court of Human Rights always apply to that discretion.

It then held that whether there is equivalent protection between EU and ECHR is not predetermined, but rather it has to be assessed on a case-by-case basis. Two factors are relevant in deciding upon 'equivalence': first, whether the Charter is applicable; and secondly, the role of the Court of Justice. This in practice means that the Court of Justice must have jurisdiction, although it does not necessarily need to have exercised it, provided that the national court's decision not to refer the matter for a preliminary ruling is not in breach of Article 6(1) ECHR.[165] On the other hand, and consistently with the earlier mentioned ruling in *Matthews*, if the Court of Justice does not have jurisdiction to annul the EU act (such as is the case with provisions having the same value as the Treaties), then the ECtHR will assert jurisdiction.

After this preliminary scrutiny, if the EU protection has been found to be equivalent to that afforded by the ECHR, then the ECtHR will scrutinize whether in the case in front of it, the protection has been manifestly deficient. The ECtHR though added a new requirement: it held that national courts are also under an ECHR obligation to assess whether applying the doctrine of mutual recognition in the case before them would risk rendering the protection afforded by EU law manifestly deficient. In particular it stated:

> In this spirit, where the courts of a State which is both a Contracting Party to the Convention and a Member State of the European Union are called upon to apply a mutual recognition mechanism established by EU law, they must give full effect to that mechanism where the protection of Convention rights cannot be considered manifestly deficient. However, if a serious and substantiated complaint is raised before them to the effect that the protection of a Convention right has been manifestly deficient and that this situation cannot be remedied by European Union law, they cannot refrain from examining that complaint on the sole ground that they are applying EU law.

The *Avotiņš* case then restricts the operationability of the doctrine of mutual trust, and in so doing ensures a stronger protection for fundamental rights. Furthermore, as we shall see, the *Avotiņš* ruling should be assessed also in relation to the ruling in Opinion 2/13.

To summarize, the ECtHR will assert jurisdiction over a mandatory provision of EU law in the following situations:

- When the protection afforded by EU law is *not* equivalent since the Charter is not applicable (Treaty level provisions) and/or there is no jurisdiction of the Court of Justice to review the contested measure (Treaty level provision) (*Matthews, Michaud, Avotiņš*).
- When the protection afforded by EU law, whilst equivalent in the abstract, has been manifestly deficient in the case at issue (*Bosphorus, Avotiņš*).
- The ECHR also imposes on national courts a duty to ensure that protection is not manifestly deficient, by examining serious and substantiated complaints to that effect (at least in mutual recognition cases) (*Avotiņš*).

5.2 **EU accession to the ECHR**

As we have seen in the previous section, even though the EU is not yet party to the ECHR, the ECtHR has accepted, in principle, to exercise jurisdiction in order to ensure that membership of the EU does not deprive individuals of protection at least equivalent to

[165] See also eg *Sanofi Pasteur v France* (Appl No 25137/16), judgment of 13 February 2020.

that provided by the Convention. This state of affairs is not, however, completely satisfactory since, lacking accession:

- the jurisdiction of the ECtHR is limited to those cases where the claimant can rebut the presumption of equivalent protection; this means that overall it is more difficult for individuals to seize the ECtHR in cases relating to EU law than it is in domestic cases;
- the EU is not party to the proceedings so that it is the Member States collectively that incur responsibility, and the EU is not bound, as a matter of Convention law, by the ECtHR ruling.[166]

It is for these reasons, together with the political considerations mentioned previously, that accession to the ECHR has been deemed desirable. That said, accession of an international organization to a Convention which was aimed at States is not without its challenges. In this respect, consider: that the EU is also the sum of its Member States; that in most cases, an EU act would also involve an act of national authorities (even in cases in which a regulation is at issue, since it is usually for national authorities to police compliance, seize goods, etc); and that, crucially, in the EU there is already a supranational court, the Court of Justice, which is the only court entrusted with the interpretation and assessment of validity of Union law.[167] The relationship between the ECtHR and the Court of Justice was then one of the points that needed clarification in the accession negotiations; furthermore, the interaction between the Member States and the EU is complex, especially in those cases where responsibility might be more difficult to ascertain. To address these issues, the first Draft Accession Agreement provided for a co-respondent mechanism and for the possibility of 'delaying' proceedings to allow the Court of Justice to assess the compatibility with fundamental rights of the contested EU measure, if it did not have the possibility to do so before the case reached the ECtHR.[168] The Court of Justice in Opinion 2/13 clarified that some of the features of the Draft Agreement were incompatible with the autonomy of EU law. In particular, the Court objected to certain features of the co-respondent mechanism (section 5.2.1); to the fact that the ECtHR would have jurisdiction in relation to the CFSP, even in those cases where the Court of Justice does not, and to the lack of recognition of the principle of mutual trust (section 5.3); and to problems raised by interparty applications and the applicability of Protocol 16 (section 5.4).

After a long pause, negotiations for accession restarted and a new Accession Agreement had been reached in 2023. Yet, the Court's objection as to the fact that the ECtHR would have jurisdiction over the CFSP whilst it itself did not, could not be overcome in the Accession Agreement since it relates to an internal constitutional problem within the EU. As a result, the process was paused; however, following the *KS and KD* ruling, which greatly expanded the Court's jurisdiction in the CFSP, the Commission has considered that all issues are now solved and has requested a new Opinion as to the compatibility of the Draft Revised Accession Agreement with the Treaties.[169] We shall

[166] De facto though, excluding Treaty level provisions, the EU would be bound by a ruling of the ECtHR finding a piece of EU law incompatible with the ECHR through the provisions of the Charter since Art 52(3) provides that Charter rights deriving from the ECHR must be given the same scope and meaning as those in the ECHR.

[167] Case 314/85 *Foto-Frost* [1987] ECR 4199, and see chapter 10.

[168] Fifth negotiation meeting between the Steering Committee for Human Rights (CDDH) ad hoc negotiation group and the European Commission on the Accession of the European Union to the European Convention on Human Rights, *Final Report to the CDDH*, doc 47+1(2013)008rev2, available at www.echr.coe.int/Documents/UE_Report_CDDH_ENG.pdf; see P Gragl, *The Accession of the European Union to the European Convention on Human Rights* (Oxford: Hart Publishing, 2013).

[169] See n 2.

look at the objections of the Court and the way they have been addressed in the new agreement.[170]

5.2.1 Co-respondent mechanism

Article 3(2) of the original draft agreement provided that, when an application was directed against a Member State of the EU, the EU may become a co-respondent if 'it appears' that the compatibility of EU law with the Convention is called into question. This provision would allow the EU to become a full party to the proceedings (at present the EU can only submit third party interventions), which also means it would become bound by the ruling of the ECtHR. Take, for instance, a case like *NS*[171] where deportation of asylum seekers to another EU Member State is made possible by an EU regulation, although Member States take the final (discretionary) decision as to whether they want to assess the asylum application themselves. If the individual brings the case against the Member State that has issued the deportation decision,[172] it seems reasonable that the EU might choose to become a co-respondent as there would be some uncertainty as to whether the potential breach has been caused by the EU legislation or by the implementing national act.

The reverse is also possible: in cases concerning a provision of the TEU or TFEU or another piece of EU primary law, Member States can become co-respondents in a case directed against the EU since, should a violation be found, they would have to act collectively to modify the Treaties or primary legislation to remedy the breach. So, for instance, in a case like *Matthews*[173] where the complaint related to EU primary law (in that case the failure to extend the franchise for the European Parliament to EU citizens resident in Gibraltar), the case would be directed against the EU as the body primarily responsible for the adoption of the contested act. However, Member States have a direct interest in a case like this, since it is they who are in charge of amending EU primary law: it therefore seems reasonable that, should they so wish, they can become co-respondents.

In order to ensure full protection for the individual, a new paragraph would be added to Article 36 Convention so that the admissibility of an application is decided without 'regard to the participation of a co-respondent in the proceedings'. As a result, the individual will not be penalized for not having correctly identified the potential responsibility of the EU in the alleged breach. For an overview, on fundamental rights and jurisdiction, see Fig. 9.1 at the end of this chapter.

The objections of the Court of Justice and the solution in the Draft Revised Accession Agreement

Even though the Court of Justice recognized that the co-respondent mechanism aimed to pursue a legitimate need, it found that it was incompatible with the Treaties, and in particular with the exclusive jurisdiction of the Court of Justice in determining the division of powers between EU and Member States. In the eyes of the Court this was the case since once either the EU or a Member State required to become a co-respondent it would be for the ECtHR to assess the 'plausibility' that a provision of EU law or a provision of

[170] *Final consolidated version of the draft accession instruments*, 18th Meeting of the CDDH ad hoc Negotiation Group on the Accession of the European Union to the European Convention on Human Rights, 46+1(2023)36, 17 March 2023. All references to the revised Accession Agreement and other instruments are to this version unless otherwise indicated.

[171] *NS* (n 66). See section 4.4.2.

[172] This would in fact be the case in *MSS v Belgium and Greece* (n 100).

[173] *Matthews v UK* (n 153). See section 5.1.1.

EU primary law is called into question,[174] hence jeopardizing the autonomy of the EU legal order.

The new agreement provides an unconditional right to Member States and to the EU to become co-respondent. Thus, new Article 3(5) Draft Revised Agreement on the Accession of the EU to the ECHR, provides that the EU or its Member States can become correspondent not only by accepting the invitation of the ECtHR but, crucially, also upon their own initiative. And, even more importantly, the decision as to whether the conditions provided for in the Draft Revised Accession Agreement for being co-respondent (for the EU the fact that proceedings might call into question the compatibility with the Convention and its protocols of a provision of EU law, and for the Member States the fact that proceedings might call into question a provision of primary EU law) are determined by the EU according to a reasoned assessment.[175] In this way, the risk that the ECtHR would be called to express an opinion as to the repartition of competences between Member States and the EU is eliminated. Some of the other parties to the Convention, however, insisted that the applicant should be given the opportunity to state their views on the joining of a co-respondent.[176] This is problematic for the EU because, pursuant to Opinion 2/13, and generally to the principle of autonomy of EU law, EU law cannot be reviewed by other courts. And, if the applicant could state their views then there would be a danger that the ECtHR might assess these views against the co-respondent decision to join, which would indirectly lead to a review of the repartition of competences between the EU and Member States. The compromise solution that has been suggested is to allow the applicant to state reasons but also clarify that the ECtHR cannot review the EU/Member State's decision to become co-applicants. In order to protect the autonomy of EU law, the new draft agreement also disposes of the possibility for the ECtHR to determine, in proceedings where there is a co-respondent, that only one party should be held responsible for the violation. In this way, once there is a co-respondent, both parties (the EU and the Member State) are always responsible, and it is a matter for the EU to determine potential allocation of responsibility.[177]

5.2.2 **The role of the Court of Justice**

As mentioned previously, in those cases in which the EU is co-respondent, that is, where EU law might conflict with the Convention, there would be the possibility to delay proceedings to allow the Court of Justice to assess for itself whether the rule is compatible with the Convention. For instance, take the case of *Stauder* where Mr Stauder complained that identification by name of those eligible for discounted butter constituted a breach of his right to private life.[178] In a case such as this, lacking a prior ruling by the Court of Justice, the ECtHR would be able to delay proceedings to allow the Court of Justice to examine the matter, possibly suggesting an interpretation which would make the measure compatible

[174] Opinion 2/13, para 224, 'Admittedly, in carrying out such a review, the ECtHR is to ascertain whether, in the light of those reasons, it is plausible that the conditions set out in paragraphs 2 and 3 of Article 3 are met, and that review does not relate to the merits of those reasons. However, the fact remains that, in carrying out that review, the ECtHR would be required to assess the rules of EU law governing the division of powers between the EU and its Member States as well as the criteria for the attribution of their acts or omissions, in order to adopt a final decision in that regard which would be binding both on the Member States and on the EU.'

[175] (New) Art 3(5), *Consolidated version of the Draft Revised Accession Agreement.*

[176] 12th Meeting of the CDDH ad hoc Negotiation Group ('47+1') on the Accession of the European Union to the European Convention on Human Rights, https://rm.coe.int/cddh-47-1-2021-16-en/1680a4c9ea.

[177] Art 3(7), Draft Revised Accession Agreement.

[178] Case 29/69 *Stauder* [1969] ECR 419, see section 2.1.

with fundamental rights (as was the case in *Stauder*, where the Court of Justice was able to provide an alternative interpretation of the (then) Community instrument so as to ensure respect for the applicant's right).

The reasons for this procedure are clear: in the case of national rules, an individual must have exhausted domestic remedies before being able to bring a complaint before the ECtHR. This ensures that fundamental rights protection is primarily the responsibility of national courts; it is only when something has been overlooked or went wrong in that forum that the ECtHR will intervene. The ECtHR is not a further court of appeal; rather, it ensures that a minimum standard of protection is applied throughout the territories of the contracting parties.

In the case of the EU, matters are more complex because, mostly, cases reach the Court of Justice through the preliminary ruling mechanism: conditions for direct access (standing) to the EU Courts to challenge the validity of EU law are strict. Since in most cases there is also a national enforcement element to the case, issues are more often examined by national courts which then decide whether a reference to the Court of Justice is appropriate.[179] In those cases, however, the parties have no control over whether the reference is made; and on which questions are asked of the Court of Justice. For this reason, it would have been unwise to include prior scrutiny by the Court of Justice as a prerequisite for the 'exhaustion' of domestic remedies under the Convention. Since individuals have no power to decide whether a preliminary reference is sought, they should not be penalized if the national court failed to refer the question to the Court of Justice. On the other hand, it was felt that in those cases it would be beneficial for the Court of Justice to have a 'first shot' at the correct interpretation of EU law and its compatibility with the Convention (and the Charter), not least since the matter might be resolved without the need for further investigation by the ECtHR. For this reason, when the EU is a co-respondent, and the Court of Justice has not yet assessed the Convention compatibility of the rules at issue, proceedings are delayed to allow the Court of Justice to examine the matter.

It is not obvious that this system would work in practice;[180] on the one hand, in straightforward cases where the national court of last instance refused to request a preliminary ruling, thereby going against the wording and the spirit of Article 267(3) TFEU, the procedure provided in both the original and more recent Draft Accession Treaty allows for 'a fix', by allowing the Court of Justice to rule on the matter despite the absence of a preliminary reference. However, it could be questioned whether such a 'fix' should not be provided in the context of the EU itself rather than through an external mechanism.

In other cases, it might be more difficult to ascertain whether the Court of Justice has already ruled on the issue: take, for instance, the ruling in *Kaba II*,[181] where the Court of Justice was also asked to assess the compatibility of EU law, and in particular the role of the Advocate General, with fundamental rights. The Court reversed the order of the questions so as to avoid examining the fundamental rights issue.[182] It is open to debate whether in those cases the ECtHR could delay the proceedings to allow the Court of Justice to have another say. Furthermore, the function of gatekeeper allocated by the

[179] See generally chapter 10.

[180] For a (more) positive assessment, see R Baratta, 'Accession of the EU to the ECHR: The Rationale for the ECJ's Prior Involvement' (2013) 50 *Common Market Law Review* 1305.

[181] Case C-466/00 *Kaba v Secretary of State for the Home Department* ('*Kaba II*') [2003] ECR I-2219.

[182] See also the case of *Michaud* (n 156), discussed in section 5.1.1, where the applicant complained about the relevant EU law breaching Art 8 ECHR. In Case C-305/05 *Order des barreaux francophones et germanophone v Conseil des Ministres* [2007] ECR I-5305, the Court of Justice examined the compatibility of the same piece of legislation (Directive 91/308 on prevention of the use of the financial system for the purpose of money laundering (OJ [1991] L166/77), as amended by Directive 2001/97 (OJ [2001] L344/76)), only with the right to fair trial as guaranteed by Art 6 ECHR (and Arts 47 and 48 Charter).

TFEU to national courts might well be compromised if individuals can then seize the Court of Justice through the ECtHR. After all, the fact that it is for the national court to decide what questions to refer, and when, is aimed at ensuring that the Court of Justice is not flooded by unmeritorious and spurious claims.

Another slight oddity is that, when the Member State is a co-respondent, the special delaying procedure is not available. Member States can be co-respondent when the issue relates to the compatibility of a piece of primary law with the Convention. The most likely reason the Court of Justice does not need to be involved in those cases is that it has no jurisdiction to declare EU primary law invalid. However, it could be argued that the compatibility of primary (hence, more general) rules with fundamental rights might depend very much on the interpretation given to such rules, an interpretation which is for the Court of Justice to provide.

The objections of the Court of Justice and the solution proposed in the Draft Revised Accession Agreement

The Court of Justice found that the mechanism for its prior involvement also infringed the autonomy of the EU legal order. In particular it found that in order for the ECtHR to decide whether the involvement of the Court of Justice was necessary, an interpretation of the case law of the Court of Justice would be required. It might be recalled that the prior involvement of the Court of Justice would be possible only when the Court did not have the chance to rule on a particular provision of EU law. Yet, the Court of Justice held that making that finding necessarily would entail allowing the ECtHR to give a binding interpretation of the case law of the EU Court.

In this case, though, the Court of Justice also suggested a potential solution: in any case pending before the ECtHR, the competent EU institution should be informed so as to decide whether the Court of Justice had already given a ruling on the matter and, if not, to arrange for the prior involvement procedure to be initiated. This suggestion was taken on board by the negotiators and the draft explanatory report clarifies that it is for the EU to determine whether it is necessary to initiate the prior involvement of the CJEU. This finding, like the decision on the co-respondent, is authoritative and determinative.[183]

5.3 **Accession, CFSP, and the special nature of EU law**

In Opinion 2/13, the Court of Justice objected to two elements of the jurisdiction of the ECtHR: first of all, the fact that the latter would have jurisdiction over the entire body of EU law, including the Common Foreign and Security Policy. This for the Court of Justice is a problem since it itself only had jurisdiction in relation to CFSP matters in very limited circumstances.[184] And yet, there is no political will to give the Court of Justice general jurisdiction over the rest of the CFSP; and, pursuant to Art 57(1) ECHR, no general reservation might be made by contracting parties so that it would not be possible to just exclude CFSP from the reach of the ECHR. As mentioned above, after significant discussions on the issue, it was decided that the matter rested with the EU constitutional system,

[183] Paras 76 and 77, Appendix 5, Draft Explanatory report to the Agreement on the Accession of the European Union to the Convention for the Protection of Human Rights and Fundamental Freedoms.

[184] Art 275 TFEU; note, however, that the Court, even before *KS and KD*, increasingly gave a narrow interpretation to the limitation to its jurisdiction under CFSP, see eg Case C-14/19 P *European Union Satellite Centre (SatCen) v KF*, EU:C:2020:492; Case C-455/14 P *H v Council, Commission and European Union Police Mission (EUPM) in Bosnia and Herzegovina*, EU:C:2016:569; Case C-439/13, *Elitaliana SpA v Eulex Kosovo*, EU:C:2015:753.

even though some proposals were made to assuage the fears of the Court (not taken on board in the final Draft Revised Agreement).[185] The solution to this impasse might have arrived thanks to the Court's interpretation of its own jurisdiction in the *KS and KD* case (see chapter 26).[186] In *KS and KD*, the claimants brought an action for the non-contractual liability of the EU in relation to Eulex Kosovo, a mission established by a CFSP decision. The General Court found that it lacked jurisdiction over the claim pursuant to Article 24(1) TEU and Article 275 TFEU, which excludes the role of the Union judicature over the CFSP, exception being given for cases of restrictive measures against natural or legal persons and for the policing of the boundaries between CFSP and other fields of EU law.[187] The Court of Justice, in a seminal ruling, found instead that the inclusion of the CFSP in the EU constitutional framework means that the basic principles of the EU legal order, including that of judicial review, apply also in relation to that field. The Court then drew a distinction between acts and omissions directly related to 'political or strategic choices' in the field of CFSP and the Common Security and Defence Policy (CSDP), over which the Court does not have jurisdiction; and acts which are not directly related to those choices, over which the Court has jurisdiction. Following the ruling in *KS and KD*, the gap in the jurisdiction of the Court is greatly reduced. Furthermore, given the mechanism guaranteeing prior involvement of the Court of Justice, the risk that the ECtHR would assess the compatibility with the Convention of a CFSP act without any prior involvement of the Court of Justice seems almost nil.

Secondly, the Court of Justice took issue with the fact that the EU would be treated similarly to a State party. This would mean ignoring the fact that some of EU secondary legislation which provides for mutual recognition of domestic decisions (such as the European Arrest Warrant) is based on the idea of mutual trust between Member States. Pursuant to this approach then, Member States are under an EU law obligation to presume that fundamental rights are respected throughout the Union. For this reason, Member States might be required to execute or give effect to EU law without assessing, bar exceptional circumstances,[188] whether fundamental rights are fully respected in the territory of another Member State (for instance, the requesting State in the case of a European Arrest Warrant).[189] The application of the ECHR to these situations would, in the eyes of the Court, affect this obligation of mutual trust in that a State might be held responsible under the ECHR for giving effect to a mutual recognition obligation set in EU law.[190]

[185] Art 1(4a), Draft Agreement (May 2022).

[186] Joined Cases C-29/22 P and 44/22 P *KS and KD v Council*, EU:C:2024:725; see also Case C-351/22 *Neves 77 Solutions SRL v Agenția Națională de Administrare Fiscală—Direcția Generală Antifraudă Fiscală*, EU:C:2024:723. See Editorial Comments 'From Opinion 2/13 to KS and KD: Confronting a legacy of constitutional tensions' (2024) 61 *Common Market Law Review* 1455; for a different solution, see E Spaventa, 'Remedying Constitutional Heresies: The Charter, Damages and Jurisdiction in the Common Foreign and Security Policy' in K Armstrong, J Scott, and A Thies (eds), *EU External Relations and the Power of Law* (Oxford: Hart Publishing, 2024) 47. On the CFSP, see further chapter 26.

[187] Case T-771/20 *KS and KD v Council and Others*, EU:T:2021:798.

[188] See case law in n 184.

[189] On mutual trust, see also E Spaventa, 'Systemic v Administrative Mutual Trust: Recomposing the Disconnection Between Mutual Trust and Fundamental Rights Protection' (2025) 32 *Maastricht Journal of European and Comparative Law* 158.

[190] We have mentioned that there are some extreme situations (systemic risks together with evidence of harm to the particular claimant) where even the Court of Justice has accepted that the doctrine of mutual trust can be limited; see eg Joined Cases C-411/10 and C-493/10 *NS v Secretary of State for the Home Department*, EU:C:2011:13905; Joined Cases C-404/15 *Aranyosi* and C-659/15 *Robert Căldăraru*, EU:2016:198; Case C-216/18 PPU *LM*, EU:C:2018:586.

To address the Court of Justice's concerns, a new provision has been added to the Draft Revised Agreement,[191] to clarify that Accession does not affect the principle of mutual trust and that 'the protection of human rights guaranteed by the Convention shall be ensured'. The Draft Report however, explicitly refers to the *Avotiņš* case, restating that the ECtHR has held that it must verify that 'the principle of mutual trust is not applied automatically and mechanically to the detriment of human rights'.[192] It is to be seen whether this compromise will be acceptable to the Court of Justice of the EU—given however, that the ECtHR has already drawn the limits of the doctrine of mutual trust, it is to be hoped that the Court of Justice will consider sufficient the new article to meet its reservations.

5.4 **Interstate litigation and Protocol 16**

Finally, there were other two main issues which constituted a bar to accession following Opinion 2/13. First of all, in the context of the ECHR it is possible for any High Contracting Party to refer to the Court alleged breaches of the Convention by another State (Art 33 ECHR). In Opinion 2/13, the Court of Justice objected to the applicability of this provision to Member States of the EU for fear that it would undermine Article 344 TFEU which confers upon it exclusive jurisdiction on Member States' disputes concerning the interpretation or application of the Treaties. Article 4(3) and (4) of the Draft Revised Accession Agreement clarify that the EU and its Member States shall not avail themselves of Article 33 ECHR (inter-party disputes) when the matter concerns the interpretation or application of EU law. In order to guarantee the autonomy of EU law, the determination of whether an inter-party dispute relates to EU law rests solely with the EU.

Secondly, the CJEU also objected to the potential clash between Protocol 16 and the preliminary reference procedure. Protocol 16, currently ratified by 14 out of the 27 Member States, allows for the highest courts in the contracting parties to request an advisory opinion from the ECtHR. The Court of Justice then feared that a highest court might request an advisory opinion which related also to EU law, hence affecting its exclusive jurisdiction under Article 267 TFEU. The Draft Revised Accession Agreement provides that, in relation to Protocol 16, the court of an EU Member State must not be considered a 'highest' court for the purposes of an advisory opinion under Protocol 16 if the matter falls within the field of application of EU law.[193]

6 **Conclusion**

The field of fundamental rights is that which has evolved more markedly with the evolution of the EU—it arose from a constitutionally limp Community, it was followed by institutional acknowledgement and progressive legislative recognition, to result eventually in full codification. Given its inextricable link with the process of deeper integration, it is not surprising that it is a field which is not only complex but also, at times, deeply contested. Some Member States would like to see more and better protection of fundamental rights in the EU, while others are deeply cautious, if not altogether sceptical, of giving the Court of Justice yet another weapon in its already powerful armoury. In particular, the fear is that fundamental rights jurisprudence will have an excessive impact on national rules and further blur the boundaries between EU and national sovereignty.

[191] Art 6, Draft Revised Accession Agreement.
[192] Appendix 5, Draft Report on Accession, 74c.
[193] Art 5, Draft Revised Accession Agreement.

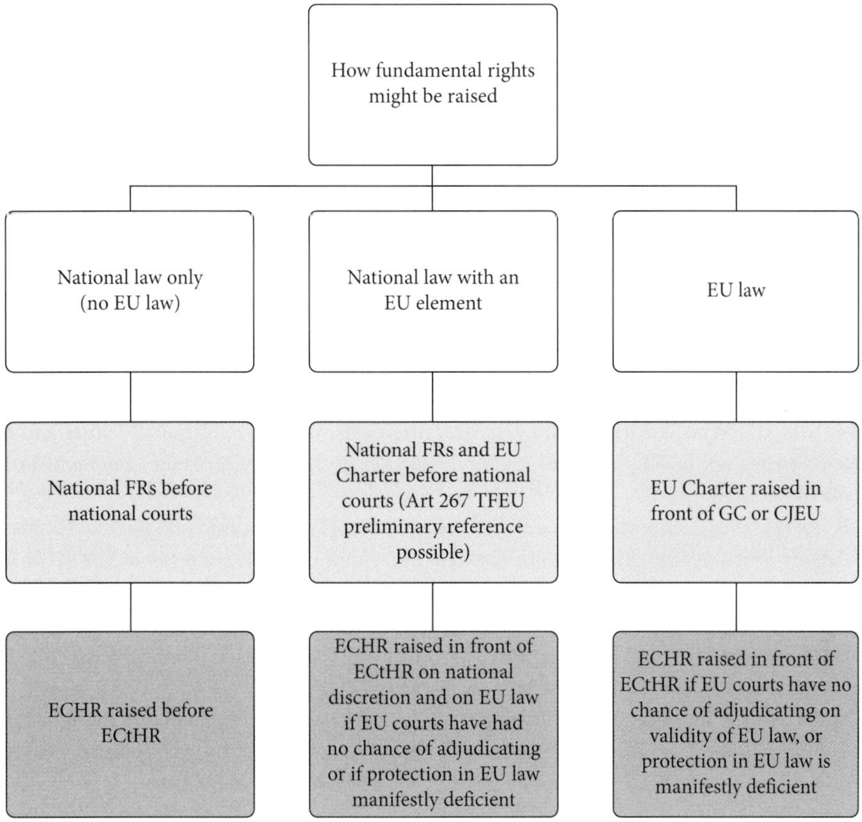

Fig. 9.1 Fundamental rights protection in the EU before the EU's accession to the ECHR

And yet, to most citizens those issues matter little: what is of value is that with every Treaty revision the rights of individuals against the EU legislature and executive (including where EU rules have been implemented by Member States) have been strengthened. Institutions that have the power to affect deeply the lives of many should be held to account: the Court, the Charter, and the Convention seek to do exactly that. Whereas it is undeniable that at times the EU falls short of expectations in the fundamental rights field, progress has indeed been made and Accession to the ECHR would ensure that the EU is subject to the same external scrutiny applicable to its Member States.

Further reading

G de Búrca, 'After the EU Charter of Fundamental Rights: The Court of Justice as a Human Rights Adjudicator?' (2013) 20 *Maastricht Journal of European and Comparative Law* 168

M Dawson, *The Governance of Fundamental Rights* (Cambridge: Cambridge University Press, 2017)

M Dougan, 'Judicial Review of Member State Action under the General Principles and the Charter: Defining the 'Scope of Union Law' (2015) 52 *Common Market Law Review* 1201

E Frantziou, *The Horizontal Effect of Fundamental Rights in the European Union: A Constitutional Analysis* (Oxford: Oxford University Press, 2019)

P Gragl, *The Accession of the European Union to the European Convention on Human Rights* (Oxford: Hart Publishing, 2013)

HCH Hofmann and BC Mihaescu, 'The Relation between the Charter's Fundamental Rights and the Unwritten General Principles of EU Law: Good Administration as the Test Case' (2013) 9 *European Constitutional Law Review* 73

K Lenaerts, 'Exploring the Limits of the EU Charter of Fundamental Rights' (2012) 8 *European Constitutional Law Review* 375

T Lock 'Rights and Principles in the EU Charter of Fundamental Rights' (2019) 56 *Common Market Law Review* 1201

S Peers, T Hervey, J Kenner, and A Ward (eds), *The Charter of Fundamental Rights: A Commentary* (2nd edn, Oxford: Hart Publishing, 2021)

A Pliakos and G Anagnostaras, 'Who Is the Ultimate Arbiter? The Battle over Judicial Supremacy in the EU' (2011) 26 *European Law Review* 109

D Sarmiento, 'Who Is Afraid of the Charter? The Court of Justice, National Courts and the New Framework of Fundamental Rights Protection in the EU' (2013) 50 *Common Market Law Review* 1267

E Spaventa, 'The Relationship between Free Movement of Persons and Fundamental Rights' in J Adams-Prassl, A Ezrachi, S Bogojević, and D Leczykiewicz (eds), *The Internal Market Idea—Essays in Honor of Steve Weatherill* (Oxford: Oxford University Press, 2024) ch 8

E Spaventa, 'Should We "Harmonize" Fundamental Rights in the EU? Some Reflections about Minimum Standards and Fundamental Rights Protection in the EU Composite Constitutional System' (2018) 55 *Common Market Law Review* 997

E Spaventa, 'The Interpretation of Article 51 of the EU Charter of Fundamental Rights' (2016) Study on behalf of the PETI Committee, European Parliament, http://www.europarl.europa.eu/RegData/etudes/STUD/2016/556930/IPOL_STU(2016)556930_EN.pdf

E Spaventa, 'A Very Fearful Court? The Protection of Fundamental Rights in the European Union after Opinion 2/13' (2015) 22 *Maastricht Journal* 35

10

Judicial protection and EU remedies

Albertina Albors-Llorens

1 Introduction

Imagine a group of Union citizens who discover that all their EU-based assets have been frozen in accordance with the provisions of an EU regulation because they are considered suspected terrorists. They will want to take action against the EU and avail themselves of the system of judicial protection set out by the Treaties. At the epicentre of this system is the Court of Justice of the European Union, which is the judicial organ of the Union and entrusted with the task of upholding the rule of law.[1] In the performance of this mandate, the Court reviews, in particular, the legality of the acts and omissions of Member States and of the EU institutions and interprets EU law at the request of the national courts.

Article 19(1) TEU provides that the Court of Justice of the European Union has three levels: the Court of Justice (generally referred to as the Court of Justice but in some quarters still as the European Court of Justice), the General Court (previously the Court of First Instance), and the specialized courts. One specialized court, the Civil Service Tribunal, was created in 2004[2] and had jurisdiction to deal with disputes between the Union and members of its staff. However, more recently, a process of judicial reform culminated, as we shall see, with a dramatic increase in the number of judges in the General Court and with the reassignment of jurisdiction in staff cases from the Civil Service Tribunal to the General Court as from 1 September 2016.[3] This entailed the dismantling of the Civil

[1] See Art 19(1) TEU.

[2] See Art 19(1) TEU. See Council Decision 2004/752 (OJ [2004] L333/7).

[3] See Regulation 2015/2422 of the European Parliament and the Council amending Protocol No 3 on the Statute of the Court of Justice of the European Union (OJ [2015] L341/14), and particularly recital 9 of the Preamble to that Regulation. See also Art 50(a) Statute of the Court.

Service Tribunal.[4] Therefore, the judicial institution of the EU currently comprises only the General Court and the Court of Justice.

This chapter will provide an overview of the various procedural avenues to the Court and will use as a template the division between two main sets of proceedings: direct actions and preliminary references (see Fig 10.1).[5] The former are brought directly either before the Court of Justice or the General Court, and they are dealt with in their entirety by these courts. By contrast, the latter proceedings begin before a national court. When this court encounters a question on the interpretation or the validity of EU law, it may (or sometimes must) make a preliminary reference on this particular point to the Court of Justice (or, for certain issues since 2024, the General Court). Once the Court of Justice or the General Court delivers a preliminary ruling on the specific issue of EU law, the national court will apply the ruling to the facts of the case and will decide on the dispute between the parties. Therefore, the intervention of the Court of Justice or the General Court is incidental—even if, as we shall see, the impact of this intervention has proved crucial to the formation and evolution of EU law as well as to the solution of disputes by national courts. This chapter will explore the structure of these two different sets of proceedings, will show how they interact, and will consider some key issues, such as whether they really ensure a complete system of judicial protection.[6]

2 The structure and jurisdiction of the Court of Justice of the European Union at a glance

The Court of Justice currently consists of 27 judges (one judge from each Member State)[7] and 11 Advocates General[8] who deliver impartial and independent Opinions in cases that raise new points of law.[9] The Advocates General are members of the Court but their Opinions reflect their personal views on how a case should be decided and the freedom that they enjoy stands in contrast with the constraints to achieve consensus under which the judges operate. While the Opinions are not legally binding on the Court, they provide invaluable assistance in the analysis of cases and have been extremely influential in the development of EU law.[10] The Court generally sits in chambers of three or five judges,[11]

[4] See Regulation 2016/1192 of the European Parliament and of the Council on the transfer to the General Court of jurisdiction at first instance of disputes between the European Union and its servants (OJ [2016] L200/137).

[5] This chapter focuses on the main procedural avenues to the Court in the context of challenges to the compatibility of the actions of Member States and of EU institutions with EU law. For the constitutional role of the Court in EU law, see chapter 3, and for its role in the context of international law, see chapter 7.

[6] See Case 294/83 *Parti écologiste 'Les Verts' v European Parliament* [1986] ECR 1339, para 23 and Case C-583/11 P *Inuit Tapiriit Kanatami v European Parliament and Council*, EU:C:2013:625, para 92.

[7] Art 19(2) TEU. The number of judges sitting in the Court of Justice decreased to 27 on the day of the UK's withdrawal from the EU.

[8] Art 252 TFEU. Council Decision 2013/336 (OJ [2013] L179/92) increased the number of Advocates General from 8 to 9, with effect from 1 July 2013 and to 11, with effect from 7 October 2015. Following the withdrawal of the United Kingdom from the European Union, the remaining five largest Member States (France, Italy, Spain, Germany, and Poland) have a permanent Advocate General while the other six Advocates General rotate among the other Member States.

[9] See Art 20 Statute of the Court.

[10] On the significance of Opinions, see further A Dashwood, 'The Advocate General in the Court of Justice of the European Communities' (1982) 2 *Legal Studies* 202; K Mortelmans, 'The Court under the Influence of Its Advocates General: An Analysis of the Case Law on the Functioning of the Internal Market' (2007) 24 *Yearbook of European Law* 127; and T Tridimas, 'The Role of the Advocate General in the Development of Community Law: Some Reflections' (1997) 34 *Common Market Law Review* 1349.

[11] Arts 251 TFEU and 16(1) Statute of the Court.

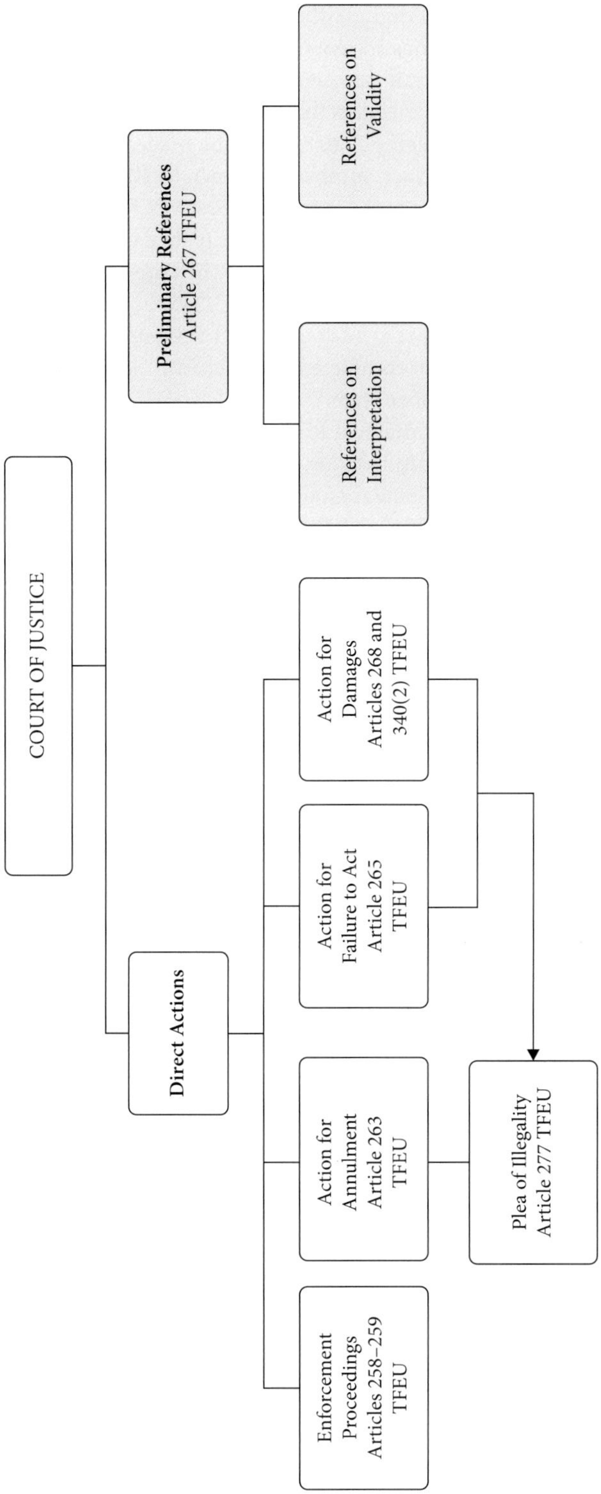

Fig. 10.1 Avenues to the Court of Justice and the General Court

but may sit in a Grand Chamber of 15 judges when a Member State or an institution of the Union that is party to the proceedings so requests[12] or depending on the importance or difficulty of a case.[13] More unusually, it may sit as a Full Court in a number of cases provided in the Treaties[14] and where it considers that a case is of exceptional importance.[15]

According to the Treaty, the General Court should be made up of at least one judge from each Member State with the exact number laid down by the Statute of the Court.[16] Until 25 December 2015, it was made up of 28 judges. However, following concerns relating to the workload of the General Court, the Court of Justice exercised its right of legislative initiative under Article 281(2) TFEU to request the amendment of the Statute of the Court. This led to the adoption of Regulation 2015/2422,[17] which provided for the number of judges in the General Court to be doubled by 1 September 2019 in a three-stage process.[18] This process has now been completed and there are currently 54 judges in the General Court, two from each Member State.[19]

There are no Advocates General attached to the General Court, but members of this Court may be called upon to perform the role of Advocate General,[20] a possibility that has been rarely used to date. The General Court normally sits in chambers of three or five judges but may also exceptionally sit as a Grand Chamber, as a Full Court, or even be constituted by a single judge.[21]

As explained earlier, in this chapter we will examine the main procedural routes to the Union judicature, taking as a starting point the basic division between direct actions and preliminary references. On the one hand, there are four main types of direct actions: infringement (or enforcement) proceedings (Articles 258 to 260 TFEU), the action for annulment (Articles 263 and 264 TFEU), the action for failure to act (Articles 265 and 266 TFEU), and the action for damages (Articles 268 and 340(2) and (3) TFEU). The plea of illegality (Article 277 TFEU) is brought directly before the Court but is used to plead the illegality of an EU act in an *incidental* way, that is, in the course of proceedings pending before the Court under another provision—generally, but not always, annulment proceedings under Article 263 TFEU.[22] Consequently, it cannot be brought independently but is always attached to a direct action and, therefore, it will be considered in this chapter within the same framework as the direct actions. In connection with any of these direct actions, the Court may also grant interim relief, which is also provided in the Treaty (Articles 278 and 279 TFEU).

The objectives of these actions could be summarized as follows. Enforcement proceedings are brought by the Commission or a Member State against a Member State that has failed to comply with its obligations under EU law. The action for annulment and the action for a failure to act are used, respectively, to challenge illegal acts and omissions of the institutions, bodies, and agencies of the EU. Finally, the action for damages is used to obtain

[12] Art 16(2) and (3) Statute of the Court.

[13] See Art 60 Rules of Procedure of the Court (OJ [2012] L265/1).

[14] See Art 16(4) Statute of the Court and Arts 228(2), 245(2), 247, and 286(6) TFEU. These provisions concern the power of the Court to dismiss the Ombudsman, or compulsorily to retire members of the Commission or of the Court of Auditors in the event of misconduct or failure to fulfil the obligations arising from their offices.

[15] For an example, see Case C-370/12 *Pringle v Ireland*, EU:C:2012:756 on the legality of the European Stability Mechanism Treaty.

[16] Arts 19(2) and 254(1) TFEU.

[17] See n 3.

[18] See Art 48 Statute of the Court as amended by Art 1 of Regulation 2015/2422 (see n 3).

[19] As with the number of judges in the Court of Justice, however, the withdrawal of the UK from the European Union had an effect on the final number of judges in the General Court.

[20] Art 49 Statute of the Court.

[21] Art 50 Statute of the Court.

[22] Technically, the plea of illegality could also be attached to an action for a failure to act or to an action for damages but, in practice, this is very rare.

compensation for damage or loss suffered as a result of an unlawful Union act. Therefore, while enforcement proceedings aim to ensure the compliance of *Member States* with EU law, the other direct actions and the plea of illegality aim to provide protection against illegal acts and omissions of the *EU institutions*. On the other hand, there are two types of references for preliminary rulings provided in Article 267 TFEU: on the interpretation and on the validity of EU law. A representation of this structure can be found in Fig 10.1.

Direct actions and preliminary rulings are naturally imbued with a different philosophy in terms of the role played by the Court. In direct actions, the Court adjudicates on the dispute between the parties, whereas in preliminary rulings it simply gives advice on a specific point of EU law, leaving the final resolution of the dispute to the national court.

Notwithstanding the differences between these two sets of proceedings, there are also areas of interaction between them. It is therefore important to see the system of judicial protection provided in the Treaty as an integrated whole in order to understand how it really operates. A prominent example of this is the relationship between the action for annulment, the plea of illegality, and preliminary rulings on validity,[23] which will be considered in more detail later in this chapter.[24] Thus, a private applicant may bring annulment proceedings or a plea of illegality to challenge the legality of a Union act *directly* before the Union judicature but, as we shall see, stringent standing conditions attached to the action for annulment have meant that these have so far been unpromising options for private parties in large areas of the case law. However, it might be possible to challenge a national act implementing a Union act before a national court, which may then make a preliminary reference on the validity of the Union act on which the national one is based. If available,[25] this second avenue will provide a similar result to the one that a successful action for annulment or plea of illegality would have produced. While the Treaty of Lisbon introduced some important changes to the standing conditions that apply to private parties wishing to bring an action for annulment, some questions still remain as to whether the combination offered by these remedies guarantees *complete* judicial protection for natural and legal persons against illegal acts of the institutions,[26] in the sense mandated by Article 47 of the Charter of Fundamental Rights of the European Union.[27]

Turning to the jurisdiction of the Court of Justice, it might be helpful to examine first the *areas* of EU law over which the Court has jurisdiction and then to consider the *functional division* of jurisdiction between the Court and the General Court. The Court of Justice now has full jurisdiction in most matters covered by EU law, including on the provisions in the area of freedom, security, and justice but with the restrictions imposed by Article 276 TFEU.[28] However, the Court has no jurisdiction in common foreign and security policy matters, with the two exceptions provided in Article 275 TFEU.[29] Some restrictions also apply to the jurisdiction of the Court to review acts of the European Council or the Council determining that a Member State has committed a serious and persistent breach of the fundamental values of the Union set out in Article 2 TEU, or that there is 'a clear risk of a serious breach' of those values.[30]

[23] See *Les Verts* (n 6) para 23. [24] See section 6, case study 10.1.

[25] As explained later, this avenue is frequently, but not always, available. See section 3.2.4.

[26] See section 4.2.1. [27] See chapters 8 and 9.

[28] According to Art 276 TFEU, the Court shall have no jurisdiction to review the validity or proportionality of operations carried out by the police or other law enforcement services of a Member State or the exercise of Member States' responsibilities regarding the maintenance of law and order and the safeguarding of internal security.

[29] Under Art 275(2) TFEU, the Court shall have jurisdiction to monitor compliance with Art 40 TEU and to rule on annulment proceedings brought against Council decisions providing for restrictive measures against private parties in the field of the common foreign and security policy. On the Court's interpretation of this exception, see chapter 26.

[30] See Art 269 TFEU and Art 7 TEU.

In terms of the division of functions between the Court and the General Court, the latter has jurisdiction principally to hear, in the first instance, direct actions brought by private applicants, direct actions brought by Member States against the Commission,[31] and direct actions brought by Member States against certain acts of the Council.[32] All other direct actions—which are mainly infringement proceedings, those dealing with interinstitutional disputes, and actions brought by Member States against EU legislative acts[33]—come before the Court of Justice.[34]

Although Article 256(3) TFEU allowed for jurisdiction to hear preliminary references in certain areas to be transferred to the General Court, the Court of Justice retained the jurisdiction over all references for preliminary rulings until very recently. However, since October 2024, jurisdiction to deliver preliminary rulings in six areas has been transferred to the General Court.[35] Finally, there is an appeal on points of law from decisions of the General Court before the Court of Justice.[36]

3 Direct actions

In this section we will examine the main categories of direct actions before the Court. Thus, we will consider infringement proceedings, the action for annulment, the action for failure to act, and the action for damages. Additionally, we will also consider the plea or

[31] This is with some exceptions. First, the narrow exception of challenges against acts or omissions of the Commission in the context of providing authorization for enhanced cooperation under Art 331 TFEU (see Art 51 Statute of the Court). Secondly, Regulation 2019/629 (OJ [2019] L111/1), amending Art 51 of the Statute of the Court, has introduced another exception in relation to actions for annulment which are brought by a Member State against an act of the Commission relating to a failure to comply with a judgment delivered by the Court under the second subpara of Art 260(2) TFEU, or the second subpara of Art 260(3) TFEU (see section 3.1.4). These actions have now been reserved exclusively to the Court of Justice. Finally, from the residual approach taken in Art 51 Statute of the Court—in combination with Art 256(1) TFEU—it follows that the General Court also has jurisdiction to hear actions based on Arts 263 and 265 TFEU brought by a Member State against acts and omissions of the European Central Bank.

[32] This applies (following Art 256(1) TFEU and Art 51 Statute of the Court) to acts of the Council where this exercises implementing powers under Art 291 TFEU and in certain instances in the fields of State aid (Art 108(2) TFEU) and anti-dumping proceedings (Art 207 TFEU). Additionally, the General Court has jurisdiction in actions based in contracts concluded by the Union which give jurisdiction to the Court (Art 272 TFEU) and in some actions concerning the EU trademark (see Art 65 of Regulation 207/2009 of the European Parliament and of the Council on the Community Trade Mark (OJ [2009] L78/1) as amended by Art 1(59) of Regulation 2015/2424 of the European Parliament and the Council (OJ [2015] L341/21)).

[33] Legislative acts are those adopted by legislative procedure: either the ordinary legislative procedure or one of the special legislative procedures (see Art 289(3) TFEU and chapter 5).

[34] See also Art 218(11) TFEU, which allows a Member State, the European Parliament, the Council, and the Commission to request an opinion of the Court of Justice as to whether an international agreement envisaged by the EU is compatible with the Treaties. This provision has great constitutional significance particularly because if the Opinion is adverse, the agreement in question cannot enter into force unless it is amended or the Treaties are revised. For an example of where the Court gave an adverse Opinion, see Opinion 2/13, discussed further in chapter 9, where the Commission had requested an Opinion from the Court of Justice on the compatibility with EU law of the first draft agreement providing for the accession of the EU to the ECHR (EU:C:2014:2454).

[35] See Regulation (EU, Euratom) 2024/2019 of the European Parliament and of the Council of 11 April 2024 amending Protocol No 3 on the Statute of the Court of Justice of the European Union (OJ [2024] L 12.8.2024). The six areas are: the common system of value added tax; excise duties; the Customs Code; the tariff classification of goods under the Combined Nomenclature; compensation and assistance to passengers in the event of denied boarding or of delay or cancellation of transport services; and the system for greenhouse gas emission allowance trading. The Court of Justice will, however, retain jurisdiction on requests for preliminary references, even when these fall within these areas, if they raise independent questions on the interpretation of primary law (including the Charter), public international law, and general principles of law.

[36] Art 256(1), second subpara, TFEU.

objection of illegality—which, as we saw previously, is always attached to a 'main' direct action. The first three actions and the plea of illegality mainly aim to obtain a declaration from the Court that either a Member State (in the case of infringement proceedings) or a Union institution (in the case of the action for annulment, the action for a failure to act, and the plea of illegality) has *breached* EU law.[37] By contrast, the action for damages is a *compensatory* action which seeks to make good the harmful consequences that an EU measure or conduct or omission by an EU institution has on an applicant.

3.1 Infringement proceedings

3.1.1 Overview

Infringement proceedings address the situation where a *Member State* has breached EU law (eg by failing to implement a directive on time or enacting legislation that is contrary to EU law). The main applicant in these proceedings is the Commission and the key provision is Article 258 TFEU. Article 259 TFEU also allows a Member State to bring infringement proceedings, but this provision has rarely been used.[38]

It is important to note that private parties *cannot* bring an infringement action before the Court.[39] This does not mean, however, that they cannot challenge illegal actions of the Member States, just that the vehicle for their challenge is a different one, namely starting an action before the national courts instead. Thus, as the Court emphasized in its seminal judgment in *Van Gend en Loos*, private parties can rely on the direct effect of EU law[40]—or, as the case may be, request that the national court makes a preliminary reference on the interpretation of EU law[41]—before their *national courts* to argue that Member States have effectively infringed EU law. Remedies are then provided at national level, subject to compliance with the principles of non-discrimination and effectiveness[42] and, following the establishment of the *Francovich* doctrine, private parties can, moreover, and as a matter of EU law, sue Member States in damages before the national courts.[43] Viewed together, all these avenues have the common aim of securing the protection of EU rights against possible infringements by Member States and national authorities.

Infringement proceedings have an administrative phase, where the Commission effectively gives a Member State an opportunity to remedy an infringement of EU law and to submit observations before resorting to litigation, and a judicial phase before the Court of Justice. A judgment of the Court finding that a Member State has failed to fulfil its obligations under EU law is binding on the Member State. If the Member State does not comply,

[37] In the case of infringement proceedings under Art 258 TFEU, this decision will take the form of a declaration that a Member State has failed to fulfil its obligations under EU law, whereas in the case of the action for annulment the Court not only might declare that an EU act is incompatible with EU law but will then go on to annul the act in question.

[38] For an early example, see Case 141/78 *France v UK* [1979] ECR 2923, but see for a more recent and high-profile one, Case C-364/10 *Hungary v Slovakia*, EU:C:2012:630.

[39] They can complain to the Commission and their complaints play an important role in alerting this institution to potential infringements of EU law but the Commission ultimately has discretion in deciding whether to initiate an Art 258 TFEU action (Case T-247/04 *Aseprofar and Edifa v Commission* [2005] ECR II-3449, para 40).

[40] Case 26/62 *Van Gend en Loos v Netherlands Inland Revenue Administration* [1963] ECR 1, 13.

[41] See eg Case C-213/89 *The Queen v Secretary of State for Transport, ex p Factortame* ('*Factortame I*') [1990] ECR I-2433. Preliminary rulings on interpretation, while technically delivered in abstract terms, have effectively provided a much-used vehicle to test the compatibility of national measures with EU law (see section 4.2).

[42] See chapter 6.

[43] Joined Cases C-6/90 and C-9/90 *Francovich v Italy* [1991] ECR I-5357, paras 33–37. See further chapter 6.

then pecuniary sanctions may be imposed on it by the Court in a subsequent action under Article 260 TFEU.

3.1.2 The elements in Article 258 TFEU

The Commission can start infringement proceedings if it considers that 'a Member State has failed to fulfil an obligation under the Treaties'. We need therefore to ascertain what constitutes a 'Member State' in this context and what it means to 'fail to fulfil an obligation under the Treaties'. In the absence of specific Treaty guidance, these terms have been given meaning in the case law of the Court.

Consistent with the expansive interpretation of the notion of 'State' followed in other areas of EU law,[44] the Court held early on in the case law that a *Member State* may incur liability under Article 258 TFEU 'whatever the agency of the State whose action or inaction is the cause of the failure to fulfil its obligations, even in the case of a constitutionally independent institution'.[45] This has been developed to mean that not only the legislative,[46] executive,[47] and judicial[48] branches of the State are covered by this umbrella but also any other public bodies, such as territorial authorities in a federated State, in a region,[49] a locality,[50] or in an autonomous community and even private entities when controlled by the State.[51] In this context, the decisive point is whether the activities or omissions leading to the potential infringement of EU law can be *attributable* to the State and thus a substantive rather than a formalistic approach has prevailed when assessing the quality of the defendant in infringement proceedings.[52] However, and irrespective of the entity which is ultimately responsible for the breach under the internal constitutional arrangements of a Member State, the defendant in an action under Article 258 TFEU is the State itself and the action is formally brought against the government of the Member State in question.[53]

The next question is what constitutes a 'failure to fulfil an obligation under the Treaties'. This expression has been understood to refer both to positive acts and omissions, and not only to obligations imposed by the Treaties themselves but also those imposed by secondary legislation, international agreements,[54] and by the general principles of law.[55] Classic examples of positive acts attracting infringement proceedings would be the enactment of national legislation[56] or the pursuance of sustained administrative practices[57] that are contrary to EU law.

[44] See eg the broad interpretation of the notion of 'State' in the context of the case law on direct effect of directives (Case C-188/89 *Foster v British Gas* [1990] ECR I-3313, para 20).

[45] Case 77/69 *Commission v Belgium* [1970] ECR 237, para 15.

[46] See Case 178/84 *Commission v Germany* [1987] ECR 1227, where proceedings were brought by the Commission against German laws intended to protect the purity of beer, but which were contrary to Art 34 TFEU.

[47] See Case 40/82 *Commission v UK* [1982] ECR 2793, where the UK government-imposed restrictions on the importation of poultry products.

[48] Case C-129/00 *Commission v Italy* [2003] ECR I-14637, paras 29–41.

[49] Case C-2/90 *Commission v Belgium* [1992] ECR I-4431, where the measure contrary to EU law was a decree issued by the regional council of Wallonia.

[50] See Case 45/87 *Commission v Ireland* [1988] ECR 4929, where Dundalk Urban District Council was responsible for an infringement of EU law.

[51] Case C-325/00 *Commission v Germany* [2002] ECR I-9977, paras 17–21.

[52] See Case 249/81 *Commission v Ireland* ('*Buy Irish*') [1982] ECR 4005, paras 10–15.

[53] See Case C-95/97 *Région Wallonne v Commission* [1997] ECR I-1787, para 7.

[54] See Case C-61/94 *Commission v Germany* [1996] ECR I-3989, para 15.

[55] See eg the principle of equal treatment in Case 61/81 *Commission v UK* [1982] ECR 2601, para 14.

[56] See eg *Commission v Germany* (n 46).

[57] See eg Case 21/84 *Commission v France* [1985] ECR 1355, where the French authorities refused, without adequate justification, to approve postal franking machines from other Member States, thus contravening Art 34 TFEU.

The 'rule of law crisis'

In recent years, a repeated series of high-profile infringement proceedings triggered in response to the 'rule of law crisis' in Poland and Hungary have demonstrated both the efficacy of this mechanism to ensure compliance with EU law—particularly when coupled with orders of interim relief[58]—and the breadth of the meaning of the expression 'an obligation under the Treaties' in Article 258 TFEU.

In relation to the first dimension, it bears noting that the activation of the Article 7(2) TEU procedure, which enables the European Council, acting by unanimity, to determine the existence of a serious and persistent breach by a Member State of the Article 2 TEU values—which include the 'rule of law' as one of the values on which the Union is founded—is plagued with political and legal difficulties. Against this background, infringement proceedings have emerged as an efficient mechanism to pursue not only specific infringements but also systemic violations of the 'rule of law'.[59]

As for the second dimension, the plethora of infringement proceedings brought against Poland and Hungary have revealed the true scope of the 'obligation under the Treaties' component in Article 258 TFEU and particularly of the nature of the legal obligations enshrined in Article 2 TEU. Thus, the Article 258 TFEU actions against Poland mainly concerned judicial reforms that threatened the independence of the national judiciary and thus were contrary to Article 2 TEU. These reforms included a national law that lowered the retirement age of the judges in the Supreme Court with both retroactive and prospective effect,[60] a law that established a different retirement age for men and women who were judges or public prosecutors in Poland and which also lowered the retirement age for judges in ordinary courts,[61] and a law adopting a new disciplinary procedure for Polish judges.[62]

Until relatively recently, the values contained in Article 2 TEU had appeared rather vague in terms of their judicial enforceability. However, a preliminary ruling delivered in 2018 by the Grand Chamber of the Court in *Associação Sindical dos Juízes Portugueses v Tribunal de Contas*[63] explained that Article 19 TEU (considered above) gave 'concrete expression to the value of the rule of law stated in Article 2 TEU'[64] and cemented the essential nature of judicial independence of national courts and tribunals as a requirement for the delivery of effective judicial protection of EU rights mandated by Article 47 of the Charter.[65] The links between these three provisions—Articles 2 TEU, 19 TEU, and 47 of the Charter—then became the key feature of the reasoning of the Court in its judgments on the infringement proceedings against Poland.[66] There, they were consistently used to find in each case a breach of EU law, thus conveying the reach of the 'obligations under the Treaties' that their combined reading was capable to embrace.

Similarly, a series of infringement proceedings against Hungary illustrate the use of Article 258 TFEU actions as a mechanism to uphold some of the other values in Article 2, particularly the protection of fundamental human rights and freedoms—and, implicitly therefore, the rule of law in the EU. In some of these cases, the Court of Justice held that Hungary was in breach *both* of Treaty provisions on free movement and of specific

58 See section 5.

59 See further M Schmidt and P Bogdanowicz, 'The Infringement Procedure in the Rule of Law Crisis: How to Make Effective Use of Article 258 TFEU' (2018) 55 *Common Market Law Review* 1061.

60 Case C-619/18 *Commission v Poland*, EU:C:2019:531.

61 Case C-192/18 *Commission v Poland*, EU:C:2019:924.

62 Case C-791/19 *Commission v Poland*, EU:C:2021:596.

63 Case 64/16, EU:C:2018:117. 64 Ibid, para 32. 65 Ibid, paras 35–44.

66 See Case C-619/18 (n 60) paras 47–59; Case C-192/18 (n 61) paras 98–107; Case C-791/19 (n 62) paras 50–62.

provisions of the Charter.[67] They therefore demonstrate an increased reliance on the provisions of the Charter as imposing independent 'obligations under the Treaties' in the context of enforcement proceedings.

Infringement proceedings were also brought against an intensely controversial Hungarian Law on Higher Education that made the exercise of teaching activities in Hungary by higher education institutions situated outside the EEA subject to the existence of an international treaty between Hungary and the relevant third country.[68] There, the Court relied, inter alia, on Hungary's failure to comply with its obligations under the General Agreement on Trade in Services (GATS) concluded under the framework of the World Trade Organization (WTO), and hence by implication, under EU law.[69]

More recently, the Commission has brought infringement proceedings before the Court against Hungary over national legislation that discriminated against people on the basis of their sexual orientation and gender identity.[70] Again, the Commission has contended that the relevant legislation violates the internal market rules[71] and the fundamental human rights of individuals (particularly of LGBTQI people). [72] Crucially, however, the Commission has argued a breach of Article 2 TEU as a self-standing plea in addition to the violation of the other rules of EU law. This is the groundbreaking aspect of the case. It raises directly the issue of the justiciability of this provision which has, in turn, been examined in painstaking detail in the compelling Opinion delivered by Advocate General Capeta in June 2025.[73]

After highlighting that Article 2 TEU is not a mere statement of values but contains legal obligations of result, the Opinion refers to the role of Article 258 TFEU as a mechanism for the Court to find that a Member State has breached its 'obligations under the Treaties'.[74] It then dismisses the traditional argument that the values in Article 2 TEU are too general for the purposes of the judicial review of national legislation in infringement proceedings.[75] While in the case at hand the Opinion considers the infringement of Article 2 TEU linked to the infringements of other EU rules, it concludes that the purpose of finding a self-standing breach of Article 2 TEU lies in demonstrating the significant divergence of the national rules 'from the model of a constitutional democracy, which respects human rights, reflected in Article 2 TEU'.[76]

It remains to be seen what position will be taken by the Court. However, this case has the potential to prove that the perceived abstraction of the values enumerated in Article 2

[67] See Case C-235/17 *Commission v Hungary*, EU:C:2019:432, where, in relation to a Hungarian law that cancelled usufructuary rights over agricultural land held by nationals of other Member States, the Court found a breach of Art 63 TFEU on the freedom of movement of capital and of Art 17 of the Charter on the right to property. See also Case C-78/18 *Commission v Hungary*, EU:C:2020:476, concerning the restrictions imposed by Hungarian law on the financing of civil organizations by persons established in other Member States, where again the Court found a breach of Art 63 TFEU and of Arts 7, 8, and 12 of the Charter on the rights to respect for family life, to protection of personal data, and to freedom of association.

[68] Case C-66/18 *Commission v Hungary*, EU:C:2020:792.

[69] As in the cases mentioned above (n 67), the Court also found in that case a breach of a free movement provision (Art 49 TFEU on the freedom of establishment) *and* of Arts 13, 14(3), and 16 of the Charter, which protect, respectively, the right to academic freedom, the right to found academic establishments, and the freedom to conduct a business.

[70] Case C-769/22 *Commission v Hungary* (2023/C 54/19), currently pending before the Court).

[71] These include Art 56 TFEU on the freedom to provide services and four internal market directives.

[72] The Commission has argued the breach of Art 21 (prohibition of discrimination on grounds of sex and sexual orientation), Art 11 (freedom of expression and information), and Art 7 (respect for private and family law) of the Charter.

[73] Opinion of AG Capeta in Case C-769/22, EU:C:2025:408, paras 4 and 150 *et seq.*

[74] Ibid, para 192. [75] Ibid, paras 201–218. [76] Ibid, paras 233 and 273.

TEU may not be an obstacle to their enforceability in situations where these values have been seriously and systemically undermined by a Member State.

Omissions by Member States

While the most typical omission by a Member State that attracts infringement proceedings is a failure to implement a directive, the net of Article 258 TFEU has been cast widely by the Court. A high-profile example of this is *Commission v France* ('*Strawberries*').[77] There, the Commission brought proceedings against the French government after the French authorities stood by and did nothing to prevent the continuous and systematic destruction of Spanish and Belgian agricultural produce by French farmers for a period of over ten years. While the disruption to the free movement of goods was, in reality, attributable to private parties, the failure of the French government to take any kind of action against such a sustained and grave violation of EU law amounted to a failure of the State to fulfil its Treaty obligations contrary to Article 34 TFEU[78] and Article 4(3) TEU.

3.1.3 **Procedure**

As explained earlier, there is an administrative phase and a judicial phase in infringement proceedings, both of which are reflected in the letter of Article 258 TFEU. It is important to understand, at the outset, that the Commission is an institution that acts in the public interest. A reflection of this is the discretion that it enjoys to decide whether and when to initiate both the administrative and the judicial phase in the proceedings.[79] Inevitably, this means that it will rank its priorities when deciding to pursue infringements of EU law and that it will not take up many of the complaints that it receives. Naturally, concerns soon arose about the lack of scrutiny over the Commission's exercise of its discretion in the context of Article 258 TFEU proceedings. In more recent times, some initiatives have sought to address a number of the deficiencies of this process. In particular, the 2002 Commission Communication to the European Parliament and the Council on relations with complainants in infringement proceedings[80]—which arose in response to criticisms from the Ombudsman when the Commission shelved a private complaint against the violation of public procurement rules by the Greek authorities[81]—aimed to increase the transparency and accountability of the Commission's decision-making process when dealing with complaints. This Communication has now been revised and updated by a 2012 Communication.[82] However, substantially—and despite these procedural safeguards—the broad discretion of the Commission remains uncontested.

The first formal step in the administrative—or pre-litigation—phase of the proceedings is the letter of formal notice, whereby the Commission defines the subject matter of the dispute and provides the basis for the Member State in question to submit observations. The Member State is given a reasonable period to respond and, following the submission of observations, the Commission may deliver a reasoned opinion describing the infringement of EU law and will then give the Member State a reasonable time limit—in practice generally two months—to comply with the opinion. While the reasoned opinion may develop in more detail the points set out in the normally concise letter of formal notice, it cannot change the subject matter of the Commission's original complaint against the

[77] Case C-265/95 [1997] ECR I-6959. See also chapter 12.

[78] Further discussion of Art 34 TFEU can be found in chapter 12.

[79] See Case 247/87 *Star Fruit Co SA v Commission* [1989] ECR 291, paras 11 and 12.

[80] OJ [2002] C244/5.

[81] Decision of the European Ombudsman on complaint 995/98/OV against the European Commission, available at www.ombudsman.europa.eu/mt/decision/en/1088.

[82] COM (2012) 154 final.

Member State or enlarge its scope.[83] If the Member State fails to comply with the opinion, the Commission may then decide to bring the matter before the Court of Justice, thus triggering the initiation of the judicial phase and the subject matter of its application must be the same or narrower than the subject matter of the reasoned opinion. The judgment of the Court will be a declaratory one, namely stating whether the Member State has breached EU law. During the course of the judicial proceedings, the Court may also decide to grant interim measures.[84]

Member States have deployed a variety of defences to explain their failures. The case law on this point shows clearly that the Court has given short shrift to these arguments and that, with very limited exceptions (eg *force majeure*[85]) the Court will concentrate on the objective existence of a violation of EU law and remain unmoved by any explanations from the Member States as to the reasons why they failed to comply with EU law. A few of these unsuccessful defences were arguments that internal or practical difficulties stood in the way of their compliance with EU law,[86] that Union institutions or other Member States had also acted in breach of EU law,[87] or that unlawful legislation was in fact obsolete and not applied by the Member State.[88]

3.1.4 **Sanctions**

The Maastricht Treaty amended the TFEU (then the EEC Treaty) to enable the Court to impose sanctions on Member States that fail to comply with a judgment of the Court under Articles 258 and 259 TFEU finding them in breach of EU law. This involved a repetition of the whole procedure, comprising both the administrative and judicial phase, coupled with an application from the Commission to the Court for the imposition of a penalty and/or a lump sum.[89] Following the entry into force of the Lisbon Treaty, Article 260 TFEU has been amended with the aim of expediting the application of pecuniary sanctions. Essentially, the Lisbon changes are as follows.

First, as provided in Article 260(2) TFEU, the pre-litigation procedure has been simplified in all cases where a Member State does not comply with the judgment of the Court. Thus, the Commission no longer needs to issue a second reasoned opinion but just a letter of formal notice—which will constitute the basis for the Member State to submit observations. The Commission has provided, and regularly updates, guidance on the determination of the applicable penalties.[90] This takes into account the seriousness of the

[83] See Case 51/83 *Commission v Italy* [1984] ECR 2793, paras 6–8.

[84] See eg Cases 31/77 and 53/77 R *Commission v UK* [1977] ECR 921, where the UK had granted temporary aid to pig producers which was prima facie contrary to EU law and where the Commission applied for and obtained a decision from the Court ordering this Member State to cease the application of the aid with immediate effect.

[85] See Case 101/84 *Commission v Italy* [1985] ECR 2629, where the Italian government argued that its failure to compile certain statistical information required under an EU directive was due to a bomb attack on its data processing centre. While the Court accepted that *force majeure* could be a valid defence, it made it clear that it would interpret it restrictively (para 16).

[86] Case 254/83 *Commission v Italy* [1984] ECR 3395.

[87] Joined Cases 90/63 and 91/63 *Commission v Luxembourg and Belgium* [1964] ECR 625, 631, and Case 232/78 *Commission v France* [1979] ECR 2729, para 9, respectively.

[88] See Case 167/73 *Commission v France* [1974] ECR 359.

[89] There have been cases where *both* a lump sum and a periodic penalty payment have been imposed (eg Case C-304/02 *Commission v France* [2005] ECR I-6263). See also Case C-270/11 *Commission v Sweden*, EU:C: 2013:339. Penalties can also be imposed in interim relief cases: Case C-441/17 R *Commission v Poland*, EU:C:2017:877, para 118.

[90] See the 2005 Commission Communication on the application of Art 260 TFEU (SEC (2005) 1658), updated in 2010 (SEC (2010) 923). The 2010 Communication provided that the relevant macroeconomic data should thereafter be subject to annual revisions in line with inflation and GDP movements.

infringement, its duration, and the deterrent effect of a sanction as well as the Member State's ability to pay. These sanctions may run to many thousands of euros.

Secondly, for the *specific* case where a Member State has failed to notify measures[91] transposing a *legislative* directive[92] on time, special arrangements set out in Article 260(3) TFEU will apply. In particular, the Commission may, even at the stage of the *original* infringement proceedings, suggest the penalty that the Court could set on a defaulting Member State in the judgment delivered at the end of the Article 258 TFEU proceedings. In other words, the need for a second set of proceedings is obviated. Clearly, and as the Commission acknowledged in a Communication on the implementation of Article 260(3) TFEU published in 2011, the purpose of this provision is to give yet another powerful incentive to Member States to implement directives on time and to protect individual rights against such a clear and generally indefensible violation of EU law.[93] The 2011 Communication also provides specific guidance as to the calculation of penalties in this particular situation but this is very similar to the mode of calculation used in Article 260(2) TFEU cases. In July 2019, the Court gave judgment, for the first time, on a case under the combined Article 258/260(3) TFEU procedure.[94]

3.2 **The action for annulment**

3.2.1 **Overview**

The action for annulment and the action for a failure to act represent two dimensions of the same remedy, namely one that addresses the situation where an EU institution has either adopted an illegal act (eg enacting a directive that breaches a general principle of law) or has failed to act when it had an obligation to act under EU law (eg the Commission does not respond at all when an undertaking complains of a violation of the Treaty competition rules). Both avenues aim to obtain a decision from the Court that an act or that the failure to act of an institution, respectively, contravene EU law.

Article 263 TFEU sets out the principles and structure underlining annulment proceedings. Essentially, there are four pivotal points that the Court will examine when an action for annulment is brought. These are:

(a) compliance with the time limit for bringing the action;

(b) the reviewability of the act;

[91] The Court has interpreted the obligation to 'notify measures transposing a directive' as meaning that a Member State must 'state, for each provision of the directive, the national provision or provisions ensuring its transposition' (Case 658/19 *Commission v Spain*, EU:C:2021:138, para 30).

[92] The special arrangements provided in Art 260(3) TFEU do not apply to cases where the directive in question has not been adopted by legislative procedure. There, the general provisions in Art 260(2) TFEU apply.

[93] OJ [2011] C12/1, at para 7. This approach is in harmony with the vigorous stance that the Court has taken in other areas, such as in the development of the doctrines of direct effect of directives and State liability in damages, which created effective deterrents to prevent Member States from failing to implement directives on time (see chapter 6).

[94] Thus, in Case C-543/17 *Commission v Belgium*, EU:C:2019:573, the Court imposed a daily penalty of €5,000 on Belgium for the partial failure of this Member State both to transpose a directive that aimed to facilitate the roll-out of high-speed electronic communication networks and to notify the national implementing measures to the Commission. This decision is important because since the procedure under Arts 258–260(3) TFEU was introduced, most cases under these provisions had been withdrawn from the Court due to the complete transposition of directives by the relevant Member States—sometimes at a very late stage in the proceedings. In 2017, the Commission published a Communication (*EU law: Better results through better application*) (OJ [2017] C/18/02) where it indicated that it hereafter would systematically ask the Court to impose both a lump sum and a periodic penalty payment in cases brought under Art 260(3) TFEU.

(c) the standing of the applicant—where the applicable rules vary significantly depending on whether the applicant is classified as 'privileged', 'semi-privileged', or 'non-privileged';

(d) the existence of possible grounds for the annulment of the act.

The first three refer to the *admissibility* of the action whereas the last one refers to the *substantive* challenge to the act. In the text that follows we will explore the action for annulment using as a basic structure the four key issues just outlined.

3.2.2 **Time limit**

The time limit for bringing an action for annulment provided in Article 263(6) TFEU is two months. This is deliberately very short to ensure that the legality of EU measures is uncertain for only a limited period. This time limit begins to run from the date of publication of the measure or of its notification to the applicant or, in the absence thereof, of the day on which it comes to the knowledge of the applicant. Even though this requirement is found in the final paragraph of Article 263 TFEU, it is of great practical importance and, logically, the first to be examined when proceedings are brought. Annulment actions brought outside the time limit are automatically inadmissible.

3.2.3 **Reviewable acts**

It follows from the first paragraph of Article 263 TFEU that the essential quality for an act to be reviewable is that it should be *legally binding*. This is demonstrated by the fact that this provision covers the review of acts of the institutions and of the offices or agencies of the Union intended to produce legal effects—and that it explicitly excludes recommendations and opinions.

In the post-Lisbon classification found in Articles 289 to 291 TFEU, both legislative acts (ie those adopted by legislative procedure) and non-legislative acts (by default those not adopted by legislative procedure, such as decisions adopted directly on the basis of the Treaties, delegated and implementing acts) that produce legal effects,[95] are reviewable. Most frequently, actions for annulment will be brought against regulations, directives, and decisions—which are the three types of binding legal acts listed in Article 288 TFEU. In these cases, therefore, the requirement for reviewability will be automatically fulfilled. However, the Court has taken a non-formalistic approach when deciding the binding nature of EU acts. Thus, where acts have not been formally identified as belonging to one of the Article 288 TFEU categories, it has looked at the substance of the act and the intention of those who drafted it and has concluded that an act will be reviewable, irrespective of the form it takes or the title it receives, as long as it is capable of affecting an applicant by bringing about a distinct change in its legal position.[96]

A frequently cited example that reflects the spirit of this line of case law is the decision of the Court in *IBM v Commission*,[97] a competition case. The Commission is the enforcer at EU level of the main competition provisions in the Treaty, Articles 101 and 102 TFEU,[98] and the procedural steps that it takes when it decides to pursue an investigation about a possible breach of these provisions are now set out in Regulation 1/2003,[99] which entered

[95] See chapter 5.

[96] For an early example, see Joined Cases 8–11/66 *Société anonyme Cimenteries CBR Cementsbedrijven NV v Commission* [1967] ECR 75, 91 and for a clear statement from the Court of the prevalence of substance over form when deciding the binding nature of an act, see Case 60/81 *IBM v Commission* [1981] ECR 2639, para 9. For a more recent example of this consistent line of case law, see Case C-362/08 P *Internationaler Hilfsfonds v Commission* [2010] ECR I-669, para 52.

[97] Case 60/81 (n 96). [98] See chapter 17. [99] OJ [2003] L1/1.

into force in 2004. Its predecessor was Regulation 17/62, which applied for over 40 years, and which was in force when the *IBM* case was decided. Despite the existence of very important differences between these two instruments, they have in common that one of the stages in the Commission's enforcement procedure is the provision of a statement of objections, where the Commission—generally following a fact-finding phase and on the basis of the available evidence—delivers its *preliminary* findings as to the existence of an infringement of Articles 101 and/or 102 TFEU. The purpose of this statement is to give an opportunity to the parties to prepare their defence against the objections raised by the Commission before it reaches a final decision. In *IBM*, the undertaking addressee of the statement of objections sought to challenge the statement before the Court. Given that the statement was not formally classified as a 'decision' in the Treaty terminology, the Court examined whether in substance it produced legal effects. The Court concluded that the statement did not *in itself* produce legal effects but merely paved the way for the final decision of the Commission that would—if the Commission concluded, after hearing the observations of the parties, that an infringement had taken place—produce such effects.[100]

However, and in line with the non-formalistic view taken by the Court, each measure will always be scrutinized individually to see whether it produces legal effects, even when it is part of a series of procedural stages leading to a final decision. As a result, there have been cases where such measures have been held to be reviewable. For example, if the Commission decides not to afford confidentiality to certain documents in the course of a competition investigation and to disclose them to third parties, the undertakings under investigation can challenge such a measure because it creates an immediate change in their legal position that has independent consequences which cannot be reversed by challenging the final decision of the Commission. In this situation, the Court has taken the view that such decisions may be challenged.[101]

In addition to the requirement that the act should be legally binding, Article 263(1) TFEU also provides that it should emanate from one of the bodies subject to review. This includes the institutions of the Union—with the exception of the Court of Justice of the EU and the Court of Auditors—and the agencies, offices, and bodies of the Union. Since Article 263 TFEU concerns the actions of the EU institutions, Member States can never be defendants in these proceedings.

3.2.4 **Standing**

We can classify applicants for judicial review into three main categories depending on the standing requirements that they must satisfy in order to bring annulment proceedings:

- privileged;
- semi-privileged; and
- non-privileged.

These will be examined in turn. The standing of the applicants classified in the first two categories is straightforward, but the strict standing conditions imposed on non-privileged applicants have generated one of the most intricate and controversial bodies of case law emanating from the Court.

[100] *IBM* (n 96) paras 10–12.

[101] See Case 53/85 *AKZO Chemie BV and AKZO Chemie UK Ltd v Commission* [1986] ECR 1965, paras 17–21.

Privileged and semi-privileged applicants

According to Article 263(2) TFEU, the *privileged* applicants are the Member States,[102] the Parliament, the Commission, and the Council. They are privileged because they have an automatic right to bring proceedings and therefore they do not have to satisfy any *locus standi* conditions.[103] The Parliament is today a fully-fledged privileged applicant but it is remarkable that—unlike the other privileged applicants—it only acquired this status fairly recently, at the time of the Treaty of Nice.[104] Both the limited role that the Parliament played in the legislative procedure until the introduction of what is today the ordinary legislative procedure and its historical lack of standing to challenge acts of the other institutions were among the arguments traditionally deployed to argue that a democratic deficit existed in the EU.

Post-Lisbon, the *semi-privileged* applicants are the Court of Auditors, the European Central Bank, and the Committee of the Regions. Unlike privileged applicants, semi-privileged applicants do not have an automatic right of action and can only bring proceedings when their prerogatives are at stake (eg they have not been consulted in a particular procedure).[105]

Non-privileged applicants

Natural and legal persons[106] are commonly referred to as non-privileged applicants in the context of annulment proceedings. This is because Article 263(4) TFEU imposes strict standing conditions on them when they wish to challenge a potentially unlawful EU act, which means that their chances of securing access to the action for annulment are limited. Following the Lisbon amendments, there are three situations when natural or legal persons will have *locus standi* to bring an Article 263 TFEU action. These are:

- if they are the *addressees* of the act in question, they will have *automatic standing*;
- if they are *not the addressees* of the act, they will have to show that they are *directly and individually* concerned by it (*general test of standing*); *but*
- if they are *non-addressees* and the act they wish to challenge is a *regulatory act*, they will have to show that they are *directly concerned* by it and that the act does *not entail implementing measures* (*special standing test* or *Lisbon test*). Importantly, in this scenario, there is no need for applicants to show that they are individually concerned, which, as we shall see, is the most stringent of all the standing conditions imposed on private parties.

[102] In this context, the notion of Member State refers to the *central* government authorities. Thus, autonomous communities and local and regional authorities do not enjoy the status of privileged applicants but are generally classified as legal persons that have to satisfy the standing requirements that apply to non-privileged applicants (see eg Case C-180/97 *Regione Toscana v Commission* [1997] ECR I-5245, paras 6–10 and Case T-238/97 *Comunidad Autónoma de Cantabria v Council* [1998] ECR II-2271, paras 42 and 43).

[103] See Case 45/86 *Commission v Council* [1987] ECR 1493, para 3.

[104] The Parliament had first no status at all as an applicant until the seminal judgment of the Court in Case C-70/88 *European Parliament v Council* (*'Chernobyl'*) [1990] ECR I-2041, where the Court treated it as a semi-privileged applicant, a finding that was later incorporated in Art 263 TFEU (then Art 173 EEC) by the Maastricht Treaty.

[105] Art 263(3) TFEU.

[106] These include both EU and non-EU nationals and companies (see ie Case T-526/10 *Inuit Tapiriit Kanatami v Commission*, EU:T:2013:215), where most of the applicants were companies, associations, and natural persons established or residing in Canada. In relation to legal persons, the Court has held that third countries would be regarded as non-privileged applicants under Art 263(4) TFEU (Case C-872/19P *Venezuela v Council*, EU:C:2021:507).

The first scenario is straightforward. If a private applicant is the addressee of an EU act (eg the addressee of a Commission decision withdrawing an agricultural aid previously awarded to the applicant), then it can automatically challenge it, as long as the action is brought within the time limit set out in Article 263(6) TFEU.

The second and third situations, which apply to non-addressees are, however, more problematic. The main reason for this is that the Treaty does not define the notions of 'direct and individual concern', of 'regulatory act', or of 'implementing measures' in this context. Therefore, the unenviable task of giving meaning to these important concepts, the application of which ultimately decides the fate of private parties in annulment proceedings, fell to the Court of Justice. This entailed, among other things, striking a balance between securing direct access to justice for private parties, whose rights and interests had been affected by EU measures, and the more practical, but important, consideration of preventing an opening of the floodgates of litigation. The result has been a complex body of case law, where the requirement of individual concern has been very narrowly—and not always consistently—applied, rendering many actions brought by private parties inadmissible.

In the text that follows, we will grapple with the development of the case law interpreting these difficult notions. To this end, we will consider first the general standing test (direct and individual concern) and then the special or Lisbon test that applies to the challenge of regulatory acts that do not entail implementing measures. Logically it would seem that, post-Lisbon, an applicant would always try to satisfy the special or Lisbon test *first* because this is more lenient—crucially, there is no need to show individual concern. Only if the Lisbon test is inapplicable, would a non-addressee resort to fulfilling the general standing test which now applies residually to all other situations not covered by the Lisbon test—and these are still numerous. The general and special standing tests are represented in Fig 10.2. Historically, however, the general standing test was the original standing test, and we will examine it first because it provides the necessary backdrop for tackling the fresh issues that are raised by the new Lisbon test.

The general standing test: acts of direct and individual concern to the applicant

According to Article 263(4) TFEU, a non-addressee can challenge an 'act' which is of 'direct and individual concern' to the applicant. The pre-Lisbon version of this provision referred specifically to *decisions* as the only acts that could be challenged by private

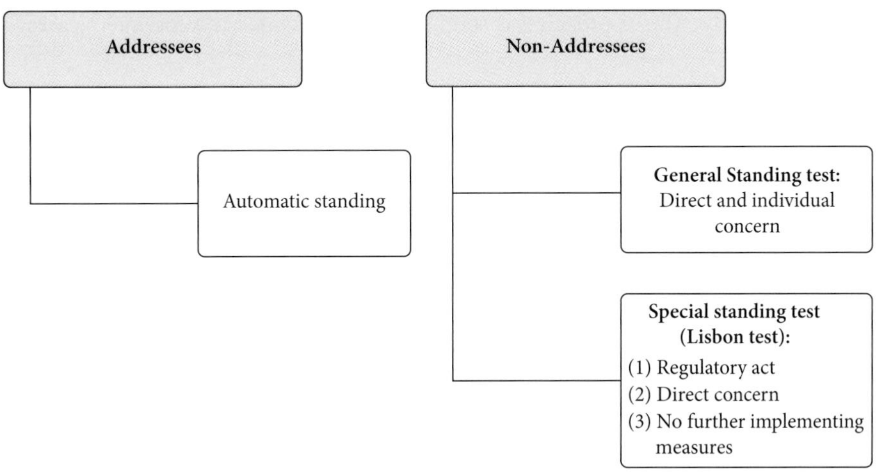

Fig. 10.2 Locus standi of private applicants after Lisbon: Article 263(4) TFEU

parties and there was a long-drawn-out debate—in the face of somewhat unclear case law—as to whether non-privileged applicants could challenge general acts, such as regulations and directives, as well as decisions.[107] The Lisbon Treaty has now settled this point and the current wording of Article 263(4) TFEU uses the all-embracing term of 'acts', which encompasses both general and individual acts (whether or not listed in Article 288 TFEU) as long as they produce legal effects. In other words, non-privileged applicants can now clearly challenge not only decisions but also regulations and directives and, effectively, any *sui generis* acts that produce legal effects.[108]

Individual concern

This leads us to the notions of individual and direct concern. The Court had a first opportunity to interpret 'individual concern' in the seminal *Plaumann* case.[109] There, Plaumann, a German company that imported clementines from countries outside the EU (then the EEC), challenged a decision of the Commission addressed to Germany refusing authorization to suspend partially the application of a customs duty set out in the Common Customs Tariff in relation to this fruit. Naturally, Plaumann's economic interests were affected by the Commission decision but since the company was not an addressee of the decision, it had to demonstrate individual and direct concern. The Court had begun its analysis in the judgment by pointing out that the right of interested parties to bring an action should 'not be interpreted restrictively'.[110] Paradoxically, however, it went on to construe the test of individual concern very narrowly by stating that non-addressees would be individually concerned if an act affects them 'by reason of certain attributes that are peculiar to them or by reason of circumstances in which they are *differentiated from all other persons* and by virtue of these factors distinguishes them individually *just as in the case of the person addressed*'.[111] The degree of individualization required to satisfy this test was therefore very high because an applicant effectively had to demonstrate that it was a de facto addressee.

In *Plaumann*, the Court implicitly provided a practical template to assess this degree of individualization. Thus, it held that Plaumann was not individually concerned because it was affected by the decision 'by reason of a commercial activity which may, at any time, be practised by any person'.[112] In other words, Plaumann was a member of an 'open category' of people because anyone could at any time (at least in theory) become an importer of clementines. Consequently, the fulfilment of the test of individual concern would seem to necessitate that the applicant is a member of a 'closed category' of people, that is, a category the membership of which is already formally fixed and ascertained *when the act in question enters into force*. This approach was soon explicitly reiterated in subsequent cases[113]

[107] In some cases, the Court had applied a triple admissibility test when private applicants brought annulment proceedings against regulations or directives. This included, as well as the tests of direct and individual concern, the application of the *abstract terminology test* to decide that the contested act was not really a regulation but a decision in substance (see eg Joined Cases 789/79 and 790/79 *Calpak v Commission* [1980] ECR 797). In these cases, the application of this practically insurmountable test meant that most actions were dismissed as inadmissible. In other cases, the Court simply applied the tests of direct and individual concern, thus implicitly acknowledging that regulations could, in principle, be challengeable by private parties (see eg Case C-152/88 *Sofrimport v Commission* [1990] ECR I-2477). The decision of the Court in *Codorníu v Council* (Case C-309/89 [1994] ECR I-1853) settled this divergence and from then onwards the Court acknowledged that true regulations could be challenged by private parties as long as these satisfied the general standing test.

[108] See, in very clear terms, Case C-583/11 P *Inuit Tapiriit Kanatami and Others* (n 6) para 56.

[109] Case 25/62 *Plaumann v Commission* [1962] ECR 95.

[110] Ibid, 107. [111] Ibid (emphasis added). [112] Ibid, 107.

[113] See eg Joined Cases 106/63 and 107/63 *Toepfer and Getreide-Import Gesellschaft v Commission* [1965] ECR 405, 411 and Case 62/70 *Bock v Commission* [1971] ECR 897, para 10.

and today still constitutes the main criterion to demonstrate individual concern[114]—but as we shall see, not the only one.

The *Plaumann* construction means, therefore, that carrying out a particular economic activity affected by the measure does not suffice to satisfy the test of individual concern. This is so even where the applicant is gravely affected by the measure[115] or when, at the time the measure was enacted, the applicant was effectively one of very few—or even the only one—carrying out that activity, as long as others could decide to undertake that activity *in the future* (ie after the date of the adoption of the act).[116] The Court's interpretation is, therefore, intensely formalistic not only because it seems dependent on demonstrating the existence of circumstances that have happened *before* the act in question was adopted, but also because it is detached from the actual effect that a measure has on an applicant and hence from economic reality. While those belonging to the closed category will generally suffer an adverse economic effect as a result of the measure, others outside the closed class may *also* experience such an effect and will nonetheless be deprived of standing.[117] A representation of the *Plaumann* test can be found in Fig 10.3.

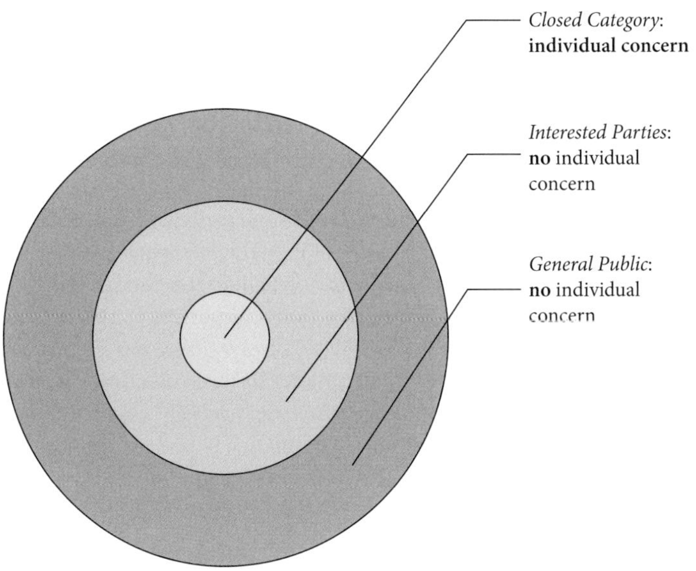

Fig. 10.3 The Plaumann test for individual concern

[114] For more recent examples, see Case T-585/93 *Stichting Greenpeace Council (Greenpeace International) v Commission* [1995] ECR II-2205, paras 53–55; Case T-16/04 *Arcelor v Parliament and Council* [2010] ECR II-211, paras 106–115; and Joined Cases C-71/09 P, C-73/09 P, and C-76/09 *Comitato 'Venezia vuole vivere' v Commission* [2011] ECR I-4727, para 52; Case C-132/12 P *Stichting Woonpunt and Others v Commission*, EU:C:2014:100, para 57; Case T-560/17 *Fortischem v European Parliament and Council*, EU:T:2018:764, para 55; and Case C-565/19 P *Carvalho v European Parliament and Council*, EU:C:2021:252, paras 35–52.

[115] Case T-173/98 *Unión de Pequeños Agricultores v Council* [1999] ECR II-3357, para 50.

[116] See eg Case 1/64 *Glucoseries réunies v Commission* [1964] ECR 413, 417 and Case C-209/94 P *Buralux v Council* [1996] ECR I-615, paras 28 and 29.

[117] See eg Case 11/82 *Piraiki-Patraiki v Commission* [1985] ECR 207, where a Commission measure imposing quotas on the importation of Greek cotton yarn into France was challenged by two groups of Greek exporters. On the one hand, it was challenged by Greek traders, who had pending contracts *at the time the measure was adopted* and, on the other, by Greek traders who normally exported cotton to France but who had no pending contracts at the time. While the first group was accorded standing (partly) on the basis that the traders were members of a closed class, the second group of exporters were denied standing, despite the fact that the measure clearly had an adverse effect on their economic interests.

Moreover, several issues have arisen in the application of the *Plaumann* test. First, it became necessary to illustrate what circumstances would propel an applicant into the 'magic circle' of a closed category. Looking at the case law, examples of applicants that satisfied the closed category test include those who—*before* the measure was adopted—had pursued an individual course of action such as applying for licences[118] or export refunds,[119] or having pending contracts[120] or goods in transit.[121]

Secondly, while the closed category test is the main indicator of individual concern, the case law has provided, on a case-by-case basis, a number of exceptions, which have unavoidably brought uncertainty to the application of the test. Most of them refer to special cases where the Court obviously found compelling reasons why the individuals should be granted *locus standi*—even if these reasons were not always fully articulated.

For example, in *Codorníu v Council*,[122] a leading Spanish manufacturer of sparkling wine, which had held a trademark including the term 'crémant' since 1924, challenged a Council regulation that reserved the use of this term for certain sparkling wines manufactured in France and Luxembourg. The Court did not specifically refer to the closed category test but explained instead that the regulation effectively prevented Codorníu from using its trademark,[123] a circumstance that later case law has construed as meaning that the applicant had a 'specific right' acquired before the measure entered into effect that had been affected by it[124] and which the Court seemed to consider as a separate basis for individual concern alongside the closed category test. While applicants have repeatedly tried to demonstrate individual concern on the basis of the *Codorníu* test, they have hardly ever been successful.[125]

Another example was the well-known decision in *Les Verts v European Parliament*,[126] where members of a new political party challenged a decision of the European Parliament allocating funds to prepare for elections to parties *already* present in the Parliament. The applicants were clearly not part of a closed class as new political parties could be constituted in the future, but the Court effectively set aside this test to give standing to the applicants as any other situation would give rise 'to inequality in the protection afforded by the Court to the various groups competing in the same elections'.[127] This judgment seemed, therefore, a rare case of triumph of substance over form.

[118] See eg *Toepfer and Getreide-Import Gesellschaft* (n 113). But, for those who applied for licences *after* the measure was adopted, individual concern was not found (see Case 38/64 *Getreide-Import Gesellschaft v Commission* [1965] ECR 203, 208).

[119] Case 100/74 *CAM v Commission* [1975] ECR 1393, paras 15–17.

[120] See eg *Piraiki-Patraiki* (n 117) para 19.

[121] *Sofrimport* (n 107) para 11.

[122] Case C-309/89 (n 107).

[123] Ibid, para 21. On the impact of *Codorníu*, see further A Arnull, 'Private Applicants and the Action for Annulment since *Codorníu*' (2001) 38 *Common Market Law Review* 7.

[124] See Case C-87/95 P *Cassa Nazionale di Previdenza ed Assistenza a favore degli avvocati e dei Procuratori v Council* [1996] ECR I-2003, para 36 and Case T-99/94 *Asociación Española de Empresas de la Carne v Council* [1994] ECR II-871, para 20. More recently, see Case T-560/17 (n 114) para 56.

[125] For an example where parallels can be drawn implicitly with the approach in *Codorníu*, see Case T-33/01 *Infront v Commission* [2005] ECR II-5897, paras 158–169 and confirmed on appeal in Case C-125/06 P *Commission v Infront* [2008] ECR I-1451. In this case, the applicants were found to be individually concerned because the decision in question had the specific purpose of altering the broadcasting rights acquired by the applicants before the measure had been enacted. However, in most situations, the invocation of the *Codorníu* test has proved unsuccessful. Eg see Case T-640/14 *Beul v European Parliament and Council*, EU: T:2015:907, para 48.

[126] Case 294/83 (n 6).

[127] Ibid, para 36.

Furthermore, there have been specific areas of the case law, notably in competition,[128] State aid, and anti-dumping and anti-subsidy proceedings,[129] where the Court has taken not only a more flexible but also a more consistent approach to individual concern. These areas have in common the fact that basic procedural or enforcement regulations[130] set out in detail the rights of participation of interested parties in the administrative procedure leading to the adoption of an EU measure, which is generally a Commission decision (in the case of competition and State aid) or Council and Commission regulations (eg in the field of anti-dumping). There, the Court has consistently found applicants individually concerned when these have participated in the proceedings—for example, by submitting a complaint to the Commission that triggered the investigation[131] or by providing observations[132] during the procedure leading to the adoption of the contested measure or even in some case where they simply *had the right* to participate but they did not do so.[133]

In some isolated cases, the Court went even further and, exceptionally, found applicants individually concerned not on the basis of their procedural involvement but because of the substantial adverse economic effect that a particular measure had on them. The leading decision is *Extramet v Council*,[134] where the largest importer of calcium metal into the EU challenged a Council regulation imposing anti-dumping duties on the importation of that product. The applicant was found to be individually concerned because of its position as the leading importer of calcium metal into the EU and because its economic activity had been seriously affected by the contested regulation. These were arguments, which, as we saw previously, had been consistently rejected, in the mainstream case law on individual concern[135] and it is therefore unsurprising that some applicants tried thereafter to extrapolate the *Extramet* findings in order to prove their *locus standi*. However, the Court

[128] See chapter 17.

[129] EU anti-dumping policy addresses the situation where undertakings outside the EU export products to the EU at prices below the normal value of those products on their domestic market—or, in other words, 'dump' the products in the EU market causing injury to the market. The EU anti-dumping Regulation (currently Regulation (EU) 2016/1036 (OJ [2016] L176/21)) sets out the procedure that applies to the imposition of anti-dumping measures. This Regulation works alongside EU anti-subsidy measures—see Regulation (EU) 2016/1037 (OJ [2016] L176/55), which sets out the procedure for countervailing any direct or indirect subsidies granted by a government for the manufacture or export of a product originating outside the EU but intended for release in the EU.

[130] See eg in the context of competition proceedings, Regulation 1/2003 (OJ [2003] L1/1); in the context of State aid, Council Regulation (EU) 2015/1589 (OJ [2015] L248/9), and in the context of anti-dumping and anti-subsidy proceedings, see Regulation 2016/1036 and Regulation 2016/1037 (n 129).

[131] See, in competition proceedings, Case 26/76 *Metro SB-Großmärkte GmbH & Co KG v Commission* ('*Metro I*') [1977] ECR 1875, para 13, where a competitor of an undertaking to whom a Commission decision was addressed had complained to the Commission. For an example in the field of anti-dumping, see Case 264/82 *Timex Corporation v Council and Commission* [1985] ECR 849, paras 13 and 14, and for an example in the field of State aid, see Case 169/84 *Compagnie française de l'azote (Cofaz) SA v Commission* [1986] ECR 391, para 25.

[132] See, in competition proceedings, Case 75/84 *Metro SB-Großmärkte GmbH & Co KG v Commission* ('*Metro II*') [1986] ECR 3021, paras 21–23. Here, the applicant had not complained to the Commission but had submitted observations during the procedure leading to the adoption of the Commission decision.

[133] See eg in the field of mergers, Case T-12/93 *Comité Central d'Entreprise de la Société Anonyme Vittel and Comité d'Etablissement de Pierval and Fédération Générale Agroalimentaire v Commission* [1995] ECR II-1247, paras 23 and 24.

[134] Case C-358/89 [1991] ECR I-2501, para 17.

[135] It could be argued that although the decision in *Codorníu* (n 107) was crafted in later case law in terms of the existence of a 'specific right', some parallels can be drawn with the ruling in *Extramet* because both in *Codorníu* (implicitly) and in *Extramet* (explicitly), the Court alluded to the grave effect that the measures in question would have on the economic interests of the applicants.

justified its approach in *Extramet* by referring to the 'exceptional circumstances' applying in that case and has been unwilling to extend it to other cases.[136]

Finally, there have been a small number of cases where the Court appeared to base its assessment of individual concern on a *cumulative* test, seemingly requiring the applicants not only to be members of a closed category but also to show that the institution enacting the measure had a duty imposed by higher ranking rules of EU law to take into account the situation of the applicants which it had failed to observe. This can be seen in *Sofrimport*.[137] There, Sofrimport, an importer of Chilean apples into the EU, brought annulment proceedings against three Commission regulations that suspended the issue of import licences for dessert apples with immediate effect. A *parent*—or basic—Council regulation[138] setting out the conditions and the framework within which the Commission could apply protective measures for fruit and vegetables included a provision that obliged the Commission to take into account the position of traders with goods in transit when adopting these measures. The Commission, however, failed to do so in this instance. At the time the regulations were adopted, Sofrimport had applied for an import licence and had a consignment of apples in transit to the EU. On arrival at the port of Marseilles, the French authorities refused to issue an import licence to Sofrimport.

The Court held that Sofrimport was individually concerned, first, because it was a member of a closed class[139]—it had applied for a licence and had goods in transit when the measures were adopted—and, secondly, because the Commission had failed to observe the duty imposed by the higher ranking EU rule.[140] An illustration of the factual background in *Sofrimport* can be found in Fig 10.4.[141] The obvious observation here is that if the applicant is a member of a closed class, it seems unnecessary to have to prove *additionally* the existence of a duty on the part of the institution. However, there is evidence in the case law that in those cases where the Court decided to apply the cumulative *Sofrimport* approach, it required the fulfilment of *both* elements, thus suggesting that membership of a closed class was not enough in itself.[142] In more recent years, this cumulative construction has been rarely applied by the Court.[143]

In many cases where private applicants did not satisfy the *Plaumann* test, the Court referred to the alternative possibility of indirectly challenging EU measures by bringing proceedings before the national courts in the hope that a preliminary reference on validity (considered in section 4.2) would be made to the Court of Justice.[144]

Given the difficulties and unpredictability associated with the application of the test of individual concern, it is unsurprising that repeated calls for a reformulation of the test were made. The most high-profile call for reform came from the Opinion of Advocate General Jacobs in *Unión de Pequeños Agricultores (UPA) v Council*,[145] where a Spanish trade association representing small agricultural producers challenged a Council

[136] See eg Case T-598/97 *British Shoe Corporation v Council* [2002] ECR II-1155, paras 48–50. See also Case C-312/00 P *Commission v Camar* [2002] ECR I-11355, paras 77–80, which indicated that being the main importer of a particular product was not, in itself, sufficient to determine individual concern.

[137] Case C-152/88 (n 107). See also section 6, case study 10.2. For another, earlier example, see *Piraiki-Patraiki* (n 117).

[138] This Regulation, post-Lisbon, would be classified as a legislative measure.

[139] *Sofrimport* (n 107) para 11.

[140] Ibid, paras 12 and 13.

[141] See also section 6, case study 10.2.

[142] See Case T-489/93 *Unifruit Hellas v Commission* [1994] ECR II-1201, para 25 and Case C-451/98 *Antillean Rice Mills v Council* [2001] ECR I-8949, paras 61 and 62.

[143] In fact, some decisions appear to suggest that the key element in those cases was the membership of a closed category, which closely aligns with the *Plaumann* construction (see *Fortischem* (n 114) para 55).

[144] See further section 4.2.

[145] Case C-50/00 P [2002] ECR I-6677.

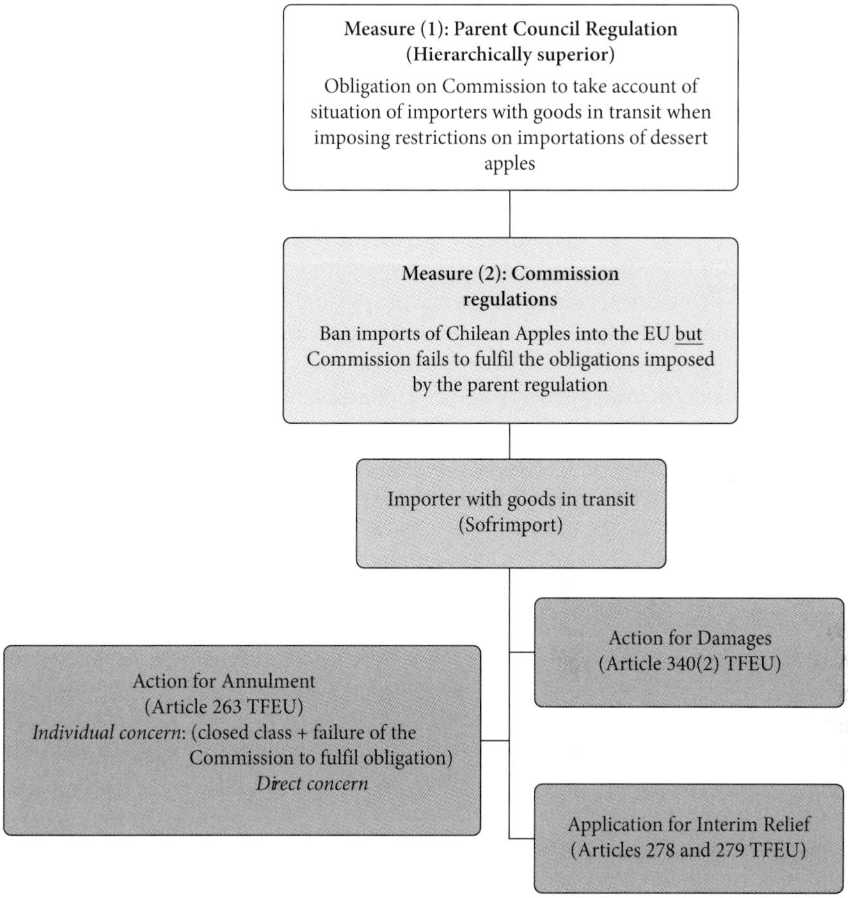

Fig. 10.4 The Sofrimport litigation

regulation that discontinued certain types of agricultural aid for small producers. Under the *Plaumann* test, the applicants were not individually concerned given that they were members of an open category of people. However, Advocate General Jacobs proposed a test that would render an applicant individually concerned where an EU measure 'has or is liable to have, a substantial adverse effect on his interests'.[146] In other words, he shifted the focus from a formalistic test to one based on the economic impact of an EU measure.

At the core of Advocate General Jacobs's submissions was the argument that it is not *automatic* that a private applicant who lacks standing to bring annulment proceedings can *always* obtain a remedy by bringing an action before the national court and hope that it will make a reference on validity to the Court of Justice.[147] This was his platform to argue for a relaxation of the test of individual concern because it effectively demonstrated that maintenance of the status quo could lead to situations of denial of justice,[148] a result at variance with the idea that the Treaty provides a *complete* system of judicial protection. *UPA* was a prime example of that kind of scenario, because the absence of implementing measures at national level—that is, the aid schemes were automatically discontinued as

[146] Ibid, paras 60 and 103 of the AG's Opinion.

[147] Ibid, paras 36–49 of the Opinion.

[148] Ibid, paras 38–44.

a result of the regulation without the need for any national intervention—meant that the applicants could not bring proceedings before the national court and therefore that the alternative of a preliminary ruling on validity was simply unavailable.

A couple of months later, the General Court in *Jégo-Quéré v Commission*[149] followed Advocate General Jacobs and took the unprecedented step of also proposing a relaxation of the *Plaumann* test. The facts of this case showed a slightly different angle than in *UPA* in terms of the availability of national proceedings. A fishing company challenged a Commission regulation that imposed minimum mesh sizes for different net-fishing techniques. The measure required no implementation at national level. The right of action before the national court—and hence the possibility of a preliminary reference on validity—could be exercised there but *only* if the applicant infringed the requirements of the Commission regulation or, in other words, only if it breached the EU measure. This was not only a risky strategy (why does an applicant have to break the law to get a remedy?) but also one that is inconsistent with the principles of effective judicial protection. Therefore, both the proceedings in *UPA* and in *Jégo-Quéré* demonstrated the weakness of the argument that the route through the national courts *always* offers a satisfactory alternative to private applicants when these are not able to satisfy the standing conditions in Article 263(4) TFEU.[150] However, the Court of Justice in *UPA* did not follow these leads and confirmed the traditional construction of individual concern;[151] a position that the CJEU takes to this day.[152]

The more recent and high-profile decision of the Court in *Carvalho v Parliament and Council*[153] has confirmed the steadfast adherence of the Court to the *Plaumann* formula. There, private applicants—mainly natural persons—from a range of Member States and third countries operating in the agricultural and tourism sectors sought the annulment of a Union legislative package on the grounds that the targets for the reduction of greenhouse gas emissions by 2030 were insufficient. The applicants had argued before the General Court that the legislative package infringed their fundamental human rights, including the right to life, the right to the integrity of the person, the rights of the child, the right to property, and the freedom to choose an occupation. In particular, they had contended that the infringement of each of these rights would be 'unique to and different for each individual'[154] and hence that they should be regarded as individually concerned by the contested measures. In the alternative, they had argued for a relaxation of the condition of individual concern, which appeared to be unsuitable in environmental cases, where the harmful effects of Union acts are widespread and where satisfaction of the closed category test seems particularly inviable.[155] On appeal, the Court of Justice remained unmoved and reiterated settled case law that a claim that an EU act may

[149] Case T-177/01 [2002] ECR II-2365, paras 49–51. The test proposed by the General Court in this case was slightly more restrictive than the one suggested by the AG in *UPA* but still more lenient than the closed category test. In particular, the Court suggested that an applicant would be individually concerned where 'the measure in question affects his legal position, in a manner which is both definite and immediate, by restricting his rights or by imposing obligations on him' (para 51).

[150] See further section 4.2 on the limitations of the system of preliminary rulings on validity.

[151] *UPA* (n 145) paras 44–45.

[152] See Case T-18/10 *Inuit Tapiriit Kanatami v European Parliament and Council* ('Inuit I') [2011] ECR II-5599, paras 88–94 and Case C-132/12 P *Stichting Woonpunt and Others* (n 114) para 57.

[153] Case C-565/19 P (n 114).

[154] Case T-330/18 *Carvalho and Others v European Parliament and Council*, EU:T:2019:324, paras 31–32.

[155] Some of these arguments had already been unsuccessfully rehearsed in older cases concerning the challenge of EU acts with an environmental impact; see Case C-321/95 P *Greenpeace Council (Greenpeace International) v Commission*, EU:C:1998:153, paras 17–18 and Case T-585/93 *Greenpeace Council (Greenpeace International) v Commission*, EU:T:1995:147, para 34.

infringe fundamental human rights was 'not sufficient in itself' to guarantee standing for private parties.[156] It then went on to confirm the dismissal of the action on the grounds that the applicants did not satisfy the exacting standards of the test of individual concern laid down in *Plaumann*, from which the Court was clearly not prepared to depart.[157]

Direct concern

By contrast, the test of direct concern has been less problematic. Essentially, this test has been construed as satisfied when there is a direct causal relationship between the act in question and the effect that it has on the applicant.[158] In practical terms, the Court has taken the view that the main situation when this causal link could be interrupted would be where the addressee of the measure had discretion as to how to implement the measure—and thus the ability to change the course of its application. In this case, the effect on the applicant would be caused by the measure adopted by the addressee rather than by the EU measure. Thus, in *Les Verts v European Parliament*, the Court explained that the European Parliament's decision was of direct concern to the applicants because the decision constituted 'a complete set of rules which are sufficient in themselves and which require no implementing provisions since the calculation of the share of the appropriations to be granted to each of the political groupings concerned is automatic and leaves no room for any discretion'.[159] Therefore, an applicant would be directly concerned where an act has a direct impact on them and, as result of this, the act requires no implementation or, even if it does, the addressee of the act has no discretion as to how to implement it.[160]

Further, in interpreting the existence of discretion for the purposes of the application of the test of direct concern, the Court has taken the view that *even* if some discretion is left to the addressee, the measure can still be of direct concern to a non-addressee where the use of the discretion is 'entirely theoretical'. This is because there is no doubt as to the intention of the addressee to implement the EU measure in a particular way. For example, if a Commission decision *authorizes* a Member State to impose import restrictions, theoretically the Member State could decide not to use the authorization. However, if the Member State actually applied to the Commission for authorization to impose the restrictions, there is little doubt that they intend to use it.[161]

Conclusion

This section has shown the difficulties inherent in the application of the general standing test. In *UPA*,[162] the Court made it clear that it would not broaden the test of individual concern and that any changes should come through political agreement between the Member States in the form of an amendment of Article 263(4) TFEU.[163] It therefore came as no surprise that the Lisbon Treaty introduced a new standing test for private parties that would coexist with the general standing test with a view to making it easier for non-privileged applicants to secure standing under Article 263(4) TFEU. The key question, however, is whether this new test has resolved all the problems created by the general standing test.

[156] Case C-565/19 P (n 114), paras 48–49. [157] Ibid, paras 67–80.

[158] Joined Cases 41–44/70 *International Fruit Co v Commission* [1971] ECR 411, paras 23–28.

[159] *Les Verts* (n 6) para 31. [160] Ibid.

[161] See eg *Piraiki-Patraiki* (n 117) paras 7–9. See, more recently and in clear terms, Case C-466/16 P *Council v Marquis Energy*, EU:C:2019:156, para 44.

[162] Case C-50/00 P (n 145). [163] Ibid, para 45.

The Lisbon test

Following the Lisbon amendments, Article 263(4) TFEU allows a non-privileged applicant, who is not an addressee of a contested measure, to challenge a 'regulatory act, which is of direct concern to the applicant and does not entail implementing measures'. Given that no requirement of individual concern needs to be satisfied, this test promised to improve the ability of private parties to challenge EU acts. However, the implications of the test could not be fully appraised until three issues were resolved. First, the notion of 'regulatory act' needed to be clarified. Secondly, a question arose as to whether the concept of direct concern in the Lisbon test would be construed in the same way as in the established case law on the general standing test. Finally, it was necessary to elucidate, in this context, what it meant that the act in question 'does not entail implementing measures.

What constitutes a regulatory act?

After much speculation, the first issue was addressed by the General Court in *Inuit I*,[164] where it defined a 'regulatory act' as an act 'of general application apart from legislative acts'.[165] This definition was upheld, on appeal, by the Court of Justice.[166] The term 'regulatory act' therefore encompasses two cumulative elements: (1) the act must be, by default, non-legislative—that is, not adopted by ordinary or special legislative procedure—*and* (2) it must be of general application.

Regulatory acts are therefore *non-legislative* acts, such as for example—but not exclusively—general implementing and delegated acts adopted under Articles 290 and 291 TFEU. By contrast, *legislative* regulations and directives—those adopted under the ordinary or special legislative procedures—do not come under this definition and are subjected to the general standing test and therefore to the rigours of the *Plaumann* test of individual concern.[167] Since the act under review in *Inuit I* was a legislative regulation, the Lisbon test was inapplicable and the general test applied instead, with the result that the applicants were denied standing, mainly due to their failure to satisfy the test of individual concern.[168]

Furthermore, regulatory acts must have a second characteristic: they must be of *general application*. In principle, this would clearly include acts that, according to Article 288 TFEU, are of a general nature, namely (non-legislative) regulations and directives. However, the case law has also included (non-legislative) decisions of general application, such as those that are addressed to Member States. Thus, only a few weeks after its decision in *Inuit I*, the General Court delivered judgment in a second key case: *Microban v Commission*.[169] This was the first time that the Lisbon test was fully satisfied in a set of circumstances where the applicant probably would not have satisfied the general test of standing due to lack of individual concern. There, an American manufacturer of antibacterial additives challenged a Commission decision addressed to the Member States removing triclosan, a chemical substance, from the list of additives that could be employed in the manufacture of plastics used with foodstuffs, which had been drawn up by a previous Commission directive. The General Court found that the Commission decision was a regulatory act because it was a non-legislative act. Moreover, the act was also implicitly understood to be an act of general application. The explanation for this seems to be that, although the act was a decision—and therefore nominally an individual act according to the terminology used by Article 288 TFEU—it was addressed to all the

164 Case T-18/10 (n 152). For a discussion of the *Inuit* litigation, see section 6, case study 10.1.

165 Ibid, para 56. 166 Case C-583/11 P (n 6) paras 50–61. 167 Ibid.

168 Case T-18/10 (n 152) paras 57–67 and (on appeal) Case C-583/11 P (n 6) paras 68–77.

169 Case T-262/10 [2011] ECR II-7697.

Member States and hence it could be categorized as an act of general application in the territory of these States. However, not all decisions addressed to Member States have been *automatically* understood to be of a general nature.[170]

When is a regulatory act of 'direct concern' to an applicant?

In *Microban*, the General Court held that the Commission decision was of direct concern to the applicant because no discretion over its implementation was left to the Member States. The Court explained that the interpretation of direct concern would not be *stricter* in the context of the Lisbon test than in the context of the general standing test.[171] As a result, the judgment seemed to leave scope for a more generous construction of the test of direct concern in the framework of the Lisbon test. However, more recent case law has interpreted the notion of direct concern in exactly the same manner as in the context of the general standing test, that is, referring to the absence of 'real' or 'substantive' discretion on the part of the addressee.[172] Finally, the General Court also took the view that the decision of the Commission in *Microban* did not entail implementing measures since it effectively introduced a direct prohibition on the use of triclosan in all the Member States—which were not required to take any further action to implement the prohibition. Microban thus became the first private applicant to satisfy the Lisbon test of standing.

Of course, the *Microban* decision showed the enhanced possibilities that the Lisbon test offered to private parties, but it did not solve all the concerns generated by the case law in this area. In particular, the *Microban* decision did not entirely clarify the meaning to be given to the expression that the regulatory act must 'not entail implementing measures'—or the degree of differentiation between this limb of the test and the satisfaction of the test of direct concern. These issues were addressed by later decisions.

What does it mean that the regulatory act must not entail implementing measures?

The Court has clarified that the rationale behind this requirement is that if a regulatory act requires further implementation at national level or (less frequently) at EU level, then, there are other avenues for the challenge of the implementing measure that should be used instead. In the first case, the national implementing measure can be challenged before the national court—thus opening the possibility of a preliminary reference on validity. In the second case, the EU implementing measure can be challenged before the General Court by means of an action for annulment—with the further possibility of a plea of illegality being brought in relation to the regulatory act.[173] It is therefore clear from this approach that this requirement effectively limits the application of the Lisbon test to cases where further challenge at either national or EU level is precluded.

Some of the difficulties that were left unresolved by the decision in *Microban* in relation to this limb of the test have now been addressed by the case law. In *Palirria Souliotis*

[170] See Case C-33/14 P *Mory SA and Others v Commission*, EU:C:2015:609, para 92. This case concerned a decision addressed to France stating that the recovery of unlawful State aid that had been ordered by a previous Commission decision was not to be extended to two particular companies that had since taken over two of the companies that were part of the original group of recipients of the aid. The Court considered this to be an *individual* act and not a general one, with the result that the Lisbon test of standing could not be applied. However, this case can be distinguished from the situation in *Microban* because, although the decision in *Mory* was addressed to a Member State, it really dealt with the individualized situation of two companies, rather than being of general application in the territory of this Member State.

[171] See Case T-262/10 (n 169) para 32.

[172] See Case T-380/11 *Palirria Souliotis v Commission*, EU:T:2013:420, para 44 and Case C-84/14 P *Forgital v Council*, EU:C:2015:517, para 44.

[173] Case C-274/12 P *Telefónica SA v Commission*, EU:C: 2013:852, paras 28–29 and Case C-456/13 P *T & L Sugars Ltd and Sidul Açúcares, Unipessoal Lda v Commission*, EU:C:2015:284, paras 30–31.

v Commission,[174] the General Court explained that the test of direct concern—which, as established in the case law, refers to the absence of 'real' or 'substantive' discretion on the part of the addressee—is different from the requirement that the act should not entail implementing measures, which appears to relate to whether or not further measures are necessary to put an EU act into effect.[175] These two issues have therefore been confirmed as distinct. It is quite possible to imagine a situation where an EU act does not leave any discretion to its addressee (ie a Member State) but where an addressee still needs to adopt a measure to put the act into effect. This would be the case, for example, of a Commission implementing decision addressed to the Member States setting out a levy on the production of sugar but where the national authorities are tasked with collecting the levy. This decision does not leave any discretion to the Member States—and hence it could be argued that it would be of direct concern to a sugar producer who must pay the levy and wishes to challenge the decision. However, technically, it could be argued that the national authorities must still take some steps to put the Commission decision into effect—ie collecting the levy—and hence that these further steps could constitute implementing measures. Of course, the difficulty here lies in whether the concept of 'implementing measure' should be interpreted in a formalistic way—ie including purely mechanical acts such as collecting a levy—or whether it should be interpreted in a more substantive way—ie involving more significant steps, such as for instance the adoption of general administrative acts.

In *Telefónica v Commission*,[176] the Court of Justice adopted what seemed a fairly formalistic interpretation of the notion of implementing measures. Thus, it held that the absence of implementing measures means the absence of *any* measure to be taken by the addressee of the measure—that is, a Member State—to put the regulatory act into operation or, in other words, the absence of any measure that generates 'specific consequences' for the applicant.[177] The rationale behind this approach is consistent with the Court's interpretation of the purpose of the third limb of the Lisbon test that we discussed earlier. If *any* measure is required at national level, theoretically there should be an opportunity to challenge it before a national court and hence the possibility of a preliminary ruling on validity. However, this interpretation has also the effect of significantly limiting the opening provided for private parties by the Lisbon test because a great proportion of EU measures require some action, even if of an entirely mechanical nature, at national level.

This construction of the third limb of the Lisbon test also raises further issues. For example, prima facie it might exclude non-legislative directives—for example, a Commission directive that amends or implements a Parliament and Council directive[178]—from the ambit of the Lisbon test. Thus, while it is possible for directives to leave little or no *discretion* to the Member States in their implementation (thus, the test for direct concern would be satisfied), they generally require *implementing* measures (thus, the test for 'not entail[ing] implementing measures' would not be satisfied). The direct challenge to these directives under Article 263 TFEU would therefore always seem to be subject to the general test on standing (which is unlikely to be satisfied due to the difficulties in showing the existence of individual concern). In practice, therefore, a challenge to these acts would

[174] *Palirria Souliotis* (n 172). [175] Ibid, para 44. [176] *Telefónica SA* (n 173).

[177] Ibid, paras 35 and 36. This approach has now been confirmed in a series of cases. See Case C-132/12 P *Stichting Woonpunt v Commission* (n 114) paras 50–54; Case C-456/13 P *T & L Sugars Ltd and Sidul Açúcares, Unipessoal Lda v Commission* (n 173) paras 40–41; Case T-601/11 *Dansk Automat Brancheforening v Commission*, EU:T:2014:839, paras 57–59; and, more recently, see Case C-244/16 P *Industrias Químicas del Vallés v Commission*, EU:C:2018:177, paras 39–77.

[178] For an example of a non-legislative directive, see Commission Directive 2012/47/EU (OJ [2013] L31/43) amending Parliament and Council Directive 2009/43/EC on the terms and conditions of transfers of defence related products within the Union (OJ [2009] L146/1).

regularly have to be made indirectly via the national route and then a preliminary reference on invalidity.

Conclusion

It follows from the line of case law where the Court has given meaning to the conditions attached to the Lisbon test that the test has allowed some private applicants to secure standing in cases where the application of the general standing test would have rendered their applications inadmissible.[179] However, this test still emerges as a partial gap-plugging mechanism in the system of judicial protection afforded by the Treaties.

As we have seen, not only is the Lisbon test designed to apply in cases where an alternative route for judicial review is unavailable—due to the lack of implementing measures—but also it may not *always* be available in some of those cases. In particular, the interpretation followed by the General Court and Court of Justice on the notion of regulatory acts excludes legislative acts from the Lisbon test. This means that the general standing test applies in relation to these acts and hence that situations of denial of justice could still arise where the preliminary reference avenue is not available (see section 4.2). In other words, a *UPA*-type situation could still arise today for applicants trying to challenge a legislative act, who are unable either to pursue their claim before the national court or to satisfy the general test of standing.[180] In *UPA*, the Court had indicated that it could not alter the wording of the Treaty and that it was the responsibility of the Member States to ensure the existence of national avenues for bringing proceedings before the national court, where a preliminary reference on validity could be made; a finding that is now strengthened by the wording of Article 19(1) TFEU.[181] This shift of responsibility towards the national legal systems in the context of the review of EU acts, has strongly resurfaced in the judgment of the Court of Justice in *Inuit I*.[182] However, this devolutionist approach of the Court stands in contrast with its approach in other contexts, such as the development of the doctrine of direct effect and creation of the principle of State liability in damages. There, the Court, guided by the need to guarantee effective legal protection for private parties against Member State action contrary to EU law did not hesitate to create, respectively, a principle and a remedy—as a matter of EU law—that could be invoked before national courts against Member States that acted in breach of EU law.

The standing of associations and interest groups

The case law on Article 263(4) TFEU offers several examples of actions brought by associations created for the promotion of collective interests (eg trade associations)[183] or interest groups (eg environmental associations).[184] So far, the prospects for associations having

[179] See *Microban* (n 169). However, the general standing test, as seen, continues to apply (with a residual character) where one of the conditions in the Lisbon test is not fulfilled, see Case T-512/14 *Green Source Poland v Commission*, EU:T:2017:299, paras 22–25.

[180] In its decision in *Inuit Tapiriit Kanatami* (n 6) the Court of Justice dismissed the argument that the exclusion of legislative acts from the Lisbon test created a gap in the system of judicial protection contrary to Art 47 of the Charter and held that 'Article 47 of the Charter does not require that an individual should have an unconditional entitlement to bring an action for annulment of European Union legislative acts directly before the Courts of the European Union' (para 105).

[181] For a very interesting study of the concerns that arise as a result of the Court's strategy of devolving responsibility for providing judicial review to the national courts, see A Arnull, 'Judicial Review in the European Union' in A Arnull and D Chalmers (eds), *The Oxford Handbook of European Union Law* (Oxford: Oxford University Press, 2014) 376.

[182] Case C-583/11 P (n 6) paras 98–107. See also, for a more implicit form of this reasoning, Case C-467/17 P *Società agricola Taboga Leandro v Parliament* and *Council*, EU:C:2017:916, paras 26–30.

[183] Case T-122/96 *Federolio v Commission* [1997] ECR II-1559.

[184] Case T-585/93 (n 155).

standing have been rather bleak. In *Federolio*,[185] a case brought by a trade association, the General Court identified the three alternative situations when these actions would be admissible:

(a) where a legal provision grants the association a series of procedural rights;
(b) where the association represents members who would themselves have standing to bring proceedings;
(c) where the own interests of the association are affected, and in particular its position as negotiator is affected by the EU act in question.[186]

These conditions are notably difficult to satisfy, especially because outside the specific fields of competition, State aid, and anti-dumping proceedings it is rare for the procedural rights of associations to be laid down by legislation[187] or for associations to be active negotiators (in the sense of interlocutors of the EU institutions)[188] in the adoption of EU measures. Most actions for annulment refer to EU measures taken in the context of the common agricultural policy, where it is infrequent that trade associations are formally granted any procedural rights in the process leading to the adoption of legislative and non-legislative acts.[189]

Similar parameters applied to applications brought by interest groups. Thus, in the *Greenpeace* litigation,[190] where three environmental associations and several private individuals challenged a number of Commission decisions authorizing the granting of aid for the construction of two power stations in the Canary Islands, the General Court and the Court of Justice applied very similar criteria to those in *Federolio* with the result that the actions were dismissed as inadmissible. However, the effects of the *Greenpeace* line of case law in relation to the standing of environmental associations have been somewhat mitigated today following the Union's signature and conclusion of the UN Economic Commission for Europe (UNECE) Convention on Access to Information, Public Participation in Decision-Making and Access to Justice in Environmental Matters (the Aarhus Convention) in 1998 and the adoption of Directive 2003/4/EC on public access to environmental information,[191] which have enhanced the standing of environmental associations before national courts.[192]

In the aftermath of the Lisbon reforms, the new special standing test has had an impact on the formulation of the standing conditions applicable to associations in relation to the second situation set out in *Federolio*—that is, where the association has standing if it represents the interests of members who would themselves have standing. There, the case law has now helpfully clarified that this would cover not only the case where members

[185] Case T-122/96 (n 183).

[186] Ibid, para 61. There have been some instances where the standing of associations has been eased further on the basis of the effect of the decision on their own interests *or those of its members*. See Case C-319/07 P *3F v Commission* [2009] ECR I-5963, for an interesting decision in the field of State aid, where a trade union was given standing to challenge a Commission decision finding that an aid scheme was prima facie compatible with EU law under the preliminary review procedure set out in Art 108(3) TFEU.

[187] For an example in anti-dumping proceedings, see Case 191/82 *Fediol v Commission* [1983] ECR 2913, paras 28–30.

[188] For an example in the field of State aid, see Case C-313/90 *CIRFS v Commission* [1993] ECR I-1125, paras 28–30.

[189] See eg *Federolio* (n 183) para 63.

[190] Case T-585/93 *Greenpeace* (n 155) and (on appeal) Case C-321/95 P (n 155).

[191] OJ [2003] L41/26.

[192] See also Arts 10–12 Council Regulation 1367/2006 (OJ [2006] L264/13), as amended by Regulation (EU) 2021/1767 of the European Parliament and of the Council (OJ [2021] L356/1).

of the association are directly and individually concerned (and hence satisfy the general standing test) but also where they are challenging a regulatory act that is of direct concern to them and that does not entail implementing measures (and hence satisfy the special standing test).[193]

3.2.5 **Grounds for annulment and effects of a successful action for annulment**

Once an applicant has managed to prove standing it is furthermore necessary to show that there is a suitable ground to challenge the legality of an EU act. Article 263(2) TFEU lists four grounds of annulment, which will be briefly examined in turn.

The first ground is lack of competence. The EU institutions are subject to the principle of conferral,[194] that is, they are only empowered to act in the specific areas provided by the Treaties. As a result, if an EU institution lacked the power to adopt an act—that is, there was no appropriate legal basis under the Treaty for its action—the act might be annulled by the Court due to lack of competence.[195] This ground will also be applicable where there has been an excessive delegation of power to an EU agency or institution[196] or where an institution implementing an EU act has not respected the limits of its powers or has gone beyond the mere implementation of a legislative act.[197]

The second ground is infringement of an essential procedural requirement. It applies whenever an EU institution has not complied with a rule of procedure in the adoption of the contested act. This would include, for example, failure to consult the European Parliament before adopting a measure where consultation is mandated by the Treaty,[198] failure to provide adequate reasons for the adoption of an act,[199] or infringement of the rights of the defence of the addressees of a Union act or of interested parties.[200]

The third ground for review is infringement of the Treaty or of any rule of law relating to its application. This has been understood to encompass a breach of the primary sources of EU law. Thus, it mainly includes Treaty provisions, international law provisions binding on the EU,[201] provisions contained in a measure of secondary legislation, which is hierarchically superior to the contested act,[202] and general principles of law.[203] Infringement of general principles of law—which are understood in the broadest sense of the expression[204] and naturally include the rights provided in the EU Charter of Fundamental Rights—is a frequently argued ground in the context of the action of annulment.

Finally, the fourth ground is misuse of powers, which, although frequently argued, has rarely been successful because the required standard of proof is very difficult to meet. In particular, the applicant needs to show that the institution in question used its powers for

[193] Case T-454/20 *Garment Manufacturers Association in Cambodia v Commission* (EU:T:2021:833), para 21.

[194] Art 5(2) TEU.

[195] See Case C-376/98 *Germany v Parliament and Council* ('*Tobacco Advertising*') [2000] ECR I-8419. See further chapter 5.

[196] Case 9/56 *Meroni v High Authority* [1957–8] ECR 133, 150–152.

[197] Case 22/88 *Industrie-en Handelsonderneming Vreugdenhil BV v Minister van Landbouw en Visserij* [1989] ECR 2049, paras 16–26.

[198] Case 138/79 *Roquette Frères v Council* [1980] ECR 3333.

[199] See Case 18/57 *Nold v High Authority* [1959] ECR 41, 51–53.

[200] See Case C-291/89 *Interhotel v Commission* [1991] ECR I-2257.

[201] Joined Cases 21–24/72 *International Fruit Co NV v Produktschap voor Groenten en Fruit* [1972] ECR 1219.

[202] See eg Joined Cases 113–118/77 *NTN Toyo Bearing Co Ltd v Council* [1979] ECR 1185.

[203] See eg *Codorníu* (n 107).

[204] See chapters 8 and 9.

a purpose other than that for which the powers were conferred or to evade a procedure specifically provided by the Treaties.[205]

If an action for annulment is well founded, the Court will annul the act in question[206] and such a declaration will have an *erga omnes* and *ex tunc* effect unless the Court decides otherwise. In other words, the act will be treated as if it had never existed.[207]

3.3 **The action for failure to act**

The action for failure to act—set out in Articles 265 and 266 TFEU—represents the natural complement to the action for annulment. It is applicable where an institution, instead of acting illegally, failed to act when it had an obligation to do so. Given that the two actions represent two sides of effectively the same remedy, they share some important characteristics. However, there are also some special issues relating to the action for failure to act that should be considered separately. Of these, the most significant is an admissibility requirement, namely that *before* an action for a failure to act can be brought before the Court, the institution in question must have been called upon to act. Only if it has then failed to define its position within two months can an action be brought.[208] This is therefore an essential *pre*-litigation requirement.

Furthermore, three other issues should be examined in connection with this means of redress. First, the time limit for bringing an action under Article 265 TFEU is two months, which starts to run after the end of the pre-litigation procedure.[209] Secondly, according to Article 265(1) TFEU, an action can be brought against the failure of an institution or of a body, office, or agency of the Union to adopt an act. While it is clear from the wording of Article 265(3) TFEU that such an act would have had to be a legally binding one when the action is brought by private parties, such a requirement is not laid down in Article 265(1) TFEU for the situation when this action is brought by a Member State or a Union institution. This suggests that, in this case, the action could be brought against the failure of a Union institution to adopt a non-legally binding act.[210] Thirdly, post-Lisbon, Article 265 TFEU recognizes two categories of applicants: privileged and non-privileged. The first category encompasses the Member States and the EU institutions. The second refers to private parties. Again, and as with Article 263 TFEU, the conditions are exacting. A natural or legal person can only bring an action where an institution, body, office, or agency of the Union has 'failed to *address* to that person an act other than a recommendation or an opinion'. In fact, this is an even more restrictive wording than that in Article 263(4) TFEU. This is because it does not seem to cover the situation where the act in question would have been addressed to a third party but would have been of direct and individual concern to the applicant. In this respect, the wording of Article 265 TFEU has not been amended since the founding Treaties and fails to create a mirror image of the Lisbon test

[205] See eg Case 8/55 *Fédération Charbonnière de Belgique v High Authority* [1954–6] ECR 292, 303 and for a more recent example, see Case C-442/04 *Commission v Spain* [2008] ECR I-3517, paras 46–51. For a rare successful challenge in a case dealing with actions brought by civil servants of the EU, see Case 105/75 *Giuffrida v Council* [1976] ECR 1395.

[206] Art 264(1) TFEU.

[207] But see Art 264(2) TFEU, which allows for certain limitations to this principle.

[208] Art 265(2) TFEU. [209] Ibid.

[210] On this point, see the observations by K Lenaerts, I Maselis, and K Gutman, *EU Procedural Law* (Oxford: Oxford University Press, 2014), who give as an example an action for failure to act brought by the Parliament against the Commission when the latter has failed to submit a legislative proposal. They explain that the rationale for including the failure to adopt a non-binding act in this situation would be that, in that situation, the proposal of the Commission would be a necessary requisite for the 'Council and the Parliament to play their respective roles in the legislative process' (at 425).

in Article 263(4) TFEU applicable to the action for failure to act. However, this divergence does not appear to be significant in practical terms. This is because the Court has recognized that the action for annulment and the action for failure to act effectively constitute two sides of the same remedy and therefore it follows from this that the same (mirrored) requirements of standing should apply to private parties under both actions.[211] It is just somewhat surprising that the drafters of the Lisbon Treaty did not take the opportunity, in the interests of clarity, to align Articles 263 and 265 TFEU on this particular point.

3.4 **The plea of illegality**

The plea of illegality is provided in Article 277 TFEU and although it is brought directly before the Court, it constitutes an incidental mechanism of review attached to a 'main' direct action. Thus, it allows an applicant who has brought a direct action before the Court—most frequently under Article 263 TFEU[212]—to plead the illegality of a general EU act (ie a regulation or a directive or a general decision) that constitutes the basis of the act the annulment of which is sought in the main action pending before the Court.[213] A typical example would be a case where a Commission implementing regulation is being challenged before the Court by means of Article 263 TFEU proceedings. During these proceedings, the applicants may wish to bring a plea of illegality against the parent legislative regulation (ie a Parliament and Council regulation) that constituted the basis of the implementing Commission regulation.[214]

There are therefore two important limitations to the use of Article 277 TFEU proceedings: they can only be brought against an *act of general application* and they are *dependent on the existence of another action pending before the Court.*[215] According to the literal wording of Article 277 TFEU, *any* party may bring a plea of illegality[216] but historically it has been brought mostly by private parties attempting to escape the stringent standing conditions that applied to the direct challenge of general acts in the context of Article 263(4) TFEU.[217] As we have seen, their chances of success were very limited, particularly because the application of the tests of direct and individual concern frequently acted as a barrier to the admissibility of the main action of annulment—without which the plea of illegality could not prosper. In this sense, the Lisbon reforms to Article 263(4) TFEU offer an interesting new dimension to the use of the plea of illegality, because in those cases where the Lisbon test now applies, the use of the Article 277 TFEU action might be more viable. Case study 10.1 shows precisely this in the context of the *Inuit* litigation.[218]

Finally, the grounds for the annulment of the act of general application are the same as those that apply in the context of the action for annulment.

[211] See Case C-68/95 *T Port v Commission* [1996] ECR I-6065, para 59. The rationale offered by the Court was that 'the possibility for individuals to assert their rights should not depend upon whether the institution concerned has acted or failed to act' (ibid).

[212] eg see Case T-526/10 *Inuit Tapiriit Kanatami v Commission* ('*Inuit II*'), EU:T:2013:215 and, on appeal, Case C-398/13 P *Inuit Tapiriit Kanatami and Others v Commission*, EU:C:2015:535.

[213] See in this respect, the observations of the Court in Case 92/78 *Simmenthal v Commission* [1979] ECR 777, para 36.

[214] For an illustration on how this mechanism operates, see Fig 10.6, which describes the *Inuit* litigation.

[215] See eg Joined Cases 87/77, 130/77, 22/83, 9/84, and 10/84 *Salerno v Commission and Council* [1985] ECR 2523, para 36.

[216] For an example of where an institution has brought a plea of illegality, see Case C-11/00 *Commission v European Central Bank* [2003] ECR I-7147, paras 76–78. See further M Vogt, 'Indirect Judicial Protection in EC Law: The Case of the Plea of Illegality' (2006) 31 *European Law Review* 364, 369–370. For an example, where a Member State was able to bring a plea of illegality, see Case C-442/04 *Spain v Council*, EU:C:2008:2760, para 22.

[217] See *Simmenthal* (n 213) para 41.

[218] See section 6, case study 10.1.

3.5 **The action for damages**

The action for damages is set out in Articles 268 TFEU and 340(2) TFEU. It covers the situation where an applicant has suffered damage or loss as a result of illegal action by a Union institution or by its civil servants. It is an independent action[219] and its aim is to obtain an award in damages.[220] Therefore, unlike the other direct actions that we have considered so far, it is not a declaratory action.[221] In theory, any party (eg a Member State) may bring an action for damages but in practice actions have been brought by natural and legal persons. No standing conditions are attached to the action and the Statute of the Court provides a time limit of five years from the occurrence of the event giving rise to liability.[222] Despite these apparently generous conditions, private applicants have had limited success when bringing this action, mainly as a result of a restrictive interpretation of the requirements necessary to show liability on the part of the EU institutions.

In *Lütticke*,[223] the Court laid down three conditions to establish liability. These are:

(a) the existence of an unlawful act or conduct on the part of the institution;

(b) actual damage suffered by the applicant; and

(c) a causal link between the illegality of the act and the damage suffered by the applicant.

While these basic conditions have remained essentially unaltered since they were first introduced, an important case law evolution has taken place in the interpretation of the first one. Thus, and in the specific context of actions for damages brought against illegal Union acts,[224] the Court has shifted the parameters for the assessment of the nature and degree of that illegality.

Initially, a formalistic and very narrow approach prevailed in the early decision of the Court in *Aktien-Zuckerfabrik Schöppenstedt v Council*,[225] where the Court held that where the illegality stemmed from a *legislative* act 'involving measures of economic policy', the institutions would not incur liability unless 'a sufficiently flagrant violation of a superior rule of law for the protection of the individual has occurred'.[226] Suffice to say, this formula was extremely difficult to satisfy[227] and the case law on actions for damages arising from EU regulations and directives at the time showed that only in the most extreme of circumstances would private applicants manage to reach this formidable threshold of illegality.[228] In the case of individual acts, such as decisions, this enhanced ceiling of illegality did not apply.

[219] Case 4/69 *Lütticke v Commission* [1971] ECR 325, para 6.

[220] In practice, and notwithstanding the independence of the action for damages, applicants frequently bring together an action for annulment and an action for damages. See section 6, case study 10.2.

[221] As AG Sharpston pointed out in her Opinion in Case C-131/03 *RJ Reynolds Tobacco Holdings* [2006] ECR I-7795 referring to the Court's case law: 'A remedy for damages does not fall within the system of judicial review. Rather, it is an autonomous form of action, with a particular purpose to fulfil within the system of legal remedies. . . . An action for damages depends on a measure or on unlawful conduct having adverse material consequences for the applicant, whereas an action for annulment depends on it having legal consequences' (para 74).

[222] Art 46 Statute of the Court.

[223] Case 4/69 (n 219) para 10.

[224] While this section focuses on liability arising from illegal binding Union acts, see for an example of an action for damages against illegal *conduct* of the institutions, the *Adams* case (Case 145/83 [1985] ECR 3539).

[225] Case 5/71 [1971] ECR 975.

[226] Ibid, para 11.

[227] See eg Case C-143/77 *Koninklijke Scholten-Honig v Council and Commission* [1979] ECR 3583.

[228] See, for rare, successful examples, section 6, case study 10.2 and case study 10.3.

A turning point in the case law, however, was the decision of the Court in *Bergaderm*,[229] where a private applicant sought compensation for damage arising from the restrictions on the use of certain ingredients in cosmetic products introduced by an EU directive and which had the effect of preventing the sale of one of the applicant's products. Although the applicant was unsuccessful, the ruling of the Court was highly relevant. First and foremost, it aligned the requirements of liability that apply, as a matter of EU law, when a Member State has infringed EU law and which were introduced by the *Francovich* line of case law[230] with those that apply where the liability emanates from an unlawful EU act.[231] This means that liability for unlawful acts under Articles 268 and 340(2) TFEU now arises where the rule of law infringed by the act was intended to confer rights on individuals, the breach is sufficiently serious, and there is a causal link between the breach attributable to the institution and the damage suffered by the applicant.

Furthermore, in the interpretation of the second condition—in parallel with cases on State liability—the Court drew a distinction depending *not* on the form of the act (eg general or individual)[232] but on a substantive criterion, namely whether the enacting institution enjoys discretion in the adoption of the measure. If the institution has discretion, that condition is fulfilled only if the institution in question has 'manifestly and gravely disregarded the limits of its discretion'.[233] However, where the institution has reduced or no discretion in the adoption of the act, the mere infringement of EU law suffices to establish liability.[234]

While the requirements to establish liability arising from discretionary acts are still demanding, *Bergaderm* has the merit of adopting a substantive rather than a formalistic approach in the determination of liability arising from EU acts and of introducing consistency in the tests for suing the Member States and the Union institutions in damages. While there have been suggestions in other areas of EU law that the Court tends to be more deferential towards the EU institutions than towards the Member States—for example when appraising the legality of their actions in light of the principle of proportionality[235]—the ruling in *Bergaderm* sends a message of coherence and equality in the assessment of the parameters of liability arising from illegal acts.

An interesting development stems from the judgment of the Court of Justice in the *Ledra Advertising* case,[236] decided against the background of the Eurozone crisis.[237] The case originated in the actions for annulment and actions for damages brought by some Cypriot citizens and a company established in Cyprus in relation to a measure that had been agreed in 2013 between the Commission and the European Central Bank, on the one hand, and the Cypriot Government, on the other. This measure had resulted in the granting of financial assistance to Cyprus by the European Stability Mechanism to address the serious financial difficulties experienced by a number of Cypriot banks in 2012. However, as a result of the application of this measure, the applicants in these cases experienced a

[229] Case C-352/98 P *Laboratoires pharmaceutiques Bergaderm SA and Jean-Jacques Goupil v Commission* [2000] ECR I-5291. See further T Tridimas, 'Liability for Breach of Community Law: Growing Up and Mellowing Down?' (2001) 38 *Common Market Law Review* 301.

[230] See, in particular, Joined Cases C-46/93 and C-48/93 *Brasserie du Pêcheur and Factortame* [1996] ECR I-1029, considered in chapter 6.

[231] *Laboratoires pharmaceutiques Bergaderm SA* (n 229) paras 41 and 42.

[232] Ibid, paras 46 and 47. [233] Ibid, para 43. [234] Ibid, para 44.

[235] See chapter 8.

[236] See, on appeal, the decision of the Court of Justice in Case C-8/15 P *Ledra Advertising Ltd and Others v Commission and European Central Bank (ECB)*, EU:C:2016:701. See also the decision of the General Court in the first instance in Case T-289/13 *Ledra Advertising v Commission and ECB*, EU:T:2014:981.

[237] See chapter 19.

significant reduction in the value of their bank deposits and this resulted in their attempt to challenge the 2013 measure and to seek compensation for their losses.

The Court took the view that the actions of the Commission and of the ECB were outside the scope of EU Law in the sense that they concerned the European Stability Mechanism alone—which is an intergovernmental mechanism created by an international agreement. Therefore, an action for the annulment of the measure in question was inadmissible because there was no EU 'act' as such that could be the subject of annulment proceedings under Article 263 TFEU. However, the Court took the view that it had jurisdiction to consider the actions for damages[238] because, although the measure was outside the scope of EU Law, the Commission maintained its role as guardian of the Treaties within the framework of the European Stability Mechanism and thus still had a duty to ensure that measures in which it was involved were consistent with the principles governing EU Law. Although the Court then found that the conditions to attract non-contractual liability were not satisfied and ultimately dismissed the actions for damages brought by the applicants, its decision showed that even where EU institutions act outside the framework of EU Law, they can, in some cases, still incur liability for damage or loss caused as a result of their actions.

4 Preliminary references

As explained previously, the preliminary reference procedure is a very different judicial avenue from direct actions. The parties in the case bring their action before the national court, rather than before the Court of Justice. At some stage in these proceedings, the national court makes a reference to the Court of Justice[239] on a point of either the interpretation or the validity of EU law that is relevant to the case. The Court of Justice delivers a preliminary ruling, which is then applied to the facts of the case by the national court. From the standpoint of the Court of Justice, this is therefore (unlike the direct actions) a non-contentious procedure, where the parties in the main action have no right of initiative and are merely invited to be heard.[240] The preliminary reference mechanism is seen by the Court as the ultimate manifestation of the relationship of cooperation between the national courts and the Court of Justice[241] and as a reflection of their role as equal partners in the development of EU law. As a result, the Court has repeatedly construed the system of preliminary references as based not on the hierarchically infused relationship existing between a court of first instance and a court of appeal but on a separation of tasks between the national courts and the Court of Justice. While the role of the Court is to interpret or decide on the validity of EU law, that of the national court is to take cognizance of the facts of the case and of the applicable national law, to decide on the need and grounds for a reference and to apply the ruling of the Court to the case in hand.[242] However, as we shall see, the development of the case law has occasionally cast some doubt on this outwardly neat division of responsibilities.

[238] The General Court had taken the opposite view, namely, that it had no jurisdiction to consider the actions for compensation (see Case T-289/13 (n 236) para 47).

[239] As mentioned above (see section 2 and n 35), the General Court has, since October 2024, acquired jurisdiction to deliver preliminary rulings in six areas of the case law. Therefore, the current section also applies to the specific preliminary references made to the General Court.

[240] Case 44/65 *Hessische Knappschaft v Maison Singer* [1965] ECR 965, 971.

[241] See Case 283/81 *CILFIT and Lanificio di Gavardo SpA v Ministry of Health* [1982] ECR 3415, para 7.

[242] Case 6/64 *Flaminio Costa v ENEL* [1964] ECR 585, 593 and Case 35/76 *Simmenthal SpA v Ministero delle Finanze italiano* [1976] ECR 1871, para 4. On this separation of functions, see further the Recommendations to national courts and tribunals in relation to the initiation of preliminary ruling proceedings (OJ [2016] C439/1) paras 1–11.

In the words of the Court, the essential function of Article 267 TFEU is to ensure that EU law is applied uniformly by the national courts.[243] This objective extends both to situations where a national court is confronted with the application of EU law[244] and to those where it is faced with disputes as to the validity of EU acts[245]—which generate, respectively, preliminary references on interpretation and preliminary references on validity. Additionally, the preliminary reference procedure performs other related functions stemming from this primary goal. Thus, it contributes to the coherent development of EU law[246] and it acts as an indirect mechanism for the review of the legality of EU acts.[247]

The procedure is set out in Article 267 TFEU. Post-Lisbon, that provision is divided into four paragraphs, which delineate the key features of the system of preliminary references. Thus, Article 267(1) TFEU determines the existence of two kinds of preliminary references: on the interpretation and on the validity of EU law. The second and third paragraphs establish a difference between two types of national courts: those which have the discretion to refer and those which have an obligation to refer. Thus, whereas any national court or tribunal *may* make a reference to the Court, only those against whose decisions there is no judicial remedy *must* make a reference to the Court if a relevant question of EU law needs to be decided in order to give their judgment. Finally, the Lisbon Treaty added a fourth paragraph to the text of Article 267 TFEU in order to reflect the urgent preliminary ruling procedure[248] (PPU, as an acronym for the French denomination of this procedure), for cases where a reference is made for a person in custody.[249] We will consider these issues in turn.

4.1 What constitutes a 'court or tribunal of a Member State'?

The entire system of preliminary references rests on the entitlement or the obligation (as the case may be) of *national courts and tribunals* to ask questions on the interpretation or on the validity of EU law to the Court of Justice. The initiative to request a preliminary reference belongs exclusively to a national court or tribunal and it is therefore essential to ascertain which national bodies fit this specification. The Treaty did not define what constitutes a national court or tribunal for these purposes, but a rich body of case law now gives us the characteristics that must be present, as a matter of EU law, for a national referring body to be classified as such. For example, in *Syfait I*[250] the Court provided a

[243] Case 66/80 *International Chemical Corporation v Amministrazione delle finanze dello Stato* [1981] ECR 1191, para 11. See also Case 166/73 *Rheinmühlen-Düsseldorf v Einfuhr-und Vorratsstelle für Getreide und Futtermittel* [1974] ECR 33, para 2.

[244] See eg *Van Gend en Loos* (n 40).

[245] Case 314/85 *Foto-Frost v Hauptzollamt Lübeck-Ost* [1987] ECR 4199, para 15.

[246] Thus, some of the fundamental principles and doctrines in EU law—such as direct effect; supremacy; vertical direct effect of directives; State liability in damages; or procedural autonomy, equivalence, and effectiveness—have all been developed through preliminary rulings.

[247] See eg Case C-263/02 P *Commission v Jégo-Quéré* [2004] ECR I-3425, para 30.

[248] See further C Barnard, 'The PPU: Is It Worth the Candle? An Early Assessment' (2009) 34 *European Law Review* 281.

[249] The Court has interpreted the wording in Art 267(4) TFEU broadly to include other cases, ie the wrongful removal of a child. See eg Case C-403/09 PPU *Detiček* [2009] ECR I-12193.

[250] See Case C-53/03 *Synetairismos Farmakopoion Aitolias & Akarnanias (Syfait) v GlaxoSmithKline plc and GlaxoSmithKline AEVE* ('*Syfait I*') [2005] ECR I-4609, para 29. On the requirement of independence and that the referring body is one acting as a third party in relation to the authority which adopted the decision under appeal, see Case C-24/92 *Corbiau v Administration des contributions* [1993] ECR I-1277, concerning a reference made by a tax authority, para 15 and *Syfait I*, above, involving a reference made by the Greek competition authority, paras 21–38. In both cases, the Court declined to give a reference because the referring bodies were not courts or tribunals within the meaning of Art 267 TFEU.

helpful summary of the main *cumulative* factors that determine this classification. Thus, the body must be:

(a) established by law;
(b) have a permanent existence;
(c) exercise binding jurisdiction;
(d) its procedure must be *inter partes*;
(e) must apply the rule of law; and
(f) be independent.[251]

Additionally, a national court may refer a question to the Court only if:

(a) there is a case pending before it; and
(b) it is called upon to give judgment in proceedings intended to lead to a decision of a judicial nature.[252]

In many cases, it will be obvious that a national body fulfils these characteristics but there have been some instances where the particular features of a national referring body have provided interesting opportunities for the Court to assess whether they were national courts or tribunals within the meaning of Article 267 TFEU.[253]

4.2 **Types of preliminary references: references on the interpretation and references on the validity of EU law**

According to the first paragraph of Article 267 TFEU, there are two types of preliminary rulings: interpretative rulings and rulings on the validity of EU law. Preliminary references on the *interpretation* of EU law can request the interpretation of Treaty provisions;[254] general principles of law; or of acts of the institutions, bodies, or agencies of the Union. The latter encompass not only legally binding acts such as regulations, directives, and decisions but also non-legally binding acts such as recommendations and opinions[255] or even judgments of the Court.[256] According to the principle of separation of functions that permeates the preliminary reference procedure,[257] the Court of Justice can only interpret EU law but not decide on the legality of national law.[258] This is true inasmuch as questions on the interpretation of EU law are formulated in abstract terms and the Court

[251] The requirement of independence has been repeatedly emphasized as essential in more recent case law (Case C-274/14 *Proceedings brought by Banco de Santander*, EU:C:2020:17, para. 57, and some parallels have been drawn between the requirement of the independence of the judiciary as construed in the 'rule of law crisis' cases and in the interpretation of the condition of independence in the context of Art 267 TFEU (see Case C-274/14, para 59). On the interesting ramifications of this trend, see M. Broberg and N. Fenger, 'The European Court of Justice's Transformation of its Approach towards Preliminary References from Member States Administrative Bodies' (2022) 24 *Cambridge Yearbook of European Legal Studies* 169–200.

[252] See *Syfait I* (n 250) para 29.

[253] See eg the case law on the position of national arbitral tribunals, ie Case 102/81 *Nordsee Deutsche Hochseefischerei GmbH v Reederei Mond Hochseefischerei Nordstern* [1982] ECR 1095, where an arbitrator appointed privately by the parties which did not fulfil *all* these criteria, was not considered a court or tribunal for Art 267 TFEU purposes.

[254] See eg *Van Gend en Loos* (n 40).

[255] Case C-322/88 *Grimaldi v Fonds des maladies professionnelles* [1989] ECR I-4407.

[256] Case 135/77 *Bosch GmbH v Hauptzollamt Hildesheim* [1978] ECR 855.

[257] See section 4.

[258] Case C-373/89 *Caisse d'assurances sociales pour travailleurs indépendants 'Integrity' v Rouvroy* [1990] ECR I-4243, para 9.

will not directly conclude that a specific national measure is illegal. However, in practice, most interpretative questions are, essentially, about the compatibility of national measures with EU law and, in many of these cases, the application of preliminary rulings on interpretation will leave the national courts with no alternative other than to declare that a national measure or principle is contrary to EU law.[259]

Preliminary references on *validity* can *only* concern legally binding acts of the institutions, bodies, or agencies of the Union. One fundamental aspect of this type of reference—which is, surprisingly, not reflected in the Treaty—was developed by the Court of Justice in its seminal decision in *Foto-Frost v Hauptzollamt Lübeck-Ost*.[260] There, one of the questions referred to the Court was whether a national court could review the legality of an EU measure. The Court developed its reasoning on the basis that the essential purpose of the Article 267 TFEU procedure is to ensure a uniform application of EU law, which is of course indispensable for the functioning and survival of the Union legal order. If national courts could declare the invalidity of EU acts, this uniformity would be immediately lost. Therefore, the Court concluded that, while national courts could always *confirm the validity* of EU acts and not make a reference to the Court—as this would not jeopardize the unity of the Union legal system—*only the Court of Justice has the power to declare an EU act invalid*. Hence, a preliminary reference on validity is *always* mandatory where a national court has some doubts about the legality of a Union measure.[261] The finding of the Court in that case was further supported by the need to ensure a coherent system of judicial protection. Thus, given that the Court has exclusive jurisdiction to declare EU acts void under Article 263 TFEU, the power to rule that EU acts are invalid must also be reserved to the Court of Justice.[262]

4.2.1 **The relationship between annulment proceedings and preliminary references on validity**

Preliminary rulings on validity offer private parties wishing to challenge the legality of EU acts an attractive alternative to the rigours of the standing tests imposed by Article 263 TFEU, as the Court itself has frequently pointed out.[263] A representation of the relationship between these two avenues can be found in Fig 10.5. However, the preliminary reference avenue does not *always* guarantee a remedy for private parties unable to satisfy the Article 263 TFEU conditions. Thus, in his Opinion in *UPA*[264] Advocate General Jacobs persuasively argued the insufficient value of this mechanism as an alternative to a direct challenge of an EU act under annulment proceedings. Apart from pointing out some procedural disadvantages and the fact that the decision on whether to refer and on the appropriate grounds of invalidity rest with the national court, he referred to cases where it would be less than straightforward for national proceedings—in the context of which a reference could be made—to be triggered. These would include cases where the EU measure in question did not require implementing measures at national level (the facts of *UPA* itself), cases where an applicant would have to break the law first in order to challenge sanctions and thus set off proceedings (as would have been the case with *Jégo-Quéré*)[265] or cases where national law requirements would make it excessively difficult or impossible to challenge national measures implementing EU law.[266]

[259] See, for some high-profile examples, Case C-271/91 *Marshall v Southampton and South-West Hampshire Area Health Authority* [1993] ECR I-4367 or *Factortame I* (n 41).

[260] Case 314/85 (n 245). [261] Ibid, paras 14–16. [262] Ibid, para 17.

[263] See eg Case C-321/95 P *Stichting Greenpeace Council* (n 155) para 33.

[264] Case C-50/00 P (n 145). [265] Ibid, para 102 of the Opinion.

[266] See eg Case C-432/05 *Unibet (London) Ltd and Unibet (International) Ltd v Justitiekanslern* [2007] ECR I-2271 and A Arnull, 'The Principle of Effective Judicial Protection in EU Law: An Unruly Horse?' (2011) 36 *European Law Review* 51.

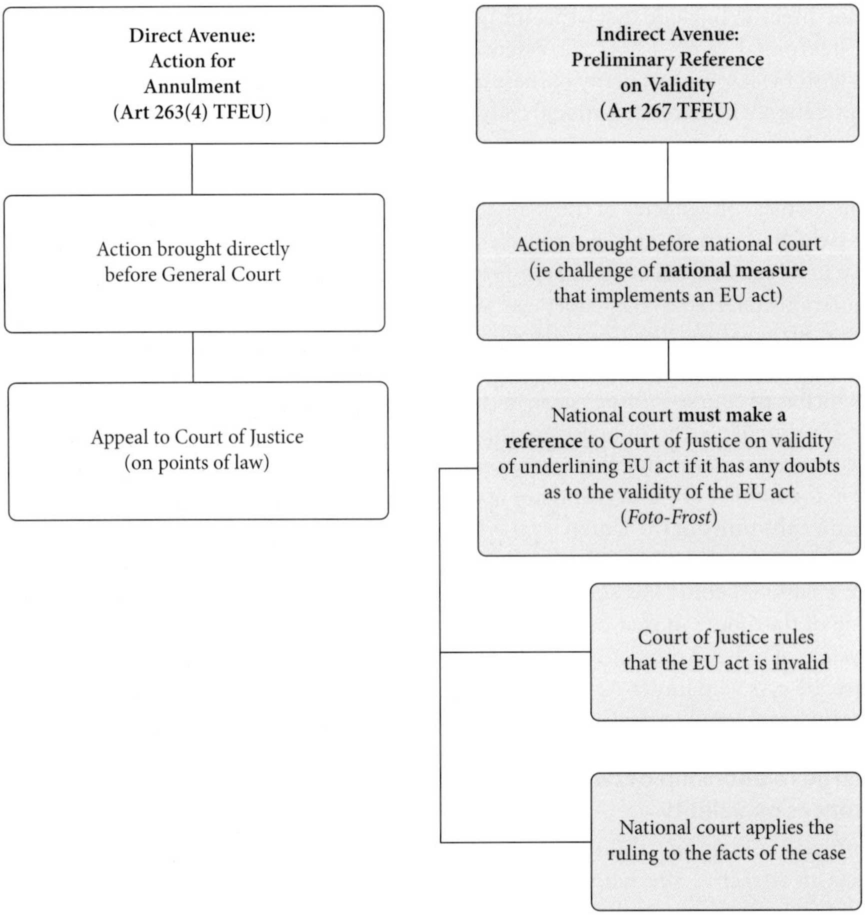

Fig. 10.5 Private parties and the challenge of EU acts: the relationship between annulment proceedings and preliminary rulings on validity

While the introduction of the Lisbon test in Article 263(4) TFEU has somewhat mitigated these objections, it is argued that a watertight system between these two remedies has not yet been fully achieved because, as we saw previously, the Lisbon test does not apply to legislative measures.[267] Thus, in the—admittedly rare—case of a legislative measure that does not require implementation (eg a hypothetical Council and Parliament regulation imposing a direct prohibition on the use of a particular substance), it is still conceivable that neither a direct challenge nor a preliminary reference on validity might be available to a private applicant. The compatibility of this result with Articles 47 and 51 of the EU Charter of Fundamental Rights seems doubtful. Nevertheless, in its decision in *Inuit I*, the Court of Justice intimated that the burden is on the national legal systems to ensure that an avenue to make a preliminary reference to the Court of Justice *is* available under national law. The Court achieved this by using the second subparagraph of Article 19(1) TEU to emphasize the responsibility of the national courts to provide remedies that ensure effective judicial protection in fields covered by EU law.[268] Future case law is

[267] See section 3.2.4, The Lisbon test.

[268] See *Inuit Tapiriit Kanatami* (n 6) paras 100–104 and, more recently, Case C-456/13 P (n 177) paras 44–52 and Case C-467/17 P (n 182) paras 26–30.

necessary to elaborate how this approach might apply in cases involving the challenge of EU legislative measures that do not require any kind of implementation at national level.

An interesting dimension of the relationship between the action for annulment and preliminary rulings on validity was developed by the Court in *TWD Textilwerke Deggendorf GmbH v Bundesrepublik Deutschland*.[269] There, the Court provided a rule to prevent the evasion of time limits when an applicant had the evident possibility of securing standing when bringing an action for annulment. Essentially, if an applicant would *clearly* have had standing to bring a direct action for annulment under Article 263 TFEU but did not do so within the time limit, the Court will not entertain a reference on validity if the applicant subsequently brings proceedings before the national court. In fact, the practical application of this rule is rather limited. First, and with the exceptions of where an applicant was the addressee of an act and a few other (rare) instances where consistent lines of case law indicate that an applicant would have certainly had standing to bring annulment proceedings,[270] it will normally be uncertain that an applicant would have had standing.[271] Depending on how the Court interprets the Lisbon text, this qualification may change if clear case law emerges on the standing of private parties to challenge regulatory acts.[272] Secondly, nothing prevents an applicant from bringing simultaneous proceedings before the Court of Justice—within the time limit set out in Article 263(6) TFEU—and before the national court, with the hope that a preliminary reference on validity will be made to the Court, even if this may not be an ideal outcome from the point of view of a judicial institution beset by the rising number of cases brought before it.

4.3 **Discretion to refer and limits to this discretion**

According to Article 267(2) TFEU, *any* national court or tribunal *may* make a reference to the Court when a case is actively pending before it if it considers that a decision on a question of EU law is necessary to enable it to give judgment. Thus any national court, however low in the judicial echelons of a Member State, has the broadest discretion to make a reference to the Court.[273] The separation of functions that underlines the preliminary reference procedure determines that only the national court can make these decisions and that the Court of Justice should not interfere in the exercise of this discretion.

However, as the caseload of the Court increased dramatically, the Court began to set what prima facie could be construed as limitations on this unfettered discretion by declaring the inadmissibility of some references from national courts that did not comply with certain criteria. Thus, there are broadly four main categories of cases where references have been rejected on this basis.[274]

[269] Case C-188/92 [1994] ECR I-833.

[270] This could be the case, eg in competition, State aid, and anti-dumping proceedings. The *TWD* case concerned the challenge of a decision in the field of State aid.

[271] See eg Case C-241/95 *The Queen v Intervention Board for Agricultural Produce, ex p Accrington Beef* [1996] ECR I-6699.

[272] On the one hand, in some post-Lisbon cases, the Court seems to have skipped the consideration of the standing barrier and addressed directly the substance of the arguments put forward by the parties. This could be understood as meaning that it was clear beyond doubt that the applicants had standing to bring an action (see eg Case T-544/13 *Dyson v Commission*, EU:T:2015:836). On the other hand, however, there are also indications that there continue to be situations where it is uncertain whether individuals would have had standing to bring annulment proceedings (see, in this respect, the Opinion of AG Kokott in Case C-389/14 *Esso Italiana and Others*, EU:C:2015:754, paras 189–205).

[273] *Rheinmühlen-Düsseldorf* (n 243) para 4.

[274] See C Barnard and E Sharpston, 'The Changing Face of Article 177 References' (1997) 34 *Common Market Law Review* 1113.

First, the Court held in *Foglia v Novello*[275] that it would not entertain a reference where there is evidence that the parties before the national court have no genuine dispute and have contrived proceedings with the exclusive purpose of triggering a reference on a particular point of EU law. In that case, it appeared that the motive of the parties was to obtain a ruling from the Court that could then be applied to find the incompatibility of a French tax with Article 110 TFEU. Clearly, the function of the Court under Article 267 TFEU is to deliver rulings that will be applicable to a real dispute between the parties in national proceedings rather than provide advisory opinions. However, the controversial aspect of this decision rests in the conclusion that the Court of Justice should effectively have the power to question the *appropriateness* of the decision to refer—when the national court alone had direct knowledge of the facts and still decided to make a reference.[276]

Secondly, the Court has declined to give a reference in cases where it has found that the question referred was irrelevant, namely that it bore no relation to the actual case or to the subject matter of the action,[277] and, thirdly, where questions submitted were judged to be hypothetical.[278] Considering the constraints under which the Court operates, it makes sense to avoid a proliferation of references that technically do not satisfy the terms of Article 267 TFEU because they are not really necessary to give judgment. On the one hand, it could be argued that only the national court can decide that a reference is not necessary. By virtue of the Court taking on this role instead, an erosion of the principle of separation of functions between the national courts and the Court and interference on the discretion of the national court under Article 267(2) TFEU could be said to have occurred. On the other, the approach of the Court in these cases could simply be seen as a question of jurisdiction. Thus, it could be posited that if the question referred is not necessary for solving the dispute, the Court simply has no jurisdiction under the terms of Article 267 TFEU and that the Court is only verifying in these cases whether it has jurisdiction or not.

Fourthly, and much less controversially because there is no real interference on the discretion of the national court, the Court may declare references inadmissible where the national court has not articulated the questions properly[279] or has failed to submit sufficient information on the factual and legal background to the case.[280] If the Court is to give a helpful ruling, it needs the national courts to provide the necessary platform to do so. The main formal requirements that national courts should follow when formulating references are set out in Article 94 of the Rules of Procedure of the Court of Justice.[281] These include setting out clearly the factual and legal background to the main proceedings, the relevant provisions of national law, and a statement of the reasons that prompted the national court to make a reference.

[275] Case 104/79 [1980] ECR 745.

[276] See further G Bebr, 'The Existence of a Genuine Dispute: An Indispensable Precondition for the Jurisdiction of the Court under Article 177 EEC Treaty [now Art 267 TFEU]' (1980) 17 *Common Market Law Review* 525. While the *Foglia* approach has not been broadly applied by the Court, in more recent years, the decision in Case C-318/00 *Bacardi-Martini SAS and Cellier des Dauphins v Newcastle United Football Co* [2003] ECR I-905 shows some similarities with that decision. The reference was also dismissed as inadmissible. However, there has also been support for the approach of the Court in *Foglia*, see D Wyatt, '*Foglia (No 2)*: The Court Denies It Has Jurisdiction to Give Advisory Opinions' (1982) 7 *European Law Review* 186.

[277] Case 126/80 *Salonia v Poidomani and Giglio* [1981] ECR 1563, para 6 and Case C-343/90 *Lourenço Dias v Director da Alfândega do Porto* [1992] ECR I-04673, para 18.

[278] Case C-83/91 *Meilicke v ADV/ORGA FA Meyer AG* [1992] ECR I-4871, paras 30–34, where a lengthy set of questions concerning the interpretation of an EU company law directive were held to be hypothetical.

[279] Ibid.

[280] Joined Cases C-320–322/90 *Telemarsicabruzzo v Circostel* [1993] ECR I-393.

[281] Rules of Procedure of the Court of Justice (OJ [2012] L265/1).

4.4 **The duty to refer and the exceptions to this duty**

Article 267(3) TFEU imposes an obligation to refer on national courts 'against whose decisions there is no judicial remedy' when a question on the validity or interpretation of EU law which is necessary to give judgment arises before them. These courts, as the Court has clarified,[282] include not only the highest courts in the judicial system of a Member State, such as the Supreme Court in the United Kingdom, but also those courts against whose decision there is no remedy *in the particular case*. This is relevant, for example, where small sums of money are involved and hence there is no possibility of appeal against the decision of a lower court[283] or in the case of appellate courts. The case law has established that if the decisions of an appellate court can be challenged before a supreme court, then the appellate court will not be a court of last resort in the sense of Article 267(3) TFEU.[284] However, if the appellate court has the power to prevent a further appeal, then it will be classified as a court of last resort and must make a reference.

The duty to refer questions imposed on courts of last resort seems to be an absolute one under the terms of Article 267(3) TFEU. However, the Court has created three main exceptions to this duty. The first is where the question referred is not relevant.[285] The second is where the question referred is materially identical to a question that has already been answered in a preliminary ruling[286] or where the points of law have already been dealt with by the Court in a previous ruling.[287] While the national court may still seek a ruling in this case, the Court has held that it has no obligation to do so.[288]

The third exception is more controversial and was laid down in the Court's landmark judgment in *CILFIT*.[289] There, the Court held that a national court of last resort does not have an obligation to seek a ruling from the Court 'where the correct application of Union law may be so obvious as to leave no scope for any reasonable doubt as to the manner in which the question raised is to be resolved'.[290] This is known as the *acte clair* doctrine. The reason why this exception is problematic[291] is because it could be technically open to abuse. In particular, national courts of last resort might not make a reference to the Court by arguing that the interpretation of EU law is clear beyond doubt in circumstances where a reference is, in fact, necessary.

On the one hand, this argument has been traditionally countered by the view that in *CILFIT* the Court imposed draconian requirements on national courts before these could decide that a reference was not necessary. Thus, they had to compare the different language versions of the provision of EU law at stake, take account of the peculiar EU law terminology and of the different meaning of legal concepts in EU law and in the national legal systems, and place every provision of EU law in its context and interpret it in light of EU law as a whole and of its particular state of evolution.[292] A rigorous application of these conditions therefore has been understood to act as a very reliable safeguard against the misuse of this exception and to prevent an incorrect interpretation of EU law by the national courts.

[282] *Flaminio Costa* (n 242) 592. [283] Ibid.

[284] Case C-99/00 *Criminal Proceedings against Kenny Roland Lyckeskog* [2002] ECR I-4839, para 16.

[285] The national court does not have an obligation to refer questions that are not necessary to give judgment (Case 283/81 *CILFIT* (n 241) para 10). This stems from the letter of Art 267(2) and (3) TFEU.

[286] Joined Cases 28–30/62 *Da Costa v Nederlandse Belastingadministratie* [1963] ECR 31, 38.

[287] *CILFIT* (n 241) para 14. [288] Ibid, para 15. [289] Ibid. [290] Ibid, para 16.

[291] The *CILFIT* decision attracted a great deal of attention in the academic literature and different views were formed as to its value and implications. See, among others, A Arnull, 'The Use and Abuse of Article 177 EEC [now 267 TFEU]' (1989) 52 *Modern Law Review* 622 and H Rasmussen, 'The European Court's *Acte Clair* Strategy in *CILFIT*' (1984) 9 *European Law Review* 242.

[292] *CILFIT* (n 241) paras 17–20.

On the other hand, it has also been argued that it is difficult to monitor the proper application of these conditions by the national courts and hence that a careless use of *CILFIT* could ultimately result in a flawed application of EU law at the national level. Such objections are rooted in the idea that the decision in *CILFIT* ultimately dilutes the mandatory character of references under Article 267(3) TFEU and devolves too much autonomy to the national courts to take decisions that can affect the uniform and consistent development of EU law. Furthermore, two decisions of the Court of Justice added to the controversy that surrounded the *acte clair* doctrine. Thus, the judgments of the Court in *X and van Dijk*[293] and *Ferreira da Silvia e Brito*[294] were interpreted as relaxing the *CILFIT* conditions for the application of the *acte clair* doctrine and in doing so, as posing a threat to the uniform interpretation of EU law by increasing the possibility that national courts of last resort might not make a reference to the Court of Justice in situations where a reference may actually be necessary.[295] The application of the doctrine of State liability in damages, which the case law extended to breaches of EU law by national courts of last resort,[296] therefore appeared as the only—but rather uncertain—mechanism available to parties before a national court of last resort to prevent an abuse of the *CILFIT* doctrine.[297]

However, the more recent and interesting decision of the Court in *Consorzio Italian Management*,[298] while not altering substantially the *acte clair* parameters in *CILFIT*,[299] has highlighted the obligation of a national court of last resort to provide a statement of reasons[300] to substantiate its decision not to make a reference to the Court of Justice.[301] In doing so, the Court relied on Article 47 of the Charter, which as we have seen, has also begun to feature prominently in the case law of the Court concerning direct actions. This is a subtle, yet important, development because it means that the requirements stemming from the principle of effective judicial protection have now been explicitly bound to the exercise of the *acte clair* exception. Further case law may develop this point but the clear implication is that a court of last resort will need to justify its decision not to make a reference to the Court, which should act not only as a mechanism to ensure the accountability of such courts in these situations but also, indirectly, to prevent the abuse of the *CILFIT* doctrine.

4.5 **Effects of a preliminary ruling**

A preliminary ruling on interpretation delivered by the Court of Justice is binding on the national referring court[302] but other national courts and public authorities should treat the ruling as authoritative.[303] A preliminary ruling on validity, while technically only

[293] Joined Cases C-72/14 and C-197/14 *X v Inspecteur van Rijksbelastingdienst and TA van Dijk v Staatssecretaris van Financiën*, EU:C:2015:564.

[294] Case C-160/14 *João Filipe Ferreira da Silva e Brito and Others v Estado português*, EU:C:2015:565.

[295] See A Kornezov, 'The New Format of the Acte Clair Doctrine and Its Consequences' (2016) 53 *Common Market Law Review* 1317–1342.

[296] See Case C-224/01 *Köbler v Republik Österreich* [2003] ECR I-10329.

[297] In theory, the Commission or another Member State could also bring infringement proceedings under Arts 258 and 259 TFEU respectively.

[298] Case C-561/19 *Consorzio Italian Management and Catania Multiservizi v Rete Ferroviaria Italiana*, EU:C:2021:799.

[299] This cautious approach was in contrast with the rather far-reaching Opinion of AG Bobek, who suggested that the duty to refer of courts of last resort should be reaffirmed and that the *CILFIT* line of case law ought to be revisited (see the Opinion of the AG in Case C-561/19 *Consorzio Italian Management*, EU:C:2021:291, paras 131–180).

[300] This is a point which had also been raised by the AG in his proposal for a reformulation of the *CILFIT* case law, at paras 166–172 of his Opinion.

[301] *Consorzio Italian Management* (n 298) para 51.

[302] Case 52/76 *Benedetti v Munari* [1977] ECR 163, para 26.

[303] *Da Costa* (n 286).

addressed to the referring court, gives ground for any other national court to regard the act as void for the purposes of any judgment they are supposed to give.[304] Thus, effectively, there is little difference between the outcome of a successful action for annulment and that of a preliminary ruling on validity.

5 Interim relief

In the previous sections we considered the basic division between direct actions and preliminary references, and we examined their characteristics and mode of application. One very important aspect to both sets of proceedings is how to protect the interests of parties affected while the main actions are pending before the Court of Justice and the national court respectively. This raises the question of the regulation of interim measures. Three main scenarios can be distinguished.

First, in relation to *direct actions*, interlocutory relief is provided in the Treaty itself. Thus, Articles 278 and 279 TFEU respectively allow the Court to award negative and positive interim measures in connection with a main direct action pending before the Court. The conditions for interim relief are set out in the Rules of Procedure of the Court of Justice[305] and refer to the existence of a prima facie case and of circumstances giving rise to urgency—which is normally appraised considering whether there is a threat of 'serious and irreparable damage to the applicant'.[306] A third step has emerged in many cases, where the Court has also carried out a balance of interests concerned.[307]

Secondly, in the case of *preliminary references on interpretation*, and particularly when the compatibility of national measures with EU law is at stake before the national court, interim relief will be granted according to the rules of national law while a reference is pending as long as these rules are both effective and non-discriminatory. For instance, in *Factortame I*[308] national principles on the application of interim relief were contested before the Court of Justice, while the main substantive reference on the interpretation of EU law—which, in practice, sought to ascertain the compatibility of UK legislation with EU law—was pending before the Court.[309]

Finally, where a *preliminary reference on validity* is pending before the Court, interim relief is not provided in the Treaty, but common principles were developed by the Court

[304] *International Chemical Corporation* (n 243) para 13.

[305] See Art 160 of the Rules of Procedure of the Court of Justice and Art 104 of the Rules of Procedure of the General Court and section 6, case study 10.1 and case study 10.2.

[306] Case 20/81R *Arbed*, EU:C:1981:61, para 13.

[307] Case C-404/04 P-R *Technische Glaswerke Ilmenau v Commission*, EU:C:2005:267, para 10. In connection with the high-profile enforcement proceedings brought by the Commission against Poland for the adoption of legislation lowering the retirement age for judges in the Polish Supreme Court (n 60), the Commission submitted an application for interim relief under Arts 278 and 279 TFEU for the suspension of the application of the legislation until the Court reached a final decision in the Art 258 TFEU action. This led first to the Vice-President of the Court provisionally awarding interim measures in Case C-619/18 R *Commission v Poland*, not published (EU:C:2018:852). However, the Vice-President of the Court, applying Art 161(1) of the Rules of Procedure of the Court of Justice, exceptionally referred the application for interim relief to the Court of Justice, which, in the light of the importance of that case, assigned it to the Grand Chamber. This resulted in an Order from the Court granting interim relief (Case C-619/18 R *Commission v Poland*, EU:C:2018:1021) which, inter alia, suspended the application of the Polish legislation. The Order of the Court contains a very thorough and helpful examination of the conditions for the grant of interim relief, with the requirements of a prima facie case, urgency, and balancing of interests all fully considered. Note also that penalties can be imposed in interim relief cases: Case C-441/17 R *Commission v Poland*, EU:C:2017:877, para 118.

[308] See *Factortame I* (n 41).

[309] Case C-221/89 *Factortame II* [1991] ECR I-3905.

of Justice as a natural consequence of the *Foto-Frost*[310] decision. Thus, in *Zuckerfabrik*[311] the Court held that a national court could suspend the enforcement of a *national measure* based on an EU measure the validity of which is being questioned before the Court of Justice (negative interim relief) and in *Atlanta*[312] that a national court could grant interim measures pending the ruling on validity from the Court of Justice (positive interim relief). While this is still *national* interim relief from a procedural point of view, binding conditions for granting interlocutory relief were developed in these judgments as a matter of EU law. These conditions are that a reference on validity must have been made to the Court, that there is urgency or the threat of serious and irreparable damage to the applicant, and that the national court takes account of the EU's interests.[313]

6 The relationship between the Treaty remedies

As explained at the beginning of this chapter, it is important to understand how the system of remedies provided in the Treaty operates as an integrated whole. In this section, we will use three brief examples to illustrate how they interact in concrete cases.

Case study 10.1: Seal products, animal welfare, and hunting for subsistence: the *Inuit* litigation

Following concerns expressed by the European Parliament and by citizens and consumers in the EU on the application of cruel methods for the hunting of seals, several initiatives were taken at Union level to restrict the importation of seal products into the EU. In 2009, the Council and the European Parliament adopted Regulation 1007/2009[314]—under what is, post-Lisbon, the ordinary legislative procedure[315]—based on Article 114 TFEU with the aim of harmonizing national rules across the EU concerning the commercialization of seal products in the EU. According to the Preamble, the main aim of the Regulation was to eliminate the fragmentation of the internal market caused by different national rules and to take into account animal welfare considerations.[316] Essentially, the Regulation only allowed the placing in the Union market of seal products where these were the result of traditional methods of hunting by Inuit communities and contributed to their subsistence.[317]

The litigation originated by this Regulation provides an interesting example of the interplay between the action for annulment, the plea of illegality, and the application for interim relief (connected with the direct actions provided in the TFEU) (see Fig 10.6). In *Inuit I*,[318] several applicants including associations representing the Inuit people, seal hunters, trappers, and companies involved in the processing of seal products brought annulment proceedings against the Regulation under Article 263 TFEU. While the main action was pending, the applicants also applied for negative interim relief under Article 278 TFEU,[319]

[310] Case 314/85 (n 245).

[311] Case C-143/88 *Zuckerfabrik Süderdithmarschen AG v Hauptzollamt Itzehoe* [1991] ECR I-415.

[312] Case C-465/93 *Atlanta Fruchthandelsgesellschaft mbH v Bundesamt für Ernährung und Forstwirtschaft* [1995] ECR I-3761.

[313] *Zuckerfabrik* (n 311) para 33.

[314] OJ [2009] L286/36.

[315] Then Art 251 EC and post-Lisbon Art 294 TFEU.

[316] See recitals 1–10 in the Preamble to the Regulation.

[317] See Art 3(1) Regulation 1007/2009 and the additional limited exceptions in Art 3(2).

[318] Case T-18/10 (n 152). See also sections 3.2 and 3.4.

[319] Case T-18/10 R *Inuit Tapiriit Kanatami v European Parliament and Council* [2010] ECR II-75. A second application for interim relief, also dismissed, was brought in Case T-18/10 R II [2010] ECR II-235.

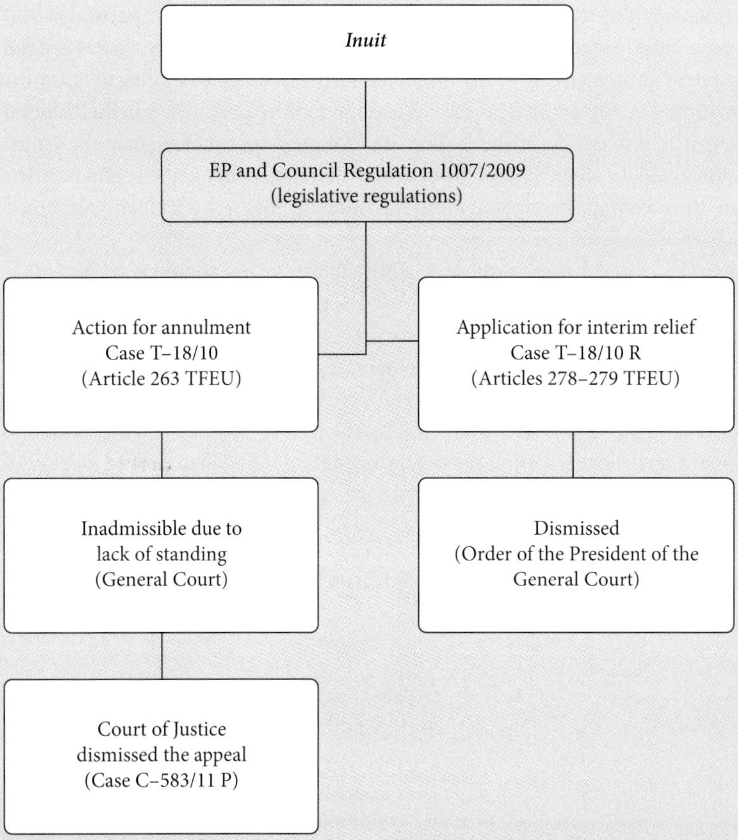

Fig. 10.6 The Inuit litigation ('Inuit I') (Case T-18/10 and Case C-583/11 P)

asking for the suspension of the Regulation. The application for interim relief was rejected by the General Court because the existence of urgency, one of the conditions for the grant of interim relief, was not present. In September 2011, the General Court issued its Order in *Inuit I*, where it concluded that the special Lisbon standing test was inapplicable given that Regulation 1007/2009 was a genuine legislative act and hence not within the meaning given to the notion of 'regulatory act' by the Court in that same case.[320] As a result, the General Court went on to apply the general standing test, found that the applicants were not individually concerned, and dismissed the action for annulment as inadmissible. The Court of Justice subsequently upheld the General Court's interpretation on appeal in *Inuit Tapiriit Kanatami*.[321]

In August 2010, the Commission—which had been given implementing powers by Regulation 1007/2009 (the 'parent regulation')[322]—adopted Regulation 737/2010[323] (the 'implementing regulation') laying down detailed rules for the implementation of the parent regulation. Undoubtedly aware of the possible standing difficulties that they might encounter in the direct challenge of the parent regulation in *Inuit I*—which was pending at the time—several

[320] See section 3.2.4, The Lisbon test.
[321] Case C-583/11 P (n 6) and section 3.2.4, The Lisbon test.
[322] OJ [2009] L286/36.
[323] OJ [2010] L216/1.

of the applicants who had brought the annulment action in *Inuit I*, brought a second action for annulment before the General Court in *Inuit II*.[324] This time, they directly challenged the Commission implementing regulation and simultaneously raised a plea of illegality against the parent regulation (see Fig 10.7). This case offered a good opportunity for the General Court to reaffirm its construction of the Lisbon standing test—especially since the Commission regulation could, in all likelihood, be classified as a 'regulatory act'[325]—and perhaps even to elucidate the meaning of 'implementing measures' in that test which still remained uncertain even after *Microban*.[326]

The General Court skipped the question of admissibility in its judgment in *Inuit II*[327] and instead considered directly the substantive grounds put forward to claim the illegality of both the parent and implementing regulations. All grounds put forward by the applicant—which included lack of legal basis, infringement of proportionality, and protection of fundamental human rights and misuse of powers—were dismissed as unfounded. However, *Inuit II* showed the enhanced possibilities offered by the plea of illegality[328] after Lisbon—used there to mount a challenge against the parent regulation which ha[illegible] so elusive in *Inuit*. An appeal against the decision of the General Court in *Inuit II* was later dismissed by the Court of Justice.[329]

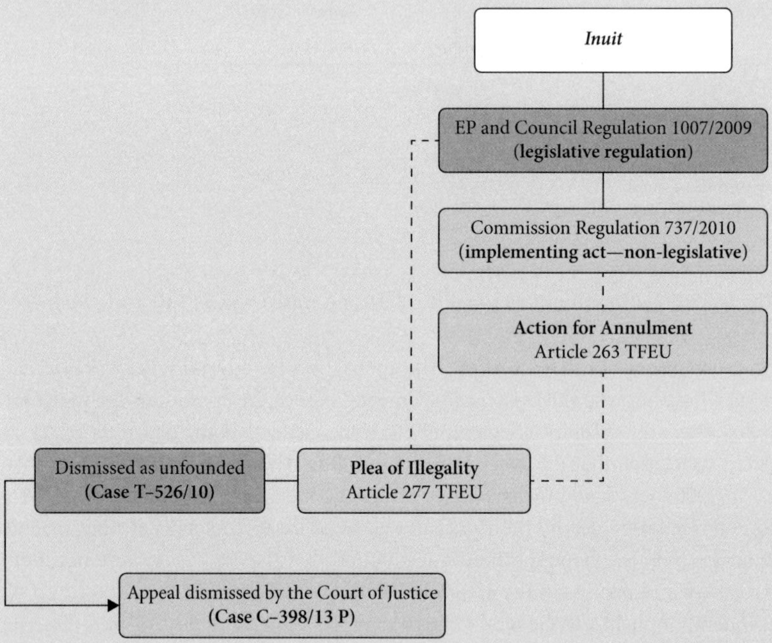

Fig. 10.7 The Inuit litigation ('Inuit II') (Case T-526/10 and Case C-398/13 P)

[324] Case T-526/10 (n 212).

[325] See section 3.2.4, The Lisbon test.

[326] Case T-262/10 (n 169).

[327] Case T-526/10 (n 212) paras 18–21.

[328] Pre-Lisbon it is very unlikely that the applicants would have satisfied the test of individual concern either in the challenge of the parent regulation or in the challenge of the implementing regulation. Therefore, the use of the plea of illegality to challenge incidentally the former regulation in the context of a direct challenge to the latter would not have been possible.

[329] Case C-398/13 P *Inuit Tapiriit Kanatami and Others v Commission* (n 212).

Case study 10.2: Perishable cargo and a rare success story for a private applicant: the *Sofrimport* litigation

Considering the well-documented difficulties that private parties have generally encountered when directly challenging the legality of EU acts and the EU institutions in damages, the *Sofrimport* litigation[330] offers a rare glimpse of a case where a private applicant was successful in annulment proceedings, in securing interim measures and in suing the Commission in damages (see Fig 10.4). There, a French importer of Chilean apples who had a consignment of apples in transit to the EU, brought an action for annulment against three Commission regulations that suspended with immediate effect the issue of import licences for dessert apples without taking into account the position of traders who had goods in transit to the Union at the time the regulations were adopted. A parent or basic Council regulation in this area, which had given powers to the Commission to adopt protective measures, had imposed on the Commission an obligation to take account of the potential impact of these measures on traders with goods in transit before adopting them. The applicant also brought an action for damages under Article 340(2) TFEU against the Commission in the same set of proceedings.

The applicant also applied for interlocutory relief under Articles 278 and 279 TFEU[331] while the main actions were pending, citing, inter alia, the high storage costs, the impossibility of transporting the apples elsewhere without incurring very high costs, and the reduction in the value of the apples due to their loss of freshness. The Court ordered the suspension of the regulations in relation to the consignment of apples shipped by Sofrimport, and at the time stored in transit at the port of Marseilles, since there was a prima facie case and the threat of serious and irreparable damage to the applicant. Essentially, on the facts, there was a risk that Sofrimport might even have to cease trading because of the impact of the Commission's measures.

As regards the action for annulment, and as we saw earlier in this chapter, the applicant managed to secure standing under Article 263(4) TFEU[332] and the Court went on to annul the Commission regulations on the basis that the Commission had breached the principle of legitimate expectations. The action for damages was also successful. Given that *Sofrimport* was decided before the ruling in *Bergaderm*, and since the regulations were acts of general application that involved choices of economic policy, the *Aktien-Zuckerfabrik Schöppenstedt*[333] formula was applied by the Court. Thus, the Court considered whether a 'sufficiently serious breach of a superior rule of law for the protection of the individual' had occurred. Even though this formula has proved to be notably difficult to satisfy in many cases, the Court found that liability did arise in this case. It identified the breach of the principle of legitimate expectations of the applicants as the superior rule of law and found that the Commission's total disregard of its obligation to take account of the position of traders with goods in transit amounted to a sufficiently serious breach and that the damage suffered by the applicant went beyond the limits of the economic risks inherent in their business. The EU was therefore ordered to compensate Sofrimport for its losses.

[330] *Sofrimport* (n 107).
[331] Case C-152/88 R *Sofrimport v Commission* [1988] ECR 2931.
[332] See section 3.2.4.
[333] See section 3.5.

Case study 10.3: Milk quotas and legitimate expectations: the *Mulder* litigation

In response to the chronic oversupply of milk products in the EU, the Council introduced several measures in the 1970s and 1980s in the context of the Common Agricultural Policy. Thus, a first Council regulation enacted in 1977 introduced a system of premiums that would be given to farmers who undertook not to market milk products for a five-year period and a second Council regulation imposed a levy on the treating or processing of milk products. Mr Mulder, a Dutch farmer, agreed not to deliver milk or dairy products for a period of five years from 1 October 1979. In 1984, the Council and the Commission adopted two further regulations designed to counteract the ever-present surplus of milk and introduced a system of quotas for the production of milk, whereby farmers had to apply to the relevant national authorities for reference quantities for the production of milk on the basis of which additional levies would be calculated. In particular, these measures provided that those reference quantities would be calculated on the basis of the quantities of milk produced in a particular year, which in the Netherlands was 1983. Mr Mulder had, of course, not produced any milk in the year 1983 following the undertaking that he gave as a result of the 1977 Council regulation. When he applied to the relevant national authority for a reference quantity of milk in 1984, his application was rejected on the basis that he had not produced any milk in 1983.

This set of facts indicated a fairly clear breach of the principle of legitimate expectations. When Mr Mulder agreed not to produce any milk between 1979 and 1984, following the provisions of the 1977 Council regulation, there was no indication that this would later prevent him from resuming his normal activity and the 1984 Council and Commission measures did not make any provisions for those who had not produced milk in the reference year of 1983. However, given that Mr Mulder was a private party, it was important to ascertain which avenue he would use to challenge the legality of the 1984 Council and Commission regulations.

In theory, the applicant had two options. The first would have been to bring a direct action for annulment under Article 263 TFEU before the Court. Had he decided to do this, Mr Mulder would have had to overcome the standing barrier in Article 263 TFEU. At the time, it was not even clear whether true regulations could be challenged by private parties and in some cases the Court still added the abstract terminology test[334] to the already formidable tests of individual and direct concern. This meant that the prospects of securing standing in the challenge of general measures under Article 263 TFEU were rather bleak. The second option, which was the one chosen by the applicant, was to challenge before the national court the decision of the national authority rejecting Mr Mulder's application for a reference quantity of milk on the basis of the 1984 regulations. In the course of these national proceedings, the national court made a preliminary reference on the validity of the 1984 regulations to the Court of Justice under Article 267 TFEU, which led to the decision in *Mulder v Minister van Landbouw en Visserij* ('*Mulder I*').[335] There, the Court gave a preliminary ruling holding these regulations invalid on the ground of breach of legitimate expectations because they did not provide for the allocation of reference quantities to farmers in Mr Mulder's position.

This case therefore shows the possibilities that a preliminary reference on validity might offer an alternative to a direct action for annulment. A few years later, and armed with the declaration of invalidity of the 1984 measures in *Mulder I*, the applicant and others in a similar position brought a direct action for damages before the Court under Article 340(2) TFEU against the Council and Commission for the losses that they sustained as a result of those measures. This led to the decision in *Mulder v Council and Commission* ('*Mulder II*'),[336] where the Court found the conditions for liability to be satisfied and awarded compensation to the applicants.

[334] See n 107. [335] Case 120/86 [1988] ECR 2321.
[336] Joined Cases C-104/89 and C-37/90 [1992] ECR I-3061.

7 Conclusion

This chapter has viewed the composite of judicial avenues to the Court of Justice as a set of remedies that interact with a twofold purpose: to provide a system of protection against illegal action of the Member States and Union institutions and to secure a uniform and consistent interpretation and application of EU law at the national level. It has considered the main proceedings that come before the Court, both those that start and finish before the Court (direct actions) and those that start and finish before the national court but where the Court intervenes to address a question on the validity or interpretation of EU law (preliminary references). In other words, it has focused on what we could term the 'centralized' system of protection provided in the Treaty that has at its apex the Court of Justice. Of course, in order to appreciate the full extent and depth of the judicial protection offered by the Treaties, it is necessary to remember that this centralized system constitutes only one dimension of the remedial system.

A second and essential tier is the role performed by the national courts, which became a reality from the moment that the Court laid down the principles of direct effect and primacy. This is a 'decentralized' dimension because the task of applying EU law falls on the national judiciaries. Thus, when national courts apply EU law by virtue of the doctrine of direct effect and use national remedies (subject to the principles of non-discrimination and effectiveness) and/or apply the doctrine of State liability in damages, they also protect natural and legal persons against violations of EU law by national public authorities and/or private parties.[337]

We have seen in this chapter that within the centralized system of remedies available before the Court, there are aspects of horizontal interaction—that is, between some of the direct actions like annulment proceedings, the plea of illegality, or the action for damages. There are also elements of vertical (though not in a hierarchical sense) interaction—that is, between the national courts and the Court of Justice where the former raise preliminary references on interpretation to question the compatibility of national legislation with EU law or where preliminary references on validity are made to attain the same result as annulment proceedings. Likewise, there are synergies between the centralized and decentralized tiers mentioned previously. For example, the enforcement of EU law before the national courts through the principles of direct effect and primacy often has a similar goal as enforcement proceedings before the Court. This second, decentralized aspect of judicial protection, is covered elsewhere in this book[338] but a panoramic view of judicial protection in EU law is only acquired when these two tiers are considered together and examined in light of their objectives.

In this chapter, one of the key themes has been whether the Treaty system of remedies at EU level is truly a complete one. In relation to the protection afforded to private parties against potentially illegal measures adopted by the EU institutions—where only the Court has jurisdiction to annul or declare them invalid—it can be argued that while the Lisbon reforms have certainly narrowed the existing gaps, particularly by introducing the new special standing test that applies to the challenge of regulatory acts, it is not clear that *all* the gaps have been plugged.

A trend that has emerged strongly in recent cases is that the Court of Justice understands that national courts have a shared responsibility in ensuring that a comprehensive system of judicial protection exists across the EU. Not only must they guarantee the review of the illegal action of Member States at the instance of private parties—and the corresponding existence of effective and non-discriminatory national remedies—but *also* ensure the possibility of review of EU acts that cannot be challenged directly before

337 See chapter 6.   338 Ibid.

the Court of Justice due to lack of standing of the applicants, by providing avenues at national level that can be used to trigger preliminary references on validity.

Further reading

A Albors-Llorens, 'Remedies against the EU Institutions after Lisbon: An Era of Opportunity?' (2012) 71 *Cambridge Law Journal* 507

A Arnull, 'Judicial Architecture or Judicial Folly? The Challenge Facing the European Union' (1999) 24 *European Law Review* 516

S Balthasar, '*Locus Standi* Rules for Challenges to Regulatory Acts by Private Applicants: The New Article 263(4) TFEU' (2010) 35 *European Law Review* 542

C Barnard and E Sharpston, 'The Changing Face of Article 177 References' (1997) 34 *Common Market Law Review* 1113

N Burrows and R Greaves, *The Advocate General and EC Law* (Oxford: Oxford University Press, 2007)

P Craig, *EU Administrative Law* (3rd edn, Oxford University Press, 2018)

M Dougan, 'The Treaty of Lisbon 2007: Winning Minds, Not Hearts' (2008) 45 *Common Market Law Review* 617

F Hilpert, 'An Old Procedure with New Solutions for the Rule of Law Crisis' (2019) 2 *Nordic Journal of European Law* 1

C Hilson, 'The Role of Discretion in EC Law on Non-Contractual Liability' (2005) 42 *Common Market Law Review* 677

S Kartalova, 'Trust and the Procedural Requirements of Article 7(2) TEU: When More than One Bad Apple Spoils the Barrel' (2024) 25 *German Law Journal* 128

J Komarek, 'In the Court(s) We Trust? On the Need for Hierarchy and Differentiation in the Preliminary Ruling Procedure' (2007) 32 *European Law Review* 467

A Kornezov, 'The New Format of the Acte Clair Doctrine and Its Consequences' (2016) 53 *Common Market Law Review* 1317

K Lenaerts and T Corthaut, 'Judicial Review as a Contribution to the Development of European Constitutionalism' (2003) 22 *Yearbook of European Law* 1

L Prete and B Smulders, 'The Coming of Age of Infringement Proceedings' (2010) 47 *Common Market Law Review* 9

M Schmidt and P Bogdanowicz, 'The Infringement Procedure in the Rule of Law Crisis: How to Make Effective Use of Article 258 TFEU' (2018) 55 *Common Market Law Review* 1061

T Tridimas, 'Knocking on Heaven's Door: Fragmentation, Efficiency and Defiance in the Preliminary Reference Procedure' (2003) 40 *Common Market Law Review* 9

J Usher, 'Direct and Individual Concern: An Effective Remedy or a Conventional Solution?' (2003) 28 *European Law Review* 575

S Weatherill, *Cases and Materials on EU Law* (12th edn, Oxford: Oxford University Press, 2016) chs 7 and 8

Chapter acknowledgements

I am grateful to Anthony Arnull, Catherine Barnard, Nabil Khabirpour, Alexander Kornezov, and the anonymous referees for their invaluable comments on previous drafts of this chapter. Any errors remain entirely my own.

11

The internal market and the philosophies of market integration

Jukka Snell

1 Introduction

The building of a European market has been at the heart of the European integration project from the very beginning. In fact, 'common market' was for a long time used as a synonym for what is now the EU; when the British voted in a referendum on European Economic Community membership in 1975, they voted on whether they wanted to be a part of a 'common market'. What is unclear is the exact nature of the European market, which the Treaties today call the 'internal market'. It is the aim of the present chapter to examine this question, as well as to analyse the tools that the Treaties have created for the achievement of the internal market.

The main theme of the chapter is that the nature of the internal market is contested, lacks clarity, and has varied from time to time. This may at first glance appear surprising. After all, we have now had nearly 70 years to work out what the internal market means, and in fact the internal market is one of the very few concepts the Treaties actually define. According to Article 26(2) TFEU, 'the internal market shall comprise an area without internal frontiers in which the free movement of goods, persons, services and capital is ensured'. Unfortunately, the definition is somewhat circular.[1] In order to understand it, we need to understand the free movement of goods, persons, and so on. Yet when we seek to explore the meaning of the four freedoms, we quickly discover that they need to be understood against the background of the internal market. In other words, to understand the internal market, the four freedoms have to be understood, and vice versa.

[1] See the chapter by S Weatherill in M Adams, J Meeusen, G Straetmans, and H de Waele (eds), *Judging Europe's Judges: The Legitimacy of the Case Law of the European Court of Justice Examined* (Oxford: Hart Publishing, 2013).

The present chapter begins by setting out three possible ways an internal market could be organized. Those models are host country control, the harmonized model, and home country control. Each represents a very different approach to, or philosophy of, economic integration. They entail differing consequences for the division of power between the EU and its Member States, and between courts and legislatures. They are also likely to result in different balances being struck between economic and non-economic interests; in other words, one may benefit trade while potentially undermining social or environmental protection, while another may do the opposite.

The chapter continues by examining how the nature of European market integration has changed in the course of the history of the EU. It will argue that the original common market paradigm set out in the Spaak Report[2] and incorporated into the Treaty of Rome gradually gave way to the single market paradigm first initiated by the European Court of Justice and subsequently embraced by the political institutions. Further, it will be argued that we may now be moving towards yet another paradigm change, where the internal market is influenced by the need to create a true economic union. The contentious nature of market integration is illustrated by a case study exploring how it can both build support for the European project and undermine it.

Finally, in sections 4 and 5 the chapter moves to investigate the principal tool the Treaty has created for the achievement of the internal market, namely Article 114 TFEU. First, the extent of the power that this provision puts in the hands of the EU legislature is analysed, partly through the use of a case study. Secondly, the use of this power is explored, with focus on two techniques of approximation of the laws of the Member States: minimum and total harmonization.

A word of caution: the present chapter is only able to offer a partial picture of the internal market. To obtain a fuller view, the chapters on the four freedoms need to be consulted.[3] Here, I will seek to set out the broad context and to examine the power of the EU political institutions actively and positively to push for the creation or perfection of the internal market. Yet the ability of the Court to disapply national laws that violate the free movement of goods, persons, services, or capital is equally fundamental in the shaping of the internal market.

2 The nature of the internal market: three models

All markets need freedom. Suppliers of products and inputs need to be able to sell and buy. In the EU, the four freedoms of goods, services, persons, and capital provide this. However, all markets also need rules and the European internal market is no exception. Rules create the market in the first place: they establish property rights and contracts without which a market would not exist. They regulate what things can be sold and bought, and what things cannot.[4] Rules set out health and safety requirements that products must meet to be lawfully marketed, or qualifications that service providers must possess to trade legally. The fundamental question then is: who is to set the rules for the European internal market?

[2] Report of the Heads of Delegation to the Foreign Ministers at the Messina Conference, 21 April 1956.

[3] Chapters 12, 13, 14, and 15.

[4] eg sale of human body parts.

2.1 Three models of market integration

In theory, three different ideal models of organizing an internal market can be envisaged.[5] It is to be stressed that these are ideals; they help us to think about the issue, but do not exist in pure form anywhere. Each of the three models has different implications for the power structure of the EU, and for the balance between different interests.

The first possible model is *host country control*. This means that the rules of the country where the economic activity takes place apply. If a good is produced in country A but then sold in country B, it has to comply with the requirements of the latter State. If a worker from country C goes to work in country D, it is again the laws of the latter State that apply. Host State control is, of course, the normal situation when it comes to trade between independent countries. However, by committing to the internal market, the EU has decided to move further. This means that the host country control has to be tempered at least with a rule of non-discrimination. In other words, the rules of the host country apply, but those rules cannot discriminate against things or people from the other Member States.

The second possibility is a *harmonized model*. Here the conditions of a single unitary State are replicated at the EU level. For each issue, there is only one rule, which has been produced by the EU. All products and factors of production must comply with it, but can then be sold and bought freely in the territory of the entire Union.

The final model is *home country control*. This is the mirror image of host country control. The rule that applies to any given product or input is the rule of its country of origin, not the rule of the country where it is sold. For example, if a good is produced in country A and sold in country B, it is the rule of the first State (A) that applies. If a worker from country C goes to country D, it is again the rules of the former State (C) that regulate the activity. In other words, there is an EU rule of mutual recognition. For this kind of model to work, there has to be a significant level of trust between the countries.[6] Country B has to be confident that the goods produced in country A are safe. Country D has to trust that qualifications the worker obtained in country C render them competent to engage in the activity they are planning to undertake. In the real EU, such absolute trust does not exist. Instead, where mutual recognition does apply, it is tempered with exceptions that allow the host country to deny recognition in certain cases.

2.2 The implications of the different models

2.2.1 Consequences for sovereignty

The three models outlined in the previous section have different implications for the sovereignty of Member States.[7] The model of *host country control* is likely to impose the fewest constraints on the autonomy of each State to regulate its own affairs, although much will depend on how the rule of non-discrimination is applied. The second, *harmonized model* entails a vertical transfer of power from the State level to the EU level. Member States lose their power to regulate their own affairs; instead the laws come from the EU. However, it needs to be remembered that Member States are well represented in the EU legislature;

[5] M Poiares Maduro, *We the Court* (Oxford: Hart Publishing, 1998). Maduro uses the terms decentralized model, centralized model, and competitive model. KA Armstrong, 'Mutual Recognition' in C Barnard and J Scott (eds), *The Law of the Single European Market: Unpacking the Premises* (Oxford: Hart Publishing, 2002) employs the same terminology as the present chapter.

[6] See eg K Nicolaïdis, 'Trusting the Poles? Constructing Europe through Mutual Recognition' (2007) 14 *Journal of European Public Policy* 682.

[7] See generally eg J Snell, 'Who's Got the Power? Free Movement and Allocation of Competences in EC Law' (2003) 22 *Yearbook of European Law* 323.

in particular they form the Council.[8] In other words, under the harmonized model the Member States to a degree are pooling their sovereignty: they exercise it jointly. The *home country control model* involves a reassignment of sovereignty between the Member States. Each State loses its power to control matters within its own territory in certain circumstances. At the same time, the rules of each country extend further than they did before and now apply to circumstances outside its borders.

2.2.2 **Institutional consequences**

The different models also have different institutional consequences.[9] The balance between the power of the legislature and the power of the judiciary may be struck differently. In the *host country control model* the (national) legislatures are likely to play a dominant role, although it should be noted that courts may be highly influential as well, depending on how the rule of non-discrimination is applied. If only overt or direct discrimination[10] is caught, their influence is likely to be small. However, if a far-reaching standard that also outlaws indirect or covert discrimination is adopted, the judiciary may become a much more important actor. In extreme cases, the distinction between host and home country control may even evaporate under the glare of a non-discrimination rule: it can be argued that a failure of a host country to take into account the fact that a product or an input has already been the subject of regulation in its home State and now must comply with a second set of rules is itself a form of discrimination. After all, a product or an input of the host country has to deal with only one set of rules and can enter the market unchanged, while one coming from another Member State is subject to a double burden and needs to be altered to enter the new market.[11]

In the *harmonized model* it can be expected that the (EU) legislature is the dominant player, but again this is not necessarily so. The natural way of creating a harmonized set of rules is that they are promulgated by the central legislature. However, the judiciary can also engage in harmonization, in two ways. It can create a deregulated, liberal, laissez-faire market by striking down rules in the name of the four freedoms.[12] Alternatively, it can be more selective and target national rules that differ markedly from a European consensus.[13] For example, if Member States A, B, and C have very similar laws, while the law of D is very different, the Court might advance harmonization by disapplying the rule of D, thus encouraging its legislature to fall into line.

In the third, *home country control model*, the role of the judiciary is likely to be pronounced. It will have to ensure that mutual recognition takes place. It may also have to set the reach of mutual recognition in two ways, if the legislature has not done so. First, which rules are subject to mutual recognition in the first place? For example, if a worker from country A moves to country B, their qualifications may be recognized. But what about the salary levels—are they also set by the legislation or collective agreements of the home country? Secondly, mutual recognition is typically subject to exceptions that allow the host country to insist on the application of its own rules,[14] for example in the name of public policy. For home country control to work, the use of these exceptions needs to be carefully monitored by a judicial institution.

[8] See further chapter 4. [9] Snell, 'Who's Got the Power?' (n 7).

[10] For definitions of direct and indirect discrimination, see chapter 13.

[11] For the classic account, see G Marenco, 'Pour une interpretation traditionelle de la notion de mesure d'effet equivalent a une restriction quantitative' (1984) 19 *Cahiers de Droit Européen* 291.

[12] See N Bernard, 'The Future of European Economic Law in the Light of the Principle of Subsidiarity' (1996) 33 *Common Market Law Review* 633, 637.

[13] Poiares Maduro, *We the Court* (n 5) 72–76 calls this 'majoritarian activism'.

[14] It is not a coincidence that in Case 120/78 *Rewe v Bundesmonopolverwaltung für Branntwein* ('*Cassis de Dijon*') [1979] ECR 649 the Court both insisted on mutual recognition and created additional justifications for Member States.

2.2.3 Welfare considerations

Each model obviously aims at improving the welfare of our societies, that is, making citizens better off. However, they do so in very different ways, with different consequences. The *host country control model* allows trade to take place, and basic economic theory tells us that this makes all participants wealthier.[15] It also allows for the protection of other interests. For example, the host country is free to set whatever environmental or consumer protection standards it sees fit, as long as it avoids discrimination. Different countries are able to maintain different levels of protection. This is important if the preferences vary from country to country. The citizens of State A may place a high value on a clean environment, while citizens of B may place a higher value on material things. Under host country control, each State is able to set its level of protection accordingly.

The *harmonized model* brings with it significant economic benefits, too, in particular in terms of economies of scale. There is only one rule that economic actors need to comply with, in contrast with the patchwork of national rules that host country control allows. This reduces various compliance and transaction costs, and may allow companies to produce more efficiently. Often, it is cheaper per unit to produce a large number of products than a small number. For example, a large factory with a long assembly line may be able to churn out goods more cheaply than a smaller enterprise. If there is only one product standard for a company to worry about, rather than a multitude of different standards, these economies of scale can be achieved. In practice, this is an argument that has often been put forward in Europe, and in particular it has been claimed that without unification European companies will struggle to compete against companies from countries with large home markets,[16] such as the US or China.

Under the harmonized model, other interests such as the environment can also be protected by appropriate rules being adopted at the EU level. However, there are at least three problems. By necessity, an EU-wide rule cannot take diversity into account: one rule has to fit all countries, even if their preferences vary. The more diverse the Member States are, the less likely it is that a compromise satisfying all can be found. Secondly, it can be doubted whether the EU legislature would in practice be capable of producing rules in sufficient quantity and quality to afford non-economic interests, such as the environment, appropriate protection. Finally, rules adopted at the EU level may prove inflexible, rigid, and difficult to change. The EU legislative process tends to be lengthy, and involves numerous actors, veto points, and supermajority requirements. When a particular piece of EU law has been adopted, it may not be easy to amend if circumstances change or if it proves less than completely satisfactory.[17]

The welfare implications of *home country control* are the most difficult to assess. This is because they introduce a complex element of regulatory competition into the mix.[18] Regulatory competition means that in addition to the competition between firms that all models of internal market entail there is also competition between legislatures. Each country will try to attract valuable assets, for example by creating policies designed to encourage inward investment and prevent capital flight. They supply policies in the same manner as companies supply products. Economic actors then choose among the offerings of the competing countries. For example, consumers in country A may buy products

[15] See in the EU context, eg W Molle, *The Economics of European Integration: Theory, Practice, Policy* (5th edn, Aldershot: Ashgate, 2006).

[16] See eg P Cecchini et al, *The European Challenge 1992: The Benefits of a Single Market* (Aldershot: Wildwood House, 1988).

[17] FW Scharpf, 'The Joint-Decision Trap: Lessons from German Federalism and European Integration' (1988) 66 *Public Administration* 239.

[18] See eg W Kerber, 'Interjurisdictional Competition within the European Union' (2000) 23 *Fordham International Law Journal* 217.

produced in, and according to the standards of, country B. They vote with their purse. This will benefit the producers based in country B, and will be a matter of concern for producers and the government of country A. It may be inclined to amend the rules of country A to make products coming from country A more attractive and to counteract the risk of capital flight. As another example, country C may wish to attract capital by imposing low taxes on corporate profits and creating a favourable regulatory climate. This may increase the flows of international inward investments to country C as investors vote with their feet, potentially forcing country D to reconsider its fiscal policies.

Economists teach us that regulatory competition can have many beneficial effects.[19] First, it increases choice. A consumer can choose between products manufactured according to the specifications of many different jurisdictions. A worker can choose whether to live in a country of high salaries and relentless rat race, or lower income but good quality of life. Secondly, it creates a discovery mechanism.[20] Countries innovate to produce attractive rules and policies. They are tested in the marketplace for regulations. Some of these prove successful and are copied. Others fail to achieve the desired effect and are abandoned. This creates valuable information about which public policies actually work and which ones do not. In a way, each State acts as a laboratory of democracy.[21] Thirdly, regulatory competition may counteract the predatory tendencies of public officials. If they impose excessive taxes or oppressive rules, there is the option of exit. For example, an entrepreneur hit with a confiscatory tax may relocate to another jurisdiction to escape it. This possibility makes the imposition of such taxes less likely. Thus, regulatory competition may help to tame the leviathan.[22]

Unfortunately, regulatory competition can also prove detrimental.[23] This is incontestable in situations where the costs and the benefits of a policy fall on different jurisdictions. For example, assume that prevailing winds carry emissions from country A to country B. The government of country A would have no incentive to adopt appropriate environmental standards—after all, the benefits of the industrial activity fall on country A while the pollution falls on country B. In the language of economics, there are externalities, which render regulatory competition harmful. Further, it is sometimes supposed that regulatory competition leads more generally to an uncontrolled race to the bottom. The worry is that countries, in order to attract capital, will start competitively lowering their standards of labour or environmental protection (since people tend to be less mobile than capital) in a destructive cycle that leaves each with zero regulation. Emotive words such as social or environmental dumping are often used in this context. Whether a race to the bottom is a real danger associated with home country control is fiercely contested. There are arguments that such fears are unfounded or at least unlikely to materialize in practice. At any rate, empirical evidence is scarce.[24]

[19] See already CM Tiebout, 'A Pure Theory of Local Expenditures' (1956) 64 *Journal of Political Economy* 416.

[20] This aspect of competition is emphasized in FA Hayek, 'Competition as a Discovery Procedure' (2002) 5 *Quarterly Journal of Austrian Economics* 9.

[21] The expression was coined by Justice Brandeis of the US Supreme Court in *New State Ice v Liebmann*, 285 US 262 (1932).

[22] This is a prime concern of public choice theory. See eg G Brennan and JM Buchanan, *The Power to Tax: Analytic Foundations of a Fiscal Constitution* (Indianapolis, IN: Liberty Fund, 1980).

[23] See J-M Sun and J Pelkmans, 'Regulatory Competition in the Single Market' (1995) 33 *Journal of Common Market Studies* 67 for an attempt at cost–benefit analysis.

[24] See on a global scale, DW Drezner, *All Politics is Global: Explaining International Regulatory Regimes* (Princeton, NJ: Princeton University Press, 2007) who argues at 15 that: 'There are anecdotal examples that support the idea of a race to the bottom, but the bulk of the evidence strongly suggests that these assertions are flatly wrong.'

2.2.4 Democratic concerns

The previous paragraphs have considered the effects of different models of integration on the welfare of citizens as passive rule-takers. It is also important to consider the matter from the point of view of citizens as active rule-makers. In other words, do the different models have particular pitfalls from the perspective of democracy?

All three models have been subject to democratic criticism, from different perspectives. The argument against the *host country control model* has been that it is under-inclusive. Laws are formulated by the citizens of the host State, or their representatives. They do not take into account the interests of outsiders, such as companies or workers of other Member States, who do not have a voice in the political process of the host country. Yet the laws also affect these outsiders. Thus, it is argued, the host country control model suffers from the weakness that some affected interests are not represented at all.[25] The *harmonized model* is vulnerable to the entire gamut of democratic deficit criticism that the EU is regularly subjected to.[26] This is covered elsewhere in this book.[27] The *home country control model* is open to criticism as well. A particular worry is that it distorts national democracy by favouring capital over workers.[28] Under home country control, actors have the option of exit. A factory owner who does not like the regulatory climate of country A can relocate their production facility to country B, or at least threaten to do so. The same exit option is also available for workers, in theory. In practice, the different factors of production, capital, and labour, have differing levels of mobility. Liquid capital can be sent to another jurisdiction at the press of a button, while human beings with family ties and fluent in their native language only will find the prospect of relocation daunting. Thus, the threat of capital flight tends to be more credible than the threat of loss of skilled workers, forcing national legislatures to pay particular heed to the demands of capital. The result could be, for example, that the tax burden on the mobile factor, capital, is lowered, while the burden on the less mobile factor, labour, is increased.[29]

Where does the discussion leave us? It shows that there are profoundly different philosophies of economic integration. The approaches have different consequences for fundamental features of our societies, such as distribution of power, institutional balance, welfare of citizens, and democracy. The creation of the internal market is not a value-neutral technical project that can be left to the experts to manage, but must be an object of wider debate and contestation. The next section will show that, as the theory predicts, in the real world the nature of the internal market has been fought over. It has not remained stable, but has fluctuated and continues to fluctuate, displaying features of all three models that have been outlined previously.

[25] See eg C Joerges, 'What Is Left of the European Economic Constitution? A Melancholic Eulogy' (2005) 30 *European Law Review* 461, 488.

[26] See for discussion, eg J Snell, 'European Constitutional Settlement, and Ever Closer Union, and the Treaty of Lisbon: Democracy or Relevance' (2008) 33 *European Law Review* 619.

[27] See esp chapters 2 and 4.

[28] M Kumm, 'Constitutionalising Subsidiarity in Integrated Markets: The Case of Tobacco Regulation in the European Union' (2006) 12 *European Law Journal* 503.

[29] J Vella, *Nominal vs Effective Corporate Tax Rates Applied by MNEs and an Overview of Aggressive Tax Planning Tools, Instruments and Methods* (IP/A/TAXE/2015–07, PE 563.450) finds at 12–14 a decline in effective corporate tax rates between 1999 and 2015.

3 The nature of the internal market: the historical experience

This section explores the evolution of the internal market of the EU.[30] It argues that there have been different paradigms of market integration. The initial paradigm was the common market. As envisaged in the Spaak Report, which prepared the ground for the Treaty of Rome and the early years of integration, the European marketplace would combine freedom and fairness, and would largely be achieved by the legislative activity of the EU. The planned common market had some affinities with the harmonized model discussed earlier. The common market paradigm was replaced by the single market paradigm in the course of the 1970s and 1980s. Under this paradigm, the European Court of Justice became a more important actor, and the substance of the law shifted towards a more competitive model where home country control had a larger role to play. However, it will be argued, the single market paradigm suffered from instability and weaknesses. Instead, a new economic union paradigm may be emerging. Finally, a case study will explore how the European Commission has sought to use the internal market to bolster the legitimacy of the EU, while the Brexit referendum demonstrated that it can also foster discontent.

A note about terminology: the original Treaty of Rome used the term common market. The Single European Act of 1986 inserted the term internal market, which coexisted with common market in the language of the Treaty. In the political discussions, the term single market was often preferred. The Lisbon Treaty, which came into force in 2009, replaced all references to the common market with internal market. The Court has tended to use all three concepts interchangeably. For example, in *Gaston Schul* it stated that the common market 'involves the elimination of all obstacles to intra-Community trade in order to merge the national markets into a single market bringing about conditions as close as possible to those of a genuine internal market'.[31] However, legal scholars have insisted that the common market and the internal market were different concepts.[32]

3.1 The common market

The common market was at the heart of the Treaty of Rome of 1957 that established the European Economic Community. The EEC was a response to the failure of a more ambitious attempt to integrate Europe.[33] In 1952, treaties for the European Defence Community and the European Political Community of 'supranational character' had been put forward. They did not survive the national ratification process, and were killed off by the French Parliament in 'an atmosphere of riot'.[34] A more modest approach was called for, and a Benelux proposal for a common market was chosen as a vehicle to move integration forward despite the ratification crisis. The groundwork for the common market was laid down in the Spaak Report,[35] which was produced under the chairmanship of Paul-Henri Spaak, the Belgian foreign minister. He had also been the author of the European Political

[30] See also P Craig, 'The Evolution of the Single Market' in Barnard and Scott, *The Law of the Single European Market* (n 5); M Egan, 'Single Market' in E Jones, A Menon, and S Weatherill (eds), *The Oxford Handbook of the European Union* (Oxford: Oxford University Press, 2012); and LW Gormley, 'The Internal Market: History and Evolution' in N Nic Shuibhne (ed), *Regulating the Internal Market* (Cheltenham: Edward Elgar, 2006).

[31] Case 15/81 *Gaston Schul* [1982] ECR 1409, para 33.

[32] See eg LW Gormley, 'Competition and Free Movement: Is the Internal Market the Same as a Common Market?' [2002] *European Business Law Review* 517.

[33] For an excellent short summary of the developments, see D Dinian, *Europe Recast: A History of European Union* (Basingstoke: Palgrave Macmillan, 2004).

[34] Ibid, quoting J Lacouture, *Pierre Mendès-France* (New York: Holmes and Meier, 1984).

[35] See n 2.

Community Treaty, but with the common market project he expunged supranationalism from his vocabulary and focused on producing a blueprint for a treaty that would be acceptable for all parties, in particular France.[36]

The Spaak Report argued for the merger of separate national markets into a common market to arrest and reverse the perceived international decline of Europe. The key benefits were thought to be the increasing division of work that would lead to efficiencies, achievement of economies of scale, and greater competition. Three sets of actions were proposed. First, national protections creating obstacles to trade had to be suppressed. This involved the abolition of customs duties and quotas as well as those national regulations that resulted in the practical elimination or control of foreign competition. At the same time, however, it was recognized that common European-level regulations would be needed in the public interest or due to the nature of production or particular markets. Secondly, distortions of competition needed to be dealt with, whether they resulted from business practices, State aid, or disparities between national legislations. Thirdly, conditions for common growth had to be ensured by helping underdeveloped regions, by assisting business in adjusting to competition and modern production methods, and by freeing the circulation of factors of production: labour and to a degree also capital. The practical realization of the common market required the creation of institutions that would apply competition law, ensure State compliance with Treaty obligations, coordinate national policies, and provide parliamentary or judicial control.

The EEC Treaty followed closely the blueprint set up by the Spaak Report. For goods, there were rules on elimination of customs duties and quotas, and also a new provision outlawing measures of equivalent effect that apparently followed from a query by a mid-ranking customs official.[37] For persons and services, tools and a process for liberalization were established. There were to be issue- or sector-specific initiatives, with the Commission proposing and the Council adopting common rules that would realize free movement. For capital, a more modest degree of liberalization was envisaged, again following legislative initiatives. A harmonization mechanism was also created for the purposes of eliminating distortions of competition, and the Commission was charged with applying competition law and policing State aid. There was some coordination of economic policies, and the European Social Fund and the European Investment Bank were established to shelter the workforce, to help underdeveloped regions, and to assist business modernization. Following French concerns that its higher social costs would undermine French companies, social provisions were included declaring, inter alia, the need to improve and harmonize working conditions and standards of living for workers, as well as setting out the principle that men and women should receive equal pay for equal work.

The common market was a carefully calibrated mix of freedom and fairness. On paper, it had affinities with the harmonized model discussed in section 2.1. Markets would be opened, but in a controlled fashion. There would be no creative destruction, but instead a managed process of adjustment, adaptation, and fair competition. All the key concerns of France were addressed. This proved a recipe for political success. The Treaty sailed through the French Parliament just three years after the death of the European Defence and Political Communities.

The early years of market integration proceeded successfully. Customs duties and quotas were indeed eliminated. However, the harmonization of national rules did not proceed as planned. The empty chair crisis and Luxembourg Accords of the mid-1960s

[36] P-H Laurent, 'Paul-Henri Spaak and the Diplomatic Origins of the Common Market, 1955–1956' (1970) 85 *Political Science Quarterly* 373.

[37] A Prate, *Quelle Europe?* (Paris: Commentaire Julliard, 1991) 55 and A Moravcsik, *The Choice for Europe: Social Purpose and State Power from Messina to Maastricht* (London: UCL Press, 1999) 146.

had replaced the planned majority voting rules in the Council with the requirement of unanimity.[38] This made it difficult to engage in successful harmonization. Further, the task of creating a common market was probably greater than had been anticipated. Even for goods, non-tariff barriers proved prevalent. In the words of one observer, 'the lowering of tariffs has, in effect, been like draining a swamp. The lower water level has revealed all the snags and stumps of non-tariff barriers that still have to be cleared away'.[39] Further, technical and other developments meant that ever more issues needed to be dealt with[40] and laws that actually had been successfully adopted at the EU level required frequent revision.

3.2 **The single market**

The paradigm began to change in the 1970s.[41] The European Court of Justice stepped forward to take the lead. In the early 1970s, it found in a series of cases that the four freedoms, with the exception of capital, were directly effective. They could be applied even in the absence of the legislative activity that the Treaty had envisaged.[42] Starting in the late 1970s, it reinforced this by creating the principle of mutual recognition.[43] The Treaty freedoms went beyond simple non-discrimination rules and also required that the host country accepts goods, services, or economic actors that fulfil the requirements of the home country on its markets, unless the host State has a good reason to oppose such market access and does so in a proportionate fashion. In other words, the principle is that a product good enough for, say, French consumers, is also good enough for, say, German consumers, unless Germany can convincingly show otherwise. To use the language of section 2.1, the Court moved the European market towards the home country model.[44] At the same time, institutionally, it occupied a key position in advancing economic integration.[45]

The Commission sought to capitalize on the rulings of the Court. It issued a Communication setting out a far-reaching interpretation of the principle of mutual recognition.[46] The initial reaction of the Member States was hostile. However, over time they

[38] See eg J Gillingham, *European Integration 1950–2003: Superstate or New Market Economy?* (Cambridge: Cambridge University Press, 2003) 68–72.

[39] R Baldwin, *Non-Tariff Distortions of International Trade* (Washington DC: Brookings Institution, 1970), quoted in MP Egan, *Constructing a European Market: Standards, Regulation, and Governance* (Oxford: Oxford University Press, 2001) 41.

[40] In recent years, this has affected in particular the EU's attempts to come to grips with the digital revolution and has resulted in numerous legislative initiatives; see D Adamski, 'Lost on the Digital Platform: Europe's Travails with the Digital Single Market' (2018) 55 *Common Market Law Review* 719 for an overview.

[41] See also AJ Menéndez, 'The Existential Crisis of the European Union' (2013) 14 *German Law Journal* 453, 471–484.

[42] See eg P Craig, 'Once upon a Time in the West: Direct Effect and the Federalization of EEC Law' (1992) 12 *Oxford Journal of Legal Studies* 453, 463–467.

[43] Case 120/78 *Rewe v Bundesmonopolverwaltung für Branntwein* [1979] ECR 649. See further chapter 12.

[44] See W-H Roth, 'Mutual Recognition' and A Saydé, 'Freedom as a Source of Constraint: Expanding Market Discipline through Free Movement', both in P Koutrakos and J Snell (eds), *Research Handbook on the Law of the EU's Internal Market* (Cheltenham: Edward Elgar, 2017) on mutual recognition and on its relationship to national treatment.

[45] See, on the role of the Court, T Horsley, 'Institutional Dynamics Reloaded: The Court of Justice and the Development of the EU Internal Market' in Koutrakos and Snell (eds), *Research Handbook on the Law of the EU's Internal Market* (n 44).

[46] Communication from the Commission concerning the consequences of the judgment given by the Court of Justice on 20 February 1979 in Case 120/78 ('*Cassis de Dijon*') (OJ [1980] C256/2). See KJ Alter and S Meunier-Aitsahalia, 'Judicial Politics in the European Community: European Integration and the Pathbreaking *Cassis de Dijon* Decision' (1994) 26 *Comparative Political Studies* 535.

became more receptive.[47] A national experiment at socialism had failed in France, and the French government moved from autarkic policies to support internal market liberalization. The Britain of Margaret Thatcher was pushing forward a programme of liberalization, and the Christian Democrats had replaced the Social Democrats in government in Germany. European businesses were lobbying hard for more economic integration to strengthen their position against US and Japanese competitors. The result was a relaunch of integration under the banner of the single market.[48]

The most visible element of the single market was the adoption of a new Treaty to amend the Treaty of Rome, the Single European Act (SEA), which followed an important Commission White Paper on the completion of the internal market[49] and entered into force in 1987. This document set out the aim of achieving the internal market by the end of 1992. The internal market was defined as 'an area without internal frontiers in which the free movement of goods, persons, services and capital is ensured'. For this aim to be realized, the SEA brought forward a new rule that allowed internal market legislation to be passed by qualified majority voting, rather than by unanimity (see section 4).

The SEA was supported by innovations in the Commission's approach to harmonization. Under the so-called 'new approach', harmonization would be focused on those national rules that survived the direct application of the Treaty. In other words, if the host country had to recognize the product of the home country under the four freedoms anyway, there was no need for the EU to legislate. Only if the host country was able to oppose the importation, for example on grounds of health and safety, was there a need for the EU legislature to engage. Further, the type of legislation would be different. Instead of detailed harmonization of rules on narrow sectors, broader directives would be adopted that would seek to harmonize only the essential health, safety, environmental, and other requirements. The details would be left for the European standardization process undertaken by bodies such as CEN (the European Committee for Standardization) and CENELEC (the European Committee for Electrotechnical Standardization). Finally, an early warning system was established that required Member States to notify new technical regulations to the Commission, so that it could take preventative action.[50]

The single market paradigm had a number of advantages. It aligned the Treaty, harmonization, and standardization. It abandoned unachievable ambitions for complete harmonization. It left room for experimentation and local differences. Most importantly, it was realistic. The measures that needed to be adopted were by and large passed; the deadline of 1992 was for the most part met. The single market was created in a workable form. Importantly, this does not mean that the project was finished in 1992. New challenges arise all the time: for example, the digital transformation of the economy has engendered a need to develop rules for issues that were not on the radar in the early 1990s. In this sense, the single market will never be completed but will always remain work in progress.

[47] See A Moravcsik, 'Negotiating the Single European Act: National Interests and Conventional Statecraft in the European Community' (1991) 45 *International Organization* 19 and W Sandholtz and J Zysman, '1992: Recasting the European Bargain' (1989) 42 *World Politics* 95 for classic studies of the impetus behind the single market project.

[48] According to K Nicolaïdes, 'Kir Forever? The Journey of a Political Scientist in the Landscape of Recognition' in M Poiares Maduro and L Azoulai (eds), *The Past and Future of EU Law: The Classics of EU Law Revisited on the 50th Anniversary of the Rome Treaty* (Oxford: Hart Publishing, 2010) 448: 'When I recently asked Lord Cockfield, Commissioner for the internal market, what he considered the greatest achievement of his career, he answered without a beat: to have exported Cassis from the European Court of Justice and goods to the single market Europe 1992 programme.'

[49] Commission White Paper, 'Completing the internal market', COM(85) 310 final.

[50] See J Pelkmans, 'The New Approach to Technical Harmonization and Standardization' (1987) 25 *Journal of Common Market Studies* 249.

However, the success of the single market was a qualified one and the paradigm was never fully stable. When things such as convergence in labour productivity, wage dispersion, or trade within countries as opposed to between countries are measured, the European market does not appear well integrated. In the words of the International Monetary Fund (IMF), '[t]rade integration in the European Union is higher than in other regional agreements, but only a fraction of the level observed among states in the United States'.[51] In the same way, most predictions of the long-term economic effects of Brexit forecasted substantially reduced growth for the UK due to the loss of full access to the single market, but '[n]one of the models predict anything like the year-on-year falls in output that were experienced during 2008' at the height of the financial crisis.[52] Trading on World Trade Organization (WTO) terms would be significantly worse than being in the single market—but not catastrophically so.[53] The lack of EU integration is most pronounced in services, which of course dominate modern economies but only occupy a small slice of intra-EU trade.[54] The economic shortcomings of the single market have been highlighted in recent high-level reports.[55]

Despite its theoretical attractiveness, the single market paradigm did not really satisfy many of the key stakeholders. First, from the business perspective the approach was less than perfect. While mutual recognition was fine in theory, in practice its application left a lot to be desired. National authorities were still left as guardians of market access, and could deny mutual recognition on the basis of the derogations written in the Treaty, such as the needs of public policy, or on the basis of exceptions developed in the case law, such as consumer or environmental protection. In other words, an attempt by a company to penetrate the market of another country was often frustrated by the insistence of host State officials that local rules be obeyed because the rules of the home country did not in their view sufficiently protect non-economic interests. Whether such a requirement was lawful depended on the proportionality of the host country rule. This was very difficult to predict in advance and could only be tested in costly and lengthy litigation. As a result, for a company it would often be easier just to follow the local rule than to rely on European rights.[56]

For national governments, the single market model created at least two types of difficulty. The national publics expect States to protect them from environmental degradation, substandard products, and so on. If there is a problem, for example a food scandal, the national government may get blamed. Yet those governments have now given up their ability fully to control products that are sold in their country. They might end up bearing

[51] International Monetary Fund, 'Regional Economic Outlook: Europe' (April 2024), 18. See R Raudla and A Spendzharova, 'Challenges to the European Single Market at Thirty: Renationalisation, Resilience, or Renewed Integration?' (2022) 44 *Journal of European Integration* 1 on the recent dynamics across various sectors of the economy.

[52] G Tetlow and A Stojanovic, *Understanding the Economic Impact of Brexit* (London: Institute for Government, 2018) 23.

[53] However, at the time of writing the multilateral trading system may be in the process of collapsing due to trade wars unleashed by the US and trading practices adopted by China, so WTO terms may not be on offer. See eg MBG Froman, 'After the Trade War: Remaking Rules from the Ruins of the Rules-Based System' *Foreign Affairs*, 11 August 2025.

[54] See eg European Commission, 'Annual Single Market and Competitiveness Report 2025', COM (2025) 26 final, 6–7.

[55] See especially E Letta, 'Much more than a market' (April 2024), at www.consilium.europa.eu/media/ny3j24sm/much-more-than-a-market-report-by-enrico-letta.pdf.

[56] J Pelkmans, 'Mutual Recognition in Goods: On Promises and Disillusions' (2007) 14 *Journal of European Public Policy* 699, 708–711. The EU has put forward various initiatives to improve the functioning of mutual recognition, in particular European Parliament and Council Regulation (EU) 2019/515 on the mutual recognition of goods lawfully marketed in another Member State (OJ [2019] L91/1).

the responsibility for things that they cannot affect. Further, the kind of competition the single market model entails may be branded unfair. National companies on the losing end might blame their lack of success on the various 'unfair' regulatory advantages that foreign competitors enjoy, such as lower standards or wages, and demand protection. Under European law such protection is likely to be illegal. This could leave the national decision-makers between the rock of domestic public opinion that expects the government to protect local companies and the hard place of EU rules that outlaw it.

For organized interest groups, such as trade unions or environmental groups, the principle of mutual recognition at the heart of the single market represented a threat. As discussed in section 2.2, the principle potentially allows regulatory competition to take place. This could undermine the labour or environmental standards that the groups were committed to. Even if fierce regulatory competition failed to start, the balance of power between organized interest groups and industry was altered. The industry was provided with the ability to threaten relocation in the absence of domestic reforms. In other words, the industry could tell the government or trade unions that without changes, such as greater labour market flexibility, future investment decisions would be directed at other parts of the EU.[57]

For the advocates of further integration, the single market was insufficient. It was a construct of logic and economic advantage. It lacked emotional pull; it did not instil Europatriotism in citizens. In the words of Jacques Delors, the President of the Commission during the single market project, 'It is difficult to fall in love with the single market.' In fact, quite the opposite: some of the bitterest resistance to the European project has been due to attempts to extend the single market.

In this context, the enlargement of the Union is a significant factor. The expansions of 2004 and thereafter brought into the EU a large number of countries that were at quite a different level of economic development from the existing Member States. This created political problems. An attempt to enhance the effectiveness of the single market in the services sector by the adoption of a directive with a country-of-origin principle met fierce resistance and resulted in the watering down of the directive. Judgments of the Court of Justice on the kinds of actions trade unions could take to oppose competition from the new Member States[58] entered into political discussion, for example in the context of the Irish referenda on the Lisbon Treaty, just as the threat of Polish plumbers 'stealing' the jobs of French plumbers had been invoked in debates on the Constitutional Treaty in France. In the UK, the resistance to the free movement of workers from Eastern Europe is thought to have been one of the key factors behind the Leave vote, as explored in case study 11.1. Behind these phenomena was the economic insecurity that heightened competition created, in particular when the labour-cost differences between some of the new and old Member States were very substantial. Further, the single market with its mutual recognition requires mutual trust, and with enlargement that trust was at least temporarily undermined.[59]

The pressures described previously have had an impact on legal developments. As mentioned, the attempt to liberalize services markets in one fell swoop using the country-of-origin principle was abandoned.[60] The Commission has in certain areas moved

[57] See generally C Barnard, 'Social Dumping and the Race to the Bottom: Some Lessons for the European Union from Delaware?' (2000) 25 *European Law Review* 57.

[58] See further chapters 13 and 20.

[59] For an empirical assessment, see J Delhey, 'Do Enlargements Make the European Union Less Cohesive? An Analysis of Mutual Trust between EU Nationalities' (2007) 45 *Journal of Common Market Studies* 253. For details of the cases referred to here, see chapter 13.

[60] K Nicolaïdis and SK Schmidt, 'Mutual Recognition "On Trial": The Long Road to Services Liberalization' (2007) 14 *Journal of European Public Policy* 717.

away from the idea of divergent but coordinated national systems and instead returned to an approach based on more complete harmonization of rules.[61] The Commission has also contributed to uniformity at the level of implementation by working quietly to shift away from directives that need to be transposed by Member States to regulations that do not.[62] There have been attempts to emphasize social Europe and non-economic issues to appease disgruntled citizens, rather than leaving the matters for regulatory competition. This was expressed forcefully in the report for the Commission on the relaunch of the single market by Professor Monti. He advocated the creation of a stronger single market but also noted the need to build consensus to support it as 'today the single market . . . is seen by many Europeans . . . with suspicion, fear and sometimes open hostility'.[63] It also finds an expression in the Lisbon Treaty, which commits the EU to the goal of a 'social market economy' and, in a gesture full of symbolism, relegates the EU's commitment to undistorted competition from the first Articles of the Treaty to a Protocol. The current Commission President identified 'an economy that works for people' where 'the *social* and the *market*' are reconciled as her priorities.[64] In other words, some of the single market paradigm's basic features have been checked or challenged.

3.3 **Economic union?**

It is possible that we are now witnessing another paradigm shift for the internal market. The weakened, unstable single market paradigm may be giving way to an economic union paradigm. The proximate cause for this is the need to ensure the success of the single currency, the euro, which has been battered by the financial crisis that began in 2007. Further pressure in this direction may be coming from global developments that are leading towards a more geoeconomic world order, where the world economy is becoming more fragmented due, in large part, to the great power rivalry between China and the US.

The internal market and the economic and monetary union (EMU) complement each other, as was already recognized in the Commission's slogan 'one market, one money'. In fact, a single currency only makes sense in the context of an internal market. A decision to adopt a single currency is always an exercise in balancing its benefits against its costs,[65] and a well-functioning internal market increases the former and reduces the latter.

At least four points need to be made. First, the advantages of a single currency in terms of lower transaction costs, greater transparency, and the elimination of exchange-rate risk are only felt if there is trade and investment, and a single currency can in turn be expected to provide a further boost for them. A strong internal market increases the benefits of the single currency, which in turn strengthens the internal market.

Second, the problem with a single currency is that it reduces flexibility: an individual Member State can no longer respond to economic developments by changing interest rates or the value of its currency. However, a well-functioning internal market may reduce

[61] European Commission Green Paper on the Review of the Consumer Acquis, COM(2006) 744 final. See generally S Weatherill, 'Maximum versus Minimum Harmonization: Choosing between Unity and Diversity in the Search for the Soul of the Internal Market' in N Nic Shuibhne and LW Gormley (eds), *From Single Market to Economic Union: Essays in Memory of John A Usher* (Oxford: Oxford University Press, 2012).

[62] According to Internal Market Scoreboards, as of December 2024, 1,000 directives and at least 4,603 regulations were in force to ensure the functioning of the single market. This contrasts with 1,490 directives and only 275 regulations in 2001. See J Pelkmans and A Correia de Brito, *Enforcement in the EU Single Market* (Brussels: CEPS, 2012) 107.

[63] M Monti, 'A New Strategy for the Single Market: At the Service of Europe's Economy and Society', May 2010.

[64] U von der Leyen, 'A Union that strives for more: My agenda for Europe', available at https://ec.europa.eu/info/sites/default/files/political-guidelines-next-commission_en_0.pdf.

[65] P Krugman, 'Revenge of the Optimum Currency Area' (2012) 27 *NBER Macroeconomics Annual* 439.

the need for independent action by Member States if it brings with it an alignment of business cycles.[66] If every Member State experiences booms and busts simultaneously, a centralized monetary policy will work well—there is simply less need for national autonomy.

Third, in the literature on optimum currency areas, labour mobility has been identified as one of the key factors for a successful currency union.[67] Free movement of labour assumes a greater significance under a single currency. If one Member State is experiencing fast growth while another is suffering a slowdown, the workers may move from the latter to the former. This compensates for the loss of independence in interest and exchange-rate setting—it offers flexibility. The problem for Europe is that free movement of workers remains largely words on paper, with only a small percentage of EU nationals taking advantage of their right to move to another country for employment.[68] In fact, the low level of actual labour mobility in Europe was a factor that was frequently raised in the original debates on the desirability of the euro.[69]

In the same vein, well-functioning European capital and credit markets could better smooth economic shocks, which is particularly important as there are no substantial fiscal transfers—public risk sharing can be replaced by private risk sharing. Shocks would not affect just one country with potentially devastating consequences but would be absorbed more widely, reducing their impact and smoothing their effects on individuals. A European Commission study from 2016 estimated that in the US the fully integrated markets meant that less than 20 per cent of shocks went unsmoothed.[70] The smoothing was primarily the result of private risk sharing through markets. By contrast, in the EU over 75 per cent of shocks went completely unsmoothed. Private risk sharing only amounted to little over 20 per cent. This is why the Commission has identified the creation of a Capital Markets Union as a key priority.

Fourthly, and more broadly, a well-functioning internal market allows the real exchange-rate channel to work. What this means is that a country whose economy is overheating due to low real interest rates, which result from a centrally set nominal interest rate and a high level of inflation, is automatically cooled down. Due to the high inflation, its goods and services become more expensive so its export sector suffers. The weakening export sector stabilizes the system. By contrast, in a country that is experiencing a slowdown due to an excessively high real interest rate, which results from a centrally set nominal interest rate coupled with low inflation, the export sector is going to accelerate. The low inflation will make its goods and services cheaper, and its export performance will be boosted. This again stabilizes the system automatically. The problem for the EU is that weaknesses in the internal market which, for example, still covers services only partially, have meant that the real exchange-rate channel has not operated with sufficient force to counteract localized overheating and bubbles.[71] It is no accident that serious proposals for dealing with the euro crisis tended to call for the strengthening of the internal market.[72]

[66] JA Frankel and AK Rose, 'The Endogeneity of the Optimum Currency Area Criteria' (1998) 108 *Economic Journal* 1009.

[67] RA Mundell, 'A Theory of Optimum Currency Areas' (1961) 51 *American Economic Review* 657.

[68] See further chapter 13. According to the Commission, 'Annual report on intra-EU labour mobility' (2024), there are only 10 million working age long-term EU-movers, while the EU's total population is 450 million. Further, the countries with the largest groups of movers, Romania and Poland, are not in the eurozone.

[69] See eg OJ Blanchard and LF Katz, 'Regional Evolutions' (1992) *Brookings Papers on Economic Activity* 1.

[70] See European Commission, 'Cross-Border Risk Sharing after Asymmetric Shocks: Evidence from the Euro Area and the United States' (2016) 15 *Quarterly Report on the Euro Area* 7.

[71] The dominance of the real interest-rate channel over the real exchange-rate channel has been described well in H Enderlein et al, *Completing the Euro: A Road Map towards Fiscal Union in Europe—Report of the 'Tommaso Padoa-Schioppa Group* (Paris: Notre Europe, 2012).

[72] See eg H Van Rompuy et al, 'Towards a Genuine Economic and Monetary Union', available at www.consilium.europa.eu/uedocs/cms_data/docs/pressdata/en/ec/134069.pdf, at 10.

More broadly still, it can be questioned how well the basic idea of a competitive single market model, and the original EMU more broadly, where each Member State is responsible for its own economic policies and then competes with others, fits with the reality of the single currency. The divergences between Member States that are perfectly acceptable in a single market are deeply problematic in a single currency area. In the past, when Germany's productivity growth was high and Italy's low, Italy could always respond by devaluing the lira. That is no longer an option. Instead, a painful internal devaluation looms.

The crisis has also shown that eurozone countries are highly interconnected. When a number of countries got into trouble, this proved to be a problem for the entire eurozone; ultimately the stronger countries and the European institutions decided not to let the weaker ones drown but came forward with various rescue mechanisms. Further, within the eurozone, problems of one country can rapidly infect other States. If there are question marks over the health of the banks of one country, markets quickly become worried about the financial institutions of the other countries as well; if the ability of one Member State to stay within the euro is questioned, the markets quickly start to worry about the other countries. In other words, it is in the interest of all euro States to ensure that every euro State is economically healthy. It is not simply a matter of each State looking after its own performance and competing with the others.[73] This has been recognized in some of the reforms and many of the reform proposals. For example, the important Five Presidents' Report of 2015 called for a new convergence process towards the best performance and practices to achieve sound policies and similarly resilient economic structures throughout the euro area under the mantra that the success of monetary union anywhere depends on its success everywhere. Binding EU convergence legislation was suggested primarily for labour markets, competitiveness, business environment and public administrations, as well as certain aspects of tax policy,[74] areas which thus far have largely been beyond the reach of harmonization.[75]

The crisis also demonstrated the need for profound changes in the field of financial services, one of the most important sectors of modern economies. First, the crisis led to a re-fragmentation of the single financial market, as companies repatriated some of their activities, often at the behest of national supervisors. This meant that some of the most tangible gains of the internal market were lost. It also meant that the conditions of competition for non-financial firms diverged, as the availability and cost of capital could vary dramatically between countries. Further, the monetary policy decisions of the European Central Bank lost some of their effectiveness as, for example, the cutting of interest rates might not result in a lower cost of finance on the ground. More broadly, the financial crisis exposed the unhealthy relationship between many Member States and their banks. When individual banks got into trouble, their home States had to rescue them. This increased their national debt and made investors doubt the solvency of countries such as Ireland and Spain. It also weakened national banks further, as they often have large holdings of

[73] For a succinct review of the issues, see Communication from the Commission, 'A blueprint for a deep and genuine economic and monetary union: launching a European debate', COM(2012) 777 final.

[74] The report, titled 'Completing Europe's Economic and Monetary Union', was authored by Commission President Juncker in close cooperation with the presidents of the European Council, Eurogroup, European Central Bank, and European Parliament, and is available at https://ec.europa.eu/commission/publications/five-presidents-report-completing-europes-economic-and-monetary-union_en.

[75] Arguably, the EU's response to Covid-19 was informed by its experiences with the financial crisis. There were concerns that the pandemic could cause significant damage to the internal market and the single currency, but a robust EU response, in particular in the form of the Covid recovery plan, was able to deal with the threats. See generally eg B de Witte, 'The European Union's COVID-19 Recovery Plan: The Legal Engineering of an Economic Policy Shift' (2021) 58 *Common Market Law Review* 635.

their government's bonds. In other words, national banking and fiscal problems fed into each other. In sum, the single market model where banks and financial service providers were largely regulated, supervised, and ultimately supported by their home countries but operated on a pan-European scale has proven unsustainable.[76]

The move away from the single market paradigm can be seen graphically precisely in the case of financial regulation. This was a sector where the principle of home country control at one time reigned supreme. Every Member State regulated its own financial institutions, which then traded in the whole EU using the single passport that the home country had provided them.[77] The new financial services rules that have been adopted since the financial crisis have abandoned the idea of home country control and moved to a centralized approach with a single rulebook rather than a number of competing and mutually recognized national rules.[78] The banking union, while still incomplete, already includes the Single Supervisory Mechanism where bank supervision has been lifted from individual Member States to the European Central Bank, and also a system of bank rescue and resolution that entails risk mutualization and burden sharing across national borders.[79] The ongoing Capital Markets Union project has been described as embodying 'a set of policy actions to push European policies beyond the mutual recognition'.[80]

It is thus possible that through a process of spillback the 'remorseless logic' of monetary integration requires an internal market fit for an economic union[81]—a market that works better and is more uniform and centralized than the one contemplated under the single market paradigm. If so, an acute dilemma emerges. How to manage the relationship between those Member States that have signed up to the euro, and those that have not?[82] We have already got a small taste of this in the context of the EU banking union, which is compulsory for euro countries and voluntary for others. Non-participating Member States were deeply concerned about the possibility that in practice the euro countries would impose their view on the future shape of the internal market on the whole EU. A partial solution for this concern was found in the shape of a complex double majority decision-making mechanism that sought to safeguard the interests of the outs.[83] The same tension can also be seen in the case law, where the attempt by the European Central Bank to insist that companies involved in certain clearing operations had to be based in the eurozone was successfully contested by the UK, supported by Sweden.[84] However, the matter was not fully settled and similar concerns are likely to emerge elsewhere,[85] perhaps

[76] See Communication from the Commission, 'A blueprint for a deep and genuine economic and monetary union: launching a European debate', COM(2012) 777 final.

[77] See further chapter 14.

[78] For critical overviews, see M Andenas and IHY Chiu, 'Financial Stability and Legal Integration in Financial Regulation' (2013) 38 *European Law Review* 335 and N Moloney, 'EU Financial Market Regulation after the Global Financial Crisis: "More Europe" or More Risks?' (2010) 47 *Common Market Law Review* 1317.

[79] See generally eg K Alexander, 'A Legal and Institutional Analysis of the Single Supervisory Mechanism and the Single Resolution Mechanism' (2015) 40 *European Law Review* 154.

[80] D Valiante, 'CMU and the Deepening of Financial Integration' in D Busch et al (eds), *Capital Markets Union in Europe* (Oxford: Oxford University Press, 2018) 13.

[81] See further on the relationship between 'microeconomic and macroeconomic constitutions', K Tuori and K Tuori, *Eurozone Crisis: A Constitutional Analysis* (Cambridge: Cambridge University Press, 2014).

[82] See New Settlement for the United Kingdom within the European Union, EUCO 1/16, 12–15, for an attempt to deal with the issues. However, this lapsed following the result of the Brexit referendum.

[83] Regulation 1022/2013 (OJ [2013] L287/5), Art 44 as amended.

[84] Case T-496/11 *UK v ECB*, EU:T:2015:133.

[85] See generally on the limits of market integration in the context of different models of capitalism, J Snell, 'Varieties of Capitalism and the Limits of European Economic Integration' (2010–11) 13 *Cambridge Yearbook of European Legal Studies* 415.

in particular in the context of the ongoing Capital Markets Union project,[86] mentioned earlier. This is an internal market initiative designed to encompass all of the Member States but also a part of the EMU's 'Financial Union' that is meant to increase risk sharing across eurozone countries. It may well prove that while relatively loose arrangements would suit States that do not participate in the euro, the eurozone would prefer a tighter, more centralized Capital Markets Union.[87]

Finally, the current external challenges that the EU faces may be pushing in the same direction. Both recent high-level reports on Europe's economy and the Commission are calling for a reinvigoration of the internal market as a response to the geopolitical challenges and trade tensions that the EU is facing. There is a hope of a rally-around-the-flag effect, where external threats and crises result in temporary shelving of differences between Member States and political groups to facilitate a united response.[88]

To sum up, the nature of market integration has changed in the course of the development of European integration. In the beginning, what was contemplated was a common market that would balance freedom and fairness, and where the political institutions would play the leading role in creating the common market through harmonization. This did not work. The institutions proved unequal to the task. Instead, the Court seized the initiative in cooperation with the Commission and with the eventual support of the Member States. The result was a single market that was based less on harmonization and a level playing field and more on home country control and competition. However, it may be that we are now once again witnessing a shift in the internal market paradigm. The tensions inherent in the single market and the need to support the EMU may be pushing economic integration in a new, more centralized direction.[89]

Case study 11.1: Internal market as a source of legitimacy and discontent

It has been a theme of this chapter that the internal market is not a technical value-free project but rather reflects contentious political choices. This case study seeks to illustrate this by focusing on two developments: the Commission's drive for the 'Europe of results'[90] and Brexit.

The Commission has increasingly sought to rely on the internal market as a source of legitimacy for European integration. In particular, it has attempted to focus on specific projects capable of producing tangible benefits that can be portrayed as examples of the EU working for its citizens. Rather than seeking to advance the internal market on a broad front in the name of economic efficiency, like it did for example with the 1985 White Paper or the original proposal for the Services Directive, it has increasingly concentrated on key sectors or themes that preferably also resonate among the public.[91] The Digital Single Market provides a recent example.

[86] See J Payne and E Howell, 'The Creation of a European Capital Market' in Koutrakos and Snell (eds), *Research Handbook on the Law of the EU's Internal Market* (n 44).

[87] See generally N Moloney, 'Capital Markets Union: "Ever Closer Union" for the EU Financial System?' (2016) 41 *European Law Review* 307.

[88] See eg Commission, 'The Single Market: our European home market in an uncertain world', COM (2025) 500 final and A Herranz-Surrallés, C Damro, and S Eckert, 'The Geoeconomic Turn of the Single European Market? Conceptual Challenges and Empirical Trends' (2024) 62 *Journal of Common Market Studies* 919, 927–928.

[89] See for a discussion of the themes in the previous sections from the perspective of European economic constitution, K Tuori, *European Constitutionalism* (Cambridge: Cambridge University Press, 2015) esp ch 5.

[90] The phrase was used by Commission President Barroso in 2006, in the aftermath of the demise of the Constitutional Treaty, see http://europa.eu/rapid/press-release_SPEECH-06-286_en.htm.

[91] See eg Commission Communication, 'Single Market Act II Together for new growth', COM(2012) 573 which outlined 12 'key actions' and was accompanied by a 'Citizen's summary'.

A Digital Single Market sought to achieve three things: improve access to digital goods and services, create a regulatory environment favourable to digital networks and services, and use digitalization as a driver for growth. The initiatives were expressly framed with deliverables in mind, such as cross-border access to music, movies, and sport on electronic devices, and the creation of jobs in particular for younger job-seekers.[92] Ensuring that Europe is fit for the digital age remains a priority for the Commission, and significant legislative steps have been taken.[93]

However, the internal market has also served to fuel discontent. As discussed earlier, there has been a widespread worry that the social dimension of the EU project has lagged behind its market dimension. The EU has opened markets and brought greater competition. As with any competition, there are winners and losers. The concern has been that the interests of those on the losing side have been ignored.

This emerged particularly strongly in the debates on the UK's position in the EU and the free movement of workers and the referendum result.[94] Hundreds of thousands of migrant workers, in particular from countries such as Poland and Romania, had entered the British labour market relying on the EU freedoms. From their perspective, as well as from the perspective of many well-off Britons, this was a boon. Migrant workers were able to benefit from opportunities not available in their home countries. British businesses had access to cheap labour and the middle classes could employ builders and nannies at an affordable cost. However, for many unskilled British workers the immigrants were perceived as a source of competition and a force that kept their earnings down and a burden on pressed public services such as housing and public health.[95]

The UK government sought to deal with the discontent by negotiating exceptions to free movement prior to the referendum. Some limitations were indeed agreed,[96] but for the most part the other EU countries stood firm on the need to safeguard the principle that has been a part of the integration project from the very beginning.[97]

The issue surfaced again during the withdrawal negotiations. For the UK, full control of immigration was a red line.[98] The EU defended the indivisibility of the internal market, namely the idea that the freedoms of goods, persons, services, and capital constitute an inseparable whole, with the result that the UK could not pick and choose.[99]

From an economic perspective, maintaining all four freedoms is generally thought to be optimal. Under them, both products (goods and services) and factors of production (labour and capital) can flow in an efficient fashion.[100] Further, the different freedoms are

[92] Commission Communication, 'A Digital Single Market Strategy for Europe', COM(2015) 192 final. However, see Adamski (n 40) 737 for a pessimistic take on the first achievements.

[93] See https://digital-strategy.ec.europa.eu/en/policies/digital-services-act-package for an overview of the Digital Services Act and the Digital Markets Act. See further chapter 14.

[94] See eg MJ Goodwin and O Heath, 'The 2016 Referendum, Brexit and the Left Behind: An Aggregate-Level Analysis of the Result' (2016) 87 *Political Quarterly* 323, 331, and SO Becker, T Fetzer, and D Novy, 'Who Voted for Brexit? A Comprehensive District-Level Analysis' (2017) 32 *Economic Policy* 601, 605.

[95] Since 2007 the UK had experienced one of the largest falls of real average wages of any rich country. See *OECD Employment Outlook 2017*, 213, available at www.oecd-ilibrary.org/employment/oecd-employment-outlook-2017_empl_outlook-2017-en.

[96] EUCO 1/16, 19–24.

[97] See 'Cameron Pins Brexit on EU Failure to Grant UK Brake on Migration', *Financial Times*, 29 June 2016.

[98] https://brexitcentral.com/theresa-mays-speech-lancaster-house/.

[99] Statement following an informal meeting of 27, available at www.consilium.europa.eu/en/press/press-releases/2016/06/29-tusk-remarks-informal-meeting-27/, para 4.

[100] In a currency union, the free flow of labour is particularly important as noted above.

often factually connected. However, history is full of trade arrangements that do not involve all four elements, and even within the EU some of the freedoms are, and always have been, more developed than others.[101] So in principle, if all parties were to agree, a pick and choose would be possible.[102] But therein lies the rub: all parties are unlikely to agree. For example, why would eastern Europeans wish to grant the UK full access to their goods and services markets, if the UK denies their citizens the access to its labour market? And more broadly, if all EU countries were free to select only those elements of the four freedoms that happen to suit them at a given moment, there would be no internal market.

As a result, since the UK was unwilling to grant free movement of workers, it could not be a part of the internal market. This ruled out the Norwegian model,[103] under which the UK would have left the EU but remained in the EEA, like Norway. Norway is a part of the internal market, but it cannot limit the number of migrant workers from the EU. The relationship between the UK and the EU would have to be more distant.

Ultimately, the UK and the EU ended up with a Trade and Cooperation Agreement that entered into force in 2021.[104] It facilitates trade and economic cooperation but does not come close to replicating a membership in the EU's internal market. The tension underlying much of the negotiations was the UK's desire to diverge freely from EU standards while maintaining access to the EU market, while the EU was only prepared to grant such access if the UK stuck to EU standards in fields such as environmental and social protection. The kinds of concerns about lightly regulated (UK) firms enjoying unfair advantages over their (continental) competitors that were discussed earlier in the chapter were a key element in the negotiations. The final agreement is a complex compromise seeking to balance the competing concerns.

In sum, economically the internal market makes the EU as a whole richer. Yet this has not proved enough on its own to legitimize integration. The Commission has sought to remedy this by concentrating on projects that can create tangible results which can be put on display—a prominent example from the recent past is the battle it has waged against mobile phone roaming charges. However, there is a concern that the internal market may serve to exacerbate social divisions within the Member States. This was observable in the UK referendum, where in particular the less well-off voted for Brexit. The likely result is disappointment. The UK has had to settle for a less ambitious trading relationship with the EU. The economic consequences of this may well overwhelm any benefits that the exclusion of cheap migrant labour might bring to unskilled British workers.[105]

[101] See S Weatherill, 'The Several Internal Markets' (2017) 36 *Yearbook of European Law* 125.

[102] See, however, Editorial Comments in (2019) 56 *Common Market Law Review* 1189 for an argument that the indivisibility of the four freedoms is a principle of EU law.

[103] See on the various models, eg J-C Piris, 'Which Options Would Be Available for the United Kingdom in the Case of a Withdrawal from the EU?' in PJ Birkinshaw and A Biondi (eds), *Britain Alone!* (Alphen aan den Rijn: Kluwer, 2016).

[104] OJ [2021] L149/10. For analysis, see eg P Craig, 'Brexit a Drama, the Endgame—Part II: Trade, Sovereignty and Control' (2021) 46 *European Law Review* 129. See also chapter 27.

[105] See already S Clarke, *A Brave New World: How Reduced Migration Could Affect Earnings, Employment and the Labour Market* (London: Resolution Foundation, 2016). For a comprehensive survey of the various economic predictions, see Tetlow and Stojanovic (n 52). At the time of writing, the 2025 estimate of the UK's Office for Budget Responsibility is that UK productivity will be 4 per cent lower and its trade 15 per cent lower than if it had remained in the EU; see https://obr.uk/forecasts-in-depth/the-economy-forecast/brexit-analysis/#assumptions.

4 The law of the internal market: the power to harmonize

In practice, the law needs to supply two things to establish the internal market. First, there needs to be rules on free movement. These are the subject of other chapters in this book.[106] Secondly, there needs to be a rule that allows the EU to legislate for internal market purposes. In the actual EU of today, there are a number of such rules. The most important among them is Article 114 TFEU.[107] This is the topic of the present section. It will discuss the extent of the power Article 114 TFEU gives to the EU, and the exceptions the same provision contains.[108]

4.1 The power

The wording of Article 114(1) TFEU is as follows:

> Save where otherwise provided in the Treaties, the following provisions shall apply for the achievement of the objectives set out in Article 26. The European Parliament and the Council shall, acting in accordance with the ordinary legislative procedure and after consulting the Economic and Social Committee, adopt the measures for the approximation of the provisions laid down by law, regulation or administrative action in Member States which have as their object the establishment and functioning of the internal market.

There are a number of points that can be made about this. The first three can be taken quickly. First, Article 114 TFEU is a residual provision. It can only be used if other legal bases are not available.[109] For example, Article 50 TFEU contains a specific legal basis for the right of establishment. Secondly, the procedure under Article 114 is the ordinary legislative procedure, which means majority voting in the Council. This was the key innovation of the SEA. However, the second paragraph of the same provision states that this does 'not apply to fiscal provisions, to those relating to the free movement of persons nor to those relating to the rights and interests of employed persons'. These matters were considered too sensitive by the Member States. Thirdly, Article 114 allows the EU to adopt 'measures'. This means that the legislature has the discretion to choose the legal instrument most suitable for the issue in hand; it is not bound to employ only directives, as is the case under a number of other legal bases.

Fourthly, the measures adopted must have as their object the establishment and functioning of the internal market,[110] as defined in Article 26 TFEU. Harmonization cannot be pursued for its own sake. The crucial question is how far this power reaches.[111] After all, almost everything has some kind of impact on the market. The extent of the power is particularly salient given that it operates under majority voting. In effect, Article 114 TFEU represents a bargain among the Member States: they gave up their vetoes, but only in the specific area of the internal market.

[106] See especially chapters 12–15. See R Schutze, '"Re-Constituting" the Internal Market: Towards a Common Law of International Trade?' (2020) 39 *Yearbook of European Law* 250 on the interplay between the harmonization powers and free movement rules.

[107] According to Art 4(2) TFEU, the internal market is a shared competence between the EU and the Member States.

[108] See on the issue of the choice of legal basis in the context of Art 114 TFEU, C Barnard, *The Substantive Law of the EU: The Four Freedoms* (8th edn, Oxford: Oxford University Press, 2025) ch 14.

[109] See eg Case C-533/03 *Commission v Council* [2006] ECR I-1025 for an illustration.

[110] See G Davies, 'Democracy and Legitimacy in the Shadow of Purposive Competence' (2015) 21 *European Law Journal* 2 for a critical examination.

[111] For a more recent exploration, see S Weatherill, 'The Competence to Harmonise and Its Limits' in Koutrakos and Snell (eds), *Research Handbook on the Law of the EU's Internal Market* (n 44).

By way of comparison, in the US the Commerce Clause of the Constitution, which gives the Congress the power 'to regulate commerce ... among the several states' has been used as the basis of very broad legislation, including the New Deal that was the response to the Great Depression of the 1930s and the Civil Rights Act of 1964. This federal legislative activity has been at the expense of the powers of the states. Between 1937 and 1995 the Supreme Court accepted all measures put forward by the Congress under the Commerce Clause, but more recently it has begun to exercise some control over the power, for example striking down the Gun-Free School Zones Act that made it a federal criminal offence to carry a firearm near a school. The Congress had adopted the Act on the basis of the power to regulate interstate commerce, but the Court found the nexus between commerce and the possession of firearms near schools too tenuous.[112] In other words, the power to regulate commerce can be interpreted as an almost unlimited legislative power; it depends on the attitude of the judiciary whether this is sustainable.[113]

The reach of Article 114 TFEU was confronted in the case of *Tobacco Advertising*.[114] This case is considered in detail in case study 11.2. The key points bear repeating. Article 114 does not provide a general power to regulate the economy. This would go against the very idea of the EU with limited powers. Instead, measures adopted under it must genuinely seek either to establish the internal market or to improve its functioning. This boils down to two things: either the measure must eliminate obstacles or it must deal with appreciable distortions of competition. As the Tobacco Advertising Directive on the facts did neither, the Court annulled it.

Tobacco Advertising sent an important signal. Article 114 TFEU was not without limits, and the Court was prepared to police them. However, it did not lead to a more general wave of successful litigation. The Court's attitude remains permissive to the EU institutions. Particularly instructive in this respect is the ruling in *Swedish Match*.[115] It concerned a Directive adopted under Article 114 that banned all tobacco for oral use, except tobacco for chewing or smoking. This ban included snus, a type of tobacco placed between lip and gum popular in Sweden. It was argued by Swedish Match that the Directive did not in fact contribute to the internal market: how could the ban of a product establish or improve the internal market? The Grand Chamber of the Court rejected the argument. It ruled that national laws concerning tobacco for oral use were developing in different directions, which was creating obstacles to trade. This justified action by the EU legislature, which could, if appropriate, even prohibit the marketing of a product. One possible way of explaining the ruling is that the Court upheld the ban of a particular type of product to allow the circulation of others. A directive might, for example, prohibit dangerous widget types so that only safe widgets remain on the market and can be traded freely. On the facts, this does not seem a convincing explanation, however. All oral tobacco products were banned, apart from smoking or chewing tobacco. It is not easy to see how this improved trade. When *Swedish Match* is looked at together with other cases decided after *Tobacco Advertising*, it seems that the practical limits of Article 114 are very wide indeed.[116] In fact, in the context of Treaty reform, the remit of Article 114 was singled out

[112] *United States v Lopez*, 514 US 549 (1995).

[113] See EA Young, 'Protecting Member State Autonomy in the European Union: Some Cautionary Tales from American Federalism' (2002) 77 *New York Law Review* 1612 for a comparison between the US and the EU.

[114] Case C-376/98 *Germany v European Parliament and Council* [2000] ECR I-8419.

[115] Case C-210/03 *Swedish Match* [2004] ECR I-11893.

[116] See D Wyatt, 'Community Competence to Regulate the Internal Market' in M Dougan and S Currie (eds), *50 Years of the European Treaties: Looking Back and Thinking Forward* (Oxford: Hart Publishing, 2009).

as a key question,[117] although in the end the Lisbon Treaty did not amend it. However, the fact that the Court has failed to police the competence limits of Article 114 TFEU strictly does not mean that there is no judicial control of harmonizing measures at all; in recent years the Court has begun to scrutinize vigorously the compliance of EU legislation with fundamental rights.[118]

Case study 11.2: Tobacco advertising

Can the EU ban tobacco advertising in Member States in order to achieve or improve the internal market, or would this go beyond the remit of Article 114 TFEU? Behind this question are important issues of principle: is the EU competent to regulate all economic activity, even against the objections of an individual Member State, given the majority voting under the provision? How far can the EU go in the name of the internal market in matters related to human health and other non-economic issues, given that the Treaty sets strict limits on its powers to regulate, for example, public health as such?

The idea of regulating tobacco advertising at the level of the EU has been around since 1984. However, it was only in 1998 that the EU legislature produced a Directive to tackle the issue generally.[119] Essentially the Directive banned all tobacco advertising. The legal basis selected was Article 114 TFEU. This meant that Germany, which opposed the Directive, could not veto it, but was outvoted. Germany, after losing the political battle, began a legal battle and challenged the validity of the Directive on a number of grounds, including the ground that it could not be validly adopted under Article 114 at all. This was not a surprise. Already in the legislative process it had been suggested that Article 352 TFEU, which requires unanimity in the Council, would be the correct legal basis; reportedly this was also the view of the Council Legal Services.[120]

The first argument that the Court confronted was that the Directive was in reality a health protection measure, not an internal market one, and that the Treaty specifically excluded any harmonization for the protection of human health. The Court acknowledged that the ban on health harmonization should not be circumvented. However, this does not mean that an internal market measure could not have any effect on health. In fact, health requirements have to be taken into account in all EU policies, and Article 114(3) expressly requires that a high level of human health protection be ensured. In other words, the Court explicitly recognized that in the internal market economic and non-economic issues are inextricably intertwined. When the market is regulated, this always impacts on other concerns; yet it does not make market regulation health regulation.

While the Court accepted that health reasons could even be 'decisive'[121] in an internal market directive, it did not accept that Article 114 TFEU gave the EU legislature a general power to regulate the market. Such a finding, said the Court, would be incompatible with the principle of conferred powers in Article 5 TEU. This was important. In the past, no one

[117] See the Laeken Declaration on the Future of the European Union, adopted by the European Council on 15 December 2001.

[118] See in particular Case C-293/12 *Digital Rights Ireland*, EU:C:2014:238, discussed in chapter 9.

[119] European Parliament and Council Directive 98/43/EC on the approximation of the laws, regulations and administrative provisions of the Member States relating to the advertising and sponsorship of tobacco products (OJ [1998] L213/9).

[120] See para 17 of the Opinion of AG Fennelly in *Tobacco Advertising* (n 114).

[121] *Tobacco Advertising* (n 114) para 88. In the same vein, the Court decided in Case C-482/17 *Czech Republic v European Parliament and Council*, EU:C:2019:1035 that the EU was entitled to amend an earlier harmonizing measure to increase further the protection of interests such as safety.

had been particularly concerned about the exact limits of the EU's powers. This was because the legislative process had operated under unanimity. When only measures that all Member States supported could pass, the precise limitations of EU competences had seemed an insignificant issue, and certainly no Member State had a reason to bring an action. With the abolition of national vetoes this changed. Member States that could no longer exercise complete control over the EU's political process suddenly became much more conscious of the legal limits.[122] This was something national courts had also picked up on.[123] In its ruling the Court responded.

Instead of a general power to regulate the economy, the Court continued, Article 114 TFEU provided two specific powers. First is the competence to establish the internal market, in other words to eliminate obstacles to free movement. The second is the competence to improve the functioning of the internal market, in other words to eliminate distortions of competition. The question to decide was whether the Directive did either of these things.

Elimination of obstacles is a familiar concept in internal market law. What exactly is an obstacle to one of the four freedoms is the central issue of EU economic law and is discussed elsewhere in the book.[124] The key point to note here is that the Court created a direct linkage between Article 114 TFEU and provisions such as Article 34 TFEU on free movement of goods: the wider the reading of the notion of obstacle, the wider the power to harmonize. In *Tobacco Advertising*, the Court added a couple of further points. Article 114 can be used to prevent the emergence of future obstacles to trade that could arise if national laws developed in different directions. It is not only for the elimination of existing barriers. However, the mere finding of disparities between national laws and an abstract risk of obstacles is not sufficient to justify the use of Article 114, and if it is future obstacles that are targeted, their emergence must be likely. On the facts, there was indeed a danger that barriers could arise, for example for the free movement of magazines or newspapers. A newspaper including tobacco advertisements legal in one country could be denied access into the market of another country that banned such advertisements. However, the Directive went much further than this. It also banned things such as umbrellas or ashtrays containing the logo of a tobacco company, and advertisements in cinemas. This did not facilitate trade. The Directive also failed to provide that products complying with it could move freely. Instead, Member States remained free to ban even those few goods that did conform to it.

For distortions of competition, the Court emphasized that only the elimination of appreciable distortions could justify recourse to Article 114 TFEU. Otherwise, the powers of the EU legislature would in practice be unlimited. After all, any differences between national rules can be said to affect conditions of competition at least indirectly. The Court accepted that differences between the laws of Member States on tobacco advertising could in certain circumstances indeed distort competition appreciably. For example, the organizers of a car race might decide to move the event to a country where sponsorship by tobacco companies was legal. However, the Directive was not limited to these kinds of issues but went much further. In this context, the argument that advertising agencies established in countries with the fewest restrictions had a competitive advantage was rejected by the Court. While such companies might enjoy increased profits, the effects were remote and indirect, and could not be deemed appreciable.

[122] JHH Weiler, *The Constitution of Europe: 'Do the New Clothes Have an Emperor?' and Other Essays on European Integration* (Cambridge: Cambridge University Press, 1999) 39–74.

[123] *Brunner* [1994] 1 CMLR 57.

[124] See further chapters 13 and 15.

The result was that the Tobacco Advertising Directive was annulled by the Court. For the first time, a general EU legislative measure was struck down for a lack of competence. This was not the end, however. A few years later, a new Directive was adopted.[125] It was much more closely tailored to the internal market concerns.[126] Again, Germany challenged it. This time the Grand Chamber of the Court, noting the more limited reach of the second Directive, allowed it to stand.[127] In other words, the EU can regulate those aspects of tobacco advertising that can have implications for free movement or lead to real distortions of competition, but it cannot just ban all tobacco advertising in the Member States in the name of the internal market.[128]

The fifth point about Article 114(1) TFEU is that it only gives the power for 'the approximation of the provisions laid down by law, regulation or administrative action in Member States'. In other words, under the provision the EU can bring national laws closer to each other, to harmonize. It does not give the EU the competence to create something new that is unrelated to pre-existing[129] or anticipated[130] national laws. Thus, national trademark laws could be harmonized under Article 114, but a new EU-wide trademark could not be established using it.[131] While national company laws were approximated using internal market powers, a new European public limited company form, Societas Europaea, was based on Article 352 TFEU.[132]

The issue may resurface in the context of the so-called 28th Regime Initiative.[133] The idea is to create an EU legal framework for innovative companies. This would not replace national laws, but would offer an option that companies could select instead of complying with the rules of one of the Member States. It is hoped that this initiative could provide a major boost for the EU's competitiveness. However, much may depend on whether the planned legal regime can be adopted on the basis of Article 114, or requires the use of Article 352 TFEU. It is feared that in the latter case unanimous decision-making could lead to delays and compromises that water down the initiative.

The Court had to confront the precise limits of the requirement of approximation in *ENISA*.[134] The EU legislature had established ENISA, the European Network and Information Security Agency, under Article 114 TFEU. This followed a series of earlier directives that regulated electronic communication networks and services. The role of the agency was to help the Commission and the Member States on network and information security matters, ensuring the smooth functioning of the internal market.

[125] European Parliament and Council Directive 2003/33/EC on the approximation of the laws, regulations and administrative provisions of the Member States relating to the advertising and sponsorship of tobacco products (OJ [2003] L152/16).

[126] See generally S Weatherill, 'The Limits of Legislative Harmonization Ten Years after *Tobacco Advertising*: How the Court's Case Law Has Become a "Drafting Guide"' (2011) 12 *German Law Journal* 827.

[127] Case C-380/03 *Germany v European Parliament and Council* [2006] ECR I-11573.

[128] Tobacco-related cases have continued to emerge, eg as unsuccessful challenges to Directive 2014/40/EU on the manufacture, presentation and sale of tobacco and related products (OJ [2014] L127/1), which bans menthol cigarettes, imposes limitations on e-cigarettes, and sets out requirements for health warnings etc on cigarette packets.

[129] Case C-436/03 *European Parliament v Council* [2006] ECR I-3733, para 44.

[130] Case C-58/08 *Vodafone* [2010] ECR I-4999, which adopts a particularly permissive approach.

[131] Opinion 1/94 [1994] ECR I-5267, para 59.

[132] Council Regulation (EC) No 2157/2001 on the Statute for a European company (OJ [2001] L294/1).

[133] See eg Commission, 'A Competitiveness Compass for the EU', COM(2025) 30 final, 4.

[134] Case C-217/04 *UK v European Parliament and Council* [2006] ECR I-3789. See also eg Case C-66/04 *UK v European Parliament and Council* [2005] ECR I-10553 (smoke flavourings).

Its tasks included the identification of risks, the development of common methodologies for the prevention of security issues, the promotion of the exchange of best practice, and generally enhancing cooperation in the area of network and information security. The UK argued that Article 114 only allowed the harmonization of national laws, not the creation of new EU bodies. The test in the view of the UK was whether the result of the measure could be achieved if all Member States produced identical laws. The UK argued that since the establishment of ENISA was beyond the capacity of individual Member States, it did not qualify as a harmonizing measure. The Grand Chamber of the Court, disagreeing with Advocate General Kokott, held that the regulation setting up the agency was valid. The Court reasoned that the legislature was entitled to establish a body to contribute to the harmonization process when the adoption of various supporting measures would help the uniform implementation and application of other harmonizing measures. However, the tasks of such a body had to be closely related to the previous EU internal market legislation. On the facts, the Court decided that this was the case.

The ruling in *ENISA* is important. Without it, the creation of new agencies would have to be based on the cumbersome Article 352 TFEU, which requires unanimity.[135] The EU legislature has taken advantage of the relatively permissive attitude of the Court.[136] In the context of the financial crisis that began in 2007, it has established a set of important new financial supervisory authorities to deal with banks, securities and markets, and insurers and occupational pension providers. While ENISA's tasks concerned advice and cooperation, the European supervisory authorities have much wider powers, including the power to impose binding decisions.[137] Again, a legal challenge proved unsuccessful, with the Court holding that Article 114 TFEU could confer on the European Securities and Markets Authority (ESMA) the power to take binding measures directed at specific natural or legal persons and overriding national decisions.[138]

4.2 **The exceptions**

So far, this section has discussed the power that Article 114 TFEU gives the EU. We finally turn to the qualifications contained in the same Article.[139] Essentially, these qualifications represent a compromise. The countries with high standards in matters such as health and safety or the environment were concerned that under majority voting Article 114 could result in the lowering of the level of protection. The price for the acceptance of majority voting was a commitment to high standards, incorporated into Article 114(3), and possibilities for derogation, now found in paragraphs 4 to 10.

Article 114(4) TFEU provides a derogation for *pre-existing* national rules. It allows a Member State to maintain a higher level of protection than envisaged in a harmonization measure. This is subject to two qualifications. Only major needs listed in Article 36 TFEU or the protection of the environment or the working environment can justify a derogation, and the Commission must be notified. Article 114(5) provides a derogation for *new* national rules that have been adopted after harmonization. Again, a number of

[135] See on 'agencification', HCH Hofmann 'European Regulatory Union? The Role of Agencies and Standards' in Koutrakos and Snell (eds), *Research Handbook on the Law of the EU's Internal Market* (n 44).

[136] For another example, see Commission Proposal for a Regulation of the European Parliament and of the Council on a Common European Sales Law, COM(2011) 635 final.

[137] See E Fahey, 'Does the Emperor have Financial Crisis Clothes? Reflections on the Legal Basis of the European Banking Authority' (2011) 74 *Modern Law Review* 581.

[138] Case C-270/12 *UK v European Parliament and Council*, EU:C:2014:18. Specifically, the relevant regulation gave ESMA the power to prohibit the short selling of securities.

[139] See generally I Maletić, 'Derogations from the Regulation of Free Movement: Article 114 TFEU' in Koutrakos and Snell (eds), *Research Handbook on the Law of the EU's Internal Market* (n 44).

conditions, which are cumulative, need to be fulfilled.[140] There needs to be new scientific evidence. The evidence must relate to the environment or the working environment. There must be a problem that is specific to the relevant Member State and that has arisen after harmonization. Again, the Commission must be notified. Article 114(6) sets out the procedure that the Commission must follow when it receives a notification. In most cases it will have six months to decide whether to approve or reject the national measure. The criterion is whether the national measure is a means of arbitrary discrimination or a disguised restriction on trade between Member States and whether it constitutes an obstacle to the functioning of the internal market. It is important to note that the national rule is unenforceable against an individual relying on the direct effect of an EU harmonizing measure until Commission approval has been gained.[141] In other words, the Commission decision has a constitutive effect. If recourse to a derogation proves justified, the Commission is under an obligation to consider whether the existing harmonization measures need to be adapted or new ones adopted. In this way, the experiences of individual Member States can serve to inform EU harmonization.

The introduction of derogations to Article 114 TFEU was originally met with grave concern.[142] The worry was that Member States would routinely turn to them, frustrating the whole objective of Article 114. These fears have not materialized.[143] It seems that the Member States have been committed to the internal market, the standards of protection have generally been sufficiently high, and the onerous conditions for the derogations have discouraged reliance on them.

To sum up, Article 114 TFEU gives the Union the crucial power to harmonize in the name of the internal market. Its use does not require unanimity. In practice, it has been utilized frequently. The power is a wide one, but not without limits. In particular, it does not give the EU legislature a general competence to regulate the economy, only the competence to deal with obstacles or appreciable distortions of competition. It is only available for approximation, not for the creation of things such as new EU intellectual property rights or company forms unrelated to national laws. It is also subject to tightly circumscribed derogations that made the majority voting palatable for high-standard countries.

5 The law of the internal market: the types of harmonization

The final issue to be addressed in this chapter concerns the types of harmonization employed by the EU, and their legal implications. What kinds of measures are adopted under Article 114 TFEU and under other internal market legal bases? Various typologies could be offered. The present section concentrates on total and minimum harmonization,[144] which form the two paradigm cases,[145] and which represent quite different approaches.

[140] See eg Joined Cases C-439/05 and 454/05 P *Land Oberösterreich* [2007] ECR I-7141.

[141] Case C-319/97 *Kortas* [1999] ECR I-3143. However, if the Commission fails to adopt a decision within the time limit, the national provisions are deemed to have been approved.

[142] See eg P Pescatore, 'Some Critical Remarks on the "Single European Act"' (1987) 24 *Common Market Law Review* 9.

[143] See eg Barnard, *The Substantive Law of the EU* (n 108) ch 14.

[144] Similarly, M Dougan, 'Minimum Harmonization and the Internal Market' (2000) 37 *Common Market Law Review* 853.

[145] An analytically more precise typology would be to contrast total with partial harmonization, and maximum with minimum harmonization, based on a distinction between the coverage and the level of regulation. See also M Klamert, 'What We Talk About When We Talk About Harmonisation' (2015) 17 *Cambridge Yearbook of European Legal Studies* 360, 362. However, in practice, total and maximum harmonization entail similar legal consequences, as do partial and minimum harmonization.

Total harmonization was the predominant method of approximation in the early years of the EU, and is still employed today. In fact, as discussed in section 3.2, in some areas it has enjoyed something of a renaissance.[146] Total harmonization takes place when an EU measure, such as a directive, regulates something exhaustively, not leaving any room for divergent rules of the Member States. For example, a directive on widgets could lay down all the features and characteristics that widgets must comply with. Given that it is a directive, Member States would have to transpose its contents into their national law. However, they would not be entitled to add further conditions for widgets to meet.[147] In other words, the directive has pre-empted Member State activity; it has occupied the field.

Total harmonization has another important legal consequence: a national rule that complies with an EU measure totally harmonizing something is no longer open to challenge on the basis of the four freedoms of the Treaty.[148] The Member State can defend its national law against such a challenge by simply saying that the law is fully in line with the EU measure. Any challenge would have to demonstrate that the law somehow fails to respect the relevant EU measure.

Nevertheless, an EU measure harmonizing an area totally is not immune to legal scrutiny. A challenge could be brought on the grounds that the EU measure itself violates some higher-ranking rule or principle of EU law. However, the crucial difference is that the question would be whether the EU measure violates EU law, not whether a national measure violates EU law. In these kinds of circumstances, the Court of Justice has traditionally taken a hands-off attitude and only struck down EU measures if they manifestly infringe the Treaty.[149]

Minimum harmonization sets the floor below which no Member State may go, but leaves them free to adopt more demanding rules. In this way, it is respectful of the national diversity that total harmonization suppresses. For example, the widget directive could just specify the minimum safety features that every widget must at the very least meet, but give the Member States the option to impose more stringent requirements. Minimum harmonization has often been used in the context of issues such as the protection of the environment or consumers, where some Member States have wished to impose or maintain tougher rules than the others.

A national law that goes beyond the requirements of the minimum harmonization measure would not enjoy immunity from the Treaty. Rather, any national rule would be open to challenge on the ground that it violates a Treaty free movement provision.[150] In this way, the Treaty forms the ceiling above which the Member States are not permitted to go. The mere fact that, say, a directive has authorized Member States to adopt more stringent rules on widgets, does not mean that those rules acquire immunity from the four freedoms if they are applied in a cross-border context.

Unfortunately, it is not necessarily easy in practice to decide whether a particular EU act seeks to bring about total harmonization or to leave Member States free to adopt stricter rules or to rely on grounds not listed in the measure. For example, the Services Directive,[151] which is an important piece of EU legislation that was designed to improve

[146] See also eg European Parliament and Council Directive 2011/83/EU on consumer rights (OJ [2011] L304/64) and European Parliament and Council Directive 2019/771/EU on certain aspects concerning contracts for the sale of goods (OJ [2019] L136/28).

[147] See eg Case 5/77 *Tedeschi* [1977] ECR 1555.

[148] See eg Case C-324/99 *DaimlerChrysler* [2001] ECR I-9897.

[149] See eg Case C-233/94 *Germany v European Parliament and Council* [1997] ECR I-2405.

[150] See eg Case C-382/87 *Buet* [1989] ECR 1235.

[151] European Parliament and Council Directive 2006/123/EC on services in the internal market (OJ [2006] L376/36).

the operation of the single market in services, lists a number of grounds that Member States may use to limit service provision. However, there was a debate about whether these are the only grounds Member States can still rely on, which would correspond with the idea of total harmonization, or whether they are still free to invoke other reasons as well.[152] Ultimately, the matter boils down to the interpretation of the relevant harmonization measure,[153] and this may not always be an easy task. In fact, in the context of the Services Directive the Court chose to dodge the issue.[154]

To sum up, the EU legislative process produces different types of measures; the two paradigm cases are total and minimum harmonization. The legal consequences of the different types of harmonization vary. Member State compliance with a measure of total harmonization means that it cannot be criticized on the basis of the four freedoms, while a Member State going beyond the requirements of minimum harmonization must ensure that its national law is in line with the Treaty free movement rules.

6 **Conclusion**

The internal market has been at the heart of the European integration project from the beginning. However, there is no consensus on its fundamental nature and it has changed over time. Three possible ideal models can be distinguished: host country control, harmonized model, and home country control, based on the allocation of legislative power. The models represent fundamentally different philosophies of market integration, and entail different consequences for sovereignty, the balance of legislative and judicial powers, the protection of public policy interests, and democracy. In the historical experience of the EU, no model has been adopted in a perfect form. Nevertheless, when the integration moved from the original common market model to single market it did take a step towards the home country model and away from the harmonized model. The single market paradigm has not proven stable. In practice, the ideas of mutual recognition and regulatory competition have encountered resistance and created only limited market integration. It is possible that the internal market is shifting towards an economic union paradigm.

Whatever the model or the paradigm of the internal market, legally two things are needed: there need to be rules on free movement and a conferral of legislative power to the EU. The latter was the subject of this chapter. The key provision is Article 114 TFEU that gives the EU the competence to harmonize in order to achieve or improve the internal market. This is a broad power but not without its limits. The Court of Justice has found that it allows the EU legislature to deal with obstacles to trade and with appreciable distortions of competition. Another limit is that the power is there for the approximation of national rules, not for the creation of new free-standing EU rights or things unrelated to Member State laws. The exact contours of this are subject to an important debate. It needs to be noted that the harmonization that the EU engages in can take different forms. Particularly important types are total and minimum harmonization, which entail different legal consequences.

152 See eg C Barnard, 'Unravelling the Services Directive' (2008) 45 *Common Market Law Review* 323, 367.

153 See eg Case 148/78 *Ratti* [1979] ECR 1629.

154 Case C-179/14 *Commission v Hungary*, EU:C:2016:108, para 116.

Further reading

F Amtenbrink et al (eds), *The Internal Market and the Future of European Integration* (Cambridge: Cambridge University Press, 2019)

L Azoulai, 'The Complex Weave of Harmonization' in D Chalmers and A Arnull (eds), *The Oxford Handbook of European Union Law* (Oxford: Oxford University Press, 2015)

C Barnard, *The Substantive Law of the EU: The Four Freedoms* (8th edn, Oxford: Oxford University Press, 2025)

C Barnard and J Scott (eds), *The Law of the Single European Market: Unpacking the Premises* (Oxford: Hart Publishing, 2002)

G Davies, 'Democracy and Legitimacy in the Shadow of Purposive Competence' (2015) 21 *European Law Journal* 2

M Dougan, 'Minimum Harmonization and the Internal Market' (2000) 37 *Common Market Law Review* 853

N Dunne, 'Liberalisation and the Pursuit of the Internal Market' (2018) 43 *European Law Review* 803

M Egan, 'Single Market' in E Jones, A Menon, and S Weatherill (eds), *The Oxford Handbook of the European Union* (Oxford: Oxford University Press, 2012)

S Garben and I Govaere (eds), *The Internal Market 2.0* (Oxford: Hart Publishing, 2020)

A Herranz-Surrallés, C Damro, and S Eckert, 'The Geoeconomic Turn of the Single European Market? Conceptual Challenges and Empirical Trends' (2024) 62 *Journal of Common Market Studies* 919

M Klamert, 'What We Talk About When We Talk About Harmonisation' (2015) 17 *Cambridge Yearbook of European Legal Studies* 360

P Koutrakos and J Snell (eds), *Research Handbook on the Law of the EU's Internal Market* (Cheltenham: Edward Elgar, 2017)

I Maletić, *The Law and Policy of Harmonisation in Europe's Internal Market* (Cheltenham: Edward Elgar, 2013)

M Poiares Maduro, *We the Court: The European Court of Justice and the European Economic Constitution: A Critical Reading of Article 30 of the EC Treaty* (Oxford: Hart Publishing, 1998)

J Snell, 'Varieties of Capitalism and the Limits of European Economic Integration' (2010–11) 13 *Cambridge Yearbook of European Legal Studies* 415

S Weatherill, *The Internal Market as a Legal Concept* (Oxford: Oxford University Press, 2017)

S Weatherill, 'The Several Internal Markets' (2017) 36 *Yearbook of European Law* 125

S Weatherill, 'Maximum versus Minimum Harmonization: Choosing between Unity and Diversity in the Search for the Soul of the Internal Market' in N Nic Shuibhne and LW Gormley (eds), *From Single Market to Economic Union: Essays in Memory of John A Usher* (Oxford: Oxford University Press, 2012)

S Weatherill, 'The Limits of Legislative Harmonization Ten Years after *Tobacco Advertising*: How the Court's Case Law Has Become a "Drafting Guide"' (2011) 12 *German Law Journal* 827

12

Free movement of goods

Martín Martínez Navarro

1 Introduction

The aim of the internal market in goods is to enable European manufacturers to sell the same product in all Member States, thereby fostering competition, achieving economies of scale, and creating greater prosperity throughout the Union. The aims of the internal market, however, go beyond purely economic considerations, as its original seeds can be traced back to the Schuman Declaration:

> Europe will not be made all at once, or according to a single plan. It will be built through concrete achievements which first create a de facto solidarity.[1]

The goal of such de facto solidarity was to make war in Europe 'not merely unthinkable, but materially impossible'.

The Treaty of Rome of 1957 established the 'common market'.[2] In its seminal judgment in *Gaston Schul*, the Court held:

[1] Declaration by Robert Schuman, Foreign Affairs Minister of France, of 9 May 1950.

[2] The 'common market', the 'single market', and now the 'internal market' appear to be largely interchangeable concepts, although for some scholars they may differ; see chapter 11.

> The concept of a common market as defined by the Court in a consistent line of decisions involves the elimination of all obstacles to intra-Community trade in order to merge the national markets into a single market bringing about conditions as close as possible to those of a genuine internal market.[3]

At present, Article 3(3) TEU provides: 'The Union shall establish an internal market.' The internal market is defined in Article 26(2) TFEU[4] as follows:

> The internal market shall comprise an area without internal frontiers in which the free movement of goods, persons, services and capital is ensured in accordance with the provisions of the Treaties.

As a result, the Court frequently finds national measures to be contrary to the TFEU, even though they have, of course, been enacted by democratically elected governments. By signing and ratifying the various successive Treaties, the Member States have given their blessing to this. Nevertheless, it can sometimes raise the hackles of Member States or public opinion—as where the Germans were told that their centuries-old Purity Law was unlawful so that the sale of drinks as 'beer' had to be allowed even if they contained such proscribed ingredients as rice or maize, which were commonly used for making beer in other Member States.[5] Italian national pride suffered a similar blow when the Court ruled that their country's ban on the sale of pasta containing soft wheat was in breach of Article 34 TFEU.[6] The Member States tolerate such occasional upsets for the simple reason that they are outweighed by the benefits, namely allowing goods made in their own territory free access to the markets in the other Member States (and the States of the European Economic Area (EEA)).

Despite the impressive achievements of the internal market, the recent Letta and Draghi reports make clear that there is still room for improvement.[7]

This chapter will consider the Treaty provisions on the free movement of goods: the so-called *non-fiscal* rules (or non-tariff barriers) as well as the *fiscal* rules on customs duties and discriminatory internal taxation. Together these rules form the basis of the EU's customs union.

2 The customs union

2.1 The concept of a customs union

By virtue of Article 28(1) TFEU, the EU constitutes a customs union covering all trade in goods. According to a widely received definition, a customs union, in contrast to a free trade area, does not merely involve liberalization of trade between the parties; it

[3] Case 15/81 *Gaston Schul* [1982] ECR 1409, para 33. See further chapter 11.

[4] This provision was first introduced into the Treaties, albeit in a slightly different form, by the Single European Act in 1987.

[5] Case 178/84 *Commission v Germany* ('*Beer*') [1987] ECR 1227.

[6] Case 90/86 *Zoni* [1988] ECR 4285.

[7] Letta's report, 'Much more than a market', of 2024 recommends the prioritization of regulations to fully harmonize the internal market rules (instead of relying on minimum harmonization directives) and points out that energy markets are insufficiently integrated. Draghi's report, 'The future of European competitiveness', of 2024 suggests that the remaining barriers to trade within the internal market may cost around 10 per cent of potential growth in GDP.

also entails the establishment of uniform rules for goods coming from third countries.[8] Consequently, a customs union has an *external* and an *internal* dimension.

The *external* dimension of the EU as a customs union is reflected in the adoption of uniform common rules which apply to products originating from third countries: a common customs tariff (Article 31 TFEU) and the common commercial policy in trade with third countries (Article 207 TFEU). These matters fall outside the scope of the present chapter, which focuses instead on the *internal* dimension of the customs union.

The establishment of the customs union involves the prohibition of the following *internal* barriers to trade in goods between Member States:

(a) customs duties and charges of equivalent effect or CEEs (Article 30 TFEU);

(b) quantitative restrictions and measures of equivalent effect or MEEs (Articles 34 to 36 TFEU); and

(c) discriminatory and protective internal taxation (Article 110 TFEU).

Although the latter provision is not part of the Title of the TFEU relating to the internal market, it has in practice become assimilated to it. All these provisions are directly effective.[9]

Articles 30 and 110 apply to fiscal rules (ie an obligation to pay a sum of money), Articles 34 to 36 apply to non-fiscal rules (ie an obligation to comply with other types of requirement).

The counterpart to these prohibitions is a vast body of EU legislation harmonizing national laws so as to enable goods to flow more freely between Member States. That legislation will be considered in chapters 11, 21, and 23.

2.2 **Goods originating in a Member State and goods in free circulation**

By definition, the provisions on free movement apply to goods originating in any Member State. For good measure, this is stated explicitly in Article 28(2) TFEU. The same paragraph also establishes that those provisions extend to products coming from third countries which are in free circulation in the Member States; that is the necessary consequence of the fact that the EU is a customs union. The same principle applies to Article 110 TFEU, although this is not spelt out anywhere in the Treaty.[10]

Pursuant to Article 29 TFEU, products originating in a third country are considered to be in free circulation if the import formalities have been complied with and any customs duties due have been levied in a Member State, unless they have benefited from a total or partial drawback. In practice, this simply means that third-country goods must have been cleared through customs, whether or not customs duties have actually been paid.[11]

In *Donckerwolcke*, it was held that goods originating in third countries and placed in free circulation 'are definitively and wholly assimilated to products originating in Member States'.[12] Consequently, the free movement rules are applicable without distinction to goods originating in the EU and to those which have been put in free circulation in

[8] Opinion of the Permanent Court of International Justice of 1931 in the 'customs system between Germany and Austria', Compendium of Consultative Decrees, Directives and Opinions, Series A–B, no 41, p 51, and Art XXIV(8)(A) of the GATT 1947. See also Case C-125/94 *Aprile* [1995] ECR I-2919, para 32 and Case C-126/94 *Cadi Surgelés* [1996] ECR I-5647, para 14.

[9] Case 33/76 *Rewe-Zentralfinanz* [1976] ECR 1989, para 5 (Art 30); Case 74/76 *Iannelli v Meroni* [1977] ECR 557 (Art 34 TFEU); Case 83/78 *Redmond* [1978] ECR 2347 (Arts 34 and 35); and Case 7/65 *Lütticke* [1966] ECR 293 (Art 110).

[10] Case 193/85 *Co-Frutta* [1987] ECR 2085, paras 24–29.

[11] The customs authorities may allow payment of customs duties to be deferred: Arts 105, 108–114, 195, and 201 of Regulation 952/2013 laying down the Union Customs Code (OJ [2013] L269/1).

[12] Case 41/76 *Donckerwolcke* [1976] ECR 1921, para 17.

one Member State.[13] Thus a consignment of widgets from the US which is cleared through customs in Antwerp (Belgium) is in free circulation in that Member State, and is assimilated to Belgian goods for the purposes of Articles 30, 34 to 36, and 110. These widgets can subsequently move freely to other Member States. A particularly clear illustration of this principle is to be found in *Commission v Ireland*, where it was held that the defendant State (Ireland) had infringed Article 34 TFEU by imposing an import licensing system for potatoes originating in Cyprus (which was then outside the EU) but in free circulation in the UK (which was then in the EU).[14]

3 The meaning of 'goods'

The English version of the TFEU uses the terms 'goods' (eg Article 28(1)) and 'products' (eg Articles 28(2) and 29). Although several other language versions also employ two different words, they plainly bear the same meaning in this context. What is more, Articles 34 and 35 TFEU speak of 'imports' and 'exports' respectively without referring to 'goods' or 'products'; but there is no doubt whatsoever that imports and exports of *goods* are meant.

The *locus classicus* is *Commission v Italy*, where the Court defined 'goods' to mean 'products which can be valued in money and which are capable, as such, of forming the subject of commercial transactions'.[15] On this basis, it held that works of art constituted goods, rejecting Italy's contention that 'goods' meant only 'ordinary merchandise'. Had the Court accepted Italy's position, restrictions on trade in works of art would have fallen outside the Treaty altogether, which would have been unthinkable.[16] In any case, that does not prevent Member States from imposing restrictions on the free movement of works of art under certain conditions.

The definition in *Commission v Italy* is not exhaustive.[17] For instance, waste is to be regarded as goods, whether or not it has any intrinsic commercial value.[18] The analysis of the case law suggests that goods are normally tangible, perhaps with the exception of electricity, which has also been held to constitute goods.[19] Finally, human corpses and body parts arguably fall within this concept as well.[20]

On the other hand, transactions covered by the other three fundamental freedoms do not relate to goods. Thus, broadcasting is a service, not a product,[21] as is the operation of a lottery.[22] The same applies to intangibles other than electricity.[23] Similarly, coins and banknotes do not constitute goods, provided that they are still legal tender somewhere in the world.[24]

[13] Ibid, para 18.

[14] Case 288/83 *Commission v Ireland* [1985] ECR 1761; see also Case C-216/01 *Budejovický Budvar* [2003] ECR I-13617, para 95.

[15] Case 7/68 *Commission v Italy* ('*Works of art*') [1968] ECR 423, 428.

[16] Subsequently, the Court held that the Treaty aims to 'ensure that all economic activity falls within the scope of the four freedoms' (Case C-452/04 *Fidium Finanz* [2006] ECR I-9521, para 32).

[17] AG Fennelly in Case C-97/98 *Jägerskiöld* [1999] ECR I-7319, 7328.

[18] Case C-2/90 *Commission v Belgium* ('*Walloon waste*') [1992] ECR I-4431.

[19] Case C-393/92 *Almelo* [1994] ECR I-1477. See AG Fennelly's comment in *Jägerskiöld* (n 17) para 20: 'To my mind, electricity must be regarded as a specific case, perhaps justifiable by virtue of its function as an energy source and, therefore, in competition with gas and oil.'

[20] See generally Case C-203/99 *Veedfald* [2000] ECR I-3569. However, this does not mean that no restrictions can be imposed.

[21] Case 155/73 *Sacchi* [1974] ECR 409 and Case 52/79 *Debauve* [1980] ECR 833.

[22] Case C-124/97 *Läärä* [1999] ECR I-6067.

[23] See *Jägerskiöld* (n 17) (concerning fishing rights and permits).

[24] Case 7/78 *Thompson* [1978] ECR 2247 (coins) and Case C-358/93 *Bordessa* [1995] ECR I-361 (banknotes). See further chapter 15.

4 Nationality and residence

The Treaty provisions considered in this chapter apply regardless of the nationality of the trader,[25] or the purchaser. Similarly, the residence of the legal and natural persons involved is irrelevant. The only relevant criteria are the EU origin of the goods and, if they originate in a third country, whether they have been put into free circulation in the EU. In this regard, the free movement of goods differs from the other fundamental freedoms (considered in chapters 13 to 16) for which nationality and/or residence are relevant factors.

5 Interstate element, internal borders, and purely national situations

According to the traditional approach, the rules on the free movement of goods do not cover situations which are internal to a Member State; they require an interstate element.[26] That approach was based on the text of Articles 28(1), 30, 34, 35, and 110 TFEU, which refer explicitly to Member States. Thus, the factor which triggered the application of the prohibition of customs duties and CEEs, as well as quantitative restrictions and MEEs, was the crossing of a border *between* Member States. By the same token, reverse discrimination (which consists of a Member State treating its own domestic products less favourably than imports) was also thought to fall outside the scope of the Treaty.[27]

However, subsequent case law indicates that the free movement rules may be invoked to eliminate internal borders. For instance, the imposition of a charge on a good crossing an internal border has been regarded as a CEE under Article 30. In *Lancry*,[28] certain French overseas territories imposed charges on 'imports' of whatever provenance, including continental France. Relying on a teleological interpretation, the Court held that a charge levied at a regional border undermines the unity of the customs union and creates an obstacle to the free movement of goods as serious as a charge levied at a national border. The same rationale underpinned *Carbonati Apuani*,[29] where the local authorities of Carrara (Italy) imposed a charge on marble transported from the town towards any other part of Italy or the EU. The Court stated that the Treaty defines the internal market as an area without internal frontiers, without drawing any distinction between interstate frontiers and frontiers within a State.

Similarly, as regards MEEs, the more recent case law suggests that traders in domestic products may rely on a breach of Article 34, even if all the facts of the specific case are confined to the territory of a single Member State.[30]

The evolution of the case law indicates that the circumstances in which a situation can be considered as being purely internal for the purposes of the EU free movement rules on goods have become very limited in practice.[31]

[25] Case 2/69 *Sociaal Fonds voor de Diamantarbeiders* ('*Diamonds*') [1969] ECR 211, paras 24–26 (Art 30 TFEU); Case C-402/09 *Tatu* [2011] ECR I-2711, para 36 (Art 110 TFEU).

[26] See Case 314/81 *Waterkeyn* [1982] ECR 4337; Case 286/81 *Oosthoek* [1982] ECR 4575; and Case 355/85 *Cognet* [1986] ECR 3231.

[27] Opinion of AG Jacobs in Case C-321/94, *Pistre* [1997] ECR I-2343, para 35.

[28] Case C-363/93 *Lancry* [1994] ECR I-3957, paras 25ff.

[29] Case C-72/03 *Carbonati Apuani* [2004] ECR I-8027, para 23.

[30] See Case C-321/94 *Pistre* [1997] ECR I-2343, paras 41ff and Case C-448/98 *Guimont* [2000] ECR I-10663, paras 13ff, where the Court observed that the contested measures could apply at least potentially to intra-Union trade.

[31] See also chapter 13.

6 Entities bound by the free movement of goods rules

Having examined issues pertaining to the material and territorial scope of application of the rules on free movement of goods, we need to consider now their personal scope of application: against whom can those rules be invoked? The straightforward answer is that, first and foremost, Member States are bound by the rules on free movement, which have vertical direct effect.[32] That includes the legislative, the executive, and even the judicial branch of government.[33] It also covers all levels of government, including national, regional, and local authorities.[34] The *Buy Irish* case shows that actions undertaken by bodies set up, directed, and/or financed by the public authorities may trigger the application of the rules on free movement of goods (even where they are non-binding, such as a promotional campaign).[35] Furthermore, the rules on free movement of goods can be clearly invoked against professional bodies, which may enjoy an explicit or implicit delegation of powers from public authorities to regulate the exercise of a profession.[36]

Although it is questionable whether the provisions on free movement of goods may be invoked against the acts of individuals or strictly private parties (horizontal direct effect),[37] it is possible to challenge an omission and an implicit authorization by public authorities in connection with the acts of private parties, as the *Strawberries* case[38] and *Schmidberger*[39] illustrate. Finally, *AGM-COS.MET* provides guidance as to the dividing line between the acts of officials in their public capacity, which are attributable to the State, and those in their private capacity.[40]

7 Quantitative restrictions and measures of equivalent effect

According to Article 34 TFEU, quantitative restrictions (QRs) and MEEs on imports between Member States are prohibited. Article 35 TFEU lays down a corresponding prohibition as regards QRs and MEEs on exports. These provisions are intended to eliminate non-tariff barriers to trade between Member States. Finally, Article 36 TFEU is an exception clause which provides that QRs or MEEs falling under Articles 34 or 35 may be justified in certain circumstances as being for the general interest.

[32] See chapter 6 on direct effect in general, chapter 14 specifically on free movement of persons and services, and chapter 15 on free movement of capital.

[33] See, by analogy, Case C-55/18 *Federación de Servicios de Comisiones Obreras (CCOO)*, EU:C:2019:402, para 70, recognizing the obligation of national courts to change their established case law if it is based on an interpretation of national law which is incompatible with EU law.

[34] Case C-1/90 *Aragonesa de Publicidad* [1991] ECR I-4151, para 8 (regional authorities) and Case 45/87 *Commission v Ireland (Dundalk)* [1987] ECR 1369, para 12 (local authorities).

[35] Case 249/81 *Commission v Ireland* ('*Buy Irish*') [1982] ECR 4005, paras 21ff.

[36] Case 266/87 *Royal Pharmaceutical Society of Great Britain* [1989] ECR 1295, paras 14–16.

[37] If a household or a private company decide to buy only domestic products to support the national economy, this can hardly be regarded as an MEE on imports. It seems equally unconceivable that the acts of such private parties may fall within the concepts of internal discriminatory taxation or CEEs.

[38] Case C-265/95 *Commission v France* ('*Strawberries*') [1997] ECR I-6959, paras 30ff, concerned the interception and violent damaging of agricultural products originating from Spain by French farmers which took place for years. The Court held that Member States are responsible for ensuring that free movement of goods is respected, including by maintaining public order and internal security.

[39] Case C-112/00 *Schmidberger* [2003] ECR I-5659, paras 51ff, concerning a demonstration with environmental aims, notified to the Austrian authorities, which closed a major motorway for 30 hours. Without prejudice to the possibility of a justification based on fundamental rights (freedom of expression and assembly), the Court ruled that the implicit authorization was a measure attributable to the State.

[40] Case C-470/03 *AGM-COS.MET* [2007] ECR I-2749.

7.1 **Quantitative restriction: imports and exports**

The TFEU does not define the concept of QRs. However, the Court of Justice has held that 'the prohibition on quantitative restrictions covers measures which amount to a total or partial restraint of, according to the circumstances, imports, exports or goods in transit'.[41] A 'total restraint' in this context is a total prohibition on imports or exports; a 'partial restraint' is a system of import or export quotas (eg a restriction on importing or exporting more than 10,000 widgets per year).

While the concept of QRs is the same whether imports or exports are at stake, the definition of MEEs on imports is fundamentally different from that of MEEs on exports. These two concepts will now be considered in turn. A diagram showing which national measures are permitted is set out in Fig. 12.1.

7.2 **Measures of equivalent effect: imports**

7.2.1 **The evolution of the concept in the case law**

The definition of MEEs under Article 34 has caused a great deal of ink to flow and given rise to a considerable amount of case law over the years. The big question is: to what extent, if at all, does a measure have to *discriminate* against imports for this provision to be engaged? In other words, how far does the Treaty encroach on the decisions of the Member States? Article 34 uses the word 'restrictions' but does not mention discrimination at all.

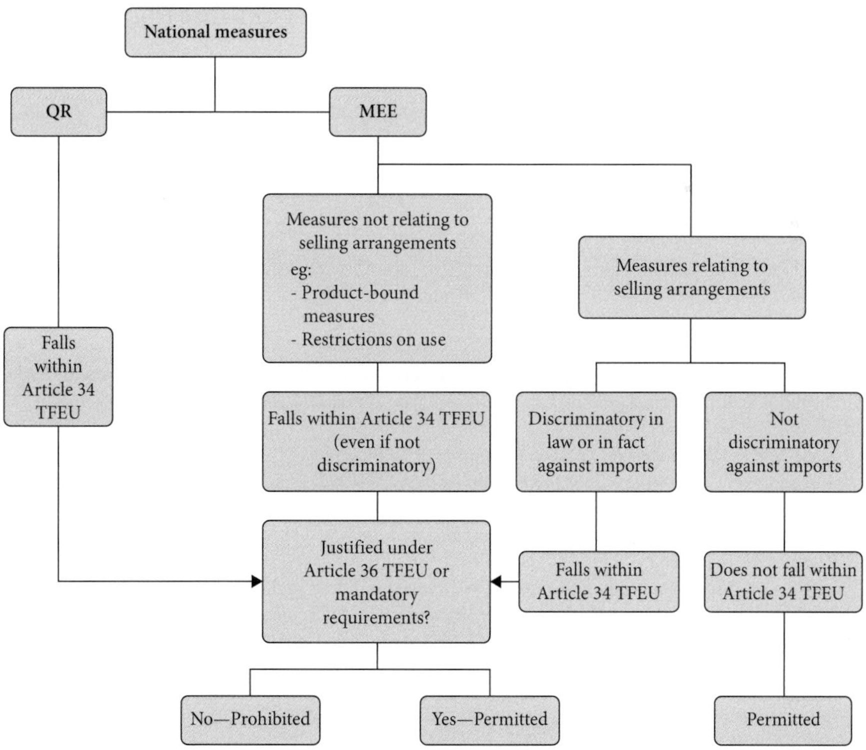

Fig. 12.1 When national measures are permitted in relation to QRs and MEEs

[41] Case 2/73 *Geddo* [1973] ECR 865, 879.

The best way to examine the case law is to follow a chronological approach, considering in turn each of the four principal judicial milestones *Dassonville*[42] (1974), *Cassis de Dijon*[43] (1979), *Keck*[44] (1993), and finally *Commission v Italy* ('*Trailers*')[45] and *Mickelsson*[46] (2009).

Dassonville

The classic definition of MEEs is to be found in *Dassonville*, a case concerning imports of Scotch whisky manufactured in the UK and in free circulation in France into Belgium. According to the Belgian legislation, imported goods bearing a designation of origin had to be accompanied by a certificate of origin (in this case, from the UK authorities). Such requirement did not apply to domestic products. In that context, the Court famously held:

> All trading rules enacted by Member States, which are capable of hindering, directly or indirectly, actually or potentially, intra-Community trade are to be considered as measures having an effect equivalent to quantitative restrictions.[47]

This definition has been repeated in nearly every subsequent case, albeit with certain variations.[48] In particular, the word 'trading' is usually omitted,[49] so no importance can be attached to this word.

Even though the case concerned a discriminatory measure,[50] the most striking feature of the *Dassonville* formula is its great breadth. Just how broad it is can be seen from the ruling in *Commission v France* ('*Foie gras*').[51] In that case, the Commission alleged that France had infringed Article 34 TFEU by laying down standards for goods sold under the trade description *foie gras*. The defendant argued that the infringement was purely hypothetical, since this product was produced only in very small quantities in other Member States and products from those States generally complied with the French standards in any event. The Court dismissed this argument:

> Article [34] applies . . . not only to the actual effects but also to the potential effects of legislation. It cannot be considered inapplicable simply because at the present time there are no actual cases with a connection to another Member State.[52]

Since the *Dassonville* formula involves an examination of the 'actual or potential, direct or indirect effect' of the measure in question, the Court considers it unnecessary to rely

[42] Case 8/74 *Dassonville* [1974] ECR 837. See P Oliver, '*Dassonville* and Non-Tariff Barriers to Trade' in P Craig and R Schütze (eds), *Landmark Cases in European Union Law* (Oxford: Hart Publishing, 2025), vol 2, ch 1.

[43] Case 120/78 *REWE-Zentral* ('*Cassis de Dijon*') [1979] ECR 649.

[44] Joined Cases C-267/91 and 268/91 *Keck and Mithouard* [1993] ECR I-6097.

[45] Case C-110/05 *Commission v Italy* ('*Trailers*') [2009] ECR I-519.

[46] Case C-142/05 *Mickelsson* [2009] ECR I-4273.

[47] *Dassonville* (n 42) 852.

[48] eg the Court has been known to speak of 'a direct or indirect, real or potential hindrance to imports between Member States' (Case 4/75 *Rewe-Zentralfinanz* [1975] ECR 843, para 3).

[49] eg Case C-368/95 *Familiapress* [1997] ECR I-3689, para 7 and Case C-67/97 *Bluhme* [1998] ECR I-8033, para 18.

[50] Discrimination took place at two levels: first, between imported products and domestic products (which were not subject to the requirement of a certificate of origin) and, secondly, between products directly imported from the country of origin (in which case the direct importer may obtain the certificate of origin more easily) and products indirectly imported (in which case the importer may face serious difficulties to obtain the required certificate).

[51] Case C-184/96 *Commission v France* ('*Foie gras*') [1998] ECR I-6197.

[52] Ibid, para 17.

on any economic or statistical analysis regarding the impact on imports.[53] This is neatly illustrated by *Buy Irish*.[54] The defendant contended that the contested advertising campaign encouraging the public to buy domestic goods in preference to imports was not an MEE because imports had actually risen since the campaign began. The Court gave this argument short shrift, pointing out that imports might have increased even more in the absence of the campaign.[55] What is more, reliance on statistical data would lead to perverse results, as the legality of a measure might vary from year to year, or even from month to month.

Equally, it is inherent in the *Dassonville* formula that some measures do not constitute even potential or indirect hindrances to imports and therefore fall outside the *Dassonville* formula altogether. In *Krantz*,[56] a German company had sold a machine on instalment terms to a company established in the Netherlands. Before it had been fully paid, the purchaser went bankrupt. Under Dutch bankruptcy law, the seller's reservation of property pending the payment of the final instalment could not be invoked against the Dutch tax authorities. The seller claimed that the Dutch law infringed Article 34 TFEU, since it operated as a disincentive to traders in other Member States to sell goods by instalment to the Netherlands. The Court dismissed this argument on the ground that the effects of such a rule were 'too uncertain and indirect to warrant the conclusion' that it was 'liable to hinder trade between Member States'.[57] Following *Krantz*, the Court has held in a line of cases that measures fell outside Article 34 TFEU on the ground that the possibility of their affecting imports was too 'uncertain and indirect',[58] which in effect is a rule of remoteness.[59]

Ever since its ruling in *van de Haar*, the Court has refused to apply a *de minimis* rule, unlike in the area of EU competition law, by holding that national measures can constitute MEEs even if 'the hindrance is slight'. [60] An interesting illustration of this principle can be seen in *Bluhme*, where a ban on keeping certain species of bee applicable to an island representing less than 1 per cent of Danish territory was nevertheless held to fall under Article 34.[61]

A further obvious characteristic of the *Dassonville* formula is that it refers exclusively to the *effects* of a measure, not its purpose; and the overwhelming thrust of the subsequent case law confirms this. That is scarcely surprising: Article 34 TFEU speaks of 'measures of

[53] That is without prejudice to the need to consider the impact of price restrictions in order to determine whether they constitute MEEs: eg Case 65/75 *Tasca* [1976] ECR 291, para 13 and Case 13/77 *GB-Inno* [1977] ECR 2115, paras 52ff.

[54] *Buy Irish* (n 35).

[55] Ibid, paras 22 and 25; see also Case C-405/98 *Gourmet International* [2001] ECR I-1795, para 22 and Case C-463/01 *Commission v Germany* ('*Mineral water*') [2004] ECR I-11705, para 65.

[56] Case C-69/88 *Krantz* [1990] ECR I-583.

[57] J Stuyck has pointed out that cases in which the Court has followed this approach have frequently related to private law ('Is *Keck* Still Alive and Kicking?' in L Gormley, P Nihoul, and E van Nieuwenhuyze (eds), 'What Standard after *Keck*?' (2012) *European Journal of Consumer Law* 343, 345),

[58] eg Case C-379/92 *Peralta* [1994] ECR I-3453; Case C-96/94 *Centro Servizi Spediporto* [1995] ECR I-2883; Case C-140/94 *Bassano di Grappa* [1995] ECR I-3257; and Case C-134/94 *Esso Española* [1995] ECR I-4223. In all these cases, the facts were extreme. Eg, in *Peralta*, the captain of a ship discharged into the sea water used to clean tanks which had contained harmful chemicals. During the criminal proceedings brought against him, Captain Peralta claimed that the legislation constituted an MEE as it made imports of chemicals more expensive, an argumentation swiftly rejected by the Court.

[59] However, AG Kokott has pointed out that the criteria of 'uncertainty and indirectness' are 'difficult to clarify and thus do not contribute to legal certainty' (para 46 of her Opinion in *Mickelsson* (n 46).

[60] Joined Cases 177/82 and 178/82 *van de Haar* [1984] ECR 1797, para 14.

[61] *Bluhme* (n 49). See also Case C-309/02 *Radlberger* [2004] ECR I-11763, para 68. As mentioned in section 8, Art 30 TFEU is not subject to a *de minimis* rule either.

equivalent *effect*' to quantitative restrictions. Although the Court has referred to the aim of a national measure in several instances,[62] it is not easy to find a single case in which a measure has been held to fall within the scope of Article 34 solely for this reason.

Cassis de Dijon

What the Court did not do in *Dassonville* was to give any indication as to whether discrimination is a necessary ingredient of an MEE.

The early cases, including *Dassonville*, all concerned so-called 'distinctly applicable' measures (those which discriminate against imports on their face).[63] The Court first encountered indistinctly applicable measures in the celebrated case of *Cassis de Dijon*.[64] The claimants, who sought to import the French blackcurrant-based drink of that name, contested the validity of a provision of an indistinctly applicable German law requiring spirits to have a minimum alcohol content (25 per cent for fruit liqueurs), since Cassis de Dijon had a lower alcohol content (between 15 and 20 per cent). The Court ruled for the first time that a non-discriminatory measure constituted an MEE and established the fundamental principle of mutual recognition. According to this principle, in the absence of harmonization at EU level, goods lawfully produced in one Member State can be marketed in other Member States irrespective of their compliance with the domestic rules of the latter, and vice versa. In so doing, Member States mutually recognize in principle that their respective rules equally protect the general interests being pursued.[65] Effectively, *Cassis de Dijon* enshrines the principle of home country control,[66] tempered with the exceptional possibility for the host country to impose its regulatory standards when justified under Article 36 or the (newly developed) mandatory (now increasingly called public interest) requirements.[67] In view of the quite exceptional importance of this judgment, the Commission took the then unprecedented step of issuing a formal Communication on it.[68]

Cassis de Dijon was followed by a large number of similar rulings relating to other indistinctly applicable measures.[69] In all these cases, the measures in issue did not discriminate against imports on their face; but a more subtle form of discrimination was at work. The provisions at issue in these cases reflected the long-standing characteristics of domestic products (alcohol content, ingredients, etc), whereas producers in other Member States wishing to export to another Member State needed to adapt their products specifically for the latter's market, with all the added costs which this entailed. This may be regarded as a form of discrimination in fact.

What about measures which do not discriminate against imports at all? This issue came to a head in *Torfaen v B & Q*,[70] a reference from the UK concerning the legality of

[62] *Keck* (n 44) paras 12 and 14; Case C-379/92 *Peralta* [1994] ECR I-3453, para 24; and *Trailers* (n 45) para 37.

[63] This widely used term is not employed by the Court itself.

[64] *Cassis de Dijon* (n 43).

[65] In the same judgment, the Court broadened the rules on justification of MEEs; see section 7.4.2.

[66] See chapter 11.

[67] See section 7.4.

[68] OJ [1980] C356/2.

[69] eg Case 788/79 *Gilli* [1980] ECR 2071 (ban on sale of cider vinegar); *Beer* (n 5) (ban on use of generic name 'beer' for drinks made with rice or maize); Case 216/84 *Commission v France* [1988] ECR 793 (ban on sale of substitute milk powder); and *Zoni* (n 6) (ban on sale of pasta containing soft wheat).

[70] Case C-145/88 *Torfaen* [1989] ECR 3851. See also the other Sunday trading cases: Case C-312/89 *CGT v Conforama* [1991] ECR I-997; Case C-332/89 *Marchandise* [1991] ECR I-1027; and Case C-169/91 *Stoke-on-Trent v B & Q* [1992] ECR I-6635.

the then ban on Sunday trading. The measures in that case did not involve any discrimination against imports in any shape or form; nor were they aimed at imports in any sense. Although the judgment of the Court appeared to seek a path indicating that Sunday trading laws were acceptable under EU law, its reasoning has been described by some commentators as unclear.[71]

Keck

Four years after *Torfaen*, the Court found a conceptual framework to limit the broadness of Article 34 TFEU and refined the applicable legal test in *Keck*, a case on a French prohibition to resell at a loss. It divided measures into two types:

(a) so-called 'product requirements', which concern the inherent characteristics of a product such as designation, form, size, weight, composition, presentation, and labelling;[72] and

(b) measures relating to 'certain selling arrangements'.[73]

As to the former category, the Court confirmed its earlier (*Dassonville* and *Cassis de Dijon*) case law. With respect to the latter category, a major change was announced: such measures fall outside the scope of Article 34 provided that (i) they did 'apply to all affected traders operating within the national territory'[74] and (ii) did not discriminate against imports 'in law' or 'in fact'.[75]

As the Court explained in paragraph 17 of its judgment, the rationale behind *Keck* is that, so long as conditions (i) and (ii) are fulfilled, selling arrangements—such as the Sunday trading rules or the prohibition on reselling at a loss—are less restrictive of free trade than product requirements because they do not oblige traders in other Member States to produce goods to particular specifications just for the Member State in question. In practice, this amounts to injecting a dose of host country control back into the system, namely as regards rules concerning the marketing of products. In the view of this author, this approach is entirely sound.

Having said that, paragraphs 15 and 16 of the judgment in *Keck* could have been better drafted and the judgment overlooked some crucial points. The concept of measures relating to 'selling arrangements' was not defined in *Keck* itself, but has subsequently been held to cover the following categories of measures:

- restrictions on when goods may be sold;[76]
- restrictions on where or by whom goods may be sold;[77]

[71] L. Gormley, 'Case 145/88, *Torfaen Borough Council v. B&Q PLC (formerly B&Q Retail Ltd)*, Preliminary reference under Art 177 EEC by the Cwmbran Magistrates' Court on the interpretation of Arts 30 & 36 EEC' (1990) 27 *Common Market Law Review* 149.

[72] *Keck* (n 44) para 15. The term 'product-bound' is not used by the Court itself.

[73] This term is used by the Court in para 16.

[74] A very rare example of this limb of para 16 being applied is Case C-198/14 *Visnapuu*, EU:C:2015:751, paras 103ff.

[75] As to the concept of discrimination 'in fact' in this context, see Case C-391/92 *Commission v Greece (Infant milk)* [1995] ECR I-1621 and Case C-322/01 *DocMorris I* [2003] ECR I-14887.

[76] Joined Cases C-401/92 and 402/92 *'t Heukske* [1994] ECR I-2199 and Case C-69/93 *Punto Casa* [1994] ECR I-2355.

[77] *Commission v Greece* (n 75) (ban on selling processed milk for infants except in pharmacies) and *DocMorris I* (n 75) (ban on selling pharmaceuticals on the internet).

- advertising restrictions;[78] and
- price controls.[79]

Identifying a 'selling arrangement' is not always easy, however, as AG Poiares Maduro pointed out in *Alfa Vita*.[80] This case concerned so-called 'bake-off' products, namely bread which is first half-baked, then frozen and transported to the point of sale (typically a supermarket), where the baking process is completed. The contested Greek legislation required vendors of such goods, whether domestic or imported, to comply with all the standards and have all the equipment required for traditional bakeries. Quite obviously, this legislation was designed to make 'bake-off' products prohibitively expensive so as to protect local bakeries. The Court ruled—correctly, it is submitted—that the contested measure did not relate to a 'selling arrangement'. Rules relating to the production process are not 'selling arrangements', even if they take effect at the point of sale.

In any case, when any doubt exists as to whether a measure is product-bound or relates to a selling arrangement, the Court inclines towards the former,[81] although this has never been spelt out in the case law.

Another problem with the wording of the judgment in *Keck* was that the term '*certain* selling arrangements' in paragraph 16 suggested that some selling arrangements were not subject to the new test. However, it has long been clear that all selling arrangements are concerned.

Another major weakness in *Keck* is that it overlooked a crucial point: many MEEs are neither product requirements nor 'selling arrangements'. The measure in issue in *ANETT* is a clear example. That case concerned a Spanish ban on tobacco retailers directly importing tobacco into the country; instead, they were required to purchase their supplies from authorized wholesalers. Unsurprisingly, this measure, which by its very nature is liable to restrict imports, was held to be an MEE;[82] but it is equally clear that it was neither a product requirement nor a 'selling arrangement'. Similarly, restrictions on use do not fall into either category.[83]

Consequently, it is scarcely surprising that *Keck* has been widely criticized over the years both by Advocates General[84] and by scholars,[85] as it is said to create an artificial and largely unworkable distinction. For a long time, the Court remained impervious to such criticism except in one respect: the distinction between 'selling arrangements' and 'product requirements' gradually mutated into a distinction between 'selling arrangements' and *all* other measures, so that only the former were subject to a discrimination test;[86] but this has never been explicitly stated by the Court. Measures which cannot be categorized

[78] Case C-292/92 *Hünermund* [1993] ECR I-6787; Case C-412/93 *Leclerc-Siplec* [1995] ECR I-179; Case C-34/95 *De Agostini* [1997] ECR I-3843; and Case C-405/98 *Gourmet International* [2001] ECR I-1795.

[79] *Keck* itself related to a prohibition on reselling goods at a loss, which is a form of price control. See also Case C-531/07 *LIBRO* [2009] ECR I-3717. But in this regard *Keck* did not change the pre-existing case law: it has always been the case that price controls only constitute MEEs if they discriminate against imports (P Oliver et al, *Oliver on Free Movement of Goods in the European Union* (5th edn, Oxford: Hart Publishing, 2010) paras 7.87ff).

[80] Case C-158/04 *Alfa Vita* [2006] ECR I-8135, paras 24ff.

[81] Case C-470/93 *Mars* [1995] ECR I-1923 and *Familiapress* (n 49).

[82] Case C-456/10 *ANETT*, EU:C:2012:241, para 44.

[83] See following subsection.

[84] Especially AG Jacobs in *Leclerc-Siplec* (n 78); AG Poiares Maduro in *Alfa Vita* (n 80) paras 24ff; and AG Bot in *Trailers* (n 45).

[85] Among the vast body of critical literature, see L Gormley, 'Inconsistencies and Misconceptions in the Free Movement of Goods' (2015) 40 *European Law Review* 925.

[86] Case C-473/98 *Toolex* [2000] ECR I-5681 (restriction on use); Case C-390/99 *Canal Satélite Digital* [2002] ECR I-607 and Case C-244/06 *Dynamic Medien* [2008] ECR I-505 (market authorization requirements).

as either product requirements or as selling arrangements were therefore found to be MEEs whether they were discriminatory or not.

Finally, while advertising restrictions are still considered to be 'selling arrangements', 'outright bans' on advertising a certain product are considered to be discriminatory per se.[87] That is because of the central importance of advertising for market integration: even if a product is a household name in (say) Finland, the manufacturers have little chance of marketing it successfully elsewhere in the EU unless it can be advertised.[88]

Trailers and Mickelsson

In *Trailers* and *Mickelsson*, the Court had to analyse restrictions on the use of products: *Trailers* concerned a ban on the use of trailers on the back of motorbikes, while *Mickelsson* related to a ban on the use of jet-skis other than in general navigable waterways or on specially designated waters. Although nothing suggested initially that these may become landmark cases, the Opinion of Advocate General Kokott in *Mickelsson* altered the course of events[89] by proposing that restrictions on use be subject to a discrimination test, like selling arrangements.[90] Effectively, Advocate General Kokott proposed to make restrictions on use subject to host country control.[91] However, the Court did not follow that proposal. Recognizing that restrictions on use can have a considerable impact on consumer behaviour, the Court ruled that measures prohibiting the specific purpose for which products are intended or greatly restricting their use are to be regarded as MEEs irrespective of discrimination.[92] It follows that only the most significant restrictions on use are caught by Article 34.[93]

In *Trailers*, the Court finally succumbed to the widespread criticism of *Keck*, but in an ambiguous way. It appeared to confirm the pre-existing case law, but then, in order to assess restrictions on use, added that 'any other measure which hinders access to the market' also constitutes an MEE[94]—language which broadly reflects the test proposed by many critics of *Keck*.

Unfortunately, the term 'market access' could not be more nebulous. Snell has stated that 'the notion of market access obscures rather than illuminates',[95] while Gormley points

[87] Case C-34/95 *De Agostini* [1997] ECR I-3843 (ban on television advertising targeted at children) and Case C-45/98 *Gourmet International* [2001] ECR I-1795 (alcohol). In *Gourmet*, a prohibition on advertising alcoholic drinks was treated by the Court as an 'outright ban' although it was subject to two minor exceptions. However, in Case C-190/20 *DocMorris II*, EU:C:2021:609, which concerned a prohibition on pharmacies to organize advertising campaigns in the form of prize competitions, the Court held that the *De Agostini/Gourmet* case law did not apply because the prohibition did not concern 'the promotion of a particular [medicinal] product . . . but . . . the sale by mail order of all kinds of medicinal products, both from Germany and from other Member States' (para 42); in reality, the measure was not intended to influence the customer's choice of a given medicinal product but the choice of the pharmacy (para 21).

[88] Paras 19ff of AG Jacobs' Opinion in *Leclerc-Siplec* (n 78).

[89] *Trailers* (n 45), an infringement case brought by the Commission against Italy, was originally assigned to a regular chamber of the Court, there was no hearing and AG Léger delivered his Opinion, in which he considered that Italy had infringed its obligations, without signalling that the case raised any novel issues. In view of the Opinion of AG Kokott in *Mickelsson* (n 46), however, the Court reassigned the *Trailers* case to the Grand Chamber, organized a hearing, and asked AG Bot to deliver a new Opinion.

[90] Unless the measure is a general prohibition on use or it only allows a marginal possibility for use, in which case AG Kokott considered that it would prevent market access and should be regarded as an MEE.

[91] One may, indeed, take the view that, if Member States can decide how goods are marketed in their territory, they should be able determine similarly how products are to be used therein.

[92] *Trailers* (n 45) para 56 and *Mickelsson* (n 46) para 28. The judgment in *Mickelsson*, delivered shortly after *Trailers*, follows the latter's approach.

[93] Consequently, restrictions such as speed limits on roads and bans on playing loud music at night fall outside the scope of Art 34 and do not need to be justified under Art 36 or the mandatory requirements.

[94] *Trailers* (n 45) para 37.

[95] J Snell, 'The Notion of Market Access: A Concept or a Slogan?' (2010) 47 *Common Market Law Review* 437, 470.

out that this concept 'adds nothing at all to the basic *Dassonville* principle'[96] and Barnard[97] has demonstrated that 'market access' can bear a wide range of different meanings.

In any case, over 17 years after *Trailers* and *Mickelsson*, it is questionable whether they changed anything at all. Reports that *Keck* was dead or even experiencing a 'progressive demise'[98] have proved to be greatly exaggerated. The fact is that, as Advocate General Szpunar asserted in *Deutsche Parkinson*, '*Keck* is still alive',[99] although it is rarely mentioned in the judgments: in some cases decided since *Trailers* and *Mickelsson*, *Keck* has played a central role in the reasoning of Advocates General[100] or of the Court itself.[101] Accordingly, *Keck*, as fundamentally adapted by the subsequent case law discussed earlier, is clearly not dead or even moribund.

Moreover, it is hard to identify a single case decided after *Trailers* and *Mickelsson* in which the Court has reached a different *result* from that which it would have reached prior to those judgments,[102] even though the term 'market access' is frequently employed.[103]

In short, the case law has divided non-tariff barriers to imports into several categories:

- Measures relating to 'selling arrangements', which only constitute MEEs if they discriminate against imports 'in law' or 'in fact'.

  BUT,

  – advertising differs from other 'selling arrangements' in that 'outright bans' on advertising goods are regarded as discriminatory in fact and therefore constitute MEEs.

- All other non-fiscal measures on imports constitute MEEs whether or not they are 'product requirements' and whether or not they discriminate against imports.

  BUT,

  – restrictions on use only constitute MEEs if they have the effect of preventing people from using goods 'for the specific and inherent purposes for which they were intended or of greatly restricting their use'.[104]

Of course, this case law is not perfect, but a more satisfactory approach has yet to be found.

7.2.2 Some examples of MEEs on imports

MEEs come in a very wide variety of forms. We can only give a few examples here. In addition to those mentioned previously, the following deserve a particular mention:[105]

- import licences, even if they are granted automatically;[106]
- inspections and controls;[107]

[96] Gormley (n 85) 928.

[97] See C Barnard, *The Substantive Law of the EU: The Four Freedoms* (8th edn, Oxford: Oxford University Press, 2025) 25ff.

[98] I Lianos, 'In Memoriam *Keck*: The Reformation of EU Law on the Free Movement of Goods' (2015) 40 *European Law Review* 225.

[99] Opinion in Case C-148/15 *Deutsche Parkinson Vereinigung*, EU:C:2016:776, para 23.

[100] eg AG Szpunar in *Deutsche Parkinson* (n 99) and AG Hogan in Case C-400/19 *Commission v Hungary*, EU:C:2021:194 (agricultural and food products), paras 95ff.

[101] See *Visnapuu* (n 74) para 103 and *DocMorris II* (n 87) paras 35ff.

[102] In stark contrast, *Keck* itself reversed a number of earlier judgments (n 44).

[103] eg *ANETT* (n 82) para 37.

[104] *Mickelsson* (n 46) para 28.

[105] For a more thorough account, see Oliver et al (n 79) ch 7.

[106] Case 51/71 *International Fruit Co* [1971] ECR 1107 and Case 41/76 *Donckerwolcke* [1976] ECR 1921.

[107] *Rewe-Zentralfinanz* (n 48) and Case 35/76 *Simmenthal* [1976] ECR 1871.

- the obligation to produce a certificate;[108]
- prohibition on the sale of goods containing particular ingredients;[109]
- requirements as to presentation or packaging;[110]
- labelling requirements;[111]
- encouragement to purchase domestic products in preference to imports;[112]
- restrictions on use;[113]
- restrictions on possession[114] or storage;[115] and
- restrictions on health-care coverage.[116]

The first category (import licences) is distinctly applicable by definition. The other categories of measure listed here constitute MEEs even if they are indistinctly applicable.

7.3 **Measures of equivalent effect: exports**

Export restrictions are rare, since Member States are usually motivated to promote exports: the Court has decided many hundreds of cases on Article 34 TFEU, but only a small number concern Article 35 TFEU. However, there are several reasons why a State might take such a step:

- a desire to ensure supplies in times of shortage;[117]
- the protection of jobs in processing industries, in which case the export restriction will cover the raw material or component part, but not the finished product;[118]
- the maintenance of the quality or reputation of exports;[119] or
- the preservation of works of art for the nation.[120]

108 Case 251/78 *Denkavit* [1979] ECR 3369 and Case C-205/89 *Commission v Greece* [1991] ECR I-1361.

109 *Cassis de Dijon* (n 43); *Gilli* (n 69); and *Commission v France* ('*Substitute milk powder*') (n 69).

110 Case 261/81 *Rau v De Smedt* [1982] ECR 3961 (requirement that margarine be sold in cubic packaging to distinguish it from butter) and Case C-366/04 *Schwarz* [2005] ECR I-10139 (prohibition on selling chewing gum from vending machines without a wrapper).

111 Case 27/80 *Fietje* [1980] ECR 3839 (language requirement) and *Mars* (n 81).

112 *Buy Irish* (n 35) and Case C-325/00 *Commission v Germany* ('*Quality label for domestic agricultural produce*') [2002] ECR I-9977.

113 *Toolex* (n 86) and *Mickelsson* (n 46).

114 Case C-293/94 *Brandsma* [1996] ECR I-3159 and Case C-400/96 *Harpegnies* [1998] ECR I-5121.

115 Case 13/78 *Eggers* [1978] ECR 1935.

116 Case C-120/95 *Decker* [1998] ECR I-1831.

117 As in Case 68/76 *Commission v France* ('*Export licences for potatoes*') [1977] ECR 515 and Case C-648/18 *ANRE*, EU:C:2020:723 (electricity). Similarly, when the Covid-19 pandemic broke, several Member States imposed export restrictions on medical equipment; see Communication from the Commission on a Coordinated economic response to the Covid-19 crisis, COM(2020) 112 final, pp 3–4; see P Oliver, 'COVID-19 and the Free Movement of Goods: Reaching for the Placebo of Protectionism' in D Utrilla and A Sabbir (eds), *EU Law in Times of a Pandemic: An Overview of the EU's Response to the Covid-19 Crisis* (EU Law Live SA, 2021) ch 28.

118 Case C-203/96 *Dusseldorp* [1998] ECR I-4075 (restriction on exporting waste for reprocessing in another Member State).

119 Case 53/76 *Bouhelier* [1977] ECR 197 (obligation to supply quality certificates for exported watches only was in breach of Art 35 TFEU) and Case C-388/95 *Belgium v Spain* ('*Rioja*') [2000] ECR I-3123 (rule that wine could only be sold as 'Rioja' if it was produced and *bottled* in the eponymous region was an MEE).

120 Measures adopted for this purpose will be justified under Art 36 if they constitute 'national treasures possessing artistic, historic or archaeological value'.

The definition of MEEs under Article 35 is radically different from that under Article 34. The Court has consistently held that Article 35 covers only measures which discriminate against goods intended for export in favour of those destined for the domestic market.[121] However, the formulation of this definition is not always consistent. The test which the Court actually applies is that set out in *Belgium v Spain* ('*Rioja*'), where Article 35 was held to apply to measures which have 'the effect of specifically restricting patterns of exports . . . and thereby of establishing a difference of treatment between trade within a Member State and its export trade'.[122] In *Groenveld*, the Court had stated that it was necessary to show that the measure provided 'a particular advantage for national production or for the domestic market of the State in question at the expense of the production or of the trade of other Member States';[123] but in practice the final limb of that test ('at the expense of . . .') appears to be redundant.

Having said all that, in at least two cases relating to restrictions on transit (which fall under both Articles 34 and 35), the Court has applied the same test to both provisions;[124] but the measures at issue in those cases discriminated against goods intended for export in any event.

The rules on the free movement of goods differ markedly from those governing the other fundamental freedoms, where a unitary approach is followed: 'import' restrictions (barriers to incoming transactions) and 'export' restrictions (barriers to outgoing transactions) are subject to the same test.[125] The rationale behind the Court's narrow interpretation of Article 35 appears to be that that provision should not be extended to cover restrictions on production (eg planning constraints on the construction of factories).[126] Nevertheless, it is sometimes claimed that the test is too narrow, at least as regards marketing restrictions.[127]

This prompted Advocate General Trjstenjak in *Gysbrechts*[128] to advise the Court to transpose its case law on Article 34 in its entirety to Article 35. The proceedings concerned a Belgian rule precluding vendors in a distance-selling contract from requesting the details of the purchaser's credit card before the expiry of the period during which the latter enjoyed a statutory right to withdraw from the contract for seven working days. In view of the obstacles to bringing legal proceedings in another Member State against defaulting consumers, this constituted de facto discrimination against goods intended for export. Despite the Advocate General's entreaties, the Court stood by its traditional approach and maintained the requirement of discrimination,[129] even though the ruling at least makes it plain that de facto discrimination will suffice to bring a measure under Article 35 TFEU.[130]

[121] eg Case 15/79 *Groenveld* [1979] ECR 3409 and Case 155/80 *Oebel* [1981] ECR 1993 (prohibition on baking at night not an MEE).

[122] *Rioja* (n 119) para 41.

[123] *Groenveld* (n 121) para 7.

[124] *Schmidberger* (n 39) and Case C-320/03 *Commission v Austria* ('*Brenner I*') [2005] ECR I-9871.

[125] Case C-415/93 *Bosman* [1995] ECR I-4921 and Case C-18/95 *Terhoeve* [1999] ECR I-345 (workers); and Case C-384/93 *Alpine Investments* [1995] ECR I-1141 (services).

[126] If planning laws discriminate against other EU nationals, they fall under Art 49 TFEU on the freedom of establishment; see chapter 14.

[127] AG Jacobs in *Alpine Investments* (n 125) 1157, and AG Trstenjak in Case C-205/07 *Gysbrechts* [2008] ECR I-9947, paras 42ff.

[128] *Gysbrechts* (n 127).

[129] For the view that the ruling in *Gysbrechts* did broaden the definition of MEEs on exports, see A Dawes, 'A Freedom Reborn? The New Yet Unclear Scope of Article 29 EC' (2009) 34 *European Law Review* 639 and Barnard, *The Substantive Law of the EU* (n 97) 103–104.

[130] That, however, was never in doubt: see Case C-350/97 *Monsees* [1999] ECR I-2921, where a measure which discriminated de facto against goods intended for export was held to fall foul of Art 35. See also Case C-15/15 *New Valmar*, EU:C:2016:464.

7.4 Justification under Article 36 and the mandatory requirements

7.4.1 Justification under Article 36

Article 36 TFEU provides:

> The provisions of Articles 34 and 35 shall not preclude prohibitions or restrictions on imports, exports or goods in transit justified on grounds of public morality, public policy or public security; the protection of health and life of humans, animals or plants; the protection of national treasures possessing artistic, historic or archaeological value; or the protection of industrial and commercial property.
>
> Such prohibitions or restrictions shall not, however, constitute a means of arbitrary discrimination or a disguised restriction on trade between Member States.

Since exceptions to the rules on free movement are the subject of chapter 16, there is no need to attempt an exhaustive discussion of Article 36 TFEU in this chapter. However, a brief overview of some key issues is set out here.

As its wording makes clear, Article 36 TFEU lays down exceptions to both Articles 34 and 35 TFEU. Article 36 does not constitute an exception to any other provisions of the Treaty.[131]

Whether imports or exports are at stake, Article 36 applies in the same way.

As an exception to a fundamental principle, Article 36 is to be construed narrowly.[132] One manifestation of this is that the party seeking to show that a measure is justified bears the burden of proof.[133]

7.4.2 The status of the mandatory requirements

The 'mandatory requirements' are grounds of justification not mentioned in Article 36 TFEU. They first made their appearance in *Cassis de Dijon*,[134] where the Court recognized three such public interest exceptions: the prevention of tax evasion,[135] the prevention of unfair competition, and consumer protection.[136] Others followed, including environmental protection,[137] the improvement of working conditions,[138] and fundamental rights.[139]

The mandatory requirements (now increasingly called public interest requirements) recognized in *Cassis* related to important policy concerns which were not relevant or prominent when the Treaty of Rome was drafted in 1957. So, their introduction has not been the source of any controversy simply because it suits the Member States. Nevertheless, their existence is in direct contradiction with the principle that Article 36 TFEU is to be construed narrowly. In an attempt to square this circle, the Court has traditionally held that only indistinctly applicable measures can be justified on the basis of the mandatory requirements.[140] However, this has led to various contortions.[141] Perhaps partly due to

131 *Works of art* (n 15).

132 Ibid.

133 *Denkavit* (n 108) and Case C-265/06 *Commission v Portugal* [2008] ECR I-2245, para 39, plus literally hundreds of other cases.

134 *Cassis de Dijon* (n 43).

135 See also *GB-Inno* (n 53).

136 See also *Gilli* (n 69) and *Gysbrechts* (n 127).

137 Case 302/86 *Commission v Denmark* ('*Returnable bottles*') [1988] ECR 4607; *Walloon waste* (n 18); *Brenner I* (n 124); and Case C-28/09 *Commission v Austria* ('*Brenner II*'), EU:C:2011:854.

138 *Oebel* (n 121).

139 *Schmidberger* (n 39).

140 Case 113/80 *Commission v Ireland* [1982] ECR 1625; Case C-1/90 *Aragonesa de Publicidad* [1991] ECR I-4151, para 13 and *Walloon waste* (n 18) para 34.

141 An obvious example is *Walloon waste* (n 18), where the Court argued that the restriction on imports of waste into Wallonia was not discriminatory even though waste generated in other Member States was undisputably treated differently (paras 34–36).

the fact that MEEs on exports—by definition discriminatory—could never be justified by mandatory requirements under this approach and partly in response to various calls from the Advocates General,[142] the Court has therefore begun to treat the mandatory requirements in precisely the same way as the grounds of justification spelt out in Article 36 TFEU.[143] Unfortunately, the Court has never provided an explicit explanation for this and has never formally renounced its traditional approach. The widespread view today is that the latter approach is clearly preferable:[144] a measure may be objectively justified on (say) environmental grounds, even if it is distinctly applicable.[145]

Consequently, references in this chapter to Article 36 TFEU should be taken to include the mandatory requirements, unless otherwise indicated.

7.4.3 The grounds of justification

To the extent that exhaustive guarantees are laid down in EU legislation for a specific matter (eg preventing the spread of a particular disease), reliance on Article 36 TFEU is no longer possible because national measures differing from that legislation are not necessary.[146] Otherwise, the whole purpose of the EU adopting harmonizing legislation would be defeated. This is not to say, however, that every Directive necessarily provides exhaustive guarantees so as to oust the application of Article 36. Whether the guarantees provided by a Directive are exhaustive will depend on its wording, context, and purpose.[147] By definition, where a Directive only lays down minimum standards, it is not exhaustive.[148]

Purely economic considerations cannot justify restrictions falling under Article 34 or 35 TFEU:[149] objectives such as the promotion of employment or investment, curbing inflation, and controlling the balance of payments fall outside Article 36 TFEU. Otherwise, the internal market would be wholly undermined. However, some grounds of justification do contain an economic element, although normally not a protectionist one.[150] Examples include intellectual property (called 'industrial and commercial property' in Article 36 TFEU)[151] and the preservation of the financial balance of social security and health-care systems (a mandatory requirement).[152]

[142] eg AG Jacobs in *Dusseldorp* (n 118) paras 89–90 and Case C-379/98 *Preussen Elektra* [2001] ECR I-2099, paras 225–226; AG Geelhoed in *Brenner I* (n 124) paras 104–107.

[143] *Brenner I* (n 124) para 70 (restrictions on goods in transit, which trigger both Arts 34 and 35); Case C-54/05 *Commission v Finland* [2007] ECR I-2473, para 38 (discriminatory restrictions on imports under Art 34); *Gysbrechts* (n 127) para 45 and *New Valmar* (n 130) para 48 (the latter two cases concern discriminatory restrictions on exports under Art 35).

[144] This view has been expressed by two members of the Court: Judge Rosas, '*Dassonville* and *Cassis de Dijon*' in M Poiares Maduro and L Azoulai (eds), *The Past and Future of EU Law: The Classics of EU Law Revisited on the 50th Anniversary of the Rome Treaty* (Oxford: Hart Publishing, 2010) 444–445, and Judge Timmermans, 'Creative Homogeneity' in N Wahl and U Bernitz (eds), *Liber Amicorum in Honour of Sven Norberg* (Brussels: Bruylant, 2006) 472, 475 *et seq*. See also Oliver et al (n 79) paras 8.04–8.16; and see chapter 16, section 3.1 of this book.

[145] That was the situation in *Walloon waste* (n 18).

[146] Case 148/78 *Ratti* [1979] ECR 1629 and *Toolex* (n 86) para 25.

[147] Case C-324/99 *DaimlerChrysler* [2001] ECR I-9897, para 42.

[148] *Rewe-Zentralfinanz* (n 48); and *Toolex* (n 86) paras 26–33.

[149] Case 7/61 *Commission v Italy* [1961] ECR 317, 329 and Case C-416/00 *Morellato* [2003] ECR I-9343, paras 40–41. See P Oliver, 'When, If Ever, Can Restrictions on Free Movement Be Justified on Economic Grounds?' (2016) 41 *European Law Review* 147.

[150] For a quite fact-specific exception to this rule of thumb, see Case 72/83 *Campus Oil* [1984] ECR 2727, para 35, concerning restrictions on imports of refined oil products into Ireland in order to ensure the viability of the only existing refinery in the country, which was justified on grounds of public security.

[151] *Rioja* (n 119).

[152] *Decker* (n 116).

Public (human) health deserves particular attention: as one would expect, it has been held to 'rank first among the interests protected by Article 36'.[153] It is also by far the most important ground of justification in terms of the number of cases decided by the Court.

Case study 12.1: How does the Court decide complex public health issues?

Many free movement cases before the Court raise complex public health issues. In infringement proceedings, the Court is required to decide these issues. In contrast, when delivering preliminary rulings, the Court is not meant to decide questions of fact, but in practice it often comes very close to doing so.[154]

Sometimes no assessment of scientific data is involved. For instance, *Commission v Germany* concerned a measure requiring each hospital to obtain all its supplies from the same pharmacy; since emergency supplies were included, it followed that the pharmacy had to be within a few kilometres of the hospital, thereby excluding pharmacies in other Member States in nearly all cases.[155] Similarly, in *Humanplasma* the Court was called upon to rule on whether Austrian legislation restricting the marketing of human blood was justified on public health grounds; under that legislation, blood could not be distributed in Austria if any money had been paid to the donors, even to cover their travel costs.[156]

However, in many public health cases a profusion of scientific data is laid before the Court. For example, often it has had to rule on the legality of measures restricting, or fixing maximum thresholds for, certain vitamins, minerals, or additives in foodstuffs.[157]

Needless to say, the judges do not normally have any scientific training.[158] These cases place them in a difficult position: on the one hand, the Court attaches the utmost importance to public health; on the other hand, it has encountered a large number of dubious arguments based on public health. Sometimes this is blatant. For instance, in *Cassis de Dijon* the Court had no difficulty in rejecting Germany's argument that the *minimum* alcohol requirement was justified so as to prevent a proliferation of low-alcohol drinks on the market, which would induce a tolerance to alcohol.[159] But usually the questionable nature of public health arguments will not be so obvious. Sometimes the Court is faced with conflicting scientific evidence submitted by the parties. In order to cope with these complex issues, the Court has developed some rules of thumb, such as the principle that the party seeking to show that a measure is justified on public health grounds bears the burden of proof.[160] If that party makes out a reasonably convincing case on justification, then the burden shifts to the other party.[161]

[153] Case 104/75 *De Peijper* [1976] ECR 613, para 15.

[154] On the difference between these types of proceedings, see chapter 10.

[155] Case C-141/07 *Commission v Germany* ('*Hospitals*'), EU:C:2008:492. This measure was held to be justified to ensure the reliability and speed of supply to hospitals.

[156] Case C-42109 *Humanplasma* [2010] ECR I-12869.

[157] eg Case C-192/01 *Commission v Denmark* [2003] ECR I-9693; Case C-95/01 *Greenham* [2004] ECR I-1333; and Case C-333/08 *Commission v France* [2010] ECR I-757.

[158] The Court can commission an expert's report (Art 70 of its Rules of Procedure). But this procedure is very rarely used; and it would be unthinkable on a reference for a preliminary ruling where the Court is not required to rule on the facts!

[159] *Cassis de Dijon* (n 43) paras 10 and 11. See also Case C-319/05 *Commission v Germany* [2007] ECR I-9811 where Germany had classified garlic capsules as medicinal products; this meant that a market authorization was required before they could be sold!

[160] See n 133 and the accompanying text.

[161] eg *Beer* (n 5) and Case C-55/99 *Commission v France* [2000] ECR I-11499, paras 34–36.

Article 36 TFEU is purely permissive. Accordingly, it is up to Member States to decide how far they wish to go in protecting public health.[162] Thus a national measure may be justified even if no other Member State has adopted such a stringent rule,[163] although this may be an indication that the measure is disproportionate.[164]

The Court also attaches considerable importance to the position taken by other international organizations. For instance, in *Beer*,[165] the Court relied on recommendations of the World Health Organization as well as the UN's Food and Agriculture Organization; and in *Humanplasma*, it did likewise with a recommendation of the Council of Europe.[166]

The judgment in *Deutsche Parkinson Vereinigung* is a good illustration of how these principles are applied.[167] The claimant was a support group for patients suffering from Parkinson's disease, which offered its members bonuses on prescription pharmaceuticals purchased from DocMorris, an online pharmacy based in the Netherlands.[168] These bonuses were found to be incompatible with the fixed prices imposed by German legislation. After ruling that the price controls were caught by Article 34, the Court turned to Article 36. First, it considered Germany's claim that this measure was justified to 'ensure a safe and high-quality supply of medicinal products', especially to remote areas, and rejected the argument as unsubstantiated. In particular, it held that price competition could benefit patients insofar as it would allow for prescription medicines to be offered at more attractive prices. Therefore, the Court concluded that the measure was unjustified.[169]

7.4.4 **The general principles governing Article 36 TFEU**

Proportionality

The principle of proportionality, which is a general principle of EU law, also applies in the context of Article 36.[170] It imposes two main requirements: first, the restrictions must be 'appropriate' to achieve a legitimate public interest goal; secondly, they must be 'necessary'.[171]

The first aspect of the principle of proportionality requires verification that the restriction is suitable to achieve the legitimate goal. For instance, in *LEGO*, a mesure seeking to promote the use of renewable energy sources to generate electricity was deemed suitable

[162] *Commission v Germany* ('*Hospitals*') (n 155) para 51 and *Humanplasma* (n 156) para 39. Eg a particularly strict measure may be justified by the dietary habits of the population of a Member State. Case 53/80 *Eyssen* [1981] ECR 409 concerned a ban on the use of a particular additive in cheese in the Netherlands; the additive was harmless in small doses, but the ban was held to be justified, even though most other Member States are less strict in this regard. The Court's conclusion was based in part on the high consumption of cheese in that Member State.

[163] *Eyssen* (n 162).

[164] *Commission v France* (n 157) para 105 and *Humanplasma* (n 156) para 41.

[165] eg Case C-178/84 (n 5) paras 44 and 52.

[166] *Humanplasma* (n 156) para 44.

[167] *Deutsche Parkinson* (n 99) paras 28 *et seq*. See also A Alemanno, 'Balancing Free Movement and Public Health: The Case of Minimum Unit Pricing of Alcohol in *Scotch Whisky*' (2016) 53 *Common Market Law Review* 1037.

[168] Following the ruling in *DocMorris I* (n 82), which concerned the same Dutch pharmacy, Germany had repealed its ban on the sale of pharmaceuticals on the internet.

[169] *Deutsche Parkinson* (n 99) paras 37–45.

[170] One of earliest references to the content of this principle in the context of Art 36, although without using the expression 'principle of proportionality', is in *De Peijper* (n 153), paras 16–17. See also *Simmenthal* (n 107) para 19. See further chapter 16.

[171] *Trailers* (n 45) para 59; Case C-662/21 *Booky.fi*, EU:C:2023:239, para 37 and Case C-624/22 *BP France*, EU:C:2024:640, para 65.

for the protection of the environment and public health insofar as it contributes to the reduction of greenhouse gas emissions.[172] In contrast, in *Humanplasma*, a prohibition to reimburse travel costs of blood donors (eg bus journey) was ruled to be unsuitable to encourage blood donations.[173]

Moreover, if the measure is not applied in a consistent and systematic manner, it will be deemed inappropriate. This is neatly illustrated by *Commission v Portugal*, a case concerning a ban on affixing tinted film to car windows, which was allegedly justified to fight crime and to enable the police to see whether seat belts were being worn. This argument was dismissed when it emerged that there was no restriction in Portugal on marketing cars fitted with tinted windows from the outset.[174]

As for the second requirement of the principle of proportionality, the measure must not go beyond what is necessary to achieve the legitimate goal. There must be no alternative less restrictive means to achieve the objective. Frequently, the Court identifies an alternative measure which would achieve the desired aim without affecting interstate trade to the same degree.[175] For instance, an adequate labelling requirement has often been held to constitute a suitable substitute for a sales ban.[176] However, the Court has occasionally softened the standard of proof in this regard,[177] relying sometimes on the Member States' margin of discretion.[178]

Another aspect of proportionality relating to the necessity of the measure is the principle of *mutual recognition*, which is also an application of the obligation of sincere cooperation under Article 4(3) TEU. As mentioned earlier,[179] mutual recognition made its first appearance in the case law in *Cassis de Dijon*: it was held there that the sale of goods lawfully produced and marketed in one Member State may not be restricted in another Member State without good cause.[180] However, this test must not be read narrowly: it appears to suffice for the goods to have been lawfully produced *or* marketed in the first Member State;[181] and the principle extends to goods produced outside the EU, if it is lawful to produce and market them in the Member State where they were first put into free circulation.[182] In short, the importing Member State cannot prohibit the sale of goods meeting equivalent standards to its own, even if they are not identical, and it cannot unnecessarily duplicate controls carried out in other Member States.[183]

[172] Case C-242/17 *LEGO*, EU:C:2018:804, paras 64–65.

[173] *Humanplasma* (n 156) para 37.

[174] *Commission v Portugal* (n 133) para 43; similarly, see *New Valmar* (n 130) paras 58–59.

[175] eg Case C-387/99 *Commission v Germany* [2004] ECR I-3751, para 81.

[176] *Cassis de Dijon* (n 43) para 13 and *Gilli* (n 69) para 7.

[177] In *Trailers* (n 45), the Court ruled that Member States are not required to prove that no other conceivable measure could enable the objective to be equally attained (para 66).

[178] Ibid, para 65 and *Humanplasma* (n 156) para 39.

[179] See the text accompanying n 67.

[180] *Cassis de Dijon* (n 43) para 14. See the Commission's Communications on mutual recognition, COM(1999) 299 and OJ [2003] C265/2. This was followed by the adoption of Regulation 764/2008 of the European Parliament and the Council on mutual recognition (OJ [2008] L218/21), which was subsequently amended and partially replaced by Regulation 2019/1020 of the of the European Parliament and the Council (OJ [2019] L169/1). It has now become a general principle of Union law: M Möstl, 'Preconditions and Limits of Mutual Recognition' (2010) 47 *Common Market Law Review* 405 and W-H Roth, 'Mutual Recognition' in P Koutrakos and J Snell (eds), *Research Handbook on the Law of the EU's Internal Market* (Cheltenham: Edward Elgar, 2017) 427.

[181] *Canal Satélite Digital* (n 86) para 37; AG La Pergola in *Foie Gras* (n 51) para 28. See P Oliver, 'Mutual Recognition: Addressing Some Outstanding Conundrums' in A Albors-Llorens, C Barnard, and B Leucht (eds), *Cassis de Dijon: 40 Years On* (Oxford: Hart Publishing, 2021) ch 8.

[182] Case C-525/14 *Commission v Czech Republic* (*Hallmarking*), EU:C:2016:714. See Oliver, *Mutual Recognition* (n 181).

[183] *Canal Satélite Digital* (n 86) paras 36ff.

However, *Dynamic Medien*, a case concerning the approval for viewing by children in Germany of DVDs which had already been subject to a classification procedure in the UK, makes clear that the principle of mutual recognition does not require the importing Member State to simply accept the classification chosen by the Member State of origin.[184] That is because each Member State has a margin of discretion to determine its own level of protection, which may be higher than in other Member States. [185]

Arbitrary discrimination and disguised restriction on trade

The last sentence of Article 36 TFEU provides that restrictions constituting arbitrary discrimination or disguised restrictions on trade may not be accepted. 'Arbitrary discrimination' refers to disparate treatment which cannot be objectively justified.[186] A justification is much harder to prove when the measure is discriminatory, but it is not impossible.[187]

7.5 **Remedies**

As already mentioned, Articles 34 and 35 TFEU are directly effective.[188] Consequently, persons who are affected by a breach of those provisions are entitled to an effective remedy before the courts. Occasionally, this has been spelt out in judgments relating to these provisions,[189] but in any case it follows from the right to effective judicial protection, which is now enshrined in Article 19(1) TEU as well as Article 47 of the Charter of Fundamental Rights of the European Union.[190] In appropriate circumstances, the ordinary remedies should be available: annulment, injunctions (interim and final), as well as damages.

8 Customs duties and charges of equivalent effect

The prohibition of customs duties is set out in Article 30 TFEU:

> Customs duties on imports and exports and charges having equivalent effect shall be prohibited between Member States. This prohibition shall also apply to customs duties of a fiscal nature.

[184] It would be different, however, if the substantive standards were established by EU law or were equivalent national standards.

[185] *Dynamic Medien* (n 86) paras 44 and 49. The Court reached the same conclusion in *Booky.fi* (n 171) paras 56–60. In relation to the freedom of establishment relating to gambling which also involves issues of public morality, see also Case C-316/07 *Stoss* [2010] ECR I-8069, paras 112–113.

[186] For examples of arbitrary discrimination, see Case 121/85 *Conegate* [1986] ECR 1007, paras 15–16 (prohibition on imports of pornographic materials without a corresponding prohibition on manufacturing such goods domestically) and *Bouhelier* (n 119) para 15 (quality standard certificates required for exports of watches alone, not for domestic marketing).

[187] Besides the successful justification of restrictions on exports, all of which are discriminatory measures, see *Rewe-Zentralfinanz* (n 48) para 8 (phytosanitary inspections on imports of apples may be justified if other effective measures are taken in relation to domestic apples; eg surveillance of domestic production which allows treating the apple trees themselves) and *Commission v Germany* (n 155) paras 47–57 (requirement that pharmacies supplying hospitals be located in the latter's area to ensure reliability and speed of supply).

[188] See n 9 and accompanying text.

[189] *Denkavit* (n 108) para 3 and Case C-46/93 *Brasserie du pêcheur* [1996] ECR I-1029, para 23.

[190] OJ [2007] C303/1.

8.1 **Customs duties**

The abolition of customs duties between Member States was an essential element in the establishment of the internal market since they are among the most blatant obstacles to trade. Customs duties are charges levied on goods by reason of the fact that they cross a frontier between Member States. Perhaps unsurprisingly, the Court has not had the opportunity to consider customs duties on many occasions due to the clear and unambiguous prohibition established by the Treaty. *Van Gend en Loos*[191]—the celebrated case where the Court first laid down the principle of direct effect[192]—is one of the relatively few judgments concerning customs duties. The Court took the opportunity to state that the prohibition of customs duties is an 'essential provision' and constitutes one of the foundations of the EU.

8.2 **Charges of equivalent effect**

Article 30 TFEU also prohibits CEEs, as otherwise it would be very easy for Member States to circumvent the prohibition on customs duties. The Treaty contains no definition of CEEs, so the task of defining this concept was left to the Court.

The landmark ruling on the definition of CEEs is the *Diamonds* case.[193] Belgium had established a Social Fund for Diamond Workers. All imports of unworked diamonds were subject to a contribution intended to enable the fund to fulfil its tasks. The contribution amounted to 0.33 per cent of the value of the unworked diamonds imported. The Court ruled:

> any pecuniary charge, however small and whatever its designation and mode of application, which is imposed unilaterally on domestic or foreign goods by reason of the fact that they cross a frontier, and which is not a customs duty in the strict sense, constitutes a charge having equivalent effect within the meaning of Articles [28] and [30] of the Treaty, even if it is not imposed for the benefit of the State, is not discriminatory or protective in effect or if the product on which the charge is imposed is not in competition with any domestic product.[194]

The following aspects of this definition should be highlighted. First, a CEE is a *pecuniary* charge; in other words, an obligation to pay a sum of money.

Secondly, the charge must be imposed on domestic or foreign goods by reason of the fact that they cross a frontier.[195]

Thirdly, it is irrelevant that the amount of the charge is minimal, as was the case in the underlying dispute (0.33 per cent). As the Court indicated, the justification for this is that any charge, however small, constitutes an obstacle to the free movement of such goods. (As mentioned in section 7, Articles 34 and 35 TFEU are not subject to a *de minimis* rule either.)

Fourthly, the designation and mode of application are also irrelevant.

[191] Case 26/62 *Van Gend en Loos* [1963] ECR 1.

[192] See further chapter 6.

[193] *Diamonds* (n 25); see also Joined Cases 2/62 and 3/62 *Commission v Luxembourg and Belgium* [1962] ECR 813.

[194] *Diamonds* (n 25) paras 15–18.

[195] Case C-402/14 *Viamar*, EU:C:2015:830 concerned a car registration tax, which is usually a form of internal taxation. However, this tax was not reimbursed even if vehicles were re-exported without ever being registered in the Member State concerned. Consequently, the Court found that the tax was imposed solely by virtue of the fact that the goods crossed the frontier and thus constituted a CEE prohibited by Art 30.

Fifthly, the concept of CEEs is not confined to charges imposed for the benefit of the State (although this is probably the most frequent situation) but extends to those which finance another entity such as a social fund. Moreover, CEEs are prohibited independently of any consideration of the purpose for which they were introduced and the destination of the revenue obtained.

Sixthly, charges may constitute CEEs even if they are not discriminatory or protective. A charge imposed on both imports and exports (but not on domestic products sold on the market of the Member State concerned) can be a CEE. What is more, a charge may be caught by Article 30 TFEU even if there is no domestic production of the goods in question: although Antwerp is one of the world's major diamond trading centres, Belgium has no diamond mines.

Furthermore, in *Istanbul Lojistik*, the Court held that 'a charge which is imposed not on a product as such, but on a necessary activity in connection with' it may be a CEE.[196] Accordingly, a Hungarian charge imposed on Turkish lorries each time they entered or left the country if their laden weight exceeded 12 tonnes, was held to be a CEE—even though the charge was not imposed on the cargo as such but on the vehicles.[197]

Finally, the Court has consistently held that the prohibition of customs duties and CEEs constitutes a fundamental rule which does not permit of any exceptions.[198] The *Works of art* case is particularly interesting in relation to this issue.[199] The Court declared that the elimination of all obstacles to the free movement of goods by the abolition of customs duties and CEEs is a fundamental principle; and that exceptions to this fundamental rule must be strictly construed. Thus, the grounds of justification recognized in Article 36 TFEU cannot be invoked in the context of Article 30 TFEU. If a Member State wishes to protect its artistic treasures, it can only do so by adopting *MEEs* on exports which are compatible with Article 36.[200]

8.3 **Permissible charges**

Despite the strict approach adopted by the Court to customs duties and CEEs, there are two situations which may escape the prohibition contained in Article 30 TFEU, namely (a) where the payment is consideration for a service rendered, or (b) where it relates to inspections required by EU law. These are not exceptions to the prohibition on CEEs: such charges are not CEEs at all. However, attempts to show that a charge falls within one of these two situations rarely succeed.

8.3.1 **Services rendered**

According to the case law, the service must confer a specific advantage on the importer or exporter and the charge must be proportionate to the benefit conferred.[201] In *Statistical levies*,[202] Italy had imposed a small charge on imports and exports of goods. Italy argued, inter alia, that the charge constituted consideration for a service rendered, namely the

[196] Case C-65/16 *Istanbul Lojistik*, EU:C:2017:770, para 43. The same principle applies to Art 110: see section 9.

[197] The case concerned the provisions on the partial customs union with Turkey, but the Court applied Art 30 by analogy (para 44).

[198] eg *Diamonds* (n 25) paras 19–21.

[199] *Works of art* (n 15).

[200] See section 7.4 for more details on Art 36 TFEU.

[201] Case 132/82 *Commission v Belgium* [1983] ECR 1649, para 8.

[202] Case 24/68 *Commission v Italy* [1969] ECR 193.

availability of accurate statistics on imports and exports. The Court rejected this argument on the ground that the statistical information was beneficial to the economy as a whole, but not to the individual importer or exporter.[203]

8.3.2 Inspections required by EU law

Where health inspections are *required* by EU law, Member States are entitled to recover the costs, subject to certain conditions.[204] In *Commission v Germany*, the conditions were stated to be as follows:

(a) the charge must not exceed the actual cost of the inspection;

(b) the inspections in question must be obligatory and uniform for all products in the EU;

(c) the inspections must be required by EU law; and

(d) they must facilitate the free movement of goods by eliminating obstacles which could arise from unilateral measures of inspection adopted by Member States in accordance with Article 36.[205]

In contrast, where EU law merely *permits* Member States to carry out the inspections, Article 30 applies.[206]

8.4 Remedies

The consequence of breaching the prohibition is that the Member State concerned must eliminate the CEE. Furthermore, where charges have been unlawfully levied, the persons concerned have a right to be reimbursed by the Member State in question.[207] Repayment will be subject to the conditions and procedures established by domestic law, which cannot be less favourable than those relating to similar claims regarding national charges (principle of equivalence) and cannot render it virtually impossible or excessively difficult to obtain repayment (principle of effectiveness).[208] However, in order to ensure that traders are not unjustly enriched, repayment may be excluded when the charges levied unlawfully have been incorporated into the price of the goods and passed on to consumers.[209]

9 Discriminatory or protective internal taxation

The purpose of Article 110 TFEU is to prevent Member States from circumventing the prohibitions in Articles 30 and 34 to 36 TFEU by introducing internal taxes which are liable to make goods imported from other Member States less attractive than domestic products.[210] As we saw in section 8.2, the Court held in *Co-Frutta*[211] that this provision extends to goods originating in third countries but in free circulation in the Member States.

[203] See also Case 87/75 *Bresciani* [1976] ECR 129.

[204] Case 46/76 *Bauhuis* [1977] ECR 5. The inspections themselves are MEEs; see section 7.

[205] Case 18/87 *Commission v Germany* [1988] ECR 5427, para 8.

[206] Case 314/82 *Commission v Belgium* [1984] ECR 1543.

[207] Case 199/82 *San Giorgio* [1983] ECR 3595, para 12. Art 30 TFEU is directly effective; see n 9.

[208] *San Giorgio* (n 207).

[209] Ibid, para 13. This idea was further developed in Joined Cases C-192–218/95 *Comateb* [1997] ECR I-165.

[210] *Tatu* (n 25) paras 52 and 53.

[211] Case 193/85 (n 8).

Article 110 TFEU refers to 'products from other Member States', which may suggest that it only prohibits discrimination against imported products. Nevertheless, it is now clear that discrimination against exports in favour of products intended for domestic consumption is also contrary to this provision.[212] This makes perfect sense, since the Treaty also prohibits customs duties, CEEs, QRs, and MEEs on exports.

If Article 110 TFEU were confined to taxes on goods themselves, then many types of discriminatory tax would fall outside the Treaties altogether, even though they constitute serious barriers to the internal market. Accordingly, the Court has consistently held that this provision 'must be interpreted widely so as to cover all taxation procedures which, directly or indirectly, conflict with the principle of equality of treatment of domestic products and imported products'.[213] Thus in *Bergandi*,[214] the legality of a tax on the *use* of automatic gaming machines was assessed under this Article. Similarly, discriminatory fees for health inspections[215] and port duties[216] were found to be in breach of Article 110 TFEU. Finally, in *Frohnleiten* the same was held to apply to a discriminatory levy on dumping imported waste on a landfill site.[217]

Two separate prohibitions are in issue: a prohibition under the first paragraph of Article 110 on internal discriminatory taxation in favour of similar domestic products; and a prohibition under the second paragraph on internal taxation affording protection to other domestic products in competition with imported products. It cannot be sufficiently stressed that Member States can impose any taxes they like on products as long as they are not discriminatory or protective.[218]

9.1 Article 110(1) TFEU: discrimination against similar imported products

The prohibition laid down in Article 110(1) applies where two cumulative conditions are met: first, the relevant imported product and the relevant domestic product must be similar; and, secondly, there must be discrimination (unjustified differential treatment).

9.1.1 Similar products

In its early case law, the Court relied on a rather rudimentary criterion for determining whether products are similar, namely whether they were in the same fiscal, customs, or statistical classification.[219] However, probably due to the inherent limitations of this formalistic approach, the Court soon started to develop a test based on the products' characteristics and consumers' needs: a comparison must be made between products which, at the same stage of production, have similar characteristics and satisfy the same consumer needs.[220]

This is illustrated by *Johnnie Walker*, which concerned a Danish system of differential taxation of Scotch whisky and fruit wine of the liqueur type.[221] The Court stated that, in order to establish whether two products are similar, it is necessary to begin by considering

[212] Case 142/77 *Larsen* [1978] ECR 1543, paras 24–26. For the sake of simplicity, the remainder of this chapter will simply refer to imported products.

[213] Case C-252/86 *Bergandi*, EU:C:1988:112, para 25 and Case C-221/06 *Frohnleiten* [2007] ECR I-2613, para 40.

[214] *Bergandi* (n 213).

[215] Case 29/87 *Dansk Denkavit* [1988] ECR 2965.

[216] Case C-90/94 *Haahr Petroleum* [1997] ECR I-4085.

[217] *Frohnleiten* (n 213). Waste constitutes goods for the purposes of the Treaty: *Walloon waste* (n 18); see section 3.

[218] *Bergandi* (n 213) para 24.

[219] Case 27/67 *Fink-Frucht* [1968] ECR 223, 232.

[220] Case 45/75 *Rewe-Zentrale* [1976] ECR 181, para 12.

[221] Case 243/84 *John Walker & Sons* [1986] ECR 875.

certain objective characteristics of the beverages, such as their origin, method of manufacture, organoleptic properties (taste, smell, etc), and alcohol content. Then it must be established whether the two beverages are capable of satisfying the same consumer needs. In the case at hand, it was held that the two beverages had manifestly different characteristics (eg different manufacturing methods, different alcoholic strengths) and therefore could not be regarded as 'similar products'.[222]

Further examples of the interpretation of this concept may be found in *Commission v France* (*'Cigarettes'*), in which the Court held that light-tobacco cigarettes and dark-tobacco cigarettes should be regarded as similar,[223] and in *X* (*'Cars'*), where the Court set out detailed guidance as to the specific criteria to be taken into account in order to establish whether two motor vehicles can be regarded as similar (eg price, size, performance, comfort, etc).[224]

In conclusion, the concept of similarity has been interpreted broadly by the Court, but its precise boundaries remain somewhat unclear. Although it is usual to carry out a systematic and rigorous analysis inspired by economic concepts to define the relevant product market in competition law, there has been no attempt to draw inspiration from this for the purposes of Article 110.[225]

9.1.2 **Discrimination**

Member States must ensure that their taxation systems are 'neutral' between imported and domestic products and do not treat the latter more favourably. As is clear from its wording, Article 110(1) prohibits both direct and indirect discrimination (without prejudice to the possibility of establishing a system of differentiated taxation based on legitimate criteria).[226]

Direct discrimination arises when the tax scheme differentiates explicitly on the basis of the origin of products. The most obvious examples are where the tax burden imposed on imported products is heavier than that imposed on domestic products,[227] or where only domestic products may benefit from a reduction.[228] The same applies where domestic products are subject to a flat tax and imports to a progressive tax[229]—or vice versa[230]—if that leads, at least in some cases, to a higher rate being levied on imports. Direct discrimination also occurs where domestic producers are given longer time limits for the payment of the tax[231] or where the penalties applied for infringing the tax legislation are more severe for imported products than for domestic products.[232]

222 Ibid, paras 11–14.

223 Case C-302/00 *Commission v France* (*'Cigarettes'*) [2002] ECR I-2055.

224 Case C-437/12 *X* (*'Cars'*), EU:C:2013:857.

225 See chapter 17. Given the broad interpretation of the concept of similarity, it is arguable that two products may be regarded as similar for the purposes of Art 110 TFEU, even if they are not part of the same relevant product market for the purposes of competition law. Compare Case 112/84 *Humblot* [1985] ECR 1367, where the Court rejected the suggestion that luxury motor vehicles were not similar to their more humble counterparts for the purposes of Art 110(1), and the Commission's decision in Case No COMP/M.5518—Fiat/Chrysler, where the Commission indicated that it might be appropriate to segment the relevant market between luxury motor vehicles and others.

226 See section 9.4.

227 *Haahr Petroleum* (n 216).

228 Case 148/77 *Hansen* [1978] ECR 1787 (tax reductions for certain fruit spirits and for spirits from small distilleries not available for imports) and Case 21/79 *Commission v Italy* (*'Regenerated oil'*) [1980] ECR-1 (reduction to promote the recycling and regeneration of petroleum products not available for imports).

229 Case 127/75 *Bobie* [1976] ECR 1079.

230 Case C-213/96 *Outokumpu Oy* [1998] ECR I-1777.

231 Case 55/79 *Commission v Ireland* [1980] ECR 481.

232 Case 299/86 *Drexl* [1988] ECR 1213.

Indirect discrimination arises where the tax scheme does not explicitly differentiate by reason of the origin of the products but in fact imposes a heavier tax burden on imported products. An illustrative example is *Humblot*, where an individual challenged the French annual road tax on cars.[233] Under the scheme, France imposed a progressive tax on cars with 16 CV (fiscal horsepower) or less. In contrast, cars with a higher horsepower were subject to a flat-rate tax, which was considerably higher. The Court noted that Member States were free to establish a progressive tax system which increased the rate depending on an objective factor such as horsepower. However, they must ensure that the system does not have any discriminatory effect. Although the scheme did not formally differentiate on the basis of the origin of the products, it was deemed to be discriminatory because only imported cars were subject to the higher flat-rate tax. Moreover, the increase from the progressive tax to the flat-rate tax was much higher than any of the increases in the various steps existing within the progressive tax (the flat-rate tax was almost five times higher than the highest progressive tax rate).

In *Cigarettes*,[234] the Court examined the French excise duty on cigarettes. The system did not differentiate on the basis of the origin of the cigarettes. However, the tax on light-tobacco cigarettes was higher than that on dark-tobacco cigarettes. The Court noted that the system was designed in such a way that the products falling within the most favourable tax category (dark-tobacco cigarettes) were almost all produced domestically, whereas almost all imported products came within the least favoured category (light-tobacco cigarettes). The scheme was therefore discriminatory. It was irrelevant that a very small fraction of imported cigarettes came within the most favoured category and that a certain proportion of domestic production were within the least favoured category.

Finally, in line with the traditional principle that the Treaty does not prohibit *reverse* discrimination,[235] Article 110(1) does not preclude Member States from imposing higher internal taxes on domestic products than on imported products.[236]

9.2 **Article 110(2) TFEU: protection of domestic competing products**

The prohibition enshrined in Article 110(2) TFEU applies if two cumulative conditions are met: first, the imported product and the domestic product must be in competition with one another; secondly, the tax must protect the domestic product. Both conditions are more easily satisfied than those in Article 110(1) TFEU. But it is also fair to say that the boundaries of legal test applicable to the two conditions of Article 110(2) ('competing products' and 'protection') are more imprecise than the conditions of Article 110(1).

In *Fink-Frucht*, the Court indicated that Article 110(2) does not require the imported product and the domestic product to be in *direct* competition. However, their competitive relationship cannot be merely fortuitous, but must be lasting and characteristic.[237]

The leading case in this area is the *Commission v UK* ('*Wine and beer*') saga.[238] These proceedings, which concerned a differentiated tax scheme for beer (essentially a domestic product) and wine (all of which was imported), were brought by the Commission against

[233] *Humblot* (n 225).

[234] *Cigarettes* (n 223).

[235] See section 5 and Case 35/82 *Morson* [1982] ECR 3723. For a detailed discussion on reverse discrimination, see Barnard, *The Substantive Law of the EU* (n 97) 90–91.

[236] Case 86/78 *Peureux* [1979] ECR 897, paras 32 and 33.

[237] *Fink-Frucht* (n 219).

[238] Case 170/78 *Commission v UK* [1980] ECR 417 (interlocutory judgment) and [1983] ECR 2265 (final judgment).

the UK exclusively on the basis of Article 110(2). In its interlocutory judgment, the Court took the unusual step, in view of the significant uncertainties as to whether beer and wine were in competition and whether the tax scheme had protective effects, of ordering the parties to re-examine the case and to make new submissions by a fixed date.

In its final judgment, the Court emphasized that Article 110(2) applies to products which, without being 'similar', are in partial or potential competition. To a certain extent, wine and beer were capable of meeting identical consumer needs and thus there was a degree of mutual substitution. On the other hand, the Court acknowledged the substantial differences between their manufacturing processes and their natural properties. Ultimately, in view of the substantial differences in quality and price of wines, the Court found that the products which should be regarded in competition were beer and the lightest and cheapest varieties of wine.[239]

Next, the Court considered whether the British tax scheme protected beer. The parties disagreed as to the relevant method of comparison, namely the assessment of the tax burden by reference to (a) the volume of the beverage, (b) the alcoholic strength, or (c) the price of the products. Applying all three criteria, the Court ruled that the tax on cheaper wines was several times higher than on beer. Thus, the British tax system had the effect of stamping wine with the hallmarks of a luxury product, which would not constitute a genuine alternative to domestic beer in the eyes of consumers.[240] Consequently, the UK had infringed Article 110(2) TFEU.

The outcome of these proceedings stands in contrast to that in the subsequent Swedish case, which concerned the same products.[241] As in the UK *Wine and beer* case, the Court concluded that strong beers and the lightest wines were in competition. However, although it recognized that the tax burden on wine was higher (up to 50 per cent) than that on beer, it concluded that the differential tax treatment was unlikely to influence consumer behaviour, probably due to the modest amount of the tax.[242] Thus Article 110(2) was not infringed.

9.3 **The holistic approach to Article 110 TFEU**

The determination as to whether two products are 'similar' within the meaning of Article 110(1) TFEU may often be difficult in practice, since the precise boundaries of this concept remain blurred. Accordingly, in certain cases the Court has followed what might be called a 'holistic' approach to Article 110, namely an approach which does not distinguish between the first and the second paragraphs.

This can be observed in the *Spirits* cases.[243] The French *Spirits* case concerned a tax scheme which differentiated between spirits obtained from wine or fruit (eg cognac, Armagnac, and calvados) and those based on cereals (eg whisky, gin, and vodka). The former category was predominantly French, whereas spirits in the latter category were overwhelmingly imported. After indicating that it was necessary to interpret the concept of 'similar products' with sufficient flexibility, the Court emphasized that the relevant criterion should not be the strictly identical nature of the products but that of their 'similar and comparable use'. The Court noted that it was impossible to disregard the fact that all the relevant products had certain common features (eg they were distilled and contained

239 Ibid, final judgment, paras 7–12.

240 Ibid, paras 13–28.

241 Case C-167/05 *Commission v Sweden* ('*Wine and beer*') [2008] ECR I-2127, paras 40ff.

242 The impact of the tax differential in the final selling price amounted to around €0.50 per litre.

243 Case 168/78 *Commission v France* [1980] ECR 347; Case 169/78 *Commission v Italy* [1980] ECR 385; and Case 171/68 *Commission v Denmark* [1980] ECR 447.

alcohol), but also had their own characteristics (the raw materials used, flavourings, or manufacturing processes). It found that some spirits were 'similar' to one another within the meaning of Article 110(1) TFEU, although it might be difficult to decide this in specific cases. In any event, spirits had sufficiently common characteristics to consider that they were at least in partial competition for the purposes of Article 110(2) TFEU.[244] Accordingly, in view of the difficulties of establishing whether certain products should be regarded as 'similar', the Court found that France had infringed Article 110 taken as a whole.

It is submitted, however, that this approach can be problematic, due to the fact that Article 110(1) prohibits discrimination, while Article 110(2) prohibits protectionism. Indeed, while Article 110(1) prevents (unjustified) differential treatment, Article 110(2) allows for differential treatment as long as it is not protectionist.[245] In more recent times, the Court has avoided applying the two paragraphs cumulatively.

9.4 **Legitimate differentiation/justification**

Systems of differentiated taxation are common across the world. Such systems are compatible with Article 110 TFEU if they are justified by an objective and legitimate policy reason (eg environmental protection, social policy, economic policy), so long as they are not discriminatory or protective.[246]

An interesting example is *Chemial Farmaceutici*, in which Italy had adopted a differentiated tax scheme applicable to ethyl alcohol obtained from fermentation (derived from agricultural products) and to synthetic ethyl alcohol (derived from oil).[247] Even though the two categories of ethyl alcohol were based on quite different raw materials, their chemical properties were identical. The Court held that differentiated tax schemes are permissible if three conditions are met. First, the criteria must be objective. Secondly, the differentiation must pursue legitimate objectives. Thirdly, the detailed rules must avoid any form of direct or indirect discrimination against imported products and any form of protection of competing domestic products.[248] The Court found that all three conditions were fulfilled in that case. In particular, it ruled that a policy favouring agricultural over manufactured products was legitimate.

It follows that, although measures caught by Article 110 TFEU cannot be justified on the grounds set out in Article 36 or the mandatory requirements,[249] it may be possible to put in place a system of differentiated taxation which does not infringe Article 110.

9.5 **Remedies**

The consequences of infringing Article 110(1) TFEU are different from the consequences of a breach of Article 110(2) TFEU: in the case of a discriminatory tax (Article 110(1)) the Member State must equalize the taxes imposed on similar products; but with a protective

[244] *Commission v France* (n 243) paras 11–13.

[245] See section 9.5.

[246] See *Hansen* (n 228) (tax differentiation to promote the use of certain raw materials, the production of spirits of high quality, or the continuance of certain classes of undertakings); *Regenerated oil* (n 228) (tax scheme promoting environmental protection); and Case C-132/88 *Commission v Greece* (*Cars*) [1990] ECR I-1567.

[247] Case 140/79 *Chemial Farmaceutici* [1981] ECR 1.

[248] Ibid, para 14.

[249] See, to that effect, Opinion of AG Bot in *Visnapuu* (n 74), para 57 and Opinion of AG Saugmandsgaard Øe in Case C-855/19 *Dyrektor Izby Administracji Skarbowej w Bydgoszczy*, EU:C:2021:222, para 59.

tax (Article 110(2)) it is required to eliminate the protectionist effect, without necessarily equalizing the tax.[250] Persons who have paid undue tax by reason of a breach of either paragraph of Article 110 may recover the sums concerned according to the same principles as those applying to infringements of Article 30.[251]

10 The boundaries between the provisions on free movement of goods

In *Iannelli v Meroni*, the Court held: 'However wide the field of application of Article [34] may be, it nevertheless does not include obstacles to trade covered by other provisions of the Treaty.'[252] Consequently, it ruled that Articles 30 and 34 TFEU are mutually exclusive.[253] For the same reason, Articles 34 and 110 TFEU are also mutually exclusive.[254] It follows that Article 34 never applies to taxes.[255] Beyond any doubt, Article 35 TFEU cannot be applied cumulatively with Article 30 or 110 TFEU either. Equally, a tax or charge can be caught either by Article 30 or 110 TFEU, but not both.[256]

The rationale behind these principles is spelt out in the following passage of Advocate General Jacobs's Opinion in *De Danske Bilimportører*:

> If a charge is caught by Article [30] it must be abolished, whereas if it is caught by Article [110] then only the discriminatory or protective element need be removed. A measure caught by Article [34] may be permitted if it pursues one or more justified aims in a manner proportionate to their achievement, whereas the scope for justification under Articles [30] or [110] is very much more limited. On the other hand, those two articles apply only in a limited set of circumstances, always involving a charge or tax, whereas Article [34] is capable of applying to a very wide variety of measures which may hinder trade.[257]

10.1 The two *Danish cars* judgments

In *Commission v Denmark* ('*Cars*'),[258] the Commission sought a ruling from the Court that Denmark had infringed Article 110 TFEU with its very high registration taxes for new vehicles. The Court ruled that that provision could not be infringed because there was no domestic production of new motor vehicles in Denmark. This Article, it held, could not be relied on to challenge the allegedly excessive level of national taxes unless they could be regarded as discriminatory or protective.[259] However, the Court suggested that, although

[250] That is how the UK put an end to the infringement in *Wine and beer* (n 238).

[251] Case 68/79 *Hans Just* [1980] ECR 501.

[252] *Iannelli* (n 9) para 9. See also Case C-228/98 *Dounias* [2000] ECR I-577, para 39.

[253] See Case C-78/90 *Compagnie Commerciale de l'Ouest*, EU:C:1992:118 and Case C-383/01 *De Danske Bilimportører* [2003] ECR I-6065, para 32.

[254] *Fink-Frucht* (n 219) and *Iannelli* (n 9).

[255] Accordingly, the ruling in Case C-591/17 *Austria v Germany*, EU:C:2019:504, is highly anomalous: it was held that there a road tax imposed de facto only on passenger vehicles registered abroad was a breach of inter alia Art 34, although clearly that measure should have been assessed under Art 30 (unfortunately, however, Austria had not relied on that provision).

[256] Case C-234/99 *Nygård* [2002] ECR I-3657, para 17 and *De Danske Bilimportører* (n 253) para 33.

[257] *De Danske Bilimportører* (n 253) para 31 of the Opinion.

[258] Case C-47/88 *Commission v Denmark* ('*Cars*') [1990] ECR I-4509 (2016).

[259] Ibid, para 10.

the Commission's action must fail because it was based exclusively on Article 110 TFEU, it might be possible to challenge the tax on the basis of Article 34 TFEU.[260]

A decade later, this rather unusual assertion led an association of importers of motor vehicles to contest the high registration tax imposed on new motor vehicles (frequently exceeding 200 per cent!) on the basis of Article 34.[261] However, the Court found that that provision was not applicable because the measure was of a fiscal nature. The only relevant provision was Article 110 since the measure was part of a scheme of internal taxation and, in the absence of domestic production of new cars, there could be no discrimination. Nevertheless, it appeared to suggest that, if the tax was so high as to render imports of cars prohibitive (which was not the case), then it might be contrary to some other provision of the Treaty;[262] but the Court did not mention a specific provision.

In sum, if a Member State requires compliance with certain rules, that measure is to be assessed under Article 34 or 35. In contrast, if a Member State imposes an obligation to pay an amount of money, that measure falls to be analysed under Article 30 or 110.

10.2 **CEEs and discriminatory internal taxation**

The dividing line between Articles 30 and 110 TFEU is as follows: the former applies to charges imposed due to the fact that products cross a frontier, whereas the latter applies to taxes imposed within a Member State.[263] Thus, the chargeable event for taxes caught by Article 110 is an internal transaction, unconnected as such with the importation or exportation of the goods.[264]

Two types of situation deserve to be briefly mentioned here: the cases in which the charge is imposed on goods of a kind which is not produced in the Member State in question; and so-called 'parafiscal' charges.

As regards the cases in which there is no domestic production of the relevant goods, this fact is irrelevant for the characterization of the charge.[265] The charge may be a CEE[266] or an internal tax[267] depending on the chargeable event. If it is imposed by reason of the fact that goods cross a frontier (for instance by reference to the origin or destination of the goods), it will be a CEE; but it will constitute internal taxation if it is part of a general system of internal dues, even if there is no domestic production.

The phenomenon of 'parafiscal' charges relates to situations in which the proceeds are used to provide a benefit to the domestic industry. Usually, the charge is imposed both on imported and domestic products. Parafiscal charges fall within the scope of Article 30 or Article 110 depending on whether the advantage granted to the domestic production wholly or partly offsets the burden of the charge. In the first case, the parafiscal charge

[260] Ibid, paras 12 and 13.

[261] *De Danske Bilimportører* (n 253).

[262] Ibid, para 40.

[263] *Commission v Denmark* ('*Cars*') (n 258). If a charge is imposed on domestic and imported goods at the same marketing stage and the chargeable event is identical in both cases, it will be regarded as part of the internal taxation system and will be analysed under Art 110. In contrast, if a charge is imposed on products intended for export on the grounds that products consumed domestically are subject to a similar charge, it will be treated as a CEE under Art 30. See Case C-305/17 *FENS*, EU:C:2018:986, paras 36–41.

[264] For an unusual case, see *Viamar* (n 195).

[265] Otherwise the same type of measure applied in two different Member States would be characterized differently, depending on whether there is domestic production of the goods in question. Moreover, the existence or otherwise of domestic production may change over time, which would create legal uncertainty.

[266] See *Diamonds* (n 23); see section 8.2.

[267] See *Co-Frutta* (n 10), in which Italy applied a tax on the consumption of bananas. Although an extremely small quantity of bananas was being produced in Italy, the Court considered that the tax should be assessed under Art 110.

will be regarded as a CEE, whereas the second case will be regarded as discriminatory internal taxation.[268]

10.3 What if there are two distinct, but closely linked measures?

Finally, there are situations in which two distinct measures may nevertheless be closely linked. This is clearly illustrated by the cases in which imports and/or exports are subject to health inspections, and a charge is imposed for those inspections. The inspections constitute MEEs under Articles 34 and 35 TFEU (which may be justified), while the charges are CEEs under Article 30 TFEU.[269]

11 Conclusion

Free movement of goods was the first of the four freedoms to flourish and mature. As the reader will be aware, the Treaty of Rome which established the EEC came into force on 1 January 1958. All the provisions discussed in this chapter became effective by the end of 1969, but some had already done so before then. Without prejudice to the substantive body of harmonizing rules adopted by the EU legislature, this chapter shows unequivocally the fundamental role played by the case law of the Court of Justice in the crystallization of the rules on free movement of goods, which tend to gravitate around the principle of home country control (subject to certain qualifications). Notwithstanding the specificities of the Treaty rules on free movement of goods (which contain separate provisions for fiscal measures and for non-fiscal measures), the evolution of this freedom has paved the way for the development of the other fundamental freedoms and thus it is often possible to identify similar milestones along the road: a trend from prohibiting discrimination towards tackling non-discriminatory obstacles to trade; the need to respect the principle of proportionality when it comes to justification; the recognition of mandatory requirements or public interest requirements, alongside the Treaty grounds of justification; etc. Accordingly, it is submitted that those who are familiar with the rules on free movement of goods are well equipped to master the subtleties and complexities of the internal market as a whole.

The case law of the Court of Justice on free movement of goods is mature by now and sound. Therefore, whatever improvements this area of law may still require (such as those called for in the Draghi and Letta reports), in the author's view, these will necessarily require further harmonization measures[270] as the possibilities stemming from *negative* integration appear to have been exhausted already.

Further reading

C Barnard, *The Substantive Law of the EU: The Four Freedoms* (8th edn, Oxford: Oxford University Press, 2025) chs 1–5

Commission, 'Guide on Articles 34–36 TFEU' (2021 OJ C100/38)

[268] Case 77/72 *Capolongo* [1973] ECR 611; Case 77/76 *Cucchi* [1977] ECR 987; *Compagnie Commerciale de l'Ouest* (n 253); Case C-28/96 *Fazenda Pública* [1997] ECR I-4939; *Nygård* (n 256); and Case C-517/04 *Koornstra* [2006] ECR I-5015.

[269] *Bauhuis* (n 204) paras 12 and 13.

[270] Also known as *positive* integration.

S Enchelmaier, '*Moped Trailers, Mickelsson & Ross, Gysbrechts*: The ECJ's Case Law on Goods Keeps on Moving' (2010) 29 *Yearbook of European Law* 190

L Gormley, 'Inconsistencies and Misconceptions in the Free Movement of Goods' (2015) 40 *European Law Review* 925

P Oliver, 'Mutual Recognition: Addressing Some Outstanding Conundrums' in A Albors-Llorens, C Barnard, and B Leucht (eds), *Cassis de Dijon: 40 Years On* (Oxford: Hart Publishing, 2021) ch 8

P Oliver et al, *Oliver on Free Movement of Goods in the European Union* (5th edn, Oxford: Hart Publishing, 2010)

R Schütze, *From International to Federal Market* (Oxford: Oxford University Press, 2017) chs 3–4

J Snell, 'The Notion of Market Access: A Concept or a Slogan?' (2010) 47 *Common Market Law Review* 437

E Spaventa, 'The Classic Freedom? The Free Movement of Goods' in S Garben and I Govaere (eds), *The Internal Market 2.0* (Oxford: Hart Publishing, 2020) ch 5

S Weatherill *The Internal Market as a Legal Concept* (Oxford: Oxford University Press, 2017) especially ch 6

Chapter acknowledgements

The author writes here in his personal capacity. A previous version of this chapter was written together with Peter Oliver.

13

Free movement of natural persons and citizenship of the Union

Catherine Barnard

1 Introduction

1.1 The Treaty provisions and their use

Any reader of this book, who is an EU national, is likely to have exercised rights of free movement within the EU: as a tourist on holiday in Italy, as a student studying on an Erasmus programme in Germany, as a ski instructor in the French Alps, or as a recipient of services provided by Amazon in Luxembourg. All of these situations are covered by one of the following provisions of EU law:

- Article 45 TFEU on the free movement of workers, which allows EU nationals to work in another Member State in an employed capacity (dependent labour) on a permanent basis. This also covers frontier workers who live in one Member State but work in another;
- Article 49 TFEU on freedom of establishment, which allows EU nationals to work in another Member State in a self-employed capacity on a permanent basis (independent labour);
- Articles 56 and 57 TFEU on the free movement of services, which allow EU nationals to provide or receive services in another Member State (independent labour).

These three types of movement, all included in the Treaty of Rome, presuppose that migrant EU nationals are 'economically active' (as a worker, a self-employed person, or as a provider/receiver of services). They contribute to the economy of the host State (ie the State in which they work), through their labour and by paying taxes. They were thus seen by the Treaty drafters as a benefit to the host State.[1] However, since the Maastricht Treaty in 1992, 'Every person holding the nationality of a Member State shall be a citizen of the Union' (now Article 20 TFEU),[2] which, according to Article 21 TFEU, gives them certain rights to free movement, whether they are economically active or not. While EU citizenship, granted by the EU, was introduced to give a greater sense of EU identity to EU nationals, receiving States became increasingly concerned about 'benefit tourism', namely individuals moving with a view to obtaining (better) social welfare benefits in other States. It was the (receiving) States and their taxpayers that were footing the bill.

The Treaty rights on free movement of persons (Articles 45, 49, 56, and 21 TFEU) have been elaborated by the EU legislature, notably by the Citizens' Rights Directive (CRD) 2004/38[3] and, for workers, by Regulation 492/11[4] and the Enforcement Directive 2014/54.[5] The advent of EU citizenship has produced some surprise twists and turns in the case law[6] and has, at least in the past, helped to shape the Court's interpretation of the secondary legislation.

The right to free movement of persons, especially Article 45 TFEU, has proved the most controversial of the four freedoms. For some, free movement is an article of faith, the defining feature of the EU. For others, it is a destructive force, with migrants competing with nationals for jobs and other limited resources (housing, maternity services, schooling), ultimately leading to a hollowing out of national identity. The EU enlargements in 2004 and 2007 brought countries into the EU where wages were significantly lower than those in Northern Europe, leading to a significant increase in the numbers of those exercising free movement rights which had not, in fact, occurred prior to 2004. Transitional arrangements were put in place by a number of countries to stop the sudden arrival of a large number of people moving from the Central and Eastern European countries; these arrangements expired seven years after the enlargement.

The UK (together with Ireland and Sweden) did not impose transitional arrangements in 2004. It proved a magnet for about six million EU workers coming to the UK to work. The economy benefited but, for many voters, especially in small, economically deprived towns, the arrival of many Eastern European workers was seen as a threat. As the *Economist* noted, where foreign-born populations increased by more than 200 per cent between 2001 and 2014, a Leave vote followed in 94 per cent of cases.[7] Controlling immigration was the principal reason for a vote to Leave the EU.

1.2 **Themes**

With this context in mind, four themes/questions will shape this chapter. First, one of the indicators of national sovereignty is the ability for a State to 'control its own borders' or rather control who comes into its country and for what purpose. The EU rules on the four freedoms pose a direct challenge to this. Some say that if the EU is becoming more

[1] For background on the origins of free movement of workers, C Barnard and S Fraser Butlin, 'Ceding Control and Taking It Back: The Origins of Free Movement in EU Law' (2022) 51 *Industrial Law Journal* 643.

[2] Art 20 TFEU continues: 'Citizenship of the Union shall be additional to and not replace national citizenship.'

[3] OJ [2004] L8/17. [4] OJ [2011] L141/1. [5] OJ [2014] L128/8.

[6] See eg Case C-138/02 *Collins v Secretary of State for Work and Pensions* [2004] ECR I-2703; Case C-184/99 *Grzelczyk* [2001] ECR I-6193; Case C-413/99 *Baumbast and R v Secretary of State for the Home Department* [2002] ECR I-7091.

[7] www.economist.com/britain/2016/07/08/britains-immigration-paradox.

like the United States of Europe then people should be able to move as freely between Bucharest and Berlin as they do between New York and San Francisco. Others say that the EU is far from (and should never become) a United States of Europe and so controls are needed. This raises the question of whether economic migration is beneficial for the host State and its (non-migrant) citizens. If not, should States be able to control the number of economic migrants coming into their country?[8] And what about the sending States? Are they losing some of their brightest and best? What can and should they do to encourage their citizens to stay?[9]

Secondly, the CRD and decisions of the Court of Justice, have broadened the net of beneficiaries of free movement to include those who are not (so) economically active (work-seekers, students, persons of independent means—the 'semi-economically active') as well as the economically inactive (eg the unemployed). Why should the non-economically active be able to migrate? Does a shared EU citizenship entitle them to move and, if so, enjoy social security benefits in the host State? Might this serve to undermine, rather than strengthen, any nascent solidarity upon which EU citizenship is based? At what price does this come to already overburdened social welfare systems in the host States?

Thirdly, the extension of the rights of free movement to the semi- and non-economically active is an illustration of a broader dynamic witnessed elsewhere in EU law: an increasing reference to, and reliance on, human rights.[10] EU free movers are no longer seen simply as factors of production contributing to the economy of the host State but also as the bearers of human rights. This means that, in principle, they should enjoy a certain standard of living in the host State, as should their family members, irrespective of the nationality of those family members. The Court has used the advent of EU citizenship to reinforce the link between migration and human rights—whether derived from the European Convention on Human Rights (ECHR) or from the EU Charter (see section 8). Does it mean that the right to free movement, itself a fundamental right in the Treaty and the Charter, applies not only to the young, fit, and well educated but also to groups viewed less favourably by society, including the Roma from Romania[11] and travelling football fans?[12] Further, do third-country nationals (TCNs), also human beings but not EU citizens, benefit from these rights?

Fourthly, should a single set of rules apply across the free movement of persons provisions? At first sight, the answer to this question is yes: Articles 45, 49, 56, and 21 TFEU all concern natural persons who move from one EU State to another. Often it is difficult to police the boundaries between one provision and another (see section 3). It therefore makes sense to apply common principles. However, if this analysis is correct, why have separate Treaty provisions at all? This suggests that there are differences between the Treaty provisions, but, if so, what might they be?

The aim of this chapter is to give an overview of the EU rules on free movement of natural persons; chapter 14 considers the free movement rules in respect of legal persons. The rules on free movement of persons cover a vast area of law, so this chapter is inevitably

[8] C Barnard and F Costello, 'The Darker Side of the Internal Market Ideal: EU Migrant Workers Living in a Coastal Town' in J Adams-Prassl et al (eds), *The Internal Market Ideal: Essays in Honour of Stephen Weatherill* (Oxford: Oxford University Press, 2024) 315.

[9] F Strumia, 'Supranational Citizenship's Enablers: Free Movement from the Perspective of Home Member States' (2020) 45 *European Law Review* 507. See also the Letta report, Enrico Letta—Much more than a market (April 2024), 15, which introduces the idea of 'freedom to stay': 'The Single Market should empower citizens rather than create circumstances where they feel compelled to relocate in order to thrive.'

[10] See further chapter 9.

[11] M Dawson and E Muir, 'Individual Institutional and Collective Vigilance in Protecting Fundamental Rights in the EU: Lessons from the Roma' (2011) 48 *Common Market Law Review* 751.

[12] *Gough and Smith v Chief Constable of Derbyshire* [2002] 2 CMLR 11.

selective both in its choice of subject matter and the cases discussed. The analysis that follows will be structured round seven questions which are considered in some form in most free movement of persons cases:

(a) Does EU law apply at all (section 2)? If yes,
(b) Which Treaty provision is engaged (section 3)?
(c) Does EU law apply to this particular person or entity ie are they bound by the obligations under EU law (section 4)? If yes,
(d) What rights do EU free movers enjoy under the secondary legislation (section 5)?
(e) What rules or practices breach the Treaty (section 6)?
(f) Can that breach be justified (section 7)? If yes,
(g) Is the breach compatible with human rights and are the steps proportionate (section 8)?

We begin with the most fundamental question: does EU law apply at all?

2 Does EU law apply at all?

2.1 Introduction

Various attempts have been made, usually by defendants, to argue that the case falls outside the scope of EU law and so should be judged by the standards of *national* law only, which they consider to be more favourable. The leading case of *Viking* provides a good example of this.[13] Viking Line, the Finnish owners of a passenger ferry which plied the route between Helsinki in Finland and Tallinn in Estonia, wanted to reflag the vessel as Estonian. The Finnish Seamen's Union (FSU), fearing that Finnish seamen's jobs were at stake, threatened strike action, which would have been lawful under Finnish law. The International Transport Federation (ITF) also told its members to black (ie not service) any Viking vessel. Viking Line argued that the action by FSU and ITF breached Article 49 TFEU on the freedom of establishment.

The first question for the Court of Justice was whether EU law applied at all. The trade unions and some governments argued not. For example, the Danish government argued that the right of freedom of association, the right to strike, and the right to impose lockouts fell outside the scope of the fundamental freedom laid down in Article 49 TFEU since, in accordance with Article 153(5) TFEU, the EU does not have competence to regulate those matters. The Court disagreed:[14]

> even if, in the areas which fall outside the scope of the Union's competence, the Member States are still free, in principle, to lay down the conditions governing the existence and exercise of the rights in question, the fact remains that, when exercising that competence, the Member States must nevertheless comply with [Union] law (see, by analogy, in relation to social security (*Decker and Kohll*);[15] in relation to direct taxation (*Commission v France* and *Marks & Spencer*)).[16]

[13] Case C-438/05 *International Transport Workers' Union Federation et al v Viking Line ABP* [2007] ECR I-7779. See also chapter 20.

[14] Ibid, para 40.

[15] Case C-120/95 *Decker* [1998] ECR I-1831, paras 22 and 23 and Case C-158/96 *Kohll* [1998] ECR I-1931, paras 18 and 19.

[16] Case C-334/02 *Commission v France* [2004] ECR I-2229, para 21 and Case C-446/03 *Marks & Spencer v Halsey* [2005] ECR I-10837, para 29.

In other words, even in areas such as social security, taxation, and strike action, where the EU has no—or highly circumscribed—competence to legislate (positive integration), the Treaty provisions on the four freedoms will still apply to national action (negative integration).

That said, there are three significant limitations on the application of the free movement provisions which the Court has, more or less consistently, upheld. The Treaty provisions apply only to those who:

(a) hold the nationality of a Member State;
(b) have moved to another Member State; and
(c) (in the case of Articles 45, 49, and 56 TFEU) have been, or are, engaged in some economic activity in the Member State they have moved to.

If one of these conditions is not satisfied, EU law will not apply. We shall consider these conditions in turn.

2.2 **EU nationality**

The free movement rights under Articles 45, 49, 56, and 21 TFEU apply to nationals of a current[17] EU Member State only; they do not apply to TCNs unless they are family members of the migrating EU national (see section 5.2.2). So who, then, is a national of a Member State? It had long been thought that this was purely a matter of national law.[18] However, the position has become muddied by the decisions in *Rottmann*[19] and now *Commission v Malta*,[20] where the Court focused not on Article 21 TFEU but on Article 20 TFEU which establishes 'Citizenship of the Union'. Specifically, Article 20 TFEU says 'Every person holding the nationality of a Member State shall be a citizen of the Union. Citizenship of the Union shall be additional to and not replace national citizenship.'

Rottmann, an Austrian national, was being investigated for serious fraud in Austria. During the investigations, he moved to Germany where he acquired German nationality, with the result that, under Austrian law, he lost his Austrian nationality.[21] When the German authorities discovered his past (which they had not known at the time of his naturalization) they tried to deprive him of his German citizenship. The Court said that even where a matter fell within the competence of the Member States, 'in situations covered by European Union law' the national system had to have 'regard for EU law'.[22] Because the decision of the German authorities risked rendering him stateless, and thus depriving him of 'the status [of citizen of the Union] conferred by Article [20 TFEU] and the rights attaching thereto', the Court said that this situation did fall 'within the ambit of European Union law'.[23] EU law principles, including proportionality, therefore applied.[24] This meant the German authorities had to take into account the consequences

[17] Case C-673/20 *EP v Préfet du Gers*, EU:C:2022:449, para 83: UK nationals lost EU citizenship due to Brexit.

[18] Case C-192/99 *R v Secretary of State, ex p Kaur* [2001] ECR I-1237, although cf Case C-369/90 *Micheletti v Delegación del Gobierno en Cantabria* [1992] ECR I-4239. See also Declaration No 2 on nationality of a Member State, annexed by the Member States to the final act of the Maastricht Treaty on European Union.

[19] Case C-135/08 *Rottmann v Freistaat Bayern* [2010] ECR I-1449.

[20] Case C-181/23 *Commission v Malta*, EU:C:2025:283.

[21] See C-118/20 *Wiener Landesregierung* (*Revocation of an assurance of naturalisation*), EU:C:2022:34 for the duties on the State of origin.

[22] Ibid, para 41. [23] *Rottmann* (n 19) para 42.

[24] Ibid, para 55. See also Case C-221/17 *Tjebbes and Others v Minister van Buitenlandse Zaken*, EU:C:2019:189; Case C-689/21 *Udlændinge- og Integrationsministeriet* (*Loss of Danish nationality*), EU:C:2023:626.

deprivation of German citizenship entailed for Rottmann and members of his family and 'whether that loss [of German nationality] [was] justified in relation to the gravity of the offence committed by that person, to the lapse of time between the naturalisation decision and the withdrawal decision and to whether it [was] possible for that person to recover his original nationality'.[25]

While *Rottmann* concerned the loss of nationality and thus the benefits of EU citizenship, *Commission v Malta* concerned the opposite: the acquisition of the nationality of a Member State through investment (eg a payment of €750,000 to the Maltese government). In a decision rich with rhetorical flourish[26] and constitutional implications,[27] the Court found that Malta had breached Article 20 TFEU and the principle of sincere cooperation in Article 4(3) TEU. It said that a Member State 'manifestly disregards' the requirement for 'a special relationship of solidarity and good faith, characterised by the reciprocity of rights and duties between the Member State and its nationals, and thus breaks the mutual trust on which Union citizenship is based' when it 'establishes and implements a naturalisation scheme based on a transactional procedure' by which Maltese nationality and, therefore, the status of Union citizen, is 'essentially granted in exchange for predetermined payments or investments'.[28] The Court concluded:

> A programme of that sort amounts to the commercialisation of the granting of the status of national of a Member State and, by extension, Union citizenship, which is incompatible with the conception of that fundamental status that stems from the Treaties.[29]

Thus, under EU law States cannot sell their nationality to the wealthy because this has implications for EU citizenship. Member States still have a broad discretion in the choice of the criteria to be applied for determining nationality,[30] recognizing that 'the bedrock of the bond of nationality of a Member State is formed by the special relationship of solidarity and good faith between that State and its nationals and the reciprocity of rights and duties'.[31] But any decision may now be subject to review under EU law, particularly via the principle of proportionality and presumably the Charter.

2.3 **The interstate element**

Not only must the individual be a national of a Member State but, according to the orthodoxy, he or she must have moved, be in the course of moving, or be likely to move between one Member State and another,[32] or returning to his or her State of origin after a period of time resident in a host State.[33] If there is no interstate element—the so-called wholly internal situation—then national law only applies.[34] This is more than a technicality. It is about division of competence: EU free movement law applies where there is an interstate element, national law applies otherwise.

[25] See also Case C-118/20 *JY v Wiener Landesregierung*, EU:C:2022:34, para 74: it is disproportionate to deprive an individual of nationality based on administrative traffic offences giving rise to a mere pecuniary penalty.

[26] M van den Brink, 'Why Bother with Legal Reasoning? The CJEU Judgment in *Commission v Malta (Citizenship by Investment)*' (2 May 2025) Robert Schumann Centre, https://globalcit.eu/why-bother-with-legal-reasoning-the-cjeu-judgment-in-commission-v-malta-citizenship-by-investment/.

[27] Ibid. [28] Para 99. [29] Para 100. [30] Para 98. [31] Para 96.

[32] See eg Art 3(1) CRD and Case C-434/09 *McCarthy v Secretary of State for the Home Department* [2011] ECR I-3375.

[33] See eg Case C-370/90 *Surinder Singh* [1992] ECR I-4265.

[34] See eg Case 175/78 *R v Saunders* [1979] ECR 1129.

Yet despite the solid constitutional foundations for the rule, it brings with it legal, political, and practical problems. First, the wholly internal rule can give rise to so-called 'reverse discrimination'. This means that EU citizens who migrate may be in a more favourable position than those who stay at home. So, for example, EU nationals who move from one Member State to another can invoke EU rights to bring their TCN spouse into the host State and reside with them there.[35] Those who do not exercise EU rights of free movement can rely only on national law and may find that national law denies admission to the TCN spouse.[36]

Secondly, if the EU is about creating a single market, barriers created internally within a Member State should logically also be removed. This is the position that the Court took in respect of Article 30 TFEU on customs duties.[37] It also formed part of Advocate General Sharpston's reasoning in the *Walloon* case[38] that the wholly internal rules should be abolished, at least in respect of the devolved or federal situation where one devolved region (eg Flanders in Belgium) offers a benefit to its residents (and to EU nationals who work there) but not to residents from elsewhere in the same country (eg to those living in the Walloon region but working in Flanders). The Court firmly rejected the AG's arguments and reiterated that the wholly internal rule continued to apply in the field of free movement of persons.

Thirdly, despite the Court's determination to uphold the wholly internal rule when it is pressed specifically on the point, the Court has been somewhat cavalier in maintaining the orthodoxy in individual cases. So, for example, in *Carpenter*[39] the Court said that EU law applied where a British man went—only occasionally—to another Member State to provide services (selling adverts in medical journals). This meant his wife, a Filipino national, was able to argue that her deportation (for overstaying her visa) would interfere with *his* free movement right, contrary to Article 56 TFEU, since without her there would be no one to look after his children from a previous marriage.

Carpenter suggests that it takes very little movement for EU law to apply. This point was recognized by Advocate General Sharpston in *Ruiz Zambrano*.[40] The case concerned a failed Colombian asylum seeker living in Belgium. While his claim was being processed, he and his Colombian wife had two children (Diego and Jessica) who acquired Belgian nationality under Belgian law. When the Belgian authorities tried to deport him, he invoked EU law to stop his deportation from the territory of the EU. His (legal) problem: he was a TCN and, in respect of Diego and Jessica, their situation was a wholly internal situation. Therefore, according to the orthodoxy, EU law should not apply.

On the question of the wholly internal rule, Advocate General Sharpston said:

> If one insists on the premise that physical movement to a Member State other than the Member State of nationality is required before residence rights as a citizen of the Union can be invoked, the result risks being both strange and illogical. Suppose a friendly neighbour had taken Diego and Jessica on a visit or two to Parc Astérix in Paris, or to the seaside in Brittany. They would then have received services in another Member State. Were they to seek to claim rights arising from their 'movement' it could not be suggested that their situation was 'purely internal' to Belgium. Would one visit have sufficed? Two? Several? Would a day trip have been enough; or would they have had to stay over for a night or two in France?

[35] *Surinder Singh* (n 33). [36] *McCarthy* (n 32).

[37] Case C-72/03 *Carbonati Apuani Srl v Commune di Carrara* [2004] ECR I-8027. See further chapter 12.

[38] Case C-212/96 *Government of the French Community and Walloon Government v Flemish Government* [2008] ECR I-1683.

[39] Case C-60/00 [2002] ECR I-6279.

[40] Case C-34/09 [2011] ECR I-1177.

In other words, the wholly internal rule, as interpreted by the Court in cases such as *Carpenter*, was flawed.

The Court did not consider the wholly internal rule. It adopted a different approach entirely. Following the approach in *Rottmann*, it focused not on Article 21 TFEU but Article 20 TFEU:[41]

> Article 20 TFEU precludes national measures which have the effect of depriving citizens of the Union of the genuine enjoyment of the substance of the rights conferred by virtue of their status as citizens of the Union.

It continued that a refusal to grant a Belgian right of residence to Mr Ruiz Zambrano, a TCN with dependent minor Belgian children, and also a refusal to grant him a work permit, had the effect of depriving the *children* of the genuine enjoyment of the substance of their EU rights. Mr Ruiz Zambrano was therefore able to stay in Belgium to look after his children, relying on rights derived from their citizen status.

This case is an example of the creative use of the citizenship provisions of the Treaty to deliver justice to the Ruiz Zambrano family. The decision precipitated a large number of claims brought by TCNs in various Member States wishing to rely on *Ruiz Zambrano* to be allowed to stay in the EU. Subsequent case law appears to have limited *Ruiz Zambrano* to its unique facts (ie the de facto removal from the territory of the EU as a whole, of dependent, young children who are EU citizens).[42]

Rottman and *Ruiz Zambrano* suggest the wholly internal rule does not apply to Article 20 TFEU. Subsequently, in *O and B*[43] the Court addressed Advocate General Sharpston's concerns about the length of time in the host State necessary to trigger EU free movement rights in respect of cases decided under Articles 45, 49, and 56 TFEU. It said that the EU citizen's residence in the host State had to be 'sufficiently genuine so as to enable that citizen to create or strengthen family life in that state'.[44] Drawing on the different periods of residence laid down by the Citizens' Rights Directive (CRD) 2004/38 (section 5), the Court said that EU citizens who migrated for three months or less did not intend to settle in the host State. So, in such a case, the refusal to confer on the TCN family members a derived right of residence, when the EU citizen returns to the home State (as in the fictitious example of a friendly neighbour taking Diego and Jessica on a visit to Parc Astérix in Paris) would 'not deter such a citizen from exercising his rights under Article 6'.[45] By contrast, those EU citizens residing in the host State for three months or more (under Articles 7 and 16 CRD) did establish genuine residence and so could return to the home State with their TCN family members.[46]

2.4 **Economic activity**

Finally, in respect of the original Treaty provisions (Articles 45, 49, and 56 TFEU), the migrant workers, self-employed, and service providers must be engaged in economic activity. This, according to the Court in *Jundt*,[47] is 'the decisive factor' which brings an activity within the ambit of the provisions of the Treaty. In many cases, the existence

[41] Ibid, para 42.

[42] See eg *McCarthy* (n 32); Case C-256/11 *Dereci* [2011] ECR I-11315; Case C-40/11 *Iida v Stadt Ulm*, EU:C:2012:691; Joined Cases C-420/22 and C-528/22 *NW and PQ v Országos Idegenrendészeti Főigazgatóság*, EU:C:2024:344, para 60.

[43] Case C-456/12 *O and B v Minister voor Immigratie, Integratie en Asiel*, EU:C:2014:135, para 61.

[44] Ibid, para 51. [45] Ibid, para 52. [46] Ibid, paras 54–56.

[47] Case C-281/06 *Jundt v Finanzamt Offenburg* [2007] ECR I-12231, para 32.

of economic activity is assumed, particularly where the individual or company is being remunerated for the activity performed. However, it does become an issue with voluntary or semi-voluntary activities, especially those undertaken as part of a rehabilitation programme.[48] In *Jundt* the Court emphasized that 'the activity must not be provided for nothing' for Article 56 TFEU to apply, albeit that there is no need for the service provider 'to be seeking to make a profit'.[49]

The position is different under Article 21(1) TFEU. There, the link between free movement rights of the non-economically active and economic activity has been severed. The Court made this clear in *Baumbast*:[50]

> The Treaty does not require that citizens of the Union pursue a professional or trade activity, whether as an employed or self-employed person, in order to enjoy the rights provided in Part Two of the [TFEU] on citizenship of the Union.

Therefore, in the case of citizens wishing to exercise their rights under Article 21(1) TFEU, it is sufficient that they merely hold the nationality of one of the Member States; unlike individuals wishing to invoke Article 45, 49, or 56 TFEU, they need not be engaged in an economic activity. However, as we shall see (section 5.2), the significance of this severing of the link with economic activity is reduced by the Court's subsequent interpretation of the CRD, especially by its decision in *Dano*.[51]

3 **Which Treaty provision is engaged?**

Once it has been decided that EU law applies in principle, the next question is what Treaty provision is engaged: Article 45 TFEU on workers, Article 49 TFEU on establishment, Articles 56 and 57 TFEU on services, or Article 21 TFEU on citizenship? This question is not merely a semantic one of classification. While there are common principles underpinning all four articles, there are, as we shall see, some important differences in the levels of justification required when a breach of the Treaty is established. These issues will be considered in section 6. First, we look at the elements which distinguish the different freedoms.

3.1 **Free movement of workers**

3.1.1 **The definition of workers**

Workers are essentially dependent labour. The Treaty has not defined the term but in *Lawrie-Blum*[52] the Court said that the essential feature of an employment relationship is that:

> for a certain period of time a person performs services for and under the direction of another person in return for which he receives remuneration.

Both the sphere of employment and the nature of the legal relationship between employer and employee, whether involving public law status or a private law contract, are immaterial. Therefore, on the facts of the case, the Court found that a trainee teacher had to be regarded as a worker for the purpose of Article 45(1) TFEU. In subsequent

[48] Case 344/87 *Bettray v Staatssecretaris van Justitie* [1989] ECR 1621, para 17.

[49] *Jundt* (n 47) para 33.

[50] Case C-413/99 (n 6) para 83.

[51] Case C-333/13 *Elisabeta Dano and Florin Dano v Jobcenter Leipzig*, EU:C:2014:2358.

[52] Case 66/85 *Lawrie-Blum v Land Baden-Württemberg* [1986] ECR 2121.

cases, the Court has made clear that the individual must be engaged in a 'genuine and effective' economic activity which is not on such a small scale as to be 'purely marginal and ancillary'.[53] This is of particular relevance to part-time workers and others working in the gig economy.[54]

3.1.2 The position of work-seekers

The term 'workers' also includes work-seekers who will enjoy the status of worker for a reasonable period.[55] The period allowed for the worker to remain in the host Member State looking for work depends on the rules of the particular Member State but the worker must be allowed a reasonable time in which to apprise themselves of offers of employment corresponding to their occupational qualifications and to take, where appropriate, the necessary steps in order to be engaged.[56] A declaration recorded in the Council minutes when two pieces of secondary legislation on free movement were adopted in the 1960s[57] talked about a three-month period but the Court rejected this document as an interpretative tool since no reference was made to it in the secondary legislation itself.[58] The Court also rejected the link with the three-month period under the Social Security Regulation 883/2004 in which the migrant can claim benefits while in the host State. The Court therefore concluded that a period of six months, such as that laid down in the national legislation at issue, was sufficient but with the important caveat that if, after the expiry of that period, the person concerned produced evidence that he was continuing to seek employment and that he had genuine chances of being engaged, he could not be required to leave the territory of the host Member State.[59] This line of case law is now reflected in Article 14(4)(b) CRD.[60]

3.1.3 Those deemed workers or self-employed

Finally, the CRD also provides that an individual retains worker (or self-employed) status in the host Member State in four prescribed situations:[61]

(a) He/she is temporarily unable to work as the result of an illness or accident.

(b) He/she is in duly recorded involuntary unemployment after having been employed for more than one year and has registered as a job-seeker with the relevant employment office.

(c) He/she is in duly recorded involuntary unemployment after completing a fixed-term employment contract of less than a year or after having become involuntarily unemployed during the first 12 months and has registered as a job-seeker with the relevant employment office. In this case, the status of worker shall be retained for no less than six months.

(d) He/she embarks on vocational training. Unless he/she is involuntarily unemployed, the retention of the status of worker shall require the training to be related to the previous employment.

[53] Case 53/81 *Levin* [1982] ECR 1035, para 17. The Court said that the rules relating to free movement of workers also applied to part-time workers, even where they earned less than the minimum wage of a particular Member State.

[54] Ibid.

[55] Case C-292/89 *R v IAT, ex p Antonissen* [1991] ECR I-745.

[56] Ibid, para 16.

[57] OJ [1968] English Special Edition, Series II, p 485.

[58] *Levin* (n 53) para 18.

[59] Ibid, para 21.

[60] In Case C-710/19 *GMA v État belge*, EU:C:2020:1037 para 51: the host Member State can require job-seekers to provide evidence that they are seeking employment during the reasonable period; after the expiry of that period, the host Member State may require job-seekers to show not only that they are continuing to seek employment but that they have a genuine chance of being engaged.

[61] Art 17(3).

3.2 **Establishment**

While Article 45 TFEU concerns dependent labour, Article 49 TFEU concerns *in*dependent labour, namely the self-employed (and companies).[62] As the Court said in *Gebhard*:[63]

> the concept of establishment within the meaning of the Treaty is therefore a very broad one, allowing a [Union] national to participate, on a stable and continuous basis, in the economic life of a Member State other than his state of origin and to profit therefrom, so contributing to social and economic penetration within the [Union] in the sphere of activities as self-employed persons.

Many self-employed people move to provide services in a professional or semi-professional capacity (eg lawyers, hairdressers, accountants). This may create confusion in respect of classification with service providers moving under Article 56 TFEU who are also self-employed. The essence of the distinction between the two situations lies in the language of *Gebhard* concerning permanence: if the service provision is 'on a stable and continuous basis', Article 49 TFEU on freedom of establishment will apply. If the service provision is *temporary* then Article 56 TFEU on the free movement of services applies (see section 3.3). The distinction is important because it determines which State takes primary responsibility for regulating the activities of the service supplier: if it is a case of freedom of establishment then the *host* State is the principal regulator (this is also the case with workers moving under Article 45 TFEU). If it is a case of service provision under Article 56 TFEU then it will be the *home* State which is the principal regulator, and any additional regulation by the host State will have to be carefully justified (see further section 7.2).

3.3 **Services**

3.3.1 **Freedom to provide services**

As we have seen, the distinguishing feature of Articles 56 and 57 TFEU on the free movement of services is that the service, which is 'normally provided for remuneration' (emphasizing the need for economic activity—see section 2.4), is *temporary*. Neither the Treaty nor the case law give any quantitative guidance as to what constitutes 'temporary'. However, in *Gebhard*[64] the Court said the temporary nature of the provision of services is to be determined in light of 'its duration, regularity, periodicity and continuity'. Providers of services may also equip themselves in the host Member State with the infrastructure necessary for the purposes of performing the service in question.[65]

While the early cases concerned lawyers seeking to provide services temporarily in other Member States,[66] more recent cases have involved companies providing services and taking their own workforce with them to do the particular job.[67] These workers, described as posted workers, essentially bring their own labour law system with them. This means that they are employed under the terms and conditions of employment of the *home* State, not the host State where the work is performed. Where the service providers come from Eastern Europe and the work is performed in Northern Europe, the service providers enjoy a competitive advantage in terms of wage costs. To Northern European trade unions this looks like social dumping and something to be prevented; to the Eastern

[62] Case C-221/89 *R v Secretary of State for Transport, ex p Factortame* [1991] ECR I-3905, para 20. See further chapter 14.

[63] Case C-55/94 [1995] ECR I-4165. [64] Ibid, para 39. [65] Ibid.

[66] See eg Case 33/74 *Van Binsbergen* [1974] ECR 1299.

[67] Case C-341/05 *Laval* [2007] ECR I-987. See further chapter 20.

Europeans it looks like taking advantage of their competitive position and something to be exploited.[68]

This tension between the two perspectives came to the fore in *Laval*.[69] The case concerned a Latvian company (Laval) which won a contract to refurbish a school in Sweden using its own Latvian workers, who earned about 40 per cent less than comparable Swedish workers. The Swedish construction union wanted Laval to apply the Swedish collective agreement (an agreement between Swedish employers and Swedish trade unions on terms and conditions of employment) but Laval refused, in part because the collective agreement was unclear as to how much Laval would have to pay its workers. There followed serious industrial action against Laval which eventually led to its bankruptcy.

Laval successfully argued that this industrial action was contrary to *Union* law, in particular Article 56 TFEU on freedom to provide services, and the Posted Workers Directive 96/71.[70] Directive 96/71 had been introduced—in part—to combat social dumping (ie States taking advantage of their low labour costs).[71] It required *host* States to impose some of their labour law rules on posted workers but only in the areas listed in Article 3(1) of the Directive, which included minimum rates of pay. However, the Court said, in effect, that because Article 3(1) was an exception to the general rule that home State rules apply, it had to be interpreted narrowly and all of the detailed rules surrounding its operation had to be complied with to the letter. Because that was not the case on the facts, the Directive did not apply, and any industrial action taken to enforce the Directive was therefore also unlawful under Article 56 TFEU.

Important revisions to the Posted Workers Directive 96/71 were made by Directive 2018/957.[72] This Directive provides that for the first 12 months host State rules in the areas listed in Article 3(1) of the Directive will apply, including a revised provision on remuneration. After 12 months (but with the possibility of the service provider requesting an extension to 18 months), all host State labour law rules will apply to the posted worker. This suggests that after 12 months posted workers under Article 56 TFEU will be treated in much the same way as migrant workers under Article 45 TFEU.[73]

3.3.2 **Other situations**

So far, we have talked about freedom to *provide* services. Although the Treaty talks only of the provision of services, the case law and the secondary legislation make clear that Article 56 TFEU also applies to EU nationals wishing to travel to receive services[74] and to provide services electronically where no one travels.[75] In the case of natural persons, the right to travel to receive a service has become particularly important: they

[68] This issue was expressly recognized in the Monti Report, 'A New Strategy for the Single Market', May 2010, https://www.europarl.europa.eu/meetdocs/2009_2014/documents/empl/dv/empl_monti_report_/empl_monti_report_en.pdf.

[69] Case C-341/05 *Laval un Partneri Ltd v Svenska Byggnadsarbetareförbundet, Svenska Byggnadsarbet areförbundets avdelning*, EU:C:2007:809.

[70] This Directive is now complemented by Directive 2014/67 (OJ [2014] L159/11) on the enforcement of Directive 96/71/EC concerning the posting of workers in the framework of the provision of services.

[71] Speech of Vladimir Spidla, then EU Employment, Social Affairs and Equal Opportunities Commissioner, IP/06/423.

[72] OJ [2018] L173/16.

[73] This is one of the reasons why the Directive was challenged—ultimately unsuccessfully—in Case C-626/18 *Poland v Parliament and Council of the European Union*, EU:C:2020:1000 and Case C-620/18 *Hungary v Parliament and Council of the European Union*, EU:C:2020:1001.

[74] Cases 286/82 and 26/83 *Luisi and Carbone* [1984] ECR 377.

[75] See by analogy Case 352/85 *Bond van Adverteerders v Netherlands* [1988] ECR 2085.

can travel as tourists,[76] to receive medical treatment,[77] and education.[78] Service recipients enjoy protection not only under the Treaty but also under the Services Directive 2006/123.[79]

3.4 Union citizens

3.4.1 Economically, semi-economically, and non-economically active EU migrants

Article 21 TFEU provides: 'Every citizen of the Union shall have the right to move and reside freely within the territory of the Member States, subject to the limitations and conditions laid down in the Treaties and by the measures adopted to give them effect.' Not only are the *economically* active (workers, the self-employed, and service providers/recipients) citizens of the Union but so are the *semi-economically* active—students, and persons of independent means (PIMs)—whose position was first recognized by directives in the early 1990s, directives which have now been repealed and replaced by provisions in the CRD. Students and PIMs enjoy the right to free movement provided they have comprehensive sickness insurance and sufficient resources. The CRD (see section 5.2) also permits *non-economically* active citizens to enjoy the right to reside in the host State but only for the first three months. After that, they can reside lawfully in the host Member States only if they satisfy the conditions of those who are economically active (ie working in some form) or semi-economically active (ie having sufficient resources and sickness insurance), or they are genuinely looking for work under Article 14(4)(b) CRD.

3.4.2 Non-migrant EU citizens

While this chapter concentrates on those EU citizens enjoying the rights to free movement under Articles 45, 49, 56, and 21 TFEU, it should not be forgotten that vast numbers of EU citizens have never exercised free movement rights (other than, perhaps, through tourism). Nevertheless, they enjoy certain EU rights (eg social rights,[80] consumer protection, to petition the European Parliament, and apply to the Ombudsman[81]) which are not contingent on their exercising rights of free movement. As *Rottmann* and *Ruiz Zambrano* make clear, in exceptional cases they may also enjoy some rights under Article 20 TFEU (see sections 2.2 and 2.3) but generally the rights under EU free movement law do not apply to them.

4 Does the EU measure apply to this particular person or entity?

Once an assessment has been made as to the applicable Treaty provision (Article 45, 49, 56, or 21 TFEU), the next question is whether it can be invoked by the claimant against this particular person or entity. The early case law made clear that the Treaty provisions on persons have vertical direct effect and so could be invoked against the State.[82]

[76] *Luisi and Carbone* (n 74).
[77] Ibid. Case C-157/99 *Geraets Smits v Stichting Ziekenfonds* [2001] ECR I-5473. See further chapter 21.
[78] Case C-109/92 *Wirth v Landeshauptstadt Hannover* [1993] ECR I-6447.
[79] Arts 20 and 21 of Directive 2006/123 (OJ [2006] L376/76). See further chapter 14.
[80] See chapter 20. [81] Art 24.
[82] Art 45 TFEU—Case 167/73 *Commission v France* ('*French Merchant Seamen*') [1974] ECR 359; Art 49 TFEU—Case 33/74 *Reyners* [1974] ECR 1299; Art 56 TFEU—*Van Binsbergen* (n 66); Art 21 TFEU—*Baumbast* (n 6). For a full discussion on direct effect, see chapter 6.

However, *Walrave and Koch*,[83] which said that 'the rule on non-discrimination applies in judging *all legal relationships*', suggested that the free movement of persons provisions had horizontal direct effect as well and so could be invoked against 'private', that is, non-State, actors. Yet, subsequent cases suggested a narrowing of this approach. These cases concerned action taken by public authorities[84] or professional regulatory bodies, such as the Bar Council.[85] This suggested an extended form of vertical direct effect. Yet in *Angonese*[86] the Court said that the prohibition of discrimination in Article 45 TFEU applied both to agreements intended to regulate paid labour collectively and to contracts between individuals[87]—in other words, horizontal direct effect. This raises the question whether the principle in *Angonese* applied to Articles 49 and 56 TFEU as well. There are hints in *Viking*[88] that Article 49 TFEU has horizontal direct effect[89] but equally hints that the trade unions were liable only because of their collective power, thereby suggesting some form of extended vertical direct effect.

If the provision is directly effective, it can be enforced in the national court. Article 3 of the Enforcement Directive 2014/54 requires States to provide judicial procedures for the enforcement of rights under Article 45 and Regulation 492/2011.

5 What rights do EU free movers enjoy?

5.1 Introduction

Once resident in a host State, EU migrants enjoy a wide range of rights. The precise nature of those rights varies depending on the classification of the individual (worker, self-employed, citizen, etc), the duration of residence (0 to 3 months, 3 months to 5 years, and 5 years and beyond), (see Fig. 13.1).

In respect of workers, the Workers Regulation 492/11, repealing and replacing the original Regulation 1612/68, and the CRD are both relevant; for the self-employed, it is only the CRD. Service providers under Article 56 TFEU are not expressly covered by the CRD but they could fall within Article 6 CRD (in the same way as any EU national) and Article 7 CRD (as a self-employed person or as a person of independent means (PIM)). For periods beyond five years, the individual may no longer be considered a service provider but instead be seen as established in the host State. However, the Treaty remains the hierarchically superior rule and on some occasions the Court chooses to apply the Treaty provision but not the relevant secondary legislation to which it makes no reference. This tends to suggest that, as far as economically active migrants are concerned, the Court may view the secondary legislation as merely fleshing out the meaning of the Treaty.

For those who are not economically active and move to another Member State (students, PIMs, and others), their position is more heavily regulated by the CRD. In the past, the Court has also applied the Treaty but since *Dano* (considered later)[90] this seems less likely.

This chapter cannot be comprehensive about the rights enjoyed by migrants.[91] It will therefore focus on certain key protections, in particular the right of residence and the principle of equal treatment.

[83] Case 36/74 [1974] ECR 1405.
[84] Case 41/74 *Van Duyn* [1975] ECR 1337.
[85] Case 71/76 *Thieffry* [1977] ECR 765.
[86] Case C-281/98 [2000] ECR I-4139.
[87] Ibid, para 34.
[88] Case C-438/05 (n 13).
[89] Ibid, para 55; see also para 58.
[90] *Dano* (n 51).
[91] For further details, see C Barnard, *The Substantive Law of the EU: The Four Freedoms* (8th edn, Oxford: Oxford University Press, 2025) chs 6–9.

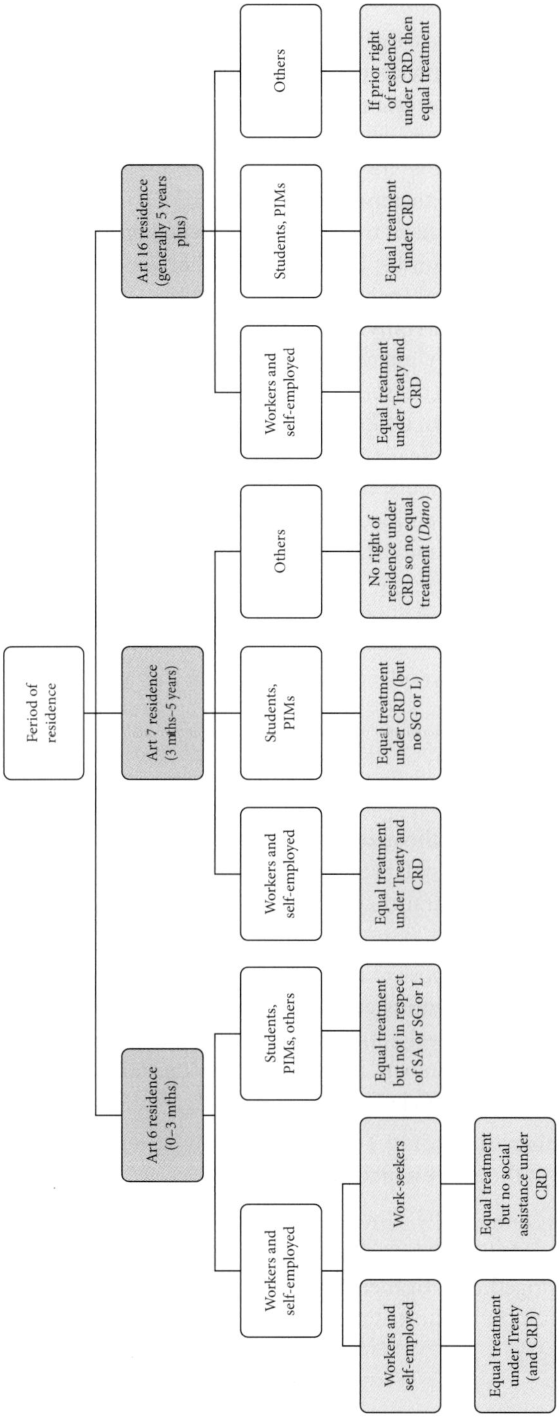

Fig. 13.1 Length of residence and entitlement to equal treatment

5.2 The right of residence for EU migrants and their family members, and the principle of equal treatment

5.2.1 Periods of residence

The CRD adopts a tiered approach to legal rights: the longer migrants are resident, the greater the rights they enjoy. It envisages three periods: up to three months, three months to five years, and five years and beyond. We shall examine the rights associated with each period in turn.

The right of residence for those entering for up to three months (Article 6)

Union citizens and their family members (see section 5.2.2), irrespective of the nationality of those family members, have the right of residence on the territory of another Member State for up to three months. In this period, they are not subject to any conditions (eg as to resources, medical insurance) or formalities other than holding a valid identity card or passport (passport only in the case of TCN family members). In principle, all EU migrants and their family members enjoy equal treatment with nationals under Article 24(1) CRD from day one (but see the discussion of the equal treatment principle at section 5.2.3 and its application in *Collins*).[92]

For those who are not economically active (ie those who are not workers[93] or the self-employed) and their family members, they can move to another Member State and enjoy equal treatment but they are not entitled to equal treatment in respect of social assistance (SA), [94] a term discussed in section 5.2.4), subject to the Charter,[95] or student grants or loans (SG or L) (see Fig. 13.1).

The 'right of residence' in the period three months to five years (Article 7)

Union citizens have a 'right of residence' in the territory of another Member State for more than three months if they:

- are an employed person; or
- are a self-employed person; or
- have sufficient resources for themselves and their family members not to become a burden on the social assistance system in the host Member State during their stay and have comprehensive sickness insurance cover in the host Member State (Article 7(1)(b)); or
- are enrolled at a private or public establishment, accredited or financed by the host State for the principal purpose of following a course of study, including vocational training, and they have comprehensive sickness insurance and assure the national authority (by means of a declaration) that they have sufficient resources for themselves and their family members not to become a burden on the social assistance system of the host State (Article 7(1)(c)); or
- are family members (including TCNs) accompanying or joining a Union citizen who falls in one of the above situations.[96]

Thus, those who are economically active (workers/self-employed) or semi-economically active EU migrants (students, PIMs both needing comprehensive sickness insurance and sufficient resources), together with their family members, are entitled to a right of residence after three months in the host State.

[92] Case C-138/02 (n 6).

[93] There is a longer period of exclusion for work-seekers under Art 14(4)(b).

[94] Case C-299/14 *Vestische Arbeit Jobcenter Kreis Recklinghausen v Jovanna García-Nieto and Others*, EU:C:2016:114.

[95] Case C-709/20 *CG v The Department for Communities in Northern Ireland*, EU:C:2021:602.

[96] There is a narrower list of family members who can join a migrant student: Art 7(4).

Those who are *not* economically active (EU migrant 'others' in Fig. 13.1) are not entitled to a right of residence under the CRD. They can only hope for a liberal interpretation of the *Treaty* provisions on citizenship by the Court of Justice to allow them to stay in the host State or to get the benefit they seek.[97] However, the decision in *Dano*[98] now makes this more unlikely.[99]

Ms Dano was a Romanian migrant living in Germany on a residence certificate of unlimited duration issued to EU nationals. She had limited education and had never worked in Germany. She lived with her sister while raising a young child. She was refused particular special non-contributory cash benefits, a decision upheld by the Court of Justice, on the ground that she did not satisfy the requirements laid down in Article 7(1)(b) CRD that she had to have sufficient resources. As the Court said:[100]

> To accept that persons who do not have a right of residence under Directive 2004/38 may claim entitlement to social benefits under the same conditions as those applicable to nationals of the host Member State would run counter to an objective of the directive, set out in recital 10 in its preamble, namely preventing Union citizens who are nationals of other Member States from becoming an unreasonable burden on the social assistance system of the host Member State.

The Court added that 'Article 7(1)(b) of Directive 2004/38 seeks to prevent economically inactive Union citizens from using the host Member State's welfare system to fund their means of subsistence.'[101] In other words, benefit tourism will not be encouraged under EU law.

Dano therefore suggests, at least in cases with similar facts, that a lawful right of residence under Article 7 is a *precondition* to the enjoyment of the principle of equal treatment. Equal treatment cannot be used to provide the sufficient resources to give a right to residence. This means that non-economically active migrant EU citizens ('others' on Fig. 13.1) cannot enjoy the right of residence under EU law beyond three months.

Economically *active* migrant EU citizens enjoy equal treatment with nationals (subject to the principles shown in Fig. 13.2).

Semi-economically active migrant EU citizens (PIMS, students) with sufficient resources and comprehensive sickness insurance will also enjoy equal treatment with nationals, except in respect of SG or L. Further, since students and PIMs are meant to be self-sufficient financially, they should not need access to the SA systems of the Member States. This requirement of self-sufficiency, combined with the exclusion of SG or L from the equality principle, means that for the semi-economically active access to social benefits is in practice curtailed for the first five years of their stay in the host State.

Those with a 'right of permanent residence' (Articles 16 and 17 CRD)

Those EU migrant citizens with permanent residence are in the most favourable situation. They are seen to be integrated into the host State and so they enjoy equal treatment with nationals without exception (ie no exclusions for SA or SG or L) (see Fig. 13.1). The principles in Fig. 13.2 continue to apply but given the Directive is premised on the fact that those with five years' residence are fully integrated, it is unlikely that a host State rule requiring more than five years' residence in order to be entitled to a particular benefit would be either justifiable or proportionate.

[97] cf *Martínez Sala* (n 126); Case C-456/02 *Trojani v CPAS* [2004] ECR I-7573 (considered in case study 13.1).

[98] *Dano* (n 51).

[99] Cf Case C-673/16 *Coman v Inspectoratul General pentru Imigrări and Ministerul Afacerilor Interne*, EU:C:2018:385.

[100] *Dano* (n 51) para 74.

[101] Ibid, para 76.

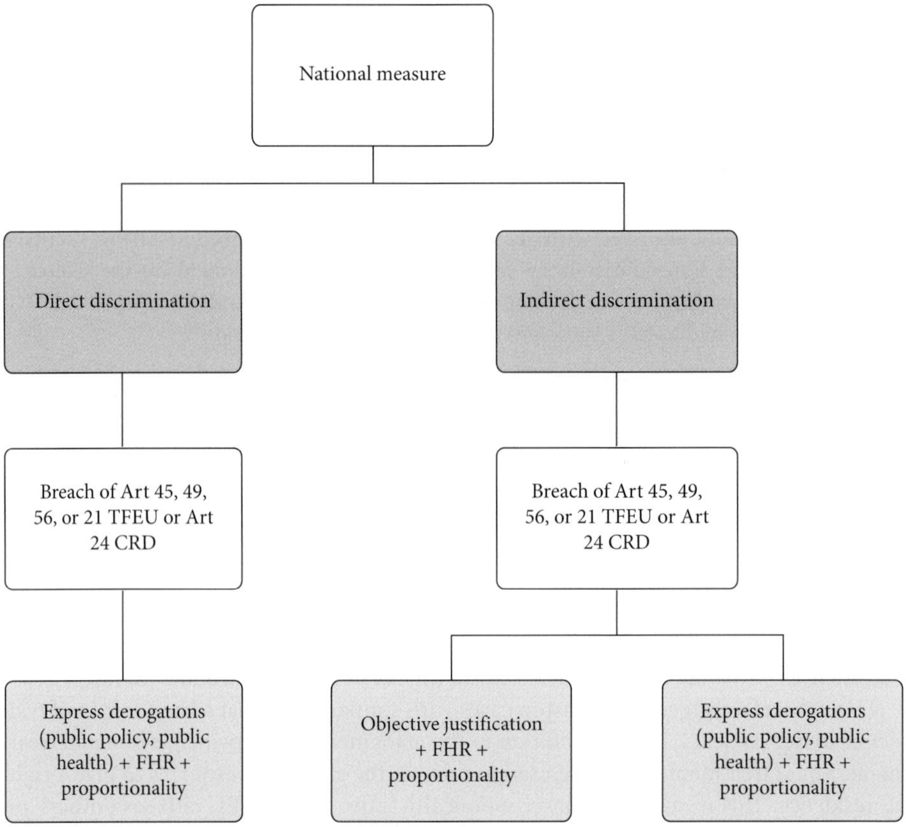

Fig. 13.2 The principle of equal treatment

There are two ways of acquiring permanent residence. First, Article 16 provides that those EU citizens residing in the host State for more than five years (workers, the self-employed, students, and PIMs, and their family members including those who are not nationals but who have resided with the Union citizen for five years) will have the right of permanent residence. None of the conditions applicable to students and PIMs concerning sufficient resources and medical insurance apply to those with permanent residence. However, students and PIMs must have satisfied the conditions laid down in Article 7 in order to accrue the five years of residence in the first place.[102]

Secondly, Article 17(1) provides that *workers and the self-employed* have the right to permanent residence in the host State in three additional situations:

(a) retirement at the pension age or through early retirement, provided they have been employed in the host State for the preceding 12 months and resided in the host State continuously for more than three years;

(b) incapacity, provided they have resided for more than two years in the host State and have ceased to work due to some permanent incapacity;

(c) frontier workers, provided after three years of continuous employment and residence in host State A, they work in an employed or self-employed capacity in State B, while retaining their residence in State A to which they return each day or at least once a week.

[102] Joined Cases C-424/10 and C-425/10 *Ziolkowski v Land Berlin*, EU:C:2011:866; Case C-378/12 *Nnamdi Onuekwere v Secretary of State for the Home Department*, EU:C:2014:13; and Case C-400/12 *MG*, EU:C:2014:9.

The conditions as to length of residence and employment in (a) and (b) do not apply if the worker/self-employed person's spouse or partner[103] is a national of the host State or has lost the nationality of the host State through marriage to the worker/self-employed person.[104] Special provisions apply to the worker's family members.

5.2.2 **Family members**

As we have seen, EU migrants can migrate with their family members, including TCNs. Family members fall into two groups: (a) those who must be admitted[105] and (b) those whose entry and residence the host State must merely facilitate.[106] In respect of the first group, family member means:[107]

(a) spouse;

(b) the partner with whom the Union citizen has contracted a registered partnership, on the basis of the legislation of a Member State, if the legislation of the host Member State treats registered partnerships as equivalent to marriage and in accordance with the conditions laid down in the relevant legislation of the host Member State;

(c) direct descendants who are under the age of 21 or are dependants and those of the spouse or partner as defined in (b);

(d) dependent direct relatives in the ascending line and those of the spouse or partner as defined in (b).

In respect of the second group (those whose admission must be facilitated), two sorts of family members fall into this category:[108]

(a) any other family members, not falling under Article 2(2) who, in the country from which they have come, are dependants or members of the household of the Union citizen having the primary right of residence, or where serious health grounds strictly require the personal care of the family member by the Union citizen;[109]

(b) the partner with whom the Union citizen has a durable relationship, duly attested.[110]

TCN spouses could either accompany the migrant spouse when moving from State A to B, or join the migrant spouse in State B directly from a third country. This was confirmed in *Metock*[111] where the Court also recognized that the CRD gave rights not only to pre-existing couples (family reunification) but also to couples that meet in the host State (family formation).[112]

What about those who have entered a same-sex marriage? Article 2(2)(b) requires the host State to admit the couple if the marriage is recognized in both the home and host States. But what if it is not? This was the issue in *Coman*[113] concerning a gay couple, the

[103] Partner as defined in Art 2(2)(b) CRD. [104] Art 17(2). [105] Art 3(1).

[106] Art 3(2). [107] Art 2.

[108] Art 3(2) CRD. See also Case C-83/11 *Secretary of State for the Home Department v Rahman*, EU:C:2012:519.

[109] The fact that these conditions are satisfied must be proved by a document issued by the relevant authority in the country of origin or country from which they are arriving in the case of those seeking residence under Art 7: Arts 8(5)(e) and 10, for TCNs.

[110] By contrast, the fact that a 'durable relationship, duly attested' exists is satisfied merely by 'proof' for those seeking residence under Art 7: Arts 8(5)(f) and 10, for TCNs.

[111] Case C-127/08 *Metock* [2008] ECR I-6241, para 70.

[112] Ibid, para 99.

[113] Case C-673/16 *Coman v Inspectoratul General pentru Imigrări and Ministerul Afacerilor Interne*, EU:C:2018:385. See also Case C-490/20 *VMA v Stolichna obshtina, rayon 'Pancharevo'*, EU:C:2021:1008 the Bulgarian authorities had to give an identity card to a Bulgarian child born to married mothers (Bulgarian and British) in Spain, even though Bulgaria did not recognize same-sex marriage. See also Case C-713/23 *Cupiak-Trojan* EU:C:2025:917

Union citizen being Romanian, his husband American. They had been living in Belgium but wished to return to Romania. The Romanian authorities did not allow them to live permanently in Romania because Romania did not recognize same-sex marriage. The Court ruled that following Coman's genuine residence in Belgium under Directive 2004/38, where 'family life is created or strengthened', the 'effectiveness of the rights conferred on the Union citizen by Article 21(1) TFEU requires that that citizen's family life in that Member State may continue when he returns to the Member State of which he is a national, through the grant of a derived right of residence to the third-country national family member concerned'. Note how the Court has used Article 21(1), that is, the Treaty right, to strengthen the protection provided by the Directive.

Family members, once lawfully resident, have the right, irrespective of their nationality, to engage in gainful activity[114] and, subject to the same limitations as for EU nationals, the right to equal treatment.[115] Children have the right to go to school.[116]

5.2.3 **The meaning of equal treatment**

As we have already seen, EU migrants enjoy equal treatment with nationals in certain situations (see Fig. 13.2). Although the principle of equal treatment sounds positive in nature, in fact the law gives effect to it through the negative concept of non-discrimination. This means national rules should be neither directly nor indirectly discriminatory. *Direct* discrimination arises where the migrant is, or may be, differently[117] and usually less favourably treated on the grounds of nationality. So in *Bosman*[118] the Court found that UEFA's so-called 3+2 rule,[119] approved by the Commission, that there could be no more than three foreign and two 'acclimatized' players (ie foreign players who had been in the host State for at least five years) in any football team, breached Article 45 TFEU because it was directly discriminatory against foreign players. According to the orthodoxy, directly discriminatory measures can, however, be justified but only by reference to the express derogations (public policy, public security, and public health) (see further section 7.1 and Fig. 13.2), as well as any additional derogations found in the relevant secondary legislation such as language requirements for workers in Article 3(1) of Regulation 492/11. This was not satisfied in this case and so UEFA's rule was unlawful.

An *indirectly discriminatory* measure focuses on the discriminatory effect of the rule on the migrant. As *O'Flynn*[120] made clear, that effect can be actual or potential:

> 18. [C]onditions imposed by national law must be regarded as indirectly discriminatory where, although applicable irrespective of nationality, they affect essentially migrant workers or the great majority of those affected are migrant workers, where they are indistinctly applicable but can be more easily satisfied by national workers than by migrant workers or where there is a risk that they may operate to the particular detriment of migrant workers.

The Court continued:

> 19. It is otherwise only if those provisions are justified by objective considerations independent of the nationality of the workers concerned, and if they are proportionate to the legitimate aim pursued by national law.

Thus, an indirectly discriminatory rule—in this case a British requirement for the impecunious to be buried in the UK if the UK government was to pay for the funeral, a rule

[114] Art 23. [115] Art 24(1). [116] Art 10 of the Workers Regulation 492/11.
[117] Art 7(1) of the Workers Regulation 492/11. [118] Case C-415/93 [1995] ECR I-4921.
[119] UEFA is the Union of European Football Associations, and the governing body of football in Europe.
[120] Case C-237/94 [1996] ECR I-2617.

which was liable to disadvantage migrants who might want to be buried in their State of origin—could be justified by the State invoking not only the express derogations but also by the judicially developed 'objective justifications' (also referred to as 'public interest' requirements or 'overriding requirements in the general interest' (section 7.2)). These are State interests, considered to be valid under EU law, which take precedence over free movement rights, provided the steps taken to achieve the interests are proportionate.

On the facts, the UK argued that its rule on the location of the burial was justified on the grounds of the prohibitive cost and practical difficulties of paying the allowance if the burial or cremation took place outside the UK. Surprisingly, the Court did not reject the justification on the basis that it was purely economic (see section 7.2) but on the facts: Leaving aside transportation, the Court thought the costs for burial in the UK or abroad would be broadly the same.[121] For good measure, the Court said that there was nothing to prevent the UK from limiting the allowance to a lump sum or reasonable amount fixed by reference to the normal cost of a burial or cremation within the UK.[122]

Rules generally considered to be indirectly discriminatory include: residence requirements, length of service requirements, and registration requirements. Such rules tend to favour the national to the detriment of the migrant. The Court does, however, allow such rules to be justified on the grounds of, for example, the protection of ethics of the profession,[123] and consumer protection,[124] provided that the steps taken are compatible with fundamental human rights (FHR) and are proportionate (see section 8).

A particularly important justification is the need to show a genuine link with the territory of the host State, at issue in *Collins*.[125] He was an Irish national who claimed jobseeker's allowance within a week of his arrival in the UK. He was refused the benefit on the ground that he was not habitually resident in the UK. Requirements as to habitual residence are indirectly discriminatory. However, the Court found that such requirements could be objectively justified by the need to ensure that there was a genuine link between an applicant for an allowance and the geographic employment market in question; whether the habitual residence requirement was also proportionate was left to the national court.

By allowing host States to justify the requirements that have to be fulfilled prior to obtaining a particular domestic benefit, but also ensuring that those requirements are proportionate, the Court struck a balance between (a) facilitating free movement (there might be an entitlement to a social welfare benefit in the future and any disproportionate restrictions should be removed) and (b) preventing the national welfare systems from being burdened by individuals like Mr Collins who had neither made contributions to the social welfare system in the UK nor had resided in the UK for a sufficient period to justify receiving benefits in the host State as part of the security blanket of national solidarity.[126] Increasingly, States are turning to indirectly discriminatory requirements to protect their social welfare systems and then running an argument to justify the residence requirement based on the need for a genuine link between the claimant and the territory of the host State. *Collins* therefore makes clear that the right to equal treatment is not absolute.

Under the non-discrimination model, the corollary of the prohibition of discrimination is that rules which do *not* discriminate are lawful. So a requirement that a tax applied to all those receiving the bulk of their income in State A, whether they are nationals of State

121 Ibid, para 28. 122 Ibid, para 29.

123 Joined Cases 110/78 and 111/78 *Van Wesemael* [1979] ECR 35.

124 Case C-180/89 *Commission v Italy* ('*Tourist guides*') [1991] ECR I-709.

125 Case C-138/02 *Collins v Secretary of State for Work and Pensions* [2004] ECR I-2703.

126 cf Case C-85/96 *Martínez Sala* [1998] ECR I-2691.

A or EU migrants, would be lawful under the non-discrimination approach. However, as we shall see in section 7, the rise of the market access approach has cast doubt on this basic assumption. For now, it is sufficient to note that where the Court decides cases under the CRD or the Workers Regulation 492/11 it tends to use the equal treatment approach as described in this section and illustrated in Fig. 13.2, and not the market access approach.

5.2.4 **Equal treatment and social and tax advantages**

While citizens in general enjoy the rights under the CRD, *workers* are in a more favourable position because they benefit from the rights in the Workers Regulation 492/11 as well. There is considerable overlap between the two measures; where there are differences, it is likely that the worker will be able to rely on the most advantageous provision. This is particularly important in respect of receipt of *social advantages*. Workers, including work-seekers,[127] enjoy equal treatment in respect of social advantages under Article 7(2) of Regulation 492/11 from day one of their arrival in the host State (albeit that host States can impose proportionate, justified residence requirements that the migrant establish a real link with the labour market of the host State,[128] which may, as in *Collins*, delay the worker from receiving the social advantage until a genuine link with the host territory, via residence, has been realized); non-economically active citizens can be denied *social assistance* for the first three months altogether. So how, then, do these terms differ?

The term 'social *assistance*', as used in the CRD, is not defined. However, in *Brey*[129] the Court said that the phrase social assistance means:

> all assistance introduced by the public authorities, whether at national, regional or local level, that can be claimed by an individual who does not have resources sufficient to meet his own basic needs and the needs of his family and who, by reason of that fact, may become a burden on the public finances of the host Member State during his period of residence which could have consequences for the overall level of assistance which may be granted by that State.

This definition suggests that social assistance benefits are those intended to protect against destitution.

In *Even*[130] the Court defined 'social *advantages*' broadly to include all benefits:[131]

> Which, whether or not linked to a contract of employment, are generally granted to national workers primarily because of their objective status as workers ***or by virtue of the mere fact of their residence on the national territory*** and the extension of which to workers who are nationals of other Member States therefore seems suitable to ***facilitate their mobility*** within the [Union].

The Court has interpreted the phrase to include benefits granted as of right[132] or on a discretionary basis,[133] and those granted after employment has terminated.[134] It also covers

[127] *Collins* (n 125).

[128] Joined Cases C-22/08 and 23/08 *Vatsouras* [2009] ECR I-4585, para 40.

[129] Case C-140/12 *Pensionsversicherungsanstalt v Brey*, EU:C:2013:565, para 61.

[130] Case 207/78 *Criminal Proceedings against Even* [1979] ECR 2019.

[131] Ibid, para 22 (emphasis added).

[132] See eg Case C-111/91 *Commission v Luxembourg* [1993] ECR I-817; *Martínez Sala* (n 126), para 28.

[133] Case 65/81 *Reina v Landeskreditbank Baden-Württemberg* [1982] ECR 33, para 17.

[134] See eg Case C-57/96 *Meints v Minister van Landbouw, Natuurbeheer en Visserij* [1997] ECR I-6689, para 36 (payment to agricultural workers whose employment contracts are terminated).

benefits not directly linked to employment, such as language rights,[135] death benefits,[136] and rights to be accompanied by unmarried companions.[137]

This case law suggests that social advantages are used to facilitate migration—of workers and their family members—and to encourage integration into the labour market of the host State. In *Vatsouras*[138] the Court confirmed that 'Benefits of a financial nature which, independently of their status under national law, are intended to facilitate access to the labour market cannot be regarded as constituting "social assistance" within the meaning of Article 24(2) of Directive 2004/38.' They are therefore likely to be social advantages under the Workers Regulation. So it is in an individual's interests to argue that he or she is a worker and that the benefit concerns labour market integration and is thus a social advantage to which the principle of equal treatment applies (see Fig. 13.2) and not social assistance (which is excluded from the scope of the equality principle for the first three months, at least for those who are not economically active and for job-seekers whose right of residence in the host Member State is based solely on Article 14(4)(b) CRD[139]).

Not only do migrant workers enjoy equal treatment in respect of social advantages but they also enjoy it in respect of tax advantages. In the UK, this meant that, when it was a Member State, low-paid migrant workers were entitled to tax credits (essentially topping up low wages) in the same way as UK nationals.

5.2.5 **Other areas of equal treatment for the economically active and their family members**

So far, we have concentrated on the application of the equal treatment principle to social welfare benefits. However, the Workers Regulation 492/11 is quite expansive in the areas in which equal treatment is required. These include any conditions of employment and work, in particular remuneration, dismissal, and, should the worker become unemployed, reinstatement or re-employment;[140] vocational training;[141] access to housing;[142] and trade union membership.[143] There is no reason why these rights to equal treatment across such a broad range of areas would not also apply to other economically active citizens under the general principle of equal treatment in the CRD and/or the Treaty.

Originally, the principle of equal treatment also applied to qualifications.[144] However, this proved more of a hindrance than an asset. If a lawyer, who has spent six years qualifying in State A, wanted to work in State B but discovered that she can practise there only after requalifying as a State B lawyer with a further six years of study of State B law (ie equal treatment as regards the training which a State B lawyer would also have had to undergo), this would be a considerable disincentive to her free movement. So the Court developed the principle of mutual recognition of qualifications, borrowing directly from the *Cassis de Dijon* line of case law.[145] In *Vlassopoulou*[146] the Court ruled that:[147]

[135] Case 137/84 *Criminal Proceedings against Mutsch* [1985] ECR 2681, para 18 (criminal proceedings in the defendant's own language).

[136] *O'Flynn* (n 120) (social security payments to help to cover the cost of burying a family member).

[137] Case 59/85 *Netherlands v Reed* [1986] ECR 1283, para 28.

[138] Joined Cases C-22/08 and 23/08 (n 128) para 45.

[139] Case C-181/19 *Jobcenter Krefeld v JD*, EU:C:2020:794, para 67. Where the social assistance, such as a disability allowance, is granted to a direct relative in the ascending line, this constituted for the migrant worker a 'social advantage' 'since that direct relative in the ascending line is dependent on that worker: Case C-488/21 *GV v Chief Appeals Officer*, EU:C:2023:1013.

[140] Art 7(1). [141] Art 7(3). [142] Art 9. [143] Art 8.

[144] Case 11/77 *Patrick v Ministre des affaires culturelles* [1977] ECR 1199.

[145] See further chapter 12. [146] Case C-340/89 [1991] ECR I-2357.

[147] Ibid, para 15 (emphasis added). See also Case C-19/92 *Kraus v Land Baden-Württemberg* [1993] ECR I-1663, para 32.

> national requirements concerning qualifications may have the effect of *hindering nationals of the other Member States in the exercise* of their right of establishment guaranteed to them by Article [49 TFEU]. That could be the case if the national rules in question took no account of the knowledge and qualifications already acquired by the person concerned in another Member State.

This meant that the host State had to compare a migrant's qualifications and abilities with those required by the national system to see whether the applicant had the appropriate skills to join the equivalent profession. If they were equivalent, then the host State was obliged to recognize the diploma. If they were not, then the host Member State could require the applicant to demonstrate that she had acquired the relevant knowledge and qualifications, which then had to be taken into account.[148]

Vlassopoulou effectively pre-empted the 'diabolically complex and completely unnecessary'[149] directives adopted in the late 1980s and early 1990s, now repealed and replaced by Directive 2005/36.[150] Nevertheless, in respect of the occupations covered by the Directive, the Directive applies, not the case law.

5.3 **Other rights specifically attached to EU citizens *qua* citizens**

As we have seen, EU citizens can be migrant and non-migrant. Both groups can enjoy—as EU citizens *qua* citizens (not as workers, the self-employed, or service providers)—certain rights under the Treaty which are found in Part Two TFEU entitled 'Non-discrimination and citizenship of the Union'. These rights include the right to petition the European Parliament, to apply to the European Ombudsman, and to address the institutions and the advisory bodies of the Union in any of the Treaty languages and to obtain a reply in the same language. Further, as a result of Article 20(2) TFEU, which provides that 'Citizens of the Union shall enjoy the rights and be subject to the duties provided for in the Treaties', all citizens will enjoy the rights under the Charter, subject to the limits on the application of the Charter laid down in the horizontal clauses in Articles 51 and 52 Charter, as well as various other rights, including to equal pay for men and women under Article 157 TFEU.

In addition, migrant EU citizens[151] enjoy the right to vote in local and European elections (but not national elections) (Article 22 TFEU) and stand for election and membership of a political party[152] and the right to diplomatic and consular protection from the authorities of any Member State in third countries (Article 23 TFEU). Most importantly, migrant citizens will enjoy the right to equal treatment more generally, as the leading

[148] *Vlassopoulou* (n 146) paras 17–21.

[149] J Lonbay, 'Picking Over the Bones: The Rights of Establishment Reviewed' (1991) 16 *European Law Review* 507, 516.

[150] OJ [2005] L255/22. See further chapter 21. An amendment directive has been adopted: Directive 2013/55 (OJ [2013] L354/132). See also the Proportionality Directive 2018/958 (OJ [2018] L173/25).

[151] But not UK citizens resident in an EU Member State post-Brexit: *EP* (n 17) para 83. They 'no longer enjoy . . . the right to vote and to stand as a candidate in municipal elections in their Member State of residence'.

[152] Case C-808/21 *Commission v Czech Republic* (*Ability to stand for election and membership of a political party*), EU:C:2024:962; Case C-814/21 *Commission v Poland* (*Ability to stand for election and membership of a political party*), EU:C:2024:963, paras 112 and 113. In *Commission v Malta* (n 20), para 89 the Court said: 'In exercising the political rights conferred on them by Articles 10 and 11 TEU, Union citizens participate directly in the democratic life of the European Union. Its functioning is founded on representative democracy, which gives concrete expression to democracy as a value, which is, under Article 2 TEU, one of the values on which the European Union is founded.'

case of *Grzelczyk*[153] (considered in case study 13.1) makes clear. The right to equal treatment is derived from a combined reading of Articles 21, 20(2), and 18 TFEU (the latter being the non-discrimination provision). Prior to the adoption of the CRD, this was the only way for non-economically active citizens to gain access to the equality principle. Now with the CRD, Article 24(1) CRD will cover much the same ground as the Treaty protection. However, as we have seen (see section 5.2.4 and Fig. 13.1), there are significant limitations on the equality principle under Article 24(2) CRD in respect of social assistance and SG or L for the non-economically active (EU migrant 'others' in Fig. 13.1), as well as for new and recent arrivals. *Dano*, considered earlier, has emphasized the importance of those restrictions.

Case study 13.1: *Grzelczyk* and the golden days of EU citizenship?

Grzelczyk was a French student studying in Belgium. He worked during the first three years of his studies to help to support himself financially. He stopped working in his fourth and final year and applied to the Belgian authorities for the minimex, a minimum income guarantee. This does not count as student finance but it is a social advantage.[154] He was refused the benefit on the ground that he was not Belgian. Could EU law help him?

The Court said that, as a citizen of the Union lawfully resident in Belgium who has exercised his right of free movement, Grzelczyk was entitled to equal treatment under Article 18 TFEU[155] because, as the Court famously said:

> Union citizenship is destined to be the fundamental status of nationals of the Member States, enabling those who find themselves in the same situation to enjoy the same treatment in law irrespective of their nationality, subject to such exceptions as are expressly provided for.[156]

Although equal treatment applied in principle to Grzelczyk, as we saw in section 5.2.3, it is not absolute. Article 21 TFEU is read subject to the express derogations and, in the case of students and PIMs, to the conditions concerning sufficient resources and sufficient medical insurance.[157] The Belgian government argued that because Grzelczyk was asking for financial support, by definition he did not have sufficient resources, and so he could be denied equal treatment and removed from the territory.

The Court disagreed. It said that students needed to declare that they had sufficient resources for themselves and their family only when they started their course.[158] If they ran out of money and sought financial help during their course, the State could withdraw a student's residence permit or not renew it, but 'in no case may such measures become the automatic consequence of a student who is a national of another Member State having recourse to the host Member State's social assistance system'.[159] For good measure, the Court then suggested that Grzelczyk should be entitled to some State support as long as he did not 'become an "unreasonable" burden on the public finances of the host Member State'.[160] This is because, in adopting the original 1990 residence directives on students and PIMs (now repealed and replaced by Article 7 CRD), the States accepted 'a certain degree of financial solidarity between nationals of a host Member State and nationals of other Member States, particularly if the difficulties which a beneficiary of the right of residence encounters are temporary'.

153 Case C-184/99 (n 6).
154 Case 249/83 *Hoeckx* [1985] ECR 973.
155 *Grzelczyk* (n 6) para 36.
156 Ibid, para 31.
157 Ibid, para 37.
158 Ibid, paras 41, 42, and 45.
159 Ibid, para 43.
160 Ibid, para 44.

In the subsequent case of *Baumbast*,[161] the Court offered some more clarity in its reasoning. This time a German citizen, a PIM, did have sufficient resources (he worked in third countries) but did not have comprehensive sickness insurance for himself and his family in the UK where he was living, including for emergency treatment, although he did have that insurance in Germany. Could the UK refuse to renew his residence permit? No, said the Court: he enjoyed a free-standing right to reside in the UK under Article 21(1) TFEU,[162] albeit subject to the limitations and conditions laid down by the TFEU and by the measures adopted to give it effect, namely (what is now) the CRD. However, the Court said that those 'limitations and conditions must be applied in compliance with the limits imposed by [Union] law and in accordance with the general principles of that law, in particular the principle of proportionality'.[163]

The Court then highlighted certain facts of Mr Baumbast's case: that he had sufficient resources, he had worked and therefore lawfully resided in the UK for several years, during that period his family also resided in the UK and remained there even after his activities as an employed and self-employed person in that State had come to an end, neither Mr Baumbast nor the members of his family had become burdens on UK public finances, and both Mr Baumbast and his family had comprehensive sickness insurance in Germany. Under those circumstances, the Court concluded, 'to refuse to allow Mr Baumbast to exercise the right of residence which is conferred on him by Article [21(1) TFEU] by virtue of the application of the provisions of [the CRD] on the ground that his sickness insurance does not cover the emergency treatment given in the host Member State would amount to a disproportionate interference with the exercise of that right'.[164]

Extending the *Baumbast* reasoning to the facts of *Grzelczyk*, Grzelczyk had completed three out of four years of his degree. It would be disproportionate to interfere with his free movement rights by denying him access to the minimex. Conversely, extending the *Grzelczyk* reasoning to *Baumbast*, Baumbast was sufficiently integrated into UK society that there was a sufficient degree of solidarity between UK taxpayers and sick Germans and their families that Mr Baumbast and his family should be entitled to emergency medical treatment in the UK.

The striking feature of these two cases is that the Court used EU citizenship law to establish the right to equal treatment. It also used EU citizenship rules to impose limits on the limits to equal treatment. It was enough for students and PIMs to have *sufficient* sickness insurance and resources, not comprehensive insurance and resources.[165] The cases also established that the concept of EU citizenship was a dynamic tool which could be used to achieve quite radical surgery on the secondary legislation.

The Court has, in the past, also used the Treaty provisions on citizenship, in cases such as *Trojani*,[166] to give certain protection to migrant EU citizens who are not economically active, including the homeless and others on the margins of society. Trojani was a French national who arrived in Belgium and lived on various campsites for over a year before being given a place in a Salvation Army hostel where, in return for board and lodging and some pocket money, he did various jobs for about 30 hours a week as part of a personal 'socio-occupational reintegration programme'. Like Grzelczyk, he was turned down for the minimex. Unlike Grzelczyk and Baumbast, he was not entitled to a right to reside in Belgium, due to his lack of sufficient resources. The denial of a right to reside was, the Court found, proportionate. However, the Court did say that there was another way of achieving EU rights. Because he

161 Case C-413/99 (n 6). 162 Ibid, para 84. 163 Ibid, para 91. 164 Ibid, para 93.
165 See also *Brey* (n 129). 166 Case C-456/02 (n 97).

was lawfully resident in Belgium for a certain period of time under *Belgian law*, with or without a residence permit,[167] he could therefore enjoy the right to equal treatment under Article 18 TFEU.

The principle of EU citizenship, and its interpretation by the Court in the cases discussed in this section, has served to be an effective source of rights for migrants. However, for Member States the effect of these cases is EU control over ever more of their decisions in areas, such as social security, still largely matters for national competence and an issue of considerable political sensitivity. This has contributed to making interior ministries of a number of Member States suspicious of the Court of Justice. As we saw earlier, the Court responded in *Dano* where, at least in the case of access to benefits, it apparently reversed its approach in *Grzelczyk* et al and instead insisted that there needed to be prior lawful residence under EU law (specifically under Article 7 CRD for semi/non-economically active migrants), not under national law, *before* the principle of equal treatment under Article 18 TFEU/Article 24 CRD was engaged. In other words, equal treatment of migrants can no longer be invoked to deliver the benefits which will enable the migrant to have sufficient resources to stay in the host State. At no stage in its reasoning did the Court refer to the fact that Ms Dano had a residence permit issued by the German authorities. More specifically, it did not mention the decisions such as *Trojani*[168] where the Court suggested that an EU national lawfully resident in another EU Member State under *national* law enjoyed rights under EU law including the principle of non-discrimination under Article 18 TFEU. Nor did the Court engage in any of the creative gymnastics with the citizenship and equal treatment provisions of the Treaty to deliver equality for the Dano family.

Dano provides a strong hint of the (cold) winds of change, at least for poor migrant citizens. The CRD will not, it now seems, always be read in the light of Article 21 TFEU, nor will any interpretation of the Directive be subject to a further check under Article 21 TFEU.[169] *Dano* suggests that the strict words of the Directive will be adhered to—and enforced.

The *Dano* decision came as a relief to some Member States, not least because it was followed by *Alimanovic*[170] where the Court said that while those residing under Article 14(4)(b) CRD as job-seekers, both as first-time job-seekers and those who have lost their job and were seeking further employment, were entitled to equal treatment in respect of access to social assistance, the host State could rely on the derogation under Article 24(2) CRD not to grant that assistance during the first three months.[171] No individual assessment had to be made in this case.[172] That said, there are hints in *Jobcenter Krefeld*[173] that the Court may be willing to temper some of the effects of *Dano. Dano*, it said, concerned 'nationals of a Member State who were economically inactive and who had exercised their freedom of movement with the *sole aim* of receiving social assistance from another Member State and who had no right of residence in the host Member State based on Directive 2004/38 or on any other provision of EU law'. Where, as in this case, the benefit claimant and his daughters had other EU rights of residence (eg under Article 10 of Regulation 492/11) they could enjoy social advantages under Article 7(2) of Regulation 492/11.[174]

[167] Ibid, para 43. [168] Ibid.

[169] cf Case C-287/05, *Hendrix*, EU:C:2007:494 and more recently *Coman* (n 99).

[170] Case C-67/14 *Jobcenter Berlin Neukölln v Alimanovic*, EU:C:2015:597, para 45. See also Case C-308/14 *Commission v UK*, EU:C:2016:436.

[171] *Alimanovic* (n 170) para 57.

[172] Ibid, para 59. [173] Case C-181/19 *Jobcenter Krefeld v JD*, EU:C:2020:794, para 68.

[174] Ibid, para 79.

However, in *CG*[175] the Court reverted to its tough *Dano* line: 'a Member State has the possibility, pursuant to Article 7 of Directive 2004/38, of refusing to grant social benefits to economically inactive Union citizens who exercise their right to freedom of movement and who do not have sufficient resources to claim a right of residence under that directive'. It concluded that 'the financial situation of each person concerned should be examined specifically, without taking account of the social benefits claimed, in order to determine whether he or she meets the condition of having sufficient resources laid down in Article 7(1)(b)' CRD. As Anderson puts it, 'Across Europe, citizenship is increasingly cast as being deserved by hard-working, self-reliant individuals prepared to take responsibility for themselves.'[176]

Grzelczyk et al may hark back to more ambitious days of EU-State building when the Court was leading the process of using entitlements to benefits, enforceable against not the EU itself, but against the host State, as a means of integrating migrant EU citizens. In the UK, this case law had, paradoxically, a disintegrative effect. Post-Brexit, it seems there is little appetite for the Court to return to the 'golden days' of *Grzelczyk* et al. The rhetoric of fundamental status is still there,[177] as we saw in *Commission v Malta*,[178] but the substance and radical appetite for transformation of the lives of poor migrants is now much less obvious.

6 What rules/practices breach the Treaty?

6.1 Introduction

So far we have been talking about the principle of equal treatment which underpins the secondary legislation. However, a number of factual situations have arisen which fall outside the scope of the CRD and Regulation 492/11, and the Court has applied the Treaty to these cases instead. It is to these cases that we shall now turn.

The principle of equal treatment or, more specifically, non-discrimination, also underpins the Treaty provisions on free movement of persons (see Fig. 13.3). This is particularly clear in respect of Article 49 TFEU, which says that 'Freedom of establishment shall include the right to take up and pursue activities as self-employed persons and to set up and manage undertakings . . . *under the conditions laid down for its own nationals by the law of the country where such establishment is effected*.'[179] Discriminatory national rules will always breach the Treaty unless justified. However, according to the orthodoxy, non-discriminatory rules are lawful.[180]

Yet, as this section will show, non-discriminatory rules which nevertheless hinder market access have increasingly been considered 'restrictions' to free movement, using the language in Articles 49 and 56 TFEU, or 'obstacles' to free movement, using the wording of the original Article 3 EEC. The language of removing restrictions or obstacles, also

[175] Case C-709/20 *CG v The Department for Communities in Northern Ireland*, EU:C:2021:602, para 78.

[176] B Anderson, '"Heads I Win, Tails You Lose": Migration and the Worker Citizen' (2015) 68 *Current Legal Problems* 179, 195.

[177] See eg Case C-709/20 *CG* (n 175) para 62. See also Case C-535/19 *A v Latvijas Republikas Veselības ministrija*, EU:C:2021:595, para 59: a host Member State could make affiliation to its public sickness insurance system of an economically inactive Union citizen, residing in its territory on the basis of Art 7(1)(b) of Directive 2004/38 subject to conditions intended to ensure that that citizen did not become 'an unreasonable burden on the public finances of that Member State'.

[178] (n 20) para 92.

[179] Art 49(2) TFEU.

[180] Case 221/85 *Commission v Belgium* [1987] ECR 719.

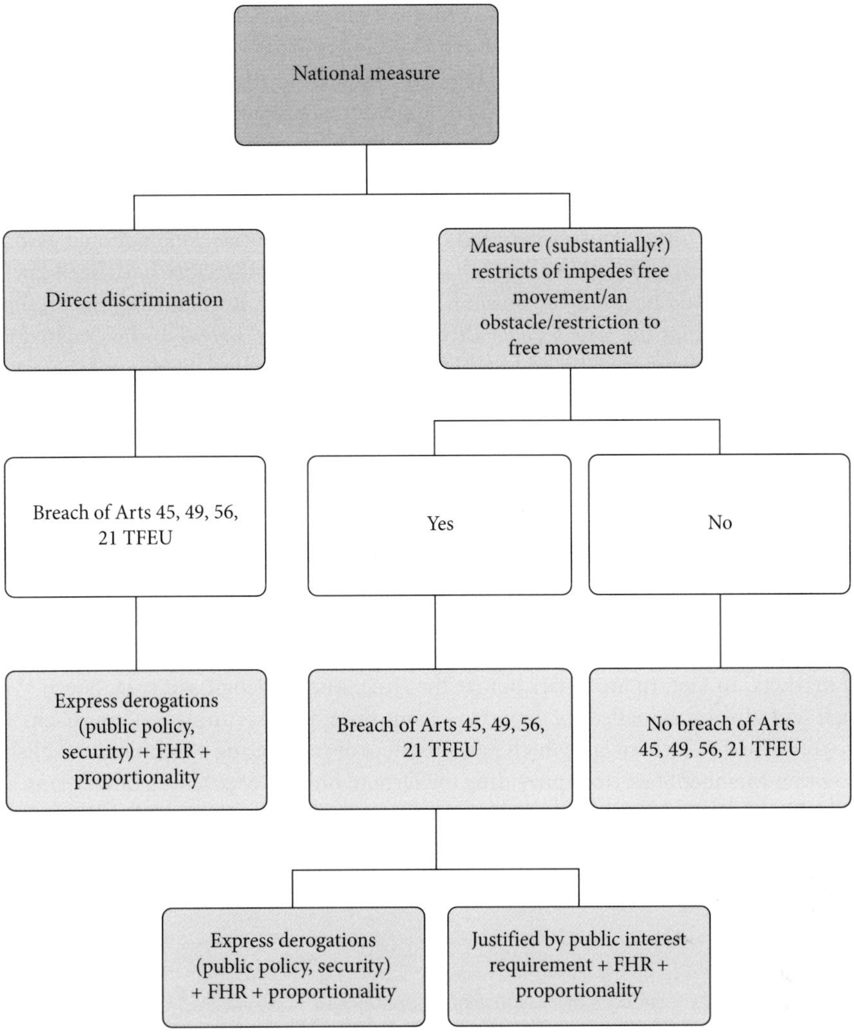

Fig. 13.3 The restrictions model

referred to as the 'market access' approach (section 6.2), has become influential in shaping the Court's approach under the Treaty, particularly (but not exclusively[181]) in respect of Articles 49 and 56 TFEU, where the secondary legislation has been less important.

6.2 **The shift to market access**

The move away from the pure non-discrimination approach started in the 1990s. First, the Court became conscious, not only in the field of persons but also in goods, that the non-discrimination approach was not always sufficient to address a particular obstacle to free movement. The transfer rule at issue in *Bosman*[182] provides a good example of this

[181] Case C-40/05 *Lyyski v Umeå universitet* [2007] ECR I-99 (on Art 45 TFEU); Case C-192/05 *Tas-Hagen v Raadskamer WUBO van de Pensioen-en Uitkeringsrad* [2006] ECR I-10451 (on Art 21 TFEU).

[182] Case C-415/93 (n 118).

problem. Under the then UEFA rules, a football player out of contract could be transferred to another club on condition that the receiving club paid a transfer fee to the selling club. For players in the dusk of their career, they might, like Mr Bosman, find that the fee was set too high and so the buying club could not, or would not, pay it, leaving the player without employment. As the Court noted, the rules were genuinely non-discriminatory: they applied not only to international transfers but also to transfers between clubs belonging to different national associations within the same Member State and were similar to the rules governing transfers between clubs belonging to the same national association. Under the discrimination approach, such rules would therefore have been lawful. However, this would have left Mr Bosman without a remedy. Recognizing this problem, the Court noted that the UEFA rules 'directly affect players' access to the employment market in other Member States and are thus capable of impeding freedom of movement for workers'. They thus breached Article 45 TFEU and needed to be justified (which was not possible on the facts).

In reaching this conclusion, the Court confirmed its earlier decision in *Alpine Investments*,[183] where the Court said that the Dutch prohibition on cold-calling (ie unsolicited telephone calls to individuals) both in and out of the Netherlands by financial firms operating in the Netherlands breached Article 56 TFEU since the rule, while non-discriminatory, 'directly affects access to the markets in services in the other Member States and is thus capable of hindering intra-Union trade in services'.[184] The rule was, however, justified on the ground of protecting investor confidence in the Dutch financial markets. In fact, in an earlier but, at the time, under-recognized case, *Säger*,[185] the Court had already signalled its departure from the non-discrimination approach. The case concerned a German law which had the effect of prohibiting a company established in another Member State from providing to German holders of patents a monitoring and renewal service in respect of those patents in Germany. This was because the German law reserved such tasks exclusively to those possessing a particular professional qualification, such as that of patent agent. The Court said that Article 56 TFEU required:[186]

> ***not only*** the elimination of all discrimination against a person providing services on the ground of his nationality ***but also*** the abolition of any restriction, even if it applies without distinction to national providers of services and to those of other Member States, when ***it is liable to prohibit or otherwise impede*** the activities of a provider of services established in another Member State where he lawfully provides similar services. (Emphasis added)

The Court said that rules, such as those at issue in *Säger*, which hindered market access or created a restriction on free movement, breached Article 56 TFEU unless justified by reference to the public interest requirements or the express derogations (see section 7). On the facts, the Court found that the rule could be justified on the ground of consumer protection but the law was not proportionate because the task of the service provider was essentially administrative (eg notifying patent agents when renewal fees had to be paid) and so did not require a qualified person to deliver it.

Subsequent cases made clear that *Säger*, far from being an aberration, in fact marked a turning point.[187] For example, in *Gebhard*[188] the Court had to consider whether an Italian rule, requiring lawyers to be registered with the local Bar before they could use the title *avvocato*, breached Article 49 TFEU. The Court said:[189]

[183] Case C-384/93 *Alpine Investments v Minister van Financien* [1995] ECR I-1141.

[184] Ibid, para 38.

[185] Case C-76/90 *Säger* [1991] ECR I-4221, para 12.

[186] Ibid (emphasis added). See also Case C-55/94 *Gebhard* (n 63) para 37 on Art 49 TFEU.

[187] See eg *Kraus* (n 147).

[188] Case C-55/94 *Gebhard* (n 63) para 37.

[189] Ibid, para 39.

> national measures liable to hinder or make less attractive *the exercise of fundamental freedoms* guaranteed by the Treaty must fulfil four conditions: they must be applied in a non-discriminatory manner; they must be justified by imperative requirements in the general interest; they must be suitable for securing the attainment of the objective which they pursue; and they must not go beyond what is necessary to attain it. (Emphasis added)

It is striking that the Court talks of 'the exercise of fundamental freedoms' and not just Article 49 TFEU, thereby suggesting a generalization of the principle in *Säger* to Articles 45 and 49 TFEU as well as to Article 56 TFEU (see Fig. 13.3). The Court also changed the language from measures 'liable to prohibit or otherwise impede' in *Säger* to 'national measures liable to hinder or make less attractive the exercise of fundamental freedoms'. These terms are synonymous. The differences turn on quirks of translation and, sometimes, the context.

The formula used in *Säger* tends to apply when the rules of the *host* State are at issue. When *home* State rules are at stake, the formula differs. In *Kranemann*,[190] for example, a case concerning a German rule that trainees who did their practical legal training in Germany were entitled to reimbursement of all their travel expenses but not if they did their training in another Member State, the Court said:

> the Treaty provisions relating to freedom of movement for persons ... preclude measures which might place [Union] nationals at a disadvantage when they wish to pursue an economic activity in the territory of another Member State.[191]

The Court continued that the German rule therefore constituted 'an obstacle' to the free movement of workers even if applied without regard to the nationality of the workers concerned.[192] Further, the rule could not be justified: aims of a purely economic nature (such as 'budgetary considerations') could not constitute pressing reasons of public interest justifying a restriction on the fundamental freedom.[193]

6.3 **The advantage of the market access approach**

As *Kranemann* and *Säger* show, the Court concluded that the national rules were a 'restriction' or an 'obstacle' to free movement. In *Graf*,[194] considered in section 6.5, the Court made the link between the obstacles/restrictions approach and the concept of market access when it said that 'in order to be capable of constituting such an *obstacle*, [the provisions] must affect *access of workers to the labour market*'. This is why the *Säger* test is now often referred to as the market access approach. The focus of the market access test is not on whether the migrant and national are being treated differently on the grounds of nationality but on whether there is a barrier—which may have nothing to do with nationality—which interferes with the ability of the free mover to get on to the market of the host State or, as the Court made clear in *Gebhard*, to exercise that freedom once on the market.[195]

The advantage of the market access approach is that it catches a multitude of national rules in its net, rules often built up over decades which may well have lost their original *raison d'être* but continue to interfere with the creation of a single market. Although the

[190] Case C-109/04 *Kranemann v Land Nordrhein-Westfalen* [2005] ECR I-2421, para 25.
[191] Ibid, para 25. [192] Ibid, para 26. [193] Ibid, para 34.
[194] Case C-190/98 *Graf v Filzmoser Maschinenbau GmbH* [2000] ECR I-493, para 23 (emphasis added).
[195] Ibid, paras 31 and 32.

States have the possibility of justifying those rules, in many cases the justification may not be made out by the State (as in *Kranemann*) or the national rules may be disproportionate (as in *Säger*). For this reason, the market access approach is perceived as deregulatory: it generates a bonfire of State regulation.

6.4 **The criticisms of the market access approach**

6.4.1 **Constitutional criticisms**

But the market access approach has its critics. First, there are those who criticize it from a constitutional perspective: why is it legitimate for the EU to interfere with national rules adopted by democratically elected governments? The effect of the market access approach is to undermine the diversity of national rules and thus the essence of competitive federalism in the EU (where States compete with one another to attract the highest skilled migrants).[196] Even those who see the benefit of the market access approach fear it has reached—or has the potential to reach—too deeply into the national systems. For example, as we have already seen, in *Viking* and *Laval* the Court used the market access approach to declare strike action—which was lawful under national law—to breach Articles 49 and 56 TFEU respectively (and so needed to be justified and the steps taken proportionate).

6.4.2 **Legal and economic criticisms**

The second criticism of the market access test is essentially legal/economic: the phrase 'market access/restriction' is ill-defined. Spaventa offers three possible interpretations.[197] The first, and narrowest, is that barriers to market access are those created by circumstances or legislation that make it more costly for individuals to enter a particular job or profession. Such rules might include the need to register with the local Bar, as in *Gebhard*, when the individual is already registered in their home State. Such rules might be considered indirectly discriminatory and so would be caught under either the discrimination or the market access test.

The second, and much broader, approach to market access is that *any* regulation can be seen as a potential barrier to market access, since *any* regulation imposes and implies compliance costs. This approach was particularly evident in the field of taxation, where at times the Court came close to saying that the higher tax rate in another Member State constituted an obstacle to the free movement of persons.[198] Such a rule therefore breached the Treaty; and justification proved difficult because economic justifications are not permitted.

The third approach is what Spaventa describes as 'intuitive': rules which interfere with intra-Union trade should be subject to judicial scrutiny while rules considered neutral as regards intra-Union trade should not. Many think that this is the test the Court is applying in practice. It can probably explain the decision in *Carpenter*.[199] It will be recalled that the UK wanted to deport Mrs Carpenter, the Filipino spouse of a UK national service provider, on the ground that she had overstayed her visa to remain in the UK. She argued that her deportation would interfere with her husband's ability to provide services since she looked after his children from a previous marriage while he was away providing those services. The Court said:[200]

[196] See further chapter 11. See also C Barnard, 'Restricting Restrictions: Lessons for the EU from the US?' (2009) 68 *Cambridge Law Journal* 575.

[197] 'From *Gebhard* to *Carpenter*: Towards a (Non-)Economic European Constitution' (2004) 41 *Common Market Law Review* 743, 757–758.

[198] Case C-168/01 *Bosal v Staaatssecretaris van Financiën* [2003] ECR I-9409.

[199] Case C-60/00 (n 39). [200] Ibid, para 45.

> It is clear that the separation of Mr and Mrs Carpenter would be detrimental to their family life and, therefore, to the conditions under which Mr Carpenter exercises a fundamental freedom. That freedom could not be fully effective if Mr Carpenter were to be deterred from exercising it by obstacles raised in his country of origin to the entry and residence of his spouse.

Her deportation therefore breached Article 56 TFEU unless justified by public interest requirements (see sections 7 and 8).

6.4.3 **Linguistic criticisms**

The third criticism of the 'market *access*' approach is linguistic because it focuses on the initial entry to the market. However, restrictions can occur not just at the stage of initial market access but also during the *exercise* of that freedom once on the market. Further, the language of market access sits increasingly uncomfortably in the world of free movement of natural persons. As the case law on citizenship shows, these are very human situations where individuals want to use EU law to ensure they can reside in another State and have access to opportunities there. They do not see themselves as gaining access to any market.

6.5 **The response to the criticisms**

There are signs that the Court has paid some (inconsistent) heed to its critics. First, in the field of taxation there are indications that the Court has reverted to the discrimination approach. This can be seen in *Weigel*,[201] a case concerning a German husband and wife who transferred their residence to Austria where Mr Weigel had a job. They both brought their cars with them, which had to be re-registered in Austria, for which a hefty tax was charged. The Court rejected their arguments that this tax breached Article 45(2) TFEU, noting that the Austrian rule applied 'without regard to the nationality of the worker concerned to all those who registered a car in Austria and, accordingly, it is applicable without distinction'.[202] The Court then added that 'It is true that [the tax] is likely to have a negative bearing on the decision of migrant workers to exercise their right to freedom of movement.'[203] Under the *Säger* formula, this observation would have been enough for a finding of a breach of Article 45 TFEU, which Austria would then have had to justify. However, in *Weigel* the Court resorted to the pure non-discrimination approach and said that, provided that national and migrant workers were treated in the same way, the fact that the tax regimes of the different Member States were different was compatible with Union law.[204]

Secondly, the Court has recognized that a threshold requirement may need to be added to the market access test to avoid the test from becoming all-embracing. For example, in the commercial context of *Commission v Italy* ('*Motor insurance*'),[205] the Court said that the obligation on an insurance company to provide third party cover to every potential customer constituted a 'substantial' interference on the operators' freedom to contract,[206] and that the obligation was likely to lead, in terms of organization and investment, to '*significant* additional costs for such undertakings'.[207]

[201] Case C-387/01 *Weigel v Finanzlandesdirection für Vorarlberg* [2004] ECR I-4981.

[202] Ibid, para 52. [203] Ibid, para 54.

[204] Ibid, para 55. See also Case C-365/02 *Lindfors* [2004] ECR I-7183 (Art 21 TFEU).

[205] Case C-518/06 [2009] ECR I-3491. For parallels, see Case C-110/05 *Commission v Italy* ('*Trailers*') [2009] ECR I-519 discussed in chapter 12.

[206] *Motor insurance* (n 205) para 66 (emphasis added).

[207] Ibid, para 68.

While *Motor Insurance* used an economic threshold, *Graf*[208] introduced a tortious one. Mr Graf, who worked in Austria, resigned to take up a job in Germany. By resigning, he lost the chance of being dismissed and so could not claim a termination payment for his dismissal. He argued that the loss of a chance of being dismissed, and so being paid, interfered with his free movement rights. The Court disagreed. It noted that the entitlement to compensation on termination of employment was 'not dependent on the worker's choosing whether or not to stay with his current employer but on a future and hypothetical event, namely the subsequent termination of his contract without such termination being at his own initiative or attributable to him'. It continued:

> Such an event is *too uncertain and indirect* a possibility for legislation to be capable of being regarded as liable to hinder free movement for workers where it does not attach to termination of a contract of employment by the worker himself the same consequence as it attaches to termination which was not at his initiative or is not attributable to him.

While often not successful, States have increasingly relied on the 'too uncertain and indirect' formula to argue that EU law does not apply to the situation at issue.[209]

7 Can the breach be justified?

As the net of EU law is cast ever wider, through the application of the market access approach, an increasing number of national rules are caught by the prohibition under EU law and so need justification. The general approach to derogations/justifications is discussed in detail in chapter 16. This chapter will therefore merely outline some of the issues that arise in respect of derogations in the context of free movement of natural persons.

7.1 Express derogations

7.1.1 General express derogations

The basic rules

Refusal of entry or deportation and any measures which are directly discriminatory can be justified only by one of the three express derogations in the Treaty: public policy, public security, and public health. These are listed in Article 45(3) TFEU (workers) and Articles 52 and 62 TFEU (establishment and services), and elaborated in the CRD. Common principles apply to these derogations as well as to the other derogations found in the Treaty. These are established by the Court in the free movement of capital case *Église de Scientologie*:[210]

- Derogations from the fundamental principle of free movement have to be interpreted strictly, so that their scope cannot be determined unilaterally by each Member State without any control by the Union institutions.
- Derogations cannot be misapplied so as, in fact, to serve purely economic ends.
- Any person affected by a restrictive measure based on such a derogation has to have access to legal redress.
- Derogations are subject to the principle of proportionality.

208 Case C-190/98 (n 194) (emphasis added).

209 See eg Joined Cases C-11/06 and C-12/06 *Morgan v Bezirksregierung Köln* [2007] ECR I-9161.

210 Case C-54/99 [2000] ECR I-1335.

However, overlaying these rules are the requirements laid down by the CRD which make it increasingly difficult for individuals to be refused entry/removed from a host State.

Up to three months' residence

For the first three months, individuals can be refused entry or deported on any one of the three express grounds: public policy, public security, and public health. According to Article 27(2) CRD, 'Measures taken on grounds of public policy or public security shall comply with the principle of proportionality and shall be based exclusively on the personal conduct of the individual concerned. Previous criminal convictions shall not in themselves constitute grounds for taking such measures.' So the key issue for the public policy and public security derogations is personal conduct. Article 27(2) explains that 'The personal conduct of the individual concerned must represent a genuine, present and sufficiently serious threat affecting one of the fundamental interests of society. Justifications that are isolated from the particulars of the case or that rely on considerations of general prevention shall not be accepted.' This definition is derived from early decisions of the Court.[211]

As far as public health is concerned, Article 29(1) CRD provides: 'The only diseases justifying measures restricting freedom of movement shall be the diseases with epidemic potential as defined by the relevant instruments of the World Health Organisation and other infectious diseases or contagious parasitic diseases if they are the subject of protection provisions applying to nationals of the host Member State.' This derogation became highly significant in the light of the Covid-19 pandemic.[212]

In respect of all three derogations, the Member State must also consider whether the exclusion/deportation is proportionate and compatible with fundamental rights.

Finally, individuals refused entry or deported have the right at least to the minimum procedural protection provided by the Directive. This includes the right to receive notification of the reasons for the decision refusing them entry or deporting them,[213] generally a period of up to one month to leave,[214] and, according to Article 31, access to judicial and, where appropriate, administrative redress procedures in the host Member State to appeal against or seek review of any decision taken against them. If they are excluded from the State, they have the right to submit an application for the lifting of the exclusion order after a reasonable period and in any event after three years.[215]

Three months to five years

Between three months and five years of residence, the only grounds which the State can invoke to justify deportation are public policy and public security.[216] For those deported during this period, States must take into account not only questions of human rights and proportionality but also the individual's degree of integration into society (eg how long the individual concerned has resided on its territory, his or her age, state of health, family and economic situation, social and cultural integration into the host Member State, and the extent of his or her links with the country of origin).[217]

[211] eg Case 6/74 *Bonsignore v Obersdirektor of the City Cologne* [1975] ECR 297 (deportation order could not be made to make an example of the individual); Case 2/74 *Van Duyn v Home Office* [1974] ECR 6311 (scientology) (past association is irrelevant, present association is relevant; the activity does not have to be illegal in the host State).

[212] Case C-128/22 *Nordic Info*, EU:C:2023:951.

[213] Art 30(1). [214] Art 30(3). [215] Art 32. See further chapter 16.

[216] Art 29(2). [217] Art 28(1).

Five years and beyond

For those with permanent residence status and who have resided in the host State for between five and ten years, they can be deported but only for *serious* grounds of public policy (which presumably means that the individual must represent a seriously serious threat to a fundamental interest of society).[218]

For those resident for ten years or more, and those who are minors, an expulsion decision may not be taken against Union citizens, unless the decision is based on imperative grounds of public security, subject again to tests based on the degree of integration and human rights. It was originally thought that the threshold set for this final category was so high that only in truly exceptional circumstances (terrorism, murder) would an individual be deported. However, in *Tsakouridis*[219] the Court appeared to lower the bar. Although the Court emphasized that Article 28(3) 'considerably strengthens' the protection against expulsion enjoyed by individuals,[220] it concluded that 'the fight against crime in connection with dealing in narcotics as part of an organised group' was capable of being covered by the concept of 'imperative grounds of public security'.[221]

7.1.2 **Specific exception: employment in the public service and the exercise of official authority**

In addition to the general exceptions, the Treaty provides for a specific exception for employment in the public service for workers (Article 45(4) TFEU) and the exercise of official authority for establishment and services (Articles 51 and 62 TFEU). This allows States to reserve certain jobs which require a 'special relationship of allegiance to the state'[222] to nationals only. Given that this provision allows States to discriminate directly, and thereby artificially reduce the pool from which they can select the best workers, the Court has taken a restrictive line on the scope of the derogation. For example, the Court adopts a functionalist rather than institutional (organic) approach. So it looks at the nature of the tasks performed by the individual rather than allowing entire sectors to be excluded.[223] The Court has also said that the derogation applies only at the moment of recruitment to the post, not to the terms and conditions of employment in that post.[224] Generally, the Court finds that most cases fall outside the scope of the derogation.[225]

7.2 **Public interest justifications**

In addition to the express derogations, the Court has recognized a range of public interest requirements to justify indirectly discriminatory rules (section 5.2.3) and those which hinder market access (section 6.2). In *Gouda*,[226] as in *Cassis de Dijon* in the field of goods, the Court brought the public interest requirements together for the first time. It recognized the following 'imperative reasons in the public interest':

- professional rules intended to protect the recipients of a service;
- protection of intellectual property;

[218] Art 28(2).

[219] Case C-145/09 *Tsakouridis* [2010] ECR I-11979, para 28.

[220] Ibid. [221] Ibid, para 56.

[222] Case 149/79 *Commission v Belgium* [1980] ECR 3881; and follow-up [1982] ECR 1845.

[223] Case 152/73 *Sotgiu* [1974] ECR 162. [224] Ibid.

[225] eg teaching post in a State school (*Levin* (n 53)), state nurse (Case 307/84 *Commission v France* [1986] ECR 1725), foreign language assistant in a university (Case 33/88 *Allué and Coonan v Universita degli studia di Venezia* [1989] ECR 1591).

[226] Case C-288/89 *Gouda* [1991] ECR I-4007.

- protection of workers;
- consumer protection;
- conservation of the national historic and artistic heritage;
- turning to account the archaeological, historical, and artistic heritage of a country and the widest possible dissemination of knowledge of the artistic and cultural heritage of a country.

This rather eclectic list is not exhaustive: well over 50 other justifications have since been recognized by the Court. What they have in common is that the State has identified an interest, which has also been recognized by the Court as worthy of protection, that should take precedence over the free movement of persons. As we have seen, purely economic justifications have not been recognized. However, this category has now been generally confined to cases where Member States are essentially advocating pure protectionism.[227]

There is, however, one key difference in respect of the application of the justifications under Article 56 TFEU compared to those under Articles 45 and 49 TFEU. If a host State tries to invoke a justification to extend its law to the service provider, account must first be taken of the level of protection already provided by the home State. This reflects the idea, outlined in section 3.2, that the activities of service providers are primarily regulated by the home State. This is also referred to as the country of origin principle or the principle of home State control, which underpins the most controversial provisions of the Services Directive 2006/123 (considered in chapter 14).

8 Fundamental rights and proportionality

Once a breach of an EU rule has been established, and a Member State has invoked an exception, derogation, or justification, it must be read subject to the principles of fundamental human rights (FHR) and proportionality (see Fig. 13.3). The decision in *Carpenter*[228] provides a good example of how the Court's reasoning works in free movement of persons cases. As noted previously (section 6.4.2), Mrs Carpenter successfully argued that her deportation would constitute an obstacle to Mr Carpenter's ability to provide services under Article 56 TFEU.[229] However, the Court recognized the UK's right to 'invoke reasons of public interest to justify a national measure which is likely to obstruct the exercise of the freedom to provide services',[230] namely the need to ensure the respect for UK immigration law. It then said that the measures nevertheless had to be 'compatible with the fundamental rights whose observance the Court ensures', the right to respect for Mr Carpenter's family life within the meaning of Article 8 ECHR.

The Court then used the proportionality principle to strike a balance between the State's interest in the maintenance of its immigration laws and Mrs Carpenter's interest in her family life. It said a decision to deport Mrs Carpenter did 'not strike a fair balance between the competing interests, that is, on the one hand, the right of Mr Carpenter to respect for his family life, and, on the other hand, the maintenance of public order and public safety'.[231] It stated that although Mrs Carpenter had infringed UK immigration

[227] Case C-157/99 *Geraets-Smits v Stichting Ziekenfonds and Peerbooms v Stichting CZ Groep Zorgverzekeringen* EU:C:2001:404.

[228] Case C-60/00 (n 39).

[229] Ibid, para 39.

[230] Ibid, para 40.

[231] Ibid, para 43.

laws, her conduct otherwise had been good. The Court therefore found that 'the decision to deport Mrs Carpenter constitutes an infringement which is not proportionate to the objective pursued'.[232]

9 Conclusion

The decision in *Carpenter* illustrates, in microcosm, a number of the facets of free movement of natural persons highlighted by this chapter: the erosion of the requirement of an interstate element before the EU rules on free movement apply, how little it takes to establish an obstacle to free movement and thus a breach by the State of EU law, the need for the State to establish a justification in order to preserve State interests, but what the State can do to protect that interest is curtailed by the principles of human rights and proportionality. The generous reading of human rights in *Carpenter*, in particular the right to family life, also suggests that sometimes the Court views cases on the free movement of natural persons through a citizenship lens and thus is more willing to embrace a human rights dimension to its analysis than would be in cases on free movement of legal persons, which are considered in chapter 14.

The introduction of EU citizenship, with its aspiration to create a strong bond between the EU and its peoples, has broken down the stark dichotomy found in the original Treaty of Rome between the economically active who could migrate and the economically inactive who could not. We now know that the economically semi-active (students, PIMs) and the economically inactive can migrate in the same way as the economically active. However, the basic divide is still visible in the politically and economically sensitive context of welfare benefits: those who are economically active and economically contributing (through paying taxes) enjoy equal treatment in all matters from day one (subject to the non-discrimination principles set out in Fig. 13.2). The economically *in*active are denied social assistance for the first three months and, in principle, cannot have recourse to social welfare benefits for the first five years, given the requirements of self-sufficiency. After five years, all migrants—economically active or not—are deemed to have sufficient ties to the host State that they enjoy full equal treatment with nationals. By introducing this sliding scale, the legislature has tried to strike a balance between the EU interests in facilitating free movement, on the one hand, and the preservation of national social security schemes (and addressing concerns of national taxpayers), on the other.

But while the legal position on immigration is clear, EU free movement law cannot address the problem of the hostility felt by (some) locals fearing that EU migrants are taking 'their' jobs and housing. The only realistic response to this is prosperity. In the current economic climate, those halcyon days seem a long way off. Reforms to the banking system, financial regulation, and economic governance more generally will put the eurozone on a firmer economic footing and thus may eventually lead to greater growth but the financial crisis, the cost of living crisis, the pandemic, the geo-political context, and the consequences of climate change are imposing significant burdens on States.[233] There is little that the Court can do apart from sit on the sidelines and deal with the cases which come before it. Which it does, guided by the objectives laid down by the Treaty: to facilitate migration, ensuring that it is as easy to move between Poznan and Paris as it is between Rome and Rimini.

[232] Ibid, para 45.
[233] See further chapters 11 and 19.

Further reading

C Barnard and A Ludlow, '"Undeserving" EU Migrants "Milking Britain's Benefits"? EU Citizens Before Social Security Tribunals' [2019] *Public Law* 260

C Barnard, F Costello, and S Fraser Butlin, *Low Paid EU Migrant Workers: The House, The Street, The Town* (Bristol: Bristol University Press, 2024)240, ISBN 978-1529229578

Commission v Malta: the analysis and reflections section of the (2025) 50(4) *European Law Review* is devoted to a discussion of this case

ACL Davies, 'One Step Forward, Two Steps Back, The *Viking* and *Laval* Cases in the ECJ' (2008) 37 *International Law Journal* 126

M Everson, 'The Legacy of the Market Citizen' in J Shaw and G More (eds), *New Legal Dynamics of the European Union* (Oxford: Clarendon Press, 1995)

E Guild, S Peers, and J Tomkin, *The Citizens' Rights Directive* (Oxford: Oxford University Press, 2019)

E Hancox, 'Judicial Approaches to Norm Overlaps in EU law: A Case Study on the Free Movement of Workers' (2021) 58 *Common Market Law Review* 1057

K Hylten-Cavallius, 'Who Cares? Caregivers' Derived Residence Rights from Children in EU Free Movement Law' (2020) 57 *Common Market Law Review* 399

N Nic Shuibhne, 'The "Social Freedom"? The Free Movement of Persons in EU27' in S Garben and I Govaere, *The Internal Market 2.0* (Oxford: Hart Publishing, 2020)

N Nic Shuibhne, 'Reconnecting Free Movement of Workers and Equal Treatment in an Unequal Europe' (2018) 43 *European Law Review* 481

N Nic Shuibhne, 'The Resilience of EU Market Citizenship' (2010) 47 *Common Market Law Review* 1597

C O'Brien, 'The Great EU Citizenship Illusion Exposed: Equal Treatment Rights Evaporate for the Vulnerable' (2021) 46 *European Law Review* 801

C O'Brien, 'Real Links, Abstract Rights and False Alarms: The Relationship between the ECJ's "Real Link" Case Law and National Solidarity' (2008) 33 *European Law Review* 643

F Ristuccia, 'Ties that Bind and Ties that Compel: Dependency and the *Ruiz Zambrano* Doctrine' (2023) 60 *Common Market Law Review* 1227

E Spaventa, 'Seeing the Wood Despite the Trees? On the Scope of Union Citizenship and Its Constitutional Effects' (2008) 45 *Common Market Law Review* 13

F Strumia, 'Supranational Citizenship's Enablers. Free Movement from the Perspective of Home Member States' (2020) 45 *European Law Review* 507

M Tecqmenne, 'Migrant Jobseekers, Right of Residence and Access to Welfare Benefits: One Step Forward, Two Steps Backwards' (2021) 46 *European Law Review* 765

B Van Leeuwen, Legal Empathy in the Internal Market: Free Movement Law as a Comparative Dialogue (2021) 46 *European Law Review* 625

14

Free movement of legal persons and the provision of services

Catherine Barnard with Jukka Snell

1 Introduction

Google Inc is a Californian firm with subsidiaries in various EU Member States. The search engine and all other services are run directly by Google Inc in the US. In the EU, they have a group of companies that are incorporated under local law and wholly owned by Google Ireland. Google Ireland has data centres in Belgium and Finland.[1] The US company Amazon, the world's biggest online retailer, has similarly complex arrangements. In the past, it has said that it has its European headquarters in Luxembourg; corporate offices in France, Germany, Italy, Slovakia, and the UK; development centres in Germany, Ireland, the Netherlands, Romania, and the UK; 'fulfilment centres' in France, Germany, Italy, Spain, and the UK which supply the goods; and customer services centres in Germany, Ireland, and the UK.[2] More recently, it has said that it has branches in Spain, Netherlands, Sweden, and Poland.[3] Although both Google and Amazon are secretive about the precise nature of their legal structure and what is done in each location,[4] the fact is that EU law is engaged whether, for example, Amazon Europe has subsidiaries (with separate legal personality) or branches (with no separate legal personality) or any other form of establishment in the other Member States.

[1] See the AG's Opinion in Case C-131/12 *Google Spain SL, Google Inc v Agencia Española de Protección de Datos (AEPD), Mario Costeja González*, EU:C:2013:424, para 62. See also www.google.com/about/datacenters/locations/dublin/.

[2] To get an idea of the scale of its operation, see www.amazon.jobs/content/en/locations.

[3] www.aboutamazon.eu/news/policy/amazon-pays-millions-of-euros-in-corporate-tax-across-europe.

[4] See the AG's Opinion in *Google Spain SL* (n 1) para 62.

The aim of this chapter is to consider the EU rules which apply to a legal person's establishment rights under Article 49 TFEU and its rights to provide services under Articles 56 and 57 TFEU. The right of establishment, under Article 49 TFEU, implies the migrating company has a permanent link with the host Member State, while the freedom to provide services under Articles 56 and 57 TFEU envisages a much more temporary relationship between the provider/receiver and the host State. This distinction is reflected in the approach taken by the EU legislator and the Court of Justice: generally the host State controls the activities of the migrant person/company in the case of freedom of establishment, whereas the home State (country of origin) controls the activities of the migrant person/company in the case of free movement of services. But complications arise when a company wants to relocate from State A to B. To what extent can the home and the host States interfere with the corporate decision? This thorny question is considered in section 3 on the relationship between national company law and the EU rules on free movement.

Three themes run through this chapter. First, to what extent can and should legal persons be treated in the same way as natural persons? Although they are subject to common Treaty provisions, are the policy issues different? For example, do companies benefit from human rights protection in the same way as natural persons?[5] Does (or should) the concept of EU citizenship affect legal persons?

Secondly, to what extent has the distinction between home State control (service providers) and host State control (establishment) actually been delivered on in the case law and the secondary legislation and what does this mean in the new digital world in which many of these goods and services are being provided through online intermediaries?

Thirdly, has secondary legislation made a difference in this field or has the Treaty, as interpreted by the Court, been left to do the real heavy lifting? If so, has the Court got the balance right between protecting State (and often consumer) interest, on the one hand, and the interests of migrating/service providing companies, on the other?

This chapter is divided into three parts. First, it discusses the Treaty provisions on freedom of establishment and free movement of services (section 2). These Treaty provisions are essentially negative: they prevent Member States from interfering with free movement, subject to the possibility of the State justifying its national rules for various public interest reasons. Secondly, the chapter considers some key pieces of secondary legislation adopted in the field of freedom of establishment and free movement of services, legislation intended to facilitate the operation of the freedoms in respect of legal persons (section 3). Some of the legislation, notably the Services Directive 2006/123, builds on the case law of the Court under Articles 49 and 56 TFEU and requires Member States to remove national laws which interfere with the free movement of services and which cannot be justified. Other legislation requires Member States to adapt their rules to accommodate EU obligations. This legislation is harmonizing and is seen as imposing positive obligations on States. There is, for example, much harmonization in the field of company law and this is considered in section 3.2. There are, however, significant gaps in the EU's programme of corporate law harmonization, especially in respect of migrating companies, and it is here that the Treaty has been used to fill the holes. Finally, reference will be made to the major new developments in the field concerning the EU's regulation of the digital single market.

[5] See Case T-367/23 *Amazon EU v Commission*, EU:T:2025:1038.

2 The Treaty requirements

2.1 Introduction

As we saw in chapter 13, the following questions need to be answered in most free movement cases where the Treaty is engaged:

(a) Does EU law apply at all (section 2 of chapter 13)? If yes,

(b) Which provision of the Treaty is engaged (section 2.2 of chapter 14)?

(c) Who/what are the subjects of Articles 49 and 56 TFEU (section 2.3 of chapter 14)?

(d) Has national law infringed the Treaty provision (section 2.4 of chapter 14)? If yes,

(e) Can that breach be justified and are the steps taken proportionate (section 2.5 of chapter 14)?

This chapter builds on the analysis in chapter 13 and provides additional commentary specific to the case of legal persons. Assuming EU law is engaged (ie the legal person holds the 'nationality' of a Member State which in the case of a legal person is the location of its corporate seat)[6] and there is sufficient interstate element (section 2 of chapter 13), the next question is what Treaty provision is engaged.

2.2 Which provision of the Treaty is engaged?

Identifying the relevant Treaty provision is not as straightforward as would first appear. In the section that follows, we examine the main Treaty provisions (Articles 49 and 56 TFEU) but also their interaction with the free movement of capital under Article 63 TFEU (on which, see further chapter 15).

2.2.1 Freedom of establishment

The relevant Treaty provisions

Article 49 TFEU concerns the establishment of EU natural persons and companies, branches, and agencies in other Member States on a permanent or semi-permanent basis. It provides:

> Within the framework of the provisions set out below, restrictions on the freedom of establishment of nationals of a Member State in the territory of another Member State shall be prohibited. Such prohibition shall also apply to restrictions on the setting-up of agencies, branches or subsidiaries by nationals of any Member State established in the territory of any Member State.
>
> Freedom of establishment shall include the right to take up and pursue activities as self-employed persons and to set up and manage undertakings, in particular companies or firms within the meaning of the second paragraph of Article 54, under the conditions laid down for its own nationals by the law of the country where such establishment is effected, subject to the provisions of the Chapter relating to capital.

[6] Case 270/83 *Commission v France* ('*Tax credits*') [1986] ECR 273, para 18. However, sometimes it can equate with its fiscal residence: V Edwards, *EC Company Law* (Oxford: Oxford University Press, 1999).

Article 54 TFEU talks specifically about companies:

> Companies or firms formed in accordance with the law of a Member State and having their registered office, central administration or principal place of business within the Union shall, for the purposes of this Chapter, be treated in the same way as natural persons who are nationals of Member States.
>
> 'Companies or firms' means companies or firms constituted under civil or commercial law, including cooperative societies, and other legal persons governed by public or private law, save for those which are non-profit-making.

Article 55 TFEU adds:

> Member States shall accord nationals of the other Member States the same treatment as their own nationals as regards participation in the capital of companies or firms within the meaning of Article 54, without prejudice to the application of the other provisions of the Treaties.

Primary and secondary establishment

Looking at the Treaty provisions, we can say that Article 49 TFEU covers two situations. First, it covers the right for natural or legal persons to set up and manage undertakings, in particular companies and firms, in other Member States. This is known as primary establishment. In *Cadbury Schweppes*[7] the Court said that Article 49 TFEU presupposes (a) actual establishment of the company in the host State (ie permanent presence), and (b) the pursuit of a genuine economic activity there. Both conditions need to be satisfied. This can be seen in *Stauffer*.[8] An Italian charitable foundation had commercial premises in Germany which it rented out, the letting being managed by a German property agent. The Court said that Article 49 TFEU did not apply because, while holding immovable property indicated permanent presence, there was no genuine economic activity because the property was not actively managed; Article 63 TFEU on free movement of capital applied instead (see further chapter 15).

Secondly, Article 49 TFEU provides the right for legal persons to set up agencies, branches, or subsidiaries in another Member State. This is known as secondary establishment. The Treaty does not define these terms but in *Somafer*,[9] a case on the interpretation of similar terms in the then Brussels Convention, the Court ruled:

> the concept of branch, agency or other establishment implies a place of business which has the appearance of permanency, such as the extension of a parent body, has a management and is materially equipped to negotiate business with third parties so that the latter, although knowing that there will if necessary be a legal link with the parent body, the head office of which is abroad, do not have to deal directly with such parent body but may transact business at the place of business constituting the extension.

It does not even matter if the establishment cannot be formally classed as a branch or agency, Article 49 will still apply to the entity. So in *Commission v Germany* ('*Insurance*')[10] the Court said that an insurance undertaking of another Member State which maintained

[7] Case C-196/04 *Cadbury Schweppes v Commissioners of the Inland Revenue* [2006] ECR I-7995.
[8] Case C-386/04 *Centro di Musicologia Walter Stauffer* [2006] ECR I-8203, para 19.
[9] Case 33/78 *Somafer SA v Saar-Ferngas AG* [1978] ECR 2183.
[10] Case 205/84 [1986] ECR 3755.

a permanent presence in the host State came within the scope of Article 49 TFEU even if that presence did not take the form of a branch or agency, but 'consists merely of an office managed by the undertaking's own staff or by a person who is independent but authorized to act on a permanent basis for the undertaking, as would be the case with an agency'.

The Court has been keen to ensure that the right to secondary establishment is effective. This can be seen in *Commission v Italy* ('*Foreign securities dealing*').[11] In order to set up as a securities dealer in Italy, Italian law required the dealer to be constituted in the form of a limited company with its registered office in Italy. The Commission successfully argued that this requirement prevented dealers from other Member States from making use of other forms of establishment, especially branches or agencies, and discriminated against them by obliging them to bear the expense of setting up a new company. The Court said that Article 49 TFEU expressly left traders free to choose the appropriate legal form in which to pursue their activities in another Member State[12] and so Italian law breached Article 49 TFEU. In seeking to justify the breach, the Italian authorities argued that the requirement to have a registered office in Italy was necessary for supervising and effectively sanctioning the dealer in question. The Court disagreed, reasoning that Italy had failed to show that this was the 'only means' of achieving the objective.

The fact that the Treaty encourages secondary establishment raises questions as to whether those wishing to form a company can take advantage of EU rules by incorporating a company in State A which has lenient incorporation rules and then, relying on Articles 49 and 54 TFEU, set up a branch or agency in State B, thereby avoiding State B's more onerous rules of incorporation. Early cases on services suggested that this tactic would fail since it is a well-established principle that EU law cannot be relied on for abusive or fraudulent ends.[13] However, in *Centros*,[14] considered in case study 14.1, the Court shifted its approach and said that simply taking advantage of EU law rights did not constitute abuse.

Moving beyond primary and secondary establishment

Although the Treaty covers only the two situations of primary and secondary establishment, more recent case law shows that the Court is willing to use Articles 49 and 54 TFEU to achieve freedom of establishment more generally, without attempting to shoehorn the facts into either the primary or secondary establishment box. For example, the Court has said that Article 49 TFEU applies to individuals or companies from State A acquiring a majority shareholding in a company established in State B, without making reference to the type of establishment.[15] *SEVIC*[16] provides another example. It concerned an inbound merger[17] by acquisition (the absorption of a Luxembourg company (SVC) by a German company (SEVIC)). However, German law on company transformations allowed for mergers only between companies established in Germany. While the Advocate General

[11] Case C-101/94 *Commission v Italy* ('*Re Restrictions on Foreign Securities Dealing*') [1996] ECR I-2691. See also *Tax credits* (n 6); Case 79/85 *Segers v Bedrijfsvereniging voor Bank-en Verzekeringswegen, Groothandel en Vrije Beroepen* [1986] ECR 2375.

[12] *Tax credits* (n 6) para 22.

[13] See eg Case 33/74 *Van Binsbergen v Bedrijfsvereniging Metaalnijverheid* [1974] ECR 1299, para 13; Case C-23/93 *TV10 v Commissariaat voor de Media* [1994] ECR I-4795.

[14] Case C-212/97 [1999] ECR I-1459.

[15] Case C-251/98 *Baars* [2000] ECR I-2787, paras 21 and 22, and Case C-208/00 *Überseering* [2002] ECR I-9 919, para 77. Art 49 TFEU also applies to national rules which affect relations within a group of companies: Case C-446/04 *Test Claimants in the FII Group Litigation v Commissioners of Inland Revenue* ('*FII (No 1)*') [2006] ECR I-11753, para 118; Case C-231/05 *Oy AA* [2007] ECR I-6373, para 23.

[16] Case C-411/03 *SEVIC Systems* [2005] ECR I-10805.

[17] ie the acquisition of a foreign company by a domestic company.

worked hard to show how an inbound merger could actually be viewed, from the German company's point of view, as the equivalent to setting up a secondary establishment in Luxembourg,[18] the Court did not bother with such analysis. Instead, it made the general observation:[19]

> the right of establishment covers all measures which permit or even merely facilitate access to another Member State and the pursuit of an economic activity in that State by allowing the persons concerned to participate in the economic life of the country effectively and under the same conditions as national operators.

The Court therefore said that cross-border mergers (making no express distinction between inbound and outbound mergers) constituted an exercise of the freedom of establishment. Since such mergers could not be registered in the German commercial register, this was likely to deter the exercise of freedom of establishment.[20] The Court recognized that while the national rules could be justified on the grounds of protecting the interests of creditors, minority shareholders, and employees, as well as protecting the effectiveness of fiscal supervision and the fairness of commercial transactions, the German law was nevertheless disproportionate because it involved a general refusal to register a merger between an in-State and out-of-State company, even where the protection of public interests, such as shareholder protection, was not threatened.[21]

SEVIC is therefore a good illustration of how the Court has used Article 49 TFEU to stop national rules interfering with corporate decisions on, for example, company transformation operations, to restructure their company in the way that they see fit to meet market conditions.[22]

2.2.2 **Free movement of services**

The previous discussion shows that the concept of establishment is broad: it requires economic activity together with a degree of permanence by the company in the host State.[23] The question of permanence distinguishes Article 49 TFEU from Article 56 TFEU on services.

The relevant Treaty provisions

Article 56(1) TFEU provides:

> Within the framework of the provisions set out below, restrictions on freedom to provide services within the Union shall be prohibited in respect of nationals of Member States who are established in a Member State other than that of the person for whom the services are intended.

Article 57 TFEU then gives a partial definition of services:

> Services shall be considered to be 'services' within the meaning of this Treaty where they are normally provided for remuneration, in so far as they are not governed by the provisions relating to freedom of movement for goods, capital and persons.
>
> Services shall in particular include: (a) activities of an industrial character; (b) activities of a commercial character; (c) activities of craftsmen; (d) activities of the professions.

[18] AG Tizzano in *SEVIC* (n 15) paras 35–37. [19] *SEVIC* (n 16) para 18.

[20] Ibid, para 22. [21] Ibid, para 30.

[22] See also Case C-438/05 *International Transport Workers' Federation and Finnish Seamen's Union v Viking Line ABP and OÜ Viking Line Eesti* [2007] ECR I-10779 on the reflagging of a vessel.

[23] Case C-221/89 *R v Secretary of State for Transport, ex p Factortame* ('*Factortame II*') [1991] ECR I-3905, para 20.

> Without prejudice to the provisions of the Chapter relating to the right of establishment, the person providing a service may, in order to do so, temporarily pursue his activity in the Member State where the service is provided, under the same conditions as are imposed by that State on its own nationals.

The principle of non-discrimination emphasized in Article 57(3) TFEU is repeated in Article 61 TFEU:

> As long as restrictions on freedom to provide services have not been abolished, each Member State shall apply such restrictions without distinction on grounds of nationality or residence to all persons providing services within the meaning of the first paragraph of Article 56.

Finally, Article 58 TFEU adds:

1. Freedom to provide services in the field of transport shall be governed by the provisions of the Title relating to transport.
2. The liberalisation of banking and insurance services connected with movements of capital shall be effected in step with the liberalisation of movement of capital.

The elements of service provision

From this, it can be seen that for Articles 56 and 57 TFEU to be engaged three conditions must be satisfied. First, there must be a *service*. Article 57 TFEU (cited earlier) provides some examples of services; the case law has gone considerably beyond this traditional definition and has said that 'services' include:

- the provision of people by an employment agency;[24]
- medical services such as the termination of a pregnancy;[25]
- education;[26]
- the provision of a television signal;[27]
- the transmission of programmes and advertisements from broadcasters in one Member State to cable networks in another;[28]
- lotteries;[29]
- building loans provided by banks;[30]
- judicial recovery of debts.[31]

Secondly, the service must *normally be provided for remuneration*, that is, it constitutes consideration for the service in question.[32] This excludes voluntary services from the scope of the Treaty.[33] The remuneration does not need to be paid directly by the recipient of the service. This can be seen in *Skandia*.[34] The case concerned contributions by

[24] Case 279/80 *Webb* [1981] ECR 3305.
[25] Case C-159/90 *SPUC v Grogan* [1991] ECR I-4685. [26] Ibid.
[27] Case 62/79 *Coditel v Cine Vog Films* [1980] ECR 881.
[28] Case 352/85 *Bond van Adverteerders v Netherlands* [1988] ECR 2085; *TV10* (n 13).
[29] Case C-275/92 *Customs and Excise v Schindler* [1994] ECR I-1039.
[30] Case C-484/93 *Svensson and Gustafsson* [1995] ECR I-3955.
[31] Case C-3/95 *Reisebüro v Sandker* [1996] ECR I-6511.
[32] Case 263/86 *Belgian State v Humbel* [1988] ECR 5365, para 17. [33] *SPUC v Grogan* (n 25).
[34] Case C-422/01 *Försäkringsaktiebolaget Skandia (publ) and Ola Ramstedt v Riksskatteverket* [2003] ECR I-6817.

an employer to a pension scheme on behalf of an employee. The Court said 'the premiums which Skandia pays are the consideration for the pension which will be paid to Mr Ramstedt when he retires. It is irrelevant that Mr Ramstedt does not pay the premiums himself, as Article [57 TFEU] does not require that the service be paid for by those for whom it is performed.' It continued, 'Moreover, the premiums unquestionably represent remuneration for the insurance companies which receive them.'[35] This case also shows that the remuneration and the service need not coincide in time: indeed they may be separated by years, even decades.

Thirdly, the services must be *temporary*, with the temporariness being assessed, according to *Schnitzer*,[36] 'in the light not only of the duration of the provision of the service but also of its regularity, periodical nature or continuity'. The Court added that service providers can equip themselves 'with some form of infrastructure in the host Member State (including an office, chambers, or consulting rooms) in so far as such infrastructure is necessary for the purposes of performing the services in question'.[37] It concluded:[38]

> Thus, 'services' within the meaning of the Treaty may cover services varying widely in nature, including services which are provided over an extended period, even over several years, where, for example, the services in question are supplied in connection with the construction of a large building. Services within the meaning of the Treaty may likewise be constituted by services which a business established in a Member State supplies with a greater or lesser degree of frequency or regularity, even over an extended period, to persons established in one or more other Member States, for example the giving of advice or information for remuneration.

Finally, despite the suggestion in Article 57 TFEU that services is a residual category, and applies only where the Treaty provisions on goods, capital, and persons do not, the Court roundly rejected this view in *Fidium Finanz*.[39]

The material scope of Articles 56 and 57 TFEU

Articles 56 and 57 TFEU apply in three situations. First, they apply to *the freedom to (travel to) provide services*. This was the situation envisaged by the Treaty.[40] Case law has also made clear that companies performing services can bring their own staff to perform the contract. These staff are referred to as posted workers and the rules governing the terms and conditions of employment are laid down in the Posted Workers Directive 96/71.[41]

Secondly, Articles 56 and 57 TFEU cover *the freedom to travel to receive services* (eg tourism and education services). This situation was not envisaged by the Treaty but it was covered by early secondary legislation[42] and this has now been confirmed by the case law.[43]

Thirdly, Articles 56 and 57 TFEU cover the situation where *neither provider nor recipient travels*. This was also not expressly envisaged by the Treaty but since the Court has

[35] Ibid, para 24. The Court cited the health-care cases on this point, namely Case C-157/99 *Smits and Peerbooms* [2001] ECR I-5473, para 58, discussed in chapter 21.

[36] Case C-215/01 [2003] ECR I-14847. [37] Ibid, para 28. [38] Ibid, para 30.

[39] Case C-452/04 *Fidium Finanz AG v Bundesanstalt für Finanzdienstleistungsaufsicht* [2006] ECR I-9521. See further chapter 15.

[40] *Van Binsbergen* (n 13).

[41] This Directive, and the amendments, are discussed further in chapters 13 and 20.

[42] Art 1(b) of Directive 73/148 (OJ [1973] L172/14) required the abolition of restrictions on the movement and residence of 'nationals wishing to go to another Member State as recipients of services'.

[43] Joined Cases 286/82 and 26/83 *Luisi and Carbone* [1984] ECR 377 (Italians travelling to Germany to receive medical and tourism services); Case 186/87 *Cowan v Le Tresor Public* [1989] ECR 195 (Englishman mugged on French metro. As a recipient of a service, he was entitled to receive criminal injuries compensation as a French man would). See also *Smits and Peerbooms* (n 35).

ruled that service provision includes electronic provision of services (where the service moves but not the provider or recipient), the Treaty applies here too.[44]

Finally, for the Treaty to apply the entity must be connected to one Member State but be providing services in another Member State (this threshold is set fairly low: a potential interstate element will suffice).[45]

2.2.3 **The relationship between Articles 49, 56, and 63 TFEU**

So far, we have examined the different material scope of Articles 49 and 56 TFEU. A further complication arises when Article 63 TFEU on free movement of capital (considered in chapter 15) is added to the mix. The issue is important because the territorial scope of the provisions is different:

- Articles 49 and 56 TFEU apply only to movements of the self-employed and companies within the EU/EEA;
- Article 63 TFEU applies to movements of capital within the EU/EEA and between the EU/EEA *and* third countries.

Yet, the provisions on capital have, in particular, a close link with the free movement of services, a link recognized in Article 58(2) TFEU, which provides that the liberalization of banking and insurance services connected with movement of capital were to be effected in step with the liberalization of movement of capital. It has fallen to the Court to distinguish the material, and thus territorial, scope of the three fundamental freedoms.

The guidance the Court has offered has not always been clear. In early decisions, the Court favoured deciding cases without reference to the free movement of capital provision.[46] In other cases, the Court considered the rule under two provisions.[47] This was fine as long as there was no third country element to the problem, since the free movement rules of the Treaty would apply in any event. But what if there is? In that case, the free movement rules would apply only if capital movements were involved, but would not if establishment or services were at stake.

Services and capital

The Court was forced to address the services/capital divide in *Fidium Finanz*, where it was asked whether a company established in a non-Member State (Switzerland) could, in the context of granting credit on a commercial basis to residents of Germany, rely on the free movement of capital rules laid down in Article 63 TFEU, or whether the preparation, provision, and performance of such financial services were covered solely by the freedom to provide services laid down in Article 56 TFEU.

The Court recognized that the rules on granting credit on a commercial basis could equally involve service provision and capital movement. However, having looked at the context of the German rules (they formed part of the German legislation on the supervision of undertakings which carried out banking transactions and offered financial services) it adopted a centre of gravity approach: 'the predominant consideration [was] freedom to provide services rather than the free movement of capital'. Therefore, a

[44] See eg Case C-384/93 *Alpine Investments BV v Minister van Financien* [1995] ECR I-1141 (cold-calling by Dutch company offering financial services in other Member States).

[45] For issues connected with the interstate element, see chapter 13.

[46] Case C-1/93 *Halliburton Services* [1994] ECR I-1137; Case C-410/96 *Criminal Proceedings against André Ambry* [1998] ECR I-7875, para 40; Case C-118/96 *Safir* [1998] ECR I-1897, para 35; Case C-200/98 *X and Y* [1999] ECR I-8261.

[47] See eg *Svensson and Gustafsson* (n 30) (capital and services).

company in a non-Member State could not rely on Article 56 TFEU to challenge the detail of those rules, in particular the requirement to be authorized before trading in Germany.

Establishment and capital

The borderline between freedom of establishment and free movement of capital has also proved difficult. Generally, the Court looks at the object and purpose of the rule;[48] where that does not work, it will consider the facts of the case.[49] Generally, it has said:

- National legislation intended to apply only to those shareholdings which enable the holder to exert a definite influence on a company's decisions and to determine its activities (ie where the voting rights go beyond the 10 per cent threshold) falls within the scope of Article 49 TFEU on freedom of establishment.[50]
- National provisions which apply to shareholdings acquired solely with the intention of making a financial investment without any intention to influence the management and control of the undertaking (so-called portfolio investment) must be examined exclusively in light of the free movement of capital.[51]

2.3 **Who/what are the subjects of Articles 49 and 56 TFEU?**

Having established the material and territorial scope of Articles 49 and 56 TFEU, we turn now to the question as to who/what are subject to these provisions. The case law is clear: they have vertical direct effect. This means that they apply to the Member States[52] and also to regulatory bodies.[53] Less clear is the extent to which these Treaty provisions apply to private bodies (in other words, whether they have horizontal direct effect). There are hints in *Viking*[54] that the rules do have horizontal application but the Court also recognized that the problem in this case was not the behaviour of individuals but the collective power of the trade union (the Finnish trade union (FSU), which was threatening strike action when it learned that the Finnish shipping company was planning to reflag its vessel in Estonia):

> the collective action taken by FSU and ITF [International Transport Workers Federation] is aimed at the conclusion of an agreement which is meant to regulate the work of Viking's employees collectively, and, that those two trade unions are organisations which are not public law entities but exercise the legal autonomy conferred on them, inter alia, by national law.

This paragraph tends to locate the Court's decision—that Article 49 TFEU could be relied on by a private undertaking against a trade union or an association of trade unions—more firmly in the frame of an extended form of vertical direct effect. However, the question remains open.

[48] *Cadbury Schweppes* (n 7) paras 31–33; Case C-374/04 *Test Claimants in Class IV of the ACT Group Litigation* [2006] ECR I-11673, paras 37 and 38; Case C-524/04 *Test Claimants in the Thin Cap Group Litigation* [2007] ECR I-2107, paras 26–34.

[49] *FII (No 2)* (n 111) para 94.

[50] *FII (No 1)* (n 15) para 37; Case C-81/09 *Idrima Tipou* [2010] ECR I-10161, para 47.

[51] Joined Cases C-436/08 and 437/08 *Haribo Lakritzen Hans Riegel and Österreichische Salinen* [2011] ECR I-305, para 35.

[52] *Van Binsbergen* (n 13) paras 26 and 27.

[53] Case 36/74 *Walrave and Koch* [1974] ECR 1405, para 17. On the concept of direct effect, see further chapter 6.

[54] Case C-438/05 (n 22) para 58, where the Court cited the well-known case of Case 43/75 *Defrenne* [1976] ECR 455, paras 31 and 39 which gave horizontal direct effect to Art 157 TFEU on equal pay. See also chapter 13.

2.4 **Has national law infringed the Treaty provision?**

2.4.1 **Introduction**

Once a claimant company has established that the national rule it wishes to challenge falls in the scope of Article 49 or 56 TFEU, it must then show that the rule breaches that Treaty provision. As we saw in chapter 13, at first the Court said that only discriminatory national rules breached the Treaty; subsequent cases suggested that the Court now adopts a broader approach and prohibits any rule that interferes with free movement (chapter 13, section 6.2). The burden then shifts to the Member State to justify the rule and show that steps taken to achieve that objective are proportionate and, where appropriate, compatible with fundamental human rights (chapter 13, sections 7 and 8). A similar shift in direction can be seen in the case law on legal persons. First, however, we consider the right of a company to leave a State where it was established.

2.4.2 **The right of a company to exit the host state**

It might seem obvious that a company can exit a state: free movement would suggest that there is a right to leave one State[55] and to enter another. In fact, it is more complicated than that. In *Daily Mail*[56] the Court refused to recognize an unrestricted right of exit for companies. Having pointed to the wide variety of national laws on the factors providing a connection to the national territory and the absence of coordination directives, the Court concluded that neither Article 49 TFEU nor Article 54 TFEU conferred on companies incorporated in State A the right to transfer—without any restriction or impediment from State A—their central management, control, and administration to State B while at the same time retaining their status as companies in State A.[57] This judgment does not mean that companies cannot move their residence but that—at the present stage of development of Union law—national restrictions, particularly those concerning taxation at issue in *Daily Mail*, could be imposed on emigrating companies by the home State.

With the development of the 'restrictions' case law (see section 2.4.3 and especially the decisions in *Centros* and *SEVIC*), some commentators asked whether the position might now be different. However, in *Cartesio*[58] the Court affirmed its decision in *Daily Mail* but emphasized it applied only where the seat of a company incorporated under the law of one Member State was transferred to another Member State with *no* change as regards the law which governed that company. As Szydło points out,[59] companies are creatures of national law; they must exist under such law before they can enjoy any rights under freedom of establishment. That existence is therefore a preliminary matter which, in principle, is a matter of national company law alone.

While *Daily Mail* concerned a company which moved its operations to the Netherlands but continued operating as a company under UK law, something possible under UK law which subscribes to the incorporation theory (which says that a company is governed by the law of the State in which it is formally incorporated, regardless of whether it is connected to that State in any other way (eg plant, premises, or staff)), *Polbud*[60] concerned the opposite situation: a Polish company which decided to keep its premises and real head office in Poland but to reincorporate under the law of Luxembourg, where the company transferred its registered office.[61] The company's place of business remained in

[55] See eg Case C-10/90 *Masgio v Bundesknappschaft* [1991] ECR I-1119, paras 18 and 19; Case C-415/93 *Bosman* [1995] ECR I-4921, para 104.

[56] Case 81/87 [1988] ECR 5483.

[57] Ibid, para 24.

[58] Case C-210/06 *Cartesio Oktató és Szolgáltató bt* [2008] ECR I-9641.

[59] Szydło (n 61) 1564–1565.

[60] Case C-106/16, EU:C:2017:804.

[61] M Szydło, 'Cross-Border Conversion of Companies under Freedom of Establishment: *Polbud* and Beyond' (2018) 55 *Common Market Law Review* 1549.

Poland—there was no physical conversion. Polbud asked for its name to be removed from the Polish commercial register. Its application was refused because it had not produced the relevant documents; Polbud said it did not need to produce the documents because it was not being wound up.

The Court ruled that all measures (such as requiring the winding up of the company) which prohibited, impeded, or rendered less attractive[62] the outbound exercise of freedom of establishment amounted to restrictions under Articles 49 and 54 TFEU.[63] However, it found that the requirement of compulsory winding up of an outbound company under Polish law could, in principle, be justified on the grounds of ensuring the interests of creditors, minority shareholders, and employees of a company, but the measure was not proportionate because no consideration had been given to the actual risk of detriment to those groups.[64] *Polbud* suggests that the Court is increasingly making it more difficult for home States to impose unjustified restrictions on outbound movements.

2.4.3 **The right not to be discriminated against or subject to restrictions**

Discrimination approach

In the early days, the Court, following the language of the Treaty, prohibited direct and indirect discrimination on the grounds of nationality (see Fig. 13.2) both in respect of initial access to the market in the host State and to exercise of the activity once on that market.[65] As we saw earlier, in the case of a company, its 'nationality' equates with the location of its seat.

Direct discrimination concerns less favourable treatment on the grounds of origin. According to the orthodox view, direct discrimination can be saved by the express derogations only (see section 2.5).[66]

Direct discrimination was at issue in *Factortame II*.[67] Under the British Merchant Shipping Act 1988, a fishing vessel could be registered and thus entitled to fish in UK waters only if (a) the vessel was British-owned;[68] (b) the vessel was managed, and its operations directed and controlled from within the UK; and (c) any charterer, manager, or operator of the vessel was a qualified (British) person or company.[69] Inevitably, with the overt nationality requirement, the Court found that these rules breached Article 49 TFEU and could not be justified. This led to substantial claims for damages against the British State.[70]

Indirect discrimination concerns a rule, such as a residence requirement of the corporate headquarters, which, on its face, applies to all companies but in fact disadvantages those with only a branch in the host State.[71] Such rules can, however, be objectively

[62] On the facts the Polish rules were in fact discriminatory: the conversion of a Polish company from one form into another did not trigger an obligation to liquidate and wind up the company but this was ignored by the Court: see Szydło (n 61) 1561.

[63] *Polbud* (n 60) para 46.

[64] Ibid, paras 55–58.

[65] Case 197/84 *Steinhauser v City of Biarritz* [1985] ECR 1819.

[66] Case C-288/89 *Gouda* [1991] ECR I-4007, paras 10 and 11.

[67] Case C-246/89 *Commission v UK* ('*Factortame*') [1991] ECR I-3125; *Factortame II* (n 23).

[68] According to s 14(2), a fishing vessel was deemed to be British-owned if the legal title to the vessel was vested wholly in one or more qualified persons or companies and if the vessel was beneficially owned by one or more qualified companies or, as to not less than 75 per cent, by one or more qualified persons.

[69] According to s 14(7), 'qualified person' meant a person who was a British citizen resident and domiciled in the UK and 'qualified company' meant a company incorporated in the UK and having its principal place of business there, at least 75 per cent of its shares being owned by one or more qualified persons or companies and at least 75 per cent of its directors being qualified persons.

[70] Joined Cases C-46/93 and C-48/93 *Factortame III* [1996] ECR I-01029.

[71] *Tax credits* (n 6); Case C-330/91 *Ex p Commerzbank* [1993] ECR I-4017, para 15.

justified/justified on public interest grounds as well as saved by the express derogations (see section 2.5.2).[72]

In the context of the free movement of services, direct discrimination covers not only less favourable treatment on the grounds of nationality but also on the basis of establishment in another Member State. This was confirmed by the Court in *Svensson and Gustafsson*, which concerned Swedish nationals resident in Luxembourg (at a time when Sweden was not yet an EU member) who were refused an interest rate subsidy on a building loan because they had borrowed the money from a (Belgian) institution which did not satisfy the requirement of being established in Luxembourg. The Court said:[73]

> the rule in question entails ***discrimination based on the place of establishment***. Such discrimination can only be justified on the general interest grounds referred to in Article [52 TFEU], to which Article [62 TFEU] refers, and which do not include economic aims.

This decision has caused problems because a rule which concerns discrimination based on the place of establishment (direct discrimination) could equally be cast as a rule requiring residence in the host State which has been considered indirectly discriminatory and so can be objectively justified.

The move to market access

The corollary of the discrimination approach is that rules which do not discriminate do not breach the Treaty. But what about rules which are non-discriminatory but nevertheless hinder market access? This was at issue in *Alpine Investments*.[74] The case concerned a Dutch rule prohibiting cold-calling by the Dutch financial services industry both within and outside the Netherlands. It was argued that since this rule was non-discriminatory, EU law would not apply, following the principles laid down in *Keck*.[75] The Court disagreed: it said the Dutch rule breached Article 56 TFEU since although non-discriminatory,[76] it 'directly affects access to the markets in services in the other Member States and is thus capable of hindering intra-Union trade in services'.[77]

The decision in *Alpine Investments* presaged a broader shift towards the so-called market access/restrictions approach.[78] In fact, this change had already been signalled in the earlier case of *Säger*,[79] where the Court said that Article 56 TFEU required:

> ***not only*** the elimination of all discrimination against a person providing services on the ground of his nationality ***but also*** the abolition of any ***restriction***, even if it applies without distinction to national providers of services and to those of other Member States, when ***it is liable to prohibit or otherwise impede*** the activities of a provider of services established in another Member State where he lawfully provides similar services.

Thus national rules which are 'liable to prohibit or otherwise impede the activities of a provider of services' breach Article 49 or 56 TFEU unless they can be justified by the Member States and shown to be proportionate (see section 2.5). Sometimes the Court uses slightly different language for services, particularly when the rule being challenged is set by the home, not host State. So, for example, in *Skandia*[80] the Court said:

[72] *Gouda* (n 66) paras 12 and 13. [73] *Svensson and Gustafsson* (n 30), emphasis added.
[74] Case C-384/93 (n 44).
[75] Joined Cases C-267/91 and 268/91 *Keck and Mithouard* [1993] ECR 1–6097. See further chapter 12.
[76] *Alpine Investments* (n 44) para 35. [77] Ibid, para 38.
[78] For a discussion of the terminology, see further chapter 13.
[79] Case C-76/90 *Säger* [1991] ECR I-4221, para 12. [80] Case C-422/01 (n 34).

> 26. In the perspective of a single market and in order to permit the attainment of the objectives thereof, Article [56 TFEU] precludes the application of any national legislation which has the effect of making the provision of services between Member States more difficult than the provision of services purely within one Member State.

Thus, while the discrimination approach compares the treatment of the in-State and out-of-State company and finds illegality where there is a difference in treatment, with the market access approach the Court looks at a particular rule only from the perspective of the out-of-State company/service provider: is there a rule in the home or host State which is liable to interfere with its access to the market? The fact that the rule treats national service providers in just the same way is irrelevant: the question is the impact the rule has on the out-of-State provider. In subsequent cases, the Court simplified the language of the market access approach to reflect the terminology of the Treaty: it says the Treaty prohibits 'obstacles' or 'restrictions' to free movement. This change of approach can be seen in *Viking*, where the Court said that proposed strike action to be taken by members of the Finnish Seamen's Union in protest at the Finnish company's decision to reflag its vessel as Estonian was a 'restriction' on freedom of establishment and so in principle contrary to Article 49 TFEU.

So what, then, is a 'restriction'? The Court has recognized a range of rules as restrictions on freedom of establishment and free movement of services. These include:

- authorization requirements,[81] especially where they come without clear procedures;[82]
- rules restricting the number of establishments in a particular area;[83]
- residence requirements;[84]
- conditions relating to maximum/minimum staffing levels;[85]
- obligations to lodge guarantees with the relevant authorities;[86]
- rules setting compulsory minimum fees, or at least permitting control by the relevant authorities of the fees charged;[87]
- advertising restrictions.[88]

Whether the Court describes these rules as restrictions on free movement or hindrances to market access seems to make little difference. In the context of legal persons, at least, the Court uses the terms interchangeably. This can be seen in *Commission v Italy* (*'Motor insurance'*),[89] where the Court found that an Italian 'obligation to contract' imposed on all insurance companies operating in the field of third party liability motor insurance and in relation to all vehicle owners, irrespective of risk, constituted a restriction on freedom of establishment and freedom to provide services. It said the imposition by a Member State of an obligation to contract 'constitutes a *substantial* interference in the freedom to contract which economic operators, in principle, enjoy'.[90] It continued that in a sector

[81] Case C-189/03 *Commission v Netherlands* (*'Private security firms'*) [2004] ECR I-9289, para 17; Case C-439/99 *Commission v Italy* (*'Trade fairs'*) [2002] ECR I-305, para 39.

[82] Case C-333/21 *European Superleague Company v FIFA*, EU:C:2023:1011.

[83] Case C-134/05 *Commission v Italy* (*'Extra-judicial debt recovery'*) [2007] ECR I-6251, para 64.

[84] *Ex p Commerzbank* (n 71).

[85] Case C-465/05 *Commission v Italy* (*'Private security activities'*) [2007] ECR I-11091, para 105.

[86] Ibid, para 109.

[87] Ibid, para 127.

[88] Case C-405/98 *Gourmet* [2001] ECR I-1795, para 39; Case C-429/02 *Bacardi v Télévision Française 1 SA* [2004] ECR I-6613.

[89] Case C-518/06 [2009] ECR I-3491.

[90] Ibid, para 66 (emphasis added).

like insurance, 'such a measure affects the relevant operators' access to the market, in particular where it subjects insurance undertakings not only to an obligation to cover any risks which are proposed to them, but also to requirements to moderate premium rates'.[91] It concluded that 'Inasmuch as it obliges insurance undertakings which enter the Italian market to accept every potential customer, that obligation to contract is likely to lead, in terms of organisation and investment, to significant additional costs for such undertakings.'[92] The rules therefore breached the Treaty but could be justified on the grounds of social protection for victims of road traffic accidents. The Court also said the rules were proportionate.

These cases demonstrate that while the restrictions approach is effective at challenging any national rules which interfere with free movement, it also reaches deeply into the national systems and challenges legitimate regulatory choices and policy decisions taken by democratically elected national governments. The Court is alert to this problem and has some tools to limit the reach of the restrictions approach, notably:

- that the effect of the national rule on free movement is too uncertain and indirect (ie a remoteness test);[93]
- some sort of *de minimis* test (ie an economic threshold) as was suggested in the *Motor insurance* case,[94] where the Court talked of a '*substantial* interference in the freedom to contract'.[95]

Although the Court of Justice and the national courts now have the tools to limit the effect of the market access case law, the Court has not applied them consistently and generally the Court finds that most national rules do, in principle, interfere with free movement and so need to be justified by the State and shown to be proportionate (see Fig. 13.3). There are two exceptions to this general observation: rules concerning the exit of companies, considered in section 2.4.2, and national rules on taxation to which we now turn.

2.4.4 **The special case of taxation**

Introduction

Taxation is a necessary evil: without it there would be no public services. That said, large companies employ armies of lawyers and accountants to establish complex corporate arrangements to reduce their tax liability. The restrictions approach appeared to add a new tool to the lawyers' armoury. It had the potential to enable them to bring challenges to all sorts of tax rules, including differential rates of taxation (eg where corporation tax rates are higher in State B than State A, companies in State A might argue that these higher rates are likely to deter them from establishing themselves in State B; State B's rules thus constitute a restriction on freedom of establishment).[96] The restrictions approach, combined with the Court's uncertain approach to justifications, made it almost impossible for finance ministries to draft any tax laws which could not, at least in principle, be challenged under EU law. Going back to the corporation tax example, had

[91] Ibid, para 67. [92] Ibid, para 68.

[93] Case C-602/10 *SC Volksbank România v CJPC*, EU:C:2012:443, para 81, where the Court found that the effect of a national rule prohibiting credit institutions from levying certain bank charges was too indirect and uncertain to be regarded as liable to hinder intra-Union trade.

[94] *Motor insurance* (n 89).

[95] Ibid. See also Case C-442/02 *CaixaBank France v Ministère de l'Économie, des Finances et de l'Industrie* [2004] ECR I-8961, especially the AG's Opinion.

[96] Although cf the early decision in Case C-336/96 *Gilly v Directeur des services Fiscaux du Bas-Rhein* [1998] ECR I-2793, para 34, where the Court appeared to reject such arguments.

a non-discrimination model been applied then State B's rules would not have breached Article 49 TFEU because they would have applied equally to all companies/subsidiaries established in State B (assuming that they did) or, if they did not, this was because the two situations (domestic and cross-border) were not in fact alike and so should have been treated differently. This would have resolved many problems. Yet the blanket application of the restrictions model in the early 2000s appeared to rule out space for a discrimination approach and led to the 'unplanned destruction' of national systems.[97]

Furthermore, the Court's application of the restrictions model overlooked two key points. The first point is practical: by definition companies established in State A would never challenge tax rates in State B which were *lower* than those in State A.[98] So essentially the companies would cherry-pick the rules they wished to challenge and the Court, by accepting these challenges, disregarded the fact that tax policy is a package: some rates are higher (eg personal tax) and some are lower (eg corporation tax) and that the choice how to strike that balance is made by democratically elected governments. The restrictions model was thus being used to unpick those democratic choices and ultimately risked the unravelling of whole schemes of taxation.[99] This would not be so serious if the EU was in fact capable of reregulating in the field of taxation. While it has competence to legislate (eg under Article 113 TFEU on harmonization of legislation concerning turnover taxes, excise duties, and other forms of indirect taxation or Article 115 TFEU on rules directly affecting the establishment or functioning of the internal market[100]), the unanimity requirement in the legal basis and the refusal by certain Member States to countenance EU-level tax legislation have resulted in the almost total absence of EU harmonization legislation, especially in the field of direct taxation. The restrictions approach adopted by the Court thus risked creating a legal vacuum.

The second point is that, again in the absence of any meaningful harmonization of tax rules at EU level, taxation policy is national but reflects internationally agreed norms (see below) on which, the Court recognized in the early case of *Gilly*,[101] it was reasonable for Member States to base their practice. The application of the restrictions approach thus risked undermining international standards without the EU having the realistic possibility of replacing those rules with standards of its own.

Under public international law of taxation Member States remain free to identify:[102]

- the tax base (ie the nature and quantum of the receipts it wishes to tax and the identification of the entitlement to and nature of tax reliefs);
- the tax rate (ie the level(s) at which the tax would be set);
- how they wish to administer, assess, collect, and recover tax;
- the tax unit.

[97] J Tiley and G Loutzenhiser, *Advanced Topics in Revenue Law* (Oxford: Hart Publishing, 2013) 11. See also chapter 21 for a good discussion of the issues raised by the case law of the Court of Justice in the tax field.

[98] See AG Geelhoed's Opinion in *FII (No 1)* (n 15) on this point.

[99] eg when the Court struck down the national rule in Case C-168/01 *Bosal Holding BV* [2003] ECR I-9409 it was estimated that the direct costs of the case amounted to €1.2 billion between 2003 and 2010. Even after changing its legislation, it is estimated that the cost to the Netherlands was €0.55 billion a year to comply with the judgment: S Kingston, 'The Boundaries of Sovereignty: The Court's Controversial Role Applying the Internal Market Rules to Taxation' (2006–7) 9 *Cambridge Yearbook of European Legal Studies* 287.

[100] Art 114(2) says 'Paragraph 1 [general internal market legal base with qualified majority voting] shall not apply to *fiscal* provisions. . . .'

[101] Case C-336/96 (n 96) paras 30 and 31.

[102] J Ghosh, *Principles of the Internal Market and Direct Taxation* (Oxford: Key Haven, 2007) 1–14. See also *Test Claimants in Class IV of the ACT Group Litigation* (n 48) para 50.

We shall focus on the question of the tax unit, that is those over whom States wish to assert legislative fiscal jurisdiction. Generally, this means that resident companies are taxed on their worldwide profits ('unlimited taxation'), while non-resident companies are taxed only on profits arising from sources located in that taxing State ('limited taxation').[103] This is known as the principle of territoriality. The distinction between residents and non-residents, while suspect under general EU internal market law, is the bedrock of international taxation.

The corollary of the principle of territoriality is that generally the State of residence grants taxpayers tax advantages, for example tax relief (tax credits), because their financial interests are centred there and so the State of residence can best assess the taxpayers' ability to pay tax.[104] But one of the consequences of the principle of territoriality is that a company resident in State A but receiving profits in State B risks being taxed twice: once by the source State (State B) and then again in the State of residence (State A), where it is taxed on worldwide profits. To avoid this problem, a huge network of bilateral Double Taxation Conventions (DTCs), based on a model OECD convention, have been drawn up between States agreeing on which State enjoys priority in cross-border situations.[105] International tax principles lay down the general rule that priority of taxation lies with the source State, meaning that it is up to the home State (State A) to alleviate the double taxation. But what if State A refuses to do so? While the early cases might have suggested this constituted a restriction on freedom of establishment, more recently the Court has realized that the risk of double taxation is the inevitable consequence of the parallel existence of 27 national systems and the Court has now recognized that the home State is not obliged to alleviate the double taxation.[106] This line of case law marked an important shift towards recognizing that the EU's restrictions case law should not trample over internationally agreed norms.

Return to a discrimination-based approach

At the same time as the Court was beginning to realize the significance of international rules on taxation, in two Grand Chamber decisions, *FII (No 1)*[107] and *ACT Group Litigation*,[108] the Court showed signs that it was rejecting a pure restrictions approach in favour of a discrimination model.

ACT concerned 'outgoing' dividends, that is, dividends paid by a UK subsidiary to a non-UK parent. Consistent with the principles of international tax, the non-UK parent was not liable for UK tax on the dividends but nor was it entitled to a UK tax credit on those dividends. By contrast, UK parents receiving 'upstream' dividends from UK subsidiaries would have received a tax credit for the advance corporation tax paid by the UK subsidiary.

FII (No 1) concerned the reverse situation—'incoming' dividends payable by a non-UK subsidiary to a UK parent. The UK parent company was liable to UK corporation tax on the incoming dividends. It was granted tax relief for any foreign tax which the non-UK subsidiary had paid on the dividends abroad but was not otherwise entitled to a UK tax credit on them. By contrast, a UK parent receiving dividends from a UK subsidiary would

[103] A point the Court recognized in Case C-446/03 *Marks & Spencer plc v Halsey (Her Majesty's Inspector of Taxes)* [2005] ECR I-10837, para 39.

[104] Case C-279/93 *Finanzamt Köln-Altstadt v Schumacker* [1995] ECR I-225, para 32.

[105] S Kingston, 'A Light in the Darkness: Recent Developments in the ECJ's Direct Tax Jurisprudence' (2007) 44 *Common Market Law Review* 1321, 1331.

[106] Case C-194/06 *Orange European Smallcap Fund* [2008] ECR I-3747, paras 37–41.

[107] Case C-446/04 (n 15).

[108] Case C-374/04 (n 48). This section draws on C Barnard, *The Substantive Law of the EU: The Four Freedoms* (5th edn, Oxford: Oxford University Press, 2016).

not be liable to corporation tax on the dividends and would have received a tax credit for the advance corporation tax which the UK subsidiary had paid. In both *ACT* and *FII (No 1)* the claimants argued that the UK rules breached Article 49 TFEU.

In *ACT* the Court found that the UK rules were compatible with Article 49 TFEU. The Court said that the situation of a UK parent and a non-UK parent was not comparable because the non-UK parent was not subject to the tax charge while the UK parent was subject to the charge.[109] Therefore, the UK rules did 'not constitute discrimination prohibited by Article [49 TFEU]'.[110] By contrast, in *FII (No 1)* the Court found that the rules did breach Article 49 TFEU because in this case the two UK parent companies were in a comparable situation but the rules were discriminatory because the UK parent with the resident subsidiary got the tax credit, while the UK parent with the non-resident subsidiary did not. As the Court put it:[111]

> Article [49 TFEU] precludes a national measure which allows a resident company which has received dividends from another resident company to deduct the amount of ACT [advance corporation tax] paid by the latter company from the amount of ACT for which the former company is liable, whereas a resident company which has received dividends from a non-resident company is not entitled to make such a deduction in respect of the corporation tax which the last-mentioned company is obliged to pay in the State in which it is resident.

In *FII (No 2)* the Court expressly confirmed the discrimination approach:[112]

> It should be noted in this regard that, since European Union law, as it currently stands, does not lay down any general criteria for the attribution of areas of competence between the Member States in relation to the elimination of double taxation within the European Union . . . each Member State remains free to organise its system for taxing distributed profits, provided, however, that the system in question does not entail discrimination prohibited by the FEU Treaty.

In the absence of any discrimination there is no breach of EU law and so the national tax regime is lawful.

More recent case law has also adopted a more sophisticated and nuanced approach to justifications where discrimination was established.[113] It is to the subject of derogations and justifications more generally that we now turn.

2.5 **Can that breach be justified and are the steps taken proportionate?**

Once a rule has been classified as a restriction or an obstacle to free movement, the question is whether Member States can justify that rule. The Treaty lays down an exhaustive list of derogations which apply across all four freedoms; the case law has supplemented those with judicially developed justifications.[114]

[109] *ACT Group Litigation* (n 48) para 58. For a further example, see Case C-282/07 *Etat belge—SPF Finances v Truck Center SA* [2008] ECR I-10767, para 49.

[110] *ACT Group Litigation* (n 48) para 72.

[111] *FII (No 1)* (n 15) para 94. For a further example of discrimination between nationally sourced dividends and foreign sourced dividends, this time in the method used for calculating the tax, see Case C-35/11 *Test Claimants in the FII Group Litigation v Commissioners of Inland Revenue ('FII (No 2)')*, EU:C:2012:707, para 65.

[112] *FII (No 2)* (n 111) para 40.

[113] See eg *Marks and Spencer v Halsey* (n 103); *Cadbury Schweppes* (n 7).

[114] See further chapter 16.

2.5.1 **Express derogations**

Articles 52(1) and 62 TFEU allow Member States to derogate from the rules on freedom of establishment and the free movement of services on the grounds of public policy, public security, and public health. The general rules which apply to these derogations are set out in *Église de Scientologie*[115] (considered in chapter 13).

In addition to the express general derogations, there is a special exception from the free movement rules for the 'exercise of official authority' (Article 51(1) TFEU on establishment; Article 62 TFEU extends this to services). The nature of what constitutes official authority was considered in *Reyners*.[116] The Court said that Article 51 TFEU had to be narrowly construed: it applied only to those activities which had a 'direct and specific connection with official authority'.[117] In *Commission v Belgium ('Security guards')*[118] the Court said that the activities of private security firms, security-systems firms, and internal security services were not normally directly and specifically connected with the exercise of official authority.

Thus it seems that the derogations under Articles 51 and 62 TFEU must be restricted to activities which, in themselves, are directly and specifically connected with the exercise of official authority; functions that are merely auxiliary and preparatory, especially when carried out by a private body, which are supervised by an entity which effectively exercises official authority by taking the final decision, are excluded from the definition of the exercise of official authority.[119]

2.5.2 **Public interest justifications**

'Public interest' or 'objective justifications' exist for indirectly discriminatory and non-discriminatory national measures which impede the activities of a provider of services and any other measure which hinders market access. Also known in the case law as 'imperative reasons in the public interest',[120] objective justifications have covered a wide range of public concerns such as:

- the need to safeguard the reputation of the Dutch financial markets and to protect the investing public;[121]
- preventing gambling and avoiding the lottery from becoming the source of private profit (see further case study 14.2);[122]
- avoiding the risk of crime or fraud;[123]
- avoiding the risk of incitement to spend, with damaging individual and social consequences;[124]
- maintenance of pluralism of the press;[125]
- fiscal cohesion;[126]
- combating money laundering;[127]

[115] Case C-54/99 *Église de Scientologie* [2000] ECR I-1335.

[116] Case 2/74 [1974] ECR 631. [117] Ibid, para 45.

[118] Case C-355/98 *Commission v Belgium* [2000] ECR I-1221, para 26. See also Case C-283/99 *Commission v Italy* [2001] ECR I-4363, para 20; *Private security activities* (n 81) para 40.

[119] Case C-404/05 *Commission v Germany ('Inspection of organic production')* [2007] ECR I-10239, para 38; Case C-438/08 *Commission v Portugal ('Vehicle inspection')* [2009] ECR I-10219, para 37.

[120] See also the ORRPI in the Services Directive 2006/123 (discussed in section 3) which serve an equivalent function in the context of the Directive.

[121] *Alpine Investments* (n 44). [122] *Schindler* (n 29). [123] Ibid. [124] Ibid.

[125] *Gouda* (n 66) para 23.

[126] Case C-300/90 *Commission v Belgium* [1992] ECR I-305, para 14.

[127] Case C-212/11 *Jyske Bank Gibraltar Ltd v Administración del Estado* EU:C:2013:270.

- protection of the interests of creditors, minority shareholders, and employees;[128]
- the effectiveness of fiscal supervision.[129]

Once a Member State has made out a justification, it must then show that the steps taken to achieve that objective are proportionate (ie suitable and no more restrictive than necessary) and, where appropriate, are compatible with human rights.[130] An examination of how these various requirements interrelate can be seen in case study 14.1.

Case study 14.1: The application of the restriction/justification/proportionality approach and its effect on the *siège reel* doctrine

The important decision of *Centros*[131] provides a good example of how the establishment of breach (the restrictions or obstacles approach), justification, and proportionality fit together. Centros Ltd was a private company incorporated in the UK (then a Member State) by two Danish citizens, Mr and Mrs Bryde, who were its sole shareholders. With a view to trading in Denmark, they applied to have a branch of the company registered in Denmark. At the time of the registration request, Centros had never traded in the UK, and for this reason the Danish registrar of companies refused to register the branch. He considered that the company was actually seeking to register its principal business establishment in Denmark and not just a branch, and that the Brydes were seeking to evade Danish law on minimum capital requirements by establishing in the UK. In Denmark companies had to have at least DKr 200,000 (approximately £20,000) when they were formed; the UK had no rules on minimum capital requirements.

The Court ruled that the registrar's refusal to grant the registration request constituted an *obstacle* to the freedom of establishment,[132] saying that it was 'immaterial' that the company was formed in the UK only for the purpose of establishing itself in Denmark where its main or entire business was to be conducted.[133] It also said that this was not a case of abuse because the national rules which the Brydes were trying to avoid were rules governing the formation of companies and not rules concerning the pursuit of certain trades, professions, or businesses.[134] In other words, they were not fraudulently taking advantage of the provisions of Union law[135] because they were doing what the Treaty expressly permits, namely incorporating in one Member State and setting up a secondary establishment in another.[136]

The Danish government sought to *justify* the refusal to register on the ground of the need to maintain its rules on minimum capital requirements. It said that the rules served two purposes: first, to reinforce the financial soundness of companies in order to protect public creditors against the risk of seeing the debts owed to them become irrecoverable (since, unlike private creditors, they could not secure debts by means of guarantees); and, secondly, the law aimed at protecting all creditors from the risk of fraudulent bankruptcy due to the insolvency of companies whose initial capitalization was inadequate.

The Court ruled that the first justification offered was inadequate because it was inconsistent—the vital factor in the registrar's refusal to grant the registration request was the failure of the company to trade in the UK. This was immaterial to the protection of creditors since

[128] *Überseering* (n 15) para 92.

[129] Case C-55/98 *Bent Vestergaard* [1999] ECR I-7641, para 23.

[130] See P Oliver, *The Fundamental Rights of Companies: EU, US and International Law Compared* (Oxford: Bloomsbury, 2018).

[131] *Centros* (n 14). [132] Ibid, paras 29 and 30. [133] Ibid, para 17, citing *Segers* (n 11).

[134] Ibid, para 26. [135] Ibid, para 24.

[136] Ibid, para 27. See also *Cadbury Schweppes* (n 7) para 36.

they would have been no better off had the company previously traded in the UK and been able to register its branch in Denmark.[137] Furthermore, EU company information disclosure directives put Danish creditors on notice that Centros Ltd was not a company governed by Danish law. The refusal to register was not only unjustifiable, it was also *disproportionate*. The Court said that the Danish authorities could have adopted less restrictive measures by, for example, making it possible in law for public creditors to obtain the necessary guarantees.

The Court did, however, recognize the validity of the second justification put forward by the Danish government about abuse. It said that its ruling did not prevent Denmark from adopting measures for preventing or penalizing fraud, either in relation to the company itself or to its members, where it had been established that the members were in fact attempting to evade their obligations towards private or public creditors by means of the formation of the company. However, the Court added that combating fraud did not justify a practice of refusing to register a branch of a company which had its registered office in another Member State[138]—but did not suggest what steps States could take to combat fraud which would be compatible with Union law.

Not only does the *Centros* case neatly show how the restrictions/justification/proportionality approach works, but it also highlights another more profound tension created by EU law. As noted above, English law applies the incorporation theory: it permits companies to be incorporated in the UK to have their residence or main operations in another Member State. This outcome would not be permitted by Member States which operate the *siège réel* (real seat) doctrine which applies in the majority of Member States, including France and Germany. This says that a company is to be established under the law of the State in which its operational headquarters is situated, even though it might be formally incorporated in another Member State. The Court, by ruling, in *Centros*, that the Danish registrar's refusal to recognize the branch constituted an unjustified obstacle to the UK company's freedom of establishment, implicitly called into question the status of the *siège réel* doctrine under EU law and created a market for incorporations under EU law. Becht et al note that the UK experienced a 400 per cent increase in incorporations of companies that had their headquarters in other Member States after *Centros*.[139]

A permutation on *Centros* arose in *Überseering*,[140] which raised the question whether a company incorporated under one legal regime (State A) but which then transferred its principal place of business to another (State B) could retain its legal status as a company in State A and have that status recognized in State B. Überseering, a Dutch company, sued a German company, NCC, for defective work carried out by NCC on Überseering's behalf in Germany. Prior to bringing the proceedings, all the shares in Überseering had been acquired by two German nationals. The German court found that, since Überseering had transferred its centre of administration to Germany, as a company incorporated under Dutch law it did not have legal capacity in Germany because it had not been formed according to German law and so could not bring proceedings.[141] German law thus refused to recognize the legal personality which Überseering enjoyed under Dutch law (and continued to enjoy under Dutch law even after its centre of administration had been moved),[142] with the result that the German courts effectively denied the company access to justice in Germany.

[137] *Centros* (n 14) para 35. [138] Ibid, para 38.

[139] M Becht, C Mayer, and HF Wagner, 'Where Do Firms Incorporate?' [2008] *Journal of Corporate Finance* 241, 242 cited in J Borg-Barthet, 'Free at Last? Choice of Corporate Law in the EU Following the Judgment in *VALE*' (2013) 62 *International and Comparative Law Quarterly* 502.

[140] Case C-208/00 (n 15). [141] Ibid, para 9. [142] Ibid, paras 63 and 71.

The Court said that because Überseering was a company validly incorporated under the law of the Netherlands, where its registered office was established, the company had no alternative under German law but to reincorporate in Germany if it wished to enforce its rights under a contract before a German court.[143] This contravened Articles 49 and 54 TFEU,[144] a breach which could not be justified.[145]

The effect of this judgment may be to erode the *siège réel* doctrine still further. It requires German courts to recognize companies validly formed under Dutch law, even though they would not be recognized under German law. Indeed, a company with its 'registered office, central administration or principal place of business within the [Union]' cannot be denied access to any other Member State. This does not necessarily mean that the Court is privileging the incorporation theory; rather that it is paying more attention to the State in which the company has been incorporated.

In the context of free movement of services, one extra factor needs to be taken into account in respect of justifications raised by the host State: the extent to which the interest at stake in the host State is already protected in the home State. The Court made this clear in *Gouda*,[146] where it said that national restrictions came within the scope of Article 56 TFEU:

> if the application of the national legislation to foreign persons providing services is not justified by overriding reasons relating to the public interest or if the requirements embodied in that legislation are already satisfied by the rules imposed on those persons in the Member State in which they are established.

This is a weak form of the country of origin principle (which is considered further in the discussion on the Services Directive in section 3.2).

However, the Court is prepared to override the country of origin principle where serious issues of public interest are at stake. This can be seen in *Jyske Gibraltar*,[147] concerning a Spanish rule requiring credit institutions providing services but not established in its territory, to forward directly to the Spanish financial intelligence unit (FIU) their reports on suspicious operations and any other information requested by the FIU. The Court found this rule was a restriction on the free movement of services. However, the Court said the breach could be justified, inter alia, on the grounds of combating money laundering and terrorist financing.[148]

The Court also said the steps taken were proportionate. They were *suitable* because, since the Spanish authorities had exclusive jurisdiction with regard to the criminalization, detection, and eradication of offences committed on its territory, information concerning suspicious transactions carried out in Spain could be forwarded to the Spanish FIU.

The rules were also *no more restrictive than necessary* because, although there was provision in EU secondary law for the credit institution to provide information to the FIU of its home State which could then be shared with the FIU in the host State, there were deficiencies in the procedure. In particular, because disclosure relating to suspicious transactions was carried out in the home State FIU there was no obligation under the EU legislation for that information to be forwarded automatically to the host State FIU (Spain). This meant that the Spanish FIU might not have information corroborating

143 Ibid, para 79.
144 Ibid, paras 80 and 81.
145 Ibid, paras 92 and 93.
146 Case C-288/89 (n 66) para 13.
147 Case C-212/11 (n 127).
148 Ibid, para 62.

the suspicions so as to send a request for information to the FIU of the Member State of origin. Therefore, the Court said that even though disclosure to the Spanish FIU gave rise to additional expenses and administrative burdens on the part of service providers, those burdens were relatively limited given that the credit institutions already had to establish infrastructure necessary for information to be forwarded to the home State's FIU.

Case study 14.2: The special case of gambling

All Member States impose significant controls on gambling: who can offer it, where and how it can be done (in person or online), who can participate, what happens to the winnings. This is widely regarded as an area of great sensitivity for Member States and the Court has therefore applied a fairly relaxed level of scrutiny to national rules. Indeed, in the first major case which came before it, *Schindler*,[149] a reference from the UK, the Court so fell over itself to be accommodating to the UK (which was trying to defend its blanket ban on national lotteries despite the fact that the National Lotteries Bill was going through Parliament at the time, setting up the national lottery) that it failed to consider the question of proportionality at all.

Since then, the cases have followed a more orthodox pattern (restriction/justification/proportionality), albeit still with a light-touch review at either or both the justification and proportionality stage. So the Court tends to find that the rules imposing limitations on gambling are restrictions on free movement. This has been the case with, for example:

- rules restricting the right to operate games of chance or gambling solely to casinos in permanent or temporary gaming areas;[150]
- rules prohibiting the installation of computer games in venues other than casinos;[151]
- national rules restricting the provision of gambling activities to public and private monopolies;[152]
- rules confining off-course betting to a single company which was closely controlled by the State;[153]
- rule prohibiting—on pain of criminal penalties—the pursuit of activities in the betting or gaming sector without a licence or police authorization;[154]
- rules prohibiting Italian intermediaries from facilitating the provision of betting services on behalf of a British supplier.[155]

Having brought the rules within the purview of Article 49 or 56 TFEU, the Court considers whether they can be justified on the grounds of various public interests outlined previously (eg preventing gambling and the incitement to spend).

The focus then shifts to proportionality. As we saw in *Centros*, the proportionality review is usually fairly rigorous. This has not been so with the gambling cases: in *Schindler*, the

[149] Case C-275/92 (n 29).

[150] Case C-6/01 *Anomar v Estado português* [2003] ECR I-8621, para 66.

[151] Case C-65/05 *Commission v Greece* [2006] ECR I-10341, para 56.

[152] Case C-46/08 *Carmen Media Group v Land Schleswig Holstein* [2010] ECR I-8149 and Case C-258/08 *Ladbrokes Betting & Gaming v Stichting de Nationale Sporttotalisator* [2010] ECR I-4757, respectively.

[153] Case C-212/08 *Zerturf Ltd v Premier Ministre* [2011] ECR I-5633. Rules prescribing the legal form and amount of share capital or the holder of a company may also constitute restrictions: Case C-347/09 *Dickinger* [2011] ECR I-8185; Case C-64/08 *Engelmann* [2011] ECR I-8219.

[154] Joined Cases C-338/04, C-359/04, and C-360/04 *Placanica* [2007] ECR I-1891, paras 42 and 44.

[155] See also Joined Cases C-316/07 and C-358–360/07 *Stoß v Wetteraukreis* [2010] ECR I-8069.

Court did not consider proportionality at all when upholding the national rule banning the sale of lottery tickets in an out-of-State lottery; in *Läärä*[156] the Court did examine proportionality but its approach was remarkably hands-off.[157] The case concerned a Finnish law granting exclusive rights to run the operation of slot machines to a public body, with the revenue raised going into the public purse. This rule had the effect of preventing a British company from operating its slot machines in Finland. The Court said the Finnish rules could be justified,[158] and the steps taken were proportionate.[159] The Court said that it was for the Member States to decide whether to prohibit the operation of such machines or only to restrict their use.

However, the Court has increasingly insisted that Member States at least be consistent in the application of their policies towards gambling. So where, as in *Carmen*, a Member State justified the restriction on free movement by reference to the need to prevent incitement to squander money on gambling and to combat gambling addiction, while at the same time encouraging the development of other games of chance which posed higher risks of addiction with a view to maximizing revenue, the Court said that the restriction was not suitable for attaining the objective in 'a consistent and systematic manner'.[160] Similarly, in *Lindman*[161] the Court ruled that a Finnish law, which taxed lottery winnings when the lottery took place in another Member State but not when they occurred in Finland, was not appropriate to achieve the objective of preventing wrongdoing and fraud, the reduction of social damage caused by gaming, the financing of activities in the public interest, and ensuring legal certainty. The Court said that the file transmitted by the referring court disclosed 'no statistical or other evidence which enables any conclusion as to the gravity of the risks connected to playing games of chance or, *a fortiori*, the existence of a particular causal relationship between such risks and participation by nationals . . . in lotteries organised in other Member States'.[162]

Generally, however, the Court will intervene only if the value judgements of the Member State appear manifestly unfounded. This might help to explain why, in *Gambelli*,[163] the Court indicated that an Italian law imposing criminal penalties, including imprisonment, on private individuals in Italy who collaborated over the web with a British bookmaker to collect bets—an activity normally reserved to the Italian State monopoly CONI—was disproportionate, although the Court said it was ultimately for the national court to decide, bearing in mind that betting was encouraged in the context of games organized by licensed *national* bodies[164] and that the British supplier was already regulated in the UK.[165]

[156] Case C-124/97 [1999] ECR I-6067.

[157] See also Case C-36/02 *Omega* [2004] ECR I-9609 and Joined Cases C-94/04 and C-202/04 *Cipolla v Fazari* [2006] ECR I-2049; Case C-250/06 *United Pan Europe Communications v Belgium* [2007] ECR I-11135.

[158] *Läärä* (n 156) para 33.

[159] Ibid, para 42. See also Case C-42/07 *Liga Portuguesa de Futebol Profissional (CA/LPFP) v Departamento de Jogos da Santa Casa da Misericórdia de Lisboa* [2009] ECR I-7633, where the Court found the Portuguese ban on operators established in other Member States from offering gambling over the internet was also proportionate to the objective of the fight against crime.

[160] *Carmen* (n 152) para 71. However, controlled expansion may be consistent: *Zerturf* (n 153).

[161] Case C-42/02 *Lindman* [2003] ECR I-13519.

[162] Ibid, para 26.

[163] Case C-243/01 *Gambelli* [2003] ECR I-13031.

[164] Ibid, para 72.

[165] Ibid, para 73.

3 Secondary legislation in the field of freedom of establishment and the free movement of services

3.1 Introduction

So far we have considered the application of the Treaty provisions on freedom of establishment and free movement of services and how, outside the gambling sector, they are often used to strike down national laws which interfere with free movement. We turn now to consider some examples of how the EU has (re)regulated at EU level, laying down EU rules to facilitate freedom of establishment and free movement of services. We shall start with an examination of a piece of horizontal legislation, the Services Directive 2006/123, which applies across all sectors, before considering case study on special provisions on financial services (14.3), and then take a look at the regulation of the digital single market.

3.2 The Services Directive 2006/123

3.2.1 Introduction

The Services Directive 2006/123[166] was highly controversial at the time, with critics conjuring up 'the spectre of the immigrant "Polish plumber" undercutting the wages of locals'.[167] It was intended to open up the market in services, which accounts for over two-thirds of Europe's gross domestic product (GDP). Chapter III of the Directive, which concerns the establishment of service providers, codifies much of the Court's case law. Chapter IV of the Directive concerns the free movement of services and was the most controversial part of the Directive.

The Directive is built round four pillars:

- easing freedom of establishment and the freedom of provision of services in the EU;
- administrative simplification (requiring States to simplify all the procedures used in creating and establishing a service activity; formal requirements such as the obligation to submit original documents, certified translations, or certified copies to be removed, except for certain cases; from December 2009, undertakings and individuals to be able to carry out all the necessary formalities online using points of single contact) and administrative cooperation between States;
- strengthening rights of recipients of services as users (the rights here are fairly rudimentary, reiterating simply that consumers have the right to receive services and the right to information about those services);
- promoting the quality of services (this is the least-well-developed part of the Directive and focuses mainly on encouraging voluntary certification of activities or drawing up quality charters and European codes of conduct).

We shall focus on the first, and for the purposes of this chapter, most important, pillar of the Directive (see section 3.2.4). However, we begin by looking at the vexed question of the scope of the Directive and the exclusions from that scope.

3.2.2 Scope

According to Article 2(1), the Directive applies to 'services supplied by providers established in a Member State'. Services are defined in accordance with the General Agreement on Trade in Services (GATS): '"Service" means any self-employed economic activity,

[166] OJ [2006] L376/36.

[167] S Fleming, 'Who killed Europe's single market dream?', *Financial Times*, 14 December 2025.

normally provided for remuneration, as referred to in Article [57 TFEU].'[168] The list of services found in Article 57 TFEU has been updated by the Directive to include:

- business services such as management consultancy, certification, and testing; facilities management, including office maintenance; advertising; recruitment services; and the services of commercial agents;
- services provided both to businesses and to consumers, such as legal or fiscal advice; real estate services such as estate agencies; construction, including the services of architects; distributive trades; the organization of trade fairs; car rental; and travel agencies;
- consumer services such as those in the field of tourism, including tour guides; leisure services, sports centres, and amusement parks; and, to the extent that they are not excluded from the scope of application of the Directive, household support services, such as help for the elderly.[169]

The striking feature about this list is that the services identified are relatively uncontroversial and are often provided by small operators (SMEs). It is estimated that the Directive covers a wide group of service activities which represent around 40 per cent of the EU's GDP and employment. The case law has expanded the definition to include, for example, the retail sale of goods.[170]

Assuming the activity is a service within the meaning of the Directive then the Directive can be used to challenge 'requirements which affect access to or the exercise of a service activity'.[171] The word 'requirement' is broadly construed by Article 4(7) of the Directive:

> any obligation, prohibition, condition or limit provided for in the laws, regulations or administrative provisions of the Member States or in consequence of case-law, administrative practice, the rules of professional bodies, or the collective rules of professional associations or other professional organisations, adopted in the exercise of their legal autonomy.

Thus, the Directive is underpinned by notions of market access rather than discrimination (see section 2.4.3).

3.2.3 **Exclusions**

Although the potential scope of the Directive is broad, in fact the effectiveness of the Directive is limited by the significant exclusions found mainly in Article 2(2) and (3).[172] The list is long and broad, and includes important sectors such as health-care services,[173] financial services,[174] electronic communication services and networks,[175] temporary work agencies,[176] and private security services.[177] Further, services of general interest,[178] audiovisual services,[179] gambling activities,[180] including lotteries, gambling in casinos, and betting transactions, are excluded from the scope of the Directive. Specific provision is also made in respect of social policy, including strike action, which is intended to fall outside the Directive. All these excluded sectors and activities remain subject to specific legislation, where it exists, or the Treaty rules (ie Articles 49 and 56 TFEU).[181]

[168] Art 4(1). [169] Recital 33.

[170] Joined Cases C-360/15 and C-31/16 *X and Visser*, EU:C:2018:44, para 97. [171] Recital 9.

[172] The objective of protecting or promoting cultural or linguistic diversity in Art 1(4) is also not within the scope of the Directive: Case C-366/24 *Amazon EU (Minimum charges for the delivery of books)*, EU:C:2025:990, para 42.

[173] Art 2(2)(f). [174] Art 2(2)(b). [175] Art 2(2)(c). [176] Art 2(2)(e).

[177] Art 2(2)(k). [178] Art 2(2)(a). [179] Art 2(2)(g).

[180] Art 2(2)(h). See also recital 25 of the Preamble.

[181] Case C-366/24 *Amazon EU (Minimum charges for the delivery of books)*, EU:C:2025:990, para 42.

3.2.4 **Easing of freedom of establishment and freedom to provide services**

Member States also had to screen existing legislation to remove legal and administrative barriers to the provision of services. This had to be done by December 2009. Different obligations apply depending on whether the rules concern establishment (Chapter III) or services (Chapter IV). The Court now uses the provisions to establish whether there is a breach of the Directive.

Establishment

The establishment chapter specifically deals with two groups of rules: (a) authorization schemes, and (b) 'other' requirements which are either prohibited or subject to evaluation. Authorization schemes are permitted provided that:

- they do not discriminate (either directly or indirectly) against the provider in question;
- the scheme is justified by an overriding reason relating to the public interest (ORRPI);[182]
- the objective pursued cannot be attained by means of a less restrictive measure (eg monitoring the activities of the service provider or making a simple declaration).

According to Article 10(2), criteria for granting authorization must also satisfy these requirements, together with the obligations to be clear and unambiguous, objective, made public in advance, transparent, and accessible.[183] This was at issue in *Cali Apartments*[184] concerning prior authorization requirements for Airbnb. The Court said it was lawful for French law to give powers to local authorities to require authorization before accommodation was turned into Airbnb premises (ie accommodation 'repeatedly for short periods to a transient clientele which does not take up residence there'), permission being granted according to 'the characteristics of the local housing markets and the need to avoid exacerbating the housing shortage, making those authorisations subject, if necessary, to an offset requirement in the form of the concurrent conversion of non-residential premises into housing', provided that those requirements satisfied the criteria in Article 10(2) and were transparent and accessible.

The Directive concerns not only authorization schemes but also 'other requirements'. In respect of 'other requirements', Article 14 lists eight requirements which are *prohibited*. This means that there are no ORRPI justifications or derogations available to Member States.[185] Reflecting the Court's case law, the prohibited requirements include nationality requirements for the provider, its staff, individuals holding the share capital, or members of the provider's management or supervisory bodies;[186] or a rule forbidding a provider from having an establishment in more than one Member State.[187]

[182] Art 4(8) refers to ORRPIs recognized as such in the case law of the Court of Justice, including the following grounds: public policy (which includes issues relating to human dignity, the protection of minors and vulnerable adults, and animal welfare); public security; public safety; public health; preserving the financial equilibrium of the social security system; the protection of consumers, recipients of services, and workers; fairness of trade transactions; combating fraud; the protection of the environment and the urban environment; the health of animals; intellectual property; the conservation of the national historic and artistic heritage; social policy objectives and cultural policy objectives.

[183] Art 10(2).

[184] Joined Cases C-724/18 and C-727/18, EU:C:2020:743, para 108.

[185] In Case C-593/13 *Rina Services and Others*, EU:C:2015:159 the Court confirmed that at least in respect of Art 14, the Directive was an exhaustive harmonization measure which meant that the State could not invoke the Treaty justifications to defend its use of a prohibited requirement.

[186] *Factortame II* (n 23).

[187] Case 96/85 *Commission v France* [1986] ECR 1475.

In addition, Article 15(2) identifies a further eight requirements, a number of which have already been considered 'restrictions' on freedom of establishment in the Court's case law, which are 'suspect'. These include quantitative or territorial restrictions (ie limiting the number of establishments generally or in a particular area),[188] and an obligation on a provider to take a specific legal form (eg a company or partnership). Unlike the prohibited requirements, the Directive requires Member States to evaluate whether these 'suspect' requirements are subject to the requirement of 'necessity'[189] and proportionate. Only if they satisfy these tests will they be allowed to continue.[190]

New national legislation introduced in respect of freedom of establishment after 2009 has to be notified to the Commission.[191]

Services

The provisions on services proved to be the most controversial aspect of the Directive. The original version of the Directive contained a strong country of origin principle ('Member States shall ensure that providers are subject only to the national provisions of their Member State of origin which fall within the coordinated field'). This meant that services should be regulated by the country in which the service provider was established and only exceptionally by the country in which the service was being provided (the host country), as permitted by the derogations.

Such overt recognition of the country of origin principle proved too controversial for some Member States and the language of the later version of the Directive was changed. Article 16 now provides:

> Member States shall respect the right of providers to provide services in a Member State other than that in which they are established.
>
> The Member State in which the service is provided shall ensure free access to and free exercise of a service activity within its territory.

This is followed by a list of seven particularly suspect requirements largely based on the Court's case law (including an obligation on the provider to have an establishment in the territory of the host State;[192] a ban on the provider setting up a certain form or type of infrastructure, including an office or chambers;[193] and the application of specific contractual arrangements between the provider and the recipient preventing or restricting service provision by the self-employed). These requirements, while frowned upon, can, however, be saved by the express derogations in Article 17, the case-by-case derogations in Article 18,[194] and by a narrow list of public interest requirements provided for by the Directive.

But how great, in fact, is the difference between the country of origin principle and the freedom to provide services? Under the country of origin principle, the principal regulator would have been the home State, reinforced by the presumption that the host State could not impose any additional requirements unless there were very good reasons for

[188] See eg Case C-503/23 *Centro di Assistenza Doganale (Cad) Mellano Srl v Agenzia delle Dogane e dei Monopoli—Agenzia delle Dogane—Direzione Interregionale per la Liguria*, EU:C:2024:933.

[189] Art 15(3)(b). The language of necessity is confusing when what is actually meant is objective justification, the language used in, eg Art 10(2)(b).

[190] See eg Case C-593/13 *Rina Services and Others*, EU:C:2015:399, para 33 and Case C-209/18 *Commission v Austria (Civil engineers, patent agents and veterinary surgeons)*, EU:C:2019:632, para 80).

[191] Art 15(7).

[192] *Van Binsbergen* (n 13).

[193] Case C-55/94 *Gebhard* [1995] ECR I-4165.

[194] This leads to the result that the physical safety of consumers can be protected under Art 18 but the economic interests of consumers cannot be protected under Art 16(1) or 16(3).

this. The approach in Article 16 appears to reverse this: it accepts that the host State can impose its own restrictions on the service provider, where there are good reasons for so doing, account being taken of the protection already provided in the home State.

The current approach therefore broadly reflects the case law of the Court where, as section 2.5.2 shows, the country of origin principle is not as firmly embedded in respect of services as it is in goods. It does exist, but not in terms of establishing the breach (as is the case for goods), but in terms of justifying the breach where the Court requires the host State to take into account requirements already imposed by the home State.[195] In practice, the difference may well be one of emphasis rather than substance: the country of origin principle raises a strong presumption of illegality of the host State measure; the current approach raises a weaker presumption of illegality. In practical terms, it means that service providers will continue to have to investigate the rules in each State in which they provide services and this creates significant barriers to trade. In 2024, the International Monetary Fund (IMF) estimated that Europe's internal barriers in services were equivalent to a tariff of 110 per cent.[196] This is one of the reasons why the *Financial Times* described the single market in services as half-baked.[197]

Case study 14.3: Financial services

Financial services have for a long time been seen as a key sector for European economic integration.[198] There are at least two substantive reasons for this. First, financial services are a large and important sector where services can actually be traded across frontiers. The problem with many services, from hairdressing to care of the elderly, is that they do not travel well. They cannot be provided remotely and it is rare that either the provider or the recipient would wish to move to another country for the service activity. Partly as a result, the internal market in services is much less developed than that in goods. By contrast, in the field of financial services many services can be offered remotely, for example using the telephone or the internet. Further, companies operating in the field have often been eager to expand abroad, for example by establishing branches or subsidiaries. Thus, financial services are well suited for the creation of an internal market in services.

Secondly, through the free movement of financial services, a deep and liquid European capital market can be attained. This means easier access to capital for all European companies. For an individual, free movement may bring access to financial products such as loans from a wide variety of European providers. Financial service integration promises cheaper and more readily available capital, for the benefit of the entire EU economy.

Unfortunately, the financial services sector is as dangerous as it is beneficial. Again, two key issues should be highlighted. Economists would call these (a) information asymmetries and (b) externalities.[199] First, many financial products are complex: it is difficult for a buyer

[195] See eg *Säger* (n 79) para 15: 'the freedom to provide services may be limited only by rules which are justified by imperative reasons relating to the public interest and which apply to all persons or undertakings pursuing an activity in the State of destination, *in so far as that interest is not protected by the rules to which the person providing the services is subject in the Member State in which he is established*' (emphasis added).

[196] 'Europe's Choice: Policies for Growth and Resilience', cited in B Moens et al, 'The lone bread maker: Europe's half-baked single market in services', *Financial Times*, 8 December 2025.

[197] Ibid.

[198] See eg already Commission White Paper, 'Completing the internal market', COM(85) 310 final, 27–29.

[199] See further eg C Goodhart, 'How Should We Regulate Bank Capital and Financial Products? What Role for "Living Wills"?' in A Turner et al (eds), *The Future of Finance: The LSE Report* (London: London School of Economics and Political Science, 2010) 167.

to understand all the features and risks involved. Financial advice may be of limited help; in practice, problems with the quality of advice have been common, sometimes due to conflicts of interests of the adviser. And the stakes are high: when something goes wrong, the consequences can be devastating for an individual—life savings can be lost, families ruined.

Secondly, there is the issue of financial stability[200] and in particular the various systemic externalities (contagion) relating to it. Banking has always been recognized as a particularly risky activity. Banks borrow short and lend long, meaning that they have to pay to depositors on demand but the loans they have issued will only be repaid gradually. This mismatch has resulted in bank runs when panicked depositors, fearing the bank's inability to pay them money they have on deposit, try to withdraw their funds from a bank, all at the same time, causing the bank to collapse (think of the scene in the film *Mary Poppins* where the little boy's demand for his 'tuppence' back led to a run on the bank where his father worked). States have tried to reduce such risks by various devices, including central banks as lenders of last resort, capital requirements, and deposit guarantees. A further complication that is more pressing today is that many financial services providers are highly interconnected. They owe money to each other. If one collapses, others take a hit, which in turn may put their solvency in question—there is a danger of contagion. In such circumstances, States have often come to the rescue, spending taxpayers' money to bail out failing banks. Thus private debt becomes public debt and, during the financial crisis, in the case of Ireland and Spain, put the State in a vulnerable position because its own lending costs became higher. And because there has been no EU pot of tax money that could be used to bail out the banks, it is the home State that has had to intervene, even if the bank's operations have been on a pan-European scale. This is sometimes called the 'international in life, national in death' phenomenon.

The EU legislative framework

The unique desirability of financial service integration and the risks that it involves have resulted in a complex and evolving framework. It quickly became apparent that the freedoms that the Treaty set out were not sufficient for the creation of an internal market in this sector. In *Casati*[201] it was established that the free movement of capital lacked direct effect, and in a series of cases on insurance services it was found that Member States were entitled to restrict free movement on public interest grounds.[202] Due to the risks involved, Member States could place limitations on free movement of services, even though some harmonizing directives had been adopted.

The EU legislature responded by adopting a set of directives, such as the Investment Services Directive,[203] that were designed to create an internal market utilizing the device of mutual recognition.[204] The directives established the *minimum* standards that each country had to apply. The Member States could grant so-called passports to their financial services providers, which could then operate in the whole EU. The idea was home country control: companies based in one State were authorized and supervised there, and this was

[200] See on the connection between legal integration and financial stability, M Andenas and IHY Chiu, 'Financial Stability and Legal Integration in Financial Regulation' (2013) 38 *European Law Review* 335.

[201] Case 203/80 *Casati* [1981] ECR 2595.

[202] See eg *Insurance* (n 10). See further chapter 15.

[203] Council Directive 93/22/EEC on investment services in the securities field (OJ [1993] L141/27), repealed and replaced by Directive 2004/39/EC (OJ [2004] L145/1) which in turn was replaced by Directive 2014/65/EU (OJ [2014] L173/349) (see n 207).

[204] See further chapters 12 and 13.

recognized by the other States.[205] As we have seen, this was consistent with the ideas underpinning Article 56 TFEU.

The system was overhauled following the creation of an ambitious Financial Services Action Plan at the end of the 1990s.[206] The directives went from minimum to full harmonization: they no longer sought to establish just the minimum standards, but attempted to regulate comprehensively. For example, the Investment Services Directive was replaced by MiFiD.[207] Each Member State still granted passports to its firms, but now using fully harmonized EU rather than national rules.[208]

The financial crisis that began in 2007 ushered in a new phase.[209] In practice, the integrated financial market that had been created re-fragmented, with many firms retreating from some of their overseas operations, often at the behest of their national supervisors. At the same time, the EU adopted a new, more centralized, mode of regulation. Both the scope (ie the subject matter covered) and the intensity of its activities have grown. Examples of the former are the regulations on credit rating agencies and the Hedge Funds Directive.[210] An example of the latter is the EU's involvement not only in law-making but also in supervision. New EU agencies have been established under the European System of Financial Supervisors, covering banking, securities markets, insurance, and occupational pensions. They have powerful roles in preparing the detailed rules of the 'single rulebook' that put into effect the more general EU legislation, they oversee the supervisory activities of national authorities, and they can, in certain circumstances, even impose binding decisions on individual companies. The reformed system proved resilient and robust when it faced its first significant test, namely the economic shock and financial stability risks brought by the Covid-19 pandemic in 2020.[211]

In 2015 the EU launched a further initiative with the aim of building a single market for capital: a Capital Markets Union.[212] The underlying idea was to reduce Europe's reliance on bank lending and move towards more market-based finance. After two action plans and a multitude of individual measures, progress has been achieved. However, a true single capital market still remains an aspiration. In many cases, 'agreement . . . has come at the cost of substantial dilution of the level of ambition',[213] or the key barriers relate to sensitive areas of national law that remain resistant to integration, such as taxation or insolvency. Nevertheless, further capital markets integration is still seen as a key priority. A well-functioning EU-

[205] See eg E Lomnicka, 'Home Country Control Principle in the Financial Services Directives and the Case Law' in M Andenas and W-H Roth (eds), *Services and Free Movement in EU Law* (Oxford: Oxford University Press, 2002).

[206] Commission Communication, 'Implementing the framework for financial markets: action plan', COM(1999) 232. See on the evolution R Veil, 'History' in R Veil (ed), *European Capital Markets Law* (Oxford: Hart Publishing, 2022).

[207] European Parliament and Council Directive 2004/39/EC on markets in financial instruments (OJ [2004] L145/1), as amended. This is now the recast Directive 2014/65/EU (OJ [2014] L173/349).

[208] V Hatzopoulos, *Regulating Services in the European Union* (Oxford: Oxford University Press, 2012) 235–236.

[209] See N Moloney, 'EU Financial Market Regulation after the Global Financial Crisis: "More Europe" or More Risks?' (2010) 47 *Common Market Law Review* 1317.

[210] European Parliament and Council Regulation (EC) No 1060/2009 on credit rating agencies (OJ [2009] L302/1), as amended, and European Parliament and Council Directive 2011/61/EU on alternative investment fund managers (OJ [2011] L174/1), as amended.

[211] N Moloney, 'EU Financial Market Regulation a Decade after the Financial-Crisis-Era Reforms: Crisis, Uncertainty, and Capacity' (2023) 42 *Yearbook of European Law* 169.

[212] Commission Communication, 'Action Plan on Building a Capital Markets Union', COM/2015/0468 final.

[213] 'Capital markets union—reboot: a policy discussion on the future of the capital markets union' at 2, available at https://eu2019.fi/documents/11707387/15400298/CMU+Reboot+Informal+ECOFIN+final+Issues+Note+2019-09-09_S4.pdf.

wide capital market would offer vital support for the broader European priorities of green transition, digital transformation, competitiveness, and defence, all of which require significant private sector investments. The Commission has refocused and rebranded the initiative and continues to push it under the new name of the Savings and Investments Union.[214]

Efforts have been underway to go even further in the context of the eurozone and to establish a full banking union.[215] As we have seen in case study 14.3, the financial crisis demonstrated dangerous negative loops between Member States and their banks. If a bank gets into trouble, its home country has typically had to rescue it. This can put a strain on its public finances. This in turn lowers the value of its bonds, which are often held by domestic banks. This may require further rescue operations, which further undermine government bonds, and so on. When this happens, other Member States may in the end have to come to the aid of the Member State itself. To break this negative loop, the European Central Bank (ECB) has become the direct supervisor for the most significant banks in the eurozone, and participates in the single supervisory mechanism that covers all banks in the euro area.[216] It is thought that the ECB can adopt a more objective view of banks than national supervisors, which may get too close to their charges. To complement the system of supervision, a single resolution mechanism and a single resolution fund have been set up.[217] The fund is financed by payments from the banks themselves. It is hoped that this will allow failing banks to be resolved in an orderly manner, without the involvement of public money.[218] However, the third pillar of a full banking union—a European deposit insurance scheme—has proven too controversial politically and has not advanced in the legislative process.[219]

3.3 **The Digital Single Market**

Much of EU regulation to date has been about the physical provision of goods and services. Yet, as the Commission notes, the rapid and widespread development of digital services has created new ways to communicate, shop, or access information online have appeared, and they are constantly evolving.[220] However, while the EU is keen to encourage innovation through online platforms, it also recognizes the risks associated with platforms: the platforms themselves can dominate the market, keeping out new market entrants; and users of those platforms can sell dangerous goods, post hate speech, and exploit children. The EU has legislated extensively[221]—too extensively for some—to address these issues, and it has tried to square a circle between innovation and protection, while also

[214] Commission Communication, 'Savings and Investments Union: A Strategy to Foster Citizens' Wealth and Economic Competitiveness in the EU', COM/2025/124 final.

[215] See Communication from the Commission, 'A blueprint for a deep and genuine economic and monetary union: launching a European debate', COM(2012) 777 final. See also chapter 19. While the banking union applies to euro countries, non-euro countries are also allowed to join.

[216] Council Regulation (EU) No 1024/2013 conferring specific tasks on the European Central Bank concerning policies relating to the prudential supervision of credit institutions (OJ [2013] L287/63).

[217] Regulation (EU) No 806/2014 of the European Parliament and of the Council establishing uniform rules and a uniform procedure for the resolution of credit institutions and certain investment firms in the framework of a Single Resolution Mechanism and a Single Bank Resolution Fund (OJ [2014] L225/1), as amended.

[218] Directive 2014/59 of the European Parliament and Council establishing a framework for the recovery and resolution of credit institutions and investment firms (OJ [2014] L173/190), as amended.

[219] Commission Proposal for a Regulation to establish a European Deposit Insurance Scheme, COM(2015) 586 final.

[220] https://digital-strategy.ec.europa.eu/en/policies/digital-services-act-package.

[221] European Commission, *A Europe fit for the digital age* (2019). Available at: https://commission.europa.eu/strategy-and-policy/priorities-2019-2024/europe-fit-digital-age_en.

respecting fundamental rights. For the purposes of this chapter, we shall consider two major pieces of legislation (regulations) that have been adopted:[222] the Digital Markets Act (DMA)[223] and the Digital Services Act (DSA).[224]

The DMA applies to 'gatekeepers' such as online marketplaces, operating systems, social networks, cloud services, or online search engines. It defines quantitative thresholds as a basis for defining presumed gatekeepers. They include Amazon, Apple, Meta,[225] and Bytedance (TikTok).[226] These gatekeepers are subject to a number of obligations ('dos') and prohibitions ('don'ts').[227] The 'dos' include: allowing third parties to interoperate with the gatekeeper's own services in certain specific situations; allowing their business users to access the data that they generate in their use of the gatekeeper's platform; providing companies advertising on their platform with the tools and information necessary for advertisers and publishers to carry out their own independent verification of their advertisements hosted by the gatekeeper; and allowing their business users to promote their offer, and conclude contracts with their customers outside the gatekeeper's platform.

The 'don'ts' are targeted at unfair practices such as treating services and products offered by the gatekeeper itself more favourably in ranking than similar services or products offered by third parties on the gatekeeper's platform; blocking users from uninstalling any pre-installed software or apps; preventing consumers from linking up to businesses outside their platforms; and tracking end users outside the gatekeepers' core platform service for the purpose of targeted advertising, without effective consent having been granted. Sanctions for non-compliance include fines of up to 10 per cent of the gatekeeper's worldwide turnover.

The DSA, of particular relevance to this chapter, covers[228] a range of intermediary services offering network infrastructure including hosting services such as cloud and webhosting services. It draws a distinction between:

- Online platforms bringing together sellers and consumers such as online marketplaces, app stores, collaborative economy platforms, and social media platforms.
- Very large online platforms and very large online search engines[229] which pose particular risks in the dissemination of illegal content and societal harms such as Meta and X. They are subject to additional obligations.

All online intermediaries offering their services in the single market, whether they are established in the EU or outside, have to comply with the DSA. In other words, these

[222] There is a significant body of other consumer-focused regulation which also deals with online service provision which is discussed in chapter 23.

[223] Regulation 2022/1925 (OJ [2022] L265/1). The DMA builds on Regulation (EU) 2019/1150 on promoting fairness and transparency for business users of online intermediation services known as the Platform to Business (P2B) Regulation (OJ [2019] L186/57).

[224] Regulation 2022/2065 (OJ [2022] L277/1.

[225] European Commission, *Digital Markets Act: Commission designates six gatekeepers* (2023), https://ec.europa.eu/commission/presscorner/api/files/document/print/en/ip_23_4328/IP_23_4328_EN.pdf.

[226] In Case T-1077/23 *Bytedance v Commission*, EU:T:2024:478, the General Court upheld the Commission's assessment of Bytedance as a gatekeeper. It satisfied the quantitative criteria set out in the DMA, including its substantial global market value and the considerable number of TikTok users in the EU.

[227] The following is drawn from this: https://digital-markets-act.ec.europa.eu/about-dma_en.

[228] https://digital-strategy.ec.europa.eu/en/faqs/digital-services-act-questions-and-answers. It builds on the E-Commerce Directive 2000/31 (OJ [2000] L178/1).

[229] For a list of VLOPs and VLOSEs, see https://digital-strategy.ec.europa.eu/en/policies/list-designated-vlops-and-vloses. Amazon unsuccessfully challenged its designation in Case T-367/23 *Amazon EU v Commission*, EU:T:2025:1038.

rules have extra-territorial effect, which Anu Bradford describes as the 'Brussels effect',[230] with EU rules shaping behaviour both inside and outside the territory of the EU. This is now seeing significant pushback, not least from the tech giants in the US. The argument is that 'such legislation is seen as not just protectionist in outlook but also outdated in a world where the EU—which had failed to create its own techgiants—was an increasingly marginal player'.[231]

The obligations in the DSA fall into two main parts. Chapter II, headed 'Liability of providers of intermediary services', is in fact mainly about immunity from liability for information society services, and therefore is about encouraging innovation. As the Commission put it when the legislation was still in draft:[232]

> Clarified liability and efficient compliance mechanism:
>
> - Apply and further clarify the conditions for liability exemptions which had previously been in the E-Commerce Directive 200/31:[233] Platforms and other intermediaries are not liable for users' unlawful behaviour unless they are aware of illegal acts and fail to remove them.
> - Rules for the liability exception will now be harmonised and uniform across the EU thanks to a directly applicable Regulation.
> - New clarifications on how these conditions apply for consumer protection liability.
> - Solving the paradox of voluntary measures taken by small platforms: diligent platforms are not liable for illegal content they detect themselves.
> - More legal certainty on interaction with authorities: platforms will have to cooperate with authorities that issue legal orders that have minimum common criteria.

Chapter III is about protecting users, including minors. The Commission summarizes this as follows:[234]

> - Transparency in content removals - If your content is removed or suspended, platforms must explain why this has been done.
> - Options to appeal to content moderation decisions - If you disagree with a content moderation decision taken by a platform, you can appeal it through the platform itself or an out-of-court dispute settlement body, which is faster and cheaper than going to court.
> - Easy flagging of illegal content - You can report illegal content, goods or services via an easy-to-use mechanism directly on the platform you are using. Platforms must respond to your reports and offer options to appeal their decisions.
> - Enhanced protection for minors - Platforms must take measures to safeguard minors on their services, such as reducing the risks of exposure to age-inappropriate content like gambling or pornography. The DSA also introduces a complete ban on showing targeted advertisements to children. . . .
> - Ad transparency - Ads must be clearly labelled as such and include information like who is placing them and why you are seeing them, while very large online platforms are required

[230] *The Brussels Effect: How the European Union Rules the World* (Oxford: Oxford University Press, 2020), especially ch 5.

[231] P Foster and B Moens, 'How the "Brussels effect" backfired', *Financial Times*, 14 December 2025.

[232] https://digital-strategy.ec.europa.eu/en/faqs/digital-services-act-questions-and-answers.

[233] See further Case C-492/234 *X v Russmedia Digital*, EU:C:2025:935.

[234] https://digital-strategy.ec.europa.eu/en/policies/digital-services-act.

to store ad information in a publicly accessible repository. Platforms can no longer show you ads based on your sensitive data, such as sexual orientation, religion, or race.

- Ban on dark patterns - Deceptive design tactics, such as aggressive pop-ups or confusing and misleading consent buttons, are now prohibited.
- Verified sellers - Marketplaces must verify and display the contact details of sellers, so you have clear information about whom you're buying goods or services from.

At the core of Chapter III lies 'TAR' principles: *T*ransparency (eg over why content has been removed), *A*ccountability (eg options to appeal content moderation decisions), and *R*emedies (individuals can bring claims, Member States have the primary role, supported by a new European Board for Digital Services; and for very large online platforms and very large online search engines, supervision and enforcement by the Commission). The Commission's sanctioning powers are significant. For example, it can apply fines up to 6 per cent of the worldwide annual turnover in the case of breach of DSA obligations, failure to comply with interim measures, and a breach of commitments. The Commission has fined X €120 million for breaching its transparency obligations under the DSA, including 'the deceptive design of its "blue checkmark", the lack of transparency of its advertising repository, and the failure to provide access to public data for researchers'.[235]

Eifert et al say that with the DMA and the DSA, the Commission has 'aimed for the stars', defining the ground rules for today's platform economy by (a) specifying the special obligations that come with the intermediary, regulatory, and information-spreading function that platforms assume and (b) by binding the most powerful platforms to a code of conduct, which is intended to ensure that markets remain open wherever feasible.[236] The backlash from the US and elsewhere may see the wings of the DSA/DMA being clipped. The AI Act is already being subject to the EU's simplification agenda.[237]

4 **Conclusion**

The free movement of legal persons is firmly entrenched in the EU system. Big companies like Amazon and Google make use of it. Some of this may be to do with the fact that Member States are keen to host such companies and the tax and employment opportunities they bring, without the stick of EU law. However, compliance with national corporate rules is onerous for smaller companies wishing to expand their operations to other Member States. The Court, through its case law, has precipitated some important changes, most notably in forcing the recognition of companies established in other Member States. Here the driving force has not been developing the higher ideals of citizenship and human rights, as with natural persons, but the more hard-headed imperative of ensuring that companies can take full advantage of the opportunities that the single market has to offer.

The single market has been a powerful force in opening up national markets to competition from providers in other Member States. The EU legislative programme has obviously been of assistance. However, the Services Directive has so far failed to live up to its potential, in part because some Member States remain resistant to applying single

[235] https://digital-strategy.ec.europa.eu/en/news/commission-fines-x-eu120-million-under-digital-services-act.

[236] M Eifert et al, 'Taming the Giants: The DMA/DSA Package' (2021) 58 *Common Market Law Review* 987, 1024.

[237] COM(2025) 836.

market rules to the services sector.[238] Further, the services logic, based on home State control, applied in the 1990s to the financial services sector, proved insufficiently robust in the face of the crisis. And the crisis has forced a more general rethink as to the balance of interests between the Member States and private interests. This can be seen most acutely in *EFTA Surveillance Authority v Iceland*,[239] concerning the Icelandic government's failure to ensure payment of compensation (as required by Articles 7 and 10 of the then Directive 94/19 on deposit guarantees) to depositors holding deposits in Icesave branches in the UK and the Netherlands, an Icelandic bank which went bust.[240] The EFTA Court said[241]

> that the Directive does not envisage that the defendant itself must ensure payments to depositors in the Icesave branches in the Netherlands and the United Kingdom, in accordance with Articles 7 and 10 of the Directive, in a systemic crisis of the magnitude experienced in Iceland.

Here it is the troubled State's interest that has prevailed. Pragmatism sometimes triumphs over principle.

However, the EU legislator, albeit playing catch-up, has intervened to try to prevent such systemic failures happening again: most importantly through the agreed revisions to the Deposit Guarantee Directive[242] and the Bank Failure Directive,[243] which, together with the Capital Requirements Directive IV package implementing the new global standards on bank capital and liquidity,[244] comprise 'key pillars of the single rulebook necessary for the stability and integrity of the EU's internal market in financial services', which in turn 'provides a common foundation which allows a move to the banking union without any risk of fragmenting the single market'.[245]

Meanwhile attention has turned to the digital single market. The developments in this field will shape practice in the EU and beyond for the next decade. Online services will change and the regulation will have to adapt but the DSA and DMA are important markers for the EU to put down to show the need to balance the obligations of the big online players and their customers.

Further reading

M Andenas and W-H Roth (eds), *Services and Free Movement in EU Law* (Oxford: Oxford University Press, 2002)

[238] B Moens et al, 'The lone breadmaker: Europe's half-baked single market in services', *Financial Times*, 8 December 2025.

[239] Case E-16/11 *EFTA Surveillance Authority v Iceland* [2013] EFTA Ct Rep 4.

[240] OJ [1994] L135/5.

[241] *EFTA* (n 239) para 178.

[242] See Directive 2014/49/EU of the European Parliament and of the Council on deposit guarantee schemes (OJ [2014] L173/149).

[243] Directive 2014/59 of the European Parliament and Council establishing a framework for the recovery and resolution of credit institutions and investment firms (OJ [2014] L173/190).

[244] Regulation (EU) No 575/2013 on prudential requirements for credit institutions and investment firms and amending Regulation (EU) No 648/2012 (OJ [2013] L176/1); and Directive 2013/36/EU on access to the activity of credit institutions and the prudential supervision of credit institutions and investment firms, amending Directive 2002/87/EC and repealing Directives 2006/48/EC and 2006/49/EC (OJ [2013] L176/338).

[245] European Commission, 'A Roadmap towards a Banking Union', COM(2012) 510 final, p 5, http://eur-lex.europa.eu/LexUriServ/LexUriServ.do?uri=COM:2012:0510:FIN:EN:PDF.

C Barnard, *The Substantive Law of the EU: The Four Freedoms* (8th edn, Oxford: Oxford University Press, 2025) chs 8 and 11

N Boeger (ed), *Perspectives on Corporate Social Responsibility* (Cheltenham: Edward Elgar, 2008)

J Borg-Barthet, *The Governing Law of Companies in EU Law* (Oxford: Hart Publishing, 2012)

V Edwards, *EC Company Law* (Oxford: Oxford University Press, 1999)

M Eifert, A Metzger, H Schweitzer, and G Wagner, 'Taming the Giants: The DMA/DSA Package' (2021) 58 *Common Market Law Review* 987

M Graetz and A Warren, 'Dividend Taxation in Europe: When the ECJ Makes Tax Policy' (2007) 44 *Common Market Law Review* 1577

V Hatzopoulos, *Regulating Services in the European Union* (Oxford: Oxford University Press, 2012)

S Kingston, 'The Boundaries of Sovereignty: The ECJ's Controversial Role Applying the Internal Market Rules to Taxation' (2006–7) 9 *Cambridge Yearbook of European Legal Studies* 287

N Moloney, 'Resetting the Location of Regulatory and Supervisory Control over the EU Financial Markets: Lessons from Five Years On' (2013) 62 *International and Comparative Law Quarterly* 955

N Moloney, 'EU Financial Market Regulation after the Global Financial Crisis: "More Europe" or More Risks?' (2010) 47 *Common Market Law Review* 1317

J Snell, 'Non-Discriminatory Tax Obstacles in Community Law' (2007) 56 *International and Comparative Law Quarterly* 339

T Tridimas, 'EU Financial Regulation: Federalization, Crisis Management, and Law Reform' in P Craig and G de Búrca (eds), *The Evolution of EU Law* (2nd edn, Oxford: Oxford University Press, 2011)

B de Witte, 'The Freedom to Provide Services: The Controversial Freedom' in S Garben and I Govaere (eds), *The Internal Market 2.0* (Oxford: Hart Publishing, 2020)

Chapter acknowledgements

I am grateful to Julian Ghosh, Chris Kuner, Marios Koutsias, Steve Peers, and Vassilis Hatzopoulos for their advice. Jukka Snell kindly provided the section on financial services.

15

Free movement of capital

Leo Flynn

1 Introduction

From the signature of the Treaty of Rome in 1957 until 31 December 1992, the focus of European integration was the common market, later known as the internal market. Since the signature of the Maastricht Treaty in 1992, and arguably for the foreseeable future, the focus of European integration has become the development of the eurozone, as the chief incarnation of economic and monetary union (EMU).[1] Free movement of capital is central to both market integration and to EMU. Without it, neither is possible.

EU law on the free movement of capital was, relative to the other internal market freedoms, comparatively underdeveloped until the end of the 1980s. Since then, however, there has been a major shift in its role. The completion of the single market, targeted for 31 December 1992, involved a liberalization of the rules on capital movement. Shortly afterwards, with the entry into force of the Maastricht Treaty, those liberalized rules became a core element of a new step in European integration—the creation of the single currency and the institutions charged with managing EMU.

This chapter will first consider the development of the current rules on capital, focusing on their material scope, direct effect, and role in relation to third countries. It will then explain how the concept of restrictions, which is a feature of all internal market freedoms, operates in relation to capital. The chapter will next deal with the power of Member States to limit capital flows between different parts of the Union, as well as into and out of the Union. Finally, it will examine the effects of case law regarding capital movement in relation to philanthropic and charitable activities, in order

[1] See more generally chapter 19.

to see how the free movement of capital affects the ability of Member States to design the instruments by which they organize the delivery of services they consider are in the public interest.

Two themes will be evident in this chapter. One of them is the extent of the role of free movement of capital in EMU and the resulting differences for that particular free movement when compared with the other freedoms which only have a part to play in the creation of the internal market. The other, which applies to all of the freedoms underpinning the internal market, is the extent to which national conceptions of public interest must be recalibrated in order to take account of constraints which the free movement of capital places on the choices and priorities of the Member States. When national authorities view public interest objectives primarily in the framework of the national territory, does the case law on free movement of capital force them into either abandoning those goals or else 'Europeanizing' them?

2 The legal framework and its origins

2.1 The evolution of the original rules on capital

For free movement of capital and EMU in EU law, many of the key developments in that field have economic, as opposed to legal origins, most of which have their foundations in the international monetary system. In order to see why certain features of the law on free movement of capital take the form they do, it is worth surveying that evolution.

2.1.1 Bretton Woods and the post-Second World War international monetary environment

The original Treaty of Rome establishing the EEC included only minor provisions for monetary cooperation between its six founding Member States. They all participated in the Bretton Woods international monetary system set up in 1944. That system established fixed exchange rates with a mechanism for adjustments when necessary. Since it was intended to create monetary stability in the world economy, a parallel system in Europe seemed unnecessary.

2.1.2 The pre-Maastricht rules on capital

The rules in the EEC Treaty on capital and payments were in two separate parts of the Treaty. Capital was governed by Articles 67 to 73 EEC, while payments were dealt with in Article 104 EEC.

Article 67(1) EEC obliged Member States to 'progressively abolish between themselves all restrictions on the movement of capital belonging to persons resident in Member States and any discrimination based on nationality or on the place of residence of the parties or on the place where such capital is invested'. However, that obligation was a qualified one: Article 67(1) EEC laid down the duty of abolition 'to the extent necessary to ensure the proper functioning of the common market'. There was no express standstill clause, prohibiting the introduction of new restrictions. The Court relied on those limitations when it ruled in *Casati* in 1981 that Article 67(1) EEC did not have direct effect, in contrast with its counterparts on goods, workers, establishment, and services.[2]

[2] Case 203/80 *Casati* [1981] ECR 2515.

Article 69 EEC provided a legal base for directives for the progressive implementation of Article 67 EEC. There was significant legislative activity in the early 1960s:

- the First Capital Directive[3] was adopted in 1960; and
- the Second Capital Directive[4] was adopted in 1962.

Those Directives sorted transactions involving capital into different categories, in the form of a Nomenclature divided into four lists. Transactions within List A were to be completely liberalized while national restrictions were permitted for those in the other parts, with the limitations varying in permissible intensity. In that early period, the trend was for the Capital Directives to introduce greater liberalization of capital movements.

2.1.3 The growth of monetary instability from the 1960s onwards and European responses

In the late 1960s, currency instability became an increasing feature in international monetary relations. As a result, in December 1969, at the Hague Summit, the heads of State and government decided to make EMU an explicit goal of the Community and set up a high-level group to examine how to achieve it, chaired by Luxembourg's Prime Minister, Pierre Werner.

The resulting Werner Report, issued in October 1970, proposed a three-stage plan to create an economic and monetary union within a decade. The principal economic as well as monetary policy decisions would be taken at Community (now Union) level. In addition to fixing currency conversion rates and the creation of a single currency and a single monetary policy, EMU would foster harmonization and ultimately unification of economic policies at Community level. It would include control over the essential features of Member States' national budgets, and involve the creation of a Committee of Central Bank Governors and a body to take decisions regarding economic policy, politically responsible to a reformed European Parliament.

In 1971, the Bretton Woods system effectively collapsed, ending the fixed exchange-rate regime and bringing about a wave of instability on foreign exchanges. The EMU project was temporarily abandoned. Instead, in April 1972, the six Member States set up a so-called 'snake in the tunnel' mechanism to narrow the fluctuation margins between the Community currencies (the snake) in relation to fluctuations against the US dollar (the tunnel).

Against the background of growing international monetary turmoil from the mid-1960s onwards, although the Commission proposed greater liberalization of capital movement, the Council could not agree on such measures. A draft Third Capital Directive was proposed in 1964, amended in 1967, and after almost a decade of stasis was withdrawn by the Commission in 1976. Indeed, in 1972 the Council adopted Directive 72/156, based on Articles 70 and 103 EEC, which allowed for *greater* restrictions to be introduced on capital movements.

2.1.4 The foundations of EMU: the SEA and the Delors Report

In 1978, following a Franco–German initiative, the Community decided to relaunch monetary integration at the Brussels European Council by creating a European Monetary System (EMS), with the objectives of stabilizing exchange rates, reducing inflation, and preparing for monetary integration. The EMS entered into force in March 1979.

[3] First Directive of 11 May 1960 for the implementation of Article 67 of the Treaty (OJ [1960] L9/21; English Special Edition, Series I, Chapter 1959–62, p 49).

[4] Second Council Directive 63/21/EEC of 18 December 1962 adding to and amending the First Directive for the implementation of Article 67 of the Treaty (OJ [1963] L9/62; English Special Edition, Series I, Chapter 1963–4, p 5).

As part of the drive to complete the internal market which began with the adoption of the 1985 White Paper, legislative moves to liberalize capital movement were relaunched. In 1988 the Third Capital Directive[5] was adopted, repealing the first two Directives of the 1960s. That Directive shared the structure of its predecessors, with a nomenclature annexed to the Directive which set out various transactions involving capital. However, it introduced full liberalization, along with a series of exceptions on specific grounds. The Court ruled in *Bordessa* that the prohibition on restrictions on capital movements in the Third Capital Directive was directly effective.[6]

With the adoption of the Single European Act (SEA) in 1986, monetary cooperation was included as a new area of Community competence. The establishment of the internal market brought a new stimulus to the idea of a single currency. At Hanover in June 1988 the European Council concluded that 'in adopting the Single Act, the Member States of the Community confirmed the objective of progressive realisation of economic and monetary union'. A committee was set up under the chairship of Commission President Jacques Delors with 'the task of studying and proposing concrete steps leading towards this union'.

The following year, in April 1989, the Delors Report set out a plan to introduce EMU over three stages, including an institutional framework to allow policy to be decided and executed at the Community level in economic areas of direct relevance for the functioning of EMU. It included the creation of a monetary institution, namely a European System of Central Banks (ESCB), which would become responsible for formulating and implementing monetary policy as well as managing external exchange-rate policy. Unlike the Werner Plan, the Delors Report envisaged that the coordination of economic policy could be carried out within the existing institutional framework.

Most of the ideas set out in the Delors Report later formed the basis for the EMU provisions agreed in the Maastricht Treaty. The Delors Report was adopted by the Madrid European Council, which decided to launch the first stage of EMU on 1 July 1990.[7]

When the EEC Treaty was amended by the Maastricht Treaty, in order to allow for Stages Two and Three of EMU as envisaged by the Delors Report, the Treaty's authors took the provisions of the Third Capital Directive and rewrote them in the form of what are now Articles 63 to 66 TFEU. As a result, the Court continues to refer to the Third Capital Directive in litigation relating to those new provisions.

2.2 **Overview of the current provisions**

The provisions relating to free movement of capital are in Title IV of the TFEU, in Articles 63 to 66 TFEU. Those provisions are significantly more liberal than their predecessors in the EEC Treaty, Articles 67 to 73 EEC, which were repealed by the Treaty of Amsterdam.

Article 63 TFEU prohibits all restrictions on the movement of capital, as well as on payments, between Member States and between Member States and third countries. By virtue of free movement of capital, individuals and companies can, for example, transport cash; open, make deposits into and withdrawals from, and close bank accounts; take out loans; register mortgages; buy and sell shares; receive dividends; or obtain and give gifts. They can invoke the free movement of capital to carry out any of those transactions across borders—and, unusually for the four freedoms, that border need not be the frontier between two Member States: it can be between a Member State and a third country.

5 Third Capital Directive 88/361/EEC (OJ [1988] L178/5).

6 Joined Cases C-358/93 and 416/93 *Bordessa* [1995] ECR I-361.

7 See further chapter 19.

Several limitations then follow the basic principle of free movement set out in Article 63 TFEU—a 'grandfather clause'[8] relating to third country-directed restrictions (Article 64 TFEU) and an exceptions clause (Article 65 TFEU).

Article 64(1) TFEU allows Member States and the Union to keep in place specific types of rules affecting free movement of capital to and from third countries that were already in place on a certain cut-off date (31 December 1993 for all Member States except Bulgaria, Estonia, and Hungary, for which the relevant date was 31 December 1999, while for Croatia it was 31 December 2002) even though those rules contravene Article 63 TFEU. For example, if Spain had legislation dating to 1980 that prevented foreigners from purchasing real estate in certain regions, it would be entitled to maintain those rules, but only in respect of third country nationals.

Article 64(1) TFEU provides that Article 63 TFEU:

> shall be without prejudice to the application to third countries of any restrictions which existed on 31 December 1993 under national or Union law adopted in respect of the movement of capital to or from third countries involving direct investment—including in real estate—establishment, the provision of financial services or the admission of securities to capital markets. In the cases of Bulgaria, Estonia and Hungary, the relevant date is 31 December 1999. In respect of restrictions existing under national law in Croatia, the relevant date shall be 31 December 2002.

Article 65 TFEU is similar to Articles 36, 45(3), and 52 TFEU. It sets out grounds for an express exception to the basic principle of free movement. Article 65(1)(a) TFEU allows the Member States to apply provisions of their tax law which distinguish between taxpayers who are not in the same situation with regard to their place of residence or with regard to the place where their capital is invested. Article 65(1)(b) TFEU permits Member States to, inter alia, take measures which are justified on grounds of public policy or public security.

Article 66 TFEU allows safeguard measures to be taken by the Council in order to deal with exceptional circumstances in which movements of capital to or from third countries cause, or threaten to cause, serious difficulties for the operation of EMU. Such measures with regard to third countries may last for up to six months and must be strictly necessary.

Prior to the entry into force of the Lisbon Treaty in 2009, the rules on capital set out powers relating to freezing of assets, within Article 60 EC. That provision is now to be found, as Article 75 TFEU, in the part of the TFEU concerning freedom, security, and justice.

3 Material scope of the capital rules

3.1 Defining capital

The TFEU contains almost no elements indicating what comes within the material scope of the free movement of capital, unlike, for example, the indications offered in Article 57 TFEU about services.[9] However, we now know that capital movements cover, in essence, those resources used for, or capable of, investment intended to generate revenue. That term covers, for example, cash, bonds and other debt instruments, and shares.

[8] A grandfather clause is a provision in which an old rule continues to apply to some existing situations, while a new rule will apply to all future cases.

[9] See further chapters 13 and 14.

However, it not only covers resources in the form of money but also in kind, such as a gift of a washing machine[10] or the loan of a car.[11] The notion of capital is, in that context, opposed to that of 'current payments', which covers all financial dealings relating to trade in goods and services between the residents of a country and individuals residing in the rest of the world. The distinction between capital and current payments was accepted in *Luisi and Carbone*,[12] in which the Court referred to the existence of different Treaty provisions dealing with each of those notions.

The Court has given indications of what is meant by 'capital'. In some cases, it rules on the point without providing any particular reasoning. However, the Court has more often invoked the provisions of the Third Capital Directive, together with the Nomenclature annexed to that Directive, to define what constitutes a capital movement.[13] Relying on the Third Capital Directive, the Court has classified the following situations as implicating the free movement of capital:

- investments in and transfers of immovable property;[14]
- acquisition of shares or securities in the capital markets;[15] and
- receipt of dividends.[16]

Advocate General Colomer severely criticized that feature of the Court's reasoning in his joint Opinion on *UK Golden Shares* and *Spanish Golden Shares*, when he stated that:

> in order to give substance to the terms 'movements of capital' and 'payments', the Court of Justice must turn to the hallowed techniques of interpretation. To my mind it is particularly inappropriate to use secondary legislation for the purposes of ascertaining the meaning of one of the fundamental freedoms laid down in the Treaty.

However, the Court did not let his admonition deflect it from maintaining its approach.[17]

3.2 **Relationship with other Treaty freedoms**

It can be difficult to establish a 'bright line' separating free movement of capital from the other Treaty freedoms. However, the significance of such a division has diminished greatly with the development of case law on capital which is extremely similar to that of its counterparts, most notably through the market access/restrictions approach.[18] Even so, on at least two points, the division may be quite important:

- first, until it is clear whether the rules on capital are horizontally directly effective, in actions between private law persons, knowing whether the relevant EU rules are those on free movement of persons, for example, and not capital, could be crucial.

[10] Case C-318/07 *Persche* [2009] ECR I-359.

[11] Joined Cases C-578–580/10 *van Putten, Mook and Frank*, EU:C:2012:246; Case C-274/20 *Prefettura di Massa Carrara*, EU:C:2021:1022.

[12] Case 286/82 [1984] ECR 377, paras 21 and 22.

[13] Case C-222/97 *Trummer and Mayer* [1999] ECR I-1661, paras 20 and 21.

[14] Case C-302/97 *Konle* [1999] ECR I-3099, para 22; Joined Cases C-519–524/99 and C-526–540/99 *Reisch* [2002] ECR I-2157, para 30; Case C-562/22 *JD* (*Residence condition*) EU:C:2024:55.

[15] Case C-98/01 *Commission v UK* [2003] ECR I-4641, paras 39–41.

[16] Case C-35/98 *Verkooijen* [2000] ECR I-4071, paras 27–30; Case C-319/02 *Maninen* [2004] ECR I-7477.

[17] See *Commission v UK* (n 15) para 39 and Case C-463/00 *Commission v Spain* [2003] ECR I-4581, para 52, where the Court indicated that the method of interpretation criticized by the AG was in line with 'settled case-law'.

[18] See the discussion on that point in chapter 13.

- secondly, because free movement of capital, unlike all other internal market freedoms, potentially applies to movements to and from third countries, it can again be vital to determine which Treaty freedom(s) can be invoked.

The Treaty does not exclude the concurrent application of free movement of capital and other Treaty freedoms. Indeed, Article 65(2) TFEU implicitly allows an overlap between the freedoms:

> The provisions of this chapter [on capital and payments] shall be without prejudice to the applicability of restrictions on the right of establishment which are compatible with the Treaty.

That overlap will be discussed in the next sections.

3.2.1 Capital and payments/goods

The relationship between free movement of goods and free movement of capital is relatively unexplored. As noted earlier, the Court has clarified that the tax treatment of charitable gifts is covered by free movement of capital, even if they are made in kind in the form of everyday consumer goods.[19] The Court had already analysed the tax treatment of gifts to third persons resident in another Member State in the context of inheritances and legacies,[20] ruling that the tax treatment of transferred assets, which can include both sums of money and movable and immovable property, comes within Article 63 TFEU. It therefore rejected the claim which the Greek government had advanced with particular strength in *Persche*, that a gift of consumer goods should be analysed in relation to free movement of goods.

The cleavage between goods and payments, on the other hand, has been well examined. In *Thompson*,[21] the Court ruled that 'means of payment are not to be regarded as goods falling within the provisions of Articles [34 to 37 TFEU]'. The same view was taken in *Bordessa*, where the Court ruled that banknotes do not constitute goods.

3.2.2 Capital and payments/persons

The relationship between free movement of capital and free movement of persons gives rise to discussion mainly in relation to freedom of establishment. However, issues relating to the free movement of workers can surface in a case on capital. For example, as a result of the Second Capital Directive, savings repatriated by migrant workers returning to their home Member State appeared in List A of the original Nomenclature.

In *Barbier*, dealing with an assessment of the value of a non-resident's estate for inheritance tax purposes, the Court, having analysed under the rubric of capital a rule limiting favourable treatment of the value of immovable property to residents, stated:

> It . . . is not necessary to examine the questions referred for a preliminary ruling in so far as they concern freedom of movement for persons. Suffice it to point out in that regard that the tax consequences in respect of inheritance rights are among the considerations which a national of a Member State could reasonably take into account when deciding whether or not to make use of the freedom of movement provided for in the Treaty.[22]

[19] *Persche* (n 10) paras 25 and 29. For discussion of the goods provision, see chapter 12.

[20] See eg Case C-364/01 *Barbier* [2003] ECR I-15013; Case C-513/03 *van Hilten-van der Heijden* [2006] ECR I-1957; Case C-11/07 *Eckelkamp* [2008] ECR I-6845; Case C-43/07 *Arens-Sikken* [2008] ECR I-6887; Case C-67/08 *Block* [2009] ECR I-883.

[21] Case 7/78 *R v Thompson* [1978] ECR 2247, paras 25–27.

[22] *Barbier* (n 20) para 75.

3.2.3 Capital and payments/establishment and services

The freedoms to provide services (whether on a permanent basis, under Article 49 TFEU, or on a temporary basis, under Article 56 TFEU) and of capital movement are the hardest to separate of all the market freedoms.[23]

As to the *freedom of establishment*, the judgments of the Court are often ambiguous as to when the rules on capital, establishment, or both should be applied. There is an unusual degree of clarity in *Reisch*, where the Court stated that:

> as is apparent from Article [50(2)(e) TFEU], the right to acquire, use or dispose of immovable property on the territory of another Member State, which is the corollary of freedom of establishment, . . . generates capital movements when it is exercised.[24]

However, in cases that do not involve immovable property, the Court's position has been less categorical.

The Court initially avoided addressing issues relating to free movement of capital in cases which also concerned freedom of establishment. Greater certainty seems to have emerged on the question of how those freedoms are to be divided, to the extent that the Court could deal with it by means of a reasoned order in one case.[25] In several rulings the Court has reiterated that the rules on establishment cover national provisions that concern shareholdings which give rise to a certain influence on the decisions of the company and help to determine its activities. If such national rules have restrictive effects on the free movement of capital, such effects are to be considered as the inescapable consequence of the possible restriction on the freedom of establishment and so there is no need to examine those rules in light of Articles 63 to 65 TFEU.[26]

Holböck[27] and *Scheunemann*[28] show how the dividing line between capital movement and establishment is determined.

In *Holböck*, an Austrian taxpayer in receipt of dividends from a Swiss company objected to the taxation of those dividends in Austria at the full income tax rate when dividends distributed to natural persons by companies established in Austria were subject to tax at half the average rate. The Court noted that the Austrian legislation in question was not intended to apply only to those shareholdings which enable the holder to have a definite influence on a company's decisions and to determine its activities. Such legislation could, therefore, fall under free movement of capital or freedom of establishment.

That ruling can be contrasted with *Scheunemann* regarding a German taxpayer who had inherited her father's shares in a Canadian firm of which he was sole shareholder. She sought to benefit from exemptions on inheritance tax available if a legacy in the form of shares made up more than one-quarter of the total shares in a firm and if the legatee retained those shares for more than five years. She argued that the rule was intended to deal with capital movements (in the form of inheritances). The Court accepted the argument of the German government that the threshold of one-quarter of the shares in a firm ensured that only persons running a business obtained the tax exemption. Since it was decisive to have control over the firm, the freedom of establishment was relevant (which is not applicable to situations involving third countries).

[23] See Art 65(1)(a) and (2) TFEU, as well as the second sentence of Art 49 TFEU. See also chapter 14.

[24] *Reisch* (n 14) para 29.

[25] Case C-268/03 *De Baeck* [2004] ECR I-5961.

[26] See Case C-196/04 *Cadbury Schweppes and Cadbury Schweppes Overseas* [2006] ECR I-7995, para 33; Case C-524/04 *Test Claimants in the Thin Cap Group Litigation* [2007] ECR I-2107, para 34.

[27] Case C-157/05 *Holböck* [2007] ECR I-4051.

[28] Case C-31/11 *Scheunemann*, EU:C:2012:481.

As to the *freedom to provide and receive services*, there are extremely close links between the Treaty chapters on services and on capital and payments. For example, Article 58(2) TFEU provides that the liberalization of banking and insurance services connected with movement of capital shall be effected in step with liberalization of movement of capital. On the other hand, the personal scope differs between the Treaty provisions on services and on capital. Free movement of capital grants the same rights to EU citizens and third country nationals.[29] The freedom to provide services does not. Unlike the free movement of capital, the services rules can be relied on only by Union citizens.

In *Safir*, Advocate General Tesauro expressed concern that the cumulative application of provisions relating to two or more freedoms might undermine the framework for each one envisaged by the Treaty, as a result of the distinctions between them.[30] He proposed to the Court that it should resolve the problem by focusing on the monetary nature or otherwise of the restriction. Thus, if the measure at issue directly affected the transfer of capital, rendering it impossible or more difficult, the rules on capital would apply. In opposition, if the rule only indirectly restricted movement of capital and primarily constituted a non-monetary restriction on the freedom to provide services, the rules on services would apply.[31]

The Court simultaneously applied the services and capital rules in *Italian recruitment agencies*,[32] where the Commission claimed that requiring undertakings that provide temporary workers to lodge a guarantee with a bank having its seat or a branch in Italy violated both the capital and services rules. Having stated that the guarantee requirement was in itself a restriction on employment agencies' freedom to provide services, the Court ruled that the obligation to lodge the guarantee with a bank established in Italy was both a restriction on capital movement from the employment agency's perspective and discrimination, within the meaning of Article 56 TFEU, against banks established in other Member States. Thus, the same rule was, from the standpoint of the two different groups affected by it, a violation of both freedoms. That analysis dispels disquiet about the concurrent application of the two freedoms because they are applied to different aspects of the rule's material effects.[33]

In *Fidium Finanz*, the Court again had to examine the relationship between the two freedoms.[34] German legislation provided that any person carrying out banking activities in Germany had to obtain written authorization from the Bundesanstalt für Finanzdienstleistungsaufsicht (the BaFin). Such authorization was to be refused to companies that did not have their central administration or a branch in Germany. Fidium Finanz was a company incorporated under Swiss law with its registered office and central administration in Switzerland. It granted small loans over the internet to clients abroad, most of whom were in Germany. Fidium Finanz did not have the authorization required to carry on those activities in Germany. Consequently, the BaFin prohibited it from carrying on lending activities targeted at customers in Germany.

The Court held that such rules fall within the provisions on the freedom to provide services, not the free movement of capital. Companies established in non-member countries are not entitled to rely on the freedom to provide services. The Court acknowledged that

[29] Case C-484/93 *Svensson and Gustavsson* [1995] ECR I-3955.

[30] Case C-118/96 *Safir* [1998] ECR I-1897, Opinion of AG Tesauro, points 9–19.

[31] For an approach similar to that proposed by AG Tesauro, see Case C-602/10 *SC Volksbank România*, EU:C:2012:443.

[32] Case C-279/00 *Commission v Italy* [2002] ECR I-1425, paras 37 and 38.

[33] See also, for a similar approach, Case C-531/06 *Commission v Italy* ('*Italian pharmacies*') [2009] ECR I-4103 and Case C-233/09 *Dijkman and Dijkman-Levaleije* [2010] ECR I-6649.

[34] Case C-452/04 *Fidium Finanz* [2006] ECR I-9521.

the activity of granting credit on a commercial basis concerns, in principle, the rules on both services and capital. Consequently, it considered to what extent the German rules affected the exercise of those two freedoms. It held that the requirement of approval and the fact that it is impossible to get such approval if the company does not have its main administration or a branch in Germany effectively impeded access to the German financial market for companies established in non-member countries.

However, such rules primarily affect the freedom to provide services. It is certainly possible that by making financial services offered by companies established in non-member countries less accessible for clients established in Germany, there will be a reduction in cross-border financial traffic relating to those services. However, that restrictive effect on capital movements was merely an unavoidable consequence of the restriction imposed as regards the provision of services. Since Article 56 TFEU cannot be invoked by natural or legal persons from outside the Union, and since the freedom to provide services was the only relevant freedom for examining the German legislation, it was not necessary to examine the compatibility of the German rules with the free movement of capital.

4 Personal and geographical scope of the capital rules

4.1 Against whom can the capital rules be invoked?

As the prohibition contained in Article 63(1) TFEU is framed in a clear and imperative way, it obviously lends itself to creating direct effects. Indeed, it is clearer than its counterpart in the Third Capital Directive, Article 1, which was ruled by the Court in *Bordessa* to be capable of direct effect. The Court was, therefore, willing to hold that Article 63(1) TFEU had direct effect in relation to third country capital movements in *Sanz de Lera*.[35] In *Pension funds communication* the Court, in relation to the Treaty rules on capital, services, and establishment, stated that:

> while those provisions, which have direct effect, prohibit imposing unjustified restrictions on the freedoms concerned, they are not sufficient in themselves to ensure the elimination of all obstacles to free movement of persons, services and capital.[36]

It is, therefore, clear that the free movement of capital is capable of vertical direct effect.

By contrast, the issue of horizontal direct effect of the capital rules is not settled. Most case law on capital deals with legislative and administrative measures adopted by the Member States. As for acts of the Member States which are unrelated to their official authority, the Member States deal with assets that constitute capital in the same way as any private person would, as a promoter, borrower, lender, guarantor, or other non-regulatory participant on the security markets. The Belgian government argued in *Belgian Eurobonds* that a Eurobond issue, to which Belgian residents were prohibited from subscribing, was a market transaction in which it had acted as a private borrower, not as a public authority.[37] It argued that in limiting access to a Eurobond issue to investors who did not reside in Belgium, it had behaved in the same way as any borrower so as to maintain a standard feature of such issues, the waiver of withholding tax on interest. It claimed that there had, therefore, been no 'restriction'. The Court held that because

[35] Joined Cases C-163/94, 165/94, and 250/94 *Sanz de Lera* [1995] ECR I-4821.

[36] Case C-64/95 *Commission v France* [1997] ECR I-627, para 20.

[37] Case C-478/98 *Commission v Belgium* [2000] ECR I-7587, paras 22–26.

the waiver of tax was provided for in a regulatory measure that only the State as a public authority could take, that claim was not made out.[38] Therefore, on the facts before it, the Court was dealing with a classic situation of vertical direct effect.

In *Federconsumatori*, the Court was asked about provisions in Italy's company law legislation which allowed public authorities holding shares in a company that had previously been publicly owned directly to appoint one or more members of the company's board.[39] Investors in a formerly publicly owned firm opposed a proposal by the municipality of Milan, which held shares in that firm, that it be entitled to name a proportion of the firm's directors based on the proportion of shares it held. That proposal was accepted by the firm's shareholders at its general meeting.

The Court, however, considered (based on the findings of the national court which had referred the issue to it) that the municipality's entitlement was a derogation from standard company law, in that it could only be granted to the State or public bodies holding shares in a firm. It was not removed from the field of application of Article 63 TFEU merely because that entitlement had been placed by the national legislator in the company law code. Admittedly, the right of nomination was not conferred by statute directly on the public bodies in question since it depended on a decision of the shareholders in a general meeting. However, it was only by reason of the statutory provision that a public shareholder could, unlike a private shareholder, obtain the right to participate in the company's board with greater influence than its shareholding would ordinarily allow.[40] As a result, the Court again refused to accept that the national rule was only the result of private law.

The manner in which Article 63 TFEU applies to measures which are not dependent on public law powers has thus not been resolved, and the closely entwined issue of horizontal direct effect for Article 63 TFEU is also open.

4.2 **When can an EU national invoke the capital rules against their own Member State?**

To date, the Court has never applied free movement of capital to a fact situation which is entirely within a single Member State ('a wholly internal situation'). On that basis, the Court ruled in *Fisher* that a transfer of assets between Gibraltar and the United Kingdom was outside the scope of Article 63 TFEU, as a wholly internal situation.[41] However, as with the other freedoms, once a cross-border element is in place, a national of a Member State is free to invoke the Treaty's provisions against their own national authorities. This can be seen in *Barbier*, where the Court examined the Treaty's impact on Dutch legislation on the assessment of tax due by a Dutch taxpayer on the inheritance of immovable property.

In the Netherlands, the tax authorities were required to reduce inheritance tax where the deceased person holding legal title had been under an unconditional obligation to transfer the property to another person who had financial ownership of that property but only if, at the time of his death, the owner of the legal title resided in that Member State. As a result, the heirs of Mr Barbier, a Dutch national holding property in the Netherlands and resident in Belgium at the time of his death, were not entitled to carry out such a reduction. The cross-border element here was the investment in property in the Netherlands

38 See also *Commission v UK* (n 15) paras 48 and 49.

39 Joined Cases C-463/04 and C-464/04 *Federconsumatori* [2007] ECR I-10419.

40 See also Case C-112/05 *Commission v Germany* [2007] ECR I-8995.

41 Case C-192/16 *Fisher*, EU:C:2017:762.

from Belgium and the Court stated that 'the rights . . . are not subject to the existence of other cross-border elements'.[42]

4.3 **Third countries**

The free movement of capital is applicable throughout the entire territory of the Union. The persons invoking it need not be nationals of a Member State, as can be seen from *Svensson and Gustaffson* and *Bordessa*, in both of which third country nationals invoked that freedom in the EU; nor is it necessary that the currencies be those of a Member State.

Article 63 TFEU is unique among the internal market freedoms in that it clearly covers third country transactions, treating capital movements into, out of, and within the Union in the same way.

Although the basic freedom enunciated in Article 63(1) TFEU deals with external capital movements in the same broad terms as are used for intra-Union capital movements, the existence of Articles 64 and 66 TFEU clearly creates a less liberalized framework. Even so, that limitation did not prevent the Court from ruling that ex Article 73B(1) EC was capable of direct effect with regard to third country capital movements in *Sanz de Lera*.

On the other hand, the Court seems careful not to venture views on third country currencies unnecessarily; for example, although in *Trummer and Mayer* the question referred by the national court was drafted in terms of 'foreign currencies', the Court transformed it to 'currency of another Member State'.[43] Such a re-characterization of the factual context at issue before the Court proved quite important in *Maninen*, where Member States argued that practical difficulties in obtaining information about the tax treatment of dividends issued in another country justified limiting a tax credit system designed to prevent double taxation of dividends issued by Finnish companies.[44] The Court responded that the case before it did not in any way concern the free movement of capital between Member States and non-member countries.

As we saw in section 3.2.3, the main arguments in *Fidium Finanz* turned on the fact that the free movement of capital provisions apply to third countries as well as to the Member States. When it challenged Germany's authorization requirement, the Swiss-established firm, Fidium Finanz, could invoke only the EU provisions governing the free movement of capital. Because the Court based its review of the German authorization requirement on the right to provide services and not on the right of free movement of capital, it denied any extension of free movement rights to the Swiss firm.

The Court returned to the issue in *A*, a reference on Sweden's tax treatment of dividends received in that country which originated from a company in Switzerland.[45] Dividends distributed in the form of shares in a subsidiary of the company making the dividend could be exempt from income tax in Sweden. Sweden only granted the exemption where the distributing company was established in a European Economic Area (EEA) country or a third country with which Sweden had concluded an information-exchange agreement. It did not have such an agreement with Switzerland. In the ensuing case before the Court it was argued that Article 63 TFEU only had direct effect as regards third countries in relation to categories of capital movement not covered by Article 64(1) TFEU.

The Court disagreed, holding that Article 64(1) TFEU did not affect the direct effect of the capital rules. It was also argued that the concept of restriction should be treated differently in relation to third countries than in relation to Member States. The Court did not

[42] *Barbier* (n 20) para 59.

[43] *Trummer and Mayer* (n 13). See also Case C-367/98 *Commission v Portugal* [2002] ECR I-4731.

[44] *Maninen* (n 16).

[45] Case C-101/05 *A* [2007] ECR I-11531.

accept the view that for movement between Member States, free movement of capital was linked to the completion of the internal market, while for movement to and from third countries it was related to economic and monetary union.

The same concept of 'restriction' therefore applies whether the movement is between Member States or between a Member State and a third country. However, the Court noted that whether a restriction is justified may vary depending on whether it applies to intra-Union capital movements or movements involving third countries. It went on to hold that since the award of the exemption was dependent on certain conditions being fulfilled and since third countries were not bound to provide information which would allow the national tax authorities to verify if the taxpayer met those conditions, it was justifiable to impose such a restriction on capital movements from Switzerland.

Article 64 TFEU acts as a 'shelter', shielding existing restrictions on capital movements to and from third countries from Article 63 TFEU. It does not prevent national law from abolishing a previously existing restriction on free movement of capital to a third country. By contrast, if the Member State makes the existing rules on capital movement from a third country more stringent, Article 64 TFEU does not shield the new national measure from Article 63(1) TFEU. If a new national rule widens or changes the logic of an existing restriction on third country capital movements, that initial restriction will not come within the scope of Article 64 TFEU even if the Member State later repeals that new national rule, unless the provisions of the new national rule never took effect in the Member State's legal order before the repeal.[46]

4.3.1 Defining a 'third country'

Finally, the question of what constitutes a 'third country' has also surfaced. In *Ospelt*, the Court was faced with the argument that Liechtenstein was a third country for the purpose of Article 64 TFEU so that legislation restricting free movement of capital as regards that country could be maintained insofar as it had been, in substance, in force on 31 December 1993.[47] The cases concerned a refusal to allow a Liechtenstein-resident owner of farmland in Austria to transfer her property to a foundation also established in Liechtenstein because the foundation would not farm the land itself. The Court ruled that since 1 May 1995, the date on which the EEA Agreement entered into force in respect of Liechtenstein, Member States could no longer invoke that provision vis-à-vis that country because the provisions in that agreement on free movement of capital and discrimination are identical to those under Union law with regard to relations between the Member States. 'Third country', at least for those purposes, thus does not seem to cover Iceland, Liechtenstein, and Norway from the time when the EEA Agreement entered into force there.

On the other hand, in *Fokus Invest*, the Court held that a company formed under Swiss law could not, through a company established under Austrian law, claim an entitlement to purchase real estate in that Member State.[48] Article 64 TFEU allowed the Austrian authorities to retain a restriction on the acquisition of immovable property in the form of an authorization regime.

Lastly, the situation of overseas countries or territories (OCTs), was examined in *Prunus and Polonium* (in that case the British Virgin Islands). In line with previous internal market rulings, the Court confirmed that OCTs only benefit from provisions of EU law in the same manner as Member States when EU law expressly provides that they are to be treated in such a manner. As such, OCTs are treated by Article 64 TFEU as non-Member States.[49]

[46] Case C-135/17 *X (Intermediary firms established in third countries)*, EU:C:2019:136, paras 46–51.

[47] Case C-452/01 *Ospelt* [2003] ECR I-9743.

[48] Case C-541/08 *Fokus Invest* [2010] ECR I-1025.

[49] Case C-384/09 *Prunus and Polonium* [2011] ECR I-3319, para 37.

5 Restrictions

5.1 Equal treatment and non-discrimination

Article 63(1) TFEU prohibits 'restrictions' on the movement of capital and the related provisions on capital only refer to discrimination in Article 65(3) TFEU when limiting the scope of available exceptions. The long-standing debate on restrictions/discrimination which has been a feature in relation to the other Treaty fundamental freedoms[50] does not resonate here. Nevertheless, as will be seen, the case law can be broken down into a typology of measures which is familiar from the jurisprudence on other freedoms.

The Court was directly confronted with the discrimination/restriction distinction in the litigation relating to golden shares.[51] In *UK Golden Shares* the Court reiterated its ruling in *Portuguese Golden Shares*[52] and in *French Golden Shares*[53] that the prohibition laid down in Article [63 TFEU] goes beyond the mere elimination of unequal treatment, on grounds of nationality, as between operators on the financial market.[54]

Thus, the fact that a rule does not discriminate as regards nationals of other Member States and applies without distinction on grounds of nationality does not place it outside the scope of Article 63(1) TFEU.[55]

As a result, the Court has generally refrained from qualifying national measures as being either discriminatory (in relation to the persons involved) or distinctly applicable (in relation to currency in which the capital is denominated or the place where an investment is made). A 2011 ruling on a tax amnesty instituted by Portugal in 2005 illustrates the Court's reluctance to go beyond restriction in most cases.[56] Portugal sought to encourage taxpayers who had not declared their assets to regularize their tax situation, and established an amnesty for previously undeclared assets that were declared to the tax authorities. The declared assets would be subject to a one-off payment of 5 per cent of their value. However, a lower payment (2.5 per cent) would be imposed if those assets were Portuguese State securities or if the proceeds of the assets were repatriated to Portugal and invested in such State securities. By treating Portuguese bonds more favourably than the securities issued by other Member States, Portugal had breached Article 63 TFEU. Limiting the preferential tax treatment to taxpayers holding public debt securities issued by Portugal was held by the Court to be a restriction on free movement of capital, without any comment on its discriminatory character.[57]

[50] See further chapter 13.

[51] 'Golden shares' refer to a series of control mechanisms used by public authorities in relation to firms which were previously State-owned after their privatization. The classic example would be a single share held by the minister which gives him or her special rights over decisions taken by the firm.

[52] *Commission v Portugal* (n 43) para 44.

[53] Case C-483/99 *Commission v France* [2002] ECR I-4781, para 40.

[54] *Commission v UK* (n 15) para 43.

[55] See also Case C-42/01 *Portugal v Commission* ('*Cimpor takeover*') [2004] ECR I-6079, para 44.

[56] Case C-20/09 *Commission v Portugal* [2011] ECR I-2637.

[57] The same approach can be seen in the 2018 ruling on Belgium's system of taxation of rented properties, in Case C-110/17 *Commission v Belgium*, EU:C:2018:250. For properties located in Belgium, the tax base was set using the cadastral value of the property. For properties outside Belgium the calculation was based on the actual rental value of the property, which is a higher base than the cadastral value. The Court said that the use of two methods was a restriction since it resulted in a difference of treatment liable to discourage Belgian residents making investments in real estate in other parts of the Union or the EEA.

5.2 **What constitutes a restriction?**

As already noted, the case law on capital restrictions categorizes measures in a manner familiar from the jurisprudence on other freedoms.

As with the other Treaty market freedoms, a *total ban* will constitute a restriction. In *Belgian Eurobonds*, the Court ruled that a prohibition on Belgian residents acquiring securities of a loan on the Eurobond market was a restriction on the movement of capital.[58]

A *prior authorization system* will also constitute a restriction, one which, moreover, will face difficulties in being considered compatible with the Treaty. In *Reisch*, when faced with a prior authorization regime for purchases of land, the Court stated bluntly that, 'those measures . . . restrict, by their very purpose, the free movement of capital'.[59] They remain restrictive even where authorization is deemed to have been granted if the transaction is not deferred by the public authorities within a relatively brief period or if failure to request authorization attracts no penalty.[60]

The Court has also treated *excessive fines* as a restriction on the free movement of capital. In *Chmielewski*, the Court looked at the level of fines imposed under Hungarian law giving effect to Regulation 1889/2005, which requires travellers entering or leaving the Union to declare if they are carrying more than €10,000 in cash. Mr Chmielewski failed to declare the amount of cash he was carrying (€147,492 in a combination of Bulgarian leva, Turkish lira and Romanian lei), and was fined the equivalent of 60 per cent of the undeclared cash. The Court held that the amount of any fines for that administrative offence must be proportionate, although proportionality did not necessarily require the national authorities to take account of the individual circumstances of the cases such as intention or recidivism.[61] The fine for Mr Chmielewski went beyond what was necessary to ensure compliance with the obligation to make the declaration, especially given that Regulation 1889/2005 allowed the national authorities to detain the undeclared cash while investigating its provenance and its intended use.

Moving away from specific examples, what features must a national measure have in order to be considered a restriction? In general, the Court's analysis of an alleged restriction turns on the effect of national provisions, notwithstanding the remarks in *Reisch* about purpose. In *Barbier*, the Court offered two independent reasons as to why measures constituted restrictions:

- They discouraged the purchase of immovable property situated in the Member State concerned and the transfer of financial ownership of such property to another person by a resident of another Member State.
- They also had the effect of reducing the value of the estate of a resident of a Member State other than that in which the property is situated who is in the same position as Mr Barbier.[62]

The dissuasive effect or discouragement inherent in the rule has been the principal basis on which the Court has identified restrictions. In *Verkooijen*, the Court developed the practical application of the dissuasion test.[63] It examined Dutch legislation which refused to extend an exemption from tax to dividends received from shares held in foreign firms,

[58] *Commission v Belgium* (n 37) para 27. See also Case C-78/21 *PrivatBank and others*, EU:C:2023:137, para 50.

[59] *Reisch* (n 14) para 32.

[60] Case C-54/99 *Église de Scientologie* [2000] ECR I-1335, para 15.

[61] Case C-255/14 *Chmielewski*, EU:C:2015:475.

[62] *Barbier* (n 20) para 62. See also *Trummer and Mayer* (n 13).

[63] *Verkooijen* (n 16).

looking at its effects on capital supply and demand. For the provider of the capital, the potential shareholder resident in the Netherlands, it:

> has the effect of dissuading nationals of a Member State residing in The Netherlands from investing their capital in companies which have their seat in another Member State.

For the recipient of the capital, such a provision:

> also has a restrictive effect ... [I]t constitutes an obstacle to the raising of capital in The Netherlands because the dividends ... receive less favourable tax treatment ... so that their shares are less attractive to investors residing in The Netherlands than shares in companies which have their seat in that Member State.[64]

On the few occasions it has used the additional costs approach, the Court has expressly confirmed that no *de minimis* rule exists as regards free movement of capital.[65]

The central role of deterrence or discouragement can be seen in the infringement action brought by the Commission in respect of the 'VW law'.[66] Under German company law, each share in a public limited company carries one vote. However, the VW law provided that the voting rights of any individual shareholder in the Volkswagen firm were limited to 20 per cent irrespective of the number of shares actually held. The Commission claimed that the VW law constituted an unjustified restriction on the free movement of capital.

The Court accepted that capping shareholders' rights was a recognized instrument of company law. However, it pointed to the key difference between a cap decided on by shareholders themselves and one imposed by means of national legislation from which they could not derogate. Although the cap applied without distinction, it limited the possibility for other shareholders to participate in the company with a view to creating or maintaining lasting and direct economic links with it which would make possible direct participation in the management of the company or in its control. Because of its effects, the VW law was liable to deter investors from other Member States.[67]

6 Exceptions and justifications

6.1 Treaty-based limitations and exceptions

In common with the other internal market freedoms, the basic prohibition on restrictions on the free movement of capital is accompanied by exception clauses. All exceptions to the freedoms are to be interpreted in a narrow fashion and can only be used in a manner that respects the principle of proportionality. The grounds set out in the Treaty on which Member States may limit free movement are essentially common to all the freedoms. It is possible to transpose the reasoning of the Court in relation to those matters from one area to another.[68]

[64] See also *Commission v Portugal* (n 43) para 45; *Maninen* (n 16) paras 22 and 23; and Case C-242/03 *Weidert and Paulus* [2004] ECR I-7379, paras 13 and 14.

[65] *Dijkman and Dijkman-Levaleije* (n 33) para 42. See also Case C-78/21 *PrivatBank and others*, EU:C:2023:137, para 53..

[66] *Commission v Germany* (n 40).

[67] For similar rulings, see Case C-212/09 *Commission v Portugal* ('*GALP*'), EU:C:2011:737.

[68] See further chapters 13 and 16.

Article 65 TFEU allows action to be taken to limit the free movement of capital within the Union and in relation to third countries. It also covers freedom of payments.

6.1.1 Article 65(1)(a) TFEU: fiscal matters

Article 65(1)(a) TFEU deals with fiscal matters, stating that the provisions of Article 63 shall be without prejudice to the right of Member States to apply the relevant provisions of their tax law between taxpayers who are not in the same situation with regard to their place of residence or with regard to the place where their capital is invested. It must be read in light of Declaration No 7 on the Treaty of European Union in which the 1991 Intergovernmental Conference affirmed that the Member States would apply that exception only with respect to the relevant provisions of their tax law which existed at the end of 1993. However, that Declaration is itself limited to capital movements between the Member States and payments effected between Member States.

The exception has not been invoked very often, but Article 65(1)(a) TFEU was extensively argued in *Verkooijen*, where the Dutch government and the Member States intervening in its support argued that the limitation of a fiscal exemption to those dividends paid on shares in companies established in the Netherlands came within its scope. The Court excluded the applicability of that exception on the basis that the facts in the principal case arose prior to the entry into force of the Maastricht Treaty.[69] However, in an obiter observation, it went on at paragraph 43 to say:

> the possibility granted to the Member States by Article [63(1)(a) TFEU] of applying the relevant provisions of their tax legislation which distinguish between taxpayers according to their place of residence or the place where their capital is invested has already been upheld by the Court. According to that case-law, before the entry into force of Article [63(1)(a) TFEU], national tax provisions of the kind to which that article refers, insofar as they establish certain distinctions based, in particular, on the residence of taxpayers, could be compatible with [EU] law provided that they applied to situations which were not objectively comparable . . . or could be justified by overriding reasons in the general interest, in particular in relation to the cohesion of the tax system.

The Court, therefore, treats that clause in the way its drafters seem to have intended: as embodying such case law as *Bachmann*[70] and *Schumacker*.[71] *Verkooijen* confirms that the principle of proportionality would, in any event, apply whenever the clause is invoked. The Court thereby dismissed the argument raised by some Member States in that case, that the terms of Article 65(3) TFEU—'The measures and procedures referred to in paragraphs 1 and 2 shall not constitute a means of arbitrary discrimination or a disguised restriction on the free movement of capital'—make clear that the limitation does not apply to Article 65(1)(a), which speaks of 'provisions', rather than 'measures and procedures', of national tax law.

That analysis was further developed in *Maninen*, where the facts arose after Article 65(1)(a) TFEU became applicable. The Court pointed out that it is subject to a restrictive interpretation. It went on to draw a distinction between unequal treatment, which is permitted under Article 65(1)(a) TFEU, and arbitrary discrimination, which is prohibited under Article 65(3) TFEU. In order for unequal treatment of revenue from national dividends and revenue from foreign dividends to be lawful, the Court held that such

[69] *Verkooijen* (n 16) para 42.

[70] Case C-204/90 *Bachmann* [1992] ECR I-249. See also Case C-300/90 *Commission v Belgium* [1992] ECR I-305 relating to fiscal cohesion.

[71] Case C-279/93 *Schumacker* [1995] ECR I-225.

treatment must concern situations which are not objectively comparable or be justified by overriding reasons in the general interest, with any justification being subject to a strict proportionality test.

In that respect, the situation of a Finnish taxpayer receiving dividends from a Finnish firm was the same as that of a Finnish taxpayer receiving dividends from a Swedish firm; both sources of income could be subject to double taxation because of how the two tax systems were structured. Moreover, while the principle of territoriality which had been accepted by the Court in relation to freedom of establishment[72] was not relevant in *Maninen*, the Court held that in any event that principle cannot justify different treatment of dividends distributed by Finnish firms and those paid by firms established in other Member States, if the categories of dividends concerned share the same objective situation. The Court went on to reject a justification based on cohesion of the national tax system, as well as to exclude the reduction of tax receipts as a basis for justifying unequal treatment which was not based on objective differences.

6.1.2 **Article 65(1)(b) TFEU: general**

Article 65(1)(b) TFEU allows Member States to take all requisite measures to prevent infringements of national law and regulations, in particular in the field of taxation and the prudential supervision of financial institutions. It also allows them to lay down procedures for the declaration of capital movements for purposes of administrative or statistical information. Finally, under that provision a Member State may take measures which are justified on grounds of public policy or public security. Article 65(1)(b) TFEU is, in effect, a combination of Article 4 of the Third Capital Directive and Articles 36 and 52 TFEU: the first two sets of exemption come from the Directive, while the final one, relating to public policy and public security, is inspired by the other Treaty provisions.

'[T]o prevent infringements of national law and regulations, in particular in the field of taxation and the prudential supervision of financial institutions'

Nothing similar to that formula is to be found in the other Treaty exception clauses; as such it underlines the very sensitive nature of the free movement of capital. The Member States' power to prevent infringement of national law is set out in a non-exhaustive fashion. In *Bordessa*, the Court, interpreting the equivalent term found in Article 4(1) of the Third Capital Directive, ruled that Member States could take measures necessary to combat illicit activities that are of comparable gravity to those in the fields of fiscal matters and the supervision of financial institutions, such as money-laundering, drug-trafficking, and terrorism. It is open to question whether they would now be considered as falling under the final limb of Article 65(1)(b) TFEU, on public policy and public security.[73]

If public policy and public security are the appropriate bases on which to uphold restrictive national measures outside the field of tax and banking supervision, then the Court might now take a narrower approach to the phrase 'to prevent infringements of national law and regulations' than it took in *Bordessa*. Irrespective of the scope of legislation covered by Article 65(1)(b) TFEU, it is clear from *Konle* that Member States' power to take 'requisite' measures to prevent infringement of laws limits permissible restrictions on capital to those necessary to achieve the goal pursued.

[72] Case C-250/95 *Futura Participations and Singer* [1997] ECR I-2471.

[73] Case C-78/21 *PrivatBank and others*, EU:C:2023:137, para 69.

'[T]o lay down procedures for the declaration of capital movements for purposes of administrative or statistical information'

Another example of the relatively broad freedom given to Member States by Article 63(1)(b) TFEU is found in the fact that Member States are expressly authorized to have systematic controls in relation to capital for administrative and statistical purposes. For the other freedoms, no such leeway has been accorded under the Treaty.[74]

'[T]o take measures which are justified on grounds of public policy or public security'

Although the final limb of Article 65(1)(b) TFEU echoes the other exemption clauses in the Treaty, it contains a shorter list of grounds which may be invoked by the Member States. There are no references to public morality or public health, or to official authority. A basic problem that arises here is that the Court traditionally took the view that such provisions should be strictly interpreted and were confined to matters of a non-economic nature. However, many public interest grounds that might be relevant in relation to capital movements could involve economic concerns.

Église de Scientologie, in which a French court asked if a refusal to authorize proposed direct foreign investment in France by adherents of the Church of Scientology was compatible with the Treaty, provided an opportunity to clarify the scope of public policy.[75] Although the national court did not raise that specific point in its reference, the Court followed Advocate General Saggio, who considered it necessary to examine that question when identifying the conditions under which a system of prior authorization could permissibly restrict the free movement of capital. He considered that the jurisprudence developed around that concept in the fields of workers and goods could be transposed to that of capital. As a result, the term would be strictly interpreted, would exclude typically economic interests, and would be subject to control by the Union institutions and by the national courts.

As for public security, that ground arose in *Albore*,[76] in which an Italian court asked if legislation requiring nationals of other Member States to obtain authorization for the acquisition of buildings situated in zones declared to be of 'military importance' while its own nationals had no such obligation was compatible with the freedoms of establishment and capital. The Court, relying on case law related to free movement of goods, stated that public security extends to the external security of the Member State but noted that the concept was subject to the principle of proportionality and could not, in any event, permit arbitrary discrimination. It went on to say that a mere reference to requirements of defence of the national territory could not suffice to bring a national rule that discriminates against nationals of other Member States in access to the property market in some or all of that Member State within the scope of Article 345 TFEU. The position would be different only if it were demonstrated, for each area to which the restriction applied, that non-discriminatory treatment of the nationals of all the Member States would expose the military interests of the Member State concerned to real, specific, and serious risks which could not be countered by less restrictive procedures. The Court left it to the national court to decide, in the case before it, whether there was sufficient justification for the contested restriction.

Public security also arose in *Belgian Golden Shares*.[77] The golden shares in question entitled Belgian authorities to oppose any transfer, use as security, or change in intended

[74] Compare Case 42/82 *Commission v France* [1983] ECR 1013, para 64 (goods) and Case 321/87 *Commission v Belgium* [1989] ECR 997, para 15 (persons).

[75] *Église de Scientologie* (n 60).

[76] Case C-423/98 *Albore* [2000] ECR I-5965.

[77] Case C-383/98 *Commission v Belgium* [2002] ECR I-4809.

use of various strategic assets held by energy distribution firms, and to oppose certain management decisions which were contrary to guidelines on the country's energy policy. The Court held that the objective pursued, of safeguarding energy supplies in the event of a crisis, fell within the ambit of a legitimate public interest and specifically within the public security justification in Article 65(1)(b) TFEU. It then examined if the legislation properly responded to a genuine and sufficiently serious threat to a fundamental interest of society and found that, because no less restrictive measures could have been taken to attain the objective, it was justified.

The Court used the same analysis in *French Golden Shares*,[78] in relation to the safeguarding of petroleum supplies in the event of a crisis, the justification for the controls on the acquisition of holdings in the privatized Elf-Aquitaine. However, in that case, the French legislative provisions did not reflect the limited nature of the justification invoked, since neither the prior authorization regime nor the opposition procedure in the legislation was limited by reference to such circumstances. Unlike the Belgian legislation, it was not based on any precise, objective criteria and so went beyond what was necessary to achieve the goal.[79]

6.2 **Justifying restrictions**

Cassis and its equivalent rulings in relation to the other internal market freedoms introduced what was, in effect, a regulatory function for the Court of Justice. That regulatory role arises because the Court has been led to indicate when a restriction on internal market freedoms is justified in ruling on infringement actions against the Member States and, more controversially, in answering questions submitted to it by national courts for a preliminary ruling. Under that jurisprudence, national measures liable to hinder or make less attractive the exercise of fundamental freedoms guaranteed by the Treaty can be justified only if they fulfil four conditions:

- they must be applied in a non-discriminatory manner;
- they must be justified by overriding reasons based on the general interest;
- they must be suitable for securing the attainment of the objective which they pursue; and
- they must not go beyond what is necessary in order to attain that objective.

Even in relation to Article 67 EEC, the Court had indicated in *Veronica Omroep* that the maintenance of pluralism within a Member State's television market could justify limits on investment in a channel operating under foreign law and so permit restrictions on free movement of capital.[80] It did not take long for the case law on that question to develop along similar lines to that followed for the other freedoms.

As regards the present provisions of the Treaty, the Court first considered the question in detail in *Trummer and Mayer*, where Finland argued that the rule at issue before the Austrian courts in that case was based on an 'overriding factor serving the public interest', namely ensuring the predictability and transparency of the mortgage system.[81] The Court accepted that such public interests could be legitimately pursued by means selected under the law of the State in which that objective was to be attained.

78 Case C-483/98 *Commission v France* [2002] ECR I-4781.
79 See also *Commission v Spain* (n 17).
80 Case C-148/91 *Veronica Omroep* [1993] ECR I-487, paras 13 and 14.
81 *Trummer and Mayer* (n 13).

By the time it came to give judgment in *Reisch*, the Court was able to express its position in a clear fashion:

> restrictions may nevertheless be permitted if the national rules pursue, in a non-discriminatory way, an objective in the public interest and if they observe the principle of proportionality, that is if the same result could not be achieved by other less restrictive measures.[82]

6.2.1 **Grounds of justification**

As to the grounds that have been accepted as 'objectives in the public interest' or as 'overriding requirements of the general interest' in the context of free movement of capital, they are reminiscent of the other freedoms. They include:

- protection of creditors (by means of the transparency of a mortgage registration system);[83]
- maintenance of a permanent population and stable economic activity in rural or mountainous regions;[84]
- protection of the environment;[85] and
- 'preserving agricultural communities, maintaining a distribution of land ownership which allows the development of viable farms and sympathetic management of green spaces and the countryside as well as encouraging a reasonable use of the available land by resisting pressure on land, and preventing natural disasters'.[86]

However, the Court requires more than a general reference to goals that are in the public interest. In consequence, in *Spanish Golden Shares* the Court made it clear that a generic reference to 'strategic imperatives and the need to ensure continuity in public services' was not a sufficient basis on which to invoke such overriding requirements of general interest. That Spanish legislation failed to establish how the undertakings involved (a tobacco producer and a group of commercial banks) took responsibility for a public service function.[87]

Against that background, we can look to see how the Court evaluates grounds of justification as legitimate or otherwise.

In *VW law*,[88] the German government argued that the VW law was justified by the protection of workers' interests and the protection of minority shareholders. The Court found that, as regards the protection of workers' interests, the national authorities had been unable to explain why, in order to protect that firm's employees, it was appropriate and necessary for the federal and regional authorities to hold a strengthened and immovable position in the capital of Volkswagen. As to the protection of minority shareholders, the Court repeated its scepticism and noted that in some instances the public authorities might use their enhanced powers to defend general interests which might be contrary to the economic interests of the company and so contrary to the interests of its other shareholders.

The protection of public health arose as a ground of justification in relation to capital and establishment (Articles 63 TFEU and 49 TFEU) in *Italian pharmacies*.[89] Italian legislation excluded non-pharmacists from owning and operating pharmacies—in the case

[82] *Reisch* (n 14) para 33. [83] *Trummer and Mayer* (n 13) para 30. [84] *Konle* (n 14) para 40.
[85] *Reisch* (n 14) para 35.
[86] *Ospelt* (n 47) para 39. See also Case C-370/05 *Festersen* [2007] ECR I-1135, para 28.
[87] *Commission v Spain* (n 17) para 70. [88] *Commission v Germany* (n 40).
[89] *Italian pharmacies* (n 33).

of legal persons, only those which were controlled by a natural person qualified as a pharmacist could operate pharmacies. While it was a non-discriminatory restriction affecting the two freedoms equally, the Court accepted that public health could be used to justify that restriction, noting the importance of the objective of ensuring that the provision of medicinal products to the public is reliable and of good quality.

The fight against tax evasion was accepted by the Court in *Établissements Rimbaud*[90] as a ground which could properly be invoked. However, it stated that such a justification could be permissible only if it was targeted against purely artificial contrivances and that any general presumption of evasion was not permitted. Here, the Court confirmed that the legislation was appropriate to combat tax evasion because it was directed against practices the sole aim of which was to enable natural persons to avoid paying tax on capital in France.[91]

Finally, the 2011 ruling on a tax amnesty instituted by Portugal in 2005 confirms that purely economic grounds cannot be used to justify a restriction.[92] The Court rejected Portugal's claim that payment of a lower amount by taxpayers holding Portuguese State bonds took account of the benefit to the State which did not exist where the taxpayer had invested in securities from other Member States. That argument was, it held, in reality an attempt to justify a measure restricting free movement of capital by pursuit of an objective that is economic in nature, namely offsetting the Member State's lost tax revenue.

Although only the Court can ultimately decide whether a ground of justification is legitimate, the Commission in its role as 'guardian of the Treaties' sometimes has to take a view on those matters. Its perspective can be particularly important where a new issue arises and there has not yet been time for a preliminary reference to be made to the Court. For example, in the early part of 2013, Cyprus imposed a series of capital controls to prevent the uncontrollable outflow of bank deposits, which could lead to the banks' collapse and the immediate risk of the failure of the country's financial system. The Commission took the view that the stability of financial markets and of the banking system in that Member State was 'a matter of overriding public interest and public policy justifying the imposition of temporary restrictions on capital movements'.[93] That evaluation shows the potential breadth of grounds of justification, but it has yet to be examined by the Court.

6.2.2 **Proportionality**

The *Cassis de Dijon* case law allows traders and the Commission to attack national measures that do not discriminate but which could have a restrictive effective on trade. Under that Court-developed test, the national measure will be allowed to stand only if the restrictive effect on the internal market freedom is an inescapable side product of the pursuit, by proportionate means, of a public interest goal. In order for the contested measures to be considered proportionate, the rule must be suitable and necessary. However, the approach to necessity has been more nuanced than that bare description might suggest.

Moreover, difficult procedural questions arise in order to determine whether a given restriction is necessary. Adjudication on the acceptability of national rules when measured against the internal market freedoms raises the issue of how closely courts should review the evaluation of the decision-making which adopted the contested rules.

[90] Case C-72/09 *Établissements Rimbaud* [2010] ECR I-10659.

[91] See also Case C-451/05 *ELISA* [2007] ECR I-8251.

[92] *Commission v Portugal* (n 56).

[93] Commission Press Release IP/13/298, 28 March 2013.

Suitability

Proportionality requires that the measures under scrutiny be suitable for securing the attainment of the objective that they pursue. In a few rather unusual cases the Court looks only to the suitability requirement because that test is not satisfied, so there is no need to see if less restrictive means are available. For example, in *Trummer and Mayer* the Court stated that even if creditor protection was at the heart of the national system at issue in the case, the rules in place were not suitable to achieve that goal. They required registration of all mortgages, with the value of the secured debt denominated either in the national currency or as an amount of gold. There was predictability for lower-ranking creditors, by fixing the value of debt secured against the mortgage. However, that benefit was gained at the price of lack of predictability for higher-ranking creditors whose secured debts had been given in foreign currencies. Moreover, some insecurity was inherent in the national legislation because it allowed for the value of the mortgage to be expressed in terms of the price of fine gold, a measure of value also subject to fluctuation in the same way as foreign currencies. While that legislative provision had fallen into disuse, it had not been formally repealed. Thus, the Court applied the criterion relating to the national rule's suitability to set aside creditor protection as a justification for those rules.

Another example can be found in *SEGRO*.[94] Hungary changed its law to prohibit the creation of rights of usufruct over agricultural law and abolish existing usufruct rights except where the usufructuary was a close family member of the landowner. It argued that the ban sought to facilitate the creation of properties of a sufficient size to be viable and competitive farms, preventing fragmentation of ownership of agricultural land. The Court observed that the requirement of close family relationship between the holders of preserved or new usufruct rights and the landowner did not appear appropriate to secure, in a consistent manner, the public interest objectives pursued—which prevented the restriction on free movement of capital being justified on that basis.[95]

Absence of any less restrictive means

Suitability is a floor, a threshold control on the measure's status. The greater hurdle for national authorities is to show the absence of less restrictive means of achieving the legitimate goal that is the measure's object. That second requirement is at the heart of the proportionality principle.

The absence of less restrictive means can be well illustrated by the case law on prior authorization regimes that subject a proposed transaction to *ex ante* administrative review. Such regimes were at the heart of both *Bordessa* and *Sanz de Lera*, as regards controls on currency exports. In *Bordessa*, the Court took the view that a prior authorization procedure for the export of currency was incompatible with Article 4 of the Third Capital Directive, the predecessor to Article 63 TFEU. Such a procedure excessively limited the free movement of capital because it suspended the export of banknotes and submitted the free circulation of capital to the discretion of the national administration. In *Sanz de Lera*, the Court indicated that a declaration procedure, setting out the transaction's nature and the identity of the parties to it, was sufficient to ensure the genuine use of currency exports to third countries without impermissibly hindering movement of capital.

[94] Joined Cases C-52/16 and C-113/16, *SEGRO*, EU:C:2018:157. Following on from the *SEGRO* ruling, the Court said in Case C-177/20 *'Grossmania'*, EU:C:2022:175 that those deprived under Hungarian law of their rights of usufruct had to be able to claim restoration of those rights or compensation, even if they had not challenged the unlawful deletion of those rights before the national courts.

[95] On the further consequences, see Case C-419/23 *Nemzeti Földügyi Központ*, EU:C:2024:1016.

However, prior authorization regimes in different contexts may have other purposes. If intended to fulfil a preventive function, *ex ante* controls may respect the proportionality requirement. It is potentially the case as regards the prior authorization requirements for purchase of immovable property.

The Court stated in *Konle* that a Member State may justify its requirement of prior authorization for the purchase of building land by invoking an object of general interest where, inter alia, the same result cannot be achieved by other less restrictive procedures.[96] The need for a prior authorization procedure was not shown in *Konle*. A procedure simply involving a declaration would suffice where, as in that case, there would be adequate repressive measures if a breach of the agreed declaration was duly established after the property had been acquired. The restriction in question was not, therefore, 'essential'.[97]

By contrast, in *Ospelt* the Court took a more favourable view of such regimes in relation to agricultural land.[98] It accepted that the objective of maintaining viable agriculture required keeping land intended for agriculture in use and continuing to make use of it under appropriate conditions. Prior supervision is legitimate to ensure that transfer of such land does not lead to change of use which would be incompatible with long-term agricultural use. Moves to restore the *status quo* would be inadequate to ensure that the land's suitability for such use is not irretrievably impaired. However, the Court indicated that one condition applied in that system was unnecessary. There was no justification for the exclusion of transfers to persons who, although they will not farm the land themselves, will lease it to farmers. Such limitations cannot be justified because they are over-broad.

The status of a prior authorization regime as regards foreign direct investment is less clear. In *Église de Scientologie*, the Court followed Advocate General Saggio, who had taken the view that prior authorization was potentially licit in respect of direct foreign investment. In his view, there are forms of investment that would be difficult to dislodge in an expeditious fashion. Therefore, EU law should permit, he argued, resort to prior authorization. The Court agreed: a prior declaration system might be inadequate to counter the dangers of a genuine and sufficiently serious threat to public policy and public security.

Though the proportionality principle arose in the 'golden shares' cases, the measures' proportionality was not examined in most of them because the Court found that the systems were incapable of satisfying another criterion. Thus, in *Portuguese Golden Shares* there was no need to examine the proportionality of that system because the grounds of justification invoked (the State's financial interests) did not constitute an overriding requirement of general interest.[99] In *French Golden Shares*, the basis of the authorization system was insufficiently clear, as was part of the system in *Spanish Golden Shares*.

The fate of the rules at issue in *Belgian Golden Shares* shows that an opposition system is likely to be viewed more favourably than a prior authorization system. The Court upheld the compatibility of the Belgian regime with Article 63 TFEU. It took account of the *ex post facto* nature of the powers of intervention, the strict time limits within which they were to be exercised, and the limited nature of the measures that could be taken (veto in respect of decisions concerning strategic assets and specific management decisions).

Italian pharmacies,[100] on Italian legislation which excluded non-pharmacists from owning and operating pharmacies, is of interest here as well. The Court accepted that the protection of public health could be invoked to justify that legislation, which was a restriction both on free movement of capital and the freedom of establishment. In light of the risks to individuals' health from inappropriate medicinal products, and to the

[96] *Konle* (n 14). [97] See also *Reisch* (n 14). [98] *Ospelt* (n 47).
[99] *Commission v Portugal* (n 43). [100] *Italian pharmacies* (n 33).

financial balance of social security systems which pay for drugs, the Court found that restricting who could own and operate a pharmacy was an appropriate means of achieving that goal. It considered that while both pharmacists and non-pharmacists providing that service were motivated by profit, the former group had a training and responsibility which the latter did not have and which moderated their conduct. A Member State was, therefore, entitled to find that such an exclusion rule was a suitable means of achieving that goal, even if other Member States did not find it necessary. The Court went on to find that the Commission had not demonstrated that there were less restrictive means of achieving the same goal.

Because the free movement of capital applies in principle to third countries as well as to intra-Union movements, the issue arises whether justifications will be accepted in the same manner for a restriction relating to a third country as to a Member State. That point came up in *Établissements Rimbaud*, where the Court held that the case law on intra-Union restrictions cannot be transposed in its entirety to movements of capital between Member States and third countries, because such movements take place in a different legal context.[101] While the Court had ruled previously regarding the French legislation in issue in *Établissements Rimbaud* that a taxpayer established in another Member State had to be able to present evidence showing that the company was not a screen behind which a natural person subject to capital tax in France was sheltering,[102] the same possibility did not have to be given to non-resident taxpayers established in Lichtenstein. As between Member States there is a Directive from 1977 which allows Member States to verify administrative information in relation to tax matters; there is no counterpart to that Directive as regards Lichtenstein. As such, France was not required to examine the situation of a taxpayer established in Lichtenstein on a case-by-case basis.

That absence of a framework for cooperation with third countries may not be relevant for certain rules applied by Member States to movements of capital, as can be seen from *Welte*.[103] Mr Welte, a Swiss national resident in Switzerland, inherited land in Düsseldorf and the proceeds in bank accounts in Germany and in Switzerland on the death of his spouse. He was allocated a tax-free allowance of €2,000 by the German tax authorities on that inheritance. If either he or his spouse had been resident in Germany on the date of the death, the allowance in question would have been €500,000. The Court unsurprisingly noted that the situation was not a purely domestic situation and that the inheritance at issue was a movement of capital. It was also evident that the relevant German rule on inheritance taxes restricted free movement of capital. Rejecting Germany's reliance on the grandfathering clause in Article 64 TFEU (preserving the legality of rules affecting non-member countries which exist on 31 December 1993) the Court held that that provision can only be applied to real estate where the national rule concerns investments in real estate related to the carrying out of an economic activity. Article 64 TFEU cannot be applied to investments in real estate of a patrimonial nature made for private purposes unconnected with the carrying out of an economic activity.

The Court went on to hold that as regards the amount of inheritance tax payable in Germany, there is no objective difference between situations in which neither person resides in Germany and the situation where at least one of them resides there. In both situations, German law considers the heir to be a taxable person. In both situations, the amount of inheritance tax is calculated on the basis of the value of the property and of the personal link between the deceased and the inheritor, neither of which depends on the place of residence of those two individuals. German law therefore treated inheritances

[101] See also Case C-540/07 *Commission v Italy* [2009] ECR I-10983 and *A* (n 45).

[102] *ELISA* (n 91).

[103] Case C-181/12 *Welte*, EU:C:2013:662.

in both situations in the same manner, except for the amount of the tax-free allowance awarded. There was therefore no objective difference and the situation of Mr Welte was held to be comparable to the situation of any heir inheriting an immovable property located in Germany from their deceased spouse who was residing in Germany, as well as being comparable to the situation of any heir residing in Germany who acquires by inheritance an immovable property located in Germany from their deceased spouse who was not residing there.

Finally, the Court rejected justification based on the effectiveness of fiscal supervision. It accepted that a Member State can refuse to grant a tax advantage if requirements on which the advantage depends can only be verified by obtaining information from the authorities of a non-member country where it proves impossible to obtain such information from that country. However, the information required in relation to the inheritance rules concerned death certificates and proof of family relationships. They can be issued by or forwarded by the heirs and they do not require complex evaluation. Moreover, the €500,000 allowance was available to any heir residing in Germany inheriting an immovable property located in Germany from their deceased spouse who was not residing there. In those circumstances Germany was willing to accept the kind of documents which Mr Welte would have to provide. As such, the Court rejected the claim that the measure was justified by the need to preserve the effectiveness of fiscal supervision, even though there was no specific framework for cooperation with the Swiss tax authorities.

6.3 **Procedural requirements applied to justifications and exceptions**

In recent years, the Court has developed a set of procedural requirements relating to the justifications and exceptions invoked by national authorities. Some of the precursors of that development relate to the Treaty-based exceptions. However, for the most part that phenomenon has been seen in relation to the mandatory requirements and overriding requirements of general interest. The national measure must allow traders, investors, purchasers, or other persons invoking the freedom to be sure that any restriction will not be applied in a discriminatory manner, as well as being clear when a particular form of restriction will be applied. If those requirements are not satisfied, the Court has ruled that the Treaty precludes such a measure and may do so without examining its proportionality.

The clearest statement of the Member States' obligations in relation to the procedural aspect of justifying a restriction on a freedom can be found in *Église de Scientologie*. The Court had confirmed that a prior authorization regime could be acceptable in relation to foreign investment, but then stated:

> 21. [T]he essence of the system in [the present case] is that prior authorisation is required for every direct foreign investment which is 'such as to represent a threat to public policy [and] public security', without any more detailed definition. Thus, the investors concerned are given no indication whatever as to the specific circumstances in which prior authorisation is required.
>
> 22. Such lack of precision does not enable individuals to be apprised of the extent of their rights and obligations deriving from Article [63 TFEU]. That being so, the system established is contrary to the principle of legal certainty.[104]

[104] On this point, also contrast *Commission v France* (n 74) and *Commission v Spain* (n 17) with *Commission v Belgium* (n 74).

6.4 **The limits of restrictions**

In relation to free movement of capital, the broad scope of the dissuasion test articulated in the case law to date raises the question whether the interpretation of 'restriction' may catch too much. If so, that 'over-inclusion' could create pressure for a supple approach to justification. There would be an attendant risk that such flexibility would in turn generate problems when applied to 'hardcore' restrictions on free movement of capital. The issue surfaced in *UK Golden Shares*, where the UK government argued that the measures at issue, rules in a privatized company's articles of association which prevent any investor acquiring shares in that firm carrying the right to more than 15 per cent of the votes, did not restrict access to the market within the meaning of *Keck*.[105] The Court stated that the measures in issue were not comparable with rules concerning selling arrangements. It noted that although the relevant restrictions on investment operations applied without distinction to both residents and non-residents, they affected the position of a person acquiring a shareholding as such; they were liable to deter investors from other Member States from making such investments and thus affected access to the market. The analysis leaves free movement of capital in a position similar to the freedom to provide services in the wake of *Alpine Investments*, in which the Court refused to apply *Keck* to the rule before it, but did not exclude its potential applicability to that Treaty freedom.

Case study 15.1: Capital movements in the public interest

SOCIAL SERVICES OF GENERAL INTEREST AND NATIONAL IDENTITY

Social services such as health and long-term care, childcare, social housing, and the care and social inclusion of vulnerable groups are very important to individuals' and communities' feelings of identity—for example, if you consider the differing conceptions between countries in the Nordic, Central European, and Mediterranean regions (as well as between countries in those regions) as to what is the appropriate role of the individual, the family, the local community, and the State in relation to all those activities, you will see that such services are intimately connected with the sense of what makes a given society distinctive or gives it a particular character.[106]

Those services operate on the basis of the solidarity principle (or to put it another way, they are provided outside the logic of a market system), are intended to protect those considered most vulnerable, are not for profit, and are strongly rooted in local cultural traditions. The free movement of capital can have a significant impact on the mechanisms by which such services are delivered. This case study seeks to examine the impact of that freedom on the provision of social services in the Member States. In doing so, we will be looking at the impact of the legal issues considered in this chapter—at the material scope of 'capital', at the concept of 'restriction', at the scope of the exceptions laid down by the Treaty, at how grounds of justification can be developed, at the role of proportionality, and at differences between justification in relation to capital moving between Member States as opposed to between Member States and third countries. The main theme examined here can be summarized by the question: is there an emerging Union-level view of when capital movements are in the public interest?

[105] *Commission v UK* (n 15) para 43.

[106] See also chapter 18 on public services and EU law.

THE *PERSCHE* RULING

If the Member State decides that in addition to (or instead of) direct provision of such a social service by public law bodies, private law operators will be made responsible (possibly only in part) for delivery of that service, it can use a wide variety of financing mechanisms. For example, it may seek to facilitate or encourage private financing by means of tax breaks; they could be given to persons who make donations to service providers. Such fiscal mechanisms raise issues regarding free movement of capital. The Court was first confronted with the issue of funding of those services and its connection with free movement of capital in *Persche*.[107] Mr Persche claimed as an exceptional tax-deductible expense his donation of bedlinen and towels, and also Zimmer frames and toy cars for children, to the Centro Popular de Lagoa (a retirement home to which a children's home had been added) in Portugal. The German authorities rejected his request because the recipient of the donation was not established in Germany.

The Court first clarified that the taxable treatment of such gifts came within the scope of the rules on capital, even if they were made in kind in the form of everyday consumer goods. It then noted that the inability in Germany to deduct gifts to bodies recognized as charitable if they were established in other Member States was likely to affect the willingness of German taxpayers to make gifts for the benefit of those bodies. As such, the German legislation restricted the free movement of capital. In order for the German legislation to be compatible with the Treaty, the difference in treatment would have to concern situations which are not objectively comparable or would have to be justified by an overriding reason in the public interest (and be proportionate in the pursuit of the legislation's objective).

Was there indeed an objective difference between donations to German charities and donations to Portuguese charities?

The Court started by recognizing that it was for each Member State to determine whether it would provide for tax advantages in favour of bodies which concerned themselves with activities that it recognized as being charitable and taxpayers who made gifts to those bodies. However, where a Member State decided to grant tax advantages to bodies pursuing certain charitable purposes, the Court held that it could not restrict the benefit of such advantages only to bodies established in that Member State.

There are, however, some counterarguments to the idea that tax breaks for charitable gifts must extend to donations outside the Member State:

- A right for taxpayers to deduct the value of gifts from their tax bill decreases the Member State's tax revenues, and the Member State should have to allow that fall in its income only if there is also a reduction in its expenses by the taxpayer taking over a burden (eg providing for the elderly) that would otherwise fall on the State.
- Such tax advantages allow the Member State to discharge some of its duties, and those responsibilities do not exist beyond its borders since they are an expression of the bonds of solidarity within that society.
- Giving such tax advantages for charitable gifts outside the Member State cannot be effectively controlled to ensure that the taxpayer is genuinely giving to charity (as opposed to reducing her tax bill by bogus means).

The Court acknowledged that providing tax breaks for charitable donations could encourage charitable bodies to substitute themselves for the public authorities in assuming certain

[107] Case C-318/07 (n 10).

responsibilities, which was an aspect of the first counterargument listed. However, it went on to hold, in line with the case law examined on justification, that the need to prevent a reduction of tax revenues was neither among the objectives in Article 65 TFEU nor was it capable of constituting an overriding reason in the public interest.

As regards the second counterargument, the Court accepted that there was no requirement in Union law for a Member State automatically to confer on foreign bodies recognized as having charitable status in their Member State of origin the same status in their own territory. Member States had discretion as to what goals or activities they wish to consider charitable. However, the Court did not uphold that counter-argument: Germany's freedom to define the interests of the general public it wished to promote did not allow it to refuse equal treatment to a body recognized as having charitable status in Portugal which satisfied the requirements imposed by German law and the object of which was to promote the very same interests of the general public. In other words, is it likely that body would be recognized as having charitable status in the Member State of the taxpayer? If the activities of the Centro Popular benefit children and old people, that element is decisive to establish if it is comparable with an identical body established in Germany. There is no relevance to the fact that those children and elderly persons are Portuguese or reside in Portugal.

The Court went on to dismiss the third counterargument, based on a need to safeguard the effectiveness of fiscal supervision. As shown regarding grounds of justification, national authorities can require a taxpayer to provide such proof as they consider necessary to determine whether the conditions for deducting expenses had been met. However, the mere fact that the taxing authorities might be faced with administrative disadvantages could not justify a blanket refusal to grant taxpayers advantages which they could obtain in respect of gifts to national bodies of the same kind. The Court also held that Germany could not exclude the grant of tax advantages for gifts made to a body established and recognized as charitable in Portugal purely because, in relation to such bodies, the German tax authorities were unable to check, on the spot, compliance with requirements imposed by their tax legislation. Even in relation to national charitable bodies, an on-the-spot inspection was not usually required. Moreover, the provision of information in the framework of mutual assistance between tax administrations under Directive 2011/16 would normally suffice to check that the recipient body fulfilled the conditions imposed by German legislation.

On that final point, the Court distinguished the situation of charitable bodies in third countries, because non-member countries are not under any international obligation to provide information. It was therefore as a rule legitimate for the Member State of taxation to refuse to grant such a tax advantage to charitable bodies in a third country.[108]

THE *WONINGSTICHTING SINT SERVATIUS* RULING

In 2011, the Court moved on in *Woningstichting Sint Servatius*[109] to deal with how a Member State organizes delivery of a social service. The Dutch Constitution requires the government to promote adequate housing. Dutch law creates a system of housing associations which are non-profit-making, must operate exclusively in the public housing sector and in a designated geographical area, and are answerable to the minister. The minister has the power to authorize housing associations to construct experimental projects which she believes to be in the

[108] The Court has also explored the questions of tax breaks for private funding of charities and of activities in the public interest in other recent cases: compare the ruling in *Persche* with Case C-25/10 *Missionswerk Werner Heuchelbach* [2011] ECR I-497 and Case C-10/10 *Commission v Austria* (*'University donations'*) [2011] ECR I-5389.

[109] Case C-567/07 [2009] ECR I-9021.

interests of public housing, even where that would depart from the general regime governing such associations. Servatius was an approved association operating in the Maastricht area; it sought to build housing as part of a mixed-use development (commercial, rented dwellings, owner-occupied, parking) in Liège, some 30 km from the Dutch border, and was prepared to use some of the funds it had obtained at favourable rates because of its status as an approved association. Servatius sought the minister's permission to carry out that project. The minister refused to approve it on the basis of the project's location in Belgium. As a climax to litigation in the national courts challenging that refusal, the Dutch Council of State referred a series of questions regarding, inter alia, free movement of capital to the Court.

In light of its long-standing case law on prior authorization systems for the purchase of real estate, the Court found that the requirement for those institutions to obtain prior authorization from the competent minister before investing in immovable property in other Member States constituted a restriction on the free movement of capital.[110] The Dutch authorities had either to bring the national legislation within the scope of one of the Treaty's exceptions or to justify the measure.

As to the claim that the promotion of social housing is covered by the notion of 'public policy' in Article 65 TFEU, the Court was brisk and to the point: even if housing associations fail to comply with their statutes and divert the funds they receive for other purposes, that behaviour cannot amount to a genuine and sufficiently serious threat to a fundamental interest of society. On the other hand, the Court was quite willing to accept that requirements related to public housing policy in a Member State and to the financing of that policy could constitute overriding reasons in the public interest and therefore justify the restriction at issue.[111] Indeed, apart from the inherent importance of that policy for any Member State, specific features of the Dutch housing market reinforced the significance of the ground invoked, namely a structural shortage of accommodation and a particularly high population density.[112] As ever, once a legitimate ground of justification has been raised to defend a national rule that restricts free movement of capital, the decisive question is whether the measure is proportionate. The Court left that issue to the national court.[113]

THE *HUIJBRECHTS* RULING

A final example of a Member State using tax rules to encourage public interest activities, and how those practices interact with free movement of capital, is the *Huijbrechts* ruling.[114] Belgian law gave a tax advantage (an exemption from inheritance tax) for inherited woodland on condition that the wooded area was subject to a 'sustainable management plan', but only if the area in question was in Belgium. Mr Huijbrechts inherited woodland in the Netherlands from a Belgian taxpayer, and sought to have his inheritance exempted from tax. On a reference, the Court held that the goal of protecting the environment could not justify the restriction on capital created by the requirement for the woodland to be in Belgium. The limitation meant that the Belgian rule was not appropriate, because sustainable management

[110] Ibid, paras 22–24.

[111] See also Joined Cases C-197/11 and C-203/11 *Libert and others*, EU:C:2013:288, para 52.

[112] *Woningstichting Sint Servatius* (n 109) para 30.

[113] A comparable approach was taken by the Court to a similar social service, the provision of pensions and severance payments, in *Polish OPFs* (see Case C-271/09 *Commission v Poland*, EU:C:2011:855, para 75) and *VBV—Vorsorgekasse* (see Case C-39/11, EU:C:2012:327, para 31). Member States argued that they were guaranteeing the stability and security of assets managed by the funds responsible for those payments by requiring them to invest only in their home Member State. In both cases the Court found the rule was a restriction on free movement of capital and was sceptical about the claims that it could be justified.

[114] Case C-679/17 *Huijbrechts*, EU:C:2018:940.

of a wooded area situated on the adjoining territories of two Member States is a cross-border environmental issue not confined to the territory of one of them alone.

SUMMARY

Free movement of capital rules can severely limit what Member States traditionally thought of as their freedom in an area of particular sensitivity for local, regional, and national identity. First, free movement of capital constrains the choices which Member States can make where the providers are of social services financed through the tax system, whether by relieving them of fiscal burdens imposed on other taxpayers or by inducing taxpayers to make contributions directly to them. Secondly, at the other end of the financial cycle, the power of Member States to direct providers of those services to offer a wider or narrower range of services is also affected by free movement of capital.

7 Conclusion

The development of free movement of capital since it joined the ranks of the other internal market freedoms, after the Maastricht Treaty came into force, has seen the Court align it closely with those other freedoms. There has also been a significant increase in the extent to which it is litigated: in the period from 2008 to 2017, there were some 158 cases before the Court in which that freedom was invoked, compared with 77 cases in the preceding decade, while there have been 88 additional such cases in the past five years. Moreover, because of its role in EMU, which involves a different and deeper level of integration among the Member States than the creation of the internal market, and because of its special role as regards non-member countries, the free movement of capital will always be particularly sensitive.

Further reading

L Flynn, 'Coming of Age: The Free Movement of Capital Case Law 1993–2002' (2002) 39 *Common Market Law Review* 773

S Grundmann and F Möslein, 'Golden Shares—State Control in Privatised Companies: Comparative Law, European Law and Policy Aspects' [2004] 1 *Euredia* 623

S Peers, 'Free Movement of Capital: Learning Lessons or Slipping on Spilt Milk?' in C Barnard and J Scott (eds), *The Law of the Single European Market: Unpacking the Premises* (Oxford: Hart Publishing, 2002)

J Snell, 'Non-Discriminatory Tax Obstacles in Community Law' (2007) 56 *International and Comparative Law Quarterly* 339

J Usher, *The Law of Money and Financial Services in the European Community* (2nd edn, Oxford: Oxford University Press, 2000)

Chapter acknowledgements

Leo Flynn is an Official of the European Commission. The views expressed in this text are personal.

16

Exceptions to the free movement rules

Niamh Nic Shuibhne

1 Introduction

The free movement rights conferred on natural and legal persons are at the heart of both Union citizenship and the internal market. However, these rights are not absolute. Freedom of movement is a core Union objective, but it is recognized that other interests and values should sometimes take precedence. This means that, in certain circumstances, free movement rights can be restricted in compliance with EU law if (a) for discriminatory (distinctly applicable) restrictions, a derogation ground expressly provided for in the Treaties can be engaged; (b) for indirectly or non-discriminatory (indistinctly applicable) restrictions, a legitimate objective in the public interest that is capable of justifying a restriction of the Treaty freedoms can be established; and (c) in both cases, the restriction also satisfies a proportionality test, being demonstrated to be both appropriate and necessary for achieving the relevant objective.

This chapter explores derogation, justification, and proportionality. It asks when Member States can lawfully displace the obligations placed on them by the Treaty requirements on freedom of movement. The approach taken is to explain how the derogation and justification systems work by exploring the principles that underpin their application, rather than to examine various public interest grounds in a substantive sense.[1] The chapter also outlines the specific rules that apply to derogations from the free movement of persons, which are underpinned by the status of Union citizenship and codified in EU legislation.

[1] For comprehensive discussion of the different grounds of public interest, see C Barnard, *The Substantive Law of the EU: The Four Freedoms* (8th edn, Oxford: Oxford University Press, 2025) chs 5 and 11.

The topic of exceptions to the Treaty's free movement rules reflects an important theme that shapes much of EU law: how to balance the acknowledged need for common citizenship and internal market standards that apply uniformly in all Member States, on the one hand, with appropriate recognition of national regulatory diversity and the limits of Union competence, on the other. A secondary theme is that while the frameworks applicable to derogation and justification can, at one level, be presented in a relatively systematic way, there is inevitable inconsistency with respect to their application in case law practice.

2 The Treaty framework: derogations

Following a brief overview of the role and purpose of derogation in free movement law, and of the broader Treaty framework that shapes these questions, this section then outlines the express derogation grounds provided for in the Treaty.

2.1 The role of derogation and the broader legal framework

The EU Treaties establish a complex system in which many objectives, interests, and values are accommodated, but then need to be balanced against each other. For example, Article 3(3) TEU provides that 'The Union shall establish an internal market.' But it goes on to list a series of other tasks and objectives: sustainable development, balanced economic growth and price stability, a highly competitive social market economy, full employment, social progress, protection and improvement of the quality of the environment, equality between women and men, protection of the rights of the child, and respect for cultural and linguistic diversity. Similarly, while Article 4(2) TEU requires that 'competences not conferred upon the Union in the Treaties remain with the Member States' and that the Union 'shall respect the equality of Member States . . . as well as their national identities', Article 4(2) TFEU confirms that the internal market is an area for which regulatory competence between the Union and the Member States is shared.

The fact that States can legitimately restrict free movement rights in certain circumstances—on the basis that another interest should take precedence over free movement objectives—is one expression of the resulting regulatory balance.[2] An important challenge for the Court of Justice is to ensure the achievement of effective market integration while enabling more localized regulatory diversity that reflects the constitutional mandate of shared EU/Member State competence.[3]

To resolve disputes connected to freedom of movement, the Court of Justice addresses three distinct questions:

(a) Is there a *restriction* of the free movement rights guaranteed by the Treaty?

(b) If there is, can it be *justified*?

(c) If it can, is it *proportionate*?

It has been shown in several chapters of this book that it is not difficult to establish an actual or potential restriction of free movement rights within the meaning of the Treaty. For example, in *CaixaBank*, the Court defined restrictions on freedom of establishment

[2] AG Bot expressed it in this way in Case C-141/07 *Commission v Germany*, EU:C:2008:218: 'The rules surrounding the exercise of [a Member State's] reserved powers mean that if its legislation causes a restriction of one of the fundamental freedoms of movement it must be in a position to provide a legitimate reason . . . to justify this' (para 83 of the Opinion). [3] See also chapter 11.

as 'All measures which prohibit, impede or render less attractive the exercise of that freedom.'[4] A national measure that satisfies this definition must be disapplied unless it can be shown that the measure is justifiable and proportionate. However, even an overtly discriminatory restriction of free movement can be 'saved' if a Member State can demonstrate that there is a good—that is, justifiable and proportionate within the limits of EU law—reason for it.

2.2 **Derogation and EU legislation**

Where EU legislation establishes harmonized regulatory standards, no derogation is permitted unless expressly provided for in the legislation itself. The basic rule is that 'A national measure in a sphere which has been the subject of exhaustive harmonisation at [Union] level must be assessed in the light of the provisions of the harmonising measure and not those of the Treaty.'[5] This means that any permitted derogations will need to be accommodated within the legislation from the outset. EU legislation can provide for (a) a general derogation clause, empowering the Commission to examine, on a case-by-case basis, difficulties that a Member State might encounter when implementing the measure and to permit that State to derogate from the relevant obligation for a specified period; or (b) specific derogation clauses, establishing a particular exception for a Member State vis-à-vis part of the measure's requirements. Examples of both mechanisms can be found in Directive 2005/36/EC, which regulates the recognition of professional qualifications in order to facilitate freedom of establishment and the provision of cross-border professional services.[6]

Article 114 TFEU, the legal basis used for most internal market harmonization measures, establishes a post-adoption derogation procedure on grounds of either the objectives specified in Article 36 TFEU (see section 2.3) or the protection of the environment or the working environment.[7] Legislation adopted during the Covid-19 pandemic provides an example of entire measures focused on limiting free movement to protect public health.[8]

Where EU legislation provides for minimum harmonization, States remain free, in principle, to adopt more stringent standards to protect the public interest at national level. In the classic language of minimum harmonization, the standards prescribed by Union legislation constitute only the 'floor', that is, the threshold that national measures must implement and respect. However, following the first *Tobacco Advertising* case,[9] EU minimum harmonization measures must include a free movement clause too. In the revised version of the Tobacco Advertising Directive[10]—adopted after the Court of Justice annulled the original measure—Article 8 provides that 'Member States shall not prohibit

[4] Case C-442/02 *CaixaBank France v Ministère de l'Économie, des Finances et de l'Industrie*, EU:C:2004:586, para 11.

[5] Case C-322/01 *Deutscher Apothekerverband eV v 0800 DocMorris NV and Jacques Waterval*, EU:C:2003:664, para 64.

[6] Directive 2005/36/EC of 7 September 2005 on the recognition of professional qualifications (OJ [2005] L255/22); Art 61 of the Directive is the general derogation clause; for a specific derogation clause, see eg Art 33(a).

[7] See Art 114(4) and (5) TFEU.

[8] eg with Art 21 TFEU as the legal basis, Regulation 2021/953/EU on a framework for the issuance, verification and acceptance of interoperable COVID-19 vaccination, test and recovery certificates (EU Digital COVID Certificate) to facilitate free movement during the COVID-19 pandemic (OJ [2021] L211/1).

[9] Case C-376/98 *Germany v Parliament and Council*, EU:C:2000:544.

[10] Directive 2003/33/EC of 26 May 2003 on the approximation of the laws, regulations, and administrative provisions of the Member States relating to the advertising and sponsorship of tobacco products (OJ [2003] L152/16).

or restrict the free movement of products or services which comply with this Directive.' In such circumstances, national measures going beyond the standards mandated by the Directive can still be tested against the derogation and justification framework established by the Treaty and the case law. Thus, while EU legislation marks the 'floor' for public interest protection, the Treaty represents the 'ceiling' for national regulatory discretion.

However, for most areas of free movement law, the question of derogation normally arises when there is no relevant Union legislation in the first place, that is, in the context of negative integration.[11] In such situations, national measures are tested against the limits built into the Treaty freedoms or, in the absence of direct discrimination, within the justification framework developed by the Court of Justice.

2.3 **Treaty-based derogation grounds**

The derogation grounds in the Treaty can be used to defend State action taken for a variety of public interest reasons protected as Union concerns, as Table 16.1 shows.

As these provisions demonstrate, the Treaty freedoms may be derogated from for reasons connected to, broadly speaking, public policy, public security, or public health. The protection of public health is the Treaty-based derogation raised most frequently in case law on free movement restrictions, especially for the free movement of goods. The Court considers that 'the health and life of humans rank foremost among the assets and interests protected by the Treaty'.[12] In recognition of that special position, it also acknowledges that:

> it is for the Member States to determine the level of protection which they wish to afford to public health and the way in which that level is to be achieved. Since the level may vary from one Member State to another, Member States must be allowed discretion.[13]

There is some variation of approach to derogation across the freedoms, with a more extended list of grounds for Article 36 TFEU and also for the free movement of capital. Article 36 TFEU further requires that 'Such prohibitions or restrictions shall not . . . constitute a means of *arbitrary discrimination* or a *disguised restriction* on trade between Member States.'[14] This proviso means that derogation arguments will not normally be accepted if the State has not placed comparable restrictions on goods produced domestically.[15] Although the proviso in Article 36 TFEU is not expressly part of the derogation provisions for other Treaty freedoms, the underlying principle is more generally applicable.[16]

[11] This point has been expressed by the Court as the precondition that 'there are no [Union] harmonising measures providing for measures necessary to ensure the protection of [the relevant] interests' (Case C-112/05 *Commission v Germany*, EU:C:2007:623, para 72).

[12] Case C-171/07 *Apothekerkammer des Saarlandes*, EU:C:2009:316, para 19. See further chapter 12.

[13] Ibid. For an example of public health concerns that potentially permitted a discriminatory restriction on free movement rights, see eg Case C-73/08 *Bressol and Chaverot v Gouvernement de la Communauté française*, EU:C:2010:181.

[14] Emphasis added. See similarly, Art 65(3) TFEU: 'The measures and procedures referred to in paras 1 and 2 shall not constitute a means of arbitrary discrimination or a disguised restriction on the free movement of capital and payments as defined in Article 63.'

[15] eg in the context of arguments based on public morality, compare Case 121/85 *Conegate Ltd v HM Customs & Excise*, EU:C:1986:114, where a prohibition on certain imported goods was not matched by a prohibition on their domestic manufacture, with the earlier case of Case 34/79 *R v Henn and Darby*, EU:C:1979:295.

[16] On the absence of comparable restrictions placed on nationals in the sphere of freedom of establishment, see eg Case 115/81 *Adoui and Cornuaille v Belgian State and City of Liège*, EU:C:1982:183.

Table 16.1 Summary of Treaty derogations for the four freedoms

Treaty: rights	Treaty: derogation	Grounds
Article 21 TFEU *Citizenship*: movement/ residence rights	*Article 21 TFEU*	'limitations and conditions laid down in the Treaties and by the measures adopted to give them effect'
Articles 34 and 35 TFEU *Goods*: quantitative restrictions on imports/exports	*Article 36 TFEU*	'public morality, public policy or public security; the protection of health and life of humans, animals or plants; the protection of national treasures possessing artistic, historic or archaeological value; or the protection of industrial and commercial property'
Article 45 TFEU *Workers*	*Article 45(3) TFEU*	'limitations justified on grounds of public policy, public security or public health'
	Article 45(4) TFEU	'employment in the public service'
Article 49 TFEU	*Article 51 TFEU*	'exercise of official authority'
Establishment	*Article 52 TFEU*	'grounds of public policy, public security or public health'
Article 56 TFEU *Services*	*Article 62 TFEU*	Article 52 TFEU grounds ie 'public policy, public security or public health'
Article 63 TFEU *Capital*	*Article 65 TFEU*	'exercise of official authority'; 'public policy or public security' plus taxation and 'prudential supervision of financial institutions'

Article 30 TFEU provides that 'Customs duties on imports and exports and charges having equivalent effect shall be prohibited between Member States. This prohibition shall also apply to customs duties of a fiscal nature.' Exceptionally, no corresponding derogation grounds are provided for in the Treaty. A charge that is imposed purely because goods have crossed a frontier will fall outside the scope of Article 30 only in very limited circumstances established through case law:

> such a charge escapes that classification if it relates to a general system of internal dues applied systematically and in accordance with the same criteria to domestic products and imported products alike, if it constitutes payment for a service in fact rendered to the economic operator of a sum in proportion to the service, or again, subject to certain conditions, if it attaches to inspections carried out to fulfil obligations imposed by [Union] law.[17]

[17] Case C-389/00 *Commission v Germany*, EU:C:2003:111, para 23 (confirming Case 18/87 *Commission v Germany*, EU:C:1988:453, para 6); for further discussion these exceptions, see Barnard, *The Substantive Law of the EU* (n 1) ch 2.

The concept of public policy might be construed as a generic notion that could offer considerable leeway to Member States. However, the Court of Justice has interpreted its scope very strictly in practice.[18] This narrow approach was of particular importance before the Court had fully developed the broader justification framework (outlined in section 3) that goes beyond the public interest grounds in the Treaty. In early case law, States sought recognition of public interest concerns, such as protection of the environment or consumers, which were simply not recognized as important public interest grounds by the Treaty's drafters in the 1950s. However, the Court declined to expand the concept of public policy to include emerging public interest considerations.[19]

How restrictions on the movement and residence rights of EU citizens may be limited is distinctive, in the sense that such rights are subject not only to the derogation grounds listed in the Treaty (ie public policy, public security, or public health) but also to 'measures adopted' to give effect to the Treaty, that is, to limits established in secondary legislation. The way in which Articles 20 and 21 TFEU are constructed thus marks an exception to the idea that secondary law cannot take priority over primary law. This point becomes particularly important for the discussion in section 6, which focuses on the provisions of Directive 2004/38/EC on the free movement of Union citizens and their family members that govern expulsion decisions.[20]

Additionally, Article 45(4) TFEU provides that 'The provisions of this Article shall not apply to employment in the public service.' Similarly, for freedom of establishment (and also, through Article 62 TFEU, freedom to provide services), Article 51 TFEU states that 'The provisions of this Chapter shall not apply, so far as any given Member State is concerned, to activities which in that State are connected, even occasionally, with the exercise of official authority.' Again, however, the Court curtailed the potential breadth of both exclusions. The scope of 'employment in the public service' has been interpreted to mean only:

> posts which involve direct or indirect participation in the exercise of powers conferred by public law and duties designed to safeguard the general interests of the State or of other public authorities and thus presume on the part of those occupying them the existence of a special relationship of allegiance to the State and reciprocity of rights and duties which form the foundation of the bond of nationality.[21]

Similarly, the 'exercise of official authority' as it relates to establishment and services 'must be restricted to activities which in themselves are *directly and specifically* connected with the exercise of official authority' and, conversely, 'does not extend to certain activities that are auxiliary or preparatory' in that context.[22]

The Court has rationalized its narrow interpretative approach on the basis that these concepts set exceptions to the 'fundamental character' of free movement rights and, as such, they 'cannot be given a scope which would exceed the objective' for which they were included in the Treaty in the first place.[23]

[18] Case 231/83 *Cullet v Centre Leclerc*, EU:C:1985:29, para 30.

[19] See eg Case 177/83 *Kohl KG v Ringelhan & Rennett SA and Ringelhan Einrichtungs GmbH*, EU:C:1984:334, on consumer protection.

[20] OJ [2004] L158/77.

[21] Case C-405/01 *Colegio de Oficiales de la Marina Mercante Española v Administración del Estado*, EU:C:2003:515, para 39 (confirming Case 149/79 *Commission v Belgium*, EU:C:1982:195, para 10).

[22] Case C-61/08 *Commission v Greece*, EU:C:2011:340, paras 77 and 78 (emphasis added).

[23] Case 2/74 *Reyners v Belgian State*, EU:C:1974:68, para 43.

3 The justification framework: public interest requirements

As explained in previous chapters, restrictions on free movement rights can be (a) directly discriminatory on the grounds of nationality (ie discriminatory in law), (b) indirectly discriminatory (ie not discriminatory in law, but discriminatory in result or effect), or (c) non-discriminatory (ie not discriminatory in law or in effect, but still restrictive of free movement).

Section 2 introduced the basic rule for derogation from free movement: directly discriminatory restrictions can be defended *only* by recourse to the grounds provided for expressly in the Treaty. However, to defend indirectly discriminatory and non-discriminatory—that is, indistinctly applicable—restrictions of free movement, States can raise virtually any public interest argument that they wish, without being confined to policy objectives predetermined by the Treaty's derogation provisions. Their arguments may not be successful; but the critical point is that there are few subject matter limitations on the kinds of public interest concerns that States can assert when they seek to justify the retention of national rules or practices that restrict free movement. This open-ended justification framework will now be outlined in more detail, followed by consideration of whether the distinction between discriminatory and other types of restriction still holds. Other limits that constrain the scope of State discretion—for example, that arguments based on economic rationales are normally not permitted—are then discussed in section 4.

3.1 From 'mandatory requirements' to 'overriding requirements in the public interest'

To defend indistinctly applicable national measures, Member States can submit justification arguments based on any public interest grounds that they consider to be relevant. This open-ended justification route could be glimpsed in early free movement case law.[24] It was more substantively developed as the doctrine of 'mandatory requirements' for Article 34 TFEU in *Cassis de Dijon*.[25] In that case, the Court considered that:

> Obstacles to movement within the [Union] resulting from disparities between the national laws relating to the marketing of the products in question must be accepted in so far as those provisions may be recognized as ***being necessary in order to satisfy mandatory requirements*** relating ***in particular*** to the effectiveness of fiscal supervision, the protection of public health, the fairness of commercial transactions and the defence of the consumer.[26]

In this way, the Court accommodated genuine policy concerns that were not relevant or prominent when the Treaty of Rome was drafted, such as the protection of consumers (and, in subsequent cases, protection of the environment[27]) without the need for Treaty amendment to expand the express derogations. The rather awkward concept of 'mandatory requirements' is rarely used in case law anymore. Instead, the Court advises that

[24] Case 33/74 *Van Binsbergen v Bestuur van de Bedrijfsvereniging voor de Metaalnijverheid*, EU:C:1974:131, para 12: 'specific requirements imposed on the person providing the service cannot be considered incompatible with the Treaty where they have as their purpose the application of professional rules *justified by the general good*' (emphasis added).

[25] Case 120/78 *Rewe-Zentrale AG v Bundesmonopolverwaltung für Branntwein* ('*Cassis de Dijon*'), EU:C:1979:42.

[26] Ibid, para 8 (emphasis added).

[27] Case 302/86 *Commission v Denmark* [1985] ECR 4607.

[28] Case C-110/05 *Commission v Italy* ('*Trailers*'), EU:C:2009:66, para 59.

national measures may be justified 'in order to meet imperative requirements'[28] or by 'overriding reasons in the public interest capable of justifying restrictions on the fundamental freedoms guaranteed by the Treaty'.[29] The ruling in *Gebhard*, which concerned the dividing line between freedom of establishment and provision of services, articulates a classic statement of the restriction/justification formula that operates across the different sectors of free movement law:

> national measures liable to hinder or make less attractive the exercise of fundamental freedoms guaranteed by the Treaty must fulfil four conditions: they must be applied in a non discriminatory manner; they must be justified by imperative requirements in the general interest; they must be suitable for securing the attainment of the objective which they pursue; and they must not go beyond what is necessary in order to attain it.[30]

Some examples of the numerous public interest justification grounds that the Court has recognized in principle include:

- combating drug tourism;[31]
- combating criminality linked to betting and gambling;[32]
- ensuring road safety;[33]
- maintaining press diversity;[34]
- protecting the recipients of legal services and the proper administration of justice;[35]
- protecting national or regional socio-cultural characteristics;[36]
- ensuring the effective collection of tax;[37]
- promoting the use of renewable energy sources;[38]
- protecting workers and encouraging employment.[39]

The justification framework is not premised on public interest concerns protected as Union interests in the same way as the Treaty-set grounds for derogation (considered in section 4). Rather, it has stronger potential to recognize more national or local understandings of, and concerns related to, the public interest. Through the logic of public interest justification, the Court has created, in other words, a merits-based system where national concerns can be examined and evaluated on a case-by-case basis. The Court's assessment of the public interest can evolve over time, in tune with how conceptions of public interest evolve generally.[40] It has acknowledged that certain justification arguments overlap with

[29] Case C-384/08 *Attanasio Group Srl v Comune di Carbognano*, EU:C:2010:133, para 50.

[30] Case C-55/94 *Gebhard v Consiglio dell'Ordine degli Avvocati e Procuratori di Milano*, EU:C:1995:411, para 37.

[31] eg Case C-137/09 *Josemans v Burgemeester van Maastricht*, EU:C:2010:774, para 82.

[32] eg Case C-375/14 *Laezza*, EU:C:2016:60, para 32.

[33] eg Case C-55/93 *Criminal Proceedings against van Schaik*, EU:C:1994:363, para 19.

[34] eg Case C-368/95 *Vereinigte Familiapress Zeitungsverlags—und vertriebs GmbH v Heinrich Bauer Verlag*, EU:C:1997:325, para 26.

[35] eg Case C-807/23 *Plavec v Rechtsanwaltskammer Wien*, EU:C:2025:234, para 36.

[36] eg Case C-169/91 *Council of the City of Stoke-on-Trent and Norwich City Council v B&Q plc*, EU:C:1992:519, para 11.

[37] eg Case C-83/21 *Airbnb Ireland and Airbnb Payments UK*, EU:C:2022:1018, para 63.

[38] eg Case C-573/12 *Ålands Vindkraft AB v Energimyndigheten*, EU:C:2014:2037, para 82.

[39] eg Case C-201/15 *AGET Iraklis*, EU:C:2016:972, paras 74–75.

[40] eg Case C-244/06 *Dynamic Medien*, EU:C:2008:85, para 44.

[41] eg on protection of a State's official language, see Case C-391/09 *Runevič-Vardyn and Wardyn*, EU:C:2011:291, para 86; Case C-202/11 *Las*, EU:C:2013:239, para 26.

respect for a State's national identity, as provided for in Article 4(2) TFEU.[41] The Court has also confirmed that national measures protecting fundamental rights can constitute valid justification grounds, as discussed in more detail in section 4.4.1.

The development of the justification framework is also, of course, a striking example of the Court's significant law-shaping powers in the field of free movement, since it has, in effect, recognized significantly more public interest grounds than the limited categories in the Treaty. On the other hand, the Member States have never stepped in to regain constitutional ownership of the issue through Treaty amendment since *Cassis de Dijon* and it is arguable that there is implicit (but nonetheless legitimizing) political acceptance of the Court's approach for that reason.

At one level, the flexibility extended to Member States through the combination of Treaty derogation and case law justification is remarkable. They can raise even the most singular, local, or esoteric, but nonetheless genuine, public interest arguments without the need to shoehorn their concerns artificially into the limited grounds in the Treaty; as we see below, the Court has insisted that the meaning of 'public policy' in the Treaty must be interpreted very narrowly on its own terms. However, while States may *submit* a greater number of justification arguments in principle, this does not mean that they have had notable success in restricting free movement rights in reality.[42] This point highlights the importance of both the standard of proof that Member States must reach when shaping their arguments and the principle of proportionality, considered in sections 4 and 5 respectively.

3.2 **Does the distinction between discriminatory and non-discriminatory restrictions still matter?**

Formally, the distinction introduced in section 1 still stands: directly discriminatory restrictions cannot be justified for reasons other than the derogation grounds specified expressly in the Treaty (see Fig. 13.1). However, it is increasingly difficult to sustain the reliability of that distinction by reference to case law practice. For example, in *Petruhhin*, the relevant national rules established protection against extradition for home State nationals only (ie a directly discriminatory rule). Nevertheless, the Court stated that such a restriction of Article 21 TFEU could be justified 'where it is based on objective considerations and is proportionate to the legitimate objective of the national provisions'.[43]

Initially, a particular point of strain emerged when States sought to justify directly discriminatory restrictions of free movement on grounds of environmental protection. In such cases, the Court endeavoured, not altogether convincingly, to classify the national measure as non-discriminatory (or indistinctly applicable)[44] to enable the defendant State's arguments based on the public interest requirement of environmental protection to be heard. Attention has been drawn to the confusing case law that developed in consequence,[45] since the Court neither explicitly confirmed that the justification framework

[42] See eg the comparative study of relevant judgments from 1984, 1994, and 2004 in C Barnard, 'Derogations, Justifications and the Four Freedoms: Is State Interest Really Protected?' in C Barnard and O Odudu (eds), *The Outer Limits of European Union Law* (Oxford: Hart Publishing, 2009) 295.

[43] Case C-182/15 *Petruhhin v Latvijas Republikas Generālprokuratūra*, EU:C:2016:630, para 34.

[44] See esp Case C-2/90 *Commission v Belgium* ('*Walloon waste*'), EU:C:1992:310. In Case C-28/09 *Commission v Austria* ('*Brenner II*'), AG Trstenjak described the Court's approach in *Walloon waste* as 'work[ing] around' the rule on discriminatory restrictions and Treaty-based derogations (EU:C:2010:770, fn 34 of the Opinion).

[45] See AG Jacobs in Case C-379/98 *PreussenElektra AG v Schhleswag AG, in the presence of Windpark Reußenköge III GmbH and Land Schleswig-Holstein*, EU:C:2000:585, paras 222–238 of the Opinion; AG Trstenjak in *Brenner II* (n 44) paras 79–91 of the Opinion.

can also be applied to save directly discriminatory measures nor clarified the basis on which such a step might be taken. It has never, for example, reversed the narrow interpretation applied to public policy in a way that would enable protection of the environment to fit within it.

In more recent case law, the Court has continued to circumvent the issue by sidestepping the nature of the restriction at issue and avoiding the language of discrimination altogether. In *Commission v Austria* ('*Brenner II*'),[46] the Court was asked to review a ban that precluded vehicles weighing over 7.5 tonnes from carrying certain goods, affecting a motorway route with significant implications for transalpine traffic. Even though the Commission had argued that the measure was discriminatory, the judgment of the Grand Chamber stated very briefly that the contested national rule was a measure having equivalent effect to a quantitative restriction and was therefore precluded by Article 34 TFEU—with no discussion at all of what *kind* of restriction this actually was. In contrast, the exclusion of local and regional traffic from the scope of the ban informed the Commission's classification of the measure as discriminatory.[47]

There are also several examples of public interest requirements other than environmental protection being considered in cases that involve distinctly applicable restrictions of free movement. The issue is no longer, in other words, confined to the potentially special nature of environmental protection. In *Commission v Finland*,[48] the Court found that 'it is clear from settled case-law that national legislation which constitutes a measure having equivalent effect to quantitative restrictions can be justified by one of the reasons of public interest laid down in Article [36 TFEU] *or by imperative requirements*'[49]—even though the contested procedural requirements were imposed on imported cars only. Similarly, in *Fachverband der Buch—und Medienwirtschaft*, concerning pricing restrictions imposed only on imported books, the Court first confirmed the narrow scope of 'protection of national treasures possessing artistic, historic or archaeological value' in Article 36 TFEU; but then stated that 'the protection of books as cultural objects can be considered as an overriding requirement in the public interest capable of justifying measures restricting the free movement of goods'.[50] Neither is the issue confined to the free movement of goods.[51]

Even in the early stages of this confusing case law, Advocate General Jacobs had already highlighted the weakening distinction between derogation grounds and the broader justification framework established by case law. In *PreussenElektra*, concerning restrictions on the free movement of goods, he noted, first, that the Court had 'not formally abandoned the rule that imperative requirements cannot be invoked in connection with directly

[46] Case C-28/09, EU:C:2011:854.

[47] Even more strikingly, the Court stated in *Austria v Germany* that, with reference to Art 18 TFEU, 'the protection of the environment constitutes a legitimate objective for the purposes of justifying a difference in treatment on ground of nationality' (Case C-591/17, EU:C:2019:504, para 75). However, when discussing the contested national measure as a breach of Art 34 TFEU specifically, the Court framed the issue in terms of indirect discrimination and restrictions on market access (paras 120–132).

[48] Case C-54/05, EU:C:2007:168. [49] Ibid, para 38 (emphasis added).

[50] Case C-531/07 *Fachverband der Buch—und Medienwirtschaft v LIBRO Handelsgesellschaft mbH*, EU:C:2009:276, paras 32–34.

[51] eg outlining the varied approaches in case law on national restrictions placed on gambling, affecting freedom to provide services, see AG Mengozzi in Case C-153/08 *Commission v Spain*, EU:C:2009:472, paras 77–81 of the Opinion. In another example, relating to Arts 21 and 49 TFEU, in Case C-524/06 *Huber v Bundesrepublik Deutschland*, EU:C:2008:724, a case concerning aspects of a data processing system that applied only to nationals of other Member States, the Court considered the objective of fighting crime as an element of protecting public order; but it did not discuss that objective in the Treaty-set language of public policy or public security.

discriminatory measures' but also, secondly, that 'In view of the fundamental importance for the analysis of Article [36] of the Treaty of the question whether directly discriminatory measures can be justified by imperative requirements, the Court should, in my view, clarify its position in order to provide the necessary legal certainty.'[52] Weatherill has argued that 'There is strong normative appeal to a model whereby all types of justification are in principle available, but according to which the presence of discrimination would make the job of the regulator in showing that the chosen scheme is lawful particularly onerous.'[53] Similarly, in *Brenner II*, Advocate General Trstenjak supported 'in principle' the idea that protection of the environment (at least) should be available as an overriding reason in the public interest to justify discriminatory measures 'under any circumstances'.[54] She suggested that 'the discriminatory character of a measure restricting the free movement of trade can be taken into account in a proportionality test in which the necessity and reasonableness of such measures in particular can be examined more closely'.[55]

If the Court were to reverse the convention that the justification of directly discriminatory measures is confined to the grounds provided for in the Treaty—whether for protection of the environment only or, as suggested by its case law, for any public interest requirements on a case-by-case basis—it would result in a merits-based justification framework across the board. This would, in turn, obviate the need for the Court to distinguish between *types* of discrimination, which is not always a straightforward exercise.[56] Nevertheless, to collapse the distinction between derogation and justification more definitively would challenge the significance of having a limited pool of public interest grounds stipulated in the Treaty in the first place. It would also simply push many of the complexities that we encounter in free movement law to the third stage of analysis, that is, the determination of proportionality—a stage of review that is not free from complexity or controversy on its own terms, as discussed further in section 5.

4 Application of the derogation and justification frameworks

For both Treaty-based derogation and case law-driven justification, this section addresses the Court's general approach to, and role in, the determination of public interest (section 4.1); the relevant burden and standard of proof (section 4.2); and specific issues relating to the justification of free movement restrictions based on the protection of fundamental rights (section 4.3).

4.1 General principles

4.1.1 Conceptualizing exceptions in free movement law

Derogation and justification arguments seek to establish an exception to the free movement rights guaranteed by the Treaty. In section 2, it was seen that the Court generally interprets Treaty rights widely and defines any exceptions to them as narrowly as possible, having regard to the 'fundamental character' of the Treaty freedoms. On the other hand,

52 AG Jacobs in *PreussenElektra* (n 45) paras 228 and 229 of the Opinion.

53 S Weatherill, 'Free Movement of Goods' (2012) 61 *International and Comparative Law Quarterly* 541, 544.

54 AG Trstenjak in *Brenner II* (n 44) paras 83 and 89 of the Opinion respectively.

55 Ibid, para 90.

56 On this point, see AG Sharpston in *Bressol and Chaverot* (n 13) paras 43–76 of the Opinion (EU:C:2009:396). The Commission raised the same question in Case C-308/14 *Commission v UK*, EU:C:2016:436 (see para 23 of the Opinion of AG Cruz Villalón, EU:C:2015:666) but the point was not addressed by the Court.

we saw in section 3 that the justification framework has evolved and expanded over time. Adjudication of the extent to which public interest arguments can supersede free movement rights therefore constitutes a prime space within which debates about the character of the internal market, and about the EU more broadly, are aired and progressed.

The Court rarely excludes issues from the scope of the Treaty at the stage of establishing a restriction of free movement rights because of the subject matter involved.[57] Instead, it navigates moral and other complexities at the stages of justification and proportionality. For example, the Court's softer approach to proportionality review in cases involving national restrictions on gambling is usually connected to the moral sensitivities associated with this activity, which clearly differ across the Member States.[58] This point is explained in more detail in section 5, in the context of proportionality review.

A similarly generous approach, emphasizing that discretion should be allocated to the Member States in determining the measures that need to be put in place to ensure the effective protection of the public interest, can be seen in the *Trailers* case. Here, the Court considered that the contested national rules, which restricted the use of goods, were justified on the ground of road safety and proportionate to the achievement of that objective, against the views of two Advocates General.[59] In its judgment, however, the Court also widened the scope of Article 34 TFEU to catch non-discriminatory restrictions, which suggests that the Court's 'margin of appreciation' approach to justification and proportionality was in fact compensating for the greater number of national measures that would

Case study 16.1: Derogating on grounds of public health

When addressing the compatibility of national restrictions on the operation of pharmacies with the Treaty provisions on establishment and services, the Court held in *DocMorris* (section 2.2) that 'the health and life of humans rank foremost among the assets and interests protected by the Treaty and that it is for the Member States to determine the level of protection which they wish to afford to public health and the way in which that level is to be achieved. Since the level may vary from one Member State to another, Member States must be allowed discretion.'[60] That statement would appear to suggest a devolved regulatory space within which the Member States can determine and implement their own responses to public health concerns. In reality, however, the requirements of EU law are much more prescriptive and public health defences rarely succeed before the Court.

First, a State must demonstrate that any alleged risks to public health are genuine.[61] Where scientific data is relied upon, it must be 'the results of international scientific research' and the 'latest scientific data available at the date of the adoption of [the national] decision' in order for the State's arguments to be persuasive enough to merit a restriction of free move-

[57] eg Case C-159/90 *Society for the Protection of Unborn Children Ireland Ltd (SPUC) v Stephan Grogan*, EU:C:1991:378, para 21: 'medical termination of pregnancy, performed in accordance with the law of the State in which it is carried out, constitutes a service within the meaning of . . . the Treaty'; Case C-268/99 *Jany v Staatssecretaris van Justitie*, EU:C:2001:616, para 49: 'prostitution is a provision of services for remuneration which . . . falls within the concept of economic activities'. For an exception, when the activity in question was unlawful in *all* of the Member States, see *Josemans v Burgemeester van Maastricht* (n 31) para 41.

[58] eg F de Witte 'The Constitutional Quality of the Free Movement Provisions: Looking for Context in the Case Law on Article 56 TFEU' (2017) 42 *European Law Review* 313.

[59] cf the decision in *Trailers* (n 28) with the Opinions of AG Léger and AG Bot (EU:C:2006:646).

[60] *Apothekerkammer des Saarlandes* (n 12) para 19; confirmed in Case C-333/14 *Scotch Whisky Association*, EU:C:2015:845, para 35.

[61] eg Case 90/86 *Criminal Proceedings against Zoni*, EU:C:1988:403, para 13.

ment.[62] Where contested national legislation is not yet in force, a national court reviewing that legislation for compliance with EU free movement law 'must take into consideration any relevant information, evidence or other material of which it has knowledge [on the date on which it gives its ruling] under the conditions laid down by its national law', an assessment being 'all the more necessary in a situation . . . where there appears to be scientific uncertainty as to the actual effects of the measures provided for by the national legislation'.[63] The Court has acknowledged that:

> an assessment of the risk could reveal that scientific uncertainty persists as regards the existence or extent of real risks to human health. In such circumstances . . . a Member State may, in accordance with the precautionary principle, take protective measures without having to wait until the existence and gravity of those risks are fully demonstrated.[64]

But the Court also emphasized that 'the risk assessment cannot be based on purely hypothetical considerations'.[65]

Secondly, for natural persons, and reflecting the implications of—and the level of protection that attaches to—the status of Union citizens, restrictions of freedom of movement on the grounds of public health are strictly delimited by the requirements of Directive 2004/38/EC, Article 29 of which provides:

1. The only diseases justifying measures restricting freedom of movement shall be the diseases with epidemic potential as defined by the relevant instruments of the World Health Organization and other infectious diseases or contagious parasitic diseases if they are the subject of protection provisions applying to nationals of the host Member State.[66]
2. Diseases occurring after a three-month period from the date of arrival shall not constitute grounds for expulsion from the territory.
3. Where there are serious indications that it is necessary, Member States may, within three months of the date of arrival, require persons entitled to the right of residence to undergo, free of charge, a medical examination to certify that they are not suffering from any of the conditions referred to in paragraph 1. Such medical examinations may not be required as a matter of routine.

Finally, in the case law on access to health-care services, the Court has been willing to review aspects of the structure of national health-care systems—even though these kinds of national policy choices are closely connected to models of social solidarity and to the allocation of national financial resources, case law returned to in section 4.1.2.[67] This point links to the broader principle that 'whilst it is established that EU law respects the power of the Member States to organise their social security systems and that, in the absence of harmonisation at EU level, it is for the legislation of each Member State to determine the conditions for the grant of social security benefits, the fact nevertheless remains that, when exercising that power, Member States must comply with EU law'.[68]

[62] Case C-95/01 *Criminal Proceedings against Greenham and Abel*, EU:C:2004:71, paras 40 and 42.

[63] *Scotch Whisky Association* (n 60) paras 63–64.

[64] *Greenham and Abel* (n 62) para 43. [65] Ibid.

[66] Applying the requirments of the Directive in light of travel restrictions imposed at national level during the Covid-19 pandemic, see Case C-128/22 *Nordic Info BV v Belgische Staat*, EU:C:2023:951.

[67] eg Case C-158/96 *Kohll v Union des caisses de maladie*, EU:C:1998:171; Case C-368/98 *Vanbraekel v Alliance nationale des mutualités chrétiennes (ANMC)*, EU:C:2001:400; Case C-372/04 *Watts v Bedford Primary Care Trust and Secretary of State for Health*, EU:C:2006:325, paras 103 and 104.

[68] Case C-527/13 *Cachaldora Fernández*, EU:C:2015:215, para 25; confirming *Watts* (n 67) para 92.

[69] Case C-35/98 *Staatssecretaris van Financiën v BGM Verkooijen*, EU:C:2000:294, para 48.

now be caught by Article 34 TFEU in the first place. This example demonstrates the intricate connection between how restrictions are defined and how they are, in turn, defended.

The Court does not distinguish between or rank different public interest concerns in a formal or systematic way although, as noted earlier, nuanced differences in approach can nevertheless be detected in the case law. However, a more generous approach to a Member State defence at the conceptual level does not mean that the Court will not thoroughly scrutinize the persuasiveness of the State's claims, as case study 16.1 on public health derogations shows.

4.1.2 **Economic justifications**

It is a central premise of free movement law that 'aims of a purely economic nature cannot constitute an overriding reason in the general interest justifying a restriction of a fundamental freedom guaranteed by the Treaty'.[69] This principle has clear roots in the ambitions as well as the logic of closer integration. Extending equal opportunities to the nationals of other Member States—for example, in the context of employment, or the provision of public goods and services—costs money. If States could plead economic concerns to defend restrictions placed on free movement, there is a risk that the whole purpose of the internal market could be negated.

However, another case law thread establishes that 'none the less . . . *interests of an economic nature*'[70] can provide a legitimate defence to free movement restrictions. This line of reasoning emerged initially in case law on access to medical services. In *Kohll*, the Court accepted that:

> the objective of maintaining a balanced medical and hospital service open to all . . . although *intrinsically linked* to the method of financing the social security system, may also fall within the derogations on grounds of public health . . . in so far as it contributes to the attainment of a high level of health protection.[71]

In *Vanbraekel*, the economic premise seemed to stand more autonomously, with the statement that:

> it cannot be excluded that the risk of seriously undermining the financial balance of a social security system might constitute an overriding reason in the general interest capable of justifying a barrier to the principle of freedom to provide services.[72]

This perforation of the economic objective exclusion remains a consistent feature of case law on medical services,[73] and has crept outwards into public spending issues more generally—for example, the funding of education[74] and the coordination of social security benefits.[75]

In many of these cases, the apparently economic aim is arguably not of a *purely* economic nature. In *FKP Scorpio*, for example, an accepted justification argument based on 'the need to ensure the effective collection of income tax' embodies broader systemic or structural objectives too.[76] But it is difficult to distinguish the economic and other

[70] *Commission v Germany* (n 2) para 60 (emphasis added).

[71] *Kohll* (n 67) para 50 (emphasis added). [72] *Vanbraekel* (n 67) para 47.

[73] eg Case C-243/19 *A v Veselības ministrija*, EU:C:2020:872, para 47.

[74] eg Joined Cases C-11/06 and 12/06 *Morgan and Bucher*, EU:C:2007:626, para 36.

[75] eg Joined Cases C-396/05, C-419/05, and C-450/05 *Habelt, Möser and Wachter v Deutsche Rentenversicherung Bund*, EU:C:2007:810, para 83.

[76] Case C-290/04 *FKP Scorpio Konzertproduktionen GmbH v Finanzamt Hamburg-Eimsbüttel*, EU:C:2006:630, para 35.

objectives discussed in many of the judgments that veer into economic territory—especially in cases on access to publicly-funded services. The Court expresses its understanding of the distinction as follows: while 'grounds of a purely economic nature cannot constitute overriding reasons in the public interest justifying a restriction of a fundamental freedom guaranteed by the Treaties', on the one hand, 'national legislation may constitute a justified restriction on a fundamental freedom when it is dictated by reasons of an economic nature in the pursuit of an objective in the public interest', on the other.[77] Nevertheless, how this 'economic justification +' case law has evolved does suggest an exception from the conventional approach to economic exceptions that has not been confronted directly.[78]

Finally, the impact of justifications having an economic character in the case law on Union citizenship should also be noted. The conditions under which a State may deport a Union citizen on economic grounds—concerning the lack of financial resources of that citizen—are outlined in section 6.2. At a more general level, the Court has accepted that 'the exercise of the right of residence for citizens of the Union can be subordinated to the legitimate interests of the Member States—[to] the protection of their public finances'.[79] Protection of State finances as a public interest reason has been applied both to the conditions and limitations placed on the right to move and reside freely by provisions of Directive 2004/38[80] and to the justification of restrictions put in place at national level.[81] The relevant case law is closely connected to the complex balance between free movement rights, lawful residence, and equal treatment.[82]

4.1.3 The horizontal scope of the Treaty

At the level of establishing a restriction of free movement rights, the Court of Justice has conceived different levels of horizontality in the case law to date: (a) rules that regulate freedom of movement in a collective manner even if not adopted by a public body (establishment, services, and workers);[83] (b) Member State responsibility for private actions that impede free movement (goods);[84] (c) rules adopted by a private law body that has power to regulate in reality (goods);[85] and (d) full horizontal reach (workers).[86]

If the Treaty can, in certain circumstances, catch the actions of private bodies and even private individuals, it then becomes important to ask whether such bodies and individuals can also rely on the derogation and justification frameworks outlined in the Treaty and developed in the case law respectively. In *Fra.Bo*, Advocate General Trstenjak identified two approaches to this question in the case law.[87] First, she observed that 'in most judgments',

[77] Joined Cases C-105–107/12 *Essent and Others*, EU:C:2013:677, paras 51–52.

[78] For further analysis and discussion, see P Oliver, 'When, If Ever, Can Restrictions on Free Movement Be Justified on Economic Grounds?' (2016) 41 *European Law Review* 147; S Arrowsmith, 'Rethinking the Approach to Economic Justifications under the EU's Free Movement Rules' (2015) 68 *Current Legal Problems* 307.

[79] Case C-140/12 *Brey*, EU:C:2013:565, para 55.

[80] Ibid, paras 53–56.

[81] *Commission v UK* (n 56) para 80.

[82] See also, Case C-333/13 *Dano*, EU:C:2014:2358 and Case C-67/14 *Alimanovic*, EU:C:2015:597; for discussion, see chapter 13.

[83] Case 36/74 *Walrave and Koch*, EU:C:1974:140 and Case C-415/93 *Bosman*, EU:C:1995:463.

[84] Case C-265/95 *Commission v France* ('*Spanish strawberries*'), EU:C:1997:595.

[85] Case C-171/11 *Fra.bo SpA Deutsche Vereinigung des Gas—und Wasserfaches eV (DVGW)—Technisch—Wissenschaftlicher Verein*, EU:C:2012:453.

[86] Case C-281/98 *Angonese v Cassa di Risparmio di Bolzano SpA*, EU:C:2000:296; confirmed in Case C-94/07 *Raccanelli*, EU:C:2008:425.

[87] AG Trstenjak in *Fra.Bo* (n 85, EU:C:2012:176) paras 38 and 39 of the Opinion.

[88] eg *Angonese* (n 86) para 42.

[89] Citing eg Case C-325/08 *Olympique Lyonnais SASP v Olivier Bernard and Newcastle UFC*, EU:C:2010:143, para 38.

the Court simply applies the usual justification standard—establishing an overriding reason in the public interest—to private bodies and individuals as well.[88] However, secondly, she also identified a limited case law thread on 'special grounds in the private interest'.[89] In case law on the regulation of sporting activities, for example, the Court has considered justification based on grounds such as the recruitment and training of young players.[90]

In general, the idea of *legitimate* interest beyond *public* interest can be rationalized by the limited capacity of private actors to affect or to influence the kinds of policy issues affected and influenced by State authorities. If the scope of the Treaty reaches into private market behaviour in the field of free movement, then it seems inevitable that the corresponding scope of justification arguments has to be altered too.

4.2 **The jurisdiction of the Court of Justice**

The role of the Court is necessarily different in direct actions and indirect actions. In infringement proceedings against a Member State under Article 258 or 259 TFEU, it must decide directly on all aspects of the case—including the outcome of any justification and proportionality arguments submitted. However, for preliminary rulings:

> It is one of the essential characteristics of the system of judicial cooperation established under Article [267 TFEU] that the Court replies in rather abstract and general terms to a question on the interpretation of [Union] law referred to it, while it is for the referring court to give a ruling in the dispute before it, taking into account the Court's reply.[91]

In essence, this means that the Court of Justice resolves questions of law, but the referring court retains authority over questions of fact. In most cases, then, the final view on justification—and especially proportionality—should be left to the national court.[92]

In reality, though, the extent of the Court's review in preliminary rulings does vary and there are examples in free movement case law where the Court exceeds the baseline of resolving relevant questions of law and effectively resolves the case itself. The very detailed 'guidance' provided for the referring court in *Laval* provides a useful, and controversial, example.[93] There, the Court concluded, unambiguously, that:

> collective action such as that at issue in the main proceedings cannot be justified in the light of the [protection of workers] where the negotiations on pay, which that action seeks to require an

[90] The Court provided general guidance in Case C-650/22 *Fédération internationale de football association (FIFA) v BZ*, EU:C:2024:824, para 95: 'Measures of non-State origin may be permitted even though they are liable to impede a freedom of movement enshrined in the FEU Treaty, if it is proved, first, that their adoption pursues a legitimate objective in the public interest which is compatible with that Treaty and which is therefore other than of a purely economic nature and, second, that they observe the principle of proportionality, which entails that they are suitable for ensuring the achievement of that objective and do not go beyond what is necessary for that purpose.'

[91] Case C-162/06 *International Mail Spain SL v Administración del Estado and Correos*, EU:C:2007:681, para 24. See further chapter 10.

[92] eg Case C-14/09 *Genc v Land Berlin*, EU:C:2016:247, para 32: 'The national court alone has direct knowledge of the facts giving rise to the dispute and is, consequently, best placed to make the necessary determinations.'

[93] Case C-341/05 *Laval*, EU:C:2007:809. See further chapters 13 and 20.

[94] *Laval* (n 93) para 110.

undertaking established in another Member State to enter into, form part of a national context characterised by a lack of provisions, of any kind, which are sufficiently precise and accessible that they do not render it impossible or excessively difficult in practice for such an undertaking to determine the obligations with which it is required to comply as regards minimum pay.[94]

On one view, more definitive Luxembourg rulings reflect the Court's understandable intention to provide the referring court with a genuinely 'useful answer' to the dispute before it.[95] More detailed responses are also likely to appeal to national courts for that reason. But not even the acknowledged virtues of procedural economy and judicial cooperation displace the fact that constitutional boundaries written into Article 267 are overridden when the Court of Justice delivers overly prescriptive rulings and makes definitive findings on all aspects of a referred case. Nor do these kinds of responses ensure that national courts will assume responsibility for the analysis of cases through an EU legal prism themselves, which would help to embed EU law more seamlessly into national legal orders than has arguably happened to date.[96]

4.3 **The burden and standard of proof**

Whether a public interest argument is made on derogation grounds or as an overriding public interest requirement, the *burden* of proof falls on the Member State seeking to establish that defence.[97] The required *standard* of proof is more difficult to pin down, since the procedural rules for proceedings before the Court of Justice—whether for direct or indirect actions—contain very little detail on the issues of evidence and proof.[98] Two general principles can, however, be extracted from guidance provided in the case law.

First, it is not sufficient for States merely to assert the relevance of a public interest objective to defend a contested national restriction. Relatedly, generalizations will not be enough to meet the required standard of proof. Instead, States must present evidence to support and demonstrate their claims.[99] Secondly, that evidence must be sufficiently 'precise' in order to 'substantiate' the arguments submitted.[100] The Court has described the nature of 'precise' evidence in different ways—for example, 'specific evidence',[101] 'appropriate evidence',[102] 'conclusive evidence'[103]—but the common requirement is that it must *substantiate* the Member State's arguments. The Court increasingly discusses the required standard of proof that Member States should meet in its free movement case law.[104]

[95] Case C-142/05 *Åklagaren v Mickelsson and Roos*, EU:C:2009:336, para 41.

[96] See further H van Harten, 'Proportionality in Decentralized Action: The Dutch Court Experience in Free Movement of Services and Freedom of Establishment Cases' (2008) 35 *Legal Issues of Economic Integration* 217.

[97] However, in *Commission v UK* (n 56), the Court appeared to reverse that position; see para 85: 'the Commission, which has the task of proving the existence of the alleged infringement and of providing the Court with the evidence necessary for it to determine whether the infringement is made out . . . has not provided evidence or arguments showing that such checking does not satisfy the conditions of proportionality, that it is not appropriate for securing the attainment of the objective of protecting public finances or that it goes beyond what is necessary to attain that objective'.

[98] The Rules of Procedure of the Court of Justice are published at OJ [2012] L265/1. See also, Amendments to the Rules of Procedure of the Court of Justice, OJ [2024] L2024/2094.

[99] Case C-333/08 *Commission v France*, EU:C:2010:44, para 97.

[100] Case C-161/07 *Commission v Austria*, EU:C:2008:759, paras 36 and 37.

[101] Case C-147/03 *Commission v Austria*, EU:C:2005:427, para 63.

[102] Case C-319/06 *Commission v Luxembourg*, EU:C:2008:350, para 51.

[103] Case C-400/08 *Commission v Spain* ('*Shopping centres*'), EU:C:2011:172, para 62.

[104] See eg the extensive discussion of proof with respect to justification and proportionality arguments in *Bressol and Chaverot* (n 13) and *Scotch Whisky* (n 60).

4.4 **Fundamental rights as limits to free movement**

Two important questions arise in the context of balancing freedom of movement and fundamental rights when considering the principles that govern exceptions in free movement law: whether it is appropriate or effective to treat arguments based on fundamental rights in the same way as 'normal' derogations or justifications (section 4.4.1); and whether the Lisbon Treaty, and especially the binding nature of the Charter of Fundamental Rights, altered how free movement disputes are resolved by the Court (section 4.4.2).

4.4.1 **Fundamental rights as derogations and justifications**

Fundamental rights are protected in EU law both as general principles of EU law and through the Charter of Fundamental Rights, which has 'the same legal value as the Treaties' (Article 6(1) TEU). As a general rule, 'A Member State may invoke reasons of public interest to justify a national measure which is likely to obstruct the exercise of [free movement rights] only if that measure is compatible with the fundamental rights whose observance the Court ensures.'[105] The intensity of review that the Court will apply in these circumstances is considered in section 4.4.2. It may be noted as a preliminary point here, however, that while Article 52(1) of the Charter establishes the criteria against which limitations on Charter rights should be assessed in general (provided for by law; respect the essence of those rights and freedoms; subject to the principle of proportionality; genuinely meet objectives of general interest recognized by the Union or the need to protect the rights and freedoms of others), Article 52(2) provides that '[r]ights recognised by this Charter for which provision is made in the Treaties shall be exercised under the conditions and within the limits defined by those Treaties'. Thus, for example, although the right of Union citizens to move and reside freely is codified in Articles 20 and 21 TFEU and also in Article 45 of the Charter, the general system for derogation and justification developed for Treaty, not Charter, rights will apply.[106]

In some cases, however, Member States seek to defend a restriction of free movement on the ground that the contested national measure *exists* to protect fundamental rights. Here, potentially different levels of protection in national systems, often required by national constitutions, raise a persisting point of contention between the Union and its Member States, and especially between the Court of Justice and national constitutional courts.

The protection of fundamental rights by a Member State can be a legitimate basis on which to restrict the free movement rights guaranteed by the Treaty. In *Omega*, a case involving restrictions on laser killing games in Germany on the basis of the protection accorded to human dignity by the German Constitution, the Court stated that:

> since both the [Union] and its Member States are required to respect fundamental rights, the protection of those rights is a legitimate interest which, in principle, justifies a restriction of the

[105] Case C-60/00 *Carpenter v Secretary of State for the Home Department*, EU:C:2002:434, para 40.

[106] See eg Case C-390/12 *Pfleger and Others*, EU:C:2014:281, on freedom to provide services (Art 56 TFEU) and the rights protected by Arts 15 and 17 of the Charter (freedom to choose an occupation, right to engage in work, and freedom to conduct a business). See, however, S Prechal, 'Fundamental Rights and Treaty Freedoms: The "Derogation Situation" and Infringement Proceedings' in J Adams-Prassl, A Ezrachi, S Bogojević, and D Leczykiewicz (eds), *The Single Market Ideal: Essays in Honour of Stephen Weatherill* (Oxford: Oxford University Press, 2024).

[107] Case C-36/02 *Omega Spielhallen—und Automatenaufstellungs-GmbH v Oberbürgermeisterin der Bundes stadt Bonn*, EU:C:2004:614, para 35.

[108] Ibid, para 34.

> obligations imposed by [Union] law, even under a fundamental freedom guaranteed by the Treaty such as the freedom to provide services.[107]

Importantly, the Court underlined that ensuring respect for human dignity was a requirement of *Union* law, 'it being immaterial in that respect that, in Germany, the principle of respect for human dignity has a particular status as an independent fundamental right'.[108] However, the Court clearly had regard to the specific level of protection provided for under German law in its light-touch assessment of the proportionality of the restrictions. The use of proportionality to accommodate national differences in this way is returned to in section 5.

The earlier judgment in *Schmidberger* is generally considered to offer a useful template for how fundamental rights protection should be managed in free movement cases. There, a decision by an Austrian public authority to authorize an environmental protest—resulting in the closure of a major interstate motorway for just over 30 hours—was challenged as a restriction on the free movement of goods. In its judgment, the Court presented the nature of the decision that it needed to make as raising:

> the question of the need to reconcile the requirements of the protection of fundamental rights in the [Union] with those arising from a fundamental freedom enshrined in the Treaty and, ***more particularly***, the question of the respective scope of freedom of expression and freedom of assembly, guaranteed by Articles 10 and 11 of the ECHR, and of the free movement of goods, where the former are relied upon as justification for a restriction of the latter.[109]

Having established that freedom of expression and freedom of assembly are rights that can be limited in certain circumstances under the system of European Convention on Human Rights (ECHR) law, the Court concluded that 'the interests involved *must be weighed* having regard to all the circumstances of the case in order to determine *whether a fair balance was struck* between those interests'.[110] The Court added that:

> The competent authorities enjoy a wide margin of discretion in that regard. Nevertheless, it is necessary to determine whether the restrictions placed upon intra-[Union] trade are proportionate in the light of the legitimate objective pursued, namely, in the present case, the protection of fundamental rights.[111]

The Court's approach to the balancing of the different interests at stake where free movement rights and fundamental rights need to be 'reconciled' was considered to have broken down, however, in the controversial rulings in *Viking Line*[112] and *Laval*. There, the Court confirmed, for the first time, that the right to take collective action is a fundamental social right protected by EU law, on the basis that the protection of workers constitutes an overriding public interest requirement. But the outcomes in the cases, which privileged freedom of establishment and the free provision of services respectively, seemed to dilute the normative significance attached to fundamental rights in cases like *Omega* and *Schmidberger*. In that light, Barnard questioned whether the fundamental social rights invoked in these cases can ever have the capacity to displace free movement rights since

[109] Case C-112/00 *Schmidberger, Internationale Transporte und Planzüge v Republik Österreich*, EU:C:2003:333, para 77 (emphasis added).

[110] Ibid, para 81 (emphasis added). [111] Ibid, para 82.

[112] Case C-438/05 *International Transport Workers' Federation and Finnish Seamen's Union v Viking Line ABP and OÜ Viking Line Eesti*, EU:C:2007:772.

[113] C Barnard, 'Social Dumping or Dumping Socialism' (2008) 67 *Cambridge Law Journal* 262, 264.

'The moment collective action is found to be a "restriction" . . . the "social" interests are on the back-foot, having to defend themselves from the economic.'[113]

Both the realization of free movement objectives and the protection of fundamental rights are provided for in EU primary law. In reality, it falls to the Court of Justice to reconcile these interests in individual cases in the absence of clear signals about their relative weighting in the Treaty itself. Reflecting the language in *Schmidberger* and *Omega*, Advocate General Trstenjak has argued against seeing fundamental freedoms and fundamental rights as being in a 'hierarchical relationship'—emphasizing the role of proportionality to effect case-by-case assessments and considering that 'a restriction on a fundamental freedom is justified, when that restriction arose in the exercise of a fundamental right and was appropriate, necessary and reasonable for the attainment of interests protected by that fundamental right'.[114]

However, the protection of fundamental rights was enhanced in many respects by the Lisbon Treaty, especially through the binding status conferred on the Charter. Advocate General Mengozzi is among those who interpreted these developments as signalling *legal* change:

> As a result of the entry into force of the Treaty of Lisbon, when working conditions constitute an overriding reason relating to the public interest justifying a derogation from the freedom to provide services, they must no longer be interpreted strictly. In so far as the protection of workers is a matter which warrants protection under the Treaties themselves, it is not a simple derogation from a freedom, still less an unwritten exception inferred from case-law. To the extent that the new primary law framework provides for a mandatory high level of social protection, it authorises the Member States, for the purpose of safeguarding a certain level of social protection, to restrict a freedom, and to do so without European Union law's regarding it as something exceptional and, therefore, as warranting a strict interpretation.[115]

The Court has re-emphasized the 'fair balance' method in post-Lisbon cases.[116] However, criticism that free movement goals are (still) unduly privileged, at the expense of fundamental rights protection, must be acknowledged.[117]

4.4.2 **Review of national measures 'implementing' Union law**

The extent to which Member State derogation and justification arguments can be scrutinized for their compatibility with EU standards of fundamental rights protection is another important question. On one view, when a Member State is trying to extract itself from its obligations under free movement law, a credible argument can be made that the national measure should be treated as, in effect, falling outside the scope of Union law altogether. However, in *ERT*, the Court ruled that:

> where a Member State [seeks] to justify rules which are likely to obstruct the exercise of the freedom to provide services, such justification, provided for by [Union] law, must be interpreted in the light of the general principles of law ***and in particular of fundamental rights***.[118]

[114] AG Trstenjak in Case C-271/08 *Commission v Germany*, EU:C:2010:183, paras 186 and 189 of the Opinion.

[115] AG Mengozzi in Case C-211/08 *Commission v Spain*, EU:C:2010:88, para 53 of the Opinion.

[116] eg Case C-283/11 *Sky Österreich*, EU:C:2013:28, para 60; *AGET Iraklis* (n 39) para 90.

[117] eg S Weatherill, 'Use and Abuse of the EU's Charter of Fundamental Rights: On the Improper Veneration of "Freedom of Contract"' (2014) *10 European Review of Contract Law* 167; critiquing the judgment in Case C-426/11 *Alemo-Herron and Others*, EU:C:2013:521.

[118] Case C-260/89 *Elliniki Radiophonia Tileorassi AE (ERT) v Dimotiki Etairia Pliroforissis*, EU:C:1991:254, para 43 (emphasis added). [119] Emphasis added.

On this understanding of exceptions to free movement law, the frameworks of derogation and justification are *themselves* part of Union law, and relevant national measures therefore fall within the scope of EU law for the purposes of fundamental rights review.

Article 51 of the Charter seemed to indicate a retreat from the position established by *ERT*. It states that 'The provisions of this Charter are addressed . . . to the Member States *only when they are implementing* Union law.'[119] This wording arguably conveys Member State action in a positive or active sense only, such as measures adopted to implement an EU directive. However, in the post-Lisbon case law, the Court continued to interpret the concept of 'implementing' Union law broadly—and, for present purposes, as still capturing Member State measures taken to derogate from or justify restrictions of free movement rights. In *Åkerberg Fransson*, the Court referred to the explanations attached to the Charter,[120] which do not have binding effect but have influenced the Court's interpretation of the Charter in accordance with Article 6(1) TEU's instruction that it should have 'due regard' to them, to establish that 'fundamental rights guaranteed by the Charter must . . . be complied with where national legislation *falls within the scope of* European Union law'.[121] In *Pfleger*, the pre-Lisbon position on derogation and justification, as established in *ERT*, was confirmed.[122] In other words, 'The use by a Member State of exceptions provided for by EU law in order to justify an obstruction of a fundamental freedom guaranteed by the Treaty must, therefore, be regarded as "implementing Union law" within the meaning of Article 51(1) of the Charter.'[123]

5 Proportionality

5.1 Overview of the proportionality test

Even if the Court of Justice accepts that a national measure may legitimately restrict free movement in principle, proportionality then becomes critical since 'a restriction on the fundamental freedoms enshrined in the Treaty may be justified only if the relevant measure is *appropriate* to ensuring the attainment of the objective in question and does not go beyond what is *necessary* to attain that objective'.[124] The first—appropriateness—test is also expressed as an assessment of *suitability*. It is more debated whether what is normally referred to as proportionality *stricto sensu* (ie the greater the impact on free movement, the greater the importance attached to satisfying the public interest objective on which the Member State relies) is a distinct third test or is absorbed by the test of necessity.[125] In general, however, the Court articulates proportionality as a two-step test in free movement law.

The Court sends mixed messages on the need to submit empirical evidence to establish the proportionality of a national measure to justify a restriction of free movement rights. For example, in *Stoß*, which concerned restrictions on gambling, the Court noted that 'the referring courts are in doubt as to whether, in order to justify restrictive measures . . . the national authorities *must be able to produce a study* supporting the proportionality of those measures which was prior to their adoption'.[126] It then considered that:

[120] OJ [2007] C303/17.

[121] Case C-617/10 *Åkerberg Fransson*, EU:C:2013:280, para 21 (emphasis added).

[122] *Pfleger* (n 106) paras 31–36.

[123] *AGET Iraklis* (n 39) para 64.

[124] *Attanasio Group* (n 29) para 51 (emphasis added).

[125] See AG Poiares Maduro in Case C-434/04 *Criminal Proceedings against Ahokainen and Leppik*, EU:C:2006:462, para 26 of the Opinion.

[126] Joined Cases C-316/07, C-358–360/07, C-409/07, and C-410/07 *Stoß*, EU:C:2010:504, para 70 (emphasis added).

[127] Ibid, para 71 (emphasis added), referring to Case C-227/06 *Commission v Belgium*, EU:C:2008:160, paras 62 and 63.

> if a Member State wishes to rely on an objective capable of justifying an obstacle to the freedom to provide services arising from a national restrictive measure, ***it is under a duty*** to supply the court called upon to rule on that question with ***all the evidence of such a kind*** as to enable the latter to be satisfied that the said measure does indeed fulfil the requirements arising from the principle of proportionality.[127]

But it was conceded that 'it cannot ... be inferred ... that a Member State is deprived of the possibility of establishing that an internal restrictive measure satisfies those requirements, *solely on the ground that that Member State is not able to produce studies* serving as the basis for [its] adoption'.[128] On balance, however, States have a far greater chance of success if they can submit appropriate evidence to substantiate proportionality claims.

Linking back to the points made in section 4.2 about the role of the Court of Justice within the preliminary reference procedure, its task in such cases is to provide a coherent guiding structure for the application of proportionality so that the referring court can then determine the outcome—after all, that court is the judicial body closest to the dispute itself, to the facts of the case, to the detail and discussion of the evidence submitted, and to the nuances of the public interest conceptions at stake.[129] National courts have distinct responsibilities in that respect; in their judgments, they should demonstrate, through clear reasoning and engagement with relevant EU case law, that they have reached their conclusions on proportionality in accordance with the guidance provided by the Court of Justice, which they are required to follow even if different kinds of proportionality tests or criteria are applicable under national law.

In reality, however, the division of functions between national courts and the Court of Justice is more complex. For example, we saw both a prescriptive assessment of proportionality in *Laval* alongside a more devolved 'margin of discretion' approach in *Omega* in section 4.4.1. The reticence of the Court to engage in more extensive proportionality review was also noted in section 4.1.1 for the *Trailers* case, even though Advocate General Bot had argued persuasively that less restrictive measures could be put in place to achieve the justifiable road safety objective.[130] We return to this complexity in section 5.4.

5.2 **Appropriateness**

Restrictive national measures taken in the public interest will be considered to be appropriate if 'the means which they employ are suitable for the purpose of attaining the desired objectives'.[131] That standard has also been expressed as confirming that the national measure is 'appropriate to ensuring attainment of the objective pursued only if it genuinely reflects a concern to attain it in a consistent and systematic manner'.[132] This limb of the proportionality test, which is essentially a procedural review, is normally addressed very briefly, with the Court often simply stating that the measure 'is' (or is not[133]) appropriate, without providing detailed reasoning.[134]

[128] *Stoß* (n 126) para 72 (emphasis added).

[129] For recognition of this by the Court, see eg Case C-405/98 *Konsumentombudsmannen (KO) v Gourmet International Products AB (GIP)*, EU:C:2001:135, para 33.

[130] AG Bot in *Trailers* (n 59) paras 167–171 of the Opinion; cf the judgment of the Court (n 28) at paras 65–67.

[131] Case C-463/01 *Commission v Germany*, EU:C:2004:797, para 78.

[132] *Attanasio Group* (n 29) para 71.

[133] eg Case 124/81 *Commission v UK* ('*UHT milk*'), EU:C:1983:30, para 32: 'It has not been shown that public health in the United Kingdom has been affected in the slightest by such imports.'

[134] eg *Trailers* (n 28) para 64.

[135] eg Case C-443/10 *Bonnarde v Agence de Services et de Paiement*, EU:C:2011:641, para 35: 'Whilst the requirement ... does indeed appear to be ... appropriate for the attainment of the objectives of protecting the environment and combating fraud, it must however be verified that it is necessary to attain those objectives and that there are no other less restrictive means of doing so.'

5.3 **Necessity**

Assessment of the necessity of a national measure normally involves more substantive consideration of whether alternative measures that can achieve the stated public interest objective but have less restrictive effects on EU trade can be conceived.[135] Assessing the proportionality of a national measure in this sense involves consideration of whether alternative measures could be *equally* effective in terms of achieving the public interest objective that has been accepted as legitimate in principle, but *less* restrictive having regard to their effect on EU trade.[136]

The Court has confirmed that 'the burden of proof cannot be so extensive as to require the Member State to prove, positively, that *no other conceivable measure* could enable that objective to be attained under the same conditions'.[137] At a general level, the Court requires that 'If a Member State has a choice between various measures to attain the same objective it should choose the means which least restricts [free movement].'[138] Sometimes, it gauges the proportionality of national measures by engaging in a comparative review of solutions adopted in other States.[139] But 'the fact that one Member State imposes less strict rules than another Member State does not mean that the latter's rules are disproportionate'.[140] What does seem clear is that the resolution of questions about proportionality is the most evidently 'case-by-case' dimension of free movement law, more closely connected to the facts of individual cases as well as to the arguments that the parties actually submit.

5.4 **Proportionality as a tool for mediating public interest**

Public interest concerns often differ across the Member States. Where it can be argued, using appropriate evidence, that a contested national measure is both suitable and necessary to achieve legitimate public interest objectives, the restriction of free movement rights can be defended. However, when the Court delves into the detail of proportionality, States rarely succeed in persuading it that the measures under review satisfy the necessity test. In free movement law, it is essential to study judgments of national courts as much as possible too—whether or not a preliminary reference was made—in order to understand the calibration of proportionality in a more complete and also realistic sense.

It is also important to remember that proportionality assessments are at the fringes of law itself. They often require scientific or other expert, such as economic, evidence to be understood and interrogated by legal practitioners and, sometimes, the outcome seems to suggest a subjective value judgement more than a neutral legal assessment.[141] The underpinning concern is to distinguish genuinely held—and genuinely pursued—public interest *protection* from more problematic national *protectionism*.

[136] eg Case C-205/07 *Gysbrechts and Santurel Inter BVBA*, EU:C:2008:730, para 53.

[137] *Trailers* (n 28) para 66 (emphasis added).

[138] Case 261/81 *Walter Rau Lebensmittelwerke v De Smedt PVBA*, EU:C:1982:382, para 12.

[139] eg Case C-126/91 *Schutzverband gegen Unwesen in der Wirtschaft v Yves Rocher*, EU:C:1993:191, para 18.

[140] *Commission v Germany* (n 2) para 51; recalling eg Case C-384/93 *Alpine Investments BV v Minister van Financiën*, EU:C:1995:126, para 51 and *Omega* (n 107) para 108.

[141] For discussion and illustration of these points in an applied context, see C Barnard, 'A Proportionate Response to Proportionality in the Field of Collective Action' (2012) 37 *European Law Review* 117.

CASE STUDY 16.2: Navigating public moralities through proportionality review

The value of a clear, coherent, and predictable body of case law is obvious when considered from the perspective of legal certainty. It is not, however, the only relevant consideration in the development of EU law.

In section 4.1, we saw that the unlawfulness, or restricted lawfulness, of an activity within a Member State will not remove the subject matter from the material scope of the Treaty—or, in consequence, from possible review by the Court of Justice if national regulatory measures are challenged as a restriction of free movement. The regulation of gambling activities provides a good example of behaviour that is perceived and therefore regulated in different ways by different Member States, reflecting divergent national conceptions of the morality, or otherwise, of such activities. Things become especially interesting when States have to confront the limits potentially imposed on their regulatory discretion by the demands of EU law and the internal market: can they continue to prohibit their own nationals and economic operators from participating in an activity that they seek to proscribe or restrict within their borders that is lawfully and often more freely accessible in other States—moreover, at the click of a mouse in the online age?

In *Schindler*, which concerned advertising restrictions in the UK relating to a lottery organized in Germany, the Court was mindful of arguments about the social harm that gambling can create or exacerbate, but it declined to take an overtly paternalistic stance. Applying its standard approach, it held that 'Even if the morality of lotteries is at least questionable, it is not for the Court to substitute its assessment for that of the legislatures of the Member States where that activity is practised legally.'[142]

However, such restrictions will almost always be justifiable in principle to protect the national public interest, especially where a State can show that it clearly takes a 'consistent and systematic' policy approach to the restriction of gambling.[143] In *Liga Portuguesa*, Advocate General Bot rationalized the Court's approach as follows:

> the national authorities must be allowed a sufficient margin of discretion to determine the requirements entailed by the protection of gamblers and, more generally, taking account of the social and cultural characteristics of each Member State, the preservation of public order, with regard to the organisational arrangements of gaming and betting and the amount of stakes, as well the use made of the profits to which they give rise. The Member States are therefore free to set the objectives of their policy on betting and gaming and, where appropriate, to define in detail the degree of protection sought.[144]

In that light, the intensity of proportionality review becomes critically important and in the gambling case law, there is consistent evidence of lighter-touch assessment from the Court of Justice. For Advocate General Bot, proportionality review of gambling restrictions 'should consist in ascertaining that the State in question has not manifestly exceeded its margin of discretion in the context in which those measures were adopted and applied.'[145]

This 'deference' to national discretion is typically described in the academic commentary as a more procedural than substantive assessment of the appropriateness and necessity of national measures.[146] It is also more likely that the Court will refrain from making a definitive

[142] Case C-275/92 *Her Majesty's Customs and Excise v Schindler*, EU:C:1994:119, para 32.

[143] eg Case C-42/07 *Liga Portuguesa de Futebol Profissional and Bwin International Ltd v Departamento de Jogos da Santa Casa da Misericórdia de Lisboa*, EU:C:2009:519, para 61; Case C-49/16 *Unibet International*, EU:C:2017:491, para 40.

[144] AG Bot in *Liga Portuguesa* (n 143) para 67 of the Opinion (EU:C:2008:560).

[145] Ibid, para 258.

[146] eg F de Witte, 'Sex, Drugs and EU Law: The Recognition of Moral, Ethical and Cultural Diversity in EU Law' (2013) 50 *Common Market Law Review* 1545.

pronouncement on proportionality in the cases that reach it through the preliminary reference procedure.[147] However, while the regulation of gambling activities must reflect and accommodate moral sensitivities, review of restrictions on access to the gambling market must also recognize that it is a lucrative trade sector. On one view, the reticence of the Court to get involved more substantively in reviewing national gambling restrictions makes it difficult to ascertain how, and the extent to which, the rights of citizens and economic actors who wish to participate in such activities are being restricted in different parts of the supposedly border-free EU market. The resulting space created for meaningful regulatory diversity in a sensitive policy area showcases, on the other hand, how the elasticity inherent in proportionality review can be used to enable a spectrum of divergent, and genuinely held, moral and social views.[148]

However, it should not be forgotten that the Court is itself, in a sense, making moral and social decisions about these questions too. In prescribing the level of proportionality review that should be applied according to the relevant subject matter, the Court is essentially communicating its own view on when free movement rights conferred by the Treaty should prevail over other interests and values, and when they should not. Choices made about the application of proportionality may, therefore, be merited and they may prove to be effective when viewed in wider social and constitutional perspectives; but they are not neutral.

The discussion in this chapter has also pointed to instances of varying *intensity* of proportionality review. In section 4, for example, it was noted that areas of particular sensitivity can attract less intensive review from the Court. This message is apparent in the Court's instructions back to referring courts, as explored in more detail in case study 16.2 on gambling restrictions.

6 Derogating from the free movement of persons

It was observed in section 2 that the free movement rights of natural persons holding Member State nationality—irrespective of the purpose for which they have moved, that is, whether to exercise economic activity (eg working) or not (eg moving to study or for holidays)—are connected to the status of Union citizenship. These rights are subject to conditions and limits laid down in secondary legislation as well as by the Treaty. Union citizenship adds a distinct element to the issue of derogation since it imbues the nature of the free movement rights conferred on Member State nationals in the first place. The Court has consistently asserted that Union citizenship is 'destined to be the fundamental status of nationals of the Member States, enabling those who find themselves in the same situation to enjoy the same treatment in law irrespective of their nationality, subject to such exceptions as are expressly provided for'.[149] EU legislation can, therefore, shape the exercise of free movement and residence rights, and in accordance with the wording of Articles 20 and 21 TFEU, it can attach conditions and limits to their exercise. However, it cannot undermine the existence of those rights. In *Baumbast*, the Court was clear on this point:

[147] See eg Case C-258/08 *Ladbrokes Betting & Gaming Ltd and Ladbrokes International Ltd v Stichting de Nationale Sporttotalisator*, EU:C:2010:308, para 50; but cf more recently, *Unibet International* (n 143) and Case C-3/17 *Sporting Odds Ltd v Nemzeti Adó- és Vámhivatal Központi Irányítása*, EU:C:2018:130.

[148] Considering these issues in a recent ruling, see the judgment of the Court in Joined Cases C-475–482/20 *Admiral Gaming Network and Others*, paras 48–55.

[149] Case C-184/99 *Grzelczyk v Centre public d'aide sociale d'Ottignies-Louvain-la-Neuve*, EU:C:2001:458, para 31.

[150] Case C-413/99 *Baumbast and R v Secretary of State for the Home Department*, EU:C:2002:493, para 86.

> the application of the limitations and conditions acknowledged in Article [21(1) TFEU] in respect of the exercise of that right of residence is subject to judicial review. Consequently, any limitations and conditions imposed on that right do not prevent the provisions of Article [21(1) TFEU] from conferring on individuals rights which are enforceable by them and which the national courts must protect.[150]

Reflecting that understanding, Directive 2004/38 tightly curtails the extent to which Member States can lawfully expel EU citizens from their territories. The rules codified by the Directive capture and strengthen principles developed through case law over many years, two elements of which will be outlined in this section: the general provisions of the Directive that govern derogation from free movement rights in the form of expulsion orders against EU citizens (section 6.1), and the specific issue of expulsion on economic grounds (section 6.2).

6.1 Expulsion and Directive 2004/38: general principles

Member States may only restrict the movement and residence of EU citizens and their family members on grounds of public policy, public security, or public health.

The limited scope of the public health derogation was already outlined in section 4.1. Article 27(2) of the Directive requires that decisions based on public policy or public security 'shall comply with the principle of proportionality and shall be based exclusively on the personal conduct of the individual concerned'. This means that expulsion decisions taken in respect of groups of EU citizens without due consideration of the circumstances or behaviour of each individual member of the group or that are preventive in motivation are not permitted under EU law. The Directive also delimits the meaning of personal conduct as 'represent[ing] a genuine, present and sufficiently serious threat affecting one of the fundamental interests of society'.[151]

Other provisions of Directive 2004/38 establish a net of procedural protection for individuals subject to expulsion decisions, establishing conditions that relate to the notification of decisions (Article 30); administrative and judicial review redress procedures, as appropriate (Article 31); the duration of exclusion orders, including the opportunity to submit an application for the lifting of such an order after a 'reasonable period' (Article 32); and limitation of expulsion as a 'penalty or legal consequence of custodial penalty' (Article 33).[152]

For all expulsion decisions, Article 28(1) requires a Member State to take into account 'considerations such as how long the individual concerned has resided on its territory, his/her age, state of health, family and economic situations, social and cultural integration into the host Member State and the extent of his/her links with the country of origin'. In many respects, these criteria reflect the more general requirement of respect for family life guaranteed by Article 8 ECHR and Article 7 of the Charter.[153] Article 28 of the Directive also enshrines enhanced protection against expulsion relative to the degree of connection

[151] Reflecting pre-citizenship case law, eg Case 30/77 *R v Bouchereau*, EU:C:1977:172, para 35.

[152] The procedural guarantees in Arts 30 and 31 of Directive 2004/38 also apply in situations where a Union citizen or their family members are expelled from a host State without enjoying a right of residence there under EU law; see eg Case C-94/18 *Chenchooliah*, EU:C:2019:693. In *Nordic Info*, the Court considered that Arts 30–32 of the Directive 'give effect to the principle of legal certainty, the principle of good administration and the right to an effective judicial remedy' (n 66, para 70).

[153] These factors are applied by analogy in situations involving the expulsion of family members who reside in a Union citizen's home State on the basis of the *Ruiz Zambrano* case law: see Case C-304/14 *CS*, EU:C:2016:674. Case C-34/09 *Ruiz Zambrano*, EU:C:2011:124 is discussed in chapter 13.

established between the citizen and the host State. Where a Member State national or their family members acquire permanent residence rights in a host State in accordance with the conditions in Articles 16 to 18 of the Directive, they can only be expelled on *serious* grounds of public policy or public security under Article 28(2). According to Article 28(3), only *imperative* grounds of public security can justify an expulsion decision against a Union citizen who has either resided in the host State for the previous ten years

Case study 16.3: Expulsion and criminal convictions

Article 27(2) of Directive 2004/38 codifies principles first developed in case law: 'Previous criminal convictions shall not in themselves constitute grounds for taking' expulsion decisions. The requirement that an individual must continue to represent 'a genuine, present and sufficiently serious threat affecting one of the fundamental interests of society' is relevant in this context. The judgment in *Calfa*, in which a lifelong ban from Greece imposed as a result of a conviction for a drugs-related offence (which attracted a three-month term of imprisonment) was successfully challenged on the basis of the prospective impact on the applicant's free movement rights, demonstrates that proportionality is important here too, since, 'as the Court has repeatedly stated, the public policy exception, like all derogations from a fundamental principle of the Treaty, must be interpreted restrictively'.[154]

Expulsion can never be the *automatic* consequence of a criminal conviction; and neither can preventive expulsion decisions be taken following a criminal conviction unless a real risk of reoffending can be demonstrated.[155] In other words, 'the existence of a previous criminal conviction can justify an expulsion only in so far as the circumstances which gave rise to that conviction are evidence of personal conduct constituting a *present* threat to the requirements of public policy'.[156]

In *Tsakouridis*, the Court of Justice was asked 'whether and to what extent criminal offences in connection with dealing in narcotics as part of an organised group' amounted to 'serious' or 'imperative' grounds of public security.[157] Ultimately, the Court left the decision to the referring court; but against a backdrop of the 'devastating effects' of dealing in narcotics and the 'serious evil for the individual' as well as 'social and economic danger to mankind' of drug addiction, the Court did provide detailed guidance on the scope of Article 28 and the other interests that national decision-makers should consider:

> In the application of Directive 2004/38, a balance must be struck more particularly between the exceptional nature of the threat to public security as a result of the personal conduct of the person concerned . . . by reference in particular to the possible penalties

[154] Case C-348/96 *Criminal Proceedings against Calfa*, EU:C:1999:6, para 23.

[155] In the Withdrawal Agreement between the EU and the UK, there is greater scope for national discretion with respect to undertaking criminality checks under applicable national rules; see Arts 18(1)(p) and 20. The Withdrawal Agreement is discussed in chapter 27.

[156] Joined Cases C-482/01 and C-493/01 *Orfanopoulos and Oliveri v Land Baden-Württemberg*, EU:C:2004:262, para 67 (emphasis added). However, in the context of acts referred to in Art 1F of the Geneva Convention (commission of a crime against peace, a war crime, or a crime against humanity), the Court confirmed in Joined Cases C-331/16 and C-366/16 *K and HF*, EU:C:2018:296, para 56 that 'while, in general, the finding of a genuine, present and sufficiently serious threat affecting one of the fundamental interests of society, within the meaning of the second subparagraph of Article 27(2) of Directive 2004/38, implies the existence in the individual concerned of a propensity to repeat the conduct constituting such a threat in the future, it is also possible that past conduct alone may constitute such a threat to the requirements of public policy'.

[157] Case C-145/09 *Land Baden-Württemberg v Panagiotis Tsakouridis*, EU:C:2010:708, para 39.

> and the sentences imposed, the degree of involvement in the criminal activity, and, if appropriate, the risk of reoffending . . . on the one hand, and, on the other hand, the risk of compromising the social rehabilitation of the Union citizen in the State in which he has become genuinely integrated . . . The sentence passed must be taken into account as one element in that complex of factors.[158]

The Court further emphasized the need for the referring court to take both the requirements of proportionality and the fundamental rights of the individual concerned into account, highlighting the right to respect for family life.

However, in *PI*, the gradation between 'serious' and 'imperative' grounds became blurred. The applicant was convicted and sentenced to a term of seven years' imprisonment for sexual assault offences committed over a period of 11 years, the victim of which was his former partner's daughter. While again reciting the case law on taking decisions on a case-by-case basis and ensuring adequate respect for fundamental rights and procedural safeguards, the Court indicated that:

> it is open to the Member States to regard criminal offences . . . as constituting a particularly serious threat to one of the fundamental interests of society, which might pose a direct threat to the calm and physical security of the population and thus be covered by the concept of 'imperative grounds of public security', capable of justifying an expulsion measure under Article 28(3), as long as the manner in which such offences were committed discloses particularly serious characteristics, which is a matter for the referring court to determine on the basis of an individual examination of the specific case before it.[159]

While fully appreciating the grave nature of the offences and the seriousness of the impact of the crimes committed for the victim, commentators have questioned whether the legislative intention underpinning imperative grounds of public security should have applied in *PI* in the absence of risk to the security of broader State society.[160] Advocate General Bot perhaps gives an indication of the concern that shaped the decision at paragraph 62 of his Opinion: 'To acknowledge that Mr I. may derive from his criminal conduct the right to the enhanced protection provided for in Article 28(2) and (3) of that directive would, in my view, conflict with the *values* on which citizenship of the Union is based' (emphasis added).

More generally, the Court considers that while a period spent in prison in the host State can break the individual's integrative links with that society for the purposes of eligibility for enhanced protection under Article 28(3)(a) of the Directive, this is the case only 'in principle' and therefore 'may–*together with the other factors going to make up the entirety of relevant considerations in each individual case*–be taken into account by the national authorities responsible for applying Article 28(3) [of the Directive] as part of the overall assessment required for determining whether the integrating links previously forged with the host Member State have been broken, and thus for determining whether the enhanced protection provided for in that provision will be granted'.[161] More recently, though, the Court has also underlined the rehabilitative dimension of imprisonment for

[158] Ibid, paras 51 and 52.

[159] Case C-348/09 *PI v Oberbürgermeisterin der Stadt Remscheid*, EU:C:2012:300, para 33.

[160] See G Anagnostaras, 'Enhanced Protection of EU Nationals against Expulsion and the Concept of Internal Public Security: Comment on the *PI* Case' (2012) 37 *European Law Review* 627; L Azoulai and S Coutts, 'Restricting Union Citizen's Residence Rights on Grounds of Public Security—Where Union Citizenship and the AFSJ Meet: *PI*' (2013) 50 *Common Market Law Review* 553.

[161] Case C-400/12 *MG*, EU:C:2014:9, para 36 (emphasis added).

the purposes of undertaking such overall assessments, observing that 'the attitude of the person concerned during his detention may, in turn, reinforce that disconnection [from host State society] or, conversely, help to maintain or restore links previously forged with the host Member State with a view to his future social reintegration in that State'.[162]

In expulsion case law, we see, once again, the recurring tension between the narrow approach taken to exceptions from free movement rights, on the one hand, and more obviously circumstance-specific rulings in certain cases, on the other. From the latter, it is harder to extract principles of general application for future cases.

or is a minor, unless expulsion can be shown in the latter case to be 'necessary for the best interests of the child'.

Through the levels of protection established by Article 28, the EU legislator clearly intended to strengthen the residence rights acquired by Union citizens in host States over time, noting the progression from 'serious' to 'imperative' grounds of public policy and/or public security. However, this distinction has been less meaningful in practice, as case study 16.3 on expulsion and criminal convictions suggests.

6.2 **Expulsion on economic grounds**

Article 27(1) of Directive 2004/38 provides that public policy, public security, or public health may not be invoked 'to serve economic ends'. However, the link between expulsion and financial resources is more complex in reality.

For residence rights in a host State beyond an initial (and essentially unregulated) stay of three months, Article 7 of the Directive establishes the conditions of 'sufficient resources . . . not to become a burden on the social assistance system of the host Member State' and 'comprehensive sickness insurance' for Union citizens who are neither working nor self-employed there. Recital 16 of the Directive's Preamble provides more nuance:

> As long as the beneficiaries of the right of residence do not become an ***unreasonable*** burden on the social assistance system of the host Member State they should not be expelled. Therefore, ***an expulsion measure should not be the automatic consequence of recourse to the social assistance system***. The host Member State should examine whether it is a case of temporary difficulties and take into account the duration of residence, the ***personal circumstances*** and the amount of aid granted in order to consider whether the beneficiary has become an ***unreasonable*** burden on its social assistance system and to proceed to his expulsion. In no case should an expulsion measure be adopted against ***workers, self-employed persons or jobseekers*** as defined by the court of justice save on grounds of public policy or public security.[163]

Article 14(3) of the Directive confirms that 'An expulsion measure shall not be the *automatic* consequence of a Union citizen's or his or her family member's recourse to the social assistance system of the host Member State.'[164] But the inverse of this position

[162] Joined Cases C-316/16 and C-424/16 *B and Vomero*, EU:C:2018:256, para 74.

[163] Emphasis added.

[164] Emphasis added.

[165] The lawfulness of this course of action is confirmed in eg *Grzelczyk* (n 149) para 42: 'That interpretation does not, however, prevent a Member State from taking the view that a student who has recourse to social assistance no longer fulfils the conditions of his right of residence or from taking measures, within the limits imposed by Community law, either to withdraw his residence permit or not to renew it.'

is that recourse to the host State's social assistance system *can* be a legitimate basis for expulsion decisions in appropriate cases.[165] The irony of the fact that this exception to the general rule on economically-driven exceptions is applied to the rights attached to the most 'fundamental status' that Member State nationals enjoy is self-evident. It is one of the starkest disconnects between the conceptual potential of Union citizenship, on the one hand, and the legal constraints placed on its realization, on the other.

The Court has established that 'mere physical departure' from a host State following an expulsion decision in circumstances of non-compliance with the Directive's conditions for lawful residence is not sufficient; rather, the Union citizen concerned must have 'genuinely and effectively terminated his or her residence' before there can be any question of returning to claim residence rights there in the future.[166] Additionally, while Article 15(1) of the Directive requires that the procedures in Articles 30 and 31 apply in cases of expulsion for non-compliance with the Directive's conditions, it does not extend the scope of other protective provisions to such decisions. A generous approach was arguably signalled in *Rendón Marín*, where the Court indicated that 'in order to determine whether an expulsion measure is proportionate to the legitimate aim pursued, *in the present instance* protection of the requirements of public policy or public security, account should be taken of the criteria set out in Article 28(1) of Directive 2004/38'.[167] However, in *Chenchooliah*, the Court confirmed that Articles 27 and 28 apply 'only if the person concerned currently derives from [the Directive] a right of residence in the host Member State which is either temporary or permanent'.[168]

Linking back to the discussion on protection of State finances in section 4.1.2, it is arguable that the free movement of persons has become more vulnerable over time; that the appropriate balance between the rights conferred and permitted exceptions is out of kilter. While events overtook the proposals negotiated in February 2016 in the context of the UK's referendum on withdrawal from the EU, restrictions agreed as part of that process would have restricted the free movement of workers, presumed to be the most protected cohort of persons in EU law.[169] Moreover, while the relevant Decision stated that 'Encouraging recruitment, reducing unemployment, protecting vulnerable workers and averting the risk of seriously undermining the sustainability of social security systems are reasons of public interest recognised in the jurisprudence of the Court of Justice', the proposed restriction on in-work benefits was framed in directly discriminatory language ('EU workers'), bringing a new dimension to the eroding distinctions between different *forms* of free movement restriction discussed in section 3.2. However, the Court of Justice subsequently pulled no punches on the legality of the other proposed restriction, that is, indexing exported family benefits to the State in which an EU worker's family members reside: 'if such an amendment had been adopted by the EU legislature, it would have been invalid under Article 45 TFEU'.[170]

[166] Case C-719/19 *FS v Staatssecretaris van Justitie en Veiligheid*, EU:C:2021:506, para 81.

[167] Case C-165/14 *Rendón Marín*, EU:C:2016:675, para 62 (emphasis added).

[168] *Chenchooliah* (n 152) para 87.

[169] See Section D of the Decision of the Heads of State or Government, meeting within the European Council, concerning a new settlement for the United Kingdom within the European Union, 18–19 February 2016.

[170] Case C-328/20 *Commission v Republic of Austria*, EU:C:2022:468, para 57.

[171] AG Bot in *Trailers* (n 59) para 101 of the Opinion.

7 Conclusion

This chapter has provided an overview of the Treaty-based derogation system and the broader justification framework that enable Member States to restrict free movement rights in certain circumstances. The Court of Justice interprets the public interest concerns that underpin free movement restrictions as narrowly as possible, mindful of the fact that rights protected by EU primary law are at stake. National measures taken in the public interest are thus subject to a two-step proportionality review that assesses both the suitability and necessity of any restrictions imposed. As Advocate General Bot pointed out in the *Trailers* case, 'It is . . . the review of proportionality which enables the Court to weigh the interests associated with attainment of the internal market against those relating to the legitimate interests of the Member States.'[171] Both the derogation/justification and proportionality elements of a defendant State's public interest submissions must be properly supported with appropriate evidence.

Notwithstanding the strictness of the scrutiny applied to reviewing exceptions to free movement rights in general, however, there are also clear examples of a more hands-off approach in certain sectors of the case law—normally, when sensitivities are involved vis-à-vis the substantive public interest concerned either in a general sense or specifically for the Member State in question. Other points of case law incoherence include (a) the inherently pliable nature of public interest and, especially, proportionality through the process of legal adjudication; (b) the dissolving distinction between Treaty-based derogations and broader public interest arguments; and (c) the difficult question of the extent to which national public finances should be accommodated as a legitimate defence for free movement restrictions.

The search for the optimal balance between uniform EU free movement rights and respect for more local expressions of regulatory diversity clearly continues.

Further reading

C Barnard, 'Derogations, Justifications and the Four Freedoms: Is State Interest Really Protected?' in C Barnard and O Odudu (eds), *The Outer Limits of European Union Law* (Oxford: Hart Publishing, 2009)

I Govaere 'Internal Market Dynamics: On Moving Targets, Shifting Contextual Factors and the Untapped Potential of Article 3(3) TEU' in S Garben and I Govaere (eds), *The Internal Market 2.0* (Oxford: Hart Publishing, 2020)

P Koutrakos, N Nic Shuibhne, and P Syrpis (eds), *Exceptions from EU Free Movement Law: Derogation, Justification and Proportionality* (Oxford: Hart Publishing, 2016)

N Nic Shuibhne and M Maci, 'Proving Public Interest: The Growing Impact of Evidence and Proof in Free Movement Case Law' (2013) 50 *Common Market Law Review* 965

S Reynolds, 'Explaining the Constitutional Drivers behind a Perceived Judicial Preference for Free Movement over Fundamental Rights' (2016) 53(3) *Common Market Law Review* 643

V Velyvyte, *Judicial Authority in EU Internal Market Law. Implications for the Balance of Competences and Powers* (London: Hart Publishing, 2022)

17

Competition law

Alison Jones

1 Introduction

This chapter examines the two core TFEU competition rules governing anticompetitive agreements (and other forms of collusion) between independent firms[1] (Article 101) and abuse of a dominant position (Article 102). Despite several changes in the EU Treaties, and their evolution from Treaties with largely economic goals to a much more integrated social and economic system, the competition law provisions remain largely unchanged since the original Treaty of Rome 1957. That does not mean that the interpretation of these provisions has stood still, however. As with many other norms, competition rules, and their interpretation, have been impacted by evolving factors, economic and sociopolitical. Thus, it is seen in section 2 that although early case law of the EU Courts indicated that the objectives of the competition law rules were relatively broad, from the end of the 1990s, a growing view emerged that the competition laws should, principally at least, pursue an economic objective—the maximization of consumer welfare. Increasing concern about European competitiveness, environmental issues and the rising private and economic power of a number of large firms, especially digital platforms and the big technology companies (Big Tech) has, however, reignited the debate as to whether competition law should now pursue a more egalitarian vision, taking account of a broader set of objectives or whether it should at least adapt to reflect these developments.

As support for a consumer welfare objective gained momentum, there was a push to move away from the form-based interpretation of the rules manifested in some early jurisprudence, towards a more effects-based economic approach. This chapter focuses on these two themes (the goals of EU competition law; and the move to a more economic,

[1] In fact, Art 101 TFEU refers to three different kinds of collusion: agreements and concerted practices between undertakings (see further section 4) and decisions of associations of undertakings. In this chapter the word 'agreements' is used to refer to all three of these collectively: see further section 6.2.

effects-based competition analysis) when discussing Articles 101 and 102 and considering who these competition law rules apply to, when they apply, and to which types of conduct.

2 Overview of EU competition law

2.1 EU competition law

Approximately 140 jurisdictions around the world now have a competition law system in place (or antitrust laws as they are known in the US).[2] Such systems are, essentially, designed to protect the process of competition, and to deal with market imperfections arising, in a free market economy. Without competition law rules, firms may be free to distort the process of competition by, for example, colluding or merging with their competitors. Further, firms which win the competitive battle or 'natural' monopolies may be free to act without any competitive restraint being exercised over their behaviour.

The original EEC Treaty (the Treaty of Rome) incorporated competition laws. Indeed, the activities of the EEC included, among other things, not only the creation of an internal market but also 'a system ensuring that competition in the internal market is not distorted'.[3] This provision embedded the principle of undistorted competition in the fundamental provisions of the Treaty and provided the foundation for the specific competition rules set out therein, including:

- an article prohibiting restrictive agreements between undertakings[4] (now Article 101 TFEU):
  - Article 101(1) prohibits 'all agreements between undertakings, decisions by associations of undertakings and concerted practices which may affect trade between Member States and which have as their object or effect a prevention, restriction or distortion of competition within the common market';
  - such agreements are prohibited and restrictive provisions within them are void (see Article 101(2))[5] unless the agreement satisfies the four criteria for legal exception, or exemption, set out in Article 101(3)—broadly where specified benefits are passed on to consumers and offset the restrictive effects. Agreements satisfying the conditions of a block exemption regulation (see section 6.3.5) are automatically exempted from Article 101(1) unless and until the benefit of the block exemption is withdrawn;
- an article prohibiting 'any abuse by one or more undertakings of a dominant position' held within a substantial part of the internal market 'in so far as it may affect trade between Member States' (now Article 102 TFEU);
- rules to prevent Member States maintaining in force measures contrary to these and other Treaty rules (now Article 106 TFEU);
- rules prohibiting Member States granting unlawful State aid to undertakings so as to distort competition (now Articles 107 to 109 TFEU) (see chapter 18).

In addition, to ensure that the EU competition system is comprehensive and effective, merger control rules have been added to the competition law arsenal by Council regulation.[6]

[2] In contrast, 'Until the mid 20th century less than 10 competition regimes existed worldwide', https://unctad.org/publication/united-nations-set-principles-and-rules-competition-implementation-after-40-years).

[3] Art 3(f) later Art 3(1)(g) EC Treaty. Following Lisbon, this provision was amended and removed to Protocol 27 to the Treaties.

[4] See section 4.1.

[5] As interpreted by Case 56/65 *Société Technique Minière v Maschinenbau Ulm GmbH*, EU:C:1966:38.

[6] See now Regulation 139/2004 (OJ [2004] L1/1).

This chapter focuses on Articles 101 and 102, the rules governing anticompetitive agreements, and conduct of dominant undertakings.

2.2 **Objectives of EU competition law**

The EU Treaties do not define the core concepts set out in the competition law rules, such as a restriction of competition or an abuse of a dominant position, or explicitly articulate their goals. It has therefore been for the EU Courts to interpret these provisions. A question which is fundamental to their interpretation, however, is what is the intended objective of the rules? The case law makes it clear that Articles 101 and 102 both have the same aim(s).[7]

Several goals have been proposed. The main ones are Ordoliberalism, consumer welfare, and integration of the internal market. Ordoliberalism is a school of thought born of a group of economists and lawyers from Freiburg, Germany. Although its precise contours and impact are disputed, very broadly Ordoliberalism perceives a direct link between competition law and democracy and supports the view that competition law should protect individual economic freedom of action as a value in itself and the restraint of undue economic power, which constitutes a threat to a democratic State.[8] This freedom is viewed as a political (even human) right. It includes the freedom for firms to compete with others without powerful firms interfering to restrict them. Competition rules pursing this goal therefore focus on eliminating cartels, the market power of single firms, and contracts creating unjustified limits on firms' competitive autonomy. Ordoliberals welcome efficiency, but they 'would prefer a state of inefficiency coupled with freedom rather than a totalitarian, but efficient, state'.[9] Although this objective appears to have influenced the development of the case law and decisional practice in the past, Ordoliberalism does not today garner widespread support, even if apparent references to this goal can, arguably, still be gleaned from EU Court case law.[10] Indeed, the Commission received considerable criticism for following this type of approach in the early years of its application of Articles 101 and 102, and at the end of the 1990s it set about significantly 'modernizing' its interpretation and application of the EU competition law rules.

Following modernization, the Commission expounded the view that the appropriate goal for Articles 101 and 102 is 'to protect competition on the market as a means of enhancing consumer welfare and of ensuring an efficient allocation of resources'.[11] Under this approach, broadly, competition (which theoretically delivers lower prices, greater choice, innovation, and efficiency) is undermined, when the conduct at issue allows or will allow the relevant undertaking or undertakings to exercise *market power*, that is,

[7] Case 6/72 *Europemballage Corporation and Continental Can Company Inc v Commission*, EU:C:1973:22, paras 24 and 25.

[8] See eg W Möschel, 'The Proper Scope of Government Viewed from an Ordoliberal Perspective: The Example of Competition Policy' (2001) 157 *Journal of Institutional and Theoretical Economics* 4 and P Behrens, 'The Ordoliberal Concept of "Abuse" of a Dominant Position and Its Impact on Article 102 TFEU' in P Nihoul and I Takahashi, *Abuse Regulation in Competition Law*, Proceedings of the 10th ASCOLA Conference (2015).

[9] L Lovdahl Gormsen, *A Principled Approach to Abuse of Dominance in European Competition Law* (Cambridge: Cambridge University Press, 2010) 43.

[10] Case C-1/12 *Ordem dos Técnicos Oficiais de Contas (OTOC) v Autoridade da Concorrência*, EU:C:2013:127, paras 92 and 93 (Art 101); Joined Cases 6/73 and 7/73 *Istituto Chemioterapico Italiano SpA and Commercial Solvents Corporation v Commission*, EU:C:1974:18 (Art 102).

[11] Commission guidelines on the application of Article 81(3) [now Art 101(3)] of the Treaty (Art 101(3) Guidelines) (OJ [2004] C101/97) para 13.

the ability to maintain prices above competitive levels for a significant period of time or to maintain output in terms of product quantities, product quality and variety or innovation below competitive levels for a significant period of time.[12]

This recognition led to a 'more economic', or an effects-based, approach to interpretation of the laws and their enforcement,[13] and to the efficiency objective growing in importance. Despite the central role played by the Commission in the development of EU competition policy, the interpretation of the Treaties is a matter for the EU Courts (rather than the Commission). Although many more recent Court judgments place emphasis on consumer welfare as a goal and endorse the pursuit of efficiency as the primary goal of EU competition enforcement,[14] some have also stressed the importance of protecting 'not only the interests of competitors or of consumers, but also the structure of the market and, in so doing, competition as such'[15] or fair competition.[16]

It will be seen from some of the cases discussed later in this chapter that the rules have also been applied as a mechanism to ensure the functioning of the internal market—that is, to prohibit conduct which 'might tend to restore the national divisions in trade between Member States'[17] as this could frustrate the most fundamental objectives of the EU, the creation of an internal market. This goal is not pursued in most other competition laws around the world, but its importance is still reiterated in the jurisprudence.[18]

A recurring, ongoing, and current, debate is nonetheless whether the competition law rules should pursue a purely consumer welfare goal or whether other public interest or policy goals can also be taken into account when applying them. Indeed, some support has been reignited for the view that, given the importance placed upon teleological and contextual readings of the EU Treaties, the impact of an agreement or conduct on certain public policy goals, especially environmental protection, privacy, and data protection, should be taken into account in competition law assessments.[19] For example, Article 11 TFEU states that 'Environmental protection requirements must be integrated into the definition and implementation of the Union's policies and activities, in particular with a view to promoting sustainable development.'[20] Indeed, in the last few years concerns

[12] Art 101(3) Guidelines (n 11) para 25.

[13] Described in A Witt, *The More Economic Approach to EU Competition Law* (Oxford: Hart Publishing, 2016).

[14] See eg Case C-209/10 *Post Danmark v Konkurrencerådet*, EU:C:2012:172 (judgment of the Grand Chamber of the Court focusing heavily on the effects of the conduct on consumers), Case C-67/13 P, *Groupement des cartes bancaires (CB) v European Commission*, EU:C:2014:2204, Case C-413/14 P *Intel v Commission*, EU:C:2017:632, and Case C-377/20 *Servizio Elettrico Nazionale*, EU:C:2022:379 (see further n 221 and text).

[15] *Post Danmark* (n 14) para 63. See also Case C-8/08 *T-Mobile Netherlands BV v Raad van Bestuur van de Nederlandse Mededingingsautoriteit*, EU:C:2009:343, para 38.

[16] See eg. Case T-612/17 *Google and Alphabet v Commission* (*Google Shopping*) EU:T:2021:763, paras 433–434.

[17] Joined Cases 56/64 and 58/64 *Établissements Consten and Grundig-Verkaufs v Commission*, EU:C:1966:19.

[18] Cases C-501, 513, 515, and 519/06 P *GlaxoSmithKline Services Unlimited v Commission*, EU:C:2009:610, para 61 (Art 101); Joined Cases C-468–478/06 *Sot Lélos kai Sia EE v GlaxoSmithKline AEVE Farmakeftikon Proïonton*, EU:C:2008:504, paras 65 and 66 (Art 102). See also eg Cases AT.40632, *Mondelēz* 23 May 2024 and AT.40642, *Pierre Cardin* 28 November 2024.

[19] See C Townley, *Article 81 EC and Public Policy* (Oxford: Hart Publishing, 2009) ch 2; S Kingston, *Greening EU Competition Law and Policy* (Cambridge, Cambridge University Press, 2011); F Costa-Cabral and O Lynskey, 'Family Ties: The Intersection between Data Protection and Competition in EU Law' (2017) 54 *Common Market Law Review* 11. See also Case C-519/04 P *Meca Medina v Commission*, EU:C:2006:492, para 45; Case C-309/99 *Wouters v Algemene Raad van de Nederlandse Orde van Advocaten*, EU:C:2002:98, paras 97 *et seq*; and Case T-193/02 *Laurent Piau v Commission*, EU:C:2005:22, para 102.

[20] See further section 6.3.5 and chapter 22.

about climate change, economic and wealth inequality, the well-being and competitiveness of national and EU industries, the benefits of international trade, and the mounting power of the Big Tech companies, have renewed some support for the view that competition law should not just pursue a purist-efficiency based goal but should embrace broader objectives such as the ones set out above.[21]

Although the Commission has resisted arguments that EU competition law can and should be applied directly in furtherance of discrete policy goals such as data privacy or sustainability, a slight move away from its strict commitment to efficiency-maximization and effects-based analysis can be detected, at least in some spheres. In particular, the Commission places increasing emphasis on the importance of 'fair' competition,[22] especially as it has sought to challenge the rising power of the Big Tech giants. A Commission Policy Brief issued in 2023 thus asserted that 'EU competition policy is able to pursue multiple goals, such as fairness and level-playing field, market integration, preserving competitive processes, consumer welfare, efficiency and innovation, and ultimately plurality and democracy.'[23] Further, the Commission has indicated that it is prepared to apply the rules flexibility to accommodate conduct that might deliver more sustainable products and services to consumers (eg agreements to phase out or withdraw non-sustainable products and processes), so enhancing technical development, consumer choice, and benefits.[24]

3 Enforcement and consequences of infringement

Articles 101 and 102 are enforced:

(a) publicly, by a network of competition authorities (the European Competition Network (ECN)), comprised of the Commission and the national competition authorities (NCAs) of the Member States; and

(b) privately, through civil litigation in the national courts.

This section starts by examining EU public and private enforcement methods (respectively, sections 3.1 and 3.2). This is followed by a discussion on the extent to which Articles 101 and 102 can, or should, be applied consistently by all of these public and private actors.

3.1 Enforcement by the Commission and NCAs

Council Regulation 1/2003[25] confers significant powers on the Commission to enforce Articles 101 and 102, including the power to investigate, in an administrative procedure, violations of the provisions, to issue decisions, and to impose significant fines upon undertakings found to be in breach (fines of up to 10 per cent of their worldwide turnover). Although this enforcement structure confers considerable power on the Commission

[21] See eg European Parliament, *Report on the Annual Report on Competition Policy*, available at www.europarl.europa.eu/doceo/document/A-8-2018-0474_EN.pdf?redirect, para 7 and Commission's Draft Guidelines on the appraisal of mergers, 30 April 2026.

[22] N Dunne, 'Fairness and the Challenge of Making Markets Work Better' (2021) 84 *Modern Law Review* 230.

[23] European Commission Competition Policy Brief, 'A dynamic and workable effects-based approach to abuse of dominance,' Issue 1, March 2023, p 1.

[24] See especially Commission Guidelines on the applicability of Article 101 to horizontal co-operation agreements (OJ [2023] C259/01), section 9 and e.g. the Commission's Draft Guidelines on the appraisal of mergers, 30 April 2026.

[25] OJ [2003] L1/1. The Commission is in the process of reviving the EU antitrust procedural rules, see https://ec.europa.eu/info/law/better-regulation/have-your-say/initiatives/14729-EU-antitrust-procedural-rules-revision-_en.

(which acts as integrated decision-maker investigating, prosecuting, and deciding an individual case), the case law of the European Court of Human Rights suggests that, as the Commission's decisions are subject to review by the EU Courts,[26] the structure is compatible with Article 6 of the European Convention on Human Rights (ECHR), and in particular satisfies the investigated undertaking's right '[i]n the determination of his civil rights and obligations or of any criminal charge against him' to a 'fair and public hearing within a reasonable time by an independent and impartial tribunal' (the 'right to a fair trial').[27] Because, however, Articles 101 and 102 proceedings may culminate in the imposition of punitive fines (criminal charges for the purposes of Article 6(1) ECHR), 'the presumption of innocence resulting in particular from Article 6(2) of the ECHR . . . applies to the procedures relating to infringements of the competition rules'.[28] The burden is therefore on the Commission, or other person, alleging an infringement of Article 101(1) or 102, to establish 'sufficiently precise and coherent proof'[29] of an infringement.[30] Only when this is established does the burden shift to those seeking to justify the conduct.[31]

Initially the Commission played the central role in the enforcement process. This was partly because, from 1962 to 2004, it had the exclusive right to rule on the compatibility of an individual agreement with Article 101(3) and so to exempt individual agreements from the Article 101(1) prohibition (following the notification of the agreement to the Commission).[32] Although *block exemptions* (see section 6.3.5), granted by EU regulation, exempt certain categories of agreement from Article 101(1), this set-up meant that it was difficult for NCAs and national courts to play a meaningful role in the enforcement process when an agreement infringed Article 101(1) but a block exemption did not apply. From 1 May 2004, however, Regulation 1/2003 removed the Commission's exclusive right to apply Article 101(3),[33] so paving the way for the NCAs to be able to apply both Articles 101 and 102 in their entirety. A key aim of this change was to allow greater enforcement of the rules at the national level. Regulation 1/2003 requires that designated NCAs should have power to apply Articles 101 and 102, but leaves it to the Member State to determine which national body enforces the competition rules and the mechanisms for investigating infringements and enforcement. This framework has now been augmented by the ECN+ Directive, which is designed to ensure NCAs have the necessary independence, resources, and enforcement and fining powers to be able to apply Articles 101 and 102 effectively.[34] Although some NCAs enforce under a judicial model, many have the power to fine undertakings in breach of Article 101 or 102 (and/or national equivalents) following an administrative procedure similar to that followed by the Commission.

In some Member States, there is provision for sanctions beyond corporate fines—including for individuals (such as imprisonment or fines) as well as undertakings (such as exclusion or debarment from public procurement processes)—whether in civil or criminal procedures.

[26] See Regulation 1/2003, recital 33 and Art 31; and Arts 261 and 263 TFEU.

[27] See especially *A Menarini Diagnostics SRL v Italy* (Appl No 43509/08), ECtHR, 27 September 2011.

[28] Case C-199/92 P *Hüls AG v Commission*, EU:C:1999:358, paras 149 and 150.

[29] Joined Cases 29/83 and 30/83 *Compagnie Royale Asturienne des Mines SA and Rheinzink GmbH v Commission*, EU:C:1984:130. The standard of proof in private litigation is a matter for the national courts of the relevant Member State.

[30] Joined Cases C-89/85 etc *Re Wood Pulp Cartel: Ahlström Osakeyhtiö v Commission* ('*Wood Pulp II*'), EU:C:1993:120, para 127.

[31] See Regulation 1/2003, Art 2, and discussion of objective justification in section 7.3.4.

[32] Regulation 17 (OJ [1959–62] English Special Edition, p 87), Art 9(1).

[33] Regulation 1/2003, recitals 6–8 and Arts 5 and 6.

[34] Directive (EU) 2019/1 of the European Parliament and of the Council of 11 December 2018 to empower the competition authorities of the Member States to be more effective enforcers and to ensure the proper functioning of the internal market (OJ [2019] C11/3), see especially Art 1(1).

3.2 **Private enforcement through civil litigation in the national courts**

A claimant that has been, or is being, injured by an agreement or conduct that infringes Article 101 or 102 may rely on such an infringement in private proceedings before a national court and seek a declaration of nullity, an injunction, and/or damages to compensate loss suffered as a consequence. EU law requires national courts to protect the rights which individuals derive from directly effective provisions of EU law and even, in certain circumstances, to award damages to those who have been injured by a breach.[35] Nonetheless, up until a decade ago there was relatively little 'antitrust litigation' brought by private individuals before national courts. In 2013, the Commission noted that 'in only 25% of all antitrust infringement decisions the Commission took in the past seven years did victims seek to claim compensation'.[36]

Although private litigation has grown dramatically in some Member States, it is clear that private litigation in others has been, and is still being, deterred by a number of obstacles. The Commission has sought to tackle some of these. Among other things, an EU directive which is designed has sought to facilitate damages actions in the national courts by removing the main obstacles to full compensation for victims of antitrust violations and ensuring that private and public enforcement operate harmoniously together.[37] The Directive has been transposed into law in all of the Member States. The Commission has also recommended non-binding principles for the introduction of collective redress systems for damages actions in the Member States, designed to encourage group or class actions in competition litigation.[38] The Commission also offers assistance to the national courts in individual cases.

3.3 **The consistent enforcement of Articles 101 and 102 in the EU?**

As noted earlier, a key benefit of the decentralized enforcement regime created by Regulation 1/2003, allowing Member State courts and NCAs to apply Article 101 in its entirety, was that there would be more enforcement of the competition laws. On the other hand, the Commission (as well as many firms and others) feared that this might lead to their inconsistent enforcement.

Features of the 'modernized' system promote the consistent application of Articles 101 and 102 by EU competition agencies. For example, the ECN regularly meets to discuss EU competition policy and enforcement and may debate different viewpoints. Further, Regulation 1/2003 contains mechanisms designed to encourage consistent enforcement. In particular, it permits, and in some cases requires, NCAs to apply Articles 101 and 102 in addition to their national competition laws and provides that national competition laws must largely be applied in conformity with Articles 101 and 102 (although there is more scope for divergence regarding Article 102) (Article 3).[39] In addition, NCAs must notify the Commission (Article 11) about cases that they are investigating; and before they take a decision. This information, combined with an ultimate power conferred on the Commission to relieve an NCA of competence in a case by initiating proceedings (Article

[35] Case C-453/99 *Courage Ltd v Crehan*, EU:C:2001:465. See also Joined Cases C-295–295/04 *Manfredi v Lloyd Adriatico Assicurazioni SpA*, EU:C:2006:461.

[36] Commission Press Release IP/13/525, 'Commission proposes legislation to facilitate damages claims by victims of antitrust violations', 11 June 2013.

[37] Directive 2014/104/EU of the European Parliament and of the Council of 26 November 2014 on certain rules governing actions for damages under national law for infringements of the competition law provisions of the Member States and of the European Union Text with EEA relevance (OJ [2014] L349/1).

[38] More details can be found at https://eur-lex.europa.eu/EN/legal-content/summary/a-framework-for-collective-redress-class-actions.html.

[39] See further n 67 and accompanying text.

11(6)), allows the Commission to prevent 'inconsistent' decisions from being adopted by NCAs (although this power has never actually been exercised, it can be seen that its very existence gives the Commission considerable leverage over an NCA, for example if it were to disapprove of a decision an NCA was about to adopt). More recently, the Commission has become concerned that different procedural rules in the Member States, and different institutional structures for NCAs, might also undermine the consistent enforcement of Articles 101 and 102. The ECN+ Directive seeks to address this problem by better aligning processes.[40]

As regards the Member States courts, they have the ability (and sometimes, where they are a court or tribunal of a Member State against whose decisions there is no judicial remedy under national law, a duty), to refer questions of interpretation of the EU Treaties to the Court of Justice of the European Union (Article 267 TFEU). This includes the competition rules.

4 Who do Articles 101 and 102 TFEU apply to and when do they apply?

4.1 Undertakings

Articles 101 and 102 apply to 'undertakings'. The term is not defined in the EU Treaties but the case law has settled that it 'encompasses every entity engaged in an economic activity, regardless of the legal status of the entity and the way in which it is financed' (*Höfner*).[41] It has been defined in the same way under both Articles 101 and 102.[42]

4.1.1 Economic activity

The definition of undertaking set out in *Höfner* requires that the entity be engaged in *economic activity*, that is, the offering of goods and services on a market. In principle, such an offer could 'be carried on by a private undertaking in order to make a profit'[43] (even if it does not in fact).[44] The concept of an *entity* has been interpreted expansively to cover natural persons (including sole traders), legal persons (companies, partnerships, and cooperatives), and even State entities. As the notion of undertaking focuses on the nature of the activity carried out by the entity concerned, it is clear that 'a given entity might be regarded as an undertaking for one part of its activities while the rest fall outside the competition rules'.[45] Thus 'the fact that, for the exercise of part of its activities, an entity is vested with public powers does not, in itself, prevent it from being classified as an undertaking . . . in respect of the remainder of its economic activities'.[46] For example, activities which fall within a State's public powers (eg maintaining and improving air navigation safety)[47] are not considered to be of an economic nature; whereas, when an entity acts outside these areas, such as when they provide employment procurement services, this is economic activity.[48]

[40] See n 34 and accompanying text.

[41] Case C-41/90 *Höfner and Elsner v Macrotron*, EU:C:1991:161, para 21.

[42] Case T-68/89 *Società Italiano Vetro*, EU:T:1992:38, para 358.

[43] Case C-67/96 *Albany International v Stichting Bedrijfspensioenfonds Textielindustrie*, EU:C:1999:28, AG Jacobs, para 311.

[44] eg in ibid, the German State did not charge for its service of helping people to find work.

[45] Case C-475/99 *Firma Ambulanz Glöckner v Landkreis Südwestpfalz*, EU:C:2001:284, AG Jacobs, para 72.

[46] Case C-49/07 *Motosykletistiki Omospondia Ellados NPID (MOTOE) v Elliniko Dimosio*, EU:C:2008:376, para 25.

[47] Case C-113/07 *SELEX Sistemi Integratei v Commission*, EU:C:2009:191, para 70. Note that the question of what are 'public powers' is one of EU law: *Jean Claude Becu* (n 47) para 31.

[48] *Höfner and Elsner* (n 41) paras 22 and 23.

Economic activity focuses on the supply function. Thus it is not enough that a State is merely purchasing goods, 'the subsequent use of the purchased goods [must also] amount to an economic activity'.[49] Further, consumers consuming, that is, purchasing in a personal capacity, are not considered to be engaged in economic activity.[50]

4.1.2 Entities and single economic units

A line of case law makes it clear that a single undertaking is not necessarily synonymous with natural or legal personality,[51] but denotes an 'economic unit' which may be comprised of one or more persons, natural or legal.[52] For example:

- Employees are not considered to be separate undertakings[53] but as constituent elements of an undertaking.
- Agents are not considered to be entities separate from their principal, but rather to form an integral part of the principal's undertaking,[54] where they bear no, or insignificant, financial and commercial risks on the contracts they conclude/negotiate. Relevant risks include those that relate to the contracts concluded or negotiated by the agent on behalf of the principal and risks related to market-specific investments.[55]
- The single economic entity, or economic unit, doctrine also potentially expands the notion of an undertaking to entire corporate groups. This means that agreements concuded between members of the group may fall outside the scope of Article 101.[56] In the context of parent–subsidiary relationships, the entities will constitute a single economic unit if the subsidiary 'enjoys no economic independence'[57] or 'has no real freedom to determine its course of action on the market',[58] but carries out the instructions issued by the parent company controlling it. The question of when exactly a parent is able to, and does actually, exercise decisive influence over its subsidiary, so the latter does not enjoy real autonomy or independence in determining its course of action in the market,[59] has proved controversial, especially as the doctrine is now frequently relied upon as a mechanism for attributing liability to a parent (or other member of the economic unit) for the conduct of another entity within that economic unit that has violated the rules.[60] The cases establish

[49] Case C-205/03 P *Federación Española de Empresas de Tecnología Sanitaria (FENIN) v Commission*, EU:C:2006:453, para 26.

[50] Case C-180/98 *Pavel Pavlov*, EU:C:2000:428, paras 76–82, by implication.

[51] Commission Decision, *Pre-insulated Pipe Cartel* (OJ [1999] L24/1), para 154.

[52] Case 170/83 *Hydrotherm Gerätebau GmbH v Compact de Dott Ing Mario Adredi & CSAS*, EU:C:1984:271, para 11 and Case C-97/08 P *Akzo Nobel v Commission*, EU:C:2009:536, para 55.

[53] Case C-22/98 *Jean Claude Becu*, EU:C:1999:419, para 26.

[54] See especially Case C-279/06 *CEPSA Estaciones de Servicio SA v LV Tobar e Hojos SL* ('*CEPSA*'), EU:C:2008:485, paras 33–44; Case C-217/05 *Confederación Española de Empresarios de Estaciones de Servicio (CEES) v Compañia Española de Petróleos SA*, EU:C:2006:784, paras 38–63. Contrast *Consten and Grundig* (n 17) 340.

[55] *CEES* (n 54) paras 46 and 51. See also Commission guidelines on Vertical Restraints (OJ [2010] C130/01), paras 12–21.

[56] *Consten and Grundig* (n 17) 340.

[57] Case 22/71 *Béguelin Import Co v SAGL Import Export*, EU:C:1971:13, para 8.

[58] Case 15/74 *Centrafarm BV and Adriaan De Peijper v Sterling Drug Inc*, EU:C:1974:114, para 41. See generally WPJ Wils, 'The Undertaking as Subject of EC Competition Law and the Imputation of Infringements to Natural or Legal Persons' (2000) 25 *European Law Review* 99.

[59] Case 48/69 *Imperial Chemical Industries v Commission* ('*Dyestuffs*'), EU:C:1972:32, paras 125–146.

[60] See Case C-882/19 *Sumal, SL v Mercedes Benz Trucks España, SL*, EU:C:2021:800, and eg A Jones, 'The Boundaries of an Undertaking in EU Competition Law' (2012) 8 *European Competition Journal* 301 and S Daly and A Jones, 'The Undertaking and Single Economic Entitry Concepts in EU and UK Competition Law: Proposals for a Refined Approach' in F Thépot and A Tzanaki, *Research Handbook on Competition and Corporate Law* (Cheltenham: Edward Elgar, 2025) 128.

that where a parent holds a 100 per cent shareholding in a subsidiary, or an insignificant amount less,[61] a rebuttable presumption that the parent does in fact exercise decisive influence over the commercial policy and conduct of its subsidiary applies.[62] Further, that the ability of, and actual exercise of, decisive influence can be ascertained even where the parent holds only a majority or minority interest in a subsidiary[63] where the 'factual evidence, including, in particular, any management power exercised by the parent company or companies over their subsidiary'[64] supports such a finding.

4.2 May (appreciably) affect trade between Member States

The Court of Justice has held that 'in order to come within the prohibition imposed by Article [101(1)], the agreement must affect trade between Member States and the free play of competition to an appreciable extent'.[65] To fall within the scope of Articles 101 and 102, agreements or conduct must therefore have a minimum level of cross-border effects. This jurisdictional test sets out the external reach of the provisions and 'the boundary between the areas respectively covered by Community law and the law of the Member States'.[66] In addition, Regulation 1/2003 clarifies that when applying national competition laws to conduct which appreciably affects trade between Member States, NCAs and national courts must also apply Articles 101 and/or 102 and may not apply national rules governing agreements more strictly (they cannot prohibit an agreement infringing national competition law if it does not infringe Article 101).[67]

The Court has confirmed that for conduct to be capable of affecting trade between Member States, it must be possible to foresee with a:

> sufficient degree of probability, on the basis of a set of objective factors of law or of fact, that they have an influence, direct or indirect, actual or potential, on the pattern of trade between Member States in such a way as to cause concern that they might hinder the attainment of a single market between Member States [the EU internal market] . . . Moreover, that influence must not be insignificant.[68]

Alternatively, that the competition is liable to interfere with the structure of competition in the common market.[69] In making the required assessment, the question is whether the arrangement or practice as a whole distorts trade; it is not necessary that the anticompetitive elements affect trade or that trade is affected adversely. It could be sufficient therefore that the conduct increases the volume of trade.[70]

[61] See eg Case C-508/11 *Eni SpA v Commission*, EU:C:2013:289.

[62] *Akzo Nobel* (n 52) para 60. It is for the parent to rebut the presumption and the Commission is obliged to consider the rebuttal evidence, see eg Case T-185/06 *L'Air liquide SA v Commission*, EU:C:2011:275.

[63] Case T-141/89 *Tréfileurope Sales SARL v Commission*, EU:C:1995:62. See also *Commercial Solvents* (n 10) (parent and subsidiary in which the parent held a 51 per cent shareholding were to be treated as an economic unit).

[64] Case T-132/07 *Fuji Electric System Co Ltd v Commission*, EU:C:2011:344, para 181.

[65] *Béguelin Import* (n 57). The text of Art 101(1) and Art 102 does not explicitly require that the effect on competition or trade should be appreciable.

[66] Case C-238/05 *Asnef-Equifax v Asociación de Usuarios de Servicios Bancarios*, EU:C:2006:734, para 33.

[67] Regulation 1/2003, recital 8 and Art 3(1). There are also limits on the result they can come to at national law, when Arts 101 and 102 are triggered, recital 8 and Art 3(2).

[68] *Asnef-Equifax* (n 66) para 34. Also, Commission guidelines on the effect on trade concept contained in Articles 81 and 82 of the Treaty (Guidelines on the effect on trade concept) (OJ [2004] C101/81).

[69] Case 6–7/73 *Istituto Chemioterapico Italiano SpA and Commercial Solvents Corp v Commission*, EU:C:1974:18, paras 5 and 30–35.

[70] *Asnef-Equifax* (n 66) para 38.

Despite the insertion of an appreciability element in the test, the effect on trade test has been construed widely so many agreements and much single firm conduct operating within the EU have an appreciable effect on trade.[71] Some, by their very nature, reinforce the partitioning of markets on a national basis, thus impeding the economic interpenetration that the EU Treaties aim to generate.[72] For example, where national agreements concern undertakings from other Member States[73] or incorporate restraints on cross-border trade or where a dominant firm charges different prices in different Member States. This latter conduct is likely to increase trade of the relevant product from the low-priced State to the high-priced one.

Agreements relating only to the marketing of products or services in a single Member State may also affect trade between Member States.[74] For example, an agreement precluding a buyer from purchasing goods from a competing supplier may affect trade by prohibiting the buyer from contracting with competitors in other Member States.

There may even be an appreciable effect on trade between Member States where an undertaking, located outside the EU, agrees to distribute products there and not to import them into the EU.[75]

4.3 **Exclusions**

Although Articles 101 and 102 do not contain any express exclusions, in practice several exclusions exist from one or both of these provisions by virtue of, for example, Treaty provisions, the EU Courts' case law, or EU regulation. These may be rooted in public policy grounds. Exclusion avoids a need to balance these objectives *within* the framework of Articles 101 and/or 102.[76] For example:

- Article 346(1)(b) TFEU provides that the provisions of the EU Treaties, including the competition rules, do not preclude a Member State from taking measures that it considers 'necessary for the protection of the essential interests of its security which are connected with the production of or trade in arms, munitions and war material'. Such measures shall not adversely affect the conditions of competition in the internal market regarding products which are not intended for specifically military purposes.
- In *Albany*,[77] the Court excluded from the ambit of Article 101 certain agreements belonging to the realm of social policy. This case concerned an agreement between employers and labour which aimed to improve the conditions of work and employment in the Dutch textile industry. Although the arrangements potentially seemed to breach Article 101, they also appeared to be in accordance with EU social provisions, which encourage collective bargaining.[78] The Court, by reading the EU Treaties as a whole, permitted social policy objectives to trump the competition law ones and held that these agreements fell outside the scope of Article 101(1) altogether.

[71] eg Joined Cases C-215/96 and 216/96 *Carlo Bagnasco v Banca Popolare di Novara soc coop arl and Cassa di Risparmio di Genova e Imperia SpA*, EU:C:1999:12 and Guidelines on the effect on trade concept (n 68).

[72] *Asnef-Equifax* (n 66) para 37.

[73] Ibid, paras 35 and 66.

[74] See eg Case C-128/21 *Lietuvos notarų rūmai v Lithuanian Competition Authority*, EU:C:2024:49 and Guidelines on the effect on trade concept (n 68) para 77.

[75] Case C-306/96 *Javico International and Javico v Yves Saint Laurent Parfums*, EU:C:1998:173.

[76] See section 2.2.

[77] Case C-67/96 (n 43) para 59. See also discussion of the *Wouters* exception, in section 6.3.4.

[78] See TFEU, Art 151 etc.

- Article 42 TFEU gives some precedence to the Common Agricultural Policy objectives (listed in Article 39 TFEU, such as ensuring a fair standard of living for the agricultural community) over the competition ones. In line with Article 39, derogations apply in relation to certain agricultural agreements.[79]

5 Identifying anticompetitive agreements and conduct

5.1 The use of economic analysis

It has been seen that the prevailing view is that a core goal of the competition laws is to prohibit and prevent conduct which will harm consumer welfare and efficiency. This is not an easy objective to achieve, however, as it means that complex economic principles and tools generally lie at the heart of providing a coherent framework for analysing whether conduct infringes the rules. These may not always establish a clear outcome for a case. For example, it has been seen that the applicability of the law frequently requires an assessment of whether or not a particular firm has market power.[80] The answer to this question leaves considerable scope for disagreement on a number of issues, such as:

- How can the existence of market power be identified? Can it be measured directly, or can it only be identified indirectly through use of proxies such as an analysis of market shares and other factors such as barriers to entry into the market? EU law has generally used indirect mechanisms for assessing market power, requiring the relevant market to be identified (from both a product and geographic perspective (and sometimes a temporal one)) and an assessment of the conditions of competition on that market.[81]
- What market (product, geographic, and temporal) does the undertaking(s) operate on?[82] Does a producer of sparkling water, for example, operate on a market for sparkling water, bottled water, fizzy drinks, soft drinks, or another product market and is the market local, national, or broader? And how are relevant markets identified in scenarios where firms (such as a newspaper or digital platform) operate on multi-sided markets providing goods or services to two or more different sets of customers (eg readers/users on one side of the market and advertisers on the other)?
- Does the firm compete vigorously with rival on the market and do barriers to entry exist[83] which prevent other undertakings from entering that market and challenging that firm's position on the market?
- What is the theory of harm raised in a given case (what are the consumer welfare implications of the practices), and, for example, how are actual or potential anticompetitive effects to be identified and weighed against pro-competitive ones or efficiencies, especially those which might only be achieved in the longer run?

Clearly, in addition to being complex, such analysis is time-consuming, expensive, and difficult to apply in practice. Although therefore competition law should be guided by economics, it cannot always replicate economists' (frequently conflicting) views.[84]

[79] See Regulation 1184/2006 (OJ [2006] L214/7) and Regulation 1308/2013 (OJ [2013] L347/671).

[80] See section 2.2.

[81] See especially section 7.2. But see eg 'Special Issue: Louis Kaplow's Why (Ever) Define Markets' (2012) 57 *Antitrust Bulletin*, and J Farrell and C Shapiro, 'Antitrust Evaluation of Horizontal Mergers: An Economic Alternative to Market Definition' (2010) 10 *The BE Journal of Theoretical Economics* 1.

[82] See section 7.2. [83] Ibid.

[84] See eg Justice Breyer's dissenting judgment in *Leegin Creative Leather Products Inc v PSKS, Inc, DBA Kay's Kloset*, 551 US 877 (2007).

5.2 Form and effects: type 1 and type 2 errors

Competition law systems have, therefore, to consider how to construct legal rules or standards which can reflect the law's economic underpinnings and distinguish anticompetitive conduct which will harm consumer welfare from pro-competitive conduct in a way which will be both sufficiently:

(a) clear—enabling firms to comply with them and courts or other decision-makers to administer them; and

(b) accurate—identifying and prohibiting anticompetitive conduct while permitting (and not deterring) that which may promote competition.

Although the view could be taken that, in order to ensure accuracy, anticompetitive effects should be identified and balanced against any pro-competitive benefits in every competition case, such an approach is likely to impose too high a burden on firms, competition agencies (and other claimants), and/or courts, creating a risk that pro-competitive agreements will be deterred and/or too little enforcement/condemnation of harmful agreements will occur. In selecting the optimal approach for a given case, a trade-off may therefore need to be made between more complex standards, requiring detailed factual and economic analysis, which are more difficult and costly to apply, and simpler, clearer, bright-line rules, which require less sophisticated analysis and less emphasis on expert economic evidence but which may, consequently, be less accurate (or even inaccurate) in some cases.

It may also be necessary to consider whether an approach which is over-inclusive and may sometimes condemn legitimate business practices (false positives—so-called 'type 1' errors) and so potentially chill pro-competitive conduct is a lesser or greater evil than one which may sometimes be under-inclusive and may allow anticompetitive practices to escape antitrust prohibitions (false negatives—so-called 'type 2' errors).[85]

In seeking to set out accurate, administrable, consistent, objective, and transparent rules, most competition law systems, including the EU system, accept that some sorting of agreements and other conduct into categories is required, distinguishing between and affording different treatment to, for example:

- conduct which is very likely to cause anticompetitive effects and unlikely to have offsetting benefits—where a *presumption* of incompatibility with the rules may be applied (see eg the discussion of agreements that restrict competition by object in section 6.3.2);
- conduct which is very unlikely to cause anticompetitive effects—in some systems, such conduct may benefit from a safe harbour or a presumption of compatibility with the rules (see eg the discussion of EU block exemptions in section 6.3.5, which provide a safe harbour for agreements assumed to be compatible with Article 101); and
- conduct the effects of which are more ambiguous—which require closer individual scrutiny of anticompetitive and pro-competitive effects.

This is so even though the EU competition laws are not drafted in a 'form-based' way (where a prohibitory approach is based on the form of that agreement or conduct). A controversial issue which the existence of these categories creates, however, is what type of conduct should go into each.

[85] See eg OECD, 'Policy Roundtables: Resale Price Maintenance (2008)', DAF/COMP(2008)37, www.oecd.org/daf/competition/43835526.pdf.

6 Article 101 TFEU

6.1 Introduction

Article 101 has two substantive parts. Article 101(1) contains the core prohibition of arrangements and other joint conduct between separate undertakings which restrict competition, while appreciably affecting trade between Member States. Article 101(3) provides a legal exception for agreements achieving offsetting benefits. The burden is on the Commission, or other person alleging an infringement of Article 101(1), to establish sufficient proof of an infringement.[86] Only if established does the burden shift onto the undertakings claiming the benefit of exemption to demonstrate that Article 101(3) is fulfilled.[87]

The concepts of undertaking and effect on trade have already been considered. This section consequently focuses on the question of what constitutes joint conduct targeted by Article 101 and which agreements etc restrict competition and are prohibited by it.

6.2 Agreements, concerted practices, and decisions

Article 101(1) prohibits joint, not individual, conduct. The reference to 'agreements between undertakings, decisions by associations of undertakings and concerted practices' thus requires some element of 'collusion', cooperation or joint conduct between independent undertakings. The different types of collusion referred to in Article 101(1) are distinguishable from each other only by their intensity and the forms in which they manifest themselves and must be understood in light of the concept inherent in the Treaties' competition rules that each economic operator must determine independently the policy which it intends to adopt on the market.[88]

In many Article 101 cases, the existence of an agreement is not in doubt. There may be doubt, however, as to the precise terms of the agreement or as to whether the terms can be said to restrict competition. In other cases, frequently where it is suspected that a serious violation of the competition rules has been committed (eg price fixing by competitors), evidence that independent undertakings agreed or concerted to fix prices may, effectively, prove a violation of Article 101(1).[89] If detected, heavy sanctions may be imposed on the undertakings proved to have been party to the infringement. In such cases, the colluding undertakings often cooperate in more amorphous ways or try to conceal their collusion rather than attempt to try to defend the legitimacy of the practices under Article 101(3). The challenge in such scenarios is to uncover such covert operations and, where evidence is skimpy, to determine whether or not the behaviour on the market results from collusion, which is prohibited under Article 101, or independent behaviour, which is not.

6.2.1 Agreement

The term 'agreement' encompasses situations where undertakings have 'expressed their joint intention to conduct themselves on the market in a specific way'[90] or where there is 'a concurrence of wills between economic operators on the implementation of a policy,

[86] See section 3.1.

[87] See Regulation 1/2003, recital 5 and Art 2. In Cases C-204/00 P etc *Aalborg Portland A/S v Commission* ('*Cement*'), EU:C:2004:6, para 78.

[88] Case C-238/05 *Asnef-Equifax* (n 66).

[89] Where the agreement has as its 'object' the restriction of competition and its anticompetitive 'effect' does not need to be demonstrated, see section 6.3.

[90] Case T-41/96 *Bayer AG v Commission* [2000] ECR II-3383, para 67, aff'd on appeal Cases C-2 and 3/01 P, EU:C:2004:2. See also Case C-49/92 *Commission v Anic Partecipazioni*, EU:C:1999:356, paras 79 and 122.

the pursuit of an objective, or the adoption of a given line of conduct on the market'.[91] As long as there is a concurrence of wills, constituting the faithful expression of the parties' intention,[92] its form or nature is unimportant—it can catch agreements: whether horizontal (between competitors operating at the same level of the economy, eg two brewers or two manufacturers of vitamins) or vertical (between non-competitors operating at different levels of the economy, eg a brewer and a publican or café owner or a manufacturer of electronic products and a retailer of electronic products),[93] whether or not they are intended to be legally binding, whether or not sanctions are provided for a breach, and whether they are written or oral.[94] An agreement may also be found where an offer to collude is accepted tacitly, for example where an undertaking participates in meetings at which anticompetitive agreements are concluded, without manifestly opposing them.[95]

6.2.2 **Concerted practices**

The term 'concerted practice' catches looser forms of collusion. It does not require an agreement or even a plan or a meeting of minds, but catches reciprocal coordination which 'knowingly substitutes practical co-operation' between the undertakings 'for the risks of competition',[96] so precluding 'any direct or indirect contact between such operators, the object or effect whereof is either to influence the conduct on the market of an actual or potential competitor or to disclose to such a competitor the course of conduct which they themselves have decided to adopt or contemplate adopting on the market'.[97] Where firms engage in conduct designed to remove strategic uncertainty about each other's future conduct on the market, for example through a direct, or even indirect,[98] exchange[99] or disclosure[100] of strategic information, they may be found not to be acting independently or unilaterally and so their conduct is subject to Article 101.

6.2.3 **Decisions by associations of undertakings**

The reference to decisions by associations of undertakings facilitates holding associations liable for the anticompetitive behaviour of their members. In *Wouters v Algemene Raad van de Nederlandse Orde van Advocaten*,[101] Advocate General Léger stated that the concept:

> seeks to prevent undertakings from being able to evade the rules on competition on account simply of the form in which they coordinate their conduct on the market. To ensure that this principle is effective, Article [101(1)] covers not only direct methods of coordinating conduct between undertakings (agreements and concerted practices) but also institutionalised forms of cooperation, that is to say, situations in which economic operators act through a collective structure or a common body.[102]

[91] Case T-41/96, *Bayer AG* (n 90). [92] Ibid, para 69. [93] *Consten and Grundig* (n 17).

[94] See eg Case 28/77 *Tepea BV v Commission*, EU:C:1978:133.

[95] Case C-204/00 *Aalborg Portland A/S* (n 87) para 81.

[96] Case 48/69 *ICI v Commission* (n 96) paras 64 and 65.

[97] Joined Cases 40/73 etc *Re the European Sugar Cartel: Coöperatieve Vereniging 'Suiker Unie' UA v Commission*, EU:C:1975:174, para 174.

[98] But see *Wood Pulp II* (n 30) (no collusion established where undertakings had announced their price increases in advance and the information had been rapidly transferred between both buyers and sellers by means of publication in the trade press).

[99] Case C-8/08 *T-Mobile Netherlands* (n 15) paras 54–62.

[100] See eg *Re the European Sugar Cartel* (n 97); and Joined Cases T-202/98 etc *Tate & Lyle, Napier Brown and British Sugar*, EU:T:2001:185, aff'd Case C-359/01 P *British Sugar*, EU:C:2004:255.

[101] Case C-309/99 (n 19). [102] Ibid, para 62, AG Léger.

This concept has thus been interpreted broadly to catch recommendations,[103] rules, and other schemes[104] designed to coordinate the member undertakings' behaviour on the market and/or to exclude competitors.

6.2.4 Joint not unilateral conduct

In some cases, the EU Courts have annulled a Commission decision for failing to provide adequate evidence of an agreement, decision, or concerted practice. For example, no agreement was found in the *Bayer/Adalat* case. Although Bayer in this case had pursued a policy designed to try to stop French and Spanish wholesalers from selling products into the UK, the EU Courts found that the Commission had *not* shown that Bayer had sought to obtain agreement or acquiescence from its wholesalers to adhere to its policy or that the wholesalers had acquiesced explicitly, or implicitly, in it.[105] In addition, in *Wood Pulp II*,[106] the Court of Justice held that even if it can be established that all suppliers on a market have acted in parallel (eg by making identical transaction prices), parallel behaviour alone cannot be relied upon to furnish proof of a concerted practice between the suppliers to fix prices unless concertation is the only plausible explanation for the conduct.

6.3 Identifying which agreements infringe Article 101 TFEU

6.3.1 Categories of analysis

To determine whether an agreement is prohibited by Article 101, a claimant must first identify the anticompetitive aspects of an agreement—it must establish a restriction of competition, whether by object or effect within the meaning of Article 101(1). Where an agreement infringes Article 101(1), it is prohibited unless it can be established that the agreement satisfies the conditions of Article 101(3).

6.3.2 Agreements which restrict competition by object

Certain agreements considered to have as their purpose the restriction of competition are *assumed* to restrict competition—to be restrictive by object. The question whether or not an agreement is restrictive of competition by object thus has a critical impact on the likelihood of a violation being established and the burden of proof. Where it is shown that the object of an agreement is to restrict competition (and the other conditions of Article 101(1) are satisfied), there is no need to demonstrate anticompetitive effects—a violation of Article 101 is proved unless the person denying the breach can demonstrate that the agreement satisfies the Article 101(3) criteria. Where the object of the agreement is not found to restrict competition, however, the significant burden of proving that this is its actual or potential *effect* is on the person alleging the breach.

The Court of Justice has held that in order to determine whether conduct is 'by its very nature' injurious to competition (ie a restriction by object), 'regard must be had inter alia to the content of its provisions, the objectives it seeks to ascertain and the economic and legal context of which it forms part'.[107] Because a finding of restriction by object exempts the Commission (or other claimant) from the burden of demonstrating the restrictive effects of the agreement, however, the Court in *Groupement des Cartes Bancaires (CB) v Commission*[108] stressed that the category must be interpreted restrictively; it is

[103] See eg Commission Decision, *FENEX* (OJ [1996] L181/28).

[104] See eg *Stichting Certificatie Kraanverhuurbedrijf and Federatie van Nederlandse Kraanbedrijven* (OJ [1995] L312/79) and Joined Cases T-213/95 and T-18/96 *Stichting Certificatie Kraanverhuurbedrijf and Federatie van Nederlandse Kraanbedrijven v Commission*, EU:T:1997:157.

[105] *Bayer AG* (n 90) paras 66–185.

[106] Joined Cases C-89/85 etc (n 30).

[107] Case C-501/06 P *GlaxoSmithKline* (n 18) para 58.

[108] Case C-67/13 P, EU:C:2014:2204.

reserved exclusively for agreements which inherently reveal a sufficient degree of harm to competition.

Content

Jurisprudence illustrates that agreements containing certain, established restraints (see Table 17.1) are liable in principle to be restrictive of competition by object.[109]

Table 17.1 Agreements highly likely to be found to restrict competition by object

Horizontal agreements (or 'cartels')—collusion between competitors:	Vertical agreements:
To fix prices, limit non-price competition or output, share markets, rig bids, reduce capacity.[110]	To fix or set the minimum prices at which retailers can sell the contract product (resale price maintenance).[111]
To exchange information designed, directly or indirectly, to fix purchase or selling prices[112] to exclude rivals.[113]	To confer absolute territorial protection (ATP) on a distributor or otherwise partition national markets.[114]

There is a fairly broad consensus that competition law systems should treat cartel activity between competitors as an automatic violation of the rules (see further case study 17.1 on the *Marine Hoses* case). More controversial, however, is the fact that this category of 'established' restrictions (set out in Table 17.1) also includes vertical restraints. Since vertical agreements are not made between competitors but between providers of complementary goods and services, they are less obviously anticompetitive than horizontal arrangements and provide greater scope for efficiencies.

In *Consten and Grundig*, for example, the parties complained that the Commission had been wrong to find a restriction by object as the vertical agreement conferring the exclusive right on Consten to sell Grundig products in France had been essential to enable Grundig (a German manufacturer of consumer electronics) to penetrate the French market: Consten (Grundig's appointed exclusive distributor in France) would not have proceeded without the territorial protection from other distributors (and Grundig itself) which could otherwise have taken a 'free ride' upon Consten's promotional and investment efforts. Even though, therefore, the agreement resulted in the existence of only one distributor of Grundig products in France (there was a restriction on competition between distributors of Grundig products—*intra-brand competition*), the agreement led to an increase in competition for consumer electronics products in France (there was an increase in *inter-brand competition* because Grundig products had not been sold in France before). Although this approach gained support from Advocate General Roemer, the Court of Justice upheld the Commission's decision. The agreement, giving Consten the exclusive right of sale of Grundig products in France, had as its *object* the restriction of competition so that an assessment of its *effect* was unnecessary. The Court has reiterated

[109] But see further eg A Jones, B Sufrin, and N Dunne, *Jones and Sufrin's EU Competition Law* (7th edn, Oxford: Oxford University Press, 2019) ch 4.

[110] See eg Joined Cases T-374/94 etc *European Night Services v Commission*, ECR:T:1998:198, para 136, Case C-209/07 *Competition Authority v Beef Industry Development Society Ltd (BIDS)*, EU:C:2008:643.

[111] See eg Case 243/83 *SA Binon & Cie v SA Agence et Messageries de la Presse*, EU:C:1985:284, para 44.

[112] *T-Mobile Netherlands* (n 15) paras 36–43.

[113] See eg Case C-333/21 *European Super League Company, SL v Union of European Football Associations (UEFA) and Fédération Internationale de Football Association (FIFA)*, EU:C:2023:1011, para 164.

[114] See eg *GlaxoSmithKline* (n 18) para 61.

this view, that vertical restraints may be restrictive by object, on several occasions—especially territorial restraints eliminating any possibility of competition between distributors in different Member States.[115] There seems little doubt that this approach is influenced by the internal market objective.

The objectives and context of the agreement

In order to ensure Article 101 analysis is in tune with the objectives underpinning it and that the risk of type I errors is minimized, 'context' also constitutes a central plank of the characterization exercise and in identifying object restraints. The contextual analysis here is, however, limited and confined 'to what is strictly necessary . . . to establish the existence of a restriction of competition by object'.[116] Although fact- and context-specific, the assessment required is not therefore as in-depth as that required to identify actual or potential restrictive effects and does not generally demand a detailed assessment of the relevant market or counterfactual scenario.[117]

The need to assess context does mean, however, that even 'established' restraints may not restrict competition by object if contextual evidence casts reasonable doubt[118] on the conclusion that the agreement by its very nature harms competition, for example because it indicates that the agreement pursues a credible, pro-competitive commercial objective.[119] Further, that in spite of its narrow nature, the category of object restraints can encompass new agreements (beyond those established in past cases) where sufficient and consistent experience and evidence exists of the inherently harmful nature of the type of agreement.[120]

6.3.3 **Agreements which restrict competition by effect**

Where it is not found that the object of the agreement is to restrict competition, the likely impact of the agreement on inter-brand competition or intra-brand competition must be determined before it can be decided whether it has restrictive effects. This requires proof that the agreement either (a) affects 'actual or potential competition to such an extent that on the relevant market negative effects on prices, output, innovation or the variety or quality of goods and services can be expected with a reasonable degree of probability',[121] or (b) restricts a supplier's distributors from competing with each other since potential competition that could have existed between the distributors absent the restraint is restricted.

In *Delimitis v Henninger Bräu*,[122] for example, the Court set out guidance for determining whether a beer supply agreement, incorporating a 'beer tie' (a commitment by the buyer to purchase beer exclusively from named suppliers—and so not from other beer suppliers) infringes Article 101(1). It held that as the purpose of the beer tie was to secure

[115] See Case C-501/06 P *GlaxoSmithKline* (n 18) and also, more generally, Case C-32/11 *Allianz Hungária Biztosító Zrt, Generali-Providencia Biztosító Zrt v Gazdasági Versenyhivatal*, EU:C:2013:160.

[116] Case C-373/14 P *Toshiba Corp v Commission*, EU:C:2016:26, para 29.

[117] Case C-591/16 P *H Lundbeck v Commission*, EU:C:2021:243, para 140.

[118] A mere unsubstantiated assertion concerning pro-competitive effects is insufficient: *Lundbeck*, ibid, para 137.

[119] Case C-307/18 *Generics*, EU:C:2020:52, para 111; Case C-228/18 *Budapest Bank*, EU:C:2020:265, paras 71–75.

[120] See Case C-67/13 P *Groupement des Cartes Bancaires (CB) v Commission*, EU:C:2014:2204.

[121] Art 101(3) Guidelines (n 11) para 24. This could be because the agreement restricts actual or potential competition between the parties or between any one of the parties and third parties that could have existed absent the agreement (paras 25 and 26).

[122] Case C-234/89, EU:C:1991:91. See V Korah, 'The Judgment in *Delimitis*: A Milestone towards a Realistic Assessment of the Effects of an Agreement or a Damp Squib' (1992) 14 *European Intellectual Property Review* 167.

advantages (to guarantee both an outlet for the supplier and a supply of products to the retailer, to ensure that the retailer concentrates its sales efforts on the distribution of the contract goods, and to ensure the ability of the retailer to gain access to the market on favourable terms) it could not be characterized as restrictive by object.

Whether or not the agreement had a restrictive effect depended on whether it would foreclose competitors from entering or expanding in the market. This was dependent on the relevant market, the number and size of producers operating on the market, the existence of networks of similar agreements, the saturation of the market, and brand loyalty, etc. Only if access could be said to be inhibited would it be necessary to assess whether the agreement in question (which is taken to mean the agreements of that particular producer or brewer) contributes appreciably to that situation. In effects cases, therefore, it is crucial to assess contractual restraints, not abstractly as restraints, but in the context in which they operate, before their effect can be determined.

In *Société Technique Minière v Maschinenbau Ulm GmbH* ('*STM*'),[123] the Court held that an agreement appointing an exclusive distributor in France which, in contrast to that concerned in *Consten and Grundig*, did not confer ATP (or complete exclusivity over the right to distribute in France) on the distributor did not have as its object a restriction of competition. Rather, accepting similar arguments to those raised by the parties in *Consten and Grundig* (which was handed down two weeks after *Société Technique Minière*), it indicated that an exclusive distribution agreement would not restrict competition if the appointment of an exclusive distributor was necessary in order to enable a manufacturer to penetrate a new market. Before it could be determined whether the agreement restricted competition, the agreement should be examined in light of the competition which would occur *if the agreement in question were not or had not been made*. In this case, it seemed that the economic justifications for the agreement might outweigh the territorial restrictions inherent in the agreement.

6.3.4 **Ancillary restraints and the *Wouters* exceptions**

Two distinct lines of cases hold that agreements incorporating certain contractual restraints fall outside of Article 101.

'Ancillary restraints' cases establish that contractual restraints which are objectively necessary, or ancillary, to a main operation or activity that has positive or neutral effects in terms of competition, are not covered by Article 101(1) if it is not possible to dissociate them from the main operation or activity of which they form part without jeopardizing the latter's existence or aims (the agreement is impossible to implement without them).[124]

A separate line of cases also establish that contractual restraints necessary to the pursuit of legitimate objectives in the public interest do not fall within the scope of Article 101(1) so long as their inherent effect of restricting competition does not go beyond what is necessary (the restrictions are proportionate)—often referred as the *Wouters* exception.[125] In *Wouters v Algemene Raad van de Nederlandse Orde van Advocaten*[126] itself, the Court of Justice was asked how it was to be determined whether professional rules which prohibited members of the Bar practising in full partnership with accountants in the Netherlands restricted competition. Although the rules restricted services that could be offered and reduced scope for efficiencies, the Court concluded that they would not restrict competition if it was not unreasonable for the Bar Council to take the view that they were necessary for the proper practice of the legal profession (that they were required to achieve ethical or principled objectives relating to the regulation of a professional activity).[127]

[123] Case 56/65 (n 5). [124] See eg Case C-382/12 P *MasterCard*, EU:C:2014:2201.
[125] Case C-650/22 *Fédération Internationale de Football Association v BZ*, EU:C:2024:824, para 149.
[126] Case C-309/99 (n 19). [127] Contrast *OTOC* (n 10) 9.

The *Wouters* exception has also been invoked in some cases as a means of justifying prima-facie restrictive sporting rules, for example where the rules are inherent in, and justified by, a legitimate sporting objective, such as safeguarding the fairness, integrity, and objectivity of the conduct of competitive sport and upholding its integrity (rules relating to the organization of competitive sport fall outside the application of Article 101(1)).[128] At the end of December 2023, the Court of Justice gave three judgments, in the *International Skating Union (ISU)*, the *European Super League (ESL)*, and the *Royal Antwerp Football Club* cases,[129] considering application of the doctrine. In *ISU* and *ESL*, the relevant sporting governing bodies at issue not only organized their own events but also were entrusted with power to authorise third-party, competing events. Although the Court considered that this structure was not inherently problematic, insofar as the authorization powers were exercised in a transparent, objective, non-discriminatory, and proportionate way,[130] it had no hesitation in finding in both cases that the rules at issue (a) did not satisfy these conditions and so restricted competition by object; and (b) could not benefit from the *Wouters* exception, as the doctrine did not apply to conduct revealing a degree of harm to competition justifying a finding that it has as its very object the restriction of competition.[131]

6.3.5 **Agreements of minor importance**

The Court of Justice had held that EU law is not concerned with agreements which have an 'insignificant effect on the market, taking into account the weak position which the persons concerned have on the market of the product in question'.[132] 'Thus an exclusive dealing agreement, even with absolute territorial protection, may, having regard to the weak position of the persons concerned on the market in the products in question in the area covered by the absolute protection, escape the prohibition laid down in Article [101(1)].'[133] Although the Court in *Völk* thus indicated that even agreements containing object restraints may be of minor importance if the parties' market shares were very low,[134] in *Expedia* the Court held that an agreement which is restrictive of competition by object is so injurious to competition that it always constitutes an appreciable restriction of competition.[135]

Because of the huge practical importance of the concept of appreciability, the Commission has provided clarification, by Notice,[136] of when, in its view, an agreement is likely to be of minor importance: essentially where it does not contain object restraints[137] and the parties' market shares do not exceed 10 per cent (where the agreement is between competitors (actual or potential)) or 15 per cent (where it is between non-competitors).

6.3.6 **Article 101(3) TFEU**

Any agreement which infringes Article 101(1) may in principle benefit from Article 101(3) (including agreements containing object restraints),[138] whether by individually satisfying its criteria or by satisfying the conditions of a block exemption. In practice, it is a

[128] See eg Case C-519/04 P *Meca-Medina v Commission*, EU:C:2006:492.

[129] Case C-124/21 P *International Skaters Union v Commission*, EU:C:2023:1012 (relating to COMP/40.208, *ISU* 8 December 2017, aff'd Case T-93/18, EU:T:2020:610), Case C-333/21 *European Super League*, EU:C:2023:1011 and Case C-680/21 *Royal Antwerp FC v Royal Belgian FA*, EU:C:2023:1010.

[130] *ISU* (n 129), paras 125–132.

[131] Case C-333/21, EU:C:2023:101, para 186, Case C-124/21 P, EU:C:2023:1012, para 113.

[132] See section 4.2. [133] Case 5/69 *Völk v Vervaecke*, EU:C:1969:35.

[134] See J Faull and A Nikpay, *Faull and Nikpay: The EC Law of Competition* (3rd edn, Oxford: Oxford University Press, 2014) para 3.494.

[135] Case C-226/11 *Expedia Inc v Authorité de la Concurrence*, EU:C:2012:795, para 38.

[136] Commission Notice on agreements of minor importance which do not appreciably restrict competition under Article 101(1) (*De Minimis* Notice) (OJ [2014] C291/1).

significant burden to establish that its four cumulative criteria are met in an individual case. To do so, it must be established that:

- the agreement leads to an improvement in the production or distribution of goods or the promotion of technical or economic progress. The Commission's view is that this criterion requires the parties to establish that, despite the fact that the agreement restricts competition, it will lead to efficiency gains, cost efficiencies, and/or qualitative efficiencies, creating value in the form of new or improved products (dynamic efficiencies) (there must be a causal link between the agreement and the claimed efficiencies).[139]

  A controversial issue is whether Article 101(3) also permits the parties to rely on broader public policy benefits (eg environmental benefits) achieved by the agreement. Although a sole consumer-welfare objective would suggest that such considerations should not be assessed, others argue that a teleological interpretation would allow Article 101(3) to be interpreted broadly against the backdrop of the wider EU aims and objectives so that its application does not produce results inconsistent with other EU policies (see section 2.2.). In *European Super League*,[140] however, the Court of Justice referred to the need, under the first condition of Article 101(3), for it to be demonstrated that the agreement in question 'makes it possible to achieve efficiency gains'[141] that may 'compensate for the disadvantages caused in competition terms by the rules at issues in the main proceedings, on the other'.[142] It is possible nonetheless that, for example, sustainability benefits may be manifested in the form of broad qualitative or cost efficiencies (eg cleaner production or distribution technologies or less pollution) that benefit consumers and outweigh the increase in cost of more sustainable processes:[143]

- the agreement allows consumers a fair share of the benefit: by showing that there is a pass-on of the cost and quality efficiencies to consumers;[144]
- the agreement only contains restrictions which are indispensable to the achievement of the benefits shown to result from the agreement. This criterion is often difficult to establish, particularly where object restrictions are incorporated within the agreement. The Commission takes the view that restrictions will not be indispensable if the efficiencies specific to the agreement can be achieved by other practicable and less restrictive means, or if individual restrictions are not reasonably necessary to produce the efficiencies;
- the agreement as a whole must not afford the parties the possibility of eliminating competition. 'Ultimately the protection of rivalry and the competitive process is given priority over potentially pro-competitive efficiency gains which could result from restrictive agreements.'[145]

Parties will be spared the difficult task of determining whether these criteria apply to their agreement individually if it meets the conditions, and so falls within the 'safe harbour', of

[137] Ibid, para 13. The Notice thus endorses the view that the Court in *Expedia* effectively overrules the judgment of *Völk* on this point.

[138] Case T-17/93 *Matra Hachette SA v Commission*, EU:T:1994:89, para 85.

[139] Art 101(3) Guidelines (n 11) paras 45 and 64–72.

[140] Case C-333/21, EU:C:2023:1011, para 196.

[141] Case C-333/21 *European Super League*, EU:C:2023:1011, para 190.

[142] Ibid, para 196.

[143] Guidelines on the applicability of Article 101 to horizontal co-operation agreements (OJ [2023] C259/01), section 9.

[144] Ibid, paras 83–104. See discussion of the different ways that consumers can benefit from a sustainability agreement in the Horizontal Co-operation Guidelines (OJ [2023] C259/01), 9.4.3.

[145] Ibid, para 105.

one of the block exemptions set out in an EU regulation. These regulations grant 'exemption' from Article 101(1) to categories of agreements that satisfy their conditions and their benefit can only be withdrawn prospectively.[146] Some pertain to specific sectors (eg transport). Others apply more generally, for example to vertical (Regulation 2022/720[147]), horizontal cooperation (Regulations 2023/1066[148] and 2023/1067[149]), or technology transfer (Regulation 2026/877[150]) agreements. As the block exemptions are directly applicable,[151] agreements falling within their ambit benefit from the legal certainty that they are automatically exempt from the Article 101(1) prohibition (unless and until it is withdrawn). Most of the block exemptions now contain market-share thresholds and a list of 'hardcore restraints' which, if included within the agreement, preclude the application of the block exemption. The list of hardcore restraints closely mirrors the established object restraints[152] discussed previously, reflecting the Commission's view that agreements containing such restraints are highly likely to be anticompetitive and unlikely to produce countervailing efficiencies, and so cannot benefit from a block exemption. For example, the Vertical Block Exemption Regulation, applies only where:

- the supplier's and buyer's market shares do not exceed 30 per cent of the relevant market; and
- the agreement does not incorporate any hardcore restraints—which include, for example, provisions: fixing or setting minimum selling prices to be adhered to by the buyer; or imposing (with some exceptions) restrictions on the territory into which, or of the customers to whom, the buyer may sell the contract goods or services.

Case study 17.1: Cartels and the Marine Hose cartel

Parties to cartels—including anticompetitive agreements and other collusive arrangements between competitors to fix prices, make rigged bids (collusive tenders), establish output restrictions or quotas, or share or divide markets[153]—deliberately set out to interfere with free competition. Such cartels 'diminish social welfare, create allocative inefficiency and transfer wealth from consumers to the participants in the cartel'.[154] The formation and successful operation of a cartel is easier for firms operating in an oligopolistic market—a market in which there are only a few players—where it is simpler to coordinate conduct and where each firm's profits are strongly dependent upon the course of action chosen by its competitors.

There is a fairly general consensus that cartel activity poses a serious threat to economies and consumers and, as one of 'the most egregious'[155] violations of competition law and require clear competition law rules against them. Debate now focuses on how best to reflect the seriousness of the offence and to ensure that cartel activity is detected, deterred, and punished. The Marine Hoses[156] cartel illustrates both the way in which business peo-

[146] See Regulation 1/2003 (OJ [2003] L1/1), Art 29(1), (2) and Regulation 330/2010 (OJ [2010] L102/1), recital 15 and Art 6.

[147] OJ [2022] L134/4. [148] OJ [2023] L143/9. [149] OJ [2023] L143/20.

[150] OJ [2026] L2026/87. [151] Art 288 TFEU.

[152] They are not identical, however, as, as has been explained, there is no fixed list of restrictions of competition by object, which can be identified only after an analysis of context, context, and objectives.

[153] 'Recommendation of the Council Concerning Effective Action against Hard Core Cartels', OECD Publication C(98)35/FINAL, 25 March 1998, available on the OECD's website.

[154] Commission, XXXIInd Report on Competition Policy (2002), part 26.

[155] OECD Publication C(98)35/FINAL (n 153).

[156] Commission Press Release IP/09/137, 'Commission fines marine hose producers €131 million for market sharing and price-fixing cartel' (*EUROPA*, 28 January 2009).

ple may go about rigging the market, and interfering with the free play of competition on it, and the different views as to how such conduct should be detected, deterred, and punished. In both the US and the UK, criminal proceedings were pursued. In the EU, the Commission imposed hefty sanctions on the undertakings involved for violation of Article 101.

The case concerned several companies involved in the manufacture and sale on a global basis of marine hoses—used principally for the transportation of oil from remote places offshore. These manufacturers operated a bid-rigging, price-fixing, and market-sharing allocation agreement designed to suppress and eliminate competition between them. The cartel was managed and facilitated by Peter Whittle, who essentially designated a champion or winner for each job on which the conspirators 'bid' and provided others with instructions on how to bid on the job with the objective of ensuring that the designated champion would win it. Cartel members went to great lengths to conceal its existence, meeting clandestinely in locations around the world and using code names.

In 2006, however, one of the conspirators, the Yokohama Rubber Co Ltd, disclosed details of the cartel to the US, EU, and Japanese competition authorities. When the cartel members next met in Houston, the meetings were monitored and the individuals involved were arrested. The US competition agency cooperated with some of its counterparts in the EU (including the Commission and UK competition agency[157]—the UK was then an EU Member State), and at the same time as the arrests were occurring in the US, surprise unannounced inspections were made both at the conspirators' premises and the homes of an individual in Europe. Each competition authority thus investigated the activities of the cartel insofar as the cartel had effects in its jurisdiction. The operation of the cartel in the end proved costly to the companies and individuals involved:

- plea agreements and criminal convictions were made in the US under criminal antitrust laws;
- class actions for damages were launched in the US;
- under the US plea agreements, three British nationals (Peter Whittle, Bryan Allison, and David Brammer) were returned to the UK, pleaded guilty to committing a criminal (cartel) offence in the UK, and were sentenced to prison;[158]
- the European Commission imposed fines of €131,510,000 on five groups of companies involved in the cartel for entering into a single and continuous agreement which had as its object the restriction of competition;[159] and
- Japanese and Australian competition authorities also found violations of their competition law rules.

In an interview, Mr Allison subsequently stated: 'I would never ever do it again, and I wouldn't recommend to anyone that they do it. The loss to you in terms of your life is too great.'

[157] See speeches by SD Hammond, 'Recent Developments, Trends, and Milestones in the Antitrust Division's Criminal Enforcement Program', Department of Justice, 56th Annual Spring Meeting, Washington, DC, 26 March 2008, and A Nikpay, 'Cartel Enforcement: Past, Present and Future', Law Society Anti-Trust Section, London, 11 December 2012.

[158] *R v Whittle, Brammar and Allison* [2008] EWCA Crim 2560.

[159] Commission Press Release IP/09/137; one fine was reduced on appeal, Case T-146/09 *Parker ITR Srl v Commission*, EU:T:2013:258, but judgment set aside and referred back to the General Court, Case C-434/13 P, EU:C:2014:2456.

CASE STUDY 17.2: Selective distribution and *Pierre Fabre v Président de l'Autorité de la concurrence*

Selective distribution systems are distribution systems 'where the supplier undertakes to sell the contract goods or services, either directly or indirectly, only to distributors selected on the basis of specified criteria and where these distributors undertake not to sell such goods or services to unauthorised distributors'.[160] Many selective distribution systems in the EU do not infringe Article 101, either because they meet the conditions, and so benefit from the safe harbour of the EU block exemption applicable to vertical agreements (Regulation 2022/720) or because they do not have as their object or effect the restriction of competition. In particular, they will not infringe Article 101(1) where the selective distribution system is necessary to maintain a specialist trade capable of providing suitable services for high-quality and/or technically complex products and where resellers are chosen on the basis of objective and qualitative criteria applied in a non-discriminatory way.

Pierre Fabre[161] concerned a selective distribution system operated by Pierre Fabre for the distribution of its cosmetics and personal care products in France. The agreements stipulated that sales of these products had to be made in a physical space, meeting specified requirements, and that a qualified pharmacist had to be present. The French competition authority found that the agreement was not compatible with the competition law rules. Rather, this agreement violated Article 101 as the obligation for a pharmacist to be physically present at sale operated as a de facto ban on internet selling. Consequently, the ability of the distributor to sell the contractual products outside its contractual territory was considerably reduced.

Following an appeal, the French cour d'appel de Paris made a reference to the Court of Justice which subsequently held that:

(a) as the de facto ban eliminated cross-border trade, the restraint at issue was 'liable to restrict competition'.[162] It was restrictive of competition by object as the restriction was not a proportionate means of pursuing a legitimate aim—individual advice from a pharmacist was not necessary in the context of non-prescription medicines or to maintain Pierre Fabre's prestigious brand image;

(b) because the agreement incorporated a 'hardcore' restraint—it precluded (through incorporation of the de facto ban on internet selling) active or passive sales to end-users by the retailers within the selective distribution system—the verticals block exemption then in force did not apply. It was not necessary to adopt a broad interpretation of the block exemption provisions as undertakings have the option of asserting that Article 101(3) applies on an individual basis to their agreement (see section 6.3.5, agreements can individually satisfy the conditions of Article 101(3) even if they do not satisfy the conditions of a block exemption regulation);

(c) it did not have sufficient information before it to provide guidance to the referring court on the question of whether the agreement individually satisfied the criteria of Article 101(3).

When the matter reverted to the French court, applying the guidance set out by the Court, it upheld the fine that had been imposed on Pierre Fabre by the French competition authority.

[160] Regulation 2022/720, Art 1(1)(g).

[161] Case C-439/09, EU:C:2011:649.

[162] Ibid, para 38.

7 Article 102 TFEU

7.1 Introduction

Article 102 prohibits any abuse by one or more undertakings of a dominant position. Although not set out in the wording of Article 102, the EU Courts have consistently held that a dominant undertaking may provide objective justification for behaviour that is otherwise liable to be found abusive and caught by the prohibition under Article 102.

Like Article 101, it applies to undertakings and to conduct that has an appreciable effect on trade between Member States. This section consequently focuses on the concepts of dominance and abuse. The dominant position must be in the internal market, or in a substantial part of it.

7.2 Dominance

Article 102 only applies where an undertaking[163] holds a dominant position. In *Hoffmann-La Roche*, the Court of Justice held that a dominant position relates to a position of economic strength enjoyed by an undertaking:

> which enables it to prevent effective competition being maintained on the relevant market by affording it the power to behave to an appreciable extent independently of its competitors, its customers and ultimately of the consumers. Such a position does not preclude some competition.[164]

Although this definition focuses on the concept of independence, rather than the power of the firm to exercise market power and maintain supra-competitive prices,[165] the General Court in *AstraZeneca* explicitly equated this notion of 'independence' with the market power of a dominant firm and its ability to maintain high prices.[166]

It has been seen that market power is frequently identified indirectly in EU competition law. Indeed, the Court has defined two steps in assessing dominance. First, the relevant market must be identified (from both a product and geographic perspective). This is difficult and complex.[167] Secondly, it must be determined whether the undertaking is dominant on the relevant market. This is done by looking both at market shares and other factors indicating dominance.

Where market shares are very large and have been held for some time, they may provide a good proxy for market power or dominance.[168] In *AKZO*, the Court of Justice established a presumption of dominance for firms with a market share of 50 per cent or more:

> With regard to market shares the Court has held that very large shares are in themselves, and save in exceptional circumstances, evidence of the existence of a dominant position . . . That is the situation where there is a market share of 50%.[169]

[163] The Court has confirmed that Art 102 also applies where two or more undertakings are collectively dominant on a market, see eg Jones, Sufrin, and Dunne (n 109) ch 6. Only single dominance is discussed in this chapter.

[164] Case 85/76 *Hoffmann-La Roche v Commission*, EU:C:1979:36, paras 38 and 39.

[165] See eg L Ortiz Blanco, *Market Power in EU Antitrust Law* (Oxford: Hart Publishing, 2012) 47.

[166] Case T-321/05 *AstraZeneca v Commission*, EU:T:2010:266, para 267, aff'd Case C-457/10 P *AstraZeneca v Commission*, EU:C:2012:770, paras 177–181.

[167] See Commission Notice on the definition of the relevant market (OJ [2024] C1645).

[168] *Hoffmann-La Roche* (n 164) para 41.

[169] Case C-62/86 *AKZO Chemie v Commission*, EU:C:1991:286, para 60.

Dominance may also be found where market shares are below 50 per cent, although in practice a finding of dominance is unlikely if the undertaking's market share is below 40 per cent.[170]

It is important to stress nonetheless that market shares are just the starting point in dominance assessments. They provide a snapshot of how the market is at that time, but they do not indicate why the undertaking has these market shares, for example whether it is because it produces the best products more efficiently or because it is not vulnerable to new entry into its market by competitors. In addition to considering market shares, it is also important to consider:

- the undertaking's market share compared to those of its rivals[171]—an undertaking with a market share of 40 per cent is less likely to be found dominant when its nearest rival has a share of 40 per cent, than when its nearest rival has a share of 5 per cent;
- how the firm's market shares have changed over time[172]—high market shares that are sustained over time may be more suggestive of dominance;
- the dynamics of competition on the market—competition today and how the market might develop in the future (especially in markets driven by innovation);
- whether or not there are barriers to entry or expansion into the market; and
- countervailing buyer power.[173]

The question of whether there are barriers to entry or expansion is especially important. If there are no or low barriers to entry/expansion into a market, an undertaking will be deterred from increasing prices (and so be unable to exercise market power), because doing so will attract new entry into the market. Consequently, even a firm with a 100 per cent market share will not have market power if it cannot sustain supra-competitive prices.[174] In contrast, where barriers to entry/expansion are high, a (dominant) firm may be able to sustain supra-competitive prices without attracting new entrants or expansion by rivals.

An essential question is therefore what constitutes a barrier to entry or expansion. Stigler took the view that, in the absence of statutory regulation and where raw materials are available, barriers exist only when a new entrant faces higher costs than those firms already in the marketplace face, or had to face.[175] Other economists, such as Bain, define barriers to entry more broadly, as anything that makes entry more costly.[176]

Some early decisions of the EU Courts, and the Commission, were criticized for taking too broad an approach when identifying barriers to entry and 'other factors indicating

[170] See eg Case 27/76 *United Brands v Commission*, EU:C:1978:22, paras 108–129 (40–45 per cent) and Case T-219/99 *British Airways v Commission*, EU:C:2003:343, paras 189–225 (39.7 per cent).

[171] *Hoffmann-La Roche* (n 164) para 48.

[172] M Motta, *Competition Policy: Theory and Practice* (Cambridge: Cambridge University Press, 2004) 120.

[173] See ibid, 121–123 and Paper (n 177) para 18.

[174] W Baumol, J Panzar, and R Willig, *Contestable Markets and the Theory of Industry Structure* (revised edn, New York: Harcourt Brace Jovanovich, 1988).

[175] G Stigler, *The Organisation of Industry* (Homewood, IL: Richard D Irwin, 1968).

[176] J Bain, *Barriers to New Competition: Their Character and Consequences in Manufacturing Industries* (Cambridge, MA: Harvard University Press, 1956). Monti explains the differences in the following way: if newly devised planning laws prevent the construction of a factory necessary for the competitor's entry, this is an entry barrier under both definitions. On the other hand, the fact that the incumbent has an efficient distribution network is not an entry barrier under Stigler's definition because if such a network is key to market success, it is an investment which both incumbent and new entrant have to make to participate in the market. It can, however, constitute an entry barrier under Bain's definition because it is an extra cost which makes entry riskier (G Monti, 'The Concept of Dominance in Article 82' (2006) 2 *European Competition Journal* (Special edn) 31–52).

dominance'. Further, for placing too great an emphasis on market shares in its assessments of dominance so creating an exaggerated picture of an undertaking's market power and creating a risk that the rules may be applied overexpansively (leading to type 1 errors).

The Commission, however, now acknowledges that market shares only give a first indication of market structure, and that '[e]asy expansion and entry in a market limits the ability of an undertaking in that market to behave independently, as applying prices or other conditions above the competitive level would attract expansion or new entry by rivals'.[177] The Commission's Draft Guidelines on the application of Article 102 to abusive exclusionary conduct by dominant undertakings recognize that barriers to expansion or entry can result from various factors—legal and regulatory or from certain advantages:

> Legal and regulatory barriers have been found to include, for example, tariffs or quotas, planning regulations, licensing requirements and authorisation requirements, statutory monopolies and intellectual property rights. Other barriers to expansion and entry that derive from certain advantages that have been identified in the past include: (i) an established distribution and sales network[53], (ii) economies of scale[54] and scope[55], (iii)vertical integration and exclusive or preferential access to inputs or customers[56], (iv) access to critical raw materials[57], (v) inertia of doctors in their prescribing habits, (vi) brand image and brand effects[59], (vii) data-driven advantages and (viii) the existence of a first mover advantage. Other factors that may create barriers to expansion and entry are significant upfront investments and high sunk costs, as well as costs and other impediments when switching to a rival, including behavioural biases.[178]

A particularly complex issue is how market power can be assessed in markets in the digital economy. For many years there has been concern that the strong positions of a number of the big technology companies (such as Google/Alphabet, Amazon, Meta, and Apple) have become entrenched, in particular, because of (a) the tendency of many digital markets to tip to monopoly or 'winner takes all'[179] situations (competition is for, rather than on, the market); (b) the barriers to entry created by network effects;[180] (c) the difficulty of displacing such firms other than through innovation; (d) the strong incentives for dominant platforms and ecosystems,[181] fearing that markets might tilt against them, 'to engage in anticompetitive behaviour';[182] and (e) a wave of mergers which has enabled them to purchase new start-ups and to acquire control over large volumes of data, so increasing barriers to entry and significantly impeding effective competition.[183] A concern

[177] Draft Guidelines on the application of Article 102 to abusive exclusionary conduct by dominant undertakings (2024), para 29.

[178] Ibid, para 30.

[179] See eg P Barwise and L Watkins, 'The Evolution of Digital Dominance: How and Why We Got to GAFA' in M Moore and D Tambini (eds), *Digital Dominance: The Power of Google, Amazon, Facebook, and Apple* (Oxford: Oxford University Press, 2018) and contrast D Evans and R Schmalensee, 'Why Winner-Take-All Thinking Doesn't Apply to the Platform Economy', *Harvard Business Review*, 4 May 2016, https://hbr.org/2016/05/why-winner-takes-all-thinking-doesnt-apply-to-silicon-valley.

[180] Direct network effects exist where the willingness of users to switch to a new platform is dependent on the willingness of other users on the same side of the platform to switch. Indirect network effects may exist where the willingness of one group of users to switch to a new platform depends on the willingness of the group of users on the other side of the platform to switch.

[181] The Commission explains in its Notice on Market Definition (n 167) that (digital) ecosystems 'can, in certain circumstances, be thought of as consisting of a primary core product and several secondary (digital) products whose consumption is connected to the core product, for instance, by technological links or interoperability', para 103.

[182] J Crémer, Y-A de Montjoye, and H Schweitzer, 'Competition Policy for the Digital Era' (European Commission, 2019) 37.

[183] See eg Document prepared by Lear for the Competition and Markets Authority, Ex-post Assessment of Merger Control Decisions in Digital Markets, 9 May 2019 (noting that on the information available, Google, Facebook, and Amazon acquired 168, 71, and 60 companies respectively between 2008 and 2018).

nonetheless is that assessment of market power in this area is particularly challenging[184] because their features often mean that traditional competition law tools developed to assess market power are inappropriate, unworkable, or provide poor indicators of market power.[185] For example, competition in these markets often relates to quality and innovation rather than price, complexities arise as a result of their development of ecosystems and in relation to multi-sided markets where platforms deal with different customers and compete with distinct rivals on separate sides of the platform (eg the provision of search or social network services on one side and display advertising services on the other), and because in many instances services on one side of the market (searches, social media etc) are provided for 'free' (at a zero price).[186] Nonetheless, EU competition agencies have tended to rely on product and service functionalities for determining markets in this area combined with careful scrutiny of other factors, such as internal documents and barriers to entry into identified markets. In 2024 the Commission updated its market definition guidelines to reflect its practice in this area.[187]

7.3 **Identifying conduct which infringes Article 102**

Article 102 makes it clear that it is not an offence for a firm to hold a dominant position: an abuse of that dominant position must be committed. The EU Courts have consistently stressed, however, that although a finding of dominance is not a recrimination, a dominant firm does have a special responsibility 'not to allow its conduct to impair genuine undistorted competition'.[188]

7.3.1 **Abuse**

Article 102 itself sets out an illustrative, but not exhaustive, list of abuses, including 'directly or indirectly imposing unfair purchase or selling prices or other unfair trading conditions' (Article 102(a)), 'limiting production, markets or technical development to the prejudice of consumers' (Article 102(b)), and 'applying dissimilar conditions to equivalent transactions with other trading parties, thereby placing them at a competitive disadvantage' (Article 102(c)).

Although the provisions indicate that Article 102 may apply to 'exploitative' abuses (where a dominant undertaking takes advantage of its market power and exploits it) and certain price discrimination,[189] a majority of cases have focused on exclusionary abuses—'practices that cause consumers harm through their impact on competition',[190] for example predatory pricing (see case study 17.3), exclusive dealing obligations (where a buyer is obliged to purchase all of its requirements from the dominant supplier), refusal to supply/deal, margin squeeze, or tying. Indeed, in *Continental Can*,[191] the Court of Justice emphasized that the object of Article 102 is not only to protect consumers directly from

[184] See N Davidson, M Finck, and J Infranca (eds), *Cambridge Handbook on Law and Regulation of the Sharing Economy* (Cambridge: Cambridge University Press, 2018).

[185] See D Sokol and J Ma, 'Understanding Online Markets and Antitrust Analysis' (2017) 15 *Northwestern Journal of Technology and Intellectual Property* 43.

[186] See eg N Zingales, 'Product Market Definition in Online Search and Advertising' (2013) 9 *Competition Law Review* 29.

[187] See Commission Market Definition Notice (n 167).

[188] Case 322/81 *NV Nederlandsche Vanden-Industri Michelin v Commission* ('*Michelin I*'), EU:C:1983:313, para 57.

[189] See eg Case C-525/16, *Meo—Serviços de Comunicações e Multimédia*, EU:C:2018:270.

[190] *Post Danmark* (n 14) para 20. The categories of exclusionary and exploitative abuse are not mutually exclusive, however. See Jones, Sufrin, and Dunne (n 108) ch 7.

[191] Case 6/72 (n 7).

the exploitation of market power, but also to protect them from conduct which through its impact on the structure of competition is detrimental to them indirectly—in that case strengthening a dominant position and eliminating competition by taking over a competitor. Conduct may also constitute an abuse where the conduct is inimical to the internal market, so parallel trade is prejudiced.

The Court has set out general statements about the nature of the concept of an (exclusionary) abuse. In particular, it has held that it:

> is an objective concept relating to the behaviour of an undertaking in a dominant position which is such as to influence the structure of a market where, as a result of the very presence of the undertaking in question, the degree of competition is weakened and which, through recourse to methods different from that which condition normal competition in products or services on the basis of the transactions of commercial operators, has the effect of hindering the maintenance of the degree of competition still existing in the market or the growth of that competition.[192]

The emphasis on the objective nature of the concept indicates that it is not essential that fault or subjective intent to exclude competitors or weaken competition is established. The clear presence of an anticompetitive objective/intent may, however, reinforce a finding that there is an abuse of a dominant position.[193]

7.3.2 **Exploitative abuses: unfair pricing and terms and conditions**

The view could be taken that there is nothing wrong with charging supra-competitive prices which 'at least for a short period—is what attracts "business acumen" in the first place; it induces risk taking that produces innovation and economic growth'.[194] Indeed, despite Article 102's clear wording (targeting unfair prices and trading conditions), EU competition authorities have generally been cautious about tackling exploitative abuses, especially high pricing. This may be because they are reluctant to engage in price regulation—the antithesis of the free market—and also because unfairly high prices are difficult to identify (how can a *fair* selling price be determined?) and, even if identified, hard to remedy. Such conduct may therefore be considered better dealt with by regulatory agencies specialized in dealing with natural or legal monopolies (such as regulatory authorities in the Member States), through contract or consumer protection laws, or by acting decisively against exclusionary conduct designed to perpetuate a position of dominance.[195]

In its *1998 Football World Cup* decision,[196] however, the Commission looked at the distribution and sale arrangements for entry tickets to the 1998 Football World Cup which were operated by Comité français d'organisation de la Coupe du monde de football 1998 (CFO). Essentially, customers could only purchase tickets from CFO if they provided a postal address in France. Consequently, 'only by entering into wholly arbitrary, impractical and exceptional arrangements . . . could most of the general public resident outside France have obtained tickets direct from CFO'. The conduct was exploitative in the sense that it 'had the effect of imposing unfair trading conditions on residents outside France which resulted in a limitation of the market to the prejudice of those consumers'. By discriminating against customers on the grounds of nationality, the behaviour was also inimical to the internal market objective.

[192] *Hoffmann-La Roche* (n 163) para 91.
[193] *AstraZeneca v Commission* (n 165) para 359.
[194] *Verizon Communications v Law Offices of Curtis V Trinko* 540 US 398, 408 (2004), para 2 (Scalia J).
[195] XXIVth Report on Competition Policy (Commission, 1994), part 207.
[196] Commission Decision, *1998 Football World Cup* (OJ [2000] L5/55).

Further, spurred on partly perhaps by a desire to ensure that competition law addresses 'unfairness' in the system, interest in high pricing and unfair trading conditions has been mounting, especially in the health care and technology sectors and the digital economy, where it has been argued that competition and market circumstances are not delivering consumers real choice. In November 2018, for example, the OECD Competition Committee convened hearings on 'Excessive Prices in Pharmaceutical Markets'[197] and an increasing number of competition agencies, including the Commission and NCAs,[198] have become concerned about the impact on consumer welfare, public funds, and health of sudden hikes in the prices of pharmaceutical products. A core difficulty in such cases is, however, to establish 'unfairly high or excessive prices which bear no reasonable relation to the economic value of the product supplied',[199] in particular, by establishing that the difference between cost and price is excessive and that a price has been imposed which is unfair either in itself or when compared to competing goods.[200] In *Apple*,[201] the Commission also imposed a fine €1.8 billion on Apple for the imposition of unfair trading conditions contrary to Article 102; in that case through the use of anti-steering obligations, which prevented music streaming app developers from fully informing iOS users about alternative and cheaper music subscription services available outside of the app. The Commission considered that the conduct led to higher prices, and a degraded experience, for iOS users.

There has also been concern that data practices in the digital economy, involving sophisticated mechanisms for tracking and monitoring individual preferences, might involve a form of exploitation. A prominent case in this sphere is the German *Facebook* case,[202] where the German NCA, the Bundeskartellamt (BKA) found Facebook to be dominant on the German market for social networks[203] and that its data processing practices, in particular the collection and merging of user data both from Facebook and third-party websites without effective consent, infringed data protection principles and were abusive contrary to German competition law.[204] The case thus raised the question of how competition law should deal with non-compliance with data protection principles (set out in the General Data Protection Regulation (GDPR)).[205] In *Facebook v Bundeskartellamt*,[206] the Court of Justice confirmed that a competition authority could consider the question of fairness under competition law, taking account of whether a breach of the GDPR had occurred (although only relevant data authorities could decide, or advise, on the latter).

[197] See http://www.oecd.org/officialdocuments/publicdisplaydocumentpdf/?cote=DAF/COMP(2018)12&docLanguage=En hearing on 27–28 November 2018.

[198] See eg Case AT.40394, *Aspen* 10 February 2021.

[199] Case 27/76 *United Brands v Commission*, EU:C:1978:22, para 252.

[200] Although the Court of Justice has made it clear that there is no single methodology for identifying unfairly high prices and that other ways may be devised, in practice many EU competition authorities have relied on the two-prong test set out in *United Brands* in excessive prices cases.

[201] Case AT.40437, *Apple—App Store Practices (music streaming)* 4 March 2024.

[202] Case B6-22/16, *Facebook* 6 February 2019. See also in the UK, Case 1433/7/7/22, *Dr Liza Lovdahl Gormsen v Meta Platforms, Inc.*

[203] Based on the existence of high market shares, strong network, and lock-in effects.

[204] Established German authority holds that imposing unfair trading conditions, either in comparison to competitors' conditions or by imposing inappropriate contractual terms and conditions, is prohibited, see KZR 47/14, *VBL Gegenwert II* 24 January 2017. On appeal, the German Higher Regional Court held that the German authority should also have relied on Art 102 TFEU in its proceedings.

[205] Regulation (EU) 2016/679 of the European Parliament and of the Council of 27 April 2016 on the protection of natural persons with regard to the processing of personal data and on the free movement of such data, and repealing Directive 95/46/EC (OJ [2016] L119/1).

[206] Case C-252/21, EU:C:2023:537.

7.3.3 **Exclusionary abuses**

The Court of Justice's definition of abuse (set out in section 7.3.1) requires a difficult line to be drawn between unlawful exclusionary behaviour and competition on the basis of performance or competition on the merits (normal competition). For example, in the area of 'pricing' it is frequently hard to distinguish unlawful exclusionary pricing practices from aggressive but legitimate price competition (see case study 17.3).

It was often complained that the EU competition law rules developed in early cases to identify abusive behaviour were excessively broad and so chilled aggressive competition and low-cost pricing, arguably 'the very conduct the antitrust laws are designed to protect'.[207] Further, that they placed too great an emphasis on the form of the conduct, and insufficient on its effects. For example, in *Hoffmann-La Roche* both the incorporation of an exclusive purchasing obligation (a duty to purchase the contract products exclusively—or almost exclusively—from the dominant undertaking) and the use of a loyalty rebate (incentivizing the customer to engage in exclusive purchasing through discount policies which are conditional on exclusive purchasing or purchasing a percentage of requirements) were treated almost automatically as abusive conduct.[208] Further, in other cases, the Commission and the Court of Justice were criticized for being, arguably, too willing *to presume* anticompetitive effects when a competitor was excluded from the market. Thus, in *Commercial Solvents* it was held that CSC, dominant in the supply of a raw material, aminobutanol, had abused its dominant position when it ceased selling aminobutanol to Zoja, which used it to make an anti-tuberculosis drug. CSC had decided to start making this drug itself and wanted to stop supplying Zoja. The Court held that:

> an undertaking which has a dominant position in the market in raw materials and which, with the object of reserving such raw material for manufacturing its own derivatives, refuses to supply a customer, which is itself a manufacturer of these derivatives, and therefore risks eliminating all competition on the part of this customer, is abusing its dominant position.[209]

The Court did not clarify, however, why it considered this conduct to be abusive. In particular, whether it simply sought to constrain CSC's economic power, especially because of its impact on Zoja's freedom to compete on the market (a seemingly Ordoliberal goal), or whether it was concerned about the impact of the elimination of Zoja on competition downstream (and consumer welfare). If the latter, the Court simply seemed to assume the harm to competition downstream from the exclusion of Zoja without actually assessing the actual impact on it.[210]

Complaints about this type of approach triggered a vigorous debate about the nature of Article 102 which resulted in the publication of a Guidance Paper which promised a closer analysis of the effects of conduct and that the Commission would focus its resources only on cases where the exclusionary conduct of the dominant firm impairs effective competition by 'foreclosing their competitors in an anticompetitive way, thus having an adverse impact on consumer welfare'.[211] Since then, however, the Commission has, in the light of market developments, subsequent case law, and, it seems, growing concern about under-enforcement in this area, revised this Guidance in some materials ways (2023) and

[207] *Matsushita Electric Industrial Co v Zenith Radio Corp*, 475 US 574, 594 (1986).

[208] See *Hoffmann-La Roche* (n 164), but see now Case C-413/14 P *Intel v Commission*, EU:C:2017:632.

[209] *Commercial Solvents* (n 10) para 25.

[210] More recent cases are equally ambiguous, eg for the abuse of margin squeeze see Case C-52/09 *Konkurrensverket v TeliaSonera Sverige*, EU:C:2011:83, paras 22–37.

[211] Guidance on the Commission's Enforcement Priorities in Applying Article 82 of the EC Treaty to Abusive Exclusionary Conduct by Dominant Undertakings [2009] OJ C45/2 (revised in 2023, C(2023) 1923 final) para 19.

is consulting on the adoption of new Article 102 Guidelines, which would replace the Guidance.[212]

Indeed, the case law on abuse has evolved considerably since 2009. In the context of some abuses at least, the case law has displayed a less formalistic approach. In the area of refusal to supply, for example, the Court of Justice has become more cautious than it appeared in *Commercial Solvents* about declaring such conduct to be abusive, see especially its judgment in *Oscar Bronner*.[213] It now seems to be recognized that although requiring access to an upstream product or facility may facilitate competition downstream, an obligation to deal interferes with the dominant firm's right to choose its trading partner and risks discouraging investment and innovation both by the dominant firm (which has developed the asset its rival wants access to)[214] and the rival downstream ('the prospect of being expropriated of their investments discourages firms from introducing new inputs and facilities in the first place').[215] The case law now establishes that a refusal to deal by a vertically integrated dominant firm (as in *Commercial Solvents*, eg where the dominant firm supplied a raw material upstream used for the manufacture of a drug downstream) to a downstream rival will only constitute an abuse where:[216]

(a) access to its product, service, or facility is 'indispensable' for the rival to compete (there are no actual or potential substitutes for it).[217] When demonstrating that no actual or potential substitutes exist upstream and that access to the existing product or system is therefore indispensable, it is not sufficient simply to demonstrate that it is not economically viable for the rival to compete without access to the product or facility (eg the raw material). To be indispensable, it is necessary at the very least to show that it is not economically viable to create a competing scheme even if it had similar economies of scale to the dominant undertaking;[218]

(b) the refusal is likely to eliminate all competition on the secondary market (even if not imminent).[219]

Further, the Court of Justice has now clarified that there is only a presumption that exclusive dealing and loyalty rebates are abusive. Thus 'where the undertaking concerned submits, during the administrative procedure, on the basis of supporting evidence, that its conduct was not capable of restricting competition and, in particular, of producing the alleged foreclosure effects' the Commission must analyse 'first, the extent of the undertaking's dominant position on the relevant market and, secondly, the share of the market covered by the challenged practice, as well as the conditions and arrangements for granting the rebates in question, their duration and their amount; it is also required to assess the possible existence of a strategy aiming to exclude competitors that are at least as efficient'.[220] In addition, in *Servizio Elettrico Nazionale*[221] the Court of Justice stressed that the well-being of consumers had to be regarded as constituting

[212] See n 177. The final Guidelines are anticipated in 2026.

[213] Case C-7/97 *Oscar Bronner v Mediaprint Zeitungs-und Zeitschriftenverlag*, EU:C:1998:569, para 41.

[214] Arguably, there should be less concern about this issue where the firm has not developed the asset itself, but the government has developed an 'asset' and then privatized it: *Post Danmark* (n 14) para 23.

[215] Motta (n 172) 68.

[216] See especially Cases C-241/91 P etc *RTE and ITP v Commission*, EU:C:1995:98 and *Oscar Bronner* (n 213).

[217] *Oscar Bronner* (n 213) para 41.

[218] Ibid, paras 45 and 46.

[219] The EU Courts have been willing to assume that such conduct will harm the competitive structure and, possibly, consumers through the elimination of rivals on the downstream market.

[220] See especially Case C-413/14 P *Intel v Commission*, EU:C:2017:632, paras 138–139.

[221] Case C-377/20, EU:C:2022:379, paras 46–48.

the ultimate objective of Article 102. It is thus for competition authority (or other claimant) to demonstrate that the conduct of the dominant firms is likely to harm the effective competitive structure, through recourse to means other than those which govern normal competition. Where that burden is discharged, the dominant firm can escape a finding of abuse by demonstrating that the exclusionary conduct is counterbalanced, or exceeded by positive effects for consumers, particularly in terms of price, quality, choice, and innovation.

It is important to note, however, that there is no exhaustive list of abuses, a number of different practices have been found to constitute unlawful abusive behaviour, such as misleading public authorities, or denigrating a rival's products, and some commentators now complain about a *decline* in the economic approach in other more recent jurisprudence. In the digital economy, a number of such cases have focused on the conduct of dominant big technology companies which has excluded rivals in other parts of an ecosystem, in particular through techniques which make it harder to compete with the dominant company (eg through practices which favour its own business over third-party rivals' businesses, see case study 17.4).[222] The new Digital Markets Act (DMA), signed into law on 14 September 2022, also now regulates and prohibits a range of practices by core platform service providers designated as 'gatekeepers'.[223]

7.3.4 **Objective necessity and efficiencies**

Broadly, a dominant firm may provide an objective justification for its behaviour either by showing that its conduct is objectively necessary or that the abusive conduct is counterbalanced, outweighed even, by objective economic justifications—advantages in terms of efficiency that also benefit consumers.[224]

It appears that objective necessity relates to factors external to the dominant undertaking,[225] justifying conduct on technical or commercial grounds,[226] for example the conduct was required for health and safety reasons or because the buyer was a bad debtor, or has a bad credit rating. The Commission states that such justification must be proportionate and that it is normally for public authorities to set and enforce public health and safety standards.[227]

In terms of efficiencies, the dominant undertaking must show that the gains likely to result from its conduct counteract any likely negative effects on competition in the affected markets, that those gains have been, or are likely to be, brought about as a result of that conduct, that such conduct is necessary for the achievement of those gains in efficiency, and that it does not eliminate effective competition, by removing all or most existing sources of actual or potential competition. This assessment must be made on the basis of the whole circumstances of the case.[228] Furthermore, as it is an objective assessment, it does not matter that generating efficiencies was not an explicit motivation for the dominant undertaking's actions.[229] The Court of Justice has thus written into Article 102 a defence virtually identical to Article 101(3).

[222] See Case T-612/17 *Google and Alphabet v Commission*, EU:T:2021:763, Case C-48/22 P, EU:C:2024:726.

[223] Regulation (EU) 2022/1925 on contestable and fair markets in the digital sector (OJ [2022] L265/1).

[224] *Post Danmark* (n 14) para 41.

[225] Case COMP/39.525, *Telekomunikacja Polska* 22 June 2011, para 874; this decision was appealed (Case T-486/11), but not on this ground.

[226] Case 311/84 *Centre belge d'études de marché—Télémarketing v Compagnie luxembourgeoise de télédiffusion*, EU:C:1985:394, paras 26 and 27.

[227] Guidance Paper (n 211) para 29.

[228] Case C-95/04 P *British Airways v Commission*, EU:C:2007:166, para 86.

[229] *Post Danmark* (n 14) paras 42 and 43.

CASE STUDY 17.3: Predatory pricing and *AKZO Chemie v Commission*

Predatory pricing occurs where a firm with market power lowers its price with the purpose of eliminating or disciplining its competitors. The lower prices may be applied across the board or targeted at certain customers. The practice harms consumer welfare as, although prices are lowered in the short term, the dominant firm invests in a strategy which allows it to exclude its competitors and, following the predatory siege, to hurt consumers by raising prices and charging supra-competitive prices. A particular problem for competition law is how a rule or standard can be crafted to identify predatory pricing and to distinguish it from hard-nosed price competition. An overly broad rule might deter low-cost pricing and encourage complaints by less efficient rivals losing out in the competitive battle.

In 1975, in an influential article, Areeda and Turner[230] proposed a cost-based test for identifying predatory behaviour in the US. They suggested a rule that where a firm charges prices below its average variable costs (AVC—variable costs are those that vary with output, eg fuel, materials, and labour, and are distinct from fixed costs (eg management overheads and rent) which do not vary with output/how much of a good or service the firm sells), it should be held to be engaged in unlawful predatory behaviour. But a firm pricing at or above AVC should be conclusively presumed to have acted lawfully. Although there has been considerable concern expressed about the accuracy and appropriateness of this test, and in particular whether it screens out too many legitimate predatory-pricing claims, most competition systems now adopt some form of price–cost test for identifying low-cost pricing which is likely to be predatory and to exclude equally efficient competitors from the market. How any such test is constructed is likely to determine whether the rule might be over- or under-inclusive (leading to type 1 or type 2 errors). In the US, for example, the Supreme Court has held that, in addition to showing that a defendant has predated below a certain measure of costs, a claimant must show that the defendant has a dangerous probability of recouping its investment in below-cost pricing. The Supreme Court thus favours a test which will, if anything, be under-inclusive and will not deter firms, even dominant ones, from engaging in aggressive low-cost pricing. This approach prefers the risk of type 2 to type 1 errors. In the EU, in contrast, the Court of Justice has held that a presumption of predation applies where a dominant firm prices below AVC and that 'demonstrating that it is possible to recoup losses is not a necessary pre-condition for a finding of predatory pricing'.[231] Further, predatory pricing may also be demonstrated even where pricing is above AVC, if it is below average total costs (ATC—fixed and variable) and forms part of a strategy designed to eliminate a competitor from the market. These rules were established in a line of cases commencing with *AKZO*.[232]

This case concerned the conduct of AKZO Chemie BV's UK subsidiary, which produced organic peroxides—speciality chemicals used in the plastics industry and as bleaching agents for flour. Two other suppliers (ECS and Diaflex) also offered a range of flour additives in the UK. When, however, ECS decided to start supplying organic peroxides for plastics application, AKZO found out and ordered ECS to stop and threatened to harm ECS's organic peroxides sales to the flour industry if it refused. ECS did not comply, so AKZO offered organic peroxides to ECS's biggest customers in the flour industry at low prices (which were significantly lower than those charged by AKZO to its own customers). AKZO had superior financial resources to ECS and could withstand such a strategy for longer.

[230] P Areeda and DF Turner, 'Predatory Pricing and Related Practices under Section 2 of the Sherman Act' (1975) 88 *Harvard Law Review* 697.

[231] Case C-202/07 P *France Télécom SA v Commission*, EU:C:2009:214, para 113.

[232] Case C-62/86 (n 169).

The Commission found that AKZO had violated Article 102 and imposed fines of €10 million and ordered it to terminate the infringement. The Court upheld the Commission's finding that AKZO was dominant. It affirmed the Commission's finding that AKZO was dominant on the market holding that 'very large shares are in themselves, and save in exceptional circumstances, evidence of the existence of a dominant position . . . That is the situation where there is a market share of 50% such as that found to exist in this case.'

It also upheld the finding that AKZO had abused its dominant position. A dominant firm must not eliminate a competitor and thereby strengthen its own position other than by using methods which come within the scope of competition on the basis of quality. Not all competition on price can be regarded as legitimate. Rather, the Court held that:

- 'Prices below average variable costs by means of which a dominant undertaking seeks to eliminate a competitor must be regarded as abusive. A dominant undertaking has no interest in applying such prices except that of eliminating competitors so as to enable it subsequently to raise its prices by taking advantage of its monopolistic position, since each sale generates a loss, namely the total amount of the fixed costs . . . and, at least, part of the variable costs relating to the unit produced';
- 'prices below average total costs, that is to say fixed costs plus variable costs, but above average variable costs, must be regarded as abusive if they are determined as part of a plan for eliminating a competitor. Such prices can drive from the market undertakings which are as efficient as the dominant undertaking but which, because of their smaller financial resources, are incapable of withstanding the competition waged against them.'

In this case, AKZO had been selling below its ATC over a prolonged period of time with the intention of selectively targeting the customers of ECS to force ECS either to abandon them or to match a loss-making price in order to retain them. Both the Commission and the Court also rejected, on the facts, AKZO's justification that it had acted not to discipline ECS but to sell off surplus stock. Although the Court held that AKZO's behaviour was particularly serious, it reduced the Commission's fine by 25 per cent because this was the first time that the Court had clarified the law in this area.

In a later case, *Post Danmark A/S v Konkurrencerådet*,[233] the Court confirmed that prices above ATC are not predatory: Article 102 does not 'seek to ensure that competitors less efficient than the undertaking with the dominant position should remain on the market' and so precludes only pricing practices 'that have an exclusionary effect on competitors considered to be as efficient as it is itself'.[234]

Arguably, the emphasis placed in this line of cases on the need for the conduct to be able to drive from the market undertakings which are as efficient as the dominant firm, suggests that the rules in this area are not simply designed to protect smaller, even perhaps if they are less efficient, competitors (as an Ordoliberal goal might do) but are designed to protect customers from price rises once the rivals have been disciplined (to prevent conduct which will harm consumer welfare). A presumption is applied, however, that where the test is met, the dominant firm, having disciplined or excluded its competitor(s) will be able to raise prices, recoup losses made during the predatory siege, and harm consumers. The risk of consumer harm from the predatory strategy is thus assumed: in contrast to the position in the US, actual proof that the strategy is likely to be successful is not required.

[233] Case C-209/10 (n 14) para 36, but see eg the exceptional facts of Joined Cases C-395 and 396/96 P *Compagnie Maritime Belge v Commission*, EU:C:2000:132.

[234] *Post Danmark* (n 14) paras 21 and 25. See also eg Case T-671/19 *Qualcomm v Commission* EU:T:2024:626.

CASE STUDY 17.4: Self preferencing and the *Google Shopping* case

The Commission has become increasingly concerned about dominant firms (especially super-dominant firms) that give preferential treatment to their own products compared to those of competitors, mainly by means of non-pricing behaviour (self-preferencing). For example, in the landmark *Google Search (Shopping)*[235] case, the Commission found that Google had abused its dominant position in general online search in the EEA, by placing its own comparative shopping service (CSS) more favourably within its general search results pages than those of its competitor CSSs. It imposed a fine of €2.42 billion on Google and required it to treat its competitor CSSs no less favourably than its own CSS within its general search results.

In its decision, the Commission noted that, taking account of specific market circumstances, Google's discriminatory conduct (artificially manipulating its search algorithm both to promote Google Shopping and to demote rival CSSs) lead to a weakening of competition. In particular, because general search traffic was very important for CSSs, the conduct had the potential to foreclose competing CSSs, and to result in higher fees for merchants, higher prices for consumers, and less innovation.

Google strongly contested the decision on appeal, including on the basis that as its conduct was akin to a refusal to supply, the Commission should have considered whether access to its online search facility was 'indispensable' for rivals to compete before finding an abuse (see *Oscar Bronner*). Google's complaints were dismissed on appeal.[236] The Court of Justice held that the *Bronner* criteria did not apply in that case as there had been no refusal to contract. Further, that the more favourable treatment by Google of its own CSS, combined with the characteristics of the upstream market and the specific circumstances of the case, meant that the conduct did not fall within the scope of competition on the merits.

Under Article 6(5) of the DMA,[237] designated gatekeepers[238] are now specifically obliged not to treat more favourably, in ranking and related indexing and crawling, services and products offered by the gatekeeper itself than similar services or products of a third party. The gatekeeper shall apply transparent, fair, and non-discriminatory conditions to such rankings. The Commission has now opened an investigation into Alphabet's compliance with Article 6(5) in relation to its online search engine, Google. It is considering whether it treats its own services (such as shopping, hotel booking etc) more favourably in Google search than similar services offered by third parties.[239]

8 Conclusion

Articles 101 and 102 prohibit, respectively, anticompetitive agreements between two or more entities engaged in economic activity and abusive conduct of entities which hold a dominant position in the EU or a substantial part of it. The provisions apply insofar as

[235] Case AT.39740, 27 June 2017.

[236] See Case T-612/17 *Google and Alphabet v Commission*, EU:T:2021:763, aff'd Case C-48/22 P, EU:C:2024:726

[237] Regulation (EU) 2022/1925 on contestable and fair markets in the digital sector (OJ [2022] L265/1).

[238] Alphabet has been designated as providing online search engine and online intermediation core platform services, respectively (Google Search) and (Google Maps, Google Play, and Google Shopping).

[239] Case DMA.100193, *Alphabet—Online Search Engine—Google Search—Article 6(5) DMA*.

the agreement or conduct at issue appreciably affects trade between Member States. As severe consequences may flow for undertakings which violate either rule (including fines and exposure to damages claims), it is essential that they understand what conduct is prohibited by the rules and why.

For more than 20 years, the Commission has set out its view that the objective of Articles 101 and 102 should be to prohibit conduct which harms consumer welfare, a view which has gained support from the EU Courts. Nonetheless, debate still exists as to how this objective is to be achieved and whether, and if so how, competition law can or should contribute to broader policy objectives.

A core difficulty in applying Articles 101 and 102 is how to distinguish anticompetitive agreements and conduct from conduct which is neutral or pro-competitive in a way which (a) provides undertakings and decision-takers with sufficient certainty, while at the same time (b) ensuring that a coherent and accurate antitrust system is maintained. Although in the past the EU authorities have been criticized for adopting too formalistic an approach to this issue, relying on over-inclusive rules, the Commission has taken significant strides towards modernizing the interpretation and application of Articles 101 and 102 and to ensuring that an effects-based approach is adopted where feasible, focusing on the effects of the conduct in a greater number of cases. A challenge nonetheless is to ensure that the bar is not raised so high for claimants that there is a significant risk of under-inclusive rules and under-enforcement of the law.

Further reading

A Jones, B Sufrin, and N Dunne, *Jones and Sufrin's EU Competition Law* (8th edn, Oxford: Oxford University Press, 2023)

A Kalintiri, *Evidence Standards in EU Competition Enforcement* (Oxford: Hart Publishing, 2019)

M Motta, *Competition Policy* (Cambridge: Cambridge University Press, 2004)

R Whish and D Bailey, *Competition Law* (11th edn, Oxford: Oxford University Press, 2024)

18

EU law on State aid and public procurement

Okeoghene Odudu and Albert Sanchez-Graells

1 Introduction

When times get tough, business and the public look to the government for assistance. Take the case of the workers' support schemes provided during the Covid-19 pandemic. Or the financial help given during the energy crisis following the Russian invasion of Ukraine. The public also expect the State to invest in long-term infrastructure projects such as road, rail, broadband provision, and technological capacity to support things such as the development of artificial intelligence, while maintaining digital sovereignty. How governments decide to spend can create distortions in the market. What if workers' support schemes exclude migrant workers? Or, government funding is available only to those who use locally sourced materials or domestic labour? Given the huge sums of (national) taxpayers' money involved, this is an area of law that is heavily politicized, especially in the context of high-profile economic or business crises with large potential (un)employment implications, or where States seek to boost innovation in specific sectors by giving 'State aid'—most recently in the field of digital technologies.[1]

This chapter introduces rules enabling the EU to supervise the way its Member States intervene in the operation of a market economy. In general, the supervision can be, first, over the way the State raises money to finance its own activities and, secondly, over the way the State spends the money it has raised. This chapter focuses on this second type of supervision through rules on State aid and on public procurement. EU Member States typically dedicate over €180 billion annually, close to 1 per cent of their Gross Domestic

[1] M Schito, 'The Politics of State aid in the European Union: Explaining Variation in Aid Allocation among Member States' (2020) 41 *Journal of Public Policy* 277.

Product (GDP), to granting State aid.[2] Additionally, EU Member States currently spend around 14 per cent of GDP (around €2 trillion per year) on the procurement of services, works, and supplies,[3] a figure likely to increase with geopolitical developments driving increased defence spending, with NATO members (which include 23 EU Member States) committing to 5 per cent GDP defence expenditure by 2035.[4] The traditional, *negative*, role of the EU's supervision is to prevent discrimination based on the nationality of those from whom the State raises its funds and those in receipt of State expenditure.

The negative role of public expenditure control, to prevent discrimination, in more recent times has been revised to accommodate a *positive* role of public expenditure control, to (a) demonstrate probity, legitimacy, effectiveness, and fairness in the redistribution of public funds and (b) promote economic and social cohesion, as well as the green and digital 'twin transition'.[5] There are thus a broad array of exemptions, exceptions, and systems to authorize the granting of State aid where it pursues legitimate goals and/or policy goals endorsed by the EU. Three-quarters of aid expenditure in 2024 related to EU policy objectives,[6] such as environmental protection, energy saving, research, development and innovation, and regional development; with the rest dedicated to crisis support (primarily linked to the Russian invasion of Ukraine).[7]

This chapter sets out the broad policy considerations at play (section 2) before outlining the EU rules on State aid (section 3) and public procurement (section 4). The chapter also explains how these rules have applied in the context of the provision of public services, in particular health care, a key social policy, especially during the Covid-19 crisis, as well as on the (financial) support to environmental sustainability.

2 The policy issues

2.1 The role of government expenditure in economic integration/State intervention in the economy

States award contracts for the completion of works in public infrastructure (such as roads, public Wi-Fi networks, or supercomputers), the supply of goods or the provision of services needed in the delivery of public services (such as hospital consumables, or health-care IT services), or to outsource specific services to private providers (such as the management of prisons or detention centres). As a major purchaser of certain goods or services, the criteria used to determine from whom the State purchases can shape the market and deliver various public policy aims.[8] States may also influence the operation

[2] European Commission, '2024 State Aid Scoreboard', https://ec.europa.eu/competition-policy/state-aid/scoreboard_en. The Scoreboard contains information about all State aid measures in favour of industries and services (including agriculture, fisheries, and aquaculture), for which the Commission has either adopted a formal decision or received a summary information sheet from the Member States for measures qualifying for exemption under the GBER or sectoral block exemptions (see section 3.3).

[3] European Commission, 'Public procurement', https://single-market-economy.ec.europa.eu/single-market/public-procurement_en.

[4] NATO, 'Defence expenditures and NATO's 5% commitment', www.nato.int/cps/en/natohq/topics_49198.htm.

[5] See chapter 22. See also S Verschuur and C Sbrolli, 'The European Green Deal and State Aid: Regions, State Aid and the Just Transition' (2021) 20 *European State Aid Law Quarterly* 587.

[6] See the joined approach to the management of the European Structural and Investment Funds.

[7] 2024 State Aid Scoreboard (n 2) 15.

[8] Commission Notice, 'Guidance on Innovation Procurement', C(2021) 4320 final; European Commission, 'Green Public Procurement', https://green-forum.ec.europa.eu/green-public-procurement_en; Commission Notice, 'Buying Social: a guide to taking account of social considerations in public procurement (2nd edition)', C(2021) 3573 final.

of the market by providing firms with funds or subsidies, tax exemptions, selling them public assets, or concluding contracts for goods or services.[9] State-owned assets, such as land dedicated to military uses, may be sold to facilitate their renovation and reuse in a new context, such as housing development. State intervention may occur to accelerate the speed at which certain products, such as renewable energy or environmentally sustainable products, come to market, or to secure the provision of important services, such as health care or education, which would be under-consumed if the State did not bear at least some of the cost. State intervention may also occur to: promote domestic firms or industries believed to be strategically important (such as airlines); promote the hiring of the long-term unemployed; attract inward investment in a region; or to support the economy more generally, such as in the aftermath of the 2008 financial crisis, the 2020 coronavirus pandemic, or the 2022 Russian invasion of Ukraine.

2.2 **The need to monitor government expenditure**

The way States raise revenue or allocate expenditure may confer economic advantages on national or domestic operators that are not based on the superior skill, quality, or other features of the products or services provided or promoted. The risk is of firms operating on an uneven playing field, where inferior (national) firms in receipt of aid thrive at the expense of superior (foreign) firms not in receipt of aid. This not only results in allocative inefficiencies, but also reduces the likelihood of successful innovation occurring. *Rules on public contracting (or procurement)* seek to establish a level playing field for the award of public contracts in the internal market in order to prevent discrimination on the basis of nationality in the award of contracts financed with public funds.[10] Such rules prevent the use of contract awards to channel financial support to specific economic operators under the fiction of buying services.[11]

Rules on State aid aim to supervise the way Member States otherwise intervene in the economy by expenditure, generally prohibiting measures that distort competition in the *internal market*.[12] However, the EU is also concerned with subsidies granted by third countries to firms trading in the EU market, which has led the EU recently to adopt rules on foreign subsidies distorting the internal market.[13] New rules on third-country access to the EU's public contracts market and a five-year ban on the procurement of medical devices of Chinese origin have been adopted to address a similar concern.[14] Rules are also

[9] All of these are potential forms of State aid; see Commission Notice on the notion of State aid as referred to in Article 107(1) of the Treaty on the Functioning of the European Union (OJ [2016] C262/1).

[10] For a general description and entry point to European Commission resources, see European Commission, 'Public procurement', https://single-market-economy.ec.europa.eu/single-market/public-procurement_en.

[11] Case T-116/01 *P & O European Ferries (Vizcaya) v Commission*, EU:T:2003:217, paras 113–137.

[12] Art 107(1) TFEU and Notice on the notion of State aid (n 9). For a general description and entry point to European Commission resources, see European Commission, 'State Aid Overview', https://competition-policy.ec.europa.eu/state-aid/overview_en.

[13] Regulation (EU) 2022/2560 of the European Parliament and of the Council of 14 December 2022 on foreign subsidies distorting the internal market (OJ [2022] L330/1). See Lena Hornkohl, 'Protecting the Internal Market From Subsidisation With the EU State Aid Regime and the Foreign Subsidies Regulation: Two Sides of the Same Coin?' (2023) 14(3) *Journal of European Competition Law & Practice* 137.

[14] Regulation (EU) 2022/1031 of the European Parliament and of the Council of 23 June 2022 on the access of third-country economic operators, goods and services to the Union's public procurement and concession markets and procedures supporting negotiations on access of Union economic operators, goods and services to the public procurement and concession markets of third countries (International Procurement Instrument—IPI) (OJ [2022] L173/1) and Commission Implementing Regulation (EU) 2025/1197 of 19 June 2025 imposing an International Procurement Instrument measure restricting the access of economic operators and medical devices originating in the People's Republic of China to the European Union public procurement market for medical devices pursuant to Regulation (EU) 2022/1031 of the European Parliament and of the Council (OJ [2025] L2025/1197).

in place to prevent third countries from pressuring the EU or a Member State into making a particular choice by applying, or threatening to apply, measures affecting trade or investment.[15]

3 State aid

3.1 Introduction

The legal framework governing the regulation of State aid under EU law is set out in Article 107 TFEU. Article 107 is divided into three parts. Article 107(1) TFEU contains what is known as the *general prohibition* against State aid:

> Save as otherwise provided in the Treaties, any aid granted by a Member State or through State resources in any form whatsoever which distorts or threatens to distort competition by favouring certain undertakings or the production of certain goods shall, in so far as it affects trade between Member States, be incompatible with the internal market.

The general prohibition contains four elements which are discussed at section 3.2.

Article 107(2) TFEU contains a short list of *exceptions* which concern aid deemed compatible with the internal market and falling outside the general prohibition; while Article 107(3) TFEU provides a mechanism to determine whether specific beneficial effects outweigh the harm of any aid granted, and so an *exemption* can be provided. Both are discussed at section 3.3.

3.2 General prohibition

The general prohibition can be divided into four constituent elements:

(a) the granting of an economic advantage to an undertaking;
(b) financing the economic advantage through State resources;
(c) the selectivity of the measure; and
(d) its effect on competition and trade between Member States.[16]

The first two conditions concern the *existence* of aid. The second two conditions determine the *impact* the aid has on the operation of the internal market. The four requirements are cumulative, meaning the failure to satisfy any single element prevents the prohibition from applying.[17]

3.2.1 Economic advantage (aid)

The first condition to be satisfied is the existence of an economic advantage. The Treaty does not provide a definition of economic advantage, but as part of the 2012 State Aid Modernisation programme, in May 2016, the Commission published a Notice on the notion of aid.[18] The economic advantage, as Article 107(1) makes clear, may take 'any form whatsoever' so long as the economic burden of carrying out the relevant economic activity is

[15] Regulation (EU) 2023/2675 of the European Parliament and of the Council of 22 November 2023 on the protection of the Union and its Member States from economic coercion by third countries (OJ [2023] L2023/2675).
[16] Notice on the notion of State aid (n 9) para 5.
[17] Case C-345/02 *Pearle v Hoofdbedrijfschap Ambachten*, EU:C:2004:448, para 32.
[18] Notice on the notion of State aid (n 9).

reduced.[19] The classic form of State aid is a direct subsidy. The Commission and the CJEU use a concept of aid that is much broader than subsidy and captures the grant of any economic advantage 'which . . . would not have obtained under normal market conditions'—that is, in the normal course of business.[20] An economic advantage may be conferred positively, for example by a grant or subsidy, or negatively, for example by an exemption from taxation[21] or by not charging rent for the use of public premises.[22] Other examples of an economic advantage are loans below the market rate of interest; the disposal of land or buildings below the market rate; and not taking action to recover debts. An economic advantage may be directly or indirectly conferred. So, for example, aid to consumers to enable them to purchase from an identifiable group of undertakings is an indirect form of aid.[23]

The essence of State aid is that it confers an economic benefit on the recipient. For example, in *Syndicat Français de l'Express International (SFEI) v La Poste*, free commercial and logistical assistance was provided by the State.[24] While the conferral of gratuitous benefits clearly constitutes aid, aid also exists if some consideration is given but the consideration does not match the value of the benefit conferred. The existence of an economic advantage is then identified by conducting a counterfactual analysis to establish the expected financial situation under normal market conditions.[25] The benchmark is set by identifying the terms on which a non-State entity would make the investment, loan, sale, or purchase. The Commission views all these as manifestations of the market economy operator test,[26] and the CJEU has stressed that the assessment of the conditions in which an advantage is granted is, in principle, carried out by applying the market economy operator principle.[27] Under this test, no economic advantage is conferred if no more is given than the firm would obtain in the market. This may be established, for example, if private operators participate in the transaction on the same terms as the public operator (or *pari passu*), or the sale or purchase of assets, goods, and services are organized though market process.[28] In that regard, the CJEU has recently confirmed that the assessment of a State aid measure requires assessment of procurement compliance when this is linked to the object of the aid at issue.[29]

Does making support available, even when not called upon, confer an economic advantage or 'psychological aid'? This was the view of the Commission in relation to a €9 million shareholder loan made available to France Télécom but which it did not call upon.[30] The General Court seemed to reject the notion of psychological aid, but, because the economic advantage conferred need not be the same magnitude as the cost to the State of conferring the advantage, the Court of Justice left the question open.[31]

[19] For discussion, see P Papandropoulos et al, 'Selectivity, Economic Advantage, Distortion of Competition and Effect on Trade' in J Derenne and M Merola (eds), *Economic Analysis of State Aid Rules: Contributions and Limits* (Berlin: Lexxion, 2007) 119–155, 145ff.

[20] Case C-39/94 *Syndicat Français de l'Express International (SFEI) v La Poste* ('*SFEI*'), EU:C:1996:285, para 60.

[21] Ibid, para 58.

[22] Case C-710/22 P *JCDecaux Street Furniture Belgium v Commission*, EU:C:2024:787.

[23] Case T-177/07 *Mediaset v Commission*, EU:T:2010:233, para 177.

[24] *SFEI* (n 20).

[25] Ibid, para 61 and Notice on the notion of State aid (n 9) para 67.

[26] Notice on the notion of State aid (n 9) para 75.

[27] Joined Cases C-746/23 and C-747/23 *Cividale and Flag*, EU:C:2025:171, para 42.

[28] Notice on the notion of State aid (n 9) paras 84ff and 97ff. See GS Ølykke, 'The Notice of the Notion of State Aid and Public Procurement Law' (2016) 15 *European State Aid Law Quarterly* 508.

[29] Case C-59/23 P Austria v Commission (Centrale nucléaire Paks II), EU:C:2025:686, paras 66ff).

[30] Commission Decision 2005/709/EC of 2 August 2004 on the State aid implemented by France for France Télécom (OJ [2005] L269/30).

[31] See Joined Cases T-425/04, T-444/04, T-450/04, and T-456/04 *France and Others v Commission*, EU:T:2010:216, paras 234–240 and 288–289, annulled in Joined Cases C-399/10 P and C-401/10 P *Bouygues SA v Commission*, EU:C:2013:175. Further developments are seen in Joined Cases T-425/04 RENV and T-444/04 RENV *France v Commission*, EU:T:2015:450 and Case C-486/15 P *Commission v France and Orange*, EU:C:2016:912.

The recipient of the economic advantage must be an undertaking, a concept explored elsewhere in this volume.[32] The requirement for the beneficiary of the aid to be an 'undertaking' is common to the other elements of EU competition law and it had long been thought that the concept of an undertaking under Article 107 was the same as that under the competition law provisions in Articles 101 and 102 TFEU. In *ACEA-Electrabel*, however, the Court confirmed that 'the concept of an economic unit in State aid matters can differ from that applicable in other areas of competition law'.[33] Nonetheless, the CJEU has also has stressed that 'it is settled case-law of the Court that the concept of "undertaking" within the meaning of Article 107(1) TFEU covers any entity engaged in an economic activity, regardless of its legal status and the way in which it is financed, and that any activity consisting in offering goods or services on a given market constitutes an economic activity'.[34] Whilst the concept of an undertaking in State aid *can* deviate from the concept used more generally in competition law, the extent to which it *does* deviate is unclear. This has proven particularly problematic when applying the rules to public undertakings, and undertakings providing social security or welfare services (see section 3.2.3).

3.2.2 State origin (imputability and State resources)

The economic advantage (aid) must have been granted by the State and conferred using State resources. In relation to both the entity conferring the advantage and the origin of the resources used to confer the advantage, the CJEU has adopted a broad definition of the State to capture central, regional, and local government.[35] In those same broad terms, and in relation to judicial activities, the CJEU has stated that 'the condition of imputability of an aid measure is satisfied in the event of "involvement" of "public authorities" in the adoption of that measure'.[36] If the economic advantage is not granted by the State, the question is whether the measure is 'imputable' to the State. The requirement is met when the State has a sufficient degree of control over the funds used to finance the economic advantage conferred. In *Stardust Marine*, the CJEU said that 'the imputability to the State of an aid measure taken by a public undertaking may be inferred from a set of indicators arising from the circumstances of the case and the context in which that measure was taken'.[37] This approach generally requires an analysis of the degree of control the State could exercise to either grant, or block, the aid measure under consideration, even if it was formally administered or decided upon by a private entity.[38]

The 'State resources' requirement is satisfied when conferring the economic advantage results in a diminution in State resources, though it is not always clear that the State has suffered detriment. Article 107(1) TFEU is intended to cover:

[32] See section 4 of chapter 17. Cf A Bartosch, 'Economic vs Non-Economic: A Long and Winding Road' (2021) 20 *European State Aid Law Quarterly* 507, W Sauter, *Coherence in EU Competition Law* (Oxford: Oxford University Press, 2016) 75–78 and O Odudu, 'Economic Activity as a Limit to Community Law' in C Barnard and O Odudu (eds), *The Outer Limits of European Union Law* (Oxford: Hart Publishing, 2009) ch 10.

[33] Case C-480/09 P *AceaElectrabel Produzione SpA v Commission*, EU:C:2010:787, para 66.

[34] Case C-325/22 *Ministar na zemedelieto, hranite i gorite*, EU:C:2023:793, para 29.

[35] Notice on the notion of State aid (n 9) para 48.

[36] Case C-701/21 P *Mytilinaios v DEI and Commission*, EU:C:2024:146, para 91.

[37] Case C-482/99 *France v Commission* ('*Stardust Marine*'), EU:C:2002:294, para 55. On those factors, see Notice on the notion of State aid (n 9) para 43.

[38] Although the CJEU case law is not particularly clear concerning situations where the State failed to block, or implicitly authorized, an aid measure; see Case C-677/11 *Doux Élevage and Coopérative agricole UKL-ARREE*, EU:C:2013:348, paras 30ff.

all the financial means by which the public authorities may actually support undertakings, irrespective of whether or not those means are permanent assets of the public sector. Therefore, even if the sums corresponding to the measure in question are not permanently held by the Treasury, the fact that they constantly remain under public control, and therefore available to the competent national authorities, is sufficient for them to be categorised as State resources.[39]

This issue has often arisen when seemingly private funds are used, such as in the context of mandatory purchase requirements, which are particularly common in the renewable energy sector.[40]

3.2.3 **Selectivity**

The third condition to be satisfied in order that the prohibition applies is that the economic advantage conferred is selective. Article 107(1) TFEU requires the aid to favour 'certain undertakings or the production of certain goods'. General measures favouring the whole economy, such as the lowering of tax or interest rates, do not create a selective benefit.[41] If all companies in State A pay a tax rate of 10 per cent, they are at a competitive advantage in relation to companies in State B, which imposes a tax rate of 15 per cent. There is, however, no *selective* advantage as the question is whether a selective benefit is conferred against all others operating in the market of a single Member State, and not as against those operating in other Member States.

The selectivity condition can be difficult to apply and has been referred to as one of the most controversial issues in State aid.[42] Though measures of general application are not prohibited, measures that are seemingly general may operate selectively. To determine whether a measure is general or selective, a two-stage process is often taken.[43] This involves:

(a) defining the 'reference framework' that will provide a benchmark; and
(b) identifying differential treatment in relation to the benchmark.[44]

In relation to measures *designed* to be selective, it is not necessary to establish a reference framework. The simple fact that an economic advantage is conferred generates the presumption that the measure is selective.[45] In other cases, a reference framework is required and may be the whole Member State's economy. As an example, if the Member State enables lower airport charges at only one regional airport, airlines using that airport are recipients of a selective advantage from the Member State. If, however, a regional authority approves a schedule of charges for airports in its region that is lower than charges levied by other regions in the State, so that airlines using that regional airport face lower airport charges than those using other airports, the appropriate reference framework would be limited to the area over which the entity has autonomous authority.[46]

[39] *Stardust Marine* (n 36) para 37. On those factors, see Notice on the notion of State aid (n 9) paras 47–65.

[40] Case C-405/16 P *Germany v Commission*, EU:C:2019:268, paras 60ff. See case study 18.2.

[41] Notice on the notion of State aid (n 9) para 118. Case C-453/23 *Prezydent Miasta Mielca*, EU:C:2025:285, paras 46–50.

[42] Opinion of AG Wathelet in Joined Cases C-20/15 P and C-21/15 P *World Duty Free Group v Commission*, EU:C:2016:624, para 5 and Opinion of AG Wahl in Case C-524/14 P *Commission v Hansestadt Lübeck*, EU:C:2016:693, para 3.

[43] Notice on the notion of State aid (n 9) para 128.

[44] Ibid, para 132.

[45] Ibid, para 126.

[46] Case C-524/14 P *Commission v Hansestadt Lübeck*, EU:C:2016:971, paras 62–64.

Within the reference framework, the second stage is to consider whether the measure confers an advantage as compared to what would occur in its absence. A measure is selective, if, 'within the context of a particular legal regime, it has the effect of conferring an advantage on certain undertakings over others, in a different sector or the same sector, which are, in the light of the objective pursued by that regime, in a comparable factual and legal situation'.[47] For example, the Commission has found measures available only to the manufacturing sector and not to the service sector to be selective.[48] One factor that can make a measure selective is if there is discretion as to whether the measure will be applied. A measure is not of general application merely because there are a (large) number of eligible undertakings, or a large and diverse number of economic sectors benefit from the measure. Nor is a measure of general application merely because recipients of its benefit cannot be defined in advance.[49] Conversely, a measure may be of general application even if it benefits only one sector of the economy or only some undertakings within a sector of the economy (eg only operators of digital terrestrial television platforms in a specific region),[50] as the given sector or region may be the relevant reference framework. The selective advantage may result from successive decisions by the State, or from the interaction between different State interventions.[51]

Compensation for the provision of a public service

As seen above, State aid does not exist unless the undertaking is in receipt of a selective advantage. An important problem confronted by the Court is how to analyse a situation in which (a) the State puts the undertaking at a disadvantage and then (b) compensates the undertaking to remove that disadvantage. Such a situation arises when, say, a local authority looking to the private sector to provide services for care for the elderly requests an outcome in terms of objective quality, safety, affordability, equal treatment, or universal access that would not be supplied (or would be supplied under different conditions) by the market without public intervention.[52] This describes the provision of services of general economic interest (SGEIs) and captures services such as health care, education, and other welfare services, depending on how the Member States regulate them. The Treaty contains distinct provisions to protect SGEIs (Articles 14 and 106 TFEU). Article 106(2) TFEU provides:

> Undertakings entrusted with the operation of services of general economic interest . . . shall be subject to the rules contained in the Treaties, in particular to the rules on competition, ***in so far as the application of such rules does not obstruct the performance, in law or in fact, of the particular tasks assigned to them.*** The development of trade must not be affected to such an extent as would be contrary to the interests of the Union.

[47] Case C-70/16 P *Comunidad Autónoma de Galicia and Retegal v Commission* (*Retegal*), EU:C:2017:1002, para 61; Case C-588/22 P *Ryanair v Commission*, EU:C:2024:935, para 102.

[48] State Aid E/2/98 Ireland, Proposal for appropriate measures under Article 93(1) of the EC Treaty concerning Irish corporation tax (ICT) 98/C 395/09.

[49] Notice on the notion of State aid (n 9) para 118.

[50] *Retegal* (n 46) para 61.

[51] On the former point, see Case C-15/14 P *Commission v MOL*, EU:C:2015:362, paras 92 and 93; Joined Cases C-399/10 P and C-401/10 P *Bouygues and Bouygues Télécom v Commission and Others and Commission v France and Others*, EU:C:2013:175, paras 103 and 104, and on the latter point, see Case C-131/15 P *Club Hotel Loutraki and Others v Commission*, EU:C:2016:989, para 75.

[52] Communication, 'A Quality Framework for Services of General Interest in Europe', COM(2011) 900 final, 3. For detailed conceptual discussion, see W Sauter, *Public Services in EU Law* (Cambridge: Cambridge University Press, 2014) 9–20. See also AM Collins and M Martínez Navarro, 'Economic Activity, Market Failure and Services of General Economic Interest: It Takes Two to Tango' (2021) 21 *Journal of European Competition Law & Practice* 380–386.

The interaction between Article 106(2) TFEU and whether a selective advantage has been provided contrary to Article 107(1) TFEU was clarified by the CJEU in its seminal *Altmark* judgment.[53] There, the Court considered that a selective economic advantage is not granted to an undertaking that is obliged to provide an SGEI if four conditions are met:[54]

(a) the recipient undertaking is actually required to discharge public service obligations and those obligations have been clearly defined;
(b) the parameters on the basis of which the compensation is calculated have been established beforehand in an objective and transparent manner;
(c) the compensation does not exceed what is necessary to cover all or part of the costs incurred in discharging the public service obligations, taking into account the relevant receipts and a reasonable profit for discharging those obligations; and
(d) where the undertaking which is to discharge public service obligations is not chosen in a public procurement procedure, the level of compensation needed has been determined on the basis of an analysis of the costs which a typical undertaking, well run and adequately provided with material means so as to be able to meet the necessary public service requirements, would have incurred in discharging those obligations, taking into account the relevant receipts and a reasonable profit for discharging the obligations.

The *Altmark* conditions ensure that the recipient of the selective economic advantage received no more than is required to enable it to discharge the additional obligations it has by virtue of being entrusted with the provision of an SGEI. When the *Altmark* conditions are satisfied, there is no overcompensation and, ultimately, no selective economic advantage for the undertaking entrusted with SGEI provision.[55]

The application of *Altmark* is complex, not least because legacy entrustments of SGEI provision (eg arrangements predating a States' EU accession) and exceptions to the obligation to tender a public contract under the applicable rules (see section 4)[56] mean that a procurement procedure is not always used to select the undertaking entrusted to provide SGEI. Conflicting case law makes assessing the likely outcome of any given case particularly difficult. For example, in the *German abattoirs* case,[57] payments to an undertaking to maintain reserve capacity to facilitate a response to an epizootic disease outbreak (such as bird flu) did not benefit from *Altmark* because a procurement procedure was absent, even when the payments were for net costs only and did not include a profit component. Conversely, in *Spezzino*,[58] the CJEU sidestepped the *Altmark* test when contracts for ambulance services were awarded to not-for-profit associations without tender, so long as

[53] Case C-280/00 *Altmark Trans and Regierungspräsidium Magdeburg* ('Altmark'), EU:C:2003:415. It should be stressed that *Altmark* did not concern Art 106 TFEU, but rather sectoral State aid rules for the transport sector. However, it is broadly seen as a clarification of the interaction between public sector obligations and State aid rules, directly applicable to analysis under Art 106(2) TFEU, as the CJEU has relied on *Altmark* in Art 106(2) cases.

[54] *Altmark* (n 52) para 95. It should be noted that the specific wording of the paragraphs setting each of the conditions (paras 89–93) is slightly different.

[55] Case C-660/15 P *Viasat Broadcasting v European Commission*, EU:C:2017:178, para 25.

[56] Directive 2014/24/EU (OJ [2014] L94/65). See GS Ølykke, 'Commission Notice on the Notion of State Aid as Referred to in art 107(1) TFEU: Is the Conduct of a Public Procurement Procedure Sufficient to Eliminate the Risk of Granting State Aid?' (2016) 25 *Public Procurement Law Review* 197.

[57] Case C-446/14 P *Germany v Commission*, EU:C:2016:97, para 36.

[58] Case C-113/13 *Azienda sanitaria locale n 5 'Spezzino' and Others*, EU:C:2014:2440. For discussion, see the special issue in (2016) 11(1) *European Procurement & Public Private Partnership Law Review.*

the 'legal and contractual framework in which the activity of those associations is carried out actually contributes to the social purpose and the pursuit of the objectives of the good of the community and budgetary efficiency on which that legislation is based'.

3.2.4 Effect on competition and trade

The fourth element of the general prohibition is the existence of an effect on (a) competition and (b) trade. Competition is distorted when the economic advantage strengthens an undertaking's position vis-à-vis its competitors. State aid law has not embraced the more economic approach that infuses competition law. It is therefore not necessary to define relevant markets or carry out an empirical examination of a measure's likely impact. It is normally presumed that competition is distorted merely by receipt of the economic advantage (although this need not be the case in all circumstances, see section 3.2.1). Quantification is, however, necessary in order to recover the aid. The likelihood of the effect on trade is assessed similarly to the analysis under Articles 101 and 102 TFEU, and there does exist a *de minimis* requirement.[59]

3.3 Exceptions, and block exemption regulations

3.3.1 Exceptions and exemptions

While the TFEU starts from the general prohibition of State aid discussed in section 3.2, it recognizes that there are situations where the granting of State aid should not be prohibited, either at all, or when specific conditions are met. Article 108(2) TFEU grants the Commission the exclusive competence to assess the compatibility of an aid measure with the internal market. Article 108(3) TFEU requires Member States not only to notify State aid measures to the Commission before their implementation, so that the Commission can carry out that assessment, but also to await the outcome of the Commission's investigation before implementing notified measures (standstill obligation). A breach of the standstill obligation will make the aid unlawful, and thus potentially recoverable if found incompatible with the internal market (see section 3.4). There are exceptions in Article 107(2) TFEU which are mandatory and exemptions in Article 107(3) which are discretionary.

Article 107(2) TFEU lists three (mandatory) exceptions from the general prohibition (emphasis added):

> 2. The following *shall* be compatible with the internal market:
>
> (a) aid having a social character, granted to individual consumers, provided that such aid is granted without discrimination related to the origin of the products concerned;
>
> (b) aid to make good the damage caused by natural disasters or exceptional occurrences;
>
> (c) aid granted to the economy of certain areas of the Federal Republic of Germany affected by the division of Germany, in so far as such aid is required in order to compensate for the economic disadvantages caused by that division. Five years after the entry into force of the Treaty of Lisbon, the Council, acting on a proposal from the Commission, may adopt a decision repealing this point.

[59] Commission Regulation (EU) 2023/2831 (OJ [2023] L2023/2831). However, it should be acknowledged that this is a variable parameter heavily influenced by policy decisions of the European Commission, such as their post-financial crisis attempt to recalibrate State aid enforcement to be 'big on big, and small on small'. S Cnossen and G Dictus, 'Big on Big, Small on Small: A Never Ending Promise? A Critical Assessment of the Commission Decision Practice with Regard to the Effect on Trade Criterion' (2021) 20 *European State Aid Law Quarterly* 30.

The first two exceptions are the most used,[60] with Article 107(2)(b) TFEU offering a legal basis for the adoption of significant State aid packages in the aftermath of the 2020–2021 coronavirus pandemic.[61] The application of these exceptions solely requires demonstrating that the conditions in, for example, Article 107(2)(b) are met, although there are procedural obligations for the Member States seeking to rely on the exception.

Article 107(3) TFEU lists the grounds for possible (discretionary) exemption of specific types of State aid (emphasis added):

> 3. The following *may* be considered to be compatible with the internal market:
>
> (a) aid to promote the economic development of areas where the standard of living is abnormally low or where there is serious underemployment, and of the regions referred to in Article 349, in view of their structural, economic and social situation;
>
> (b) aid to promote the execution of an important project of common European interest or to remedy a serious disturbance in the economy of a Member State;
>
> (c) aid to facilitate the development of certain economic activities or of certain economic areas, where such aid does not adversely affect trading conditions to an extent contrary to the common interest;
>
> (d) aid to promote culture and heritage conservation where such aid does not affect trading conditions and competition in the Union to an extent that is contrary to the common interest;
>
> (e) such other categories of aid as may be specified by decision of the Council on a proposal from the Commission.

Two points are worth noting. First, the list in Article 107(3) TFEU is open-ended; the Council can consider Commission proposals to extend it (Article 107(3)(e) TFEU). Secondly, while some of the exemptions have not been used in the past, in particular Article 107(3)(b) TFEU, they have more recently formed the legal basis for the adoption of temporary State aid frameworks after the 2008 financial crisis,[62] the onset of the coronavirus pandemic,[63] and in the aftermath of the Russian invasion of Ukraine[64]—which channelled significant amounts of public funds under rather relaxed State aid control rules.

[60] However, it should be noted that the exception concerning disadvantaged areas of Germany has not been used since the mid-1990s, Parliamentary Answer given by Ms Vestager on behalf of the Commission on 17 October 2017; www.europarl.europa.eu/doceo/document/E-8-2017-005568-ASW_EN.html.

[61] P Nicolaides, 'Application of Article 107(2)(b) TFEU to Covid-19 Measures: State Aid to Make Good the Damage Caused by an Exceptional Occurrence' (2020) 11 *Journal of European Competition Law & Practice* 238; A Rosanò, 'Adapting to Change: COVID-19 as a Factor Shaping EU State Aid Law' (2020) 5 *European Papers* 621.

[62] Temporary Community framework for State aid measures to support access to finance in the current financial and economic crisis (OJ [2009] C16/1); see RM D'Sa, '"Instant" State Aid Law in a Financial Crisis: A U-Turn?' (2009) 8 *European State Aid Law Quarterly* 139.

[63] Temporary Framework for State aid measures to support the economy in the current COVID-19 outbreak, informal consolidated version, https://ec.europa.eu/competition-policy/system/files/2021-11/TF_consolidated_version_amended_18_nov_2021_en_2.pdf; see I Agnolucci, 'Will COVID-19 Make or Break EU State Aid Control? An Analysis of Commission Decisions Authorising Pandemic State Aid Measures' (2022) 13 *Journal of European Competition Law & Practice* 3.

[64] Temporary Crisis and Transition Framework for State Aid measures to support the economy following the aggression against Ukraine by Russia, consolidated text, https://eur-lex.europa.eu/legal-content/EN/TXT/?uri=CELEX%3A02023XC0317%2801%29-20240502.

3.3.2 **Block exemption regulations**

Individual assessment under Article 107(3) of all State aid measures adopted by the 27 Member States would be unworkable. Consequently, Article 109 TFEU allows the Council, on a proposal from the Commission and after consulting the European Parliament, to adopt category-based block exemption regulations.[65]

Block exemption regulations (BERs) provide pre-established compatibility with the internal market, without the need for an explicit or individualized decision by the Commission, when the conditions set out in the instrument are met. Over the years, a thick network of BERs has emerged, some of a horizontal nature, and some with a sector-specific approach. The most important horizontal exemption instrument is the General Block Exemption Regulation (GBER),[66] which establishes rules for 17 different types of aid, including regional aid, aid to small and medium enterprises (SMEs), aid for environmental protection, and aid for broadband infrastructures. There are also a number of sector-specific block exemption regulations, such as for fisheries,[67] or agriculture and forestry in rural areas.[68]

The strength of the *presumption* of compatibility generated by a BER can be seen in relation to, for example, the GBER, where Article 3 establishes that 'Aid schemes, individual aid granted under aid schemes and ad hoc aid *shall be compatible with the internal market* within the meaning of Article 107(2) or (3) of the Treaty and *shall be exempted from the notification requirement* of Article 108(3) of the Treaty provided that such aid fulfils all the conditions laid down' in the GBER (emphasis added). To avoid abuses of the GBER by the Member States, Article 10 establishes a mechanism for the withdrawal of the benefit of the block exemption, whereby a Member State that is found to have granted aid allegedly exempted without fulfilling the applicable conditions can be forced to notify all future aid of the same type to the Commission. This shows that BERs operate on the basis of mutual trust between the Commission and the Member States.

Some types of aid are unsuited to BER treatment, such as the most controversial type of State aid: rescue and restructuring aid.[69] This type of aid measure seeks to prop up an ailing business and, as such, is the most selective and potentially most anticompetitive type of State aid. For types of aid not covered by a BER, the Commission also publishes sectoral guidelines specifying the conditions under which it will take positive decisions on aid compatibility. The guidelines function as a half-way house between an open-ended assessment of a specific type of aid measure and a block exemption regulation, in that the guidelines lay down compatibility criteria that the Commission is bound to follow in its decision-making. This is the case, for example, of the Guidelines on State aid for climate, environmental protection and energy 2022,[70] which identify 'a number of categories of environmental protection and energy measures in respect of which State aid may be compatible with the internal market under Article 107(3), point (c), of the Treaty under certain conditions'.

[65] At least concerning horizontal aid, the power to make block exemptions is now also partly delegated to the European Commission. See Council Regulation (EU) 2015/1588 of 13 July 2015 (codification), http://data.europa.eu/eli/reg/2015/1588/2018-12-27.

[66] Commission Regulation No 651/2014 of 17 June 2014 declaring certain categories of aid compatible with the internal market in application of Articles 107 and 108 of the Treaty (consolidated version), http://data.europa.eu/eli/reg/2014/651/2023-07-01. The GBER is currently under review.

[67] Commission Regulation No 2473/2022 (consolidated version), http://data.europa.eu/eli/reg/2022/2473/2023-12-13.

[68] Commission Regulation No 702/2014 (consolidated version), http://data.europa.eu/eli/reg/2014/702/2020-12-10.

[69] Guidelines on State aid for rescuing and restructuring non-financial undertakings in difficulty (OJ [2014] C249/1), as prolonged by the respective Communication (OJ C, C/2025/5428, 13.10.2025).

[70] COM(2022) 481 (OJ [2022] C80/1).

To facilitate the application of the *Altmark* test (considered at section 3.2.3), the Commission adopted a package of measures for SGEI aid,[71] a specific *de minimis* rule,[72] a BER for State aid in the form of public service compensation granted to certain undertakings entrusted with the operation of SGEIs,[73] a Communication on the application of the State aid rules to compensation granted for the provision of SGEIs,[74] and a general framework for the assessment of State aid in the form of public service compensation.[75] These instruments are explained in a dedicated guide to the application of the European Union rules on State aid, public procurement, and the internal market to SGEIs.[76] The assessment of a selective economic advantage granted to an entity entrusted to provide an SGEI is thus carried out in the following sequence:[77]

1. check whether the amount exceeds the SGEI *de minimis* threshold of €750,000; if so
2. check whether the aid meets the *Altmark* conditions, as specified in the Communication on the application of the State aid rules to compensation granted for the provision of SGEIs; if not
3. check whether the measure is covered by the SGEI BER; if not
4. check whether the measure meets the requirements of the general framework for the assessment of State aid in the form of public service compensation.

It should be stressed that steps 1 to 3 are carried out by the Member State seeking to grant aid to the undertakings they entrust with SGEI provision, while step 4 can be carried out only by the Commission upon notification by the Member State. Of course, incorrect assessment under steps 1 to 3 by the Member States can lead to an investigation by the European Commission, either of its own motion or following a complaint. This is discussed in section 3.4. The application of the rules is also exemplified in case study 18.1.

3.4 **Enforcement and compliance with State aid rules**

State aid law functions on the basis of mutual trust. Member States themselves assess whether notification to the Commission is required in relation to a specific aid measure and self-police the standstill obligation. Abusing that trust can lead to loss of the benefits of State aid BERs, and breach of the duty to notify and await the Commission's assessment can make aid unlawful, triggering an obligation to re-establish the situation that existed on the market prior to the granting of the aid.[78]

The procedure for assessing a notified State aid measure, or for the investigation of a suspected unlawful measure, is regulated in detail.[79] The ultimate beneficiary of the aid does not take part in proceedings and complainants have very limited rights.[80] This

[71] A Sanchez-Graells, 'The Commission's Modernization Agenda for Procurement and SGEI' in E Szyszczak and J van de Gronden (eds), *Financing Services of General Economic Interest: Reform and Modernization* (The Hague: TMC Asser Press/Springer, 2012) 161–181.

[72] Commission Regulation (EU) 2023/2832 of 13 December 2023 on the application of Articles 107 and 108 of the Treaty on the Functioning of the European Union to de minimis aid granted to undertakings providing services of general economic interest (OJ [2023] L2023/2832).

[73] OJ [2012] L7/3 (the 'SGEI BER'). [74] OJ [2012] C8/4.

[75] OJ [2012] C8/15. [76] SWD(2013) 53 final/2.

[77] JL Buendía Sierra and JM Panero Rivas, 'The Almunia Package: State Aid and Services of General Economic Interest' in Szyszczak and van de Gronden (n 70) 132.

[78] Commission Notice on the recovery of unlawful and incompatible State aid (OJ [2019] C247/1).

[79] Council Regulation 2015/1589 laying down detailed rules for the application of Article 108 of the Treaty on the Functioning of the European Union (OJ [2015] L248/9).

[80] European Ombudsman, Decision of the European Ombudsman in case 1179/2014/LP on the involvement of 'interested parties' in State aid investigations carried out by the Commission.

reflects the 'intergovernmental' nature of the procedure, which makes it prone to politicization. Commission decisions are open to challenge before the General Court under Article 263 TFEU,[81] with a further appeal to the Court of Justice. Again, the procedural rights of intended beneficiaries of an aid measure (especially intended beneficiaries of an aid scheme) are extremely limited owing to the operation of Article 263 TFEU.[82]

The European Commission's partial enforcement monopoly, and its ability to grant exemptions from the general State aid prohibition under Article 107(3) TFEU, diminishes the role of complainants and national courts.[83] Some of the State aid rules do have direct effect and it is also possible to challenge action a Member States takes to bring itself back into compliance (eg when it breaches the standstill obligation) before the national courts. Though there are limited opportunities for direct intervention in the State aid procedure before the Commission, increasingly we see the private enforcement of the State aid rules by the courts of the Member States.[84] There is specific guidance, recently revised, on the role of national courts in State aid proceedings.[85]

Case study 18.1: State aid related to the promotion of renewable energy

Spain wished to support the generation of electricity from renewable energy sources (RES). It did so by imposing a charge on all final electricity consumers and using the income generated to subsidize those using RES.[86] The charge imposed significant costs on energy-intensive companies, such as those in the textile-weaving or flat-glass manufacturing sectors, which considered themselves to be at a significant disadvantage compared to those manufacturing in jurisdictions without RES charges. To protect the competitiveness of its energy-intensive industries, the Spanish government provided a discount (or rebate) of up to 85 per cent of the RES charges paid by those in energy-intensive industries.

The Spanish government considered that the RES rebate triggered the operation of the general prohibition of Article 107(1) TFEU since:

(a) the beneficiaries of the measure were undertakings;

(b) the measure was to be enacted in secondary legislation, and so imputable to the State;

(c) the RES rebate was financed with public funds, as it lowered the proceeds of RES charges received by the Treasury;

(d) the measure was selective, as not all undertakings qualified as operating in energy-intensive industries (the conditions being laid down in secondary legislation);

(e) there was a risk of distorting competition and trade within the internal market; and

(f) the measure was expected to provide millions of euro in any given year of operation of the scheme to any individual manufacturer in an energy-intensive industry, and so could not be considered *de minimis*.

[81] See further chapter 10.

[82] Case C-274/12 P *Telefónica v Commission*, EU:C:2013:852.

[83] This can be contrasted with the fully decentralized enforcement architecture underpinning the general competition rules in Arts 101 and 102 TFEU under Regulation 1/2003. See section 3 of chapter 17.

[84] F Pastor-Merchante, 'The Private Enforcement of State Aid Law' in L Hancher and JJ Piernas López (eds), *Research Handbook on European State Aid Law* (2nd edn, Cheltenham: Edward Elgar, 2021) 226–248.

[85] Commission Notice on the enforcement of State aid rules by national courts (OJ [2021] C305/1).

[86] This is a simplified version of Case State Aid SA.54558 (2020/N)—Spain (Compensation for EIUs for the cost of financing of RES, CHP, and non-peninsular territories in Spain).

To comply with Article 108(3) TFEU, in February 2020, Spain notified the proposed measure to the Commission, making the case that the measure complied with Article 107(3)(c) TFEU, inasmuch as it sought to promote the development of certain (energy-intensive) economic activities within the European Union. The Commission assessed the RES rebate in relation to guidelines it had issued in relation to this type of State aid and, in particular, the Guidelines on State aid for environmental protection and energy 2014–2020 (EEAG).[87] Having confirmed that Spain had complied with the standstill obligation (ie the RES charge rebate scheme was not yet in operation) the Commission confirmed that the EEAG-authorized reductions in contributions levied on energy-intensive companies active in certain sectors and exposed to international trade, in order to ensure their global competitiveness. On the basis of the information provided by Spain, both in the initial notification and in response to additional requests, the Commission found the rebate would be granted only to energy-intensive manufacturers exposed to international trade, in line with EEAG requirements, and ensure the global competitiveness of energy-intensive users and promote EU energy and climate goals without unduly distorting competition. On this basis, the Commission concluded that the measure was in line with EU State aid rules and authorized its implementation until 31 December 2022.

3.5 **Summary**

Bringing this all together, when the four elements of the prohibition in Article 107(1) TFEU are satisfied (section 3.2), it is necessary to consider whether any exemptions or exceptions to the general prohibition are applicable (section 3.3). The assessment is conducted in the following sequence (see Fig. 18.1):

1. check whether the amount exceeds the *de minimis* threshold (ie is the aid 'worth' more than €300,000 over any period of three fiscal years); if so
2. check whether any of the exception grounds in Article 107(2) TFEU apply; if not
3. check whether the aid measure is covered by a BER and complies with its conditions; if not
4. check whether the aid measure is covered by guidelines and complies with their conditions; if not
5. check whether the aid measure can still be considered compatible with the internal market (eg despite not meeting all conditions in the applicable guidelines);
6. if there is no exception or exemption, the aid is unlawful.

It should be stressed that steps 1 to 4 are carried out by the Member State seeking to grant the aid, while steps 5 and 6 can only be carried out by the Commission upon notification of the aid measure by the Member State. Incorrect assessment under steps 1 to 4 by the Member States can lead to an investigation by the European Commission, either of its own motion or as a result of a complaint. To grant aid, States should notify the Commission. Aid should not be distributed until the Commission has given authorization (section 3.4).

[87] OJ [2014] C200/1. Please note these guidelines have now been replaced by the Guidelines on State aid for climate, environmental protection and energy 2022 (n 69).

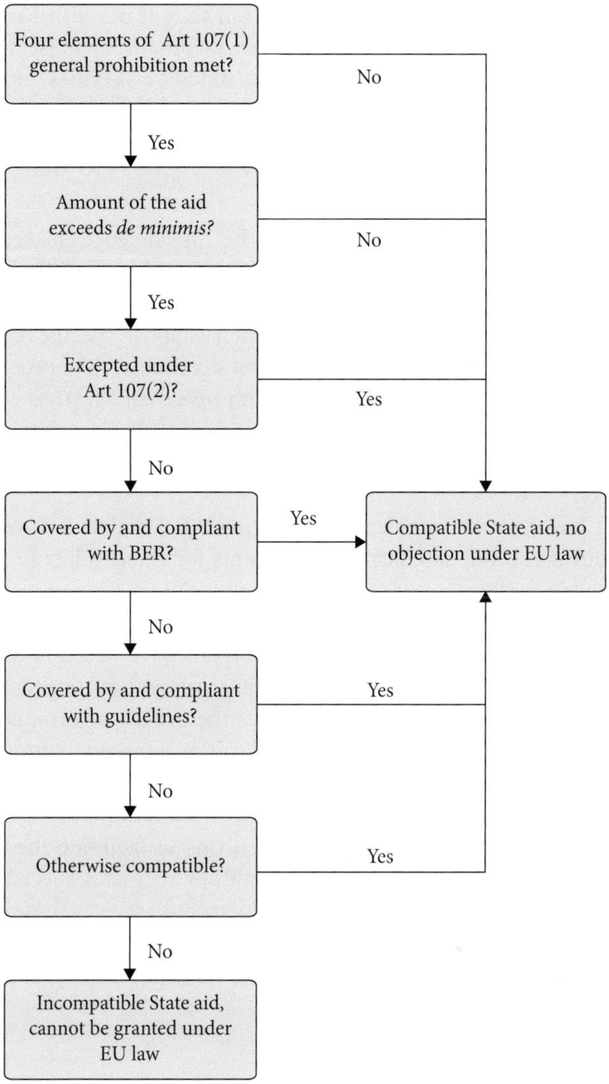

Fig. 18.1 Decision-tree for the application of State aid rules

4 **Public procurement rules**

Much like State intervention in the form of aid, States can generate an uneven playing field through the award of contracts to their domestic economic operators on a preferential basis. The discriminatory award of a public contract could amount to State aid (see section 3.2), but the rules on State aid have been considered insufficient to regulate the matter in all circumstances. Further, the EU must comply with its international obligations under the World Trade Organization Government Procurement Agreement. EU law thus includes a set of rules on public procurement with the main objective of ensuring free movement of goods and the freedom to provide services, and the opening up of undistorted competition in all the Member States.[88] This section provides an overview

[88] Case C-3/19 *Asmel*, EU:C:2020:423, para 58. A Sanchez-Graells, 'Competition and Procurement Regulation' in C Risvig Hamer et al (eds), *Into the Northern Light—In memory of Steen Treumer* (Copenhagen: Ex Tuto Publishing, 2022) 65–81.

of the rules, stressing the flexibility and discretion they leave with Member States to implement policies such as innovation, green, or social procurement (section 4.1). It then clarifies the interaction between the procurement and State aid rules, picking up on the discussion of *Altmark* (section 4.2).

4.1 **General rules**

EU public procurement law currently comprises the 2009 defence and security procurement Directive;[89] the 2014 Public Procurement Package, inclusive of (directives on public sector procurement,[90] utilities procurement,[91] and the procurement of concessions[92]); as well as the procurement remedies directives,[93] which establish specific regulation for the administrative and judicial review of procurement decisions.[94] The procurement directives are currently under review, with the goal to improve their effectiveness[95] or facilitate a more integrated internal market for defence procurement.[96] The review is also likely to create a future 'EU preference' for procurement for strategic sectors, such as defence or digital industries.[97]

Procurement law does not regulate *what* to buy,[98] but rather *how* to buy, and sets detailed procedural and documentary requirements for the conduct of public tenders. Procurement law generally requires public buyers to *facilitate effective competition for the public contract* through the advertisement of contract opportunities. It then imposes a set of constraints seeking to ensure proportionate qualitative selection requirements for tenderers (eg based on systems of mutual recognition of qualifications, previous experience), neutral technical specifications (eg requires the use of performance-based specifications, and of international or European standards as opposed to domestic standards which favour local contractors), and suitable and proportionate award criteria against which to evaluate the tenders (eg selection on merit, value for money).

Procurement law also includes several mechanisms to facilitate the delivery of EU *horizontal policy goals*. For example, procurement law regulates special procedures to facilitate public–private co-creation of new products and services (innovation partnership); it includes flexibility for the consideration of the environmental impact of procurement (such as through life-cycle costing methods, or requirements concerning quality

[89] Directive 2009/81/EC (OJ [2009] L216/76).

[90] Directive 2014/24/EU (OJ [2014] L94/65).

[91] Directive 2014/25/EU on procurement by entities operating in the water, energy, transport and postal services sectors (utilities) (OJ [2014] L94/243).

[92] Directive 2014/23/EU (OJ [2014] L94/1).

[93] Council Directive 89/665/EEC on remedies for the public sector, as repeatedly amended, http://data.europa.eu/eli/dir/1989/665/2014-04-17; and Council Directive 92/13/EEC on remedies for the utilities sector, as repeatedly amended, http://data.europa.eu/eli/dir/1992/13/2014-04-17.

[94] S Weatherill, 'EU Law on Public Procurement: Internal Market Law Made Better' in S Bogojević, X Groussot, and J Hettne (eds), *Discretion in EU Public Procurement Law* (Oxford: Hart Publishing, 2019) 21–49.

[95] This follows from the European Court of Auditor's Special Report 28/2023: Public procurement in the EU—Less competition for contracts awarded for works, goods and services in the 10 years up to 2021, www.eca.europa.eu/en/publications/SR-2023-28.

[96] Proposal for a Directive of the European Parliament and of the Council amending Directives 2009/43/EC and 2009/81/EC, as regards the simplification of intra-EU transfers of defence-related products and the simplification of security and defence procurement, COM(2025) 823 final.

[97] Communication, 'A Competitiveness Compass for the EU', COM(2025) 30 final.

[98] There are, however, sectoral rules imposing mandatory requirements on the procurement of specific products or components of products, see Willem A Janssen, Study into the external coherence between the public procurement directives and other legislative instruments regulating public procurement (July 2025) https://data.europa.eu/doi/10.2873/7419429.

assurance and environmental management standards); it allows for the inclusion of social requirements (eg 'social value' as an award criterion); and requirements relating to the employment conditions of the workers involved in the delivery of the contract (through contract performance clauses). Procurement law also allows for the exclusion of economic operators that cannot be considered reliable or adequate partners for the public buyer, such as those that have infringed tax or social security laws, environmental laws, competition rules, or have been involved in criminal procedures (including cases of conviction of members of the management team).

Given the importance of procurement in the context of public services, there are special rules for social and other services (such as health care and education), which are subject to a light-touch regime. Features of the light-touch regime include the ability to ring-fence public contracts for certain types of market operators which are either not-for-profit or distribute profits on the basis of participatory considerations (eg charities, NGOs, or mutuals).

4.2 **Interaction with State aid rules**

As mentioned in section 3.2.3, carrying out a public procurement exercise for the selection of the provider of an SGEI, or an economic operator otherwise entrusted with a public service obligation (PSO), has been required by the CJEU case law as a safeguard against the selectivity of the award, as well as a mechanism to ensure that the terms of the contract reflect market conditions and thus confer no economic advantage. This has been the general approach since the 2003 *Altmark* decision. However, successive reforms of the EU procurement rules, in 2004 and 2014, extended the flexibility and discretion available to the design of tender procedures and award criteria. These reforms loosened the constraints that a procurement exercise imposed when *Altmark* was originally decided. The current generation of procurement rules contains a large number of exceptions that could result in the direct or negotiated award of a contract for the provision of an SGEI, as well as the possibility of taking non-economic considerations into account as predominant evaluation and decision-making factors. As such, the 'objectivity' of the procurement exercise can be jeopardized or, less controversially, there is scope for the outcome of a procurement exercise that does not reflect 'normal market conditions'.[99] This has led the Commission to issue additional guidance on the types of procurement procedures and the acceptable mechanisms that allow for the presumption of compliance with State aid and SGEI rules that derive from *Altmark*.[100] Only procurement procedures meeting those narrow requirements will trigger the presumption, with all other (legally compliant) procedures requiring additional benchmarking under the general State aid guidance. This need for additional benchmarking can be seen as restrictive of the public buyer's discretion, to the extent that State aid risks can influence (and limit) the extent to which contracting authorities avail themselves of the flexibilities within the procurement rules—although the CJEU has confirmed that it is possible to show that even a direct award does not involve State aid where the SGEI compensation is within standard market parameters.[101]

[99] A Sanchez-Graells, 'State Aid and EU Public Procurement: More Interactions, Fuzzier Boundaries' in Hancher and Piernas López (n 83) 329–346.

[100] Notice on the notion of State aid (n 9) paras 84ff.

[101] Case C-186/22 *Sad Trasporto Locale*, EU:C:2023:795.

Case study 18.2: Financing hospitals in the Brussels Capital Region

As part of the restructuring of the management and financing of hospitals in Brussels, the relevant authorities decided to create a network of hospitals (IRIS-H), restructure them, and modify the ways they were funded.[102] The restructuring of the Brussels public hospitals also consisted of a financial part. More specifically, the Brussels Capital Region granted a loan of approximately €100 million over a period of 20 years to the public hospitals to cover part of their financial liabilities. In 1996, the Brussels Capital Region decided not to demand repayment of the loan and interests, on the condition that the hospital restructuring agreements were fully implemented and the financial plans respected.

The condonation of the loan and interests was challenged as State aid by complainants in 2005. In 2009, the Commission initially decided not to raise objections, but this was appealed to the General Court, which annulled the decision in 2012, and the case was sent back to the Commission for a fresh assessment, which restarted in 2014.

In its 2016 decision, the Commission found that all cumulative requirements of the Article 107(1) TFEU prohibition were present. This was particularly important regarding the analysis whether the hospitals should be classed as undertakings. The crucial issue here was the need to take into account a distinction between, first, national health systems managed by ministries and other bodies and that operate according to the principle of solidarity, and, secondly, those run by management bodies responsible for the provision of hospital care against remuneration in a competitive environment.[103] The Belgian system was an example of the latter and, consequently, Belgian IRIS-H hospitals were classed as undertakings.

The Commission then proceeded to assess aid compatibility in relation to Article 106(2) TFEU. The measure exceeded the SGEI *de minimis* threshold and could not be exempted following *Altmark* because the IRIS-H had not been selected via public procurement procedures for the public service obligations with which they are entrusted according to the Belgian authorities, so the Commission proceeded to consider whether the aid met the conditions of the SGEI BER.[104] Ultimately, the Commission concluded that this was the case, in particular because IRIS-H hospitals were entrusted with SGEI obligations beyond those of 'ordinary' Belgian hospitals, creating a 'social healthcare SGEI' specific to IRIS hospitals that generated significant additional costs. The State aid in the form of compensation of the deficits of the Brussels public IRIS hospitals by the Brussels municipalities was declared compatible with the internal market on the basis of Article 106(2) TFEU.

One of the interesting issues raised by the case, other than the very detailed assessment of compliance with the SGEI BER, comes from considering what would have been the implications of the opposite finding by the Commission. Given that the aid that formed the basis of the complaint was granted in 1996, if the Commission had concluded that the aid was incompatible, it should have mandated its recovery, together with interest for the intervening 20 years. This would have had significant financial consequences for the hospitals and possibly threatened their viability.

[102] This is a simplified version of Case SA.19864–2014/C (ex 2009/NN54)—Belgium (IRIS hospitals).

[103] D Gallo, 'State Aids, Social Services and Healthcare in EU Law' in B Nascimbene and A Di Pascale (eds), *The Modernisation of State Aid for Economic and Social Development* (Cham: Springer, 2018) 267, 272.

[104] The analysis required assessing part of the support in relation to the earlier 2005 version of the SGEI BER.

5 **Conclusion**

Both State aid rules and public procurement laws have as the primary goal the creation of a level playing field and the promotion of competition within the internal market. A significant theme is the existence of mechanisms that facilitate a balance between economic and other (often competing) policy goals. EU law has created a complex set of rules that seek to achieve such balance in a flexible manner. These are, however, highly politicized decisions and can reflect different economic and legal approaches to the regulation of the market. When Member States are compelled by their populations to respond to certain matters, compliance with State aid and procurement obligations is not often the foremost thought. Similarly, the intention to have competition in the award of public contracts, evaluate bids on a level playing field, and maximize probity and value for money in the award of public contracts seem to be in permanent tension with the reality of the political context in which expenditure occurs.

Two important reports, one by the former Italian prime minister, Enrico Letta, and the other by former President of the European Central Bank, Mario Draghi, were published in 2024.[105] The reports highlight the misuse of State aid as a considerable distortion of competition, while recognizing the need for considerable investment to spur innovation and improve EU competitiveness. They call for stricter enforcement of State aid regulations, and propose reforming the State aid process so that the rules measure the impact on Union, rather than national, initiatives.[106] The extent to which EU Member States are willing to pool such sovereignty remains to be seen.[107]

Further reading

S Arrowsmith, *The Law of Public and Utilities Procurement: Regulation in the EU and UK* (3rd edn, London: Sweet & Maxwell, vol I 2014 and vol II 2018)

K Bacon, *European Union Law of State Aid* (3rd edn, Oxford: Oxford University Press, 2017)

M Cyndecka, *The Market Economy Investor Test in EU State Aid Law: Applicability and Application* (Alphen aan den Rijn: Kluwer Law International, 2016)

J Grandia and L Volker (eds), *Public Procurement. Theory, Practices and Tools* (Cham: Palgrave Macmillan, 2023)

L Hancher, T Ottervanger, and PJ Slot, *EU State Aids* (6th edn, London: Sweet & Maxwell, 2021)

C Quigley, *European State Aid Law and Policy (and UK Subsidy Control)* (4th edn, Oxford: Hart Publishing, 2022)

A Semple, *A Practical Guide to Public Procurement* (Oxford: Oxford University Press, 2015)

[105] Available respectively at www.consilium.europa.eu/media/ny3j24sm/much-more-than-a-market-report-by-enrico-letta.pdf and www.consilium.europa.eu/en/press/press-releases/2024/11/08/the-budapest-declaration and https://ec.europa.eu/commission/presscorner/detail/en/ip_25_339.

[106] Letta report, p 11; Draghi report, p 68

[107] See M Chang, 'The Letta and Draghi Reports: Economic Efficiency Versus Political Exigency' (2025) 63 *Journal of Common Market Studies*, https://doi.org/10.1111/jcms.70013.

19

Economic and Monetary Union

Alicia Hinarejos

1 Introduction

The Economic and Monetary Union (EMU) is one of the most important and best-known aspects of EU integration; it is also one of the most controversial. It envisages a single monetary policy, conducted by a single monetary authority; a single currency, the euro; and coordination of national economic policies. Not all Member States of the EU participate in all phases of EMU: as of October 2025, 20 Member States have entered the last stage of EMU and adopted the euro as their currency; these countries constitute the 'eurozone' or 'euro area'. The number has now increased to 21, as Bulgaria joined the euro area on 1 January 2026.

Centralized monetary policy for the euro area is conducted by an EU institution, the European Central Bank (ECB), assisted by the national central banks; all together they form the European System of Central Banks (ESCB). At the same time, economic policy remains in the hands of Member States, within certain limits. There is thus an underlying tension within EMU between a centralized monetary policy and essentially decentralized economic and fiscal policy. Ultimately, this asymmetric design of EMU proved to have certain flaws that contributed to the euro area government debt crisis and made it more difficult to address said crisis. This chapter will explain how EMU was set up, and the flaws within the system. It will also give a brief overview of the euro crisis and its relationship to, and consequences for, EMU. Finally, the chapter will look to the current debate on the future of EMU and the EU.[1]

[1] Certain sections of this chapter draw on material included in A Hinarejos, 'The Euro Area Crisis and Constitutional Limits to Fiscal Integration' (2012) 14 *Cambridge Yearbook of European Legal Studies* 243; A Hinarejos, *The Euro Area Crisis in Constitutional Perspective* (Oxford: Oxford University Press, 2015). I am grateful to the Social Sciences and Humanities Research Council of Canada for its support in the course of this research (Insight Grant 2022–2026).

2 History and design of EMU

States normally control their monetary policy (matters such as the production of currency and interest rates) alongside their fiscal policy (the acquisition of public funds through, for example, taxation or debt, as well as the allocation of those funds through public spending or the creation of a social insurance system). Monetary and fiscal policies are traditionally considered two sides of the same coin. The term 'economic policy' is potentially broader than these two policies taken together—as it may also cover all instances of intervention in the economy through the use of regulation (eg concerning wages or other aspects of labour law).

The EMU was part of the project of European integration dating back to the early 1970s.[2] Its formal legal origins lie with the Treaty on European Union, adopted in 1991, which granted the (then) European Community the competence to establish an economic and monetary policy which would include the fixing of exchange rates leading to the introduction of a common currency, a central monetary and exchange rate policy conducted with a view to maintaining price stability, and limited coordination of national economic policies. After exchange rates were indeed fixed in 1998,[3] a new common currency, the euro, was introduced in 1999.[4] Euro banknotes and coins were introduced in 2002. As noted, as of early 2026, 21 Member States (since Bulgaria joined on 1 January 2026) have entered the last stage of EMU and adopted the euro as their currency; these countries constitute the 'eurozone' or 'euro area'.[5] The remaining Member States, apart from Denmark,[6] are committed to adopting the euro when their economies satisfy a set of pre-established requirements, or convergence criteria, set out in the Treaty and a Protocol.[7] These criteria seek to limit inflation, annual public deficit, and total accumulated public debt. Countries are also required to have maintained stable exchange rates and long-term interest rates for a certain period of time before joining EMU. There are no express provisions in the Treaty on terminating EMU as a whole, or on a Member State leaving EMU, voluntarily or otherwise—presumably unless the Member State decides to leave the EU altogether, pursuant to Article 50 TEU.

The creation of an economic and monetary union was considered the next logical step of economic integration, after the establishment of the internal market.[8] What is most significant about this area of Union competence is its asymmetry, or the fact that monetary

[2] For an overview of its historical origins prior to the TEU: F Snyder, 'EMU-Integration and Differentiation: Metaphor for European Union' in P Craig and G de Búrca (eds), *The Evolution of EU Law* (2nd edn, Oxford: Oxford University Press, 2011).

[3] Council Regulation (EC) 2866/98 on the conversion rates between the euro and the currencies of the Member States adopting the euro (OJ [1998] L359/1).

[4] Council Regulation (EC) 974/98 on the introduction of the euro (OJ [1998] L139/1).

[5] These countries are: Austria, Belgium, Croatia, Cyprus, Estonia, Finland, France, Germany, Greece, Ireland, Italy, Latvia, Lithuania, Luxembourg, Malta, the Netherlands, Portugal, Slovakia, Slovenia, and Spain.

[6] The UK also had an opt-out when it was a Member State. Both opt-outs are set out in protocols attached to the Treaties: Protocol No 15 on certain provisions relating to the United Kingdom of Great Britain and Northern Ireland; Protocol No 16 on certain provisions relating to Denmark.

[7] Based on what is nowadays Art 140 TFEU and Protocol No 13 on the convergence criteria.

[8] Economists have traditionally distinguished the following progressive stages: Free Trade Area, Customs Union, Common Market, Monetary Union, Economic Union, Political or Full Union. B Balassa, *The Theory of Economic Integration* (London: Allen and Unwin, 1961). See also C Barnard, *The Substantive Law of the EU: The Four Freedoms* (5th edn, Oxford: Oxford University Press, 2016) 8ff; P Verloren van Themaat, 'Some Preliminary Observations on the IGC: The Relations between the Concepts of a Common Market, a Monetary Union, an Economic Union, a Political Union and Sovereignty' (1991) 28 *Common Market Law Review* 291.

policy has been separated from fiscal policy (and from the broader national economic policy):[9] EMU includes a full monetary union, defined and conducted at the EU level, while economic/fiscal policies are still conducted at the national level.

Indeed, the EU has exclusive competence in monetary policy for the Member States whose currency is the euro, according to the Treaties.[10] Monetary policy is defined and implemented for the whole eurozone by the ESCB: this system includes the national central banks (eg the Deutsche Bundesbank, De Nederlandsche Bank, etc), and has the European Central Bank at its helm.[11] The ESCB and all its components are supposed to be independent and free from political influence.[12]

EMU, however, does not include a full fiscal or economic policy conducted at the EU level. Instead, Member States remain in control of their own fiscal policies, and of their broader economic policies, within certain limits that will be discussed later. So far, EMU has merely given Member States a framework to coordinate these policies to a certain degree:[13] Article 2(3) TFEU marks economic policy as an area where the EU's competence is a coordinating one; that is, where the Union is merely supposed to provide arrangements to facilitate coordination of policies that remain national in nature. Coordinating competences were introduced in the Treaty of Lisbon (in force 1 December 2009) and, although they seem to hover somewhere between shared and supporting competences, their constitutional character is not fully defined yet.[14] It seems safe to say, nevertheless, that the Union has no proper legislative competence at the moment to generate an independent economic or fiscal policy.

The design of EMU, then, gives great predominance to the monetary component, while integration of economic policies lags much further behind. This final design was the result of a debate in the 1960s and 70s between 'monetarists' and 'economists': The first ones believed that the starting point of EMU should be fixing exchange rates or the introduction of a common currency, and that coordination of economic policies would then follow. On the contrary, the 'economists' believed that coordination of economic policies should happen prior to the introduction of a common currency. Needless to say, the 'monetarists' prevailed;[15] as a result, while all members of the euro area are bound to each other through a common currency, each of them is free to conduct their own fiscal and economic policies, within certain limits. The next section will turn to the nature and effectiveness of these limits.

[9] The issue of economic governance within an asymmetric EMU has been discussed for many years. For a historical review: N Jabko, 'Which Economic Governance? Facing up to the Problem of Divided Sovereignty', SIEPS Report 2011/02. For a historical analysis of the Franco–German debate concerning the appropriate EMU architecture: J Pisani-Ferry, 'Only One Bed for Two Dreams: A Critical Retrospective on the Debate over the Economic Governance of the Euro Area' (2006) 44 *Journal of Common Market Studies* 823.

[10] Art 3(1)(c) TFEU. On the concept of exclusive EU competences, see further chapter 5.

[11] On the design of the ESCB and ESM, see R Smits, The European Central Bank: Institutional Aspects (The Hague: Kluwer, 1997); F Antembrink, 'The Democratic Accountability of Central Banks: A Comparative Study of the European Central Bank' (Oxford: Hart Publishing, 1999).

[12] Art 130 TFEU. On this requirement, see also Joined Cases C-202/18 and C-238/18 *Rimšēvičs v Latvia*, EU:C:2019:139; A Hinarejos, 'The Court of Justice Annuls a National Measure Directly to Protect ECB Independence: *Rimšēvičs*' (2019) 56 *Common Market Law Review* 1649.

[13] On economic coordination (before the euro area crisis), see eg I Harden, 'The Fiscal Constitution of EMU' in P Beaumont and N Walker (eds), *The Legal Framework of the Single European Currency* (Oxford: Hart Publishing, 1999) 71–93; D Hodson and I Maher, 'The Open Method as a New Mode of Governance: The Case of Soft Economic Policy Co-ordination' (2001) 39 *Journal of Common Market Studies* 719; I Maher, 'Economic Governance: Hybridity, Accountability and Control' (2007) 1 *Colombia Journal of European Law* 679.

[14] For more on the concept of coordinating competences, see chapter 5.

[15] See historical overview pieces in n 9.

3 The Stability and Growth Pact and measures of coordination before the crisis

The limits imposed on national fiscal policies were initially laid down in the Treaties and in the Stability and Growth Pact, based on Articles 121 and 126 TFEU.[16] Member States agreed to keep their annual deficit and debt below a certain percentage of their Gross Domestic Product (GDP), or the value of all goods and services produced within their national borders in a year. With the Stability and Growth Pact, States agreed to keep their annual deficit below 3 per cent of their GDP, and their debt below 60 per cent of their GDP. This was the 'preventive arm' of the Pact; there was also a 'corrective arm', or excessive deficit procedure, allowing the Council, on a recommendation from the Commission, to penalize and even impose fines on euro area Member States that did not abide by the rules.

In practice, however, the need for political agreement within Council in order to impose sanctions meant that the corrective arm of the Pact lacked effectiveness. In 2002 and 2003, the Commission initiated excessive deficit procedures against Germany and France, respectively. These countries adopted measures to address the situation, but the Commission did not consider them effective enough. Accordingly, the Commission urged the Council to pursue more forceful action.[17] In both cases, the Council voted and decided not to follow the Commission's recommendations. The Commission then challenged the legality of the resulting Council measures before the Court of Justice of the EU.[18] The judgment was complex; what is most relevant for the current discussion is that the Court rejected the Commission's claim that the Council's failure to adopt the Commission's recommendation was in itself a decision, and one that should be annulled.[19] Ultimately, the Commission could not require the Council to pursue further action against France, Germany, or any other country that breached the Pact. Recurring breaches without significant consequences were likely to diminish the credibility of the Pact further. As a consequence, it was considered preferable to reform the Pact in 2005: its rules were made more flexible, allowing for even greater discretion.[20] In general, the Pact appeared to have lost its teeth.

Aside from the Pact, Member States were—and still are—also supposed to follow the Broad Guidelines on Economic Policy, issued by the Council every three years with a view to coordinating national economic policies (and affecting fiscal policy, but also regulation of the economy more broadly).[21] The guidelines are not legally binding: States make

[16] The origins of the Stability and Growth Pact lie in a Resolution from 1997 (Resolution of the European Council on the Stability and Growth Pact, 17 June 1997). This spawned two regulations (preventive and corrective arm, respectively): Council Regulation (EC) 1466/97 on the strengthening of the surveillance of budgetary positions and the surveillance and coordination of economic policies (OJ [1997] L209/1); and Council Regulation (EC) 1467/97 on speeding up and clarifying the implementation of the excessive deficit procedure (OJ [1997] L209/6). The excessive deficit procedure is further detailed in Protocol No 12 attached to the Treaties.

[17] The Commission recommended to the Council that deadlines be set, that specific measures be imposed on France and Germany, and that the Council's recommendations be made public.

[18] Case C-27/04 *Commission v Council* [2004] ECR I-6649.

[19] For more information on this and other aspects of the judgment: F Snyder, 'EMU—Integration and Differentiation: Metaphor for European Union' in P Craig and G de Búrca (eds), *The Evolution of EU Law* (2nd edn, Oxford: Oxford University Press, 2011); I Maher 'Economic Policy Coordination and the European Court: Excessive Deficits and ECOFIN Discretion' (2004) 29 *European Law Review* 831.

[20] Council Regulation (EC) 1055/2005 amending Regulation (EC) 1466/97 (OJ [2005] L174/1); Council Regulation (EC) 1056/2005 amending Regulation (EC) 1467/97 (OJ [2005] L174/5).

[21] On the basis of Art 121 TFEU.

certain commitments in order to comply with these recommendations,[22] and then they report annually on their progress.[23] Additionally, members of the eurozone also seek to coordinate their policies within the Eurogroup, an informal gathering of the finance ministers of all euro countries, together with the Commission Vice-President for Economic and Monetary Affairs, and the President of the ECB.[24]

To sum up: the assumption at the heart of EMU was always that a central monetary policy and a single currency necessitate effective coordination of economic and fiscal policies, yet this coordination may have turned out to be more difficult than anticipated. This imbalance between the different sides of EMU is related to the so-called euro area crisis, which the next section will discuss.

4 The euro area crisis and its relationship to EMU

The effects of the financial crisis that erupted in 2007 were felt globally. In the European Union, these effects were amplified by certain flaws in the design of EMU: in 2010, it became clear that the economies of several euro area members were in serious trouble, and that the euro area had a government debt crisis (also called sovereign debt crisis) on its hands.[25] Although the most obvious symptoms of the crisis affected specific countries, the crisis had a much broader scope. From a political or constitutional perspective, the crisis cast doubt not only on the viability of a mechanism of integration such as the one envisaged in EMU, but also on the future of the EU as a political project in the face of citizens' growing disaffection.

What is a sovereign debt crisis, and how does it start? Countries continuously refinance their public or sovereign debt, which means that they pay debts that have matured by borrowing new money from the markets. To this end, a country sells financial instruments (eg bonds) that yield interest; this interest compensates investors for the time during which they are not able to use their money, as well as for the risk they take in lending it. Prior to the outbreak of the crisis, the cost of funding for most euro area economies was similar, with Greece paying a small risk premium compared to Germany. The crisis changed this: once the markets paid more attention to the specifics of each euro economy, they started to have doubts as to specific countries' credibility as debtors. Typically, this lack of confidence leads to rising costs of borrowing and refinancing, since a country in this situation needs to compensate investors with a higher risk premium. As its borrowing costs rise inexorably, the troubled country risks being shut out of private markets; as a result of the vicious circle just described, State default—the situation where a State is not able to repay its debts—becomes a more likely possibility.[26]

In the case of the euro area, markets started to doubt the ability of some euro countries (Ireland, Portugal, and Greece, initially) to repay their debt, for different reasons. All three countries received financial assistance after committing to the implementation

[22] eg the 2015 guidelines included the following recommendation: 'continuing to reform labour markets and social security systems in order to increase growth and employment while ensuring universal access to social benefits and services, alongside their quality, affordability and sustainability': Council Recommendation (EU) 2015/1184 of 14 July 2015 on broad guidelines for the economic policies of the Member States and of the EU (OJ [2015] L192/27).

[23] On the guidelines and their effect, D Hodson, *Governing the Euro Area in Good Times and Bad* (Oxford: Oxford University Press, 2011) ch 5 ('Why the BEPGs Failed to Bite').

[24] Art 137 TFEU and Protocol No 14 on the Eurogroup.

[25] For a concise overview of the crisis: House of Lords (EU Select Committee), 'The Euro Area Crisis', 25th Report of Session 2010–12, HL Paper 260.

[26] Rather, a default on private debt is inevitable in the absence of official sector financing.

of strict austerity measures. These 'bailouts'—which are, strictly speaking, loans—came from the International Monetary Fund[27] and from two different European emergency mechanisms.[28] While the bailouts seemed to ameliorate the situation in Ireland and Portugal, the Greek problem was of a much greater scale; the country was revealed to have long misrepresented the volume of its debt and, in general, the state of its finances, in order, at least at first, to be able to join the euro.[29] Market fears spread to other countries as well, especially Spain and Italy, which meant that these countries too saw their economy threatened by the rising cost of borrowing money under the worsening conditions offered by a wary market.

The imbalance between EU monetary policy, on the one hand, and national fiscal/economic policies, on the other, was relevant to the crisis in several respects. First, some economists believe that different national economic policies fostered competitive asymmetries between the euro area members;[30] when left unchecked, these asymmetries put certain members in a position that was more vulnerable to the global economic crisis.[31] Secondly, the monetary union meant that, initially, certain eurozone members were able to borrow money from the markets much more cheaply than they should have, creating a certain incentive for running up national debt.[32] Thirdly, individual euro countries were not able to use the tools of monetary policy, by now out of their hands: for example, they were not able to produce more money (quantitative easing) in order to alleviate their debt, or alternatively to devalue their currency, so as to make their exports cheaper and foster economic growth. Fourthly, the perception that some euro countries may default affected the value of the common currency and thus the economies of all members of the euro area; more specifically, there was a risk of contagion as the risk of default in one State made investors wary of the same happening in others. And finally, independent fiscal policies meant that better-off members of the euro area were (justifiably) reticent to bail out members in risk of default, since the latter might not alter their behaviour in the absence of an incentive for fiscal responsibility. For the same reason, better-off euro countries are equally reluctant to pool their public debt in the future, for example by having the whole euro area issuing bonds jointly.[33] In short, the asymmetry at the heart of EMU has arguably contributed to the fiscal problems of some euro countries, or at least allowed them to happen; it has exposed all euro area members to the problems of a few; and it has made it difficult to address these problems at the EU level.[34]

[27] The IMF is an international organization. Its members (189 countries to date) contribute money to a fund which can be used to make conditional loans to struggling economies.

[28] The European Financial Stability Mechanism (EFSM), a small loan facility within the EU system, and the European Financial Stability Fund (EFSF), a much bigger, temporary vehicle created on an intergovernmental basis. There was also an ad hoc loan agreement for Greece. See further section 5.1.2.

[29] For an early overview of the Greek situation and the EU's response: Editorial Comments, 'The Greek Sovereign Debt Tragedy: Approaching the Final Act?' (2011) 48 *Common Market Law Review* 1769.

[30] This means that different members within the currency area will have different economic structures (eg some are manufacture- and export-driven, while others rely on the provision of services) and will not be equally competitive. Suboptimal labour and capital mobility add to this problem.

[31] For a brief overview, see, eg, S Micossi, 'Misguided Policies Risk Breaking Up the Eurozone and the EU' (December 2011) CEPS Policy Brief No 260, 4, electronic copy available at: www.ssrn.com/abstract=1996457.

[32] More specifically, it was the perception (in retrospect proved to be partly correct because of the extraordinary level of official sector financing provided) that other euro area economies would provide financial support if one member threatened to default.

[33] There is also a question as to whether joint bonds (sometimes called 'eurobonds') would violate the no-bailout clause in the Treaty, Art 125 TFEU (discussed in section 5.1.2). See also n 102 and corresponding main text for further discussion.

[34] This does not mean that EMU is the root of all fiscal problems; after all, some non-eurozone States have run up large deficits. Eg while it was still a member of the EU but not a euro country, the UK ran up an enormous deficit that peaked in 2009/10 and 2010/11.

Against this background, it seemed that, while a bailout or the creation of a rescue mechanism could temporarily preserve financial stability in the euro area as a whole, it was also necessary, in the longer term, to address the imbalance between the strong monetary union and the weak economic coordination between the members of the euro area. Case study 19.1 and the next two sections will discuss the bailout mechanisms, as well as the reforms undertaken to improve economic coordination since the beginning of the crisis.

Case study 19.1: Dealing with the euro crisis

Countries A, B, and C are all members of the euro area.

Before the global financial crisis, Country A's banks bought a great deal of 'toxic' financial products, which means that they are now in trouble and likely to default. Rather than facing a meltdown of its economy, Country A decides to bail out its banks. As a result, Country A now has a very large volume of public debt and faces problems of liquidity.

Country B also faces problems of liquidity, for other reasons. They already had a problem with public debt, and they are now finding that, because of the financial crisis, it has become more difficult to borrow money in the markets, either by borrowing directly from banks or by selling bonds to private investors. When their struggles become public, private investors panic and nobody wants to buy Country B bonds, because they are considered 'junk bonds' (ie not likely to be repaid when they mature). To make up for the level of risk, Country B has to offer an ever-increasing interest rate. Very soon it will be so expensive for them to borrow money through the issuing of bonds (ie they will have to offer such high interest rates in return) that they will be effectively shut out from the market, and thus unable to borrow the necessary money to refinance ('roll over') their debt. A default looks more and more likely.

When faced with this situation, all members of the euro area decide that it makes sense to bail out Countries A and B (ie lend them money in advantageous conditions). Investors are already worrying about the creditworthiness of other members of the euro area, which makes it more likely that these other countries, too, will face escalating costs when borrowing money from the markets. The economies of all euro area countries are also intertwined in other ways: Country C's banks, for example, own a great deal of Country B's debt; so much that Country C's economy would suffer a severe blow if Country B were unable to pay Country C's banks.

Of course, the citizens of different countries see a potential bailout in a very different light: the residents of Country C are not happy about sending their tax money to Country A or B. They think that they should not be paying for countries that chose to spend too much, instead of being responsible like they were. They also worry that, once Country B receives a bailout, its government will just go back to spending too much, safe in the belief that the country will be saved again if necessary.

On the other hand, citizens in Countries A and B hope for solidarity from the rest of the euro area. They start to wonder whether the Union is only a 'proper' union as long as the economy is going well. They also argue that the richer countries in the euro area (and, chief among them, Country C) have benefited from the single market and EMU for many years; in fact, they argue that these countries have benefited far more than everybody else, because of the way their industries work (they have a competitive manufacture- and export-based industry). Accordingly, they think, these rich countries should now be willing to share some of the wealth.

In the end, the bailouts take place, and countries A and B need to comply with very strict conditions in order to receive the money. They have to make quite dramatic economic reforms and implement cutbacks across the board. The citizens of these countries perceive these conditions as draconian and unfair. People feel let down and tensions grow; the media start a campaign against the government and citizens of Country C, who do not understand the backlash and feel like everybody else in the Union is taking advantage of them.

In order to keep this sort of thing from happening again, there is a consensus that the way in which EMU works needs to change.

First, Country A's troubles could have been avoided if the behaviour of banks had been better regulated; accordingly, the EU decides to work towards a better, more harmonized approach to regulation in this area.

Secondly, it is agreed that no member of the euro area should be allowed to get in a situation as bad as that of Country B before the bailout. In principle, the Stability and Growth Pact should have stopped Country B from accumulating such volume of debt, but the Pact has never been properly enforced and everybody knows it. Accordingly, the Member States want to give teeth to the Pact, and to do so they adopt new measures to make sure that sanctions are applied whenever a euro country goes above the level of debt or deficit set out in the Pact. Further, there is a feeling that more detailed and substantive measures are needed; after all, the problem is not only the level of spending, but the fact that some economies in the euro area are less competitive than others.

A set of measures designed to improve surveillance is adopted: this means that, every year, members of the euro area have to send reports on the state of their economy, as well as their draft budgets for the next year, to the Commission. The Commission produces a report for each country with specific recommendations (eg 'you should reform your pension system', or 'you need to cut salaries in the public sector'). If a country is perceived to be in serious trouble, either because of their excessive deficit or because of imbalances in their economy, they will be placed under special monitoring and, if they fail to address the situation, sanctions may be imposed.

Certain governments start voicing their discontent with what they perceive as undemocratic interference from the Commission, and citizens grumble about Brussels. On the other hand, other members of the euro area, together with the Commission, reason that this sort of control has been proven necessary by the crisis, and that EMU and the euro have no future without it.

5 Addressing the crisis

Several factors made the euro area crisis particularly difficult to address. As you will remember from section 2, there is an imbalance at the heart of EMU: the powers of the EU vary widely between monetary policy, where it has an exclusive competence for the euro area, and economic policy, where it merely has a coordinating competence and where policy decisions are made at a national level. This was one of the causes of the crisis, and it is also one of the factors that made this crisis difficult to address. The EU tried to tackle the problem while staying within its limited powers—this is not easy, and the danger is always that the EU can be perceived to be either overstepping into very delicate national matters, on the one hand, or simply ineffective, on the other. In addition, Member States also tried to address the crisis by acting collectively outside the legal framework of the EU.

It was discussed earlier that the design of EMU followed the 'monetarist' line of economic argument, according to which, once monetary policy had been centralized, sufficient economic coordination would follow—an assumption that has not been borne out by facts. There are further reasons why economic and fiscal policy was left to the Member

States: these are very sensitive areas, and the feeling, to date, was that they were most appropriately discussed and conducted within the national political process. These areas have to do with the allocation of limited resources in our societies, our understanding of the role of the State, and the role and boundaries of solidarity between citizens; decisions taken here concern, for example, tax rates, public-sector salaries, or the level of pensions. Understandably, the idea of a growing role for the EU in these areas is typically met with concern; one of the arguments most often put forward is that the Union does not (yet?) have the necessary democratic legitimacy to decide in matters such as taxation, pensions, or the boundaries of the welfare state.[35] These concerns have not only been expressed in the political discussion; in fact, several national constitutional courts believe that there are necessary limits to European integration. In particular, the German Federal Constitutional Court has been quite vocal in its position that a full economic and fiscal policy would be beyond those limits.[36]

Because of all this, the EU is limited in what it can do in this area, and it has to be very careful in negotiating its actions. With this in mind, we will now discuss the measures adopted to address the crisis.

The EU's response to the crisis was multifaceted.[37] First, we have seen that a quick intervention was necessary in order to stabilize the situation of euro countries (section 5.1). To this end, several loan facilities were created, and the European Central Bank also played an important role in calming down the markets. Secondly, several measures were adopted in order to improve budgetary surveillance and economic coordination (section 5.2). Thirdly, the EU has undertaken, and is still in the process of undertaking, important reforms aimed at the creation of a stronger financial framework, and a so-called 'banking union' for the euro area (section 5.3). This is because, as we have seen, the euro area crisis is connected to the global financial crisis that started in 2007, and which had inadequate financial regulation as one of its causes.

5.1 Stabilization: the ECB and bailouts

As we have seen, several euro countries have been in acute financial trouble and in need of assistance. This assistance came mainly from two sources: from the European Central Bank, and from loan facilities created for this purpose.

5.1.1 The evolving role of the ECB

The European System of Central Banks is tasked with conducting the Union's monetary policy, with the primary objective of maintaining price stability (Article 127(1) TFEU). The ECB is able to work towards its primary objective through a series of measures that include the setting of interest rates and the supply of liquidity to the banking system (ie to banks and credit institutions) against appropriate collateral. What it is not able to do, according to the Treaties, is to provide liquidity directly to the EU or to the Member States: the Treaties were worded in such a way as to preclude the possibility of the ECB becoming direct lender of last resort to any Member State, or to the EU institutions.[38] This is another manifestation of the tension within EMU highlighted earlier: while there is a central monetary policy and an institution such as the ECB, decentralization in the areas of economic and fiscal policy means that Member States are supposed to remain responsible for their own debts.

35 On the democratic legitimacy of the EU, see further chapters 3 and 4.

36 Decision of 30 June 2009, BVerfGE 123, 267 (the Lisbon decision), esp [175]–[252].

37 The distinction between the three following aspects of EU action comes from C Barnard, 'The Financial Crisis and the Euro Plus Pact: A Labour Lawyer's Perspective' (2012) 41 *Industrial Law Journal* 98.

38 Art 123(1) TFEU.

Nevertheless, the ECB has had to adjust its role due to the crisis:[39] it has intervened in the markets in order to assist euro countries in trouble, stopping short of buying their bonds directly, which is prohibited in the Treaty. It has typically acted in the secondary markets, buying sovereign bonds from investors who had bought them from the countries in trouble. It has also adopted other measures to make these bonds more attractive to investors. In September 2012, the ECB established its Outright Monetary Transactions (OMT) Scheme, announcing that if a Member State was having liquidity problems and private investors would not buy its bonds, the ECB would step in and buy these bonds in the secondary market, provided the Member State complied with certain conditions. Although the OMT was never activated, its mere existence had a strong effect on the markets. In 2015, the ECB announced another bond-buying scheme, the Public Sector Purchase Programme (PSPP),[40] a part of the Bank's quantitative easing policy.[41] Under the PSPP, the ECB acquired large quantities of Member State sovereign bonds in the secondary markets, similarly to what it had announced it would do some years earlier under the OMT programme. More recently, in 2022, the Bank announced a new purchase programme (the Temporary Protection Instrument).[42] As the role of the ECB continues to evolve and expand to address the crisis, concerns have also arisen as to the legality of its actions: both of the bond-buying schemes discussed have been the object of high-profile challenges before the German Federal Constitutional Court and the Court of Justice of the EU,[43] which have shown quite different attitudes towards the ECB and the judicial review of its decisions.

5.1.2 **The bailouts**

In 2010, specific emergency mechanisms were created in order to provide financial support to struggling euro area economies: the European Financial Stability Mechanism (EFSM), a relatively small loan facility within the EU system, and the European Financial Stability Fund (EFSF), a bigger, temporary loan vehicle created on an intergovernmental basis—ie by members of the euro area acting collectively, but outside the legal framework of the EU. After detailed negotiations, countries in specific crisis situations were able to receive funds from both mechanisms, as well as from the International Monetary Fund (IMF).[44]

[39] T Beukers, 'The New ECB and Its Relationship with the Eurozone Member States: Between Central Bank Independence and Central Bank Intervention' (2013) 50 *Common Market Law Review* 1579.

[40] Decision 2015/774 of the European Central Bank of 4 March 2015 on a secondary markets public sector asset purchase programme, as amended by Decision 2017/100 of the European Central Bank of 11 January 2017. For an overview of the programme and its legal limits, see S Grund and F Grle, 'The European Central Bank's Public Sector Purchase Programme (PSPP), the Prohibition of Monetary Financing and Sovereign Debt Restructuring Scenarios' (2016) 41 *European Law Review* 781.

[41] Quantitative easing aims at increasing liquidity and stimulating the economy; the ECB set out to do this by acquiring, among other assets, large quantities of sovereign bonds through its Public Sector Purchase Programme. The PSPP was terminated at the end of 2018.

[42] ECB Press Release, 21 July 2022, available here: www.ecb.europa.eu/press/pr/date/2022/html/ecb.pr220721~973e6e7273.en.html.

[43] On the OMT: Case C-62/14 *Gauweiler*, EU:C:2015:400; BVerfG, Judgment of the Second Senate of 21 June 2016, 2 BvR 2728/13, 2 BvE 13/13, 2 BvR 2731/13, 2 BvR 2730/13, 2 BvR 2729/13. On the PSPP: Case C-493/17 *Heinrich Weiss and Others*, EU:C:2018:1000; BVerfG, Judgment of the Second Senate of 5 May 2020, 2 BvR 859/15, 2 BvR 980/16, 2 BvR 2006/15, 2 BvR 1651/15. Both cases and their significance will be discussed in section 6.2. Additionally, the ECB also adopted a Public Emergency Purchase Programme (PEPP) to address the effects of the Covid-19 pandemic; the legality of this programme was also challenged before the German Federal Constitutional Court (2 BvE 7/20, 2 BvR 420/21, pending).

[44] See n 27.

This, however, was not sufficient to reassure the markets. Both the EFSF and the EFSM were temporary in nature, and had limited lending power. There were also doubts as to the legality of these facilities.[45] In short, a Treaty amendment was considered necessary.

In March 2011, the European Council amended Article 136 TFEU using a simplified amendment procedure, introducing a new paragraph (3) that affirmed the Member States' power to create a permanent crisis mechanism to safeguard the stability of the euro.[46] Even before this amendment was ratified, the members of the euro area had already signed an international agreement creating the European Stability Mechanism (ESM). This is a permanent and more powerful intergovernmental mechanism, established outside the framework of the EU Treaties, which may grant financial assistance to countries in difficulties, subject to stringent conditions. Several challenges at the national level delayed the entry into force of the ESM Treaty until 27 September 2012 for 16 signatories to the Treaty, and a few days later for Estonia.[47] Since the beginning of its operations in October 2012, the ESM is the main instrument to finance new programmes of financial assistance.

The intergovernmental nature of the ESM is a manifestation of a wider trend since the beginning of the crisis: that of Member States attempting to address different aspects of the sovereign debt crisis through intergovernmental means, at times completely outside the EU legal order, yet still using the EU institutions.[48] This is the case of the ESM Treaty, but also of the Treaty on Stability, Coordination, and Governance (sometimes called the 'fiscal compact'), which will be discussed in the next section. The rise of this brand of intergovernmentalism has spurred very different concerns. First, acting in this way could be ineffectual due to the lack of effective enforcement,[49] wasting precious time that should be used to address the crisis. And secondly, serious concerns arise regarding lack of transparency, judicial control, and democratic legitimacy, since, typically, negotiations in an intergovernmental setting are conducted behind closed doors, and involving only national executives. Indeed, the worry that Member States were trying to avoid using EU mechanisms in order to circumvent control was at the heart of the challenge to the legality of the ESM brought before Irish courts and the CJEU in *Pringle* (see case study 19.2). There have been recent attempts to incorporate the ESM into the EU framework, but they have been unsuccessful so far.[50]

[45] The EFSM, in particular, was created on the basis of Art 122 TFEU, which states that the EU may help a State in 'extraordinary circumstances'; some interpreted this provision to exclude circumstances brought about by a country's own behaviour (through, eg, flawed fiscal or economic policies). More generally, it was questionable whether both emergency mechanisms were compatible with the 'no-bailout clause' set out in Art 125 TFEU, which states that a Member State's debt shall not be assumed by either the Union or other Member States. Some interpreted this clause as a ban on any form of financial assistance, including the creation of loan facilities.

[46] European Council Decision 2011/199/EU amending Art 136 of the TFEU with regard to a stability mechanism for Member States whose currency is the euro (OJ [2011] L91/1). The amendment was based on Art 48(6) TEU, which provides for a simplified Treaty amendment procedure that could be used because it did not enlarge EU competence (since the resulting mechanism is not part of the EU, but intergovernmental in nature). For an overview: B de Witte, 'The European Treaty Amendment for the Creation of a Financial Stability Mechanism', SIEPS, *European Policy Analysis* 6 (2011) 1. On Treaty amendment procedures, see chapter 5.

[47] Three further Member States, Latvia, Lithuania, and Croatia, acceded to the ESM subsequently (in 2014, 2015, and 2023, respectively), bringing the total of members to 21 as at January 2026.

[48] S Peers, 'Towards a New Form of EU Law? The Use of EU Institutions Outside the EU Legal Framework' (2013) 9 *European Constitutional Law Review* 37.

[49] See chapter 5 on decision-making and chapter 6 on the nature of EU law.

[50] 'Further Steps Toward Completing Europe's Economic and Monetary Union: A Roadmap', COM(2017)821 final. The package included the Commission's proposal to reform the ESM and turn it into a European Monetary Fund (European Commission, 'Proposal for a Council Regulation on the establishment of the European Monetary Fund', COM(2017)827 final). The proposal has been abandoned and a less ambitious reform of the ESM (which does not envisage its incorporation into EU law) has been agreed. See further section 6, nn 100–101.

Case study 19.2: The ESM and the *Pringle* decision

One of the challenges to the legality of the ESM Treaty before national courts was brought by Mr Pringle, a member of the Irish Parliament.[51] Mr Pringle argued, among other things, that the simplified procedure should not have been used to amend the TFEU, and that the ESM Treaty itself was contrary to several provisions of the EU Treaties, mostly concerning the Economic and Monetary Union. The Irish Supreme Court made a reference for a preliminary ruling to the Court of Justice of the European Union. In the unsurprising but momentous *Pringle* decision, the CJEU sitting in a Full Court of all 27 judges—which is exceedingly rare—rejected all challenges and confirmed the legality of the ESM Treaty.[52] The decision is significant for various reasons. First, it clarified, to a degree, the relationship between an intergovernmental mechanism such as the ESM and the EU Treaties. Secondly, it shed light on whether the Member States can allocate tasks to the EU institutions outside the EU framework. Finally, it provided a purposive and dynamic interpretation of EMU provisions; most importantly, of the no-bailout clause.

The first question posed to the Court of Justice in *Pringle* concerned the use of the simplified procedure to amend the TFEU. This procedure can only be used to amend Part Three of the Treaty, and the Court had to consider whether the amendment, formally of a provision within that Part Three, nevertheless affected in substance the nature and scope of the Union's competence in monetary and economic policy (set out in Part One of the Treaty). The Court decided that the ESM fell outside the EU's exclusive monetary policy competence because of its different aim and instruments. The ESM seeks to safeguard the stability of the euro area, whereas the objective of the eurozone's monetary policy is price stability. Moreover, the ESM would operate through the granting of financial assistance, which is not an instrument of monetary, but economic policy.

Having decided that the ESM was an instrument of economic policy, the Court went on to find that this mechanism complemented the EU's competence in economic policy without encroaching on it. This is because the Union only has a coordinating competence in the area, and it would lack the power to establish a permanent emergency mechanism like the ESM. Member States, however, are able to create such a mechanism themselves, as long as they comply with EU law in doing so. The Court was satisfied that this compliance with EU law is ensured by the fact that financial assistance from the ESM will only be granted following compliance with strict conditions by the relevant Member States. The Court concluded that the TFEU amendment did not grant any new powers to the EU—something that could not have been done through the simplified procedure either. In the Court's view, Article 136(3) TFEU simply clarified a pre-existing competence of the Member States.

Next, the Court had to deal with a series of questions concerning the compatibility of the ESM Treaty itself with several provisions of the EU Treaties. The Court reaffirmed its position that the ESM would not subvert the EU's coordinating competence in economic policy. It considered the ESM a financial mechanism, not a mechanism for the coordination of economic policies; and that the aim of the conditionality attached to ESM assistance is not to coordinate national economic policies, but to ensure compliance with EU law—more specifically, with the EU's coordinating economic measures, and with the EU Treaties' no-bailout clause.

[51] This section draws on material included in A Hinarejos, 'The Court of Justice of the EU and the legality of the European Stability Mechanism' (2013) 72 *Cambridge Law Journal* 237.

[52] Case C-370/12 *Pringle v Ireland*, EU:C:2012:756.

This brings us to one of the most difficult questions that faced the court in *Pringle*: whether the no-bailout clause in the TFEU precluded the creation of a mechanism of financial assistance such as the ESM. The Court adopted a purposive reading of the no-bailout clause. This provision, according to the Court, has two aims: the first one is to encourage prudent budgetary policy in the Member States by ensuring that they remain responsible to their creditors, thus submitting Member States to market discipline. The second, more general aim is to safeguard the financial stability of the euro area.

The Court inferred from this that the no-bailout clause does not cover all forms of financial assistance; more specifically, it does not preclude a mechanism such as the ESM as long as it is only activated when necessary to safeguard the financial stability of the euro area as a whole, the Member State that receives assistance remains responsible to its creditors, and the assistance is subject to conditions that prompt the Member State to implement a prudent budgetary policy.

The Court also had to consider the legality of the allocation of tasks to the EU institutions outside the framework of the EU, particularly as the ESM Treaty allocated tasks to the European Central Bank, the Commission, and the Court itself. The Court concluded that this allocation was not problematic, so long as it was not done in an area of exclusive EU competence and it did not alter the essential character of the institutions' powers under the EU Treaties. Interestingly, the Court did not mention the consent of all Member States as a requirement for this use of the institutions; although consent had been given in this particular case, clarification of this point may have been useful for the future. Furthermore, it had been argued that Member States should only be allowed to task EU institutions when using the enhanced cooperation mechanism set out in the EU Treaties (ie the procedure which allows a group of Member States to go ahead and adopt EU law measures without some other Member States).[53] The Court rejected this argument, at least as regards cases such as the present one, where enhanced cooperation cannot be used because the EU does not have the prerequisite competence to act. This left open the question of whether it is possible to confer powers to the EU institutions outside the context of enhanced cooperation in an area of (non-exclusive) EU competence.

In addition, it had been argued that placing the ESM outside the EU framework breached the right to legal protection, guaranteed in Article 47 of the EU Charter of Fundamental Rights. The Court's response was that, when creating the ESM, the Member States were not implementing EU law, which meant that they were acting outside the scope of the Charter. Accordingly, the Member States do not have to comply with the Charter when acting pursuant to the ESM Treaty; questions remained, though, concerning the application of the Charter to EU institutions when they are acting in the context of the ESM Treaty. As we shall see later, some of these questions have since been answered.

Overall, the *Pringle* judgment brought few surprises. Some of the measures intended to address the euro area crisis may have been adopted in a legal grey area, but few would argue that they were unnecessary. While the ESM may not be perfect, few expected the Court of Justice to stand in the way of an emergency mechanism that had political support, and the demise of which would likely have sent the euro area back into the acute phase of the crisis. The degree of deference shown by the Court to the political process in *Pringle* is not surprising, and it is arguably justified in such exceptional circumstances. EMU provisions in the Treaties were designed to prevent a crisis, but not to manage one; as such, they needed to be interpreted in a purposive and dynamic manner to ensure that the EU's legal framework

[53] For more on enhanced cooperation, see chapter 5.

does not become obsolete and that the eurozone is capable of dealing effectively with this crisis of confidence.

As to the aftermath of *Pringle*, certain questions regarding the judicial accountability of the ESM were left open by the judgment, and have since been answered. In *Ledra Advertising*,[54] the Court clarified that EU institutions are always subject to EU law and the Charter, even when acting under the ESM. This is significant because of the conditionality attached to ESM aid, which typically requires the receiving Member State to effect cutbacks that impact citizens' rights. The legality of these conditions, normally set out in a 'memorandum of understanding', has been questioned before the Court of Justice on several occasions; for a long time, the Court declined jurisdiction, claiming the lack of a link to EU law.[55] Recently, there have been some signs of change in this regard.[56] In any event, even if ESM acts remain outside the scope of EU law, the involvement of EU institutions in the adoption of those acts may give rise to the Union's liability in damages.[57]

[54] Joined Cases C-8–10/15 P *Ledra Advertising*, EU:C:2016:701; see also Joined Cases C-105–109/15 P *Mallis*, EU:C:2016:702 and further references in n 57.

[55] In the Romanian cases, Romania had signed a Memorandum of Understanding (MoU) in order to receive Balance of Payments assistance (which may be granted by the EU to non-euro countries under Art 143 TFEU) together with IMF and World Bank assistance: Cases C-434/11 *Corpul Naţional al Poliţiştilor*, order of 14 December 2011; C-134/12 *Corpul Naţional al Poliţiştilor*, order of 10 May 2012; and C-369/12 *Corpul Naţional al Poliţiştilor*, order of 15 November 2012. In the Portuguese cases, Portugal had negotiated an MoU in order to receive EFSF and EFSM (together with IMF) assistance: Cases C-128/12 *Sindicato dos Bancários do Norte and Others*, order of 7 March 2013; C-264/12 *Sindicato Nacional dos Profissionais de Seguros e Afins*, order of 26 June 2014; C-665/13 *Sindicato Nacional dos Profissionais de Seguros e Afins*, order of 21 October 2014. In all these cases, the Court claimed the lack of a link to EU law, even when the MoU conditions had been implemented into a Council decision. See further D Sarmiento, 'Who's Afraid of the Charter? The Court of Justice, National Courts and the New Framework of Fundamental Rights Protection in Europe' (2013) 50 *Common Market Law Review* 1267, 1273, and ff; C Kilpatrick, 'Are the Bailouts Immune to EU Social Challenge Because They Are Not EU Law?' (2014) 10 *European Constitutional Law Review* 393–421.

[56] In more recent case law, the Court of Justice has considered that some MoUs fall within the scope of EU law; crucially, however, the MoUs in question were adopted in the context of financial mechanisms that are part of the EU legal system (Balance of Payments assistance and EFSM), and it is doubtful that this will extend, for the time being, to MoUs adopted in the context of mechanisms outside the EU framework (ie ESM or EFSF). In *Florescu*, the Court considered an MoU adopted within the EU's Balance of Payments assistance and its implementation within the scope of EU law and subject to the Charter: Case C-258/14 *Florescu and others*, EU:C:2017:448. The later decision in *Portuguese Judges* also resulted in national implementation of EFSM conditionality being subject to the Court's jurisdiction, although through different means (the MoU was considered subject to Art 19(1) TFEU because it affected judges' independence): Case C-64/16 *Associação Sindical dos Juízes Portugueses*, EU:C:2018:117.

[57] Thus, while the ESM acts themselves cannot be challenged through the action for annulment, individuals can try to get damages. This will still be very difficult, given the high threshold required. Joined Cases C-8/15–10/15 P *Ledra Advertising*, EU:C:2016:701; Joined Cases C-105–109/15 P *Mallis*, EU:C:2016:702. For analysis, see eg R Repasi, 'Judicial Protection against Austerity Measures in the Euro Area: *Ledra* and *Mallis*' (2017) 54 *Common Market Law Review* 1123; S Laulhé Shaelou and A Karatzia, 'Some Preliminary Thoughts on the Cyprus Bail-In Litigation: A Commentary on *Mallis* and *Ledra*' (2018) 43 *European Law Review* 249; A Poulou, 'Financial Assistance Conditionality and Human Rights Protection: What Is the Role of the EU Charter of Fundamental Rights?' (2017) 54 *Common Market Law Review* 991. More recently, the Court has decided that the Eurogroup is not an 'institution' (within the meaning of Art 340(2) TFEU) whose actions may trigger the EU's liability in damages in the context of the ESM: Joined Cases C-597–598/18 P, C-603/18 P, and C-604/18 P *Council v K Chrysostomides & Co and Others*, EU:C:2020:1028. See further A Karatzia and M Markakis, 'Financial Assistance, Conditionality and Effective Judicial Protection: *Chrysostomides*' (2022) 59 *Common Market Law Review* 501.

5.2 **Budgetary and economic coordination measures**

Bailouts, while essential, were only one factor in addressing the euro area crisis. In the longer term, it seems necessary to address the imbalance between the strong monetary union and the weak economic coordination between the members of the euro area. This is what the Member States have tried to do through the adoption of several measures or packs of measures since the beginning of the crisis. Some of these measures are EU instruments; these generally focus on strengthening budgetary and economic surveillance at the EU level. On other occasions, Member States have adopted instruments that are formally outside the EU legal order. This section will first consider EU legislation (the so-called Six-Pack and the Two-Pack), followed by measures adopted by Member States outside the EU framework (the Treaty on Stability, Coordination, and Governance, part of which is known as the 'fiscal compact'). Additionally, the Member States also adopted measures of EU soft law, most significantly the so-called 'Euro Pact',[58] which did not impose enforceable legal obligations; it remains largely dormant and it will not be discussed further in this chapter.[59]

5.2.1 **EU Legislation: the Six-Pack and the Two-Pack**

Since the beginning of the crisis, the EU has legislated in order to enhance different aspects of economic and budgetary surveillance. Very broadly speaking, Member States have to share a great deal of information regarding their budget and their economy with the Commission, which analyses countries' reports and gives them specific recommendations. The Commission is supposed to ensure, among other things, that Member States comply with a strengthened Stability and Growth Pact. If a Member State runs an excessive deficit, it will be under special obligations to report and follow recommendations; the Council may impose sanctions on euro countries. The Commission will also control to ensure that Member States' economies do not suffer macroeconomic or competitiveness imbalances (concerning, for example, liabilities of the financial sector, level of unemployment, or house prices)[60]—if that is the case, the euro country in trouble will, again, have special obligations, and sanctions may be imposed. In general, the EU has legislated to regulate the different aspects of EU surveillance and correction of the budgetary and economic policies of all Member States, and especially of eurozone members.

The first measures adopted by the EU in this regard constitute the Six-Pack: this is a package of measures (five regulations and one directive) adopted in November 2011,[61]

[58] Adopted at the European Council Meeting of 24–25 March 2011 by the heads of State or government of the euro area, plus six other Member States: www.consilium.europa.eu/uedocs/cms_data/docs/pressdata/en/ec/120296.pdf.

[59] The Pact was a political declaration focused on four areas: competitiveness, public finance, employment, and financial stability. The participating Member States agreed on economic objectives, which they undertook to pursue with their own policy-mix. On the Pact losing traction with the Member States and becoming dormant: European Commission, European Political Strategy Centre Strategic Notes, Issue 3 (8 May 2015), 1.

[60] There is a scoreboard containing 14 indicators (including the three mentioned here) that are used to determine the existence of an imbalance.

[61] Regulation 1173/2011 on the effective enforcement of budgetary surveillance in the euro area (OJ [2011] L306/1); Regulation 1174/2011 on enforcement measures to correct excessive macroeconomic imbalances in the euro area (OJ [2011] L306/8); Regulation 1175/2011 on the strengthening of the surveillance of budgetary positions and the surveillance and coordination of economic policies (OJ [2011] L306/12); Regulation 1176/2011 on the prevention and correction of macroeconomic imbalances (OJ [2011] L306/25); Council Regulation 1177/2011 on speeding up and clarifying the implementation of the excessive deficit procedure (OJ [2011] L306/33); Council Directive 2011/85/EU on requirements for budgetary frameworks of the Member States (OJ [2011] L306/41).

with a view to improving the framework for surveillance of budgetary positions and economic policies. These measures create an annual cycle of policy coordination called the 'European Semester' and a procedure for the prevention and correction of macroeconomic imbalances;[62] the measures also strengthen the enforcement of the Stability and Growth Pact by, among other things, creating an enhanced system of sanctions for members of the euro area.[63] Although these sanctions stop short of being automatic, a system of reverse qualified majority voting has been introduced whereby a qualified majority in the Council would be necessary to avoid the imposition of a sanction, rather than in order to impose it.[64] As mentioned above, the Six-Pack also created a procedure for the prevention and correction of macroeconomic imbalances.[65] In serious cases, the Member State in trouble will be placed under special surveillance from the Commission and will have to submit a corrective action plan. In the case of euro countries, interest-bearing deposits and fines may be imposed, also by reverse qualified majority voting.

In May 2013, the so-called Two-Pack was adopted in order to further strengthen surveillance of euro countries. It consists of two regulations: the first one creates an enhanced surveillance mechanism of draft budgetary plans, building on the preventive arm of the Stability and Growth Pact. It requires euro countries to introduce and adhere to a common budgetary timeline, and to create independent fiscal bodies that monitor compliance with fiscal rules. Euro countries also need to submit their draft budgetary plans to the Eurogroup and the Commission.[66] The second regulation creates a system of enhanced surveillance for euro area countries that face financial difficulties, of automatic application to those countries that receive certain types of financial assistance (including from the ESM).[67]

At the time of writing, the EU has just adopted a series of measures to update its economic governance framework. These include a directive relating to the budgetary frameworks of Member States which amends the relevant part of the Six-Pack and incorporates into EU law commitments that Member States made under international law (the Treaty on Stability, Coordination and Governance, to be discussed in the next section);[68] further reforms aim at modernizing and clarifying fiscal rules and the excessive deficit

[62] Until now, several Member States have been found to experience excessive macroeconomic imbalances, but no corrective action has been adopted.

[63] Regulation 1173/2011 (n 61) creates gradual financial sanctions for euro area countries; this covers both the preventive and the corrective arm of the Stability and Growth Pact. Regulation 1174/2011 (n 61) foresees the imposition of enforcement measures to correct excessive macroeconomic imbalances in the euro area.

[64] The vast majority of Member States have been subject to some stage of an excessive deficit procedure (EDP), but no sanctions have ever been imposed at the time of writing. Two of these EDPs resulted in the launching of sanction procedures, namely against Portugal and Spain (July 2016). Fines were determined and then immediately cancelled: 'Council Implementing Decision on imposing a fine on Portugal for failure to take effective action to address an excessive deficit', 11554/16 (5 August 2016); 'Council Implementing Decision on imposing a fine on Spain for failure to take effective action to address an excessive deficit', 11555/16 (5 August 2016).

[65] Regulation 1176/2011 on the prevention and correction of macroeconomic imbalances (OJ [2011] L306/25).

[66] The Commission then issues an opinion on the draft budgetary plans and may request a revised plan if there is 'particularly serious non-compliance' with the Stability and Growth Pact obligations.

[67] Based on Arts 136 and 121 TFEU, and of application to euro countries. Regulation 473/2013 on common provisions for monitoring and assessing draft budgetary plans and ensuring the correction of excessive deficit of the Member States in the euro area (OJ [2013] L140/11); Regulation 472/2013 on the strengthening of economic and budgetary surveillance of Member States in the euro area experiencing or threatened with serious difficulties with respect to their financial stability (OJ [2013] L140/1).

[68] Council Directive 2024/1265 amending Directive 2011/85/EU on requirements for budgetary frameworks of the Member States (OJ [2024] L1265).

procedure, and at enhancing economic coordination and the Macroeconomic Imbalance Procedure.[69]

5.2.2 The Treaty on Stability, Coordination and Governance

In December 2011, the European Council agreed on the need for a new fiscal Treaty or fiscal compact that would foster budgetary discipline further and that would allow the members of the euro area to 'move towards a stronger economic union',[70] and to 'work towards a common economic policy'.[71] The first intention was to adopt such a Treaty within the framework of the EU. Ultimately, the UK's refusal thwarted this plan, and it was agreed that the new Treaty would be a purely intergovernmental instrument adopted outside the EU framework, albeit with institutional ties to it. The resulting Treaty on Stability, Coordination and Governance in the EMU (TSCG) was signed on 2 March 2012 by all Member States apart from the UK and the Czech Republic, as well as Croatia, which joined the EU subsequently. The Treaty entered into force on 1 January 2013 for the 16 Member States that had ratified it prior to this date.[72]

The TSCG has two clearly distinguishable parts: one dealing with budgetary discipline, and one concerning economic convergence and cooperation.[73] We will only discuss the part dealing with budgetary discipline (commonly referred to as the 'Fiscal Compact'), as it turned out to be the most significant. In this area, the Treaty set out certain balance rules on fiscal stance for Member States to implement at the national level, and it imposed limits on the size of public debt and structural deficit, covering similar ground to previous instruments such as the Stability and Growth Pact and the Six-Pack.[74] The most important addition in this respect was the obligation to implement rules on budgetary discipline into national law,[75] and the signatories' agreement to grant jurisdiction to the Court of Justice of the EU to monitor compliance with this duty (although the TSCG was outside the EU legal system).[76]

The TSCG was another manifestation of a trend that has been discussed already in this chapter: the rise of intergovernmentalism in dealing with the eurozone crisis, and the willingness to act formally outside the EU legal order when necessary, while still

[69] Council Regulation 2024/1264 amending Regulation 1467/97 on speeding up and clarifying the implementation of the excessive deficit procedure (OJ [2024] L1264); Regulation 2024/1263 of the European Parliament and of the Council on the effective coordination of economic policies and on multilateral budgetary surveillance and repealing Council Regulation 1466/97 (OJ [2024] L1263).

[70] Statement by the euro area Heads of State or Government, 9 December 2011, 1.

[71] Ibid, 5.

[72] For subsequent ratifiers, the Treaty entered into force on the first day of the month following their ratification. At the time of writing, the Treaty has been ratified by all 25 signatories; additionally, Croatia and the Czech Republic acceded to the Treaty in 2018 and 2019 respectively, bringing the total of participating Member States to 27.

[73] The Treaty also deals with governance of the euro (concerning eg regular meetings of the euro area and their organization); this will not be discussed here either.

[74] National budgets must be in balance or surplus; this requirement would be met if the annual structural government deficit does not exceed 0.5 per cent of GDP at market prices.

[75] This is for the first time a legally binding obligation. For an analysis, see Editorial, 'The Fiscal Compact and the European Constitutions: "Europe Speaking German"' (2012) 8 *European Constitutional Law Review* 1; F Fabbrini, 'The Fiscal Compact, the "Golden Rule", and the Paradox of European Federalism' (2013) 36 *Boston College International and Comparative Law Review* 1.

[76] This is made possible by the TFEU itself, Art 273.

[77] Art 16 TSCG.

[78] 'Further Steps Toward Completing Europe's Economic and Monetary Union: A Roadmap', COM(2017) 821 final. The package includes a proposal to incorporate the (reformed) obligations of the Fiscal Compact into EU law: 'Proposal for a Council Directive laying down provisions for strengthening fiscal responsibility and the medium-term budgetary orientation in the Member State', COM(2017) 824 final. The proposal stalled and has now been superseded by later reforms (n 79).

using or allocating tasks to some of the EU institutions (which the Court of Justice considered in accordance with EU law in *Pringle*). Notably, there was a commitment in the TSCG to incorporate it into EU law within five years of its entry into force,[77] a period that ended in January 2018. Attempts to incorporate the Treaty into EU law were largely unsuccessful,[78] until a package of reforms to the economic governance framework in 2024 incorporated much of the substance of Title III of the TSCG (rules on budgetary discipline) into EU law.[79]

5.3 **Financial regulation and banking union**

The global financial crisis that started in 2007 was the precursor to the euro area sovereign debt crisis: in some cases, euro countries amassed unmanageable debt because they had to bail out their banks. More generally, the financial crisis worsened the economic problems of certain euro countries, and made it more difficult for them to borrow money. So it is natural that part of the EU's response to the crisis has been to seek better regulation of the financial markets, in order to avoid a similar financial crisis in the future.[80] Some of these reforms apply to the whole EU financial sector, not just within the euro area. These EU-wide reforms include the setting-up of a new European System of Financial Supervision comprised of a new European Banking Authority and other supervisory bodies with significant powers delegated to them,[81] as well as the progressive building of a 'single rulebook',[82] a single set of common rules that would apply to all financial institutions operating in the EU. At the moment, the single rulebook comprises, inter alia, stricter rules on capital requirements for financial institutions,[83] revised harmonizing rules on national deposit guarantee schemes,[84] and common rules on recovery and resolution tools to deal with banks in difficulty within the single market.[85]

[79] Council Directive 2024/1265 amending Directive 2011/85/EU on requirements for budgetary frameworks of the Member States (OJ [2024] L1265).

[80] N Moloney, 'EU Financial Market Regulation after the Global Financial Crisis: "More Europe" or More Risks?' (2010) 47 *Common Market Law Review* 1317; E Ferran, 'Crisis-Driven Regulatory Reform: Where in the World Is the EU Going?' in E Ferran, N Moloney, JA Hill, and JC Coffee (eds), *The Regulatory Aftermath of the Financial Crisis* (Cambridge: Cambridge University Press, 2012).

[81] Apart from the European Banking Authority, the framework includes a European Insurance and Occupational Pensions Authority, a European Securities and Markets Authority, and a European Systemic Risk Board. Regulation 1093/2010 establishing a European Supervisory Authority (European Banking Authority) (OJ [2010] L331/12); Regulation 1094/2010 establishing a European Supervisory Authority (European Insurance and Occupational Pensions Authority) (OJ [2010] L331/48); Regulation 1095/2010 establishing a European Supervisory Authority (European Securities and Markets Authority, or ESMA) (OJ [2010] L331/84); Regulation 1092/2010 on European Union macro-prudential oversight of the financial system and establishing a European Systemic Risk Board (OJ [2010] L331/1).

[82] Conclusions of the European Council of 18–19 June 2009, 11225/2/09.

[83] Directive 2013/36/EU on access to the activity of credit institutions and the prudential supervision of credit institutions and investment firms (OJ [2013] L176/338), as amended most recently by Directive 2019/878 (CRD V) (OJ [2019] L150/253) and Directive 2024/1619 (CRD VI) (OJ [2024] L1619); Regulation (EU) No 575/2013 on prudential requirements for credit institutions and investment firms (OJ [2013] L176/1), as amended most recently by Regulation (EU) 2019/876 (CRR II) (OJ [2019] L150/1) and Regulation 2024/1623 (CRR III) (OJ [2024] L1623).

[84] Directive 2014/49 on deposit guarantee scheme (recast) (OJ [2014] L173/149).

[85] Directive 2014/59 establishing a framework for the recovery and resolution of credit institutions and investment firms (OJ [2014] L173/190), as amended by Directive 2024/1174 (OJ [2014] L1174). These rules are applicable to the whole EU single market, while the Single Resolution Mechanism, discussed later on in the same section, is part of the banking union and thus applies, in principle, within the euro area (although non-euro countries can join).

[86] Conclusions from the European Council of 27–28 June 2013, EUCO 104/2/13; Communication from the Commission to the European Parliament and the Council: a Roadmap towards a Banking Union, COM(2012) 510 final.

The reforms discussed apply to the whole of the EU. Other, more ambitious reforms would apply in principle to the euro area, although they are open to other Member States wishing to join: the intention is to create a so-called 'banking union',[86] to provide common mechanisms to supervise banks and, if necessary, react when they fail. So far, the banking union consists of two main pillars: a Single Supervisory Mechanism (SSM) for banks, led by the ECB,[87] and a Single Resolution Mechanism (SRM), in order to deal with the failure of banks within the euro area in a centralized manner.[88] The legality of the parts of the banking union that are already in place (SSM and SRM) was challenged without success before the German Constitutional Court.[89] Finally, the Commission has also proposed the creation of a European Deposit Insurance Scheme, which would constitute a third and final pillar to the banking union;[90] this proposal, however, has stalled.[91]

6 The future of EMU

So what next for EMU? The intentions behind the post-crisis measures adopted by the EU and the Member States were, one, to bring the euro area out of the acute phase of the crisis, and two, to improve the way in which economic coordination happens in the future. At the time of writing, the measures seem to have achieved the first objective; only time will tell how effective they are in achieving the second one.

The crisis, however, also prompted a more general and ongoing discussion as to the future of EMU, and even as to the future of the EU as a political project. Does EMU need more than just economic coordination to be sustainable? Do we think that it is the 'destiny' of EMU to lead to a full economic union—and, if so, does this presuppose a full political union too?

It may be possible for EMU to continue to rely on economic coordination of national policies. But this would mean there is a natural limit to how far integration can go within EMU, and it is likely that economic shocks—such as the global financial crisis or the euro area crisis—would continue to threaten it. It may be possible to avoid this by finding new ways to foster discipline among Member States, perhaps by giving the EU more power

[87] Council Regulation (EU) 1024/2013 conferring specific tasks on the ECB concerning policies relating to the prudential supervision of credit institutions; Regulation (EU) 1022/2013 of the European Parliament and of the Council amending Regulation (EU) 1093/2010 establishing a European Supervisory Authority (ESA) as regards the conferral of specific tasks on the ECB pursuant to Council Regulation (EU) 1024/2013. The CJEU has had to clarify certain aspects of the ECB's role in the SSM, adopting a rather centralized approach: see eg Case C-450/17 *Landeskreditbank Baden-Württemberg v ECB*, EU:C:2019:372; Case C-219/17 *Berlusconi and Fininvest*, EU:C:2018:1023. On standing to challenge the ECB in this area, see Joined Cases C-663/17 P, C-665/17 P, and C-669/17 P *Trasta Komercbanka*, EU:C:2019:923.

[88] Regulation 806/2014 establishing uniform rules and a uniform procedure for the resolution of credit institutions and certain investment firms in the framework of a Single Resolution Mechanism and a Single Resolution Fund and amending Regulation 1093/2010, (OJ [2014] L225/1), consolidated version as of 14 November 2024.

[89] Decision of 30 July 2019, BVerfG, 2 BvR 1685/14 and 2631/14. The German Court considered the Banking Union (SSM and SRM) in accordance with the German Constitution, as long as the SSM and SRM rules are interpreted restrictively. This, however, contradicts the approach taken by the CJEU in this area so far (see n 87).

[90] Proposal for a Regulation of the European Parliament and of the Council amending Regulation (EU) 806/2014 in Order to Establish a European Deposit Insurance Scheme, COM/2015/0586 final.

[91] A genuine European Deposit Insurance Scheme would entail large and potentially open-ended financial commitments, and it is uncertain when or whether Member States will be ready to adopt this final third pillar and complete the banking union. See eg R Herring, 'The Danger of Building a Banking Union on a One-Legged Stool' in F Allen et al (eds), *Political, Fiscal and Banking Union in the Eurozone?* (Philadelphia, PA: FIC Press, Wharton Financial Institutions Center, 2013) 25.

over national fiscal and economic policies, so that, while the Union does not have its own resources, it would gain progressively more power to tell Member States what to do with theirs. There are several problems with this approach: for example, it is not clear that focusing on discipline alone is effective, and there are concerns about democratic legitimacy and a potential 'hollowing out' of national parliaments. Alternatively, the EU—or rather the euro area—could acquire its own fiscal capacity, so that it has the tools to try to prevent economic shocks or address them, once they happen (the literature refers to these tools at times as stabilization mechanisms). This could happen to different degrees, from granting the EU the competence to raise taxes and spend them freely, to more cautious proposals for a modest budget to be spent only in particular ways. There is, in the end, a clear divide between those who think that EMU should remain mostly about discipline, and those who think that the future of EMU necessarily entails more sharing of resources.

In terms of enhancing discipline, it has been mentioned already that the EU has adopted in 2024 a legislative package that reforms its economic governance framework. The measures aim at strengthening national budgetary requirements, streamlining and clarifying fiscal rules and the excessive deficit procedure, and enhancing economic coordination and the macroeconomic imbalance procedure.[92] These discussions were complex, some feel the reforms did not go far enough, and disagreements remain; there are very different opinions among Member States about what the substance of fiscal rules should be, and how much flexibility should be left to Member States and in what circumstances (eg should there be extra leeway when it comes to Member States making 'green investments', and what should 'green' mean for this purpose?). Strong geopolitical factors have also been at play in this context: notably, the ongoing Russian invasion of Ukraine and the EU's push to strengthen its defence capacity have resulted in more flexibility to incentivize Member States to make 'strategic' investments in this area.[93] Overall, then, the discussions on the discipline side of EMU are far from straightforward; and yet the disagreements are starker when it comes to the sharing of resources.

Various institutional actors have stated that further economic and fiscal integration will be necessary to ensure the resilience of EMU and have put forward various overarching proposals for the short, medium, and long term, with varying degrees of detail.[94] While all of these proposals continue to emphasize the importance of discipline, many of them consider the building of a fiscal capacity for the euro area—in different ways and to different degrees—as a necessary next step. The fact that political reforms would be necessary is commonly acknowledged too. In 2015, the 'Five Presidents' (of the Commission, the Euro Summit, the Eurogroup, the ECB, and the European Parliament) published a joint report (the 'Five Presidents' Report') that set out an ambitious plan to complete EMU in three stages, and that would include the future creation of a euro area treasury.[95]

[92] See nn 68–69.

[93] Activation of a national escape clause to deviate from the fiscal rules for Member States who solicit it (16 at the time of writing), in order to make room for defence spending; see also the White Paper for European Defence—Readiness 2030, presented by the Commission and High Representative on 19 March 2025.

[94] Commission's 'Blueprint for a deep and genuine economic and monetary union: launching a European debate', COM/2012/0777 final; and the so-called 'Four Presidents' Report', prepared by President of the European Council Herman Van Rompuy in cooperation with the Presidents of the Commission, ECB, and Eurogroup, 'Towards a genuine economic and monetary union', 5 December 2012. For recent non-institutional proposals, see the 'Fourteen Experts' Report': 'Reconciling risk sharing with market discipline: A constructive approach to euro area reform', Centre for Economic Policy Research, Policy Insight No 91, January 2018.

[95] 'Completing Europe's Economic and Monetary Union', Report by Jean-Claude Junker, in close cooperation with Donald Tusk, Jeroen Dijsselbloem, Mario Draghi, and Martin Schulz ('The Five Presidents' Report'), June 2015.

Since then, the Commission has also issued various proposals bearing on the future of EMU,[96] and envisaging further pooling of resources in this area. In 2017, it put forward a package that included a proposal for the reform and incorporation of the ESM into EU law;[97] under the proposed reform the ESM would have acquired a broader role, potentially also as a stabilization mechanism (thus increasing risk-sharing). The proposal lacked political support and was abandoned.[98] Instead, a far more modest reform of the ESM—one that does not aim at incorporating it into EU law or turning it into a stabilization mechanism—was agreed.[99]

In general, it has become clear in recent years that, while some Member States call for ambitious reforms and pooling of resources, other Member States are very resistant to the idea; many of them would still rather focus on discipline or risk-limiting, rather than risk-sharing.[100] Until the Covid-19 pandemic, it was only possible to agree on very limited reforms of this kind: in 2019, the euro area agreed on the creation of a 'Budgetary Instrument for Competitiveness and Convergence'[101]—a small structural fund to encourage countries to invest long-term—and to continue debating the matter in the future. Other instruments that would require greater sharing of resources remained elusive: there were many proposals for the creation of 'eurobonds' as a way to mutualize debt among euro countries,[102] for example; or for different versions of a basic European unemployment insurance scheme.[103]

[96] The European Commission's 'Reflection Paper on the deepening of the Economic and Monetary Union', COM(2017) 358, 28 June 2017, and 'Further Steps Toward Completing Europe's Economic and Monetary Union: A Roadmap', COM(2017) 821 final; the Fourteen Experts' Report, 'Reconciling risk sharing with market discipline: A constructive approach to euro area reform', Centre for Economic Policy Research, Policy Insight No 91, January 2018.

[97] 'Further Steps Toward Completing Europe's Economic and Monetary Union: A Roadmap', COM(2017) 821 final. The package includes the Commission's proposal on the creation of an EMF (European Commission, 'Proposal for a Council Regulation on the establishment of the European Monetary Fund', COM(2017) 827 final).

[98] A Hinarejos, 'A Possible European Monetary Fund and the Future of the Euro Area' (2019) 38 *Yearbook of European Law* 119.

[99] Agreement amending the Treaty Establishing the ESM, signed on 27 January and 8 February 2021 (to enter into force on the date when all signatories have deposited instruments of ratification, approval, or acceptance). The reform will allow the ESM to act as a backstop to the Single Resolution Fund, will make it easier to access its precautionary credit lines, and will give the institution a greater role in negotiating and monitoring euro area support programmes.

[100] In 2018, France's President Macron put forward ambitious risk-sharing proposals that failed to convince other euro countries, notably Germany and the so-called New Hanseatic League (the first statement of this group was signed by Denmark, Estonia, Finland, Ireland, Latvia, Lithuania, the Netherlands, and Sweden in March 2018; in broad terms, they lobby for more discipline and surveillance and are opposed to significant risk-sharing). France and Germany reached an agreement on (very watered-down) proposals (Meseberg Declaration, No 2014/18, 19 June 2018) that were then endorsed by the Eurogroup: Euro Summit Statement, 14 December 2018, EURO 503/18.

[101] Agreed in the Eurogroup meeting in inclusive format of 9 October 2019: www.consilium.europa.eu/media/41173/summing-up-letter-eg-9-october-2019.pdf.

[102] These bonds would be issued by either a single euro country or the whole eurozone (there are different versions of the proposal); all members of the eurozone would be liable for the debt. There have been many different iterations of the idea: 'Blueprint for a deep and genuine economic and monetary union: launching a European debate', COM/2012/0777 final, 30 and ff. The Four Presidents' Report refers to common debt too: 'Towards a genuine economic and monetary union', Interim Report by President of the European Council Herman Van Rompuy, Brussels, 26 June 2012; Final Report by President of the European Council Herman Van Rompuy, Brussels, 5 December 2012, 5 and ff. These have also been put forward in the literature in different guises: see J Delpla and J von Weizsäcker, 'The Blue Bond Proposal'; J Delpla and J von Weizsäcker, 'Eurobonds'.

[103] This tool would allow the euro area to prevent certain economic shocks and absorb them more efficiently and in a more centralized manner. See eg M Beblavy, G Marconi, and I Maselli, 'A European Unemployment Benefit Scheme: The Rationale and Challenges Ahead', CEPS Special Report, August 2015. See also the European Commission's Reflection Paper on the deepening of the Economic and Monetary Union, COM(2017) 358, 28 June 2017, 26.

In the midst of this discussion, the Covid-19 pandemic started in 2020 and had an unparalleled effect on Member States' economies. This prompted responses such as the suspension of budgetary obligations for Member States—given the enormous spending involved in grappling with the crisis and recovering from it—and ECB measures to help them in their efforts.[104] But it also prompted an unprecedented effort to pool resources at EU level to deal with the crisis collectively.

First, a European Instrument for temporary Support to mitigate Unemployment Risks in an Emergency (SURE) was created.[105] This is a fund from which Member States can obtain loans to deal with shocks to their employment market; it is funded from Member States' voluntary contributions. But far more significant—given its size and nature—was the adoption of NextGenerationEU,[106] a recovery package that encompasses the creation of a very sizeable (€750bn at 2018 prices) pot of money to help Member States rebuild their economy after the pandemic. This is to be funded through EU borrowing; the Commission has been authorized to borrow money in the private markets in the EU's name. Slightly more than half of the money will be given to Member States as grants (ie without the need to pay back), the rest as loans. The EU will be responsible for paying back the money disbursed as grants, through its own budget, by 2058. In order to make this possible, it is foreseen that the EU will create new genuine own resources (eg through the creation of new taxes or levies). If this does not prove possible, Member States will have to step in and pay back the borrowed money through their own, much larger contributions to the EU budget. NextGenerationEU is significant because of its size and nature: such pooling of resources that is unprecedented among Member States, both in terms of its scale and workings. It is supposed to be exceptional and temporary, but it will remain a milestone in the debate on the creation of a more stable central fiscal capacity. First, because the recovery package does entail an agreement and roadmap to create ways for the EU to raise new own resources. And secondly and more importantly, as a precedent that may have shifted our perspective on pooling resources and a blueprint for future action in this area.

Indeed, recent developments have prompted calls for the further pooling of resources in a post-pandemic and geopolitically unstable world: Russia's invasion of Ukraine in 2022 underscored the need for the EU to boost its own defence and, more generally, to have the necessary fiscal capacity to address collective shocks of any kind, including geopolitical

[104] Communication from the Commission to the Council on the activation of the general escape clause of the Stability and Growth Pact, COM(2020)123 of 20 March 2020. More broadly, the pandemic lent much currency to an already ongoing debate about the permanent reform of fiscal rules: see eg P Dermine, 'The EU's Response to the COVID-19 Crisis and the Trajectory of Fiscal Integration in Europe: Between Continuity and Rupture' (2020) 47 *Legal Issues of Economic Integration* 337. Finally, the ECB put in place a series of measures that include the adoption of a Pandemic Emergency Purchase Programme (PEPP) to lower borrowing costs and increase lending in the euro area, and a series of decisions to increase the funds that banks can borrow from it, as well as to make the conditions to do so easier.

[105] Council Regulation (EU) 2020/672 of 19 May 2020 on the establishment of a European instrument for temporary support to mitigate unemployment risks in an emergency (SURE) following the Covid-19 outbreak.

[106] Council Regulation 2020/2094 of 14 December 2020 establishing a European Union Recovery Instrument to support the recovery in the aftermath of the COVID-19 crisis (OJ [2020] L433 I/23); Council Decision 2020/2053 of 14 December 2020 on the system of own resources of the European Union and repealing Decision 2014/335/EU, Euratom (OJ [2020] L424/1); Regulation 2021/241 of the European Parliament and of the Council of 12 February 2021 establishing the Recovery and Resilience Facility (OJ [2021] L57/17). For details on the nature and significance of NextGenerationEU, see B de Witte, 'The European Union's COVID-19 Recovery Plan: The Legal Engineering of an Economic Policy Shift' (2021) 58 *Common Market Law Review* 635. For a rather critical appraisal, see P Leino-Sandberg and M Ruffert, 'Next Generation EU and its Constitutional Ramifications: A Critical Assessment' (2022) 59 *Common Market Law Review* 433.

ones. As a result, there have been renewed calls for joint borrowing and investment tools to build this fiscal capacity as a matter of urgency.[107]

In general, however, and apart from the significant effects that NextGenerationEU and the invasion of Ukraine have had on this debate, it has always been difficult to get euro countries to pool resources to a large degree, for different reasons. Some are pragmatic reasons: richer countries (or their citizens) think it is unfair to pay for (what they perceive to be) other countries' mistaken economic policies. Other reasons are more abstract: there are concerns that the creation of a significant fiscal capacity for the euro area would need corresponding reforms in the political realm in order to be democratically legitimate, or that there is a limit to how much you can push integration in this area without 'diluting' the State. The next two sections will focus on these concerns.

6.1 **Democratic legitimacy**

A significant obstacle to a full-fledged EU fiscal policy is democratic legitimacy: the question is to what extent an overarching capacity to determine the amount and provenance of public resources and their uses (thus including taxation, but also for example social insurance mechanisms) can be decoupled from national politics, in the absence of a comparable degree of democratic legitimacy at the EU level. This problem seems much more acute when considering the direct redistribution of wealth that comes with fiscal policy than when considering purely regulatory policies, such as the single market. In the latter, the above-mentioned decoupling from national politics has already occurred, to a certain degree.[108]

The debate concerning the democratic deficit of the EU has been going on for years; it is a nuanced, varied debate to which this chapter can only nod briefly. One of the generally accepted premises of the debate is that, although the role of the European Parliament has grown over the years, the EU cannot claim to have the degree of representative democracy that States have. Where opinions diverge is to what extent this is a fatal flaw. Some argue that because only limited competences have been delegated to the EU the Union needs less democratic legitimacy than a State, and that it derives enough indirect legitimacy from national politics.[109] Many argue that the EU is able to generate democratic legitimacy of

[107] See eg the Commission's 'Communication on Orientations for a Reform of the EU Economic Governance Framework', COM/2022/583 final, which pointed to the war in Ukraine as one of the systemic shocks that require stronger common fiscal tools. More recently, see the White Paper for European Defence—Readiness 2030 (n 93); Editorial Comments, 'ReArm Europe/Readiness 2030: European Defence in Times of War' (2025) 62 *Common Market Law Review* 1019. For a broader analysis of the effects of this conflict on the EU legal system: F Fabbrini, *The EU Constitution in Time of War* (Oxford: Oxford University Press, 2025).

[108] See eg C Joerges, 'The Market without the State? The "Economic Constitution" of the European Community and the Rebirth of Regulatory Politics' (1997) 1 *European Integration Online Papers*. More generally, on 'disembedded' market and politics, K Polanyi, *The Great Transformation: The Political and Economic Origins of Our Time* (Boston, MA: Beacon Press, 2011); C Joerges and J Falke (eds), *Karl Polanyi, Globalisation and the Potential of Law in Transnational Markets* (Oxford: Hart Publishing, 2011).

[109] Either through the involvement of national executives in law-making, or because of the original consent given to the Treaties, or a combination of both. See A Moravcsik, 'In Defence of the "Democratic Deficit": Reassessing Legitimacy in the EU' (2002) 40 *Journal of Common Market Studies* 603; A Moravcsik, 'Preferences and Power in the European Community: A Liberal Intergovernmental Approach' (1993) 31 *Journal of Common Market Studies* 473; G Majone, *Regulating Europe* (London: Routledge, 1996); G Majone, 'Europe's "Democratic Deficit": The Question of Standards' (1998) 4 *European Law Journal* 5; G Majone, *Dilemmas of European Integration* (Oxford: Oxford University Press, 2005); P Lindseth, *Power and Legitimacy: Reconciling Europe and the Nation-State* (Oxford: Oxford University Press, 2010). On different intellectual approaches to democratic legitimacy in the EU: AJ Menéndez, 'The European Democratic Challenge: the Forging of a Supranational Volonté Générale' (2009) 15 *European Law Journal* 277.

its own through mechanisms that are different from the ones typically found within the national framework, such as deliberative democracy, and through the protection of outsiders whose interests are not represented within—but affected by—national politics.[110]

Convincing as these arguments may be, it is still arguable that a fiscal policy, encompassing matters such as the redistribution of wealth through taxation and the organization of the welfare system, for instance, would require a higher degree of democratic legitimacy than the establishing and functioning of the single market does, even with all the latter's ramifications. Fiscal measures, with taxation as the paramount example, speak very directly to the link between the citizen and the State. The power to impose the positive obligation on citizens to contribute taxes (as well as the general power to determine how this wealth is going to be distributed)[111] seems to necessitate a degree of political contestation and of connection between the citizen and the State that is currently lacking at the EU level, either through representative or deliberative democracy. Equally, a full fiscal policy would be essential and too wide-ranging to be characterized as a part of a limited delegation of powers to the Union, with sufficient indirect legitimacy being derived from national politics.[112]

6.2 **'Reserved domains' and the disappearing State**

A connected concern is the extent to which taking steps towards a full economic/fiscal union would threaten essential aspects of the Member States' identity as States. While this question may seem a bit theoretical, it has an important practical side: it is unlikely that national constitutional courts would allow integration to proceed to a stage that threatens or does away with an important aspect of their State's constitutional identity, however defined. 'Constitutional identity' is the term used by the German Constitutional Court, but several national constitutional courts have made largely similar remarks to the effect that there must be limits to European integration—imposed by the national constitutions that they enforce—because certain areas are too integral to the sovereignty or the identity of the State.[113]

The German Constitutional Court has been most vocal on the question of limits to integration, which it addressed explicitly in its decision on the Lisbon Treaty.[114]

[110] See eg AJ Menéndez (n 109) 15; D Curtin, 'Framing Public Deliberation and Democratic Legitimacy in the European Union' in S Besson et al (eds), *Deliberative Democracy and Its Discontents* (Aldershot: Ashgate, 2006); D Halberstam, 'The Bride of Messina: Constitutionalism and Democracy in Europe' (2005) 30 *European Law Review* 775. On the EU as a corrector of national political processes, see also: M Maduro, *We, the Court* (Oxford: Hart Publishing, 1998) 168ff; M Poiares Maduro, 'Europe and the Constitution: What If This Is as Good as It Gets?', 2000/5 ConWeb—Papers on Constitutionalism & Governance beyond the State, 11.

[111] While the law of the single market may have a bearing on some of these decisions, what is discussed here is a general power to adopt these decisions even when there is no connection to the single market; there is a crucial difference of degree.

[112] Moravcsik's argument is based on the fact that the EU is limited to a 'modest subset of the substantive activities pursued by modern states'. He explicitly excludes taxation and the setting of fiscal priorities, among other essential areas: Moravcsik, 'In Defence of the "Democratic Deficit" (n 109) 607.

[113] See eg: Case K32/09 *Treaty of Lisbon*, Judgment of Polish Constitutional Tribunal of 24 November 2010; *Re Constitutionality of Framework Decision on the European Arrest Warrant* (Czech Constitutional Court) [2007] 3 CMLR 24; Ratification of the Lisbon Treaty (French Constitutional Council) Case 2007-560 [2010] 2 CMLR 26. For an overview, see D Chalmers, 'Democratic Self-Government in Europe' (May 2013) Policy Network Paper.

[114] Decision of 30 June 2009, BVerfGE 123, 267. For comments on this case, see D Thym, 'In the Name of Sovereign Statehood: A Critical Introduction to the Lisbon Judgment of the German Constitutional Court' (2009) 46 *Common Market Law Review* 1795; M Payandeh, 'Constitutional Review of EU Law after *Honeywell*: Contextualising the Relationship between the German Constitutional Court and the EU Court of Justice' (2011) 48 *Common Market Law Review* 9.

The German Court went on to ground the existence of these limits to European integration on the need for democratic legitimacy (which takes us back to the previous section). It stated that the 'constitutional identity' of Germany required legitimate democratic government. Building on its seminal *Maastricht* decision,[115] the German court then drew a link between certain areas of competence, real democratic legitimacy, and the State.[116] It contended that, in order to regulate or govern these areas legitimately, democratic representation of the kind that is found only in a State is necessary. The court concluded that, unless things changed dramatically in the future (that is, unless the Member States were willing to change the current constitutional settlement and, one assumes, create a federal State at the EU level that would have the representative democratic legitimacy of a State),[117] there would always be certain areas of competence that needed to remain the purview of national democracy. Transferring these competences in the current circumstances would go against the 'constitutional identity' of Germany: neither the German Constitution nor the German court would allow this. Crucially for our discussion here, these special competences, or 'reserved domains' highlighted in the Lisbon judgment include 'fundamental fiscal decisions on public revenue and expenditure, [and] decisions on the shaping of the social state'.[118] This statist conception of democracy and demos has attracted some criticism in the literature.[119]

The German Court has relied on its conception of democracy and on the notion of constitutional identity to protect national parliamentary powers in its decisions concerning the legality of measures adopted to address the crisis,[120] including its assessment of the legality of two ECB programmes (the OMT in *Gauweiler* and the PSPP in *Weiss*).[121] As mentioned earlier, *Gauweiler* was the first time that the German Court asked the Court of Justice for a preliminary ruling, and the closest the two courts had come to an open conflict in recent years. A clash was ultimately avoided in that instance, as the German Court was (grudgingly) satisfied with the interpretation provided by the CJEU.[122] The clash did come, unexpectedly, in the subsequent case of

[115] Decision of 12 October 1993, BVerfGE 89, 155.

[116] Decision of 30 June 2009, BVerfGE 123, 267 [175].

[117] In its decision, the German court equates democratic legitimacy with the legitimacy that emanates from representative democracy, without considering other concepts of democracy that have been put forward as being more adequate for the EU and also potentially capable of legitimizing government (see n 114).

[118] Decision of 30 June 2009, BVerfGE 123, 267 [252].

[119] See eg Thym (n 1154); S Theil, 'What Red Lines, If Any, Do the Lisbon Judgments of European Constitutional Courts Draw for Future EU Integration?' (2014) 15 *German Law Journal* 599.

[120] The German court's later decisions on the constitutionality of the Greek bailout and Germany's guarantees to the EFSF which insisted on the need for parliamentary approval in every individual instance, refer once more to budgetary powers (the exercise of which is legitimized through representative democracy) as part of the constitutional identity of Germany: Decision of 7 September 2011, BVerfG, 2 BvR 987/10; 2 BvR 1485/10; 2 BvR 1099/10. On the German court's judgment and its relationship to the EU response to the euro crisis, see Editorial, 'The Euro Crisis: Storm, Meet Structure' (2011) 7 *European Constitutional Law Review* 349. Several months later, the German court rejected that a parliamentary committee consisting of nine members could give the necessary parliamentary approval: Decision of 28 February 2012, BVerfG, 2 BvE 8/11. When considering the legality of the ESM Treaty, the German court considered again that national parliamentary approval was necessary for any increase in Germany's contribution to the fund: Decision of 12 September 2012, BVerfG, 2 BvR 1390/12; 2 BvR 1421/12; 2 BvR 1438/12; 2 BvR 1439/12; 2 BvR 1440/12; 2 BvE 6/12. This concerned the legality of both the ESM Treaty and the TSCG.

[121] See n 43.

[122] On the German reference, see eg T Beukers, 'The Bundesverfassungsgericht Preliminary Reference on the OMT Program: "In the ECB We Do Not Trust. What About You?"' (2014) 15 *German Law Journal* 343. On the CJEU decision, see eg D Adamski, 'Economic Constitution of the Euro Area after the Gauweiler Preliminary Ruling' (2015) 52 *Common Market Law Review* 1451.

Weiss.[123] Although most commentators expected both courts to tread similar lines, the German Court refused to accept the Court of Justice's assessment of the ECB's PSPP scheme in *Weiss* and declared the latter's judgment ultra vires. Following the decision, the ECB sought to address the German court's concerns by demonstrating the proportionality of the PSPP programme in various ways, including by releasing relevant meeting minutes. In June 2020, the German government and the Bundestag stated that they were satisfied that the ECB had complied with the requirements set out by the German Court in *Weiss*, clearing the way for ongoing German participation in the PSPP. The German Constitutional Court agreed.[124] So while the specific clash was patched over, at least for the time being, the German decision in *Weiss* remains of historical significance—both for EMU and the relationship between the two courts—and the dialogue is set to continue: for example, the Covid-19 recovery package discussed earlier in this chapter (NextGenerationEU) was also challenged before the German Constitutional Court, which considered it lawful.[125]

Moving forward, any significant move towards further fiscal and economic integration will be carefully monitored by the German Constitutional Court. As we have seen, the latter already conducted an ultra vires review in *Weiss*, with explosive results. Additionally, a hypothetical transfer of power to the EU to create its own fiscal policy, or a dramatic development in this direction, would tread into some of the domains identified by the German court as part of its country's constitutional identity, and it seems safe to assume that other national constitutional courts would also be troubled by these developments.[126] Whatever form they take—as ultra vires review, constitutional identity review, or any other—further constitutional challenges are bound to remain a constant in this area.

7 Conclusion

The elements of Economic and Monetary Union include a centrally conducted monetary policy, a common currency for those countries within the euro area, and coordination of fiscal and economic policies that remain national in nature. This chapter has provided an introduction to the historical origins and set-up of EMU, and it has shown that there is an imbalance between the more centralized part of this Union (monetary policy) and the decentralized part (fiscal and economic policy). This tension has been a constant of EMU since its inception, and it is related to the sovereign debt crisis in the euro area.

EMU has evolved in recent years due to the need to address the immediate effects of the euro area crisis and to avoid future ones. This chapter has distinguished between three different approaches taken by the EU and its Member States in this regard: (1)

[123] The German court asked again for a preliminary ruling, this time on the legality of the PSPP programme: Case C-493/17 *Heinrich Weiss and Others*, EU:C:2018:1000. The German court disagreed with the result: BVerfG, Judgment of the Second Senate of 5 May 2020, 2 BvR 859/15, 2 BvR 980/16, 2 BvR 2006/15, 2 BvR 1651/15. See eg A Bobic and M Dawson, 'Making Sense of the "Incomprehensible": The PSPP Judgment of the German Federal Constitutional Court' (2020) 57 *Common Market Law Review* 1953; F Amtenbrink and R Repasi, 'The German Federal Constitutional Court's Decision in Weiss: A Contextual Analysis' (2020) 45 *European Law Review* 757.

[124] In 2021, the German Constitutional Court was asked to produce an order of execution relating to its judgment in *Weiss*; the applicants argued that the requirements set out by the court in its previous decision had not been satisfied. The court disagreed and the application was rejected. BVerfG, Order of 29 April 2021, 2 BvR 1651/15, 2 BvR 2006/15.

[125] BVerfG (Second Senate), Judgment of 6 December 2022, 2 BvR 547/21, 2 BvR 798/21. A challenge to the legality of the ECB's PEPP programme is still pending before the same court: 2 BvE 7/20, 2 BvR 420/21, pending.

[126] See n 113.

stabilization through the evolving role of the ECB and the creation of bailout mechanisms, (2) the creation of further budgetary and economic coordination measures, and (3) further financial regulation for the whole of the EU and steps towards an eventual banking union in the euro area.

While the measures adopted by the EU and the Member States brought the euro area out of the acute phase of the crisis, it remains to be seen how successful they will be in improving economic coordination in the future and addressing the tension at the heart of EMU. More generally, the crisis also prompted a general debate on the future of EMU and of the EU as a political project. Since then, the question has remained whether EMU should move beyond economic coordination and towards more sharing of resources and a full economic union; and, crucially, whether—or to what degree—this move would require turning the EU into a full political union.

Economic and fiscal policy are very sensitive areas, where important decisions are taken concerning the allocation of resources in society. These decisions touch upon our understanding of social justice, solidarity, and the role of the State. Accordingly, many still feel that these policies are most appropriately debated and conducted within the national political process. The idea of a growing role for the EU in these areas is often met with concern, and the argument that the EU does not have, at this moment, the necessary democratic legitimacy to decide on matters such as taxation or the size and features of the welfare state. So while it may seem necessary for EMU to evolve, the euro area countries and the institutions of the EU find themselves in uncharted, and extremely uncertain, waters. The Covid-19 pandemic and the common efforts to address its economic effects have had a lasting effect on this debate; other, more recent developments—notably the war in Ukraine and the need to strengthen the EU's defence capacity in times of geopolitical instability—are also likely to have a bearing on the future shape of EMU.

Further reading

D Adamski, 'Economic Constitution of the Euro Area after the *Gauweiler* Preliminary Ruling' (2015) 52 *Common Market Law Review* 1451

A Bobic and M Dawson, 'Making Sense of the "Incomprehensible": The PSPP Judgment of the German Federal Constitutional Court' (2020) 57 *Common Market Law Review* 1953

A Hinarejos, *The Euro Area Crisis in Constitutional Perspective* (Oxford: Oxford University Press, 2015)

M Markakis and P Dermine, 'Bailouts, the Legal Status of Memoranda of Understanding, and the Scope of Application of the EU Charter: *Florescu*' (2018) 55 *Common Market Law Review* 643

MA Panascì, 'Unravelling Next Generation EU as a Transformative Moment: From Market Integration to Redistribution' (2024) 61 *Common Market Law Review* 13

A Poulou, 'Financial Assistance Conditionality and Human Rights Protection: What Is the Role of the EU Charter of Fundamental Rights?' (2017) 54 *Common Market Law Review* 991

B de Witte and T Beukers, 'The Court of Justice Approves the Creation of the European Stability Mechanism outside the EU Legal Order: *Pringle*' (2013) 50 *Common Market Law Review* 805

20

Labour and equality law

Mia Rönnmar and Jenny Julén Votinius

1 Introduction

Labour and equality law is central to the functioning of society and economy—but also to the everyday life of individuals. Labour law regulates the individual employment relationship and employment rights, as well as the labour market more generally, and the relations between the State, employers and employees, and their representatives—the social partners. Equality law nowadays is a central part of labour law, but also extends its reach beyond working life. Both the development and content of EU labour and equality law throughout the years—and still today—reflect a tension between the EU and national sovereignty, economic and social integration, and market and human rights discourses.

Labour and equality law is regulated by a complex mix of Treaty provisions, fundamental rights, and general principles of EU law, secondary law, collective agreements at EU level, case law from the Court of Justice, and soft law measures. To this we can add regulation at national level. A selection of key labour and equality law issues are discussed in this chapter, such as restructuring of enterprises; information, consultation, and worker participation; fundamental Treaty freedoms and national collective labour law; flexible work and working conditions; the EU and national labour law in times of crisis; and gender equality, comprehensive equality, and protection against discrimination on other grounds.

Section 2 presents the legal framework and evolution of EU labour and equality law. Section 3 provides a discussion on some central issues in EU labour law. Section 4 continues with a similar discussion on EU equality law. Section 5 contains some concluding remarks.

2 The legal framework and evolution of EU labour and equality law

2.1 The evolution of EU labour and equality law and Treaty developments

Social policy is often understood to include areas connected to the welfare state, such as social security, social assistance, health care, and housing. At EU level most of the (hard law) regulation in the area of social policy refers to EU labour and equality law.[1] Together they form part of the EU social model, an often-used, but rather vague, concept. Values such as democracy, individual rights, collective bargaining, the market economy, equality of opportunity, and flexicurity (ie combining flexibility for employers and security for employees) are said to be central to the European Social Model, a model which is recognized by all EU institutions.[2] Despite a (common) European Social Model there is still great variety among the Member States' labour law and industrial relations systems, as regards, for example, the importance of constitutional principles, the balance between legislation and collective bargaining, the degree of State intervention or voluntarism, the role of the courts and case law, and the degree of trade union organization and forms of workers' representation.

Traditionally reference has been made to the three models of industrial relations in the Member States: the Romano-Germanic system, the Anglo-Irish system, and the Nordic system of industrial relations. In the Romano-Germanic system, the State plays a central and active role in industrial relations, and an emphasis is put on constitutional and statutory regulation of employment rights. In several countries belonging to this system, collective agreements can be extended to all employees and employers. Within the Romano-Germanic system the southern Mediterranean States display some specific characteristics, as do the countries which joined the EU as part of the enlargement since 2004. The Anglo-Irish system, in line with voluntarism or collective laissez-faire, provides a limited role for the State. Collective agreements are not legally binding, and there is no extensive statutory regulation, although there is a trend towards increasing legislative activity and greater State involvement in more recent years. Similarly, the Nordic system builds on voluntarism and statutory non-intervention. Collective agreements are an important legal source, and set wages and working conditions. The trade union organization rates are high, as well as the collective bargaining coverage rate. However, today there is also quite extensive statutory regulation, often providing for derogations by way of collective agreements.[3]

EU labour and equality law aims for a partial harmonization of the different labour law and industrial relations systems in the Member States, reflected in the fact that the personal scope of most EU labour and equality law directives is defined in relation to the different notions of a worker, developed and existing in each of the Member States. However, in

[1] The substantive content of social security is a matter for the Member States and national legislation. However, the coordination of social security between the Member States was implemented early on as a way to facilitate the free movement of workers; see now Regulation 883/2004 (OJ [2004] L166/1). Through soft law and the open method of coordination, not only employment policy but also aspects linked to social security have been further developed. Social security aspects will, in principle, not be discussed here. Aspects on free movement of workers, discrimination on grounds of nationality, and EU citizenship are also excluded here, see chapter 13.

[2] The concept of the 'social dimension of the EU' refers—in contrast to the economic dimension—to the part of EU politics and legal regulations connected to the citizen's social needs, social protection, and social integration, see A Numhauser-Henning and M Rönnmar (eds), *Normative Patterns and the Legal Development of the Social Dimension of the EU* (Oxford: Hart Publishing, 2013).

[3] See eg C Barnard, *EU Employment Law* (4th edn, Oxford: Oxford University Press, 2012) 58 *et seq* and B Hepple and B Veneziani (eds), *The Transformation of Labour Law in Europe: A Comparative Study of 15 Countries 1945–2004* (Oxford: Hart Publishing, 2009).

the area of free movement of workers, EU law contains a separate, autonomous, and far-reaching notion of a worker. This uniform notion of a worker has, through the case law of the Court of Justice, 'spread' into other areas of labour and equality law, such as equal pay and working time.[4] Furthermore, in several recent EU labour law directives, for example the Directive on Transparent and Predictable Working Conditions,[5] a 'hybrid' notion of worker has been introduced, which refers both to national and EU notions of a worker.[6]

There is no comprehensive coverage of EU labour and equality law, nor does it replicate national labour law in this area. Furthermore, EU labour law emphasizes and regulates issues of a cross-border nature and the intersection between the internal market and fundamental freedoms and national labour law.[7]

The legal framework for the adoption of EU rules on labour and equality law has changed a number of times, and Treaty competence has gradually expanded (from the single provision on equal pay in the Treaty of Rome,[8] where labour law was seen mainly as a domestic issue and the focus was on economic integration and free movement, to the current elaborate Treaty support, through important revisions in, for example, the Maastricht, Amsterdam, and Lisbon Treaties).[9] Secondary law is now well developed, and a large number of directives have been adopted in this area. The development has not been linear, however. There have been phases of activity, such as in the 1970s, when a number of directives, for example in the area of equality law and restructuring of enterprises, were adopted with reference to the 1974 Social Action Programme, and the Court of Justice delivered a number of important judgments. On the other hand, we have also witnessed phases of inactivity or stagnation, such as at the beginning of the 1980s.

EU labour and equality law is an area of shared competence, and the principles of subsidiarity and proportionality are thus important.[10] Article 3(3) TEU states that:

> The Union shall establish an internal market. It shall work for the sustainable development of Europe based on balanced economic growth and price stability, a highly competitive social market economy, aiming at full employment and social progress, and a high level of protection and improvement of the quality of the environment. . . . It shall combat social exclusion and discrimination, and shall promote social justice and protection, equality between women and men, solidarity between generations and protection of the rights of the child.

The Lisbon Treaty thus introduced *social market economy* as one of the main aims of the EU, which implies a combination of economic and social integration within the EU and confirms the EU's economic *and* social objectives.[11]

[4] See Case C-66/85 *Lawrie-Blum v Land Baden-Württemberg* [1986] ECR 2121, C-53/81 *Levin v Secretary of State for Justice* [1982] ECR 1035 and Case C-428/09 *Union syndicale Solidaires Isère* [2010] ECR I-9961. See also M Freedland and N Kountouris, *The Legal Construction of Personal Work Relations* (Oxford: Oxford University Press, 2011).

[5] Directive 2019/1152/EU (OJ [2019] L186/105).

[6] Thus, Art 1(2) of the Directive on Transparent and Predictable Working Conditions says that '[t]his Directive lays down minimum rights that apply to every worker in the Union who has an employment contract or employment relationship as defined by the law, collective agreements or practice in force in each Member State with consideration to the case-law of the Court of Justice'. See further section 3.3.2.

[7] See eg A Davies, *EU Labour Law* (Cheltenham: Edward Elgar, 2012) 3 *et seq.*

[8] Art 119.

[9] See the chapters by Barnard and Bell in P Craig and G de Búrca (eds), *Evolution of EU Law* (3rd edn, Oxford: Oxford University Press, 2021) on the evolution of EU labour and equality law and a close examination of the Treaty developments in this area.

[10] After the Lisbon Treaty expressly stated in Art 4(2)(6)TFEU.

[11] For a discussion on social market economy and the previous 'decoupling' of economic and social integration, see eg F Scharpf, 'The European Social Model: Coping with the Challenges of Diversity' (2002) 40 *Journal of Common Market Studies* 645.

The centrality of the attainment of equality is also emphasized by the Treaty: according to Articles 8 and 10 TFEU the EU must adopt a *mainstreaming* approach in relation to equality and non-discrimination. This means that in *all* its activities and policies (not just those in the social field) it must aim to eliminate inequalities, to promote equality between men and women, and to combat discrimination. In the social field more particularly, Article 151 TFEU provides that the Union and the Member States, having in mind fundamental social rights,[12] shall have as their objective:

> the promotion of employment, improved living and working conditions, so as to make possible their harmonisation while the improvement is being maintained, proper social protection, dialogue between management and labour, the development of human resources with a view to lasting high employment and the combating of exclusion.

However, even though the competence of the EU covers labour and equality law areas such as non-discrimination;[13] equality between men and women;[14] flexible work and working conditions, including working time and health and safety; employment protection; and information, consultation, and worker participation,[15] the competence of the EU is still limited.[16] Central aspects of national labour law and industrial relations systems, including pay, the right of association, the right to strike, and the right to impose lock-outs, are expressly excluded from the EU's competence to adopt directives[17]—though not from the scope of EU law, a question to which we will return later in the discussion of *Viking* and *Laval* and the right to collective action, and the Directive on adequate minimum wages in the EU.[18]

2.2 **Law-making and legal sources in EU labour and equality law**

The traditional 'Community method', whereby the Commission proposes legislative measures and the Council and European Parliament adopt them, is important in EU labour and equality law. The main body of EU labour and equality law is made up of directives, which provide flexibility and adaptability in relation to the variety of national labour law and industrial relations systems in the EU. Directives must be implemented in the Member States by legislation or by the social partners (employers' organizations and trade unions) and collective bargaining; however, in the latter case it remains the responsibility of the Member States to guarantee that individuals are afforded the rights and full protection provided by the directive.[19]

In national labour law and industrial relations systems, the social partners are often consulted and involved in the legislative process, and collective agreements regulate working conditions and other labour law issues. The Maastricht Treaty, and the Social Policy Agreement (signed by all Member States except the UK), subsequently integrated into the Treaty through the Treaty of Amsterdam (and thereafter applied to the UK), incorporated a similar process at EU level: the *European social dialogue* and collective

[12] Set out in international human rights sources such as the Council of Europe's European Social Charter and the EU's Community Charter of the Fundamental Social Rights of Workers.

[13] Art 19 TFEU. [14] Arts 157 and 153(1)(i) TFEU.

[15] Art 153(1) TFEU. The predecessors to Art 153 TFEU were Art 137 EC and Art 118a EEC.

[16] To adopt directives on the basis of Arts 19 and 153(1)(c), (d), (f), and (g) unanimity is required, while to adopt directives on the basis of Art 157 TFEU and the other parts of Art 153 qualified majority is required.

[17] Art 153(5) TFEU. [18] Directive 2022/2041/EU (OJ [2022] L 275/33).

[19] cf Art 155 TFEU. See Case C-187/98 *Commission v Greece* [1999] ECR I-7713 and Case 143/83 *Commission v Denmark* [1985] ECR 427.

route to legislation at Union level.[20] The Commission is charged with the task of promoting the consultation of management and labour at Union level. Before submitting proposals in the social policy field, the Commission must consult the European social partners on the possible direction of Union action (the first consultation). If, after such consultation, the Commission considers Union action advisable, it must consult the European social partners regarding the content of the envisaged proposal (the second consultation).[21] They may then inform the Commission of their wish to initiate the process provided for in Article 155 TFEU, possibly resulting in contractual relations and European collective agreements (also called framework agreements).

Social dialogue takes place at both cross-industry and sectoral levels. The actors at the general cross-industry level include the European Trade Union Confederation (ETUC), representing employees, and BusinessEurope (formerly UNICE) and SGI Europe (formerly CEEP), representing employers.[22] A number of agreements have been reached at cross-industry level: for example, agreements on parental leave, part-time work, and fixed-term work. These agreements can be implemented either through a decision by the Council and a directive, or by the social partners themselves. There is no substantive role for the European Parliament in this process.[23] In recent years, however, the European social dialogue at cross-industry level seems to have stagnated. To address this, a number of initiatives have been taken by the Commission and the European social partners to strengthen social dialogue, including, most recently, the Council Recommendation on social dialogue.[24]

Soft law measures are increasingly important in EU labour and equality law—both as a complement and alternative to hard law regulation. Since the insertion of the Employment Title into the Treaty of Amsterdam and the development of the European Employment Strategy (EES) labour law is seen as an integrated part of employment policy, which in turn is subject to the Integrated Guidelines and the Europe 2020 Strategy (replacing the Lisbon Strategy in 2010). The Europe 2020 Strategy puts forward three mutually reinforcing priorities: smart growth, sustainable growth, and inclusive growth. The EES integrates the flexicurity strategy where national systems are supposed to combine workforce flexibility with employment security. Employment policies in the Member States are coordinated through the so-called *open method of coordination* and the European Semester, using guidelines, benchmarking, targets, National Reform Programmes, and recommendations. The economic crisis has led to stricter economic and employment policy coordination within the EU. The European Semester, introduced in 2010, is the EU's annual cycle of economic policy coordination, where the Commission analyses the Member States' plans for budgetary, macroeconomic, and structural reforms and provides recommendations. The Commission's country-specific proposals to the Member States regarding their National Reform Programmes within the context of the European

[20] See C Welz, *The European Social Dialogue under Articles 138 and 139 of the EC Treaty* (Dordrecht: Kluwer Law International, 2008). Art 152 TFEU now also states that the EU recognizes and promotes the role of the European social partners, and shall facilitate dialogue between the social partners.

[21] Art 154 TFEU.

[22] cf Case T-135/96 *UEAPME* [1998] ECR II-2335. At sectoral level, sectoral dialogue committees have been established.

[23] Art 155(2) TFEU—in relation to the issue of implementation of agreements resulting from the European social dialogue, the Court of Justice in Case C-928/19 P *European Federation of Public Service Unions (EPSU) v European Commission*, an appeal of a judgment from the General Court, clarified that the Treaty provisions and the objective of promoting the role of social partners and social dialogue did not imply an obligation on the part of the Commission and the Council to give effect to a joint request by the social partners to implement their agreement at the EU level.

[24] Council Recommendation C/2023/1389 of 12 June 2023 on strengthening social dialogue in the European Union.

Semester and the European Employment Strategy have, following the economic crisis, contained deregulatory elements targeted at, for example, wage-setting and employment protection, and caused controversy and opposition (section 3.4).

In 2017, the European Pillar of Social Rights was adopted.[25] It aims to deliver new and more effective rights for citizens and to express a number of essential principles to support well-functioning and fair labour markets and welfare systems. The Pillar relates to the wider notion of social policy, and contains 20 principles that are divided into three main groups: equal opportunities and access to the labour market; fair working conditions; and adequate and sustainable social protection. So far, principles from the European Pillar of Social Rights have been integrated into the European Semester and a number of legal initiatives have been taken, including, for example, the adoption of the Directive on Transparent and Predictable Working Conditions,[26] the Work-life Balance Directive,[27] the Whistleblowing Directive,[28] the establishment of the European Labour Authority,[29] and the Directive on adequate minimum wages in the EU.[30] However, the European Pillar of Social Rights has also been debated, especially concerning its reference to areas such as housing over which the EU has no legal competence to act.

Finally, the Court of Justice has played a central role in the development of EU labour and equality law. The principles and rules developed by the Court in case law have often—not least in equality law—been codified later in secondary law and directives. The Court has frequently strengthened the protection of individual employees but, when faced with a conflict between economic integration (the free movement rules) and employment rights, it has favoured free movement (section 3.2.2).

2.3 **The Charter of Fundamental Rights of the European Union and the constitutionalization of EU labour and equality law**

At an early stage, respect for fundamental rights and freedoms became part of EU law, and the jurisprudence of the Court of Justice on fundamental rights and general principles of EU law developed with reference to constitutional traditions common to the Member States and from international conventions, most especially the European Convention on Human Rights (ECHR).[31] The Lisbon Treaty implies a new emphasis on fundamental rights, and a further *constitutionalization* of EU labour and equality law. According to Article 6 TEU, the Charter of Fundamental Rights of the European Union is made legally binding and part of primary law, and the EU is to accede to the ECHR.[32] The Charter encompasses rights, freedoms, and principles of great relevance to EU labour and equality law, such as respect for private and family life (Article 7), freedom of expression (Article 11), freedom of assembly and of association (Article 12), equality before the law (Article 20), non-discrimination (Article 21), equality between men and women (Article

[25] See European Commission, Communication from the Commission to the European Parliament, the Council, the European Economic and Social Committee and the Committee of the Regions, 'Launching a consultation of a European Pillar of Social Rights', COM(2016) 127 final.

[26] Directive 2019/1152/EU (OJ [2019] L186/105).

[27] Directive 2019/1158/EU (OJ [2019] L188/79).

[28] Directive 2019/1937/EU (OJ [2019] L305/17).

[29] Regulation (EU) 2019/1149 (OJ [2019] L186/21).

[30] Directive 2022/2041/EU (OJ [2022] L 275/33).

[31] See further chapter 9.

[32] However, the Court of Justice in its Opinion 2/13, delivered in December 2014, concluded that the draft accession agreement is not compatible with Art 6(2) TEU or with Protocol (No 8) relating to Art 6(2), and thus put (at least a temporary) stop to the accession process, see Opinion 2/13, ECHR, EU:C:2014:2454. In 2020, negotiations between the European Commission and the Member States of the Council of Europe on EU accession were resumed.

23), right to information and consultation within the undertaking (Article 27), right of collective bargaining and collective action (Article 28), protection in the event of unjustified dismissal (Article 30), and fair and just working conditions (Article 31).[33]

The provisions of the Charter are 'addressed to the institutions, bodies and offices and agencies of the Union with due regard for the principle of subsidiarity and to the Member States only when they are implementing Union law'.[34] According to the explanations to the Charter, the requirement to respect fundamental rights is binding on the Member States when they act within the scope of Union law. According to settled case law of the Court, general principles of EU law, including fundamental rights, apply when Member States implement, derogate from, and act within the scope of EU law.[35] The Charter does not extend the field of application of EU law beyond the powers of the Union or establish any new power or task for the EU.[36] There has been a dynamic case law development in the important area of the direct horizontal effect of Charter rights—that is, their application in relations between individuals, such as employers and employees. In the *Egenberger* case[37] on discrimination on grounds of religion, the Court of Justice afforded direct horizontal effect to Articles 21 (on non-discrimination) and 47 (access to justice), and in the joined cases *Bauer et al*[38] direct horizontal effect was afforded to Article 31 (on the right to paid annual leave). We will return to the Charter throughout this chapter, for example in relation to collective action, information and consultation, working time, and equality law.

3 Labour law

3.1 Restructuring of enterprises and information, consultation, and worker participation

We now turn to a substantive discussion on some key labour law issues. The discussion starts with transfers of undertakings, collective redundancies, and employer insolvency (the three areas outside sex equality first regulated by the EU in the 1970s), and continues with a consideration of information, consultation, and worker participation.

3.1.1 Transfers of undertakings, collective redundancies, and employer insolvency

Transfer of undertakings

The Transfers of Undertakings Directive,[39] the Collective Redundancies Directive,[40] and the Employer Insolvency Directive[41]—often referred to as the 'Restructuring Directives'—were adopted as part of the 1974 Social Action Programme. The Directives address social

[33] According to Art 52, a distinction is to be made between *rights* and *principles* when it comes to interpretation and application (where principles, eg, will not be directly effective in the national courts). This in turn relates to the traditional distinction between civil and political rights and economic and social rights, respectively. However, the Court has not always adhered strictly to this distinction; see eg *Viking* and *Laval*, considered in section 3.2.2.

[34] Art 51 Charter.

[35] See Case C-5/88 *Wachauf* [1989] ECR 2609; Case C-260/89 *ERT* [1991] ECR I-2925; and Case C-309/96 *Annibaldi* [1997] ECR I-7493. Cf also Case C-617/10 *Åklagaren v Hans Åkerberg Fransson*, EU:C:2013:280. See also Barnard, *EU Employment Law* (n 3) 28 *et seq*.

[36] Art 51(2). Art 52(1) clarifies that limitations on the exercise of Charter rights and freedoms must be provided for by law and respect the essence of those rights and freedoms. See further chapter 9.

[37] Case C-414/16 *Vera Egenberger v Evangelisches Werk für Diakonie und Entwicklung eV*, EU:C:2018:257.

[38] Joined Cases C-569/16 and C-570/16 *Stadt Wupperthal v Maria Elisabeth Bauer et al*, EU:C:2018:871. See further chapter 9.

[39] Directive 2001/23/EC (OJ [2001] L82/16), first adopted as Directive 77/187/EEC (OJ [1977] L61/126).

[40] Directive 98/59/EC (OJ [1998] L225/16), first adopted as Directive 75/129/EEC (OJ [1975] L48/29).

[41] Directive 2008/94/EC, first adopted as Directive 80/987/EEC (OJ [1980] L283/23).

consequences of restructuring and economic change, and aim to increase the protection of employees and to promote industrial democracy and worker participation. They are still of considerable relevance today.

The Transfers of Undertakings Directive 2001/23 aims at safeguarding the rights of employees when a business is transferred, and to provide rights to information and consultation for workers' representatives. The Directive applies to 'any transfer of an undertaking, business, or part of an undertaking or business to another employer as a result of a legal transfer or merger'. The extensive case law of the Court of Justice on the crucial concept of a transfer of an undertaking has been codified in the revised Directive, and Article 1(1)(b) now contains the following definition:

> a transfer of an economic entity which retains its identity, meaning an organised grouping of resources which has the objective of pursuing an economic activity, whether or not that activity is central or ancillary.[42]

This definition of a transfer of an undertaking in principle includes contracting out. In the case of *Rask*,[43] Philips and ISS had made an agreement according to which ISS would assume full responsibility for the running of Philips's canteens, including menu planning, preparation of food, and recruitment and training of staff. For this Philips agreed to pay ISS a fixed monthly sum and authorized ISS to use, free of charge, Philips's premises. The Court clarified that the Directive applied to a situation in which the owner of an undertaking by contract assigns to the owner of another undertaking the responsibility for running a facility for staff, previously operated directly, in return for a fee and various other benefits determined by the agreement between them. Thus, in a process of contracting out account must be taken of protecting employees' rights in accordance with Directive 2001/23.

The Directive provides that the employment relationship and the transferor's rights and obligations arising from a contract of employment (or an employment relationship) are automatically transferred on the date of the transfer to the transferee.[44] The transferee must continue to observe the terms and conditions agreed in any collective agreement on the same terms applicable to the transferor under that agreement, until the date of expiry of the collective agreement or application of another collective agreement.[45] The Directive also provides some employment protection. The transfer of the undertaking does not in itself constitute grounds for dismissal by the transferor or the transferee. However, this does not stand in the way of dismissals due to economic, technical, or organizational reasons, entailing changes in the workforce.[46]

[42] See eg Case 24/85 *Spijkers v Benedik* [1986] ECR 1119; Case 287/86 *Ny Mølle Kro* [1987] ECR 5465; Case C-392/92 *Schmidt v Spar und Leihkase* [1994] ECR I-1311; Case C-13/95 *Süzen v Zehnacker Gebäudereinigung GmbH Krankenhausservice* [1997] ECR I-1259; and Case C-101/10 *Scattolon v Ministero dell'Istruzione, dell'Universita et della ricerca* [2011] ECR I-5951.

[43] See Case C-209/91 *Rask and Christensen v ISS Kantineservice A/S* [1992] ECR I-5755.

[44] Art 3(1).

[45] Art 3(3). The Member States may limit the period for observing such terms and conditions, but not less than one year. In the much-debated *Alemo-Herron* case (Case C-426/11, EU:C:2013:82), Art 3 of the Directive, the application of collective agreements, and the freedom to conduct a business according to Art 16 of the Charter were in focus. The Court concluded that Art 3 precluded a Member State from providing that so-called dynamic clauses were enforceable against a transferee, where the transferee did not have the possibility of participating in the negotiation process of such collective agreements concluded after the date of the transfer. The Court's reasoning can be criticized for a number of reasons, such as failing to balance the fundamental right of the freedom to conduct a business to other fundamental rights of relevance to employees, such as the right of collective bargaining in Art 28. See further J Prassl, 'Freedom of Contracts as a General Principle of EU Law? Transfers of Undertakings and the Protection of Employer Rights in EU Labour Law. Case C-426/11 *Alemo-Herron and others v Parkwood Leisure Ltd*' (2013) 42 *Industrial Law Journal* 434. See, however, also Joined Cases C-680/15 and C-681/15 *Asklepios*, EU:C:2017:317, partly modifying the impact of *Alemo-Herron*.

[46] Art 4.

The Employer Insolvency Directive

The Employer Insolvency Directive applies to employees' claims from employment contracts or employment relationships against employers which are in a state of insolvency.[47] The Member States are required to put in place an institution which guarantees employees the payment of their outstanding claims for remuneration for a specific period.

Information and consultation provisions of the Transfers of Undertakings and Collective Redundancies Directives

As well as an obligation to notify the competent public authority of large-scale redundancies,[48] the Collective Redundancies Directive contains an obligation to inform and consult workers' representatives. This emphasis on information and consultation can also be found in the Transfers of Undertakings Directive. Today, EU labour law clearly emphasizes worker participation, and aims for a partial harmonization of provisions regarding information, consultation, and worker participation which is also afforded protection by Article 27 of the Charter of Fundamental Rights.[49] When employers are contemplating collective redundancies—a larger number of dismissals for one or more reasons not related to the individual workers concerned—they must begin consultations with the workers' representatives in good time with a view to reaching agreement.[50] These consultations must, at least, cover ways and means of avoiding collective redundancies or reducing the number of workers affected, and of mitigating the consequences. To enable workers' representatives to make constructive proposals, the employer must, in good time during the course of the consultations, supply workers' representatives with all relevant information, and notify them in writing of pertinent information, for example the reasons for the projected dismissals and the criteria proposed for the selection of workers to be made redundant.[51]

The Transfers of Undertakings Directive also provides that both the transferor and the transferee are required to inform the representatives of affected employees of certain matters, for example the date and reasons of the transfer and the legal, economic, and social implications of the transfer. Where the transferor or the transferee envisages measures in relation to the employees, it must consult the workers' representatives with a view to reaching an agreement.[52]

3.1.2 **European Works Councils and a general framework for information and consultation**

The Transfers of Undertakings and Collective Redundancies Directives made provision for information and consultation in the specific contexts of a transfer or collective redundancies. What about a more general duty to inform and consult workers? Within the EU, the national systems of information, consultation, and worker participation display clear

[47] Art 1. See Art 2(1) for a definition of insolvency.

[48] Arts 2 and 3, respectively.

[49] cf B Bercusson, *European Labour Law* (2nd edn, Cambridge: Cambridge University Press, 2009).

[50] Art 2.

[51] See for discussions on the timing of information and consultation, Case C-44/08 *Akavan Erityisalojen Keskusliitto AEK ry v Fujitsu Siemens Computers Oy* [2009] ECR I-8163 and Case C-12/08 *Mono Car Styling SA, in liquidation v Dervis Odemis* [2009] ECR I-6653. See also Joined Cases C-235–239/10 *Claes v Landsbanki Luxembourg* [2011] ECR I-1113 on the links between collective redundancies and employer insolvency and Case C-201/15 *AGET Iraklis*, EU:C:2016:972 on the relation between collective redundancies, freedom of establishment, and Art 16 of the Charter.

[52] A critical issue is the definition of workers' representatives. This was considered by the Court in two landmark decisions brought by the Commission against the UK; see Case C-382/92 [1994] ECR I-2435 and Case C-383/92 [1994] ECR I-2497.

differences. The legal basis varies, and there are differences in the ways in which worker participation is delivered. In *single-channel systems*, worker participation is channelled only through trade unions, while in *dual-channel systems* worker participation is channelled both through trade unions and work councils. EU law in this area has developed chronologically starting with worker participation relating to specific questions (transfers of undertakings and collective redundancies (considered in section 3.1.1)), then to worker participation in transnational companies (European Works Councils), and finally to a general framework for information and consultation at workplace level (Directive 2002/14).[53] The subject matter of information and consultation varies, and the degree of involvement varies from simple information, to consultation, and, most intense of all, consultation with a view to reaching an agreement (as with the Transfers of Undertakings and Collective Redundancies Directives).

In respect of transnational companies, several attempts to establish procedures for transnational information and consultation in the EU were made prior to the adoption of the European Works Council Directive in 1994.[54] The Preamble to the European Works Council Directive emphasizes that procedures for informing and consulting employees, regulated at national level, often are not geared to the transnational structure of the entity which makes the decisions affecting those employees. The purpose of the Directive is thus to improve the right to information and consultation of employees in Union-scale undertakings and Union-scale groups of undertakings. To that end, a European Works Council or a procedure for informing and consulting employees must be established. The Directive set up a two-stage procedure for establishing a European Works Council: first, voluntary negotiation and, secondly, mandatory (subsidiary) provisions.[55] Central management must negotiate in a spirit of cooperation with employee representatives with a view to reaching an agreement on the detailed arrangements for information and consultation of employees.

The European Works Council Directive was revised in 2009 in order, for example, to modernize the legislation, to increase the number of European Works Councils established, and to remedy the lack of legal certainty resulting from some of its provisions or the absence of certain provisions.

In respect of a general framework for information and consultation, after much discussion and political compromise the Council of Ministers finally adopted the Information and Consultation Directive in 2002.[56] The purpose of the Directive is to establish a general framework which sets out minimum requirements for the right to information and consultation of employees in undertakings or establishments within the Union. The practical arrangements for information and consultation must be defined and implemented in accordance with national law and industrial relations practices in individual Member States. Furthermore, the social partners in the Member States may, at the appropriate level, negotiate agreements, thereby 'customizing' these arrangements. The employer and employees' representatives must work in a spirit of cooperation, and the Directive provides different rules on information and consultation, such as an obligation to consult

[53] There are also further directives in the area of information, consultation, and worker participation, such as Directive 2001/86/EC supplementing the Statute for a European company with regard to the involvement of employees; Directive 2003/72/EC supplementing the Statute for a European Cooperative Society with regard to the involvement of employees; and Directive 2005/56/EC on cross-border mergers of limited liability companies.

[54] Directive 2009/38/EC (Recast), first adopted as Directive 1994/45/EC.

[55] This subsidiary provision clarifies the composition and operating methods of the European Works Council and requires that an annual information and consultation shall be held.

[56] Directive 2002/14/EC.

with a view to reaching an agreement on decisions likely to lead to substantial changes in work organization or contractual relations.[57]

3.2 **Freedom to provide services, freedom of establishment, and national collective labour law**

Cross-border issues are central to EU labour law. We will now explore the important relationship—and as it turns out, conflict—between the internal market and fundamental freedoms and national collective labour law.

3.2.1 **Freedom to provide services and posting of workers**

The free movement of services is one of the fundamental Treaty freedoms,[58] and Article 56 TFEU states that:

> restrictions on freedom to provide services within the Union shall be prohibited in respect of nationals of Member States who are established in a Member State other than that of the person for whom the services are intended.

Posting of workers—the transnational provision of services whereby a company sends ('posts') workers from one Member State (the home State) to another Member State (the host State) to fulfil a contract—raises the question of what wages and working conditions are to be applied to posted workers.[59] Should they be governed by the laws of the host State or the State of origin (home State)? If home State laws apply, then this puts services providers from a State with lower labour costs (eg one of the newer Member States) at an advantage over contractors established in the host State which must pay higher labour costs. If host State laws apply to the posted worker, this competitive advantage is lost. Famously the Court suggested in *Rush Portuguesa* that host State law would apply:

> [Union] law does not preclude Member States from extending their legislation, or collective labour agreements entered into by both sides of industry, to any person who is in employment, even temporarily, within their territory, no matter in which country the employer is established; nor does [Union] law prohibit Member States from enforcing those rules by appropriate means.[60]

However, some argued that the application of the entire body of host State law to posted workers would constitute a restriction of the free movement of services. According to the *Säger*[61] market-access line of case law, such a restriction may be accepted only if justified by overriding reasons of public interest, and if proportional—that is, if the measure is

[57] The *AMS* case (Case C-176/12, EU:C:2014:2) concerned the relationship between the Information and Consultation Directive and Art 27 of the Charter of Fundamental Rights on the right to information and consultation. The Court of Justice concluded that Art 27 could not, by itself or in conjunction with provisions of the Directive, be invoked in a dispute between individuals to conclude that a national provision contravening the Directive should not be applied.

[58] See further chapters 13 and 14.

[59] A posted worker is a worker who 'for a limited period, carries out his work in the territory of a Member State other than the State in which he normally works', Art 2 of the Posted Workers Directive. Cf Case C-815/18 *Federatie Nederlandse Vakbewegin v Van den Bosch Transporten BV, Van den Bosch Transporte GmbH, Silo-Tank kft*, EU:C:2020:319 on the concept of posted worker.

[60] Case C-113/89 *Rush Portuguesa* [1990] ECR I-1417.

[61] cf Case C-76/90 *Säger* [1991] ECR I-4221, para 12 and Case C-55/94 *Gebhard* [1995] ECR I-4165. See also C Barnard, '*Viking* and *Laval*: An Introduction' (2007–08) 10 *Cambridge Yearbook of European Legal Studies* 463.

suitable for securing the attainment of the objective pursued and does not go beyond what is necessary in order to attain it.

Article 56 TFEU is supplemented by the Posted Workers Directive 96/71,[62] adopted under a free movement Treaty base.[63] It has a twofold (and conflicting) aim: to enable the free movement of persons and services, and to provide protection for posted workers.

Article 3 of the Posted Workers Directive lays down the nucleus of mandatory rules for minimum protection, which the host Member State must ensure (regardless of the law applicable to the employment relationship) that the undertakings guarantee to workers posted to their territory. The terms and conditions in question can be laid down by law, regulation, or administrative provision, and/or by collective agreements or arbitration awards declared universally applicable within the meaning of Article 3(8). The nucleus of mandatory rules covers, for example, maximum work periods and minimum rest periods; minimum paid annual holidays; the minimum rates of pay; health, safety, and hygiene at work; and equality of treatment between men and women and other provisions on non-discrimination. Article 3(7) states that the Directive will not prevent the application of terms and conditions of employment which are more favourable to workers. Lastly, according to Article 3(10), the Directive allows Member States, in compliance with the Treaty, to apply terms and conditions of employment on matters other than those covered by the nucleus of mandatory rules for minimum protection in the case of public policy provisions, on a basis of equality of treatment.

Controversial case law developments in this area, such as *Laval*,[64] *Rüffert*,[65] and *Commission v Luxembourg*,[66] and the debate they caused, displayed a tension and difference of perspective between the old and new Member States, and Member States which are receiving and sending posted workers, respectively. This case law clarified that the Posted Workers Directive establishes only a minimum protection of a nucleus of mandatory rules, and does not provide for equal treatment of domestic and foreign employees, as a means of combating social dumping. In other words, the host State can apply its labour law rules to posted workers but only in the areas listed in Article 3(1); in all other areas home State law applies. The position in *Rush Portuguesa* is therefore no longer good law. Further, the cases showed that despite the suggestions in Article 3(7) and (10), the Directive is a *maximum* directive, establishing a 'ceiling' for the terms and conditions of employment that a trade union or a State may require foreign service providers to apply to employees. The Posted Workers Directive has subsequently been revised, for example as regards the regulation of pay (see section 3.2.2).

3.2.2 **The right to collective action**

Increasing European integration, enlargement, and cross-border activity highlight free movement and economic freedoms—as well as the need for social protection and the need to protect against social dumping. Important case law from the Court of Justice—*Viking* and *Laval*—addresses these issues (see case study 20.1). They concern, on the one hand, the EU fundamental Treaty freedoms, free movement of services, and freedom of establishment and, on the other hand, national collective labour law and fundamental trade union rights, such as the right to collective action, freedom of association, and right to collective bargaining.

Another important development post-*Laval* and *Viking* has been the reorientation of the European Court of Human Rights (ECtHR) case law regarding freedom of association, and the resulting, possibly conflicting, case law of the Court of Justice and the ECtHR. In two landmark decisions from 2008 and 2009 respectively—the case of *Demir and Baykara*

[62] Directive 96/71/EC (OJ [1997] L18/1).
[63] Arts 57(2) and 66 EC.
[64] Case C-341/05 *Laval* [2007] ECR I-11767.
[65] Case C-346/06 *Rüffert* [2008] ECR I-1989.

Case study 20.1: *Viking* and *Laval*

The *Viking* case[67] was referred by the Court of Appeal of England and Wales to the Court of Justice for a preliminary ruling. It concerned a dispute between the International Transport Workers' Federation (ITF) and the Finnish Seamen's Union (FSU) on the one hand, and Viking, a ferry operator, and its subsidiary (Viking Eesti), on the other. Viking wanted to reflag one of its vessels, the *Rosella*, from the Finnish flag to the Estonian flag, in order to reduce wage costs. As long as *Rosella* was under the Finnish flag, under Finnish law and the terms of a collective agreement Viking was obliged to pay the crew wages at the same level as those applicable in Finland. Estonian wages for crew were lower than Finnish wages. Reflagging the vessel as Estonian would enable Viking to enter into a new collective agreement. Since the ITF was running a campaign opposing such 'flags of convenience',[68] it sent out a circular to its affiliates asking them, in the name of solidarity, to refrain from entering into negotiations with Viking. The FSU gave Viking notice of a strike.

The *Laval* case[69] was referred by the Swedish Labour Court to the Court of Justice for a preliminary ruling. In May 2004, Laval, a Latvian company, posted workers from Latvia to work on Swedish building sites. The work was undertaken by a subsidiary company, and included the renovation and extension of school premises. In June 2004, Laval and the Swedish Building Workers' Union started negotiations with a view to concluding a collective agreement.[70] Laval later signed collective agreements with a *Latvian* trade union, regulating the work at the site. Consequently, no agreement was reached between Laval and the *Swedish* Building Workers' Union. In November, the Swedish Building Workers' Union started collective action in the form of a blockade at all Laval building sites, and another Swedish trade union took sympathy action. After work on the site had been interrupted for some time, the subsidiary company became bankrupt. The Latvian workers posted by Laval returned to Latvia.

Viking addressed questions on the compatibility of the right to take collective action with the freedom of establishment (Article 49 TFEU), while *Laval* addressed questions on the free movement of services (Article 56 TFEU), the right to take collective action, and the Swedish implementation of the Posted Workers Directive. Here, we leave aside the issue of the Posted Workers Directive which was considered in section 3.2.1.

In both *Viking* and *Laval*, the Court declared that collective action fell within the scope of the Treaty (even though the right to strike is excluded from the EU's competence to adopt directives according to Article 153(5) TFEU), and that Articles 56 and 49 TFEU could be invoked against trade unions. The Court, with reference to Article 28 of the Charter, also recognized the right to take collective action as a fundamental right which formed an integral part of the general principles of Union law. However, the exercise of the right to collective action could be restricted, as on the facts of these cases.

The Court then turned to the question of whether there was a breach. Although in both cases the Court emphasized that the Union not only has an economic but also a social pur-

[66] Case C-319/06 *Commission v Luxembourg* [2008] ECR I-4323. Cf also Case C-271/08 *Commission v Germany* [2010] ECR I-7091, dealing with the implementation of public procurement rules for pension services based on collective agreement.

[67] Case C-438/05 *Viking* [2007] ECR I-10779.

[68] The term 'flag of convenience' refers to the practice of registering a ship in a State different from that of the ship's owner, to reduce operating costs and avoid the regulation (labour law etc) of the State of the ship's owner.

[69] Case C-341/05 (n 64).

[70] A so-called 'application' agreement to the collective agreement for the building sector.

pose, it concluded in *Laval* that the collective action constituted a restriction on the free movement of services. It said that such a restriction was warranted only if it pursued a legitimate objective compatible with the Treaty, and was justified by overriding reasons of public interest. If that was the case, the restriction had to be suitable for securing the attainment of the objective which it pursues and could not go beyond what was necessary in order to attain this objective (the *Säger* market-access approach). The Court declared that the right to take collective action for the protection of the workers of the host State against social dumping could constitute an overriding reason of public interest. However, the specific obligations linked to the signing of the collective agreement in the building sector in *Laval* (which also went beyond the nucleus of mandatory rules for minimum protection in Article 3(1) of the Directive) could not be justified as necessary to attain such an objective.

Similarly, in *Viking* the Court found that the collective action constituted a restriction on the freedom of establishment. When it came to justification and proportionality, the Court left the assessment to the national court. However, it provided some guidance, requiring the national court to consider whether the jobs and conditions of employment of the trade union members on board the *Rosella* were jeopardized or under serious threat and, if so, whether, under the national rules and collective agreements, the trade union had other means at its disposal which were less restrictive on freedom of establishment. Only if these conditions were satisfied would the strike action be justified and proportionate. Due to the application of the *Säger* market-access approach, both *Viking* and *Laval* have been interpreted as putting fundamental Treaty freedoms and economic integration first, and trade union rights and social integration, second.[71]

The cases prompted huge and critical debate. At national level, some Member States, such as Sweden and Denmark, with an emphasis on autonomous collective bargaining, had to reform their laws on collective action and posted workers.[72]

At EU level, in 2012 the Commission put forward a proposal for a directive to improve the enforcement of the Posted Workers Directive.[73] The Enforcement Directive[74] was adopted in 2014 and established a common framework of provisions, measures, and control mechanisms necessary for better and more uniform implementation, application, and enforcement of the Posted Workers Directive. Furthermore, in 2016 the Commission presented a proposal for a targeted revision of the Posted Workers Directive to address unfair practices leading to social dumping by ensuring that the same work in the same place is rewarded by the same pay.[75] In 2018, a Directive revising the Posted Workers Directive was finally adopted.[76] This Directive addresses, for example, the rate of pay a posted worker is entitled to, long-term

[71] See eg A Davies, 'One Step Forward Two Steps Back? The *Viking* and *Laval* Cases in the ECJ' (2008) 38 *Industrial Law Journal* 126.

[72] On the legal implications of *Viking* and *Laval* in different national contexts, see eg M Freedland and J Prassl (eds), *Viking, Laval and Beyond: EU Law in the Member States* (Oxford: Hart Publishing, 2014), including M. Rönnmar, 'Sweden'.

[73] A proposal for a Monti II Regulation on the exercise of the right to take collective action in the context of freedom of establishment and the freedom to provide services was also put forward but later withdrawn, see COM(2012) 130 and COM(2012) 131. See The Adoptive Parents, 'The Life of a Death Foretold' in Freedland and Prassl (n 72).

[74] Directive 2014/67/EU (OJ [2014] L159/11).

[75] See COM(2015) 610 final and COM(2016) 128 final.

[76] Directive 2018/957/EU (OJ [2018] L173/16). The validity of the Directive was unsuccessfully challenged by Hungary and Poland: Case C-620/18 *Hungary v European Parliament and Council of the European Union*, EU:C:2020:1001.

posting,[77] and temporary work agencies. The subject matter and scope of the Posted Workers Directive is clarified, and the relationship between the Posted Workers Directive and fundamental rights, including trade union rights, is addressed.[78] In relation to pay, the Directive implies an important shift from minimum rates of pay to a broader notion of remuneration and equality of treatment between posted workers and workers in the host country.[79]

v Turkey and the case of *Enerji Yapi-Yol Sen v Turkey*[80]—the ECtHR aligned its case law with the International Labour Organization (ILO) Conventions No 87 on freedom of association and protection of the right to organize, and No 98 on the right to organize and collective bargaining, as well as the Council of Europe's European Social Charter. The freedom of association, as protected by Article 11 ECHR, is now said to comprise the right to bargain collectively and the right to industrial action.

The ILO Committee of Experts, in response to a complaint by the trade union in the *BALPA* case (a British industrial dispute which showed how trade unions could face the threat of employer claims for massive damages if they went on strike without complying with the ruling in *Viking* and *Laval* to the letter), observed with '*serious concern* the practical limitations on the effective exercise of the right to strike of the BALPA workers in this context' and declared that 'the doctrine that is being articulated in these judgements is likely to have a significant restrictive effect on the exercise of the right to strike in practice in a manner contrary to the Convention'.[81]

These different developments at the international level prompt the important question: are *Viking* and *Laval* and EU law compatible with international labour law, such as ILO Conventions, the ECHR, and the European Social Charter?[82]

3.3 **Flexible work and working conditions**

EU labour law also regulates important issues which affect the individual employment relationship. We now turn to a discussion of the regulation of flexible work and working conditions, such as health and safety and working time.

[77] When the duration of a posting exceeds 12 months, the posted workers shall be guaranteed, on the basis of equality, all the applicable terms and conditions of employment which are laid down in the Member State where the work is carried out: Art 3(1a).

[78] The Directive shall not affect the exercise of fundamental rights, such as the right to take collective action (including strike) and the right to negotiate, conclude, and enforce collective agreements: Art 1(1)(a).

[79] Posted workers are entitled to remuneration, including overtime rates, as well as conditions of workers' accommodation and allowances or reimbursement of expenditure to cover travel, board, and lodging expenses for workers away from home for professional reasons. Art 3 now also specifies that for the purposes of the Posted Workers Directive 'the concept of remuneration shall be determined by national law and/or practice of the Member State to whose territory the worker is posted and means all the constituent elements of remuneration rendered mandatory by national law, regulation or administrative provision, or by collective agreements or arbitration awards which, in that Member State, have been declared universally applicable or otherwise apply in accordance with paragraph 8'. Cf also Case C-396/13 *Sähköalojen ammattiliitto ry v Elektrobudowa spólka Akcyjna*, EU:C:2015:86.

[80] Judgment of 12 November 2008 and judgment of April 2009. See eg KD Ewing and J Hendy, 'The Dramatic Implications of *Demir and Baykara*' (2010) 39 *Industrial Law Journal* 2.

[81] cf also in 2013, the similar opinion of the ILO Committee of Experts in relation to the Swedish post-*Viking* and *Laval* legislation and the final judgment by the Swedish Labour Court in the *Laval* case, stating damage liability for the trade unions.

[82] See also the decision of the European Committee of Social Rights to Complaint No 85/2012 *Swedish Trade Union Confederation (LO) and Swedish Confederation of Professional Employees (TCO) v Sweden*, Decision on admissibility and merits, 3 July 2013, public on 20 November 2013.

3.3.1 **Part-time, fixed-term, and temporary agency work**

The process of flexibilization of the labour market has led to an increase in flexible work, such as fixed-term work, temporary agency work, self-employment, and digital platform work (see also section 3.3.2). EU labour law and employment policy have been influenced by a *flexicurity* agenda (inspired, eg, by the practice in the Netherlands and Denmark). Flexicurity is about combining flexibility for employers and security for employees, and aims at reducing labour market segmentation and increasing economic growth.[83] Flexicurity is partly about deregulation of employment protection combined with equal treatment of various forms of flexible employment, but it is also about effective active labour market policies, reliable and adaptable systems for lifelong learning, and modern social security systems. The Council has adopted Common Principles of Flexicurity and these have been integrated into the EES and the Europe 2020 Strategy, principles which have been criticized for focusing predominately on labour market flexibility and deregulation rather than employment security.

The Part-Time Work Directive,[84] Fixed-Term Work Directive,[85] and Temporary Agency Work Directive[86] form part of this flexicurity agenda. The Part-Time Work and Fixed-Term Work Directives result from the European social dialogue (considered in section 2.2). The aims of the Directives differ in part. The purpose of the Part-Time Work Directive is to provide for the removal of discrimination against part-time workers and to improve the quality of part-time work, while facilitating the development of part-time work on a voluntary basis and contributing to the flexible organization of working time in a manner which considers the needs of employers and workers.[87] The purpose of the Temporary Agency Work Directive is to ensure protection of temporary agency workers and to improve the quality of temporary agency work, while also taking into account the need to establish a suitable framework for use of temporary agency work with a view to contributing effectively to the creation of jobs and to the development of flexible forms for working.[88] The Fixed-Term Work Directive is more restrictive as regards flexibility, and its purpose is to improve the quality of fixed-term work by ensuring the application of the principle of non-discrimination, and to establish a framework to prevent abuse arising from the use of successive fixed-term employment contracts or relationships.[89] Thus, the first two Directives want to encourage this type of flexible work, while the third Directive has an emphasis on the protection of these flexible workers.

The principle of non-discrimination and equal treatment has not been given a coherent design in the Directives. In the Part-Time Work Directive and the Fixed-Term Work Directive, there is a *principle of non-discrimination*, which states that in respect of employment conditions, part-time/fixed-term workers must not be treated in a less favourable manner than comparable full-time/permanent workers solely because they work part-time/have a fixed-term contract or relation, unless that different treatment is justified on objective grounds.[90] In these two Directives, the principle of non-discrimination is

[83] See COM(2007) 359 final.

[84] Directive 97/81/EC (OJ [1998] L14/9).

[85] Directive 99/70/EC (OJ [1999] L175/43).

[86] Directive 2008/104/EC (OJ [2008] L327/9).

[87] Cl 1.

[88] Art 2. A temporary agency worker is a worker with a contract of employment or an employment relationship with a temporary-work agency with a view to being assigned to a user undertaking to work temporarily under its supervision and direction, Art 3(1)(c). See Case C-681/18 *JH v KG*, EU:C:2020:823, on the temporary nature of temporary agency work; Case C-533/13 *AKT*, EU:C:2015:173, on Art 4 and review on prohibitions or restrictions on the use of temporary agency work; and Case C-441/23 *LM v Omnitel Comunicaciones*, EU:C:2024:916 on the application of the Directive to any entity assigning workers under supervision to a user company, regardless of formal agency status.

[89] Cl 1.

[90] Cl 4 in both Directives.

limited in that it requires that any unfavourable treatment of the part-time worker or fixed-term worker must relate *solely* to the part-time work or fixed-term employment contract. It also enables the employer to justify such unfavourable treatment with objective grounds.[91] By contrast, in the Temporary Agency Work Directive the principle of equal treatment states that for the duration of their assignment at a user undertaking, the basic working and employment conditions of temporary agency workers (not all terms and conditions of employment) must be at least those which would apply if the workers had been recruited directly by that undertaking to occupy the same job.[92] There is no possibility of justifying different treatment but there are some important exceptions to the rule, including allowing States the possibility of not applying the principle of equal treatment for a certain period (see also section 4.3.2).

Employment protection is only partly regulated in these Directives.[93] For example, the Fixed-Term Work Directive prevents abuse arising from the use of successive fixed-term employment contracts or relationships. The Member States must introduce one or more of the following measures, in a manner which takes account of the needs of specific sectors and/or categories of workers:

- objective reasons justifying the renewal of such contracts or relationships;
- the maximum total duration of successive fixed-term employment contracts or relationships;
- the number of renewals of such contracts or relationships.[94]

3.3.2 **Flexible work, transparent and predictable working conditions, and digital platform work**

In 2019, a new Directive on Transparent and Predictable Working Conditions was adopted, replacing the Terms and Conditions Directive[95] from the early 1990s. The Directive aims to increase the protection for workers—including new and precarious groups of flexible workers, such as digital platform workers (or gig workers), on-demand workers, and workers with zero hours contracts. The aim of the Directive is to improve working conditions by promoting more transparent and predictable employment while ensuring labour market adaptability. In addition to the existing obligation to inform employees of their terms and conditions of employment, the Directive introduces a number of substantive provisions on, for example, a maximum duration of six months for probationary periods, requirements for minimum predictability for workers with unpredictable work patterns,

[91] Case C-313/02 *Nicole Wippel v Peek & Cloppenburg GmbH & Co KGK* [2004] ECR I-9483 is central, and discusses the aspect of comparability. Denying fixed-term workers the right to be informed of dismissal reasons is an example of discrimination, Case C-715/20 *KL v X sp z oo*, EU:C:2024:139, as is requiring part-time workers to exceed full-time hours before qualifying for overtime pay (this may also constitute indirect sex discrimination), Joined Cases C-184/22 and C-185/22 *IK and CM v KfH*, EU:C:2024:637.

[92] Art 5. The Directive provides for certain exemptions from the principle of equal treatment. These exemptions constitute adjustments to specific national contexts, and Art 5(3) provides, eg, for exemptions in collective bargaining as long as the overall protection of temporary agency workers is respected.

[93] Furthermore, Art 30 of the EU Charter of Fundamental Rights states that '[e]very worker has the right to protection against unjustified dismissal, in accordance with Community law and national laws and practices'. Employment protection aspects are also regulated by the Transfers of Undertakings and Collective Redundancies Directives, as well as different Equality Directives, which ban discriminatory dismissals.

[94] Cl 5. The Court has developed a substantial case law in relation to this provision, see eg Case C-212/04 *Adeneler* [2006] ECR I-6057; Joined Cases C-378–380/07 *Angelidaki* [2009] ECR I-3071; Case C-586/10 *Kücük*, EU:C:2012:39; and Case C-760/18 *MV and Others v Organismos Topikis Aftodioikisis (OTA)* ('*Dimos Agiou Nikolaou*'), EU:C:2021:113. Note, however, that the Directive does not introduce any requirement for objective reasons for the parties' first entry into a fixed-term employment contract.

[95] Directive 1991/533/EEC (OJ [1991] L288/32).

and measures to prevent abusive practices in relation to on-demand contracts. The scope of the Directive is linked to the notion of worker in the Member States, but consideration should be given to the EU law notion of a worker and case law from the Court of Justice (cf also section 2.1 for a discussion on this 'hybrid' notion of a worker).[96]

In recent years, there has been a growth in digital platform work, or gig work, as well as increased public debate and academic research on these workers and their working conditions.[97] A central issue in this debate has been whether digital platform workers, such as Uber drivers, are workers and thus fall within the scope of labour law protection.[98] In October 2024, the Parliament and the Council adopted the Platform Directive to improve the working conditions in platform work.[99] The Directive introduces a presumption of worker status, subject to national implementation, and lays down the first binding EU-level provisions governing algorithmic management, applicable to both employees and self-employed persons. The EU Artificial Intelligence (AI) Act, adopted in 2024, complements these developments by regulating the use of high-risk AI systems, including in the workplace where such systems affect working conditions and rights.[100] The Commission has also issued guidelines clarifying the application of EU competition law to collective agreements of solo self-employed persons.[101]

3.3.3 **Health and safety, working time, and minimum wage**

Working conditions—and their improvement—is an important aspect of EU labour law. The area of health and safety has a long-standing tradition. Two types of directives are relevant here: directives related to the harmonization of Member State regulation in the area of free movement of goods and the character and control of different products to ensure the goods are safe (so-called Product Directives); and directives related to health and safety and the working environment in the workplace (so-called Workplace Directives). The Framework Directive on Health and Safety[102] aims at introducing measures to encourage improvements in the health and safety of workers at work, and lays down minimum standards in this area.[103] It stipulates general principles on the prevention of occupational risks, the protection of health and safety, the elimination of risk and accident factors, and consultation of workers and their representatives. The employer has a duty to ensure the safety and health of workers in every aspect related to work.

In addition to the general health and safety directives, the EU has adopted one particular directive as a health and safety measure which has proved highly controversial: the Working Time Directive.[104] The aim of the Directive is to lay down minimum health and

[96] Art 1(1). See also Preamble, para 8.

[97] See eg J Prassl, *Humans as Service* (Oxford: Oxford University Press, 2018) and A Aloisi and V De Stefano, *Your Boss Is an Algorithm: Artificial Intelligence, Platform Work and Labour* (Oxford: Hart Publishing, 2022).

[98] Disputes on the worker status of digital platform workers have been brought to national courts, and some judgments from the Court of Justice have addressed legal issues related to digital platform workers, including Case C-692/19 *Yodel*, EU:C:2020:288, Case C-434/15 *Über*, EU:C:2017:981, and Case C-390/18 *AirBnB*, EU:C:2019:1112.

[99] Directive (EU) 2024/2831 (OJ [2024] L 11.11.2024).

[100] Regulation (EU) 2024/1689 (OJ [2024] L 12.7.2024).

[101] One aspect of these draft guidelines is a codification of existing case law from the Court of Justice in this area; see Case C-67/96 *Albany*, EU:C:1999:430 and Case C-413/13 *FNV Kunsten*, EU:C:2014:2411. In relation to digital platform work, AI, and labour law, see also the European social partners' Framework Agreement on Digitalisation from 2020, and the proposal for an AI regulation, COM(2021) 206 final.

[102] Directive 89/391/EEC (OJ [1989] L183/1).

[103] On the basis of the Framework Directive, a number of more specific 'daughter directives' have been adopted, cf Art 16(1).

[104] Directive 2003/88/EC (OJ [2003] L299/9). The UK unsuccessfully challenged the legal basis of the Directive (Art 118a EEC). See further Case C-84/94 *UK v Council* [1996] ECR I-5755.

safety requirements for the organization of working time. The Directive contains provisions on, for example, daily rest, breaks, weekly rest periods, maximum weekly working time, annual leave, and night work. The Directive also provides for adaptations through the use of collective agreements, as well as an 'opt-out' for Member States in relation to Article 6 and the maximum 48-hour week.[105]

According to Article 7 every worker is entitled to paid annual leave of at least four weeks, in accordance with the conditions for entitlement to, and granting of, such leave laid down by national legislation and practice. This minimum period of paid annual leave may not be replaced by an allowance in lieu, except where the employment relationship is terminated. Article 31 of the Charter on fair and just working conditions also states every worker's right to an annual period of paid leave. The Court of Justice has delivered a series of judgments in relation to paid annual leave, for example in relation to sick leave. The Court has emphasized that 'the entitlement of every worker to paid annual leave must be regarded as a particularly important principle of European union social law from which there can be no derogations'.[106] The Working Time Directive is controversial, and has been difficult to align with the demands of certain sectors, particularly health care. The Court's highly controversial rulings on the definition of working time—including stand-by time where that time is spent on the employer's premises—has increased the pressure to reform the Directive.[107] Several attempts have been made to revise the Working Time Directive, but so far they have proved unsuccessful.

The other highly controversial measure more recently adopted is the Directive on adequate minimum wages in the EU.[108] It establishes a framework for setting adequate levels of minimum wages, and access of workers to minimum-wage protection, in the form of wages set out by collective agreements or, where it exists, in the form of a statutory minimum wage, and includes provisions to promote collective bargaining. The Directive is seen as an important measure to improve working conditions and strengthen collective bargaining. However, it has also met with criticism, particularly from governments and social partners in Denmark and Sweden, where it is seen as exceeding the legislative competence of the EU (cf Article 153(5) TFEU). Subsequently, Denmark brought an action for annulment of the Directive, arguing that the Directive unlawfully intrudes on autonomous collective bargaining and wage formation at Member State level, and partly falls outside the legislative powers of the EU. In its judgment of November its judgment of November 2025, the Court of Justice largely dismissed the action, holding that the Directive pursues the objective of improving working conditions within the meaning of Article 153(1)(b) TFEU and does not, as such, regulate pay within the meaning of Article 153(5) TFEU. At the same time, the Court annulled parts of Article 5, holding that certain provisions interfered with pay and the autonomy of the social partners within the meaning of Article 153(5) TFEU, thereby, reigniting the debate on competence and subsidiarity in EU labour law.[109]

105 Art 22(1).

106 See eg Case C-173/99 *BECTU* [2001] ECR I-4881; Joined Cases C-350/06 and C-520/06 *Schultz-Hoff* [2009] ECR I-179; and Case C-282/10 *Dominguez*, EU:C:2012:33. See also Joined Cases C-569/16 and C-570/16 *Stadt Wupperthal v Maria Elisabeth Bauer et al*, EU:C:2018:871 discussed in section 2.3.

107 See eg Case C-303/98 *Simap* [2000] ECR I-7963; Case C-241/99 *CIG v Sergas* [2001] ECR I-5139; Case C-151/02 *Jaeger* [2003] ECR I-8389; Case C-344/19 *DJ v Radiotelevizija Slovenija*, EU:C:202:182; and Case C-580/19 *RJ v Stadt Offenbach am Main*, EU:C:2021:183. See also Case C-55/18, *Federación de Servicios de Comisiones Obreras (CCOO) v Deutsche Bank SAE*, EU:C:2019:402, on requirements for employers to set up a system to measure the daily working time.

108 See eg COM(2020) 682 final and L Ratti, E Brameshuber, and V Pietrogiovanni (eds), *The EU Directive on Adequate Minimum Wages: Context, Commentary and Trajectories* (Oxford: Hart Publishing, 2024).

109 Case C-19/23 *Denmark v Parliament and Council (Salaires minimaux adéquats)*, EU:C:2025:11, Opinion of AG Emiliou.

3.4 **EU and national labour law in times of crisis**

Crises, such as the global financial crisis and the Covid-19 pandemic—and the EU's and the Member States' responses—have potentially important implications for European labour markets and for labour law.

The global financial crisis, and resultant high unemployment, especially youth unemployment, had devastating effects in many EU Member States. It led to social protest and unrest, and called into question both the EU's legitimacy and its 'democratic deficit'. The responses varied among the Member States, and came in different stages. In 2008/9, many Member States first adopted crisis-related measures, such as internal flexibility, short-time working arrangements, and wage concessions. The subsequent 'eurozone' and sovereign debt crisis in 2010 led to fundamental financial and governance reforms at EU level.[110]

Since devaluation of the currency was not an option within the eurozone, focus was instead on far-reaching austerity measures (so-called internal devaluation) and deregulatory labour law reforms in many Member States.[111] These measures targeted employment protection regulation, collective bargaining, and wage-setting—at the heart of national labour law and industrial relations systems—and crucially areas which largely fall outside EU competence. The Member States that were given so-called 'bailout' packages (by the 'Troika' (the European Commission, the European Central Bank, and the IMF))—such as Greece, Portugal, and Ireland—were particularly affected. The Memoranda of Understanding accompanying the 'bailout' packages and signed by these Member States specified which labour law and labour market reforms were to be considered and introduced.

These developments were harshly criticized by the ILO, trade unions, and labour law scholars, and deep concerns were expressed, for example, as regards the disrespect for fundamental rights, the strong move towards labour market flexibilization, and the neglect of notions such as decent work and high-quality employment. These reforms were also challenged at several levels—before national constitutional courts, and before the Court of Justice, as well as before international human rights bodies, such as the ILO and the Council of Europe.[112]

The Covid-19 pandemic challenged EU integration and free movement as well as principles of human rights and solidarity. The EU put in place a comprehensive recovery plan (NextGenerationEU). Labour law, social security, and employment policy reforms—for example, as regards short-time work, health and safety and disease control, unemployment and sickness insurance benefits, and active labour market policy—were implemented at national level. Furthermore, in many Member States, collective bargaining and social dialogue played an important role in addressing the implications of the pandemic.

[110] See chapter 19, discussing the EMU and the financial governance reforms.

[111] See S Deakin and A Koukiadaki, 'The Sovereign Debt Crisis and the Evolution of Labour Law in Europe' in N Countouris and M Freedland (eds), *Resocialising Europe in a Time of Crisis* (Cambridge: Cambridge University Press, 2013).

[112] Preliminary references were made to the Court of Justice on national measures introduced as part of 'bailout' packages. In Case C-128/12 *Sindicate dos Bancários do Norte*, EU:C:2013:149, eg, salary reductions for certain public sector workers in Portugal were questioned based on the Charter of Fundamental Rights and the principles of equality and non-discrimination, and the right to fair and just working conditions. The Court, without any real explanation, found that it lacked jurisdiction, and the Court has also refused to apply the Charter in similar cases. However, Joined Cases C-8–10/15 P *Ledra*, EU:C:2016:701, related to the European Stability Mechanism (ESM), the 'bailout' package to Cyprus, and the right to property in Art 17 of the Charter of Fundamental Rights, indicated a possible change of direction. Cf also the *Pringle* case, where the ESM was challenged, but found lawful, by the Court, Case C-370/12 *Pringle*, EU:C:2012:756. See further C Kilpatrick, 'Are the Bailouts Immune to EU Social Challenge Because They Are Not EU Law?' (2014) 10 *European Constitutional Law Review* 393, and C Barnard, 'The Charter in Time of Crisis: A Case Study of Dismissal' in N Countouris and M Freedland (eds), *Resocialising Europe in a Time of Crisis* (Cambridge: Cambridge University Press, 2013) 250.

After the pandemic, there is also increased debate on working life transformation, and issues related to telework, digitalization, work–life balance, and privacy have come to the fore, provoking intense debate.

4 Equality law

4.1 Introduction to equality law

So far we have concentrated on matters considered traditionally as failing in the field of labour law. We now turn to the area where the EU has played a particularly important role, that is equality law, which has been the EU's flagship contribution to social policy. Equality law is a central and well-developed part of EU labour law—and has gradually extended its reach beyond working life. Equality law has a clear human rights basis—but also a market and economic basis. The inclusion of the equal pay provision in Article 119 EEC in the Treaty of Rome (now Article 157 TFEU) was based on an economic rationale and the concern that some Member States could gain a competitive advantage through the use of cheap female labour. In time, the human rights and social basis of equality law was strengthened. In *Defrenne (No 2)*, the Court recognized for the first time the economic *and* social aim of the Treaty provision on equal pay,[113] and in *Defrenne (No 3)* the general principle of equal treatment and non-discrimination was recognized.[114]

EU equality law first contained protection against discrimination on grounds of nationality and gender; until 1999 these were the only protected grounds. The principle of non-discrimination on the basis of nationality has been essential to European integration and the EU. EU equality law in general builds on the development and content of gender equality.[115] In 1999, through the Treaty of Amsterdam, the EU's competence in the equality field widened significantly through the inclusion of Article 13 EC (now Article 19 TFEU), which enables the EU to take appropriate action to combat discrimination based on sex, racial or ethnic origin, religion or belief, disability, age, or sexual orientation. In 2000, two important directives were adopted on the basis of Article 13 EC: the Race Directive[116] and the Employment Equality Directive,[117] covering discrimination on grounds of religion or belief, disability, age, and sexual orientation. This development is often described as a move towards comprehensive equality, which entails the protection of more and broader discrimination grounds, both within and outside working life. The Charter of Fundamental Rights in Articles 20 and 23 provides for equality before the law and equality between men and women. Article 21 contains an 'open list' of discrimination grounds and provides that:

> Any discrimination based on any ground such as sex, race, colour, ethnic or social origin, genetic features, language, religion or belief, political or any other opinion, membership of a national minority, property, birth, disability, age or sexual orientation shall be prohibited.

[113] Case 43/75 *Defrenne (No 2) v Sabena* [1976] ECR 455.

[114] Case 149/77 *Defrenne (No 3) v Sabena* [1978] ECR 1365. Cf also Case C-144/04 *Werner Mangold v Rudiger Helm* [2005] ECR I-9981 and Case C-555/07 *Seda Kücükdevici v Swedex GmbH & Co* [2010] ECR I-365. The three seminal *Defrenne* cases all concerned a female air hostess, Ms Defrenne, employed by Sabena Airlines.

[115] Later on, a more complex interplay between regulation on different grounds, and different directives, has evolved, as well as a discussion on a hierarchy of grounds, where the ban on race discrimination is the most far-reaching, while the ban on gender discrimination has firmer Treaty support and is expressed in 'stronger' legal language, see eg M Bell, 'EU Anti-Discrimination Law: Navigating Sameness and Difference' in P Craig and G de Búrca (eds), *The Evolution of EU Law* (3rd edn, Oxford: Oxford University Press, 2021).

[116] Directive 2000/43/EC.

[117] Directive 2000/78/EC.

When it comes to the development of secondary law in the area of gender equality, little happened until the 1970s, when three directives were adopted in the framework of the 1974 Social Action Programme: the Equal Pay Directive,[118] the Equal Treatment Directive,[119] and the Equal Treatment in Social Security Directive.[120] Subsequent directives included directives on occupational schemes[121] and on the self-employed.[122] All but the Equal Treatment in Social Security Directive have now been replaced by new directives: the Equal Pay, the Equal Treatment, and the Occupational Schemes Directives have all been replaced by the Recast Directive;[123] and the Self-Employed Directive has been replaced by Directive 2010/41/EU.[124] Following the Maastricht Treaty, another set of directives was adopted: the Directive on Pregnant Workers,[125] the Directive on Parental Leave,[126] and the Burden of Proof Directive.[127] The Parental Leave Directive is the result of the European social dialogue. It was first renegotiated and replaced by Directive 2010/18/EU,[128] and then in 2019 replaced by the Work-life Balance Directive.[129] In addition, in 2004 a Directive on Gender Equality in Goods and Services[130] was adopted.

From a more general perspective, Hepple has described and analysed the development of equality law in Europe since 1945 as a process from legal recognition of the right to equality in international legal instruments, to formal equality, to substantive equality, to the dawn of comprehensive and transformative equality. This development is closely connected to the protection of human rights and the value of human dignity—but also to the influence of EU law and the interventions by the Court of Justice. This development has also been intertwined with social, political, and economic developments, such as increased labour market participation for women, increased migration, a shift from standard to flexible employment, an ageing population, and restructuring and globalization.[131]

The Equality Directives are generally based on a human rights model: the prohibition against discrimination is designed as an individual right and enforced through complaints to the courts. Traditionally discrimination law was based on *formal equality*, and linked to the liberal tradition and the Aristotelian thesis of 'what is alike shall be treated alike'. Yet EU law has recognized a role for *substantive equality* (ie equality as regards outcome and results) as well, for example, by bans on indirect discrimination, rules on a reversed burden of proof, and provisions on positive action. A proactive mainstreaming approach—to aim to eliminate inequalities, to promote equality between men and women, and to combat discrimination—has also been developed and enforced, and now enjoys Treaty support.[132] The role of soft law has also been important, often paving the way for hard law measures.

Today, the Equality and Non-Discrimination Directives are aligned to a great extent and contain protection, for example by way of the prohibition on direct and indirect discrimination, harassment, and instructions to discriminate, with scope for positive action, and the reversed burden of proof. Discrimination based on gender is prohibited in employment,

[118] Directive 75/117/EEC. [119] Directive 76/207/EC. [120] Directive 79/7/EEC.

[121] Directive 96/97/EC, amending Directive 86/378/EEC (OJ [1997] L46/20).

[122] Directive 86/61/EEC (OJ [1986] L359/5). [123] Directive 2006/54/EC (OJ [2006] L204/23).

[124] Directive 2010/41/EU (OJ [2010] L180/1). [125] Directive 92/85/EEC (OJ [1992] L348/1).

[126] Directive 96/34/EC (OJ [1996] L145/4). [127] Directive 97/80/EC (OJ [1998] L14/6).

[128] Directive 2010/18/EU (OJ [2010] L68/13).

[129] Directive 2019/1158/EU (OJ [2019] L188/79). Directive 97/80/EC is now covered by the Recast Directive and work on revising the Directive on Pregnant Workers has as yet been unsuccessful.

[130] Directive 2004/113/EC.

[131] See B Hepple, 'Equality Law' in Hepple and Veneziani, *The Transformation of Labour Law in Europe* (n 3). Bell, in turn, has discussed this development in terms of widening and deepening: M Bell, 'The Principle of Equal Treatment: Widening and Deepening' in Craig and de Búrca, *The Evolution of EU Law* (n 115).

[132] Art 3(3) TEU and Arts 8 and 10 TFEU.

vocational training, occupational social security benefits, social security, and access to and supply of goods and services, while discrimination based on religion or belief, disability, age, and sexual orientation is prohibited in employment and vocational training only. The protection against race discrimination is the most far-reaching, and applies to employment, vocational training, social protection, including social security and health care, as well as social advantages, education, and access to and supply of goods and services.

4.2 **Gender equality**

4.2.1 **Evolution**

The Treaty provision on equal pay, now Article 157 TFEU, forms the starting point for EU gender equality law. Article 157 TFEU is both horizontally and vertically directly effective, and thus applies not only to the Member States but also to private employers. Article 157(3) TFEU, introduced at Amsterdam, gives the European Parliament and the Council the power to adopt measures to 'ensure the application of the principle of equal opportunities and equal treatment of men and women in matters of employment and occupation, including the principle of equal pay for equal work or work of equal value'.

Seven of the sex equality directives were recast and consolidated in the Recast Directive.[133] Sex is broadly construed: in *P v S and Cornwall County Council*,[134] the Court of Justice interpreted the concept of sex to include gender reassignment (though not sexual orientation[135]). The Recast Directive sought to bring about simplification, modernization, and improvement of EU law in this area, and the aim of the Directive is to 'ensure the implementation of the principle of equal opportunities and equal treatment of men and women in matters of employment and occupation'.[136] It applies to access to employment, including promotion, and to vocational training, to working conditions, including pay, and to occupational social security schemes.

The Directive bans direct and indirect discrimination, and discrimination here includes harassment, sexual harassment, instruction to discriminate, and any less favourable treatment of women related to pregnancy or maternity leave within the meaning of Directive 92/85/EEC (section 4.2.4).[137] Member States may maintain or adopt positive-action measures within the meaning of Article 157(4) TFEU, with a view to ensuring full equality in practice between men and women in working life, that is, *substantive equality*. *Direct discrimination*, closely related to formal equality, refers to the situation 'where one person is treated less favourably on grounds of sex than another is, has been or would be treated in a comparable situation'.[138] Direct discrimination requires no motive or intention to discriminate. It is enough if the less favourable treatment is grounded upon or caused by, in this case, gender. However, in principle, there is a need to identify an actual or hypothetical comparator.[139]

As a basic premise, direct discrimination cannot be justified. However, there are some exemptions from the equal treatment principle, such as provisions for the protection of women, especially as regards pregnancy and maternity, and as regards employment where 'by reason of the nature of the particular occupational activities concerned or the context in which they are carried out such a characteristic (eg gender) constitutes a genuine and determining occupational requirement' (GOR). So a requirement for a woman

133 Which was adopted under Art 141(3) EC, now Art 157(3) TFEU.

134 Case C-13/94 *P v S* [1996] ECR I-2143.

135 cf Case C-249/96 *Grant v South-West Trains* [1998] ECR I-621.

136 Art 1. 137 Art 2. 138 Art 2(1)(a).

139 This is, however, not the case in regard to pregnancy discrimination. See section 4.2.4.

to play Juliet and a man Romeo is likely to satisfy the GOR test, provided the objective is legitimate and the requirement proportionate.[140] Added to this is the scope for positive discrimination (eg allowing employers to appoint a woman to a job where she is equally qualified with a man but women are underrepresented).[141]

The ban on *indirect* discrimination, a step towards the realization of substantive equality, was first developed by the Court of Justice, and inspired by the concept of disparate impact in US law. The ban on indirect discrimination targets measures which are discriminatory in effect. Today, *indirect discrimination* refers to the situation:

> where an apparently neutral provision, criterion or practice would put persons of one sex at a particular disadvantage compared with persons of the other sex, unless that provision, criterion or practice is objectively justified by a legitimate aim, and the means of achieving that aim are appropriate and necessary.[142]

4.2.2 **Pay**

The early cases of indirect discrimination, such as *Jenkins* and *Bilka-Kaufhaus*,[143] related to unfavourable working conditions for part-time workers, usually women. This situation is now largely covered by the Part-Time Work Directive 97/81 discussed earlier. Article 4 of the Recast Directive contains the principle of equal pay and provides that:

> for the same work or for work to which equal value is attributed direct and indirect discrimination on grounds of sex with regard to all aspects and conditions of remuneration shall be eliminated. In particular where a job classification system is used for determining pay, it shall be based on the same criteria for both men and women and so drawn up as to exclude any discrimination on grounds of sex.

The concept of pay is broad and refers to the 'ordinary basic or minimum wage or salary and any other consideration, whether in cash or in kind, which the worker receives directly or indirectly in respect of his/her employment from his/her employer'.[144] Despite the comprehensive EU legal regulation on equal pay, the effective implementation and enforcement of the equal pay principle has continued to be a challenge. In 2023, the Pay Transparency Directive was adopted, aimed to strengthen the application of the principle of equal pay for equal work or work of equal value between men and women.[145] The Directive includes provisions on pay transparency prior to employment, in pay setting, and in pay progression policy, rights for workers to request information on their individual pay and average pay levels, employer reporting on gender pay gaps, joint pay assessment by employers and workers' representatives, and social dialogue. It also includes provisions on access to justice, remedies, and enforcement.

[140] Art 14(2).

[141] Art 3. See Case C-158/97 *Badeck* [2000] ECR I-1875, cf also Case C-450/94 *Kalanke* [1995] ECR I-3051 and Case C-409/95 *Marschall* [1997] ECR I-6363.

[142] Art 2(1)(b).

[143] Case C-96/80 *Jenkins* [1981] ECR 911 and Case C-170/84 *Bilka-Kaufhaus* [1986] ECR 1607. Cf also Case C-167/97 *R v Secretary of State for Employment, ex p Nicole Seymore-Smith and Laura Perez* [1999] ECR I-623, concerning coverage of employment protection.

[144] Art 2(1)(e). See also eg Case C-427/11 *Kenny*, EU:C:2013:122. See further Barnard, *EU Employment Law* (n 3) 298 *et seq* on, eg, the scope for objective justification and the concept of pay.

[145] Directive 2023/970/EU (OJ [2023] L132/21), also introducing a provision on intersectional discrimination in EU law.

4.2.3 **Harassment**

Harassment is defined as unwanted conduct related to the sex of a person with the purpose or effect of violating the dignity of a person, and of creating an intimidating, hostile, degrading, humiliating, or offensive environment,[146] while *sexual harassment* is defined as 'where any form of unwanted verbal, non-verbal or physical conduct of a sexual nature occurs, with the purpose or effect of violating the dignity of a person, in particular when creating an intimidating, hostile, degrading, humiliating or offensive environment'. This is per se discriminatory.

4.2.4 **The reversed burden of proof and remedies**

The protection and efficiency of equality law has been increased by the reversed burden of proof, developed by the Court, and subsequently codified in secondary law (first in the Burden of Proof Directive, now in the Recast Directive). When 'persons who consider themselves wronged because the principle of equal treatment has not been applied to them establish before a court or other competent authority, facts from which it may be presumed that there has been direct or indirect discrimination, it shall be for the respondent to prove that there has been no breach of the principle of equal treatment'.[147]

The Directive also contains provisions on victimization, sanctions and remedies, procedures, and the need for Member States to take adequate measures to promote social dialogue between the social partners, with a view to fostering equal treatment. The Treaty-based mainstreaming approach directed at the EU is complemented here by a similar obligation for the Member States to take equality between men and women into account when formulating and implementing law, regulations, and administrative provisions, as well as policies and activities in the areas referred to in the Directive.[148]

4.2.5 **Pregnancy, maternity, and parental leave**

While most of the EU gender equality law is premised on the idea that men and women should be treated equally, for obvious reasons this does not work in the case of pregnancy and maternity.[149] The Court first clarified in *Dekker*[150] that discrimination on grounds of pregnancy constitutes direct discrimination on grounds of sex, as pregnancy is intrinsically linked to the female sex. In these cases, there is no need for a comparator. This is now codified in the Recast Directive, according to which gender discrimination includes 'any less favourable treatment of a woman related to pregnancy'.[151] In the case law, the Court has applied this principle, for example in cases of appointment, dismissal and employment, and working conditions.[152] According to the Recast Directive, 'a woman on maternity leave shall be entitled after the end of her period of maternity leave, to return to her job or to an equivalent post on terms and conditions which are no less favourable to her

[146] Art 2(1)(c). [147] Art 19. [148] Art 29.

[149] The first Equal Treatment Directive (76/207/EEC) contained no specific provisions for rights for pregnant workers. It allowed, as does Art 28(1) of the Recast Directive, for employers to make special provisions, derogating from the principles of equal treatment, to protect pregnant workers and women on maternity leave.

[150] Case C-177/88 *Dekker v Stichting Vormingscentrum voor Junge Volwassen Plus* [1990] ECR I-3941.

[151] Art 2(2)(c).

[152] See also eg Case C-506/06 *Sabine Mayr v Bäckerei und Konditorei Gerhard Flöckner OHG* [2008] ECR I-1017 as regards *in vitro* fertilization; cf also Case C-207/98 *Mahlburg* [2000] ECR I-549 and Case C-109/00 *Tele Danmark* [2001] ECR I-6993. As regards questions of remuneration in cases of pregnancy and maternity leave, the developments have been less straightforward and the protection is in some cases weaker. See further Case C-342/93 *Gillespie v Northern Health and Social Services Boards* [1996] ECR I-475, and P Foubert, *The Legal Protection of the Pregnant Worker in the European Market* (Dordrecht: Kluwer Law International, 2002).

and to benefit from any improvement in working conditions to which she would have been entitled during her absence'.

In 1992, the Directive on Pregnant Workers was adopted, to improve safety and health at work of pregnant workers, and workers who have recently given birth or who are breastfeeding. This Directive applies to 'workers' as defined by EU law in the areas of free movement of workers and equal pay. It obliges the employer to assess health and safety risks and to take necessary measures to prevent such risks. If it is impossible to adjust the working situation, the employee has a right to leave with pay and benefits intact. In addition, workers are entitled to three specific forms of protection: first, to time off, without loss of pay, in order to attend antenatal examinations; secondly, to a continuous period of at least 14 weeks' maternity leave, of which at least two mandatory weeks before and/or after confinement (compensated at least at sick pay level);[153] and, thirdly, protection against dismissal during the period from the beginning of their pregnancy to the end of their maternity leave, save in exceptional cases not connected with their condition which are permitted under national law and practice.[154] Furthermore, any less favourable treatment of a woman related to pregnancy or maternity leave also constitutes gender discrimination according to the Recast Directive.[155]

In 1996, the European social partners at cross-industry level concluded, as a result of the European Social Dialogue (see section 2.2), their first Framework Agreement on Parental Leave, later adopted as the Parental Leave Directive, renegotiated and replaced by Directive 2010/18/EU, and in 2019 replaced by the Work-life Balance Directive. The Work-life Balance Directive lays down minimum requirements designed to achieve equality between men and women with regard to labour market opportunities and treatment at work, by facilitating the reconciliation of work and family life for workers who are parents or carers.[156] The Directive provides for individual rights related to paternity leave, parental leave and carers' leave, and flexible working arrangements for parents and carers. Fathers[157] are entitled to an individual right to paid paternity leave of at least ten working days around the time of birth of a child.[158] Both parents are entitled to an individual right to parental leave of four months to be taken before the child reaches a specified age, up to the age of eight, to be defined by each Member State or by collective agreement. Two months of parental leave must not be transferable.[159] The Directive also introduces a right to carers' leave,[160] and a right to request flexible working arrangements.[161] To conclude, while the Work-life Balance Directive strengthens parental rights and emphasizes the reconciling of parenthood and working life, many crucial issues are left to the Member States to regulate.

4.2.6 Gender equality beyond the workplace

When it comes to gender equality beyond working life, the Equal Treatment in Social Security Directive 79/7, adopted in the 1970s, aims at the progressive implementation of the principle of equal treatment for men and women in matters of social security and social protection. The ban on direct and indirect discrimination applies to the working population, including self-employed persons, and to statutory social security schemes in

[153] Arts 8 and 11.

[154] Art 10. See *Tele Danmark* (n 152), where the Court stated that the prohibition of dismissal applies both to employment contracts of an indefinite duration and to fixed-term contracts, and Case C-438/99 *Melgar (Jiménez) v Ayuntamiento de Los Barrios* [2001] ECR I-6915, where the Court recognized the direct effect of Art 10.

[155] Art 2(2)(c). [156] Art 1.

[157] Or, where and insofar as recognized by national law, equivalent second parents.

[158] Art 4. [159] Art 5. [160] Art 6. [161] Art 9.

relation to sickness, invalidity, old age, accidents at work and occupational diseases, and unemployment (and social assistance, insofar as it is intended to supplement or replace these schemes).[162]

The Directive on Gender Equality in Goods and Services adopted in 2004 on the basis of Article 13 EC, extends the scope of gender equality law to the access to and supply of goods and services. The aim of the Directive is:

> to lay down a framework for combating discrimination based on sex in access to and supply of goods and services with a view to putting into effect in the Member States the principle of equal treatment between men and women.

As with the Recast Directive, direct and indirect discrimination, harassment and sexual harassment, and instruction to discriminate are all prohibited, and these bans apply to goods and services which are available to the public in both public and private sectors, as long as they are offered outside the area of private and family life.[163] Most notable in this Directive is Article 5(1), which provides that Member States must ensure in all new contracts that the use of sex as a factor in the calculation of premiums and benefits in insurance and related financial services will not result in differences in an individual's premiums and benefits. In *Test-Achats*,[164] the Court used Articles 21 and 23 of the Charter of Fundamental Rights and the general principle of equal treatment for men and women to invalidate Article 5(2), which allowed for an exemption from the main rule and a possibility for the Member States to permit proportionate differences in an individual's premium and benefits in these cases (eg the UK relied on Article 5(2) to justify allowing the insurance industry to charge higher insurance premiums to young male drivers than to young female drivers).[165]

4.3 **Comprehensive equality and protection against discrimination on other grounds**

4.3.1 **Discrimination on grounds of racial or ethnic origin**

The Race Directive 2000/43 aims at combating discrimination on grounds of racial or ethnic origin.[166] The Directive applies in employment, vocational training, social protection, including social security and health care, social advantages, education, and access to and supply of goods and services, and contains protection against direct and indirect discrimination, harassment, and instructions to discriminate as well as the rule on a reversed burden of proof. The Directive provides scope for positive action, as well as an exemption for genuine and determining occupational requirements.

Article 2(2)(a) of the Race Directive states that direct discrimination requires *one person* to have been treated less favourably than another. Despite this, the Court found in

[162] The Self-Employed Directive complements the Recast Directive and the Equal Treatment in Social Security Directive with provisions on the principle of equal treatment between men and women engaged in an activity in a self-employed capacity, or contributing to the pursuit of such an activity.

[163] Art 3. However, the Directive does not apply to the content of media, advertising, and education.

[164] Case C-236/09 *Association Belge des Consommateurs Test-Achats ASBL v Conseil des ministres* [2011] ECR I-773.

[165] In June 2022, ten years after a proposal for a directive was first presented, the European Parliament and the Council agreed on Directive 2022/2381, improving the gender balance among non-executive directors of companies listed on stock exchanges and related measures, cf COM(2012) 614 final.

[166] Art 1. The concept of racial or ethnic origin is not defined in the Directive. However, differences of treatment based on nationality is not covered. Compare also the Preamble that states that the 'European Union rejects theories which attempt to determine the existence of separate human races. The use of the term "racial origin" in this Directive does not imply an acceptance of such theories'.

Firma Feryn[167] that a public statement by an employer that he would not recruit employees of a certain ethnic or racial origin constituted direct discrimination, even though there was no identified victim. This has been called *discrimination by declaration*.

4.3.2 **Discrimination on grounds of religion or belief, disability, age, or sexual orientation**

The Employment Equality Directive lays down a general framework for combating discrimination on the grounds of religion or belief, disability, age, or sexual orientation, as regards employment and occupation. Like the Race Directive, this Directive contains protection against direct and indirect discrimination, harassment, and instructions to discriminate, as well as a rule on a reversed burden of proof. The Directive provides a scope for positive action, as well as an exemption for genuine and determining occupational requirements. Both the Race Directive and the Employment Equality Directive contain provisions on victimization, sanctions and remedies, and procedures.

In the area of *religion or belief*, the Court of Justice has dealt with a number of cases relating to restrictions on the use of headscarves. In *Achbita*,[168] the employee was dismissed for her insistence on wearing an Islamic headscarf at work in contravention of the employer's internal rule and neutrality policy, and in *Bougnaoui*[169] the employee was dismissed for her refusal to remove her Islamic headscarf when sent on assignment to customers of her employer. The Court of Justice aligned its interpretation of the concept of religion in the context of the Directive to the interpretation of Article 9 of the European Convention on Human Rights and Article 10 of the EU Charter of Fundamental Rights, and referred also to constitutional traditions common to the Member States. In *Achbita*, the Court clarified that it is not inconceivable that the internal rule introduces a difference of treatment that is indirectly based on religion or belief if it is established that the apparently neutral obligation it encompasses results in persons adhering to a particular religion or belief being put at a particular disadvantage. Such a difference of treatment does not amount to indirect discrimination if it is objectively justified by a legitimate aim, and if the means of achieving that aim are appropriate and necessary. In this context, the Court emphasized the managerial prerogative, and its recognition in the freedom to conduct a business in Article 16 of the Charter.

In *Bougnaoui*, the Court of Justice said, in relation to Article 4(1) and the notion of a genuine and determining occupational requirement, that it is not the ground on which the difference of treatment is based, but a characteristic related to that ground, which must constitute a genuine and determining occupational requirement. The Court also emphasized that a characteristic related, in particular, to religion may only, in very limited circumstances, constitute a genuine and determining occupational requirement. Joined Cases *WABE* and *MH Müller Handels*[170] confirmed this case law, and further developed the Court's reasoning on the distinction between direct and indirect discrimination and justification of differential treatment. This case law does not establish a general ban on headscarves in the workplace. Instead, the judgments imply that employers, under certain circumstances, may ban employees from wearing headscarves. These circumstances

[167] Case C-54/07 [2008] ECR I-5187. This judgment was later confirmed by the Court of Justice in Case C-81/12 *ACCEPT*, EU:C:2013:275 and Case C-507/18 *NH v Associazione Avvocatura per i diritti LGBTI—Rete Lenford*, EU:C:2020:289.

[168] Case C-157/15 *Samira Achbita, Centrum voor gelijkheid van kansen en voor racismebestrijding v G4S Secure Solutions NV*, EU:C:2017:203.

[169] Case C-188/15 *Asma Bougnaoui, Association de défense des droits de l'homme (ADDH) v Micropole SA, formerly Micropole Univers SA*, EU:C:2017:204.

[170] Joined Cases C-804/18 and C-341/19 *IX v WABE eV and MH Müller Handels GmbH v MJ*, EU:C:2021:594.

relate, for example, to the establishment of a neutrality policy, and the genuine, consistent, and systematic application of that policy.[171] In *OP v Commune d'Ans*, the CJEU held that, in public administration, a general and neutral prohibition of visible signs of religious or philosophical belief may be justified under the legitimate aim of ensuring a fully neutral administrative environment, and not constitute indirect religious discrimination provided that the policies are appropriate, necessary, and proportionate in light of the specific context.[172]

In the area of *disability*, Article 5 regulates the issue of reasonable accommodation and states that 'employers shall take appropriate measures, where needed in a particular case, to enable a person with a disability to have access to, participate in, or advance in employment, or to undergo training, unless such measures would impose a disproportionate burden on the employer'. In *Coleman*,[173] a woman was found to have suffered discrimination when she was treated less favourably and harassed because of her son's disability, so-called 'transferred' or 'associated discrimination'. The Court held that the applicability of the ban on discrimination was not dependent on 'a particular category of persons' but by reference to the grounds protected by the Directive.[174]

The EU Member States and the EU have signed the United Nations Convention on the Rights of Persons with Disabilities. In *HK Danmark*,[175] the Court aligned its interpretation of the concept of disability with that of the UN Convention and declared that the Convention formed an integral part of the EU legal order, wherefore the Directive had to 'as far as possible, be interpreted in a manner consistent with that Convention'.[176] The Court also clarified that a reduction in working hours may constitute one of the reasonable accommodation measures referred to in Article 5.[177]

Age, as a ground for discrimination, and the legal regulation of age discrimination, stand out in some respects. The protection against age discrimination covers all chronological ages; thus, both old people and young people are protected. Discrimination on grounds of age—even direct discrimination—can be justified to a greater extent than discrimination on other grounds. This is related to the traditional role age is assigned in the labour market and in labour law. Article 6 states that Member States 'may provide that differences of treatment on grounds of age shall not constitute discrimination, if, in the

[171] See also, on discrimination on grounds of religion, Art 4(2) of the Directive and genuine, legitimate, and justified occupational requirement, Case C-414/16 *Vera Egenberger v Evangelisches Werk für Diakonie und Entwicklung eV*, EU:C:2018:257, also addressing the direct horizontal effect of Art 21 of the EU Charter (section 2.3), and Case C-148/22 *OP v Commune d'Ans*, EU:C:2023:924. See also M Bell, 'Leaving Religion at the Door? The European Court of Justice and Religious Symbols in the Workplace' (2017) 17 *Human Rights Law Review* 784.

[172] Case C-148/22 *Commune d'Ans*, 28 November 2023.

[173] Case C-303/06 [2008] ECR I-5603.

[174] Ibid, para 50.

[175] Joined Cases C-335/11 and C-337/11 *HK Danmark*, EU:C:2013:222, cf also Case C-152/11 *Odar*, EU:C:2012:772.

[176] The Court also discussed the issue of illness, and stated that 'if a curable or incurable illness entails a limitation which results in particular from physical, mental or physiological impairments which in interaction with various barriers may hinder the full and effective participation of the person concerned in professional life on an equal basis with other workers, and the limitation is a long-term one, such an illness can be covered by the concept of "notions of disability" within the meaning of Directive 2000/78' (*HK Danmark* (n 175) para 41). The Court, however, also, with reference to its earlier case and illness (see Case C-13/05 *Chacón Navas* [2006] ECR I-6488), held that 'Illness as such cannot be regarded as a ground in addition to those in relation to which Directive 2000/78 prohibits discrimination' (*HK Danmark* (n 175) para 42). Cf also Case C-354/13 *FOA*, EU:C:2014:2463. As regards the interpretation of Arts 20, 21, and 26 of the Charter of Fundamental Rights and the integration of persons with disabilities, see Case C-356/12 *Glatzel*, EU:C:2014:350.

[177] In Case C-485/20 *XXXX v HR Rail SA*, EU:C:2022:85, the Court of Justice held that reassignment to another post may also constitute a reasonable accommodation measure.

context of national law, they are objectively and reasonably justified by a legitimate aim, including legitimate employment policy, labour market, and vocational training objectives, and if the means of achieving that aim are appropriate and necessary'. There is extensive case law around age discrimination, and particularly 'old-age' discrimination. The first case was *Mangold* in 2005, which created a lot of attention and debate.[178] In this case, the Court unexpectedly declared that not only was age discrimination covered by the Employment Equality Directive, but also that EU law encompassed an (independent) general principle of non-discrimination on grounds of age which might have some form of horizontal application.[179] This was reaffirmed in 2010 in *Kücükdevici*.[180]

Many of the cases have dealt with mandatory retirement rules, and whether these are acceptable, despite the ban on age discrimination. Mandatory retirement is covered by the Employment Equality Directive, and the Court basically deems rules on mandatory retirement to be age discriminatory but can nevertheless be justifiable.[181] The Member States have been given a large margin of appreciation, and when applying Article 6 the Court has found the differences of treatment on grounds of age to be objectively and reasonably justified by legitimate aims, such as intergenerational fairness in terms of access to employment, prevention of humiliating forms of termination of employment, and a reasonable balance between labour market and budgetary concerns. In addition, the means for achieving these aims have frequently been found appropriate and necessary, especially where the individual is entitled to a pension on retirement.[182]

In the area of *sexual orientation*, the case *ACCEPT*,[183] on discrimination in recruitment of a football player and the case *NH v Associazione Avvocatura per i diritti LGBTI—Rete Lenford*,[184] on discrimination in recruitment of persons in a law firm, confirmed the case *Firma Feryn* and the principle of *discrimination by declaration*. Furthermore, in the case *Maruko*[185] the Court held that a survivor's benefit granted under an occupational pension scheme fell within the scope of Directive 2000/78/EC, and that Articles 1 and 2 precluded legislation under 'which, after the death of his life partner, the surviving partner does not receive a survivor's benefit equivalent to that granted to a surviving spouse, even though, under national law, life partnership places persons of the same sex in a situation comparable to that of spouses so far as concerns that survivor's benefit'.[186]

The Equality Directives just discussed are all premised on the principle of equal treatment. Thus, in common with the atypical work directives—Part-Time Work, Fixed-Term Work, and Temporary Agency Work Directives—the equality directives use principles of non-discrimination and equal treatment as a way of protecting employees and improving the quality of flexible work (section 3.3.1). However, neither of these principles is phrased expressly in terms of prohibitions on direct and indirect discrimination or harassment and instruction to discriminate in the atypical work directives, which would put them in line with the Recast, Race, or Employment Equality Directives. In addition, these principles

[178] Case C-144/04. [179] See further chapter 6.

[180] Case C-555/07. Cf also Case C-441/14 *Dansk Industri (DI), acting on behalf of Ajos A/S v Estate of Karsten Eigil Rasmussen*, EU:C:2016:278.

[181] eg in Case C-411/05 *Palacios de la Villa* [2007] ECR I-8531, Case C-388/07 *Age Concern England*, EU:C:2009:128, and Case C-45/09 *Rosenbladt* [2010] ECR I-09391.

[182] See further A Numhauser-Henning and M Rönnmar (eds), *Age Discrimination and Labour Law. Comparative and Conceptual Perspectives in the EU and Beyond* (Alphen aan den Rijn: Kluwer Law International, 2015).

[183] Case C-81/12 *ACCEPT*, EU:C:2013:275.

[184] Case C-507/18 *NH v Associazione Avvocatura per i diritti LGBTI—Rete Lenford*, EU:C:2020:289.

[185] Case C-267/06 *Maruko* [2008] ECR I-1757.

[186] See also Case C-258/17 *EB v Versicherungsanstalt öffentlich Bediensteter BVA*, EU:C:2019:17, on the future effects of the ban on discrimination on grounds of sexual orientation.

of non-discrimination and equal treatment display a basic difference with regard to traditional equality law. Here, equal treatment is not based on the personal characteristics of the employee (such as race, age, or sexual orientation), but instead on the employment contract and its form and content. This problem is reflected in the *Wippel* case, where full-time workers who were working under a contract which fixed a working week of 38.5 hours were found not to be comparable to Ms Wippel, who was working on a 'work-on-demand' contract.[187]

5 Conclusion

Today, EU labour and equality law enjoy elaborate Treaty support and encompass a large body of secondary law, mainly comprising directives. The Court has developed a rich case law in these areas. This chapter has dealt with many different—though not all—issues of labour and equality law, such as restructuring of enterprises; information, consultation, and worker participation; fundamental Treaty freedoms and national collective labour law; flexible work and working conditions; digitalization and AI, the EU and national labour law in times of crisis; and gender equality, comprehensive equality, and protection against discrimination on other grounds.

We have witnessed an increasing constitutionalization of EU labour and equality law, and apart from the EU Charter of Fundamental Rights the Treaty aim of a social market economy and the European Pillar of Social Rights influence current and future developments. Equality law has continuously expanded its scope beyond working life, and in recent years the Court has strengthened and clarified the protection against discrimination in different ways. At the same time, developments related to posted workers, Brexit, the Covid-19 pandemic, economic crisis, and increased division in Europe have fundamentally challenged national labour law and the EU and social Europe.

Thus, EU labour and equality law will continue to face important societal and economic challenges. The challenges also relate to developments, such as the war in Ukraine, climate change, enlargement, ageing populations, segmented labour markets, and vulnerable groups of workers. A key question will be how to find the appropriate balance between competing interests, as well as between competing rights.

Further reading

C Barnard, 'EU "Social" Policy: From Employment Law to Labour Market Reform' in P Craig and G de Búrca (eds), *The Evolution of EU Law* (3rd edn, Oxford: Oxford University Press, 2021)

M Bell, 'EU Anti-Discrimination Law: Navigating Sameness and Difference' in P Craig and G de Búrca (eds), *The Evolution of EU Law* (3rd edn, Oxford: Oxford University Press, 2021)

A Bogg, C Costello, and ACL Davies, *Research Handbook on EU Labour Law* (Cheltenham: Edward Elgar, 2016)

B Hepple and B Veneziani (eds), *The Transformation of Labour Law in Europe: A Comparative Study of 15 Countries 1945–2004* (Oxford: Hart Publishing, 2009)

C Hiessl, *EU Labour Law: A Commentary* (Alphen aan den Rijn: Kluwer Law International, 2025)

T Jaspers, F Pennings, and S Peters (eds), *European Labour Law* (2nd edn, Cambridge: Intersentia, 2024)

B teer Haar and Attila Kun (eds), *EU Collective Labour Law* (Cheltenham: Edward Elgar Publishing, 2021)

[187] Case C-313/02 *Wippel* (n 91).

21

EU health law

Tamara K Hervey

1 Introduction

EU health law is 'transversal'. Cutting across different areas of EU law, it is found in surprising places, especially to health lawyers and health policy makers.

Before the EU legislature gained formal competence to adopt health measures, it relied on implied competence, based on Article 2 EEC. Explicit competence to adopt *public* health measures, complementing national competences, was given to the EU legislature by the Treaty of Maastricht. But much of the EU's health law is based on other competence provisions, in particular those on the internal market. When the EU legislature adopts measures in other fields that affect health, it is obliged to 'take into account' 'requirements linked to . . . the protection of human health'. This 'mainstreaming' obligation is found in Articles 9 and 168(1) TFEU.

EU health law has also unfolded through 'directly effective' provisions of the TFEU, especially those on free movement of the factors of production, and on free and fair competition, and on the legislation that supports those measures. The CJEU has found that EU law on free movement of goods, services, workers, and freedom of establishment, as well as on anticompetitive agreements, and abuse of a dominant position, applies in health contexts. EU health law has thus been developed through litigation, not only through Treaty reform and EU legislation.

As we will see in this chapter, EU health law is an excellent case study illustrating many important questions for EU lawyers. What is an appropriate balance in EU law between the 'economic' (free trade, fair competition) and the 'social' (protecting human health, making provision for health care through a national welfare system)? When does public health justify limiting free movement, such as in the case of a global pandemic? Does EU law push health care systems towards an 'individual services' model, based on patient choice, and away from a 'welfare system' model, based on equitable care, and maximizing efficiency from public resources, through providing cost-effective care using public services? Where should these questions be determined? Is it appropriate that they are decided by the CJEU and national courts, through preliminary references, or should legislation be involved? Where legislative or administrative decisions affect human health, which interests should be represented in those decision-making processes, and how should they be represented? If legislation or administrative action is to be involved, should it be taken at regional, national, EU, or even global level? What, if anything, does EU law mean for global (health) equality, like access to vaccines?

This chapter will examine how key provisions of EU law examined earlier in this book interact with health. We start with the free movement of patients, perhaps the most visible but also the most controversial aspect of the impact of EU law on health.

2 Patient mobility

Three main aspects of EU law secure patient mobility: EU legislation covering migrant workers and their families; Treaty law on free movement of services; and EU legislation on 'patients' rights'. We consider each in turn.

2.1 Migrant workers: coordination of health care systems

EU legislation seeks to remove restrictions on free movement of workers that would arise from uncoordinated social security systems. There is, of course, no EU-level social security or health care system.[1] Each Member State determines its own social security and health care entitlements. However, if no EU-level law covered this situation, potential migrant workers might be reluctant to take up employment in another Member State, because, if they did, they and their families might lose access to medical treatment. The EU's response to this restriction on free movement of workers was to adopt legislation which requires the *coordination* of the separate national social security systems, including their health care systems.[2] In the relevant EU law, migrant patients are not patients as such, they are migrant workers.

EU law on migrant patients as migrant workers is covered by legislation that dates from the 1970s. Now replaced by Regulation 883/2004/EC,[3] this legislation supports migrant workers, and their families, if they need to rely on the national health care system of the host Member State, for instance in the event of an illness or disability that means they are no longer able to work. Regulation 883/2004/EC essentially covers mobility of patients in three situations:

- emergency medical treatment (relying on the European Health Insurance Card (EHIC));
- authorized medical treatment (treatment authorized by the home State, 'home State control');

[1] See also chapter 13.

[2] The relative security these administrative arrangements give to migrant workers is a significant difference between EU law on human migration and international bilateral or multilateral agreements or other arrangements such as 'points based' systems for immigrant workers.

[3] OJ [2004] L166/1–123. For a corrected version of the text, see OJ [2004] L200/1–49. This replaced Regulation 1408/71/EEC (OJ [1971] Special Edition, Series II, p 416) and entered into force on 1 May 2010.

- exceptional medical treatment (where the treatment is covered under the patient's home legislation and the treatment is not available for that patient within the time regarded as medically justifiable for obtaining that treatment in their home Member State).

First, there is an entitlement to emergency medical treatment that becomes necessary during a stay in the territory of another Member State.[4] This would cover, for example, a tourist who suffers appendicitis or a broken limb while on holiday in another EU State. Emergency medical treatment is administered through the EHIC. The EU–UK Trade and Cooperation Agreement extends a version of this entitlement to residents in the EU/UK when visiting the UK/EU.[5]

Second, a system allows Member States to authorize individual treatment in another (host) Member State.[6] The home Member State pays for the treatment, and retains control over whether to authorize it. Some nationals of Member States, particularly smaller states such as Luxembourg and Malta, are frequent users of this provision, partly through tradition and partly because medical expertise and equipment is felt to be superior in other countries. Other Member States use it rarely.

The third situation was added to the legislation following some litigation involving experimental treatment, where medical opinion was divided on the value of a therapy (in this case, hydrotherapy, a form of physiotherapy or pain management) and the patient wanted to have the treatment in another Member State.[7] Article 20(2) now requires Member States to grant authorization where the treatment (a) is covered by the health (insurance) system in the home Member State; and (b) cannot be given to the patient within a 'time limit which is medically justifiable' in the home Member State, taking into account the patient's 'current state of health and the probable course of his/her illness'. By implication, then, a patient (who may or may not be a migrant worker) may, exceptionally, rely on Article 20(2).

The key feature of Regulation 883/2004/EC is thus that, although Member States must adjust their health care systems so as to allow access to migrant workers, and in exceptional circumstances under Article 20(2) others, Member States essentially keep control over their national health systems. The numbers of migrant workers are relatively small. In any event, virtually all patients accessing medical care under the Regulation are already contributing to the national economy of the host State. They are thus contributing to the national health system in the same way as nationals (either through taxation or through 'social insurance', the two main ways in which European health care systems are financed). Although the emergency and exceptional medical treatment rules diverge from that general position, they do not constitute a major incursion into the power of the Member States to determine entitlements under their national health systems, and arrange them as they see fit. However, a second aspect of EU health law on patient mobility, based on Article 56 TFEU, disturbed that equilibrium.

2.2 **Freedom to receive health care services**

Article 56 TFEU provides that 'restrictions on freedom to provide services within the Union shall be prohibited'. Article 56 TFEU also implies an entitlement of a service *recipient* to go to another Member State to receive services.[8] 'Services' in this context must be

4 Regulation 883/2004/EC, Art 19.

5 EU–UK Trade and Cooperation Agreement, Art 488, and Protocol on Social Security Coordination, Art SSC.17.

6 Regulation 883/2004/EC, Art 20.

7 Case 117/77 *Pierek (No 1)* [1978] ECR 825; Case 182/78 *Pierek (No 2)* [1979] ECR 1977.

8 Joined Cases 286/82 and 26/83 *Luisi and Carbone* [1984] ECR 377; Case 186/87 *Cowan* [1989] ECR 195.

Table 21.1 Model of types of organization of national health care systems in the EU

Type	Bismarck	Beveridge
Underlying basis	Social insurance	Taxation
Funding source	Compulsory Insurance—paid for by employers and employees	General Taxation—paid for by tax-paying population: human beings and legal entities
Coverage	Originally, only employees (by sector) and their families. Extended to whole population	Whole population
Funding administered by	Sickness Insurance Funds (public or private entities, which hold insurance on behalf of patients)	Health Ministry (national, or sometimes regional, government)
Health care provided by	Hospitals, clinics, which may be public or private entities	Publicly owned hospitals and clinics
Access determined by	Sickness Insurance Funds contract with providers, from among which patients can choose, subject to health care professional opinion	Health care professionals, traditionally no patient choice
Patient experience, re funding	May be 'benefits-in-kind' system, where patient receives health care without awareness of funding arrangements; or may be 'reimbursement' system, where patient pays for care and is reimbursed by insurance	Patients receive benefits in kind, and are not involved in the funding arrangements

provided for remuneration. The CJEU recognized in 1984 that private medical services fall within the scope of Article 56 TFEU.[9] Remuneration for the service need not come directly from the service recipient.[10] So health care services paid for by a sickness insurance fund could fall within the TFEU's concept of services. This is so, even though sickness insurance funds are a common means by which Member States finance their national health care systems. Table 21.1 outlines the key differences between the two models[11] of health care system found in the EU, Bismarck and Beveridge.

The CJEU confirmed the principle that health care services paid for by a sickness insurance fund, as part of a national health system, fall within the TFEU's concept of services in the *Kohll* case in 1998.[12] *Kohll* concerned a patient (Mr Kohll's daughter) receiving non-hospital care (orthodontic treatment), in a situation where the home Member State (Luxembourg) operated a system of reimbursement, whereby patients pay for their treatment and are subsequently refunded by their sickness insurance fund. Ms Kohll's doctor recommended treatment by an orthodontist established in Trier, Germany, just over the

[9] Joined Cases 286/82 and 26/83 *Luisi and Carbone* [1984] ECR 377, para 16; Case C-159/90 *Society for the Protection of Unborn Children Ireland v Grogan* [1991] ECR I-4685, para 18.

[10] Case 352/85 *Bond van Adverteerders* [1988] ECR 2124.

[11] This is a *model*. No country adheres to either type in its pure form. All countries have a mix of different funding types, and variations on each type are found across the EU.

[12] Case C-158/96 *Kohll* [1998] ECR I-1931.

border. But the Luxembourg social security medical supervisors refused to authorize payment for the treatment from the social security fund. Only one orthodontist established in Luxembourg would have been able to give the treatment, hence Ms Kohll would have had a much longer wait if she had not crossed the border. Kohll challenged the refusal to authorize payment, and the national court referred to the CJEU under Article 267 TFEU as to whether this refusal was consistent with EU law.

The CJEU held that 'the special nature of certain services does not remove them from the ambit of the fundamental principle of freedom of movement'.[13] Luxembourg's defence to non-payment included the need to guarantee the quality of medical services, and the need to control health expenditure. The CJEU was not impressed. It pointed out that health professional qualifications had been harmonized by EU legislation since the 1970s. Hence, the CJEU claimed, the quality of medical services across the EU was guaranteed. Mr Kohll was seeking reimbursement only for the rate that would have been reimbursed had the treatment taken place in Luxembourg. So no threat to the financial stability of the national health system was present. In the face of Member States' reluctance to accept the logic of this reasoning, the CJEU has repeated it in numerous cases.[14]

Kohll left many questions open. Further litigation, and legislation, has clarified matters. As case study 21.1 shows, the principles in *Kohll* now apply to all types of national health care system.[15] This must be correct. Although it is common to distinguish between 'Bismarckian' social insurance health care systems and 'Beveridge' taxation systems, in reality these categories represent only ideal types (see Table 21.1). Every health care system across the EU relies on a mix of funding sources, including user charges; compulsory, social, voluntary, or private insurance; as well as public taxation. Given the budgetary constraints that all Member States face, it would be wrong for the CJEU to prevent policy experimentation that might lead to more efficient funding of national health care systems. All Member States use taxation to some extent in their health care systems, so there is no good reason to hold that Article 56 TFEU applies to 'Bismarck', but not to 'Beveridge', systems. It is also right that, in that context, the CJEU does not distinguish between hospital and non-hospital care.[16] Good medical practice can mean treating patients outside of hospitals where possible, and many Member States have health care systems based on polyclinics and other health institutions where patients do not stay overnight. It would be wrong—morally, ethically, and from the perspective of the best treatment—if the application of Article 56 TFEU inadvertently encouraged Member States to bring as much health care as possible into hospitals.

Case study 21.1: Mrs Watts' hip replacement

Mrs Watts, a wheelchair user, was told in September 2002 that she needed a double hip replacement, and that she would have to wait for around a year before she could have the treatment, under the care of Bedford Primary Care Trust (PCT), England (the UK was then a Member State). Her daughter, a journalist, knew of the *Kohll* ruling, and asked the PCT to authorize treatment abroad. The PCT refused, saying that surgery would be available in England for Mrs Watts within a reasonable time, taking account of her consultant's assessment of her medical need. In March 2003, her condition worsened. Mrs Watts decided to have the

[13] Para 20.

[14] See eg Case C-255/09 *Commission v Portugal (Non-hospital Medical Care)* [2011] ECR I-10547.

[15] Case C-157/99 *Geraets-Smits and Peerbooms* [2001] ECR I-5473; Case C-372/04 *Watts* [2006] ECR I-4325; Case C-444/05 *Stamatelaki* [2007] ECR I-3185; Case C-268/13 *Petru*, EU:C:2014:2271.

[16] Case C-368/98 *Vanbraekel* [2001] ECR I-363.

surgery in Abbeville, France. She paid the French hospital for her treatment in advance. She then asked the PCT for reimbursement of the cost, and was again refused.

Mrs Watts sought judicial review of that decision first in the High Court, which upheld the PCT's decision, and then on appeal before the Court of Appeal, which referred the case to the CJEU. The CJEU held that the *Kohll* ruling applied to the English NHS, even though hospital treatment is provided to patients who need it in England free of charge, and paid for by taxation. Although it is acceptable for cross-border hospital care to be subject to prior authorization, it was not acceptable that that prior authorization was based on a system that paid no attention to the individual patient concerned. Prior authorization could not be refused just because of hospital waiting times, where these were used as a general instrument for planning and managing hospital resources, on the basis of predetermined general clinical priorities. What was required is an individual objective assessment of the patient's medical situation, including her pain and disability at the time the authorization was sought.

The case settled before the Court of Appeal gave its final ruling. Mrs Watts was represented by Richard Stein, a well-known judicial review and human rights solicitor. For him, the case was a victory not only for Mrs Watts, but also because of the changes it forced on NHS England at the time. Rather than risk increasing numbers of patients going abroad, the NHS reduced waiting times for elective procedures such as hip replacements, by allowing PCTs to contract with private hospitals in England with unused capacity. It also meant that decisions about undue waiting times were individual medical decisions, not general administrative decisions.

But others have criticized the ruling, pointing out that Mrs Watts, and patients like her, are relatively healthy, and relatively wealthy. In the context of an NHS with limited resources, it may be that increased choice for some patients meant worse treatment for others, who are less able to exercise such choice.

Although *Kohll* applies in principle whichever two Member States are concerned, Article 56 TFEU does not require Member States to extend the 'basket of care' that is reimbursable under their health system.[17] This applies both to innovative treatments, which tend to be expensive, and also to treatments that have been excluded from coverage on ethical grounds in a particular Member State. The CJEU therefore declined to apply Article 56 TFEU in *Veselības ministrija*,[18] a case where the patient, a Jehovah's Witness, sought to have a treatment (open heart surgery) that was available in his home state (Latvia) but on terms which he could not accept on grounds of religion (involving a blood transfusion). The CJEU held that the Patients' Rights Directive (see below) had codified the CJEU's case law, and applied the Directive, interpreted in the light of Article 21 (1) of the EU Charter of Fundamental Rights, holding that treatment may not be refused in those circumstances unless justified, justification being a matter for the national court.

Moreover, a patient may not make a profit through relying on their rights to cross-border health care under Article 56 TFEU.[19] However, expenditure on the patient's board and lodging, while receiving cross-border health care, can be regarded as an integral part of the treatment itself.[20]

Where free movement of patients is concerned, the most significant aspect of the *Kohll* ruling is the exceptionally broad definition given to the term 'restriction' in that context.[21] As the CJEU has put it:

[17] Case C-173/09 *Elchinov* [2010] ECR I-8889; Case C-268/13 *Petru*, EU:C:2014:2271.

[18] Case C-243/19 *A v Veselības ministrija*, EU:C:2020:872.

[19] Case C-368/98 *Vanbraekel* [2001] ECR I-5363.

[20] Case C-8/02 *Leichtle* [2004] ECR I-2641.

[21] For a more detailed discussion on this point, see chapter 13.

> Article [56 TFEU] precludes the application of any national rules which have the effect of making the provision of services between Member States more difficult than the provision of services purely within a Member State.[22]

In terms of the relationship between Article 56 and Regulation 883/2004/EC, the CJEU has held that the rules in the Regulation on authorization must be interpreted consistently with the Treaty. The consequence is that, if national rules on prior authorization make it more difficult to have the treatment in another Member State, then those rules (even though permitted by the EU legislature) are 'restrictions' in the sense of Article 56 TFEU, and are prohibited unless justified.[23] Given that national health systems are organized on a national territorial basis, the effect is that all sorts of perfectly logical rules from the point of view of running an efficient health system, with scarce public resources, potentially fall foul of Article 56 TFEU.

Fortunately, the CJEU's jurisprudence has taken this into account. The CJEU has long recognized that the social protection provided by national social security systems can be an 'objective public interest' justifying restrictions on the free movement of services.[24] To begin with, in the context of free movement of patients, the CJEU allowed 'restrictions' on cross-border services within the context of hospital care, referring to the distinct characteristics of the hospital sector, in particular, the planning of the number of hospitals, their geographical distribution, the way in which they are organized and equipped, and the nature of the health services they offer as justifications. By 2010, the CJEU had recognized that a restriction on free movement of patients could be justified outside a hospital setting, where treatment involved the use of major medical equipment, such as 'PET' (positron emission tomography) scanners, 'MRI' (magnetic resonance imaging) scanners, hyperbaric chambers and cyclotrons, outside hospital infrastructures, again, on the basis of the planning necessary to ensure a balanced range of high-quality treatment, and at the same time control costs by avoiding wastage of resources.[25] This brings the case law into line with the legislative position in Article 8(1) of Directive 2011/24.

2.3 **The 'Patients' Rights Directive'**

Where the CJEU creates significant uncertainties for relevant actors, the governments of the Member States, acting within Council, may have a stronger incentive to adopt EU-level legislation, to clarify matters, or indeed to seek to persuade the CJEU to modify its approach. This happened with the case law on free movement of patients. The governments of the Member States called on the Commission to bring forward a specific legislative proposal responding to *Kohll*. This followed the adoption of the general Directive 2006/123/EC on services in the internal market, which does not apply to:

> healthcare services whether or not they are provided via healthcare facilities, and regardless of the ways in which they are organised and financed at national level or whether they are public or private.[26]

[22] Case C-444/05 *Stamatelaki* [2007] ECR I-3185, para 25. See also chapter 13.

[23] Case C-56/01 *Inizan* [2003] ECR I-12403; Case C-8/02 *Leichtle* [2004] ECR I-2641.

[24] Case C-272/94 *Guiot and Climatec* [1996] ECR I-1905. See further chapters 13 and 16.

[25] Case C-512/08 *Commission v France* (*Major Medical Equipment*) [2010] ECR I-8833.

[26] Directive 2006/123/EC, Art 2(2)(f). However, Directive 2006/123/EC *does* apply to social care services, such as care services provided for elderly people in care homes or day centres. See Case C-57/12 *Femarbel*, EU:C:2013:517.

A lengthy legislative process ensued, resulting in the adoption of Directive 2011/24/EU on patients' rights in cross-border health care.[27] The Commission's stated aims of the proposal[28] were as follows:

- to help patients access cross-border health care;
- to reassure patients that cross-border health care is safe;
- to foster cooperation between health systems to improve health care for all.

These aims, along with the title of the Directive, make the Directive sound highly patient-focused, bolstering patient choice and autonomy, as well as promoting high quality, and efficiently provided, health care. Actually, once analysed, the terms of the Directive are rather more about enhancing national control over cross-border health care. The scope of the Directive extends only to *health* care, defined as provided by health professionals, and not to broader social care or well-being services. It does not, therefore, affect the potentially lucrative market in such 'lifestyle services' provided by gyms or fitness/diet gurus.[29]

Directive 2011/24/EU articulates the 'general principle' that the home Member State must reimburse the costs of patients receiving cross-border health care.[30] But this rule is subject to three important exceptions:

- the 'basket' of health care provision;
- Regulation 883/2004/EC;
- Directive 2011/24/EU, Articles 8 and 9.

We examine these exceptions in turn.

First, the rule that cross-border patients are to be reimbursed by their home Member State applies *only* if the treatment concerned is among the benefits to which that patient is entitled in the home Member State.[31] Thus the home Member State controls the 'basket' of health care entitlements. A patient does not have a right to receive any health care they might wish, if that treatment is not available at home, although that provision must be interpreted consistently with the EU Charter of Fundamental Rights, including its provisions on religious equality.[32]

Second, the rule on reimbursement by the home State is subject to Regulation 883/2004/EC. Article 20(2) of the Regulation requires national authorities to authorize treatment in the home State's 'basket' of entitlements, and where the patient 'cannot be given such treatment within a time limit which is medically justifiable, taking into account his/her current state of health and the probable course of his/her illness'. Under those circumstances, prior authorization rules that refuse to reimburse a treatment carried out in another Member State, may breach EU law.[33] But if we turn this reasoning to its logical reverse, if the treatment sought does *not* correspond to the home system's 'basket', it follows that there is no obligation to authorize treatment in another Member State under the Regulation. Hence, there is no obligation to pay for such treatment under the Patients' Rights Directive either.

Third, the reimbursement rule is subject to Articles 8 and 9 of the Patients' Rights Directive. Article 8 permits Member States to have a system of prior authorization for reimbursement of the costs of cross-border health care, listing the types of health care

[27] Directive 2011/24/EU of the European Parliament and of the Council on the application of patients' rights in cross-border healthcare (OJ [2011] L88/45).

[28] COM(2008) 414 final.

[29] See Case C-57/12 *Femarbel*, EU:C:2013:517.

[30] Directive 2011/24/EU, Art 7(1).

[31] Directive 2011/24/EU, Art 7(1).

[32] *Veselības ministrija* (n 18).

[33] Case C-173/09 *Elchinov* [2010] ECR I-8889, para 62. I am grateful to the student in Aarhus University who corrected this point in previous editions.

that may be subject to such prior authorization. The list goes much further than the CJEU's jurisprudence:[34]

(a) Health care that is 'made subject to planning requirements relating to the object of ensuring sufficient and permanent access to a balanced range of high-quality treatment in the Member State concerned or to the wish to control costs and avoid, as far as possible, any waste of financial, technical and human resources and:

 (i) involves overnight hospital accommodation of the patient in question for at least one night; or

 (ii) requires use of highly specialised and cost-intensive medical infrastructure or medical equipment';[35]

(b) Health care that 'involves treatments presenting a particular risk for the patient or the population'; or

(c) Health care that is 'provided by a healthcare provider that, on a case-by-case basis, could give rise to serious and specific concerns relating to the quality or safety of the care, with the exception of healthcare which is subject to Union legislation ensuring a minimum level of safety and quality throughout the Union'.

Member States may therefore refuse to authorize reimbursement of cross-border health care under the terms of the Directive. Although in theory the CJEU could assert the entitlements of patients under the constitutionally superior Article 56 TFEU, in practice the CJEU has, since around 2010, been bringing its Article 56 TFEU jurisprudence into line with the Directive.[36] Nevertheless, there are circumstances in which Member States *must* authorize cross-border treatment. These are outlined in Article 8(5):

> when the patient is entitled to the healthcare in question in accordance with Article 7, and when this healthcare cannot be provided on its territory within a time-limit which is medically justifiable, based on an objective medical assessment of the patient's medical condition, the history and probable course of the patient's illness, the degree of the patient's pain and/or the nature of the patient's disability at the time when the request for authorisation was made or renewed.

As already noted, the provision is consistent with the system under Regulation 883/2004/EC, in that it leaves the control over the 'basket' of health care entitlements with the home Member State. Moreover, the Patients' Rights Directive contains a further protection for the national health systems of home Member States, under Article 8(6). Authorization need not be granted where:

> (a) the patient will, according to a clinical evaluation, be exposed with reasonable certainty to a patient-safety risk that cannot be regarded as acceptable, taking into account the potential benefit for the patient of the sought cross-border healthcare;
>
> (b) the general public will be exposed with reasonable certainty to a substantial safety hazard as a result of the cross-border healthcare in question;

[34] See eg Case C-157/99 *Geraets-Smits and Peerbooms* [2001] ECR I-5473; Case C-385/99 *Müller-Fauré/Van Riet* [2003] ECR I-4509.

[35] See also Case C-512/08 *Commission v France (Major Medical Equipment)* [2010] ECR I-8833.

[36] See T Hervey and J McHale, *European Union Health Law: Themes and Implications* (Cambridge: Cambridge University Press, 2015) 83–97; and see, more recently, Case C-115/24 *UJ*, EU:C:2025:694, in which the CJEU relied on EU legislation to interpret Art 56 TFEU in the context of dental telemedicine.

(c) this healthcare is to be provided by a healthcare provider that raises serious and specific concerns relating to the respect of standards and guidelines on quality of care and patient safety, including provisions on supervision, whether these standards and guidelines are laid down by laws and regulations or through accreditation systems established by the Member State of treatment;

(d) this healthcare can be provided on its territory within a time-limit which is medically justifiable, taking into account the current state of health and the probable course of the illness of each patient concerned.

So we see that, despite its name, the Patients' Rights Directive gives significant control to the national health authorities in the home (paying) Member State. Questions about the legal limits on that control will continue to be litigated in extreme instances, such as when patients do not have time to seek prior authorization because their health deteriorates rapidly.[37] But, essentially, if health care can be given in the home Member State, within a time limit that is 'medically justifiable', then the patient has no rights under the Directive to cross-border health care. The Directive has thus significantly tightened national control over the litigation processes begun by the *Kohll* case. It is not a surprise, therefore, that relatively few patients made use of the Directive. A Commission report on data from 2022[38] shows around 550,000 claims not subject to prior authorization, and around 4,500 requests, of which only 840 were refused. Data-gathering remains a problem, but even so, in the context of the Union population, these numbers are tiny. Probably the most significant aspect of the Directive is simply that it requires Member States to give more information to patients about their options to seek health care in other Member States.

3 Health care professionals

EU health law also covers health care professionals. The relevant law seeks to secure free movement of self-employed persons establishing themselves in another Member State, workers, and service providers, through mutual recognition of professional qualifications (a key component of EU law on free movement of persons). Originally, EU legislation on mutual recognition of professional qualifications took two broad approaches: a 'sectoral' approach that covers specific professions (such as dentist or midwife); and a 'general' approach that applies to other professional qualifications. The two approaches were brought together into one legislative instrument in 2005.[39] A range of problems with the relevant EU law have led to further reforms.

3.1 The 'sectoral' approach

EU internal market law on professional mobility dates from the 1970s. Some of the first professions to be regulated by the EU were in the health sector: doctors, dentists, pharmacists, midwives, and general care nurses. The aim was to promote free movement by enabling the automatic recognition in all Member States of a licence to practise a profession in one Member State. Each sector was covered by two Directives. One defined at EU level the minimum educational requirements for access to the profession. Member States aligned their national degree programmes with these requirements. The other Directive

[37] See eg Case 777/18 *WO*, EU:C:2020:745.

[38] European Commission, *Member State data on cross-border patient healthcare following Directive 2011/24/EU* (European Commission, 2024).

[39] Directive 2005/36/EC (OJ [2005] L255/22).

simply listed, by official title, all diplomas which satisfy the requirements.[40] Host Member States were allowed to ensure that health professionals had sufficient language skills to communicate with their patients.[41] But otherwise, the beauty of the sectoral system was its simplicity: it allowed for recognition of *qualifications* without the need for assessing each *individual* migrant professional.

That was the idea in theory. In practice, however, in many Member States non-nationally qualified health professionals were not universally accepted or trusted, and the minimum training requirements were seen as inadequate, as they did not cover specific content of training, or dictate the level of competence that a professional must reach. For instance, comparisons between the number of patients that trainee doctors were required to treat before qualifying showed significant differences between Member States. Worse, the need for full EU legislative agreement meant it was difficult to change educational requirements to reflect changes in scientific understanding or good practice in medical education.[42] Moreover, the sectoral system worked only for professions where there was a general consensus across the Member States about the scope and meaning of a particular professional title. This is not the case for many health professions, such as psychologists, chiropractors, osteopaths, or opticians.

3.2 **The 'general' approach**

In the late 1980s, the EU moved to a system of 'general' Directives on mutual recognition of qualifications, covering all other professions. The two systems (general and sectoral) were consolidated in Directive 2005/36/EC,[43] which remains the current applicable legislation. A further 'modernization' of the general professional mobility rules, principally in order to further liberalize services markets across the EU, promote growth through exploiting economies of scale, and make it easier for professionals to relocate and set up in another Member State, hence creating more jobs and tackling workforce skills shortages in some Member States, took place in 2013.[44] The rules include the 'Internal Market Information System' (an online system for local, regional, and national administrative authorities to share and access information about professional qualifications and services provision) and a 'European Professional Card', which is intended to facilitate the procedure for recognizing professional qualifications. It is currently available only for general care nurses, pharmacists and physiotherapists, not other health professions.

Many of the key principles of law were established through the CJEU's case law.[45] The basic logic is the idea of 'mutual recognition'. Member States must consider, on a case-by-case basis, whether a qualification from another Member State is equivalent to its own qualification. Host Member States must take into account professional qualifications, and experience of practice in another Member State, and compare the knowledge and abilities certified by the professional qualification, and experience, with those required by national rules.[46] If the qualification is not equivalent, then the Member State must decide what 'compensating measures' must be taken by a health care professional seeking to establish themselves in the host Member State. 'Compensating measures' can take the form of an aptitude test, or a period of adaptation. Health care professions differ quite

[40] These lists were updated in 2016, see Commission Delegated Decision 2016/790/EU (OJ [2016] L134/135).

[41] Confirmed in Case C-424/97 *Haim II* [2000] ECR I-5123.

[42] The European Commission now has delegated power to update these lists, see Directive 2005/36/EC, as amended, Art 21(6).

[43] OJ [2005] L255/22.

[44] Directive 2013/55/EU amending Directive 2005/36/EU and the IMI Regulation (OJ [2013] L354/132).

[45] See further chapter 13. [46] Directive 2005/36/EC, Art 12.

significantly across the EU, so Member States consider compensating measures to be justified in the vast majority of health professions.

In general, 'compensating measures' apply only to the exercise of freedom of *establishment*. Host Member States may not restrict provision of *services* for any reason relating to professional qualifications. If the service provider is lawfully established in one Member State, they must be allowed to provide services in any other.[47] The distinction between establishment and services is about permanence or temporary activity.[48] However, what is important here is that this general rule does *not* apply to health services. Directive 2005/36/EC explicitly allows Member States to check the professional qualifications of the health service provider prior to the first provision of services.[49]

Nevertheless, this ability to check qualifications of health professionals who provide cross-border services has not always been effectively used.

The 2013 legislative amendments[50] adjusted rules on training hours for medical professionals and reflected significant developments in nursing as a profession over the previous ten years or more, taking into account major differences between nursing training in Eastern and Western Europe. The amendments also expanded Member States' powers to require language skills by imposing controls on any profession with implications for patient safety.[51] Despite these attempts to improve trust between Member States, health professional mobility is still far from realized in the EU in practice.

3.3 **Concerns about EU law on health professionals**

Several problems with EU law on health professionals have been identified:

- insufficient provision for continuous professional development;
- lack of transparency on professional misconduct;
- 'regime shopping';
- no focus on quality of care.

The EU rules operate on the assumption that initial training of a health professional, at the start of their career, is an adequate guarantor of fitness to practise across a whole career. Yet medical training must include continuous professional development, to keep up with developments in medicine. Moreover, all EU Member States have systems of peer review, external evaluation, audit, and inspection: these vary significantly. For example, Germany and the Netherlands require formal revalidation every five years. EU law supports healthcare professional development only by a provision in Directive 2013/55/EU requiring Member States to ensure that migrant health professionals are able to keep abreast of professional developments. This is insufficient to tackle the diversity with its obvious problems for a notional single market in health care services. The European Accreditation Council for Continuing Medical Education provides a 'soft law' approach to bringing together best practice in continuing medical education and continuing professional development. But it is not the same as mandatory EU level legislation.

Another concern about free-moving health care professionals within the EU is the extent to which 'rogue' health professionals might rely on their free movement rights to

[47] Directive 2005/36/EC, Art 5(1). This rule is also reflected implicitly in Directive 2006/123/EC (OJ [2006] L376/36), Art 16.

[48] Directive 2005/36/EC, Art 5(2); Case C-55/94 *Gebhard* [1995] ECR I-4165. See also chapter 13.

[49] Directive 2005/36/EC, Art 7(4).

[50] Directive 2013/55/EU, amending Directive 2005/36/EU and the IMI Regulation (OJ [2013] L354/132).

[51] Directive 2005/36/EC, as amended, Art 53.

evade being barred from practice. Following the 2013 amendments to Directive 2005/36/EC, Member States must exchange information 'regarding disciplinary actions or criminal sanctions which relate to a prohibition or restriction' of professional activities,[52] and not only where the host Member State requests it.[53] Information exchange is subject to EU and national privacy and data protection law.

A third problem concerns the very different qualifications standards that must be met in order to access different health care professions across the EU. These have resulted in de facto exclusion from practice in many Member States. Despite legislative obligations seeking to impose the proportionality test more effectively,[54] the European Commission regularly brings infringement proceedings in such cases, and these increased following the Covid-19 pandemic. For example, live cases in 2025 include Germany's non-recognition of midwife qualifications;[55] Cyprus's additional training requirements for paramedics;[56] Ireland's non-recognition of nurses;[57] and an announcement that 14 Member States will be investigated for non-recognition of Romanian nurses.[58]

Many Member States, seeking to plan capacity and avoid an overproduction of qualified professionals, restrict the numbers of students who can access medical training. Some of these rules have been challenged as breaching EU law on non-discrimination on grounds of nationality.[59] The CJEU has found that indirect discrimination may be justified by the objective of 'maintaining a balanced high-quality medical service',[60] so long as a national court is satisfied that there is a real link between that need and the specific arrangements made for training of future health professionals. The CJEU has accepted that forward planning in the sector may constitute an objective public interest justification. However, in providing evidence justifying the policy, the Member State must take into account migration patterns of health professionals across the EU.

Fundamentally, the problem with EU law on health professionals is that it is not the aim of the EU provisions to protect patients or to ensure high-quality, cost-effective care. Rather, EU law seeks to promote the free movement of service providers and freedom of establishment of professionals. The relevant EU Directives do not grant individual rights to patients, and thus could not be enforced by a patient who received substandard care from a professional moving between Member States in reliance upon a Directive.

3.4 **The challenge of telemedicine**

EU law on free movement of patients, services, and healthcare professionals is ill-suited to respond to new health technologies, especially telemedicine. Telemedicine is 'the online provision of health care services without physical contact between the patient and the health provider'.[61] It is a highly lucrative, emerging global market and promises to increase efficiency in health care provision in Europe, and enhance patient choice.

52 Directive 2005/36/EC, as amended, Arts 4e, 56.

53 Directive 2005/36/EC, as amended, Art 8.

54 Directive 2018/958/EU on a proportionality test before adoption of new regulation of professions (OJ [2018] L173/25).

55 INFR(2023)4101, https://ec.europa.eu/commission/presscorner/detail/en/inf_23_3445.

56 INFR(2018)2299, https://ec.europa.eu/commission/presscorner/detail/en/inf_23_3445.

57 INFR(2023)2100, https://ireland.representation.ec.europa.eu/news-and-events/news/professional-qualifications-commission-asks-ireland-comply-eu-rules-2023-09-28_en.

58 www.eunews.it/en/2025/05/22/eu-launches-infringement-procedure-against-14-countries-including-italy-over-non-recognition-of-romanian-nurses.

59 Case C-147/03 *Commission v Austria* [2005] ECR I-7963; Case C-73/08 *Bressol* [2010] ECR I-2735.

60 *Bressol* (n 59).

61 A den Exter, 'Health Services: Telemedicine' in S Garben and L Gormley (eds), *OUP Online Encyclopaedia of EU Law* (Oxford: Oxford University Press, 2025).

Telemedicine is covered by multiple overlapping provisions of EU law: Article 56 TFEU; the Patients' Rights Directive; EU legislation on information society services, especially the e-Commerce Directive;[62] Directive 2005/36/EC on mutual recognition of qualifications; the General Data Protection Regulation;[63] and the 'European Health Data Space' Regulation 2025/327/EU.[64] These constitute an uneasy compromise between the many competing interests at play, as illustrated by the *UJ* case,[65] involving dental telemedicine services.

The case involves a product and service called 'DrSmile': invisible dental aligners. Patients/customers contract with the supplier (DNK Deutsche Zahnklinik, licensed to operate as a dental clinic in Germany) via a website. The website allows patients to request an appointment with a convenient 'partner dentist'. The 'partner dentist' takes a medical history, provides an initial consultation, takes a 3D scan of the jaw, and carries out any necessary pre-treatments. The supplier secures the product from the global health firm Urban Technology (UJ), established in Germany. Follow-up is provided through an online app, by which the patient regularly sends images of their teeth, and new supplies of dental aligners are sent accordingly.

The professional organization for dentists in Austria—the Austrian Dental Chamber—sought an injunction against UJ, claiming that UJ was participating in providing dental services in Austria with companies that were not authorized to do so in Austrian law. The case was referred to the CJEU by the Austrian Supreme Court, which asked questions about the Patients' Rights Directive; the e-Commerce Directive; Directive 2005/36; and Article 56 TFEU. In the absence of a definition for 'telemedicine' in EU legislation, the CJEU held, adopting a 'plain language'[66] and contextual interpretation, that telemedicine means a medical service where the patient and provider are not in the same place. Drawing on an earlier case involving supply of contact lenses,[67] the CJEU went on to sever the service provided by UJ from that provided by DNK Deutsche Zahnklinik, and held that UJ's service was not telemedicine, as the patient and UJ were physically present in the same place. The CJEU confirmed that, in EU law, telemedicine must be provided according to the rules of the place where the health care service provider is established. This was Germany for the service of DrSmile, but given that the initial consultation, taking place in Austria, was not 'telemedicine', EU law did not apply to it. The CJEU's approach thus protected the interests of Austria, in keeping home-state control over UJ; of Germany, in keeping home-state control over the services provided by DNK Deutsche Zahnklinik; and internal market law's exception to the rule of home-state control for service provision. However, it did so by using legal technicalities to sever what is, in effect, one medical service.

4 Health care institutions

As we saw in the *UJ* case, EU health law also applies to health care institutions. The CJEU has established that there is nothing special about these bodies that removes them from the scope of EU free movement or competition law. The organization of health systems

[62] Directive 2000/31/EC ('e-Commerce Directive') (OJ [2000] L178/1); see also Directive 2015/1535/EU on information society services (OJ [2015] L241/1).

[63] Regulation 2016/679/EU ('GDPR') (OJ [2016] L119/1).

[64] Regulation 2025/327/EU on the European Health Data Space (OJ [2025] L327), ELI: http://data.europa.eu/eli/reg/2025/327/oj.

[65] Case C-115/24 *UJ*, EU:C:2025:694.

[66] Para 62.

[67] Case C-108/09 *Ker-Optika*, EU:C:2010:725.

is a matter for each Member State, but, when exercising that power, Member States must comply with EU law. Some have claimed that EU health law therefore implies a threat to European health systems, moving them away from their historical roots based on 'solidarity' (the act of supporting the less well off in a society, through distribution of resources) between citizens within a welfare state, and towards a market and individual-choice-based system. Others offer a more nuanced interpretation. This section considers such claims, looking first at freedom of establishment and freedom to provide services; then turning to some aspects of EU competition law.

4.1 Freedom of establishment/freedom to provide services

EU law on freedom of establishment and freedom to provide services applies to health care institutions where they provide services for remuneration, including where remuneration comes from a third party, such as a social insurance fund. The scope of the provisions covers a very wide range of possible 'restrictions' on free movement.[68] Hence many national rules concerning the organization of national health systems are subject to scrutiny for their compliance with EU law. Some examples include:

- single-practice rules, prohibiting health professionals from being registered or practising in more than one Member State;[69]
- registration rules, requiring formal registration and authorization to provide certain health services;[70]
- territorial or capacity planning rules, restricting the numbers of health care professionals operating in a geographical area, or the system as a whole;[71]
- limitations on the choice of legal form (eg, where a company is established; who may be a partner or company director; who may own a company);[72]
- rules prohibiting profit-making suppliers of long-term care.[73]

Merely stating that a regulatory arrangement is part of the national health system is inadequate as a defence. Member States must show that the policy is justified by an objective public interest (such as patient safety, timely access to care, professional ethics, or financial stability of the health care system), and that the proportionality test is met.[74]

The flexibility of 'proportionality' allows the CJEU to distinguish between those health institutions which are more closely associated with a national health system and those less so.[75] The more central to a publicly funded national health system an institution, the more readily will the CJEU accept that measures restricting freedom of establishment or free provision of services across EU borders are justified. Rules restricting dental clinics[76]

[68] See further chapter 14.

[69] Case C-96/85 *Commission v France* [1986] ECR I-1475; Case C-351/90 *Commission v Luxembourg* [1992] ECR I-3945.

[70] Case C-8/96 *MacQuen* [2001] ECR I-837; Case C-294/00 *Deutsche Paracelsus Schulen v Gräbner* [2002] ECR I-6515.

[71] Case C-456/05 *Commission v Germany* [2007] ECR I-10517.

[72] Case 221/85 *Commission v Belgium (Clinical Biology Laboratories)* [1987] ECR 719; Case C-196/01 *Commission v France (Biomedical Laboratories)* [2004] ECR I-2351; Joined Cases C-171 and 172/07 *Neumann-Siewart* [2009] ECR I-4171; Case C-531/06 *Commission v Italy (Pharmacies)* [2009] ECR I-4103.

[73] Case C-70/95 *Sodemare* [1997] ECR I-3395.

[74] See also chapter 16.

[75] See T Hervey and J McHale, *European Union Health Law: Themes and Implications* (Cambridge: Cambridge University Press, 2015) 227–268.

[76] Case C-169/07 *Hartlauer* [2009] ECR I-1721.

and opticians[77] are subject to strict scrutiny; rules for hospitals,[78] laboratories,[79] and blood centres[80] much less so. Pharmacies occupy a middle ground.[81]

4.2 **Competition law**

The basic aims of EU competition law are to prevent anticompetitive behaviour and to punish it where it takes place.[82] EU competition law includes anti-cartel rules; monopolies rules; and rules regulating mergers. Enforcement is now largely undertaken by national competition authorities, although formal enforcement by individuals through courts is also possible.[83] However, often the effects of the application of competition law in the health sector come from pressure to comply, rather than formal legal sanctions. For example, in October 2011, the Italian Antitrust Authority announced that, in response to its investigation, six foreign companies offering parents storage of umbilical cord blood had agreed to change their marketing material to better inform potential consumers about scientific developments in the field.[84] The companies had targeted parents in Italy, where cryopreservation of umbilical cord blood for personal use (as opposed to as part of a public blood bank) is prohibited. The unfair commercial practices were targeted as anticompetitive collusive behaviour.

EU competition law applies to 'undertakings', and prohibits anticompetitive agreements[85] and abusive monopolies.[86] A special exemption applies to 'public undertakings and undertakings to which Member States grant special or exclusive rights'.[87] If such undertakings are 'entrusted with the operation of services of general economic interest', they are only subject to the Treaty rules, including those on competition, 'insofar as the application of such rules does not obstruct the performance, in law or in fact, of the particular tasks assigned to them'.[88]

Many institutions within EU national health systems are not 'undertakings' because they do not meet the relevant criteria.[89] For example, the Grand Chamber of the CJEU found that the Slovak state health insurer is not,[90] overturning a decision of the General Court. The ways in which EU competition law could apply to health institutions are illustrated by two high-profile cases concerning health services: *BetterCare Ltd v Director of Fair Trading*,[91] a decision of the British Competition Appeal Tribunal, and *Ambulanz Glöckner*, a decision of the CJEU.[92] These cases establish the principle that EU competition law applies to health institutions if they are 'undertakings', but that the grant of exclusive rights to such institutions may be justified as necessary to the operation of a

[77] Case C-8/96 *MacQuen* [2001] ECR I-837; Case C-140/03 *Opticians* [2005] ECR I-3177.

[78] eg Case C-157/99 *Smits/Peerbooms* [2001] ECR I-5473; Case C-512/08 *Major Medical Equipment* [2010] ECR I-8833.

[79] Case 221/85 *Commission v Belgium (Clinical Biology Laboratories)* [1987] ECR 719; Case C-196/01 *Commission v France (Biomedical Laboratories)* [2004] ECR I-2351.

[80] Case C-262/08 *CopyGene* [2010] ECR I-5053.

[81] See for a rare early example Case C-391/92 *Infant Formula* [1995] ECR I-1621; Case C-322/01 *DocMorris* [2003] ECR 14887; Case C-141/07 *Hospital Pharmacies* [2008] ECR I-6935; Joined Cases C-570 and 571/07 *Pérez Gómez* [2010] ECR I-4629.

[82] See further chapter 17.

[83] Case C-453/99 *Courage v Crehan* [2001] ECR I-6297; Joined Cases C-295–298/04 *Manfredi* [2006] ECR I-6619.

[84] https://en.agcm.it/en/media/press-releases/2011/10/alias-1968.

[85] Art 101(1) TFEU. An exemption is available under Art 101(3) TFEU.

[86] Art 102 TFEU.

[87] Art 106 TFEU.

[88] Art 106(2) TFEU. See also chapter 18.

[89] For the definition of 'undertaking', see further chapter 18.

[90] Joined Cases C-262/18 P and C-271/18 P *Dôvera zdravotná poisťovňa*, EU:C:2020:450.

[91] [2002] CAT 7.

[92] Case C-475/99 [2001] ECR I-8089.

'service of general economic interest'.[93] The EU's merger regulation[94] also potentially applies to health institutions.[95]

4.3 **Assessment**

Where a Member State operates its health system on a 'social solidarity' footing, then health care institutions will not be covered by EU law. National health systems remain within national competence. If, however, a Member State makes changes to its health system, which involve the state acting as an 'economic operator', perhaps seeking to increase management efficiency therein, then EU law will apply. For instance, countries such as the Netherlands, Hungary, and Germany have seen competition law being applied to many health institutions. EU law has been used to scrutinize hospital mergers, including the controversial Zeeland hospitals merger in the Netherlands. Zeeland is located on a relatively isolated peninsula, and the increase in patient travelling time expected after the proposed merger resulted in intense lobbying in opposition to the proposals. It was claimed that, were the merger to go ahead, there would be a significant risk of abuse of a dominant position, as the merged entity would have over 80 per cent of the relevant market. In this instance, the Competition Authority allowed the merger, subject to some behavioural conditions (a price cap, quality improvements, and enhancing the bargaining power of the hospitals' consultants).[96] But the Competition Authority has blocked hospital mergers, such as the Albert Schweitzer/Rivas Care proposal, where the market share of the new merged entity is such as to remove the disciplinary pressure of competition, and result in raised prices and lower quality.[97]

EU competition law has also been applied to social insurance bodies (the main way in which health systems are financed across the EU as a whole);[98] hospitals; pharmacies; laboratories;[99] blood and tissue banks; and dentists; as well as health professional organizations. On the one hand, this seems entirely appropriate. It is consistent with the general approach to the balance of competences between the EU and its Member States. As AG Maduro put it in *FENIN*:[100]

> the power of the State which is exercised in the political sphere is subject to democratic control. A different type of control is imposed on economic actors acting on a market: their conduct is governed by competition law. But there is no justification when the State is acting as an economic operator, for relieving its actions of all control.

On the other hand, this approach assumes that the roles and concepts of 'market' and 'state solidarity' are entirely distinct. But in practice they are not. Different types of market involve different levels of competition, and so a more subtly differentiated application

[93] See further chapter 18.

[94] Council Regulation (EC) 139/2004 on the control of concentrations between undertakings (OJ [2004] L24/1).

[95] For examples, see M Guy, *Competition Policy in Healthcare: Frontiers in Insurance-Based and Taxation-Funded Systems* (Cambridge: Intersentia, 2019).

[96] See M Canoy and W Sauter, *Hospital Mergers and the Public Interest: Recent Developments in the Netherlands*, http://papers.ssrn.com/sol3/papers.cfm?abstract_id=1470695.

[97] See Guy (n 95) 170–176.

[98] Case T-289/03 *BUPA v Commission* [2008] ECR II–81; Case C-437/09 *AG2R Prévoyance* [2011] ECR I-973; Case T-216/15 *DZP/UZP*, EU:T:2018:64, appealed in Case C-262/18 P; though contrast Joined Cases C-264/01, C-306/01, C-354/01, and C-355/01 *AOK Bundesverband* [2004] ECR I-2493, and see also Case C-185/11 *Commission v Slovenia (Non-life Insurance)*, EU:C:2012:43.

[99] Case T-90/11 *Ordre national des pharmaciens and Others v Commission*, EU:T:2014:1049.

[100] Para 26.

of EU law would be more responsive to changing policy contexts within the Member States. Member States experiment with market models, responding to the challenges of fiscal prudence, ageing populations, and increased demand for ever more expensive medical treatments.[101] Where they do so, they are unlikely to seek to move from a totally solidarity-based provision to one that is totally based on free competition within a market. Instead, they may phase in competitive elements, perhaps only within one part of the system, in order to protect the stability of the health care system as a whole, and to allow for a period of adjustment. The ways in which EU competition and free movement law are applied involve considering not health *systems*, but a set of *individual services*, which may or may not be categorized as services of general interest. Their systemic nature comes into play as an *exception* to the rule of free movement and fair competition. The structure and approach of EU health law is therefore not conducive to an effective transformation of health services to meet contemporary challenges.

5 **Medical devices and pharmaceuticals**

The EU has regulated health care products since the 1960s. Its legislation and administrative rules cover the entire 'lifecycle' of such products, from the research and bringing to the market phase, through manufacture, authority to sell, 'pharmacovigilance' (ensuring products on the market are safe, and acting on information suggesting they might not be), liability for harm, price controls, and advertising or information. Fig. 21.1 illustrates the lifecycle of such health care products.

The EU has also used competition and free movement law to seek to open up markets in these products, and enhance the global competitiveness of the European pharmaceuticals and medical devices industries, while protecting patients, and those parts of the industry that pursue innovation and rely on intellectual property law to protect the fruits of their invention. These competing objectives are not easily reconciled. An ongoing review of the EU's Pharmaceuticals Strategy,[102] launched in November 2020, illustrates the difficulties the EU has in this respect. The Covid-19 pandemic focused attention on access to medicines (vaccines), and there may be further moves towards Europeanization of this aspect of pharmaceuticals regulation in the future.[103] The European Commission has proposed a 'Critical Medicines Act' to secure supply of essential medicines to European populations.[104]

5.1 **Medical devices**

EU law treats pharmaceuticals and medical devices quite separately. Medical devices are a special category of the general system of 'CE' product safety certification, a process governed by the 'General Product Safety Directive'.[105] Product safety is determined by 'certification bodies', which are private companies. Comparison with other countries, such as

[101] SL Greer, 'The Three Faces of EU Health Policy: Policy, Markets, Austerity' (2014) 33 *Policy and Society* 13.

[102] Communication from the Commission, 'Pharmaceutical Strategy for Europe', COM/2020/761 final.

[103] See further below, and see S Baute and A de Ruijter, 'EU Health Solidarity in Times of Crisis: Explaining Public Preferences towards EU Risk Pooling for Medicines' (2022) 29(8) *Journal of European Public Policy* 1183.

[104] Proposal for a Regulation of the European Parliament and Council laying a framework for strengthening the availability and security of supply of critical medicinal products as well as the availability of, and accessibility of, medicinal products of common interest, COM(2025)102 final.

[105] Directive 2001/95/EC (OJ [2002] L11/4). See also chapter 23.

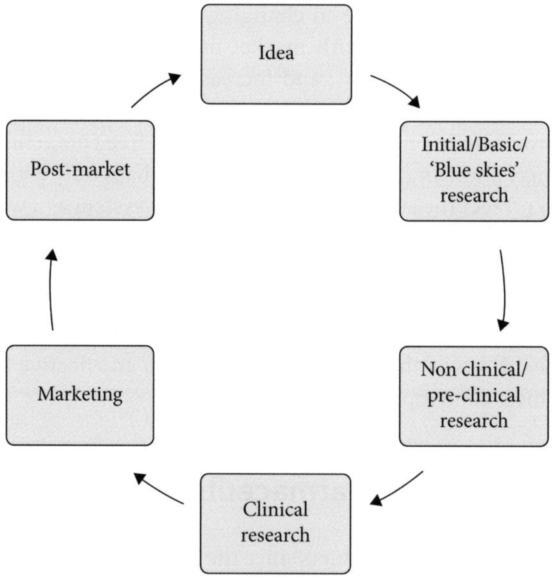

Fig. 21.1 The cycle of health technology innovation

Source: G Bache, M Flear, and T Hervey, 'The Defining Features of the European Union's Approach to Regulating New Health Technologies' in M Flear, T Hervey, AM Farrell, and T Murphy (eds), *European Law and New Health Technologies* (Oxford: Oxford University Press, 2013).

the US, has raised concerns about the appropriateness of this process for medical devices. These concerns came to a head when it was discovered that CE-marked Poly Implant Prothèse breast implants, manufactured in France, and approved by a private German certification body, TÜV-Rheinland, contained a fraudulently substituted industrial grade silicone, which caused a much higher rupture rate and consequent harm to patients.

The Poly Implant Prothèse affair led to reform of the EU's medical devices legislation.[106] The new Regulations seek to secure greater oversight of certification bodies, to pin down who is responsible for securing compliance, and ensure more effective post-market surveillance and traceability of devices. They do not, however, go as far as applying the approach EU law takes to pharmaceuticals. The Regulations provided for a staggered and transitional entry into effect, with the main provisions applying from May 2021, but other provisions coming into effect from May 2025 to May 2028.

The CJEU missed an opportunity to change the legal landscape when it declined to uphold its Advocate General in *Schmitt*.[107] As the manufacturer of her defective breast implants was insolvent, Elisabeth Schmitt sued TÜV-Rheinland for compensation. The CJEU held that tortious liability for product compliance does not extend to certified bodies. Rather, the conditions of liability of notified bodies to end users of medical devices are a matter of national law. The limitations of EU law were also illustrated in the subsequent *Allianz* case.[108] The CJEU found that a challenge brought by a German patient, 'RB', to the clause in the insurance contract held by TÜV-Rheinland with Allianz that restricted liability only to harm occurring in France, fell outside the scope of EU law.[109]

[106] Regulation (EU) 2017/745 (OJ [2017] L117/1); Regulation (EU) 2017/746 (OJ [2017] L117/176).

[107] Case C-219/15 *Schmitt*, EU:C:2017:128.

[108] Case C-581/18 *RB v TÜV Rheinland and Allianz*, EU:C:2020:453.

[109] See B Van Leeuwen, 'The Scope of Application of the Free Movement Provisions and the Role of Article 18 TFEU: Allianz' (2021) 58 *Common Market Law Review* 1249.

5.2 Pharmaceuticals

Pharmaceuticals (defined by 'presentation'[110] and by 'function'[111]) must have an advance marketing authorization (licence) before being sold in the EU. Marketing authorization can be from a national regulatory body, such as France's *Agence Nationale de Sécurité du Médicament et des Produits de Santé*,[112] or from the EU's European Medicines Agency (EMA). Authorization from the EMA is required for novel pharmaceuticals (which include vaccines), for example developed using biotechnology or other high technology processes.[113] Other 'novel' pharmaceuticals—for example, those derived from human plasma, may use the EMA procedures. In practice, this covers virtually all truly new pharmaceuticals.

The EMA operates through its scientific committees, made up of national representatives. It assesses marketing authorization applications, which must be made accompanied by a dossier of specified evidence from clinical trials, designed to demonstrate quality, safety, and efficacy. The test is whether the new pharmaceutical works better than a placebo—there is no obligation to show an improvement on existing treatments, a separate process called 'health technology assessment'. Because such existing treatments are likely to be cheaper (not least because they are likely to be off-patent), this requirement is controversial. There are also significant concerns about whether the EMA's procedures are sufficiently robust to deal with the powerful pharmaceutical industry, whose practices have been criticized for being insufficiently attentive to patient safety, as well as presenting significant burdens to national health systems which must pay for expensive new treatments that are brought to market, if they are authorized within the system. A Regulation on health technology assessment[114] requires Member States to engage in joint decision-making, using common rules and methodologies, although it will not apply to all new medicines until 2030. It does not directly affect national competences to make decisions about the pricing of medicines or access to medicines in practice, that is, which medicines will be available in national health systems.

Criticisms have also been made of the lack of transparency of the EMA, and lack of legal oversight of its work. A good example is the Nordic Cochrane Centre's attempts, described in detail by Ben Goldacre[115] and others, to gain access to data on which the EMA relied to make its decisions on two weight loss drugs, orlistat and rimonabant. Orlistat is currently approved for long-term use by the EMA, and by US and Canadian authorities; rimonabant is not, due to safety concerns. After a lengthy process, during which the EMA maintained that it could not release data because of the commercial interests of the companies concerned, or because individual patient data could not be removed from the files, the European Ombudsman recommended that the EMA release the documents.[116] The EMA agreed to do so, and the information was finally released some three years and seven months after the original request.[117]

[110] 'Any substance or combination of substances presented for treating or preventing disease in human beings'—Directive 2001/83/EC on the 'Community Code relating to medicinal products for human use' (OJ [2001] L311/67), Art 1 (2), as amended.

[111] 'Any substance or combination of substances which may be used in or administered to human beings either with a view to restoring, correcting or modifying physiological functions by exerting a pharmacological, immunological or metabolic action, or to making a medical diagnosis.'

[112] National Agency for Medicines and Health Products Safety.

[113] Regulation (EEC) No 2309/93 (OJ [1993] L214/1), as amended, Annex A.

[114] Regulation (EU) 2021/2282 (OJ [2021] L458/1).

[115] B Goldacre, *Bad Pharma* (London: Fourth Estate, 2012) 70–79.

[116] Decision of the European Ombudsman closing his inquiry into complaint 2560/2007/BEH against the European Medicines Agency, www.ombudsman.europa.eu/en/cases/decision.faces/en/5459/html.bookmark.

[117] PC Gøtzsche and AW Jørgensen, 'Opening Up Data at the European Medicines Agency' (2011) *British Medical Journal*; 342:d2686 doi: 10.1136/bmj.d2686.

The CJEU has confirmed that the general principle of access to documents may be displaced by the commercial confidentiality of information that forms part of a marketing authorization application in a case concerning a new treatment for Duchenne Muscular Dystrophy, [118] a rare muscle-wasting condition. Transparency in the EMA's decision-making became even more critical for marketing authorizations of Covid-19 vaccines, especially given widespread global vaccine denial (ie denial the vaccines are effective). The European Ombudsman investigated the EMA's refusal to make transparent detailed information about the composition and process for manufacturing the mRNA Cominarty and Moderna vaccines, which would, if released, in effect have allowed others to make the vaccines. The Ombudsman found there had been no maladministration on the part of the EMA, reasoning that public health interests did not in this instance displace the need to protect the commercial interests of the manufacturers. The Ombudsman also noted with approval that the EMA had proactively published non-clinical and clinical data about the safety and efficacy of the mRNA vaccines.[119]

The role of the EMA is considered further in case study 21.2.

Case study 21.2: Nancy Fern Olivieri and the *Deferiprone* trials

In the early 1990s, a Canadian scientist at the University of Toronto, Dr Olivieri, signed a contract with Apotex, to support a randomized clinical trial on deferiprone, a promising new treatment for thalassaemia (a blood disorder). The contract included standard confidentiality clauses, which required her to keep all trial data secret for a number of years. Olivieri had previously approached the Canadian Medical Research Council, which had declined to sponsor such trials itself, but had suggested that she apply under its 'university-industry' programme. The involvement of private industry in University research is standard practice, in Canada, and in Europe.

Initial trial data was positive, and Olivieri published a paper to that effect in 1995. However, she soon became concerned that, while the results overall looked promising, for a small subgroup of patients, outcomes were much worse. She asked Apotex if she could conduct a separate trial to investigate this, and explained that she had an ethical obligation to inform those patients, and also the University's Research Ethics Board. Apotex reviewed her data, told her that they did not agree with her interpretation of it, terminated her contract, and reminded her of the obligations under the confidentiality clauses. Academics John Abraham and Courtney Davis say that Olivieri had broken an 'unspoken code' of loyalty to the company.

Deferiprone was not granted marketing authorization from Canadian or US authorities. However, Apotex turned to the global market. In 1998, it applied to the EMA for a marketing authorization, using Olivieri's trial data, but without her signature. EMA's scientific committee reviewed the data, and recommended that EMA grant an authorization. Before the European Commission took a formal decision, Olivieri wrote to the committee members, and to the EMA, setting out her concerns. EMA reinvestigated, but granted authorization.

Olivieri sought judicial review of the Commission's decision. The General Court held that the case was inadmissible. Olivieri had not established an interest in bringing proceedings in order to protect public health or in order to defend her professional reputation. That decision, to dismiss the case on the basis of lack of *locus standi* (see chapter 10) and therefore not

[118] Case C-175/18 P *PTC Therapeutics*, EU:C:2020:23.

[119] European Ombudsman, Decision on the European Medicines Agency's (EMA) refusal of public access to documents relating to the manufacturing of mRNA vaccines against COVID-19 (case 1458/2021/MIG), www.ombudsman.europa.eu/en/decision/en/149025.

to review its substance, is highly unfortunate. There are obvious differences in opinion as to how to interpret the relevant scientific information. We might legitimately expect EU law, and the scrutiny of courts, to support processes of making scientific disagreement more visible to policymaking processes and to the public. And yet the Court's decision meant that in this instance it failed to take the opportunity of increasing transparency and accountability. Deferiprone is still on the EU market.

6 **Blood, organs, and human tissue**

The EU also regulates blood, organs, and human tissue. It does so in two main ways: by requiring Member States to set up institutions and processes of quality control to ensure patient safety; and through intellectual property law.

6.1 **Patient safety**

In the 1990s, the EU adopted soft law concerning blood safety, responding to the global AIDS epidemic, and the fact that the EU was reliant on blood from developing and transitional economies. These soft law measures set out non-binding principles for blood donation in the EU, and recommended that the Member States should 'encourage the voluntary and unpaid donation of blood or plasma',[120] as the safest source of human blood. Now Article 168(4) TFEU gives the EU competence to adopt 'measures setting high standards of quality and safety of organs and substances of human origin, blood or blood derivatives'. The EU has done so, following a standard model in its legislation,[121] which requires Member States to establish 'competent authorities', whose task is to ensure that quality assurance procedures are followed. The competent authorities manage risk in the collection, testing, processing, storage, and distribution of human materials, and collect and share information on safety.

The EU's blood safety laws fail to acknowledge sufficiently the reality of the EU market for human blood and plasma products.[122] The underlying approach stresses voluntary donation and an ethic of altruism. There is, however, some scope for out-of-pocket payments, in all of the relevant legislation.[123] The Organs Directive goes further, in that it recognizes that living organ donors might need to be compensated for loss of income.[124]

As well as EU legislation on blood and organ safety, there is CJEU case law. Legislation prohibiting importation of blood products where payment had been made for the donation of the blood breaches EU law on free movement of goods, and is not justified by the need to protect public health.[125] A Member State may not specify, in a public procurement tender for plasma-derived medicines, that plasma must be sourced only from that Member State.[126] In both decisions, the CJEU relied on permissions in EU Blood Safety legislation. Implicitly, therefore, the CJEU has accepted that EU law does not require that the donation of human material in health contexts be completely separated from the

[120] Recommendation 98/463/EC, para 14.

[121] Regulation 2024/1938/EU on substances of human origin (OJ [2024] L1938), ELI: http://data.europa.eu/eli/reg/2024/1938/oj, replacing Directives 2002/98/EC and Directive 2004/23/EC, into effect in 2027; Organs Directive 2010/53/EU (OJ [2010] L207/14).

[122] See AM Farrell, *The Politics of Blood* (Cambridge: Cambridge University Press, 2012).

[123] Regulation 2024/1938/EU, Art 54; Directive 2002/98/EC, Art 20; Directive 2004/23/EC, Art 12; Directive 2010/53/EU, Art 13(2); see Case C-421/09 *Humanplasma* [2010] ECR I-2869, para 44.

[124] Directive 2010/53/EU, Art 13(2).

[125] Case C-421/09 *Humanplasma*, EU:C:2010:760.

[126] Case C-296/15 *Medisanus*, EU:C:2017:431.

internal market. These examples have important implications for the balance between the interests of EU-wide economic development, expressed through the permissive position of internal market law, and the interests of individuals in safe health care, expressed through policies of precaution.

Similarly, the CJEU has given guidance to national courts on how to interpret the balance between human rights protection, and in particular non-discrimination on grounds of sexuality, and blood safety, in the context of a case involving a national policy permanently excluding men who have had sex with men from being blood donors. The CJEU held that such a permanent ban might not be consistent with the principle of proportionality.[127]

6.2 **Intellectual property**

The purpose of a patent is to grant the inventor of a novel product or process exclusive rights over its invention for a period of time, in exchange for full disclosure of the invention. The idea is to reward innovation, by allowing inventors to safeguard the fruits of their labours and investment. Patents can be used as a way of *indirectly* regulating behaviour, because in practice, without the safeguard of a patent right, inventors may either be discouraged from seeking new discoveries, or may seek to keep their inventions secret, inhibiting the benefits of those inventions being known more widely.

Where a novel product or process involves human material, either in the product itself, or in the process by which the product is created, questions of ethics arise. The EU has become involved in these questions.[128] Directive 98/44/EC on the legal protection of biotechnological inventions requires Member States to recognize biotechnology patents, including where human material is involved.[129] But the Directive excludes patentability of certain products or processes, where commercial exploitation would be contrary to *ordre public*, or morality.[130] In particular, the Directive provides that 'uses of human embryos for industrial or commercial purposes' shall be considered unpatentable.[131] The scope of this exclusion is not entirely clear from the text of the Directive: what counts as a 'human embryo' for these purposes?

Brüstle[132] and *International Stem Cell* give some guidance.[133] The science is complex here, and so are its legal and ethical implications. But the essence of the CJEU's purposive approach is to distinguish on the basis of whether the cells at issue 'have the inherent capacity of developing into a human being'.[134] In both cases, the CJEU ultimately left this question to the national court.

The cases illustrate well the interactions between national and EU level judicial decision-making on matters of ethical sensitivity. The CJEU articulates a strong ethic of human dignity, drawing on Europe's human rights tradition. Although the legal basis of the Directive is to create the internal market, the needs of market actors appear secondary in the CJEU's reasoning. Yet, in practice, the significant discretion left to the national court allows for patenting of inventions involving human material, at least in those Member States where national courts are willing to exercise the discretion left to them by the preliminary reference procedure accordingly. Hence, some of the more extreme predictions from the commentary surrounding the CJEU's *Brüstle* decision (for instance, that the biotechnology industry would cease to invest in the EU) turned out to

[127] Case C-528/13 *Léger*, EU:C:2015:288.

[128] See further M Flear, AM Farrell, T Hervey, and T Murphy (eds) *European Law and New Health Technologies* (Oxford: Oxford University Press, 2013); T Hervey and H Black, 'The European Union and the Governance of Stem Cell Research' (2005) 12 *Maastricht Journal of European and Comparative Law* 11.

[129] (OJ [1998] L213/13), Art 1 (1).

[130] Arts 4, 5, and 6.

[131] Art 6(2)(c).

[132] Case C-34/10 *Brüstle* [2011] ECR I-9821.

[133] Case C-364/13 *International Stem Cell*, EU:C:2014:2451.

[134] Ibid, para 27.

be unwarranted. A 2012 attempt to use the European Citizens Initiative[135] to change EU law to outlaw all research activities that involve human embryos was unsuccessful.[136]

7 **Public health**

The EU has explicit competence to take action that *complements* national competence to improve public health, through coordination and incentive measures, but not harmonization.[137] When it came to the Covid-19 pandemic, it was the Member States that took key legal decisions, including 'stay-at-home orders'; closures of shops, businesses, and schools; travel restrictions (justified in EU internal market law);[138] furlough schemes; and the like. The EU's contributions focused on coordinating and sharing information and scientific advice, through the European Centre for Disease Control, acting in partnership with national entities; and on the benefits of economies of scale of EU-level action. For example, the EU used its bargaining power to secure tests, treatments and vaccines on behalf of its Member States.[139]

Relying on soft law and deploying EU resources to tackle the pandemic is consistent with the allocation of competences in the Treaties, although the EU has been criticized for failing to act effectively, especially at the start of the pandemic.[140] There were consequent calls for changes to the EU's health competences, in the form of a 'European Health Union',[141] or at least clarification of the blurred lines between 'supporting and complementing' areas and shared competence;[142] and some institutional changes were made, in particular a new Directorate General within the European Commission, the Health Emergency Preparedness and Response Authority (HERA).[143]

Nevertheless, the EU did adopt some binding legislation in response to the pandemic. For example, marketing authorizations for Covid-19 vaccines are formally speaking European Commission decisions.[144] The mutually-recognized 'Digital Covid-19 certificate', necessary for opening up travel in 2021, was created through Regulations.[145]

Internal market law concerning trade in food, alcohol, and tobacco also has important effects on public health. For example, when Finland joined the EU, it was required to dismantle its state monopoly on alcohol sales. Following the accession of Estonia in 2004, Finland had to reduce its domestic prices in the face of cheap imports from just 'over the

[135] Art 11(4) TEU, Art 24(1) TFEU.

[136] Case C-418/18 P *Puppinck*, EU:C:2019:1113.

[137] Art 168 TFEU.

[138] I Goldner Lang, '"Laws of Fear" in the EU: The Precautionary Principle and Public Health Restrictions to Free Movement of Persons in the Time of Covid-19' (2021) 12 *European Journal of Risk Regulation* 1.

[139] See eg European Commission, 'Commission Decision of 18.6.2020 approving the agreement with Member States on procuring Covid-19 vaccines on behalf of the Member States and related procedures', C(2020) 4192 final.

[140] See further T Hervey and S Röttger-Wirtz, 'The European Union', entry for *The Oxford Compendium of National Legal Responses to Covid-19*, open access at https://lexatlas-c19.org/; V Delhomme and T Hervey, 'The European Union's Response to the Covid-19 Crisis and (the Legitimacy of) the Union's Legal Order' (2023) 41 *Yearbook of European Law* 48, yeac01.

[141] https://europeanhealthunion.eu.

[142] See S Garben 'Supporting Policies' in PJ Kuijper and F Amtenbrink (eds), *The Law of the European Union* (Alphen aan den Rijn: Kluwer Law International, 2018).

[143] Commission Decision of 16 September 2021 establishing the Health Emergency Preparedness and Response Authority (OJ [2021] C393I/3).

[144] An up-to-date list may be viewed here: www.ema.europa.eu/en/human-regulatory/overview/public-health-threats/coronavirus-disease-covid-19/treatments-vaccines/vaccines-covid-19/covid-19-vaccines-authorised.

[145] Regulation (EU) 2021/953 on the EU Digital COVID Certificate OJ [2021] L211/1; Regulation (EU) 2021/954 on the EU Digital COVID Certificate with regard to third-country nationals (OJ [2021] L211/24).

water'. The consequence was a steep rise in deaths from alcohol-related problems. Scotland's Alcohol (Minimum Pricing) Act 2012 was challenged for its consistency with Article 34 on free movement of goods, including by the Scotch Whisky Association. The CJEU held[146] that the measure might be disproportionate, but the UK Supreme Court held that it was a proportionate response to the specific public health needs of the Scottish population.[147]

In principle, the EU has considerable legal powers which could be deployed to address obesity, which has become a major European health problem since the 1990s: the Common Agricultural Policy above all, but also food regulation within the internal market. In practice, however, the food industry's links with powerful national governments have kept EU food legislation relatively low key. For example, the proposed 'traffic light' system on 'guideline daily amounts' (the proportion of an average adult recommended amount of protein, fat, sugars, salt and so on present in a food) did not survive in the final text of the 2011 EU Food Information Regulation.[148] Nonetheless, that regulation does prohibit making unjustified health claims that might mislead consumers into thinking that sugar is healthy.[149]

The EU's public health law concerning tobacco began with its 1987 'Europe against Cancer' programme.[150] Several Directives, adopted under qualified majority voting in Council, covering tobacco products and their labelling, as well as taxation, had been adopted by 1992.[151] These cover matters such as permitted tar, carbon monoxide and nicotine levels, and health warnings. The health warnings provisions were considerably tightened in 2001,[152] to include a ban on misleading product descriptions, such as 'light' and 'mild'. Further legislation on tobacco additives, labelling, and packaging, as well as on new products, in particular, 'e-cigarettes', was adopted in 2014.[153] The global tobacco industry has been persistent in its opposition to EU health law in this area. Nothing better exemplifies this opposition than the tobacco advertising example (see case study 21.3).[154] In

Case study 21.3: Tobacco advertising

Although the tobacco industry claims that its advertising is aimed at encouraging existing smokers to switch brands, banning tobacco advertising has been proven to reduce smoking. The EU banned all TV advertising of tobacco in Directive 89/552/EEC on cross-border TV services. Eventually, after years of opposition to proposals, Directive 98/43/EC introduced a more comprehensive ban on tobacco advertising across the EU.

This Directive was challenged by Germany, as well as several tobacco companies, as unlawful. The argument was that its 'legal basis' (the Treaty provision giving competence to the EU institutions to adopt the law) was insufficient. The legal basis was for internal market legislation; this was, in reality, a public health measure. Hence, to rely on internal market

[146] Case C-333/14 *Scotch Whisky Association*, EU:C:2015: 845.

[147] *Scotch Whisky Association* [2017] UKSC 76.

[148] Regulation 1169/2011/EU (OJ [2011] L304/18).

[149] See Case T-100/15 *Dextro Energy*, EU:T:2016:150.

[150] Resolution of Council and the Representatives of the Governments of the Member States on a programme of action of the European Communities against cancer (OJ [1986] C184/19).

[151] Directive 89/622/EEC on labelling (OJ [1989] L359/1); Directive 90/239/EEC on tar yield (OJ [1990] L137/36); Directive 92/41/EEC on smokeless tobacco (OJ [1992] L158/30); Directive 92/80/EEC on taxes on manufactured tobacco other than cigarettes (OJ [1992] L316/10); Directive 92/78/EEC on taxes other than turnover taxes (OJ [1992] L316/1); Directive 92/41/EEC amending labelling Directive 89/622/EEC (OJ [1992] L158/30).

[152] Directive 2001/37/EC on manufacture, presentation, and sale of tobacco products (OJ [2001] L194/26).

[153] Directive 2014/40/EU on manufacture, presentation, and sale of tobacco products (OJ [2014] L127/1). It was challenged (unsuccessfully) in Cases C-358/14 *Poland v Parliament and Council*; C-477/14 *Pillbox 38(UK)*; and C-547/14 *Philip Morris and others*, EU:C:2016:325.

[154] See also chapter 11.

competence was a misuse of power. The CJEU rejected this particular reasoning, but it did hold that the Directive was invalid. It pointed out that prohibiting tobacco advertising on items such as posters, parasols, ashtrays, which do not cross borders, or in advertising slots in cinemas, in no way facilitates trade within the internal market.

Following the ruling, a revised Directive was adopted, taking into account guidance from the earlier decision. Subsequent challenges to that Directive were unsuccessful.

Why is Germany so opposed to tobacco advertising regulation? This was a bit of a puzzle. Production of tobacco in Europe is mainly concentrated in the south of Europe. Only around 3,000 hectares are devoted to growing tobacco in Germany; compare the figure for Italy, for instance, which is some 30,000. Information that has since come to light, in part through orders made by US courts requiring access to documents, shed some light on the lobbying processes involved. It seems that the significant German technical industry producing machinery and machine parts for production of cigarettes (not the tobacco-growing industry itself) explains the German opposition to tobacco regulation, and also why the tobacco industry targeted Germany as a key component of its opposition to EU regulation.

2026, five Member States challenged the application of the UK's Tobacco and Vapes Act in Northern Ireland, arguing that it obviously breaches EU law. It does not.[155]

8 Global contexts

Health is a global concern. This much is patently obvious from the Covid-19 pandemic.

But also, patients seeking medical treatment outside of their home country do not confine themselves to the EU—global medical tourism is on the increase. A mobile world and a global food industry (food is an important disease vector, eg salmonella in eggs and pork; e-coli in beef; campylobacter in poultry) mean that tackling communicable diseases must happen on a global level. EU and national regulation of food, alcohol, and tobacco, to protect health, must fit within global trade rules for goods, governed by the World Trade Organization (WTO). Pharmaceutical companies, in particular, are influential global actors, often operating through international organizations, such as the International Conference on Harmonisation of Technical Requirements for Registration of Pharmaceuticals for Human Use (ICH). The ICH agrees technical requirements for demonstrating the quality, safety, and efficacy of new medicines. Although formally non-binding, the ICH guidelines have a 'hard' effect in practice, because, under national or EU law, compliance is necessary for clinical trials or marketing authorization. The World Bank has considered the opportunities and challenges arising from the creation of global health service markets.

How does EU health law contribute to global health?

The EU was explicitly given external Treaty competence in health fields for the first time in 1992. The Treaty of Lisbon consolidated EU external competence rules: 'The Union and the Member States shall foster cooperation with third countries and the competent international organisations in the sphere of public health.'[156] In 2003, the EU signed the World Health Organization (WHO) Framework Convention on Tobacco Control, the WHO's first binding international treaty on global health concerns. The EU negotiated—for matters within its competence[157]—the WHO Pandemic Agreement 2025.

[155] V Delhomme, A de Ruijter, T Hervey, M McKee, J Veraldi, 'Tobacco End-Game Policies and the Intrinsic Connection of health and EU market law' Health Economics Policy and Law 2026].

[156] Art 168(3) TFEU.

[157] Council Decision 2022/451/EC on the international agreement on pandemic prevention (OJ [2022] L92/1).

8.1 **Health through the common commercial policy**

There is, overall, relatively little formal EU external relations law in health fields. But the EU's 'common commercial policy' and its development cooperation policy (section 8.2) form a central platform for those aspects of its external health law that are more developed, and new law on health security (section 8.3) is emerging.

EU health policy concerning the safety of food (and feed), covered by the WTO Agreement on Sanitary and Phytosanitary Measures (SPS),[158] falls within the fields of trade in goods, and agriculture, both of which are within the EU's competences. Competence is shared with the Member States, so both the EU and the Member States have ratified the SPS Agreement. Specific public health scares, such as the BSE/vCJD ('mad cow') crisis, or dioxins in pork, have prompted international agreements with countries such as the US,[159] Australia, and New Zealand, in which the EU agreed very detailed rules on animal slaughter, sterilization, inspection and so on. The EU is associated with a more precautionary approach to risks to human health than the US.

In Opinion 2/2015 on the EU–Singapore Trade Agreement,[160] the CJEU reconfirmed that EU competence for external trade in services, and for the 'commercial aspects' of intellectual property, is exclusive. Trade in services includes trade in health services; intellectual property is crucial for development of novel health technologies. Exclusive EU competence over these aspects of trade agreements means that individual Member States no longer have a veto. Any protections for health systems, like the 'sustainable development' provisions in the Singapore Agreement, will need to be secured by the Council acting on behalf of all the Member States.

8.2 **Health through development cooperation**

The EU's development cooperation policy affects health in several ways—through the EU's contribution to the 'Sustainable Development Goals',[161] which include public health concerns and global health inequalities; through infrastructure and capacity building, including human resource development; and through specific project-based work, for instance combating HIV/AIDS, malaria, and tuberculosis. An important element of the EU's development policy concerns access to essential medicines.

'Essential medicines', according to the WHO, are those needed for the priority health needs of a population. The WHO 'essential medicines' list provides a check for governments, particularly in least developed countries. The idea is that access to these 'essential medicines', should be available, irrespective of class, race, religion, sexuality, and other 'forbidden grounds', and at a price affordable to individuals and the community.[162] Sustainable Development Goal 3 calls for 'access to safe, effective, quality and affordable essential medicines and vaccines for all'.[163] Yet it is reported that progress towards this goal is too slow, and the Covid-19 pandemic made matters worse. Many patients in least developed and developing countries do not have access to essential medicines.

[158] WTO Agreement on the Application of Sanitary and Phytosanitary Measures 1995 (OJ [1994] L336/40).

[159] Agreement between the EC and the USA with regard to the bovine and porcine fresh meat trade (OJ [1993] L68/1); Agreements between the EC and the USA on sanitary measures to protect public and animal health in trade in live animals and animal products (OJ [1998] L118/3) and (OJ [2003] L316/21); Agreement between the EC and New Zealand on sanitary measures applicable to trade in live animals and animal products (OJ [2003] L214/38).

[160] Opinion 2/15 of 16 May 2017, EU:C:2017:376. See also Case C-137/12 *Commission v Council*, EU:C:2013:675; Case C-414/11 *Daiichi Sankyo Co Ltd*, EU:C:2013:520.

[161] Successors to the 'Millennium Development Goals', a series of time-bound targets (originally with a deadline of 2015) towards ending extreme poverty, agreed at the UN in 2000.

[162] www.who.int/activities/strengthening-access-to-essential-medicines.

[163] www.un.org/sustainabledevelopment/health.

The EU uses its development law and policy inter alia to secure access to essential medicines in low- and middle-income countries. In December 2021, the EU adjusted its development budget to include supply of Covid-19 vaccines to such countries.[164] But the relatively small scale and slow pace of the EU's response have been criticized.[165]

The EU has also been criticized for supporting a global intellectual property regime that contributes to this global health inequality. Operating through the WTO's Agreement on Trade Related Aspects of Intellectual Property Rights (TRIPS), the EU has recognized a global 20-year patent for novel pharmaceuticals. During that time, generic equivalents to those pharmaceuticals may not enter the marketplace. These generics are much cheaper to produce than on-patent pharmaceuticals, because they are 'reverse engineered' from the on-patent product. The entry into force of TRIPS in 1995 put an end to the practice, in many developing countries, particularly India, of making such generics both for home markets, and for markets in other developing and least developed countries. However, in 2001, a group of 80 developing and least developed countries successfully proposed the 'Doha Declaration', which:

> reaffirms the right of WTO members to use, to the full, the provisions in the TRIPS Agreement which provide flexibility . . . to protect public health and, in particular, to promote access to medicines for all.[166]

One possibility for increasing global equal access to essential medicines is to encourage developing and least developed countries to take advantage of these TRIPS flexibilities. Some have suggested that the EU has done quite the opposite. On the other hand, EU technical assistance to developing countries in intellectual property matters puts more emphasis on incorporating TRIPS flexibilities in national law, including those flexibilities concerning public health, than technical assistance from other developed countries.

8.3 **Health as security**

Increasingly, the EU is considering health to be among its security concerns.[167] This is slowly emerging in legal form.

For example, Regulation 2022/2371/EU on serious cross-border threats to health includes the formal legal power to declare a public health emergency,[168] which, once declared, has clearly delineated (though also non-exhaustive) legal effects for the European Union institutions, such as to monitor and respond to critical medical shortages, including by joint procurement of medicines or vaccines.

However, much of the relevant law is focused on *European* health security, rather than the focus on global health security which would be necessary in the event of a future global health security crisis, such as another pandemic.[169]

[164] Commission Implementing Decision on the financing of the special measure in favour of contributing to the global immunisation efforts against the COVID-19 in low and lower-middle income countries for 2021, C(2021) 9933 final.

[165] TV Padma, 'Covid Vaccines Won't Reach Poorest Countries before 2023' (2021) 595 *Nature* 342 (15 July).

[166] The Doha Declaration on the TRIPS Agreement and Public Health, adopted by the WTO Ministerial Conference, 14 November 2001, WT/MIN(01)/DEC/2.

[167] European Commission, 'Joint Communication to the European Parliament, the European Council, the Council, the European Economic and Social Committee and the Committee of the Regions on the European Preparedness Union Strategy' (2025), JOIN(2025) 130 final.

[168] Regulation 2022/2371/EU on serious cross-border threats to health (OJ [2022] L314/55).

[169] See eg M Dukovic and T Hervey, 'Strengthening Legal Preparedness in the European Union after the Pandemic: Law, Policy and Parliamentary Accountability' in M Balestrieri and A Cauduro, (eds), *The Legal Anatomy of the Body: Health, Rights, and Politics in Time of Emergency* (Berlin: Springer, 2026).

Assessing the contribution of EU health law to overall global health is not easy. Some aspects of EU health law—such as its approach to health risks arising from trade in food—suggest a positive contribution. Yet other aspects of EU law may actually have negative effects on global health, through, for instance, supporting the TRIPS system, or focusing only on European and European neighbouring countries.

9 Conclusion

EU health law cuts across the taxonomy accepted by EU lawyers[170] as establishing the categories of EU law. In order to understand EU health law, which has a logic of its own,[171] we need to look at the health implications of many areas of EU law, including free movement law, competition law, and external relations law.

EU health law illustrates many of the key tensions of EU law in general. How should EU law balance the 'economic', such as benefits from free trade and fair competition, and the 'social', such as arrangements within welfare systems? How should EU law balance individual choice, such as patients choosing where to have medical treatment, and community solidarity, such as protecting cash-strapped national health systems from individual claims on resource? Who should decide: courts or the legislature? Which courts: national courts or the CJEU? Is it justifiable for a court, for the CJEU, to undermine a legislative settlement, for instance on coordination of national health systems for migrant patients? Where should decisions about risks to health be made, at regional, national, EU, or global level? Who should be 'at the table', to ensure such decisions are legitimate? How do we ensure sufficient transparency, and judicial scrutiny, to support decisional accountability? How, if at all, should EU law tackle global inequality? These questions will continue to be resolved through litigation and legislation, involving the EU institutions, and in interactions with national and global actors.

Further reading

A De Ruijter, *EU Health Law and Policy: The Expansion of EU Power in Public Health and Health Care* (Oxford: Oxford University Press, 2019)

K Fierlbeck (ed), *Healthcare and the Fate of Social Europe, Vol 46 of the Journal of Health Politics, Policy and Law* (Duke University Press, 2021)

S Greer, 'The Three Faces of EU Health Policy: Policy, Markets, Austerity' (2014) 33 *Policy and Society* 13

L Hancher and W Sauter, *EU Competition and Internal Market Law in the Health Care Sector* (Oxford: Oxford University Press, 2012)

T Hervey and J McHale, *European Union Health Law: Themes and Implications* (Cambridge: Cambridge University Press, 2015)

T Hervey, C Young, and L Bishop, *Research Handbook on EU Health Law and Policy* (Cheltenham: Edward Elgar, 2017)

170 Represented, eg, in the main chapter headings in textbooks on EU law, in the way in which the TEU and TFEU are organized into different parts and chapters, each covering different legal topics, and in the taxonomy according to which the EU institutions, particularly the European Commission, organize EU law.

171 T Hervey, 'Telling Stories about European Union Health Law: The Emergence of a New Field of Law' (2016) 15 *Comparative European Politics* 352.

22

Environmental law

Elisa Morgera, Kati Kulovesi, and Seita Vesa

1 Introduction

Environmental protection is an essential component of any policy aimed at improving human well-being: clean air and water, and healthy lands and seas are essential to human life and health, adequate nutrition, and cultural and recreational activities—in fact, these are essential for the protection of basic human rights,[1] as recognized by the UN General Assembly with regard to everyone's human right to a healthy environment.[2] Environmental protection also contributes to ensuring the long-term maintenance of economic activities that are based on the use of natural resources (the agricultural, fishing, and logging sectors) or depend on well-preserved natural features (the tourism sector). While traditionally environmental regulation tended to protect the environment from degradation arising from economic activities, more recently it has attempted to protect the environment and encourage sustainable economies at the same time. Thus, one of the key themes that will be explored in this chapter is how and to what extent EU environmental law has attempted to reconcile conflicting objectives, either by trying to strike a balance between competing environmental and economic objectives or by integrating environmental and economic objectives through market-based mechanisms and other innovative regulatory approaches. As environmental protection is a dynamic and ever-expanding area of international law, the other key theme explored in this chapter is the influence of international environmental law over EU environmental

[1] Report of the Special Rapporteur on the Issue of Human Rights and the Environment John Knox: Framework Principles on Human Rights and the Environment, UN Doc A/HRC/34/49 (2017).

[2] UN General Assembly Resolution 76/300 of 1 August 2022.

law, and attempts by the EU to influence the further development of international environmental law.

The EU has developed over 200 secondary legislative instruments covering a wide array of environmental issues, ranging from the conservation of nature to water, air pollution, climate change, noise, dangerous substances, genetically modified organisms, waste, and nuclear safety. This legislative activity has been highly influential on Member States, where 70–80 per cent of national environmental law is of EU origin.[3] In addition, EU environmental law has been very pervasive in seeking to 'green' other areas of EU law, such as the Common Agricultural, Transport, and Fisheries Policies. Environmental law is also an area where the EU has experimented with new concepts and approaches that have progressively become part of general EU law.[4] This is the case of the subsidiarity principle, which calls for Union action only if and insofar as the objectives to be achieved cannot be sufficiently achieved by the Member States but can be better achieved at EU level by reason of the scale or effects of the proposed action.[5] It is also demonstrated by the use of financial penalties against Member States infringing EU law, which has been progressively refined in environmental cases.[6]

This chapter will first introduce the legal framework of EU environmental policy, by explaining its historic evolution, as well as its current objectives and principles. It will then explore two representative areas of EU environmental law: nature conservation and climate change, with a view to highlighting two trends of broader relevance to the understanding of EU environmental law as a whole: the interaction between environmental protection and economic development, and the interaction between EU and international environmental law.

2 The legal framework

2.1 Evolution of EU environmental law

Given the abundance and pervasiveness of EU environmental law today, it may be surprising that initially the EEC, when it was established by the original Treaty of Rome in 1957, had no mandate to address issues related to environmental protection. It has only been over time, through successive Treaty revisions, that the EU environmental policy that we know today has emerged. The evolution of the Treaty provisions on the environment thus provides key indications as to the Union's changing approach to environmental regulation, which has to a significant extent also been shaped by concurrent developments in international environmental law (see Table 22.1).[7]

[3] L Kramer, 'Regional Economic International Organizations: The European Union as an Example' in D Bodansky et al (eds), *The Oxford Handbook of International Environmental Law* (Oxford: Oxford University Press, 2007).

[4] J Jans, 'Environmental Spill-Overs into General Community Law' (2008) 31 *Fordham International Law Journal* 1360.

[5] Art 5(3) TEU; see further chapter 5.

[6] Case C-387/97 *Commission v Greece* [2000] ECR I-5047; Case C-278/01 *Commission v Spain* [2003] ECR I-14141; Case C-304/02 *Commission v France* [2005] ECR I-6263; and Case C-494/01 *Commission v Ireland* [2005] ECR I-3331.

[7] E Morgera, M Geelhoed, and M Ntona, 'European Environmental Law' in E Techera et al (eds), *Routledge Handbook of International Environmental Law* (2nd edn, Abingdon: Routledge, 2020) and I von Homeyer, 'The Evolution of EU Environmental Governance' in J Scott (ed), *Environmental Protection: European Law and Governance* (Oxford: Oxford University Press, 2009).

Table 22.1 Summary table of the evolution of EU environmental law

	Treaty changes	Evolution of EU environmental law	Enlargements	International environmental law developments
First Phase (1958–72)	• European Coal and Steel Community (1952–2002) • Treaty of Rome (1958) Birth of the **EEC** (common market) • EURATOM Treaty (1958)	• Lack of reference to the environment in the Treaty of Rome • Incidental environmental action: eg Directive 67/548 on classification, packaging and labelling of dangerous preparations[8]	• Founding members: Belgium, Germany, France, Italy, Luxembourg, and the Netherlands	• Sporadic initiatives for the protection of natural resources at the international level
Second Phase (1973–86)		• First Environmental Action Programme (1973–76) • Case C-240/83 *ADBHU*: environmental protection as an 'essential objective' • 1979: Wild Birds Directive[9]	• 1973: UK, Ireland, and Denmark • 1981: Greece • 1986: Spain and Portugal	• 1972: Stockholm Conference on Human Environment • EC becomes party to Barcelona Convention for the protection of the Mediterranean Sea against Pollution (1978), Berne Convention on the Conservation of European Wildlife and Natural Habitats and Convention on the Conservation of the marine fauna and flora of the Antarctic (1982), Convention on the Conservation of Migratory Species and Convention on Long-range Transboundary Air Pollution (1983)
Third Phase (1987–92)	• Single European Act (1987) Elimination of remaining barriers to single market	• explicit legal basis for environmental policy • unanimous decision-making • 1992: Habitats Directive[10]		• EC becomes party to Convention for the Protection of the Ozone Layer and its Montreal Protocol (1989)

(*Continued*)

[8] OJ [1967] 191/1. [9] See n 106; discussed in section 3.1. [10] See n 107; discussed in section 3.2.

Table 22.1 (*Continued*)

	Treaty changes	Evolution of EU environmental law	Enlargements	International environmental law developments
Fourth Phase (1993–97)	• Maastricht Treaty (1993) EC and EU Economic and monetary union Cooperation in foreign and security policy	• introduced 'environment' into overarching Treaty provisions • precautionary principle and objective of promoting measures to deal with regional and worldwide environmental problems • reference to 'sustainable growth' • qualified majority voting (with exceptions) • 1996 Directive on Integrated Pollution Prevention and Control[11]	• 1995: Austria, Finland, and Sweden	• 1992: Rio Conference on the Environment and Development • EC becomes a party to UN Framework Convention on Climate Change (UNFCCC), the Convention on Biological Diversity (CBD) and Basel Convention on the Control of Transboundary Movements of Hazardous Wastes and their Disposal (1994)
Fifth Phase (1999–2008)	• Treaty of Amsterdam (1999) Fundamental rights and principles of democracy, liberty, and rule of law Area of Freedom, Security and Justice	• Sustainable development and high level of environmental protection among the overarching provisions of EC law • Environmental integration as general principles of EU law (Article 11 TFEU) • Co-decision (ordinary legislative procedure) • 2000: Water Framework Directive	• 2004 ('big-bang enlargement'): Cyprus, Czech Republic, Estonia, Hungary, Latvia, Lithuania, Malta, Poland, Slovakia, and Slovenia Environmental policy becomes formally an area to be specifically addressed in pre-accession negotiations • 2007: Romania and Bulgaria	• 2002: World Summit on Sustainable Development • EC becomes a party to the UN Convention on the Law of the Sea, UN Convention to Combat Desertification (1998); Kyoto Protocol to the UNFCCC and Cartagena Protocol on Biosafety to the CBD (2003); Stockholm Convention on Persistent Organic Pollutants and Rotterdam Convention on the Prior Informed Consent Procedure for Certain Hazardous Chemicals and Pesticides in International Trade (2004); Aarhus Convention on Access to Information, Public Participation in Decision-Making and Access to Justice in Environmental Matters (2005)

[11] Directive 2008/1/EC of the European Parliament and of the Council of 15 January 2008 concerning integrated pollution prevention and control (codified version) (OJ [2008] L24/8).

Table 22.1 (*Continued*)

	Treaty changes	Evolution of EU environmental law	Enlargements	International environmental law developments
The present (2009–)	• Lisbon Treaty (2009) • EU with legal personality (merged with EC) • Institutional amendments • EU Charter with the same legal value as Treaties (Article 6 TEU) • General integration/coherence clause (Article 7 TFEU)	• Explicit reference to climate change (Article 191(1) TFEU) • new legal basis on energy policy (Article 194 TFEU) • Environmental component of new unified legal basis for external action (Articles 3(5) and 21(2) TEU) • 2009: Climate and Energy Package 2018: 2030 Climate and Energy Framework[12] 2019 European Green Deal 2021 Regulation establishing the framework for achieving climate neutrality	• 2013: Croatia (Candidate countries: Turkey, Serbia, Montenegro, Albania, and FYR Macedonia Potential candidate countries: Bosnia and Herzegovina, and Kosovo)	• 2012: Rio+20 UN Summit 2017: Minamata Convention on Mercury 2016: Paris Agreement on climate change 2022 UN General Assembly recognized the human right to a healthy environment 2024: Advisory Opinion of the International Tribunal for the Law of the Sea on State Obligations on Climate Change 2025: Advisory Opinion of the International Court of Justice on State obligations on Climate Change

[12] See discussion in section 4.1.

Note: the year of entry into force of Treaties is provided (and in the case of multilateral environmental agreements, the date of entry into force of that agreement for the EU is indicated).

If we consider parallel international developments, it is not so surprising that the Treaty of Rome did not contain any reference to the environment: environmental issues were generally not a policy concern in the 1950s. It was only with the convening of the first global summit on environmental protection in 1972 (the Stockholm Conference on the Human Environment) that the international community (and the EEC) recognized the urgent need for environmental protection.[13] The Stockholm Conference is traditionally seen as the birth of modern international environmental law. The same year, a summit of heads of State of the EEC Member States declared that economic expansion was not an end in itself, and that European integration was ultimately to help to attenuate disparities in living conditions, including by protecting 'non-material' values such as environmental protection. The origin of EU environmental law was thus linked to human well-being, as also being a necessary goal for economic growth. On that understanding, European leaders called for an action programme to launch an EEC environmental policy.[14] The following year the First Environmental Action Programme was adopted[15] and in its aftermath EEC law was enacted to tackle differences in Member States' environmental legislation that were considered to have a (potential) detrimental effect on intra-Community trade and competition.[16] This practice permitted the adoption of EEC legislation on aquatic pollution, air pollution, industrial hazards, and toxic waste, albeit only to the extent permitted by economic considerations, in the absence of a legal basis in the Treaties for the Community to adopt measures which solely concerned the environment. EU environmental law was therefore initially aimed to develop environmental protection legislation that would also contribute to economic integration.

In 1985, however, the Court of Justice affirmed that environmental protection had become one of the Community's 'essential objectives', and that environmental protection measures, being of general interest, could justify certain restrictions to the free movement of goods as long as they were non-discriminatory and did not go beyond the inevitable restrictions justified by the pursuit of the objective of environmental protection.[17] The Court, therefore, addressed possible conflicts between environmental protection and economic objectives by sanctioning the possibility of an autonomous environmental policy of the EEC independent of the establishment of the common market.[18]

It was then the Single European Act (in force 1987) that introduced an explicit legal basis for an autonomous EEC environmental policy, setting the objectives, principles, and criteria to guide environmental law-making at EEC level.[19] Accordingly, in the field of the environment the EEC was to take legislative action to preserve and improve the quality of the environment, contribute towards the protection of human health, and ensure a prudent and rational utilization of natural resources. These powers were subject to unanimous decision-making by the Council in consultation with the Parliament. In addition, with Spain and Portugal joining the EEC in 1986, Germany and Denmark—countries with traditionally higher environmental standards—insisted on introducing in

[13] Declaration of the United Nations Conference on the Human Environment, UN Doc A/Conf.48/14/rev.1 (16 June 1972).

[14] Bulletin EC 1972, No 10 (see Table 22.1).

[15] Declaration of the Council of the European Communities and of the representatives of the Governments of the Member States meeting in the Council of 22 November 1973 on the programme of action for the European Communities on the environment (OJ [1973] C112/1).

[16] On the basis of Art 100 EEC, later Art 94 EC (now Art 115 TFEU); see also Case 92/79 *Commission v Italy* [1980] ECR 1115.

[17] Case 240/83 *ADBHU* [1983] ECR 531.

[18] M Lee, *EU Environmental Law: Challenges, Change and Decision-Making* (2nd edn, Oxford: Hart Publishing, 2014) 2.

[19] Post-SEA, Art 130r EEC.

the Treaty a provision allowing Member States to maintain or introduce more stringent environmental protection measures than might be pursued at EEC level.[20]

Following the convening of another major global summit, the 1992 United Nations Conference on Environment and Development in Rio de Janeiro, environmental law also gained more prominence at European level. The Maastricht Treaty (in force 1993) elevated environmental protection to being one of the objectives of the EC.[21] The Treaty also significantly amended the legal basis on environmental policy, by adding a reference to the precautionary principle (discussed later[22]) and the objective of promoting *international* measures to deal with regional or worldwide environmental problems.[23] In addition, the Maastricht Treaty established that the general rule for decision-making on environmental policy would be qualified majority in the Council (ie the Member States' environment ministers), thereby facilitating the adoption of new environmental law at EC level. Only certain matters remained subject to unanimity.

The Treaty of Amsterdam (in force 1999) fine-tuned the inclusion of environmental protection in the general clauses of the EC Treaty. It included the 'harmonious, balanced and sustainable development of economic activities' and a 'high level of protection and improvement of the quality of the environment' among the objectives of the EC.[24] It also upgraded a pre-existing requirement for environmental mainstreaming in other policy areas of the EU ('environmental integration') to a general principle of EU law.[25] Finally, the Treaty of Amsterdam established that co-decision was the normal decision-making procedure for environmental policy, thus ensuring a veto power for the European Parliament.[26] This procedure has remained relevant for present environmental policy (renamed the 'ordinary legislative procedure' by the Lisbon Treaty).[27] And starting with the so-called 'big-bang' enlargement of 2004 (ie the admission of ten new Member States), environmental policy formally became an area to be specifically addressed in pre-accession negotiations, given the need for 'upward pressure' to align the environmental protection policy of new Member States with that of the EU.[28]

With the latest Treaty amendments,[29] the Lisbon Treaty (in force 2009) singled out climate change as one of the global environmental issues in which the EU is expected to play a significant role at the international level,[30] thereby reflecting the political priority attached to this specific environmental problem by the EU since the early 2000s.[31] The Lisbon Treaty also added two new provisions further supporting environmental integration: one requires integrating animal welfare requirements in certain policy areas,[32] and the other has regard to the need to preserve and improve the environment in the context of EU energy policy, by promoting energy efficiency, energy saving, and the development of renewable forms of energy.[33]

[20] This Treaty rule is still in force today (Art 193 TFEU).

[21] Post-Maastricht, Arts 2 and 3(k) EC.

[22] Section 2.3.2.

[23] Post-Maastricht, Art 130r(1) EC.

[24] Post-Amsterdam, Art 2 EC.

[25] Post-Amsterdam, Art 6 EC (now Art 11 TFEU).

[26] Post-Amsterdam, Art 175 EC.

[27] Art 294 TFEU. For more details on this procedure, see chapter 5.

[28] M Soveroski, 'EC Enlargement and the Development of European Environmental Policy: Parallel Histories, Divergent Paths?' (2004) 13 *Review of European, Comparative and International Environmental Law* 127, 129.

[29] M Lee, 'The Environmental Implications of the Lisbon Treaty' (2008) 10 *Environmental Law Review* 131 and H Vedder, 'The Treaty of Lisbon and European Environmental Policy' (2010) 22 *Journal of Environmental Law* 285.

[30] Art 191(1) TFEU.

[31] E Morgera and G Marín Durán, 'The UN 2005 World Summit, the Environment and the EU: Priorities, Promises and Prospects' (2006) 15 *Review of European, Comparative and International Environmental Law* 11.

[32] ie in the areas of agriculture, fisheries, transport, internal market, research and technological development, and space policies (Art 14 TFEU).

[33] Art 194(1) TFEU.

Possibly the most significant feature of the Lisbon Treaty, from an environmental perspective, is the emphasis placed on the international dimension of the EU environmental policy. The Treaty introduced an explicit link between sustainable development and EU external relations, by clarifying that 'in its relations with the wider world, the Union shall . . . contribute to . . . the sustainable development of the Earth'.[34] Furthermore, the new legal basis on EU external action provided that the EU shall define and pursue common policies and actions, and work for a high degree of cooperation in all fields of international relations, with the specific objective of fostering the sustainable environmental development of developing countries, in order to eradicate poverty; and help to develop international measures to preserve and improve the quality of the environment and the sustainable management of global natural resources, in order to ensure sustainable development.[35]

Internationally, 2024 and 2025 represented a critical juncture when four international courts[36] were called upon to clarify the international obligations of States to take action on climate change. Both the International Tribunal for the Law of the Sea (ITLOS)[37] and the International Court of Justice (ICJ)[38] clarified that all States have binding but differentiated international legal obligations to mitigate and adapt to climate change under and beyond the 2015 Paris Agreement, including by collectively limiting the global average temperature increase to 1.5°C from pre-industrial times. Both courts highlighted obligations related to conserving and restoring nature and the ocean, preventing significant harm to the environment and related negative human rights impacts, and the duty to collaborate in good faith to these ends. Advisory Opinions are not legally binding, but provide an authoritative statement of the interpretation of existing international law. In particular, the ICJ advisory proceedings represented an unprecedented process in international law: the initiative started from a group of university students—the Pacific Islands Students Fishing Climate Change at the University of the South Pacific, who were later joined by a global youth movement. Their proposal was then supported and led by Vanuatu and other Pacific Island States, leading to a resolution of the UN General Assembly. The ICJ advisory proceedings saw the highest number of States intervening (along with the EU and several individual Member States), and eventually led to the unanimous adoption of what is largely seen as the most extensive interpretation of international environmental law the Court has ever pronounced. The ICJ Advisory Opinion also offers a clear interpretation of the interconnections between international environmental law and international human rights law. While it does not directly affect the EU legal system, the ICJ and other Advisory Opinions clarify interpretations of international law that can be relied upon to assess whether the EU is taking sufficiently ambitious and integrated action on climate change. It remains to be seen whether and how the EU institutions will take these legal interpretations into account in future climate action; and whether these opinions will be relied upon in climate litigation to seek changes to EU and Member States' climate law.

2.2 **Objectives of EU environmental policy**

The objectives of EU environmental policy are very broadly defined as:

- preserving, protecting, and improving the quality of the environment;
- protecting human health;

[34] Art 3(5) TEU. [35] Art 21(2)(d) and (f) TEU.

[36] The four international tribunals are: the International Tribunal for the Law of the Sea, the Inter-American Court of Human Rights, the International Court of Justice, and the African Tribunal on Human and Peoples' Rights.

[37] ITLOS Advisory Opinion for Case No 31 (2024).

[38] ICJ Advisory Opinion on the obligation of States in respect of climate change, 2025.

- ensuring the prudent and rational utilization of natural resources; and
- promoting measures at the international level to deal with regional or worldwide environmental problems, and in particular combating climate change.[39]

Basically, it is almost impossible to define clearly on this basis the boundaries of EU environmental policy. There is sufficient flexibility for the EU to tackle, through its environmental policy, new and emerging environmental issues. In addition, the policy permits wide discretion in the choice of environmental measures to be adopted at EU level: these may include conservation, restoration, repression, precaution, prevention, and eminently procedural environmental measures.[40]

2.2.1 **Competence and scope of EU legislation**

While there are no clear substantive limits to the exercise of EU environmental competence, this is shared with the Member States[41] and is therefore subject to the principle of subsidiarity: the EU will take action if the objectives of the proposed environmental action cannot be sufficiently achieved by the Member States and if, by reason of the scale or effects of the proposed action, these objectives are better achieved at the EU level.[42] This is not, however, 'a straight-forward technical' question as different levels of environmental regulation (EU, Member State, as well as international, regional, and national ones) may be linked in complex ways or act in isolation from one another.[43]

Furthermore, environmental competence is exercised under the decision-making procedures set out by the Treaty: generally it is subject to agreement between the Council (acting by qualified majority voting) and the European Parliament (under the ordinary legislative procedure). In certain specific areas, however, the Treaty requires unanimous decision-making by the Council in consultation with the European Parliament (ie a special legislative procedure), namely:

- provisions primarily of a fiscal nature;
- measures affecting town and country planning, quantitative management of water resources or affecting, directly or indirectly, the availability of those resources, and land use with the exception of waste management; and
- measures significantly affecting a Member State's choice between different energy sources and the general structure of its energy supply.[44]

These are areas in which Member States wish to retain a higher degree of control because of their politically sensitive nature or concerns about the preservation of national sovereignty.

As to the territorial scope of EU environmental competence, reference to worldwide and regional environmental problems in the Treaty clarifies that the EU can also take unilateral and multilateral measures targeting the environment beyond its borders, in the same way as can its Member States, within the limits imposed by international law.[45] An

[39] Art 191(1) TFEU.

[40] J Jans and H Vedder, *European Environmental Law* (4th edn, Groningen: Europa Law, 2012) 26–35.

[41] Art 4(2)(e) TFEU. For more on the concept of shared competence, see chapter 5. Note that EU measures adopted on the environment legal basis 'shall not prevent any Member State from maintaining or introducing more stringent protective measures'. Such measures must be compatible with the Treaties. They shall be notified to the Commission (Art 193 TFEU).

[42] Art 5(3) TEU. For more on the concept of subsidiarity, see chapter 5.

[43] Lee, *EU Environmental Law* (n 18) 21.

[44] Art 192 TFEU. For more on special legislative procedures, see chapter 5.

[45] Jans and Vedder (n 40) 31–36.

example, discussed in more detail later, is the regulation of the greenhouse gas emissions from international aviation.[46]

As the environmental competence of the EU is shared with the Member States, Member States can exercise their competence only as long as the EU has not exercised its competence, or has decided to cease to exercise it.[47] In this respect, it should be emphasized that the scope of EU competence vis-à-vis that of the Member States is difficult to determine, as EU environmental policy is subject to continuous evolution.[48] This has important implications on the international scene where environmental law-making is constantly taking place. If the EU adopted environmental measures internally, Member States would no longer have competence to undertake international obligations that would affect those EU rules. This is not the case, however, if the EU measures allow (as is often the case) Member States to adopt more stringent measures,[49] including in principle the possibility of undertaking more stringent international obligations. However, this flexibility for Member States is constrained by the duty of sincere cooperation enshrined in Article 4(3) TEU, according to which:

> Pursuant to the principle of sincere cooperation, the Union and the Member States shall, in full mutual respect, assist each other in carrying out tasks which flow from the Treaties.
>
> The Member States shall take any appropriate measure, general or particular, to ensure fulfilment of the obligations arising out of the Treaties or resulting from the acts of the institutions of the Union.
>
> The Member States shall facilitate the achievement of the Union's tasks and refrain from any measure which could jeopardise the attainment of the Union's objectives.

The Court has interpreted the duty as entailing enforceable substantive and procedural obligations upon Member States with a view to protecting unity in the international representation of the EU.[50]

Finally, with reference to international treaties on environmental matters, in the vast majority of cases both the EU and its Member States negotiate and conclude multilateral environmental agreements together (so-called 'mixed agreements'[51]), which entail significant internal efforts to ensure proper coordination at all stages, including that of implementation.

2.3 **Principles of EU environmental policy**

The Treaty also identifies the principles that should guide EU environmental policy, both as a guide for law-making and for interpretation. These principles are a high level of environmental protection; the precautionary principle; as well as the principles that preventive action should be taken, that environmental damage should as a priority be rectified at source, and that the polluter should pay.[52] Environmental principles also include environmental integration and sustainable development. These principles, as will be discussed in the following subsections, may play a key role in ensuring an appropriate balance between environmental protection and economic growth in the EU, in some instances.

[46] See case study 22.2 in section 4.3.
[47] Art 2(2) TFEU.
[48] Jans and Vedder (n 40) 61–64.
[49] Art 191(4) TFEU.
[50] Case C-266/03 *Commission v Luxembourg ('Inland Waterways Agreement')* [2005] ECR I-4805, para 60; Case C-433/03 *Commission v Germany ('Inland Waterways Agreement')* [2005] ECR I-6985, para 66; and Case C-246/07 *Commission v Sweden ('POPs Convention')* [2010] ECR I-3317, para 104.
[51] For more on the concept of mixed agreements, including a case study of their use in the area of environmental law, see chapter 26.
[52] Art 191(2) TFEU.

The EU legislator, however, has a significant margin of discretion in implementing the principles. Only in exceptional cases could an EU measure be annulled for insufficient regard to these principles, in cases of manifest error of appraisal by the EU legislature. The Court clarified this in a preliminary reference involving EU legislation on the protection of the ozone layer (further discussed later),[53] emphasizing that the protection of the environment necessarily presupposes complex assessments weighing the respective merits and drawbacks of any given action, taking account of a series of parameters, in particular available scientific and technical data.[54] The underlying reason for such judicial restraint is the need to strike a balance between environmental principles and other policy priorities of the EU, as well as the need to allow ample room for manoeuvre in tackling the complexity of environmental challenges. Nonetheless, the environmental principles have proven very important shaping factors in EU environmental law and assist in better understanding the various pieces of secondary EU environmental legislation, as will be shown in the following sections.

2.3.1 **'A high level of environmental protection'**

The principle of a high level of environmental protection is included among the general objectives of the EU,[55] although it is made subject to consideration of the 'diversity of situations in the various regions of the Union'.[56] While the principle prevents the EU from adopting the lowest common denominator among the Member States' environmental protection measures,[57] the Court of Justice clarified that it does not necessarily call for the highest standard that is technically possible.[58] The case involved a preliminary reference on an EU provision prohibiting the use, importation, release for free circulation, or marketing of hydrochlorofluorocarbons (a substance that depletes the ozone layer).[59] At the national level, a company using the prohibited substance in fire-fighting products raised the question whether the prohibition could be justified only if allocated absolute priority to the highest possible level of environmental protection.[60] The Court concluded that the legal basis for environmental policy does not necessarily aim to ensure absolute, immediate, and global protection of the environment and therefore allows the EU legislator to pursue a level of environmental protection that is not the highest possible. Consequently, the provision at stake was considered consistent with the Treaty because it still aimed at improving appreciably the protection of the environment.[61]

Overall, the principle of a high level of environmental protection reflects a moving target—the idea of continuous improvement of environmental protection standards across the Member States.[62] That said, the ICJ indicated in its 2025 Advisory Opinion that States have a binding international obligation to pursue the 'highest possible ambition' in their climate action.[63]

2.3.2 **'The precautionary principle'**

The precautionary principle, also a principle of international environmental law,[64] provides guidance in situations of scientific uncertainty. It has been interpreted by the Commission as a risk-management tool comprising a risk assessment leading to the establishment of precautionary measures that are:

[53] See section 2.3.1. [54] Case C-284/95 *Safety Hi-Tech Srl v S & T Srl* [1998] ECR I-4301, paras 71–73.

[55] Art 3(3) TEU. [56] Art 191(2) TFEU.

[57] L Kramer, *EU Environmental Law* (7th edn, London: Sweet & Maxwell, 2011) 12–13.

[58] *Safety Hi-Tech* (n 54).

[59] Art 5 of Council Regulation (EC) No 3093/94 on substances that deplete the ozone layer of 15 December 1994 (OJ [1994] L333/1).

[60] *Safety Hi-Tech* (n 54) para 58. [61] Ibid, paras 76–78.

[62] Kramer, *EU Environmental Law* (n 57) 12. [63] ICJ Advisory Opinion, para 246.

[64] Rio Declaration on Environment and Development, UN Doc A/CONF.151/26 (1992), vol I, principle 15.

> proportional to the chosen level of protection, non-discriminatory in their application, consistent with similar measures already taken, based on an examination of the potential benefits and costs of action or lack of action, and subject to review in the light of new scientific data.[65]

The trigger of the precautionary principle is a situation where:

> preliminary objective scientific evaluation, indicates that there are reasonable grounds for concern that the potentially dangerous effects on the ***environment, human, animal or plant health*** may be inconsistent with the high level of protection chosen for the [EU].[66]

The General Court, for instance, relied on the precautionary principle, as well as that of a high level of protection and environmental integration, to condemn the authorization of an ingredient in pesticides that had been linked in medical literature to Parkinson's disease.[67] While the CJEU has mainly emphasized the technique of risk assessment in its complex case law on the precautionary principle, notably to prioritize environmental protection and human health over economic considerations, commentators have increasingly emphasized that this principle calls not only for an analysis of available scientific evidence, but also for open and deliberative decision-making.[68]

2.3.3 **'The prevention principle'**

The 'prevention' principle, also an international environmental principle,[69] calls for taking action to protect the environment at an early stage, with a view to preventing damage from occurring rather than repairing it.[70] The main difference with the precautionary principle lies in the availability of data on the existence of a risk, although such distinction may be difficult to draw in practice. The Court of Justice, for instance, relied on the prevention principle, as well as that of a high level of protection, to review an export ban on British beef adopted in the context of the Common Agricultural Policy because of a possible—rather than certain—risk related to mad cow disease.[71] Guidance on the application of the prevention principle in EU law stresses the need to improve information for decision-makers and the public (eg through monitoring and surveying requirements), introduces procedures supporting prompt and informed decision-making on the environment such as the environmental impact assessment, and monitors implementation of adopted measures to ensure their adaptation in light of new circumstances or knowledge.[72]

2.3.4 **'Rectification at source'**

The 'rectification at source' principle means that environmental damage should as a priority be rectified at its source, and has had particular resonance in the area of waste management. The Court of Justice held that according to this principle local authorities must take measures necessary to ensure the reception, processing, and removal of their own waste, so that this waste can be disposed of as close as possible to its place of production. This interpretation allowed the Court to justify measures that discriminated against

[65] Commission, 'Guidelines on the Precautionary Principle', COM(2000) 1, para 6.

[66] Ibid, para 3 (emphasis added).

[67] Case T-229/04 *Sweden v Commission* [2007] ECR II-2437.

[68] Lee, *EU Environmental Law* (n 18) 5–11.

[69] Rio Declaration, principle 2.

[70] Jans and Vedder (n 40) 40–42.

[71] Case C-157/96 *National Farmers Union* [1998] ECR I-2211, para 64.

[72] Resolution of the Council of the European Communities and of the Representatives of the Governments of the Member States, meeting within the Council, on the continuation and implementation of a European Community policy and action programme on the environment (1982–1986) (OJ [1983] C46/1) (Third Environmental Action Programme) 6–7.

waste produced in different areas.[73] The case, therefore, represents a derogation from the normal approach to free trade in goods in EU law,[74] which is necessary in the case of irreconcilable conflict between environmental protection and economic growth.

2.3.5 'Polluter pays' principle

The 'polluter pays' principle, also an international environmental principle,[75] posits that the costs of the measure to deal with pollution should be borne by those causing the pollution, through the imposition of environmental charges, environmental standards, or environmental liability. In addition, the principle has been interpreted in the EU context so that environmental protection should not in principle depend on the granting of State aid or policies placing the burden on society, and that requirements should not target persons or undertakings for the elimination of pollution that they did not contribute to producing. Accordingly, the Court of Justice indicated that farmers are not obliged to bear all the costs of pollution by nitrates, but only those caused by their own agricultural activities. So it is up to authorities to take account of other sources of pollution and, having regard to the circumstances, avoid imposing on farmers unnecessary costs of eliminating pollution.[76] Determining actual sources of pollution, however, can be complicated, as several individuals or sectors can be responsible in a particular case, so the principle does not prevent the imposition of environmental costs on other parties than polluters.[77]

2.4 Environmental integration

The principle of environmental integration—also a principle of international environmental law[78]—is included among the general principles of EU law. It is framed in clearly mandatory wording and acts as a mechanism for the operationalization of sustainable development.[79] It reads:

> Environmental protection requirements must be integrated into the definition and implementation of the Union policies and activities, in particular with a view to promoting sustainable development.

It aims to prevent progress in environmental protection from being undermined by developments in other policy fields that disregard environmental concerns. Environmental issues should be integrated into all policies of the EU, internal and external, both at the stage of the framing of these policies and at the stage of their implementation. Environmental integration therefore requires that other EU policy areas must 'pursue' the EU environmental objectives, and 'aim at' or 'be based on' the EU environmental principles.[80] Thus, it has resulted in the application of the precautionary principle outside the environmental sphere, in the area of the protection of public health[81] and of the prevention and high level of protection principles in the area of agriculture.[82]

[73] Case C-2/90 *Commission v Belgium* [1992] ECR I-4431.

[74] See discussion of the usual approach to free movement of goods in chapter 12.

[75] Rio Declaration, principle 16.

[76] Case C-293/97 *Standley* [1999] ECR I-2603, paras 46–52.

[77] Kokott AG in Case C-378/08 *Raffinerie Mediterranee v Ministero dello sviluppo economic* [2010] ECRI-1919, para 125. See also Lee, *EU Environmental Law* (n 18) 13–15.

[78] Rio Declaration, principle 4.

[79] Art 11 TFEU.

[80] N Dhondt, *Integration of Environmental Protection into Other EC Policies: Legal Theory and Practice* (Groningen: Europa Law, 2003) 84.

[81] Jans and Vedder (n 40) 21, on the basis of Joined Cases T-74, 76, 83, 85, 132, 137, and 141/00 *Artegodan GmbH ao v Commission* [2002] ECR II-4954.

[82] *National Farmers Union* (n 71).

Nonetheless, the environmental integration principle does not assign priority to environmental concerns over other objectives of the EU, including economic objectives. Rather, it imposes a general obligation on EU institutions to reach an integrated and balanced assessment of all the relevant environmental aspects, and that the resulting decision respects the principle of proportionality—that the policy or action does not go beyond what is strictly necessary for the protection of the environment.[83] The environmental integration principle also entails that EU environmental law itself is interpreted broadly, in light of the environmental objectives, principles, and criteria of Article 191 TFEU, even when they are not explicitly incorporated in the specific secondary legislation at issue.[84]

Environmental integration has indeed resulted in significant legislative developments, both in terms of 'greening' other areas of EU law, as well as in recourse to an 'integrationist' approach in the development of EU environmental law (relying, for instance, on environmental impact assessments,[85] strategic environmental assessments,[86] and integrated pollution prevention and control[87]). The principle is also reflected in the 2019 European Green Deal,[88] which includes measures aimed at mainstreaming sustainability in all EU policies and pays particular attention to green finance and investment.

2.5 **Sustainable development**

The principle of sustainable development is among the 'objectives' of the EU both in its internal and external actions.[89] In addition, sustainable development is specifically referred to as a 'principle' in the Preamble to the TEU,[90] but notably is not mentioned as the legal basis for the environmental policy of the EU.[91] The principle of sustainable development is the product of international environmental law,[92] where it is traditionally (but not exclusively) seen as 'development that meets the need of present without compromising the ability of future generations to meet their own needs'.[93] It is generally operationalized as a balancing exercise between 'three pillars'—environmental, social, and economic development.[94] In EU law, however, the connection between sustainable development and environmental regulation is unclear and controversial. Some authors argue that sustainable development provides an opportunity to give preference to short-term economic

[83] Jans and Vedder (n 40) 17–18.

[84] Dhondt (n 80) 179, on the basis of Joined Cases C-175/98 and C-177/98 *Lirussi and Bizzaro* [1999] ECR I-6881; Joined Cases C-418/97 and C-419/97 *ARCO Chemie Nederland* [2000] ECR I-4475; and Case C-318/98 *Fornasar* [2000] ECR I-4785, where the Court adopted broad interpretations of EU waste legislation.

[85] Directive 2011/92/EU on the assessment of the effects of certain public and private projects on the environment (OJ [2012] L26/1) amended by Directive 2014/52/EU (OJ [2014] L124/1).

[86] Directive 2001/42/EC on the assessment of the effects of certain plans and programmes on the environment (OJ [2001] L197/30).

[87] Directive 2010/75/EU on industrial emissions (integrated pollution prevention and control—recast) (OJ [2010] L334/17).

[88] Commission, 'The European Green Deal', COM(2019) 640 final.

[89] Arts 3(3) and (5) and 21(2)(f) TEU. [90] TEU, recital 9.

[91] L Kramer, 'Sustainable Development in the EC' in H Bugge and C Voigt (eds), *Sustainable Development in International and National Law* (Groningen: Europa Law, 2008) 378–379.

[92] Rio Declaration, principles 3–4.

[93] World Commission on Environment and Development, *Our Common Future* (Oxford: Oxford University Press, 1987) ch 2, para 1; which was quoted in Commission, 'Towards Sustainability: A European Programme of policy and action in relation to the environment and sustainable development' (OJ [1993] C138/5).

[94] Political Declaration of the World Summit on Sustainable Development, UN Doc A/CONF.199/20 (4 September 2002), resolution 1 (WSSD Declaration), para 5.

interests and may therefore work against environmental protection.[95] In actual fact, the Court of Justice has not engaged in defining the legal implications of sustainable development,[96] and it is usually left to EU policy documents to provide guidance on sustainable development. Following the international adoption of the 2030 Sustainable Development Agenda and its Sustainable Development Goals,[97] the EU has clarified how its overarching approach to sustainable development aligns with international priorities in terms of a transition towards a low-carbon, climate-resilient, resource-efficient, circular economy that can also contribute to continued economic growth and job creation.[98] It does not make reference to increasing calls within the scientific community to respect long-term ecological limits.[99]

It remains to be verified in the details of EU environmental law and its implementation how sustainable development operates in practice—as we will see in the next sections. In that connection, the ICJ indicated that all States have obligations to protect the environment through meaningful international cooperation and through the effective regulation and monitoring of public and private actors, in accordance with the principles of sustainable development, equity, and precaution.[100]

3 Nature protection

EU law on nature protection has until recently focused on traditional conservation measures (protected areas and species[101]) that emerged in the late 1970s and early 1990s. It has developed in a 'patchy' manner, resulting in a system that is complex and ambiguous, and the components of which in part overlap.[102] Nonetheless, it is considered 'highly influential . . . [in] affecting for the first time Member States' use of land'[103] and equipped to accommodate modern challenges, such as adaptation to climate change.[104] Notwithstanding its long-standing place in EU environmental law, full and effective implementation of nature protection legislation in the EU remains a challenge.[105] In most cases, the challenge is due to conflicts with economic development projects that are resolved without sufficient attention to nature protection.

[95] Kramer, 'Sustainable Development in the EC' (n 91) 391–393; A Ross-Robertson, 'Is the Environment Getting Squeezed Out of Sustainable Development?' [2003] *Public Law* 249.

[96] Even if it had an opportunity to do so: Case C-142/95 P *Associazione degli Agricoltori della provincia di Rovigo v Commission* [1996] ECR I-6669 and Case C-371/98 *R v Secretary of State for Environment, Transport and the Regions, ex p First Corporate Shipping* [2000] ECR-I 9235.

[97] UN General Assembly Resolution 70/1 of 21 October 2015.

[98] European Commission, Communication: Next Steps for a Sustainable European Future—European Action for Sustainability, COM(2016) 739 final. See also Joint statement by the Council and the representatives of the governments of the Member States meeting within the Council, the European Parliament and the Commission (2017/C 210/01) (OJ [2017] C210/1).

[99] Lee, *EU Environmental Law* (n 18) 79–80; and D Langlet and S Mahmoudi, *EU Environmental Law and Policy* (Oxford: Oxford University Press, 2016) 46.

[100] ICJ Advisory Opinion (n 38) para 161.

[101] Although the EU has also regulated on plant health and animal welfare.

[102] N de Sadeleer, 'EC Law and Biodiversity' in R Macrory (ed), *Reflections on 30 Years of EU Environmental Law: A High Level of Protection?* (Groningen: Europa Law, 2005) 368–369.

[103] J Holder and M Lee, *Environmental Protection, Law and Policy* (Cambridge: Cambridge University Press, 2007) 627.

[104] A Trouwborst, 'Conserving European Biodiversity in a Changing Climate: The Bern Convention, the European Union Birds and Habitats Directives and the Adaptation of Nature to Climate Change' (2011) 20 *Review of European, Comparative and International Environmental Law* 62.

[105] European Parliament, Resolution on the implementation of EU legislation aiming at the conservation of biodiversity (2009/2108(INI), 21 September 2010 (OJ [2012] C50E/19)..

The cornerstones of EU nature protection law have been two directives: the Wild Birds Directive,[106] initially adopted in 1979, and the subsequent and complementary Habitats Directive,[107] which will be discussed in detail in section 3.2. The EU then recognized the need to further develop its biodiversity legal framework with the 2015 regulation on invasive alien species[108] and the 2024 Nature Restoration Regulation. The latter introduced binding targets for the restoration of degraded habitats, in particular those that have the greatest potential to contribute to capturing and storing carbon, with a view to covering all ecosystems (natural and semi-natural, on land and sea), beyond the areas protected by the Habitats and Birds Directives.[109] The Regulation aims to restore 20 per cent of the EU's degraded ecosystems by 2030 and all ecosystems in need of restoration by 2050, with a view also to seeking synergies with climate action.

The importance of nature restoration cannot be overstated: over 80 per cent of European protected areas are in an unfavourable or poor condition, the majority of European soils are degraded, and the majority of fish stocks are overfished. And yet the process of adoption of the Restoration Regulation was fraught with unprecedented difficulties due to economic interests and attempts to undermine the science underpinning the proposal.[110] Member States have discretion to determine in which areas restoration measures are taken as part of their obligation to develop national restoration plans by the end of 2026, but they need to rely on the best available knowledge.[111] However, there are tensions between the development of national restoration plans and the fast-tracking of renewable energy development as part of the EU climate policy, with a clear preference for pursuing energy security over environmental protection,[112] as discussed in the next section.

3.1 **The Wild Birds Directive**

The Wild Birds Directive has a narrow scope: it aims to protect the species of wild birds naturally occurring in the European territory of the Member States (that are mainly migratory species), because they constitute a common heritage and their effective protection is typically a trans-frontier environmental problem entailing common responsibilities.[113] The Directive aimed to implement relevant international obligations under the Ramsar Convention on Wetlands of International Importance, which protects wetlands as key habitats for migratory birds, as well as for other contributions to environmental sustainability.[114] The Directive, on the one hand, includes provisions on the protection of habitats of wild birds, including through the designation of Special Protection Areas for birds in danger of extinction;[115] and, on the other hand, it provides for the direct protection of wild bird species, including by prohibiting or regulating their deliberate killing and capture.[116]

[106] Directive 2009/147/EC on the conservation of wild birds (OJ [2010] L20/7) (codified version including subsequent amendments to the original 1979 Wild Birds Directive).

[107] Directive 92/43/EEC on the conservation of natural habitats and of wild fauna and flora (OJ [1992] L206/7).

[108] Regulation (EU) 1143/2014 on invasive alien species (OJ [2014] L317).

[109] Regulation (EU) 2024/on nature restoration (OJ [2024] L1991).

[110] G Pe'er et al, 'Role of Science and Scientists in Public Environmental Policy Debates; The Case of the EU Agrochemicals and Nature Restoration Regulations' (2025) 7 *People and Nature* 1769.

[111] F Fleurke and P Paiement, 'Are Renewables Energy Technologies Compatible with Biodiversity Conversation? The Energy-Conservation Legal Nexus' in L Reins and A Zahar (eds), *Climate Technology and Law in the Anthropocene* (Bristol: Bristol University Press, 2025) 19–51.

[112] Ibid. [113] Wild Birds Directive (n 106) Preamble.

[114] Ramsar Convention on Wetlands of International Importance, 2 February 1971, 996 UNTS 245.

[115] Wild Birds Directive, Arts 3 and 4. [116] Ibid, Arts 5–9.

Importantly for understanding how sustainable development operates in practice, the Wild Birds Directive contains a general obligation to maintain the population of the wild bird species at a level which corresponds in particular to ecological, scientific, and cultural requirements, *while taking account* of economic and recreational requirements, or to adapt the population of these species to that level.[117] However, in a series of decisions the Court of Justice emphasized that the obligation to designate Special Protection Areas must be *solely* based on objective, environmental (ornithological) criteria on the basis of Article 4 of the Directive, without consideration of economic or recreational requirements that are mentioned in Article 2 of the Directive.[118] The Court, therefore, maintained that while the Wild Birds Directive contained a general provision that could have justified a balancing of different interests, it mostly aimed at an absolute protection of nature without the need to balance scientific (ornithological) criteria with other (economic) interests.[119] This is therefore one of the rare cases in which the balance struck clearly favours environmental protection over economic development objectives.

3.2 **The Habitats Directive**

The Habitats Directive was originally adopted in 1992. While it employs the same legal technique as the Wild Birds Directive (protection of listed species and protection of habitats through the designation of protected areas), it has a markedly different approach, explicitly espousing sustainable development:

> the main aim of this Directive being to promote the maintenance of biodiversity, taking account of economic, social, cultural and regional requirements, this Directive makes a contribution to the general objective of sustainable development; . . . the maintenance of such biodiversity may in certain cases require the maintenance, or indeed the encouragement, of human activities.[120]

It also has a much broader scope than the Wild Birds Directive. This can be explained by intervening international obligations under the Convention on Biological Diversity, which aims to protect all life on earth rather than singling out a group of species, and also focuses on their sustainable use.[121] As a result, the Habitats Directive has a more ambitious and holistic approach than the Wild Birds Directive, by aiming to protect fauna and flora and their habitats and also by creating a *coherent ecological network* of protected areas—called 'Natura 2000'—that includes areas already protected under the Wild Birds Directive.[122] The Habitats Directive thus aims to maintain or restore the natural habitats and the populations of species of wild fauna and flora in the European territory at a favourable status[123]—that is, a situation that ensures their long-term maintenance and that is likely to continue to exist for the foreseeable future.[124]

Similar to the Wild Birds Directive, the Habitats Directive contains both provisions on species protection and on habitat protection. As to the former, it calls upon Member States to monitor the conservation status of all habitats and species, and to provide different degrees of protection to species and plants listed in its Annexes by prohibiting certain activities depending on the conservation status of the species.[125] As to the latter,

117 Ibid, Art 2.

118 Case C-355/90 *Santoña Marshes* [1993] ECR I-4221; Case C-44/95 *Lappel Bank* [1996] ECR I-3805; and Case C-3/96 *Commission v Netherlands* [1998] ECR I-3031.

119 Holder and Lee (n 103) 634.

120 Habitats Directive, Preamble.

121 Ibid, Arts 2(1) and 1. Convention on Biological Diversity, 5 June 1992, 1760 UNTS 79, entered into force for the EU on 29 December 1993.

122 Habitats Directive, Art 3(1).

123 Ibid, Art 2.

124 In approximation: ibid, para 1(e).

125 Convention on Biological Diversity, Arts 12–16.

the Habitats Directive provides for the designation of Special Areas of Conservation comprising sites hosting the natural habitat types listed in Annex I and habitats of the species listed in Annex II, with a view to enabling the natural habitat types and the species' habitats concerned to be maintained or, where appropriate, restored at a favourable conservation status in their natural range.[126]

On the other hand, however, the Habitats Directive offers a compromise between comprehensive nature protection and the protection of economic interests that can be damaged by limiting human activities and development opportunities in certain areas. As opposed to the Wild Birds Directive, therefore, the Habitats Directive makes it explicit that protective measures '*shall take account of* economic, social and cultural requirements and regional and local characteristics'.[127] In addition, the Habitats Directive introduces sustainable development-based provisions for the management of designated protected areas. Ordinarily, the protection regime for a designated Special Area of Conservation may be overridden on social and economic grounds. Even for priority areas, the conservation regime may be overridden, but only on the more restrictive grounds of public health, public safety, or for certain environmental reasons following an Opinion by the European Commission and subject to the adoption of compensatory measures.[128] This system of derogation from the protection of sites in the Natura 2000 network is also applicable to areas designated under the Wild Birds Directive.[129]

These provisions clearly show that the more sustainable development-focused approach of the Habitats Directive departs from the absolute preference for conservation and environmental criteria under the Wild Birds Directive. But it is only in the phase of implementation that this difference becomes significant and that it is possible to assess whether sustainable development really achieves a pragmatic and constructive approach to balancing nature conservation and economic development concerns, or whether it mostly serves as an opportunity to give more prominence to economic interests. A closer look at the application of EU nature protection law in practice, therefore, can tell us to what extent EU law has succeeded in reconciling conflicting economic and environmental objectives.

4 Climate change

Climate change is a priority for EU environmental policy and is inextricably linked to international law. This is evident from the explicit mention of it in the Lisbon Treaty:

> The Union policy on the environment shall contribute to the pursuit of the following objectives: . . . promoting measures at [the] international level to deal with regional or worldwide environmental problems, and *in particular combating climate change*.[130]

The EU has harboured global leadership ambitions in the fight against climate change since the early years of international climate change cooperation in the 1990s. EU climate law has evolved rapidly since then, in an effort not only to ensure prompt implementation of international law (as seen in the context of nature protection and water management), but also to *influence its development*.[131]

[126] Habitats Directive, Arts 3–11. [127] Ibid, Art 2(3) (emphasis added). [128] Ibid, Art 6(4).
[129] Ibid, Art 7. [130] Art 191(1) TFEU, fourth indent (emphasis added).
[131] K Kulovesi, 'Climate Change in EU External Relations: Please Follow My Example (or I Might Force You To)' in E Morgera (ed), *The External Environmental Policy of the European Union: EU and International Law Perspectives* (Cambridge: Cambridge University Press, 2012) 115.

4.1 An overview of EU climate law

The European Climate Law[132] and the Fit for 55 (FF55) Package of legislation provide the current legal basis for climate action in the EU. The latter is a comprehensive set of legal acts aimed at implementing the EU's 2021–2030 climate change mitigation contribution under the 2015 Paris Agreement. While the EU completed a comprehensive package of climate and energy legislation in 2018,[133] the next wave of profound reform began almost immediately, building on the 2019 European Green Deal roadmap. The motivation was that current climate action in the EU and globally is not in line with the Paris Agreement's goal to limit the global average temperature increase to 1.5°C.

As part of the European Green Deal, a Regulation known as the European Climate Law was adopted in 2021. It includes the goals for the EU to be climate neutral by 2050 and reduce its greenhouse gas emissions by at least 55 per cent from 1990 levels by 2030. The climate-neutrality target is a so-called net zero goal, meaning that there must be no net greenhouse gas emissions into the atmosphere from the EU by 2050, and any remaining emissions must be balanced by removals through natural or technological sinks.[134] At the end of 2025, a Commission proposal was agreed to amend the European Climate Law by enshrining a 90 per cent net emission reduction target for 2040.[135] It can be asked whether this represents the EU's globally fair contribution to implementing the Paris Agreement, given that it is planning to use up to 5 per cent of international carbon credits to achieve the 2040 target.

To ensure the 2030 climate target is met, the FF55 package of legal reforms of EU climate and energy law were largely completed in 2023.[136] Meanwhile, the war in Ukraine has underscored the need for the EU to become independent of Russian fossil fuels, leading to further legislation to accelerate the energy and green transitions, including a regulation banning imports of oil and gas from Russia from 2026 onwards.[137]

EU climate change law reflects in various ways the environmental integration principle.[138] It has evolved through successive 'packages' of legislative measures that jointly address climate change and energy,[139] and especially the FF55 package strengthened climate measures in sectors such as transport, trade, investment, and external policy.[140] Furthermore, the fact that the EU climate objectives are now enshrined in the European Climate Law means that there are more specific climate policy requirements to consider within the context of the environmental integration principle.[141] Additionally, the European Climate Law includes a provision requiring the Commission to assess whether any draft EU measures or legislative proposal, including budget proposals, are compatible with the 2050 climate-neutrality objective and the 2030 and 2040 climate targets.[142]

[132] The Regulation establishing the framework for achieving climate neutrality and amending Regulations (EC) No 401/2009 and (EU) 2018/1999 (OJ [2021] L243/1) (European Climate Law).

[133] K Kulovesi and S Oberthür, 'Assessing the EU's 2030 Climate and Energy Policy Framework: Incremental Change toward Radical Transformation?' (2020) 29 *Review of European, Comparative and International Environmental Law* 151.

[134] European Climate Law, Art 2.1.

[135] OJ [2026] L x.x.2026.

[136] S Oberthür and K Kulovesi, 'Accelerating the EU's Climate Transformation: The European Green Deal's Fit for 55 Package Unpacked' (2025) 34 *Review of European, Comparative and International Environmental Law* 7.

[137] OJ [2026] L 2.2.2026.

[138] See section 2.3.1. See also S Oberthür, K Kulovesi, and L Reins, 'Anchoring Climate Policy Integration: Progress and Limitations under the European Green Deal' (2026) *Journal of Environmental Policy and Planning* (reference to be finalised: currently re-submitted after peer-review with minor revisions).

[139] Claire Dupont et al, 'Three Decades of EU Climate Policy: Racing Toward Climate Neutrality?' (2024) 15 *Wires Climate Change* e863.

[140] Oberthür, Kulovesi, and Reins (n 138).

[141] Ibid.

[142] European Climate Law, Art 6.4.

4.2 Key components of EU climate law

Due to recent reforms, EU climate change law can now be divided into two categories: legislation that regulates EU climate and energy governance; and legislation containing substantive measures to cut greenhouse gas emissions. In the first category, the European Climate Law plays an important role, including by enshrining in law the EU's climate targets.[143] It primarily addresses the EU level and introduces obligations mainly for the Commission.[144] In addition, EU climate and energy governance has been strengthened through the 2018 Governance Regulation that includes obligations for both the Commission and the Member States, and covers planning, reporting, and monitoring of climate and energy policies.[145] Its main requirements include that each Member State prepares a National Climate and Energy Plan every ten years, and updates the plan every five years. These plans currently detail how each Member State aims to achieve its 2030 climate and energy targets, and are subject to close oversight and guidance from the Commission.[146] The Governance Regulation also seeks to promote public participation and collaboration between the Member States.

The EU Emission Trading Scheme (ETS 1) has been the cornerstone of EU climate law since 2005. It has capped greenhouse gas emissions from energy-intensive industries, including power generation, iron and steel, chemicals, oil refineries, cement and other building materials, as well as pulp and paper, and has subjected them to a carbon price. Each year, the covered installations must purchase and surrender emission allowances, known as EUAs, to the national ETS authorities corresponding to their verified greenhouse gas emissions. The use of a market-based mechanism is considered useful to allow private operators to find the most cost-effective way to comply with the EU greenhouse gas emission reduction obligations, with the understanding that 'placing a price on carbon' will send an unequivocal signal to internalize the social cost of greenhouse gas emissions and to invest in low-carbon technologies.

ETS 1 nearly halved greenhouse gas emissions in the covered sectors between 2005 and 2023.[147] Given this success, the FF55 package expanded its scope to greenhouse gas emissions from maritime transport and established a new ETS 2 for fuel used in road transport and buildings (heating), originally scheduled to start in 2027[148] but postponed until 2028. To counter the impact of increasing fuel prices resulting from ETS 2, the Social Climate Fund was created to support vulnerable households, microenterprises, and transport users.[149] It will be capitalized through revenue generated by auctioning of ETS 2 emission allowances. As a result, carbon pricing is estimated to cover three-quarters of the EU economy from 2028 onwards. Further extensions are being planned, such as the inclusion of industrial carbon removals in ETS 1.

Through the FF55 legal reforms, the sectoral reach and stringency of EU climate law have been strengthened.[150] Other key pieces of legislation complementing emissions trading include the Effort-Sharing Regulation, which includes binding emissions targets for each Member State in the so-called effort-sharing sectors not included under the ETS,

[143] K Kulovesi, S Oberthür, H van Asselt, and A Savaresi, 'The European Climate Law: Strengthening EU Procedural Climate Governance?' (2024) 36 *Journal of Environmental Law* 23.

[144] Ibid.

[145] Regulation (EU) 2018/1999 on the governance of the Energy Union and climate action (OJ [2018] L328/1) (Governance Regulation).

[146] Kulovesi and Oberthür (n 133) 153–156.

[147] Commission, 'Progress Report 2024: Climate Action' (Report from the Commission to the European Parliament and the Council), COM(2024) 498 final, 12.

[148] Directive (EU) 2023/959 (OJ [2023] L130/134) (amended ETS Directive).

[149] Regulation (EU) 2023/955 establishing the Social Climate Fund (OJ [2023] L130/1).

[150] Oberthür and Kulovesi (n 133).

including transport, buildings, agriculture, and waste.[151] The land use, land-use change, and forestry sector constitutes the third key pillar of EU climate law, assigning each Member State a net greenhouse gas removal target and making sure that greenhouse gas emissions and their removals, for example by forest sinks, are comprehensively considered and accounted for.[152]

The Renewable Energy Directive[153] was designed to increase the share of renewable energy in the EU. In addition to setting various targets, the Directive addresses issues such as national renewable energy support schemes, biofuels, green hydrogen, as well as renewable energy communities and self-producers. The Directive sets a binding target of at least 42.5 per cent of renewable energy in the EU's final energy consumption by 2030. The Directive takes a technology-neutral approach, allowing all forms of renewable energy to contribute to the EU's binding target.

EU climate law also includes the Energy Efficiency Directive, which has sought to create a comprehensive framework for enhancing energy efficiency,[154] as well as the Energy Performance of Buildings Directive, establishing the sectoral objective of a zero-emission building stock by 2050.[155] In total, the FF55 package includes 18 pieces of climate and energy legislation.[156]

Case study 22.1: Tensions between EU climate and nature protection initiatives

The EU has long regarded the expansion of renewable energy sources as an essential means to reduce greenhouse gas emissions, enhance energy security, and support economic growth.[157] Balancing these objectives with nature protection, however, has long proved difficult in EU law.[158] The Renewables Directive recognizes the need to prevent biodiversity loss and addresses ecological trade-offs, which restrict renewable energy sourcing from areas of high biodiversity value. At the same time, the Directive introduces a number of procedural innovations aimed at accelerating the deployment of renewable energy projects, including the designation of 'renewables acceleration areas' and the imposition of binding deadlines for permit-granting procedures.

Early discussions on the sustainability of biofuels revealed how policies designed to promote renewable energy could simultaneously generate indirect land-use change, loss of high-biodiversity habitats, and greater pressure on agricultural land.[159] These concerns led to the inclusion of sustainability criteria in the Renewable Energy Directive, prohibiting biofuel production from raw materials sourced from land with a high biodiversity value. Later con-

151 Regulation (EU) 2023/857 (OJ [2023] L/111/1).

152 Regulation 2023/839 (OJ [2023] L107/1).

153 Directive (EU) 2023/2413 on the promotion of the use of energy from renewable sources (OJ [2023] L2413) (Renewables Directive).

154 Directive (EU) 2023/1791 on energy efficiency and amending Regulation (EU) 2023/955 (recast) (OJ [2023] L231/1).

155 Directive (EU) 2024/1275 on the energy performance of buildings (OJ [2024] L2024/1275).

156 Discussed in more detail in Oberthür and Kulovesi (n 133).

157 See eg European Commission, 'Communication: The European Green Deal', COM/2019/640 final; European Commission, 'Communication: The Clean Industrial Deal: A joint roadmap for competitiveness and decarbonization', COM(2025) 85 final.

158 HT Anker and BE Olsen, 'EU Species Protection Law and Wind Energy: Current Challenges and Danish Experiences' (2023) 32 *European Energy and Environmental Law Review* 36.

159 See eg S Romppanen, 'Biofuels' in E Morgera and J Razzaque (eds), *Biodiversity and Nature Protection Law* (Cheltenham: Edward Elgar, 2017) 346.

troversies surrounding forest bioenergy[160] and hydropower[161] confirmed that similar trade-offs recur across renewable energy types, particularly where their impacts intersect with carbon accounting and water protection. In the case of forest biomass, concerns have centred on carbon accounting, the use of primary woody biomass, and the adequacy of safeguards for forest ecosystems.[162] Comparable challenges have emerged in relation to hydropower, which, while advancing renewable energy and energy security goals, has been linked to the deterioration of rivers and fish habitats, underscoring tensions with the Water Framework Directive's requirements to achieve and maintain good ecological status.[163]

The revised Renewable Energy Directive seeks to address some of these challenges by encouraging a more integrated approach for climate, energy, and environmental policies. It requires that Member States identify renewables acceleration areas that are suitable for renewable energy deployment and that such areas exclude Natura 2000 sites, nationally protected areas, and other areas where the renewable energy development would not have a similar significant environmental impact.[164] Member States must also establish effective mitigation measures to limit the environmental impact of renewable energy projects located within these zones.[165] However, the same Directive also introduces measures that may, in practice, weaken environmental safeguards. In particular, it establishes strict time limits for the permit-granting process—12 months in acceleration areas and 24 months elsewhere—and provides that renewable energy projects are presumed to be in the 'overriding public interest'. This presumption simplifies the application of exemptions available under environmental legislation, such as the Habitats and Birds Directives, and may thereby lower the threshold for authorizing projects that have adverse effects on protected species or habitats.

These reforms are part of a broader effort to accelerate renewable energy deployment and reduce the EU's reliance on imported fossil fuels. While the Commission has emphasized that faster permitting is essential for achieving the 2030 climate and energy targets, this urgency has sparked serious concerns about the balance between speed and sustainability. Renewable energy infrastructure is indispensable for climate mitigation, yet it can also generate significant local environmental impacts. The tension between safeguarding biodiversity and delivering large-scale renewable projects exposes a deeper misalignment between EU environmental and climate law. As Hardiman notes, the EU's legal framework still struggles to reconcile these objectives, often resorting to 'sidestepping' provisions that prioritize climate goals without fully integrating environmental safeguards.[166]

Similar tensions arise in other sectors essential to the European green transition. Growing demand for critical raw materials needed in many renewable and various other technologies (such as lithium, cobalt, and rare earth elements) led to the adoption of the Critical Raw Materials Act,[167] which also introduces fast-tracked permitting for strategic projects.[168] At the same time, however, the extraction and processing of these materials can cause significant

[160] See eg C Sasso, A Savarese, and S Vesa, 'Piecing Together the Jigsaw: Forests in the EU's Fit for 55 Package' (2025) 34 *Review of European, Comparative and International Environmental Law* 23.

[161] K Huhta, N Soininen, and S Vesa, 'The Ecological Sustainability of the Energy Transition in EU Law: Pro et Contra Hydropower' (2025) 43 *Journal of Energy & Natural Resources Law* 29.

[162] A Korosuo et al, 'The Role of Forests in the EU Climate Policy: Are We on the Right Track?' (2023) *18 Carbon Balance and Management* 1, 10.

[163] Huhta et al (n 161). [164] Renewable Energy Directive, Art 15c. [165] Ibid.

[166] A Hardiman, 'Climate, Energy—and Environment? Reconciliation of EU Environmental Law with the Implementation Realities of EU Climate Law' (2022) 12 *Climate Law* 242, 271.

[167] Regulation (EU) 2024/1252 (OJ [2024] L 3.5.2024).

[168] It is worth noting that other EU legal instruments also introduce similar provisions on permitting.

environmental and human rights impacts, including habitat loss, water pollution, and community displacement both within the EU and beyond. Although much of this occurs outside the EU, it remains closely tied to the EU's renewable energy transition. While the Act seeks to strengthen supply security, it also exposes the persistent sidelining of the need to safeguard ecosystems and human rights. This is an approach that increasingly defines the EU's broader sustainability governance,[169] and that is in clear tension with the clarifications provided by ITLOS and the ICJ on the need to take climate action that is also in line with international obligations on the protection of biodiversity and the marine environment. Achieving coherence between these fields of international and EU law requires not only streamlined procedures, but also complementarity across substantive, enforceable safeguards, and effective oversight, to ensure a high level of environmental protection and environmental integration as the indispensable basis for any approach to sustainable development.

4.3 **International reach of EU climate law**

The evolution of EU climate law has been closely linked with the evolution of international climate law and the EU's *international* agenda on climate change. For example, the ETS aims to generate climate finance within the EU and for developing countries: it requires that the revenue generated from the auctioning of emission allowances must be used for various climate-friendly purposes within the EU, as well as to finance climate actions in vulnerable third countries, including adaptation.[170]

To address concerns that the ETS will harm European industries and production and greenhouse gas emissions will shift elsewhere ('carbon leakage'), European industries exposed to the risk of carbon leakage have received their emission allowances free of charge. However, the FF55 legal reforms included the Carbon Border Adjustment Mechanism (CBAM) requiring importers of iron and steel, aluminium, cement, fertilizers, hydrogen, and electricity to purchase certificates to cover greenhouse gas emissions embedded in their products.[171] Similar mechanisms have been subject to extensive debate, including concerning their compatibility with World Trade Organization (WTO) law.[172] CBAM has also triggered a wide range of political reactions, while also driving the development of climate policies in several countries.[173]

Other examples of the international reach of EU climate law include sustainability criteria for biofuels and bioliquids that apply to imports from third countries.[174] However, not all countries have been happy with the EU approach to sustainable biofuels and these have been subject to disputes under WTO law.[175]

[169] See S Vesa, K Huhta, and N Soininen, 'Critical Raw Materials and the Law: Confronting Legal Disruption in the Transition to Sustainability' [2025] *Law, Innovation and Technology*, DOI: 10.1080/17579961.2025.2593780. See also United Nations General Assembly, Promotion and protection of human rights in the context of climate change: Note by the Secretary-General, UN Doc A/80/211 (17 July 2025).

[170] Amended ETS Directive, Art 10(3).

[171] Regulation (EU) 2023/956 establishing a carbon border adjustment mechanism (OJ [2023] L130/52).

[172] G Marín Durán, 'Securing Compatibility of Carbon Border Adjustments with the Multilateral Climate and Trade Regimes' (2023) 72 *International and Comparative Law Quarterly* 73.

[173] S Otto, 'The External Impact of EU Climate Policy: Political Responses to the EU's Carbon Border Adjustment Mechanism' (2025) 25 *International Environmental Agreements: Politics, Law and Economics* 177.

[174] J Scott, 'The Multi-Level Governance of Climate Change' (2011) 4 *Carbon and Climate Law Review* 25.

[175] See eg *European Union and certain member states—certain measures concerning palm oil and oil palm crop-based biofuels*, Panel Report, WT/DS600/R, 5 March 2024.

Case study 22.2: Influencing environmental multilateralism through EU climate regulation—international aviation emissions

In the area of climate change it is quite evident that the EU uses its internal legislation not only to implement international environmental law, but also to try to influence ongoing multilateral environmental processes. These attempts, however, do not necessarily go unchallenged by third countries. A classic example is the EU's action to include international aviation in the ETS.[176] From 1 January 2012, all airlines, including those from third countries, were expected to participate in the ETS for their flights departing from and arriving at European airports. This EU initiative needs to be understood in the context of a long-standing international impasse on whether and under which international forum (the international climate change regime or the International Civil Aviation Organization, ICAO) to take action on greenhouse gas emissions from international aviation.

US and Canadian airlines and airline associations contested the measures transposing the relevant EU Directive in the UK. A preliminary reference was then submitted to the Court of Justice to clarify whether, among other things, the Directive violated international law. The Court concluded that the Directive did not violate international law, in particular its principles of territoriality and sovereignty of third States, as the scheme was applicable only to aircraft that were physically present in the territory of the Member States (ie flying into and out of EU airports) and therefore under the jurisdiction of the EU. In addition, the Court noted that the EU was allowed to comply with the international climate change obligations in the manner and at the speed upon which it had agreed.[177] Interestingly, Advocate General Kokott noted that the EU 'could not reasonably be required to give . . . [multilateral] bodies unlimited time in which to develop a multilateral solution'.[178] Thus, the Court of Justice found that the EU can take bold climate change measures with a view to anticipating and possibly influencing legal developments at the international level, as long as it ensures a link to its territory and has provided sufficient opportunities for other countries to reach an agreement in the context of relevant international organizations.

The Court's decision, however, did not pacify the concerns of third countries. A coalition including Brazil, China, India, Russia, South Africa, and the US opposed the inclusion of international aviation emissions within the EU ETS.[179] Faced with mounting external pressures, in November 2012 the European Commission indicated that the EU had decided to 'stop the clock' for one year on the implementation of the inclusion of non-EU flights under the ETS.[180] The Commission motivated the decision by reference to intervening positive developments at the ICAO and a desire to create a positive atmosphere for international negotiations.[181] While it is difficult to determine whether the EU was recalibrating its arms with a view to effectively and constructively influencing multilateral environmental decision-making,[182] or

[176] Directive 2008/101/EC (OJ [2009] L8/3).

[177] Case C-366/10 *Air Transport Association of America*, EU:C:2011:864 (Grand Chamber).

[178] Ibid, Opinion of 6 October 2011, paras 185 and 186.

[179] International Centre for Trade and Sustainable Development, 'Opponents of EU Aviation Carbon Law Agree on Possible Countermeasures', *Bridges Weekly Trade News Digest*, 22 February 2012.

[180] 'Stopping the clock of ETS and aviation emissions following last week's International Civil Aviation Organisation (ICAO) Council', MEMO/12/854, 12 November 2012.

[181] Ibid.

[182] E Morgera and K Kulovesi, 'The Role of the EU in Promoting International Climate Change Standards' in I Govaere and S Poli, *EU Management of Global Emergencies* (Leiden: Brill, 2014) 311–336. Regulation (EU) No 421/2014 amending Directive 2003/87/EC establishing a scheme for greenhouse gas emission allowance trading within the Community (OJ [2014] L129/1), in view of the implementation by 2020 of an international agreement applying a single global market-based measure to international aviation emissions.

whether it had been subject to pressures from Member States over the economic implications of the scheme,[183] its anticipation of positive multilateral developments proved correct. The ICAO decided in 2016 to limit international aviation emissions through a global market-based measure known as the Carbon Offsetting and Reduction Scheme for Aviation (CORSIA).[184] The EU has thus maintained in place the geographical limitation created in 2012 and continues to implement the emissions trading scheme for aviation only within the European Economic Area. The Commission is, however, mandated to review the environmental integrity of CORSIA by 1 July 2026, potentially leading the EU to revert back to the scheme's original scope.

5 **Conclusion**

The EU as an environmental regulator has set for itself very broad and ambitious objectives. It has used its law-making powers abundantly to address a variety of environmental challenges and in many respects has improved its environmental regulation in a gradual fashion, learning from past mistakes and engaging in significant innovation. Nonetheless, different areas of the EU environmental *acquis* appear at different stages of development, with different approaches and degrees of implementation. The EU Green Deal recognized the need to take a more ambitious and joined-up approach to environmental regulation in order to tackle the global climate, biodiversity, and toxics crises in an integrated fashion across the EU environmental *acquis*. However, the difficulty in appropriately ensuring coherent and sufficiently ambitious environmental protection with continued economic development—a taxing aim that is embodied in the principle of sustainable development—has become an even more evident challenge.

This chapter also demonstrates that the study of EU environmental law would not be complete without an understanding of the role of the EU as a global environmental actor, proactively engaged in the development and implementation of international environmental law. To a significant extent, EU environmental law aims to fulfil the international environmental obligations of the Union and/or its Member States. In addition, as seen in the specific area of climate change, the EU increasingly develops its internal environmental regulation to anticipate or even influence the making of international environmental law.[185]

Both the EU's ambition to advance sustainable development and to act as an international environmental leader can now be carefully scrutinized in the light of the legal clarifications provided by the international tribunals on State obligations on climate change, which are intertwined with various international rules on the protection of the environment, the ocean, and human rights. As the ICJ concluded:

> [T]he questions posed by the General Assembly represent more than a legal problem: they concern an existential problem of planetary proportions that imperils all forms of life and the very health of our planet. International law, whose authority has been invoked by the General

[183] B Lewis and V Volcovici, 'US, China Turned EU Powers against Airline Pollution Law', *Reuters*, 10 December 2012, available at: www.reuters.com/article/2012/12/10/us-eu-airlines-climate-idUSBRE8B801H20121210.

[184] ICAO Resolution, A39-2 Consolidated statement of continuing ICAO policies and practices related to environmental protection—Climate change (2016) and A39-3: Consolidated statement of continuing ICAO policies and practices related to environmental protection—Global Market-based Measure scheme.

[185] H Vedder, 'Diplomacy by Directive: An Analysis of the International Context of the Emissions Trading Directive' in M Evans and P Koutrakos (eds), *Beyond the Established Legal Orders* (Oxford: Hart Publishing, 2011) 105.

Assembly, has an important but ultimately limited role in resolving this problem. A complete solution to this daunting, and self-inflicted, problem requires the contribution of all fields of human knowledge, whether law, science, economics or any other. Above all, a lasting and satisfactory solution requires human will and wisdom—at the individual, social and political levels—to change our habits, comforts and current way of life in order to secure a future for ourselves and those who are yet to come.[186]

Further reading

J Jans and H Vedder, *European Environmental Law* (4th edn, Groningen: Europa Law, 2012)

S Kingston et al, *European Environmental Law* (Cambridge: Cambridge University Press, 2017)

L Kramer, *EU Environmental Law* (8th edn, London: Sweet & Maxwell, 2016)

M Lee, *EU Environmental Law: Challenges, Change and Decision-Making* (Oxford: Hart Publishing, 2014)

G Marín Durán and E Morgera, *Environmental Integration in the EU's External Relations: Beyond Multilateral Dimensions* (Oxford: Hart Publishing, 2012)

E Morgera (ed), *The External Environmental Policy of the European Union: EU and International Law Perspectives* (Cambridge: Cambridge University Press, 2012)

J Scott (ed), *Environmental Protection: European Law and Governance* (Oxford: Oxford University Press, 2009)

G Van Calster and L Reins, *EU Environmental Law* (Cheltenham: Edward Elgar, 2018)

[186] ICJ Advisory Opinion (n 38) para 456.

23

European consumer law

Geraint Howells and Jonathon Watson

1 Introduction

From small seeds planted in the 1970s,[1] EU consumer law has grown considerably over the past half century, with few areas of national law being as heavily influenced by EU law as consumer protection. This impact at first remained contained within the specialism, but with the adoption of the Unfair Terms in Consumer Contracts Directive in 1993,[2] which introduced minimum controls on unfair terms in consumer contracts, and especially the 1999 Consumer Sales Directive,[3] which set minimum quality standards for goods, the reach of the legislation spread out to irritate[4] core areas of private law and in particular sales law, which is the cornerstone of national commercial law regimes. Indeed, the field of European private law has developed on the back of the *consumer acquis*. Whilst some

[1] Council Resolution of 14 April 1975 on a preliminary programme of the European Economic Community for a consumer protection and information policy (OJ [1975] C92/1).

[2] Directive 1993/13 (OJ [1993] L95/29).

[3] Directive 1999/44 (OJ [1999] L171/12).

[4] To borrow the language from the well-known article on good faith as a legal irritant by G Teubner, 'Legal Irritants: Good Faith in British Law or How Unifying Law Ends Up in New Divergences' (1998) 61 *Modern Law Review* 11.

even favour the development of a European Civil Code,[5] others were more modest in their goals.[6] The notion of a European system of sales law, the 'Common European Sales Law', found political support from those within the European Commission, who saw the increase in cross-border trade as a goal in its own right.[7] However, the proposed regulation was too ambitious and was withdrawn in favour of measures which were initially focused on online sales and digital content.[8] The former ultimately morphed from a measure targeted specifically at online sales into a general reform of existing EU sales law via a maximal harmonization directive, achieving therefore to some extent the ambitions of the Common European Sales Law to overcome the divergences between the Member States.[9]

One impact of the EU legislation and case law has been to remove national rules that claimed to protect consumers but acted as unjustified barriers to trade. This is considered in section 2. The rest of the chapter concerns the EU's positive harmonization agenda, which is needed not only to give the EU a social face, but also because many national consumer protection measures are justified and a harmonized approach is the only way to promote the cross-border circulation of goods and services. Section 3 provides general commentary on the EU's approach. A distinctive feature of EU consumer law is an emphasis on empowering consumers to make decisions that are in their best interests. Information duties (including the duty to not mislead which became part of a wider regulation of unfair commercial practices) and the right of withdrawal are key instruments in this approach and are reflected on in sections 4 and 5. Such rules promoting the free choice by the consumer are favoured as they promote autonomy more than substantive rules and interfere less in national private law legal systems. However, the EU also provides for substantive consumer law issues, which are considered in sections 5 to 10, with details being provided on product safety, product liability, unfair contract terms, and sale of goods and digital content law. The Commission's policy agenda has highlighted a number of key priorities, most notably the 'green transition' and the 'digital transformation' alongside the familiar topic of 'redress and enforcement of consumer rights'.[10] The Commission is currently consulting on its Consumer Agenda 2030, but similar themes remain prominent as it seeks to promote a 'fair green and digital economy'. Whereas the first two priorities will be included in the discussion of the substantive consumer law issues, 'redress and enforcement of consumer rights' will be covered separately in section 12.

[5] A Hartkamp et al (eds), *Towards a European Civil Code* (4th edn, Alphen aan den Rijn: Kluwer Law International, 2010); H Collins, *The European Civil Code: The Way Forward* (Cambridge: Cambridge University Press, 2008). Cf P Legrand, 'Against a European Civil Code' (1997) 60 *Modern Law Review* 44.

[6] H Beale, 'The Future of the Common Frame of Reference' (2007) 3 *European Review of Contract Law* 257; C von Bar, 'Coverage and Structure of the Academic Common Frame of Reference' (2007) 3 *European Review of Contract Law* 350. Cf H Eidenmüller et al, 'The Common Frame of Reference for European Private Law: Policy Choices and Codification Problems' (2008) 28 *Oxford Journal of Legal Studies* 659. On a European business code, which is still a topic of discussion, see M Lehmann, 'EU Law-Making 2.0: The Prospect of a European Business Code' (2020) 1 *European Review of Private Law* 73 and the recent report, 'The 28th Regime—A legal framework for innovation the European way', prepared in July 2025 for the European Parliament.

[7] COM(2011) 635 final, 11 October 2011.

[8] On the relevance of the distinction between a regulation and a directive, see chapter 5.

[9] See section 10.

[10] COM(2020) 696 final, 13 November 2020, 1.

2 The negative impact of EU law on national consumer protection rules

The bulk of this chapter concerns the positive consumer protection rules introduced by the EU that now pervade national consumer law.[11] However, EU law has also played an important role in removing redundant national laws. EU law might be compared to a glacier removing all national consumer protection rules that impede the development of the internal market without having any real consumer protection purpose, or at least any purpose that could not be achieved by any less restrictive means. Thus unjustified national rules limiting permitted ingredients could not be used to exclude imports from other EU Member States—the German Beer Purity Law limiting ingredients of beer to water, barley, and hops[12] and Italian rules requiring pasta to be made from durum wheat[13] were successfully challenged, as was a German ban on the importation of 'Cassis de Dijon' because it did not have a high enough alcohol content to satisfy requirements of German law.[14] Many advertising rules, especially under German Unfair Competition Law, were successfully challenged because while claiming to protect consumers they were in reality placing unfair limits on competition.[15] An illustrative example was the need for the European Court of Justice to find the cosmetic name 'Clinique' should not be banned because of the risk of confusing German consumers that the product had medicinal properties. Out of this line of cases came the EU image of the average consumer being 'reasonably well-informed and reasonably observant and circumspect, taking into account social, cultural and linguistic factors'.[16] This was a reaction to some overprotective national regimes which really did not serve the consumer well as they unduly restricted competition. The Court has, however, shown itself to be sensitive to genuine consumer needs. The ambition of a level playing field was achieved in large part by using (old) Article 30 EC (now Article 34 TFEU) with an expansive definition of 'measures having effects equivalent to quantitative restrictions'[17] and applying the concept of mutual recognition.[18]

Not all national consumer law rules could be removed in this way for the very good reason that some had legitimate consumer protection goals. Indeed, the Court was alert to genuine consumer protection needs and would refuse challenges where a genuine consumer protection concern was at stake. For instance, it upheld a French ban on the marketing of educational materials on the doorstep.[19] These national rules might be justified

[11] This statement remains partially valid even following the United Kingdom's withdrawal from the EU on 31 January 2020 ('Brexit'). Certain pieces of UK legislation which serve to implement EU directives remain in force, eg The Cancellation of Contracts made in a Consumer's Home or Place of Work etc. Regulations 2008, SI 2008 No. 1816. However, some aspects of UK consumer law are based on the EU model, yet due to Brexit have not been changed to accord with more recent EU legislation, eg the consumer's remedies for defective goods under the Consumer Rights Act 2015.

[12] Case C-178/84 *Commission v Germany* [1987] ECR 1227.

[13] Case 202/82 *Commission v France* [1984] ECR 933 and Case 90/86 *Zoni* [1988] ECR 4285.

[14] Case C-120/78 *Cassis de Dijon* [1979] ECR 649.

[15] Case C-315/92 *Clinique* [1994] ECR I-317; Case C-470/93 *Mars* [1995] ECR I-1923; Case C-210/96 *Gut Springenheide* [1998] ECR I-4657; C-303/97 *Kessler* [1999] ECR I-513; and Case C-220/98 *Estée Lauder* [2000] ECRI-117.

[16] Directive 2005/29 (OJ [2005] L149/22), recital 18. See K Purnhagen and H Schebesta, 'Island or Ocean: Empirical Evidence on the Average Consumer Concept in the UCPD' (2020) 2 *European Review of Private Law* 293.

[17] Case C-8/74 *Dassonville* [1974] ECR 837. See chapter 12.

[18] *Cassis de Dijon* [1979] (n 14).

[19] Case C-382/87 *Buet* [1989] ECR 1235. In Case C-286/81 *Oosthoek* [1982] ECR 4575 a Dutch ban on the use of free gifts to promote sales was upheld; nowadays such national bans are likely to fall foul of the Unfair Commercial Practices Directive (on which see later).

on the basis of a Treaty provision[20] or the Court-established mandatory requirements which in *Cassis de Dijon* were said to include consumer protection as a justification for national laws that would otherwise be obstacles to movement.[21] To take the glacier analogy one step further, these areas of legitimate consumer protection might be compared to the mounds left behind after the glacier has done its work. EU law then gets to work on these issues by positively harmonizing the rules that are needed for consumer protection in a way that promotes the internal market.

3 Consumer protection and the internal market

3.1 Legal basis

In the early days the internal market provisions were the only legal basis for introducing EU consumer rules. Consumer protection as an express EU competence was in fact only introduced from 1993 in the Maastricht Treaty. Article 114 TFEU, which provides for the adoption of 'measures for the approximation of the provisions laid down by law, regulation or administrative action in Member States which have as their object the establishment and functioning of the internal market' is still the basis for most EU consumer laws. Article 114(3) TFEU requires such measures to take as a base a high level of consumer protection. Article 38 of the Charter of Fundamental Rights features similar wording.[22]

Article 169 TFEU provides for a specific consumer protection provision which provides that 'In order to promote the interests of consumers and to ensure a high level of consumer protection, the Union shall contribute to protecting the health, safety and economic interests of consumers, as well as to promoting their right to information, education and to organise themselves in order to safeguard their interests.' However, when it comes to the legislative means to achieve these aims, it is content to cross-reference to Article 114 TFEU or otherwise limits the scope to 'measures which support, supplement and monitor the policy pursued by the Member States'. As a result, few EU provisions rely on Article 169 TFEU as a legal base.[23] Furthermore, Article 12 TFEU provides that consumer protection requirements shall be taken into account in defining and implementing other Union policies and activities.

The legal basis for EU activity in consumer law being based for the most part on Article 114 TFEU might explain the dominance of the internal market perspective in the European Commission's consumer policy. It was not always so. There is indeed a certain irony in that the European Commission was the most fervent advocate of consumer protection at a time when its powers in this field were limited. It had to justify intervention solely on the ground that harmonized rules were needed to promote the functioning and establishment of the internal market.[24] Once intervention was justified the European Commission had the freedom to choose the appropriate level and consumer protection objectives could come into play. Indeed, the primacy of consumer protection as the motivating force is evident in one of the first legislative measures being Directive 85/577/EEC to protect the consumer in respect of contracts negotiated away from business premises.[25] More commonly known as the 'Doorstep Selling Directive', its main focus was to protect

[20] Art 36 TFEU. [21] *Cassis de Dijon* (n 14).

[22] For detail on Art 38, see S Weatherill, 'Article 38' in S Peers et al (eds), *The EU Charter of Fundamental Rights* (2nd edn, Oxford: Hart Publishing, 2021) 1065 *et seq.* [23] eg Directive 98/6 (OJ [1998] L80/27).

[24] eg Directive 85/577 gave particular regard to Art 100 EEC. For a detailed overview of the development of EU competence for consumer protection, see S Weatherill, *EU Consumer Law and Policy* (2nd edn, Cheltenham: Edward Elgar, 2014) 1–23. On the relationship between consumer protection and the internal market, see further chapters 11 and 12.

[25] OJ [1985] L371/31.

consumers with a cancellation option for sales and services contracts concluded at the consumer's home. While a case can be made out for such legislation promoting the internal market—there are a few companies that operate doorstep selling on a pan-European basis—it is evident that the motivation for the law was the vulnerability of people buying in their homes, normally from local businesses operating high-pressure sales techniques.

Despite consumer protection featuring more prominently in Treaty amendments there has been in fact a noticeable change in tone with the emphasis being placed on the internal market impact of divergent consumer laws. While consumer law has risen up the EU's agenda and been more mainstreamed, it is possible to argue that the protection element has become less important. The internal market needs harmonized rules, but these need not necessarily be the best consumer protection rules. Those defending the EU policy would argue that they fulfil the Treaty obligation to adopt a high base of protection, but there is scope to debate what that means and certainly it is not necessarily the same as the highest level found in some Member States.

3.2 **EU consumer law as a driver for greater cross-border trade**

It should be recognized that the present Treaty still does not see consumer legislation as an end in itself. Any such laws have to be related to the internal market or support and supplement national law.[26] The major motivations are to promote active cross-border consumerism as well as encouraging businesses to trade with consumers in other Member States to make markets within the EU more competitive. Encouraging growth in cross-border trade remains one of the Commission's central arguments for harmonizing consumer law, as is readily apparent in the preambles to consumer law directives. This is especially evident in the attempts to introduce maximal harmonization in the Consumer Rights Directive[27] and subsequently (when that failed for unfair terms and sale of goods, which were removed from the initial proposal[28]) by the unsuccessful attempt to try to adopt an alternative optional regime for cross-border sales in the form of a Common European Sales Law. Eventually maximal harmonization was a key element of the reformed rules for the sale of goods and the supply of digital content.[29] The Commission has few levers to increase cross-border trade besides making the law more harmonized. This has driven the change in emphasis in EU consumer policy. The objective of European Union consumer law is no longer just to provide a platform of minimum rights so that consumers could be confident in buying anywhere in the Union. Rather, it is increasingly the policy (though this has been resisted in some areas[30]) to make the EU rules the sole source of consumer protection (maximal harmonization, ie a uniform EU law that does not permit Member States to apply lower *or* higher standards) to give traders the confidence to trade across borders. Such an approach results from a change of focus to one that prioritizes inspiring businesses with the confidence to trade across borders without the risk of being surprised by unfamiliar national laws.[31]

[26] Arts 2(5) and 114(1) TFEU.

[27] Directive 2011/83 (OJ [2011] L304/64).

[28] COM(2008) 614 final, 8 October 2008.

[29] See section 10.

[30] eg in addition to doorstep selling and distance selling contracts the initial proposal for a Consumer Rights Directive also sought the full harmonization of unfair contract terms and consumer sales: COM(2008) 614 final, 8 October 2008. The final version of the Consumer Rights Directive, adopted in 2011 after intense legislative discussion, does not include the areas of unfair contract terms and consumer sales (Directive 2011/83 (OJ [2011] L304/64)). The latest reform of sales law adopts maximal harmonization, but at the same time allows Member States discretion on available remedies. See section 10.

[31] Though the argument is sometimes invoked that consumers may be made more active in the internal market if only the EU law applies as the rules are more certain. However, it is hard to understand how the possibility that national laws might provide for better than the minimal rights can be a deterrent to cross-border shopping.

The message from the European Commission is clear: consumers have more to gain from increased competition between traders who are emboldened to supply consumers in other States than they risk from any marginal reduction in consumer protection at the national level. This is controversial and the European Commission has not managed the soft politics of this process well, with consumer organizations remaining nervous about such developments.[32] The full extent to which changes in the law actually impact on cross-border trade is unclear[33] with other factors such as language, delivery costs, and access to redress should things go wrong also being important factors.[34] Nonetheless, statistics have indicated that a slight majority of traders do indeed find it easy to comply with the consumer law in another Member State.[35]

Equally, the extent to which maximal harmonization can fulfil the Commission's ambitions is limited by the scope of harmonizing measures (for Member States retain competence in areas not harmonized, subject to EU free movement law, as discussed later) and the discretion within the laws themselves for national differences to emerge in implementation, application, and enforcement.[36] What is also missing from this debate is any consideration of the optimum amount of cross-border shopping. More seems impliedly viewed as better, but sending consumers travelling around Europe or having traders delivering goods long distances conflicts with another important EU policy of environmental protection.[37] On the other hand it is pleasing to see that the EU has taken action against unjustified geo-blocking that risked preventing consumers from taking full advantage of the single market by traders who wanted to partition markets for no justifiable reasons.[38]

3.3 **Legislative approach**

Traditionally EU legislation in the consumer protection field used directives and applied to cross-border trade and domestic trade alike. There are increased signs that both these approaches are being eroded. Regulations are becoming more frequently preferred as the legislative instrument, in particular in relation to addressing the legal challenges of digital content and services. This may be appropriate if in fact EU law gives little discretion in implementation and especially if EU law is to become the sole source of law due to the use of maximal harmonization. This may be beneficial to consumers as regulations become directly applicable and so immediately available for use by consumers. Consumers struggle to obtain rights under directives that are not implemented or not

[32] U Pachl, 'Common European Sales Law—Have the Right Choices Been Made: A Consumer Policy Perspective' (2012) 19 *Maastricht Journal of European and Comparative Law* 180, 189.

[33] eg the results of a 2018 study show that traders consider the differences in national tax regulations to be the greatest obstacle: European Commission, 'Retailers' Attitudes towards Cross-Border Trade and Consumer Protection 2018' (2019) 4.

[34] SEC(2011) 1409 final, 29 November 2011, 3. Statistics from 2018 show that there are considerable differences between the Member States with regard to cross-border purchasing by consumers, especially in Eastern European countries: European Commission, 'Consumer's Attitudes towards Cross-Border Trade and Consumer Protection: Final Report' (2019) 18.

[35] See 'Retailers' Attitudes towards Cross-Border Trade and Consumer Protection 2018' (n. 33) 3.

[36] See also discussion of open-textured norms at section 11.2. On the challenges of full harmonization, see H-W Micklitz, 'The Full Harmonization Dream' (2022) 4 *Journal of European Consumer and Market Law* 117.

[37] On the substance of environmental policy, see chapter 22. See however COM(2020) 696 final, which refers to the 'green transition' yet makes no mention of the environmental impact of cross-border trade. For discussion of these issues, see E Terryn and E Van Gool, 'The Role of European Consumer Regulation in Shaping the Environmental Impact of E-Commerce' (2021) 10 *Journal of European Consumer and Market Law* 89.

[38] Regulation 2018/302 (OJ [2018] L60I/1).

properly implemented as most of their transactions are with private parties and not emanations of the State, and directives lack 'horizontal direct effect' against private parties.[39] However, in one famous case German consumers, relying upon the principle of Member States' damages liability for their breach of EU law, did recover from the German State for losses caused by the failure to set up a compensation fund for package travel holiday insolvencies as required by EU legislation.[40]

In some areas the traditional approach of national law sitting alongside EU rules will continue. In such areas there are advantages to the use of directives as they provide the national legislator with the flexibility to create a coherent national framework.[41] In some instances, achieving coherency at national level has resulted in the 'gold-plating' of consumer law directives to avoid different rules for contracts outside the scope of the underlying directive, thereby extending the reach of EU-inspired rules in the national legal system.

There is, however, also a tendency, started in the area of access to justice, where national procedural law autonomy is fiercely protected, for EU law only to apply where there is a cross-border trade dimension. The arguments here are nuanced and need to be considered on a case-by-case basis. While some contexts may justify such a parallel regime being established, there is a danger in making the law too complex if multiple or overlapping regimes emerge.

4 **Information policy and unfair commercial practices**

Information has been a prized technique of consumer protection by the EU. Many of the national consumer protection rules that were found to be incompatible with Article 30 EC (now Article 34 TFEU) could be so held because informing the consumer about the goods or services was seen as a more proportionate way of achieving the desired consumer protection objective.[42] Also national rules restricting the provision of information in advertising have been successfully challenged.[43] Rules permitting explicit or implicit comparisons with competitors and their products ('comparative advertising') which comply with key principles is also evidence of the desire to promote competition by better informing consumers.[44]

In its positive harmonization agenda, the EU has also favoured information provision rules. This is partly out of an ideological belief in promoting consumer autonomy by rectifying the lower amount of information the consumer has in relation to the seller (so-called information asymmetry).[45] If consumers are provided with more information,

[39] Case C-91/92 *Paola Faccini Dori v Recreb Srl* [1994] ECR I-3325. For more on the nature and legal effect of directives and regulations, see chapters 5 and 6.

[40] Joined Cases C-178/94, C-179/94, C-188/94, C-189/94, and C-190/94 *Dillenkofer v Bundesrepublik Deutschland* [1996] ECR I-4845.

[41] A directive leaves the national legislator with the choice of form and method to achieve the result intended by the directive, see Art 288 TFEU.

[42] eg in *Commission v Germany* (n 12) and *Cassis de Dijon* (n 14).

[43] Case C-362/88 *GB-INNO-BM* [1990] ECR I-667; Case C-44/01 *PippigAugenoptik* [2003] ECR I-3095; S Weatherill, 'The Rôle of the Informed Consumer in EC Law and Policy' (1994) 2 *Consumer Law Journal* 49.

[44] Directive 97/55 (OJ [1997] L290/18), recital 2, now Directive 2006/114 (OJ [2006] L376/21), recital 6; Weatherill, 'The Rôle of the Informed Consumer in EC Law and Policy' (n 43) 178.

[45] S Grundmann, W Kerber, and S Weatherill (eds), *Party Autonomy and the Role of Information in the Internal Market* (Berlin: De Gruyter, 2001); G Howells, A Janssen, and R Schulze (eds), *Information Rights and Obligations: A Challenge for Party Autonomy and Transactional Fairness* (Aldershot: Ashgate, 2005).

it is hoped they will make better decisions. An information-based approach also has the practical advantage of being easier to achieve in a multi-State context than changing substantive practices or legal standards. The relevant rules cover both information in advertising and marketing and the information that has to be supplied pre-contractually, in the contractual documentation and post-contractually.

4.1 Information obligations

Some of the earliest EU consumer law measures were concerned with the provision of misleading information.[46] These are now found in the Unfair Commercial Practices Directive.[47] As well as containing a general clause controlling unfair practices, the Directive also contains 'mini-general clauses' which prohibit misleading and aggressive practices. Its ambit thus extends beyond mere information policy. In assessing conduct the legislation borrowed the concept of the average consumer from the free movement case law but amended it somewhat to take account of the needs of vulnerable consumers.[48] There is also an annex containing practices that are always to be considered unfair. The Directive was also innovative by including an obligation to promote the provision of relevant information through the rules on misleading omissions; thus introducing a positive duty on traders to provide material information.[49] Amendments now provide guidance on how this applies to the internet and new rules cover situations where traders pay for higher rankings in search results.[50] The new law also treats as misleading 'dual quality' products: where products are marketed as being identical to products marketed in other Member States, but have significantly different product characteristics.[51]

The bulk of EU rules concern positive obligations to provide specific information pre-contractually and in the contractual documentation. This has gradually become a more and more prevalent form of regulation as can be seen by contrasting the very early Doorstep Selling Directive, in which the only information obligation for the trader was to inform the consumer of the right of cancellation,[52] with the far more extensive rules in the Distance Selling[53] and Distance Marketing of Financial Services Directives.[54] The information obligations in the latter Directive totalled more than 30 and resulted from a need to satisfy all States in order to have agreement on a maximal harmonization list. The Consumer Rights Directive[55] has substantial information rules that extend to all consumer contracts falling within its scope,[56] but has specific detailed rules under which off-premises and distance contracts are treated similarly.[57] It replaced the earlier directives on doorstep and distance selling and has since been updated to include rules for online marketplaces and additional information obligations for digital content.[58]

[46] Directive 84/450 (OJ [1984] L250/17). [47] See n 16. [48] Directive 2005/29, Art 5(3).

[49] Ibid, Art 7; G Howells, H-W Micklitz, and T Wilhelmsson, *European Fair Trading Law* (Aldershot: Ashgate, 2006) 147–158.

[50] Directive 2005/29, Annex 11a. [51] Ibid, Art 6(2)(c). [52] Directive 85/577, Art 4.

[53] Directive 97/7 (OJ [1997] L144/19), Art 4. [54] Directive 2002/65 (OJ [2002] L271/16), Art 3.

[55] Directive 2011/83 (OJ [2011] L304/64). [56] Ibid, Art 3.

[57] For detail, see E Hall, G Howells, and J Watson, 'The Consumer Rights Directive: An Assessment of Its Contribution to the Development of European Consumer Contract Law' (2012) 8 *European Review of Contract Law* 139, 142–154.

[58] Directive 2019/2161, Art 4.

4.2 **Information and behavioural economics**

The extensive rules on information may be helpful to provide the consumer with a full record of what was agreed, but if the aim is to improve consumer decision-making more attention is needed to the lessons of behavioural economics and in particular the limited powers of consumers to process information.[59] This branch of research uses the insights of psychology as to how consumers actually behave to challenge traditional formal economic models that assume consumers will always act rationally when provided with information. This allows more realistic appraisals of the impact of not just contractual information obligations, but also the rules concerning advertisements and the role of warnings, for example, in relation to product safety. It is not just the amount of information that is important, but also how it is presented and the account taken of the likely reaction by consumers to the information. Behavioural economics has been used to inform tobacco policy, for example, to draft the warnings about the risks of smoking to make them relate to consumer concerns, to give them authority, and to inform their placement and rotation.[60] The amendment to require a colour photograph to be on tobacco packages is an example of how evidence of the impact of such techniques on smoking reduction can help to inform policy.[61] In the consumer credit field more might be done to take account of how consumers budget when providing information since even very high interest rates as indicated by the APRs (annual percentage rate charges) may not impact significantly on consumers' decisions if they focus more on how much has to be repaid each month. There might be scope to personalize information, for example to inform consumers about how they have actually used their bank accounts or gym membership, or to use data analytics and artificial intelligence to tailor the information to the consumer's own personal situation, demographics, mental capacity and personality.[62] The use of such highly personalized and targeted information certainly has its merits and opens the possibility for a range of innovative goods and services, but the type of consumer data needed for this purpose as well as unintended or unpredictable side-effects of artificial intelligence (such as discrimination towards certain groups of consumers) do mean that all that glitters is not always gold.[63]

The EU is showing an awareness of the impact of behavioural economics on consumer policy, but it takes time to apply this to rules where the natural tendency is to play safe and appease Member States by allowing them all to keep their national preferences. Nonetheless, guidance on the Unfair Commercial Practices Directive expressly states that national courts are to take into account behavioural economics when assessing whether a commercial practice is misleading.[64] Knowledge of consumer behaviour can,

[59] G Miller, 'The Magical Number Seven, Plus or Minus Two: Some Limits on Our Capacity for Processing Information' (1956) 63 *Psychological Review* 81; G Howells, 'The Potential and Limits of Consumer Empowerment by Information' (2005) 32 *Journal of Law and Society* 349. There are other ways in which the EU uses behavioural insights, eg by requiring that there be positive consent to any add-ons to prices, rather than pre-ticked boxes (eg when purchasing holiday insurance): see Consumer Rights Directive, Art 22.

[60] G Howells, *The Tobacco Challenge* (Aldershot: Ashgate, 2011) 272–275.

[61] Directive 2014/40 (OJ [2014] L127/1).

[62] O Bar-Gill and F Ferrari, 'Informing Consumers about Themselves' (2010) 3 *Erasmus Law Review* 93; C Busch, 'Implementing Personalized Law: Personalized Disclosures in Consumer Law and Data Privacy Law' (2019) 86 *University of Chicago Law Review* 309, 313.

[63] See, highlighting the interplay between consumer law and data protection law at an early stage, F Zuiderveen Borgesius, N Helberger, and A Reyna, 'The Perfect Match? A Closer Look at the Relationship Between EU Consumer Law and Data Protection Law' (2017) 54 *Common Market Law Review* 1427.

[64] Guidance on the interpretation and application of Directive 2005/29/EC of the European Parliament and of the Council concerning unfair business-to-consumer commercial practices in the internal market (OJ [2021] L526/1), 39. See also in particular Case C-646/22 *Compass Banca*, EU:C:2024:957, which refers to cognitive bias, para 57.

of course, be used to make consumer protection policy more effective on a number of levels, yet at the same time can be exploited by unscrupulous traders (eg to take advantage of a 'fear of missing out' by using countdown clocks or indicating limited availability of a certain good). Such practices are commonly referred to as 'dark patterns' and are exposing grey areas in EU consumer law. The Commission is currently consulting on a Digital Fairness Act to protect consumers against, inter alia, manipulative practices and personalized targeting.

5 Right of withdrawal

5.1 Justification

The EU has also promoted the right of withdrawal for particular contracts as a consumer protection technique. This shares some of the objectives of the information strategy insofar as it does not seek to challenge the substance of the deal, but rather seeks to promote more informed consumer choices. Sometimes it does this by giving the consumer the opportunity to acquire further information about the product by being able to examine and test it in person before becoming irrevocably bound to the contract, in other cases it serves as an escape route for consumers that feel pressured into a decision when, for example, accosted on their doorstep or by a telephone call without proper time to reflect on whether the goods or services truly meet their needs.

5.2 Harmonization

The right of withdrawal, which has been given various names such as cancellation or revocation, first appeared in 1985 in the Doorstep Selling Directive.[65] It has since been extended to distance selling[66] and to particular contracts where the risks of high-pressure techniques are prevalent, such as timeshare,[67] or where a rash decision may have serious consequences for consumers, for example, life assurance[68] and credit contracts.[69] These rights grew up piecemeal in EU law and the different lengths of the withdrawal periods, different times from which that withdrawal period began to run, different rules on how withdrawal could be exercised and the consequences once the right was invoked (though often these were left to national law), and different rules about the effect on the withdrawal period if information obligations were not complied with are an ideal illustration of inconsistencies in EU law.[70] The Consumer Rights Directive has standardized the procedure for distance and off-premises contracts with a 14-day withdrawal period,[71] however earlier proposals to develop an even more harmonized and

[65] Directive 85/577, Art 5; on the variety of terminology, see B Pozzo, 'Harmonisation of European Contract Law and the Need of Creating a Uniform Terminology' (2003) 6 *European Review of Private Law* 754, 764.

[66] Directive 97/7, Art 6; Directive 2002/65, Art 6.

[67] Directive 2008/122 (OJ [2008] L33/10), Art 6.

[68] Directive 2002/83 (OJ [2002] L345/1), Art 35.

[69] Directive 2008/44 (OJ [2008] L133/66), Art 14.

[70] Extensive ECJ case law has also brought further clarification, inter alia Case C-91/02 *FacciniDori* [1994] ECR I-3325; Case C-481/99 *Heininger* [2001] ECR I-9945; Case C-336/03 *easyCar* [2005] ECR I-1947; Case C-350/03 *Schulte* [2005] ECR I-9215; Case C-412/06 *Hamilton* [2008] ECR I-2383; Case C-205/07 *Gysbrechts* [2008] ECR I-9947; Case C-489/07 *Messner* [2009] ECR I-7315; Case C-227/08 *MartínMartín* [2009] ECR 11939; Case C-511/08 *HeinrichHeine* [2010] ECR I-3047; Case C-430/17 *Walter Walbusch* EU:C:2019:17; Case C-681/17 *slewo*, EU:C:2019:255; Case C-66/19 *Kreissparkasse Saarlouis*, EU:C:2020:242.

[71] Directive 2011/83, Art 9.

overarching approach to the right of withdrawal as part of a broader consolidation of EU law were not put into practice.[72]

5.3 **Effective consumer protection?**

The right of withdrawal is undoubtedly a helpful consumer protection instrument.[73] It encourages consumers to use certain distribution channels such as the internet with the confidence that they can return goods that do not meet their expectations without having to give a reason to justify their decision. It is a protection against over-forceful salespersons in some contexts where consumers may be especially vulnerable, such as in their homes.[74] It is particularly useful as it is a self-help technique consumers can use without having to invoke a formal procedure. They simply have to clearly express their intention to withdraw to escape from their contractual obligations. However, if they have paid money over and the trader does not follow his legal obligations upon receiving the returned good, a claim may be needed to recover the amounts due.

Despite these advantages the right has also faced criticisms from different corners. Some commentators argue that the differences in the underlying rationales for the right mean that the right should be mandatory only in certain situations and an optional extra in others.[75] Some consider big data can gear withdrawal rights to match personal preferences;[76] though this risks making the law less clear and assumes consumers can assess the value of the right.[77] From an economic perspective the cost of returning goods may be a practical disincentive, particularly in a cross-border situation.[78] There are also limitations on its effectiveness as in some instances it may not be possible for consumers to determine whether they have made a good choice during the withdrawal period. This is true of many financial services products. In these cases, a better solution may be to provide consumers with fair exit routes during the course of the contract. More recently the right has faced criticism from an environmental perspective not only due to the impact of returning unwanted goods, but also because the costs of bringing goods back into circulation exceed the loss incurred from disposing of them.[79]

[72] Research Group on the Existing EC Contract Law (Acquis Group), *Contract I—Pre-Contractual Obligations, Conclusion of Contract, Unfair Terms* (Munich: Sellier, 2007); *Contract II* (Munich: Sellier, 2009); *Contract III* (Munich: Sellier, 2014).

[73] P Rekaiti and R Van den Bergh, 'Cooling-Off Periods in the Consumer Laws of the EC Member States: A Comparative Law and Economics Approach' (2000) 23 *Journal of Consumer Policy* 371.

[74] G Howells, 'The Right of Withdrawal in European Consumer Law' in H Schulte-Nölke and R Schulze (eds), *European Contract Law in Community Law* (Cologne: Bundesanzeiger, 2002) 230–232; M Loos, 'Rights of Withdrawal' in G Howells and R Schulze (eds), *Modernising and Harmonising Consumer Contract Law* (Munich: Sellier, 2009).

[75] H Eidenmüller, 'Why Withdrawal Rights?' (2011) 7 *European Review of Contract Law* 1, 7–18.

[76] O Ben-Shahar and A Porat, 'Personalizing Mandatory Rules in Contract Law' (2019) 86 *University of Chicago Law Review* 255, 257.

[77] G Howells, '*Pacta sunt servanda* and the Consumer's Right of Withdrawal' in N Witzleb (ed), *Contract Law in Changing Times* (Abingdon: Routledge 2022) 156.

[78] eg the inclusion of the potential cost of return by the consumer would have to be taken into account when calculating the total cost, see G Borges and B Irlenbusch, 'Fairness Crowded Out by Law: An Experimental Study on Withdrawal Rights' (2007) 163 *Journal of Institutional and Theoretical Economics* 84, 100.

[79] E Terryn and E Van Gool, 'The Role of European Consumer Regulation in Shaping the Environmental Impact of E-Commerce' (2021) 3 *Journal of European Consumer and Market Law* 89, 94 *et seq*.

6 Rules establishing consumer expectations

The rules on information provision and the right of withdrawal, though fettering the complete freedom of traders as to how they do business,[80] essentially build on the freedom of contract model. They can be seen as reinforcing that model by ensuring the consumer enters into an agreement with full knowledge and consent. It is where the consumer is given substantive non-excludable rights[81] that the extent of freedom of contract is less and potentially ceases to be the main underlying concept. In EU law these non-excludable rights are backed up by provisions both within the Directives[82] and in EU private international law[83] that prevent consumers losing core rights granted by EU law by choosing the law of a different or non-Member State. Some have even claimed that such a regime should be viewed more like a tort law or regulatory regime; namely, a regime imposed by the law rather than a contractual regime where the premise is that the obligations are derived from the parties' mutual agreement.[84] However, many substantive rules in practice leave some margin for traders to affect the expectations of consumers by the way they market and present the products.

Some of the laws we shall consider can be seen as specialist consumer rules with limited impact on the general law—product safety, product liability, and to some extent unfair commercial practices law might be viewed in this light. By contrast the directives on unfair contract terms and, particularly, the law on the sale of goods and the supply of digital content strike more into the heartland of private law. While they could be viewed as creating specialist regimes for consumer contracts, the general nature of certain rules could serve to provide a basis for a range of contracts beyond the narrower scope foreseen in the original EU directive—that is, by 'gold-plating' the directive during the transposition into national law.[85] Out of this grew a brand of 'European private law' scholarship that sought to modernize European contract law more generally. However, some also see this as a threat to consumer protection as some European private lawyers may be prepared to sacrifice some more protective national rules to achieve their broader ambition of a modern common European contract law.[86] The substantive rights will now be outlined, before some general reflections on them are made.

7 Product safety

7.1 Public law control and consumer protection

Although most of the rules setting minimum standards are private law in nature, it should not be overlooked that there are significant public law controls aimed at protecting the consumer, for instance in the field of product safety. The EU's involvement in product

[80] Howells, Janssen, and Schulze (n 45).

[81] eg the right of withdrawal in Directive 2011/83, Art 9(1). Later a number of substantive rights affecting the core obligations towards consumers are considered.

[82] eg in Directive 93/13, Art 6(2); Directive 97/7, Art 12(2); and Directive 1999/44, Art 7(2). Note that each of these Directives precedes later rules in EU private international law.

[83] These are the rules which govern which law and jurisdiction apply, see Regulation 593/2008 on the law applicable to contractual obligations (Rome I), Art 6(2).

[84] R Brownsword, 'Regulating Transactions: Good Faith and Fair Dealing' in Howells and Schulze, *Modernising and Harmonising Consumer Contract Law* (n 74).

[85] eg F Zoll, 'The Remedies in the Proposals of the Online Sales Directive and the Directive on the Supply of Digital Content' (2016) 6 *Journal of European Consumer and Market Law* 250, 251.

[86] H-W Micklitz, 'The Targeted Full Harmonisation Approach: Looking behind the Curtain' in Howells and Schulze, *Modernising and Harmonising Consumer Contract Law* (n 74) 75–83.

safety grew out of its work on technical harmonization and the realization that many standards needed a consumer safety element. The new approach to technical harmonization[87] saw a suite of directives (eg on personal protective equipment,[88] machinery,[89] and toy safety[90]) setting general expectations of safety, backed up by an annex laying out essential safety requirements. These were then operationalized by the development of European (CEN) standards by privatized standards bodies. Traders could choose either to meet the Directive's standards in their own way or adopt the CEN standard (as transformed into a national standard) and benefit from safe harbour provisions. Compliance with standards was indicated by use of the CE marking, which indicates conformity with standards and should not be (but often is) confused with a safety mark.

7.2 General Product Safety Directive

The EU realized that some consumer products were not covered by new approach directives and in 1992 adopted a General Product Safety Directive[91] that set a general safety requirement for all consumer products that applied where there were no specific EU rules.[92] It also set out powers the Member States had to have to react to product safety concerns,[93] introduced reporting obligations to the EU on the part of Member States about product safety incidents[94] as well as an emergency procedure to allow the EU to adopt decisions on serious and immediate risks where Member States have taken different positions.[95] An important outcome of this Directive has been to ensure at least every Member State has an authority responsible for product safety. The Directive was subsequently amended[96] to clarify a number of issues, but also to place an obligation on producers to report product safety issues and to provide an express recall obligation.[97] In 2023 the Directive was replaced by the General Product Safety Regulation.[98] This modernizes the law to take account of new technology, for instance by taking into account factors relevant to AI, the Internet of Things, and cybersecurity. The reporting mechanisms are modernized through the establishment of the Safety Gate Portal. The list of economic operators is expanded to take account of internet selling by including fulfilment service providers as economic operators. Additional requirements are placed on those using distance selling and on providers of online marketplaces, which complement the rules in the Digital Services Act.[99]

8 Product liability

Product safety laws put standards in place to ensure products are safe and provide measures to remove any unsafe products that do reach the market. The Product Liability Directive,[100] however, seeks to compensate those injured by defective products. It is

[87] Council Resolution of 7 May 1985 on a new approach to technical harmonization and standards (OJ [1985] C136/1).

[88] Directive 89/686 (OJ [1986] L399/18), repealed by Regulation 2016/425 (OJ [2016] L81/51).

[89] Directive 2006/42 (OJ [2006] L157/24), amending Directive 95/16 (OJ [1995] L213/1).

[90] Directive 2009/48 (OJ [2009] L170/1), replacing Directive 88/378 (OJ [1988] L187/1).

[91] Directive 92/59 (OJ [1992] L228/24).

[92] Directive 92/59, Arts 3 and 4.

[93] Ibid, Arts 5 and 6.

[94] Ibid, Arts 7 and 8.

[95] Ibid, Art 9.

[96] Directive 2001/95 (OJ [2001] L11/4).

[97] See D Fairgrieve and G Howells, 'General Product Safety: A Revolution through Reform?' (2006) 69 *Modern Law Review* 59.

[98] Regulation (EU) 2023/988 (OJ [2023] L135/1).

[99] Regulation 2022/2065 (OJ [2022] L277/1).

[100] Directive 85/374 (OJ [1985] L210/29).

something of an outlier in the consumer *acquis*, partly due to its origins in the directorate concerned with internal market affairs rather than consumer protection.[101] Its adoption was in large measure due to the personal tenacity of Dr Taschner, a Commission official, who was convinced of the need to introduce strict product liability in response to the thalidomide disaster in the 1960s, in which many children suffered deformities as a result of their mothers taking a morning sickness preventative drug. It was hard to establish fault liability as the effects of drugs on children *in utero* were unexpected. This Directive shows the value of being able to adopt a common European approach, as Member States' legal systems were struggling with the limitations of contract (due to privity) and tort (due to fault requirement) to address product liability claims, but each feared being the first to introduce strict liability that did not require fault in case it imported a US-style litigation explosion. The 1970s had seen a product liability insurance crisis in the US with the liability risks making it hard or impossible for some producers to obtain insurance. The Directive sought in the words of the recital to provide 'liability without fault on the part of the producer' as this was viewed 'as the sole means of adequately solving the problem, peculiar to our age of increasing technicality, of a fair apportionment of the risks inherent in modern technological production'.[102] Instead of fault, liability would be based on defectiveness that is found when a product 'does not provide the safety which a person is entitled to expect'.[103] However, this standard is open-textured, in the sense that it requires a general assessment. The extent to which such assessment is based on consumer expectations or if there is a role for risk-utility analysis is moot. In England, the High Court in *A v National Blood Authority*[104] had held blood infected by Hepatitis C did not satisfy the legitimate expectations of the public and that factors to be taken into account excluded the benefits of the product and the costs of precautions. Two subsequent High Court decisions questioned the value of talking about legitimate expectations as the test was based on what a person was entitled to expect, which may be different from their factual expectations.[105] The judges in those cases would also take a wider range of factors into account such as risk, benefit, and regulatory approval. In continental courts the reasons for finding defectiveness often do not have to be spelled out in such detail and this has allowed courts to find liability where a product has simply behaved in an unexpected manner, eg a coffee machine exploding.[106] The Court of Justice has even upheld a French rule of evidence that proof of both defect and causation between a vaccine and damage did not need any evidence of medical consensus.[107] Equally the strictness of the liability regime will depend upon how the defences are interpreted and in this respect the inclusion of the (optional)[108] development risks defence is significant. This seeks to protect producers where there was no way they could have known of the defect and risks thereby returning the debate to a negligence-style analysis where what is important is the conduct of the producer rather than the condition of the product. The Court of Justice, on the one hand, interpreted the defence narrowly as being lost by the most advanced knowledge even if that did not at the time form part of the scientific consensus. Thus, as long as one researcher has identified

[101] For more on the structure of the European Commission, see chapter 3.

[102] Directive 85/374, recital 2. [103] Ibid, Art 6(1).

[104] *A v National Blood Authority* [2001] 3 All ER 289.

[105] *Wilkes v DePuy* [2016] EWHC 3096 (QB), [2018] QB 627, [2017] 3 All ER 589 and *Gee v DePuy* [2018] EWHC 1208 (QB), [2018] 5 WLUK 394.

[106] S Lenze, 'Strict Liability for Manufacturing Defects: What Proof is Needed?' (2003) *European Product Liability Review* 11/37, comments on the Austrian Supreme Court (OGH 22.10.2002 10 Ob 98/02p).

[107] Case C-621/15 *NW, LW en CW v Sanofi Pasteur MSD SNC, Caisse primaire d'assurance maladie des Hauts-de-Seine and Carpimko*, EU:C:2017:484, [2017] 4 WLR 171.

[108] The development risks defence is excluded in Finland and Luxembourg, whereas there are limitations on the defence in France, Germany, and Spain.

the risk, the defence is lost as producers would be expected to invest in further research or insurance. On the other hand, the judgment tended towards a negligence-style analysis by requiring the knowledge to have been reasonably accessible; AG Tesauro famously gave the example of research only published in Manchurian, which European producers might not be expected to know about.[109] Whether this accessibility requirement is justified is a moot point.[110] The European Court of Justice has handed down a pro-consumer decision concerning implantable medical devices. It held that it was sufficient to establish defect that the product belonged to a category of products with a potential to be defective, even if defect could not be established with respect to the particular implanted device.[111] The operation needed to remedy the defect was considered to be damage caused by death or personal injury.

The Product Liability Directive 1985 was replaced by a new directive in 2024.[112] The definition of defect now expressly states it is based either on not providing the entitled safety or breach of a requirement of EU or national law. In any event it is probably the case that compliance with legal requirements would be the minimum safety expectations. Most of the updates are to take account of technology. Software is stated clearly to be within the definition of a product. The potential defendants are broadened to include authorized representatives, fulfilment service providers, and online platforms in some circumstances. The features of AI, the Internet of Things, and cybersecurity risks are included within the definition of defectiveness. Account is taken of the ability to update and upgrade software when determining the time to assess defectiveness and the state of scientific and technical knowledge for the purpose of the development risks defence. Environmental concerns are addressed by introducing liability for substantially modified products. Damages are stated to include psychological harm and destruction or corruption of data. The expiry (long-stop limitation) period, which is normally 10 years, is extended to 25 years in the case of latent personal injury. Access to justice is promoted through rules on disclosure of evidence and the burden of proof.

9 Unfair terms

The Unfair Terms in Consumer Contracts Directive[113] was inspired by German law and is therefore restricted to non-individually negotiated terms: in effect standard form contracts.[114] This controls terms which are unfair because contrary to the requirement of good faith, they cause a significant imbalance in the parties' rights and obligations arising under the contract, to the detriment of the consumer.[115] The reference to good faith was symbolically important to many continental Member States where good faith had been an important means of controlling unfairness. However, as it is not the sole criterion of unfairness, but has to be combined with a significant imbalance, it might in fact be considered a limiter on controls by requiring procedural as well as substantive unfairness.[116]

[109] Case C-300/95 *Commission v UK* [1997] ECR I-2649.

[110] M Mildred and G Howells, 'Comment on "Development Risks: Unanswered Questions"' (1996) 61 *Modern Law Review* 570.

[111] Case C-503/13 *Boston Scientific Medizintechnik GmbH v AOK Sachsen-Anhalt—Die Gesundheitskasse*, EU:C:2015:148.

[112] Directive 2024/2853 (OJ [2024] L 18.11.2024). For criticisms, see B Gsell and A-K Mayrhofer, 'The New Product Liability Directive 2024: Missed Updates or Upgrades for the Interplay with National Liability Rules and for Service Liability' (2025) 5 *Journal of European Consumer and Market Law* 205.

[113] Directive 93/13 (OJ [1993] L95/29).

[114] Directive 93/13, Art 3(2).

[115] Ibid, Art 3(1).

[116] R Brownsword and G Howells, 'The Implementation of the EC Directive on Unfair Terms in Consumer Contracts: Some Unresolved Questions' [1995] *Journal of Business Law* 243.

The European Court of Justice in *Aziz*[117] gave a favourable pro-consumer understanding by stating that 'in order to assess whether the imbalance arises "contrary to the requirement of good faith", it must be determined whether the seller or supplier, dealing fairly and equitably with the consumer, could reasonably assume that the consumer would have agreed to the term concerned in individual contract negotiations'.

It is likely that the use of flagrantly unfair terms (eg the exclusion of liability for negligently caused death and personal injury) will be viewed as a breach of good faith per se. There is no black list of terms that are automatically unfair, but rather an annex with a non-exhaustive list of terms that are indicatively unfair. The assessment cannot, however, cover 'the definition of the main subject matter of the contract nor to the adequacy of the price and remuneration ... in so far as these terms are in plain intelligible language'.[118] This exemption from control has been broadly construed by the UK's Supreme Court in a case where bank charges were unsuccessfully challenged.[119] Many bank accounts in the UK work on the basis that the service is free of charge as long as the account is in credit, but there are heavy charges incurred if the user goes overdrawn without permission. These charges were held not to be subject to review (and also could not be controlled as penalty clauses as they were provided for in contract rather than resulting from a breach). It is unfortunate the Supreme Court considered this matter *acte claire* and therefore not needing a preliminary reference. The Court of Justice has subsequently adopted a distinction between core and ancillary terms, though its application is left to national courts.[120] However, this core term exemption runs counter to the Nordic tradition of allowing fairness of the core terms and those States' desire to retain this stronger control is an impediment to agreeing maximal harmonization in this area.

Individual consumers can challenge unfair terms, which if found to be unfair will be non-binding. The contract will continue in existence if it is possible to sever the offending terms. However, few consumers will in practice have sufficient incentive to challenge unfair terms and indeed it is important to ensure they are not included in contracts as consumers may be unaware that the terms are unfair and therefore not binding and simply follow the contract terms. Preventative controls allowing for injunctions against unfair terms were therefore included. The Unfair Terms in Consumer Contracts Directive is an early example of the EU favouring injunctions brought by public authorities or consumer groups.[121]

An important and perhaps surprising feature of this Directive is the impact it has had on procedural law. The Court of Justice has been keen to ensure that the rules are given practical effect and has forced national courts to ensure that national procedural rules do not impede its effectiveness. They have also introduced an *ex officio* doctrine requiring courts to consider the unfairness of terms on their own initiative.[122]

[117] Case C-415/11, EU:C:2013:164. [118] Directive 93/13, Art 4(2).

[119] *OFT v Abbey National plc* [2009] UKSC 6.

[120] Case C-26/13 *Árpád Kásler, Hajnalka Káslerné Rábai v OTP Jelzálogbank Zrt*, EU:C:2013:282.

[121] In Case C-153/13 *Pohotovost', sro v JánSoroka*, EU:C:2014:1854 the Court of Justice lacked jurisdiction to decide on an interesting issue: does the Unfair Terms in Consumer Contracts Directive preclude legislation of a Member State which does not allow a legal person whose purpose is the protection of consumers' rights to intervene in court enforcement proceedings?

[122] Case C-243/08 *Pannon GSM Zrt v Erzsébet Sustikné Győrfi*, EU:C:2009:350. For detail, see the guidance on the interpretation and application of Council Directive 93/13/EEC on unfair terms in consumer contracts (OJ [2019] C323/4).

10 Sale of goods

The 1999 Consumer Sales Directive[123] had introduced the principle that goods should be in conformity and introduced a hierarchy of remedies; however, its impact on national law was limited as it was a minimal harmonization directive that allowed more protective national rules to be kept in place. Some 20 years later, the 2019 Sale of Goods Directive[124] (a maximal harmonization directive) was adopted. This newer Directive defines conformity based on compliance with factors stipulated in the contract and objective requirements covering that goods should be in conformity with the contract, by which it is understood that they should:

- comply with any description;
- possess the qualities of any model or sample;
- be fit for any particular purpose known to and accepted by the seller;
- be fit for the purposes goods of the same type are normally used;
- be delivered with such accessories, including packaging, installation instructions, or other instructions as the consumer may reasonably expect to receive; and
- be of the quantity and possess the normal quality and other features, including in relation to durability, functionality, compatibility, security, and performance the consumer can reasonably expect.

In assessing the last criterion, the 1999 Directive had been innovative in, subject to certain conditions, taking into account public statements made not only by the seller but also the producer or his representative; for example, on the labelling or in advertisements. This has been maintained.

Some of these elements are included as they relate to digital content or services as the Directive also applies to such content or services when supplied with goods ('goods with digital elements'). Rules define when this directive applies and when digital content and services are covered by its sister 'Digital Content Directive' on certain aspects concerning contracts for the supply of digital content and digital services.[125] This contains rules derived from the consumer sales context, but modified to take account of the digital environment. Thus, while goods need to comply with a sample or model, the same principle is adapted to the digital environment by making reference to compliance with a trial version or preview. Equally, incorrect installation is covered but uses the terminology incorrect integration into the consumer's digital environment carried out by the supplier or due to shortcomings in the integration instructions provided to the consumer.[126] For both goods and the one-off supply of digital content and services conformity is assessed at the time of supply and the burden of proof is reversed for the first year—doubling the period originally provided in the Consumer Sales Directive. Where the digital content or services contract specifies supply over a period of time the content must be in conformity throughout that period[127] and the burden of proof is always on the supplier, unless the consumer fails to cooperate by providing necessary details about their digital environment.[128]

123 Directive 1999/44 (OJ [1999] L171/12).

124 Directive 2019/771 (OJ [2019] L136/28).

125 Directive 2019/770 (OJ [2019] L136/1).

126 Directive 2019/770, Art 9. For goods, see Directive 2019/771, Art 8.

127 Directive 2019/770, Art 11.

128 Ibid, Art 12.

The remedies regime has been the most controversial element. In particular, the issue of EU legislation concerning damages continuously meets strong resistance from the Member States and thus damages remain a matter for national law. The remedies regime provided by the Sale of Goods Directive and the Digital Content Directive follow the hierarchical approach first set by the Consumer Sales Directive.[129]

EU law has always favoured cure, with consumers under the Sale of Goods Directive having first to seek repair or replacement; this is now reinforced by a Directive specifically on the right to repair.[130] The emphasis on sustainable consumption has shifted the focus to encouraging consumers to seek repair of the goods, even beyond cases on non-conformity (such as expected wear and tear through normal use). Manufacturers are now subject to an obligation to ensure goods are repairable, though this is limited to certain goods (eg washing machines, mobile phones, and vacuum cleaners).[131]

To avoid overburdening manufacturers and to ensure they are able to perform their obligation to repair, that obligation should be limited to those goods for which and to the extent any repairability requirements are provided for in Union legal acts. Repairability requirements do not oblige manufacturers to repair defective goods themselves, but they can subcontract. Repair is not required where this is impossible. Repairers are encouraged to use a European Repair Information Form.[132]

Whereas under the Consumer Sales Directive the Member States could retain the right to reject non-conforming goods as a primary remedy, Member States now only have a discretion to retain such remedies during the first 30 days. The Digital Content Directive also provides for cure in the first instance (and is a maximal harmonization with no special rules for the first 30 days). The specific remedies of repair and replacement are not mentioned; instead the trader has the freedom to decide how to bring the content into conformity with the recital mentioning possible means being the issuing of updates or the making of a new copy.[133] For digital content and services the questions of what can and cannot be done with the digital content on termination are also regulated, in particular regarding consumer data.[134] The modification of the digital content and services are also regulated.

There are also rules on guarantees that are voluntarily provided with goods, but these do not control their content as much as ensure that they are treated as legally binding and set out the terms in plain, intelligible language (covering issues such as name and address of guarantor, procedure to implement guarantee, designation of the goods to which it applies, terms of the guarantee), and make it clear to consumers that they have remedies for non-conformity that are not affected.[135]

11 General comments on substantive rights

11.1 Goods and services

While unfair terms and unfair commercial legislation apply to any consumer contract, most of the EU legislation providing general substantive rights focuses on goods. Less has been done in the services field. The attempt to legislate for service liability is one of the few examples of the European Commission abandoning a legislative initiative.[136] On the

[129] Ibid, Art 13; Directive 2019/771, Art 13.

[130] Directive 2024/1799 (OJ [2024] L 10.7.2024). For an overview, see A Reyna and P Gautier, 'The European Take on the Right to Repair (R2R)' (2025) 3 *Journal of European Consumer and Market Law* 92.

[131] Directive 2024/1799, Art 5(1), Annex II and recital 8.

[132] Art 4.

[133] Directive 2019/770, recital 63.

[134] Ibid, Art 16(3).

[135] Ibid, Art 6.

[136] COM(90) 482 final, 9 November 1990.

one hand there are examples of EU intervention into particular services and it has been active in the field of services of general interest[137] and financial services.[138] The EU has also adopted a Services Directive,[139] which does contain some consumer protection measures on information provision, dispute resolution, and promoting voluntary measures to improve quality, but is mainly concerned with the freedom to provide services across borders.

Digital services, on the other hand, represent an area in which the EU is taking a series of measures as part of its Digital Single Market Strategy.[140] We have already come across the Digital Content Directive that regulates services. It seems ironic that digital services are being regulated more strongly than traditional services. The EU has also adopted a Digital Services Act, which seeks to ensure hosting services and online platforms operate responsibly. Additional obligations are placed on very large online platforms. Of importance for consumer protection are the rules requiring action to be taken when goods are illegal, including unsafe goods. There is an obligation on online platforms to promote compliance by design by ensuring their interfaces enable traders to comply with their pre-contractual, compliance, and product safety information obligations. There are also specific controls on advertising directed at children using such data.[141] The Digital Markets Act[142] is focused on making it easier to do business with online platforms in a fair manner by placing obligations on gatekeeper undertakings. Some the rules, however, help consumers who fall within the class of end users, such as those rules protecting the use of their data, on data portability, and granting greater freedom to use content free of restrictions limiting choice to the products and services of the platform.

11.2 **General standards**

The general standards adopted are also by their very nature open-textured and so do not provide concrete answers but require a complex assessment of the facts against the norms set out in general terms. Open standards are inevitable when setting such general norms, but create a severe risk of different interpretations emerging and in the EU context this includes national legal systems reading their traditional approach to the norms. The discretion can be structured by use of relevant guiding factors being included in the legislation, in particular in the recitals, though the recitals themselves are not legally binding. An increasingly common practice now is for the European Commission to issue guidance.[143] Court decisions are also a way of concretizing the norms' meaning through

[137] eg electricity services under Directive 96/92 (OJ [1996] L27/20), now Directive 2003/54 (OJ [2003] L176/37); postal services under Directive 97/67 (OJ [1997] L15/14), now Directive 2008/6 (OJ [2008] L52/3); conditional access services (ie where pre-authorization is needed to access, eg television and internet services) under Directive 98/84 (OJ [1998] L320/54); and particular aspects of information society services under Directive 2000/31 (OJ [2000] L178/1).

[138] eg Directive 2002/65 (OJ [2002] L271/16) on the distance marketing of consumer financial services and Directive 2007/64 (OJ [2007] L319/1) on payment services.

[139] Directive 2006/123 (OJ [2006] L376/36).

[140] COM(2015) 192 final, 6 May 2015.

[141] Regulation 2022/2065 (OJ [2022] L277/1)

[142] Regulation 2022/1925 (OJ [2022] L265/1).

[143] Guidance document on the relationship between the General Product Safety Directive (GPSD) and Certain Sector Directives with Provisions on Product Safety; Guidance on the Implementation and Application of Directive 2005/29/EC on Unfair Commercial Practices (n 64); Guidance in the interpretation and application of Council Directive 93/13/EEC (n 122); Guidance on the interpretation and application of Directive 2011/83/EU of the European Parliament and of the Council on consumer rights. In the financial services field, there is the very complex Lamfalussy procedure that allows regulators from across Europe to come together to develop rules in a consistent manner. This was named after the chairman of the committee that proposed the scheme: see 'Final Report of Committee of Wise Men on the Regulation of European Securities Markets', 15 February 2001, www.esma.europa.eu/sites/default/files/library/2015/11/lamfalussy_report.pdf.

experience. Despite one initial brave attempt to determine whether a term was unfair[144] the Court of Justice has since backed off and made it clear that the application of the unfairness test to consumer contract terms is a matter for national courts.[145] However, it still insists on its role in giving guidance and sometimes this can be quite prescriptive.[146] In fact the Court has been quite active in the unfair contract terms field. More generally it is rather rare for Court of Justice cases to give much helpful guidance on the content of the rules. The split roles, between the Court as interpreter of EU law and national courts which apply it, means that Court of Justice judgments can be rather abstract and the true impact only revealed by seeing how the judgment was received and applied in the national system, which can be difficult for lawyers from other Member States to discover. National decisions, even those not subject to a reference, can assist, but there was a need for the development of databases that allow learning to be shared and a common knowledge developed. The Commission has launched a consumer law database and hopefully this will assist.[147] However, there is a need to go beyond mere provision of information and provide for synthesis of the rules. Academic projects and textbooks might have an educative role to play, but the development of guidance based on experience might be a helpful way forward in practical terms. Such soft law risks circumventing the European Parliament and so any such guidance should ideally be explicitly provided for in legislation.[148]

11.3 **Channelling of liability**

Obligations in EU law are imposed on several actors, including the seller, producer, and importer. Sales law traditionally focuses on the seller and the Sale of Goods Directive follows this pattern save for the provisions of voluntary guarantees where the producer may well be the guarantor. The General Product Safety Directive places obligations on parties in the supply chain (ensuring someone in the EU always takes responsibility for the safety of products marketed in the EU) and manufacturers, but those on producers are normally more onerous. The Product Liability Directive channels liability to the manufacturer (but includes others when the manufacturer is based outside the Union), distributors, and in limited situations online platforms have a secondary liability when they cannot disclose the identity of their own distributor.

New technology may challenge traditional approaches to liability channelling. The number of interconnected actors involved in many products and services may make it difficult for the consumer to determine who is at fault. The EU already uses network liability to channel responsibility to parties not directly responsible for consumer harm in areas such as connected lender credit liability and package holidays. This might need to be used more widely where a range of hardware, software, and data all interact to provide a consumer product or service.[149] There also needs to be an ongoing debate about the responsibilities of online platforms.[150]

[144] Joined Cases C-240–244/98 *Océano* [2000] ECR I-4941.

[145] Case C-237/02 *Freiburger Kommunalbauten* [2004] ECR I-3403.

[146] Case C-137/08 *VB Pénzügyi Lízing Zrt v Ferenc Schneider* [2010] ECR I-10847.

[147] See https://webgate.ec.europa.eu/e-justice/591/EN/consumer_law_database.

[148] In the product liability context, see D Fairgrieve, G Howells, and M Pilgerstorfer, 'The Product Liability Directive: Time to Get Soft?' (2013) 4 *Journal of European Tort Law* 1.

[149] G Howells and C Twigg-Flesner, 'Interconnectivity and Liability: AI and the Internet of Things' in L DiMatteo, C Poncibò, and M Cannarsa (eds), *The Cambridge Handbook of Artificial Intelligence* (Cambridge: Cambridge University Press, 2022).

[150] D Fairgrieve et al, 'Product Liability and Online Marketplaces: Comparison and Reform' (2024) 73 *International and Comparative Law Quarterly* 477.

11.4 **Minimum content**

Safety requirements, product liability, unfair terms, and sales law are all seen as representing minimum non-excludable rights. However, how high the minimum content is might be debatable since, as Mr Justice Burton noted in the product liability context, there is a tension between the non-excludability of the rights and the freedom to prevent liability arising through warnings.[151] Equally, in sales law, defects that are drawn to the buyer's attention do not give rise to liability,[152] and certain actions by the consumer may exclude the right of withdrawal.[153] As no unfair terms are automatically unfair it is moot as to the extent to which even those terms which on their face are unfair can be rendered fair by transparency, though one suspects that good faith places a limit on the extent to which transparency can make good an imbalance.

Passenger rights is one area where EU law does provide minimum rights that cannot be deviated from. The advantage of such rights is that they form a minimum set of expectations on which consumers can rely. The downside is that they constrain the offerings on the market and impose minimum obligations and with them costs which all market participants have to bear and this can increase the minimum cost of products. For instance, the duty to pay compensation to airline passengers does not vary according to the price of the ticket. The same obligations flow from the delay and cancellation of a 1p ticket bought from a low-cost carrier as arise with regard to a business class seat with a flag carrier airline.

Guaranteeing non-excludable passenger rights is a classic example of minimum consumer rights potentially affecting the market choices available. Low-cost airlines may—though the impact of such costs might in fact be rather small—have to increase their fares to provide this basic cover. In effect the rules say that if you choose to operate a business flying people around Europe you need to be responsible for their welfare if they become delayed or stranded due to cancellations. The airlines become the insurer of their passengers and the EU obliges all market operators to guarantee a minimum level of customer services as the price for being allowed to be part of the marketplace. This cannot be waived in return for lower fares. This may restrict contractual freedom, but one might prefer this to the alternative of many people being stranded with no means of shelter and basic nourishment. This is one of the few true examples of collectivization of consumer risks. The provisions are currently being revised.[154]

11.5 **Extent of harmonization**

The Court of Justice determined that the Product Liability Directive was a maximal harmonization directive, meaning that Member States cannot introduce rules that go beyond the scope of the Directive.[155] The Court avoids the use of the phrase 'maximal', and the Commission prefers the terms 'full' or 'total'. However, maximal seems the better contrast with minimal harmonization where Member States retain the discretion to be more protective. 'Full' and 'total' seem misleading as even in areas where EU law allows no discretion for Member States to retain or introduce more protective rules it is common that it

[151] *A v National Blood Authority* [2001] 3 All ER 289.

[152] Directive 2019/771, Art 7(5).

[153] Directive 2011/83, Art 16.

[154] COM(2013)130, 13 March 2013, and COM(2023) 753 final, 29 November 2023.

[155] Case C-52/00 *Commission v France* [2002] ECR I-3827; Case C-154/00 *Commission v Greece* [2002] ECR I-3879; Case C-183/00 *González Sánchez* [2002] ECR I-3901; and Case C-402/03 *SkovÆg* [2006] ECR I-199.

does not cover the whole field and areas outside the scope remain within the competence of Member States. Thus, for example, while the Unfair Commercial Practices Directive is well known for adopting a maximal harmonization approach, the issues of taste and decency remain outside its scope. The General Product Safety Regulation is assumed to be maximal in character. By contrast the Unfair Terms and the 1999 Consumer Sales Directives were expressly stated to be minimal in character.[156] Indeed it was the attempt to make rules in these areas maximal when the Consumer Rights Directive was first proposed that caused that Directive to be the most debated Directive in EU history.[157] The contentious issues were, for different Member States, the potential loss of the right to reject in national sales law and loss of freedom for national law to control core terms. Whereas the Sale of Goods and Digital Content Directives, as many other consumer law directives, have adopted maximal harmonization (with some exceptions), minimal harmonization still applies for the control of unfair terms.

12 **Enforcement and redress**

Consumer protection rules may take the form of regulations typically enforced by public authorities.[158] Enforcement is at the national level and there is no equivalent enforcement role in the consumer protection field for the Commission to the one it plays in the enforcement of competition law, though the Consumer Protection Cooperation Regulation[159] affords the Commission a key role in coordinating actions. Although patterns vary between the Member States and over time, typically consumer safety, marketing practices, and unfair terms are controlled to a large extent by public enforcement. However, there has been concern that the sanctions are not dissuasive enough and, following recent amendments, certain key directives (the Unfair Commercial Practices, Unfair Terms, and the Consumer Rights Directives) will provide for the maximum sanction being at least 4 per cent of turnover where there is a widespread infringement or a widespread infringement with a Union dimension.[160]

Consumers also have a right of private redress for goods that are of poor quality or cause them harm and to challenge unfair terms. They might also in some circumstances find it more convenient to exercise their right of withdrawal to terminate the contract directly to bypass the hurdles for termination under the Sale of Goods Directive. In some States consumers also have a private right of redress when harmed by unfair commercial practices and one of the influences of Europe had been to encourage debate about expanding this remedy in States where this right is not currently enjoyed.[161] The Unfair Commercial Practices Directive has now been amended to require that contractual and non-contractual remedies should be available that include at least the possibility for the consumer

[156] Directive 93/13, Art 8 and Directive 1999/44, Art 8(2).

[157] Over 2,000 amendments were tabled in the European Parliament: see G Howells, 'European Contract Law Reform and European Consumer Law: Two Related but Distinct Regimes' (2011) 7 *European Review of Contract Law* 173; Howells and Schulze, *Modernising and Harmonising Consumer Contract Law* (n 74); H-W Micklitz and N Reich, 'Crónica de una muerte anunciada: The Commission Proposal for a "Directive on Consumer Rights"' (2009) 46 *Common Market Law Review* 471; C Twigg-Flesner and D Metcalfe, 'The Proposed Consumer Rights Directive: Less Haste, More Thought?' (2009) 3 *European Review of Contract Law* 268.

[158] In some States there has been a tradition of enforcement by consumer organizations or even trade organizations, and this mechanism has spread under the influence of European Union law.

[159] Regulation 2017/2394 (OJ [2017] L345/1).

[160] Directive 2019/2161 (OJ [2019] L328/7).

[161] OJ [2010] C46/26. For the UK debate, see Law Commission, *Consumer Redress for Misleading and Aggressive Commercial Practices* (Law Com No 332, 2012) and new rules in s 27A of the Consumer Protection from Unfair Trading Regulations 2008.

to claim damages and, where relevant, seek price reduction or terminate the contract.[162] Traditionally the private law remedies for breach of information duties have been weak,[163] but pre-contractual information now becomes a term of the contract.[164]

12.1 **Methods of enforcement**

States have a range of traditions for enforcing regulation—this may involve the criminal law or administrative sanctions. Some directives do, of course, require some specific powers to be available,[165] but for the most part the EU laws normally merely require that States should provide 'adequate and effective means' of ensuring compliance and penalties should be 'effective, proportionate and dissuasive'.[166] It has already been noted that the General Product Safety Directive forced Member States to ensure an agency responsible for consumer safety was in place. The Consumer Protection Cooperation Regulation went further and required each Member State to nominate a competent consumer authority to be part of an EU-wide enforcement network that provides for information exchange and mutual assistance. This was a development from the Consumer Injunctions Directive.[167] The idea behind that Directive was that, as well as rationalizing and embedding an EU right to seek injunctions for breach of the consumer *acquis*, cross-border infringements could be addressed by requiring States to give qualified entities (State consumer protection bodies and/or private consumer organizations) from other States access to their injunction procedures. Under the Regulation national authorities can be requested by their counterparts in other States to take all necessary enforcement measures to bring about the cessation or prohibition of the intra-EU infringement without delay.[168] It has recently been amended to make it more effective, especially in the digital age.[169] For instance, the Regulation talks of action for cessation or prohibition of infringements, but this might not capture short-term scams that frequently appear on the internet and are then removed. The wording for cessation and prohibition remains the same but it is made clear that the harmful effects of activities that have ceased should still be addressed. It also allows investigation of the flows throughout the digital value chain in order, for example, to trace where payments go. Interim measures such as taking down websites are also permitted. The new Regulation also allows for coordination where the same infringement occurs in parallel in several States, and gives the Commission a stronger coordinating role especially where the infringement is defined as being Union wide (ie affecting two-thirds of EU citizens). The provisions for seeking injunctions are now wrapped up in a broader Representative Actions Directive.[170]

162 Directive 2019/2161 (OJ [2019] L328/7).

163 C Twigg-Flesner and T Wilhelmsson, 'Pre-Contractual Information Duties in the Acquis Communautaire' (2006) 4 *European Review of Contract Law* 441, 465–468.

164 Directive 2011/83, Art 6(5).

165 eg under Directive 2001/95 Member State authorities are entitled to take a number of measures such as banning the marketing of a dangerous product and introducing the accompanying measures required to ensure the ban is complied with (Art 8(1)(e)) or ordering the actual and immediate withdrawal of a dangerous product (Art 8(1)(f)(i)).

166 As is required in, eg Directive 2011/83, Art 24; Directive 2008/48, Art 23; and Directive 2002/65, Art 11. See also P Rott, 'Effective Enforcement and Different Enforcement Cultures in Europe' in T Wilhelmsson, E Paunio, and A Pohjolainen (eds), *Private Law and the Many Cultures of Europe* (Alphen aan den Rijn: Kluwer Law International, 2007).

167 Directive 98/27 (OJ [1998] L166/51).

168 Regulation 2006/2004, Art 8(1).

169 Regulation 2017/2394 (OJ [2017] L345/1).

170 Directive 2020/1828 (OJ [2020] L409/1).

12.2 **Access to justice**

Given the relatively small amounts typically at stake and the high costs of cross-border enforcement,[171] the amount of formal litigation by consumers in this context is likely to be limited. There are EU rules that seek to assist some consumers by providing that proceedings should be brought in their home State courts[172] or ensuring they are not deprived of their home State mandatory consumer protection rules.[173] Often this protection is linked to the consumer being a passive consumer targeted by the trader; though determining when this situation arises in, say, the context of websites, is hard to determine even with some guidance having been provided by the Court.[174] Indeed if the application of these private international law rules is called into question that in itself will involve expensive satellite litigation concerning questions of jurisdiction and choice of law before the substantive issue can be addressed.

The EU has sought to address the cost of litigation. There are some obligations to provide legal aid for cross-border disputes.[175] Also the European small claims procedure[176] in principle provides for a simplified procedure for cross-border disputes which as far as possible relies on a paper-based system. However, the scheme is underused and has revealed some problems, such as language issues, that need more work to redress.[177] Consumers may also be assisted in cross-border contexts by schemes such as the European payment order procedure.[178]

12.3 **Alternative dispute resolution**

Given the difficulty consumers are likely to face with formal litigation, it is unsurprising that the European Commission has pinned a lot of its hopes on alternative dispute resolution (ADR). It adopted two recommendations on this topic[179] and established a network of advice centres to assist consumers with cross-border disputes (ECC-Net[180] and its financial services counterpart Fin-Net[181]). An important function they have is to channel consumers to appropriate national ADR bodies. The ADR Directive[182] requires that Member States at least ensure that ADR procedures are available for all consumer disputes. The EU institutions have agreed updates to this Directive that will clarify pre- and post-contractual issues, as well as issues with traders in non-EU Member States.[183] The Regulation providing for an Online Dispute Resolution platform, which sought to

[171] COM(2008) 794 final, 27 November 2008, 4.

[172] See now Regulation 1215/2012 (OJ [2012] L351/1), Art 17. Consumers will also benefit from exequatur being abolished so that foreign judgments are automatically enforceable without any special procedure being needed.

[173] For consumer contracts, Regulation 593/2008 (OJ [2008] L177/6), Art 6(2). See also eg Directive 2008/48, Art 22(4) and Directive 93/13, Art 6(2).

[174] Joined Cases C-585/08 and C-144/09 *Peter Pammer v Reederei Karl Schlüter GmbH & Co KG and Hotel Alpenhof GesmbH v Oliver Heller* [2010] ECR I-12527.

[175] Directive 2002/8 (OJ [2002] L26/41). [176] Regulation 861/2007 (OJ [2007] L199/1).

[177] X Kramer, 'Small Claim, Simple Recovery? The European Small Claims Procedure and Its Implementation in the Member States' (2011) 12 *ERA Forum* 119. See also the Commission report on Regulation 861/2007 (COM(2013) 795, 19 October 2013) and the 2015 amendment of the legislation in light of these issues (Regulation 2015/2421 (OJ [2015] L341/1)).

[178] Regulation 1896/2006 (OJ [2006] L399/1).

[179] Recommendation 98/257/EC (OJ [1998] L115/31) and Recommendation 2001/310 (OJ [2001] L109/56).

[180] https://www.eccnet.eu/.

[181] https://finance.ec.europa.eu/consumer-finance-and-payments/retail-financial-services/financial-dispute-resolution-network-fin-net/about-fin-net_en.

[182] Directive 2013/11 (OJ [2013] L165/63). [183] Council doc 13541/25, 3 October 2025.

facilitate resolution of disputes and which online traders have to notify their consumers about, was later repealed, thereby discontinuing the platform.[184]

12.4 **Collective redress**

There has been much talk about collective redress for consumers. This was sparked by proposals in the competition field[185] and at first was taken up with vigour by those within the Commission responsible for consumer protection. A 2013 Recommendation in this area dealt with both injunction and compensatory collective redress mechanisms.[186] From 25 June 2023, however, the Member States must apply the provisions of the Representative Actions Directive.[187] This Directive allows designated national organizations or public bodies representing consumers' interest to bring cross-border representative actions to seek redress measures covering, inter alia, compensation, repair, replacement, price reduction, contract termination, or price reimbursement. Key features such as whether the regime should be opt-out or opt-in are determined by the individual Member State and access to third party funding are left to the Member States. In addition to such redress mechanisms, public authorities or consumer rights organizations may also apply for injunctions as representative actions to protect consumer interests.

13 **Conclusion**

When in 1974 Lord Denning made his famous remarks about European law being, for English law, 'like an incoming tide. It flows into the estuaries and up the rivers. It cannot be held back',[188] he was talking about the EEC Treaty and probably would not have foreseen the swathes of secondary legislation which have had a positive tsunami-like effect on the national consumer law of all EU Member States. For the most part the influence has been positive with EU law allowing the best parts of traditional national consumer law to coexist with the EU imports. Even when it uprooted the UK's venerable Trade Descriptions Act 1968, EU law replaced it with an unfair commercial practices legal regime that is probably better suited to modern trading conditions.

However, there are concerns that the consumer protection character of EU law is being diluted by an obsession with maximal harmonization that threatens national legal traditions. Indeed, the Commission ultimately achieved in part its objective of maximal harmonization of certain aspects of the sale of goods, yet it is the maximal harmonization in areas of law that are not as firmly anchored in the national legal traditions that are especially noteworthy. The new legislation that has been and will be necessary to respond to the challenges brought by digitalization illustrate the problem well: the European solutions are not necessarily a patchwork of the best tried and tested approaches from the Member States, but as European solutions for the Member States as a pre-emptive measure to avoid fragmentation. From a UK perspective it remains to be seen whether the UK legislator will draw inspiration from his European counterparts in finding solutions

[184] Regulation 524/2013 (OJ [2013] L165/1), repealed by Regulation 2024/3228 (OJ [2024] L 30.12.2024).

[185] SEC(2011) 173 final, 4 February 2011; D Fairgrieve and G Howells, 'Collective Redress Procedures: European Debates' in D Fairgrieve and E Lein (eds), *Extraterritoriality and Collective Redress* (Oxford: Oxford University Press, 2012).

[186] Commission Recommendation 2013/396 on common principles for injunctive and compensatory collective redress mechanisms in the Member States concerning violations of rights granted under Union Law (OJ [2013] L201/60).

[187] Directive 2020/1828 (OJ [2020] L409/1).

[188] *HP Bulmer Ltd v J Bollinger SA* [1974] Ch 401, 418.

to common problems or indeed vice versa. The areas of digitalization and the circular economy are likely to figure heavily in future policy debates. A likely scenario is that any drift from EU law in the UK will be passive as the UK fails to keep up with the pace of EU reforms. This may not even be by choice, but simply reflects the limited capacity of one State to reform. The EU by pooling resources is a very efficient legislator.

Further reading

C Busch and A de Franceschi (eds), *Algorithmic Regulation and Personalized Law* (Munich: CH Beck, 2021)

D Fairgrieve et al, 'Product Liability and Online Marketplaces: Comparison and Reform' (2024) 73 *International and Comparative Law Quarterly* 477

A de Franceschi and R Schulze (eds), *Digital Revolution* (Munich: CH Beck, 2019)

S Grundmann, 'The Structure of European Contract Law' (2001) 4 *European Review of Private Law* 505

G Howellsand C Twigg-Flesner, 'Interconnectivity and Liability: AI and the Internet of Things' in La Dimatteo, C Poncibò, and M Cannarsa (eds), *The Cambridge Handbook of Artificial Intelligence* (Cambridge: Cambridge University Press, 2022)

G Howells and T Wilhelmsson, 'EC Consumer Law: Has It Come of Age?' (2003) 28 *European Law Review* 370

G Howells and T Wilhelmsson, 'EC and US Approaches to Consumer Protection: Should the Gap Be Bridged?' [1997] *Yearbook of European Law* 207

G Howells, C Twigg-Flesner, and T Wilhelmsson, *Rethinking EU Consumer Law* (Abingdon: Routledge, 2019)

R Schulze, 'Precontractual Duties and Conclusion of Contract in European Law' (2005) 6 *European Review of Private Law* 841

R Schulze and F Zoll, *European Contract Law* (3rd edn, Baden-Baden: Nomos, 2021)

R Schulze, E Arroyo Amayuelas, and T Garcia-Micó (eds), *EU Consumer Law* (Baden-Baden: Nomos, 2026)

D Staudenmayer and R Schulze (eds), *EU Digital Law* (2nd edn, Baden-Baden: Nomos, 2025)

P Stone, *Stone on EU Private International Law* (4th edn, Cheltenham: Edward Elgar, 2018)

J Stuyck, 'European Consumer Law after the Treaty of Amsterdam: Consumer Policy in or beyond the Internal Market?' (2000) 37 *Common Market Law Review* 367

C Twigg-Flesner (ed), *Research Handbook on EU Consumer and Contract Law* (Cheltenham: Edward Elgar, 2016)

C Twigg-Flesner, *The Europeanisation of Contract Law* (Abingdon: Routledge-Cavendish, 2008)

T Wilhelmsson, 'The Abuse of the "Confident Consumer" as a Justification for EC Consumer Law' (2004) 27 *Journal of Consumer Policy* 317

24

EU criminal law

András Csúri and John R Spencer

1 Introduction

A recurrent theme of this chapter is one of tension. Member States are torn between the practical necessity for certain problems in the area of criminal law to be dealt with at EU level, in particular in the context of transnational criminality such as terrorism, and a deep-seated ideological resistance to this happening as control over criminal law is traditionally seen as a central feature of national sovereignty.[1]

The consequence of this, as we shall see, is that the Union competence in the field of criminal law is limited, and the bulk of the legal instruments of which EU criminal law is composed are designed to help and encourage the criminal justice systems of the various Member States to work together, rather than to impose upon them uniform rules of criminal law or criminal procedure. That is, a 'horizontal approach' to the problems of trans-border criminality, rather than a 'vertical approach' of direction from the centre. A recent exception is the European Public Prosecutor's Office, which was launched in 2021 and combines elements from both approaches.

The chapter first examines what EU criminal law consists of (which is not quite what the name suggests), the reasons for its existence, and the mechanisms by which it is created. Sections 3 to 7 then describe in concrete terms the more important of its practical manifestations.

[1] For more on the principles of subsidiarity and proportionality, see chapter 5. For analysis in the context of criminal law, see J Öberg, 'Legal Diversity, Subsidiarity and Harmonization of EU Regulatory Criminal Law' in R Colson and S Field (eds), *EU Criminal Justice and the Challenges of Diversity: Legal Cultures in the Area of Freedom, Security and Justice* (Cambridge: Cambridge University Press, 2016) 106–125.

2 What is EU criminal law?

The phrase 'EU criminal law'[2] suggests a federal arrangement with a common European criminal code and criminal procedure code, and a European public prosecutor operating within a special set of EU criminal courts. But, at present, EU criminal law exists only in a looser sense, encompassing EU legislation in the field of criminal law and national criminal law that is affected by Union law.

In concrete terms, it comprises five distinct but related bodies of law.

First, there is the body of law creating and regulating a group of European Union agencies which have been set up to secure the better functioning of criminal justice within the EU. Secondly, there is a body of law designed to facilitate cooperation between the police forces and other law enforcement agencies of the different Member States. Thirdly, there is a body of law on what is called *mutual recognition*: rules requiring the criminal justice systems of all Member States to treat as valid and, if called upon, enforce rulings and decisions emanating from the others. Fourthly, there is the body of law the purpose of which is to shape, in certain respects, the substantive criminal law of all Member States. And, finally, there is a body of law by which the EU has sought to do the same with criminal procedure. Each of these five areas of EU criminal law will be examined in greater detail.

2.1 Why does EU criminal law exist?

The purposes of the EEC (as the EU formerly was) were originally economic, and so the founding treaties did not confer any criminal powers on the Community. It is therefore not necessarily obvious at first sight where and why criminal law appears on this agenda, although it is partly a consequence of the initial setting. Indeed, over time, the specific dynamics of the internal market and free movement policies, together with certain ideological objectives and political developments, have given rise to problems with implications for criminal law which have become increasingly difficult to address in the absence of adequate Union competences. It was therefore first the case law of the Court of Justice, as so often in the development of EU law, that provided significant impetus in this respect.

One such problematic issue was the protection of specific Union interests stemming from economic integration, like preventing corruption among its officials and protecting the single currency or its finances. This latter issue, the prosecution of offences against the Union budget (known as PIF crimes after the French acronym of the term (*protection des intérêts financiers*)), has shaped various aspects of EU criminal law, so that nowadays, as we will see in section 3, the EU has at its disposal the European Anti-Fraud Office (OLAF), the PIF Directive, and the European Public Prosecutor's Office (EPPO). In the past, however, the prosecution of such offences was entirely at the mercy of the Member States. This changed with the landmark *Greek maize* ruling,[3] in which the CJEU imposed a positive obligation on Member States to protect Community interests, if necessary even by activating their criminal justice systems. In the case at hand, maize exported from the third country of the former Yugoslavia to Belgium via Greek ports was fraudulently declared as being of Greek origin with the complicity of Greek officials. The agricultural levy, which would have been due to the Community's own resources when third States are involved,

[2] For more detailed information on this topic, see V Mitsilegas, *EU Criminal Law* (Oxford: Hart Publishing, 2022); S Peers, *EU Justice and Home Affairs Law* (5th edn, Oxford: Oxford University Press, 2023); A Klip, *European Criminal Law: An Integrative Approach* (4th edn, Cambridge: Intersentia, 2021).

[3] Case 68/88 *Commission v Greece* (*Greek Maize*) [1989] ECR 2965.

was therefore not collected. The Commission had referred the case to the Court of Justice because, contrary to its request, no disciplinary or criminal proceedings were brought in Greece, although this would have been possible in similar domestic cases.

Based on the principle of sincere cooperation (current Article 4(3) TEU), the Court ruled that infringements of Community law must be sanctioned under the procedural and substantive conditions applicable to comparable breaches of domestic law (principle of assimilation, now reflected in Article 325 TFEU). In other words, budgetary fraud is budgetary fraud, whether it concerns the national or the EU budget, and if such a breach of domestic law is subject to criminal prosecution (like under Greek law at the time), a similar approach should apply for the breaches of comparable Community interests. The Court held further that while Member States remain free to choose the applicable sanctions, these must be effective, proportionate, and dissuasive.[4]

This decision therefore had three consequences for national criminal laws: they had to be activated to protect similar EU interests, existing national sanctions had to be adapted to the triple threshold, and where no adequate measure existed at national level, criminal sanctions might even have to be introduced to ensure adequate protection of EU interests.

The protection and promotion of the four freedoms was another issue that affected national criminal law; as with the *Bordessa* case,[5] where criminal proceedings were brought against individuals who did not have the authorization required under Spanish law to export money above a certain threshold. The CJEU held that national authorities might require prior declaration of money transferred across their borders, but could not make this conditional upon a prior authorization subject to criminal penalties, as this effectively restricts cross-border capital movements and payments.[6] Thus, Union law takes precedence over national law, including national criminal law, where a conflicting provision would hinder the Union's broader policies and objectives.

This of course, is also true in reverse, as the Court of Justice has derived positive obligations from EU law to activate the national criminal justice system to promote the policy of free movement. In one of these cases, the French government, unwilling to offend its farmers, allowed the police to turn a blind eye to the activities of groups who took direct action against the importation of fruit and vegetables from other Member States by stopping lorries, beating up the drivers, and damaging or destroying foreign produce.[7] The Treaties prohibit quantitative restrictions on imports between Member States and all measures having equivalent effect[8] and require them to 'take any appropriate measure, general or particular, to ensure fulfilment of the obligations arising out of the Treaties or resulting from the acts of the institutions of the Union'.[9] In sum, the Court held that in the case in question, the actions taken by the private individuals had an effect equivalent to quantitative restrictions laid down by law, and that the obvious 'appropriate measure' would have been to bring the criminal justice system to bear upon the problem.[10]

Yet one of the most significant effects of the free movement of workers, services, goods, and capital on the development of EU criminal law has been one of their unintended consequences: namely, the free movement of crime and criminals. On the one hand, there has been an increase in 'trans-border' criminality—for example, smuggling and people-trafficking—where part of the offence takes place in one Member State and part of it in

[4] Ibid, para 24. [5] Joined Cases C-358/93 and C-416/93 [1995] ECR I-361.

[6] Ibid, para 31. [7] Case C-265/95 *Commission v French Republic* [1997] ECR I-6959.

[8] Art 34 TEU, ex Art 30 TEC.

[9] Art 4(3) TEU; reproducing an obligation already existing by virtue of Art 10 TEC, which in turn has implemented the principles laid down by the Court in Cases 14/83 *von Colson and Kamann* and *Greek Maize* (n 3).

[10] *Commission v French Republic* (n 7). See in particular paras 30, 31, 58.

another. On the other hand, it has also become easier for a criminal who has committed a crime in one country to decamp to another. These problems could no longer be addressed simply by activating national laws or, on the contrary, by not applying them. In other words, they went beyond the interrelationship between EU law and national criminal law. After all, to face problems with such transnational dimensions, the national criminal justice systems of the different Member States must help one another and coordinate their responses, if necessary with guidance from the centre, that is, from Union level. Over time, this has led to various initiatives in the area of EU criminal law, such as the creation of the Schengen Information System and Eurojust, or the adoption of the European Arrest Warrant (EAW) and the European Investigation Order (EIO), all of which will be examined later in sections 3, 4, and 5.

Political developments have also influenced the development of EU criminal law. For example, in 1976, following a series of terrorist attacks, the so-called TREVI group[11] was set up—outside the Community—to coordinate police activities in the fight against terrorism within the EC. Similarly, the 9/11 terrorist attacks sped up the negotiations on the adoption of the aforementioned Framework Decision on the EAW and served as a catalyst for the establishment of Eurojust.

Finally, there are ideological reasons for the growth of EU criminal law as well as practical ones. Article 67 TFEU proclaims an objective of the EU to be the creation of 'an area of freedom, security and justice' and provides for mutual recognition and, where necessary, the approximation of laws as means to this end. From the security perspective, this implies, among other things, better coordination and cooperation between police and judicial authorities, for instance through the EAW. From the point of view of freedom and justice, this is the concept of an area in all parts of which citizens can be sure that the criminal justice system will treat those who come into contact with it with a certain minimum level of humanity, consideration, and efficiency. It is in this spirit that EU instruments have sought to grant various rights to victims in criminal proceedings, while also ensuring certain minimum rights for suspects and defendants (see section 7).

2.2 **Tensions**

As we have just seen, for various reasons it has become necessary to address criminal law issues in the context of European integration. That said, a number of factors combine to make the development of EU criminal law a particularly sensitive issue for the individual Member States.

The starting point, which tends to colour the attitude of every Member State, is that there is something about criminal justice which makes it by its very nature something for the nation-State, and the nation-State alone. This is due to the traditional dual function of all criminal justice systems. Their sword function enforces societal norms and protects individuals from criminality. Their shield function, meanwhile, protects them from the misuse of legitimate violence inherent in criminal justice. Accordingly, the power to punish is a fundamental attribute of a sovereign State, and the rules determining what types of behaviour is punishable, and how, should reflect the attitudes and beliefs of the people of the State concerned.

However, national perceptions of crime and punishment can vary considerably even between groups of people as geographically close as the citizens of the different EU countries. This is because, although their legal cultures have common mediaeval roots, they have taken on distinct forms under the influence of a variety of cultural and societal

[11] The name of the group comes from the French acronym for 'Terrorisme, Radicalisme et Violence Internationale', which also refers to the iconic fountain in Rome where the first meeting took place.

factors.[12] That said, nowadays the substantive criminal law of the different Member States is largely similar.[13] But something of a cultural cleavage does exist in relation to criminal procedure.[14] Each criminal justice system has its own rules and exceptions, developed together with other requirements of the national legal system, when it comes to the principles of criminal procedure, the collection and administration of evidence, or the powers of the competent authorities.[15] This legal diversity can lead to practical difficulties when it comes to judicial cooperation between the Member States,[16] and under EU criminal law we also face new aspects of the problem, as judicial cooperation in an area of freedom, security, and justice—especially under common EU legal instruments—should not only be effective, but also to some extent comparable and coherent. This is so in particular as regards the standing of the individuals concerned, which requires a common minimum level of fairness and humanity.[17] As for the way to ease these tensions at a Union level, a key question is whether a horizontal or vertical approach would be more appropriate. In other words, should cooperation be based on legal diversity, approximated national rules, or even common European ones? As regards the legislative instruments of choice, the question is whether legal diversity can be better addressed through minimum rules in directives that must be implemented or through common rules in regulations that are directly applicable.

There are various arrangements under the current Treaty context, which aim to pay respect to legal diversity. The most obvious of these are the opt-out arrangements that granted Denmark, Ireland, and formerly the United Kingdom a special status also in the area of criminal justice matters (see section 2.3.4).[18] Then there are the legislative solutions in the TEU, such as the subsidiarity control mechanism or the possibility of enhanced cooperation, which, incidentally, also played a significant role in the creation of the EPPO. The first made it possible to compel the Commission to review its proposal (though without any fruitful results), while the second made it possible to set up the Office even without unanimity in the Council.

Looking at the relevant chapter of the TFEU, there seems to be a legislative preference for minimum approximation of laws and on 'horizontal solutions' over 'vertical solutions': legislation designed to help national criminal justice systems deal with a given problem collectively, rather than superimposing a common set of rules, or subjecting them to the authority of Union bodies. The tension between national sovereignty, legal diversity, and integration is reflected, in particular, in those articles of the chapter that confer legislative powers on the Union in the area of criminal matters. For example, Article 82, which creates a limited power to adopt EU legislation harmonizing rules of criminal procedure, provides that 'Such rules shall take into account the differences between the legal traditions and systems of the Member States.' The same Article, as

[12] R Colson and S Field, 'Legal Cultures in Europe: Brakes, Motors and the Rise of EU Criminal Justice' in R Colson and S Field, *EU Criminal Justice and the Challenges of Diversity* (n 1).

[13] For a more nuanced view on fundamental differences, see ch 5 of K Zweigert and H Kötz, *An Introduction to Comparative Law*, trans T Weir (3rd edn, Oxford: Clarendon Press, 1998); HP Glenn, *Legal Traditions of the World* (5th edn, Oxford: Oxford University Press, 2014); and PL Reichel, *Comparative Criminal Justice Systems* (7th edn, London: Pearson Education, 2017).

[14] For analysis, see M Delmas-Marty and JR Spencer (eds), *European Criminal Procedures* (Cambridge: Cambridge University Press, 2002).

[15] See also JR Spencer, 'The Problems of Trans-Border Evidence and European Initiatives to Resolve Them' (2006–2007) 9 *Cambridge Yearbook of European Legal Studies* 465.

[16] See for instance the 2016 Eurojust annual report highlighting the impact of legal diversity on admissibility of evidence in cross-border cases in the field of interception of telecommunications, p 49.

[17] See A Csúri, 'Sense and Admissibility: Cross-Border EPPO Investigations and Evidence. *Cambridge Yearbook of European Legal Studies.* (2026) doi:10.1017/cel.2026.10029 (2026) 26 *Cambridge Yearbook of European Legal Studies* 1–20.

[18] A Hinarejos, JR Spencer, and S Peers, 'Opting Out of EU Criminal Law: What Is Actually Involved?', University of Cambridge Faculty of Law Research Paper No 25/2012.

well as Article 83, which creates limited powers to adopt common minimum rules concerning the definition of criminal offences and sanctions, incorporate what is called the 'emergency brake': the right of any Member State which perceives intended legislation as affecting 'fundamental aspects of its criminal justice system' to call a halt to the process by appealing to the European Council.[19] However, unlike the veto right under the former Third Pillar, the emergency brake does not prevent the other Member States from continuing with an initiative.

2.3 Evolution and sources

2.3.1 The beginnings: Schengen—alias CISA

As criminal law matters were not among the objectives of the founding treaties, the Community had no competence in this field and cooperation between Member States in this respect continued to be based on a set of intergovernmental conventions adopted within the Council of Europe.[20] Closer cooperation, where necessary, took place outside the Community framework. For example, the aforementioned TREVI group formulated recommendations of the then 12 Member States' interior ministers, the implementation of which depended on the political will of each Member State.

The first serious moves towards what we now call EU criminal law continued to take place outside the Community legal framework. Impatient with the lack of progress towards free movement, in 1985 the transport ministers of France, Germany, Luxembourg, Belgium, and the Netherlands met at Schengen on the river Mosel and signed an agreement designed to lead to the abolition of border controls between the contracting States. In 1990 this agreement led on to a formal convention, usually known as 'CISA'—short for 'Convention Implementing the Schengen Agreement'. In the years immediately following, a number of other countries joined.[21] In 1997, the 'Schengen *acquis*'—CISA and the rules and regulations made under it—were finally 'integrated' into the framework of the EU by a Protocol attached to the Treaty of Amsterdam.[22]

In broad outline, CISA provides for the abolition of border checks on persons at the frontiers between the contracting States, together with a swathe of flanking measures intended to compensate for the resulting lack of control by facilitating and accelerating traditional police and judicial cooperation. In particular by supplementing existing Council of Europe arrangements, notably with regard to mutual legal assistance, extradition, and the application of the principle of *ne bis in idem* in a transnational context.[23] CISA has also enabled new forms of cooperation, like cross-border surveillance, which allows the continuation of such operations on the territory of another contracting party.[24] The criminal law aspects of the technical heart of the cooperation scheme, the Schengen Information System database, are explained in more detail in section 4, and the CJEU's interpretation of the principle of *ne bis in idem* in section 7.

2.3.2 Third Pillar: cooperation under Maastricht and Amsterdam

In 1992, the Maastricht Treaty created alongside the EC a new parallel body called the European Union, endowed with a range of legislative powers in the area of justice and home affairs, including cooperation in criminal matters, under a set of constitutional

[19] On the concept of the 'emergency brake', see chapter 5.

[20] These include the 1959 European Convention on Mutual Assistance in Criminal Matters, the 1957 Convention on Extradition, and the 1983 Convention on the Transfer of Sentenced Persons.

[21] See section 4.

[22] Protocol B; the version attached to the Treaties currently in force is Protocol No 19. For the text of the Schengen *acquis*, see OJ [2000] L239. On the immigration law aspects of the Schengen *acquis*, see chapter 25.

[23] Arts 53, 54, and 59 *et seq* CISA. [24] Art 40 CISA.

arrangements known as the Third Pillar.[25] These were intended to be 'intergovernmental'—meaning that the governments of the Member States, rather than the Brussels institutions, were in control. In line with that, legislative decisions were made by the Council acting unanimously, so ensuring every Member State a right of veto. And if having signed up to a Third Pillar measure a Member State then failed to ratify or implement it, it could not be made the subject of infringement proceedings in the Court of Justice. National courts could seek guidance on the meaning of Third Pillar measures by making references to the Court where the Member State in question had chosen to opt into the procedure permitting this.[26]

Initially, a further weakness in the Third Pillar arrangements was the feeble nature of the instruments that could be adopted under it.[27] But in 1997 this changed when the Treaty of Amsterdam added a new weapon to the armoury: framework decisions. These were the Third Pillar equivalent of directives adopted under the First Pillar[28] and, once available, they became the Third Pillar instrument of choice, covering various areas from terrorism and counterfeiting to victims' rights and extradition. Like directives, framework decisions required the Member States to implement the objectives set out in them, but left open the manner in which they were to do so. Unlike directives they did not have direct effect due to the distinct features of the Third Pillar, and so did not create any rights or obligations that individuals could enforce before their national courts. Furthermore, there was no legal remedy against Member States which, though in theory bound, chose to disregard them.[29] But an important change occurred with the *Pupino* case.[30] A children's nursery teacher, Mrs *Pupino*, was prosecuted in Italy for having allegedly used physical violence against children in her care. The public prosecutor asked for the children to be heard out of court considering their age and vulnerability. This was possible under the Framework Decision on the Standing of Victims in Criminal Proceedings[31] but not under the current Italian law. The Italian court therefore raised a preliminary question about the compatibility of the Italian law with the Framework Decision.

In its judgment the CJEU had established an obligation for national courts to take into consideration not only the implementing legislation, but all the rules of national law, and to interpret them, so far as possible, in the light of the wording and purpose of the Framework Decision.[32] Thus, derived from the principle of loyal cooperation, framework decisions became subject to the same rule as directives, as regards the obligation to interpret national legislation in conformity with them.[33] In the case at hand, this allowed the vulnerable victims to give testimony under an appropriate level of protection.

The decision in this way also made a clear distinction between judicial cooperation in criminal matters within the EU and public international law: although EU criminal law remained limited to intergovernmental cooperation, the main instruments used for this purpose—the framework decisions—now had a legal effect closer to that of Union legal instruments.[34]

[25] The powers relating to police and criminal justice were contained in Title VI of the old TEU, Arts 29–42 (as renumbered by the Treaty of Amsterdam). On the 'pillar' system, see further chapter 2.

[26] Art 35 TEU (pre-Lisbon version).

[27] The Council could adopt 'joint positions' and initiate 'joint actions'—and, in addition, draw up conventions, which only came into effect if all Member States chose to ratify them.

[28] On the concept of directives, see chapter 5; on their legal effect, see chapter 6.

[29] Art 34 (2)(b) TEU.

[30] Case C-105/03 *Pupino* [2005] ECR I-5285.

[31] OJ [2001] L82.

[32] *Pupino* (n 30) paras 43 and 61.

[33] Ibid, para 42. See also Case 14/83 [1984] ECR 1891.

[34] See P Csonka and O Landwehr, '10 Years After: How "Lisbonised" Is the Substantive Criminal Law in the EU?' (2019) 4 *eucrim* 262; B Hecker, *Europäisches Strafrecht* (6th edn, Berlin: Springer, 2021) 382.

Over time, the pillar structure raised further problems. As we have seen, criminal law and criminal procedure were subject to intergovernmental cooperation under the Third Pillar, as opposed to the Community powers and legislative methods of the First Pillar. This led to competency issues between the Commission and the Council, which culminated when both tabled legislative proposals—a directive[35] and a framework decision[36]—on the protection of the environment (shared competence under the First Pillar) by means of criminal law (covered by Third Pillar cooperation). On one view, the only legislative powers and competences in the area of criminal justice were those conferred on the (old-style) EU by the Third Pillar, the alternative view being that the legislative competences under the First Pillar permitted at least some criminal justice legislation to be made by the EC too. The choice of the Treaty basis has had significant consequences, affecting the power of initiative, for example, as well as the legal effects of the measure, such as direct effect and the possibility of infringement proceedings.

The case eventually came before the Court of Justice, which annulled the Framework Decision and, in another landmark decision,[37] actively conferred criminal law competences on the Community. It held that while it is generally true that neither criminal law nor the rules of criminal procedure fall within the Community's competence, this did not prevent the Community legislature from obliging Member States to adopt criminal law measures that are necessary to ensure that the rules laid down in a certain policy area are fully effective.[38]

The Treaty of Amsterdam also set the new objective to create an area of Freedom, Security and Justice inter alia by developing common actions in the field of police and judicial cooperation in criminal matters.[39] This extended the previous compensatory approach of Schengen and Maastricht with a new European dimension of criminal law. In addition, it was under the Amsterdam context that Eurojust was created and, with the aim of gradually replacing the traditional mutual legal assistance scheme, the internal market principle of mutual recognition was extended to criminal matters as well (see sections 3 and 5).

The legal instruments of EU criminal law which were adopted under the constitutional arrangements prior to the Lisbon Treaty remain in force until they are repealed or replaced. However, they still remain in force in respect of those Member States that have not joined the newly adopted ones. This is especially true concerning Denmark, which keeps out of all criminal law-related measures adopted on the basis of the Treaty of Lisbon; and is also true of Ireland, which has so far not opted into certain measures.[40]

2.3.3 **Current arrangements—general**

After Lisbon, the main powers of the EU to legislate in criminal justice matters are contained in Chapters 4 and 5 of Title V of Part Three of the TFEU—comprising Articles 82 to 89. Though reflecting the earlier provisions of the old TEU which they replace, they are clearer and more readily intelligible.[41] Importantly, the Treaty recognizes for the first time expressly the Union competence to approximate criminal laws under strict conditions as well as a vertical approach to judicial cooperation in criminal matters in form of the EPPO.

Article 82 TFEU deals (in effect) with criminal procedure (see in detail section 7). Having proclaimed the principle of mutual recognition as the 'cornerstone' of judicial cooperation in criminal matters, it provides that, to the furtherance of this end, the EU may (inter alia) 'lay down rules and procedures for ensuring recognition throughout the

[35] COM(2001) 139 final. [36] OJ [2003] L29.

[37] Case C-176/03 *Commission v Council*, EU:C:2005:542. [38] Ibid, paras 47–48.

[39] Article K.1 Treaty of Amsterdam.

[40] Protocol (No 22) on the position of Denmark and Protocol (No 21) on the position of the United Kingdom and Ireland in respect of the area of freedom, security and justice.

[41] For a detailed analysis, see Peers, *EU Justice and Home Affairs Law* (n 2) chs 2–7.

Union of all forms of judgments and judicial decisions'. And it goes on to provide that, 'to the extent necessary to facilitate mutual recognition', the EU may also adopt directives designed to 'establish minimum rules' in relation to a number of criminal procedure matters: 'mutual admissibility of evidence between Member States', 'the rights of individuals in criminal procedure', 'the rights of victims of crime', and 'any other specific aspects of criminal procedure' which the Council has agreed upon by unanimity, with the consent of the European Parliament. Such minimum rules shall not, however, prevent Member States from maintaining or introducing a higher level of protection for individuals as we will subsequently see in the *Melloni* case.

Article 83 TFEU deals (in effect) with substantive criminal law (see in detail section 6). It provides that the European Parliament and the Council may enact directives establishing minimum rules concerning the definition of criminal offences and sanctions in those areas of 'particularly serious crime' which have a cross-border dimension or need a concerted effort to deal with them. The list of 'particularly serious crime' is exhaustive and defined as 'terrorism, trafficking in human beings and sexual exploitation of women and children, illicit drug trafficking, illicit arms trafficking, money laundering, corruption, counterfeiting of means of payment, computer crime and organised crime'. That said, other types of crime may be determined in the future by the Council, acting unanimously and with the consent of the European Parliament. This power was used in 2022 to enlarge the list in order to adopt the 2024 Directive on violations of Union foreign policy sanctions (see section 6).

In addition, the EU may also adopt directives defining crimes and prescribing punishments where 'the approximation of criminal laws and regulations of the Member States proves essential to ensure the effective implementation of a Union policy in an area which has been subject to harmonisation measures'.

Article 84 is a general provision giving the EU authority to help Member States to take action in the field of crime prevention by means other than 'the harmonisation of the laws and regulations of the Member States'.

Article 85 sets out general provisions in relation to Eurojust, the agency designed to help the prosecution authorities of the different Member States coordinate their activities, and Article 86 goes on to provide the legal basis for the creation of the European Public Prosecutor's Office. More will be said about these institutions in section 3.

Articles 87 to 89, comprising Chapter 5 of Title V, confer competences in relation to police cooperation. Article 87 provides that the Union 'shall establish police co-operation', and to this end empowers the EU to legislate on 'the collection, storage, processing, analysis and exchange of relevant information', staff training, staff exchanges, and equipment, and 'common investigative techniques in relation to the detection of serious forms of organised crime'. It then provides a limited power to legislate for 'operational co-operation' between national law enforcement agencies. Article 88 contains general legislative provisions about Europol, the police coordination body, which will be discussed in greater detail in section 3. Finally, Article 89 empowers the Council, by legislation, to make rules about the operation of national police forces and similar agencies beyond their national boundaries.

The 'measures' which the EU may adopt in the exercise of these competences are those set out in Article 288 TFEU—namely regulations, directives, decisions, recommendations, and opinions.[42]

The legislative route by which the EU is authorized to make them, however, is less simple to describe. Some, like the power in Article 82(1) to legislate for mutual recognition (see section 5), may be exercised by using the ordinary legislative procedure.[43] Others, like the power to create the European Public Prosecutor's Office contained in Article 86, require a

[42] See chapter 5.

[43] On the types of EU legislative procedure, see chapter 5.

special legislative procedure under which the consent of the European Parliament is first obtained and then, in principle, a unanimous vote of the Council is required before the matter can go any further; but failing unanimity, nine or more Member States can 'go it alone' by the process known as 'enhanced cooperation'.[44] Legislation designed to harmonize national criminal law or criminal procedure follows a third type of procedure, incorporating what is usually referred to, rather dramatically, as the 'emergency brake'. Here the ordinary legislative procedure is initially followed—but where a Member State considers that a draft directive 'would affect fundamental aspects of its criminal justice system', it may refer the matter to the European Council,[45] whereupon the legislative process is suspended. If consensus on the matter is reached at the European Council, the process is resumed. If not, a group of nine or more Member States can then continue on their own.

Finally, after a transitional period of five years which ended on 1 December 2014, a further important change occurred in that the CJEU acquired full jurisdiction over all instruments of EU criminal law, including measures concerning police cooperation and judicial cooperation in criminal matters adopted before the entry into force of the Treaty of Lisbon.[46] This means (among other things) that since then the Commission is able to bring infringement proceedings before the Court against Member States that have failed to implement a measure.

2.3.4 **Current arrangements—special positions: a 'variable geometry' for EU criminal law**

Some Member States' government were critical towards the planned new arrangements in the Lisbon Treaty, which took a route of further 'Europeanizing' criminal justice; most importantly, it entailed the loss of veto in the change in decision-making and the acquisition of jurisdiction in this area by the Court of Justice. From the first of these changes, both the UK and Ireland managed to insulate themselves by Protocol No 21, excluding both States from any new measures in this area except where they expressly chose to opt in. By Protocol No 36, the UK also managed to insulate itself—under certain conditions—from the acquisition of jurisdiction in this area by the CJEU.

Another Member State, Denmark, has, under Protocol 22, entirely opted out of all EU legislation under Title V of Part Three of the Treaty (area of freedom, security, and justice), including decisions of the CJEU interpreting any such provision or measure. With regard to the Schengen *acquis* covered by this Part, Denmark may decide, within a period of six months after the Council has decided on a proposal or initiative, whether it will implement the measure in its national law. Denmark may at any time inform the other Member States that it no longer wishes to make use of all (or part of) the Protocol. In that case, it shall apply in full all relevant measures then in force within the European Union. Whether or not this will happen remains to be seen, given that the Danes voted against accepting a more flexible opt-in arrangement in a referendum held in December 2015—much like the one that applies for Ireland and formerly for the UK. Media coverage, commented on the result being a sign of unwillingness to give up further sovereignty.[47]

These special positions have far-reaching consequences. On the one hand, pre-Lisbon arrangements, continue to apply for Denmark in general, and for Ireland if it has not acceded to an EU instrument post-Lisbon On the other hand, if a measure adopted under the pre-Lisbon framework is replaced by a post-Lisbon legislative measure, Denmark is not bound by it. For instance, Denmark does not take part in the Europol Regulation

[44] On the concept of enhanced cooperation, see chapter 5.

[45] On the European Council, see further chapter 3.

[46] Art 10 Protocol No 36 on transitional provisions.

[47] 'Denmark rejects further EU integration in referendum', euractiv, 4 December 2015.

which became applicable in 2017 and, with the entry into force of the Eurojust Regulation in December 2019, which repealed the previous Eurojust Decisions adopted under the Third Pillar, the Kingdom has ceased to be a member of the Agency (see section 3.3).

3 **Organs**

3.1 **OLAF**

Article 325(1) TFEU makes the Union and the Member States jointly responsible for combating fraud and other illegal activities affecting the financial interests of the Union. At the EU level, UCLAF (acronym of its French name: 'Unité de coordination de la lutte antifraude') was set up in 1988 to this end, with primary responsibility for fraud investigations in the Member States. It was a unit within the European Commission, dependent on its instructions, and did not have explicit powers to detect fraud within the EU institutions. Following a corruption scandal that led to the resignation of the Santer Commission in 1999, the office was relaunched in 1999 as the European Anti-Fraud Office—usually known as OLAF (after its French acronym: Office de lutte anti-fraude)—with greater independence, a bigger staff, more extensive powers, and a supervisory body.

The powers and duties of OLAF are set out in a regulation, the current version of which dates from 2013.[48] The Office is based in Brussels, as is the Commission, to which it is still formally attached. OLAF conducts investigations for the purpose of fighting fraud, corruption, and any other illegal activity affecting the financial interests of the Union. To this end, the Office is equipped with broad investigative powers and may carry out external investigations in the Member States and, subject to mutual assistance agreements, in third countries and at the premises of international organizations as well.

Importantly, OLAF can only carry out administrative investigations and has no power to prosecute a fraud if one is discovered. In the final report of its investigations, it can propose disciplinary, administrative, financial, or judicial measures. However, it must leave the decision to the authorities of the Member States concerned; their perceived reluctance to take action was one of the reasons for the creation of the EPPO which is discussed in section 3.4. If the national authorities decide to investigate further, information gathered by OLAF shall be admissible in national criminal proceedings under the same conditions as administrative reports drawn up by national administrative inspectors.[49]

When OLAF was launched, a legal basis was also created for conducting internal investigations 'within the institutions, bodies, offices and agencies established by, or on the basis of the Treaties'.[50] To this end, the Office has the right of immediate and unannounced access to any relevant information and data.

While OLAF's internal critics were mainly concerned about its inability to prosecute, its external critics have highlighted its—still—awkward constitutional position, being at once part of the Commission and the organ responsible for investigating frauds and improper practices within it.[51] Another point of criticism is the occasional heavy-handedness with which it has exercised its powers—which has led to several instances of well-publicized litigation.[52]

[48] Regulation 883/2013 (OJ [2013] L248/1). An amending Regulation was adopted in 2020 as regards OLAF's cooperation with the EPPO (Regulation 2020/2223 (OJ [2020] L437/49)).

[49] Art 11 OLAF Regulation.

[50] Art 4 OLAF Regulation.

[51] See X Groussot and Z Popov, 'What's Wrong with OLAF? Accountability, Due Process and Criminal Justice in European Anti-Fraud Policy' (2010) 47 *Common Market Law Review* 605. And see the House of Lords EU Committee, 24th Report of Session 2003–04, HL Paper 139.

[52] Notably Case T-193/04 *Tillack v Commission* [2006] ECR II-3995. For this and other litigation, see Mitsilegas, *EU Criminal Law* (n 2). See also H CH Hofmann, Decision-making in EU administrative law. The problem of composite procedures Administrative Law Review 61, 2009, 199–221.

Although OLAF also supports and coordinates the anti-fraud actions of the competent national authorities in the Member States, viewed as a whole, the Office is rather an example of the 'vertical' approach to the problems of crime within the EU. In this regard, as their field of competence overlaps, in 2020 the OLAF Regulation was revised to adapt it to the creation of the EPPO, aimed at ensuring complementarity between their respective mandates and avoiding duplication of effort.[53]

3.2 **Europol**

Europol was created, as the European Police Office, by a Third Pillar convention concluded in 1995, which came into force in 1998. Since May 2016, its constitutional document has been the new Europol Regulation,[54] with important changes being introduced in its latest amendment applicable since June 2022.[55] Europol, now called the European Union Agency for Law Enforcement Cooperation, has evolved from an international organization into a Union agency with legal personality. It is based in The Hague and comprises, among others, a Management Board with a representative from every Member State, and an Executive Director (with three deputies) who manages Europol and acts as its legal representative. Each Member State establishes or designates a national unit, which is the liaison body between Europol and the competent authorities of that Member State. Further, each national unit designates at least one liaison officer to be attached to Europol. The organization and staff of the national units are determined by, and liaison officers are subject to, the national laws of the designating Member State.[56]

Though the idea of a 'European FBI' has had its supporters,[57] Europol bears little resemblance to the Federal Bureau of Investigation in the US. It is a 'horizontal' body, with no operational powers, the basic task of which is the collection, storage, analysis, and exchange of information about criminals and crimes.[58] By Article 3 of the Europol Regulation, the purpose of Europol is to 'support and strengthen action by the competent authorities of the Member States and their mutual cooperation in preventing and combating serious crime affecting two or more Member States, terrorism and forms of crime which affect a common interest covered by a Union policy, as listed [in an Annex to the Regulation]'.[59] To this end, it runs the Europol Information System, supports thousands of international investigations each year, and produces annual reports in the fields of the terrorism situation in the EU, serious and organized crime phenomena, and threats and developments in the area of cybercrime.

By Article 88 TFEU, however, Europol can also become involved in operational policing to some limited extent. First, Europol staff may participate in joint investigation teams (or JITs, see section 4).[60] Secondly, Europol has the right to formally request national authorities to initiate criminal investigations in respect of a particular case.[61] Importantly, under the 2022 amendment to the Regulation, this is possible even if only one Member State is concerned, when common interests, covered by a Union policy, are affected.

Member States that receive such a request are obliged to consider it, but not to act on it. If, however, a Member State decides not to comply with the request it must give Europol

[53] Art 1(4a) OLAF Regulation. See also the preamble and Art 101 EPPO Regulation.

[54] Regulation 2016/794 (OJ [2016] L135/53).

[55] Regulation 2022/991 (OJ [2022] L169).

[56] Arts 7 and 8 Europol Regulation.

[57] First and foremost, the former German Chancellor, Helmut Kohl: see MP Ratzel, 'Das Europäische Polizeiamt. Europol (Teil 1)' (2008) *SIAK Journal* 28.

[58] Art 4 Europol Regulation.

[59] Europol coordinated and supported, eg, the high-profile operations 'Archimedes', 'Endgame', 'Eastwood', and 'A.S.S.E.T'. See the Europol website for details.

[60] Art 5 Europol Regulation.

[61] Art 6 Europol Regulation.

its reasons, unless to do so would be 'contrary to the essential interests of the security of the Member State concerned' or 'jeopardise the success of an ongoing investigation or the safety of an individual'.[62]

Under the amended legal framework, Europol may now also propose that Member States enter information alerts in the Schengen Information System (see section 4) and can exchange personal data with third countries on a case-by-case basis. A Fundamental Rights Officer was also introduced into the Europol system.

3.3 **Eurojust**

Eurojust, the European Union Agency for Criminal Justice Cooperation, does for public prosecutors much the same as Europol does for the police. As such, it is the most ambitious of three schemes to support and coordinate their work—the others being the exchange of *magistrats de liaison* (ie public prosecutors seconded by one Member State to another),[63] and the European Judicial Network—a network of 'national contact points' located in their Member States who, like *magistrats de liaison*, can give practical advice.[64]

Eurojust was originally agreed upon at the Tampere Council in 1999 and was created by a Council decision in 2002,[65] its constitution being amended by a second Council decision seven years later,[66] its legal position then being further regulated by Articles 85 and 86 TFEU. This has since been replaced by the Eurojust Regulation,[67] which was finally adopted in November 2018 and applied from December 2019 with specific amendments from 2022, 2023, and 2025.[68]

Eurojust has its official seat in The Hague, just across from the Europol headquarters. At a formal level, it is composed of one national member seconded by each Member State, who must have the status of a prosecutor, judge, or a representative of a judicial authority of equivalent competence under their national law. The powers of the national members vary according to their respective national laws. However, the Regulation requires Member States to confer certain powers upon their national members so that they are able to fulfil their tasks. These include the ability to support the issuing or execution of any request for mutual legal assistance or mutual recognition; to contact and exchange information directly with any competent national or international authority, Union body, office, or agency (including the EPPO); and to participate in, and contribute to the establishment of, joint investigation teams.[69]

The resulting 'college' elects a President and Vice-Presidents and is assisted by an Executive Board, responsible for taking administrative decisions.[70] Eurojust has a permanent staff, headed by an Administrative Director.

If the formal powers of Eurojust are limited, its usefulness is considerable. According to Article 2(1) of the Eurojust Regulation, the mission of the Agency is to support and strengthen coordination and cooperation between national investigating and prosecuting authorities in relation to certain serious crimes falling within Eurojust's competence, which involve two or more Member States or which require a prosecution on common bases. This happens on the basis of operations conducted and information supplied by the Member States' authorities and by Europol, the EPPO, and OLAF. At the request of either

[62] Art 6 (3) Europol Regulation. [63] OJ [1996] L105.

[64] See OJ [1998] L191 and OJ [2008] L348/130. [65] OJ [2002] L63/1. [66] OJ [2009] L138/14.

[67] Regulation 2018/1727 (OJ [2018] L295/138).

[68] Regulation 2022/838 (OJ [2022] L148); Regulation 2023/2131 (OJ [2023] L 11.10.2023); and Regulation 2025/2082 (OJ [2025] L 15.10.2024).

[69] See Arts 7 and 8 Eurojust Regulation. [70] See in particular Arts 10–18 Eurojust Regulation.

the competent authority of a Member State or the Commission, Eurojust may also assist in investigations and prosecutions involving a single Member State but which have repercussions at Union level.[71] Where third countries are concerned (now including the UK), it may assist in investigations and prosecutions at the request of the competent authority of the Member State concerned.[72]

Like Europol, Eurojust has no power, as such, to require a Member State to investigate a case or institute a prosecution, much less does it have the power to do either of these things itself (although Article 85 TFEU provides a legal basis for this). This is mainly due to the coordinative and horizontal nature of Eurojust's mission.

That said, by Article 4 of the Regulation, Eurojust may 'ask' a Member State to investigate a case or institute a prosecution and, indeed, a range of other things in addition. These include asking Member States to set up JITs and, where two or more Member States are engaged in investigating or prosecuting the same person (leading to conflicts of jurisdiction), inviting some of them to 'keep off the grass'. Where Eurojust asks a Member State to take a course of action, that Member State is required to respond to the request. It is, however, at liberty to refuse to comply with the request—though, it must give its reasons—if to do so would 'harm essential national security interests, would jeopardise the success of an ongoing investigation or would jeopardise the safety of an individual'.[73]

The aforementioned amendment from 2022 extends the operational functions of Eurojust under Article 4 (1) to support Member States' action in combating core international crimes and related criminal offences, including by preserving, analysing, and storing evidence related to those crimes and enabling the exchange of such evidence with national and international authorities. This occurred the military aggression of the Russian Federation against Ukraine, which has hindered the storage and preservation of relevant evidence. To ensure future accountability, evidence had to be stored outside the country.

Eurojust, like OLAF, faced an uncertain future with the arrival of the EPPO, especially as it was initially and partly created as a horizontal alternative to the EPPO idea. The Treaty of Lisbon enshrined Eurojust's mandate in Article 85 TFEU, but in the subsequent provision, Article 86, it stipulated that the EPPO should be created *from* Eurojust. The wording sparked academic and political debates; but ultimately the Agency remains an important actor, not simply because its competence is broader than that of the EPPO,[74] but also in relation to those PIF crimes where the EPPO has no competence, decides not to exercise its competence, or where the case involves third States or Member States which do not participate in the EPPO.

In accordance with Protocol 22, Denmark ceased to be a member of Eurojust after the entry into force of the Eurojust Regulation in December 2019. This is, of course, a very sensitive issue, as Denmark, in the meantime, remains a member of the EU and the Schengen area. Therefore, an agreement was concluded which allows the Kingdom to send representatives to Eurojust to coordinate its criminal investigations and prosecutions with other Member States and with third countries that have cooperation agreements with Eurojust. Denmark continues to have access to Eurojust's information systems and may exchange data and evidence, including personal data, in the course of criminal proceedings and prosecutions in cases registered with Eurojust.[75]

[71] Art 3 and Recital 13 Eurojust Regulation.

[72] Art 3 (5) Eurojust Regulation. Eurojust's relations with the authorities of third countries are elaborated in Arts 52–54.

[73] Art 4 Eurojust Regulation.

[74] Both legal instruments explicitly regulate the fundamental principles of the relation between the two actors. See Art 50 Eurojust Regulation and Art 100 EPPO Regulation.

[75] Agreement on criminal justice cooperation between Eurojust and the Kingdom of Denmark. https://www.eurojust.europa.eu/sites/default/files/InternationalAgreements/Eurojust-Denmark-2019-10-07_EN.pdf

3.4 The European Public Prosecutor's Office

The European Public Prosecutor's Office (EPPO), the first European body with the power to initiate *criminal* investigations in the Member States, became operational on 1 June 2021. The Office represents a significant step forward in integration in criminal matters, since, as we have seen, OLAF can only conduct administrative investigations, Europol cannot initiate criminal proceedings, and Eurojust has no prosecutorial powers.

The idea of a European Public Prosecutor was first put forward in 1997 in a document commonly known as 'Corpus Juris'.[76] This came from a study group set up by the Commission to consider the problem of budgetary fraud, prosecutions for which were then a matter for the prosecuting agencies of the Member States, some of which showed little appetite for it. The CJEU decision in the *Greek maize* case enshrined the requirement of equal protection of similar national and EU interests, but legal diversity and a lack of direction from the centre continued to hamper judicial cooperation between national authorities in that respect. The study therefore proposed a single code of criminal offences concerning EU budgetary fraud, a single set of powers to collect evidence on those offences, and the much-debated idea of a European Public Prosecutor to ensure uniform application of the rules.

However, still within the context of the Maastricht regime, Member States were neither prepared nor willing to grant the EU such extensive (vertical) powers in criminal matters—one of the foundations of national sovereignty—and so a two-part 'horizontal solution' was put forward at the 1999 Tampere European Council as an alternative: a European unit to coordinate the efforts of national prosecutors (Eurojust as discussed in section 3.3), plus a system whereby the criminal courts of all Member States would, in effect, automatically recognize and enforce one another's rulings (the mutual recognition programme, which will be discussed in section 5).

Undeterred by the initial response, the Commission continued to press for a European Public Prosecutor—taking the view that, if the above changes gave national prosecutors the means to deal with budgetary fraud, they did not give them the necessary motivation. A legal basis for creating the EPPO responsible for prosecuting budgetary fraud was introduced in Article 86 TFEU, and thereafter both OLAF and the Commission did their best to ensure that the idea remained alive.[77] This brief provision left open the main features of the future office, and the years that followed saw extensive discussions about its future mandate, powers, and institutional design, the applicable law for its actions, its relations with existing EU bodies and national prosecuting agencies, and further debates about judicial control over its actions.[78]

In July 2013, the Commission published a detailed proposal[79] which triggered, for only the second time, the so-called 'yellow card procedure' in the course of the early warning

[76] M Delmas-Marty (under the direction of), *CORPUS JURIS—introducing penal provisions for the purpose of the financial interests of the European Union* (Paris: Editions Economica, 1999).

[77] In particular, by promoting a study to elaborate a set of common investigative measures for the EPPO. See https://orbilu.uni.lu/handle/10993/42085. See also K Ligeti (ed), *Toward a Prosecutor for the European Union* (Oxford: Hart Publishing, 2013).

[78] For the discussions of the possible design of the EPPO, see A Csúri, 'Naming and Shaping. The Changing Structure of Actors Involved in the Protection of EU Finances' (2012) 2 *eucrim* 79; K Ligeti, 'The European Public Prosecutor's Office: How Should the Rules Applicable to Its Procedure Be Determined?' (2011) 4 *European Criminal Law Review* 123; A Weyembergh and C Briere, 'Towards a European Public Prosecutor's Office (Policy Department C)' (2016), available at: www.europarl.europa.eu/RegData/etudes/STUD/2016/571399/IPOL_STU(2016)571399_EN.pdf.

[79] COM(2013) 534 final, 17 July 2013.

mechanism.[80] Nonetheless, the Commission maintained its original proposal[81] which was, however, substantially modified in the subsequent negotiations in the Council in the hope of keeping enough Member States onside.[82]

In the end, the EPPO was created not by unanimity but as an exercise in enhanced cooperation: at present, there are 24 participating EU countries. The Regulation was adopted and entered into force in 2017.[83] Denmark had an opt-out under Protocol 22, while Hungary, Ireland, the UK, and initially Sweden and Poland decided not to participate in the enhanced cooperation. However, the latter two countries became members of the Office in 2024.[84] Nevertheless, based on the principle of sincere cooperation and relying on mutual recognition measures as well as on mutual legal assistance, the cooperation between the EPPO and those Member States that have not joined the Office has been positive.[85]

The competence to fight EU budgetary fraud is shared between the EPPO, which can initiate its own investigations or call in cases from the national authorities, and the Member States, which can (within certain limits) initiate their own proceedings.[86] The scope of its material competence is defined by reference to the 2017 PIF Directive[87]—fraud involving EU funds of over €10,000 and serious cross-border VAT fraud involving total damage of at least €10,000,000. Article 86 TFEU provides for the possibility to expand the competence of the EPPO in the future (ideas have already been floated for environmental crimes and terrorist offences),[88] but the specificities of the Lisbon Treaty would require unanimity and a potential extension would certainly lead to new concerns and discussions in relation to the principle of proportionality.

As regards its design, while the previous drafts attempted to keep the EPPO as small as was reasonable, the Regulation introduced a set of elaborate arrangements.[89] There is one European Prosecutor per participating Member State, forming the College led by the European Chief Prosecutor. The College takes administrative and strategic decisions with a view to ensuring a consistent prosecution policy, but it has no powers to take operational decisions in individual cases. This is a structure similar to that of Eurojust but with a significant qualitative difference—decisions of the Eurojust College are taken by national members based on intergovernmental mechanisms, whereas those of the EPPO College are genuine Union decisions made by Union officials.

The European Prosecutors also form smaller Permanent Chambers, which have operational powers, including the important decisions to dismiss a case or to send it on to trial.

80 The early warning mechanism in accordance with Art 12(b) TEU is set out in Protocol (No 2) to the Treaties. Art 7(2) of the Protocol deals with the yellow-card procedure. See also KM Lohse, 'The European Public Prosecutor: Issues of Conferral, Subsidiarity and Proportionality' in L Erkelens, A Meij, and M Pawlik (eds), *The European Public Prosecutor's Office: An Extended Arm or a Two-Headed Dragon?* (The Hague: TMC Asser Press/Springer, 2015) 165.

81 COM(2013) 851 final, 13.

82 For the subsequent changes, see Presidency Notes from the Council to the Delegations 2013/0255 (APP).

83 Regulation 2017/1939 (OJ [2017] L283/1).

84 See Commission Decisions OJ [2024] L 29.2.2024 and OJ [2024] L 18.6.2024.

85 Poland was the exception, having been involved in most cases among these states, but having been reluctant to cooperate before joining the Office. See the EPPO 2021 Annual Report, 89–90. www.eppo.europa.eu/sites/default/files/2022-07/EPPO_Annual_Report_2021.pdf. Unlike Ireland, Hungary had signed a cooperation agreement with the EPPO already in April 2021, before the Office became operational.

86 Arts 26–27 EPPO Regulation.

87 Directive 2017/1371 (OJ [2017] L198/29).

88 COM (2018) 641, 12 September 2018, proposing an extension to cover terrorism. See also A Juszczak and E Sason, 'Fighting Terrorism through the European Public Prosecutor's Office (EPPO)?' (2019) 1 *eucrim* 66; F de Angelis, 'The European Public Prosecutor's Office: Past, Present, and Future' (2019) 4 *eucrim* 274–275.

89 For a detailed analysis, see A Csúri, 'The Proposed European Public Prosecutor's Office: From a Trojan Horse to a White Elephant?' (2016) 18 *Cambridge Yearbook of European Legal Studies* 122.

The actual investigations and prosecutions are then carried out by European Delegated Prosecutors in the Member States concerned, whose 'double-hatted' status gives them the same powers as their national counterparts as well as the specific powers conferred on them by the Regulation.[90]

In consequence, the final structure is complicated, with much of the Regulation being concerned with the minutiae of the relationships between the various parts of this complex body. But, despite this, the Office has already achieved significant results. By the end of December 2025, it had 3,602 active investigations, for estimated damage to the EU budget of over €67.27 billion.[91]

Given this patchwork-design, the question must be raised as to whether this efficiency is accompanied by sufficient legitimacy. One of the most significant issues in this regard is the way its cross-border investigations are organized. The Office does not employ EIOs, meaning that the approach moves away from horizontal cooperation, yet it fails to integrate a comprehensive vertical collaboration strategy. In addition to a centralized management, this would namely require the Office to have more uniform powers in the interests of fairness and legal certainty for the defendants amid significant diversity across national criminal justice systems. This legal diversity remains the same whether judicial cooperation takes place under the EIO or the EPPO. The difference is that the EIO Directive, a mutual recognition measure, provides for a number of checks—including human rights considerations—to balance diversity, which may even result in measures not being recognized or executed (Article 11 of the EIO Directive). The EPPO scheme, in contrast, offers no grounds for refusal in cross-border cases unless a measure has not been authorized (Article 31(3) of the EPPO Regulation). Therefore, it was no surprise that the first EPPO case before the CJEU (*GK and Others* (*Parquet européen*)) specifically concerned the cooperation scheme under Article 31. It will be interesting to see in what ways the EPPO Regulation, which is currently under review by the Commission and which is expected to conclude in mid-2026, might be amended in this regard.

4 Cooperation between law enforcement agencies

Instruments designed to improve cooperation in the cross-border sharing of information between national police forces, customs officials, and other law enforcement agencies account for a sizeable part of the body of EU criminal law.[92] In terms of substance, there are three main types.

The first create databases for the automated exchange of information. Prominent among these is the Schengen Information System or SIS.[93] Under this system, the competent authorities enter in their national SIS database (N.SIS) 'alerts' containing outline information—for example, that a person is missing or that a particular item such as cars, firearms, or identity documents are lost, stolen, or sought as evidence in criminal

[90] There are some restrictions, however, including that the European Delegated Prosecutors may only order or request measures in relation to offences carrying a maximum penalty of at least four years' imprisonment and that the measures ordered or requested are subject to any conditions and limitations imposed by the applicable national law (Art 30).

[91] See EPPO 2025 Annual Report: https://www.eppo.europa.eu/assets/annual-report-2025/pdfs/EPPO_Annual_Report_2025_en.pdf.

[92] See generally Peers, *EU Justice and Home Affairs Law* (n 2) ch 7.

[93] It started out as SIS in 1995 and was initially a group of articles in the Schengen Convention. The legal basis for SIS II (as regards its criminal law functions), incorporating photographs and fingerprints and which became operational in April 2013, was Council Decision 2007/533/JHA (OJ [2007] L205/63). This was replaced by Regulation (EU) 2018/1862 (OJ [2018] L312) from March 2023 (OJ [2023] L27/29). On the immigration law aspects of this system, see chapter 25.

proceedings. Importantly, the system is also the main means by which EAWs are issued and executed by indicating that a person is wanted for arrest or extradition. Alerts may also be entered on non-EU nationals suspected of being involved in terrorism and other serious crimes in order to facilitate the monitoring of their movements. The alert is sent to the central system (CS-SIS) that immediately directs it to all national systems. If authorities in other Member States get a 'hit', they can then ask the Member State that issued the alert for further details. Europol, the national members of Eurojust, and their assistants as well as the European Border and Coast Guard Agency (Frontex) can also access and search data entered in SIS.[94] In 2025 alone, the system was searched more than 17.5 billion times, averaging 49 million searches per day, 2 million searches per hour, and resulting in almost 365,000 hits that year. [95]

The SIS is in operation in all EU Member States, as well as in the four associated countries (Iceland, Norway, Liechtenstein, and Switzerland). That said, Ireland and Cyprus still have border controls in place and only have access to some SIS data. The UK lost access to the system with Brexit, and it is reported that its law enforcement authorities have since had difficulties as a result.[96]

Another such EU scheme aims to allow the authorities of one Member State to have direct access through designated national contact points to certain crime-related databases held by other Member States, including DNA, fingerprints, and vehicle registration data. The scheme is usually known as 'Prüm', after the name of the German town where the original intergovernmental convention was concluded. It was later incorporated into the EU legal framework by two Council decisions[97] and is now binding on all EU Member States. Prüm also focuses on supplying data in relation to major events with a cross-border dimension and in order to prevent terrorist offences.

The second type of instruments are schemes which give the law enforcement agencies of Member States the right to request information from those of other Member States, and impose a reciprocal duty to supply it. Foremost among these was an instrument usually called the Swedish Framework Decision, which was replaced by a directive in 2023.[98] This requires Member States to provide information and intelligence to law enforcement agencies from other Member States in the same way as one agency would make it available to another within that Member State.

Other instruments created specific schemes in relation to particular types of information; for example, a scheme known as ECRIS under which Member States are obliged on request to supply, in a standard shape and form, details of a given person's criminal convictions.[99] Following Brexit, the UK established its own UK-CRIS system. As a result, while it no longer has access to the ECRIS database, it can still exchange criminal record data with EU Member States via a simplified procedure.

In 2021, the Commission proposed a legislative package aimed at creating a 'EU Police Cooperation Code' based on Articles 87(3) and 89 TFEU to streamline, improve, and facilitate the above instruments of law enforcement cooperation between the relevant national agencies. This includes the Council Recommendation on operational law

[94] There are other schemes as well, including a Customs Information System (CIS) and a Visa Information System (VIS). On the former, see Decision (OJ [2009] L323/20), amended in 2024 (Regulation 2024/868 (OJ [2024] L 19.3.2024)); on the latter, see chapter 25.

[95] See SIS 2025 annual statistics, https://www.eulisa.europa.eu/our-publications/sis-annual-statistics-report-2025-report.

[96] JR Spencer 'The Sunny Uplands?' (2021) 1 *Archbold Review* 9–10; J Pearson, 'Loss of Access to Schengen Information System II: UK Policing Perspectives' in G Davies and H Carrapico (eds), *UK–EU Police and Judicial Cooperation Post-Brexit* (Oxford: Hart Publishing, 2025).

[97] Together referred to as Prüm decisions (OJ [2008] L210/1).

[98] OJ [2006] L386/89, replaced by Directive 2023/977 (OJ [2023] L134/1).

[99] The initial framework decision (OJ [2009] L93) was replaced by Directive 2019/884 (OJ [2019] L151/143).

enforcement cooperation,[100] which aims to address obstacles, particularly with regard to cross-border hot pursuit, cross-border surveillance, and joint patrols. Furthermore, the aforementioned Directive, which replaced the Swedish Framework Decision and a regulation, known as Prüm II,[101] were adopted in 2024. Among other things, Prüm II sets out the conditions and procedures for automated searches of DNA profiles, fingerprint data, and certain vehicle registration data. It also introduced the possibility of searching facial images and national police record databases with regard to suspects and convicted persons.

The third type of instruments provide a legal basis for cross-border operations. Of these, the best known are joint investigation teams, or JITs, under Article 13 of the EU Mutual Legal Assistance Convention of 2000.[102] JITs are set up by agreement between the competent authorities of two or more Member States for a specific purpose and a limited period. Essentially, these enable the competent authorities of one Member State to directly participate, under strict conditions, in investigations carried out in a foreign jurisdiction. Information lawfully obtained by members of a JIT may be used for the purposes for which the team has been set up and, subject to the prior consent of the Member State where the information became available, for detecting, investigating, and prosecuting other criminal offences. Over the last two decades, JITs have become a popular collaboration tool among practitioners, with a collaboration platform the technical implementation of which is ongoing, further facilitating their work through information exchange.[103] Finally, it is important to note that non-Member States can also join the scheme provided that a legal basis, such as an international agreement or national legislation, exists.[104] The UK, for instance, is therefore still very much involved in JITs based on the Council of Europe legal framework.

5 From mutual legal assistance to mutual recognition (and back?)

5.1 Mutual recognition and criminal law

In the context of EU criminal law, mutual recognition[105] means that the decisions and rulings of the courts and other competent authorities of one legal system are accepted and applied by those of another more or less automatically. This differs from the type of arrangement that traditionally operated between the different nation-States of Europe, whereby such things were a matter of discretion, legal help was given as a favour rather than a duty, and was usually subject to the ultimate control of the executive. Extradition—the traditional arrangement under which wanted persons were recovered from other countries—was in this mould, and likewise mutual legal assistance, the traditional arrangement under which lesser forms of active help (like evidence) are sought and given. With these differences in mind, mutual recognition is usually said to follow an 'order model', whereas mutual legal assistance and extradition are said to follow a 'request model'.

In a passive sense, mutual recognition means that the decision or ruling of a criminal court in another country must be given the same status as a decision of another court within the national system. In an active sense, it means that, in addition to this

100 OJ [2022] L158. 101 Regulation 2024/982 (OJ [2024] L 9.4.2024).

102 As Member States were slow ratifying the Convention, a Council Framework Decision on joint investigation teams was also adopted in 2002 (OJ [2002] L162).

103 Council Regulation (EU) 2023/969 (OJ [2023] L132). 104 Art 1 Framework Decision on JITs.

105 See generally, Peers, *EU Justice and Home Affairs Law* (n 2) ch 3; Mitsilegas, *EU Criminal Law* (n 2) ch 4. JR Spencer, 'The Principle of Mutual Recognition' in R Kostoris (ed), *Handbook of European Criminal Procedure* (Berlin: Springer, 2018).

recognition, active steps must be taken to enforce it. Both happen without real examination of the factual basis of the case. This part of the chapter deals with mutual recognition in the active sense. Three examples of mutual recognition in the passive sense will be discussed in section 7.

The principle of mutual recognition has long been applied in the context of the internal market[106] but it was only at the Tampere Council in 1999 that the EU adopted this principle as a way forward in dealing with cross-border crime in Europe (see section 3.4). Two years later, an ambitious legislative programme of mutual recognition measures[107] was announced for the gradual replacement of traditional instruments of international cooperation in criminal matters.

Since the Lisbon Treaty, this principle has been enshrined in EU primary law. On the one hand, there is Article 67(3) TFEU, which provides for mutual recognition and, where necessary, approximation of laws as the main means to achieve the objectives of the area of freedom, security, and justice. On the other hand, Article 82 TFEU declares mutual recognition to be the 'cornerstone' of judicial cooperation in criminal matters and essentially makes the promotion of this principle a prerequisite for the EU's legislative competence in criminal procedure. (Another potential source of tension in EU criminal law, since the logic of mutual recognition would not necessarily require approximation of laws: it is precisely in spite of legal diversity that we recognize and enforce final decisions of other criminal justice systems.)

At the time of writing, EU instruments now exist providing for a range of different forms of mutual recognition in the 'active' sense in relation to the different phases of criminal proceedings. These instruments include the Framework Decision on the European Arrest Warrant,[108] the Directive regarding the European Investigation Order in criminal matters,[109] a Regulation on the mutual recognition of freezing orders and confiscation orders,[110] the Framework Decision on the mutual recognition of supervision measures as an alternative to provisional detention,[111] the Framework Decision on the mutual recognition of fines,[112] the Framework Decision on the mutual recognition of probation orders and other non-custodial penalties,[113] and the Framework Decision on the mutual recognition of custodial sentences or measures involving deprivation of liberty.[114]

Of the various mutual recognition instruments, it is the European Arrest Warrant (EAW) which has had the greatest impact, while the European Investigation Order (EIO) has brought about important changes. It is therefore these two instruments that the rest of this section will mainly be concerned with.

5.2 **The European Arrest Warrant: its origins, and its main features**

A number of features of extradition in its traditional form under the Council of Europe conventions made it slow, costly, and uncertain.[115] First, to back up its request the requesting State had to produce prima facie evidence of guilt. Secondly, it was not available for 'political offences' or 'fiscal offences'. Thirdly, in its earlier history it was subject to a 'dual criminality requirement'; the requesting State had to show that the acts of which the wanted person stood accused would have been criminally punishable in the requested

[106] See Case C-120/78 *Rewe-Zentral AG v Bundesmonopolverwaltung für Branntwein* (*Cassis de Dijon*) [1979] ECR 649. See also C Janssen, *The Principle of Mutual Recognition in EU Law* (Oxford: Oxford University Press, 2013).

[107] OJ [2001] C12/10. [108] OJ [2002] L190/1. [109] Directive 2014/41 (OJ [2014] L130).

[110] Regulation 2018/1805 (OJ [2018] L303/1). [111] OJ [2009] L294/20.

[112] OJ [2005] L76/16. [113] OJ [2008] L337/102. [114] OJ [2008] L327/27.

[115] For some facts and figures, see Hinarejos, Spencer, and Peers (n 18) para 96 or JR Spencer 'The European Arrest Warrant' (2003–04) 6 *Cambridge Yearbook of European Legal Studies*, ch 9.

State had they been committed there. Fourthly, many countries refused on principle to extradite their nationals. Fifthly, the process was political as well as legal, requiring the consent of the executive as well as of the courts. And, finally, because its availability in a given case depended on the terms of the extradition Treaty (if any) between the requesting and the requested States, it was exceedingly complicated.

With travel within Europe becoming easier and more frequent, and the number of extradition requests quickly increasing, the situation became intolerable. It was to assist this problem that the EAW was introduced. Adopted rapidly in the aftermath of the 9/11 terrorist attacks, the instrument primarily promoted the security aspect of the AFSJ, providing for nearly automatic enforcement of foreign judicial decisions to meet the immediate need to combat terrorism, without much emphasis on the protection of human rights.

With the EAW things became very different. The transfer of suspects and convicted persons between EU Member States is now a purely legal matter, the final decision no longer resting with the executive. The procedure is a summary one, based on the production by the issuing State (renamed from 'requesting State') of an arrest warrant, not the evidence on the basis of which the warrant was issued. There are time limits: a final decision must be made within 10 days where the wanted person consents to surrender and 60 days where they do not. Not only have the exceptions for political or fiscal offences disappeared,[116] dual criminality has been made irrelevant for 32 categories of misbehaviour set out in what is usually called the Framework Decision List, provided they carry at least three years' imprisonment in the issuing State. And if the basic conditions are met, the executing State (the former 'requested State') is obliged to surrender the wanted person unless one of a limited number of specified 'grounds for non-execution' listed in the Framework Decision are made out. Significantly, these do not include the fact that the wanted person is a national of the executing State. And, finally, the resulting system is uniform, or nearly so, throughout the whole of the EU—thus making it much more user-friendly for those who have to operate it. The result is that, within Europe, far more wanted people are now handed over than was previously the case and the process is much faster. This is still so, notwithstanding the fact that, in recent years, the process has become somewhat slower compared to previous trends. Taking the EU as a whole, it now takes on average around 20 days to hand over a wanted person who consents to his or her surrender, and around 57 days where they do not: as against around a year, the average time it used to take under the old system.[117]

5.3 **Criticisms of the EAW**

Of the criticisms that are made about the workings of the EAW, three are the most serious. One is its excessive scope, which enables it to be used in some cases that are trivial, or stale, or both. This stems in part from the threshold conditions set out in the Framework Decision, which do not include a general requirement of proportionality—and in consequence of which there is no apparent place for such a requirement in national implementing legislation either. Under Article 2(1) of the Framework Decision, the EAW may be used, subject to the dual criminality requirement, for 'acts punishable by the law of the issuing Member State by a custodial sentence or detention order for a maximum period

[116] As between those countries that had ratified it, this had already been abolished by the European Extradition Convention of 1996.

[117] For the latest official figures see European Commission EAW statistics from 2022, 13–14, https://commission.europa.eu/document/download/32810655-fe94-44c2-9099-2813c42c9adb_en?filename=EAW%20Statistics%20Report%202022.pdf. For previous trends, see W van Ballegooij, 'European Implementation Assessment 2004–2020 on the European Arrest Warrant' (2020) 2 *eucrim* 149.

of at least 12 months or, where a sentence has been passed or a detention order has been made, for sentences of at least four months'. As shoplifting is theft, and the maximum penalty for theft is likely to exceed 12 months under every Member States' criminal law, EAWs are available for use against shoplifters as well as bank robbers.

Another part of the reason why the EAW is too often used is that, as things stand, it is the only instrument readily available. This means that a State confronted with (say) a minor theft committed by a person who has removed themselves to another Member State has a choice between issuing an EAW—an instrument designed with grave crimes and organized criminality in mind—and letting the guilty person get away with it. This problem could be solved by creating a workable system for dealing with minor criminality committed across borders. The germ of such a system is already present in a Framework Decision which enables the cross-border enforcement of fines as well as a Directive that facilitates cross-border investigations into road traffic offences and the enforcement of related sanctions.[118]

The second serious criticism of the way the EAW works in practice is the fact that it sometimes returns suspects to countries where they then spend excessive periods in prison before trial. Andrew Symeou, a British youth, experienced this when, in July 2009, he was surrendered to Greece on charges of homicide, where he spent the next two years awaiting trial, in particularly bad prison conditions. The background to the case was a fight between British youths at a resort in Greece in July 2007, during which one of them, Jonathan Hiles, was killed. Symeou opposed his extradition, arguing that the evidence against him consisted of false confessions extracted from his companions by the Greek police. When the case finally came to trial in June 2011, the court acquitted him on the recommendation of the prosecutor. Long periods of pre-trial detention are a regrettable feature of criminal justice in a number of Member States. However, the injustice of the case would have been much less if Symeou had been allowed to spend the time waiting for trial in England; in the meantime, in 2009, the EU adopted a framework decision which, in theory, allows this.[119]

The third problem is a central issue at the very heart of all mutual recognition instrument, namely 'trust' in the functioning of foreign criminal justice systems. This is the subject of the case study 24.1, which also attempt to answer the question posed in the title of the present section. Is the current cooperation arrangement undergoing a transformation?

Case study 24.1: From *Melloni* through *Aranyosi* and *Căldăraru* to *LM*

Under the principle of mutual recognition, Member States more or less automatically enforce each other's judgments and orders. This was one of the main reasons why Member States chose this principle as the way forward for cooperation in criminal matters, as it has helped to promote the security aspects of the area of freedom, security, and justice without harmonization of laws. The justification for this scheme is said to be the existence of mutual trust: the legal systems of all Member States can be trusted to act decently and fairly. But what is the nature of this 'mutual trust'? Is it a given: a state of affairs the existence of which must be officially assumed? Or is it just an aspiration, meaning that the courts of an executing State are free, in a given case, to refuse to recognize a judgment or order if they feel that to do so would be unjust? The possibility provided for in the Treaties to resort to approximation

[118] OJ [2005] L76/16 and Directive 2015/413 (OJ [2015] L68/9), since amended by Directive 2024/3237 (OJ [2024] L 30.12.2024).

[119] OJ [2009] L294.

of laws in order to promote the principle of mutual recognition suggests that this trust is more of an aspiration. Likewise, the fact that the EAW, albeit to a limited extent, provides specific grounds on the basis of which recognition of the judgment or order may be refused. As a matter of EU law, is it then open to the courts of a Member State to refuse to execute a judgment or order for reasons of fairness which are not referable to one of these specific grounds? For example, by reference to some extra ground for refusal stated in the national implementing legislation, or the constitution of the Member State concerned, or by reference to human rights law in general? This is a difficult issue which, over time, has revived some of the traditional concerns that the system of mutual recognition was designed to overcome, in contrast to previous forms of judicial cooperation.

The CJEU has also had to wrestle with these questions on a number of occasions. In an earlier decision,[120] it took a rather hard-nosed approach. This was a case that started in 1993, long before the EAW Framework Decision was adopted, when Spanish authorities supported the extradition of Italian national Stefano Melloni to Italy in order for him to be tried for bankruptcy offences. However, Melloni could not be handed over as he fled after being released on bail. He was later sentenced in his absence to imprisonment. The Italian authorities then issued an EAW (the instrument was adopted by then) to Spain for enforcement purposes.

Due to the length of the proceedings, surrender took place under different versions of the framework decision. Initially, Article 5 stated that if an EAW was issued to execute a sentence or detention order imposed by a decision rendered *in absentia* and the person concerned had not been summoned or informed of the date and place of the hearing that led to the decision, surrender could be subject to the condition of being given the opportunity to apply for a retrial in the issuing Member State and of being present at the judgement. However, the 2009 amendment stipulated that an EAW could not be refused under such circumstances if the individual was aware of the scheduled trial and had authorised a legal counsellor to defend them, and if the counsellor had in fact provided a defence at the trial. Melloni did have legal representatives whom he had selected and appointed, and who were duly informed of the details of the proceedings.[121]

According to the Spanish Constitution, and contrary to Italian law, the right to be present at trial is not just part of the right to a fair trial, but the absence of this possibility allows for a retrial. In addition, Article 47 of the Charter of Fundamental Rights of the EU provides for the right to a fair and public hearing and Article 53 states that nothing in the Charter shall be interpreted as restricting or adversely affecting human rights and fundamental freedoms as recognized, in their respective fields of application, among other things, by the Member States' constitutions.

The Spanish Constitutional Court therefore referred the case to the CJEU for a preliminary ruling. Two interconnected questions will be highlighted here. First, whether the Framework Decision precludes the executing judicial authority from making surrender conditional on the person concerned being able to apply for a retrial in the issuing Member State. Secondly, whether the different national standards of protection allow Spain to apply its own—higher—standard and make the surrender of a person sentenced *in absentia* conditional on the possibility of the judgment being reviewed in the issuing State. In other words, whether mutual trust is affected when a national law provides a higher level of protection than that of another Member State or even EU law and whether a Member State may demand a higher level of protection of fundamental rights from another Member State than that granted by EU law.

In regard to the first question, the Court held that the Spanish courts could not refuse to execute the EAW on grounds not covered by the Framework Decision and could not make the surrender conditional on a retrial of the case.[122] On the second question, the Court held

[120] Case C-399/11 *Melloni v Ministerio Fiscal* [2013] 3 WLR 717.

[121] Article 4a of Framework Decision 2009/299/JHA of 26 February 2009.

[122] *Melloni* (n 120) para 42.

that if the Spanish court were to refuse to execute the EAW on grounds not provided for in the Framework Decision but which stemmed from the Spanish Constitution, this would allow Member States not to apply EU law that is fully in compliance with the Charter where it infringes fundamental rights guaranteed by the Constitution of the State concerned. This would be contrary to the principle of the primacy of EU law.[123]

The ensuing *Aranyosi* and *Căldăraru*[124] cases brought the first important changes. Aranyosi, a Hungarian national, and Căldăraru, a Romanian national, were arrested independently in the German town of Bremen. Aranyosi was wanted in Hungary for prosecution, while Căldăraru faced a prison sentence in Romania.

In view of the significant overcrowding in prisons in both countries, as confirmed by European Court of Human Rights (ECtHR) judgments[125] and reports of international organizations,[126] and the fact that the EAW Framework Decision does not make the adequate protection of human rights a specific ground on the basis of which a State could refuse to execute an EAW,[127] preliminary questions were referred to the Court. Namely, whether in such cases the execution of the EAW may be refused or whether the executing State may make it conditional on the detention being adequate (and, if so, whether it may lay down requirements to that effect).

The CJEU, sitting as the Grand Chamber—a fairly rare event—ruled that where there was 'objective, reliable, specific and properly updated evidence' suggesting that systematic deficiencies in the detention conditions in the issuing State might cause the wanted person to suffer 'inhuman or degrading treatment' in breach of Article 4 of the EU Charter (which mirrors Article 3 of the European Convention on Human Rights (ECHR)), the court in the executing State must make enquiries of the issuing State; and if suitable reassurances are not received within a reasonable time, it 'must decide whether the surrender procedure should be brought to an end'.[128] Thus, mutual trust in respect of detention conditions became rebuttable in a two-step test based on systemic and individual risk considerations.

In the subsequent case of *Minister for Justice and Equality v LM*,[129] the CJEU broadened the grounds to refuse the execution of an EAW, this time concerning the independence of the issuing State's judiciary; that is to say, concern about a fundamental right (the right to a fair trial) not covered as a ground for refusal by the Framework Decision. The case considered an EAW issued in Poland for the purposes of prosecution. LM—the person concerned—was arrested in Ireland. He did not consent to his surrender, stating that it would expose him to a real risk of a 'flagrant denial of justice in contravention of Article 6 of the ECHR' and relying in particular on the Commission's reasoned proposal from 2017 regarding the rule of law in Poland. That proposal particularly addressed concerns over the lack of independent and legitimate constitutional review and threats to the independence of the ordinary judiciary in Poland.

The Court established a two-step test, as with *Aranyosi and Căldăraru*, and held that the executing State might bring the surrender procedure to an end 'if there is a real risk of breach of the fundamental right to a fair trial guaranteed by the second paragraph of Article 47 of the Charter, on account of systemic or generalised deficiencies so far as concerns the independence of the issuing Member State's judiciary'. The executing authority must first broadly assess the judicial system in the issuing Member State and then determine, specifically and

[123] Ibid, para 58. On this, and other related cases, see also Mitsilegas, *EU Criminal Law* (n 2).

[124] Joined Cases C-404/15 and C-659/15 PPU, EU:C:2016:198.

[125] See eg *Varga and others v Hungary* (Appl Nos 39734/15 etc), ECtHR, 2015; *Kanalas v Romania* (Appl No 20323/14), ECtHR, 2016; *Florin Andrei v Romania* (Appl No 33228/05), ECtHR, 2014.

[126] See the reports on the periodic visits of the European Committee for the Prevention of Torture and Inhuman or Degrading Treatment.

[127] Even if the Framework Decision does not alter the obligation to respect fundamental rights and fundamental legal principles as enshrined in Art 6 TEU. See Art 1(3) EAW Framework Decision.

[128] See n 124, para 105.

[129] Case C-216/18 PPU [2019] 1 WLR 1004.

precisely, whether there are substantial grounds for believing that the individual concerned will run such a risk if they are surrendered to that State.[130] If the answer is in the affirmative, the referring court asks the Court of Justice to specify the conditions which such a check must satisfy.[131] The judgment is of particular importance because mutual recognition measures such as the EAW or the EIO are based on judicial decisions. Thus, if the independence of a Member State's judiciary is called into question, the very legality of the measure issued may be called into doubt in the context of the principle of mutual recognition.

The decision in *LM* has opened a new chapter as it implies that the judicial authority of one Member State may render an opinion, with far-reaching consequences, on the functioning of another Member State's judiciary in accordance with the rule of law. It has also shown that mutual trust is not a natural virtue, and that the original automaticity of mutual recognition instruments can be limited.

5.4 **The European Investigation Order**

In 1999, the Tampere programme also floated the idea that evidence lawfully gathered in one Member State should be admissible before the courts of another, taking into account the standards that apply there.[132] The initial debates concerned whether there was any real need to move away from mutual legal assistance in the field of evidence, and whether a shift towards mutual recognition was the right direction. Those who were sceptical feared in general that the scheme, which worked well in the area of extradition, would not necessarily take hold in the context of evidence. They emphasized, in particular, the need for prior approximation of laws in order to build up trust, at least for a standard set of 'core evidence-gathering powers' that apply in transnational cases in all Member States.[133]

The Directive regarding the European Investigation Order in criminal matters (the EIO Directive) was adopted in 2014[134] and it was 2018 before the last Member State fulfilled the obligation to transpose it, making the Directive fully applicable in practice. Since then, it has been the primary means for obtaining evidence located in another Member State bound by the instrument and its practical relevance is apparent, among other things, in that the number of EIOs supported by Eurojust increased from nearly 1,000 in 2018 to over 6,712 in 2025, while such cases represent only a fraction of their total use.[135]

An EIO is a judicial decision, which has been issued or validated by a judicial authority of one Member State for the purpose of obtaining evidence in another: either by carrying out one or more specific investigative measure(s)—usually under the applicable law of the executing authority—or by transferring evidence already in the possession of the competent foreign authority.[136] The setting up of JITs is outside the scope of the Directive, as JITs are by their very nature based on common investigation and direct cooperation, where the evidence thus obtained is automatically made available to all participating authorities.[137]

[130] Ibid, para 69. Eg the issuing Member State has been the subject of a reasoned proposal adopted by the Commission pursuant to Art 7(1) TEU in order for the Council to determine that there is a clear risk of a serious breach by that Member State of the values referred to in Art 2 TEU, such as that of the rule of law, on account, in particular, of actions impairing the independence of the national courts.

[131] Ibid, para 34.

[132] Presidency Conclusions 36, Tampere European Council, 15 and 16 October 1999.

[133] JR Spencer, The Green Paper on obtaining evidence from one Member State to another and securing its admissibility: the Reaction of one British Lawyer' (2010) 9 *Zeitschrift für Internationale Strafrechtsdogmatik* 604–605.

[134] Superseding an unsuccessful earlier instrument, the European Evidence Warrant (OJ [2008] L350/72).

[135] See the Eurojust Annual Reports for 2018 and 2025 available on its website.

[136] Art 1 EIO Directive.

[137] Art 3 EIO Directive. See also J Espina Ramos, 'The European Investigation Order and Its Relationship with Other Judicial Cooperation Instruments' (2019) 1 *eucrim* 55–56.

The aim of the Directive is to accelerate the gathering and transfer of evidence in cross-border cases. Much as with the EAW, this is provided for in a comprehensive instrument with strict deadlines and formalities to comply with. But there are limits to its comprehensiveness. As the Directive does not bind all Member States, the traditional instruments of MLA remain essential when it comes to Denmark and (at present) Ireland. The Directive also only replaces the 'corresponding provisions' of the listed conventions[138] and EU legal measures[139] applicable between the Member States bound by it. In its first report on the evaluation of the application of the EIO Directive published at the end of 2020, Eurojust already drew attention to the need for guidance on the uniform or combined use of EIOs and letters of requests as well as for clarification of the precise scope and meaning of some of the provisions in the Directive, in particular those on interception of telecommunications and cross-border surveillance.[140]

Unlike MLA, issuing and executing an EIO requires equivalency and proportionality tests on both sides of the decision-making process. The equivalency tests ensure that the respective measure could be applied to the same offence under the domestic laws of both Member States concerned.[141] The proportionality test in the issuing Member State ensures that the evidence sought is necessary and proportionate for the purpose of the proceedings, the measure chosen is necessary and proportionate for obtaining that piece of evidence, and that it is necessary and proportionate to involve another Member State in the process by issuing the EIO.[142] The proportionality test in the executing State enables the authorities to use investigative measures other than those sought, if they are less intrusive and would produce the same results.[143]

As with previous mutual recognition instruments, there are grounds for refusing to recognize or execute an EIO. However, unlike those instruments, the EIO Directive explicitly provided for a new ground for refusal where executing the EIO might lead to a breach of fundamental rights.[144] Prior to any refusal, however, the parties must consult each other, which, as the Directive does not set time limits on this, might slow down proceedings in individual cases.[145] The new guarantees strengthen the position of the defendant, as the presumption of compliance with Union law and fundamental rights, which is at the heart of mutual trust, has become explicitly rebuttable in the context of legal diversity. This became increasingly clear in the *Gavanozov* case, where the question arose as to whether a Member State that issued an EIO is legally obliged to provide a remedy against the decision itself. This issue arose from the general absence of legal remedies under Bulgarian law against decisions ordering a search, seizure or the hearing of witnesses via videoconference, all of which were ordered under a specific EIO. In summary, the Court concluded that the absence of legal remedies against the investigative measures in question, as well as against the issuance of the EIO, constituted a violation of the right to an effective remedy under Article 47(1) of the Charter. This refutes the presumption of mutual trust, thereby preventing the competent authority of a Member State from issuing an EIO. Consequently, unlike the two-step test of systematic and individual risk assessment established in the *Aranyosi and Căldăraru* case, the systematic absence

[138] Art 34 (1) EIO Directive. [139] See Art 34 (2) EIO Directive.

[140] Eurojust EIO casework report, 19–20 and 44–46. Available at www.eurojust.europa.eu/sites/default/files/2020-11/2020-11_EIO-Casework-Report_CORR_.pdf.

[141] Arts 6(1) and 10 EIO Directive. [142] Recital 11 and Art 6 EIO Directive.

[143] In addition to proportionality considerations, the issuing authority may also have recourse to a different type of investigative measure if the one ordered does not exist or would not be available in a similar domestic case (Arts 6 and 10 EIO Directive).

[144] If there were substantial grounds for believing that it would be incompatible with the executing State's obligations in accordance with Art 6 TEU and the EU Charter. Art 11(1)(f) EIO Directive.

[145] A Csúri, 'Towards an Inconsistent European Regime of Cross-Border Evidence: The EPPO and the European Investigation Order' in W Geelhoed, L Erkelens, and A Meij (eds), *Shifting Perspectives on the European Public Prosecutor's Office* (The Hague: TMC Asser Press/Springer, 2018) 141–153.

of effective legal remedies, exemplified by the *Gavanozov* case, undermines mutual trust and mutual recognition to such an extent that an assessment of individual risks in specific cases becomes unnecessary.[146]

Overall, the Directive has established a horizontal cooperation regime that falls somewhere between the numerous exceptions of the traditional MLA and the automaticity of previous mutual recognition measures: another indication of the validity of the question raised in the title of this section.[147]

5.5 **Addendum: the effect of Brexit**

The UK as a former Member State—now a third country—is in a special position as it applied the EAW and the EIO before leaving the EU and still generates many cases in relation to European transnational criminal justice.[148]

It is therefore important to note that the Trade and Cooperation Agreement[149] (TCA) reached between the EU and the UK in December 2020 contains supplementary rules on judicial cooperation in criminal matters.[150] Both the EAW and the EIO are replicated. Under the surrender regime (Title VII), the time limits remain unchanged, with the decision on surrender being taken within 10 to 60 days at the latest. However, there are two significant differences compared to the EU regime: the parties can insist on double criminality (Article 601) even for offences on the Framework Decision List and there is a possibility to refuse to surrender own nationals (Article 603).

Among the key provisions of mutual assistance (Title VIII), the agreement maintains tight deadlines for cooperation, albeit slightly beyond those in the EIO Directive (Article 640 stipulates a maximum period of 45 days for deciding on whether to execute a request, and a further maximum period of 90 days for executing the request after such a decision has been made). Moreover, as regards letters of requests, the agreement provides for the possibility of creating standard templates (Article 635). Furthermore, the execution of requests is based on proportionality and equivalence tests (Article 636) with the possibility of recourse to alternative measures (Article 637), similar to the EIO Directive.

The agreement thus provides the UK with a unique approach to judicial cooperation that falls short of the rigour of the EU instruments, but is at the same time much more efficient than the traditional ones.[151]

6 Harmonization of substantive criminal law

In recent years, there has been a rapid growth of European Union instruments requiring Member States, if they have not already done so, to make various harmonized adjustments to their substantive criminal law. Article 83(1) TFEU gives the Union the power to adopt common minimum standards for particularly serious crimes with a cross-border

[146] See Recital 19 together with Article 11(1)(f) of the EIO Directive. Also see C-324/17, *Gavanozov I* and C-852/19, *Gavanozov II*, as well as Csúri, 'Sense and Admissibility: Cross-Border EPPO Investigations and Evidence' (n 17)

[147] See Csúri, 'Towards an Inconsistent European Regime of Cross-Border Evidence' (n 145). See also V Mitsilegas, 'The Limits of Mutual Trust in Europe's Area of Freedom, Security and Justice: From Automatic Inter-State Cooperation to the Slow Emergence of the Individual' (2012) 31 *Yearbook of European Law* 319.

[148] For analysis, see R Hanratty, 'The Effect of Brexit on the Fight against Crime' (2018) 4 *Archbold Review* 4–9. For the experiences of the first five years following Brexit, see Davies and Carrapico (eds), *UK–EU Police and Judicial Cooperation Post-Brexit* (n 96).

[149] OJ [2021] L149.

[150] For analysis, see Spencer, 'The Sunny Uplands?' (n 96).

[151] See also the Eurojust publication, 'Judicial cooperation in criminal matters between the European Union and the United Kingdom from 1 January 2021', available on its website.

dimension (see section 2.3.3). The provision provides an exhaustive list of offences, also known as 'EU crimes' or 'Euro crimes'. These are terrorism, trafficking in human beings, sexual exploitation of woman and children, illicit drug trafficking, illicit arms trafficking, money laundering, corruption, counterfeiting of means of payment, computer crime, and organized crime. Most of these offences were already covered by framework decisions in the pre-Lisbon era: in fact, these covered even more than the current list of EU crimes. The exhaustive nature of the list therefore also means that in certain areas where legislation already exists, such as racism and xenophobia,[152] there is currently no direct legal basis for the adoption of directives on these issues.[153] That said, the list can be extended although only by a unanimous decision of the Council with the prior consent of the European Parliament. Two such proposals have been made so far, one on hate speech (not yet agreed)[154] and the other on the violation of Union foreign policy sanctions, adopted in 2022 and followed by a directive using this new power in 2024.[155]

Regarding EU crimes, directives have been adopted on terrorism,[156] drug trafficking,[157] child sexual abuse and pornography,[158] cybercrime,[159] money laundering,[160] people-trafficking,[161] frauds in relation to electronic payments,[162] counterfeiting currency,[163] and domestic violence/violence against women.[164]

In every case, the obligation so imposed is to make a given type of antisocial behaviour punishable and further duties are usually imposed about the type and severity of punishment. However, as criminal sanctions reflect national traditions and values and are therefore a fundamental aspect of national sovereignty, the Union follows a so-called 'minimum–maximum' approach and only sets common minimum levels of the maximum sanctions for natural persons. Thus, there is no harmonization of minimum penalties, which makes it difficult to substantiate the effectiveness of the current system.[165]

Another standard provision in these instruments is an Article requiring Member States to create extra-territorial jurisdiction over these offences when committed by their nationals—a feature common in the continental systems. A further aspect of all these instruments is that they require Member States to ensure that criminal liability extends to incitement, aiding and abetting, and attempt. Liability should also extend to 'legal persons'—that is, corporations, but there is no requirement for this to be criminal. Thus, there can also be civil or administrative liability. Although the trend in the Member States is to introduce criminal liability, there have been increasing debates in recent years as to whether criminal liability is in truth more effective than administrative liability in this context.[166]

Article 83(2) TFEU grants an additional power, which allows the Union to adopt common minimum standards for the definition of criminal acts and sanctions, where these are indispensable to ensure the effectiveness of an already harmonized EU policy. This, in essence, codifies the accessory criminal law competence of the EU, developed by the CJEU in the case concerning the protection of the environment through criminal law (see section 2.3.2). However, as the chapters of this book show, EU policies are wide-ranging and cover a variety of areas, all of which are subject to the principles of subsidiarity and proportionality. So, when is it 'indispensable' to ensure the effectiveness of already harmonized EU policies by means of approximations of criminal laws? Attempting to answer

[152] OJ [2008] L328/55. [153] Csonka and Landwehr (n 34) 263–264.

[154] COM(2021) 777 final. [155] OJ [2022] L308/18 and Directive 2024/1226 (OJ [2024] L 29.4.2024).

[156] Directive 2017/541 (OJ [2017] L88/6). [157] Directive 2017/2103 (OJ [2017] L305).

[158] Directive 2011/93 (OJ [2011] L335/1). [159] Directive 2013/40 (OJ [2013] L218/8).

[160] Council Framework Decision 2001/500/JHA (OJ [2001] L182), now partly replaced by Directive 2018/1673 (OJ [2018] L284/22).

[161] Directive 2011/36 (OJ [2011] L101/1), amended by Directive 2024/1712 (OJ [2024] L 24.6.2024).

[162] Directive 2019/713 (OJ [2019] L123/18). [163] Directive 2014/62 (OJ [2014] L151/1).

[164] Directive 2024/1385 (OJ [2024] L 24.5.2024). [165] Csonka and Landwehr (n 34) 265.

[166] Ibid.

this question, the Commission adopted a communication on EU criminal policy,[167] and in particular regarding Article 83(2) TFEU, laying down some guiding principles based on the two-step approach: whether it is necessary to use criminal law in a certain policy field at all and if so what kind of criminal measures should apply. The guiding principles in this regard are that criminal law must be necessary to ensure effective implementation, the general principles of subsidiarity and proportionality must apply, fundamental rights under the ECHR and the Charter must be respected, and the sanctions must be proportionate under Article 49 of the Charter. It is no surprise, therefore, that as of today only three directives have been adopted on the basis of Article 83(2) TFEU covering such important Union interests as market abuse,[168] PIF offences,[169] and (replacing the earlier legislation) environmental crime.[170]

But are the legislative powers contained in Title V of the TFEU the limit of the Union's competence in criminal justice matters? Or could legislation in the area of criminal justice also be adopted on the basis of other Articles? Under Article 325, for example, the Union shall take 'necessary measures' to counter fraud and any other illegal activities affecting its financial interests. Could these include legislation requiring Member States to adjust their criminal law, or criminal procedure? The Commission evidently thought so, because in July 2012 it put forward the proposal for the PIF Directive with Article 325(4) as the proposed legal basis, rather than Articles contained in Title V.[171] In the area of combating fraud, Article 325 TFEU replaced the former Article 280(4) TEC, which contained the restriction that the respective measures 'shall not concern the application of national criminal law or the national administration of justice'. This wording was deleted by the Lisbon Treaty, which, in the Commission's view, made it possible to combat fraud under Article 325 TFEU by using criminal law measures.[172] From the perspective of the Commission, Article 325 had obvious advantages, since the ordinary legislative procedure would have applied and the guarantees and restrictions that hamper legislation under Title V would not have applied.[173]

But the Council and Parliament did not see the matter in the same light and challenged the Commission's stance. In their opinion, the change of wording did not extend the scope of Article 325 TFEU. Instead, they said it should be read in the context of the inclusion of the new legal basis in Article 83(2) TFEU, which applies where the EU legislator needs to harmonize substantive criminal law in order to make other (non-criminal) harmonized EU measures more effective.[174] The Directive on the fight against fraud to the Union's financial interests by means of criminal law[175] was eventually adopted, as we have seen, on the basis of Article 83(2). As a result, it fell within the scope of the opt-in/opt-out regimes of Protocols 21 and 22.

7 Harmonization of criminal procedure

Broadly speaking, the EU has adopted legislation affecting the national criminal procedure of the Member States in two different ways. The first is legislation which requires the criminal courts of Member States to take account in current criminal proceedings of steps taken by the criminal justice systems of other Member States in earlier criminal proceedings involving the same person: mutual recognition, but in a passive sense.

[167] COM(2011) 573 final. See also Csonka and Landwehr (n 34) 264.

[168] Directive 2014/57 (OJ [2014] L173/179). [169] Directive 2017/1371 (OJ [2017] L198/29).

[170] Directive 2024/1203 (OJ [2024] L 30.4.2024).

[171] COM(2012) 363 final. On the concept of 'legal basis', see chapter 5.

[172] Ibid. Explanatory Memorandum. [173] See Csonka and Landwehr (n 34) 264.

[174] Opinion of the Legal Service of 22 October 2012 (Council Doc 15309/12), points 5, 11, and 12. See also European Parliament position at first reading of 16 April 2014, Doc P7 TA(2014)0427.

[175] OJ [2017] L198/29.

The second is legislation designed to ensure minimum standards of decent treatment for those who are caught up in criminal proceedings, either as complainants or defendants: harmonization of laws. In each case, there is a connection—or perceived connection—between the legislation and free movement.

Of passive mutual recognition measures there are three. The first is a group of Articles in the CISA designed to ensure that the '*ne bis in idem*' principle, alias the rule against double jeopardy, applies where the case against the defendant has already been dealt with by the criminal justice system of another Member State. The key provision is Article 54 of the Convention, which reads as follows:

> A person whose trial has been finally disposed of in one Contracting Party may not be prosecuted in another Contracting Party for the same acts provided that, if a penalty has been imposed, it has been enforced, is actually in the process of being enforced or can no longer be enforced under the laws of the sentencing Contracting Party.

The Court of Justice has interpreted this provision widely—holding, for example, that it applies not only where the case has been finally disposed of by a court but also when a public prosecutor, avoiding court proceedings, has closed the file by a settlement (*Gözütok and Brügge*). This broad approach was said to be justified by the need to encourage free movement: which would be inhibited, it is said, if citizens thought that their criminal past, seemingly behind them, could haunt them with the threat of further punishment when they crossed a national border.[176]

On the other hand, the Court has also held that a case is not finally disposed of before it has been examined on the merits (*M*) or where it has not been referred to the courts because the proceedings are underway in another Member State (*Miraglia*).[177]

The second passive mutual recognition instrument is the Framework Decision requiring Member States to give the same weight and effect to previous convictions imposed by the courts of other Member States as they give to previous convictions imposed by their own courts.[178] So where a previous conviction exposes a recidivist defendant to the possibility of a higher penalty, this must apply to previous convictions handed down in all other parts of the EU. As with Article 54 of Schengen, the background to this instrument is the policy of free movement—but the aim here is to deal with the consequences, rather than to encourage it. Together with the ECRIS Directive requiring Member States to provide information about criminal records on demand, the objective is to make sure that repeat offenders do not transform themselves into first offenders each time they cross a national border.

The third of the passive mutual recognition measures is Article 26(1) of the Framework Decision that created the EAW. This provides that, when sentencing the person it has recovered by using an EAW, the issuing State must deduct from the sentence any period the wanted person spent in prison while the EAW was being executed.

The EU's first attempts to harmonize criminal procedures, notably by imposing minimum standards of decent treatment for the participants in criminal proceedings, were directed towards helping complainants—a group whom the legislation, like the media, insists on calling 'victims'. A Framework Decision on the standing of victims was adopted in 2001,[179] and it was this instrument which gave rise to the famous *Pupino* decision discussed in section 2.3.2. Eleven years later, this was followed by a directive establishing minimum standards on the rights, support and protection of victims of crime,[180] a more

[176] See E Sharpston and JM Fernandez-Martin, 'Some Reflections on Schengen Free Movement Rights' (2007–08) 10 *Cambridge Yearbook of European Legal Studies*, ch 15.

[177] Joined Cases C-187/01 and C-385/01 [2003] ECR I-01345; Case C 469/03 [2005] ECR I-2009; Case C-398/12 [2014].

[178] OJ [2008] L220/32. [179] OJ [2001] L82/1. [180] OJ [2012] L315.

elaborate document which replaced the earlier instrument. This contains no fewer than 22 Articles listing specific rights and protections for victims which Member States must ensure are granted by their national systems of criminal procedure.

This list is long and only a few selected ones will be mentioned here, such as the right to be heard, which is guaranteed by Article 10, and the right to a review of a decision not to prosecute, guaranteed by Article 11. Other Articles confer on victims rights to various forms of practical protection. Article 23, for example, requires Member States to provide 'measures to avoid unnecessary questioning concerning the victim's private life' and Article 24 requires interviews with child victims to be audio-visually recorded, and the resulting interviews to be admissible in evidence. In 2023, the Commission proposed amendments to the Directive, including the introduction of an EU-wide general helpline for victims and a decision on compensation to be taken only within the criminal proceedings. Other proposals included improving victim participation in criminal proceedings and enhancing the safety of vulnerable victims.[181]

In addition, the 2011 Directive on people-trafficking[182] requires Member States to ensure that those who are victims of this offence are not prosecuted for criminal offences which, having been trafficked, they were forced to commit. In light of this, in 2013 the Court of Appeal of England and Wales quashed the convictions of a group of people who appeared to fall within the scope of this provision—taking the view that a prosecution brought in such circumstances amounted to an abuse of process.[183]

To complete the picture, mention should be made of the 2004 Directive[184]—a First Pillar instrument—which requires all Member States to operate national schemes for compensating the victims of violent crime where they are visitors from other Member States.

Negotiations on a Framework Decision guaranteeing certain minimum rights for defendants began in 2003, shortly after the creation of the EAW.[185] Three years later, however, progress in this direction was abruptly halted when the British government, initially in favour, changed tack and used its political muscle to block it. The reasons for this were never publicly explained, and by the autumn of 2009 the British government had changed its mind again and was actively backing the Commission in drawing up a 'road map' of proposed new instruments designed to ensure the protection of defendants.[186]

By then, however, the Treaty of Lisbon had introduced a legal basis under Article 82(2) TFEU, which confers on the Union the competence to create legal measures (in form of directives) designed to harmonize the criminal procedure of the Member States 'to the extent necessary to facilitate mutual recognition of judgments and judicial decisions and police and judicial co-operation in criminal matters having a cross-border dimension'. Thus, the provision is understood to mean that any harmonization must follow from the need for judicial cooperation. At first sight, this might seem strange: one would have thought that, in the 'area of freedom, security and justice' which Article 67(1) proclaims, ensuring decent treatment for participants in criminal proceedings would be a valid objective in itself, irrespective of its impact (if any) on mutual recognition. However, Article 67(1) must be interpreted in light of the more specific provisions in the later Articles.

The measures to improve the position of defendants were finally adopted on the basis of Article 82(2) and the aforementioned road map on defence rights set out a legislative programme containing six measures.[187] To date, directives have been adopted relating

181 COM (2023) 424, 12 July 2023.

182 OJ [2011] L101/1.

183 *R v L (Children's Commissioner for England and Equality and Human Rights Commission intervening)* [2013] EWCA Crim 991.

184 OJ [2004] L261.

185 COM(2003) 75 final and COM(2004) 328.

186 OJ [2009] C295/1.

187 For a detailed account of the history, and the contents of the Directives adopted to date, see V Mitsilegas, *EU Criminal Law after Lisbon* (Oxford: Hart Publishing, 2018) ch 6.

to translation and interpretation for those who need it,[188] information to be given to suspects about the charges against them and their rights,[189] legal advice to arrested persons,[190] the presumption of innocence,[191] procedural safeguards for vulnerable suspects and defendants,[192] and legal aid.[193] Title (F) in the Roadmap list led to a recommendation on procedural rights of suspects and accused persons subject to pre-trial detention and on material detention conditions in late 2022.[194]

It should be noted that the 'defence rights' Directives (and indeed the Victim's Rights Directive[195]) apply not only to criminal proceedings involving persons from two different Member States, but also to criminal proceedings in a Member State which are purely national. As with other EU legislation, Member States which fail to implement these Directives properly are potentially exposed to infringement proceedings brought by the Commission; but there is also another possible mechanism for enforcement. Defendants in criminal proceedings are, it should be remembered, on the receiving end of legal proceedings brought against them by the Member State concerned—which creates the possibility of 'direct effect'. In other words, if the State in question has failed to implement the Directive, they can assert the right conferred on them in the proceedings the State has brought against them.[196]

8 Conclusion

The chapter began by pointing out that criminal law and criminal procedure are fundamental aspects of national sovereignty, traditionally confined to the territory and citizens of a particular State. The resulting legal diversity of criminal justice systems has, however, made judicial cooperation ever more complicated, especially in view of the increase in cross-border criminality in the EU.

In the first stages of European integration, even if the Treaties did not provide for corresponding competences, Community legislation and policies relating to the internal market together with the case law of the CJEU did have an impact on national criminal justice systems. Subsequently, under Maastricht and Amsterdam, the EU acquired a primarily coordinating role in this area, based on a horizontal approach to counterbalance the security shortcomings resulting from the abolition of internal border controls of persons within the Schengen area. With the Lisbon Treaty, its competences have been extended, including the possibility of harmonization of laws and vertical cooperation, which is now increasingly justified by the Treaty objective of creating an area of freedom, security, and justice.

Thus, criminal law is no longer the exclusive domain of nation-States, and EU criminal law is not an isolated entity, but exists in interaction with national law. The present situation might therefore best be described as saying that we are witnessing a shift away from traditional forms of cooperation between national criminal justice *systems* towards new transnational and supranational arrangements under a European criminal *policy*.

Because EU criminal law is currently in a state of flux, its future shape is difficult to foresee. However, it is thought that two predictions can be safely made. The first is that as long as free movement prevails within the EU, a body of EU criminal law will be necessary to deal with the unwanted consequences, and that in future there will probably be more of it, not less. The second is that there will continue to be disagreement as to whether the 'horizontal' or the 'vertical' approach should be followed.

[188] Directive 2010/64 (OJ [2010] L280/1).
[189] Directive 2012/13 (OJ [2012] L142/1).
[190] Directive 2013/48 (OJ [2013] L294/1).
[191] Directive 2016/343 (OJ [2016] L65/1).
[192] Directive 2016/800 (OJ [2016] L132/1).
[193] Directive 2016/1919 (OJ [2016] L297/1).
[194] OJ [2022] L86/44.
[195] OJ [2012] L315.
[196] eg see Case C-242/22 PPU *TL*, EU:C:2022:611, 175. On 'direct effect' generally, see chapter 6.

From the perspective of the Member States, which tend to resent EU interference with their criminal justice systems, the horizontal approach is usually preferred. However, whether criminal justice is viewed from a 'crime control' perspective or a 'human rights' perspective, there is surely much to be said in favour of the vertical approach as with the case of the EPPO. As the EU grows, so the task of coordinating the activities of the national criminal justice systems of the Member States gets harder. It is neither possible nor necessary to unify the criminal justice systems of Europe, but this chapter has aimed to demonstrate that approximation coupled with certain uniform rules is inevitable when prosecuting cross-border crimes. This is partly to eliminate worrying national shortcomings, but more importantly to ensure that the existing European toolkit functions in a more coherent and comparable—and therefore fairer—manner.

Further reading

D Chalmers, G Davies, and G Monti, *European Union Law* (3rd edn, Cambridge: Cambridge University Press, 2014) ch 14

R Colson and S Field, *EU Criminal Justice and the Challenges of Diversity: Legal Cultures in the Area of Freedom, Security and Justice* (Cambridge: Cambridge University Press, 2016)

A Csúri, *Sense and Admissibility*: Cross-Border EPPO Investigations and Evidence. *Cambridge Yearbook of European Legal Studies* (2026) doi:10.1017/cel.2026.10029

G Davies and H Carrapico (eds), *UK–EU Police and Judicial Cooperation Post-Brexit*, (1st edn, Oxford: Hart Publishing 2025).

R Hanratty, 'The Effect of Brexit on the Fight against Crime' (2018) 4 *Archbold Review* 4–9

H-H Herrnfeld, D Brodowski, and C Burchard, *The European Public Prosecutor's Office: Article-by-Article Commentary* (2nd edn, Baden-Baden: Nomos 2026)

A Klip, *European Criminal Law: An Integrative Approach* (4th edn, Cambridge: Intersentia, 2021)

R Kostoris (ed), *Handbook of European Criminal Procedure* (Berlin: Springer, 2018)

S Miettinen, *Criminal Law and Policy in the European Union* (Abingdon: Routledge, 2013)

V Mitsilegas, *EU Criminal Law* (2nd edn, Oxford: Hart Publishing, 2022)

S Peers, *EU Justice and Home Affairs Law* (5th edn, Oxford: Oxford University Press, 2023)

J Pradel, G Corstens, and G Vermeulen, *Droit pénal européen* (3rd edn, Paris: Dalloz, 2009)

Chapter acknowledgements

The latest version of the chapter, like the previous edition, is the work of András Csúri. He dedicates it to the memory of his mother, Erzsébet Szőkefalvi-Nagy.

John R Spencer read and commented on the chapter, and its plan owes much to the scheme he devised for the first two editions of this volume, of which he was the sole author, and the chapter in the third edition, which we elaborated together.

25

Immigration and asylum

Steve Peers

1 Introduction

Many non-EU citizens visit the EU for a short period, and then leave, yet others stay for longer, sometimes indefinitely. Most enter legally, but some enter without authorization. Some come to join family, to work, or to study, while others enter unwillingly, because they have been trafficked into the territory or are forced by circumstances to leave their country of origin. The EU's involvement in this field of law must not only address these diverse aspects of migration in a coherent way, but also has to manage two distinct but related conflicts: the balance between EU competence in this field and national sovereignty, and the tension between immigration control and the protection of human rights. These two conflicts overlap to the extent that national interior ministries often wish to focus on the perceived security risks of migration, while some EU institutions (at least until recently) would place a greater priority on human rights protection. The tension between these overlapping conflicts came to a head in the EU's 'refugee crisis' in 2015, which—after an initial period of diverse responses—pushed the EU towards greater harmonization in this field, entailing reduction in the level of protection for asylum seekers and irregular migrants.

2 The legal framework

The basic legal framework for the adoption of EU rules on immigration and asylum has changed a number of times, but has moved steadily towards enhanced EU competence and a greater role for the supranational 'Community method'.[1]

[1] See S Peers, 'EU Justice and Home Affairs Law (Non-Civil)' in P Craig and G de Búrca (eds), *The Evolution of EU Law* (2nd edn, Oxford: Oxford University Press, 2010) 269.

2.1 Prior to the Treaty of Amsterdam

Initially, the legal framework in this area was an 'informal intergovernmental' system,[2] during which Member States either agreed Conventions among themselves or adopted non-binding acts such as resolutions or recommendations.[3] Next, following the entry into force of the original Treaty on European Union (TEU, often referred to as the Maastricht Treaty), it became primarily a 'formal intergovernmental system',[4] which set out an official legal framework for the adoption of measures by the Council—either Conventions (which would still need to be ratified by Member States), Joint Positions, or Joint Actions.[5] The legal status of the latter two measures was not defined, and in practice no Conventions on immigration and asylum issues were adopted during this period. Instead, due to disagreements about the intensity and substance of the EU's role in this field, 'soft law' measures such as recommendations and resolutions were still widely used.[6]

The intergovernmental nature of the EU's involvement in these issues during this period was established in particular by the requirement that the Council act unanimously in all cases. Furthermore, there was no obligation even to consult the European Parliament, the Commission had to share its power to make proposals with Member States, and the jurisdiction of the Court of Justice was excluded (except as an option, as regards Conventions).[7] However, when drawing up the original TEU, the Member States favouring a purely intergovernmental approach to these issues compromised with those favouring a more supranational approach, and allowed measures concerning a uniform visa format, and a list of the countries whose nationals would need a visa to enter the EU, to be adopted by means of the 'Community' process.[8] Perhaps inevitably, there were disputes about the dividing line between the supranational and intergovernmental rules.[9]

Moreover, the fairly limited output of the EU in this field during this period stood in contrast to the successful development of a legal framework outside the EU system per se. This was the Schengen Convention, signed by a large group of Member States, which aimed to abolish internal border controls between all of the signatory States and, as a corollary, to strengthen their common external border controls. The signatory States also agreed to adopt a fully common visa policy, and to establish 'flanking' rules on the allocation of asylum applications (which were superseded by the Dublin Convention), irregular migration, and judicial and police cooperation, including the creation of a database known as the Schengen Information System.[10] The Schengen Convention was signed in

[2] On the concept of intergovernmentalism, see further chapter 2.

[3] See eg the Dublin Convention allocating responsibility for asylum requests (OJ [1997] C254/1).

[4] See Art K to K.9 of the original TEU.

[5] For examples in the immigration and asylum field, see the Joint Position on the definition of refugee (OJ [1996] L63/2) and the Joint Action on airport transit visas (OJ [1996] L63/8).

[6] See eg the Resolution on the admission of labour migrants (OJ [1996] C274/3).

[7] For analysis, see P Müller-Graff, 'The Legal Bases of the Third Pillar and Its Position in the Framework of the Union Treaty' (1994) 29 *Common Market Law Review* 493.

[8] Art 100c EC, which provided for a Commission monopoly on making proposals, consultation of the European Parliament, and a qualified majority vote in the Council.

[9] One of these cases reached the Court of Justice: Case C-170/96 *Commission v Council* [1998] ECR I-2763, in which the Court ruled that the Joint Action on airport transit visas (n 5) did not 'encroach' upon the Community's power to adopt rules on which non-EU countries' nationals would need a visa to enter the EU.

[10] See D O'Keeffe, 'The Schengen Convention: A Suitable Model for European Integration?' (1991) 11 *Yearbook of European Law* 185 and J Schutte, 'Schengen: Its Meaning for the Free Movement of Persons in Europe' (1991) 28 *Common Market Law Review* 549.

1990 and was applied from March 1995; it was not adopted as an EU measure because the UK objected in principle to the abolition of internal border checks between Member States.[11]

2.2 The Treaty of Amsterdam

In order to increase the effectiveness of the EU's action in this area, the Treaty of Amsterdam (in force 1 May 1999) applied the usual 'Community method' to the adoption of immigration and asylum measures (along with civil law measures), subject to a five-year transitional period (ending 1 May 2004) and subject to certain important exceptions.[12] During this transitional period, for most matters the Commission had to share its monopoly of initiative with Member States, the Council still voted unanimously, and the European Parliament was only consulted. After the end of the transitional period, the Commission obtained its usual monopoly over proposing legislation and, for most matters, the Council voted by a qualified majority (QMV) and the European Parliament had powers of co-decision over legislation.[13] However, an important limitation on the role of the Court of Justice in this field (only final courts of the Member States could send references for a preliminary ruling to the Court) was retained even after the transitional period.[14] Although the Council had the power, acting unanimously, to change the rules on the jurisdiction of the Court of Justice, it did not do so.[15]

In light of the reluctance of the UK, Ireland, and Denmark to approve the application of the Community method (even with these delays and exceptions) to this area, those Member States were granted an opt-out. The UK and Ireland could choose, within three months of a proposal being tabled, whether they wished to participate in negotiations. If they did not opt in, discussions continued without them. If they opted in but blocked the adoption of the measure concerned, it could be adopted without them. Even if they opted out of discussions initially, they could decide to opt in after a measure was adopted. In practice, the UK and Ireland initially opted in to most measures concerning asylum and irregular migration, but few measures concerning legal migration or visas and border controls. Subsequently, after the end of the transitional period, they opted out of most proposals concerning asylum and irregular migration as well. After Brexit, the UK is no longer bound by those EU laws in this area which it had opted in to. British citizens are instead subject to the EU laws discussed in this chapter as *non-EU citizens*. Under the Brexit withdrawal agreement, UK citizens who moved to the EU before the end of that agreement's transition period (31 December 2020) are covered by the special rules in that agreement (see further chapter 27). As for Denmark, it could not participate at all in EU measures in this area, except to the extent that they were connected to ('built upon') the Schengen Convention.

[11] Moreover, the Court of Justice ruled that there was no legal requirement under EC law to abolish such checks, in the absence of flanking measures such as those set out in the Schengen Convention: Case C-378/97 *Wijsenbeek* [1999] ECR I-6207.

[12] Arts 61–69 EC. For analysis, see D O'Keeffe, 'Can the Leopard Change Its Spots? Visas, Immigration and Asylum following Amsterdam' in D O'Keeffe and P Twomey (eds), *Legal Issues of the Amsterdam Treaty* (Oxford: Hart Publishing, 1999).

[13] The key exception was legal migration, where the Council still voted unanimously after consulting the European Parliament. As regards visas, border controls, and irregular migration, see Art 67(2)–(4) EC and the Council Decision changing the decision-making rules (OJ [2004] L396/45), applicable from 1 January 2005. On this transition, see S Peers, 'Transforming Decision-Making on EC Immigration and Asylum Law' (2005) 30 *European Law Review* 283. As regards asylum, see Art 67(5) EC, inserted by the Treaty of Nice. On the interpretation of this provision, see Case C-133/06 *European Parliament v Council* [2008] ECR I-3189.

[14] Art 68 EC.

[15] Art 67(2) EC, second indent.

On this point, the Treaty of Amsterdam integrated the Schengen Convention and measures based upon it (referred to as the 'Schengen *acquis*') into the EU legal order, without the participation of the UK and Ireland. Those two Member States had the option to participate in some or all of the Schengen *acquis*, subject to the approval of the Council, acting unanimously. In practice the Council approved the participation of both the UK and Ireland in the Schengen measures relating to irregular migration, criminal law, and police cooperation,[16] but those Member States were not interested in participating in the 'core' of Schengen, that is, the abolition of internal border controls and the connected common policies on visas and external borders. As a consequence, the Court of Justice ruled that those Member States could not participate in any EU acts 'building upon' those core Schengen rules that they opted out of, notably the creation of an EU borders agency (known in practice as Frontex), the rules on fingerprinting EU citizens who apply for a passport, and full police access to the EU's Visa Information System (on which, see more in section 3.3).[17]

2.3 **The Treaty of Lisbon**

The Treaty of Lisbon completed the process of applying the usual 'Community' method to this area. The co-decision process, including QMV, has since applied to the issue of legal migration, as well as to the issue of visa lists and visa formats (previously the European Parliament was only consulted on these visa issues). This resulted in agreement upon a number of legal migration proposals that had previously been vetoed by one or more Member State(s).[18] Furthermore, the Treaty also revised (and generally extended) the EU's competence on immigration and asylum issues (see the separate sections later in the chapter). Moreover, the Court of Justice has since had its full jurisdiction in this area, which led to an ongoing increase in the number of immigration and asylum cases referred to the Court.[19]

3 Visas and border control

3.1 **Overview and legal framework**

The EU has been more active in the fields of visas and border controls than in any other area of immigration and asylum law, due to the Schengen *acquis* in this area, integrated into EU law in 1999, and the measures which have built upon the Schengen *acquis* since. The key elements of the Schengen system are: the abolition of internal border controls (ie controls at the land, sea, and air borders between States participating in the Schengen rules); the strengthening of external borders (ie borders between Schengen States and non-Schengen States); freedom to travel between the Schengen States for any persons who are legally residing in or visiting those States; and a common short-term visa policy.

[16] OJ [2000] L131/43 (UK) and OJ [2002] L64/20 (Ireland).

[17] See Case C-77/05 *UK v Council* [2007] ECR I-11459; Case C-137/05 *UK v Council* [2007] ECR I-11593; and Case C-482/08 *UK v Council* [2010] ECR I-10413. On the other hand, the Court accepted the UK's informal association with Schengen measures while it was a Member State: Case C-44/14 *Spain v EP and Council*, EU:C:2015:554.

[18] See S Peers, 'Mission Accomplished? EU Justice and Home Affairs Law after the Treaty of Lisbon' (2011) 48 *Common Market Law Review* 661, 673. As an exception, Art 77(3) TFEU still requires unanimity for rules on documents such as passports and identity cards: see Case C-61/22 *RL v Landeshauptstadt Wiesbaden*, EU:C:2024:251.

[19] Ibid, 682–683.

The detailed rules on these issues were initially set out in the relevant provisions of the Schengen Convention and the measures implementing it, but these measures have mostly been replaced by a number of EU regulations, in particular those setting out a 'Schengen borders code', establishing an EU agency to assist with border controls (known as Frontex), creating a second-generation version of the previous Schengen Information System (SIS II), listing the third (ie non-EU) countries whose nationals do (or do not) need a visa to enter the EU, setting out a 'visa code' on the process of obtaining short-term visas valid across the Schengen States, and establishing a Visa Information System (VIS) concerning (initially) short-term visa applicants. However, the rules on freedom to travel still appear in the Schengen Convention.[20] Since 2015, these rules have been revised to apply more stringent and harmonized controls as a response to the perceived 'refugee crisis'.

3.2 **Border controls**

First of all, the Schengen borders code sets out the key rules on the control and surveillance of external borders, as well as the basic obligation to abolish internal border controls between the Member States, subject to limited exceptions.[21] Following the so-called 'Arab Spring' of 2011, concerns about the ability of some Schengen States to play their role controlling the external borders led to an amendment of the borders code to set out a process by which a group of Member States could collectively reintroduce internal border controls for some time due to concerns about (in)effective control of the external border by another Member State.[22] This law was later invoked as a response to the refugee crisis, allowing a number of Member States to continue internal border checks which they had imposed unilaterally as a result of the crisis for a further period of six months.[23] However, the CJEU ruled that once that collective reintroduction of internal border controls has expired, Member States are still constrained as to whether they can continue internal border checks indefinitely, unless there are new reasons justifying the reintroduction of those checks.[24] Also, as a response to parallel concerns about terrorist attacks, the EU decided to amend the borders code to provide for additional checks on EU and non-EU citizens at the external borders.[25] A more recent amendment provides for longer periods of reintroducing internal border controls, a more harmonized response to future pandemics, and fast-track returns of irregular migrants at internal borders (unless the Dublin rules on asylum applications apply).[26]

The application of the borders code is complemented by the Schengen Information System, originally established by the Schengen Convention, and replaced by SIS II from April 2013.[27] This provides for a system of issuing alerts for refusal of entry of third-country

[20] Arts 19–22 Schengen Convention (OJ [2000] L239).

[21] Regulation 562/2006 (OJ [2006] L105/1), later codified after many amendments: Regulation 2016/399 (OJ [2016] L77/1). Member States are obliged to let people cross the border when the relevant criteria are satisfied: Case C-575/12 *Air Baltic*, EU:C:2014:2155. On the extent of Member States' remaining power to police the internal borders without infringing the obligation to abolish internal border controls, compare Joined Cases C-188/10 and C-189/10 *Melki and Abdeli* [2010] ECR I-5667 with Case C-278/12 PPU *Adil*, EU:C:2012:508.

[22] Regulation 1051/2013 (OJ [2013] L295/1).

[23] Council Recommendation (OJ [2016] L151/8).

[24] Joined Cases C-368/20 and C-369/20 *NW*, EU:C:2022:298.

[25] Regulation 2017/458 amending Schengen Borders Code (OJ [2017] L74/1).

[26] Regulation 2024/1717 (OJ [2024] L 20.6.24).

[27] Regulation 1987/2006 (OJ [2006] L381/4), replaced by Regulation 2018/1861 ([2018] L312/14) from March 2023 (OJ [2023] L27/29). The parallel Regulation 2018/1860 regulates the use of the Schengen Information System for returns (OJ [2018] L312/1). On the uses of this system for criminal law and policing purposes, see chapter 24.

nationals who should in principle be refused entry into the entire Schengen area.[28] The EU has also legislated to set up two further systems: (a) an 'entry-exit system', applicable since October 2025, which will record the crossing of all third-country nationals across the external Schengen borders in order to determine which of them has overstayed their permitted time period to visit;[29] and (b) an electronic travel authorization system, which will require all non-EU citizens who do not need visas to apply in advance before their visit to the EU.[30]

Furthermore, the Frontex agency has a key role supplementing the Member States' border control authorities. Originally established in 2004, its budget has been hugely increased and its powers have been enlarged so that it can play a larger role, for instance coordinating return flights and sending rapid action teams to assist Member States facing particular difficulties controlling their share of the external border.[31] There are many allegations that Frontex participates in illegal actions by Member States in breach of its obligations to protect human rights, and the EU courts have confirmed on appeal that a migrant can sue Frontex for damages if such allegations can be proven.[32]

3.3 **Visa policy**

As for the common visa policy, the original visa list Regulation was adopted in 1995, but only partially harmonized the list of countries whose nationals needed visas to enter the EU for a visit of up to three months.[33] After the integration of the Schengen *acquis* (which had more fully harmonized visa policy) within the EU legal order in 1999, the Council adopted a Regulation in 2001 which completely harmonized the lists of the countries whose nationals did (or did not) require a visa to cross the external borders.[34] This legislation has been amended a number of times.[35]

The criteria to waive or impose a visa requirement are essentially political, and take into account external relations considerations (including human rights), security risks, economic benefit, and the prospect of irregular migration. Within Europe, the EU legislation permits visa-free entry for nationals of the Western Balkan countries, some neighbouring countries like Ukraine, and European micro-States, but requires visas for nationals of Russia, some other ex-Soviet countries, and Turkey. But as a compromise, the visa regime for some other nearby countries has been softened, by means of visa facilitation treaties which simplify the process and reduce the cost of obtaining Schengen visas.[36] However,

[28] There are further rules on entry bans in the EU's Returns Directive (see section 4.2). EU free movement law takes priority over the SIS, so entry bans cannot be issued or enforced as regards third-country national family members of EU citizens unless the conditions in the free movement rules for refusing entry to such persons are satisfied: see Case C-503/03 *Commission v Spain* [2006] ECR I-1097.

[29] Regulation 2017/2226 (OJ [2017] L327/20). The system is being phased in over six months (Regulation 2025/1534 (OJ [2025] L 23.7.2025), starting from 12 October 2025 (a date set by the Commission: OJ [2025] L 30.7.2025).

[30] Regulation 2018/1240 (OJ [2018] L236/1), not yet applicable in practice at the time of writing.

[31] Currently Regulation 2019/1896 (OJ [2019] L295/1). Also on this issue, there was a dispute about the legality of the rules governing Frontex coordination of Member States' border patrols in the Mediterranean; see further chapter 5. The rules on this issue are now set out in Regulation 656/2014 (OJ [2014] L189/93).

[32] Cases C-679/23 P *WS and others v Frontex*, EU:C:2025:976 and C-136/24 P *Hamoudi v Frontex*, EU:C:2025:977.

[33] Regulation 2317/95 (OJ [1995] L234/1).

[34] Regulation 539/2001 (OJ [2001] L82/1).

[35] Codified in Regulation 2018/1806 (OJ [2018] L303/39), as itself subsequently amended, including exempting UK citizens from short-term visas after Brexit: Regulation 2019/592 (OJ [2019] L103 I/4).

[36] Such treaties are in force with Armenia, Cape Verde, Belarus, and Azerbaijan. Most countries in the Western Balkans, along with Georgia, Ukraine, and Moldova, also benefited from such treaties for several years before the EU waived the visa requirement for them.

the visa facilitation treaties with Belarus and Russia have been (respectively) partially and wholly suspended due to worsening relations with the former, and the latter's invasion of Ukraine.[37]

Due to some misgivings about more recent visa waivers, since 2014 there is a visa suspension mechanism, allowing for the fast-track possibility to reimpose visa requirements in the event of a large influx of people, insufficient cooperation on readmission (in the EU's view), or certain other grounds.[38] In the Asia/Pacific region, the EU legislation requires visas for nationals of all countries except wealthy States like Japan, Australia, Korea, Taiwan, the Emirates, and New Zealand. As for the Americas, most countries are exempt from a visa requirement (Ecuador and Bolivia are exceptions). Finally, nationals of most African and Caribbean countries require visas, with the exception of some small tropical islands such as Mauritius and Bermuda. Due to concerns about its 'golden passport' scheme, the EU has suspended the visa waiver treaty with the Pacific state of Vanuatu.[39]

The conditions for obtaining a visa are now set out in the EU's visa code, which also includes provisions on the right to appeal a refusal of a visa.[40] The visa application system is now bolstered by the VIS, which became operational in 2011 and was then rolled out worldwide.[41]

On the whole, the EU has gradually stepped up the degree of harmonization of visa and border control policies and increased control of entry to EU territory, in particular by means of technical measures (the SIS and VIS) and the enhanced operational role of Frontex. On the other hand, however, the EU visa regime is becoming gradually more liberal, in particular with the waiver of visa requirements for Western Balkan countries in 2009 and 2010 (adding Kosovo in 2024) and some eastern neighbours (Moldova, Georgia, Ukraine) between 2014 and 2017. EU visa policy increasingly interacts with the EU's external policies and has even come to resemble the EU's hierarchy of trade preferences (which either give additional trade preferences or remove those preferences for what the EU considers 'good behaviour' (such as environmental measures) or 'bad behaviour' (such as forced labour)). However, the EU usually insists on a quid pro quo for the waiver of visa requirements or the conclusion of visa facilitation treaties, in the form of readmission treaties (see further section 4) and further alignment with EU migration control policy. As regards human rights, EU legislation in this field sets out general rules on this issue, but does not always specify how such rights are to be protected in the context of visas and border controls.[42]

[37] OJ [2021] L396/58 and OJ [2022] L234I/1 respectively.

[38] It was recently amended to expand its use: Regulation 2025/2441 (OJ [2025] L 10.12.2025).

[39] [2022] OJ L69/105.

[40] Regulation 810/2009 (OJ [2009] L243/1), as amended, inter alia to pressure non-EU countries to readmit their citizens: Regulation 2019/1155 (OJ [2019] L188/55). In practice, restrictions have been imposed upon two countries (The Gambia and Ethiopia) on these grounds: Council Implementing Decisions 2021/1781 and 2024/1341 (OJ [2021] L360/124 and OJ [2024] L 14.5.2024). As with the Schengen borders code, Member States are obliged to issue a visa when the relevant criteria are satisfied: Case C-84/12 *Koushkaki*, EU:C:2013:862. Appeals against refusal of a visa must be subject to review by a court (Case C-403/16 *El Hassani*, EU:C:2017:960), although the intensity of judicial review is limited (Joined Cases C-225/19 and C-226/19 *RNNS and KA*, EU:C:2020:951).

[41] Regulation 767/2008 (OJ [2008] L218/60). There will be major amendments to the system in future, although the relevant legislation is not applied yet: Regulation 2021/1134 (OJ [2021] L248/11).

[42] See Art 4 of the borders code (Regulation 2016/399 (OJ [2016] L77/1)).

4 Irregular migration

4.1 Overview and legal framework

Irregular migration (often referred to as 'illegal' migration) is a subject of great public concern, and 'illegal immigrants' are often demonized as if they were a single category of persons. However, the concept of irregular migration covers a wide variety of situations. Some migrants enter the territory without authorization, either clandestinely without showing themselves to border guards (eg on small boats) or via official crossing points, but with the use of false or stolen passports or other travel documents. Some enter the territory entirely legally, but then overstay the period of their legal short stay without authorization. Some are even legal residents whose stay on the territory after their residence permit or long-stay visa is withdrawn or not renewed, due to a criminal conviction or alleged security threat, or because the reason they were permitted to enter is no longer valid (eg they were admitted as a student but have finished their studies). Sometimes a legal resident has a right to, or at least the possibility of, the renewal of his or her residence permit, but that permit expires before it is renewed—either because the person concerned did not apply for a renewal in time, or because, even though he or she applied for a renewal by the deadline, the authorities did not process it in time. In these cases, it is likely that the 'illegal' status of the person concerned will sooner or later be remedied retroactively. Finally, some irregular migrants applied for asylum, but their application was rejected definitively, or at first instance—but in the latter case, they may have a right to stay pending appeal.

While some irregular migrants may have the intention of committing serious crimes or even threatening Member States' national security, the large majority are seeking a better life and/or protection from persecution or serious threats in their country of origin. If irregular migrants apply for asylum, their legal status changes (see section 6), although they may again be classified as irregular migrants if their application is rejected. Under some circumstances, according to the Geneva Convention on refugee status, an asylum application can excuse a prior breach of immigration law. So as with border controls, there are 'mixed flows' of irregular migrants, some of whom argue that they need international protection and some who do not claim it. Some of the former category will be successful in their claims, but others will not. Even among the latter group, some are allowed to stay by Member States, at least for a limited period, on humanitarian grounds (eg they are too ill to travel), or because it is impossible to remove them for practical reasons (eg their State of origin cannot accept their return because their nationality cannot be sufficiently proved), or for other reasons. While in principle those irregular migrants needing protection must be treated differently from those who do not, it is impossible to know in advance which irregular migrants need protection and which do not. Indeed, assessing whether a protection claim is well founded is a separate and complex issue of its own. The status of the persons concerned can change, since an irregular migrant might apply for asylum and a rejected asylum seeker will be considered to be an irregular migrant.

What has the EU done to address these issues? As for the legal framework, Article 67(2) TFEU provides that the EU 'shall frame a common policy on asylum, immigration and external border control, based on solidarity between Member States, which is fair towards third-country nationals'. More specifically, Article 79(1) TFEU sets out the EU's objectives as regards immigration:

> The Union shall develop a common immigration policy aimed at ensuring, at all stages, the efficient management of migration flows, fair treatment of third-country nationals residing legally in Member States, and the prevention of, and enhanced measures to combat, illegal immigration and trafficking in human beings.

While Article 79(1) only requires the EU to be 'fair' toward *legally resident* third-country nationals, Article 67(2) obliges the EU to be 'fair' to third-country nationals in general, not just those who are legally resident.

Article 79(2) TFEU sets out the EU's powers to regulate migration for the 'purposes' set out in Article 79(1). The EU can adopt legislation on:

(c) illegal immigration and unauthorised residence, including removal and repatriation of persons residing without authorisation;

(d) combating trafficking in persons, in particular women and children.

Also, Article 79(3) TFEU states that the EU 'may conclude agreements with third countries for the readmission to their countries of origin or provenance of third-country nationals who do not or who no longer fulfil the conditions for entry, presence or residence in the territory of one of the Member States'.

4.2 **Adopted legislation**

To achieve these objectives, the EU has adopted a number of measures concerning the prevention of irregular migration, the treatment of irregular migrants on the territory, and the expulsion of irregular migrants from the territory. The first category of acts applies in addition to the visa and border control measures discussed previously, and includes rules on carrier sanctions (ie penalizing private companies that transport irregular migrants),[43] the transfer of passenger data,[44] prohibiting and criminalizing the facilitation of irregular authorization and residence,[45] trafficking in persons,[46] and the posting of immigration liaison officers to non-EU countries.[47] The second category of measures comprises rules sanctioning the employers of irregular migrants and rules permitting the stay of victims of trafficking—but on the condition that they help to facilitate criminal prosecutions against their traffickers, and only as long as they are useful for those prosecutions.[48] The third category of measures includes the most important EU measure on irregular migration, the so-called Returns Directive, which regulates the procedure for expelling irregular migrants, including rules on detention, entry bans, and procedural rights.[49] It also includes legislation on the mutual recognition of expulsion orders,[50] transit for expulsion,[51] joint expulsion flights,[52] and travel documents for expulsion,[53] as well as readmission treaties with a number of non-EU countries.[54]

As the growing corpus of legislation indicates, the EU has been gradually harmonizing national law as regards control of irregular migration, and it has continually been increasing the degree of control of irregular entry. But, as with the EU's visas and borders

[43] Art 26 Schengen Convention (OJ [2000] L239), as supplemented by Directive 2001/51 (OJ [2001] L187/45).

[44] Directive 2004/82 (OJ [2004] L261/24), now replaced by Regulations 2025/12 and 13, (OJ [2025] L 8.1.2025).

[45] Directive 2002/90 (OJ [2002] L328/17) and Framework Decision 2002/946 (OJ [2002] L328/1). The Commission has proposed to replace these laws: COM (2023) 754, 28 November 2023.

[46] Directive 2011/36 (OJ [2011] L101/1), as amended by Directive 2024/1712 (OJ [2024] L 24.6.2024).

[47] Regulation 2019/1240 (OJ [2019] L198/88).

[48] Directive 2004/81 (OJ [2004] L261/19).

[49] Directive 2008/115 (OJ [2008] L348/98). Entry bans are entered into the SIS (see section 3).

[50] Directive 2001/40 (OJ [2001] L149/34).

[51] Directive 2003/110 (OJ [2003] L321/26).

[52] OJ [2004] L261/28. See also the role of Frontex in joint expulsions (section 3).

[53] Regulation 2016/1953 (OJ [2016] L311/13).

[54] As of 1 October 2025, there were EU readmission treaties in force with Serbia, Bosnia, North Macedonia, Montenegro, Albania, Moldova, Russia, Ukraine, Georgia, Pakistan, Sri Lanka, Hong Kong, Macao, Turkey, Cape Verde, Armenia, and Azerbaijan.

legislation, there are countervailing tendencies towards human rights protection, in this case due to the role of the Court of Justice—as case study 25.1 demonstrates. Yet the perceived liberalism of these judgments has led in turn to proposals to reduce the rights of irregular migrants by replacing the Returns Directive by a Regulation, inter alia to increase the possibility of detaining irregular migrants and creating a new possibility of removing them to countries other than their country of origin ('return hubs').[55]

Case study 25.1: Detention of irregular migrants

While States have increasingly resorted to detention of irregular migrants as a means of deterring them and ensuring they do not abscond during the expulsion procedure, such measures have been criticized on the grounds that the persons concerned have usually not committed any crime (except perhaps the criminal offence of irregular entry, which is only another mechanism of migration control), and that the persons concerned (including children) are sometimes detained for very lengthy periods in unpleasant conditions.[56]

This issue is addressed by international human rights law. Most notably, Article 5(1)(f) of the European Convention on Human Rights (ECHR) permits States to detain a migrant after a 'lawful arrest or detention . . . to prevent his [or her] effecting an unauthorized entry into the country or of a person against whom action is being taken with a view to deportation'. According to the case law of the ECtHR, detention can be justified as long as expulsion proceedings are underway and are being pursued with 'due diligence'; there is no separate need to show the 'necessity' of this detention, even though such a requirement applies to other grounds of permissible detention set out in Article 5(1) ECHR.[57] This means that detention is no longer justified if the removal is unfeasible, and if an alternative measure to prevent absconding can be applied in practice.[58]

The Returns Directive addresses these detention issues in some detail.[59] According to the Directive, persons subject to return procedures 'may only' be detained 'in order to prepare the return and/or to carry out the removal process, in particular when' there is a risk of absconding or if the person concerned 'avoids or hampers' the return or removal process, 'Unless other sufficient but less coercive measures can be applied effectively in a specific case.' Removal arrangements must be 'in process and executed with due diligence'. Detention can be ordered by administrative or judicial authorities, and must be 'ordered in writing with reasons in fact and law'. If the detention was ordered by administrative authorities, there must be some form of 'speedy' judicial review. There must be regular reviews of detention, either automatically or at the request of the person concerned. The detainee must be released immediately if there is no 'reasonable prospect of removal' or if the conditions for detention no longer exist. Conversely, detention shall be maintained as long as the conditions exist; this shall not exceed six months, except where national law permits a further period of up to one extra year because the removal operation is likely to last longer due to lack of cooperation by the person concerned or delays in obtaining documentation.

The Directive also regulates detention conditions. There must be special facilities 'as a rule' for irregular migrants, and separation from ordinary prisoners if detained in prison. Detainees have the right to contact legal representatives, family members, and consular authorities;

[55] COM(2025) 101, 11 March 2025, not yet agreed by the European Parliament and the Council.

[56] See generally D Wilsher, *Immigration Detention: Law, History, Politics* (Cambridge: Cambridge University Press, 2012).

[57] See in particular *Chahal v UK* (Appl No 22414/93), ECtHR, 1996-V1831.

[58] *Mikolenko v Estonia* (Appl No 10664/05), judgment of 8 October 2009.

[59] Arts 15–18 of the Directive (OJ [2008] L348/98).

there are rules on the situation of vulnerable persons; independent bodies must be able to visit detention facilities; and information must be given to the persons concerned. There are more detailed rules on the detention of minors and families, although Member States may derogate from certain aspects of the rules concerning speedy judicial review and detention conditions in 'exceptional' situations.

The Court of Justice has interpreted the detention rules (among others) on many occasions. First of all, in the *Kadzoev* judgment,[60] on the grounds for detention and time limits on detention, it ruled that the time limits must take into account time served as a detainee before the application of the Directive. Also, a period of detention spent while the removal decision was subject to judicial review had to count towards the time limits. The Court interpreted the concept of a 'reasonable prospect of removal', as meaning that a 'real prospect exists that the removal can be carried out successfully, having regard to' the relevant time limits, and that this prospect 'does not exist where it appears unlikely that the person concerned will be admitted to a third country, having regard to' those time limits. In any event, as the Court pointed out, this ground for releasing the person concerned is irrelevant where the time limits on detention have expired, because in that case they should be released anyway. The Court also ruled that Member States could not keep a person in detention, once the relevant time limit had expired, merely because the detainee does not possess valid documents, their conduct is aggressive, and they have no financial support or accommodation.

Next, in the *El Dridi* judgment,[61] on the grounds for detention, the Court ruled that an irregular migrant could 'only' be detained pursuant to the Directive 'where, in the light of an assessment of each specific situation, the enforcement of the return decision in the form of removal risks being compromised by the conduct of the person concerned'. This judicial rule makes it harder to justify detention than the wording of the Directive, since the Directive does not expressly require an individual assessment of detention decisions, and moreover the Directive states that detention is justified 'in particular' where there is a risk of absconding or avoiding or hampering the removal process. Since the latter two types of behaviour will constitute most or all cases where a third-country national's conduct could compromise the enforcement of a removal decision, the Court of Justice effectively removed the words 'in particular' from the wording of the Directive. This means, for instance, that a person cannot be initially detained merely because their State of origin will probably not cooperate with the removal process.

In the same judgment, the Court ruled that the returns process in the Directive was subject to a principle of 'gradation', that is, the process starts by allowing the person concerned the most liberty (a period for voluntary departure) and ends by allowing the least liberty (detention). Even detention 'is strictly regulated . . . inter alia in order to ensure observance of the fundamental rights of the third-country nationals concerned', in light of the case law of the ECtHR and 'soft law' measures of the Council of Europe. Applying these principles to the facts of the case, the Directive precluded the application of the relevant Italian law, which provided for more possibilities for detention than the Directive (as interpreted by the Court of Justice) permitted. The Court also ruled that the detention provisions of the Directive are directly effective (on the concept of 'direct effect', see chapter 6), which means that anyone detained in breach of the Directive has to be released. Furthermore, the person concerned did not fall within the option for Member States to disapply the Directive to persons who are 'subject to return as a criminal law sanction', because the underlying obligation to leave the territory stemmed from an administrative law decision. Finally, the Court examined the

[60] Case C-357/09 PPU [2009] ECR I-11189. For an overview of the case law on detention and other issues concerning the Directive, see S Peers, 'Irregular Migrants: Can Humane Treatment Be Balanced against Efficient Removal?' (2015) 17 *European Journal of Migration and Law* 289.

[61] Case C-61/11 PPU [2011] ECR I-3015.

relationship between the Directive and national criminal law, holding that while the Directive did not deprive the Member States of all competence to define criminal law offences relating to irregular migration, Member States nevertheless had to adjust their criminal law legislation to EU rules. In this case, that meant that a custodial sentence for an illegal stay following an expulsion decision could not be imposed on the person concerned before the Member State had first tried to remove them pursuant to the returns process.

The relationship between the Returns Directive and national criminal law was further explored in the Court's third judgment, *Achughbabian*, concerning detention following detection of illegal entry or stay.[62] In this case, the Court pointed out that the Directive did not regulate the initial detention of third-country nationals to determine whether their stay was lawful. National officials have a 'brief but reasonable time' to establish the identity and immigration status of the person concerned, before the rules in the Returns Directive, including the detention rules, start to apply. Once the Directive applies, the detention of the irregular migrant cannot be considered to be an expulsion measure in itself, since the person returned remains on the territory of that Member State while they are detained. As in *El Dridi*, the detention of an irregular migrant pursuant to a custodial sentence imposed due to illegal stay was a breach of the Directive, since it delayed the expulsion of the person concerned. Moreover, the Court ruled that Member States could not exclude the application of the Directive to persons who have merely committed the criminal offence of an irregular stay. However, the sentence in question could always be imposed on the person concerned if the returns process was not carried out.

Subsequently, in *Sagor*, the Court clarified these rulings by applying them to cases of home detention, but not fines.[63] Other CJEU rulings have reduced the possibility of detention for irregular migrants in the first place, due to a generous interpretation of when an irregular migrant must be given the option of voluntary departure (and therefore not be detained).[64] Equally, the Court has ruled that the Directive applies to most cases of illegal entry onto the territory, ensuring that the detention rules apply to many more irregular migrants.[65] The Court has also confirmed that immigration detainees should not normally be detained with criminals, and they cannot waive this protection.[66] Finally, it has clarified the extent of judicial review of detention.[67]

The net result of these judgments is that EU law has harmonized the issue of immigration detention fairly extensively: detention of irregular migrants is harder to justify and the time limits for detention are more likely to run out. Detention is also expressly linked to human rights protection. Further, Member States normally cannot impose custodial sentences for illegal stay or entry before they first attempt to enforce a return decision against the person concerned. But there is a catch: the irregular migrants are only protected against serving prison time for the criminal offence of illegal stay or entry if they are returned back to the country they were desperate to leave in the first place. And if they cannot be returned to that country, then they face serving that prison time in addition to any period of immigration detention which they may already have served. Finally, these rules do not apply to the detention of asylum seekers, which is regulated instead by EU asylum legislation.[68]

[62] Case C-329/11 [2011] ECR I-12695.

[63] Case C-430/11 *Sagor*, EU:C:2012:777. However, immigration detention can be justified if the irregular migrant has breached an entry ban: Case C-290/14 *Celaj*, EU:C:2015:640.

[64] Cases C-554/13 *Zh and O*, EU:C:2015:377 and C-146/14 PPU *Mahdi*, EU:C:2014:1320.

[65] Case 47/15 *Affum*, EU:C:2016:408.

[66] Joined Cases C-473/13 and C-514/13 *Bero and Bouzalmate*, EU:C:2014:2095 and Case C-474/13 *Pham*, EU:C:2014:2096.

[67] *Mahdi* (n 64). However, see Case C-383/13 PPU *G and R*, EU:C:2013:533: a violation of the right to be heard does not necessarily mean release from detention.

[68] See section 6.

5 Legal migration

5.1 Overview and legal framework

The EU's involvement in the regulation of legal migration has been more limited than its involvement in other areas of immigration and asylum law. Nevertheless, its role in this area continues to increase, and was facilitated by the switch to QMV in the Council pursuant to the Lisbon Treaty. The key elements of EU policy were set out in the conclusions of the Tampere European Council in 1999, which stated that the EU had to 'ensure fair treatment of third country nationals who reside legally on the territory of its Member States', that 'A more vigorous integration policy should aim at granting them rights and obligations comparable to those of EU citizens', that there was a 'need for approximation' of national law 'on the conditions for admission and residence of third country nationals', and that 'The legal status of third country nationals should be approximated to that of Member States' nationals', with the grant of 'uniform rights . . . as near as possible to those enjoyed by EU citizens' to a person who 'has resided legally in a Member State for a period of time to be determined and who holds a long-term residence permit'.

Following the entry into force of the Lisbon Treaty, these objectives are reflected in Article 79(1) TFEU, which provides, inter alia, that the EU 'shall develop a common immigration policy aimed at ensuring, at all stages . . . fair treatment of third-country nationals residing legally in Member States'. To this end, Article 79(2) TFEU gives the EU power to adopt legislation concerning:

(a) the conditions of entry and residence, and standards on the issue by Member States of long-term visas and residence permits, including those for the purpose of family reunification;

(b) the definition of the rights of third-country nationals residing legally in a Member State, including the conditions governing freedom of movement and of residence in other Member States.

However, these powers are limited by Article 79(5) TFEU, which specifies that Article 79 'shall not affect the right of Member States to determine volumes of admission of third-country nationals coming from third countries to their territory in order to seek work, whether employed or self-employed'. So, while in principle the EU must aim to establish a 'common immigration policy', including rules on the admission, residence, and rights of third-country nationals legally migrating to the EU, Member States remain free to regulate the numbers of economic migrants coming from third countries.

5.2 Legislation

For some time, in fact, EU legislation did not regulate economic migration at all, and a Commission proposal for comprehensive regulation of this issue was rejected by Member States.[69] Instead, the Commission adopted a 'policy plan' on economic migration,[70] which suggested as an alternative a series of piecemeal measures on this issue. This policy was then implemented by means of the adoption of general legislation on the equal treatment and procedural rights of most economic migrants (the Single Permit Directive),[71]

[69] COM(2001) 386, 11 July 2001.

[70] COM(2005) 669, 21 December 2005; and see the earlier Green Paper (COM(2004) 811, 11 January 2005).

[71] Directive 2011/98 (OJ [2011] L343/1).

as well as more detailed legislation concerning the admission of certain categories of economic migrants: the Blue Card Directive on highly-skilled migrants,[72] and Directives on intra-corporate transferees and seasonal workers.[73] The Blue Card Directive was replaced in 2021, with a view to attracting more highly-skilled migrants, and the single permit Directive was replaced in 2024 in order to reduce exploitation of migrant workers.[74]

As for other categories of legal migrants, the EU has also adopted legislation concerning admission to carry out a research project,[75] and the admission of post-secondary students, school pupils, unpaid trainees, and volunteers.[76] These two measures were merged and overhauled in 2016.[77] EU Directives also regulate family reunion with legal migrants,[78] as well as (implementing the Tampere objectives) the acquisition of EU long-term residence status for those who have resided legally for more than five years.[79] Taken as a whole, EU legislation on the initial primary admission of migrants focuses mostly on those who are relatively young, wealthy, and highly skilled, and who are therefore more likely to bring a significant net financial benefit to Member States.

5.3 **Case law**

The two key themes of this chapter—the extent of EU harmonization and the tension between human rights protection and immigration control—are clearly reflected in the case law of the Court of Justice concerning this legislation. In fact, the European Parliament sued to annul certain provisions of the Family Reunion Directive,[80] on the grounds that human rights were not sufficiently protected by the rules in the Directive allowing Member States to insist on a three-year wait for family reunion and to exclude certain categories of children from the usual rules.[81] The Court of Justice rejected this argument, assessing the Directive particularly in light of the jurisprudence of the ECtHR on Article 8 ECHR concerning the right to family life, which generally does not guarantee a right to admission of family members into the host State.[82] As a general rule, the Court said, the Directive sets a higher standard than this case law, as it guarantees a right of admission for spouses and children; but to the extent that it does not guarantee such a right, Member States are still bound by their ECHR obligations to admit family members in special situations (eg to avoid siblings growing up in different States), and must carry out a case-by-case assessment of any applications for family reunion.

Subsequently, in a case concerning a Moroccan national receiving benefits, who had waited nearly 40 years to obtain family reunion with his wife, the Court ruled that despite

72 Directive 2009/50 (OJ [2009] L155/17).

73 Directives 2014/36 on admission of seasonal workers (OJ [2014] L94/375) and 2014/66 on admission of intra-corporate transferees (OJ [2014] L157/1).

74 Directives 2021/1883 (OJ [2021] L382/1) and 2024/1233 (OJ [2024] L 30.4.2024).

75 Directive 2005/71 (OJ [2005] L289/15).

76 Directive 2004/114 (OJ [2004] L375/12). As with the visas and borders codes, students must be admitted if they meet the criteria for admission: Case C-491/13 *Ben Alaya*, EU:C:2014:2187.

77 Directive 2016/801 (OJ [2016] L132/21).

78 Directive 2003/86 (OJ [2003] L251/12).

79 Directive 2003/109 (OJ [2004] L16/44). This Directive was later amended, in order to extend its scope to refugees and persons with subsidiary protection: Directive 2011/51 (OJ [2011] L132/1).

80 Case C-540/03 *European Parliament v Council* [2006] ECR I-5769.

81 In fact, few Member States apply these rules: see the Commission's report on the implementation of the Directive (COM(2008) 610, 8 October 2008).

82 On this case law, see S Peers, 'Family Reunion and Community Law' in N Walker (ed), *Europe's Area of Freedom, Security and Justice* (Oxford: Oxford University Press, 2004) 145–149.

the apparent flexibility which the Directive gives to Member States as regards conditions for admission:[83]

> Since authorisation of family reunification is the general rule, the faculty provided for in Article 7(1)(c) of the Directive [ie the condition relating to social assistance] must be interpreted strictly. Furthermore, the margin for manoeuvre which the Member States are recognised as having must not be used by them in a manner which would undermine the objective of the Directive, which is to promote family reunification, and the effectiveness thereof.

Furthermore, 'the concept of "social assistance system of the Member State" is a concept which has its own independent meaning in European Union law and cannot be defined by reference to concepts of national law', and 'the provisions of the Directive . . . must be interpreted in the light of the fundamental rights and, more particularly, in the light of the right to respect for family life enshrined in both the ECHR and the Charter'. The Court then said that the particular Dutch rule setting a social assistance condition breached the Directive. Member States' discretion to reject admission of the family members of migrants with modest incomes was therefore somewhat curtailed.

This can be compared to some of the Court's judgments concerning the Long-Term Residents' Directive. First of all, in the case of *Kamberaj*,[84] concerning a third-country national from Kosovo applying for housing benefit in Italy, the Court ruled on the interpretation of the equal treatment rules in the Directive. While that Directive gives some effect to the Tampere principle of equal treatment of long-term residents, it conversely leaves a degree of discretion to Member States by specifying that long-term residents are entitled to equal treatment as regards 'social security, social assistance and social protection *as defined by national law*'; moreover, it permits Member States to 'limit equal treatment in respect of social assistance and social protection to core benefits'.[85]

In this case, an Italian regional government had established a different formula for paying housing benefit to third-country nationals as compared to Italian and other EU citizens. Having established that the national rule was discriminatory, the Court said that where the EU legislature 'has made an express reference to national law . . . it is not for the Court to give the terms concerned an autonomous and uniform definition under [EU] law', as this 'means that the [EU] legislature wished to respect the differences between the Member States concerning the meaning and exact scope of the concepts in question'. Nevertheless, this did not mean that Member States are free to 'undermine the effectiveness' of the equal treatment rule. Also, the Directive had to be interpreted in light of the Charter, which 'recognises and respects the right to social and housing assistance so as to ensure a decent existence for all those who lack sufficient resources, in accordance with the rules laid down by European Union law and national laws and practices'.[86]

As for the possibility to limit the application of equal treatment to 'core benefits', the preamble to the Directive specifies that this concept 'covers at least minimum income support, assistance in case of illness, pregnancy, parental assistance and long-term care', and that 'The modalities for granting such benefits should be determined by national law.' The Court pointed out that although this list did not include housing benefit, it was non-exhaustive, and the reference to 'national law' here applied only to the 'modalities' of granting benefits (the level of benefits, the conditions for receiving them, and the procedural aspects) rather than the definition of 'core benefits'. Moreover, the Italian

[83] Case C-578/08 *Chakroun* [2010] ECR I-1839, para 43.
[84] Case C-571/10, EU:C:2012:233.
[85] Art 11(1)(d) and (4), Directive 2003/109.
[86] Art 34(3). As the Court recognized, the Charter, like the Directive, refers back to national law. See further chapter 9.

government had not officially notified any derogation, and any derogations from the general rule of equal treatment had to be interpreted narrowly. So 'core benefits' were those 'which enable individuals to meet their basic needs such as food, accommodation and health'. Finally, if the benefit in question fulfilled the purpose of the right to social and housing assistance set out in the Charter, it could not be denied that it was a 'core benefit'. The Court of Justice then left it to the national court to decide if the benefit in question was indeed a 'core benefit', 'taking into consideration the objective of that benefit, its amount, the conditions subject to which it is awarded and the place of that benefit in the Italian system of social assistance'. Overall, the Court's judgment encouraged the national court to ensure equal treatment as regards housing benefit for long-term residents, and therefore to guarantee that those long-term residents with modest incomes will be able to afford housing.

Secondly, in *Commission v Netherlands*,[87] the Court was asked to rule on whether the Dutch government had breached the Directive by imposing high fees for applications for residence permits made by long-term residents or their family members, including those who exercised the right to move between Member States provided for in the Directive. Even though the Directive did not regulate the issue of application fees—and in fact the Commission's proposal to regulate this issue in its original proposal for the Directive had not been accepted—the Court ruled that Member States' 'discretion' to charge fees 'is not unlimited': Member States cannot 'apply national rules which are liable to jeopardise the achievement of the objectives pursued by a directive and, therefore, deprive it of its effectiveness'. Since the Directive created a right to obtain long-term residence status, and to the rights which stem from that status, if the procedural and substantive conditions set out in the Directive are met, the Dutch government could not charge fees at a level which had 'either the object or the effect of creating an obstacle to ... obtaining ... long-term resident status'. Applying these criteria, the level of fees being charged breached the Directive. The judgment will be of particular benefit to those long-term residents with modest incomes who would have found it harder to afford the high fees being charged for applications. Similarly, the Court has ruled that while Member States can impose integration tests on long-term residents, they are restrained in what fees they can charge.[88]

It can be seen, in light of both the continued adoption of legislation in this field and the dynamic interpretation of that legislation by the Court of Justice,[89] that the EU's role as regards legal immigration is becoming steadily more significant. The Court has a clear tendency to look for uniform interpretations of EU law, or to constrain Member States' activity by means of the principle of effectiveness where the legislation refers to national law or is silent on an issue. In the Court's view, the legislation aims to confer rights on individuals, and exceptions from those rights must be interpreted narrowly. The overriding importance of human rights also has a continuing impact, not only as regards the right to family reunion but also as regards social rights. Taken as a whole, the case law of the Court of Justice has reduced Member States' power to restrict the benefits of EU legislation on legal migration only to relatively well-off migrants.

[87] Case C-508/10, EU:C:2012:243.

[88] Case C-579/13 *P and S*, EU:C:2015:369. See similarly, as regards the family reunion Directive, Case C-153/14 *K and A*, EU:C:2015:453.

[89] See also Case C-15/11 *Sommer*, EU:C:2012:371, where the Court ruled that Member States have only a limited power to restrict third-country students' access to employment pursuant to Directive 2004/114. This judgment particularly benefits those students who need to work to pay for their studies and their other expenses.

6 Asylum

6.1 Overview and legal framework

The definition and status of refugees is set out in the first place in the 1951 UN Convention on the Status of Refugees (referred to as the Geneva Convention in EU law), along with the 1967 Protocol to that Convention.[90] This issue is also affected by other international human rights treaties, in particular the ECHR, which, according to the ECtHR, bans the return of a person to a State in which there is a real risk of suffering torture or other inhuman or degrading treatment as set out in Article 3 ECHR. Article 3 is not subject to derogations or limitations.[91] Since the Geneva Convention does not address all situations in which persons might need some form of protection from return to their country of origin, the concept of 'subsidiary protection' (ie protection outside the scope of that Convention; see its definition of 'refugee', discussed below) has been developed. EU law has focused on refugee and subsidiary protection issues, but there are other forms of protection based on national law and practice, not harmonized by EU law.[92] Member States can establish and retain such non-harmonized forms of protection, provided that there is no confusion with refugee or subsidiary protection status.[93]

Originally, the Treaty of Amsterdam granted the EU powers to set only 'minimum standards' as regards asylum law.[94] However, EU leaders soon decided, at the Tampere European Council of 1999, that the EU should aim to establish a Common European Asylum System (CEAS), starting with a first round of legislation in the 'short term' (which became known as the 'first phase' of the CEAS), with the intention to establish, 'in the longer term', a 'common asylum procedure and a uniform status for those who are granted asylum valid throughout the Union'.

The first phase of legislation to establish the CEAS was adopted between 2003 and 2005, and consisted of a Directive on the qualification for and content of refugee and subsidiary protection status (the Qualification Directive),[95] a Directive on procedures for applying for refugee status (the Procedures Directive),[96] a Directive on reception conditions for asylum seekers (the Reception Directive),[97] and a Regulation setting out rules to allocate responsibility for each asylum seeker to a single Member State (the Dublin Regulation).[98] In order to facilitate the application of the latter Regulation, there was also an earlier Regulation establishing 'Eurodac', a system for storing and comparing asylum seekers' fingerprints.[99] There is also a Directive providing for a ready-made system of EU-wide 'temporary protection' in the event of a mass influx of people, which was used for the first time in 2022 to help those Ukrainians fleeing the Russian invasion of Ukraine.[100]

[90] All Member States have ratified both measures.

[91] See generally G Goodwin-Gill and J McAdam, *The Refugee in International Law* (4th edn, Oxford: Oxford University Press, 2021).

[92] See the study by the European Migration Network, 'The Different National Practices Concerning Granting of Non-EU Harmonised Protection Statuses' (EMN, 2010), available at www.refworld.org/docid/51b05e734.html.

[93] Joined Cases C-57/09 and C-101/09 *B and D* [2010] ECR I-10979. See now Art 2(2), Regulation 2024/1347 on qualification for status (OJ [2024] L 22.5.2024).

[94] Art 63(1) and (2) EC.

[95] Directive 2004/83 (OJ [2004] L304/12).

[96] Directive 2005/85 (OJ [2005] L326/13).

[97] Directive 2003/9 (OJ [2003] L31/18).

[98] Regulation 343/2003 (OJ [2003] L50/1). The Regulation replaced the Dublin Convention (OJ [1997] C254/1).

[99] Regulation 2725/2000 (OJ [2000] L316/1). The Eurodac system began operations on 15 January 2003 (OJ [2003] C5/2).

[100] Directive 2001/55 (OJ [2001] L212/12); OJ [2022] L71/1, applied in [2022] OJ L71/1, most recently extended to March 2027 (OJ [2025] L 24.7.2025).

For the second phase of the CEAS, the EU established the twin objectives of raising the level of protection and reducing the large divergences between Member States' recognition rates (ie the percentages of persons whose application for refugee or subsidiary protection status are successful).[101] Following the entry into force of the Lisbon Treaty, the objectives agreed in Tampere are now reflected explicitly in Article 78 TFEU, which requires that:

> The Union shall develop a common policy on asylum, subsidiary protection and temporary protection with a view to offering appropriate status to any third-country national requiring international protection and ensuring compliance with the principle of *nonrefoulement*. This policy must be in accordance with the Geneva Convention of 28 July 1951 and the Protocol of 31 January 1967 relating to the status of refugees, and other relevant treaties.

To that end, the European Parliament and the Council:

> shall adopt measures for a common European asylum system comprising:
>
> - a uniform status of asylum for nationals of third countries, valid throughout the Union;
> - a uniform status of subsidiary protection for nationals of third countries who, without obtaining European asylum, are in need of international protection;
> - a common system of temporary protection for displaced persons in the event of a massive inflow;
> - common procedures for the granting and withdrawing of uniform asylum or subsidiary protection status;
> - criteria and mechanisms for determining which Member State is responsible for considering an application for asylum or subsidiary protection;
> - standards concerning the conditions for the reception of applicants for asylum or subsidiary protection;
> - partnership and cooperation with third countries for the purpose of managing inflows of people applying for asylum or subsidiary or temporary protection.

The legislation establishing the second phase of the CEAS was adopted by the summer of 2013.[102] On the whole, this legislation provides for further harmonization of national law and additional protection of human rights, taking a modest but significant step towards raising standards in this field, and potentially reducing the divergences in Member States' recognition rates somewhat.[103] Pending (and following) the adoption and implementation of this second-phase legislation, the Court of Justice became a significant actor in the field of asylum law, following the removal of the restrictions on its jurisdiction with the entry into force of the Lisbon Treaty.

However, the 'refugee crisis' beginning in 2015 led to difficulties applying this legislation uniformly and concerns about the total volume of those entering the EU and the distribution of asylum seekers between Member States. As a consequence, the EU amended its laws on border control and authorized a number of Member States to reimpose controls

[101] OJ [2010] C115.

[102] Directive 2011/95 (OJ [2011] L337/9) (Qualification Directive); Directive 2013/33 on reception conditions (OJ [2013] L180/96); Directive 2013/32 on asylum procedures (OJ [2013] L180/60); the revised Dublin Regulation (Regulation 604/2013 (OJ [2013] L180/31)); and a revised Eurodac Regulation (Regulation 603/2013 (OJ [2013] L180/1)). The EU also established a European Asylum Support Office: see Regulation 439/2010 (OJ [2010] L132/11). The 2001 Temporary Protection Directive was not updated.

[103] See S Peers, E Guild, M Garlick, and V Moreno-Lax, *EU Immigration and Asylum Law: Text and Commentary*, vol 3 (2nd edn, Leiden: Martinus Nijhoff, 2015).

on internal borders (see section 3). In the area of asylum, it adopted temporary emergency laws aiming to relocate large numbers of asylum seekers from Italy and Greece,[104] and tried to cut back migration flows via non-EU countries (the 'Western Balkans' route and the control of those coming from Turkey—for which it promised Turkey a visa waiver and gave that country funds to assist refugee support).

Ultimately in 2024, the EU adopted (in effect) a 'third phase' of EU asylum law (known as the 'asylum pact'), which further reduces divergences between Member States and (taken as a whole) lowers standards, in particular aiming to punish any asylum seekers who leave the country responsible for their application under the Dublin rules.[105] EU lawmakers have adopted further amendments to the pact, to make it easier to fast-track applicants from supposedly 'safe countries of origin' or send them to supposedly 'safe third countries'.[106]

6.2 **Qualification for international protection**

The EU's asylum legislation raises a large number of issues, starting with the definition of refugee and subsidiary protection status. As regards both types of protection, a protection need may arise following the applicant's departure from the country of origin (known as protection *sur place*).[107] Also, the 'actors of persecution or serious harm' need not be the State, but may also be private parties, if it can be 'demonstrated' that the State, or parties controlling the State, is 'unable or unwilling' to provide protection against non-State agents.[108] This rule changed the more restrictive interpretation of the Geneva Convention in several Member States, which had traditionally recognized as refugees only those persons fleeing persecution by the State. There is a parallel rule on 'actors of protection', which provides that protection can 'only' be provided by States or parties, including international organizations, controlling all or a substantial part of a State's territory, on condition that such bodies are 'willing and able to offer protection'. Such protection must be 'effective and of a non-temporary nature', and is 'generally provided' when the actors of protection 'take reasonable steps to prevent the persecution or suffering of serious harm, inter alia, by operating an effective legal system for the detection, prosecution and punishment of acts constituting persecution or serious harm, and when the applicant has access to such protection'.[109] Furthermore, Member States must apply a concept usually known as an 'internal flight alternative', if there is a part of a protection-seeker's country of origin which is generally safe,[110] and if that person 'can safely and legally travel to and

[104] Decisions 2015/1523 (OJ [2015] L239/146) and 2015/1601 (OJ [2015] L248/80). These laws were barely applied in practice. Legal challenges to the second relocation decision failed: Joined Cases C-643/15 and C-647/15 *Slovakia and Hungary v Council*, EU:C:2017:631.

[105] Regulation 2021/2303 (OJ [2021] OJ L468/1) creating an EU Asylum Agency (replacing the previous Asylum Support Office); Regulation 2024/1358 on Eurodac, which extended the scope of fingerprinting obligations as well as access to data on asylum seekers and irregular migrants; Regulation 2024/1351 replacing the Dublin III Regulation; Regulation 2024/1350 on resettlement of refugees from non-EU countries, the first EU measure in this field; Regulation 2024/1348 on asylum procedures, replacing the previous Directive; Regulation 2024/1247 replacing the previous qualification Directive; Regulation 2024/1349 creating a border return procedure; Regulation 2024/1356 on screening of migrants; Regulation 2024/1359 on crisis situations; Directive 2024/1346 recasting the reception conditions Directive (all OJ [2024] L 22.5.2024); and Regulation 2021/2303 (OJ [2021] L468/1) creating an EU Asylum Agency (replacing the previous Asylum Support Office). The bulk of the asylum pact law will apply from 12 June 2026.

[106] Regulations 2026/463 and 464, [2026] OJ L 27.2.2026.

[107] Art 5 Regulation 2024/1347. [108] Art 6 Regulation 2024/1347.

[109] Art 7 Regulation 2024/1347.

[110] Art 8 Regulation 2024/1347. More precisely, there must be 'no well-founded fear' of persecution and no 'real risk of suffering serious harm', or 'access to protection against persecution or serious harm as defined in Article 7'.

gain admittance to a part of the country of origin and can reasonably be expected to settle there',[111] taking account of the case law of the ECtHR.[112]

The core definition of a 'refugee' (copied from the Geneva Convention) is a person who has 'a well-founded fear of being persecuted for reasons of race, religion, nationality, political opinion or membership of a particular social group'.[113] EU law expands upon both the concept of persecution and the grounds of persecution.[114] On the first point, in a case concerning members of the Ahmadiyya community, who faced attacks and criminalization in Pakistan if they professed their beliefs in public, the Court of Justice clarified the concept of 'persecution'. Even though these asylum seekers could possibly have avoided persecution in their country of origin by refraining from proselytizing to believers in the dominant religion there, and from otherwise practising their beliefs in public, the Court ruled that such persons should not be expected to refrain from public displays of their religion in their country of origin.[115] The Court also ruled similarly as regards asylum seekers who might be expected to hide their sexual orientation; it has moreover ruled that Member States cannot humiliate asylum seekers who claim that they were persecuted due to being gay or lesbian.[116]

On the second point, the case law has in particular provided strong support for women arguing that they faced different types of gender-based persecution, holding that they may have been persecuted as part of a 'particular social group', as further defined by EU law (ie they share a common background that cannot be changed, and are perceived as different by society).[117]

As for the definition of subsidiary protection, it must be granted where there are 'substantial grounds . . . for believing' that the person concerned faces a 'real risk' of 'serious harm', which consists of (a) the death penalty or execution, or (b) torture or other inhuman or degrading treatment or punishment, or (c) a 'serious and individual threat to a civilian's life or person by reason of indiscriminate violence in situations of international or internal armed conflict'.[118] While the first two criteria are based on the established case law of the ECtHR,[119] the meaning of the third criterion was unclear, particularly since it is quite clearly contradictory: how could a person face an '*individual*' threat by reason of '*indiscriminate* violence'? The Court of Justice answered this question in a case about Iraqis who feared violent retaliation because they were linked to the US forces then occupying Iraq.[120] In the Court's view, an 'individual' threat could include 'harm to civilians irrespective of their identity, where the degree of indiscriminate violence characterising the armed conflict taking place . . . reaches such a high level that substantial grounds are shown for believing that a civilian, returned to the relevant country or, as the case may be, to the relevant region, would, solely on account of his presence on the territory of that

[111] Regulation 2024/1347 made this rule mandatory, but clarified it in order to raise the standards of protection and reduce divergences of interpretation.

[112] See the judgment of that Court in *Salah Sheekh v Netherlands* (Appl No 1948/04), ECtHR, 2007-I, particularly as regards the ability to travel and settle in the safe part of the country.

[113] Art 3(5) Regulation 2024/1347, echoing Art 1A(2) of the Geneva Convention.

[114] Arts 9 and 10 Regulation 2024/1347.

[115] Joined Cases C-71/11 and C-99/11 *Y and Z*, EU:C:2012:518.

[116] See respectively Joined Cases C-199–201/12 *X, Y, and Z*, EU:C:2013:720 and Joined Cases C-148–150/13 *A, B, and C*, EU:C:2014:2406.

[117] Cases C-621/21, EU:C:2024:47 (domestic violence); C-646/21, EU:C:2024:487 (women identifying with value of sex equality); and C-608/22 and C-609/22, EU:C:2024:828 (Afghan women).

[118] Arts 3(6) and 15 Regulation 2024/1347.

[119] See P Teidemann, 'Subsidiary Protection and the Function of Article 15(c) of the Qualification Directive' (2012) 31 *Refugee Survey Quarterly* 123.

[120] Case C-465/07 *Elgafaji and Elgafaji* [2009] ECR I-921.

country or region, face a real risk of being subject to the serious threat referred to in' the previous qualification Directive (the definition has not been amended by the asylum pact).

Once an applicant has been granted refugee or subsidiary protection status, he or she (along with his or her family members) is entitled to the benefits set out in EU law, which include a residence permit, access to employment and self-employment, equal treatment with nationals as regards social welfare and health care, and equal treatment with legally resident third-country nationals as regards accommodation.[121] While the first-phase Directive left Member States with an option to give fewer such rights to beneficiaries of subsidiary protection, the second-phase Directive (and now the asylum pact Regulation) only permits lower standards for such persons as regards social welfare and residence permits.[122]

6.3 Reception conditions for asylum seekers

The Directive on reception conditions regulates such issues as the employment, health care, education, and welfare of asylum seekers during the process of deciding on their application. The second-phase Directive (and to some extent the 2024 asylum pact Directive) improved standards as compared to the first-phase Directive particularly as regards employment—permitting Member States to require an asylum seeker to wait up to 6 months for employment access, whereas the first-phase Directive had permitted a wait of up to 12 months, and the second-phase Directive provided for a wait of up to 9 months.[123] Since the second-phase Directive, there are also detailed rules on detention of asylum seekers, which differ somewhat from the rules on detention of irregular migrants in the Returns Directive (see case study 25.1), in that the grounds for detention are different and there is (in most cases) no express time limit on detention. However, the rules on legal safeguards and detention conditions are quite similar.[124]

6.4 Asylum procedures

Next, the rules on asylum procedures address such issues as legal aid, interviews, the right to an effective remedy (in particular as regards the suspensive effect of appeals), and special procedural rules such as accelerated procedures, the 'safe country of origin' concept, and the 'safe third country' concept (which respectively allow Member States to presume that some countries of origin, or other countries besides the country of origin, are safe). The second-phase Directive improved standards as regards, for instance, setting a six-month time limit (subject to exceptions) to make a first-instance decision on an application, reducing the number of possible cases subject to accelerated procedures, and strengthening the right to an effective remedy. In contrast, the asylum pact Regulation (inter alia) introduced more possibilities of fast-tracking cases and extended the use of a special border procedure where asylum seekers have more limited rights.

6.5 Responsibility for applications

Finally, there has been continued controversy concerning the application of the 'Dublin' rules on responsibility for asylum applications, in part because the criteria for responsibility (which in turn assign that responsibility based on family reunion, the issue of a visa or a residence permit, or evidence of crossing a border illegally) shifted the burden of dealing with asylum applications towards the EU's external eastern and southern land

[121] Arts 20–36 Regulation 2024/1347. [122] Arts 24 and 31(2) Regulation 2024/1347.

[123] Art 17 Directive 2024/1346; 2013/33; compare to Art 11 Directive 2003/9 and Art 15 Directive 2013/33.

[124] Arts 10–13 Directive 2024/1346.

and sea borders, mostly consisting of poorer Member States. Furthermore, there were widespread concerns that some Member States were systematically not applying many of the basic standards of the Geneva Convention, the ECHR, and EU law as regards reception conditions, qualification for status, and asylum procedures. Ultimately, the ECtHR ruled that Greece breached Article 3 ECHR (the ban on torture or other inhuman and degrading treatment) due to its low standards on reception conditions (interpreting the ECHR on this point in light of the Reception Directive) and asylum procedures, and that Belgium breached Article 3 ECHR by returning an asylum seeker to Greece despite its knowledge that such breaches were taking place.[125]

In turn, interpreting the first-phase Dublin Regulation, the Court of Justice ruled that while the EU rules were based on mutual trust that each Member State would comply with its human rights obligations, it was possible that the CEAS might 'experience major operational problems in a given Member State, meaning that there is a substantial risk that asylum seekers may, when transferred to that Member State, be treated in a manner incompatible with their fundamental rights'. But the Dublin system could not be suspended following *any* breach of those human rights obligations, but rather where there 'are substantial grounds for believing that there are systemic flaws in the asylum procedure and reception conditions for asylum applicants', leading to a breach of the ban on torture or other inhuman and degrading treatment set out in Article 4 of the EU's Charter of Fundamental Rights. So EU law also prevented sending asylum seekers to Greece pursuant to the Dublin rules.[126] The main elements of the Court's judgment were transposed into the text of the second-phase Dublin Regulation.[127]

The asylum pact version of the Regulation slightly amends the responsibility criteria, speeds up the process of transferring asylum applicants between Member States (in part by reducing their appeal rights and making it easier to detain them), and introduces new rules on the prospect of 'solidarity' between Member States, setting up a process for possible relocation of asylum seekers or financial assistance to front-line Member States or even non-EU countries.[128]

As in other areas, it can be seen that the EU's role in this field is steadily increasing, and indeed is governed by a political and legal objective of establishing a 'common' policy, with a view to reducing divergences in national policy. Indeed, increasing the role of the EU was formally built into the concept of the first and second phases of asylum legislation, and now the asylum pact. The developments in legislation and the case law of the Court of Justice to date both point clearly in the direction of an increasing level of harmonization, although even after the asylum pact EU law on asylum is not fully 'uniform'.

7 Conclusion

In all four areas of immigration and asylum law, the EU's role has been growing. It began with the development of visas and borders rules outside the EU framework, which were integrated into the EU legal framework in 1999 and have been developed significantly (VIS, SIS II, Frontex, visa and border codes, other databases) since then. Moreover, since 1999 the EU has adopted two phases of legislation concerning the CEAS, then the asylum pact. In the area of legal migration, the EU began by harmonizing the non-economic aspects of the issue and subsequently addressed sundry aspects of labour migration. Much of the legislation in this area has been revised already. As for irregular migration, the EU's initial piecemeal approach has been supplemented by the adoption of the fairly comprehensive

[125] *MSS v Belgium and Greece* (Appl No 30696/09), judgment of 21 January 2011, nyr.

[126] Joined Cases C-411/10 and C-493/10 *NS and ME* [2011] ECR I-13493.

[127] Art 3(2) Regulation 604/2013.

[128] Regulation 2024/1351.

Returns Directive, possibly to be replaced by a Regulation soon. And these legislative developments have proceeded in pace with the gradual full extension of the Community method of decision-making and judicial control to this area of the law. The case law of the Court of Justice and successive legislative developments, in particular in response to the perceived 'refugee crisis', have led to more harmonization, gradually reducing the scope of discretion of Member States in this field. And the move towards harmonization has been accompanied by steep rises in EU funding in this area,[129] and the development of sanctions to induce non-EU countries to assist the EU with migration control.[130]

The position as regards the tension between human rights protection and immigration control is more mixed. EU legislation and policy on border control and irregular migration, along with technical and operational developments, points clearly towards more control of immigration, particularly since the development of the 'refugee crisis'. However, these developments are qualified by human rights exceptions in the borders code and human rights rules in the Frontex legislation (now the CJEU ruled that they are enforceable in practice). And the ongoing development of EU legislation on visas, legal migration, and asylum pointed towards a more liberal approach—until the advent of the 'refugee crisis', where the EU asylum pact, as eventually adopted (alongside the proposed Returns Regulation), moves towards a lower (and yet more fully harmonized) standard. There is a continuing struggle within and between the EU's political institutions and Courts to establish the right balance between migration control and the protection of fundamental rights, during a time when public concern about migration leads to populist objections that could threaten the existence of the EU.

Further reading

H Battjes, *European Asylum Law and International Law* (Leiden: Martinus Nijhoff, 2006)

N Coleman, *European Readmission Policy: Third Country Interests and Refugee Rights* (Leiden: Martinus Nijhoff, 2009)

G Goodwin-Gill and J McAdam, *The Refugee in International Law* (4th edn, Oxford: Oxford University Press, 2021)

K Hailbronner and D Thym, *EU Immigration and Asylum Law: Commentary* (2nd edn, Munich/Oxford/Baden-Baden: Beck, Hart, Nomos, 2016)

I Majcher, *The European Union Returns Directive and Its Compatibility with International Human Rights Law* (Leiden: Martinus Nijhoff, 2020)

V Passalacqua, 'Legal Mobilization via Preliminary Reference: Insights from the Case of Migrant Rights' (2021) 58 *Common Market Law Review* 751

S Peers, 'The New EU Asylum Laws: Taking Rights Half-Seriously?' (2024) 43 *Yearbook of European Law* 1

S Peers, *EU Justice and Home Affairs Law* (5th edn, Oxford: Oxford University Press, 2023) vol 1

S Peers, E Guild, M Garlick, and V Moreno-Lax, *EU Immigration and Asylum Law: Text and Commentary*, 3 vols (2nd edn, Leiden: Martinus Nijhoff, vols 1 and 2 2012, vol 3 2015)

A Weisbrock, *Legal Migration to the European Union* (Leiden: Martinus Nijhoff, 2010)

D Wilsher, *Immigration Detention: Law, History, Politics* (Cambridge: Cambridge University Press, 2012)

[129] For details, see S Peers, *EU Justice and Home Affairs Law* (5th edn, Oxford: Oxford University Press, 2023), vol 1, ch 2.

[130] In addition to the visa code sanctions and 2025 changes to the visa suspension mechanism (section 3 above), the EU has agreed removal of trade preferences (Council Doc 5176/26, 9 January 2026, Art 18d) and is considering reduction of development aid (COM(2025) 551, 16 July 2025, Art 12) for countries which do not readmit their citizens.

26

EU external action

Geert De Baere

1 Introduction

A January 2026 article in *The Guardian* offered the following assessment of the EU's lack of (coherent) reaction either to US military action in Venezuela and the capture of President Maduro or to the US government's designs on Greenland:[1]

> [A] little more than 24 hours after US bombers, fighter jets and helicopters attacked Caracas and special forces seized Venezuela's president, Nicolás Maduro, the European Commission posted on social media. The EU's executive said nothing about an operation that multiple national leaders outside Europe, opposition politicians inside it and pretty much every available legal expert had denounced as a gross violation of international law. Instead, it wished Europeans a safe return from their holidays and pointed out that if they could travel across borders with only their ID cards and were guaranteed refunds or compensation in the event of bus, train or plane delays, it was thanks to the EU. This stuff—free movement, consumer protection, holiday entitlements—the EU can do. Condemning a powerful, longtime ally and standing up for liberal democracy, multilateralism and the rules-based international order? Not quite so much.

[1] J Henley, 'EU reveals weak hand as Trump raids Venezuela and threatens Greenland', *The Guardian*, 7 January 2026.

Such damning assessments are by no means new. Indeed, in an article published more than 15 years ago in *Time Magazine*, Singaporean diplomat and scholar Kishore Mahbubani likewise did not pull any punches when describing the EU's position in the world:[2]

> Europe just doesn't get it. It does not get how irrelevant it is becoming to the rest of the world. And it does not get how relevant the rest of the world is becoming to its future. The world is changing rapidly. Europe continues to drift. I am not exaggerating when I say Europe's obsession with restructuring its internal arrangements is akin to rearranging the deck chairs of a sinking Titanic.

This chapter looks at how the deckchairs are currently arranged. It starts from the assumption that in order to cast judgement on whether the EU's external policies are effective and consistent (which the images of the EU revealing a weak hand, or being akin to a drifting or sinking ship, would appear to belie) and in general on how the EU has performed as an international actor, it is crucial to understand how the EU is equipped to do so. Having a clear understanding of the intricacies of the law of EU external action is also of crucial importance to reimagine the role the Union could or should play in a fast-changing—and perhaps fast-unravelling—international legal order;[3] it is as important for the UK's relationship with the EU after Brexit.[4]

This chapter therefore offers an introduction into the law governing how the EU organizes its relations with the outside world. Those relations are both broad in scope and varied in substance. The goods and services that cross the EU's external borders, most of the planes that fly across those borders, much of the pollution that comes from or enters into the EU, the fish caught by EU fishermen outside EU waters—and many more issues besides—are regulated by EU external action law.[5]

The resulting legal framework is of a complexity verging on the byzantine. That is because the Member States, in various ways, want to preserve their competence and

[2] K Mahbubani, 'Europe's Errors', *Time Magazine*, 8 March 2010. The rearranging in question appears to be a Sisyphean task as, 15 years on, the EU is still at it: see K Istrefi and P Cebulak, 'European Commission and Council of the European Union v Front Populaire pour la Libération de la Saguia El-Hamra et du Rio De Oro (Front Polisario). Joined Cases C-779/21 P And C-799/21 P. ECLI:EU:C:2024:835' (2025) 119 *American Journal of International Law* 651: 'The [Polisario II] judgment left important issues unaddressed, which creates the risks that it will amount to nothing more than rearranging the deck chairs on the Titanic . . .'.

[3] See eg P Sands, 'Trump and his ilk imagine a world without international law—but they will not achieve it', *The Guardian*, 19 November 2025; OA Hathaway, 'The Great Unraveling Has Begun', *The New York Times*, 6 January 2026. See further A Peters, *International Law and its Scholarship in the Time of Monsters*, MPIL Research Paper Series No 2025-05; M Milanovic, 'Dystopian International Law' (2026) 120 *American Journal of International Law* 107.

[4] See in particular the Trade and Cooperation Agreement between the European Union and the European Atomic Energy Community, of the one part, and the United Kingdom of Great Britain and Northern Ireland, of the other part (OJ [2021] L149/10) (EUUKTCA), on which see S Peers, 'So Close, Yet So Far: The EU/UK Trade and Cooperation Agreement' (2022) 59 *Common Market Law Review* 49. For its interpretation and application, see eg judgment of 3 April 2025, Case C-743/24 *Alchaster II*, EU:C:2025:230. See also Council Decision (EU) 2025/2376 of 4 November 2025 on the signing, on behalf of the European Union, of the Agreement between the European Union and the United Kingdom of Great Britain and Northern Ireland regarding cooperation on the application of their respective competition laws (OJ [2025] L 24.11.2025) See further chapter 27.

[5] This chapter uses the term 'external action' in the same sense as the Treaties, ie as encompassing all external policies of the Union. Those policies include both what this chapter will refer to as 'ordinary EU external action' on the one hand and the common foreign and security policy (CFSP) on the other hand, ie the former First and Second Pillars of the EU before the Lisbon Treaty (see further chapter 2). The chapter occasionally uses the term 'external relations' in the same sense when appropriate (the term is also used twice in the Treaties, ie in Arts 18(4) TEU and 355(3) TFEU, though in the latter case with respect to the Member States and not the Union as such).

control over EU external action on the one hand, but also seek to enhance the EU's external effectiveness and consistency on the other hand. These twin objectives are in obvious tension—if not conflict—but they have each manifested themselves (as has the tension between them) in the multiple rounds of Treaty amendment in various ways.

This chapter explores the resulting complex division of competences between the Member States and the Union and between the different institutions of the Union in the field of external action. The chapter also examines the applicable decision-making procedures, including the procedure for concluding international agreements, and explores the Union's composite system of external representation, illustrating the intricacies involved by looking more closely at EU external environmental policy. Furthermore, the chapter explores how the Union manages the vertical (between the Union and the Member States) and horizontal (between the different institutions and policy fields of the EU) division of its external competences.

Finally, while the position of the Union within the wider context of the international legal order and the status of international law within the EU legal order are clearly a crucial part of the story of the Union's external action,[6] this chapter (with some minor exceptions) only covers internal EU constitutional law with respect to external action.

2 The foundations of EU external action

2.1 In search of consistency and effectiveness

One of the core tasks of the key actors of the EU's external action introduced by the Lisbon Treaty, the High Representative of the Union for Foreign Affairs and Security Policy and the European External Action Service (EEAS), is to 'ensure the consistency of the Union's external action'.[7] The drafters of the Treaties clearly realized that consistency in external action would be problematic for the Union, as is evident from the fact that Article 21(3), second paragraph, TEU returns to the issue and provides for the Union to:

> ensure consistency between the different areas of its external action and between these and its other policies. The Council and the Commission, assisted by the High Representative of the Union for Foreign Affairs and Security Policy, shall ensure that consistency and shall cooperate to that effect.

Why would consistency or effectiveness be an issue for EU external action? The point of departure in answering that question must be the awareness of a crucial difference between most countries on the one hand, and the EU on the other hand: when considering a response to an international situation, the first question the EU asks itself is not how it could react most effectively, but whether it in fact has the requisite *competence* to act at all and, if so, on what legal basis in the Treaties and through what institution action should be taken. In other words, the Union gives precedence to considerations of competence over considerations of effectiveness.[8]

[6] eg J Wouters, C Ryngaert, T Ruys, and G De Baere, *International Law: A European Perspective* (Oxford: Hart Publishing, 2018) ch 4; J Wouters, F Hoffmeister, G De Baere, and T Ramopoulos, *The Law of EU External Relations: Cases, Materials, and Commentary on the EU as an International Legal Actor* (3rd edn, Oxford: Oxford University Press, 2020) chs 5 and 12.

[7] Art 18(4) TEU and Art 3(1) of Council Decision 2010/427/EU of 26 July 2010 establishing the organisation and functioning of the European External Action Service (OJ [2010] L201/30) (EEAS Decision). See further section 5.3.

[8] G De Baere, *Constitutional Principles of EU External Relations* (Oxford: Oxford University Press, 2008) 10 and the literature cited therein.

2.2 **The principle of conferral**

In essence, that is because the Union's competences are governed by the principle of conferral as laid down in Article 5(1) and (2) TEU:[9]

> 1. The limits of Union competences are governed by the principle of conferral. . . .
> 2. Under the principle of conferral, the Union shall act only within the limits of the competences conferred upon it by the Member States in the Treaties to attain the objectives set out therein. Competences not conferred upon the Union in the Treaties remain with the Member States.

This principle incorporates the idea, fundamental not only in the law of international organizations, but also in the constitutional law of many federal States, that the organization or the federal level of government (here the Union) only has those competences that the Member States have explicitly or impliedly conferred on it in the constitution (here the Treaties). Before contemplating any action, whether internal or external, the Union must therefore first determine whether it actually has competence to do so. This implies essentially two things: (a) the EU is incapable of extending its own competences and (b) it does not have general law-making capacity. Put differently, every single EU action requires one or more legal bases in the Treaties, which must be based on objective factors (including the aim and content of the measure) that are amenable to judicial review,[10] and which determine both the vertical and horizontal division of competences.[11]

Crucially, this principle of conferral applies as much to external action as to internal policies.[12] Hence, the choice of the appropriate legal basis for the Council decision on the conclusion of an envisaged agreement has constitutional significance, since, having only conferred powers, the EU must link the acts which it adopts to provisions of the TFEU which actually empower it to adopt such acts. Consequently, proceeding on an incorrect legal basis is liable to invalidate the act concluding the agreement itself, and so vitiate the Union's consent to be bound by the agreement it has signed, particularly where the Treaty does not confer on the EU sufficient competence to ratify the agreement in its entirety or where the appropriate legal basis for the measure concluding the agreement lays down a legislative procedure different from that which has in fact been followed by the EU institutions.[13]

2.3 **The distinction between ordinary EU external action and the CFSP**

Both with respect to its internal and its international action, the EU must act within the limits of the competences conferred on it by the Member States in the Treaties to attain the objectives set out in the Treaties.[14] The Member States also have the liberty to decide

[9] For more on the concept of EU competences, see chapter 5.

[10] See judgment of 3 December 2019, Case C-482/17 *Czech Republic v Parliament and Council*, EU:C:2019:1035, para 31.

[11] See judgment of 10 February 2009, Case C-301/06 *Ireland v Parliament and Council* ('*Personal data protection*'), EU:C:2009:68, para 56. Further on the choice of legal basis in EU external action: G De Baere and T Van den Sanden, 'Interinstitutional Gravity and Pirates of the Parliament on Stranger Tides: The Continued Constitutional Significance of the Choice of Legal Basis in Post-Lisbon External Action' (2016) *European Constitutional Law Review* 85, and on the concept of legal basis more generally, see chapter 5.

[12] Judgments of 25 October 2017, Case C-687/15 *Commission v Council* (*WRC-15*), EU:C:2017:803, para 48, and of 5 December 2017, Case C-600/14 *Germany v Council* ('*OTIF I*'), EU:C:2017:935, para 44.

[13] Opinion 1/19 (*Istanbul Convention*) of 6 October 2021, EU:C:2021:832, paras 199–200, on which see G Kübek, 'Facing and Embracing the Consequences of Mixity: Opinion 1/19, Istanbul Convention' (2022) 59 *Common Market Law Review* 1465.

[14] *WRC-15* (n 12) para 48, and *OTIF I* (n 12) para 80.

the manner in which they confer those competences and how much power they are willing to relinquish, which to a large extent explains why the EU still does not take a united approach to external action. Instead, the EU approaches the subject from two quite different angles, based on the distinction between two core aspects of international relations:

(a) external 'socio-economic' relations, such as external trade and development cooperation, which fall within what this chapter will refer to as 'ordinary EU external action'. The legal rules governing this area are mostly set out in the TFEU; and

(b) what is commonly called 'high politics' (diplomatic activity and security and defence issues), which fall within the Common Foreign and Security Policy (CFSP). The legal rules governing this area are mostly set out in the TEU.

That distinction also corresponds to that between the former First and Second Pillars of the EU before the Lisbon Treaty (see further chapter 2). The EU's fundamentally different approach to these two areas has persisted after Lisbon, despite the introduction of Title V of the TEU ('General Provisions on the Union's External Action and Specific Provisions on the Common Foreign and Security Policy') and Part Five of the TFEU (entitled simply 'The Union's External Action'), and despite a single set of objectives for EU external action as a whole in Articles 3(5) and 21(2) TEU.[15]

It is hardly a novelty to question the assumption that external 'socio-economic' relations can be easily separated from 'high politics'. Hill already noted more than 20 years ago that:

> the once popular distinction between 'high' and 'low' politics is no longer of much help. High politics—in the sense of serious conflict touching on the state's most basic concerns—can be as much about monetary integration as about territory and the threat of armed attack. Conversely, low politics—in the sense of routine exchanges contained within knowable limits and rarely reaching the public realm—can be observed in NATO [North Atlantic Treaty Organization] or OSCE [Organization for Security and Co-operation in Europe] multilateralism as much as (perhaps more than) in discussions over fish or airport landing rights. Thus the ***intrinsic content*** of an issue is not a guide to its level of political salience or to the way it will be handled, except in the tautological sense that any issue which blows up into a high-level international conflict (and almost anything has the potential so to do) will lead to decision-makers at the highest level suddenly taking over responsibility.[16]

Yet the distinction persists in the EU's constitutional structure, mainly because most of the Member States want to remain firmly in charge of their 'high politics', or what they choose to regard as such.

Unsurprisingly, the consistency between the various external policies of the EU and the effectiveness of EU external action as a whole remains a challenge.

2.4 **The CFSP**

As is clear from Title V TEU ('General Provisions on the Union's External Action and Specific Provisions on the Common Foreign and Security Policy'), the Lisbon Treaty has subjected the CFSP to the overall constitutional framework of the EU.[17] The formal

[15] See also Art 205 TFEU. See in general J Larik, *Foreign Policy Objectives in European Constitutional Law* (Oxford: Oxford University Press, 2015).

[16] C Hill, *The Changing Politics of Foreign Policy* (London: Palgrave, 2003) 4.

[17] See further G Butler, *Constitutional Law of the EU's Common Foreign and Security Policy: Competence and Institutions in External Relations* (Oxford: Hart Publishing, 2019).

abolition of the pillar structure, however, does not imply a complete harmonization of procedures and an integration of all policies under the former Community; instead, it essentially leaves the former Second Pillar standing in a modified manner. The post-Lisbon EU Treaty takes into account the different characters of different policies and still permits a substantial amount of differentiation as to how the Union's institutions are involved in law-making. The 2007 Intergovernmental Conference, which led to the adoption of the Lisbon Treaty, decided to drop the idea of one single Constitutional Treaty and to keep the TEU and the (renamed) TFEU as two distinct Treaties, with the CFSP and the European Neighbourhood Policy[18] as the only substantive policies in the TEU. The Lisbon Treaty therefore established a single legal order for the Union, but with a more markedly separate sub-order for the CFSP.

Moreover, while the ordinary Union framework under the TFEU is governed by the technique of detailed and specific attribution of competences,[19] the present Chapter 2 of Title V TEU on the CFSP remains characterized by an absence of any clear let alone detailed list of what precisely it encompasses. Instead, the allocation of competences in the CFSP consists of the general grant of competence in Article 24(1) TEU, which covers:

> all areas of foreign policy and all questions relating to the Union's security, including the progressive framing of a common defence policy that might lead to a common defence.

Article 42(1) TEU in addition provides that the Common Security and Defence Policy (CSDP):

> shall be an integral part of the common foreign and security policy. It shall provide the Union with an operational capacity drawing on civilian and military assets.

The CSDP is to include (Article 42(2) TEU):

> the progressive framing of a common Union defence policy. This will lead to a common defence, when the European Council, acting unanimously, so decides. It shall in that case recommend to the Member States the adoption of such a decision in accordance with their respective constitutional requirements.

The assurance that the CSDP *will* 'lead to a common defence' may at first view appear to contain a much stronger commitment than Article 24(1) TEU, which merely refers to:

> the progressive framing of a common defence policy that ***might*** lead to a common defence.[20]

However, the role of the European Council[21] and the condition that the Member States need to adopt a decision in accordance with their respective constitutional requirements make it clear that not much legal significance should be attached to the phrase 'will lead to a common defence' in Article 42(2) TEU, which should be understood as an aspirational statement of a purely political nature.

[18] Art 8 TEU.

[19] cf A Dashwood, 'The Relationship between the Member States and the European Union/European Community' (2004) 41 *Common Market Law Review* 357 *et seq.*

[20] Emphasis added. See further F Asderaki, G Panfil, A Molnár, and S Paile-Calvo, *The Common Security and Defence Policy: New developments and challenges, ESDC autumn university book 2021* (Luxembourg: Publications Office of the EU, 2025).

[21] Contrast also ex Art 17(1) TEU ('should the European Council so decide') with current Art 42(2) TEU ('when the European Council . . . so decides').

Does, then, the principle of conferral actually apply to the CFSP? Given that, under the previous Treaty framework, the principle of conferral was not explicitly enshrined in the former EU Treaty, but in the first paragraph of then Article 5 EC, some doubted whether the principle applied to the CFSP.[22] Article 5(1) and (2) TEU (see previously), as introduced by the Lisbon Treaty in Title I ('Common Provisions') of the EU Treaty, removed all doubt in that regard, and the Court confirmed as much in *KS and KD*, holding that 'the principles of conferral and of institutional balance also apply in the area of the CFSP'.[23]

2.5 **The common principles and objectives of EU external action**

Remarkably, however, the Lisbon Treaty has reinforced the contrast between attribution in ordinary EU external action and in the CFSP by deleting the specific CFSP objectives that before the Lisbon Treaty were listed in ex Article 11(1) TEU.

In removing those objectives from the CFSP chapter, the Lisbon Treaty has made the attribution within the CFSP even less detailed and specific than it was before. Instead, Article 21 TEU now contains the overall principles and objectives of EU external action. Article 21(1) TEU provides:

> The Union's action on the international scene shall be guided by the principles which have inspired its own creation, development and enlargement, and which it seeks to advance in the wider world: democracy, the rule of law, the universality and indivisibility of human rights and fundamental freedoms, respect for human dignity, the principles of equality and solidarity, and respect for the principles of the United Nations Charter and international law.

Article 21(2) TEU further elaborates these in a rather more comprehensive list of objectives. It provides that the Union is to define and 'pursue common policies and actions', and to 'work for a high degree of cooperation in all fields of international relations, in order to':

> (a) safeguard its values, fundamental interests, security, independence and integrity;
>
> (b) consolidate and support democracy, the rule of law, human rights and the principles of international law;
>
> (c) preserve peace, prevent conflicts and strengthen international security, in accordance with the purposes and principles of the United Nations Charter, with the principles of the Helsinki Final Act and with the aims of the Charter of Paris, including those relating to external borders;
>
> (d) foster the sustainable economic, social and environmental development of developing countries, with the primary aim of eradicating poverty;
>
> (e) encourage the integration of all countries into the world economy, including through the progressive abolition of restrictions on international trade;
>
> (f) help develop international measures to preserve and improve the quality of the environment and the sustainable management of global natural resources, in order to ensure sustainable development;
>
> (g) assist populations, countries and regions confronting natural or man-made disasters; and
>
> (h) promote an international system based on stronger multilateral cooperation and good global governance.

[22] See the discussion in De Baere, *Constitutional Principles* (n 8) 105.

[23] Judgment of 10 September 2024, Joined Cases C-29/22 P and C-44/22 P *KS and KD v Council and Others*, EU:C:2024:725, para 72.

While some of the old CFSP objectives re-emerge in that list (notably in (a), (b), (c), and (h)), it is important to emphasize that they are objectives common to EU external action in its entirety. That leaves the CFSP with only the most general of competence attributions in Article 24(1) TEU as covering 'all areas of foreign policy and all questions relating to the Union's security'.

Detailed and specific attribution of competences is an important aspect of the principle of conferral as it operates under the TFEU, and its absence in Chapter 2 of Title V of the EU Treaty indicates that the principle applies in a different manner in the CFSP legal order. The Lisbon Treaty has reinforced the contrast between ordinary EU external action and the CFSP in that respect.

3 The existence of EU external competences

3.1 The fundamentals

The former EC Treaty did not contain a general legal basis for external action.[24] Article 281 EC explicitly conferred legal personality on the Community,[25] but the general capacity derived from that Article did not constitute an independent legal basis for the adoption of international agreements. However, as a legal person, the Community had the capacity to exercise rights in international legal transactions and enter into obligations over the entire field of its objectives.[26] Contrary to the Community, the pre-Lisbon Union had not been explicitly endowed with legal personality. Nevertheless, ex Article 24 TEU provided the Union with a procedural framework for making international agreements within the spheres of the former Second and Third Pillars concerning the CFSP and Police and Judicial Cooperation in Criminal Matters (PJCCM), respectively, and pre-Lisbon practice tends to suggest that the EU already had legal personality.[27]

The post-Lisbon Article 47 TEU now explicitly confirms the Union's legal personality (merged with the legal personality of the former Community: see Art 1, third paragraph, TEU). Furthermore, Article 216(1) TFEU affirms the general capacity of the Union to conclude international agreements. That provision stipulates that the Union may conclude an agreement with one or more third countries or international organizations:

(a) where the Treaties so provide; or

(b) where the conclusion of an agreement is 'necessary in order to achieve, within the framework of the Union's policies, one of the objectives referred to in the Treaties, or is provided for in a legally binding Union act or is likely to affect common rules or alter their scope'.

While (a) encompasses the category of competences for the EU to act externally that have been explicitly provided for in the Treaties, (b) is intended as a codification of the Court

[24] Contrast Art 101 of the Treaty establishing the European Atomic Energy Community (consolidated version 2016) (EAEC) (OJ [2016] C203/1), which provides: 'The Community may, within the limits of its powers and jurisdiction, enter into obligations by concluding agreements or contracts with a third State, an international organisation or a national of a third State.'

[25] cf the identical Art 184 EAEC.

[26] Judgments of 31 March 1971, Case 22/70 *Commission v Council* ('*ERTA*'), EU:C:1971:32, paras 13 and 14, and of 14 July 1976, Cases 3/76, 4/76, and 6/76 *Kramer and Others* ('*Kramer*'), EU:C:1976:114, paras 17 and 18.

[27] eg Council Decision 2001/352/CFSP concerning the conclusion of the Agreement between the European Union and the Federal Republic of Yugoslavia (FRY) on the activities of the European Union Monitoring Mission (EUMM) (OJ [2001] L125/1); Council Decision 2010/53/CFSP of 30 November 2009 concerning the conclusion of the Agreement between Australia and the European Union on the security of classified information (OJ [2010] L26/30).

of Justice's[28] case law on implied external competences, which were recognized for the first time in *ERTA*.[29]

That case concerned Council proceedings of 20 March 1970 regarding the negotiation and conclusion by the Member States of the then Community, under the auspices of the United Nations Economic Commission for Europe (UNECE), of the European agreement concerning the work of crews of vehicles engaged in international road transport (ERTA in English or AETR in French). The proceedings concerned an arrangement arrived at, not by the Council as an institution of the then Community, but by the Member States meeting in the Council. The Commission requested the annulment of the proceedings, arguing that the Community as such should have concluded this agreement and not the Member States. As there were no relevant explicit external competences for the Community, the case gave the ECJ the opportunity for the first time to set out its views on whether external competences could perhaps be implied from explicitly conferred internal competences. Implied external competences will be examined more closely in the next section.

3.2 **Implied competences**

The Treaty provisions regulating external action have always been spread over the entire Treaty, as well as being incomplete. Nevertheless, the Lisbon Treaty improved the situation somewhat by introducing Part Five of the TFEU, which can be considered as a step in the direction of improved overall consistency in external action. Attempts to address the lack of explicit legal bases have been made predominantly in two ways:[30] first, explicit legal bases for external competences were added to the Treaties in subsequent amendments; and, secondly, the ECJ interpreted the existing Treaty provisions so as to allow the Union to develop a viable external action policy, resulting in what is mostly referred to as 'implied external competences'.

The doctrine of implied competences is a well-known principle of municipal constitutional law and of the law of international institutions.[31] Within the EU, implied competences have been relied on mostly with regard to external action. As noted previously, the (extensive and meandering) case law of the ECJ on implied external competences has now been codified in Article 216(1) TFEU. That provision encompasses three principles (*ERTA*, complementarity, and legally binding Union acts), which will be considered in turn. The possibility for implied competences within the CFSP will also be briefly considered.

3.2.1 **ERTA**

The Union 'may conclude an agreement with one or more third countries or international organisations ... where the conclusion of an agreement ... is likely to affect common rules or alter their scope'. This codifies the *ERTA* principle: the Member States are not allowed to act internationally in a way that would affect existing EU law, because the situation cannot be remedied by merely disapplying the infringing rule. The Member States'

[28] Under Art 19(1), first subpara TEU, the institution of the Court of Justice of the EU (CJEU) encompasses the Court of Justice (ECJ), the General Court (EGC), and specialized courts. This chapter refers to the respective courts by the abbreviations listed here or, when appropriate, as 'the Court'.

[29] *ERTA* (n 26) para 17.

[30] EU external competences can also arise from such general legal bases as Arts 114, 115, and 352 TFEU (on the latter provision, see Declarations 41 and 42 on Art 352 of the Treaty on the Functioning of the European Union (OJ [2016] C202/350–351)). See further De Baere, *Constitutional Principles* (n 8) 29–31 and 58–59.

[31] eg *M'Culloch v The State of Maryland*, 17 US 316, 407 (1819) and *Reparation for Injuries suffered in the Service of the United Nations* [1949] ICJ Rep 174, 182; *Legality of the Use by a State of Nuclear Weapons in Armed Conflict* [1996] ICJ Rep 66, para 25.

competence is thus excluded, which necessitates the existence of EU competences to compensate for the Member States' inability to act. The resulting EU competence is exclusive pursuant to Article 3(2) TFEU.[32]

3.2.2 **Complementarity**

The Union 'may conclude an agreement with one or more third countries or international organisations . . . where the conclusion of an agreement is necessary in order to achieve, within the framework of the Union's policies, one of the objectives referred to in the Treaties'. This codifies the 'complementarity principle',[33] which was spelled out in Opinion 1/76.[34]

In contrast to *ERTA*, that case concerned a situation where no internal Community legislation (here on the laying-up of barges) existed at the moment the then Community wanted to conclude an agreement with Switzerland. The Community's aim was the rationalization of the economic situation in the inland waterways sector in the Rhine and Moselle basins, and throughout all the Dutch inland waterways and the German inland waterways linked to the Rhine basin, by elimination of short-term overcapacity of the fleet. Given that vessels from Switzerland traditionally participate in navigation on these waterways, it was hard to imagine how that objective could be achieved solely by the establishment of autonomous Community common rules. It was therefore necessary to bring Switzerland into the scheme through an international agreement. Hence the rule that whenever EU law has conferred internal competences on the institutions to attain a specific objective, the Union can enter into the international commitments necessary for attainment of that objective even in the absence of an express provision to that effect.[35]

Internal Union competences are supported by the corresponding external competences only when the latter are truly 'implicit' in the former. This is the case when the internal Union competences cannot reasonably be expected to be effectively exercised without the possibility for the Union to enter into international agreements with third countries on the same subject matter. The complementarity principle as codified in Article 216(1) TFEU will be further considered in section 4.2.3 in contrast with complementarity as a ground for exclusive external competence pursuant to Article 3(2) TFEU.[36]

3.2.3 **Legally binding Union acts**

Article 216(1) TFEU also lists the prima facie rather straightforward possibility for the Union to 'conclude an agreement with one or more third countries or international organisations . . . where the conclusion of an agreement . . . is provided for in a legally binding Union act', that is to say, in a regulation, a directive, or a decision.[37] That provision will be discussed in its relationship to Article 3(2) TFEU in section 4.2.2.

[32] See Opinion 2/15, of 16 May 2017, EU:C:2017:376, on the *Free Trade Agreement between the EU and Singapore (EUSFTA)*, paras 170–172. See further section 4.2.1.

[33] A Dashwood, 'The Attribution of External Relations Competence' in A Dashwood and C Hillion (eds), *The General Law of EC External Relations* (London: Sweet & Maxwell, 2000) 127–132.

[34] Opinion 1/76 (*Agreement on the establishment of a European Laying-up Fund for Inland Waterway Vessels*) of 26 April 1977, EU:C:1977:63. But see already *ERTA* (n 26) paras 23–27 and *Kramer* (n 26) paras 30 and 33.

[35] Opinion 1/76 (n 34) para 3; Opinion 2/94 (*Accession of the Community to the ECHR*) of 28 March 1996, EU:C:1996:140, para 26.

[36] cf M Cremona, 'External Relations of the European Union: The Constitutional Framework for International Action' in P Craig and G de Búrca (eds), *The Evolution of EU Law* (3rd edn, Oxford: Oxford University Press, 2021) 460.

[37] Art 288 TFEU.

3.2.4 The CFSP

In any event, applying the doctrine of implied competences requires caution and restraint. That is even more the case with respect to the CFSP, especially because the CJEU for the most part lacks jurisdiction with respect to the provisions in the EU Treaty relating to the CFSP and with respect to acts adopted on the basis of those provisions.[38] Moreover, the nature of the attribution as regards the CFSP in Article 24(1) TEU is so broad that an application of the doctrine of implied competences implying all the competences needed for an effective CFSP would lead to an extensive grant of external action competences going far beyond what the EU Treaty permits.

4 The nature of EU external competences

4.1 The fundamentals

Three of the 'Categories and Areas of Union Competence' in Title I of Part One of the TFEU as listed in Article 2 TFEU are most relevant for the Union's external action and will be further explored here:[39] exclusive competences,[40] shared competences,[41] and the competence to define and implement a CFSP, including the progressive framing of a CSDP.[42]

The main principles on when the Union is exclusively competent have now been laid down in Article 3 TFEU, the first paragraph of which lists the five explicitly attributed or a priori exclusive competences of the Union:

(a) customs union;
(b) the establishing of the competition rules necessary for the functioning of the internal market;
(c) monetary policy for the Member States whose currency is the euro;
(d) the conservation of marine biological resources under the common fisheries policy;
(e) common commercial (ie external trade) policy (CCP).

Both the internal and the external aspects of these policies belong to the exclusive competence of the Union. In addition, the second paragraph of Article 3 TFEU provides for the Union to have exclusive competence 'for the conclusion of an international agreement when its conclusion is provided for in a legislative act of the Union or is necessary to enable the Union to exercise its internal competence, or in so far as its conclusion may affect common rules or alter their scope'.[43] While it attempts to codify the case law of the ECJ on exclusive competences, the criteria listed in Article 3(2) TFEU appear to be neither entirely clear nor sufficiently nuanced and hence in need of further judicial clarification. In practice, the ECJ has continued to apply, and elaborated upon, its previous case law on the nature of EU external competences.[44] The different instances of when the Union acquires an exclusive external competence pursuant to Article 3(2) TFEU will be examined in section 4.2.

[38] See section 5.2. [39] Art 2(3) and (5) TFEU will not be considered further in the present chapter.
[40] Art 2(1) TFEU. [41] Art 2(2) TFEU.
[42] Art 2(4) TFEU. As noted already, the categories of EU competences are fully examined in chapter 5.
[43] Art 3(2) TFEU.
[44] eg Judgment of 4 September 2014, Case C-114/12 *Commission v Council* (*'Broadcasting Rights Convention'*), EU:C:2014:2151, paras 65–67; and Opinion 1/13 (*Accession of third States to the Hague Convention*) of 14 October 2014, EU:C:2014:2303, para 71.

However, it is important to understand that the EU's competence should be presumed to be non-exclusive, unless there are clear indications to the contrary.[45] Within the category of non-exclusive competences, a distinction should be made between shared competences on the one hand and CFSP competences on the other hand. In turn, within the shared competences, a number of further subcategories can be distinguished: the shared competences that follow the basic rule, shared competences on the basis of minimum standards, and parallel competences. The coordination by the Union of Member States' competences when EU competences are shared should also be examined in that connection. All these form the subject of section 4.4.

4.2 **Exclusive external competence on the basis of Article 3(2) TFEU**

4.2.1 ***ERTA* exclusivity**

Article 3(2) TFEU provides that the Union will have exclusive competence for the conclusion of an international agreement 'insofar as its conclusion may affect common rules or alter their scope'. That reflects the possibility for an EU external competence to become exclusive through the exercise of an EU internal competence. That eventuality is called 'the *ERTA* doctrine' or '*ERTA* exclusivity', which follows the logic of the principle of primacy (ie the priority of EU law over Member States' law),[46] but imposes greater strictures on the international actions of the Member States than primacy does internally.[47]

This manner of acquiring exclusive external competences was recognized for the first time by the ECJ in the *ERTA* case and further refined, inter alia, in the *Open Skies* cases.[48] The latter cases concerned eight separate actions brought by the Commission under what is now Article 258 TFEU against the UK, Denmark, Sweden, Finland, Belgium, Luxembourg, Austria, and Germany. They concerned various breaches of then Community law arising from the conclusion by those Member States of bilateral air transport agreements with the US. That gave the ECJ the opportunity to clarify its case law according to which Member States are not to enter into international obligations outside the framework of the Union institutions if these obligations fall within the scope of the common rules, or within an area which is already largely covered by such rules, even if there is no contradiction between those commitments and the common rules.[49] The ECJ held that if the Union has achieved complete harmonization in a given area, it acquires an exclusive external competence in that area, even in the absence of any express provision authorizing its institutions to negotiate with non-Member States. This is so because the common rules thus adopted could be affected within the meaning of the *ERTA* principle if the Member States retained freedom to negotiate with non-Member States.[50] Both

[45] See, to that effect, judgments of 20 April 2010, Case C-246/07 *Commission v Sweden* ('*PFOS*'), EU:C:2010:203, para 72; *Broadcasting Rights Convention* (n 44 para 75, and of 20 November 2018, Cases C-626/15 and C-659/16 *Commission v Council* (*Antarctic MPAs*), EU:C:2018:925, para 115.

[46] For more on the concept of primacy, see chapter 6. As to whether the principle of primacy applies to the CFSP, see De Baere, *Constitutional Principles* (n 8) 201–212.

[47] De Baere, *Constitutional Principles* (n 8) 71–72.

[48] Judgments of 5 November 2002, Case C-466/98 *Commission v United Kingdom*, EU:C:2002:624; Case C-467/98 *Commission v Denmark*, EU:C:2002:625; Case C-468/98 *Commission v Sweden*, EU:C:2002:626; Case C-469/98 *Commission v Finland*, EU:C:2002:627; Case C-471/98 *Commission v Belgium*, EU:C:2002:628; Case C-472/98 *Commission v Luxembourg*, EU:C:2002:629; Case C-475/98 *Commission v Austria*, EU:C:2002:630; and Case C-476/98 *Commission v Germany*, EU:C:2002:631. The Court confirmed its approach in the judgment of 24 April 2007, Case C-523/04 *Commission v Netherlands*, EU:C:2007:244.

[49] See eg *Commission v Denmark* (n 48) para 82; *Commission v Germany* (n 48) para 108. The question of how to determine what an 'area' is and whether it is 'largely covered' is again before the ECJ: see Opinion 1/24 (*Air Transport Agreement with Oman*), pending.

[50] *Commission v Denmark* (n 48) para 84; *Commission v Germany* (n 48) para 110.

explicit and implied external competences can become exclusive through the exercise by the Union of its competences.

The principles and the complexity involved in their application are well illustrated by the situation in *Open Skies*. There, the ECJ held that the relevant Community legislation did not govern the granting of traffic rights on intra-Community routes to non-Community carriers nor operating licences of non-Community air carriers which operated within the then Community. In other words, the international commitments at issue did not fall within 'an area already covered by Community rules' and hence could not be regarded as affecting those rules. However, Community rules had indirectly but definitely prohibited air carriers of non-member countries operating in the Community from introducing new products or fares lower than the ones existing for identical products. As a consequence, the Community had acquired exclusive competence to enter into commitments with non-member countries relating to that limitation on the freedom of non-Community carriers to set fares and rates.[51] Relevant Community legislation also applied to nationals of non-member countries, where they offer for use or use a computerized reservation system (CRS) in Community territory. The Community thus acquired exclusive competence to contract with non-member countries the obligations relating to CRSs offered for use or used in its territory.[52] Finally, common rules for the allocation of slots at Community airports applied, subject to reciprocity, to air carriers of non-member countries, with the result that the Community had exclusive competence to conclude agreements in that area with non-member countries.[53]

Determining whether and to what extent the Union has exclusive external competence on the basis that the conclusion of an international agreement 'may affect common rules or alter their scope' therefore requires a detailed and often cumbersome analysis. As Advocate General Tizzano put it in his Opinion in *Open Skies*:[54]

> I must point out, however, that in order to establish that the common rules are affected it is not enough to cite general effects of an economic nature which the agreements could have on the functioning of the internal market; what is required instead is to specify in detail the aspects of the Community legislation which could be prejudiced by the agreements.

That requirement can be explained by the fact that the ECJ needs to steer a very careful course between the desire of the Member States to remain present on the international scene on the basis of their own competences and the need to allow the Union to build a viable (ie effective and consistent) external action policy.

Finally, the Court clarified in Opinion 2/15 that the concept of 'common rules' for the purposes of the *ERTA* principle must be understood as 'provisions of secondary law which the Community, now the European Union, has progressively laid down' and that, hence, a rule of primary EU law, such as notably a Treaty Article, cannot by itself be considered as laying down common rules.[55]

4.2.2 **Exclusivity on the basis of a legislative act**

Article 3(2) TFEU provides that the Union will have exclusive competence for the conclusion of an international agreement 'when its conclusion is provided for in a legislative act of the Union'.[56] The Lisbon Treaty has thereby partly codified the ECJ's case law to that effect. In Opinion 1/94, the ECJ held:[57]

[51] *Commission v Germany* (n 48), para 98. [52] Ibid, paras 102 and 103.
[53] Ibid, para 106. [54] Opinion of AG Tizzano in *Open Skies* (n 48), EU:C:2002:63, point 77.
[55] Opinion 2/15 (n 32) paras 229–235. [56] cf Art 289(3) TFEU.
[57] Opinion 1/94 (*Agreements annexed to the WTO Agreement*) of 15 November 1994, EU:C:1994:384, para 95; see also *Commission v Denmark* (n 48) para 83; *Commission v Germany* (n 48) para 109.

> Whenever the [Union] has included in its internal legislative acts provisions relating to the treatment of nationals of non-member countries or expressly conferred on its institutions powers to negotiate with non-member countries, it acquires exclusive external competence in the spheres covered by those acts.

The ECJ seemed to hold that this *automatically* implied exclusive competence for the Union. That statement does appear to merit some nuance, in particular in light of Article 4(3) and (4) TFEU, which ostensibly provide for a type of shared competence without 'pre-emption' (see section 4.4.1), whereby the Union cannot ever prevent the Member States from acting (and vice versa):

> 3. In the areas of research, technological development and space, the Union shall have competence to carry out activities, in particular to define and implement programmes; however, the exercise of that competence shall not result in Member States being prevented from exercising theirs.
> 4. In the areas of development cooperation and humanitarian aid, the Union shall have competence to carry out activities and conduct a common policy; however, the exercise of that competence shall not result in Member States being prevented from exercising theirs.

As mentioned previously, Article 216(1) TFEU grants the Union the competence to conclude an agreement with one or more third countries or international organizations where the conclusion of an agreement is 'provided for in a legally binding Union act'. The difference in language between Articles 3(2) ('provided for in a legislative act of the Union') and 216(1) TFEU ('provided for in a legally binding Union act') would seem to imply that the exclusive nature of the external competence depends on the nature of the procedure by which the internal act granting that competence was adopted:[58] if the possibility to conclude an international agreement is provided for in a legally binding Union act, the EU acquires competence to conclude that agreement on the basis of Article 216(1) TFEU. If that same possibility is provided for in a legislative act, the Union acquires *exclusive* competence to conclude that agreement. That distinction seems justified: an internal act that provides for the conclusion of an international agreement only gives rise to an exclusive external competence if that internal act was adopted in accordance with a democratic decision-making procedure at Union level. Nevertheless, it would seem that even a legislative act cannot grant the Union an exclusive external competence in those areas for which Article 4(3) and (4) TFEU explicitly provides that the Member States cannot be prevented from acting internationally.

4.2.3 **Exclusivity on the basis of necessity for the exercise of internal competence**

Article 3(2) TFEU provides that the Union will have exclusive competence for the conclusion of an international agreement when this is 'necessary to enable the Union to exercise its internal competence'. That codifies the ECJ's case law providing for the possibility of exclusivity to arise out of the fact that the internal and external aspects of a policy area can only be exercised effectively together.

The Commission had, for example, argued that such a situation was at hand in *Open Skies*. The ECJ disagreed. It held that the EC Treaty did not prevent the institutions

[58] Perhaps the distinction in wording was introduced to make it clear that this principle cannot give rise to an exclusive competence within the CFSP, given that Art 24(1), second subpara, TEU and Art 31(1) TEU exclude the adoption of legislative acts.

from arranging, through internal Community rules, concerted action in relation to the US. Furthermore, the EC Treaty equally did not prevent the institutions from prescribing the approach the Member States should take in their external relations, in order to alleviate possible discrimination or distortions of competition resulting from the implementation of the open skies agreements entered into by certain Member States with the US. The ECJ concluded that it had not been established that the aims of the EC Treaty in the area of air transport could not be achieved by establishing autonomous Community rules.[59] This was confirmed, the ECJ held, by the fact that in 1992 the Council was able to adopt a set of measures achieving the internal market in air transport services without feeling the need to enter into any international agreements with the US. That the measures adopted by the Council contained some provisions on the treatment of third-country nationals did not diminish the force of that conclusion in any way. There was, therefore, *in casu* no question of an internal competence that can only be effectively exercised at the same time as the corresponding external competence, and that would render such a competence exclusive in accordance with the ECJ's reading of Opinion 1/76.[60]

Given that the ECJ appears to have regarded Opinion 1/76 (see section 3.2) as authority both for the existence and for the exclusive nature of implied external competence, the question arises whether and, if so, how this blurring of the two issues found its way into the TFEU. In particular, how can Article 3(2) TFEU in this respect be distinguished from the fact that the Union 'may conclude an agreement with one or more third countries or international organisations ... where the conclusion of an agreement is necessary in order to achieve, within the framework of the Union's policies, one of the objectives referred to in the Treaties', pursuant to Article 216(1) TFEU.

Perhaps the distinction between existence of implied external competence under Article 216(1) TFEU and the exclusive nature of that competence under Article 3(2) TFEU can be brought back to a distinction the ECJ arguably appears to have made in part of its case law. On the one hand, there exist situations in which the Union wishes to further, on the external front, internal policy goals, the optimal use of which presupposes an external complement, but which could nonetheless arguably have been sufficiently attained with internal rules only. The Union acquires a non-exclusive external competence in those situations. This is what Opinion 2/92 seemed to say[61] and appears to correspond to Article 216(1) TFEU. On the other hand, there may be the rare factual constellations in which the objectives of EU competences could not possibly be achieved without including third countries, through international agreements, into the binding legal framework regulating the situation. The Union would acquire exclusive implied external competences in the case of such an inextricable link,[62] though it is difficult to come up with an example of a situation that would unambiguously fall within that category.[63]

That distinction can be illustrated by the Court's reasoning in Opinion 2/15 with respect to non-direct foreign investments. In particular, the Court held that because the free movement of capital and payments between Member States and third States, laid down in Article 63 TFEU, is not formally binding on third States, the conclusion of international agreements that contribute to the establishment of such free movement on a

[59] *Commission v Germany* (n 48) para 85; see also Opinion 1/03 (*New Lugano Convention*) of 7 February 2006, EU:C:2006:81, para 123.

[60] *Commission v Germany* (n 48) paras 86–89.

[61] Opinion 2/92 (*Third Revised Decision of the OECD on National Treatment*) of 24 March 1995, EU:C:1995:83, para 32.

[62] The Court omitted a reference to the need for such an inextricable link in Opinion 1/03 (n 59) para 115.

[63] cf P Eeckhout, *EU External Relations Law* (2nd edn, Oxford: Oxford University Press, 2011) 118.

reciprocal basis may be classified as necessary in order to achieve fully such free movement, which is one of the objectives of Title IV ('Free movement of persons, services and capital') of Part Three ('Union policies and internal actions') of the TFEU. The Court concluded that the competence conferred on the European Union by Article 216(1) TFEU in respect of the conclusion of an agreement relating to the protection of non-direct foreign investments was 'necessary in order to achieve, within the framework of the Union's policies, one of the objectives referred to in the Treaties'.[64] By contrast, as regards the potentially exclusive nature of that competence, the Court limited itself to the somewhat laconic statement that 'as the Commission has expressly stated in its observations submitted to the Court, the conclusion of such an agreement does not appear "necessary to enable the Union to exercise its internal competence", within the meaning of Article 3(2) TFEU', and that it followed that the EU does not have exclusive competence to conclude an international agreement with Singapore insofar as it relates to the protection of non-direct foreign investments.[65]

Nevertheless, neither Article 216(1) TFEU nor Article 3(2) TFEU sufficiently reflect the complexity of the case law on which they are based, especially with regard to the need for an 'inextricable link' in order for 'necessity' to give rise to an exclusive Union competence. The ECJ will hence have to rely on its pre-codification case law to interpret the text of those two provisions, including, inter alia, what is to be understood under 'necessary'.[66]

4.3 **Consequences of exclusive competence**

Article 2(1) TFEU provides that when the Treaties confer on the Union exclusive competence in a specific area, only the Union may legislate and adopt legally binding acts. The Member States are only able to do so themselves if they have been so empowered by the Union or for the implementation of Union acts (see the discussion of implementation by the Member States in sections 5.1 and 5.2). Specifically with respect to external action, it follows from the ECJ's case law that the exclusivity of the Union's external competence has two main consequences, which are really two sides of the same coin.[67]

(a) First, when the external competence in a certain area is exclusive, the Member States, as the ECJ put it in *ERTA*, 'no longer have the right, acting individually or even collectively, to undertake obligations with third countries'.[68] The ECJ also referred to what is now Article 4(3) TEU, enshrining the principle of loyalty and sincere cooperation, and concluded that it would be impossible for the Member States operating outside the institutional framework of the Union to assume responsibilities that might affect or alter the scope of Union rules that have been promulgated for the attainment of Treaty objectives.[69]

(b) Secondly, the ECJ pointed out in Ruling 1/78 that when external Union competence is exclusive:[70]

[64] Opinion 2/15 (n 32) paras 239–242. [65] Ibid, paras 237–238. [66] See further section 3.

[67] Exclusivity also implies the inapplicability of the principle of subsidiarity: Art 5(3), first subpara, TEU. On that principle, see further chapter 5. Also see the Opinion of AG Szpunar in Case C-600/14 *Germany v Council*, EU:C:2017:296, point 118, noting that the principle of subsidiarity 'applies to the exercise of any shared competence, whether internal or external'.

[68] *ERTA* (n 26) para 17.

[69] Ibid, para 22; see further Opinion 1/75 (*OECD Understanding on a Local Cost Standard*) of 11 November 1975, EU:C:1975:145.

[70] Ruling 1/78 (*Draft IAEA Convention on the Physical Protection of Nuclear Materials, Facilities and Transports*) of 14 November 1978, EU:C:1978:202, para 32.

> the Member States, whether acting individually or collectively, are no longer able to impose on the [Union] obligations which impose conditions on the exercise of prerogatives which thenceforth belong to the [Union] and which therefore no longer fall within the field of national sovereignty.

In other words, the Member States must not attempt to constrain the Union's exercise of its exclusive competence and must cooperate loyally with it in order to facilitate such an exercise.[71]

Exclusivity imposes an obligation on the Member States not to enter into any international agreements that could affect the Union's exclusive competences. In other words, it limits the possibility for law-making by the Member States. They are legally obliged not to exercise their competences to enter into certain international agreements.

There are three main reasons for this:

(a) first, the desire to avoid adverse consequences for the Member States' international liability in case they conclude an international agreement incompatible with EU law;

(b) secondly, the possibility that the existence of an international agreement autonomously concluded by the Member States could prejudice the integrity of the 'coherent system' of rules established by EU law;[72] and

(c) thirdly, the possibility that Member States might block the evolution of EU law by concluding international agreements the subject matter of which is covered by common rules, thus 'freezing' Union law in the state it is in at the moment the agreement is concluded. This explains why even if the intended agreement would be consistent with EU law, the Member States are not allowed to conclude it if it falls under exclusive Union competences.[73]

Moreover, it is important to understand that competence issues in principle need to be resolved before the intended international agreement is even negotiated, as it needs to be established who will negotiate. Given that, in the nature of things, there will be no final text of the agreement at that point in time, the resolution of the competence question cannot depend on the existence of an actual conflict between the agreement and the EU common rules.[74]

However, the Member States retain capacity to conduct international relations both under national and international law. Exclusive Union competences simply require them not to act autonomously. This is evident from the text of Article 2(1) TFEU, which provides for the possibility for the Union to empower the Member States to act in an area in which the Union enjoys exclusive competence. EU law can therefore authorize the Member States to act jointly on the international plane even within exclusive external Union competences. Examples of such empowerment are a number of regulations in which the Union established a procedure for the negotiation and conclusion of agreements between Member States and third countries concerning jurisdiction, recognition, and enforcement of judgments and decisions in matrimonial matters, matters of

[71] cf ibid, paras 33 and 22; *Kramer* (n 26) paras 44–45.

[72] See Opinion 1/03 (n 59) paras 122–133.

[73] See eg Opinion 1/13 (n 44) paras 85–86.

[74] Eeckhout (n 63) 86. Cf *Antarctic MPAs* (n 45) para 112, where the Court held that Art 3(2) TFEU must be interpreted, 'in order to preserve its practical effect, as meaning that, although its wording refers solely to the conclusion of an international agreement, it also applies, at an earlier stage, when such an agreement is being negotiated and, at a later stage, when a body established by the agreement is called upon to adopt measures implementing it'.

parental responsibility, and matters relating to maintenance obligations, and the law applicable to matters relating to maintenance obligations.[75] Nevertheless, the Court has clarified that the decision to empower Member States under Article 2(1) TFEU essentially allows Member States to exercise a competence which the Treaties have conferred exclusively on the EU and which the latter should, in principle, exercise alone. Such a decision therefore expresses a specific political choice between two alternatives, namely, on the one hand, that the EU alone exercises its exclusive competence and, on the other hand, that the Member States are empowered to exercise that competence.[76] Such a choice forms part of the Commission's assessment of the general interest of the EU, to which the power of initiative entrusted to that institution by Article 17(2) TEU is inextricably linked. Therefore, an amendment by the Council seeking to empower Member States to exercise an exclusive competence of the EU would distort the very purpose of a Commission proposal reflecting the choice according to which the EU alone should exercise that competence.[77]

A particular issue arises when an agenda item in an international organization relates to a subject falling within exclusive Union competence, but where the Union itself has not managed to become a member of the organization.[78] In such situations, the division of competences must equally be complied with, and Member States are not to make unilateral proposals, even for non-binding acts. The ECJ underlined as much with respect to a proposal Greece submitted to the International Maritime Organization (IMO) Maritime Safety Committee to examine the creation of check lists or other appropriate tools for assisting the contracting States of the International Convention for the Safety of Life at Sea (the SOLAS Convention) in monitoring whether ships and port facilities complied with certain requirements.[79]

4.4 **Non-exclusive competences**

4.4.1 **Shared competences**

The basic rule

'Shared competences', as provided for by Articles 2(2) and 4 TFEU (sometimes referred to as 'concurrent' competences), can be exercised by the Member States to the extent that the Union has not exercised, or has decided to cease exercising,[80] its competence. Article 2(2) TFEU therefore ties Member States' competences to the evolving exercise of EU competence over time:[81]

> When the Treaties confer on the Union a competence shared with the Member States in a specific area, the Union and the Member States may legislate and adopt legally binding acts in that area. The Member States shall exercise their competence to the extent that the Union has not exercised its competence. The Member States shall again exercise their competence to the extent that the Union has decided to cease exercising its competence.

[75] Council Regulation (EC) No 664/2009 (OJ [2009] L200/46). Cf Regulation (EC) No 662/2009 of the European Parliament and of the Council of 13 July 2009 establishing a procedure for the negotiation and conclusion of agreements between Member States and third countries on particular matters concerning the law applicable to contractual and non-contractual obligations (OJ [2009] L200/25). See Eeckhout (n 63) 162.

[76] Judgment of 22 November 2022, Case C-24/20 *Commission v Council* (*Accession to the Geneva Act*), EU:C:2022:911, paras 102–103.

[77] Ibid, paras 104–105.

[78] See further section 6.2.6.

[79] Judgment of 12 February 2009, Case C-45/07 *Commission v Greece*, EU:C:2009:81.

[80] See Declaration 18 in relation to the delimitation of competences (OJ [2016] C202/344).

[81] The Member States' unease in that regard caused them to annex to the TEU and TFEU Protocol No 25 on the exercise of shared competence (OJ [2016] C202/306).

The effect of this is often referred to as 'occupying the field' or, by analogy with US constitutional doctrine, 'pre-emption'.[82] However, the mechanism is not as generally applicable as it may seem. Apart from the parallel competences discussed further in this section, a number of shared competences preclude the EU from fully harmonizing the law in a certain area, mainly because the Union can only lay down minimum standards.

Minimum standards

A prominent example is Article 193 TFEU, which determines that the substantive environmental measures adopted on the basis of Article 192 TFEU are to be only minimum measures:

> The protective measures adopted pursuant to Article 192 shall not prevent any Member State from maintaining or introducing more stringent protective measures. Such measures must be compatible with the Treaties. They shall be notified to the Commission.

The concept of internal Union minimum standards thus involves the Union harmonizing a certain policy area on the basis of minimum requirements, while leaving the Member States free to adopt more stringent measures. As the ECJ held in Opinion 1/03, the fact that both the Union rules and the international agreement in question lay down minimum standards:[83]

> may justify the conclusion that the [Union] rules are not affected, even if the [Union] rules and the provisions of the agreement cover the same area.

The requirement that both the Union rules and the international agreement in question lay down minimum standards is necessary in order not to inhibit the development of Union law. If an international agreement lays down an absolute standard, and the Union subsequently decides to raise its minimum standards above the absolute standard of the agreement, a conflict may arise with inevitable consequences for the international responsibility of the Union. External environmental competences and the impact of the fact that they are mostly based on minimum requirements will be further explored in this chapter's case study. As will be illustrated there, the principle of sincere cooperation in Article 4(3) TEU may nevertheless restrict Member States' actions, even if they are acting within their own sphere of competence.

Parallel competences

'Parallel competences' (a term not used in the Treaties) leave both the Union and the Member States competent to act internationally without one being able definitively to prevent the other from acting. An important example of the latter category[84] is Article

[82] See the discussion of the pre-emption doctrine in G De Baere and K Gutman, 'Federalism and International Relations in the European Union and the United States: A Comparative Outlook' in E Cloots, G De Baere, and S Sottiaux (eds), *Federalism in the European Union* (Oxford: Hart Publishing, 2012) 157–165. See further more generally A Arena, 'Exercise of EU Competences and Pre-Emption of Member States' Powers in the Internal and the External Sphere: Towards "Grand Unification"?' (2016) 35 *Yearbook of European Law* 28. However, the Court has not generally adopted this term, and there is no academic consensus on its usage. Nevertheless, the term has been mentioned by Advocates General: see eg Opinion of AG Sharpston in Opinion 2/15, EU:C:2016:992, points 59, 61, and 73, and Opinion of AG Ćapeta in Case C-500/20 *ÖBB-Infrastruktur Aktiengesellschaft*, EU:C:2022:79, points 64–67, 69, 83, 88, and 99.

[83] Opinion 1/03 (n 59) paras 123 and 127. See also Opinion 2/91 (*ILO Convention No 170*) of 19 March 1993, EU:C:1993:106, para 18. The Court further clarified the impact of minimum standards in *PFOS* (n 45) para 102. See further case study 26.1.

[84] See also Art 191(4) TFEU (environmental policy) and Art 219(4) TFEU (monetary policy).

211 TFEU on development cooperation, which states that the Union and the Member States, each within their respective spheres of competence, are to cooperate with third countries and with the competent international organizations. Pursuant to Article 209(2) TFEU, the arrangements for Union cooperation may be the subject of agreements between the Union and the third parties concerned. However, Article 209(2) TFEU ends with the explicit assurance that the external competence described in that Article 'shall be without prejudice to Member States' competence to negotiate in international bodies and to conclude international agreements'. Furthermore, Article 4(4) TFEU provides for the exercise of the Union's competence in the areas of development cooperation and humanitarian aid not to result in Member States being prevented from exercising theirs, thus creating parallel competences in those areas.

Coordination of Member States' actions

The Union may in some areas of shared competences adopt measures designed to coordinate Member States' exercise of their competence and the EU's exercise of its competence. For example, in *Open Skies*, the ECJ countered the Commission's argument that the conclusion of an international agreement was necessary in order to attain objectives of the Treaty that could not be attained by establishing autonomous rules by holding that there was:

> nothing in the Treaty to prevent the institutions arranging, in the common rules laid down by them, concerted action in relation to the United States of America, or to prevent them prescribing the approach to be taken by the Member States in their external dealings, so as to mitigate any discrimination or distortions of competition which might result from the implementation of the commitments entered into by certain Member States with the United States of America under open skies agreements.

Following the judgments in *Open Skies*, the EU did indeed adopt legislation coordinating Member States' exercise of their competence with respect to international agreements with third States as regards air traffic rights.[85] Furthermore, on 30 April 2007, the then Community and its Member States and the US signed the Air Transport Agreement designed to replace the bilateral open skies agreements between the US and various EU Member States.[86] The Agreement was provisionally applied from 30 March 2008 for all EU Member States,[87] and amended by a Protocol,[88] signed and provisionally applied on 24 June 2010.[89] The Agreement aims to open access to markets and to maximize benefits for consumers, airlines, labour, and communities on both sides of the Atlantic not just between the initial parties, but also by extending the Agreement to include third countries,[90] a call to which Norway and Iceland have responded.[91]

[85] Regulation (EC) No 847/2004 (OJ [2004] L157/7).

[86] Decision 2007/339/EC of the Council and the Representatives of the Governments of the Member States of the European Union, meeting within the Council (OJ [2007] L134/1).

[87] See Art 25(1) of the EU–US Air Transport Agreement.

[88] Decision 2010/465/EU of the Council and the Representatives of the Governments of the Member States of the European Union, meeting within the Council (OJ [2010] L223/1).

[89] See Art 9(1) of the Protocol to the EU–US Air Transport Agreement.

[90] Art 18(5) of the EU–US Air Transport Agreement.

[91] Decision 2011/708/EU of the Council and of the Representatives of the Governments of the Member States of the European Union, meeting within the Council of 16 June 2011 (OJ [2011] L283/1), annulled by judgment of 28 April 2015, Case C-28/12 *Commission v Council*, EU:C:2015:282 for being an illegal so-called 'hybrid decision', ie a decision combining a Council decision (a decision by an EU institution) with a decision of the representatives of the governments of the Member States (a collective decision by the Member States). See T Verellen, 'On Hybrid Decision, Mixed Agreements and the Limits of the New Legal Order: *Commission v Council* ("*US Air Transport Agreement*")' (2016) 53 *Common Market Law Review* 1.

4.4.2 The CFSP

Finally, what type of competence is the CFSP? Could it be argued that Article 4(1) TFEU ('The Union shall share competence with the Member States where the Treaties confer on it a competence which does not relate to the areas referred to in Articles 3 and 6') implies that the CFSP is a shared competence as well? Though a literal reading of Article 4(1) TFEU would seem to have that consequence, in view of Declarations Nos 13 and 14, annexed to the Lisbon Final Act,[92] it appears highly unlikely that the Member States had the intention of subjecting the CFSP to the corollary of shared competences, namely that the Member States can exercise their competence 'to the extent that the Union has not exercised its competence' or 'has decided to cease exercising its competence'.[93]

Moreover, if the CFSP was intended to be a 'shared competence', why then create a separate category of CFSP competence in Article 2(4) TFEU instead of listing it among shared competences in Article 4(2) TFEU and adding a clause to the effect that 'the exercise of that competence shall not result in Member States being prevented from exercising theirs', as was done with regard to research, technological development, space, development cooperation, and humanitarian aid in Article 4(3) and (4) TFEU? The Member States appear to have opted specifically not to subsume the CFSP under any of the other categories of competences and to create a *sui generis* category; the reason being no doubt to emphasize once again the special nature of the competence.

5 Decision-making in EU external action

5.1 The ordinary Union method

The ordinary Union method[94] of decision-making is characterized by:

(a) the central role of the Commission in formulating proposals;[95]

(b) qualified majority voting (QMV) in the Council;[96]

(c) involvement of the European Parliament with varying intensity depending on the decision-making procedure, but since Lisbon mostly through the ordinary legislative procedure;[97] and

(d) the role of the CJEU in ensuring judicial accountability.[98]

This is not the place for an exhaustive analysis of the various aspects of the ordinary Union method.[99] However, a couple of particular points as regards its operation within the field of external action need to be made.

First, as far as autonomous acts are concerned, the Union legal instruments are, in principle, identical in internal and external policies.

Secondly, the role of the European Parliament in the Union's ordinary external action, while larger than in the CFSP (see section 5.2), is still smaller than with regard to internal

[92] OJ [2016] C202/343. These declarations emphasize that the provisions on the CFSP in the TEU do not 'affect' the responsibilities, the existing legal basis, and the powers of the Member States for the formulation and conduct of their foreign policy.

[93] Art 2(2) TFEU, which applies, eg, to the common agricultural policy; eg judgment of 12 September 2024, Case C-557/23 *SPAR Magyarország*, EU:C:2024:737, para 35. Cf Opinion of AG Sharpston in Opinion 2/15 (n 82) point 60, fn 19.

[94] This chapter uses the term 'ordinary Union method' for what formerly was usually referred to as the 'Community method'.

[95] Art 17(2) TEU. [96] Art 16(3) TEU.

[97] Arts 289(1) and 294 TFEU. [98] Art 19(1) TEU.

[99] On this issue, see chapter 3 (as regards the political institutions) and chapter 10 (as regards the Court).

Union policies. This was even more the case before the entry into force of the Lisbon Treaty. For example, in the Union's largest and most successful area of external action, the CCP, the European Parliament had no formal role in the internal decision-making procedure. The Lisbon Treaty has changed the role of the European Parliament in EU external action in quite important ways, especially with regard to ordinary EU external action (see further section 6.2). As regards the CCP, Article 207(2) TFEU now provides for the ordinary legislative procedure to apply to measures defining the framework for its implementation. Because Article 218(6)(a)(v) TFEU now provides for the Parliament's consent to be necessary for agreements covering fields to which the ordinary legislative procedure applies, the CCP is now in principle subject to full parliamentary control, both as regards autonomous measures and international agreements.

Thirdly, an all-important point of discussion regarding the ordinary Union method is the procedure followed by the Council for adopting decisions. The options range from unanimity to several forms of majority voting, mostly through QMV.[100]

Fourthly, Union measures are, in the absence of specific provisions to the contrary, to be implemented by the Member States,[101] with due regard to the principle of sincere cooperation in Article 4(3) TEU. In ordinary EU external action, if uniform conditions for implementing legally binding Union acts are required at the Union level, those acts are to confer implementing powers on the Commission, or, in duly justified specific cases, on the Council.[102] In the field of development cooperation, for example, or in programmes such as under the Neighbourhood, Development and International Cooperation Instrument—Global Europe (NDICI—Global Europe),[103] the Commission actively oversees implementation. However, the Commission needs to coordinate in that regard with the High Representative, and the EEAS is to contribute to the programming and management cycle for such instruments. That said, the EEAS has a particular role in the programming, but the management of the Union's external cooperation programmes remains under the responsibility of the Commission, which implements the Union budget[104] and retains the authority over the operational credits.[105]

Finally, the ECJ has played a crucial role in the development of Union external action through its case law and its advisory opinions. The most significant contrast with respect to the role of the ECJ between internal and external matters, apart from its generally more circumspect approach to the latter, is the specific procedure for a preliminary opinion, as laid down in Article 218(11) TFEU:

> A Member State, the European Parliament, the Council or the Commission may obtain the opinion of the Court of Justice as to whether an agreement envisaged is compatible with the Treaties. Where the opinion of the Court is adverse, the agreement envisaged may not enter into force unless it is amended or the Treaties are revised.

[100] eg Art 207(4) TFEU. On Council voting rules generally, see chapter 4.

[101] Art 291(1) TFEU. [102] Art 291(2) TFEU.

[103] Regulation (EU) 2021/947 of the European Parliament and of the Council of 9 June 2021 establishing the Neighbourhood, Development and International Cooperation Instrument—Global Europe (OJ [2021] L209/1). See also Commission Delegated Regulation (EU) 2021/1530 of 12 July 2021 supplementing Regulation (EU) 2021/947 (OJ [2021] L330/27).

[104] Art 317 TFEU.

[105] Art 9 EEAS Decision. See further on the EEAS–Commission relationship, J Wouters, G De Baere, B Van Vooren, K Raube, J Odermatt, T Ramopoulos, T Van den Sanden, and Y Tanghe, *The Organisation and Functioning of the European External Action Service: Achievements, Challenges and Opportunities* (Brussels: European Parliament, Directorate-General for External Policies of the Union, Directorate B, Policy Department, 2013) 46–57 (the EP EEAS Study).

There is no similar procedure for determining in advance whether an internal proposal is in accordance with the Treaties. The presence of this procedure with regard to external matters and its absence with respect to internal matters can be explained by the specific needs of external action. The Union cannot afford to conclude an agreement with third countries that will later be found to be infringing the Treaties.[106] For example, in Opinion 2/94, the ECJ ruled that the then Community could not accede to the European Convention on Human Rights (ECHR)[107] without amendment of the Treaties, thereby providing the necessary impetus for the drafters of the Lisbon Treaty to insert a new Article 6(2) in the EU Treaty stating that the Union is to accede to the ECHR.[108]

Moreover, the CJEU's normal jurisdiction applies to treaties concluded by the EU, as regards their interpretation and the validity of the decisions to conclude them on the EU's behalf.[109] Article 216(2) TFEU provides for agreements concluded by the Union to be 'binding upon the institutions of the Union and on its Member States'. Such agreements prevail over EU acts,[110] and their provisions form an integral part of the EU legal order as from their entry into force.[111] This has a number of important consequences.

First, EU secondary law must be interpreted, insofar as possible, in accordance with the provisions of such agreements.[112]

Secondly, a request for a preliminary ruling concerning the validity of an international agreement concluded by the Union must be understood as relating to the EU act approving the conclusion of that international agreement, yet the review of validity that the Court may be required to carry out in that context is nonetheless capable of encompassing the legality of that act in the light of the actual content of the international agreement at issue.[113] The same applies, *mutatis mutandis*, to actions for annulment.[114]

[106] The admissibility of a request for such an opinion is predicated on the Court having sufficient information on the actual content of the envisaged agreement: see Opinion 1/20 (*Modernised Energy Charter Treaty*) of 16 June 2022, EU:C:2022:485.

[107] Convention for the Protection of Human Rights and Fundamental Freedoms of 4 November 1950, 213 UNTS 221.

[108] An agreement on the EU's accession to the ECHR was reached in April 2013. However, the ECJ held that agreement to be 'not compatible with Article 6(2) TEU or with Protocol (No 8)' relating to Art 6(2) TEU on the accession of the Union to the ECHR: Opinion 2/13 (*Accession of the European Union to the ECHR*) of 18 December 2014, EU:C:2014:2454. See further chapter 9. Accession negotiations resumed in 2020, and in March 2023, the negotiators reached an agreement on a revised set of accession instruments. The Commission has asked the ECJ whether the revised agreement is compatible with the Treaties: Opinion 1/25 (*Accession of the European Union to the ECHR*), pending.

[109] See eg judgment of 21 December 2011, Case C-366/10 *Air Transport Association of America and Others* ('*ATAA*'), EU:C:2011:864, on which see G De Baere and C Ryngaert, 'The ECJ's Judgment in *Air Transport Association of America* and the International Legal Context of the EU's Climate Change Policy' (2013) 18 *European Foreign Affairs Review* 389.

[110] *ATAA* (n 109) para 50.

[111] Judgments of 30 April 1974, Case 181/73 *Haegeman*, EU:C:1974:41, para 5; *ATAA* (n 109) para 73, and of 27 February 2018, Case C-266/16 *Western Sahara Campaign UK*, EU:C:2018:118, para 46. That is eg the case regarding the EUUKTCA: cf Opinion of AG Medina in Case C-528/24 *Minister for Justice and Equality and Others*, EU:C:2025:940, point 70, fn 55.

[112] Judgments of 27 February 2024, Case C-382/21 P *EUIPO v The KaiKai Company Jaeger Wichmann*, EU:C:2024:172, para 70, and of 10 September 2025, Case T-625/22 *Austria v Commission*, EU:T:2025:869, para 187.

[113] *Western Sahara Campaign UK* (n 111) paras 50–51. Cf regarding the Brexit Agreement: judgment of 9 June 2022, Case C-673/20 *Préfet du Gers and Institut national de la statistique et des études économiques*, EU:C:2022:449, para 85.

[114] Judgments of 4 October 2024, Joined Cases C-778/21 P and C-798/21 P *Commission v Front Polisario*, EU:C:2024:833, para 206, and Joined Cases C-779/21 P and C-799/21 P *Commission v Front Polisario* ('*Front Polisario II*'), EU:C:2024:835, para 174, on which see Istrefi and Cebulak (n 2).

Thirdly, the validity of an EU act may be affected by the fact that it is incompatible with rules of international treaty law[115] when a number of conditions are fulfilled:[116]

(a) the EU must be bound by those rules;[117]
(b) the nature and the broad logic of the international Treaty in question must not preclude the CJEU from examining the validity of an EU act in light of its provisions;[118] and
(c) the Treaty provisions relied upon for the purpose of examining the validity of the EU act in question appear, as regards their content, to be unconditional and sufficiently precise,[119] that is, they contain a clear and precise obligation that is not subject, in its implementation or effects, to the adoption of any subsequent measure.[120]

These latter two conditions are also used by the Court to examine whether provisions of international agreements have direct effect.[121]

Fourthly, Member States are under an obligation, pursuant to Article 216(2) TFEU, to implement those parts of an international agreement for which the Union has confirmed its competence and, on the basis of Article 344 TFEU, not to violate the monopoly of the CJEU to interpret and apply Union law, and hence not to initiate international dispute settlement proceedings against each other in respect of those parts of the agreement.[122]

Finally, it is worth pointing out that the CJEU has been confronted with delicate problems of international law in the exercise of its normal jurisdiction over both internal and external measures. Notable examples include the relationship between UN Security Council resolutions and human rights,[123] the territorial division of Cyprus,[124] the status of Western Sahara,[125] and the territory of the State of Israel.[126]

[115] Judgment of 4 October 2024, Joined Cases C-541–555/20 *Lithuania and Others v Parliament and Council* (*Mobility package*), EU:C:2024:818, para 1034.

[116] *ATAA* (n 109) paras 52–55. On the slightly different conditions that apply to customary international law, see ibid, para 107. See further chapter 6.

[117] Judgment of 12 December 1972, Joined Cases 21–24/72 *International Fruit Company and Others*, EU:C:1972:115, para 7.

[118] *Mobility package* (n 125) para 1036.

[119] Ibid.

[120] Judgment of 18 March 2014, Case C-363/12 *Z*, EU:C:2014:159, paras 85–90, on which see G De Baere, 'Shall I Be Mother? The Prohibition on Sex Discrimination, the UN Disability Convention, and the Right to Surrogacy Leave under EU Law' (2015) 74 *Cambridge Law Journal* 44.

[121] Judgment of 29 February 2024, Case C-549/22 *Raad van bestuur van de Sociale verzekeringsbank* (*Transfer of survivors' benefits*), EU:C:2024:184, para 30.

[122] Judgment of 30 May 2006, Case C-459/03 *Commission v Ireland* ('*Mox Plant*'), EU:C:2006:345.

[123] Judgments of 3 September 2008, Joined Cases C-402/05 P and C-415/05 P *Kadi and Al Barakaat International Foundation v Council and Commission* ('*Kadi I*'), EU:C:2008:461, and of 18 July 2013, Joined Cases C-584/10 P, C-593/10 P, and C-595/10 P *Commission and Others v Kadi* ('*Kadi II*'), EU:C:2013:518. See chapter 8, case study 8.4 and chapter 9, case study 9.1. See further eg G de Búrca, 'The European Court of Justice and the International Legal Order After Kadi' (2010) 51 *Harvard International Law Journal* 1; G De Baere, 'European Integration and the Rule of Law in Foreign Policy' in J Dickson and P Eleftheriadis (eds), *Philosophical Foundations of European Union Law* (Oxford: Oxford University Press, 2012) 374–380.

[124] Judgment of 28 April 2009, Case C-420/07 *Apostolides*, EU:C:2009:271, on which see eg G De Baere (2010) 47 *Common Market Law Review* 1123.

[125] Judgments of 21 December 2016, Case C-104/16 P *Council v Front Polisario*, EU:C:2016:973; *Western Sahara Campaign UK* (n 111), *Front Polisario II* (n 114).

[126] Judgments of 25 February 2010, Case C-386/08 *Brita*, EU:C:2010:91, and of 12 November 2019, Case C-363/18 *Organisation juive européenne and Vignoble Psagot*, EU:C:2019:954.

5.2 The CFSP

5.2.1 Preparation and adoption

Under the ordinary Union method, with only a few exceptions, nothing can happen without an initiative from the Commission, which as mentioned also has the main responsibility for implementing measures that may be necessary at Union level. By contrast, the formal distinction between the preparation and the adoption of measures is not part of the CFSP, as the preparation, adoption, and implementation of measures mostly takes place within the Council and its preparatory organs.

Nevertheless, Article 30(1) TEU provides that any Member State, the High Representative, or the High Representative with the Commission's support, may refer any question relating to the CFSP to the Council and may submit to it, respectively, initiatives or proposals. In cases requiring a rapid decision, pursuant to Article 30(2) TEU, the High Representative, of his own motion, or at the request of a Member State, is to convene an extraordinary Council meeting within 48 hours or, in an emergency, within a shorter period.

Moreover, an important and specific feature of the CSDP is that the European Council has become involved not only in setting general guidelines, but in the development of a detailed policy framework.

5.2.2 Legal instruments

While the EU Treaty does not provide for a specific and detailed attribution of competence in the CFSP, it defines the legal instruments that the EU has at its disposal to conduct the CFSP, and develops a specific set of CFSP decision-making procedures. Article 25 TEU states that the Union is to conduct the CFSP by:

(a) defining the general guidelines;
(b) adopting decisions defining:
  (i) actions to be undertaken by the Union;
  (ii) positions to be taken by the Union; and
  (iii) arrangements for the implementation of the decisions referred to in points (i) and (ii); and by
(c) strengthening systematic cooperation between Member States in the conduct of policy.

Articles 24(1) and 31(1) TEU also explicitly exclude legislative acts from being adopted within the CFSP.

The possibility for the European Council to adopt 'common strategies' under ex Article 13(2) TEU has been replaced by Article 22(1) TEU, which provides for the European Council to adopt decisions 'on the strategic interests and objectives of the Union', which are to relate to the CFSP *and* to other areas of the external action of the Union. In other words, Article 22(1) TEU has opened up the possibility for strategic decisions on EU external action in its entirety and not just on the CFSP, thereby remedying the impossibility in that regard under ex Article 13 TEU, which probably played a large part in the demise of the pre-Lisbon common strategies.[127] Nevertheless, despite their potential for contributing to greater consistency in EU external action, no decision under Article 22(1) TEU has yet been adopted.

[127] De Baere, *Constitutional Principles* (n 8) 114–115.

5.2.3 Decision-making in the Council

There is a marked distinction between the CFSP and ordinary EU external action with regard to decision-making in the Council. While, pursuant to Article 16(3) TEU, QMV is to be the rule and unanimity the exception, Article 31(1) TEU reverses that order within the field of the CFSP: decisions under the CFSP are to be taken by the European Council and the Council acting unanimously, except where Chapter 2 of Title V of the TEU (ie the chapter on the CFSP) provides otherwise.

However, the TEU contains a mechanism to enable a Member State not to take part in a decision without preventing the other Member States from adopting it by unanimity. Pursuant to what is sometimes called 'constructive abstention', when a Member State decides to abstain in a vote, it has the possibility of qualifying this abstention by making a formal declaration,[128] and it will then not be obliged to apply the decision, though it must accept that the decision binds the Union. The Member State in question must also, 'in a spirit of mutual solidarity', refrain from any action likely to conflict with or impede Union action based on the decision on which it has decided to abstain. As with the sincere cooperation obligation of Article 4(3) TEU, the loyalty works both ways: the other Member States have to respect the position of the abstaining Member State. However, differentiation and opting out has its limits. If the Member States wishing to abstain on a specific matter represent at least one-third of the Member States comprising at least one-third of the population of the Union, the decision cannot be adopted. That makes political and legal sense. Council decisions—one might add, especially with regard to external action—should have the support of a substantial number of the members of the Council, or how can it plausibly be claimed that the Union has acted.[129] The mechanism was used by Cyprus, which abstained on the adoption of the Joint Action setting up the Rule of Law Mission in Kosovo[130] on the ground that it would have preferred an explicit UN Security Council authorization.[131] More recently, Austria, Ireland, and Malta constructively abstained[132] from an assistance measure under the European Peace Facility (EPF)[133] for the supply to the Ukrainian Armed Forces of military equipment, and platforms, designed to deliver lethal force.[134] Furthermore, Hungary has, as a rule, so far abstained from EPF decisions on the supply of lethal weapons to Ukraine,[135] and likewise abstained from the decision creating the Ukraine Assistance Fund (UAF) within the EPF.[136]

By derogation from the unanimity rule in the CFSP, the Council acts by QMV:[137]

[128] Art 31(1), second subpara, TEU.

[129] cf RA Wessel, *The European Union's Foreign and Security Policy: A Legal Institutional Perspective* (The Hague/Boston/London: Kluwer Law International, 1999) 144.

[130] Council Joint Action 2008/124/CFSP (OJ [2008] L42/92).

[131] Council Doc CM 448/08 of 4 February 2008.

[132] Council Doc 7282/22 of 16 March 2022.

[133] Pursuant to Art 1(1) of Council Decision (CFSP) 2021/509 of 22 March 2021 establishing a European Peace Facility (OJ [2021] L102/14), the EPF's goal is the financing by Member States of CFSP actions to preserve peace, prevent conflicts, and strengthen international security in accordance with Art 21(2)(c) TEU, in cases where, pursuant to Art 41(2) TEU, the operating expenditure arising from those actions is not charged to the Union budget. The EPF contains €17 billion, including the dedicated Ukraine Assistance Fund (UAF) of €5 billion (see www.eeas.europa.eu/sites/default/files/2025/documents/EU-peace-facility_2025_SEPT_EN.pdf).

[134] Council Decision (CFSP) 2022/338 (OJ [2022] L60/1).

[135] D Genini, 'How the War in Ukraine Has Transformed the EU's Common Foreign and Security Policy' [2025] *Yearbook of European Law* 9.

[136] Council Decision (CFSP) 2024/890 (OJ L2024/890).

[137] Art 31(2) TEU. See Case C-883/24 *Parliament v Council* ('*Voting rules for designating the targets of restrictive measures*'), pending, in which the Parliament requests the annulment of Council Decision (CFSP) 2024/2643 of 8 October 2024 concerning restrictive measures in view of Russia's destabilising activities (OJ [2024] L 9.10.2024), insofar as Art 4(1) provides for a decision 'by unanimity', thereby infringing Arts 31(2) and 40 TEU.

- when adopting a decision defining a Union action or position on the basis of a decision of the European Council relating to the Union's strategic interests and objectives, as referred to in Article 22(1);
- when adopting a decision defining a Union action or position, on a proposal which the High Representative of the Union for Foreign Affairs and Security Policy has presented following a specific request from the European Council, made on its own initiative or that of the High Representative;
- when adopting any decision implementing a decision defining a Union action or position;
- when appointing a special representative in accordance with Article 33.

The only significant extension[138] of QMV in the CFSP compared with the pre-Lisbon situation is the possibility under the second point in the list. Nevertheless, the default rule of unanimity would apply within the European Council in this situation. The same rationale applies to the other possibilities for QMV, which are all, except for the appointment of a special representative, premised on a prior decision having been taken by unanimity.[139]

Furthermore, under Article 31(2) TEU, second subparagraph, a Member State has the option of preventing a vote when it declares that, 'for vital and stated reasons of national policy, it intends to oppose the adoption of a decision to be taken by qualified majority'. The High Representative at this point attempts to avoid referral of the decision to the European Council by searching for a solution acceptable to the objecting Member State. This is to happen 'in close consultation with the Member State involved', and would amount to the High Representative trying their best to broker a unanimous decision in the Council, which would make a referral to the European Council superfluous.

Finally, pursuant to Article 31(4) TEU, the possibilities for QMV decision-making do not apply to decisions having military or defence implications.

In sum, there are four CFSP decision-making procedures available for the Council:

- unanimity, which is still the rule, as described in Article 31(1) TEU;
- QMV in the less strict version (Article 16(4) TEU): in the case described in Article 31(2), second indent EU (proposal from the High Representative);
- QMV in the stricter version (Article 238(2) TFEU): in the cases described in Article 31(2), first, third, and fourth indent TEU;
- majority of the members of the Council: for procedural questions (Article 31(5) TEU).

5.2.4 **The role of the European Parliament**

Article 36 TEU sets out a number of basic possibilities for the Parliament's involvement in the CFSP. The High Representative has to consult the Parliament regularly on 'the main aspects and the basic choices' of the CFSP and the CSDP and 'inform it of how those policies evolve'. She also has to ensure that the views of the European Parliament are 'duly taken into consideration'.[140] Special representatives may be involved in briefing the Parliament. The imprecision in formulating the High Representative's obligations,

[138] See, however, the *passerelle* in Art 31(3) TEU, which authorizes the European Council unanimously to adopt a decision stipulating that the Council is to act by a qualified majority in cases other than those referred to in Art 31(2) TEU.

[139] Art 31(1) TEU.

[140] On the relationship between the High Representative and the EEAS on the one hand and the European Parliament on the other hand, see EP EEAS Study (n 105) 58–61.

as exemplified by expressions such as 'main aspects', 'basic choices', and 'regularly' is not encouraging for the Parliament's possibilities for scrutiny. The Parliament can also address questions to the Council or the High Representative or make recommendations to them. Twice a year, it is required to hold a debate on 'progress in implementing' the CFSP, including the CSDP.[141] All in all, the Parliament is kept at a distance from any particular CFSP measure, and can only exercise influence on the general policy choices.

With respect to international agreements in the area of the CFSP, Article 218(10) TFEU provides that the Parliament is to be immediately and fully informed at all stages of the procedure for negotiating and concluding international agreements envisaged in that Article. According to the ECJ, that rule is an expression of the democratic principles on which the Union is founded, in the sense that the Parliament's involvement in the decision-making process is the reflection, at EU level, of the fundamental democratic principle that the people should participate in the exercise of power through the intermediary of a representative assembly. The information requirement laid down in Article 218(10) TFEU therefore applies to any procedure for concluding an international agreement, including agreements relating exclusively to the CFSP.[142] The aim of that information requirement is, inter alia, to ensure that the Parliament is in a position to exercise democratic control over the Union's external action and, more specifically, to verify that the choice of legal basis for a decision on the conclusion of an agreement was made with due regard to the powers of the Parliament.[143] While the purpose of the requirement to inform the Parliament fully and immediately is not to enable the Parliament to participate in the negotiation and conclusion of agreements concerning the CFSP, that requirement also allows it to exercise its own powers with full knowledge of EU external action as a whole. In that sense, the duty to inform that the other institutions owe to the Parliament under Article 218(10) TFEU contributes to ensuring the coherence and consistency between the different areas of EU external action, in accordance with Article 21(3) TEU.[144]

5.2.5 **The role of the Court**

The role of the CJEU forms perhaps the biggest contrast between the CFSP and the rest of the EU legal order: Articles 24(1) TEU and 275 TFEU simply exclude, in principle, the Court's jurisdiction in the CFSP.[145]

The Court held in Opinion 2/13 that it had 'not yet had the opportunity to define the extent to which its jurisdiction is limited in CFSP matters' as a result of the second subparagraph of Article 24(1) TEU and the first paragraph of Article 275 TFEU, simply adding that 'as EU law now stands, certain acts adopted in the context of the CFSP fall outside the ambit of judicial review by the Court', a situation described by the Court as 'inherent to the way in which the Court's powers are structured by the Treaties', which could 'only be explained by reference to EU law alone'.[146] However, the Court considered this fact to be an obstacle against accession of the EU to the ECHR, as the European Court of Human Rights (ECtHR) would be empowered to rule on the compatibility with the ECHR of certain CFSP acts, actions, or omissions and notably of those whose legality the Court

[141] Art 36, para 2, TEU.

[142] Judgments of 24 June 2014, Case C-658/11 *Parliament v Council* (*'Mauritius Pirates Agreement'*), EU:C:2014:2025, paras 81–86, and of 14 June 2016, Case C-263/14 *Parliament v Council* (*'Tanzania Pirates Agreement'*), EU:C:2016:435, paras 68–70.

[143] *Tanzania Pirates Agreement* (n 142) para 71 (see paras 68–84 for further details), and, to that effect, *Mauritius Pirates Agreement* (n 142) para 79.

[144] *Tanzania Pirates Agreement* (n 142) para 72.

[145] See further eg P Van Elsuwege, 'Judicial Review and the Common Foreign and Security Policy: Limits to the Gap-Filling Role of the Court of Justice' (2021) 58 *Common Market Law Review* 1731–1760.

[146] Opinion 2/13 (n 108) paras 251–253.

cannot review. Such a situation would, according to the Court, effectively entrust the judicial review of those acts, actions, or omissions exclusively to a non-EU body, albeit that any such review would be limited to compliance with the rights guaranteed by the ECHR. The conclusion the Court drew from that fact was that the accession agreement failed to have regard to the specific characteristics of EU law with regard to the judicial review of CFSP acts, actions, or omissions, even though that situation was the consequence of 'the way in which the Court's powers are structured at present'.[147]

Nevertheless, the second subparagraph of Article 24(1) TEU and the second paragraph of Article 275 TFEU provide for two exceptions to the Court's lack of jurisdiction within the CFSP. The Court has jurisdiction:[148]

(a) to monitor compliance with Article 40 TEU, which concerns the dividing line between the CFSP and other EU competences (on which, see section 8); and

(b) to rule on proceedings, brought in accordance with Article 263, fourth paragraph, TFEU, reviewing the legality of decisions providing for restrictive measures against natural or legal persons.

The Court has since Opinion 2/13 had the opportunity to define—at least to some extent—the extent of its jurisdiction in CFSP matters. Notably, the ECJ has held that the second subparagraph of Article 24(1) TEU and the first paragraph of Article 275 TFEU introduce a derogation from the rule of general jurisdiction which Article 19 TEU confers on the Court to ensure that in the interpretation and application of the Treaties the law is observed, and they must, therefore, be interpreted narrowly.[149] The Court has also noted that the principle that one of the EU's founding values is the rule of law follows from both Article 2 TEU, which is included in the common provisions of the EU Treaty, and Article 21 TEU, concerning EU external action, to which Article 23 TEU, relating to CFSP, refers.[150] Furthermore, the very existence of effective judicial review designed to ensure compliance with provisions of EU law is inherent in the existence of the rule of law, and it follows from Article 2 TEU that the EU is founded on values, such as the rule of law, which are common to the Member States in a society in which, inter alia, justice prevails.[151]

In *H*, the ECJ held that the EGC and, in the event of an appeal, the ECJ, have jurisdiction to review acts of staff management taken within the context of the CFSP.[152] That jurisdiction stems, respectively, as regards the review of the legality of those acts, from Article 263 TFEU and, as regards actions for non-contractual liability, from Article 268 TFEU, read in conjunction with the second paragraph of Article 340 TFEU, taking into account Article 19(1) TEU and Article 47 of the Charter of Fundamental Rights of the EU ('the Charter').[153] Accordingly, such decisions, although adopted in the context of the CFSP, do not constitute acts referred to in the second subparagraph of Article 24(1) TEU and the first paragraph of Article 275 TFEU. Consequently, they fall within the jurisdiction of the EU judicature.[154]

The Court further defined the extent of its jurisdiction in *Rosneft*, a reference for a preliminary ruling regarding the validity and interpretation of certain restrictive measures affecting Rosneft, a Russian company specializing in the oil and gas sector of which

[147] Ibid, paras 254–257.

[148] Judgments of 10 September 2024, Case C-351/22 *Neves 77 Solutions*, EU:C:2024:723, para 36; and *KS and KD* (n 23) para 63, and of 10 April 2025, Case C-238/24 *Tartisai*, EU:C:2025:258, para 20.

[149] *Neves 77 Solutions* (n 148) para 35; *KS and Others* (n 23) para 62, and *Tartisai* (n 148) para 19.

[150] Judgment of 22 June 2021, Case C-872/19 P *Venezuela v Council* (*Whether a third State is affected*), EU:C:2021:507, para 49.

[151] Ibid, para 48.

[152] Judgment of 19 July 2016, Case C-455/14 P *H v Council and Commission* ('*H*'), EU:C:2016:569, para 55.

[153] OJ [2016] C202/389.

[154] *H* (n 152) para 59.

the Russian Federation (indirectly) holds the majority of shares. The measures affecting Rosneft formed part of a set of restrictive measures taken in reaction to Russia's 2014 actions destabilizing the situation in Ukraine.[155] This required the Court to determine whether it had jurisdiction to review the legality of CFSP decisions providing for restrictive measures against natural or legal persons not just within the framework of proceedings brought in accordance with Article 263, fourth paragraph, TFEU, but also within its preliminary ruling jurisdiction based on Article 267 TFEU. In its judgment, the Court recalled the crucial importance of the rule of law as a founding value of the EU, and held that even though Article 47 of the Charter cannot confer jurisdiction on the Court where the Treaties exclude it, the principle of effective judicial protection nonetheless implies that the exclusion of the Court's jurisdiction in the field of the CFSP should be interpreted strictly.[156] The Court concluded that it had jurisdiction to give preliminary rulings on the validity of a CFSP act provided that the request for a preliminary ruling relates either to the monitoring of that decision's compliance with Article 40 TEU, or to reviewing the legality of restrictive measures against natural or legal persons.[157]

The Court clarified in *Neves 77* that the possibility provided for by the Treaties of making a reference to the Court for a preliminary ruling regarding a regulation adopted on the basis of Article 215(1) TFEU must be available in respect of all the provisions that the Council should have included in such a regulation and which form the basis for a national sanction adopted against third parties.[158] The Court therefore considered that it had jurisdiction to give a preliminary ruling under Article 267 TFEU on the interpretation of a measure of general scope contained in an act adopted in the context of the CFSP, where the Council should have implemented that measure, which serves as a basis for national sanctions imposed on a natural or legal person, by a regulation adopted under Article 215 TFEU.[159]

In *Bank Refah Kargaran*, the Court held that the principle of effective judicial protection of persons or entities subject to restrictive measures requires, in order for such protection to be complete, that the Court be able to rule on an action for damages brought by such persons or entities seeking damages for the harm caused by the restrictive measures taken in CFSP decisions, and that accordingly the EGC and, on appeal, the ECJ, have jurisdiction to rule on an action for damages insofar as it seeks to obtain compensation for the harm allegedly caused by restrictive measures taken against natural or legal persons pursuant to CFSP decisions.[160]

Finally, in *KS and KD*, the Court explained that in examining its jurisdiction to hear and determine an action concerning acts or omissions falling within the scope of the

[155] Council Decision 2014/512/CFSP of 31 July 2014 concerning restrictive measures in view of Russia's actions destabilising the situation in Ukraine (OJ [2014] L229/13); and Council Regulation (EU) No 833/2014 of 31 July 2014 concerning restrictive measures in view of Russia's actions destabilising the situation in Ukraine (OJ [2014] L229/1). Following Russia's military aggression against Ukraine starting in 2022, the EU has adopted a still growing series of further restrictive measures (eg most recently Council Decision (CFSP) 2026/1072 of 11 May 2026 amending Decision 2014/145/CFSP concerning restrictive measures in respect of actions undermining or threatening the territorial integrity, sovereignty and independence of Ukraine (OJ [2026] L 11.5.2026); and Council Implementing Regulation (EU) 2026/1055 of 11 May 2026 implementing Regulation (EU) No 269/2014 concerning restrictive measures in respect of actions undermining or threatening the territorial integrity, sovereignty and independence of Ukraine (OJ [2026] L 11.5.2026)), which give rise to regular litigation in front of the CJEU. See eg judgments of 27 July 2022, Case T-125/22 *RT France v Council*, EU:T:2022:483, and of 10 September 2025, Case T-573/23 *Positive Group v Council*, EU:T:2025:867. See further Genini (n 135) 16–20.

[156] Judgment of 28 March 2017, Case C-72/15 *Rosneft*, EU:C:2017:236, paras 72–74. See also the Opinion of AG Wathelet, EU:C:2016:381, points 64–66.

[157] *Rosneft* (n 156) para 81. [158] *Neves 77 Solutions* (n 148) para 49. [159] Ibid, para 53.

[160] Judgment of 6 October 2020, Case C-134/19 P *Bank Refah Kargaran v Council*, EU:C:2020:793, para 36.

CFSP, it is necessary to ascertain, first, whether the situation at issue falls within one of the situations provided for in the last sentence of the second subparagraph of Article 24(1) TEU and the second paragraph of Article 275 TFEU, in which that jurisdiction is expressly allowed.[161] If that is not the case, it is necessary, second, to assess whether its jurisdiction may be based on the fact that the acts and omissions at issue are not directly related to the political or strategic choices made by the institutions, bodies, offices, and agencies of the Union in the context of the CFSP, and in particular the CSDP. Thus, if the acts and omissions at issue are not directly related to those political or strategic choices, the Court has jurisdiction to assess the legality of those acts or omissions or to interpret them. By contrast, if those acts or omissions are directly related to those political or strategic choices, the Court lacks jurisdiction. It follows that the Court does not have jurisdiction to assess the legality of, or interpret, acts or omissions directly related to the conduct, definition, or implementation of the CFSP, and especially the CSDP, that is to say, in particular the identification of the Union's strategic interests and the definition of both the actions to be taken and the positions to be adopted by the EU as well as of the general guidelines of the CFSP.[162] The Court thereby arguably introduced an EU version of the 'political question' doctrine,[163] which in US constitutional law affirms that some constitutional questions lie beyond the judiciary to resolve.[164]

5.2.6 **Implementation**

As with respect to ordinary EU external action, CFSP measures are in the first place to be implemented by the Member States.[165] However, where uniform conditions for implementing legally binding CFSP acts are needed, those acts are to confer implementing powers not on the Commission, but on the Council.[166] The Council, its rotating Presidency (held in practice by each Member State in turn for six-month periods),[167] various Council bodies, and now the High Representative, have the lead in implementing adopted measures.[168] The Council therefore needed to be equipped with an infrastructure specifically designed for the development and implementation of the CFSP.

The implementation of CFSP legal instruments by the Member States takes place against the background of both the general principle of sincere cooperation in Article 4(3) TEU (see further section 7.2) and the specific principle of loyalty for the CFSP in Article 24(3) TEU:

> The Member States shall support the Union's external and security policy actively and unreservedly in a spirit of loyalty and mutual solidarity and shall comply with the Union's action in this area.

[161] *KS and KD* (n 23) para 115. [162] Ibid, paras 116–118.

[163] See G Butler, 'From Search to Discovery of the Political Question Doctrine in EU Law' (2025) 50 *European Law Review* 761–774.

[164] See further G De Baere, 'Ulysses Unbound ? Political Questions, Judicial Answers, and the Rule of Law in EU Foreign Policy: Opinion of Advocate General Jacobs in Commission v Greece (FYROM)' in G Butler and A Lazowski (eds), *Shaping EU Law the British Way: UK Advocates General at the Court of Justice of the European Union* (Oxford: Hart Publishing, 2022) 311–324.

[165] Art 291(1) TFEU. [166] Art 291(2) TFEU.

[167] On the Council Presidency, see further chapter 3.

[168] See eg Council Decision (CFSP) 2022/1968 of 17 October 2022 on a European Union Military Assistance Mission in support of Ukraine (EUMAM Ukraine) (OJ [2022] L270/85), based on Arts 42(4) and 43(2) TEU. Pursuant to Art 5, the Political and Security Committee (PSC) within the Council is to exercise the political control and strategic direction of EUMAM Ukraine under the responsibility of the Council and of the High Representative, and is authorized to take relevant decisions in accordance with Art 38 TEU. That authorization includes the powers to amend the planning documents of EUMAM Ukraine, including the Mission Plan, and the Chain of Command.

> The Member States shall work together to enhance and develop their mutual political solidarity.[169] They shall refrain from any action which is contrary to the interests of the Union or likely to impair its effectiveness as a cohesive force in international relations.
>
> The Council and the High Representative shall ensure compliance with these principles.

More particularly, the Member States have certain duties as regards the implementation of decisions defining actions to be undertaken by the Union and decisions defining positions to be taken by the Union.[170] That is notably the case as regards restrictive measures. As Advocate General Norkus pointed out, the decentralized form of applying and implementing restrictive measures takes account of the structure of the EU and of the principle of subsidiarity. It also reflects the complexity of the task faced by the EU and its Member States in the face of a multitude of cases in which persons or bodies attempt to circumvent the sanctions regime. It therefore seems appropriate to entrust responsibility for the actual application of a regulation imposing restrictive measures and, where appropriate, for the adoption of national implementing measures, to the national authorities, which are closer to the facts.[171]

In international organizations[172] and at international conferences, as well as in third countries, both the diplomatic and consular missions of the Member States and the Union delegations have to cooperate to ensure implementation of, and compliance with, the decisions defining Union positions and actions adopted pursuant to the CFSP provisions.[173] They also have to step up cooperation by exchanging information and carrying out joint assessments.[174]

5.3 **The High Representative and the European External Action Service**

The High Representative of the Union for Foreign Affairs and Security Policy, currently Ms Kaja Kallas, replaced both the pre-Lisbon High Representative for the CFSP and the Commissioner for external relations.[175] The intention is for her to form a bridge between the CFSP and the other elements of the Union's external action, which is why one of her core tasks is to 'ensure the consistency of the Union's external action'[176] However, the High Representative has to share the international scene with the President of the European Council, currently Mr Antonio Costa, who 'at his level and in that capacity', is to ensure the external representation of the Union on issues concerning its CFSP, without prejudice to the powers of the High Representative.[177] That implies that the President of the European Council is to represent the Union at the level of heads of State and government, while the High Representative ensures representation at ministerial level, which is what on the whole appears to happen in practice.

Article 27(3) TEU provides that in fulfilling her mandate, the High Representative is to be assisted by the EEAS, which is to 'work in cooperation with the diplomatic services of the Member States and shall comprise officials from relevant departments of the General Secretariat of the Council and of the Commission as well as staff seconded from national diplomatic services of the Member States'.

[169] See also Art 222 TFEU (the 'solidarity clause').

[170] Arts 28 and 29 TEU. See, with respect to Art 29 TEU, *Rosneft* (n 156) paras 56 and 71.

[171] Opinion of AG Norkus in Case C-480/24 *Čiekuri-Shishki*, EU:C:2025:672, point 37.

[172] See also Art 220 TFEU.

[173] See Art 35, first para, TEU.

[174] Art 35, second para, TEU.

[175] See Art 18 TEU. For more on the appointment of the High Representative and her position in the broader institutional context, see chapter 3.

[176] Art 18(4) TEU. See also section 2.

[177] Art 15(6) TEU.

The EEAS was established by a Council decision as a 'functionally autonomous body' of the EU, 'separate from the General Secretariat of the Council and from the Commission' and 'with the legal capacity necessary to perform its tasks and attain its objectives'.[178] This indeterminate status is the result of a compromise between those wanting the EEAS to be an essentially intergovernmental body close to or part of the Council and those preferring it to be close to or part of the Commission. The EEAS was therefore set up as a '*sui generis*' body 'equidistant' from the Council and the Commission.[179]

The inherent structural complexities of the EEAS are evident from the enumeration of its tasks in the Decision establishing the service.[180] First, the EEAS is to 'support the High Representative in fulfilling his/her mandates',[181] which include conducting the CFSP and CSDP, ensuring the consistency of the EU's external action, presiding over the Foreign Affairs Council,[182] and acting as Vice-President of the Commission. The latter capacity not only includes 'responsibilities incumbent on [the Commission] in external relations' but also 'coordinating other aspects of the Union's external action'.[183] Secondly, the EEAS must 'assist the President of the European Council, the President of the Commission, and the Commission in the exercise of their respective functions in the area of external relations'.[184] Thirdly, the EEAS is to 'support, and work in cooperation with, the diplomatic services of the Member States as well as the General Secretariat of the Council and the services of the Commission, in order to ensure consistency between the different areas of the Union's external action and between those areas and its other policies'.[185] Fourthly, it must 'extend appropriate support and cooperation to the other institutions and bodies of the Union, in particular to the European Parliament'.[186] With the exception of the CFSP/CSDP, this complex set of tasks is determined by reference to *other* EU external actors, and includes a fragile balancing act vis-à-vis ('without prejudice to the normal tasks of') the General Secretariat of the Council and the services of the Commission.[187]

Adding to this complexity are the numerous cooperative duties listed in Article 3 of the Decision. First, the EEAS must work in cooperation with Member State diplomatic services. Secondly, the EEAS and the services of the Commission are to 'consult each other on all matters relating to the external action of the Union in the exercise of their respective functions, except on matters covered by CSDP', and the EEAS is to 'take part in the preparatory work and procedures relating to acts to be prepared by the Commission in this area'.[188] Thirdly, the Union delegations,[189] that is, the Union's diplomatic representations and as such part of the EEAS, are to 'work in close cooperation and share information with the diplomatic services of the Member States'.[190] Although the reciprocal obligation to share information provided for in the initial draft does not appear in the final text of the Decision, the logic of the principle of sincere cooperation laid down in Article 4(3) TEU indicates that this cannot be only a one-way street.[191]

[178] Art 1(2) EEAS Decision.

[179] See B Van Vooren, 'A Legal Institutional Perspective on the European External Action Service' (2011) 48 *Common Market Law Review* 501.

[180] See EP EEAS Study (n 105) 18. See further G De Baere and RA Wessel, 'EU Law and the EEAS: Of Complex Competences and Constitutional Consequences' in D Spence and J Bátora (eds), *The European External Action Service: European Diplomacy Post-Westphalia* (Basingstoke: Palgrave Macmillan, 2015) 175–191.

[181] Art 2(1) EEAS Decision.

[182] ie the configuration of the Council of Ministers where, pursuant to Art 16(6), third para, TEU, EU external action is discussed.

[183] Art 18(4) TEU.

[184] Art 2(2) EEAS Decision.

[185] Art 3(1) EEAS Decision. cf Art 21(3), second para, TEU.

[186] Art 3(4) EEAS Decision.

[187] EP EEAS Study (n 105) 18.

[188] Art 3(2) EEAS Decision.

[189] Art 221 TFEU.

[190] Art 5(9) EEAS Decision.

[191] EP EEAS Study (n 105) 18–19.

6 External representation and international agreements

6.1 External representation

A distinction must be made between internal EU decision-making on the one hand and external representation on the other hand, and in particular between the institution that decides the policy line and the institution responsible for representing it externally. In that respect, a balance must be found between the policymaking functions of the Council under Article 16 TEU and Article 17 TEU, which provides that, with the exception of the CFSP and other cases provided for in the Treaties, the Commission is to ensure the Union's external representation. That competence does not depend on the exclusive or shared nature of the EU's external competence, which relates only to internal EU rules that do not bind third States or other international organizations. However, while it is true that the Treaties limit the Commission's competence to ensure the EU's external representation only in accordance with the derogations expressly mentioned in Article 17(1) TEU, the fact remains that when the EU, as a subject of international law, decides to exercise its powers they must be exercised in observance of international law. In particular, where the EU is not a member of an international organization and is therefore precluded by international law from exercising its external competence within that organization, that competence may be exercised, inter alia, by the Member States acting jointly, under the duty of sincere cooperation referred to in Article 4(3) TEU, in the interest of the EU.[192]

As will be illustrated in case study 26.1, that does not mean that the Commission necessarily decides on the content of the position to be represented. That principle even applies to non-binding external action, as the Court made clear in the context of a dispute between the Commission and the Council on the competence to sign the Addendum to the Memorandum of Understanding on a financial contribution by Switzerland to the Member States that acceded to the Union as a result of the 2004 enlargement. The Court held that the Commission not to have the right, solely by virtue of its power of external representation under Article 17(1) TEU, to sign a non-binding agreement with a third country. According to the Court, the decision concerning the signing of an agreement with a third country covering an area for which the Union is competent—irrespective of whether or not that agreement is binding—requires an assessment of the Union's interests in the context of its relations with the third country concerned, and the divergent interests arising in those relations to be reconciled, in compliance with strategic guidelines laid down by the European Council and the principles and objectives of the Union's external action laid down in Article 21(1) and (2) TEU. A decision concerning the signature of a non-binding agreement is therefore one of the measures by which the Union's policy is made and its external action planned for the purpose of the second sentence of Article 16(1) and the third subparagraph of Article 16(6) TEU. The Court concluded that, hence, in order to sign the Addendum on behalf of the Union, the Commission needed the Council's prior approval. Thus, by signing the Addendum on behalf of the Union without the Council's prior approval, the Commission had infringed the principle of distribution of powers in Article 13(2) TEU and the principle of institutional balance.[193]

[192] Judgment of 5 April 2022, Case C-161/20 *Commission v Council* (*International Maritime Organisation*), EU:C:2022:260, paras 52–53 and 69.

[193] Judgment of 28 July 2016, Case C-660/13 *Council v Commission* ('*Swiss MoU*'), EU:C:2016:616, paras 38–46.

In the CFSP, external representation is ensured by the High Representative (Article 18(2) TEU) and as mentioned previously, 'at his level and in that capacity', by the President of the European Council, without prejudice to the powers of the High Representative (Article 15(6) TEU).

Articles 17 and 27(2) TEU set a clear framework: the external representation of the EU is ensured by the High Representative in the CFSP, and by the Commission in other external action matters. However, the Member States retain their sovereignty to conduct their own foreign relations, without prejudice to the rules of the Treaty. They remain free to decide on a case-by-case basis on the modalities of their own external representation, including when acting jointly in the interest of the EU. For those purposes, there is nothing to prevent those States from mandating, from among themselves, the Member State which holds the Presidency of the Council, insofar as that Member State is acting neither individually nor in the name of the EU.[194]

Finally, the Treaties make no specific mention of the possibility for the EU to take part in international dispute settlement, or of which institution is to represent it in such fora. Nevertheless, agreements to which the Union is a party may include a dispute settlement system, most notably the Dispute Settlement Understanding in Annex 2 of the World Trade Organization (WTO) Agreement.[195] In practice, the Commission Legal Service represents the Union in such international litigation. The ECJ has held in that regard that Article 335 TFEU, although restricted to Member States on its wording, is the expression of a general principle that the Union has legal capacity and is to be represented, to that end, by the Commission. Article 335 TFEU therefore provided a basis for the Commission to represent the EU before the International Tribunal for the Law of the Sea (ITLOS).[196]

6.2 **International agreements**

Article 218 TFEU sets out one single procedure for negotiating and concluding international agreements over the entire field of Union competences.

This section describes the different stages of the procedure and the respective roles of the different EU actors involved. While for analytical purposes a distinction between several procedural stages is useful, in practice these stages are not always as clearly separable from each other. This is especially the case with regard to complex negotiations such as the Uruguay Round of the GATT (an important international trade negotiation, during which the scope of the then Community's competences were disputed) leading up to the WTO Agreement, which encompassed several consecutive phases of negotiation.[197]

6.2.1 **Negotiation**

The procedure under Article 218 TFEU starts with the Commission making a recommendation to the Council,[198] though this is often preceded by exploratory talks in the pre-negotiation stage between the Commission and potential third-country treaty-partners.[199]

[194] *International Maritime Organisation* (n 192) para 77.

[195] Agreement Establishing the World Trade Organization, 1867 UNTS 154, 33 ILM 1144 (1994).

[196] Judgment of 6 October 2015, Case C-73/14 *Council v Commission* ('*ITLOS*'), EU:C:2015:663, paras 58–59.

[197] See eg JH Jackson, *The World Trading System: Law and Policy of International Economic Relations* (2nd edn, Cambridge, MA/London: MIT Press, 1997) 44–46; P Van den Bossche and W Zdouc, *The Law and Policy of the World Trade Organization: Text, Cases and Materials* (5th edn, Cambridge: Cambridge University Press, 2021) 2.2.

[198] Art 218(3) TFEU.

[199] De Baere, *Constitutional Principles* (n 8) 79.

Where the envisaged agreement exclusively or principally concerns the CFSP,[200] the High Representative and not the Commission makes a recommendation to the Council. This is one example of how the Lisbon Treaty, despite the increased consistency due to the unified treaty-making procedure, maintains the differentiation between ordinary EU external action and the CFSP.

Given that a Commission recommendation under Article 218(3) TFEU is not a Commission proposal under Article 293(1) TFEU, the Council does not need to act unanimously to amend it. Furthermore, while the withdrawal by the Commission of a proposal under Articles 293 and 294 TFEU implies an immediate end to the ongoing ordinary legislative procedure, the same would not appear to be the case as regards the withdrawal of a recommendation under Article 218(3) TFEU. The question was at issue during the conflict between the Commission and the Council in the course of the negotiations towards a global ban on mercury, which will be discussed in the case study.[201]

If the Council deems the negotiation of the proposed international agreement in question to be opportune, it adopts a decision authorizing the opening of negotiations and, depending on the subject of the agreement envisaged, nominating the Union negotiator or the head of the Union's negotiating team.[202] Article 218(3) TFEU appears to give the Council a choice,[203] and it will therefore probably let the appointment of the negotiator depend upon what it judges to be the 'centre of gravity' of the agreement. If the Council deems it to be the CFSP, it will most likely appoint the High Representative as negotiator. The Council can also address directives[204] to the negotiator and designate a special committee (which is often a Council working party—that is, a Council preparatory committee that performs the 'ground work' in one of the EU's diverse policies, and operates under the aegis of the Committee of Permanent Representatives of the Governments of the Member States (Coreper) or another senior preparatory committee)[205] in consultation with which the negotiations must be conducted. When negotiating the agreement, the negotiator has to consult with such special committees appointed by the Council to assist it in this task, and stay within the confines of the negotiating directives given to it by the Council.[206]

[200] Art 37 TEU provides that the Union may conclude agreements with one or more States or international organizations within the CFSP area.

[201] G De Baere, 'Mercury Rising: The European Union and the International Negotiations for a Globally Binding Instrument on Mercury' (2012) 37 *European Law Review* 648.

[202] Art 218(3) TFEU. Art 218 TFEU spells out who is to submit recommendations under what circumstances, but does not explicitly determine who is to be the negotiator. See also Art 50(2) TEU, which provides that agreements on withdrawal from the Union, such as the Agreement on the withdrawal of the UK from the EU and the EURATOM (OJ (2020) L29/7) (the 'Brexit' agreement), are to be negotiated in accordance with Art 218(3) TFEU (on this, see further chapter 27).

[203] See, however, Art 207(3) TFEU (the Commission is the only possible negotiator in the field of the CCP) and Art 219(3) TFEU (the Commission is to be merely 'fully associated with the negotiations' concerning monetary or foreign-exchange regime matters).

[204] These directives do not constitute delegated powers from the Council to the Commission and the term 'mandate', though used in daily practice, is therefore inapposite: F Hoffmeister, 'Curse or Blessing? Mixed Agreements in the Recent Practice of the European Union and Its Member States' in C Hillion and P Koutrakos (eds), *Mixed Agreements Revisited: The EU and Its Member States in the World* (Oxford/Portland, OR: Hart Publishing, 2010) 253.

[205] See De Baere, *Constitutional Principles* (n 8) 131. The General Court has emphasised (in the context of restrictive measures) that the fact that working groups composed of experts from Member States' delegations are involved in the decision-making process within the Council does not cast doubt on the conclusion that it is always the Council that adopts the final decision: judgment of 3 September 2025, Case T-1117/23 *Usmanov v Council*, EU:T:2025:810, para 187.

[206] Art 218(4) TFEU. The Court has confirmed that a decision adopted on the basis of Art 218(3) and (4) TFEU 'produces legal effects as regards relations between the European Union and its Member States and between the EU institutions': *Broadcasting Rights Convention* (n 44) para 40, and judgment of 16 July 2015, Case C-425/13 *Commission v Council*, EU:C:2015:483, para 28.

6.2.2 **Signature**

The signing stage, which may include a decision on the provisional application of the agreement,[207] starts with the negotiator nominated by the Council making a proposal to that effect.[208] It is then up to the Council to decide on the signing of the agreement and hence to approve or disapprove of the negotiator's proposal, acting by QMV, or by unanimity in the same circumstances as regarding the conclusion of the agreement.[209] However, the decision authorizing the signing of an international agreement does not include the later act of the signing itself of that agreement. Hence, where the Council has authorized the signing of a non-CFSP international agreement outside the scope of 'other cases provided for in the Treaties', it is for the Commission to ensure the actual signing of that agreement. That conclusion is not undermined by the fact that, post-Lisbon, the Council has continued to designate the signatories of international agreements and regularly to choose as signatory the permanent representative of the Member State exercising the rotating Council Presidency. A practice, however consistent, cannot alter the rules of the Treaties that the institutions are obliged to respect.[210]

6.2.3 **Conclusion**

The Council concludes the agreement through a decision by QMV, acting on a proposal by the negotiator.[211] Indeed, the first subparagraph of Article 218(8) TFEU specifies that the Council is to act by QMV throughout the procedure. Nonetheless, pursuant to the second subparagraph, a number of exceptions apply. The Council acts unanimously:

(a) when the agreement covers a field for which unanimity is required for the adoption of a Union act;[212]

(b) as regards association agreements;[213] and

(c) as regards agreements establishing economic, financial, and technical cooperation[214] with candidate Member States.

A specific case in which the Council is to act unanimously concerns the agreement on accession of the Union to the ECHR.[215] Additionally, the decision concluding this agreement is to enter into force only after it has been approved by the Member States in accordance with their respective constitutional requirements.[216]

[207] cf Art 25 Vienna Convention on the Law of Treaties, 23 May 1969, UN Doc A/Conf.39/27; 1155 UNTS 331 (the Vienna Convention does not as such apply to the EU, but its provisions generally reflect international practice and, at least in part, customary international law. See eg, with respect to Art 31 VCLT, judgment of 23 April 2026, Case C-528/24 *Minister for Justice and Equality and Others*, EU:C:2026:332, para 26). See eg Art 783(2) EUUKTCA and Art 30.7(3) of the EU–Canada Comprehensive Economic and Trade Agreement (CETA), which contains quite detailed arrangements on the provisional application of the agreement; and Council Decision (EU) 2017/38 of 28 October 2016 on the provisional application of the Agreement (OJ [2017] L11/1080). The possibility for provisional application may not be a luxury regarding agreements like CETA, which, as mixed agreements, need to be approved by all competent Member State parliaments, including, where relevant, parliaments of federated entities. Eg it was the Walloon Parliament's initial refusal to approve CETA that prompted the Belgian government to submit the request for Opinion 1/17, of 30 April 2019, EU:C:2019:341, on the *Comprehensive Economic and Trade Agreement between the EU and Canada ('CETA')*.

[208] Art 218(5) TFEU. [209] Art 218(8) TFEU.

[210] Judgment of 9 April 2024, Case C-551/21 *Commission v Council* (*Signing of international agreements*), EU:C:2024:281, paras 67 and 81–82.

[211] Art 218(6) TFEU.

[212] eg in the field of external environmental law, which forms the subject of case study 26.1, unanimity is required for the limited set of environmental matters listed in Art 192(2) TFEU. On the choice between Art 192(1) and Art 192(2) TFEU as legal basis, see the judgment of 21 June 2018, Case C-5/16 *Poland v Parliament and Council*, EU:C:2018:483, paras 37–69.

[213] Art 217 TFEU. [214] Art 212 TFEU. [215] Art 6(2) TEU. See n 105. [216] Art 218(8) TFEU.

Article 207(4) TFEU, which contains a number of specific rules on the negotiation and conclusion of agreements within the sphere of the CCP, adds more exceptions. It provides that the Council acts unanimously as regards agreements in trade in services, the commercial aspects of intellectual property,[217] and foreign direct investment[218] where such agreements include provisions for which unanimity is required for the adoption of internal rules. Moreover, the Council is to act unanimously as regards agreements:

- in the field of trade in cultural, and audiovisual services, where these agreements risk prejudicing the Union's cultural and linguistic diversity; and
- in the field of trade in social, education, and health services, where these agreements risk seriously disturbing the national organization of such services and prejudicing the responsibility of Member States to deliver them.

These are all sensitive areas in which the Member States did not wish to run the risk of the EU concluding an international agreement without the possibility to stop it. An illustration of the sensitivity of audiovisual services in particular is the fact that in line with the authorizations and negotiating directives adopted by the Council, the EU excludes audiovisual services from the scope of any liberalization or regulatory commitment in cross-border trade in services, investment, and digital trade, in all its free trade agreements (FTAs).[219] Finally, with respect to agreements in the field of transport, Article 207(5) TFEU simply contains a cross-reference to the Title on transport in the TFEU.[220] Some of the international agreements in that field will be concluded on the basis of exclusive Union competence, while others will follow the format for shared competences, which will often imply that they will be concluded as mixed agreements (ie agreements to which both the EU and the Member States are parties; see section 7.1).

With respect to such agreements, as well as mixed agreements in other fields, a requirement for unanimous voting applies de facto due to the Member States' involvement in the negotiation and ratification of those treaties.

[217] The Court has held that international commitments concerning intellectual property entered into by the Union fall within 'commercial aspects of intellectual property' when they 'display a specific link with international trade in that they are essentially intended to promote, facilitate or govern such trade and have direct and immediate effects on it': Opinion 2/15 (n 32) para 112. That is eg the case of the rules in the Agreement on Trade-Related Aspects of Intellectual Property Rights, 15 April 1994, 1869 UNTS 299, 33 ILM 1197 (1994) (the TRIPS Agreement): judgment of 18 July 2013, Case C-414/11 *Daiichi Sankyo and Sanofi-Aventis Deutschland*, EU:C:2013:520, paras 52–53, on which see Y Tanghe, 'The EU's External Competence in IP Matters: The Contribution of the Daiichi Sankyo Case to Cloudy Constitutional Concepts, Blurred Borders and the Corresponding Court Jurisdiction' (2015) 22 *Columbia Journal of European Law*; I Van Damme, 'Case C-414/11 Daiichi: The Impact of the Lisbon Treaty on the Competence of the European Union over the TRIPS Agreement' (2015) 4 *Cambridge Journal of International and Comparative Law* 73. See, by contrast, Opinion 3/15 (*Marrakesh Treaty on access to published works*) of 14 February 2017, EU:C:2017:114, paras 99–100.

[218] The Court clarified in Opinion 2/15 (n 32) para 82 that the concept of 'foreign direct investment' implies that the EU 'has exclusive competence, pursuant to Article 3(1)(e) TFEU, to approve any commitment vis-à-vis a third State relating to investments made by natural or legal persons of that third State in the European Union and vice versa which enable effective participation in the management or control of a company carrying out an economic activity'.

[219] See the Answer given by Ms Malmström on behalf of the European Commission on 6 September 2019 to a question for written answer (E-002452/2019) by two members of the European Parliament. See eg Art 2(2)(a) of the Agreement on Digital Trade between the European Union and the Republic of Singapore, signed on behalf of the EU by Council Decision (EU) 2025/798 of 14 April 2025 (OJ [2025] L 25.4.2025).

[220] Title VI of Part Three TFEU.

6.2.4 **Role of the European Parliament**

Article 218(10) TFEU provides for the European Parliament to be immediately and fully informed 'at all stages of the procedure'. Furthermore, European Parliamentary involvement in the conclusion of international agreements is now the rule, with the exception of agreements relating *exclusively*[221] to the CFSP. In practice, the large majority of international agreements concluded by the Union are deemed to fall under one of the categories listed in Article 218(6)(a) TFEU and are subject to consent:[222]

(a) association agreements;

(b) the agreement on Union accession to the ECHR;

(c) agreements establishing a specific institutional framework by organizing cooperation procedures;[223]

(d) agreements with important budgetary implications for the Union;[224] and

(e) agreements covering fields to which either the ordinary legislative procedure applies[225] or the special legislative procedure where consent by the European Parliament is required.[226]

Category (e) brought about a small revolution in EU external action. Under the second paragraph of ex Article 300(3) EC, that category contained 'agreements *entailing amendment* of an act adopted under the [co-decision] procedure'.[227] Given that consent of the Parliament is now required every time the ordinary legislative procedure *applies* and given the fact that the scope of the ordinary legislative procedure has been significantly enlarged in comparison to the co-decision procedure, Article 218(6)(a)(v) TFEU implies a substantial extension of the power of the European Parliament.

The change is perhaps most dramatic in the CCP where, as mentioned previously, before Lisbon the Parliament had no formal role in internal decision-making and did not even need to be consulted with respect to international trade agreements.[228] Post-Lisbon, the European Parliament's consent is required for agreements in the CCP. That much is clear, for example, from the Parliament's refusal to consent to the highly controversial Anti-Counterfeiting Trade Agreement (ACTA).[229]

[221] Agreements under Art 218 TFEU may include both issues falling under the ordinary EU framework and falling under the CFSP; eg Council Decision (EU) 2024/1394 of 22 April 2024 on the conclusion, on behalf of the European Union, of the Strategic Partnership Agreement between the European Union and its Member States, of the one part, and Japan, of the other part (OJ [2024] L 21.5.2024), which is based on a joint legal basis of Arts 37 TEU and 212(1) TFEU, in conjunction with Art 218(6)(a) and the second subpara of Art 218(8) TFEU. See further F Naert, 'The Use of the CFSP Legal Basis for EU International Agreements in Combination with Other Legal Bases' in F Naert and J Czuczai (eds), *The EU as a Global Actor: Bridging Legal Theory and Practice. Liber Amicorum in Honour of Ricardo Gosalbo Bono* (Leiden/Boston: Brill Nijhoff, 2017) 394–423.

[222] See also chapter 4.

[223] This category probably refers to international agreements setting up an institutional structure attaining a certain level of complexity, but nonetheless not concluded under the legal basis for association agreements (Art 217 TFEU); eg Council Decision 2006/719/EC of 5 October 2006 on the accession of the Community to the Hague Conference on Private International Law (OJ [2006] L297/1).

[224] See judgment of 8 July 1999, Case C-189/97 *Parliament v Council*, EU:C:1999:366, paras 20–32 for the relevant criteria.

[225] Art 294 TFEU.

[226] Art 289(2) TFEU; eg Art 352(1) TFEU, the Union's residual competence. On the scope of the ordinary legislative procedure and special legislative procedures, see further chapter 5.

[227] Emphasis added.

[228] De Baere, *Constitutional Principles* (n 8) 75 and 85.

[229] European Parliament legislative resolution of 4 July 2012 (12195/2011—C7-0027/2012—2011/0167 (NLE)) (OJ [2013] C349E/552).

The Parliament has been keen to demonstrate its increased powers not just in the area of external trade, but in all areas in which its consent is mandatory. For example, shortly after the entry into force of the Lisbon Treaty, the Parliament underlined its greater powers by first withholding its consent to the Agreement between the European Union and the United States of America on the processing and transfer of Financial Messaging Data from the European Union to the United States for purposes of the Terrorist Finance Tracking Program (SWIFT),[230] another controversial international agreement, notably on account of its alleged infringement of the right to protection of personal data, and only agreeing to consent after it felt that its concerns had been taken into account.[231]

Furthermore, Article 218(6)(b) TFEU provides for consultation of the European Parliament to be required in all cases except those for which consent is required pursuant to Article 218(6)(a) TFEU.

6.2.5 **Legal instrument**

The internal Union instruments used to conclude international agreements are often decisions not specifying to whom they are addressed. Post-Lisbon, these are now given an explicit legal basis in the fourth paragraph of Article 288 TFEU. There would therefore be less need than pre-Lisbon to have recourse to legal instruments outside the scope of that Article. Nonetheless, regardless of whether the legal instrument by which an international agreement is concluded is listed in Article 288 TFEU or is *sui generis*, it is amenable to judicial review by the CJEU.[232]

6.2.6 **Decision-making in a body set up by an international agreement**

The conclusion by the Union of an 'association agreement' under Article 217 TFEU or another international agreement will often give rise to the establishment of its own decision-making organs within which the Union will wish to take positions. Notable examples include the association agreement with Turkey[233] and the WTO Agreement. Such bodies with the competence to take binding decisions often do so by consensus.[234] The common positions to be defended by the Union need to be established in advance of the meeting at which the decision is scheduled to be taken. Article 218(9) TFEU gives the Council the competence, on a proposal from the Commission or the High Representative, to establish the positions to be adopted on the Union's behalf in such treaty-based bodies, when such a body is 'called upon to adopt acts having legal effects', excluding, however, acts supplementing or amending the institutional framework of the agreement, that is, constitutional decisions *sensu stricto*.

[230] European Parliament legislative resolution of 11 February 2010 (05305/1/2010 REV 1—C7-0004/2010—2009/0190(NLE)) (OJ [2010] C341E/100).

[231] European Parliament legislative resolution of 8 July 2010 (11222/1/2010/REV 1 and COR 1—C7-0158/2010—2010/0178(NLE)) (OJ [2011] C351E/453). Note that in application of Art 218(11) TFEU, the Parliament requested the Court to deliver an Opinion on the agreement envisaged between Canada and the EU on the transfer and processing of Passenger Name Record Data (see Proposal for a Council Decision on the conclusion of the Agreement between Canada and the European Union on the transfer and processing of Passenger Name Record Data (COM(2013) 528 final)), concerning both the compatibility of the agreement envisaged with primary EU law and the appropriate legal basis for the Council decision concluding it. In Opinion 1/15 (*EU-Canada PNR Agreement*) of 26 July 2017, EU:C:2017:592, the Court held that the agreement had to be based jointly on Arts 16(2) and 87(2)(a) TFEU and concluded that it was incompatible with Arts 7, 8, 21, and 52(1) of the Charter. The Council subsequently authorized the Commission to open new PNR negotiations with Canada, which resulted in the Agreement between Canada and the European Union on the transfer and processing of passenger name record data (OJ [2025] L 17.1.2025).

[232] *ERTA* (n 26) para 42; *Western Sahara Campaign UK* (n 111) paras 50–51.

[233] Agreement establishing an Association between the European Economic Community and Turkey—Protocol 1: Provisional Protocol—Protocol 2: Financial Protocol—Final Act—Declarations (OJ [1964] 217/3687, [1973] C113/1, [1977] L361).

[234] eg Art IX(1) WTO Agreement.

Given that the adoption of decisions having legal effects in such international bodies amounts to a new way of making EU law, the determination of the Union position cannot be left solely to the Commission. These binding decisions do become an integral part of the EU legal system, and at least the involvement of the Council seems therefore necessary,[235] while the European Parliament is to be 'immediately and fully informed', as it is at all stages of the Article 218 TFEU procedure.[236] As regards constitutional decisions, while the Treaty does not specify how such decisions are to be taken, the logic of Article 218 TFEU would appear to indicate that they need to be taken in accordance with the procedure that brought about the international agreement in question, ie the procedure contained in that same provision to conclude or amend international agreements.[237]

The Court clarified a number of procedural aspects of Article 218(9) TFEU in the *WRC-15* case, which concerned an action for annulment brought by the Commission against the conclusions of the Council on the World Radiocommunication Conference 2015 (WRC-15) of the International Telecommunication Union (ITU). In particular, the Court held that when the Council establishes a position to be adopted on the Union's behalf in Treaty-based bodies, it must do so by way of a decision and not by way of Council conclusions, and it must indicate the legal basis of the decision.[238] Building on its earlier judgment in *United Kingdom v Council* on the EEC–Turkey Association Agreement,[239] the Court also confirmed that the procedure for adopting a decision on the basis of Article 218(9) must be determined in accordance with the combined provisions of Art 218(8) and (9) TFEU.[240]

A set of cases concerning a disagreement between Germany and the Council further gave the Court the chance to clarify some of the conditions under which Article 218(9) TFEU could be used. In *OTIF I*, the Court held that, contrary to what Germany had claimed, Article 218(9) TFEU does not limit the action of the Union to situations where it has previously adopted internal rules in accordance with the ordinary legislative procedure. The Court concluded that the items on the agenda at the 25th session of the Intergovernmental Organisation for International Carriage by Rail (OTIF) Revision Committee as regards certain amendments to the Convention concerning International Carriage by Rail (COTIF) on which the Council had established the positions to be adopted on behalf of the Union fell within the scope of the Union's external competence. Accordingly, the Council had not infringed the principle of conferral laid down in the first sentence of Article 5(2) TEU.[241]

Finally, Article 218(9) TFEU can be used to establish Union positions to be put forward in international organizations, irrespective of the question whether the Union is a member of the organization or not. Indeed, in a case concerning the International Organization

[235] eg judgment of 20 September 1990, Case C-192/89 *Sevince*, EU:C:1990:322, paras 8–11. This also implies that the Court has jurisdiction to give preliminary rulings on questions of interpretation of such (even non-binding) decisions; eg judgment of 21 January 1993, Case C-188/91 *Deutsche Shell*, EU:C:1993:24, paras 14–18.

[236] Art 218(10) TFEU.

[237] In that sense also the Opinion of AG Cruz Villalón in Case C-399/12 *Germany v Council* ('*OIV*'), EU:C:2014:289, point 75.

[238] *WRC-15* (n 12) paras 40–47.

[239] Judgment of 18 December 2014, Case C-81/13 *United Kingdom v Council*, EU:C:2014:2449, para 66.

[240] *WRC-15* (n 12) paras 48–58. The Court further clarified the voting rules applicable to decisions adopted pursuant to Art 218(9) TFEU in the judgment of 4 September 2018, Case C-244/17 *Commission v Council (Agreement with Kazakhstan)*, EU:C:2018:662, paras 25–48, and of 2 September 2021, Case C-180/20 *Commission v Council (Agreement with Armenia)*, EU:C:2021:658, paras 27–35.

[241] *OTIF I* (n 12) paras 61–73. In parallel, the Commission brought infringement proceedings against Germany: see judgment of 27 March 2019, Case C-620/16 *Commission v Germany* ('*OTIF II*'), EU:C:2019:256, and section 7.2.

of Vine and Wine (OIV),[242] the Council adopted a decision to establish the EU position with qualified majority, although the EU itself is not a party to that agreement. Germany challenged this decision, arguing that Article 218(9) TFEU could not apply to such situations. The ECJ dismissed the argument, and concluded that the OIV decision at issue had legally binding effects in the EU legal order through incorporation via secondary law in the agricultural field. By contrast, in a case concerning an action brought by the Council against the Commission for annulment of a decision to submit a 'Written statement by the European Commission on behalf of the European Union' to ITLOS,[243] the Court held that unlike the *OIV* case, which concerned the EU position in the context of its participation, through Member States, in the adoption of recommendations within the body set up by the international agreement in question, the ITLOS case concerned the determination of a position to be expressed on behalf of the Union before an international judicial body requested to give an advisory opinion, the adoption of which falls solely within the remit and responsibility of the members of that body, acting wholly independently of the parties. Article 218(9) TFEU was therefore not applicable.[244]

7 Managing the vertical division of EU external competences

How is a federal-type structure like the EU[245] to ensure that its policies, while respecting the possibilities for differentiation within and across the several levels of government, remain broadly consistent and coherent, both internally and, which is often considered as at least as important, towards the outside world?

A crucial element in understanding how the current arrangement of the deckchairs on the ship of EU external action affects the Union's ability to have a consistent and effective external policy is to grasp the fact that the Union must do so against the background of 27 Member States retaining a large part of their external sovereignty and consequently their ability to have their own foreign policies. Because of its internally differentiated constitutional structure, the EU has to strive for consistency on two fronts: horizontally between its different institutions, structures, and policies, and vertically, between the EU and its Member States. The Lisbon Treaty has tried to tackle that issue by providing an overarching constitutional framework for the EU's external action, and for the EU in general, through a set of values that are to govern all EU action,[246] as well as a single set of principles and objectives for the entire field of EU external action.[247] The Union must respect those principles and pursue those objectives in the development and implementation of the different areas of the Union's external action, as well as the external aspects of its other policies.[248] The Union must also ensure consistency between the different

[242] Judgment of 7 October 2014, Case C-399/12 *Germany v Council* ('*OIV*'), EU:C:2014:2258.

[243] In Case No 21. See *Request for Advisory Opinion submitted by the Sub-Regional Fisheries Commission*, Advisory Opinion, 2 April 2015, ITLOS Reports 2015, p 4.

[244] *ITLOS* (n 196) paras 66–67. The Court also held that determining the content of a written statement did not constitute the exercise of a policymaking function, within the meaning of Art 16(1) TEU, and that it followed that, by sending the written statement, on behalf of the Union, to ITLOS in Case No 21 without having submitted its contents to the Council for approval, the Commission did not infringe that provision (ibid, paras 68–77). It had likewise not failed to fulfil its obligation of sincere cooperation pursuant to Art 13(2) TEU (ibid, paras 84–89).

[245] See further R Schütze, *From Dual to Cooperative Federalism: The Changing Structure of European Law* (Oxford: Oxford University Press, 2009) 287–343 and De Baere and Gutman (n 82). See further chapters 3 and 4.

[246] Art 2 TEU. Cf M Cremona, *Values and Interests, Law and Power in EU External Action : Two Perspectives*, EUI, LAW, AEL, Working Paper, 2025/05.

[247] Arts 3(5) and 21 TEU, and Art 205 TFEU.

[248] Art 21(3), first subpara, TEU.

areas of its external action and between these and its other policies. The Council and the Commission, assisted by the High Representative, are to ensure that consistency and are to cooperate to that effect.[249]

In practice, the Union manages the vertical and horizontal division of external competences through a combination of pragmatism and principle. While section 8 examines the horizontal division of competences, the present section analyses two constitutional concepts of vital importance for the management of the vertical division of competences: the technique of mixity and the principle of sincere cooperation.

7.1 Mixed agreements

7.1.1 What are mixed agreements?

An introduction into the law of EU external action would not be complete without a short exploration of the peculiar species called 'mixed agreements', which can be defined as agreements that include among their parties the Union and all or some of the Member States, and which fall partly within the competence of the Union and partly within the competence of the Member States.[250] The Court has defined a mixed agreement simply as an agreement that has to be 'signed and concluded both by the European Union and by each of its Member States',[251] and has clarified that the contracting parties to a mixed agreement concluded with third countries are, first, the EU and, secondly, the Member States. When such an agreement is negotiated and concluded, each of those parties must act within the framework of its competences while respecting the competences of any other contracting party.[252]

7.1.2 Why are there mixed agreements?

As Advocate General Sharpston put it, 'the mixed agreement is itself a creature of pragmatic forces—a means of resolving the problems posed by the need for international agreements in a multi-layered system'.[253] Their lack of clarity as to the precise vertical division of competences makes mixed agreements suitable for enabling the Union to act internationally while keeping the competence situation sufficiently vague so as not to affect openly the Member States' external competences. Moreover, an overly precise determination of the respective competences of the Union and the Member States might 'freeze' the Union's competences and hinder its evolving constitutional order. However, the unwillingness of the Union to provide any clear division of competences makes it difficult, particularly for third parties, to know who should be held responsible in the event of non-compliance.[254]

The Lisbon Treaty may have reduced the need for mixed agreements. For example, contrary to under the previous Treaty framework, under Article 218 TFEU, an agreement containing CFSP and non-CFSP aspects can be concluded as one integrated Union agreement while taking into account the relevant differences in procedure.[255]

Another factor that has the potential of reducing the need for mixed agreements is Article 207 TFEU, which considerably expands the Union's exclusive competence in the

[249] Art 21(3), second subpara, TEU.

[250] J Heliskoski, *Mixed Agreements as a Technique for Organizing the International Relations of the European Community and Its Member States* (The Hague/London/New York: Kluwer Law International, 2001) 7.

[251] Opinion 2/15 (n 32) para 29.

[252] Opinion 1/19 (n 13) para 240.

[253] Opinion of AG Sharpston in Case C-240/09 *Lesoochranárske zoskupenie*, EU:C:2010:436, point 56.

[254] See Eeckhout (n 63) 262–264. See further more generally, A Delgado Casteleiro, *The International Responsibility of the European Union: From Competence to Normative Control* (Cambridge: Cambridge University Press, 2016).

[255] See n 221.

CCP.[256] It appears to be intended to cover essentially the full scope[257] of the WTO-covered agreements.[258] Not only 'trade in goods and services, and the commercial aspects of intellectual property'[259] are now covered, but also 'foreign direct investment'.[260] Nevertheless, the comprehensive and wide-ranging character of the new generation of international trade and investment agreements currently being negotiated which, while building on existing rules found in the WTO-covered agreements, often extend those rules and cover matters that are not (yet) part of those agreements, could well have as a consequence that mixed agreements will continue to be used in the area of trade *sensu lato*. For example, following Opinion 2/15,[261] in which the Court held that the Free Trade Agreement envisaged between the European Union and the Republic of Singapore (EUSFTA) fell partly within the exclusive competence of the EU and partly within a competence shared between the Union and the Member States, the EU and Singapore negotiated a Free Trade Agreement and a separate Investment Protection Agreement. Both agreements were signed on behalf of the EU in October 2018,[262] and concluded on 8 November 2019,[263] entering into force on 21 November 2019. The Investment Protection Agreement will enter into force after it has been concluded by the Council,[264] and ratified by all EU Member States according to their own national procedures.

More generally, the choice between a mixed agreement or an EU-only agreement, when the subject matter of the agreement falls within an area of non-exclusive competence, is generally a matter for the discretion of the EU legislature (and of the Council in particular), predominantly political in nature, and subject to only limited judicial review. Within the limits of the procedure laid down in Article 218(2), (6), and (8) TFEU and, where required, subject to the consent of the Parliament, the decision whether or not to act on the proposal to conclude an international agreement, and, if so, to what extent, falls within the Council's political discretion.[265]

Advocate General Wahl has nevertheless suggested a number of circumstances under which mixed agreements would or would not be appropriate.[266] In particular, a decision to proceed by way of mixed agreements may be manifestly inappropriate where, because

[256] Nevertheless, the Court has clarified that 'the mere fact that an EU act is liable to have implications for international trade' is not enough for it to fall within the CCP. An EU act falls within that policy 'if it relates specifically to international trade in that it is essentially intended to promote, facilitate or govern trade and has direct and immediate effects on trade': Opinion 3/15 (n 217) para 61.

[257] With the notable exception of transport: Art 207(5) TFEU.

[258] That is to say, the agreements listed in Appendix 1 to the WTO Understanding on Rules and Procedures Governing the Settlement of Disputes.

[259] See n 217. [260] See n 219.

[261] Opinion 2/15 (n 32). See also Opinion of AG Sharpston in Opinion 2/15 (n 82), which reached the conclusion that the EUSFTA had to be concluded as a mixed agreement.

[262] Council Decision (EU) 2018/1599 of 15 October 2018 on the signing, on behalf of the European Union, of the Free Trade Agreement between the European Union and the Republic of Singapore (OJ [2018] L267/1); and Council Decision (EU) 2018/1676 of 15 October 2018 on the signing, on behalf of the European Union, of the Investment Protection Agreement between the European Union and its Member States, of the one part, and the Republic of Singapore, of the other part (OJ [2018] L279/1).

[263] Council Decision (EU) 2019/1875 of 8 November 2019 on the conclusion of the Free Trade Agreement between the European Union and the Republic of Singapore (OJ [2019] L294/1).

[264] See Commission Proposal for a Council Decision on the conclusion of the Investment Protection Agreement between the European Union and its Member States, of the one part, and the Republic of Singapore of the other part, COM(2018) 194.

[265] 1/19 (n 13) para 252.

[266] Opinion of AG Wahl in Opinion 3/15 (*Marrakesh Treaty on access to published works*), EU:C:2016:657, points 119–123. See further L Prete, 'The Constitutional Limits to the Choice of Mixity after EUSFTA, COTIF I, MPA Antarctic and COTIF II: Towards a More Constructive Discourse?' (2020) 45 *European Law Review* 113.

of the urgency of the situation and the time required for the 27 ratification procedures at national level, it seriously risks compromising the objective pursued, or causes the Union to breach the principle of *pacta sunt servanda*. Conversely, a mixed agreement would be required, generally, where an international agreement includes a part which falls under the exclusive competence of the Union and a part which falls under the exclusive competence of the Member States, without any of those parts being ancillary to the other. However, an agreement which, because of its objective and content, is within an area of shared competence must necessarily be concluded as an EU-only agreement when that competence, by virtue of its exercise by the Union, has become exclusive externally.[267]

7.1.3 **Concluding mixed agreements**

There is no specific procedure for concluding mixed agreements, but a practice has developed by which the majority of mixed agreements are negotiated under Article 218 TFEU (see section 6.2), in combination with a more pronounced presence of Member State representatives, as well as coordination meetings during which the line to be followed by the Commission during the negotiations is decided.

A mixed agreement has to be ratified by both the Union—which requires going through the normal Article 218 TFEU procedure and, in a clear majority of the cases, includes the formal involvement of the European Parliament—and by every single Member State (if all Member States, as is usual, participate in the agreement), which will have to go through its own constitutional procedures, most often including scrutiny and approval by the Member State parliaments. It does not require much imagination to see that this is liable to be a cumbersome process.

The Union has thus had to develop a strategy to tackle the problems engendered by the potentially long timespan between the signing and the entry into force of a mixed agreement. The Council adopted the practice of only concluding a mixed agreement after all Member States have ratified, in order to avoid so-called 'partial mixity'.[268] Apart from this, the Union can also enter into an interim agreement on the Union aspects of the mixed agreement, which can be concluded by a Council decision or can have the agreement provisionally applied from the time of signature, as provided for by Article 218(5) TFEU.[269]

Mixed agreements concluded by the Union form an integral part of the EU legal order, and the ECJ has jurisdiction to give preliminary rulings concerning the interpretation of such an agreement. In particular, the ECJ has jurisdiction to define the obligations that the Union has assumed and those that remain the sole responsibility of the Member States in order to interpret the mixed agreement in question.[270]

7.2 **Sincere cooperation**

The duty of loyal cooperation or sincere cooperation, as laid down in Article 4(3) TEU, is of great importance for the Union's external action and for its entire constitutional structure.[271] It requires the Union and the Member States, in full mutual respect, to assist each

[267] In accordance with Art 3(2) TFEU. See section 4.2.1.

[268] cf Art 102 EAEC, which expressly provides for this approach.

[269] See n 209. Eg Council Decision (EU) 2025/2625 of 12 November 2025 on the signing, on behalf of the Union, and provisional application of the Protocol on the implementation of the Sustainable Fisheries Partnership Agreement between the European Union and the Government of the Cook Islands (2025–2032) (OJ [2025] L 23.12.2025).

[270] Judgment of 14 July 2022, Case C-500/20 *ÖBB-Infrastruktur Aktiengesellschaft*, EU:C:2022:563, paras 39–40.

[271] See further G De Baere and T Roes, 'EU Loyalty as Good Faith' (2015) 64 *International and Comparative Law Quarterly* 829.

other in carrying out tasks which flow from the Treaties. The Member States are to take any appropriate measure, general or particular, to ensure fulfilment of the obligations arising out of the Treaties or resulting from the acts of the institutions of the Union and to facilitate the achievement of the Union's tasks and refrain from any measure which could jeopardize the attainment of the Union's objectives. The duty of sincere cooperation is of general application and does not depend either on whether the Union competence concerned is exclusive or on any right of the Member States to enter into obligations towards non-member countries.[272]

Furthermore, in particular where the subject matter of an agreement or convention falls partly within the competence of the Union and partly within that of its Member States, it is essential to ensure close cooperation between the Member States and the EU institutions, both in the process of negotiation and conclusion and in the fulfilment of the commitments entered into. That obligation to cooperate flows from the requirement of unity in the international representation of the Union, which in turn arises from the obligation of sincere cooperation.[273]

Crucially, the duty of cooperation in Union law does not regulate the vertical or horizontal division of competences, but the exercise of those competences. Nevertheless, the ECJ has been steadily reinforcing the procedural obligations flowing from the duty of loyal cooperation: from the prohibition on submitting a case that falls within the scope of EU law to a non-EU judicial organ,[274] to that on negotiating separate treaties without as much as informing the Commission after the latter has been authorized by the Council to negotiate international agreements with the same third State(s) on the same subject matter,[275] and the prohibition for a Member State to distance itself from an agreed Union strategy by taking action within an international organization that could potentially bind the Union.[276]

The Court has further clarified the procedural duties flowing from Article 4(3) TEU in *OTIF II*. There, the Commission brought infringement proceedings asking the Court to declare that Germany, by having, at the 25th session of the OTIF Revision Committee, voted against the position laid down in a Council decision adopted on the basis of Article 218(9) TFEU establishing the position to be adopted as regards certain amendments to the COTIF—the decision at issue in *OTIF I*[277]—and having publicly declared its opposition to that position and to the arrangements for the exercise of voting rights provided for therein, failed to fulfil its obligations under that decision and Article 4(3) TEU. The Court held that Germany had allowed doubts to exist as to the Union's ability to express a position and represent its Member States on the international stage, despite the adoption of the decision at issue. More specifically, the Court took the view that the fact that Germany distanced itself from the Union's position as established in that decision ran the risk of undermining the EU's power of negotiation within the OTIF, regarding the subjects discussed during that session, as well as related subjects. The Court concluded that, by its conduct, Germany had harmed the effectiveness of the international action of the Union, as well as the latter's credibility and reputation on the international stage, and had failed to fulfil its obligations under the decision at issue and Article 4(3) TEU.[278]

The procedural duties imposed on Member States by the principle of loyal cooperation cannot be captured in a simple dichotomy of the Member States' ability or inability to act independently. It is clear that the strictures of the duty of cooperation depend crucially on the international context in which the Union and the Member States operate together.

[272] *PFOS* (n 45) paras 69–71. [273] *OTIF II* (n 241) paras 93–94. [274] *Mox Plant* (n 122).

[275] Judgments of 2 June 2005, Case C-266/03 *Commission v Luxembourg*, EU:C:2005:341, and of 14 July 2005, Case C-433/03 *Commission v Germany*, EU:C:2005:462.

[276] *PFOS* (n 45). [277] See section 6.2.6. [278] *OTIF II* (n 241) paras 92–100.

The decisive criterion is whether the action of the Member States is likely to hinder or impede the Union's action.

This operation of the duty of cooperation underscores the distinction between the scope of Union law and the scope of Union competences.[279] Indeed, Member States and the Union institutions within their respective spheres of competence are under a mutual obligation to cooperate. That is illustrated by the *PFOS* case, which is further considered in case study 26.1.

Case study 26.1: External environmental policy

As a constantly growing policy field with a complex competence structure, external environmental policy provides an excellent testing ground to see the post-Lisbon framework for EU external action in operation.[280]

Article 3(5) TEU provides that the Union is to contribute to 'the sustainable development of the Earth'. Furthermore, the protection of the environment is mentioned twice among the basic objectives of the Union's external action.[281] 'Environment' is listed as a shared competence under Article 4(2)(e) TFEU, and the Court clarified in *Mox Plant* that the Union can choose the extent to which it exercises its shared competence in external environmental matters.[282] Concern for the environment outside the Union forms part of the core objectives of EU environmental policy, as Article 191(1) TFEU provides for Union policy on the environment to contribute to the pursuit of a list of objectives that include 'promoting measures at international level to deal with regional or worldwide environmental problems, and in particular combating climate change'.[283]

The legal bases for EU external environmental law are to be found in Articles 191 and 192 in Title XX of Part Three of the TFEU.[284] Article 193 TFEU[285] further clarifies that measures taken on the basis of Article 192 TFEU cannot prevent any Member State from maintaining or introducing more stringent protective measures. More specifically, Article 191(4) TFEU provides for the Union and the Member States to cooperate with third countries and with the competent international organizations within their respective spheres of competence, adding that the arrangements for Union cooperation 'may be the subject of agreements between the Union and the third parties concerned'. As is clear from its second subparagraph, measures based on Article 191(4) TFEU leave the Member States' competence to act internationally intact, which implies a parallel competence (see section 4.4.1). However, in Opinion 2/00, the Court held that Article 191 TFEU defines the objectives to be pursued in the context of environmental policy, while Article 192 TFEU constitutes the legal basis on which Union measures are adopted.[286] As a consequence, ex Article 174(4) EC (now Article 191(4) TFEU) was abandoned as the default

[279] See M Cremona, 'Defending the Community Interest: The Duties of Cooperation and Compliance' in M Cremona and B de Witte (eds), *EU Foreign Relations Law: Constitutional Fundamentals* (Oxford: Hart Publishing, 2008) 168.

[280] For more on the detail of EU environmental law, see chapter 22. See further on EU external environmental policy, Wouters et al, *The Law of EU External Relations* (n 6) ch 10; and on international environmental law, with particular attention to the role of the EU in that regard, ibid, ch 20.

[281] Art 21(2)(d) and (f) TEU.

[282] *Mox Plant* (n 122) paras 80–121.

[283] The EU's pursuit of that objective must now be read against the background of: ICJ *Obligations of States in respect of Climate Change*, Advisory Opinion of 23 July 2025. Further on climate change: see chapter 22, section 5. See also L Smail, *Climate Change Law and Practice* (London: Bloomsbury, 2025).

[284] Ex Arts 174 and 175 EC.

[285] Ex Art 176 EC.

[286] Opinion 2/00 (*Cartagena Protocol on Biosafety*) of 6 December 2001, EU:C:2001:664, para 44. See also *Mox Plant* (n 122) para 90.

legal basis for external environmental agreements. That is, for example, clear from comparing the Commission proposal regarding the Kyoto Protocol, an international agreement linked to the United Nations Framework Convention on Climate Change, which sets internationally binding emission-reduction targets, which was based on ex Article 174(4) EC,[287] and the eventual Council decision, based on ex Article 175(1) EC (now Article 192(1) TFEU).[288] Most substantive measures will now presumably be based on Article 192 TFEU. For example, the decision concluding the Paris Agreement was indeed based on Article 192(1), in combination with Article 218(6)(a) TFEU.[289] As the Court appears to have held in Opinion 2/00, the *ERTA* doctrine does in principle apply to such measures.[290]

However, as mentioned previously (see section 4.4.1), minimum standards such as those pursuant to Article 193 TFEU normally give rise to non-exclusive EU competences. The ECJ further clarified the scope of Article 193 TFEU in the *PFOS* case.[291]

THE *PFOS* CASE

The *PFOS* case concerned infringement proceedings brought by the Commission against Sweden for having unilaterally proposed that perfluoroctane sulfonate (PFOS), part of the category of per- and polyfluoroalkyl substances (PFAS)—sometimes nicknamed 'forever chemicals'[292]—be added to Annex A to the Stockholm Convention on Persistent Organic Pollutants.[293] The Stockholm Convention is a multilateral agreement, the objective of which is to protect human health and the environment from Persistent Organic Pollutants (POPs). The first recital in the Preamble to the Convention specifies that POPs possess toxic properties, resist degradation, bioaccumulate, and are transported through air, water, and migratory species across international boundaries and deposited far from their place of release, where they accumulate in terrestrial and aquatic ecosystems. The Convention is a mixed agreement, to which the Union[294] and all Member States are parties.[295]

A Member State is free to adopt measures providing for a higher level of protection within its own jurisdiction. However, proposing such measures within the framework of an international agreement to which the Union is a party, which would imply that the Union may be bound by a more stringent measure with which it did not express its agreement, is quite a different thing and does not fall within the scope of Article 193 TFEU.[296] It is important to appreciate that Sweden was exercising its own competence when it submitted the proposal to

[287] Proposal for a Council Decision concerning the approval, on behalf of the European Community, of the Kyoto Protocol to the United Nations Framework Convention on Climate Change and the joint fulfilment of commitments thereunder, COM/2001/0579 final (OJ [2002] 75E/17).

[288] Council Decision 2002/358/EC of 25 April 2002 concerning the approval, on behalf of the European Community, of the Kyoto Protocol to the United Nations Framework Convention on Climate Change and the joint fulfilment of commitments thereunder (OJ [2002] L130/1).

[289] Council Decision (EU) 2016/1841 of 5 October 2016 on the conclusion, on behalf of the European Union, of the Paris Agreement adopted under the United Nations Framework Convention on Climate Change (OJ [2016] L282/1).

[290] See Opinion 2/00 (n 286) paras 44–46, and judgment of 26 November 2014, Case C-66/13 *Green Network*, EU:C:2014:2399, paras 24–33.

[291] See further G De Baere, '"O, Where Is Faith? O, Where Is Loyalty?" Some Thoughts on the Duty of Loyal Co-Operation and the Union's External Environmental Competences in the Light of the *PFOS* Case' (2011) 36 *European Law Review* 405.

[292] cf R Salvidge and L Hosea, 'UK failing to match EU in fight against "forever chemicals", say scientists', *The Guardian*, 17 January 2025. On how 'forever chemicals' (PFAS) and climate change are devastating the Arctic, and polar bears in particular, see B Taub, 'The Big Ice Is Sick', *The New Yorker*, 24 November 2025.

[293] Adopted on 22 May 2001, 40 ILM 532 (2001).

[294] Council Decision 2006/507/EC of 14 October 2004 concerning the conclusion, on behalf of the European Community, of the Stockholm Convention on Persistent Organic Pollutants (OJ [2006] L209/1).

[295] *PFOS* (n 45) para 19. [296] Ibid, para 102.

list PFOS. However, in doing so, the principle of sincere cooperation (now Article 4(3) TEU) required that it take into account the fact that the Union too is competent in the matter and that a strategy had been agreed within the Council.

THE INTERNATIONAL WHALING COMMISSION

However, if the Union were *not* to be bound by a more stringent measure, the Member States would arguably be free to adopt it or propose it in the relevant international fora. Such a situation would typically occur with respect to an international agreement to which the Union has not acceded, often because the international agreement in question does not permit international organizations to become a party.

An example of this would be the participation of the Member States in the International Whaling Commission (IWC),[297] the international organization competent for the conservation and management of whale stocks. It was set up by the International Convention for the Regulation of Whaling,[298] to which the EU is an observer.[299] EU regulatory activity as regards matters pertaining to whaling does not come under the exclusive common fisheries policy,[300] but under the shared competence on the environment.[301] While Union action on whaling has been taken,[302] it would go too far to say that the Union has exercised its competence to such an extent that it has replaced the Member States within the IWC and is consequently bound by its decisions. The ECJ has put the threshold for that to happen rather high: in order for the Union to be capable of being bound, it must have assumed, and thus had transferred to it, all the powers previously exercised by the Member States that fall within the convention in question.[303] Given that EU action as regards whaling most likely does not meet that threshold, it would seem legitimate for a Member State to vote in favour of any measure proposed within the IWC that would strengthen the protection of whales beyond and above the protection agreed within the Union. That would quite clearly be the case if no position on such a proposal could be reached within the Council.

Would the same count if a position had been reached? Given that the EU is not a party to the Whaling Convention and cannot be bound by the decisions taken by the IWC, it must follow from Article 193 TFEU that Member States ought to remain free to support measures enhancing the protection of whales, while being prevented from supporting any measure lowering such protection below the level guaranteed by EU law. Nevertheless, that does not diminish the duty of the Member States on the basis of Article 4(3) TEU to attempt to obtain

[297] See Wouters et al, *The Law of EU External Relations* (n 6) ch 10.

[298] Signed in Washington DC on 2 December 1946, 62 Stat 1716, 161 UNTS 72.

[299] Membership of the IWC is only open to governments that adhere to the Whaling Convention. An amendment to the Whaling Convention allowing the EU to become a member would require the ratification of a protocol by all IWC members.

[300] Art 3(1)(d) TFEU.

[301] Art 4(2)(e) TFEU. Annex I to the TFEU lists the products coming under Art 38 TFEU on the common agriculture and fisheries policy. Chapter 3 mentions 'Fish, crustaceans and molluscs', but not marine mammals. The latter are only mentioned in Chapter 15.04: 'Fats and oil, of fish and marine mammals, whether or not refined.' In any event, EU action on whaling has as a rule been taken under environmental competence. See nevertheless eg Commission Delegated Regulation (EU) 2025/2593 of 11 August 2025 amending Regulation (EU) 2019/1241 of the European Parliament and of the Council as regards the prolongation of the measures to reduce incidental catches of common dolphin (Delphinus delphis) and other small cetaceans in the Bay of Biscay (OJ [2025] L 23.12.2025).

[302] eg Council Regulation (EEC) No 348/81 of 20 January 1981 on common rules for imports of whales or other cetacean products (OJ [1981] L39/1); Council Directive 92/43/EEC of 21 May 1992 on the conservation of natural habitats and of wild fauna and flora (OJ [1992] L206/7); Council Regulation (EC) No 338/97 of 9 December 1996 on the protection of species of wild fauna and flora by regulating trade therein (OJ [1997] L61/1).

[303] *ATAA* (n 109) para 63.

a common position at EU level. Furthermore, given that, as seen above, Article 218(9) TFEU can be used to establish Union positions to be put forward in international organizations, irrespective of the question whether the Union is a member of the organization or not, that provision is the appropriate procedural legal basis for EU coordinated positions in the IWC.[304]

THE MERCURY NEGOTIATIONS

The complexity of EU external environmental competences being what it is, whether and, if so, to what extent a specific issue that forms the subject of international negotiations falls within the competence of the Union or of the Member States is often less than clear. That situation will inevitably lead to competence quarrels between the Union and the Member States and between the EU institutions, all of which are bound by the duty of sincere cooperation in Article 4(3) TEU, a specific institutional application of which is now explicitly contained in Article 13(2) TEU, which provides for the institutions to 'practice mutual sincere cooperation'.[305]

A particularly unseemly example of how things can go awry regardless is the saga surrounding the negotiations for an international binding instrument on mercury.[306] The potentially adverse effects of the presence of mercury in the environment have been well documented.[307] Limiting the spread of mercury was the objective of the negotiations under the United Nations Environment Programme (UNEP) for a global mercury treaty, and the EU wished to take part in the process.

In its recommendation of 15 July 2009,[308] the Commission suggested that mercury was a substance already regulated to a large extent by existing legislation at Community level. It requested that the Council authorize it to participate on behalf of the Community in the negotiations, in consultation with the special committee designated by the Council in accordance with the negotiating directives. However, the Council Presidency prepared a text that provided for the EU and its Member States to be represented by the Commission and the rotating Presidency.[309] The Commission took a particularly dim view of that proposed arrangement.

What emerges from the publicly available documents, is that the Commission withdrew its recommendation, which led to an unprecedented institutional crisis. The first session of the intergovernmental negotiating committee (INC) took place in Stockholm from 7 to 11 June 2010. The absence of a decision authorizing the Commission to participate in the negotiations resulted in intense and protracted discussions between the Member States and the Commission on the issue of who should take the floor at the Plenary Session, on behalf of whom, and on what basis. That gave rise to what must have been a baffling spectacle. In addition to an opening statement by the Council Presidency on behalf of the Member States, an opening statement was made by the Commission on behalf of the EU, explaining that it was not in a position to negotiate and that the Member States likewise could not negotiate an instrument that

[304] See in that sense Proposal for a Council Decision on the position to be adopted, on behalf of the European Union, at the next three meetings of the International Whaling Commission including related inter-sessional meetings and actions, COM(2017) 463 final, 9.

[305] Art 13(2) TEU also reflects the principle of institutional balance, characteristic of the institutional structure of the Union, a principle which requires that each of the institutions exercise its powers with due regard for the powers of the other institutions: *WRC-15* (n 12) para 40; *Accession to the Geneva Act* (n 76) para 83, and *KS and KD* (n 23) para 72.

[306] Further De Baere, 'Mercury Rising' (n 201) 640–655.

[307] Y Zang eta., 'Global Health Effects of Future Atmospheric Mercury Emissions' (2021) 12 *Nature Communications* 3035.

[308] Recommendation from the Commission to the Council on the participation of the European Community in negotiations on a legally binding instrument on mercury further to Decision 25/5 of the Governing Council of the United Nations Environment Programme (UNEP), SEC(2009) 983 final.

[309] Council Doc 9504/10.

affected internal EU rules. Further statements were then made partly by the Commission on behalf of the EU and partly by the Presidency on behalf of the Member States. The Commission then made it clear that if the Presidency proceeded to intervene on behalf of the Member States, it would likewise continue to take the floor on behalf of the EU. In order to avoid a further eye-wateringly undignified display of disunion, practical arrangements were subsequently agreed for the Presidency to speak on behalf of the Member States on certain topics and for the Commission to speak on behalf of the EU *and* its Member States on other topics.

A compromise was finally reached in late 2010. The Commission was authorized to participate on behalf of the Union in the negotiations on a binding instrument as regards matters falling within the Union's competence and in respect of which the Union has adopted rules.[310] The irony of this unedifying episode is that, in substance, all Member States agree that mercury should be phased out. The negotiations should therefore have been relatively easy from a technical point of view. Nevertheless, all's well that ends well, as the international mercury negotiations culminated in January 2013 in the adoption of the text of a global legally binding instrument on mercury called the Minamata Convention on Mercury,[311] which entered into force on 16 August 2017.[312]

CONCLUSION

Member States' desire to remain present on the international scene as autonomous actors appears not to have diminished post-Lisbon. The dispute in the context of the negotiations on a binding instrument on mercury between the Commission as defender of increased consistency and efficiency in EU external environmental action through a more unified external representation under its aegis and the Council as the defender of Member State interests is telling in this regard. Mixed representation would appear to be here to stay even after Lisbon, especially in areas of shared competence. The mercury saga remains one of the most flagrant failures yet of post-Lisbon unified international representation and consistent and efficient external action, and *PFOS* a telling example of the judicial reinforcement of the loyalty obligation. However, the international context within which the EU operates may also necessitate the continued presence of Member States in the external representation of EU competences, as the example of the IWC demonstrates.

8 **Managing the horizontal division of EU external competences**

The third paragraph of Article 1 TEU provides that the Union is to be founded on the EU Treaty and on the TFEU: 'Those two Treaties shall have the same legal value.'[313] Article 40 TEU prohibits any mutual invasion of territory between the 'Union competences referred

[310] Art 1 of the Council Decision on the participation of the Union in negotiations on a legally binding instrument on mercury further to Decision 25/5 of the Governing Council of the United Nations Environment Programme (UNEP), Council Doc 16632/10.

[311] 3201 UNTS 3; cf Council Decision (EU) 2017/939 of 11 May 2017 on the conclusion on behalf of the European Union of the Minamata Convention on Mercury (OJ [2017] L142/4).

[312] In accordance with its Art 31(1). As of January 2026, there were 128 signatories and 153 parties to the Convention. Most recently, the sixth Conference of the Parties to the Convention (COP6) in November 2025 concluded with an agreement to phase out dental amalgam globally by 1 January 2035. Cf Council Decision (EU) 2025/2258 of 31 October 2025 on the position to be taken on behalf of the EU at the sixth meeting of the Conference of the Parties to the Minamata Convention on Mercury as regards the adoption of decisions amending Annexes A and B to that Convention on mercury-added products and manufacturing processes in which mercury or mercury compounds are used (OJ [2025] L 10.11.2025).

[313] See also Art 1(2) TFEU.

to in Articles 3 to 6 of the Treaty on the Functioning of the European Union' (ie the former First Pillar competences) and the CFSP.

However, it is not always entirely clear how the ECJ might judge whether or not a First Pillar measure has encroached upon the CFSP, because as noted previously, the CFSP has lost its specific objectives. This makes the ECJ's pre-Lisbon objectives-based analysis in *Small Arms and Light Weapons*[314] difficult to undertake. For example, the distinction between 'preserving peace and/or strengthening international security' (CFSP) and 'social and economic development' (development cooperation) would not resolve any border conflict between ordinary external action of the Union and the CFSP. Both fall under the general objectives of the Union's external action, under Article 21(2)(c) and (d) TEU, respectively.

In the *Legal Basis for Restrictive Measures* case,[315] the ECJ rejected the European Parliament's action for annulment against a regulation[316] amending Regulation 881/2002[317] to provide for a listing procedure ensuring that the fundamental rights of the defence and in particular the right to be heard are respected, following the ECJ's judgment[318] in *Kadi I*.[319] It held that the contested Regulation was rightly based on Article 215(2) TFEU, thereby rejecting the argument that the measure ought to have been taken on the basis of Article 75 TFEU, which ensured a greater degree of parliamentary participation through the ordinary legislative procedure.[320]

In doing so, the Court refused to attach any of the objectives of Article 21 TEU specifically to the CFSP, against the advice of Advocate General Bot,[321] and left the question open of how to choose between the CFSP and ordinary external action on the basis of its indications in *Small Arms and Light Weapons*. It had the chance to clarify this issue in *Mauritius Pirates Agreement*, an action brought by the Parliament against the Council.[322] The Parliament took the view that a Council Decision, adopted within the CFSP,[323] on the conditions of transfer of suspected pirates and associated seized property from the EU-led naval force to the Republic of Mauritius and on their conditions after transfer[324] was invalid because it did not relate exclusively to the CFSP, but also to judicial cooperation in criminal matters, police cooperation, and development cooperation, covering fields to which the ordinary legislative procedure applies. Therefore, the agreement should have been concluded after obtaining the European Parliament's consent in accordance with Article 218(6)(a)(v) TFEU. Advocate General Bot reiterated his view that the objectives in Article 21(2)(a)–(c) TEU are 'among those that are traditionally assigned to the CFSP'.[325] The Advocate General also argued that Article 21(2) TEU should be read together with more specific provisions applicable to each policy in order to determine the policy to which an objective is specifically related.[326] The latter seems a plausible approach. Nevertheless,

314 Judgment of 20 May 2008, Case C-91/05 *Commission v Council* ('*Small Arms and Light Weapons*' or '*SALW*'), EU:C:2008:288. See De Baere, *Constitutional Principles* (n 8) 296–297.

315 Judgment of 19 July 2012, Case C-130/10 *Parliament v Council* ('*Legal Basis for Restrictive Measures*' or '*LBRM*'), EU:C:2012:472. See further, G De Baere, 'From "Don't Mention the Titanium Dioxide Judgment" to "I Mentioned It Once, But I Think I Got Away with It All Right": Reflections on the Choice of Legal Basis in EU External Relations after the *Legal Basis for Restrictive Measures* Judgment' (2012–13) 15 *Cambridge Yearbook of European Legal Studies* 537.

316 Council Regulation (EU) No 1286/2009 of 22 December 2009 amending Regulation (EC) No 881/2002 imposing certain specific restrictive measures directed against certain persons and entities associated with Usama bin Laden, the Al-Qaeda network, and the Taliban (OJ [2009] L346/42).

317 Regulation (EC) No 881/2002 (OJ [2002] L139/9).

318 n 123.

319 Recital 4 in the Preamble to Regulation 1286/2009.

320 Art 294 TFEU.

321 Opinion in *LBRM* (n 321), EU:C:2012:50, points 62–63.

322 *Mauritius Pirates Agreement* (n 142).

323 On the basis of Art 37 TEU in combination with Art 218(5) and (6) TFEU.

324 Council Decision 2011/640/CFSP (OJ [2011] L254/1).

325 Opinion of AG Bot in *Mauritius Pirates Agreement* (n 142), points 86–87.

326 Ibid, point 88.

Article 21(3) TEU's exhortation for the Union to 'respect the principles and pursue the objectives set out in paragraphs 1 and 2 in the development and implementation of the different areas of the Union's external action' implies that such 'reading together' ought not to be applied so as effectively to limit objectives *exclusively* to one policy. In other words, Advocate General Bot may well have been correct in arguing that certain objectives can more readily be pursued within certain policies. However, the pursuance of those objectives should not automatically lead to the conclusion that a certain policy field is applicable.[327] The Court's judgment in *Mauritius Pirates Agreement*[328] left the question of how to choose between the CFSP and ordinary EU external action mostly undecided.

More generally, unless one is willing to attach the objectives of Article 21 TEU to specific areas of EU external action, thereby sacrificing the Lisbon Treaty's clear aim to infuse more unity in the EU's external action through a set of common objectives, the absence of specific CFSP objectives makes it considerably more difficult for the Court to apply Article 40 TEU. Perhaps the Court ought to refer predominantly to the actual content of a measure instead of its objectives in order to determine its legal basis.

The Court appears to have adopted such an approach in *Tanzania Pirates Agreement*,[329] a case concerning the Agreement between the EU and Tanzania on the conditions of transfer of suspected pirates and associated seized property from the Union-led naval force to Tanzania. It held that the Agreement fell predominantly within the scope of the CFSP, and not within the scope of judicial cooperation in criminal matters or police cooperation, and that the contested decision could therefore legitimately be based on Article 37 TEU alone.[330] The Court's determination of the correct legal basis was based on a classic centre of gravity test examining both the aim and the content of the measure, focusing notably on the fact that the provisions of the agreement define the conditions and modalities for the transfer to Tanzania of persons suspected of intending to commit, committing, or having committed acts of piracy, detained by the EU-led naval force (EUNAVFOR), and associated property seized by EUNAVFOR, and for the treatment of those persons after that transfer,[331] and that the procedure of transferring persons arrested or detained by EUNAVFOR established by the agreement constituted an instrument whereby the EU pursues the objectives of the EU military operation to contribute to the deterrence, prevention, and repression of acts of piracy and armed robbery off the Somali coast ('Operation Atalanta'), namely to preserve international peace and security,[332] in particular by making it possible to ensure that the perpetrators of acts of piracy do not go unpunished.[333] The Agreement, concluded pursuant to Article 12 of Joint Action 2008/851,[334] was therefore inherently ancillary to a CFSP operation, and hence fell within the scope of that policy.

Furthermore, in the *Agreement with Kazakhstan* judgment, the Court confirmed the applicability of the centre of gravity test to the choice of legal basis between CFSP and ordinary external action legal bases,[335] contrary to the Council's argument at the hearing to the effect that such a test must not be applied from the outset where there are references to the CFSP in the agreement at issue.[336]

[327] See De Baere and Van den Sanden (n 11) 106–107.

[328] *Mauritius Pirates Agreement* (n 142).

[329] *Tanzania Pirates Agreement* (n 142).

[330] Ibid, para 55.

[331] Ibid, paras 45–47.

[332] The Court referred (at para 50) in particular to point 14 of UN Security Council Resolution 1846 (2008), UN Doc S/RES/1846 (2008).

[333] *Tanzania Pirates Agreement* (n 142), paras 48–54.

[334] Council Joint Action 2008/851/CFSP of 10 November 2008 on a European Union military operation to contribute to the deterrence, prevention and repression of acts of piracy and armed robbery off the Somali coast (OJ [2008] L301/33).

[335] *Agreement with Kazakhstan* (n 240) paras 37–38. See also *Agreement with Armenia* (n 240) paras 35–58.

[336] Opinion of AG Kokott in *Agreement with Kazakhstan*, EU:C:2018:364, point 60.

Finally, what does the equality of the TEU and TFEU (as per the third paragraph of Article 1 TEU and Article 1(2) TFEU) imply for the possibility of autonomous acts based on a combined legal basis in the EU Treaty as regards the CFSP and within the TFEU as regards the ordinary external action of the Union? In *Legal Basis for Restrictive Measures*, the ECJ noted that while Article 75 TFEU provides for the application of the ordinary legislative procedure, which entails QMV in the Council and the Parliament's full participation in the procedure, Article 215(2) TFEU entails merely informing the Parliament. In addition, recourse to Article 215(2) TFEU, unlike recourse to Article 75 TFEU, requires a previous decision in the sphere of the CFSP, the adoption of which, as a general rule, calls for unanimous voting in the Council acting alone.[337] Building on the *Titanium dioxide* line of case law, according to which recourse to a dual legal basis is not possible where the procedures laid down for each legal basis are incompatible with each other,[338] the Court then added: 'Differences of that kind are such as to render those procedures incompatible.'[339] In other words, even if the contested regulation does pursue several objectives at the same time or have several components indissociably linked, without one being secondary to the other, the differences in the procedures applicable under Articles 75 and 215(2) TFEU mean that they cannot form a combined legal basis. The Court seemed to take the CFSP procedure necessary to adopt the basic decision under the EU Treaty as integral to the procedure to adopt the subsequent decision under the TFEU. While the ECJ has thereby not necessarily a priori excluded every combination between the ordinary external action of the EU and the CFSP regarding autonomous measures, it has made such combinations rather unlikely.

Nevertheless, the limited possibility (or even impossibility) of de jure cross-pillar autonomous measures combining CFSP and non-CFSP legal bases should not be taken to exclude any de facto cross-pillar external action, that is, measures or actions that, while formally based on a single (mostly first) pillar legal basis, contain elements that could be regarded as forming part of or at least impacting upon foreign and defence policy. Examples include the establishment of the European Defence Fund,[340] the Connecting Europe Facility,[341] the Security Action for Europe,[342] the establishment of the European Defence Industry Programme,[343] and the Commission's ReArm Europe Plan/Readiness 2030 initiative.[344]

[337] *LBRM* (n 315) para 47.

[338] Judgment of 11 June 1991, Case C-300/89 *Commission v Council* ('*Titanium dioxide*'), EU:C:1991:244, paras 17–21.

[339] Ibid, para 48.

[340] Regulation (EU) 2021/697 of the European Parliament and of the Council of 29 April 2021 establishing the European Defence Fund and repealing Regulation (EU) 2018/1092 (OJ [2021] L170/149), based on Arts 173(3), 182(4), 183, and the second para of Art 188 TFEU.

[341] Regulation (EU) 2021/1153 of the European Parliament and of the Council of 7 July 2021 establishing the Connecting Europe Facility and repealing Regulations (EU) No 1316/2013 and (EU) No 283/2014 (OJ [2021] L249/38), based on Arts 172 and 194 TFEU. See in particular on military mobility: recital 23, Arts 3(2)(a)(ii), 9(2)(c), 12(1)(b) and (d), and 14(1)(k).

[342] Council Regulation (EU) 2025/1106 of 27 May 2025 establishing the Security Action for Europe (SAFE) through the Reinforcement of the European Defence Industry Instrument (OJ [2025] L 28.5.2025), based on Art 122 TFEU. See Case C-560/25 *Parliament v Council*, pending, in which the Parliament requests the annulment of the regulation, on the grounds that (a) it should have been based on Art 173 (industrial policy) rather than Art 122 (special emergency mechanisms) TFEU, and (b) the Council failed adequately to state the reasons justifying that choice of the legal basis.

[343] Regulation (EU) 2025/2643 of the European Parliament and of the Council of 16 December 2025 establishing the European Defence Industry Programme and a framework of measures to ensure the timely availability and supply of defence products ('EDIP Regulation') (OJ [2025] L 29.12.2025), based on Arts 114(1), 173(3), 212(2), and 322(1) TFEU.

[344] European Commission, White Paper for European Defence—Readiness 2030 (https://commission.europa.eu/document/download/e6d5db69-e0ab-4bec-9dc0-3867b4373019_en), on which see Genini (n 135) 15–16, 32, 36, 38, 42.

Specifically with respect to Ukraine, in December 2025, the EU adopted a number of measures under ordinary EU competence intended to bolster Ukraine's defensive capabilities. First, it adopted a measure prohibiting any direct or indirect transfer of assets or reserves of the Central Bank of Russia, or of any legal person, entity, or body acting on behalf of, or at the direction of, the Central Bank of Russia, such as the Russian National Wealth Fund.[345] Secondly, it signed the Council of Europe Convention Establishing the International Claims Commission for Ukraine.[346] Thirdly, the European Council agreed to provide a loan to Ukraine of €90 billion for the years 2026–2027 based on EU borrowing on the capital markets backed by EU budget headroom.[347]

The adoption of de facto cross-pillar acts therefore appears to have recently gained momentum, as the EU is seemingly increasingly resorting to such measures in an attempt to help fill the void left by the projected disengagement of the US with respect to Europe's defence.[348]

9 Conclusion

Rather than merely reshuffling the occasional deckchair, the Union's external action system and by extension the Union as a whole appears to be constantly and incrementally rebuilding the ship on the open sea, 'never able to dismantle it in dry-dock and to reconstruct it there out of the best materials'.[349] At the same time, Treaty amendment after Treaty amendment, the Union has seen a further development of its external competences and an elaboration of its institutional structure for external action. Furthermore, most actors in the Union have now realized that the fundamentally different approach to ordinary EU external action on the one hand and the CFSP on the other hand, forms a major obstacle to consistent and efficient external action. The need for the Union's socio-economic external action to form a part of one unified policy together with the CFSP was elegantly phrased by Dworkin, who saw it as an example of a valuable shift in political boundaries from smaller and more homogeneous political communities to larger and more diverse ones:[350]

> Both the European nations and the world will gain, I believe, if the EU is able to form a common foreign policy and execute it with the economic power of its community giving strength to its united arm.

345 Council Regulation (EU) 2025/2600 of 12 December 2025 on emergency measures addressing the serious economic difficulties caused by Russia's actions in the context of the war of aggression against Ukraine (OJ [2025] L 13.12.2025), based on Art 122(1) TFEU.

346 Council Decision (EU) 2025/2655 of 16 December 2025 on the signing, on behalf of the European Union, of the Convention Establishing the International Claims Commission for Ukraine (OJ [2025] L 23.12.2025), based on Arts 212 and 218(5) TFEU. The establishment of such a mechanism had been called for by United Nations (UN) General Assembly Resolution ES-11/5, *Furtherance of remedy and reparation for aggression against Ukraine*, UN Doc A/RES/ES-11/5.

347 European Council meeting, 18 December 2025—Ukraine (EUCO 26/25), para 8. The loan will be established by means of enhanced cooperation (Art 20 TEU) in respect of a basic instrument to be based on Art 212 TFEU.

348 cf The White House, *National Security Strategy of the United States of America* (November 2025) 27 (see www.whitehouse.gov/wp-content/uploads/2025/12/2025-National-Security-Strategy.pdf).

349 cf the metaphor by O Neurath, 'Protocol Sentences' in AJ Ayer (ed), *Logical Positivism* (Glencoe, IL: The Free Press, 1959) 201.

350 R Dworkin, *Justice for Hedgehogs* (Cambridge, MA/London: Belknap/Harvard, 2011) 382.

Yet, rebuilding the ship remains a challenge, even in the face of particularly choppy international waters[351] that urgently require addressing the evident structural problems, in particular the continued constitutional separation between ordinary EU external action and the CFSP. While the High Representative and the EEAS attempt to bridge that divide and while it cannot be denied that the post-Lisbon institutional system has created opportunities to foster consistency, effectiveness, and continuity in the EU's external action,[352] the results remain mixed.

Nevertheless, as discussed in section 8, the current US administration's policy of rather discourteous disengagement with respect to Europe's security and defence[353] in general and regarding Russia's aggression against Ukraine in particular, appears to have jolted the EU into creatively utilizing its ordinary EU competences to adopt measures with clear defence implications, thereby creating a body of what could be termed 'de facto cross-pillar measures'. Whether such creativity without addressing EU external action's continuing structural issues will suffice to stem the rapidly changing international tide remains to be seen.

Furthermore, even an area of exclusive external competence such as the CCP offers no guarantee for a forceful external policy, as the most recent trade negotiations with the United States have demonstrated. A June 2025 article in *The New York Times* offered the following assessment of how the EU's capacity as an external actor, in particular in the area of international trade, is perceived by the current US administration:[354]

> European negotiators 'move slower than a French escargot,' a recent Fox News opinion article about trade negotiations quipped, before predicting that Europeans will spend trade talks waltzing 'us through their organic, manicured gardens again with no result'. . . . Both the Treasury secretary and the commerce secretary have recently suggested that while it would be feasible to negotiate with individual countries like Germany, the E.U. bureaucracy was getting in the way of a deal.

Based on that assessment, the 'Joint Statement on a United States-European Union framework on an agreement on reciprocal, fair and balanced trade',[355] which represents, for now, the result of the negotiations, is arguably in line with expectations.

Be that as it may, from its modest beginnings as a customs union (which contains an essential external aspect by requiring the adoption of a common customs tariff in the relations of the Member States with third countries),[356] the Union has come a long way to the current array of external policies. That remains a remarkable feat, as the tension between the self-consciousness of the Member States and their constitutional relationship within the Union is especially pronounced in external action, where they remain

[351] cf A Jäger and D Daniels, 'Things Are Terrible in Europe, and They're Only Going to Get Worse', *The New York Times*, 22 December 2024: 'Where foreign policy, military affairs or energy independence are concerned, however, Europe appears more and more rudderless in a stormy world. . . .'.

[352] cf F Hoffmeister and L Havas (eds), *The High Representative of the Union for Foreign Affairs and Security Policy as a Legal Actor* (Leiden: Brill, 2025).

[353] cf the current US administration's bleak and ominous assessment of the state of the EU, including its external policies, in *National Security Strategy of the USA* (n 348) IV, 3,'C. Promoting European Greatness'.

[354] J Smialek, 'The US Right Loathes the EU How Are They Going to Negotiate Trade?', *The New York Times*, 1 June 2025.

[355] cf European Commission, *Joint Statement on a United States-European Union framework on an agreement on reciprocal, fair and balanced trade* (Brussels: DG for Trade and Economic Security, 21 August 2025); Proposal for a Regulation of the European Parliament and of the Council on the adjustment of customs duties on the import of certain goods originating in the United States of America and opening of tariff quotas for imports of certain goods originating in the United States of America, COM/2025/471 final.

[356] Art 28 TFEU.

determined to assert their status as full subjects of international law. The Union's external action therefore operates as a multi-level system, reflecting the uniqueness of the Union as a body organized along federal lines but with fully fledged States as its component political entities. The complexity this involves is, to a significant degree, unavoidable. It does, however, make the Union a sometimes frustrating and often slightly bewildering international actor for EU citizens, third parties, and students of EU external action.

Further reading

G Butler and RA Wessel (eds), *EU External Relations Law: The Cases in Context* (Oxford: Hart Publishing, 2022)

M Cremona (ed), *Structural Principles in EU External Relations Law* (Oxford: Hart Publishing, 2018)

M Cremona and A Thies (eds), *The European Court of Justice and External Relations Law: Constitutional Challenges* (Oxford: Hart Publishing, 2014)

G De Baere, *Constitutional Principles of EU External Relations* (Oxford: Oxford University Press, 2008)

H de Waele, *Legal Dynamics of EU External Relations: Dissecting a Layered Global Player* (3rd edn, Berlin: Springer, 2023)

S Duquet, *EU Diplomatic Law* (Oxford: Oxford University Press, 2022)

P Eeckhout, *EU External Relations Law* (2nd edn, Oxford: Oxford University Press, 2011)

S Keukeleire and T Delreux, *The Foreign Policy of the European Union* (3rd edn, London: Bloomsbury Academic, 2022)

P Koutrakos, *EU International Relations Law* (2nd edn, Oxford/Portland, OR: Hart Publishing, 2015)

J Odermatt, *International Law and the European Union* (Cambridge: Cambridge University Press, 2021)

R Schütze, *Foreign Affairs and the European Constitution* (Cambridge: Cambridge University Press, 2014)

T Van den Sanden, *EU Development Cooperation Policy: Between Constitutional Strictures and Policy Objectives* (Cheltenham: Edward Elgar, 2022)

T Verellen, *Foreign Relations Federalism: The EU in Comparative Perspective* (Oxford: Oxford University Press, 2023)

R Wessel and J Larik, *EU External Relations Law: Text, Cases and Materials* (3rd edn, Oxford: Hart Publishing, 2026)

J Wouters, F Hoffmeister, G De Baere, and T Ramopoulos, *The Law of EU External Relations: Cases, Materials, and Commentary on the EU as an International Legal Actor* (3rd edn, Oxford: Oxford University Press, 2020)

27

Brexit: the legal dimension

Steve Peers and Darren Harvey

1 Introduction

On 23 June 2016, the majority of those voting in a referendum in the UK decided to leave the EU, rather than remain a Member State. Having obtained the necessary statutory authorization from the UK Parliament, the UK government subsequently started the process of leaving the EU, which finished on 31 January 2020. This chapter examines the broad legal issues raised by the 'Brexit' process—most of which could also be relevant if any other Member State decides to leave the EU.

2 Withdrawing from the EU pre-Lisbon

2.1 Public international law

The founding treaties of numerous international organizations explicitly provide for a right of each Member State to withdraw from that organization.[1] In these situations, the *lex specialis* principle dictates that a State wishing to withdraw from that organization does so unilaterally in accordance with the specific procedure laid down in the withdrawal clause, which will often contain nothing more than a notification period.[2]

Much more controversial, however, is the question of whether a State may lawfully denounce an international treaty to which it is a party, or withdraw from an international

[1] Eg Constitution of the United Nations Food and Agriculture Organization (FAO), Art 19 and the North Atlantic Treaty Organization, 4 April 1949, 63 Stat 2241, 34 UNTS 243, Art 13.

[2] J Klabbers, *An Introduction to International Organizations Law* (Cambridge: Cambridge University Press, 2022) 82–83; Opinion of AG Campos Sánchez-Bordona in Case C-621/18 *Wightman* (n 10) paras 81 and 85.

organization that does not explicitly provide for such denunciation or withdrawal.[3] This was the position of the European Union (and its predecessor Communities) before Article 50 of the TEU, which governs the issue of withdrawal, was inserted in the Treaties by the Treaty of Lisbon in 2009.

For several scholars, withdrawal from international organizations remains a sovereign prerogative of States.[4] Others have even suggested that there is a unilateral right of sovereign States to withdraw from international organizations under any circumstances.[5]

In contrast, others have argued that there may be no unilateral right to withdraw from certain international organizations which purport to either be established in perpetuity (such as the United Nations[6]) or whose specific characteristics are such that permanence is deemed necessary (eg peace agreements and treaties resolving disputes over contested boundaries).[7]

The starting point for this discussion is the Vienna Convention on the Law of Treaties (VCLT).[8] The Convention provides for the general position under public international law when it comes to the termination of and withdrawal from international treaties.[9] Furthermore, as we shall see in section 3.2, it was also referred to by the Court of Justice in its *Wightman* judgment when deciding whether the UK's notification of intention to withdraw from the EU could be revoked.[10]

Article 54 VCLT provides for consensual withdrawal: a State may withdraw from a treaty in conformity with the provisions of the treaty or at any time by consent of all the parties after consultation with the other contracting States. This unanimous consent rule applies equally to withdrawals from bilateral and multilateral treaties.[11]

This is complemented by Article 56 VCLT, which sets out a general rule that a treaty which contains no provision regarding its termination and which does not provide for denunciation or withdrawal is not subject to denunciation or withdrawal. This is subject to two exceptions: (1) it is established that the parties intended to admit the possibility

[3] E Schwelb, 'Withdrawal from the United Nations: The Indonesian Intermezzo' (1967) 61 *American Journal of International Law* 661, 661; M Akehurst, 'Withdrawal from International Organisations' (1979) 32 *Current Legal Problems* 143; K Widdows, 'The Unilateral Denunciation of Treaties Containing No Denunciation Clause' (1982) 53 *British Yearbook of International Law* 83.

[4] T Christakis, 'Article 56: Denunciation of or Withdrawal from a Treaty Containing No Provision Regarding Termination, Denunciation or Withdrawal' in O Corten and V Klein (eds), *The Vienna Convention on the Law of Treaties: A Commentary* (Oxford: Oxford University Press, 2011) vol II, 1251–1276, 1275; N Singh, *Termination of Membership of International Organisations* (London: Stevens & Sons, 1958) 80–81 and 86.

[5] G Tunkin, *Theory of International Law* (Cambridge, MA: Harvard University Press, 1974) 349–350. This view has been labelled as 'straightforward' and 'not tenable'. See ND White, *The Law of International Organisations* (Manchester: Manchester University Press, 2005) 117.

[6] N Feinberg, 'Unilateral Withdrawal from an International Organization' (1963) 39 *British Yearbook of International Law* 189, 215–217.

[7] L Helfer, 'Exiting Treaties' (2005) 91 *Virginia Law Review* 1579, 1594; J Brierly, *The Law of Nations: An Introduction to the International Law of Peace* (Humphrey Waldock ed, 6th edn, Oxford: Oxford University Press, 1963) 331.

[8] Vienna Convention on the Law of Treaties (Vienna, 23 May 1969: 1155 UNTS 331).

[9] G Naldi and K Magliveras, 'The Right to Revoke Withdrawal Notices from International Organizations: The Case of Brexit and the European Union' (2021) 28 *Maastricht Journal of European and Comparative Law* 44.

[10] Case C-621/18 *Andy Wightman and Others v Secretary of State for Exiting the European Union* ('*Wightman*'), EU:C:2018:999.

[11] V Chapaux, 'Article 54: Termination of or Withdrawal from a Treaty under Its Provisions or Termination by Consent' in O Corten and V Klein (eds), *The Vienna Convention on the Law of Treaties: A Commentary* (Oxford: Oxford University Press, 2011) vol II, 1236–1245, 1239.

of denunciation or withdrawal; or (2) a right of denunciation or withdrawal may be implied by the nature of the treaty. Furthermore, Article 56(2) VCLT mandates that a State wishing to withdraw from a Treaty that does not contain a withdrawal clause shall give not less than 12 months' notice to the other members of the treaty of its intention to do so.

Therefore, from the perspective of the right of a State to withdraw from the foundational treaty of an international organization that does not contain a withdrawal clause, Articles 54 and 56 VCLT make it clear that this will only exist where: (1) all existing parties consent to such withdrawal; or (2) it is possible to read such a right of withdrawal into the treaty itself, by either interpreting the intention of the parties or because such a right is consistent with the nature of the treaty itself.[12] As such, they give effect to an explicit and implicit right to consensual withdrawal respectively.

This is to be distinguished from Article 62 VCLT which governs the right of States to unilaterally withdraw from treaties due to a fundamental change in circumstances (*rebus sic stantibus*) since the Treaty was concluded. According to Article 62(1) VCLT, this can only apply where this change 'was not foreseen by the parties', and (a) 'those circumstances constituted an essential basis of the consent of the parties to be bound by the treaty' and (b) the change 'radically . . . transform[s] the extent of obligations still to be performed under the treaty'. In contrast to Articles 54 and 56 VCLT, Article 62 VCLT governs the termination or withdrawal from a treaty regardless of the implicit or explicit consent of the other Member States, in the event of 'fundamental change in circumstances'. This rule is said to be justified on the grounds that some treaties remain in force for long periods of time, during which fundamental changes might have occurred.[13] Mention should also be made at this juncture of Article 60 VCLT, which governs the termination or suspension of the operation of both bilateral and multilateral treaties as a consequence of a 'material breach'. A material breach of a treaty for the purposes of Article 60 VCLT consists in: (a) a repudiation of the treaty not sanctioned by the VCLT; or (b) the violation of a provision essential to the accomplishment of the object or purpose of the treaty. A material breach permits other parties to the treaty to invoke that breach as a ground for terminating the treaty or suspending its operation in whole or in part. Finally, Articles 65 to 68 VCLT set down procedural rules to be followed with respect to invalidity, termination, withdrawal from, or suspension of the operation of a treaty.

When taken as a whole, the rules of public international law as laid down in the VCLT provide for the denunciation of international treaties or withdrawal from international organizations in exceptional circumstances only. As a result, withdrawal will in many cases be merely theoretical in nature rather than a viable policy option.[14] What is more, according to Article 68 VCLT, a State retains the right to revoke its notification or instrument of withdrawal from a treaty at any time prior to such withdrawal taking effect.

2.2 **The European Union**

As already noted, prior to the insertion of Article 50 into the Treaty on European Union by the Treaty of Lisbon, there was no rule in the founding EU Treaties for the withdrawal of one of its Member States. As a result, the issue of whether an EU Member State could

[12] P Athanassiou and S Shaelou, 'EU Accession from Within? An Introduction' (2014) 33 *Yearbook of European Law* 335, 335 at fn 3.

[13] See M Shaw, *International Law* (7th edn, Cambridge: Cambridge University Press, 2014) 688–690.

[14] H Hofmeister, '"Should I Stay or Should I Go?": A Critical Analysis of the Right to Withdraw from the EU' (2010) 16 *European Law Journal* 589, 591.

withdraw either in a negotiated fashion or unilaterally from the EU was contested in the literature.[15]

Prior to the Lisbon Treaty, Algeria and Greenland were two entities that belonged to EU Member States and which left the European Communities. This was given effect in both cases by Treaty amendments.[16] In practice, Algeria was incorporated into France by the French Constitution of 1848 and was thus part of Metropolitan France (at least from the perspective of French law) from the inception of both the European Coal and Steel Community and later the European Economic Community, until its independence from France in 1962. Algeria was included in the text of the EEC Treaty itself, but was only governed by that Treaty to the extent provided for under Article 227(2) EEC, which provided for the application of certain common market rules (such as the free movement of goods, services, and competition law).

After Algeria gained its independence in 1962, the legal position was ambiguous for some time. Ultimately, the EC and Algeria concluded a first bilateral agreement in 1976,[17] and the reference to Algeria in the Treaties was not formally deleted until the 1990s.[18]

As for Greenland, its withdrawal from the, then, EC provides an example of partial withdrawal of a Member State following constitutional changes to the internal division of powers within the State of Denmark.[19]

For many years, Greenland was a colony of Denmark until a constitutional amendment in 1953 made it officially part of the Danish State. This amendment gave Greenland's citizens the same rights as Danish citizens and two elected representatives in the Danish Parliament. In 1972, Greenland voted against joining what was then the European Communities, whereas Denmark voted in favour of accession with the consequence that Greenland was effectively forced to join too.[20] These events have been cited as contributing to the growing pressure for home rule for Greenland and in 1979 the Greenland Home Rule Parliament was created.[21] Following a period of increased devolution of powers from Denmark to Greenland, the people of Greenland held a referendum on EC membership in 1982 and decided to withdraw.[22]

Again, this resulted in Treaty amendment, in fact more speedily than in the case of Algeria.[23]

[15] M Dougan, *The UK's Withdrawal from the EU: A Legal Analysis* (Oxford: Oxford University Press, 2021) 21–22; A Łazowski, 'Withdrawal from the European Union and Alternatives to Membership' (2012) 37 *European Law Review* 523, 525; Athanassiou and Shaelou (n 12) 335–336; C Hillion, 'Leaving the European Union, the Union Way: A Legal Analysis of Article 50 TEU' (2016) European Policy Analysis, Swedish Institute for European Policy Studies (Sieps), 7–8; J Hill, 'The EEC: The Right of Member State Withdrawal' (1982) 12 *Georgia Journal of International and Comparative Law* 335.

[16] S Peers, 'The Future of EU Treaty Amendments' (2012) 31 *Yearbook of European Law* 17, 53.

[17] Athanassiou and Shaelou (n 12) 351.

[18] Peers, 'The Future of EU Treaty Amendments' (n 16) 58.

[19] See generally F Weiss, 'Greenland's Withdrawal from the European Communities' (1985) 10 *European Law Review* 173; A-F Tatham, '"Don't Mention Divorce at the Wedding, Darling!": EU Accession and Withdrawal after Lisbon' in A Biondi, P Eeckhout, and S Ripley (eds), *EU Law After Lisbon* (Oxford: Oxford University Press, 2012) 145–147.

[20] See generally HR Krämer 'Greenland's European Community Referendum, Background and Consequences' (1982) 25 *German Yearbook of International Law* 273.

[21] R Friel, 'Providing a Constitutional Framework for Withdrawal from the EU: Article 59 of the Draft European Constitution' (2004) 53 *International and Comparative Law Quarterly* 407, 409.

[22] 52 per cent were in favour of withdrawal and 46.1 per cent were against it: F Harhoff, 'Greenland's Withdrawal from the European Communities' (1983) 20 *Common Market Law Review* 13, 13.

[23] Treaty amending, with regard to Greenland, the Treaties establishing the European Communities ('Greenland Treaty') (OJ [1985] L29/1). See F Harhoff (n 22) 28–31.

3 Article 50 TEU: the decision to withdraw

3.1 Must Article 50 be used to withdraw?

The right of a Member State to withdraw from the EU has been settled following the insertion into the TEU by the Treaty of Lisbon of a specific provision governing withdrawal. This is Article 50 TEU, which provides as follows:

1. Any Member State may decide to withdraw from the Union in accordance with its own constitutional requirements.
2. A Member State which decides to withdraw shall notify the European Council of its intention. In the light of the guidelines provided by the European Council, the Union shall negotiate and conclude an agreement with that State, setting out the arrangements for its withdrawal, taking account of the framework for its future relationship with the Union. That agreement shall be negotiated in accordance with Article 218(3) of the Treaty on the Functioning of the European Union. It shall be concluded on behalf of the Union by the Council, acting by a qualified majority, after obtaining the consent of the European Parliament.
3. The Treaties shall cease to apply to the State in question from the date of entry into force of the withdrawal agreement or, failing that, two years after the notification referred to in paragraph 2, unless the European Council, in agreement with the Member State concerned, unanimously decides to extend this period.
4. For the purposes of paragraphs 2 and 3, the member of the European Council or of the Council representing the withdrawing Member State shall not participate in the discussions of the European Council or Council or in decisions concerning it.
5. A qualified majority shall be defined in accordance with Article 238(3)(b) of the Treaty on the Functioning of the European Union.
6. If a State which has withdrawn from the Union asks to rejoin, its request shall be subject to the procedure referred to in Article 49.

The effect of this provision has been that the process of any Member State leaving the EU is now clearly subject to the internal rules of the EU, rather than being governed by the classic norms of public international law.[24] In the run-up to the UK's referendum on EU membership, it was suggested by some that the UK, should it vote to leave the EU, could bypass the Article 50 TEU process by invoking the referendum result as a 'fundamental change in circumstances' within the scope of Article 62(1)(a) VCLT. This is to misinterpret the scope of Article 62 VCLT, which operates as a narrowly construed exception to the general rules of treaty interpretation.[25] Moreover, the decision to terminate treaty relationships will often be brought about by democratic developments such as elections or referenda. Equally, such an interpretation would empty Article 50 TEU of much of its meaning given that any decision of a Member State to withdraw from the EU is likely to stem from a democratic decision of some sort. That said, it would still be possible for the Member States to provide for the withdrawal of one or more members by amending the Treaties in order to remove references to the withdrawing State from the Preamble

[24] Article 50 TEU entails a *lex specialis* in respect of the VCLT rules, see Case C-621/18 *Wightman and Others v Secretary of State for Exiting the European Union*, Opinion of AG Campos Sánchez-Bordona, EU:C:2018:978, para 81; Hillion, 'Leaving the European Union, the Union Way' (n 15) 9.

[25] The International Court of Justice has held that 'the stability of treaty relations requires that the plea of fundamental change of circumstances be applied only in exceptional cases': *Case concerning the Gabčíkovo-Nagymaros Project (Hungary/Slovakia) (Judgment)* [1997] ICJ Rep 7, para 104.

and other relevant sections of the Treaties. It would also presumably be possible for the Member States to amend Article 50 TEU and thus the withdrawal process itself in accordance with the ordinary revision procedure enshrined in Article 48 TEU in order to provide for the possibility of an immediate withdrawal of a Member State. However, these scenarios are more complex and less plausible than simply applying Article 50 TEU.

It is important to note that the insertion of Article 50 TEU into the EU Treaties, which makes provision for the negotiation and conclusion of a withdrawal agreement between the EU and the withdrawing Member States, does not place either side under a legal obligation to conclude such an agreement.[26] While the wording of Article 50(2) TEU clearly favours 'a negotiated secession as the optimum solution', Member States nevertheless retain the right to unilaterally withdraw from the EU by notifying the European Council of their intention to do so before opting to then simply 'sit out two years before its decision becomes final'.[27] As such, Article 50 TEU represents a compromise solution: although the Member States possess a '*unilateral* right to withdraw, they do not have an *immediate* right to do so'.[28]

3.2 'Constitutional requirements'

Article 50(1) TEU provides that a Member State may withdraw in accordance with its own domestic constitutional requirements. This is immediately followed by the first sentence of Article 50(2) TEU, which provides that a Member State which decides to withdraw shall notify the European Council of its intention.

In light of these provisions, the first question to be addressed is whether EU law is applicable to a decision taken by a Member State to withdraw in accordance with its domestic constitutional requirements. In this regard, it has been noted that the distinction between the taking of a decision and the notification of that decision creates ambiguity from both a textual and a chronological perspective.[29] It is unclear whether the language of 'decision' in Article 50(1) and 'notification of intention' in Article 50(2) can be performed by a single legal action, or whether two separate legal actions are required for these purposes. Chronologically, there is no guidance in Article 50(1) and (2) TEU on whether the decision to withdraw must occur prior to any notification. Following the judgment in *Wightman*, it seems that any decision to withdraw can only be fully realized once the Article 50 TEU process has come to an end, either by the parties reaching an agreement on withdrawal, the parties not reaching an agreement and the negotiating time limit expiring, or the withdrawing Member State taking back its notification to withdraw. Until that point, any decision to leave remains only an 'intention'.[30]

On the question of the applicability of EU law to the taking of a decision under Article 50(1) TEU, the UK courts have addressed this issue in litigation pertaining to the franchise for the Brexit referendum.

Section 2 of the European Union Referendum Act 2015 set out rules governing who could vote in the EU referendum. Subject to some modifications—such as the enfranchisement of members of the House of Lords who are ordinarily prohibited from voting in elections to the House of Commons in general elections—the rules governing the franchise for the EU referendum were the same as those governing UK general elections at the

[26] Case T-458/17 *Harry Shindler and others v Council*, EU:T:2018:838, para 63.

[27] Tatham (n 21) 152.

[28] Friel (n 26) 425. See also the position of the German Constitutional Court: *Ratification of the Treaty of Lisbon*, Judgment of 30 June 2009, 2 BvE 2/08, 2 BvE 5/08, 2 BvR 1010/08, 2 BvR 1022/08, 2 BvR 1259/08, 2 BvR 182/09.

[29] Oliver Garner, 'Seven Reforms to Article 50 TEU' (2021) 46 *European Law Review* 784, 790.

[30] Case C 621/18 *Wightman* (n 10), paras 49, 57 and 59. See discussion in section 3.6. See also Garner, ibid.

time. Consequently, UK citizens, citizens of Commonwealth countries, and Irish citizens were all able to vote in the referendum, whereas the millions of EU citizens (other than citizens of Ireland, and Commonwealth States Malta and Cyprus) who had been living and working in the UK, often for decades, were precluded from doing so.[31]

Furthermore, the Act provided that UK citizens who had moved to another EU Member State and were last registered to vote in the UK more than 15 years previously could not vote in the referendum ('the 15-year rule'). The 15-year rule as it applied to UK general elections at the time had already been subject to challenge in the UK courts in *Preston*, where it was argued that the rule constituted a restriction on free movement rights.

In that case, the court held that while EU law was, in principle, applicable to rules governing the franchise for general elections, there was no restriction to the applicants' free movement rights in the case at hand.[32] It was deemed 'unrealistic to suggest that the possibility of being denied the right to vote 15 years down the line would in practice deter anyone from leaving the UK to live in another member state'.[33] Nor would the rule discourage someone who had been resident overseas for almost 15 years from staying abroad in another Member State: 'it is inherently unlikely that the loss of the right to vote would be sufficient to cause them to up sticks and return to the UK'.[34]

In *Shindler*, a similar claim was raised against the legality of the 15-year rule (this time in relation to its application in the EU referendum) by two British citizens who had been living outside the UK in another EU Member State for longer than 15 years and were thus precluded from voting. The fundamental question to be resolved by the courts was whether the concept of 'domestic constitutional requirements' enshrined in Article 50(1) TEU and applicable to a decision to withdraw from the EU were themselves subject to EU law and could thus be overturned on grounds of incompatibility with the free movement provision of the EU Treaties.

According to the English Court of Appeal, section 2 of the EU Referendum Act did not fall within the scope of EU law at all. In the view of Lord Dyson MR, the decision in *Preston* was to be distinguished from the case at hand:

> [T]he present case is not concerned with the effective operation of EU law, where it is understandable that the CJEU would wish to prevent interference by the laws of a Member State with the exercise of fundamental EU rights. Rather, it is concerned with the sovereign decision of whether or not a Member State should be bound by EU law at all. By Article 50(1) TEU, EU law has expressly provided an area where Member States may adopt their own requirements. It would be contrary to that provision if articles of another EU Treaty relating to citizenship and free movement were to intervene so as to determine the constitutional requirements to be adopted by a Member State which is deciding whether to leave the EU.[35]

According to this view:

> a decision by a Member State to withdraw from the EU is an exercise of national sovereignty of a special kind for which the TEU has made the express provision that this may be done in accordance with a Member State's own constitutional requirements. That is hardly surprising. It would have been surprising if the Member States had agreed that a Member who wishes to withdraw from the EU altogether could only do so if the decision to withdraw did not infringe

[31] European Union Referendum Act 2015, s 2(1) and (2).

[32] *R (Preston) v Wandsworth London Borough Council* [2013] QB 687.

[33] Ibid, per Munnery LJ, para 77. [34] Ibid.

[35] *Harry Shindler MBE & Jacquelyn MacLennan v Chancellor of the Duchy of Lancaster, Secretary of State for Foreign and Commonwealth Affairs* [2016] EWCA Civ 469, per Dyson MR, para 14.

> one or more fundamental EU rules. An obvious reason why a Member State might wish to withdraw is that it found such rules unacceptable and was no longer willing to be bound by them. The right of free movement is a plain example of such a rule and one which has particular resonance in the context of the proposed UK referendum. It is one thing for Member States to agree that, while they are members of the EU, they will not infringe EU law and to that extent will accept what might be described as a loss of sovereignty. It is quite a different matter for them to agree that they may only decide to withdraw from the EU if they can do so without infringing EU law. If this had been the intention of the Member States, this would surely have been expressly agreed. But they have not done so. On the contrary, they agreed Article 50(1) TEU whose plain and natural meaning does not have this effect.[36]

For these reasons, it was held that the 2015 Act regulating the franchise for the UK's referendum on EU membership did not fall within the scope of EU law, with the result that the applicants' claim failed.[37] This conclusion is identical to that of the German Constitutional Court, which ruled that '[w]hether these [constitutional] requirements have been complied with in the individual case can, however, only be verified by the Member State itself, not by the European Union or the other Member States'.[38]

3.3 **Notifying the decision**

Following the decision of the UK electorate to leave in 2016, the question arose as to who in the UK was legally empowered to notify the European Council of that decision as per Article 50(2) TEU. Notably, the European Union Referendum Act 2015 did not stipulate whether a vote to leave would constitute a 'decision' for the purposes of Article 50(1) TEU. Nor did the Act create a statutory power authorizing the government to notify the European Council of the UK's decision to withdraw in the event of a vote to leave in the referendum. Following the referendum, the UK courts were therefore required to settle the question of who, as a matter of domestic constitutional law, was empowered to notify the European Council of the decision to withdraw from the EU.[39] The core of the dispute in *Miller* was whether, as a matter of UK constitutional law, the Crown—acting through the executive government of the day—was entitled to use its prerogative powers to give notice of the UK's intention to withdraw from the EU in accordance with Article 50 TEU.

The Supreme Court of the UK ruled that a decision pursuant to Article 50 could only be notified following the enactment of an Act of Parliament, thus meaning that the executive (using the historical 'royal prerogative', which applies in particular to the conduct of foreign affairs) could not act alone to this end.[40]

This was because EU law was a special source of law which took effect via an Act of Parliament (the European Communities Act 1972), and the government may not utilize the royal prerogative in order to strip or frustrate the rights of UK citizens that they enjoy under an Act of Parliament.

[36] Ibid, para 16.

[37] Ibid, para 20. The case was further appealed to the Supreme Court, but it upheld the decision of the Court of Appeal and thus refused to rule on this issue: *R (On the application of Shindler and another v Chancellor of the Duchy of Lancaster and another* [2016] UKSC 2016/0105.

[38] German Constitutional Court, *Ratification of the Treaty of Lisbon*, Judgment of 30 June 2009, 2 BvE 2/08, 2 BvE 5/08, 2 BvR 1010/08, 2 BvR 1022/08, 2 BvR 1259/08, 2 BvR 182/09, para 330.

[39] *R (On the application of Miller and another) v Secretary of State for Exiting the European Union* [2017] UKSC 5.

[40] Ibid; see P Craig, 'Brexit: A Drama in Six Acts' (2016) 41 *European Law Review* 447, 461–463 and S Douglas-Scott, 'Brexit, Article 50 and the Contested British Constitution' (2016) 79 *Modern Law Review* 1019, 1027–1028.

Following the judgment, the UK Parliament passed the European Union (Notification of Withdrawal) Act 2017 which provided: 'The Prime Minister may notify, under Article 50(2) of the Treaty on European Union, the UKs intention to withdraw from the EU.'[41] The notification was subsequently delivered to the European Council on 29 March 2017. Notably, the UK Parliament opted not to attach any conditions or negotiating objectives for the government when passing the Act, thereby leaving the UK government a free hand to embark on the process of negotiating Brexit.

The Supreme Court ruling in *Miller and others* also ruled on the roles of the UK's devolved administrations, in Scotland, Northern Ireland, and Wales. Whereas a slim majority of the UK as a whole voted to leave the EU, the people of Northern Ireland (55 per cent) and Scotland (62 per cent) voted overwhelmingly to remain. As a result, questions have arisen as to the political legitimacy and constitutional legality of pulling nations of the UK out of the EU against their will. This issue is particularly salient in Scotland, where the promise of continued EU membership was a central plank of the campaign to keep Scotland in the UK during the 2014 Scottish Independence referendum.[42] However, according to the Supreme Court, there was no legally enforceable right for the devolved administrations to have a role in the Brexit process. Rather, there was an unenforceable political convention that they should be consulted.

3.4 **Had a decision been taken?**

Despite resolving the issue of who could send the notification of the UK's intention to withdraw from the EU in accordance with Article 50(2) TEU, the question of whether the UK had ever taken a decision for the purposes of Article 50(1) TEU remained disputed.[43]

As noted earlier, there was nothing in the provisions of the European Union Referendum Act 2015 which indicated that the result of the referendum would be legally binding and would therefore constitute a decision to withdraw for the purposes of Article 50(1) TEU. It was also clear that the outcome of the referendum did not, in itself, legally speaking constitute a decision to withdraw from the EU.[44] Moreover, the aforementioned judgment in *Shindler* had determined that the referendum was 'part of' the UK's domestic constitutional requirements for the purposes of Article 50(1) TEU, since Parliament had mandated that a referendum be held on the question of whether the UK should leave the EU.[45]

What remained unclear following the judgments in *Miller* and *Shindler*, however, was who took a decision for the purposes of Article 50(1) TEU and when was that decision taken. This question was addressed in *Webster*, where the High Court rejected the claimant's argument that in the absence of a 'decision to withdraw' from the EU, the UK's constitutional requirements had not been satisfied as required by Article 50(1) TEU. According to Lord Justice Gross, that argument was 'totally without merit', since the European Union (Notification of Withdrawal) Act 2017 not only authorized the Prime Minister to notify the UK's intention to withdraw in accordance with Article 50(2) TEU, but also 'plainly contemplated and encompassed the power to take a decision to withdraw

[41] European Union (Notification of Withdrawal) Act 2017, s 1(1).

[42] S Douglas-Scott, 'Brexit and the Scottish Question' in F Fabbrini (ed), *The Law and Politics of Brexit* (Oxford: Oxford University Press, 2017) ch 6.

[43] Dougan (n 15) 75–83; P Eeckhout and E Frantziou, 'Brexit and Article 50 TEU: A Constitutionalist Reading' (2017) 54 *Common Market Law Review* 695, 709.

[44] *R (Miller)* (n 39) paras 116–125; see also the Court of Appeal ruling in *Shindler and others* (n 37), per Elias LJ, para 19.

[45] *Shindler and others* (n 37) paras 13 and 19.

and conferred that power expressly on the Prime Minister' for the purposes of Article 50(1) TEU.[46]

We can therefore conclude that the vote to leave in the Brexit referendum, coupled with the European Union (Notification of Withdrawal) Act 2017 (which was itself necessitated by the UK Supreme Court judgment in *Miller*) and the Prime Minister's decision formed the UK's 'domestic constitutional requirements' for the purposes of Article 50 TEU.

3.5 **The timing of notification**

While Article 50 TEU obliges a Member State which has decided to leave the EU to notify that decision to the European Council, it provides no guidance as to the form (or indeed timing) that this notification must take. It has been said that since notification is the formal step that triggers the Article 50 negotiation process, such notification should be unequivocal: 'there should be a clear message from the state concerned that it intends to leave the Union, following an internal decision to that effect. Therefore, until such a message has been conveyed to the EU, and so long as the Member State continues to fulfil all its membership obligations, the withdrawal process cannot be deemed triggered.'[47] This was the position taken by the heads of State and government of the remaining 27 EU Member States who, following the referendum, stated that while '[i]t is up to the British government to notify the European Council of the UK's intention to withdraw from the Union, [t]his should be done as quickly as possible [and] [t]here can be no negotiations of any kind before this notification has taken place'.[48]

With regards to timing, in Craig's view, while there is no explicit time limit for notification, 'it is highly likely that the Court of Justice of the European Union (CJEU) would regard it as subject to some implied limit, since otherwise it would be open to a Member State post a Brexit-type referendum to equivocate for years before deciding whether to withdraw, which could have serious negative consequences for the EU'.[49] It might be wondered, given the CJEU's emphasis upon the sovereign nature of the right of withdrawal in *Wightman*, however, whether both the taking and subsequent notification of a decision to withdraw are unilateral sovereign rights to be exercised solely by the Member State concerned and which cannot, therefore, be constrained by conditions such as time limits.

Additionally, the Member States are under a duty to respect the values of the Union as enshrined in Article 2 TEU as well as to abide by the principle of sincere cooperation in Article 4(3) TEU. This arguably implies that the discretion of a Member State vis-à-vis the timing for providing an Article 50 TEU notification should not be limitless.

3.6 **Can notification be withdrawn?**

In *Miller*, both the applicants and the government agreed that the provision of notification of the UK's decision to withdraw from the EU under Article 50(2) was irrevocable. As such, once that notification had been rendered, it would put in motion a series of steps mandated in Article 50 TEU vis the negotiation and conclusion of a withdrawal agreement between the UK and the EU which could not be stopped and would ultimately lead to the removal of certain rights of EU citizens.[50] However, the Supreme Court expressly took no position on the question of whether an Article 50 TEU notification could be revoked. While the text of Article 50 TEU is silent on this point, the constitutive instruments of a

[46] *Elizabeth Webster v Secretary of State for Exiting the European Union* [2018] EWHC 1543 (Admin), per Lord Gross, paras 10 and 13.

[47] Hillion, 'Leaving the European Union, the Union Way' (n 15) 3.

[48] Statement, Informal meeting, Brussels, 29 June 2016.

[49] Craig, 'Brexit: A Drama in Six Acts' (n 40) 464 at fn 27.

[50] *R (Miller)* (n 39) para 169.

number of other international organizations (reflecting Article 68 VCLT) explicitly provide for the possibility of a notice of withdrawal to be retracted or cancelled.[51]

The issue of revocation ultimately made its way to the CJEU by way of a reference for a preliminary ruling from the Court of Session in Scotland in the case of *Wightman*.[52] The litigation in the Scottish courts was commenced by a group of petitioners consisting of Members of the UK Parliament (MPs), Members of the Scottish Parliament (MSPs), and other interested parties.

Proceedings were brought at a time when UK MPs were poised to vote on whether to accept the proposed Withdrawal Agreement that had been negotiated between Prime Minister Theresa May's government and the European Union. According to the UK government, MPs faced a simple choice: they could either vote to approve the Withdrawal Agreement and leave the EU with a deal, or vote to reject the Agreement and leave with no deal. Faced with this choice, the petitioners in *Wightman* sought a ruling on whether the UK's Article 50(2) TEU notification could be revoked as a matter of EU law. If it could, MPs would be able to cast their votes on the Withdrawal Agreement in the knowledge that there was a third option on the table.

The Court held that a Member State's notification of its intention to withdraw from the European Union could indeed be revoked as a matter of EU law. Noting that Article 50 TEU neither expressly prohibits nor expressly authorizes revocation, the Court interpreted Article 50 TEU in light of the fundamental characteristics of the EU legal order as a whole.[53] Focusing on the wording of Article 50(2) TEU, the CJEU emphasized that that provision stipulates that a Member State which decides to withdraw from the Union must notify the European Council of its 'intention' to do so. An intention, held the Court, is, by its very nature, neither definitive nor irrevocable.[54]

Furthermore, Article 50(1) TEU provides that any Member State may decide to withdraw from the EU in accordance with its own constitutional requirements and this decision does not need to be taken in concert with any other EU Member State or EU institution. Such a decision is for the Member State alone and 'depends solely on its sovereign choice'.[55] This 'sovereign nature of the right of withdrawal' supported the conclusion that a withdrawing Member State has a right to revoke its notification of its intention to withdraw from the EU.[56]

Decisive in this regard was the fact that Articles 50(2) and 50(3) TEU set down a detailed procedure to be followed for the negotiation and conclusion of a withdrawal agreement between the withdrawing Member State and the EU.[57] Article 50(3) TEU determines that the EU Treaties shall cease to apply to a withdrawing Member State from the date of entry into force of a withdrawal agreement or, failing that, two years after the date of notification from the withdrawing Member State of its intention to withdraw. This two-year period can be extended with the unanimous agreement of the withdrawing Member State and the European Council.

Article 50 TEU therefore pursues the twin objectives of enshrining the sovereign right of Member States to withdraw from the EU and establishing a procedure for ensuring that such a withdrawal occurs in an orderly fashion.[58] Provided that a withdrawal agreement has not entered into force or the two-year time limit (possibly extended) has not expired, the revocation by a Member State of its intention to withdraw 'reflects a sovereign

[51] Examples include Art 31(1) of the Constitutive Act of the African Union, 11 July 2000, 2158 UNTS 3 and Art 104(1) of the Treaty Establishing an African Economic Community, 3 June 1991, 30 ILM 1241 (1991). For discussion, see Naldi and Magliveras (n 9) 38–40.

[52] *Andy Wightman and Others v Secretary of State of Exiting the European Union* [2018] CSIH 62.

[53] *Wightman* (n 10) paras 44–47. [54] Ibid, para 49. [55] Ibid, para 50. [56] Ibid, para 57.

[57] See section 4. [58] *Wightman* (n 10) para 56.

decision by that State to retain its status as a Member State of the European Union, a status which is not suspended or altered by that notification'.[59]

The Court supported its finding of a unilateral right to revoke an Article 50(2) TEU notification with reference to the context of Article 50 TEU and the wider EU legal order of which it is a part. The EU Treaties made clear that the EU's objectives were, inter alia, that of creating an ever-closer Union among the peoples of Europe and eliminating barriers which divide Europe. The very foundations of the EU legal order were said to be formed, in part, by the values of liberty and democracy as found in Article 2 TEU and the Preamble to the Charter of Fundamental Rights.[60] Moreover, Article 49 TEU (the counterpart provision to Article 50 TEU which governs accession) indicates that all EU Member States have freely and voluntarily committed themselves to these foundational values of the EU, and that EU law operates on the basis of a fundamental premise that all Member States share those values.[61] It was also necessary to consider the impact that any withdrawal of a Member State would have upon the rights of EU citizens, including their right to free movement.[62] These factors led the Court to conclude that since a Member State cannot be forced to accede to the EU against its will, it cannot be forced to withdraw against its will: an outcome which would materialize should a Member State be precluded from revoking its Article 50(2) TEU notification prior to the expiry of the two-year negotiation period or the entry into force of a withdrawal agreement. Such an outcome would be inconsistent with the aforementioned aims and values of the European Union.[63]

The drafting history of Article 50 TEU and the Vienna Convention on the Law of Treaties further supported the conclusion that withdrawal was unilateral and voluntary. During the negotiations over the Draft Constitution for Europe, amendments to what became Article 50 TEU which sought to expel Member States for abuse of the withdrawal process and to make the withdrawal decision more difficult were rejected by the Member States. Furthermore, Articles 65, 67, and 68 VCLT make it clear that any notification of withdrawal from a treaty which explicitly authorizes withdrawal in its provisions may be revoked at any time before such withdrawal takes effect.[64]

Having addressed the question of revocation in principle, the CJEU moved to address the concerns of the Commission and the Council that a withdrawing Member State could abuse the Article 50 TEU process by revoking its notification shortly before the end of the two-year period provided for in Article 50(3) TEU. If permitted, that Member State could then notify a new intention to withdraw immediately after that period had expired, thereby commencing a new two-year negotiation period. Such a possibility would create a de facto right for any withdrawing Member State to negotiate its withdrawal without being subject to any time limit, thus rendering Article 50(3) TEU ineffective. It could also be used by a withdrawing Member State as a tactic to pressure the EU institutions into offering up more favourable terms in the negotiations.[65]

The Court rejected the argument of the Commission and Council that any revocation should be subject to the unanimous agreement of the remaining EU Member States. Such a requirement 'would transform a unilateral sovereign right into a conditional right subject to an approval procedure'.[66] However, the right of a Member State to revoke its notification of intention to withdraw from the EU was not entirely without limits. First, any revocation must be submitted in writing to the European Council. Secondly, it must be 'unequivocal and unconditional', understood as meaning that 'the purpose of that revocation is to confirm the EU membership of the Member State concerned under terms that are unchanged as regards its status as a Member State, and that revocation brings the withdrawal procedure to an end'.[67]

[59] Ibid, para 59. [60] Ibid, paras 61–62. [61] Ibid, paras 62–63. [62] Ibid, para 64.
[63] Ibid, paras 65–67. [64] Ibid, paras 68–71. [65] Ibid, paras 39–41. [66] Ibid, para 72.
[67] Ibid, para 74.

A number of questions arise from this conclusion. How should the EU institutions go about policing compliance with these conditions? What would the consequences be if such an attempt to withdraw a notification was rejected, and could this rejection be challenged in the courts? Is revocation subject to any other explicit or implicit limits in EU law? How does the possibility of rejecting a conditional attempt by a Member State to revoke its notification of withdrawal fit with the idea that the latter is exercising a unilateral, sovereign right?[68]

Despite these ambiguities, it is now beyond dispute that as a matter of EU law a Member State that has notified the European Council of its intention to withdraw from the EU may revoke that notification, subject to the time limits and conditions discussed above.

4 Article 50: withdrawal negotiations

4.1 The Article 50 process

Article 50(2) TEU refers to Article 218(3) TFEU, which stipulates that:

> The Commission, or the High Representative of the Union for Foreign Affairs and Security Policy where the agreement envisaged relates exclusively or principally to the common foreign and security policy, shall submit recommendations to the Council, which shall adopt a decision authorising the opening of negotiations and, depending on the subject of the agreement envisaged, nominating the Union negotiator or the head of the Union's negotiating team.

Furthermore, Article 50(3) provides that the withdrawing Member State leaves two years after notification, unless the withdrawal agreement sets an earlier date, or the departing State and the remaining EU Member States agree unanimously to extend this period.

So, following notification, the focus immediately shifted to the role of the EU institutions within the process of negotiating and concluding such a withdrawal agreement. This was because, while the decision to withdraw is taken in accordance with the Member States' domestic constitutional requirements, EU law governs the departure itself.[69]

What is the role of those EU institutions? First, the European Council had to agree upon the guidelines for the negotiations.[70] According to Article 15(3) TEU, 'The European Council shall meet twice every six months, convened by its President . . . When the situation so requires, the President shall convene a special meeting of the European Council.' In fact, the European Council convened special meetings several times as regards the Brexit talks.

The EU's negotiating framework was agreed in December 2016, by the remaining Member States.[71] This framework provided for the European Council to adopt the negotiation guidelines, and then following a recommendation from the European Commission

[68] For discussion, see A Cuyvers, '*Wightman*, Brexit, and the Sovereign Right to Remain' (2019) 56 *Common Market Law Review* 1303.

[69] Łazowski (n 15) 527.

[70] For more on the role of the European Council, see section 4.1.1.

[71] Informal meeting of the heads of State or government of 27 Member States, as well as the Presidents of the European Council and the European Commission, Brussels, 15 December 2016, para 2. See also Sir D Edward and D Wyatt, 'The Process of Withdrawing from the European Union', Written Evidence to House of Lords European Union Committee (HL 138, 2015–16). See similarly J-C Piris, 'Should the UK Withdraw from the EU: Legal Aspects and Effects of Possible Options' (4 May 2015) Fondation Robert Schuman Policy Paper, European issues No 355, p 5, available at: https://www.robert-schuman.eu/en/european-issues/355-should-the-uk-withdraw-from-the-eu-legal-aspects-and-effects-of-possible-options.

as required by Article 218(3) TFEU, the Council, sitting in the General Affairs Council configuration, adopted the decision authorizing the opening of the negotiations.[72]

In line with Article 218(3) TFEU, the Council was invited to nominate the European Commission as the Union negotiator, with the Commission negotiators in regular contact with the Council and European Council.

4.1.1 The European Council

The first point to note about the Article 50 TEU process is that there is no need for unanimous Member State consent before any withdrawal agreement may take effect. As Article 50(2) TEU makes clear, any agreement will be concluded following a qualified majority vote in the Council and after obtaining the consent of the European Parliament.[73]

Consequently, the Member States hold no formal veto over the process of negotiation and conclusion of a withdrawal agreement. Instead, the only instance in which the governments of the remaining Member States wield a de facto veto over aspects of the Article 50 process is 'upstream': when sitting in the European Council and setting the guidelines for the negotiations in accordance with Article 50(2) TEU. Such a veto is provided for in Article 15(4) TEU, which states that except where the Treaties provide otherwise, decisions of the European Council shall be taken by consensus.[74] As the Treaties are silent as to which decision-making procedure to use when adopting guidelines to negotiate a withdrawal agreement, the default consensus rule applied.

Note that, as Article 50(4) TEU makes clear, the UK's representatives were explicitly prohibited from taking part in the European Council deliberations on the negotiating guidelines.

4.1.2 The Council of Ministers

The Council was actively involved throughout the Article 50 TEU negotiation process, and it was the Council that concluded the withdrawal agreement on behalf of the EU following a qualified majority vote after obtaining the consent of the European Parliament. As per Article 50(4), the withdrawing State (the UK) was excluded from voting on the withdrawal agreement on the EU side. In terms of the applicable voting rules, a qualified majority for these purposes is defined in Article 238(3)(b) TFEU, which recalculates votes when some Member States do not participate in decision-making.

Two points are worthy of note here. First, as is clear from the wording of Article 50(2) TEU, the Council may not move to conclude a withdrawal agreement without having first obtained the consent of the European Parliament.[75] Secondly, the Qualified Majority Voting rule as set down in Article 238(3)(b) TFEU provides that the Council may only approve a withdrawal agreement following a vote in favour by 72 per cent of the members of the Council representing the participating Member States, comprising at least 65 per cent of the population of these States. This is to be contrasted with the classic QMV voting rule in Article 238(3)(a), which stipulates that a qualified majority is to be defined as at least 55 per cent of the members of the Council representing the participating Member States, comprising at least 65 per cent of the population of these States. Thus, while the Member States sitting in the Council do not possess a veto for the purposes of Article 50 TEU, the threshold required for it to vote in favour of any withdrawal agreement is higher than the usual rule.

[72] Informal meeting of the heads of State or government of 27 Member States, as well as the Presidents of the European Council and the European Commission, Brussels, 15 December 2016, para 2.

[73] The following points are based on arguments made in D Harvey, '"In the Light of the Guidelines": Brexit and the European Council', *European Law Blog*, 7 October 2016, no longer available online.

[74] See further P de Schoutheete, 'The European Council' in J Peterson and M Shackleton (eds), *The Institutions of the European Union* (Oxford: Oxford University Press, 2012) 50.

[75] On the role of the European Parliament in the Art 50 process, see section 4.1.3.

4.1.3 **The European Parliament**

According to a literal reading of Article 50(2) TEU, the European Parliament is to play no role in the negotiation of a withdrawal agreement, being required only to provide its consent to a deal that has already been negotiated.[76] Indeed, within the context of the requirement that the Parliament provide consent to international agreements concluded by the EU under Article 218 TFEU, it has been noted that 'the European Parliament's consent is only requisite once the agreement has already been signed, which precludes MEPs from influencing the contents of the initial version of the agreement before signature as well as from amending individual provisions thereof after signature. The agreement can only be accepted or rejected *in toto*.'[77]

Such approval could not simply be assumed, however, given the Parliament's willingness to refuse consent to treaties in the past—for example, the EU–US Agreement on the processing and transfer of Financial Messaging Data from the EU to the US for the purposes of the Terrorist Finance Tracking Program.[78] Exercising the power accorded to it by the Lisbon Treaty to provide or withhold consent from international agreements based on Article 218 TFEU, the European Parliament decided not to give consent to the agreement amid concerns related to privacy, proportionality, and reciprocity.[79] Following this veto, the original treaty was then amended, and the European Parliament then gave its consent, having been satisfied that its concerns had been satisfactorily addressed.[80]

Notwithstanding its formal role of providing or withholding consent at the end of negotiations, the European Parliament has often tried to exert informal influence over the content of treaties that the EU was negotiating, assuming that the negotiators would take account of its views in light of its power to veto the final text.[81]

The Brexit talks were no exception here.[82] Indeed, the European Parliament adopted resolutions throughout the Brexit negotiations which emphasized, inter alia, that the 'full involvement' of the Parliament was a necessary precondition for the granting of consent to any withdrawal agreement;[83] that it would not consent to any withdrawal agreement

[76] On the role of the European Parliament during the Art 50 process, see generally D Harvey, 'What Role for the European Parliament under Article 50 TEU?' (2017) 42 *European Law Review* 585.

[77] D Jancic, 'The European Parliament and EU–US Relations: Revamping Institutional Cooperation?' in E Fahey and D Curtin (eds), *A Transatlantic Community of Law: Legal Perspectives on the Relationship between the EU and US Legal Orders* (Cambridge: Cambridge University Press, 2014) 37.

[78] European Parliament legislative resolution of 11 February 2010 on the proposal for a Council decision on the conclusion of the Agreement between the European Union and the United States of America on the processing and transfer of Financial Messaging Data from the European Union to the United States for purposes of the Terrorist Finance Tracking Program (05305/1/2010 REV 1—C7-0004/2010—2009/0190(NLE)).

[79] E Fahey, 'Law and Governance as Checks and Balances in Transatlantic Security: Rights, Redress, and Remedies in EU–US Passenger Name Records and the Terrorist Finance Tracking Program' (2013) 32 *Yearbook of European Law* 368, 379; J Monar, 'Guest Editorial: Rejection of the EU–US SWIFT Interim Agreement by the European Parliament: A Historic Vote and Its Implications' (2010) 15 *European Foreign Affairs Review* 143.

[80] For an overview, see D Jančić, 'Transatlantic Regulatory Interdependence, Law and Governance: The Evolving Roles of the EU and US Legislatures' (2015) 17 *Cambridge Yearbook of European Legal Studies* 334, 339.

[81] See generally chapter 26. The European Parliament has a right under Art 218(10) TFEU to be 'immediately and fully informed at all stages of the procedure'.

[82] MB Meislova, 'The European Parliament in the Brexit Process: Leading Role, Supporting Role or Just a Small Cameo?' in T Christiansen and D Fromage (eds), *Brexit and Democracy: The Role of Parliaments in the UK and the European Union* (Cham: Palgrave Macmillan, 2019) 235.

[83] European Parliament resolution of 5 April 2017 on negotiations with the United Kingdom following its notification that it intends to withdraw from the European Union (2017/2593(RSP)), available at: www.europarl.europa.eu/brexit-steering-group/en/documents/ep-resolutions.

that did not contain a workable solution for Ireland and Northern Ireland;[84] and that its decision to consent to the withdrawal agreement would take into account experience gained and assurances given by the UK in relation to the EU settlement scheme for EU citizens and their families.[85] Ultimately, the European Parliament consented to the withdrawal agreement in January 2020.

Throughout the Brexit process, the relationship between the European Commission as negotiator and the European Parliament was significant and it is presumed that this relationship would be equally important in the event that any other Member State notifies its intention to withdraw from the Union. In light of the framework agreement on relations between the European Parliament and the European Commission, 'Parliament shall be immediately and fully informed at all stages of the negotiation and conclusion of international agreements, including the definition of negotiating directives.'[86] Furthermore, 'the Commission shall take due account of Parliament's comments throughout the negotiations' and 'the Commission shall keep Parliament regularly and promptly informed about the conduct of negotiations until the agreement is initialled, and explain whether and how Parliament's comments were incorporated in the texts under negotiations and if not why'.[87]

A final point to consider here is whether the UK–EU Withdrawal Agreement concluded under Article 50 TEU could have been referred to the CJEU for an opinion on its legality prior to its conclusion. According to Article 218(11) TFEU: 'A Member State, the European Parliament, the Council, or the Commission may obtain the opinion of the Court of Justice as to whether an agreement envisaged is compatible with the Treaties. Where the opinion of the Court is adverse, the agreement envisaged may not enter into force unless it is amended or the Treaties are revised.' An example of this procedure is the CJEU opinion on the legality of the proposed Free Trade Agreement between the EU and Singapore, which was referred for an opinion by the European Commission in accordance with Article 218(11) TFEU.[88]

While the cross-reference in Article 50(2) TEU to Article 218(3) TFEU suggests a degree of overlap between the two types of agreements, it is unclear whether any withdrawal agreement concluded under Article 50 TEU would fall within the scope of Article 218(11) TFEU as the negotiations are being conducted with a Member State, and there is no cross-reference in Article 50 TEU.[89] Ultimately, no reference on the legality of the UK–EU Withdrawal Agreement was made to the CJEU. However, if such a reference to the Court had been made (or, indeed, is made in any future withdrawal scenario), one must not discount the prospect of one of the EU institutions withholding consent from an Article 50 withdrawal agreement prior to it receiving a clean bill of health from the CJEU.

The two-year time limit enshrined in Article 50(2) TEU, and the time limits on extending the transition period in the withdrawal agreement (see section 4.3), raise the question of whether once an EU institution requests an opinion from the CJEU that time limit is suspended. In other words, does a reference to the CJEU stop a clock from ticking? If not,

84 European Parliament resolution of 18 September 2019 on the state of play of the UK's withdrawal from the European Union (2019/2817(RSP)), available at: www.europarl.europa.eu/brexit-steering-group/en/documents/ep-resolutions.

85 European Parliament resolution of 15 January 2020 on implementing and monitoring the provisions on citizens' rights in the Withdrawal Agreement, available at: www.europarl.europa.eu/brexit-steering-group/en/documents/ep-resolutions.

86 Framework Agreement on relations between the European Parliament and the European Commission (OJ [2010] L304/47), point 23.

87 Ibid, Annex III, points 3 and 4.

88 Opinion 2/15, EU:C:2017:376. On this process, see further CHAPTER 26.

89 Piris (n 71) 5–6.

it is perfectly within the realms of possibility that the deadline for reaching an agreement may expire while a case is pending before the CJEU, unless some form of extension is agreed.

4.1.4 UK legal and institutional position before and immediately after Brexit

As is clear from Article 50(4) TEU, representatives of the withdrawing Member State may not take part in Council or European Council negotiations or decision-making concerning the withdrawal agreement. However, within the Brexit context, the CJEU ruled that the UK remained otherwise bound by EU law during the period up until its departure from the EU,[90] including during any extension period.[91] To that end, the decisions on extension of UK membership (see section 4.2) provided that the UK had to take part in elections to the European Parliament in May 2019 (which it did), and referred to the UK nominating a Commissioner in late 2019 (which it did not; see further chapter 3). Equally, this meant that, since the drafters of Article 50 excluded the withdrawing State from the Council and European Council but made no corresponding rule for the European Parliament, UK MEPs continued to participate in the workings of the European Parliament and, as a consequence, voted on the Withdrawal Agreement.

Upon the entry into force of the Withdrawal Agreement on 1 February 2020, the EU Treaties ceased to apply to the UK as per Article 50(3) TEU. As the Preamble to the Withdrawal Agreement notes, the consequence of this is that the mandates of the members of institutions, bodies, offices, and agencies of the Union who were nominated, appointed, or elected in relation to the UK's membership of the European Union would also end on the date of withdrawal.[92]

While the coming to an end of the mandate of most UK officials was legally uncontroversial, litigation arose in relation to the position of Advocate General Sharpston, who had most recently had her mandate to serve on the Court renewed by the governments of the Member States from 7 October 2015 to 6 October 2021.[93] In essence, the dispute concerned the question of whether, as a matter of EU law, the mandate of an Advocate General does indeed end upon the withdrawal from the Union of the Member State that nominated them. Uncertainty arises here because Article 19(2) TEU provides that the CJEU 'shall consist of one judge from each Member State. It shall be assisted by Advocates-General. The General Court shall include at least one judge per Member State.' On the one hand, it was argued that whereas there is a clear link established between judges at the Court and the Member States, the same cannot be said for Advocates General (AGs). Not only is there no specific fixed number of AGs, because the Council has the option to appoint more than eight of them (see Article 252 TFEU), there also does not appear to be any link in Article 19(2) TEU between AGs and a nominating Member State. It was therefore argued on the basis of this textual distinction that once an AG had been appointed, the continued membership of the EU Member State that nominated that AG was not a prerequisite for said AG to be able to serve until the end of their mandate.[94] On the other hand, the counterargument is that Declaration 38 to the Treaty of Lisbon referred to a link between AGs and Member States, reflecting the

[90] Case C-327/18 PPU *RO*, EU:C:2018:733 and Case C-661/17 *MA*, EU:C:2019:53.

[91] *Wightman* (n 10).

[92] Eighth para of the Preamble to the UK–EU Withdrawal Agreement.

[93] Decision (EU, Euratom) 2015/578 of the Representatives of the Governments of the Member States of 1 April 2015 appointing Judges and Advocates General to the Court of Justice (OJ [2015] L96/11).

[94] DV Kochenov and G Butler, 'Independence of the Court of Justice of the European Union: Unchecked Member States Power after the Sharpston Affair' (2022) 27 *European Law Journal* 1–5.

long-standing practice of appointing one AG nominated by each of the larger Member States and rotating the other AG posts between smaller Member States. On 29 January 2020 (two days before the UK's withdrawal), the Conference of the Representatives of the Governments of the Member States took a view on this, adopting a Declaration on the consequences of the UK's withdrawal from the EU for the AGs of the CJEU.[95] The Declaration noted that the Treaties would cease to apply to the UK following withdrawal and the mandates of members of EU institutions, bodies, offices, and agencies nominated, appointed, or elected in relation to the UK would similarly come to an end upon withdrawal. It then continued that, as a consequence, the permanent post of AG that was assigned to the UK during its period of EU membership would, post-Brexit, be integrated into the rotation system among the Member States for the appointment of AGs. In accordance with the established protocol order, the next eligible Member State to nominate an AG would be Greece.[96] This Declaration was followed in September 2020 by a decision of the representatives of the governments of the Member States that, inter alia, appointed Mr Athanasios Rantos, a Greek national, to the CJEU as AG from 7 September 2020 to 6 October 2021.

In dismissing AG Sharpston's challenges to the validity of both the Declaration and the Decision of the Conference of the Representatives of the Governments of the Member States, the CJEU ruled that both of the acts in question were not amenable to judicial review under Article 263 TFEU.[97] This was because neither the Declaration nor the Decision were adopted by an institution, office, body, or agency of the EU.[98] By adopting these acts, the representatives of the governments of the Member States were collectively exercising the power of the Member States and were not acting in their capacity as members of the Council.[99] Furthermore, the Court found that both acts did not produce any legal effects vis-à-vis the early termination of AG Sharpston's mandate, since the Conference of the Representatives of the Member States 'merely took note of the consequences necessarily entailed by the departure of the United Kingdom from the European Union'.[100] This was because the Treaties ceased to be applicable to the UK on 1 February 2020 and, as the eighth paragraph of the Preamble to the Withdrawal Agreement states, the ongoing mandates of the members of the institutions, bodies, offices, and agencies of the EU nominated, appointed, or elected in view of the UK's membership of the EU 'automatically came to an end on that date'.[101] Although the reasoning here was terse and somewhat opaque, the CJEU seems to have confirmed that the mandate of an AG to serve at the CJEU is necessarily dependent upon the continued EU membership of the nominating State.

[95] Declaration by the Conference of the Representatives of the Governments of the Member States on the consequences of the withdrawal of the United Kingdom from the European Union for the Advocates-General of the Court of Justice of the European Union, XT 21018/20, available at: https://data.consilium.europa.eu/doc/document/XT-21018-2020-INIT/en/pdf.

[96] Ibid. The UK was given the permanent right to nominate an Advocate General to the Court by Declaration 38 to the Treaty of Lisbon.

[97] Case C-684/20 P *Eleanor Sharpston v Council of the European Union and Conference of the Representatives of the Governments of the Member States*, EU:C:2021:486; Case C-685/20 P *Eleanor Sharpston v Council of the European Union and Conference of the Representatives of the Governments of the Member States*, EU:C:2021:485.

[98] As required by Art 263(1) TFEU.

[99] Case C-684/20 P *Sharpston v Council* (n 97) paras 38–47; Case C-685/20 P *Sharpston v Council* (n 97) paras 45–51.

[100] Case C-684/20 P *Sharpston v Council* (n 97) para 48; Case C-685/20 P *Sharpston v Council* (n 97) para 54.

[101] Case C-684/20 P *Sharpston v Council* (n 97) para 49; Case C-685/20 P *Sharpston v Council* (n 97) para 53.

[102] [2019] OJ L66 I/1.

4.2 **Extending membership**

A first Withdrawal Agreement was agreed between the UK and EU in November 2018.[102] However, the UK Parliament refused to ratify this Agreement on three occasions. In order to avoid leaving the EU without a deal, there were a series of extensions of EU membership on the basis of Article 50(3), which permits an extension of membership via a unanimous vote of the European Council, with the agreement of the withdrawing Member State.

In accordance with Article 50(3), the UK had been due to leave the EU on 29 March 2019, two years after notifying its intention to withdraw. The first extension decision provided for the UK's EU membership to continue to 22 May 2019, to give the UK further time to approve the first Withdrawal Agreement. If it did not approve the Withdrawal Agreement, membership would only be extended to 12 April 2019.[103]

Since the UK did not approve the first Withdrawal Agreement at that time, a second extension decision was adopted, this time extending membership for a longer period—to 31 October 2019.[104] The UK could leave earlier if it either approved the Withdrawal Agreement or failed in its obligation to hold elections to the European Parliament in May 2019. Neither of those things happened, and in September 2019, a majority in the UK Parliament, objecting to the apparent prospect of a 'no deal' outcome, passed an Act which required the UK government to request a third extension, for a further three months, if the UK Parliament did not approve a withdrawal agreement by 19 October 2019.[105] In fact, a second version of the Withdrawal Agreement was negotiated just before that date,[106] but the UK Parliament delayed approving it and so the UK government requested a three-month extension, which the European Council then adopted.[107] Following the results of the UK election in December 2019, which delivered a Conservative majority government which had campaigned on the basis of leaving the EU with the Withdrawal Agreement, the UK Parliament approved an Act giving effect to the Withdrawal Agreement (the Withdrawal Agreement Act) in January 2020, and the Agreement was then signed and ratified by both parties, resulting in the UK leaving the EU on 31 January 2020. The Withdrawal Agreement included a transition period during which the UK was largely still subject to EU law until the end of 2020, but from that point on the main legal basis for the EU/UK relationship is the Trade and Cooperation Agreement (see section 5)—although the Withdrawal Agreement still continues to apply, and it should not be forgotten that these are two separate treaties.

4.3 **The Withdrawal Agreement**

The second version of the Withdrawal Agreement, which came into force on the date that the UK left the EU, is the same as the first version, except for changes to the protocol on Northern Ireland, discussed below.[108] This section summarizes the main legal points in the agreement.[109]

[103] [2019] OJ L80 I/1. [104] [2019] OJ L101/1.

[105] European Union (Withdrawal) (No 2) Act 2019. [106] [2019] OJ C384 I/1.

[107] [2019] OJ L278 I/1, [108] For the text, see OJ [2019] C384I/1.

[109] This section is adapted from S Peers, 'Analysis 1 of the revised Brexit withdrawal agreement: overview', *EU Law Analysis blog*, 18 October 2019: http://eulawanalysis.blogspot.com/2019/10/analysis-1-of-revised-brexit-withdrawal.html.

4.3.1 **Common provisions**

The common provisions in Part One of the Withdrawal Agreement include an obligation for the UK to confer supremacy and direct effect upon the Agreement in national law (see chapter 6).[110] The UK also had to pass an Act of Parliament to give effect to the Agreement (as noted earlier, it did so in January 2020).

All references to EU law in the Withdrawal Agreement must be interpreted in accordance with the normal rules of EU law. As for case law of the CJEU, references to EU law must be 'interpreted in conformity with' CJEU case law delivered before the end of the transition period (on which, see 4.3.4). However, the rule is different for CJEU case law after the end of the transition period: from that point, the UK courts and authorities are only required to have 'due regard' for the case law. References to EU law include that law as amended until the end of the transition period.

4.3.2 **Status of UK and EU citizens**

The status of EU citizens living in the UK at the end of the transition period and vice versa is addressed in Part Two of the Withdrawal Agreement.[111] This part provides in principle that EU27 citizens in the UK before the end of that period (and UK citizens who were in the EU27 before the end of that period) retain the same rights as those who arrived before Brexit day. To that end, it requires the two sides to keep applying certain provisions of EU free movement legislation to the people concerned, including legislation on social security coordination and the recognition of qualifications.

On the UK side, implementation of the citizens' rights part of the Withdrawal Agreement is monitored, for at least eight years after the end of the transition period, by the Independent Monitoring Authority (IMA).[112] The IMA is empowered, inter alia, to bring and intervene in judicial review proceedings against UK public bodies that fail to implement or apply the citizens' rights part of the Withdrawal Agreement.[113] It is also possible for eight years following the end of the transition period for UK courts to send references for preliminary rulings to the Court of Justice requesting an interpretation of the citizens' rights part of the Withdrawal Agreement.[114] Responses from the Court of Justice are binding on UK courts.[115] The first such reference was sent by the High Court to the CJEU in July 2025 in a case concerning the residence rights, under the Withdrawal Agreement, of dependent family members who subsequently ceased to be dependent due to domestic abuse.[116] In other cases, the UK courts have opted not to send references to Luxembourg and have decided matters for themselves, including the rights of dependent family members to work in the UK after having ceased to be dependent,[117] and whether destitute EU citizens with pre-settled status can rely on the EU Charter of Fundamental Rights before UK courts to challenge a refusal to access elements of the UK social security system.[118]

It is to be noted that not all the rights which UK and EU citizens derived from EU law continue to apply to their respective post-Brexit legal statuses. Under the Withdrawal

[110] Arts 1–8 of the Agreement.

[111] Arts 9–39. The CJEU confirmed that UK citizens lost the status of EU citizenship due to Brexit: Case C-673/20 *EP*, EU:C:2022:449.

[112] Art 159 of the Withdrawal Agreement.

[113] s 15 of and Sch 2 to the European Union (Withdrawal Agreement) Act 2020.

[114] Art 158(1) of the Withdrawal Agreement. For discussion of this point by a UK court, see *R (Ali) v Secretary of State for the Home Department* [2024] EWCA Civ 1546, paras 114–117.

[115] Art 158(2) of the Withdrawal Agreement.

[116] *R (On the application of BZ) v Secretary of State for Work and Pensions* [2025] EWHC 1814 (Admin).

[117] *R (Ali) v Secretary of State for the Home Department* [2024] EWCA Civ 1546.

[118] *SSWP v AT* [2023] EWCA Civ 1307.

Agreement, the UK or EU27 Member States could require citizens to apply to prove their right to stay on their respective territories.[119] The UK implemented this by means of a 'settled status' scheme for EU, European Economic Area, and Swiss nationals. Those citizens arriving in the UK prior to 31 December 2020 but who had not yet lived in the UK for five years were granted 'pre-settled status', whereas those who had already lived in the UK for longer than five years were granted 'settled status'. In litigation brought by the aforementioned IMA, the High Court found the UK government's position that citizens with pre-settled status had to make a second application to the EU Settlement Scheme (EUSS) or face losing their rights under Part 2 of the Withdrawal Agreement to be unlawful. As a result, those who continue to meet the relevant legal requirements will automatically obtain settled status after five years of continuous residence in the UK.

A further difference is that some categories of people previously covered by EU law (such as UK citizens returning to the UK with non-EU family members, or UK children in the sole care of one non-EU parent) are not covered by the Withdrawal Agreement, so their position is now determined by UK law. Also, the rules on family reunion in EU free movement law (which are more favourable than those under national law or EU law applicable to non-EU families) only apply where the family relationship existed before the end of the transition period, or the family member was legally resident in the same State at that time. If citizens commit a criminal offence after the end of the transition period, national rules on expulsions will apply—and they may be more stringent than EU free movement rules on this issue.

4.3.3 **Separation provisions**

Part Three of the Withdrawal Agreement sets out 'separation provisions' to address what happened at the end of the transition period,[120] such as cases involving the UK pending in the EU Courts on Brexit day, and the further consequence of any substantive EU law (besides free movement law, discussed in 4.3.2) ceasing to apply as between the UK and EU. For instance, it defines the circumstances in which European Arrest Warrants issued by the UK for fugitives in EU Member States—and vice versa—remain valid after Brexit day. More precisely, this part sets out rules for ending the application of EU law as regards 13 issues: goods placed on the market; ongoing customs procedures; ongoing VAT and excise procedures; intellectual property protection; police and criminal law cooperation; cross-border civil litigation; personal data; public procurement; Euratom; judicial and administrative procedures; administrative cooperation; privileges and immunities; and other issues, such as the European Schools.

4.3.4 **Transition period**

Part Four of the Withdrawal Agreement sets out the rules on the transition period, referred to several times above.[121] It kept most substantive EU law in place in the UK until the end of 2020; an extension of up to two years was theoretically possible, but the UK government ruled it out.

The key elements of the transition period were that EU law (including new EU law) still applied to the UK, except in areas covered by UK opt-outs (such as the single currency and justice and home affairs law). There were special rules on external relations: for instance, the EU notified non-EU countries that the UK should still be regarded as covered by EU free trade agreements, or other types of EU treaties between the EU and non-EU countries. However, the UK was not to be represented on any EU institutions or bodies—including on the CJEU, which continued to have its usual jurisdiction regarding the UK during the transition period.

[119] Art 19 of the Withdrawal Agreement. [120] Arts 40–125. [121] Arts 126–132.

4.3.5 **Financial settlement**

Part Five of the Withdrawal Agreement specifies that the UK took part in the EU's spending until the end of the budget cycle then in force (end of 2020), which matched the end of the transition period.[122] It also includes UK payments to the budget incurred because the EU often makes financial commitments in one year and then pays them out in later years (the system known as *reste à liquider*). Furthermore, it includes continued payments to 'off-budget' EU spending such as commitments to developing countries, until the current versions of those programmes expire.

4.3.6 **Final provisions**

According to Part Six of the Withdrawal Agreement,[123] as noted above, the CJEU has jurisdiction to rule on how the rules on citizens' acquired rights apply to EU27 citizens in the UK, on the basis of requests from UK courts, for eight years after the transitional period ends (ie the end of 2028).[124] There is also an independent monitoring body in the UK with power to bring court cases on their behalf. The two sides might agree to wind up the monitoring body at the end of the same time period.

Secondly, the CJEU has jurisdiction, after the end of the transitional period, over the reference to EU law in the financial settlement part of the Agreement, in references from national courts or as regards Commission infringement actions brought against the UK.

Next, a Joint Committee is set up to oversee and implement the Agreement. It meets at least once a year, and there are a number of sub-committees dealing with specific issues like Northern Ireland and citizens' rights. The Joint Committee can take certain decisions to add to the Agreement, but for all these decisions the EU and UK must both agree.

There are detailed rules on dispute settlement, providing for arguments about the Agreement to go to a panel of arbitrators if they are not settled during consultations. However, if the arbitrators have to decide an issue of EU law when settling the dispute, they will have to ask the CJEU to give a ruling. This is unavoidable, since CJEU case law insists that the EU and its Member States cannot be bound by an interpretation of EU law other than the CJEU's (see further chapter 26). Also, the CJEU has jurisdiction over part of the Protocol on Northern Ireland, as well as the Protocol on military bases in Cyprus.

4.3.7 **Protocols**

There are three Protocols, on the Irish border, Cyprus, and Gibraltar. The border Protocol proved to be the most difficult issue to negotiate; here is where the second version of the Withdrawal Agreement differs from the first version. The Protocol includes references to the UK's territorial integrity, equality rights and human rights,[125] and the common travel area between the UK and Ireland. Originally, it included a UK-wide customs union with the EU as a 'backstop', which had also included a 'level playing field', which meant some degree of continued harmonization of law relating to tax, the environment, labour law, State aid, competition, and public companies/monopolies.

In place of the UK/EU customs union backstop, the revised Protocol states that Northern Ireland is part of the UK's customs territory for international trade purposes. No customs duties are charged on goods moved from Great Britain to Northern Ireland, unless there is a risk that the goods may be sold in the EU. The further definition of what

[122] Arts 133–157. [123] Arts 158–185.

[124] At time of writing, one UK court had taken up this possibility (n 111).

[125] On the obligation of non-regression due to Brexit as regards human rights and Northern Ireland, see particularly the judgments on the Northern Ireland Troubles (Legacy and Reconciliation) Act 2023 (*Dillon and others* [2024] NIKB 11 and [2024] NICA 59, on appeal to the Supreme Court) and the Rwanda policy (*The matter of Northern Ireland Human Rights Commission, JR295 and the Illegal Migration Act 2023* [2024] NIKB 35).

that means had to be worked out by the Joint Committee by the end of the transition period.[126] There is an exemption for personal property. An Annex applies a long list of EU laws on customs, trade, and goods regulation to Northern Ireland. Customs duties charged for goods entering Northern Ireland are kept by the UK, not given to the EU.

The Protocol also retains provisions on the UK internal market, as well as lists of specific EU laws that apply in Northern Ireland: product regulation, VAT and excise tax, a single electricity market, and State aids. There is a 'safeguard' clause in the Protocol, but neither party has invoked it; the EU planned to invoke it in January 2021 as regards export of Covid vaccines, but quickly backed off before the planned law entered into force.[127]

The institutional provisions of the Protocol were retained, including the proviso that EU bodies, including the CJEU, have competence to apply or interpret the trade provisions of the Protocol. Finally, a new provision on 'consent' specifies that the members of the Northern Ireland Assembly must give continuing consent to the customs and other economic provisions of the Protocol, every four years starting from the end of 2024.[128] There is also a unilateral UK declaration related to this issue. (The absence of a power to end the previous backstop unilaterally had been controversial.)

This Protocol has been a source of continued controversy, because it provides for some checks on goods moving between Northern Ireland and Great Britain, which Northern Ireland unionists (ie supporters of the union between Northern Ireland and Great Britain) mostly object to in principle. A legal challenge to the Protocol brought by unionists failed, on the grounds of parliamentary supremacy, given that the Protocol had been implemented by an Act of Parliament.[129] On the other hand, Northern Ireland nationalists (ie supporters of Northern Ireland being unified with Ireland) and non-aligned voters tend to support the existence of the Protocol, while supporting some amendments to it. Despite campaigning in 2019 for the Withdrawal Agreement as an 'oven ready deal' and ratifying it, the UK's Conservative government soon came to express hatred of parts of the Agreement that it had championed.

Besides the provision providing that members of the Northern Ireland Assembly must vote on continuing consent to the trade parts of the Protocol every four years, there is no other provision in the Withdrawal Agreement allowing for the termination of the entire Agreement or the Protocol. Nevertheless, the Conservative UK government's objection to what it had signed manifested itself in actions which arguably intended to breach the Protocol. First of all, a draft 'Internal Market Bill' in autumn 2020 contained clauses which would have 'switched off' specific provisions of the Protocol; the UK government dropped these clauses from the bill when it reached agreement with the EU on implementing the Protocol at the end of 2020. Subsequently, the UK Conservative government tabled a 'Northern Ireland Protocol Bill' in June 2022 which would have 'switched off' even more of the Protocol, justifying this by invoking the 'defence of necessity' in international law—a legal argument which some have challenged.

Ultimately, in 2023 the EU and UK agreed a number of changes to the Protocol, renaming it the 'Windsor Framework' in the process. The Windsor Framework simplifies, but does not eliminate, the complications for internal UK trade created by the Protocol.[130]

As for the Protocol on UK military bases in Cyprus, it confirms that the bases in Cyprus remain within the EU customs territory after Brexit, and EU regulations on goods, including agricultural and fisheries laws, still apply. EU law on excise taxes and VAT also continues to apply. Goods supplied to the staff on the bases are exempt from

[126] OJ [2020] L443/1. [127] See Case T-161/21 *McCord v Commission*, EU:T:2021:910.

[128] A majority of the Northern Ireland Assembly members gave their consent to continuing these parts of the Protocol when the first such vote was held, at the end of 2024.

[129] *Allister and others* [2023] UKSC 5.

[130] For the texts, see www.gov.uk/government/publications/the-windsor-framework.

customs and taxes, and the UK and Cyprus may agree further rules on social security coordination. There are rules on checks at the border of the base areas, and a general obligation to cooperate to prevent fraud. The EU institutions, including the CJEU, have competence to apply and interpret EU law referred to in the Protocol.

Finally, the Protocol on Gibraltar mostly expired at the end of the transition period. The remaining clause provides for the UK and Spain to cooperate on workers' rights as regards the Spain/Gibraltar crossing. The status of Gibraltar is also the subject of a separate post-Brexit treaty, agreed in 2025, involving a customs union and association with the Schengen system.[131]

5 After Brexit

There was a general consensus in the literature that there would need to be a distinction drawn between the Withdrawal Agreement concluded under Article 50 TEU and any future agreement providing for future relations between the UK and the European Union.[132] Indeed, the EU consistently pushed for this distinction to be made despite the reluctance of the then-UK government to accept it. In the end, the Withdrawal Agreement does cover some post-Brexit issues, notably the transition period and the continued relationship between the EU and Northern Ireland as regards trade in goods. But, as noted above, the main elements of the post-Brexit EU/UK relationship are in the Trade and Cooperation Agreement.

5.1 Trade and Cooperation Agreement

Alongside the Withdrawal Agreement, an updated 'political declaration' on the future relationship between the UK and the EU was published in 2019.[133] The aim of both sides was to negotiate a comprehensive free trade agreement in goods and services after Brexit, with additional commitments to negotiate future relations on other issues, such as foreign policy, internal security, and research. The end product of the negotiations is the UK–EU Trade and Cooperation Agreement (TCA), which was signed on 30 December 2020, was applied provisionally as of 1 January 2021, and entered into force on 1 May 2021.[134]

The TCA goes beyond 'typical' free trade agreements that the EU has concluded with third countries, in that it not only establishes a free trade area for goods and services (in accordance with World Trade Organization (WTO) law),[135] but it also contains provisions on investment, digital trade, intellectual property, capital movements, intellectual property, public procurement, small and medium-sized enterprises, energy, aviation and road transport, social security coordination, and fisheries.[136] In addition, the TCA sets down detailed commitments on law enforcement and judicial cooperation in criminal matters,[137] cooperation in health and cyber security,[138] and participation in Union programmes.[139]

[131] COM (2026) 91, 17 February 2026. On the Schengen system, see further chapter 25.

[132] B de Witte, 'Near-Membership, Partial Membership and the EU Constitution' (2016) 41 *European Law Review* 471; C Hillion, 'Accession and Withdrawal in the Law of the European Union' in D Chalmers and A Arnull (eds), *The Oxford Handbook of European Union Law* (Oxford: Oxford University Press, 2015) 126; Edward and Wyatt (n 71) 7–9.

[133] OJ [2019] C384 I/178.

[134] Trade and Cooperation Agreement between the European Union and the European Atomic Energy Community, of the one part, and the United Kingdom of Great Britain and Northern Ireland, of the other part (OJ [2021] L149).

[135] Art 514 TCA.

[136] See TCA, Part Two—Part 2—Trade, Transport, Fisheries and Other Arrangements.

[137] TCA, Part Three. [138] TCA, Part Four. [139] TCA, Part Five.

The TCA has Article 217 TFEU as its legal basis in the EU legal order, meaning that it was concluded on the EU side as an association agreement with a third state. Given the range of different policy fields covered by the TCA, the Council's decision to sign and conclude the TCA solely as a treaty binding the EU rather than as a mixed agreement with the participation of both the EU and the Member States is somewhat unusual.[140] The Council's Decision to conclude the TCA as an EU-only agreement was premised upon the belief that the Agreement only covered areas where the EU has either exclusive or shared competences and that mixity was therefore facultative (optional) as opposed to obligatory.[141] Article 4 of Part One (Common and Institutional Provisions) provides that the provisions of the TCA and any supplementing agreement are to be 'interpreted in good faith in accordance with their ordinary meaning in their context and in light of the object and purpose of the agreement in accordance with customary rules of interpretation of public international law'.[142] The same provision provides 'for greater certainty' that neither the TCA nor any supplementing agreements obliges the UK and EU to interpret their provisions in accordance with the domestic law of either party and that any interpretation given of said agreements by the courts of either party shall not be binding on the courts of the other party.[143] This emphasis on a classic public international law as opposed to EU law-derived approach to the interpretation and legal effects of the TCA is further emphasized in Article 5, which provides that nothing in the TCA or supplementing agreements 'shall be construed as conferring rights or imposing obligations on persons other than those created between the Parties under public international law, nor as permitting this Agreement or any supplementing agreement to be directly invoked in the domestic legal systems of the Parties'.[144] Furthermore, the UK and EU are prohibited from providing for a right of action in their own domestic law against the other party on the ground that that other party has acted in breach of the TCA or any supplementing agreement.[145]

With regards to governance, a Partnership Council is tasked with overseeing the attainment of the objectives of the TCA and any supplementing agreements, and to supervise and facilitate their implementation.[146] It is co-chaired by a UK government minister and a member of the European Commission. Each party may refer matters relating to the implementation or interpretation of the TCA and supplementing agreements to the Partnership Council, which shall meet at least once per year.[147] The Partnership Council has the power to adopt legally binding decisions in respect of all matters where the TCA or any supplementing agreement so provides. It may also issue non-binding recommendations regarding the implementation and application of the TCA and any supplementary agreements.[148] In addition, both the UK and the EU may jointly through the Partnership Council adopt decisions amending the TCA or any supplementary agreement.[149] The Partnership Council is supported by a number of other committees covering different aspects of the TCA, including the Trade Partnership Committee which oversees trade-related provisions and is in turn supported by ten trade specialized committees that deal with matters such as customs cooperation, intellectual property and investment, and digital trade.[150] Beyond trade, there are a further eight committees that cover

[140] S Peers, 'So Close, Yet So Far: The EU/UK Trade and Cooperation Agreement' (2022) 59 *Common Market Law Review* 49, 58.

[141] For discussion of the legal basis issue, including the legal opinion of the Council Legal Service, see ibid, 58–60. See also chapter 26.

[142] TCA, Part One, Art 4(1).

[143] Ibid, Arts 4(2) and 4(3).

[144] Ibid, Art 5(1). There are limited exceptions for social security and (on the EU side) criminal law provisions.

[145] Ibid, Art 5(2).

[146] TCA, Part Three, Art 7(3).

[147] Ibid, Art 7(2).

[148] Ibid, Arts 7(4) and 10(1).

[149] Ibid, Art 7(4).

[150] Ibid, Art 8.

other aspects of the TCA.[151] There is also a Parliamentary Partnership Assembly consisting of Members of the European Parliament and of Members of the UK Parliament. The Assembly may request information from the Partnership Council on the implementation of the TCA and supplementing agreements and can make recommendations to the Council.[152]

Despite going beyond most free trade agreements signed by the EU and any third States, the TCA still falls well short of the level of economic integration stemming from participation in the single market and/or customs union (some non-EU countries have single market or customs union links with the EU).[153] Unlike other trade deals—which typically improve trading relations between the contracting States—the TCA is notable for increasing trade barriers and decreasing cooperation between the UK and the EU when compared to the position of EU membership.[154] Contrary to the assertions of some, leaving the EU has not resulted in the UK retaining the exact same benefits as it had during its period of membership.

In relation to trade in goods, for example, the TCA provides that, in principle, no customs duties are to be levied on any imports or exports of goods originating in either the UK or the EU.[155] In order for goods to benefit from this preferential tariff arrangement, however, complex rules-of-origin requirements must be complied with in order to prove that the good in question did originate in the UK or the EU.[156] This is a direct consequence of the UK's decision to leave the EU customs union. It has been noted that the sheer volume and complexity of the general and product-specific rules-of-origin requirements in the TCA has resulted in some traders deciding to pay the UK/EU's most favoured nation (MFN) tariff, rather than attempting to prove the origin of their goods in order to benefit from the preferential (zero) tariff.[157] With regards to non-tariff barriers (ie regulations and standards that goods must comply with in order to be placed on the market), the TCA is modelled upon the WTO legal framework, rather than that of the EU single market—which, again, the UK decided to leave.[158] Within the EU single market, the combination of harmonization, coupled with the principle of mutual recognition, have successfully reduced much of the burden of having to comply with two sets of regulations (in the home State of production and the host State of importation).[159] In contrast, the TCA's rules on technical barriers to trade (TBT) and sanitary and phytosanitary measures (SPS)—which incorporate WTO agreements on such matters—provide far greater scope for the parties to introduce and apply differing regulations and standards.[160] There is also limited scope for mutual recognition of standards and certainly nothing like the wide-ranging system of mutual recognition that exists inside the EU single market. Consequently, the shift from a trading relationship governed by the rules of the EU single market to that of the TCA means that there is now far greater scope for both the UK and the EU to subject one another's goods to domestic regulatory requirements, with resultant increases in bureaucracy and compliance costs for traders.[161]

[151] Ibid. [152] Ibid, Art 11.

[153] See House of Lords European Union Committee, 'Beyond Brexit: Trade in Goods', 24th Report of Session 2019–21 (HL 249), 10; House of Lords European Union Committee, 'Beyond Brexit: Trade in Services', 23rd Report of Session 2019–21 (HL 248), 23.

[154] P Birkinshaw, 'Brexit and the Trade and Cooperation Agreement: Endgame or Prolegomenon?' (2021) 27 *European Public Law* 229, 253–255.

[155] TCA, Part Two, Arts 21 and 22. [156] Ibid, Arts 37–68 and TCA, Annex 3.

[157] C Barnard and E Leinarte, 'Movement of Goods under the TCA' (2022) 13 *Global Policy* 106, 110.

[158] TCA, Part Two, Arts 69–87 and 88–100 set down rules on sanitary and phytosanitary measures (SPS) and technical barriers to trade (TBT) respectively.

[159] See also chapter 12.

[160] The right to regulate under the TCA is not unlimited and remains subject to general principles of WTO law such as non-discrimination. See TCA, Part Two, Arts 73 and 90.

[161] Barnard and Leinarte (n 157) 110–114.

Similarly, as regards services, while the TCA also provides for free trade in services, this also falls short of participation in the internal market. For instance, there is little in the Agreement about financial services, and audiovisual services are excluded entirely.

5.1.1 Level playing field

One of the most contentious issues during the negotiations was the agreement of so-called 'level playing field' commitments.[162] In essence, the UK and EU took differing positions on the extent to which the parties would be prohibited from lowering existing standards (non-regression) and whether one party would have to raise its standards in the event that the other party raised theirs (ratchet clauses).[163]

According to the stated principles and objectives of the level playing field provisions in the TCA, the UK and the EU 'recognise that trade and investment between the Union and the United Kingdom under the terms set out in this Agreement, require conditions that ensure a level playing field for open and fair competition between the Parties and that ensure that trade and investment take place in a manner conducive to sustainable development'.[164] The agreed commitments relating to a level playing field vary according to subject matter, with a great many substantive and procedural obligations being scattered across nine chapters dealing with, inter alia, competition, subsidies, State-owned enterprises, and taxation. The competition provisions have since been supplemented by a further agreement on cooperation between competition authorities.[165]

Specific mention can be made here of the level playing field commitments reached on labour and social standards and the environment and climate, which both contain non-regression clauses that can be enforced by trade retaliation.[166] On labour and social standards, for example, the relevant provision provides that, 'A Party shall not weaken or reduce, in a manner affecting trade or investment between the Parties, its labour and social levels of protection below the levels in place at the end of the transition period, including by failing to effectively enforce its law and standards.'[167] Labour and social levels of protection are defined broadly as encompassing matters including fundamental rights at work, occupational health and safety standards and fair working conditions, and employment standards.[168] With regards to the EU, the relevant levels of protection for labour and social laws and standards are those that are applicable to and in, and are common to, all Member States.[169] This encompasses not only EU law, therefore, but also other laws and standards that the Member States have in common which stem from international treaties such as the Council of Europe's Social Charter. On the UK side, the relevant levels of protection are all national standards, including those not derived from EU law; although it must be kept in mind that much of UK law in this area continues to be based upon EU law that has been retained post-Brexit.[170] Not every instance of reduction in levels of protection in the UK or the EU will infringe the aforementioned non-regression clause in light of the need for any lowering of standards to affect trade and investment between the parties. Following the outcome of a dispute settlement process that is specific to the labour and environmental law chapters of the TCA, it is possible for either

[162] For an overview, see PP Craig, 'Brexit A Drama, The Endgame: Part II: Trade, Sovereignty and Control' (2021) 46 *European Law Review* 129, 145–151.

[163] The disagreements were particularly pronounced in relation to labour and social standards, see https://researchbriefings.files.parliament.uk/documents/CBP-9190/CBP-9190.pdf.

[164] TCA, Part Two, Title XI, Art 355.

[165] COM (2025) 232, 19 May 2025.

[166] TCA, Part Two, Title XI, Chapters 6 and 7.

[167] Ibid, Art 387(2). For environment and climate, see similarly ibid, Art 391(2).

[168] Ibid, Art 386(1).

[169] Ibid, Art 386(2).

[170] For discussion, see Peers, 'So Close, Yet So Far: The EU/UK Trade and Cooperation Agreement' (n 140) 63–64.

side to retaliate in the form of raising tariffs in the event of a breach of the non-regression clause.[171]

In addition to non-regression obligations, the UK and EU have also agreed that either party may take 'appropriate rebalancing measures' if there are 'material impacts on trade or investment between the parties' that arise as a result of 'significant divergencies' with respect to labour and social standards, environmental or climate protection, or with respect to subsidy control.[172] Any rebalancing measures must be restricted with respect to their scope and duration to what is strictly necessary and proportionate in order to remedy the situation.[173]

5.1.2 **Dispute settlement**

As with the Withdrawal Agreement, the dispute settlement rules provide for arguments about the Agreement to go to a panel of arbitrators if they are not settled during consultations (although the two differ on points of detail, like the deadlines for the arbitrators to act). But unlike the Withdrawal Agreement, there was initially no role for the CJEU to become involved in disputes, because there was no reference to EU law in the treaty. The one exception to this rule was research programmes, where the UK signed up to participation in an EU policy, therefore the CJEU has jurisdiction if applicants for research funding bring legal challenges against the Commission's decision to recover funds.[174]

The dispute settlement system of the TCA has been used once, when the EU objected to a ban on sand eel fishing in English and Scottish waters. According to the arbitrators appointed to settle the dispute, ruling in April 2025, the Scottish ban was wholly justified, but the English ban was procedurally flawed.[175]

5.1.3 **UK/EU 'reset'**

The newly elected UK government in 2024 strove to 'reset' the relationship with the EU by negotiating closer links in certain areas. The initial consequence of this was a joint statement and a security and defence partnership agreed in 2024, effectively setting out an agenda for further negotiations for UK participation in EU defence procurement, as well as treaties to be linked to the TCA framework. In particular, there are commitments to negotiate an UK–EU youth mobility treaty,[176] along with treaties on UK alignment with the EU's carbon trading system and food standards.[177] Departing from the approach of the previous government to the TCA, the UK is now willing to agree not only on alignment with EU law in specific areas, but also to allow arbitrators to refer questions to the CJEU about the interpretation of the EU law which the UK has aligned with. The two sides also agreed to extend the TCA provisions on fishing access and energy.[178]

5.1.4 **Retaining and assimilating EU law in the UK**

Having left the EU, what happened to all the EU law (eg Treaty provisions, EU legislation, general principles of EU law etc) that was in force in the UK prior to Brexit? Initially, the UK decided to keep virtually all that law on the domestic statute book by

171 TCA, Part Two, Title XI, Arts 389 and 408–410. 172 Ibid, Art 411(1) and (2). 173 Ibid.

174 TCA, Art 728. On the details of participation, see Decision 1/2023 of the Specialised Committee on Union programmes (OJ [2023] L 5.12.2023).

175 For details of the dispute, see https://pca-cpa.org/en/cases/334/.

176 For the EU decision on its negotiating mandate, see OJ [2025] L 1.7.2025.

177 For the proposed EU negotiating mandates, see COM (2025) 408, 16 July 2025. The EU side agreed on its negotiation mandates in November 2025.

178 OJ [2025] L 20.6.2025.

enacting the European Union (Withdrawal) Act 2018. By virtue of the 2018 Act, what was once EU law became a new form of domestic law known as 'retained EU law'.[179] The EU Withdrawal Act 2018 pursued two main objectives. First, to ensure legal certainty by providing that the vast bulk of EU law in force prior to Brexit would continue to be in force immediately post-Brexit. This was achieved by preserving domestic legislation that had implemented EU obligations and by converting other parts of EU law into a domestic equivalent.[180] Secondly, to allow the UK government to decide which elements of retained EU law should be abolished, amended, or retained into the future.[181]

The 2018 Act was followed by the Retained EU Law (Revocation and Reform) Act 2023, which sought, inter alia, to revoke all or part of close to 600 pieces of legislation that were derived from EU law and had thus acquired the status of retained EU law under the European Union (Withdrawal) Act 2018.[182] Additionally, the 2023 Act renamed retained EU law, giving it the novel name of 'assimilated law'.[183] The 2023 Act also altered the legal effects that assimilated law would produce in the domestic legal order into the future,[184] as well as further empowering the executive branch of government to restate, replicate, revoke, and replace assimilated law until June 2026.[185]

Finally, one must consider the effect of CJEU case law in the UK courts post-Brexit. Since the end of the transition period (known in domestic law as 'IP completion day'), the general position is that courts and tribunals in the UK are not bound by any principles laid down, or any decisions made, on or after IP completion day by the CJEU, and they cannot make a reference for a preliminary ruling to the CJEU after IP completion day (save as provided for elsewhere, eg in the UK–EU Withdrawal Agreement).[186] However, a court or tribunal in the UK may have regard to anything done on or after IP completion day by the CJEU, another EU entity, or the EU, so far as it is relevant to any matter before the court or tribunal.[187] Any question as to the validity, meaning, or effect of any assimilated law is to be decided, so far as that law is unmodified on or after IP completion day, and so far as they are relevant to it, in accordance with any assimilated case law, that is, judgments of the CJEU handed down before IP completion day which speak to the interpretation or validity of provisions of EU law which are now assimilated law in the UK.[188] However, the UK Supreme Court, the Court of Appeal of England and Wales, and various other UK courts and tribunals are not bound by assimilated case law.[189] When deciding whether to depart from assimilated case law, the UK Supreme Court is required to use the same test as it would use when deciding to depart from its own case law, that is, if it was right to do so.[190]

[179] Retained EU law has since been renamed 'Assimilated law', see the European Union (Withdrawal) Act 2018, s 6(7).

[180] Ibid, ss 2–7.

[181] Ibid, s 8.

[182] Retained EU Law (Revocation and Reform) Act 2023, ss 1–2 and Sch 1.

[183] Ibid, s 5.

[184] Ibid, ss 3–4. Under the 2023 Act, assimilated law does not take precedence over any other domestic law, thus bringing an end to a modified version of the supremacy principle that did apply to resolve conflicts between retained EU law and other forms of domestic law under the European Union (Withdrawal) Act 2018, see s 5(A)(2) of the Act, as inserted by s 3 of the Retained EU Law (Revocation and Reform) Act 2023.

[185] Retained EU Law (Revocation and Reform) Act 2023, ss 9–16.

[186] European Union (Withdrawal) Act 2018, s 6(1).

[187] Ibid, s 6(2).

[188] Ibid, s 6(3).

[189] Ibid, s 6(4); the European Union (Withdrawal) Act 2018 (Relevant Court) (Retained EU Case Law) Regulations 2020.

[190] European Union (Withdrawal) Act 2018, s 6(5).

5.2 **Other issues**

The controversial issue of migration and asylum is addressed post-Brexit not by a treaty between the UK and EU, but between the UK and France.[191] France has agreed, on a pilot basis, to take back one Channel boat migrant from the UK for every likely asylum seeker that the UK agrees to take.

Finally, post-Brexit the UK reconsidered its relations with non-EU countries, particularly as regards trade. The UK remains a member of the WTO, although it is now separate from the EU, which negotiates as a bloc in the WTO due to the EU's exclusive competence over trade policy (see chapter 26). Also, the UK 'rolled over' the EU's free trade arrangements with non-EU countries, attempting to replicate these as far as possible, with the agreement of the non-EU countries concerned. Some of those treaties have already been replaced (or could be replaced in future). The UK has also sought free trade agreements with some other non-EU countries which the EU does not have a free trade agreement with, and to date has agreed such treaties with Australia, India, and New Zealand (although the EU and New Zealand have subsequently agreed their own free trade deal), and joined the multiparty Asia-Pacific free trade deal known as CPTPP (although it partly replicates free trade agreements which the UK and EU have with most of its parties anyway).

Case study 27.1: Data protection law and Brexit

One example of how the Brexit process works is the case of data protection law. Under the Withdrawal Agreement, the UK applied EU data protection law until the end of the transition period in that Agreement. What happened after that?

The main EU law on data protection is the General Data Protection Regulation (known as the GDPR).[192] It provides for the EU Commission to issue an 'adequacy decision' regarding non-EU countries, which simplifies flows of personal data. Without an adequacy decision, personal data is not banned from transfer, but it can be more difficult to justify transfers. Outside the scope of the GDPR, there also has to be an assessment of the UK's data protection laws to justify association with EU policing measures.

After the end of the transition period, the EU Commission adopted adequacy decisions for the UK, although such decisions are subject to review in the event that UK law changes.[193] In the event, the Commission decided in 2025 to extend the adequacy decisions even though UK data protection law had changed post-Brexit.[194] Adequacy decisions are sometimes challenged in the EU Courts, although the adequacy decision for the UK has not been challenged so far[195]

In the area of criminal law cooperation (see further chapter 24), again the previous EU rules applied throughout the transition period (with an exception for three Member States

[191] www.gov.uk/government/publications/ukfrance-agreement-on-the-prevention-of-dangerous-journeys-cs-france-no22025, in force August 2025.

[192] Regulation 2016/679 (OJ [2016] L118/1).

[193] C(2021) 4800 and 4801, 28 June 2021.

[194] https://commission.europa.eu/law/law-topic/data-protection/international-dimension-data-protection/adequacy-decisions_en.

[195] Case C-362/14 *Schrems I*, EU:C:2015:650.

which refuse to extradite their own nationals). As noted above, the separation provisions in the Withdrawal Agreement provide for winding down the relationship (eg determining what happens to pending European Arrest Warrants). But what happens after that?[196]

Case study 27.2: Criminal law cooperation and Brexit

If the UK and EU had not reached agreement on post-Brexit criminal law cooperation, criminal justice matters would have been handled on the same legal basis as they are with other non-EU countries with which no special arrangements have been made. In some cases, this would have been facilitated by the ability to fall back on collective arrangements which exist outside the framework of the EU. For extradition, for example, the UK and the remaining Member States could have used the 1957 Council of Europe Extradition Treaty: the legal framework within which extradition within Europe operated before the European Arrest Warrant was created, and which is still used by the EU Member States to extradite wanted persons to and from European countries which are contracting parties to the Convention but do not belong to the EU, in the absence of an extradition treaty with the EU.

However, these fall-back instruments are less efficient than the EU instruments (which is why the EU instruments were created to replace them). For instance, there are more grounds to refuse cooperation, and fewer deadlines imposed on the requested State to act. As we saw in chapter 24, one of the main reasons for the emergence of EU criminal law was the need to deal with the unwanted consequences of free movement—the free movement of criminals and crime. Even without free movement of people, there is still travel and communications between the UK and the remaining Member States, and so the case for criminal law cooperation still exists.

Ultimately, the TCA contains a specific part on criminal law cooperation, which does not apply EU law as such to the UK but which sets out mutual obligations which are similar to some of the laws which applied between the UK and other Member States when the UK was a Member State. For instance, there are rules as regards extradition, mutual assistance on the exchange of evidence, and the exchange of data between law enforcement authorities (eg on passenger name data).[197] However, the post-Brexit relationship is not identical to being a Member State: in addition to the institutional changes (no CJEU jurisdiction over the UK; no UK vote on new EU legislation; association with, instead of membership of, EU law enforcement agencies), there are substantive differences—notably, the UK is no longer signed up to the Schengen Information System database of law enforcement information. Also, the criminal law part of the TCA can be terminated or suspended separately; and there is a fast track to termination or suspension on grounds of data protection issues or human rights concerns. In particular, if the UK denounced the ECHR, as some UK politicians would like to do, it is likely that the EU would terminate or suspend the criminal law part of the TCA immediately.

[196] Thanks to John R Spencer and András Csúri for their contribution towards case study 27.2.

[197] The extradition rules have led to several requests from the Irish courts to the CJEU for interpretation: Cases C-479/21 PPU *Governor of Cloverhill Prison and others*, EU:C:2021:929; C-202/24 *Alchaster I*, EU:C:2024:649; and C-743/24 *Alchaster II*, EU:C:2025:230.

6 Conclusion

The Brexit process has raised a number of complex legal issues, starting with the process of deciding how to notify the UK's departure and continuing with issues about whether the UK could withdraw its notification to leave and whether an extension of membership was possible. Now that the UK has formally withdrawn from the Union, there are legal questions about the interpretation of the Withdrawal Agreement, the Trade and Cooperation Agreement, and other issues besides. These are paralleled by issues of domestic law, as the EU Withdrawal Act and the Withdrawal Agreement Act may raise a number of questions of interpretation. Brexit will have an impact on a significant proportion of laws applied in the UK. Legal issues will also arise as regards UK relations with non-EU States. The legal questions will, of course, be intertwined with political disputes and economic issues.

Finally, Brexit will impact on the remaining EU too—particularly for those who trade with or have a personal link with the UK. Some have speculated that without the UK, the EU may be more focused on the eurozone States and less inclined towards free-market economics. On the other hand, any reduction in trade with the UK may incline the EU to look to expand trade with other non-EU countries. There is no sign to date that the EU will embark upon a fundamental rethink of the integration process in light of the UK's decision to leave. However, ten years after the initial Brexit referendum vote, there is no sign of the collapse of the EU which some of its British critics had predicted was imminent.

Further reading

P Craig, 'Brexit: A Drama in Six Acts' (2016) 41 *European Law Review* 447

Sir D Edward and D Wyatt, 'The Process of Withdrawing from the European Union', Written Evidence to House of Lords European Union Committee (*HL* 138, 2015–16)

C Hillion, 'Accession and Withdrawal in the Law of the European Union' in D Chalmers and A Arnull (eds), *The Oxford Handbook of European Union Law* (Oxford: Oxford University Press, 2015) 126–151

A Łazowski, 'Withdrawal from the European Union and Alternatives to Membership' (2012) 37 *European Law Review* 523

AF Tatham, '"Don't Mention Divorce at the Wedding, Darling!": EU Accession and Withdrawal after Lisbon' in A Biondi, P Eeckhout, and S Ripley (eds), *EU Law After Lisbon* (Oxford: Oxford University Press, 2012) 128–154

Index

Introductory Note

References such as '178–9' indicate (not necessarily continuous) discussion of a topic across a range of pages. Wherever possible in the case of topics with many references, these have either been divided into subtopics or only the most significant discussions of the topic are listed. Because the entire work is about 'EU law', the use of this term (and certain others which occur constantly throughout the book) as an entry point has been restricted. Information will be found under the corresponding detailed topics.